THE GERMAN LAW OF CONTRACT

SECOND EDITION

The German Law of Contract
A Comparative Treatise

Second Edition

SIR BASIL MARKESINIS
HANNES UNBERATH
ANGUS JOHNSTON

Forewords by

Lord Bingham,
Senior Law Lord

and

Professor Dr Günter Hirsch,
Bundesgerichtshof

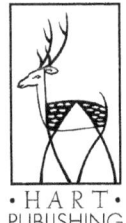

·HART·
PUBLISHING

OXFORD AND PORTLAND, OREGON
2006

Hart Publishing
Oxford and Portland, Oregon

Published in North America (US and Canada) by
Hart Publishing c/o
International Specialized Book Services
5804 NE Hassalo Street
Portland, Oregon
97213-3644
USA
Tel: +1 503 287 3093 or toll-free: (1) 800 944 6190
Fax: +1 503 280 8832
E-mail: orders@isbs.com
Web Site: www.isbs.com

Hart Publishing is a specialist legal publisher based in Oxford, England.
To order further copies of this book or to request a list of other
publications please write to:

Hart Publishing, Salter's Boatyard, Folly Bridge,
Abingdon Road, Oxford OX1 4LB
Telephone: +44 (0)1865 245533 or Fax: +44 (0)1865 794882
e-mail: mail@hartpub.co.uk
WEBSITE: http//www.hartpub.co.uk

British Library Cataloguing in Publication Data
Data Available
ISBN 13: 978–1–84113–471–0 (hardback)
ISBN 10: 1–84113–471–6 (hardback)

ISBN 13: 978–1–84113–472–7 (paperback)
ISBN 10: 1–84113–472–4 (paperback)

Typeset by Hope Services (Abingdon) Ltd.
Printed and bound in Great Britain by
CPI Group (UK) Ltd, Croydon, CR0 4YY

Foreword by Lord Bingham

There are many good reasons for a common lawyer to study a foreign law such as the German law of contract.

First and foremost, as a sustained exercise in human thinking, the product of philosophical debate, scholarly discussion and judicial application over many years, such a law deserves study in its own right. It is, like an epic poem or a symphony or a work of architecture, a refined manifestation of the human mind and spirit, commanding attention on that ground alone. Such a reason may not be very fashionable nowadays, but it should come first all the same.

The Second reason is more pragmatic. It is that by studying a foreign law such as the German law of contract the common lawyer gains valuable insights into his own law: "And what should they know of England who only England know?" On first perusing this text, the common lawyer will be struck by the familiarity (in translation) of a number of elements of the German law of contract, which may indeed be elements of any coherent law of contract. But the appearance of familiarity is to some extent deceptive, since frequently the underlying concepts are different, sometimes subtly so, sometimes substantially. Even the meaning of "contract" is not the same. These differences appear from the authors' skilful analysis, which they illuminate with references to the French Civil Code and the American and English common law.

The third reason for legislators, lawyers and judges to study a foreign law such as the German law of contract is even more pragmatic: it is to facilitate the time-honoured practice of theft. This is not, of course, to suggest that the BGB could or should be uprooted bodily and transplanted in British soil. Even if feasible, that would be absurd. But the snapping-up of well-considered trifles has a respectable legal ancestry, and when choices have to be made about the future development of an important field of law it is highly beneficial to know how the same problem has been resolved in another sophisticated and respected legal system. There are no doubt circumstances in which ignorance is bliss, but it is never folly for a lawmaker to be informed.

That leads on to a fourth and important reason. While some welcome the prospect more than others, it seems inevitable that the years ahead will bring some degree of convergence between the laws of the major European states, German and Britain prominent among them. As active trading partners, members of the European Union responsive to and bound by its legislation and as parties to important international conventions, this trend must surely grow in strength, even if falling well short of unification. It would of course be a lamentable result if this process were to lead to a common European law manifestly inferior to the national laws it replaced. So the objective of all involved must be to establish principled rules embodying the best jurisprudential products of all the great European systems. But that requires knowledge and understanding not only of one's own law but also of others with which it must be compared and blended.

When stepping into the unknown or incompletely known, even the most conscientious traveller needs a guide. It would be hard to find any guide better qualified or suited to their task than the authors of this big and important book.

Tom Bingham
House of Lords
12 April 2005

Foreword by President Hirsch

On January 1, 2002, the time-honoured German *Bürgerliches Gesetzbuch* (BGB) which came into force on January 1, 1900 underwent one of its most fundamental changes. With the *Gesetz zur Modernisierung des Schuldrechts*, not only were a number of EC Directives implemented, but the need for a modernisation of the entire law of obligations and the statutory limitation rules was also finally met. In addition, the tendency to regulate specific questions of the law of obligations by means of special statutes was brought to an end in order to retain the advantages of a comprehensive codification of the law of obligations in one singly document. A similar development can be witnessed in the case of the French *Code civil.*

The indisputable necessity to shape the law of obligations of the Member States of the European Community in such a way that it does not adversely affect trans-frontier trade can be taken into account in two ways. Either the national legislators modify their Civil Law in such a way that it is compatible with the legal systems of the other Member States, or the European legislator standardises certain fields of law within the framework of its (limited) competence—doing this as a rule by means of Directives.

Beyond the isolated steps taken in specific sectors towards an approximation of Civil Law within the European Community, the idea of an epochal project is now gaining wider recognition within the Community: a European law of contract. In 2001 the European Commission put forward four options for discussion: (1) to leave the solution of defects discovered to the market, (2) to develop common principles of the European law of contract, (3) to improve the already existing EC law of contract and (4) to lay down new regulations concerning the law of contract. With this, the development of a European law of contract has been given a new impetus. But in the short term, no quick results can be expected.

This forms the background to the work by Professor Sir Basil Markesinis, an acknowledged authority on German civil law, and his co-authors.

Civil Law is the heart of every country's legal culture. It has developed over the centuries and is an integral part of national identity of all countries.

However, today trade and tourism know no boundaries. Therefore the law also, particularly a country's law of obligations, can no longer restrict itself to providing purely national answers without any regard for other legal systems. Getting to know other legal systems and incorporating them in the interpretation and development of one's own law represents more than a cultural and intellectual enrichment. In reality it is indispensable to practice since every jurist needs to be able to see further than his own everyday problems. This is particularly true of the law of obligations which regulates the legal assessment of everyday business—a branch of the law which, these days, through e-commerce and otherwise, increasingly has a cross-border reference extending even to international business transactions.

In addition, just as a cathedral is more than the sum of the stones used to build it, and a symphony is more than the sum of its notes employed to compose it, a particular statute is more than the sum total of its paragraphs. It is the idea behind the law, the aspiration for justice connected with the law, which has to be understood if one wishes to master it.

The law of obligations is a field of law in which the cultural and social convictions of a nation are particularly clearly manifested, for instance where the binding character of obligations which have been entered into, the meaning of ownership, the freedom of the individual are concerned. It is precisely for this reason that this work by Sir Basil Markesinis, Dr Hannes Unberath and Mr Angus Johnston is so important. For, using the comparative method it goes beyond a mere description of the subject matter, making it possible not only to learn the German law of obligations but also leading to its deeper understanding. In their set task, the authors have thus done a truly magnificent job.

Professor Dr Günter Hirsch
President of the Bundesgerichtshof
Karlsruhe,
29 July 2005

Preface to the Second Edition

This is a book primarily about the German law of contract as seen by a German lawyer with a deep understanding of English law, a common lawyer with a keen interest in European law in general and German law in particular, and a comparative lawyer who has spent over thirty-five years of his professional life trying to develop a satisfactory method of presenting 'foreign' law to 'national' lawyers. Our approach to our topic is thus both different and similar. Different, since our different optics initially revealed different things to each of us as we studied the rich and complex material; similar, since our aims are the same. Prime among these has been the desire to make the richness of German legal experience available to anglo-phone jurists and, additionally perhaps, make German lawyers reflect on their own law on the basis of the impression it creates to outsiders. For, just as importantly, we all share the view that an important aim of studying law comparatively is to enhance the knowledge of the foreign system that is being studied but also to deepen the understanding of the system which the reader regards as his own. Value judgments about German law (or, conversely, Anglo-American law) have thus been omitted as having no place in a work such as this except where we felt that the reader might be helped to rethink his own ideas and solutions by being presented with the (subjective) preferences of the authors.

Designing the structure of this book has not been easy. What one of us has described as 'the art of packaging' has been practised extensively throughout its long text. Nowhere however have we consciously distorted the German rules or betrayed their spirit solely in order to make the complex material easier to absorb by 'foreign' readers. On the contrary, the point made here, reappears many times in the text in the form of warnings as to how our presentation departs from the traditional, German pattern thus emphasising to the reader the difficulties which were all-too-obvious to us as authors. This work is thus not only a book about the law of contract of an old, highly rational, and politically important legal system—the German; it is also a practical exercise in comparative methodology in line with what one of us has been writing and teaching for nearly forty years now.

The book is the natural successor of a work first conceived with Professor Dr Werner Lorenz of the University of Munich and which appeared in 1997 under the imprint of the Clarendon Press of Oxford University. Since Professor Lorenz was prevented from becoming involved in the preparation of the second edition, his widely admired modesty led him to insist that his name did not appear even on the cover page as was originally the intention and desire of the other authors. But Professor Lorenz's influence on comparative law and German law is too important to go unnoticed so all of us, having in differing ways and degrees benefited from his works and advice, gladly pay tribute to the man and scholar. The Munich Institute, which once had the great Max Rheinstein as its librarian and was made world famous by Professor Lorenz's long stewardship, has been an intellectual home for two of the three authors of this work and both proudly declare their allegiance to it as well as their gratitude to its able current Librarian Herr Rolf Riss.

But the book, as even a cursory look at the table of contents will show, is not simply a second edition but an entirely re-cast and largely rewritten account of the German law of contract necessitated by many factors, not least of which was the 'grand reform of 2001.' In preparing this edition the 'senior' author had the benefit of working with younger colleagues whom, not that long ago, he fondly regarded as 'favourite pupils'. Years later, his admiration for their learning and balanced judgment is such that he invited both of them to become involved with two (different) books of his. In the case of the present work their contribution has been such that he feels it is only fair to state that he should no longer be treated as the 'senior' author of this book (though it is, in its essentials his brainchild), but simply the 'oldest' of the three! Thus, the immense and erudite work put into this edition by Dr Unberath as well as Mr Johnston's learned and equally wide-ranging contribution, are not only noted for the record but also gratefully acknowledged. Notwithstanding the above, however, responsibility for the present edition is fully shared by all of us. For we took advantage of the marvels of computer technology and in a literally 'colourful' way put our individual imprint on a text which took longer than expected to emerge as we grappled to assess as best we could the effects of the recent law reform in Germany and then compare German law with English (and to a lesser extent, American and French law). By the way, the recent vintage of the codal text should also explain the relative paucity of 'new' decisions (at the highest level). When this case law begins to appear in significant numbers, it may-well require a significant rewrite of this account. But that will be the task of a third edition!

This book, along with its companion volume *The German Law of Torts. A Comparative Treatise*, co-authored by Basil Markesinis and Hannes Unberath and now in its fourth edition, was originally intended primarily as a student textbook. This largely remains our primary audience. But, following the growth (in sophistication and detail) of the treatment provided by the first volume, the title of the book changed in the fourth edition from *A Comparative Introduction* to a *Comparative Treatise*. Since the same (fairly) detailed treatment can also be found in this work, the same designation has been deemed appropriate for its own sub-title. Yet there is a further reason why the word 'treatise' may not be entirely inappropriate in the sub-title. For, in accordance with the declared crusade of the first of the authors, fully espoused also by the co-authors of this volume, a secondary aim of this work is to provide inspiration and, where appropriate, a guide to Common law practitioners and judges. There are some signs of a trend beginning to develop 'gently' in England and, perhaps, more so in other common law jurisdictions, judges being willing to look at foreign law for inspiration, especially where their own law is not settled or the problem they are facing is truly international and calls, perhaps, for a common approach to solve it. How far this trend will gain momentum is anyone's guess, lawyers being notoriously conservative creatures reluctant to experiment with foreign ideas, particularly if they come from a system with a different language. Nonetheless, Europeanisation and globalisation, alluded to in the first (and other chapters) of this book, is having its effect, the law of contract of national states not escaping the impact of foreign pressures and calls for greater harmonisation if not unification.

A book as detailed as this has, evidently, taken advantage of the learning of others. In keeping with the style of *The German Law of Torts* its references being limited (and included in parentheses in the text) thus do not do full justice to the extent of our intellectual debts. This is partly rectified by the inclusion of reading lists giving suggestions for further study as well as a list of often used works which are given in an abbreviated form and are mentioned at the beginning of the book. In addition to this impersonal acknowledgment, however, we also wish to thank a number of colleagues. Their names are given simply to express our gratitude but not in order to saddle them with opinions or imperfections that still remain in this book. Thanks are thus due to (in alphabetical order): Mr John Armour, Mr Stefan Arnold, Dr Matthew Conaglen, Professor Dr Stephan Lorenz and Professor Dr Gerald Mäsch. We are also deeply grateful to Professor Mark Gergen, of the Law School of the University of Texas at Austin, and Sir Roy Goode, QC, FBA, Emeritus Professor of English Law at the University of Oxford for reading an early version of the manuscript and generously giving us the benefit of their comments upon our text.

A different but, in one sense, even greater debt is owed to Kurt Lipstein, Tony Weir and Raymond Youngs for translating the bulk of the decisions of the German courts reproduced in this work. Co-authors of this work all but in name, as well as key translators of the texts found in its companion volume, they have performed a complex task magnificently and rendered a huge service to German law as well comparative law in general. The art of translation calls for very special skills and sensitivities which they all possess to the full. But since these skills also differ greatly from one person to another, we have refrained from attempting to impose any uniformity. The reader can thus choose his preferred style but, above all, appreciate the enormity of the task here undertaken.

German jurists impress by their logical analysis and (often) pulverise intellectual opponents into submission by means of structured and lengthy arguments and endless footnotes which ooze erudition. But they do not always beguile the mind nor touch the soul in the way that French juristic writing can–witness, for instance, that of the late Jean Carbonnier, and before him Georges Ripert, and before him Jean Marie Portalis. Our task was thus not just to describe the German law of contract but also to try and strip the heaviness of German legal scholarship of the outer layers which can make it so off-putting to those who do not know how to handle it. If our approach has worked, and it is for our readers to judge whether we have succeeded or not, we will have repaid an intellectual debt we all feel we owe to German legal thought but also shown Anglo-American readers why such giants of the common law as Oliver Wendell Holmes, Roscoe Pound, Karl Llewellyn, Sir Frederick Pollock, William Maitland, and Sir William Anson held the German system and its Code in such high esteem.

We have endeavoured to state the law as it was at the end of the calendar year 2004 but it is in the nature of such comparative books to be less easy to maintain fully up to date than ordinary works on national law, especially in matters of nuance. The reader, especially the practitioner, is thus accordingly warned of the very real need for continuous and detailed research, especially if using this work for professional purposes.

Basil Markesinis

London,
the Spring Equinox 2005

Table of Contents

Common-Law Cases

French Cases

German cases

European Court of Justice

Table of German Abbreviations

AcP	Archiv für die civilistische Praxis
Art	Article
BAG	Bundesarbeitsgericht
BAGGS	Bundesarbeitsgericht Großer Senat
BB	Der Betriebs-Berater
Bd.	Band (volume)
BGB	Bürgerliches Gesetzbuch
BGBl.	Bundesgesetzblatt
BGH	Bundesgerichtshof
BGHZ	Entscheidungen des Bundesgerichtshofs in Zivilsachen
BVerfG	Bundesverfassungsgericht
BVerfGE	Entscheidungen des Bundesverfassungsgerichts
CISG	Convention on Contracts for the International Sale of Goods of 11 April 1980
EGBGB	Einführungsgesetz zum Bürgerlichen Gesetzbuch
FamRZ	Zeitschrift für das gesamte Familienrecht
GBO	Grundbuchordnung
GemSOGB	Gemeinsamer Senat der Obersten Gerichtshöfe des Bundes
GesBl.	Gesetzblatt
GG	Grundgesetz
GrZS	Großer Senat in Zivilsachen
GS	Großer Senat
GVbl.	Gesetz- und Verordnungsblatt
GVG	Gerichtsverfassungsgesetz
HGB	Handelsgesetzbuch
InsO	Insolvenzordnung
JR	Juristische Rundschau
Jura	Juristische Ausbildung
JuS	Juristische Schulung
JZ	Juristen-Zeitung
KG	Kammergericht

KSchG	Kündigungsschutzgesetz
LAG	Landesarbeitsgericht
LG	Landgericht
MDR	Monatsschrift für Deutsches Recht
NJW	Neue Juristische Wochenschrift
NJW-RR	Neue Juristische Wochenschrift – Rechtsprechungs-Report Zivilrecht
Nr.	Nummer (number)
NZA	Neue Zeitschrift für Arbeits- und Sozialrecht
OLG	Oberlandesgericht
OLGZ	Entscheidungen der Oberlandesgerichte in Zivilsachen
Palandt	Palandt, Bürgerliches Gesetzbuch
RabelsZ	Rabels Zeitschrift für ausländisches und internationales Privatrecht
RdA	Recht der Arbeit
Rn., Rdn.	Randnummer (paragraph)
RG	Reichsgericht
RGZ	Entscheidungen des Reichsgerichts in Zivilsachen
RIW	Recht der internationalen Wirtschaft
S.	Seite (page); Satz (sentence)
SGB	Sozialgesetzbuch
Staudinger	Staudinger, Kommentar zum Bürgerlichen Gesetzbuch
VersR	Versicherungsrecht
VO	Verordnung
VOB	Verdingungsordnung für Bauleistungen
Vorbem.	Vorbemerkung
WM	Wertpapier-Mitteilungen
ZEuP	Zeitschrift für Europäisches Privatrecht
ZEV	Zeitschrift für Erbrecht und Vermögensnachfolge
ZfA	Zeitschrift für Arbeitsrecht
ZGR	Zeitschrift für Unternehmens- und Gesellschaftsrecht
ZGS	Zeitschrift für das gesamte Schuldrecht
ZHR	Zeitschrift für das gesamte Handelsrecht
ZIP	Zeitschrift für Wirtschaftsrecht
ZMR	Zeitschrift für Miet- und Raumrecht
ZPO	Zivilprozeßordnung

1

Introduction

Select Bibliography. The best accounts of the topics discussed in this book can be found in the classic works of Werner Flume, *Allgemeiner Teil des Bürgerlichen Rechts*, vol 2 (3rd edn, 1979, reprinted 1992); Karl Larenz, *Allgemeiner Teil des deutschen Bürgerlichen Rechts* (7th edn, 1989; 9th edn, 2004 by Manfred Wolf) and *Lehrbuch des Schuldrechts*, vol I (14th edn, 1987), vol II/1 (13th edn, 1986), vol II/2 (13th edn, 1994 by Claus-Wilhelm Canaris), and Dieter Medicus, *Allgemeiner Teil* (8th edn, 2002); *Schuldrecht*, vol I (15th edn, 2004) and vol II (12th edn, 2004); *Bürgerliches Recht* (20th edn, 2004). The literature on German contract law is extensive; we mention only a few additional books here: Reinhard Bork, *Allgemeiner Teil* (2001); Dieter Leipold, *BGB Einführung und Allgemeiner Teil* (3rd edn, 2004); Dirk Looschelders, *Schuldrecht Allgemeiner Teil* (2nd edn, 2004); Jürgen Oechsler, *Schuldrecht Besonderer Teil–Vertragsrecht* (2003); Hartmut Oetker and Felix Maultzsch, *Vertragliche Schuldverhältnisse* (2nd edn, 2004); Peter Schlechtriem, *Schuldrecht*, vol 1 (5th edn, 2003), vol 2 (6th edn, 2003). Of the smaller books one should perhaps mention Hans Brox's *Allgemeiner Teil des Bürgerlichen Gesetzbuchs* (28th edn, 2004) and Helmut Köhler's *Allgemeiner Teil des BGB* (28th edn, 2004), since both are short, clear, and will be more accessible to the foreign student. On the changes brought about by the 2001 reform of the German law of obligations, see the references given in chapter 9. We must also mention the commentary literature, which proceeds by annotating each provision of the BGB individually. To avoid repetition we indicate here (again making a selection) that the references are to the most comprehensive *Staudingers Kommentar* in its 13th edn (1993 *et seq*), the mid-sized *Münchener Kommentar* in its 4th edn, vol 1 (2001); vol 2a (2003); vol 3 (2004), and the compact *Palandt* in the 63rd edn (2004). Finally, in relation to English contract law, the reader is referred in particular to Sir Guenter Treitel's treatise, *The Law of Contract* (11th edn, 2003) and Ewan McKendrick's textbook, *Contract Law* (2003) which also contains cases and materials. Note also that in Markesinis and Unberath, *The German Law of Torts* (4th edn, 2002) we discuss a number of topics of general importance such as the organisation of the courts in civil matters, the traditional style of judgments of the *Bundesgerichtshof*, and the wider impact of the Constitution especially in the fields of family and tort law: see, especially, pp 1–13, 28–39. Of the material that exists in English one further notes: Hugh Beale, Arthur Hartkamp, Hein Kötz and Denis Tallon, *Contract Law– Ius Commune Casebooks for the Common Law of Europe* (2002); EJ Cohn, *Manual of German Law*, vol 2 (2nd edn, 1968); Werner Ebke and Matthew Finkin (eds), *Introduction to German Law* (1996); Foster, *German Legal System and Laws* (3rd edn, 2002); P Marsh, *Comparative Contract Law: England, France, Germany* (1994); Mathias Reimann and Joachim Zekoll (eds), Introduction to German Law (2nd edn, 2005); Rüster (gen ed), *Doing Business in Germany*, loose-leaf (1999); Gerhard Robbers, *An Introduction to German Law* (1998); Raymond Youngs, *Source book on German Law* (1994)—a bilingual collection of important statutes and decisions but rather poorer on contracts. Finally, of course, there is Konrad Zweigert and Hein Kötz, *An Introduction to Comparative Law* (3rd edn, 1998 translated by Tony Weir), arguably the best textbook on the subject both from its historical and dogmatic perspectives; and Hein Kötz and Axel Flessner, *European Contract Law*, vol 1 (trans Tony Weir) (1998).

1. PRELIMINARY OBSERVATIONS

In the memorable words of Tony Weir contract law is 'productive' (unlike tort law which is 'protective'). The whole institution of contract is there to increase wealth and its liberal (in the sense of classical contract law) underpinnings must not be forgotten even in a book such as this which primarily wishes to describe German law for the benefit of common lawyers by placing it in comparative juxtaposition with (mainly) the English and American ideas and solutions. Yet, starting with this observation, one is inevitably led to add six additional statements or qualifications which the reader may do well to bear in mind when reading the account of detailed rules that follow in the entire book.

Thus, first (and obviously) both in the German and the common law, the basic principle is the same since both legal families operate in what one often calls the free market system. Yet nuances (one could call them shades of capitalism and consumerism) do exist as to how far down the line one must take the free market ideas and to what extent the courts can 'intervene' and redress the balance in favour of the weaker party. Thus, German law (like French law) does not conceal a certain preference for the weaker party (invariably but not always necessarily, the consumer), just as it does not allow complete freedom to the parties to withdraw with impunity from negotiations which have not yet matured into a contract, the notions of fairness or justice here trumping that of freedom. Of course here, as in so many other cases, one must be quick to avoid lumping American law with English (private) law, since the latter has in recent times and largely under the influence of European Directives, come closer to German law than the former can ever claim to be. But the existence of differing ideological beliefs behind technical rules must nonetheless be noted straight away and always be borne in mind. To put it differently, many technical rules of the law of contract disguise (often only thinly) important political or economic choices.

Secondly, it follows from the above that German law, like most continental European legal systems, often veers towards an 'artificially' constructed equality between the parties, contrary to nature's (and the market's) preference for inequality. The result is an increased erosion of the notion of contractual freedom, especially when it comes to clauses which seek to exclude or even just limit the liability of one party. In some cases, this modern trend to assist the weaker party has also resulted in challenging traditional contractual orthodoxy: for instance, the right of consumers in certain types of contract to 'back out' of engagements already made without the need to justify this change of mind let alone for the co-contractor to agree to such an alteration. Legal orthodoxy has in these and many such cases yielded to contemporary 'socio/political' realities, and it is probably better to accept these rules on such wider socio-economic grounds rather than to try to explain them by attempting to trim or adjust classical contractual thinking. This is not to deny, however, that purists have tried to do the latter as well.

Thirdly, it could be argued that in Germany this move towards a pro-consumer/weak party position may have received some support from the so-called *Sozialstaatsprinzip*, a constitutional principle mentioned in Article 20(1) of the Constitution (Basic Law of 1949—*Grundgesetz*). This places an obligation (*Gestaltungsauftrag*) first and foremost on the legislator to shape the country's social order. The notion thus creates a (limited) legal counterbalance to positions of social and economic power. In this sense it is a new (and for some controversial) feature in Germany's constitutional history. Linking the principle to developments of a more typical private law nature is debatable—indeed the majority of private lawyers have refused to find in it the explanation for court activism let alone an underlying justification for its many incidents. Yet as stated we have not set out to write a purely descriptive book, but to also occasionally fly some academic kites, so we feel obliged to draw the attention of Anglo-American readers to the existence of this constitutional principle, not least since it is not one found in either the Anglo-American or French constitutions. A more detailed account can be found below in section 6 on the 'constitutionalisation' of private law.

It suffices here to point out that the idea of the Constitutional Court that (alleged) 'abuses of economic power' should be counterbalanced with the help of the general clauses of the German Civil Code (*Bürgerliches Gesetzbuch*, henceforth BGB in short): § 138 (public policy); § 242 (good faith), is evidently influenced by the *Sozialstaatsprinzip*—though, once again, we must stress that the dominant opinion in Germany has not gone as far as seeing in this principle the connecting link or common foundation of court activism. Yet, as we shall see in detail in chapter 5 and in section 6, p 38, contracts which (a) place an unusually heavy burden on one of the parties involved in the transaction, and (b) are the result of a 'structurally unbalanced distribution of bargaining power' are thus not acceptable under § 138 BGB. (BVerfGE NJW 1994, 36, case no 81 the seminal *Bürge*-decision, and BGH NJW 2002, 2228, case no 82.) This does not mean, as should be clear at the outset, that the legal order will or should intervene in all contractual relationships which feature some kind of inequality in the parties' respective ability to influence the negotiations; intervention for the sake of socially 'just' or 'fair' results must be balanced with legal certainty (*Rechtssicherheit*), a value in its own right. But if the contract in question falls within a category of cases typically characterised by a weakness of one party, and if this party is excessively burdened by the 'freely' negotiated result, the Constitutional Courts appear to be saying that the private legal order is called upon to intervene and to correct the outcome. The court has justified this by Article 2(1) Basic Law (protection of private autonomy), and crucially by reference to the *Sozialstaatsprinzip* though others (especially private lawyers) might choose to attribute less or no force to the principle under consideration (see for a view strongly opposing this approach of the court, eg, Adomeit NJW 1994, 2467; see also p 256 for an alternative, non-constitutional explanation of that case).

Fourthly, the move away from what one could call the nineteenth century 'liberal contractual model' has come about through a mixture of statutory intervention and judicial creativity. This is true as much of English law as it is of German law (though American law has on the whole been more reluctant to go down that path and has relied more on the courts to bring about reform). In Europe, and we now include (as one must nowadays) the UK in this term, this trend has in recent times received further impetus as a result of Community legislation. For comparative lawyers this trend may conceal consequences which national lawyers may not be inclined to notice adequately.

The following, in particular, deserve mention. One notes a trend to weaken (if not destroy) the long-hallowed distinction between English law (as being a system essentially judge-made) and continental European law (including German law) as being a system largely found in statutes, especially the Civil Code. The reader of chapters 3 and 5 will be left in no doubt about the veracity of this statement. Another consequence may be a move away from the traditional model of contract law essentially being a set of rules of a *ius dispositivum* nature and thus always subject to party agreement. We return to this point and to the limits on freedom of contract at the end of this chapter. Finally, a no less significant consequence stemming from these developments is the fragmentation of the law of contract into a law of contracts: namely, a law of business contracts, consumer contracts, national contracts, international contracts, special (and highly regulated) contracts such as employment contracts and the like. Suffice it to say, all these types of contracts are subject to different rules since they are imbued with a different socio-economic spirit. The fragmentation of modern contract law must thus not be forgotten in the account that follows, the reader always enquiring whether the rules presented in this book are appropriate to all types of contract.

The above changes have brought English law closer to the German and contemporary European protectionist and interventionist model. By so doing, it has moved contemporary English contract law closer to a variety of European notions of consensus and compromise than arguably were commonly found in the traditional or classical common law. Consequently, not everyone is happy with this 'Europeanisation' of English law. (See for instance Weir, 'All or Nothing' (2004) 78 *Tul L Rev* 511 and earlier, Professor (now Judge) Beatson's Cambridge inaugural lecture where he even asked the question whether the common law had any future; published 1997 by CUP.) Yet this phenomenon may be more interesting for the fact that it leaves wider legal circles unconcerned or plain disinterested, than for the fact that it ignores this system's considerable pedigree. For in reality, the common law has not traditionally maintained the degree of isolation which the critics of modern trends condemn having repeatedly in its past been drawn into the gravitational orbit of French (first) and German (later) legal theorising and then, having borrowed from these systems, pretended a complete originality of structure. (On this see, inter alia, the masterly analysis of Professor James Gordley, *The Foundations of Private Law: Property, Tort, Contract, Unjust Enrichment*, Part IV (2006) and the older and seminal article by Professor Brian Simpson, 'Innovation in Nineteenth Century Contract Law' (1975) 91 *LQR* 247.) Moreover, legal rules, indeed legal systems as a whole, cannot resist the pressures exerted upon them by their wider and ever-changing socio-economic environment. And this, at the turn of the twenty-first century, is very different from that which prevailed when the classical law of contract crystallised around the middle of the nineteenth century. Romantics may regret this metamorphosis but pragmatists need not fear it. For English lawyers, and indeed English politicians, need not fear losing the predominance that 'Anglo-Saxon' law has acquired in commercial matters for so long as the English language remains the *lingua franca* of commerce and this is largely controlled by 'Anglo-Saxon' financial institutions and multinational legal firms.

The above, wider comments may not convince the doubters—though here we are not trying to convince. But they may help make our readers think more broadly as they move through a book essentially devoted to explaining contemporary German law. However, they lead to our fifth broad statement namely, that contract law is not static.

To put it differently, contract rules adapt constantly to the changing backdrop of society and this backdrop is, not only consumerist in spirit, but increasingly also international in nature. This means that those who make law (in civil law systems mainly legislators but, in practice, courts as well), as well as those who teach it, are nowadays, in performing their assigned tasks, increasingly likely to be forced to look 'sideways' at what is happening elsewhere rather than backwards, ie at what old sources of law had to say about a problem. This means that growing awareness of what is happening in other legal systems as well as on the transnational 'institutional' level (European Union, international conventions, private projects of harmonisation of contract or commercial law etc) is bound to influence the future development of our subject. Though the effect this may have on national curriculum is still a matter of academic speculation (see for instance Markesinis, *Comparative Law in the Courtroom and the Classroom* (2004)), the real world of practice, upon which contract rules depend heavily, is unlikely to miss the significance of this shift. And it is this world that is giving English law its contemporary significance.

Finally, the comparison of German with English and American law calls for a special effort to be made in the presentation of the 'foreign' material. Attachment to the national method of presentation and to national concepts and terminology are likely to be so alien to lawyers from other systems that it may lead to a rapid decrease in interest in the foreign system presented to national lawyers. Such a discouragement will benefit no one (ie neither the importing or exporting system); it will only encourage the kind of insular self-sufficiency that prevailed briefly about a century ago after each European system adopted its own national codes. We believe our times call for a more open and internationalist approach and that this in turn, requires an ability to 'package' foreign law in a way that makes it attractive and user friendly to lawyers from other systems. That such an approach conceals dangers is beyond doubt (though some colleagues have made a career in proclaiming them over and over again). Here suffice it to say that all three of us have taken advantage of our different experiences in backgrounds to minimise these dangers and make a beginning at presenting to common lawyers one of the most theoretical, difficult and developed parts of German private law.

One cannot help but note the richness of contractual theorising found in German legal literature. Though English contract writing has its fair share of theorising minds—Atiyah, Burrows and Birks immediately spring to mind—it has not rivalled the kinds of writings that have emanated from the Americas in the last fifty years from the pens of such thought-provoking writers as Jules Coleman, Charles Fried, Leon Fuller, Grant Gillmore, James Gordley, AT Kronman, Stephen Smith, or Michael Trebilcok. It need hardly be stressed that the above are not meant to be taken as implying a comparative qualitative assessment of the work of learned colleagues. But it does suggest that whereas the common law writings look at the contract problems from an economic, philosophical or multidisciplinary perspective and often try to develop the author's own 'theory of contract,' the German writings are as dogmatic in content as they are singularly focused on black letter law. A different way of presenting this difference of 'style' would be to say that much German effort still goes into the writing of commentaries, treatises, and large textbooks whereas this genre of legal writing has almost disappeared in America (with the sole exception of Professor Alan Farnsworth's multi-volume treatise on contract law).

2. THE GENESIS OF THE CODE

The literature on German legal history is vast. Heinrich Mitteis's *Deutsche Rechtsgeschichte* (18th edn, 1949 (with Heinz Lieberich) 1988) and *Deutsches Privatrecht* (10th edn, 1950, again with Lieberich, 1988), are classics of a sort, though they approach their subject in purely Germanic terms. On the other hand, Paul Koschaker's *Europa und das römische Recht* (2nd edn, 1947; 1966) and Franz Wieacker's *Privatrechtsgeschichte der Neuzeit* (2nd edn, 1952; 1967, translated by Tony Weir 1996), place German legal history firmly within the wider context of the development of modern European culture. This is also emphasised by Coing, inter alia, in his 'Das Recht als Element der europäischen Kultur' HZ 238, 1984, 1. For a more recent and comprehensive review of the Roman sources of modern law, see Reinhard Zimmermann, *The Law of Obligations* (1990). Further references are given in *The German Law of Torts*, at p 24. For contemporary Anglo-American comments on the BGB, see: Maitland, 'The Making of the German Civil Code' (1906) 10 *The Independent Review* 211; E Freund, 'The New German Civil Code' 13 *Harvard LR*. 627 (1899–1900); Schuster, 'The German Civil Code' (1896) 12 *LQR*. 17 (see also his *Principles of German Civil Law* (1907)).

(a) The Tortured Path to Unity

When the German Civil Code, *Bürgerliches Gesetzbuch* (BGB) came into force on 1 January 1900 it not only coincided with the beginning of a new century, but marked the end of the long process of the unification of the German state. Legal historians would probably treat the enactment in 1495 of the *Reichskammergerichtsordnung*—the statute which regulated the establishment and organisation of the Imperial Court—as the first step towards this process. The fact that this enactment chronologically also more or less coincides with the consolidation of Habsburg hegemony, may also speak in its favour. But if indeed it really is the starting point of the unification process, it is a tenuous one at best. For the superiority of this court among the multiple courts that existed in the lands populated by Germanic people was nominal rather than real, since the emperor's own effective power over his empire was feeble. And the 'unity' of the Reich in those days was, in cultural terms, very different from the one that came three and a half centuries later; for at the close of the Middle Ages it was a union centred in the Catholic south (Austria) and not, as was later to be the case, one dominated by the Protestant north (Prussia). Still, despite these and other reservations, the enactment had a symbolic value if for no other reason than that it gave the court a fixed abode (Frankfurt) and marked the official recognition of judges trained in Roman law. In the years to come, this 'innovation' became the fashion, even in local courts. This, along with a trend-setting statute—*The Carolina* (largely influenced by the work of that remarkable man Baron von Schwartzenberg)—which was enacted in 1532, put the coping-stone on the powers of the old, lay German judges (the *Schöffen*) and marked the beginning of the Reception of Roman law. In the sixteenth and seventeenth centuries Roman law thus became known as the common law (*gemeines Recht*) of the German nation; and on the eve of the nineteenth century codification, it was still the main legal system in much of the geographic area which in post-Second World War times was known as Western Germany: ie roughly Bavaria, Hannover, Hessen, Holstein and Württemberg.

The phenomenon of the Reception has captivated legal historians, for in Germany (more so than in France) it was so massive and wholehearted that it succeeded in marginalising considerable Germanic achievements in the legal field. These achievements were all the more remarkable since they were accomplished in an otherwise fragmented and war-torn country which had suffered successive disasters (physical and man-made) since the demise of the Hohenstaufen rule in the early part of the thirteenth century.

Thus the (first) German Reich remained fragmented, despite the claim of its emperors and its people to represent the natural heirs to the Roman Empire (*Heiliges Römisches Reich Deutscher Nation*); and this fragmentation (coupled with constant wars on both its eastern and western fronts) explain both the emperor's vain attempts in the sixteenth century to repress the spread of the Reformation in the northern and eastern provinces of his empire as well as the ease with which Roman law came to be seen as the natural as well as the neutral legal system that could fill the political vacuum of the time. This political chaos, reinforced by religious wars which reached new peaks in the seventeenth century (giving Europe its first flavour of a 'world war'), ensured that legal disunity remained a feature of German political as well as legal history until the formal demise of the First Reich in 1806 at the hands of Napoleon. For by this time, as our map clearly shows, even Roman law had lost some ground; the northern and eastern provinces had fallen under the domination of the Prussian land law of 1794 (*Allgemeines Landrecht für die preußischen Staaten*)—a monstrously long enactment which covered both public and private law and represented the closest Germany ever came towards falling under the spell of the School of Natural Law. At the same time, the Rhine countries had moved legally closer to the fashionable French Civil Code. During this period, Bavaria continued to assert its legal and cultural independence by being governed by its own *Codex Maximilianus Bavaricus Civilis* of 1756, which had codified the Roman-based law of the previous century but also displayed visible signs of the legislator's belief in the tenets of the era of Enlightenment. Indeed, Bavaria has jealously guarded its 'separateness' ever since, constantly playing in Germany the kind of role that Texas enjoys in the United States, and even threatening political cessation during the early life of the Second Reich (1871), the creation of which its indebted king Ludwig had supported in exchange for the Prussian bankers servicing his debts. Finally, the Habsburg territories of Austria and Bohemia were governed by the *Allgemeine Bürgerliche Gesetzbuch* of 1811.

The nineteenth century thus became the true turning point in the process of (or progress towards) German unity. Yet the century began inauspiciously insofar as the Germany which emerged from the Napoleonic era had now opted for the form of a Confederation (*Deutscher Bund* not a *Reich*), and a loose one at that. These then were highly complex political times, where northerners were increasingly trying to dominate suspicious southerners, and politicians, men of letters, and dreamers of all kinds, urged their audiences to think of 'Germany above all'—a call that was later to acquire sinister overtones—but seeing the process that would lead to this result in very different terms. (That, at least, is what the first (and subsequently maligned) verse of Hoffman von Fallersleben's poem '*Das Lied der Deutschen*' suggests. But it is the French-inspired third verse which has survived (since 1952) as Germany's national anthem. The music, of course, was composed by Haydn for the Austrian Emperor Franz Josef on 12 February 1797, although it is better known as the theme in the second movement of the Streichquartett in C-major, Opus 76.3.)

It is in this context that the next legal battle was destined to be fought. For barely had the post-Napoleonic settlement been agreed upon than Thibaut and Savigny began their great intellectual duel. Thibaut was to fire the first shot with his pamphlet entitled *Über die Notwendigkeit eines allgemeinen bürgerlichen Rechts für Deutschland* (On the Necessity of a General Civil Code for Germany), in which he proposed that Germany should follow France's example and adopt a unifying Civil Code. It provoked Savigny's thunder in the equally forcefully expressed work *Vom Beruf unserer Zeit für Gesetzgebung und Rechtswissenschaft* (On the Vocation of our Age for Legislation and Legal Science). That Savigny's claim that the time was not ripe for a unifying code was bound to win the day seems, at any rate with hindsight, inevitable. But it is still something of a paradox that his search for the roots of German legal culture was to take him back to Roman law while ignoring the indigenous legal products. This does fit in with the fact that Roman law, as we have seen, had been adopted in the bulk of Germany in the sixteenth and seventeenth centuries. Yet this moderates only slightly the unusual direction of this cultural trend, for Savigny and his followers were not interested in the Roman law as it had been applied in Germany during the sixteenth and seventeenth centuries, but turned their attention 'back to the original sources' (*Zurück zu den Quellen*). A likelier explanation must be found in the fact that this movement was really part of the wider movement that during the nineteenth century pushed much of Germany (and the rest of Europe) to re-adopt the aesthetic ideas and ideals of classicism. But this move also had the unfortunate consequence of discarding some significant advances made on classical Roman law by the *opinio communis doctorum* and the *usus fori* (the practices of the high(er) courts of France, Germany, Italy and Spain, which were often quoted outside their respective geographical borders) during the sixteenth and seventeenth centuries. Additionally, it also had the side effect of marginalising the work which the Germanists—such as Eichhorn, Beseler, the Grimm brothers, and Otto von Gierke—were doing in order to show how important the purely Germanic elements were in the development of the cultural identity of the new country.

Yet, surprising or not, what matters is the effect that this school had on German legal science and, in some instances, the final contents of the Code. Three consequences in particular must be mentioned, if only briefly, from the very outset since they affected all of the material discussed in this book.

First, as already stated, the historical school undoubtedly stimulated an extensive study of ancient texts and shaped the minds of the legal scholars—the Pandectists—who, in one form or another dominated German legal thought throughout the nineteenth century and left their imprint on subsequent generations of lawyers. This intellectual reorientation left a strong mark on the content of the Code as a whole, and the law of contract in particular, since solutions were often adopted on the basis that they had been espoused (or, which was worse, were thought to have been espoused) nearly two thousand years earlier by Roman law.

Examples of this phenomenon abound in the Code and they are exceptionally numerous in the law of contract. We see this clearly in the approach taken towards the problem of irregularities of performance where the Code, following Mommsen's teachings ('Die Unmöglichkeit der Leistung in ihrem Einfluss auf obligatorische Verhältnisse' I, *Beiträge zum Obligationenrecht*, 1853) chose to regulate two types of such irregularity—delay (*Verzug*) and impossibility (*Unmöglichkeit*, understood in a narrow, physical sense)—but deliberately excluded what is, arguably, the most common and difficult type of 'breach', ie bad performance. (For further details see chapters 9 and 10, below.) Likewise, a misunderstanding of Roman texts, coupled with the desire (which back-fired) to protect small industrial concerns at a time of nascent industrialisation, led the draftsmen of the Code to adopt the unfortunate rule contained in § 831 BGB which makes employers liable only for their own faults (in selecting and/or supervising their employees) but not for the faults committed by these employees in the course of their employment.

There were other areas of the law where adherence to Roman doctrine gave rise to difficulties. Two more instances will be given to illustrate how oppressive the influence of the past could be on the present.

The first example comes from the Roman tendency to see even bilateral contracts as consisting of unilateral obligations which were merely brought together by occasional rules which underlined their interdependence. This gave rise to difficulties where, for instance, damages had to be quantified as a result of the purchaser's inability or refusal to pay the purchase price. In such cases, was the vendor obliged to perform his obligation to the full and then proceed against the purchaser (the so-called *Austauschtheorie*)? Alternatively, should the Roman way of looking at contractual obligations be jettisoned in favour of an approach which looked at the entire contractual transaction? This second approach, with some modifications eventually (but not without much intellectual agonising) came to be adopted by the Code and the courts (see, for instance, RGZ 50,255; BGHZ 20, 338, 343). This meant that the contract should be seen as a whole and the innocent party would be absolved from performing his obligation and instead allowed to claim only the difference between the situation that had resulted from the breach and the situation as it would have been had the contract been performed in the envisaged way (*Differenztheorie*).

Another, and for present purposes final example, relevant both to contract and to tort, can be found in the Pandectist understanding of a text from Gaius' Institutes (IV, 48) which led them to the conclusion that Roman law was unwilling to protect personal and non-material interests through the law of obligations—a view which led to the adoption of the unfortunate provision found in § 253 BGB. This led to substantial difficulties in awarding damages for violation of personality rights, which received wider recognition in the 1950s, while also impeding the award of damages for pain and suffering whenever the cause of action was contractual rather than delictual. It took more than a century to correct this by making damages for pain and suffering also available in contract claims: see now subsection two of § 253. (For further details in English see, *The German Law of Torts*, pp 44 *et seq*.)

Secondly, the return to the original Roman sources meant that any of the material that had not attracted the attention of the Roman lawyers, but had been developed by the learned doctors of the *Ius Commune*, was ignored by the nineteenth century Pandectists and left outside the Code. Only exceptionally did institutions borrowed from the commercial law manage to penetrate the Civil Code, arguably the most notable instance being the remedy of rescission. (For a fuller account see Leser, *Der Rücktritt vom Vertrag* (1975), 10 *et seq* and for further details below, chapter 9.) This meant that important parts of commercial law, such as bills of exchange, insurance contracts, the regulations of corporations, patents and copyrights (as well as strict liability in the area of tort law) were very largely ignored by the new civil Code as was, essentially, the regulation of labour relations. All these matters the *Pandektenwissenschaft* considered almost beneath its dignity and left to the representatives of the *Deutsches Privatrecht* to deal with, often with the result that they had to be regulated by separate enactments and outside the framework of the BGB. This tendency was strongly condemned by Otto von Gierke, probably the harshest critic of the new Code, and a crucial extract from his critique deserves to be quoted in full since it impinges upon the kind of education young lawyers received for a long time. In his *Die soziale Aufgabe des Privatrechts* (1889), pp 16–18, he wrote:

> [I]t is a fatal error an error committed by the draft of the German Civil Code—to think the social work can be left to special legislation so that the general private law can be shaped, without regard to the task that has thus been shifted, in a purely individualistic manner. There thus exist two systems ruled by completely different spirits: a system of the general civil law that contains the 'pure' private law, and a mass of special laws in which a private law, tarnished by and blended with public law, governs. On the one side a living, popular, socially coloured law full of inner stimulus, on the other an abstract mould, romanistic, individualistic, ossified in dead dogmatics. The real and true private law can now develop in all its logical splendour oblivious of the heretical special laws . . . *But the general law is the native soil out of which the special laws also grow. By contact with the general law our youth learn legal thinking. The judges take their nourishment from it. What a fatal abyss opens before us! What a schism between the spirit of the normal administration of justice and the administrative jurisdiction that is being extended further and further! What a . . . danger of stagnation and degeneration of jurisprudence. . . .*

The last few lines from this marvellous statement have been italicised since the criticisms that they contain may still be valid (although see the observations made in relation to modern restraints on freedom of contract, below); it may even be relevant to the way that common lawyers (both in England and the United States) teach their law of contract, often ignoring commercial, labour or social accretions to their subject, leaving them to be discussed by other colleagues in more specialised courses offered in later years of study but, invariably, only taken by a few students.

Thirdly, as will be explained more fully in the next section, this movement introduced a new methodological approach to law, spending untold effort in schematising, ordering, and integrating the concepts of Roman law and building a 'system'. As Zweigert and Kötz have put it (*An Introduction to Comparative Law*, p 140):

> Their method of treatment was once again marked by that exaggerated dogmatism which we noted in the period of the law of Reason, [ie seventeenth and eighteenth century] save that it was directed to rules of Roman law rather than particular postulates supposedly grounded in reason.

The first book of the Code, which, in its entirety, took twenty years to produce, exemplifies these ideas and their intellectual fruits. This influenced the style of the enactment as much as the style of legal reasoning and of legal education that resulted from it.

Finally, as already hinted, many of the developments and achievements of the period of the *Ius Commune* were generally discarded by the Pandectists and, in some cases, excluded by the Code. For instance, the synthesis of the Roman casuistry in the area of torts, which had led to the kind of wider formulations of tort liability found in the codes of France and the Low Countries, was abandoned in favour of a more detailed (and in some cases ludicrously narrow) regulation of the subject (see, for instance, §§ 824 and 825 BGB).

The same was true of the transformation of the Roman *actio de in rem verso* into a general action to recover losses flowing from the unjust enrichment of another person, which was one of the most interesting achievements of the Natural School of law (though the BGB eventually reached a similar breadth by adopting Savigny's approach (*System des heutigen römischen Rechts*, vol 5, ch VIII, p 503 *et seq*, and 525) of 'merging' the Roman law *condictiones* into general approach now found in para 812 BGB). It must however also be noted that other achievements of the period of *Ius Commune*, such as the gradual development of the notion of contracts in favour of third parties, the liberalisation of the law of assignment and the development of the law of agency (or, more accurately, representation: see, p 109, chapter 2), were retained by the new school. We shall discuss these points in different parts of this book but, before we do so, we must complete our sketch of the unification process by making two concluding remarks.

First, one must note that the political union, achieved as a result of the wars—first against Austria (which effectively ensured the triumph of the idea of the 'smaller Germany', ie one without the Austrian Empire within its bounds) and then against France—followed and did not precede a considerable degree of economic union which took shape from the 1830s onwards. In the beginning this too took the confrontational form of a customs union of the northern states competing with a customs union of southern states. In the end however the north triumphed in the financial arena as it had in the political one, the Austrians being almost constantly outfoxed in their manoeuvres by Bismarck.

Secondly, legal unification did not, in all respects, have to wait for political union, though it undoubtedly received a great impetus from it. Thus, the 'Law of Negotiable Instruments' (*Wechselordnung*) was unified in 1848; and in 1861 the much more important 'Commercial Code' (*Allgemeines Handelsgesetzbuch*) was agreed upon—although, like the 1848 enactment, it was left to the members of the Confederation to turn it into municipal law. A year later an attempt was even made to draft a Civil Code—the so-called *Dresdner Entwurf*—but this came to nothing. But after the establishment of the Second Reich, Imperial statutes (ie statutes applying to the whole of the Empire) were issued thick and fast by the legislature. Thus within a short period of time, important statutes imposing strict liability for carriage by rail (*Reichshaftpflichtgesetz* of 1871), the 'Law Regulating the Organisation of the Imperial Courts' (*Gerichtsverfassungsgesetz*), the law on 'Insolvency' (*Konkursordnung*) and the law on 'Civil Procedure' (*Zivilprozessordnung*) came into existence. The last to receive the Royal Assent (in 1896) and come into force on 1 January 1900 was the Civil Code (*Bürgerliches Gesetzbuch*).

The legal unification was at last complete; and as we shall note below, the document that completed this process has left a deep mark on the kind of legal education that young Germans receive to this day. On this point, Otto von Gierke's views have proved particularly prescient.

(b) The Triumph of the Learned Man

The expression belongs to the late Jack Dawson, one of the greatest comparative lawyers of our times; he used it in his Cooley Lectures (*The Oracles of the Law* (1955)) to describe the growing influence which German academics acquired in the sixteenth and seventeenth centuries in the making and not just the teaching of the law. This accounted for the reception of Roman law, already alluded to above; but it accounted for much more besides.

First, besides importing Roman law into the country, it progressively gave universities a unique role in German legal culture. For not only did they influence the development of the law, but for a while they actually shaped it by literally drafting the opinions of the courts through the machinery of dispatching of the record (*Aktenversendung*). Although this usurpation of judicial power did not prevail in quite the whole of the Empire and, in any event, subsided with the passage of time, it left a strong tradition of a dialogue which German judges to this day conduct with their academic brethren and which is clearly evidenced in their judgments, which are replete with academic citations.

A second, and related, point is that this environment encouraged the appearance in Germany of jurists with philosophical and jurisprudential leanings, something which stands in stark contrast both to the kind of pragmatic lawyers to which Napoleon was happy and, indeed, eager to entrust the future of legal education, and indeed to the English legal tradition until well into the nineteenth century. The result was the flowering in Germany of jurisprudential theories which dominated the nineteenth century and spilled over well into the twentieth. Three of these schools of thought influenced German law, its teaching and interpretation to such a great extent that they must be mentioned here. (The fourth, the so-called 'Free School' of thought, born as a reaction to the first school, had less effect on practising lawyers so it will be omitted from this brief account.)

The so-called school of the *Begriffsjurisprudenz* (the jurisprudence of notions or concepts) followed the Historical School from about the 1850s onwards and included among its proponents such eminent Pandectists as Puchta and Ihering. Its followers believed that each legal concept should be rigorously analysed and then 'fitted' into the framework of a particular legal institution (*Rechtsinstitut*) such as marriage, family, real property, inheritance and the like. All institutions, in turn formed part of the 'legal system'. The ultimate purpose was to create a complete and closed system of legal concepts that would then be capable of embracing all situations of life and provide them, almost mechanically, with a legal solution. In this world, academics were assigned pride of place since they were the system-builders. Practising lawyers—including judges—would merely have to locate the relevant facts under the appropriate concept and thus find the answer to the questions put to them. This way of thinking, so different from that found in common law systems, had a profound effect upon the style of the Code, the interpretation of legal rules, the filling of legal gaps and the development of a legal science. As we shall stress below, and note again and again in this book, this approach to law also still dictates certain thinking patterns of German lawyers.

It was not much before the enactment of the Code, however, that the excesses of this school led many jurists to feel that, in the words of Oliver Wendell Holmes, the life of the law is not merely logic but experience. Certainly, the legal judgment as a mere exercise in deductive logic taking place within a closed system soon came seriously to be questioned and a greater desire to search for the policy reasons behind judicial decisions started to emerge. So, the *Interessenjurisprudenz* emerged as a sensible reaction to this first school, arguing that life did not exist for the sake of concepts but, on the contrary, that the concepts were there to serve life's needs. This school scored a triumph of sorts when it converted Ihering to its cause, who then argued its tenets eloquently in his famous book *Der Zweck im Recht* (The Purpose in the Law) which first appeared in 1877. Philipp Heck, another of this school's later proponents, put its views clearly when he argued (in *Das Problem der Rechtsgewinnung* (1912), *Gesetzesauslegung und Interessenjurisprudenz* (1914) and in what was, arguably, his most famous work, *Begriffsbildung und Interessenjurisprudenz* (1932)) that behind all legal regulations lie certain values which lawgivers wish to assert, promote or balance against one another. It was thus wrong to pretend that the judge's role was merely an expert exercise in deductive logic. The purpose of this school thus became to discover these values and to encourage lawyers not to hide behind concepts (see RG 3.2.1914, in RGZ 84,125 where the new school scored a clear victory over the old). Legal reasoning, including judicial reasoning, was thereby considerably liberated from the strictures of the first school of thought, even though this had, by this stage, left its indelible marks on German legal culture and, just as importantly, on the image it has with foreign lawyers.

This move towards a search for values continued and even strengthened after the collapse of the Nazi regime and the end of the Second World War and led to the newest variant of the school—the jurisprudence of values or the *Wertungsjurisprudenz*. In turn, this led to a search for higher and even more abstractly expressed values in the Constitution and the entire legal order which were then 'concretised' in the realms of private law—such as contract, labour, family, and tort law—and given the form of legal rules. The creation of the so-called general right of personality (*allgemeines Persönlichkeitsrecht*) (discussed in great detail in *The German Law of Torts*, pp 74–9, 392–505), exemplifies this process. Indeed, the Constitutional Court expressly adopted this approach when it sanctioned the creation of the new 'protected interest' (under § 823 I BGB) when it said:

> Occasionally, the law can be found outside the positive legal rules erected by the state; this is law which emanates from the entire constitutional order and which has as its purpose the 'correction' of written law. It is for the judge to 'discover' this law and through his opinions give it concrete effect. The Constitution does not restrict judges to apply statutes in their literary sense when deciding cases put before them. Such an approach assumes a basic completeness of statutory rules which is not attainable in practice . . . The insight of the judge may bring to light certain values of society . . . which are implicitly accepted by the constitutional order but which have received an insufficient expression in statutory texts. The judge's decision can help realize such ideas and give effect to such values. (BVerfGE 34, 269.)

It would serve no real purpose to continue this inevitably abbreviated presentation of complicated German theories. Professor Larenz's *Methodenlehre der*

Rechtswissenschaft (6th edn, 1991) is generally regarded as containing the best account of these movements. But our common law reader may be allowed to enquire whether the end result may not reveal ideas and theories which were explored just as much by common lawyers (for instance the American realists) as they were by their German counterparts. If he is historically minded, he may even assume, often with just cause, that Germanic ideas served as starting points for American theorising. One might even go further and argue that the policy-oriented approach, found in both the German and American systems, may bring them closer together than common rumour may have us believe. Yet the style of writing, be it judicial or academic, and the reasoning processes still remain very different, as in many respects does the pedagogical purpose ascribed to the law schools of the respective countries. Contrasts thus exist and they remain sharp. The remaining part of this chapter will thus try to show how they have affected the organisation of legal material, especially as it affects the law of contracts, and how German lawyers are taught to approach their Code. The comparative lawyer is thus still forced to 'deconstruct' German law in order to make it palatable to his common law readers. The reader who manages to reach the end of this book can, in the end, decide whether we have succeeded in this aim; but this aim must remain in the sights of any common lawyer who wishes to interest his students in German law.

(c) European Contract Law?

We have, roughly a century after the entry into force of the BGB, approached an important juncture concerning the future of the law of contract. The move towards ever-stronger integration in the European Union has raised in some the hope (matched by fear and suspicion in others) that economic integration may, in the end, lead to a common codified system of private law. The debate, reminiscent in some respects of the battle between the Thibaut and Savigny schools of thought, hardly extends beyond the circles of a limited number of (mainly) comparative lawyers, yet one must only study the Commission's so called 'Action Plan for a Coherent Contract Law', COM (2003) 68, to assess how far the project of an European Code has already been advanced (in that proposal, the drafting of an 'optional' contract code is envisaged, see also COM (2004) 651). While naturally the Commission emphasises the negative effect on trade between the Member States ascribed to different systems and/or rules of national private law, the academic supporters of this project pursue a wider agenda. For them, implementing a European civil code comprising a core of common legal concepts would mean reviving a *jus commune* of Europe, only this time it would not be under the tutelage of Roman law but of legislation emanating from Brussels. The tradition of national codifications appears from this perspective as a mere interlude; in a similar vein, the influences of civil law on the common law can be underlined. See, for instance, von Bar, 'A New *Jus Commune Europaeum* and the Importance of the Common Law' in Markesinis (ed), *The Clifford Chance Millennium Lectures* (2000) 67; Basedow, 'Das BGB im künftigen europäischen Privatrecht: Der hybride Kodex' AcP 200 (2000) 445 and 'Codification of Private Law in the European Union: The Making of a Hybrid' (2001) 9 *European Review of Private Law* 35; Zimmermann, 'Europa und das römische Recht' AcP 202 (2002) 243, and Hartkamp *et al* (eds), *Towards a European Civil Code* (3rd edn, 2004). A fruit of this nourishing

European co-operation are the *Principles of European Contract Law* (in three parts, completed 2003) which represent perhaps the most comprehensive attempt so far to extract the principles shared across the common law civil law divide and, also, the *UNIDROIT Principles for International Commercial Contracts* (2004). (See the discussion by Bonell, 'UNIDROIT Principles 2004—The New Edition of the Principles of international Commercial Contracts adopted by the International Institute for the Unification of Private Law' [2004] *Uniform Law Review* 5, which also compares the Principles with the *Principles of European Contract Law*; see further, eg, Brödermann, 'Die erweiterten UNIDROIT Principles 2004' RIW 2004, 721.)

We need not speculate further on whether the idea of unified laws is gaining ground in an ever-growing European Union. Here suffice it to say that, for the near future, the *Bürgerliche Gesetzbuch* of 1896 will continue to be the major source of German contract law. It is to be hoped that making the reasoning of the German Civil Code accessible beyond the limitations imposed by its language, will contribute to the mutual borrowing between civil and common law which will lead to an organic convergence where this is desirable and needed. Thus, as already stated, this book, in addition to providing a teaching tool for those in search of wider horizons, aspires to becoming a source of inspiration for the practising lawyer where a particular national solution does not seem satisfactory or is in need of clarification or development. The obvious advantage of the BGB, if compared with scholarly distillations and compilations of principles of contract law, is that its rules have been put through the test of practical application; indeed, some of the rules discussed in this book owe their existence to the dissatisfaction of the courts with abstract codal provisions and the need to refine rules on a case-by-case basis. Accordingly, a considerable number of cases have been included, which adds to the richness of the subject and which provide an authoritative interpretation of the principles of contract law of the BGB. This trend will continue as decisions from the highest German courts begin to flesh out the recently revised codal text.

Yet, for the reasons already given at the very beginning of this book, it is impossible, even in a book on national law, to ignore the strong influence that European legislation already exerts upon private law. The focus of European law has shifted over the years. Initially, dating back to the days of the customs union, the economic freedoms (of goods, capital, workers, establishment and the provision of services), together with competition law, formed the basis for abolishing obstacles to trade and for liberalising markets. The process was an ad hoc one, aimed at reducing differences between the laws of the Member States by evaluating their negative effect on trade and prohibiting the application of those national rules whose impact upon such trade was disproportionately severe. To this list has been added a new, powerful tool. It is the harmonisation by legislation of specific sectors of trade or particular types of transactions. Of those legislative measures affecting contract law we name but a few here: Directive 85/577/EEC concerning the protection of consumers in respect of contracts negotiated away from business premises; Consumer Credit Directive 87/102/EEC; Directive 90/314/EEC on Package Travel; Directives 92/96/EEC and 92/49/EEC concerning insurance law; Directive 93/13/EEC on Unfair Terms in Consumer Contracts; Directive 1999/44/EC on Consumer Sales; Directive 2000/31/EC on Electronic Commerce; Directive 2000/35/EEC on Late Payments. It should be noted that an account of the implementation of a Directive in German law might deepen the understanding of the Directive itself. These passages may, therefore, be more directly relevant to English law than those that hold a purely comparative interest.

It would be premature to suggest that these harmonisation measures form part of a coherent overall plan leading straight to a comprehensive codification. One is almost tempted to suggest the opposite. For the fragmented and often one-dimensional (protection of the consumer, facilitating e-commerce, etc) character of this legislation is often all—too obvious. Yet it should be noted that in Germany (as also to some extent in England) specialised monographs have started to appear which seek to systematise this bulk of heterogeneous laws and discuss ways of increasing coherence. Similarly, the Commission's 'Action Plan', already referred to above, was triggered by the unsatisfactory state of the *acquis communautaire* in relation to such contractual issues. This phenomenon is an indication that European private law may be on a venture that will take it to new shores.

Further Reading. See, from the vast literature of recent years: Franzen, *Privatrechtsangleichung durch die Europäische Gemeinschaft* (1999); Kieninger, *Wettbewerb der Privatrechtsordnungen im Europäischen Binnenmarkt* (2002); Leible, *Wege zu einem Europäischen Privatrecht* (2001); Lurger, *Grundfragen der Vereinheitlichung des Vertragsrechts in der Europäischen Union* (2002); Riesenhuber, *System und Prinzipien des Europäischen Vertragsrechts* (2003).

3. THE CONTRAST WITH THE FRENCH CIVIL CODE

Even in our times of increased travel and enhanced communication facilities (including the internet) the level of knowledge most persons possess about the socio-political and cultural conditions of their neighbours is rather limited. The authors of this book, having worked for differing (but extensive) periods of time on both sides of the Channel, believe that a comparable level of ignorance extends even to 'educated' persons such as lawyers who often nourish stereotypical misapprehensions about each other's legal systems. Thus, until recently at least, widespread was the belief in England that in continental legal systems all one has to do is to turn to the codes in order to find the answer to the problem confronting him, while others have even referred to the European legal systems (as a whole) as being 'Napoleonic' in origin. In fact, though the Code Napoleon did apply (for a time) in the Rhinish states, the fact is that the German Code has distinct features from the French and a constitutional and public law jurisprudence that often brings it closer to American law than that of its southern neighbour. (Indeed, the opposite may be closer to the truth since the law of the northern two thirds of France was more Teutonic than Roman or Latin.) To remove some of these misapprehensions and, at the same time, to enhance (through contrast) the understanding of the German Code and the culture it has helped to create, an excursus into the different conditions that gave birth to the French Code might not be out of place. This, incidentally, may also put into a more accurate perspective the low regard in which (some) of the German jurists of the nineteenth century held the French Code. (We stress 'some' since others, such as the early nineteenth century German jurist Zachariae, praised the Code and by refraining from adopting an anti-French posture became himself a great influence on the Alsatian lawyers Aubry and Rau who were the first to introduce into their famous treatise on the Civil Code a 'Germanic' (in the sense of systematic) structure of treatment of their subject.)

Thus for many of the German jurists of that era, the Code was a 'rushed' affair, demonstrating serious misunderstandings of some basic Roman law texts and, moreover, in its (obviously successful) attempt to achieve stylistic elegance had given evidence of its shallow thought. The great Karl Friederich von Savigny was the first to lead the attack on the French Code, mainly because it violated his belief that legislation should emerge *slowly* and organically as a result of the study of the customary laws and traditions of a state. Windscheid, the father of the German Civil Code (BGB), likewise, condemned its style as lacking 'the true inner precision which comes from complete clarity of thought' (*Zur Lehre des Codes Napoleon von der Ungültigkeit der Rechtgeschäfte*, 1847, at V).

Savigny was both right and wrong when he (implicitly) condemned the hurried nature of the enactment of the *Code civil*. For it is true that Bonaparte, after he came to power at the coup of 18th Brumaire, personally bullied his draftsmen to produce the text of the laws which were enacted under one heading as the *Code Civil des Français* on 21 March 1804. Yet, in another sense, what became the final draft itself drew many of its ideas and even much of its text from three earlier drafts produced by Cambacérés, Napoleon's administrative 'number two', which had been the subject of prolonged discussions before different revolutionary bodies since the beginning of the Revolution in 1789. (The full story is told in masterly fashion by Halpérin, *L'impossible Code civil* (1992).) More importantly, the codification process, with its many ups and downs as well as contradictions, could be traced back at least two if not three centuries earlier when parts of French law were gradually systematised and written down in the form of specific statutes, dealing with such varied matters as commerce, procedure, bills of exchange, carriage of goods, insurance, gifts and so on.

There is another and less frequently discussed reason why the codification had to be hurried. To appreciate it fully one must immerse oneself in the French history of the time and try to see the Code as a sociological, even constitutional document that responded to the need to bring to a close a period of enormous social turbulence that followed the Revolution of 1789. (This period is beautifully sketched by Xavier Martin, *La Mythologie du Code Napoléon. Aux soubbassements de la France moderns* (2003).) And here one must note that a sizeable part of the law reform debates preceding the enactment of the *Code civil* were not, as is the case with, say, eighteenth century Scotland or late nineteenth century Germany, pre-occupied with property or obligations but with family law and succession. And in these two areas the revolutionary ideal of equality had literally played havoc with the law concerning testamentary rights, divorce and the rights of illegitimate children. By the mid-1790s French society was thus in a state of complete upheaval if not disintegration and it is a further sign of Bonaparte's genius that he sensed that the French people were willing to sacrifice everything, including a fair degree of freedom, in exchange for order and authority being returned to their lives. These ideas were shared by Portalis, the chief draftsman of the *Code civil* who, during his preceding years of political exile in Northern Germany had done much reading, acquainted himself with a wide variety of schools of thought, and had developed what can only be called a nineteenth-century liberal philosophy. (It is evidenced by his little read masterpiece *De l'usage et de l'abus de l'ésprit philosophique durant le XVIII siècle*, published posthumously in 1820 and republished in a third edition in two volumes in 1834.) One of us has sketched this complex evolutionary process elsewhere and reference to this work (and the French original sources) will, for present purposes suffice. (Thus see Markesinis, 'Two hundred years of a famous code: What should we be celebrating?' 39 *Texas International Law Journal* 561 (2004) and 'The Enduring (Double) Legacy of the Code Napoleon' (2005) 121 *LQR* 80.) But enough has been said to mitigate if not counter the accusation that the Code was a 'badly rushed' affair. Hurried, in one sense, it may have been; but in another, it has to be admitted, it had to be enacted swiftly in order to provide the *political* settlement needed by the new era. The fact that, despite its imperfections, omissions and in some cases quickly-dated ideology (eg, workers' rights, women's rights), it has survived for over two hundred years relatively intact, demonstrates that, in effect, it became the lasting constitutional charter that France's formal constitutions—13 of them since the beginning of the Revolution—never managed to provide. In this sense, therefore, the French Civil Code is very different from the German Civil Code of some ninety years later and it seems to us wrong to judge it by reference to the political conditions that prevailed in Germany in the nineteenth century and not those that obtained in France one century earlier.

The second charge levied against the French Code concerns, as we noted earlier, its style. Let us thus look briefly at article 2279 of the French Code, containing one of the most famous aphorisms of all time: 'en fait des meubles possession vaut titre' (in the case of movables, possession means title). What does possession mean? Is good faith necessary? What amounts to good faith? And when must it exist? Anyone even slightly acquainted with German legal literature of the nineteenth century knows how much these issues excited the German jurists of the period and, in that context, their criticisms of the *Code civil* (CC) must not be dismissed lightly.

The German Pandectists of the nineteenth century spent much time and effort discussing these issues. Paragraph 932 BGB was their answer. Whereas article 2279 CC amounts to seven words, its German counterpart runs to nine lines. Like most German legal writing, judicial or legislative, the wording of § 932 leaves little to the imagination. The nineteenth century German debates over the precise meaning of possession, detention and the like did not impress everyone. Of the American admirers of nineteenth-century German legal scholarship, Holmes was among the most sceptical. (On this see: G Edward White, *Justice, Oliver Wendell Holmes. Law and the Inner Self* (1993) ch. 4, and especially 134 ff.)

The entire literature on this subject has now receded into the background, its intellectual depth deprived of much of its original allure. This brief assessment of the German approach shows its strengths, especially when compared with the French legislative debates; but it also suggests some weaknesses. Among the latter, one counts the fact that it makes the exportation of a legal culture—important when export of ideas can, especially these days, be as important as the export of goods—much more difficult.

Yet this brief discussion of article 2239 CC needs one minor postscript. For, when all is said and done, what the Germans put in their code, the French judges subsequently worked out themselves, in most cases in very similar ways. And in a sense this approach has brought French law closer to English law. For the French, unlike us, attached to theory in principle, are often—like the English—willing, in practice, to move from case to case, leaving it to the judge to work out the rules needed to respond to real facts.

This is no place to compare the (real or apparent) attachment to principle rather than pragmatism or to compare drafting techniques, be it of legislation or of judgments. Yet reference, once again, must be made to Portalis's views which still deserve respect. In particular, we must guard ourselves against the danger of equating detailed legislative drafting with mature thought (which is the implication of Windscheid's statement). For the French judicial technique was not accidentally opaque but (often) deliberately broad to accommodate expansion since Portalis repeatedly stressed that 'the foresight of the legislator is limited' (Présentation au Corps législative, Expose des Motifs, Fenet (1968 reprint of the *Recueil complet des travaux préparatoires du Code civil* vol VI, 360). In this sense then the brevity of the French text was not just a generator of problems (which it undoubtedly was in many cases); it was also a source of beneficial development. For the supple wording of the texts made the growth and modernisation of French law depend very largely on the constant co-operation of the three agents of law: judges, practitioners, and academics. As we shall see in later chapters, the Germans were to discover themselves the advantages of amorphously phrased codal provisions such as § 242 BGB, though here, again, 'open-endedness' came at a price.

What has been said about the style of the French Code in general applies with equal force to its contract provisions, although here the brevity of the Code also reflects the fact that contract law was far less developed in 1800 than it was by the time the German Code came into force one century later. Contracts *inter absentes* were, in 1800, thus virtually unknown; telegraphic communications still unknown; the life insurance contract was considered immoral; and the notions of contracts in favour of third parties were virtually non-existent. Frustration, because of altered circumstances, also remained unknown; and in the second half of the nineteenth century the Cour de cassation, in the famous decision of the *Canal de Craponne* (Cass civ 6.3.1876, S 1876.1.161, D 1876.1.193), was to keep it outside the domain of *private* law. (The equally famous decision of *Gaz de Bordeaux* was to hold otherwise for contracts affecting public entities. See CE 30.3.1916, S 1916.3.17.) Overall therefore German law was, in this branch of private law, destined to find a topic worthy of its formidable intellectual vigour and, indeed, was to formulate general principles that would, as already stated, have an impact across the Channel and even the Atlantic. For it was no small thing to have attracted the admiration of such great English jurists as Austin, Pollock or Anson.

4. THE REGULATORY TECHNIQUE OF
THE GERMAN CIVIL CODE

Unlike the French Code, which divided its material following Gaius's pattern into law of persons, things and actions, the BGB has arranged its material into five books: General Part, Law of Obligations, Property Law, Family Law and Law of Succession. The First Book, the General Part, is without doubt the most original result of the Pandectist school (but for non-Germans also the most controversial). Its high degree of abstraction is the fruit of the meticulous and prolonged scholarly debates preceding the adoption of the Code. The General Part is the first and clearest mark of the Code's 'scientific' nature. The rules contained therein are deemed to be of such a general nature that they apply throughout private law, unless special reasons appropriate to that particular part of the law (eg, tort law, family law etc) require a departure from the general rule. (A good illustration is capacity, fixed at eighteen, but modified where tort or family law principles require otherwise.)

It is from the standpoint of a pragmatic common lawyer that one might doubt whether this way of organising a system of private law is really desirable, or whether in the end it might be more advantageous to adopt a less abstract and more compartmentalised approach. Before we venture to point out some advantages of a comprehensive and coherent system of abstract concepts and rules, it is readily conceded that one can question the wisdom of the fathers of the BGB as to the insertion of *particular* rules into this 'pure' general part, while leaving others to be dealt with in the special parts of the BGB. By way of illustration, we will discuss here the approach to company law and that to the law relating to mistakes.

One would expect in the General Part of private law a basic set of rules related to the concept of a natural person and that of a juridical person (First and Second Title) as the main actors of private law, as well as a definition of corporeal things (Third Title). Also, it is perfectly sensible that these sections of the Code are followed by a Fourth Title on legal transactions containing rules applicable to all legal transactions. Yet it is an inescapable consequence of this structure that associations of persons forming juridical persons are dealt with in the general part (§ 21), while other associations not constituting a juridical person, can only be based on a special contract and consequently regulated in the special part of the law of obligations namely, in Book Two (private law partnerships, § 705). From a wider perspective, however, both concepts are of equal general importance, for they form the two basic models of association of German private law from which all other incidents of company law are derived.

If we look at the section on legal transactions in the General Part it also seems only natural that they would contain rules establishing the relevance of mistake and the conditions upon which a legal transaction may be avoided for that reason (§§ 116–24, 142–4). By placing them here, the Code avoids the need of repetition in the special parts of the Civil Code. Yet, having said this, we note that this basic 'model' of mistake is subsequently qualified heavily by specific rules in the special parts of the BGB. This because, obviously, the types of mistakes that will be relevant when concluding a marriage and when entering into a contract of sale are likely to be different. It would be absurd to allow rescission of a marriage on the ground that one of the spouses did not posses a certain characteristic (§ 119 II); hence, unsurprisingly, §§ 1313 *et seq* completely replace the reasons for annulling a marriage due to deficiencies in consent. A similar phenomenon can be observed in relation to wills where, again, we find special rules governing the relevance of mistake, the person entitled to 'rescind' etc. (§§ 2078 *et seq*). Thus, the major field of application of §§ 116 *et seq* turns out to be contract law. But even here, remedies in respect of non-conformity of the subject matter of the contract—for instance termination of the contract because the goods delivered were of unsatisfactory quality—will often prevent resort to the general rules of mistake. We will discuss the latter question in more detail in chapter 6; but already some seeds of doubt may have been laid about the desirability of a general rule which is then so heavily and so frequently modified in the subsequent parts of the Code.

The reader will, of course, have observed that in the preceding passages we have been concerned with the best distribution of the material of private law in separate parts of a code, pointing out possible avenues of criticism of the placement of individual rules in the Code. These doubts should not, however, distract from the completeness of the system of rules contained in the BGB. However, the coherence of rules *in toto*, irrespective of where in the Code they have been placed, is an undoubted fact; and it accounts for much of the fascination that a codification of such highly technical nature as the BGB has provoked over the years and which still persists today.

Yet the scientific abstract approach, already evident from what we have said, has also provoked harsh criticism (see Zweigert and Kötz, *An Introduction to Comparative Law*, p 142); and as stated it is easily noticeable that the dry language of the BGB contrasts rather unfavourably with the elegant declarations of general principles in the French *Code civil*. The BGB is practically devoid of statements of principles which could be regarded as the cornerstones or the foundations of private law. The BGB is modest and technical. It contains principles and rules belonging to an 'inferior' level of deduction. The great advantage of this approach, which cannot be overestimated, is that such rules are more easily applied to individual cases. It is this balance between abstract general principles and specific stipulations which has ensured that the great majority of the provisions of the BGB have retained their field of application right up to the present day. They are sufficiently abstract to encompass new situations and concrete enough to be able to be applied by a (sufficiently trained!) lawyer arguing a case before a provincial court more than hundred years after the enactment of the BGB. The point we wish to stress here is that the provisions of the BGB, though abstract and part of a complex system of rules and concepts, are sufficiently differentiated to be applied to individual cases. If a practical example is required at this stage it can be found in comparing the delict provisions of the BGB (§§ 823 *et seq* BGB) and the equivalent articles 1382 and 1384 of the Code civil.

Another major advantage of the conceptualism of the BGB is the beneficial effect it has had upon drafting technique. The use of technical terms throughout, which regularly signify little if anything to a German lay person, has had an enormous 'economising' effect upon legal practice. Most provisions in the original text were succinct and extremely short compared with the lengthy, redundant provisions of most modern legislation. (It suffices here to give one example: contrast § 119, one of the main provisions on mistake relating to the existence of an agreement with § 355 dealing with the right to rescind pursuant to consumer Directives.) Moreover, the General Part and the general parts of the other books of the BGB provide a framework of concepts and general rules which the legislator can easily use to mould new 'special parts' of private law. The recent major reform of the BGB suggests that the tradition of legislation through abstract rules and general concepts can be successfully continued even in modern times (though it should be noted that many writers strongly opposed the idea of interfering with the substance of the Second Book, Law of Obligations, of the BGB). An example of how fundamental the reform has been is provided by the introduction into the Code of the notion of a pre-contractual relationship of obligation created by law (*culpa in contrahendo*) which previously formed part of rules established by the rich case law of the German courts. Yet this did not require more than adding two subsections to § 311 (see chapter 2, p 91).

It is thus interesting to note that the recent reform has much increased the prevalence of abstract concepts and general principles in the law of obligations even compared with the initial approach of the BGB to these matters. The system of irregularities of performance is now set out in the General Part of the law of obligations and much of the special contract law simply refers back to the general rules (eg, §§ 437, 634). We will return to this important new development in detail in chapters 9 and 10; here, it can already be stated that this new approach has simplified the law.

It cannot be denied however that many other recent insertions into the BGB can be criticised for not being capable of generalisation. One notes a number of ad hoc policy interventions or 'symbolic' acts which do not fit the conceptualism of the BGB. §§ 105a, 241a, 661a are striking examples. § 241a for instance (and similar observations could be made in relation to the other two provisions) was inserted into the Code between two major provisions of the BGB: § 241, which clarifies the availability of specific performance and governs the inference of collateral obligations, and § 242, laying down the principle of good faith—no doubt familiar as a cornerstone of German contract law, about which more will be said in chapter 3. Yet, § 241a does not contain any general principle, nor even a distinct rule which could be used beyond the microscopic scope of application of this provision. It merely allows consumers to keep, use, or destroy goods which were sent to them unsolicited and for the purpose of inducing a contract of sale and to do so without having to fear any claim whatsoever. Regulating in this way an isolated incidence of doubtful market practices has thus triggered off a gross violation of the structure of the BGB. (See the trenchant criticism of this provision by Flume, echoing Savigny's verdict that the time was not ripe for passing legislation, 'Vom Beruf unserer Zeit für Gesetzgebung' ZIP 2000, 1427.)

If any further proof were needed that the conceptualism of the BGB works in practice—at any rate for those accustomed to the Germanic thinking—one should consider the fact that generation after generation of German lawyers have been trained in this way. Ironically, as alluded to in the previous section, the term *Begriffsjurisprudenz* has somewhat pejorative connotations today and this method of 'calculating with concepts' has given way to more flexible and all-encompassing theories of *Interessen*—or *Wertungsjurisprudenz*, (as explained above) which add to the conceptual approach an increased sensitivity towards the changing demands of the legal community (*Rechtsverkehr*). Yet the way that German law is taught today closely follows the pattern of the five books of the BGB. The conceptualism of the BGB and the categorisations presupposed by the Code have thus had a profound and long-lasting influence on the way German academics approach private law as a subject of research and teaching. Textbooks and other monograph type treatments of the subject are structured accordingly, not to mention the commentary literature which, by its very nature, mirrors the structure of the BGB (the most extensive, *Staudingers*, alone fills nearly 60,000 pages). Thus, as can be seen from the bibliography at the beginning of this chapter, there are books on the General Part of the BGB, (dealing with such matters as capacity, § 104; mistake, § 119; formation, § 145; and limitation, § 195; but excluding other elements of contract law), followed by books on the General Part of the Law of Obligations (dealing for instance with the law of damages, § 249; contracts in favour of third parties, § 328; and assignment, § 398) and the Special

Part of the Law of Obligations (dealing with special types of contract: sale, § 433; lease, § 535; etc, as well as, in the same book, tort, § 823; and restitution, § 812, which to the German mind are merely special forms of obligation). Books on the law of property will discuss the details of the transfer of property and so forth. Books on 'contract law' proper are virtually absent (note also the qualifications necessary in relation to the concept 'contract' arising from the principle of separation discussed in the next section). Hence, the arrangement of topics in the present book is already anglicised. Heretically, from the perspective of the BGB, we thus bring together groups of norms taken from the first two books of the BGB as far as they bear on the coming into existence of a contract, its enforcement and death, while leaving out other examples of a relationship of obligation such as delict. In fact, so far as we can see, this book is unique, for in Germany even books bearing the title 'contract law' omit from their contents those contract law rules which are comprised in the General Part and tend to concentrate on special kinds of contracts and the issues raised by them.

This section on characteristic features of the German Civil Code would not be complete if the importance of the so-called 'general clauses' (*Generalklauseln*) were not mentioned. We will return to this topic when we discuss some of these general clauses in detail in the following chapters. Here, suffice it to point out the function of such provisions and the effect they have on the development of the law.

The most important general clauses affecting contract law are § 242 (embodying the principle of good faith) and § 138 I (declaring contracts *contra bonos mores*, good morals, public policy, void). A number of other provisions also refer to good faith, for instance the main provision dealing with interpretation of contracts: § 157. It is immediately obvious that there is a considerable gap of specificity between, on the one hand, a section such as § 145 introducing the binding nature of an offer and, on the other, the requirement that good faith or public policy must be given due consideration. The vagueness of these policy requirements is in clear contrast with the bulk of the provisions of the first two books of the BGB which, as stated, tend to be very specific. Yet these more specific rules of contract law cannot be discussed in isolation from the open-textured general clauses. For every single contract is subject to the principle of good faith and must satisfy the demands of public policy. Since the BGB itself does not define good faith or public policy except in an indirect way, the content of these principles is left to be determined by the courts.

The existence of general clauses in the BGB has three crucial implications.

First, general clauses transfer to the judge a considerable power which he would not otherwise have in a codified system such as the German. This power can be used first to mould private law and 'infer' new 'specific-abstract' rules from the general clause. An example of this is the theory of the foundation of the transaction which, though initially based on § 242, after the recent reforms has found its way into the Code as an express provision, § 313, discussed in detail in chapter 7. This function of general clauses clearly reminds one of the role equity has played in English law. The second aspect of the power bestowed on the judge by general clauses is that the 'edges' of harsh rules may be softened in individual, deserving cases. Here harsh consequences of applying the law unchanged have sometimes prompted ad hoc exceptions, such as the line of cases concerning the waiving of requirements as to form (discussed in chapter 2 under the subheading of 'formalities'). Another example can be found in the section on good faith. This will be discussed in more detail in chapter 3 but here suffice it to say that the actual wording of § 242 is limited to the manner of the performance by the debtor. The fact that the courts transcended the narrow bounds of the wording and developed a broad principle of good faith of general application indicates that general clauses have served a real (or at least perceived) need to develop the law where no other ways could be found to achieve the desired result. (As early as 1950 Hedemann described this as the 'flight into general clauses.' See, 'Fünfzig Jahre Bürgerliches Gesetzbuch' JR 1950, 1.)

Closely interrelated to the above is the second function of general clauses. The principle of good faith in particular has enabled the courts to adapt contract law to new demands of society or commerce and provide adequate regimes of liability where the existing ones appeared to fail. This partially explains why the BGB has survived, seemingly unchanged, for over a century. In other words, general clauses are essential to understand how a Code can keep up-to-date. We will thus give many examples throughout this book where the legislator has refrained from including a particular rule in the Code and instead left it to the courts to develop the law further. In some instances where the approach of the courts proved successful, the legislator subsequently transformed the rules developed on a case-by-case basis into abstract codal provisions. § 311 II has already been mentioned in this regard. Likewise, the control of standard terms was, initially, a task performed by the courts on the basis of good faith, although later supporting legislation was passed and eventually was introduced into the Code in the form of §§ 305–10 (see chapter 3, p 163 ff).

Thirdly, perhaps the most important feature which the BGB owes to the existence of general clauses is that it allows the wider political and constitutional background to infiltrate the domain of private law through the channels of good faith and public policy. General clauses are nowadays regarded as '*Einfallstore*' for value judgments, which loosely translated means that they are the gates through which policy reasons may enter the realm of private law. Viewed however from the perspective of the drafters of the BGB, the metaphor of a Trojan horse is not wholly inappropriate. For they did not foresee the (outrageous) interpretation of good faith and public policy during the Nazi period which perverted the liberal spirit of the BGB and imported into private law fascist ideology by exploiting these general clauses. Yet it would be wrong to believe that the fathers of the BGB were not aware of the dangers presented by such general clauses. Thus, in relation to § 138 I (§ 106 in the first draft), which declares void contracts contrary to *bonos mores* (*guten Sitten*), good morals or more loosely translated 'public policy', we read in the *Motive*, vol I (1888) pp 211–12:

> The provision constitutes an important step taken by the legislator which, arguably, is not without difficulties. The leeway granted to judicial discretion has hitherto been unknown in relation to such an important area of the law. (Future) errors cannot be excluded. Taking into account, however, the conscientiousness of the German judiciary, it can surely be taken for granted that the provision will, on the whole, be applied only in the manner in which it is envisaged.

With hindsight, it may seem somewhat over-optimistic to place such trust in the German judiciary. Yet during that period of national socialism legislation proved no better so it is, perhaps, too harsh to place all the blame upon the judiciary. In any event, the Basic Law (*Grundgesetz*) of 1949 drew lessons from this deeply disturbing failure and took a whole series of institutional precautions against the infringement of human rights. One of them was that it should not be left to the free discretion of the authorities whether to apply the law in 'the right spirit.' This was also soon to be realised in the field of private law. (See section 6 below on the 'constitutionalisation' of private law.)

5. CONTRACT AS PART OF THE LAW OF OBLIGATIONS

(a) Preliminary Observations

When approaching the German law of contract from the standpoint of a common lawyer one must guard against certain pitfalls. Possible misunderstandings start with the term 'contract', itself, which in German law has a different meaning from that ascribed to the term by common lawyers. The title of this book has thus been anglicised which, of course, is not something inherently wrong if it helps promote the knowledge and understanding of German law without betraying its essential characteristics. Nonetheless, a number of clarifications are necessary at the very outset of our survey of the German 'law of contract'.

Contract, as a source of voluntary obligation, is in German law expressed through the somewhat cumbersome phrase 'contractual relationship of obligation' and not simply 'contract'. In fact the concept of 'contract' is part of a whole family of concepts whose interrelationships must be explored first before we turn to the particulars of 'contract' law in the chapters that follow. These concepts are: (a) declaration of intention (*Willenserklärung*); (b) legal transaction (*Rechtsgeschäft*); (c) contract (*Vertrag*); and (d) contractual relationship of obligation (*Vertragliches Schuldverhältnis*). In fact, only the last concept encompasses the subject matter of the present book.

(b) The Different Meanings of 'Contract'

What a common law sees as a contract the BGB would describe as a contractual relationship of obligation (*vertragliches Schuldverhältnis*). Alternatively, the German lawyer would speak of a legal transaction (*Rechtsgeschäft*) that consists of two corresponding declarations of intention or declarations of 'will' (*Willenserklärung*): offer and acceptance. In the following we hope to elucidate the meaning of these three basic concepts: contractual relationship of obligation, legal transaction, and declaration of intention, and also explain the reasons for the amazing level of abstraction inherent in these concepts.

The BGB distinguishes between relationships of obligation arising from the law (*gesetzliches Schuldverhältnis*)—for instance, delict (§ 823), unjustified enrichment (§ 812), *negotiorum gestio* (§ 677)—and those created by contract (*vertragliches Schuldverhältnis*). Paragraph 311 I BGB makes it clear that to create a relationship of obligation (*Schuldverhältnis*) by means of a legal transaction (*Rechtsgeschäft*) the parties must enter into a contract (*Vertrag*). A promise becomes binding upon the promisor only on acceptance by the promisee. The view adopted in the BGB is thus that unilateral legal transactions are, as a general rule, not capable of creating a relationship of obligation. (See from a comparative and historical perspective

Zimmermann, 'Vertrag und Versprechen' *Festschrift Heldrich* (2005) 467). The Code contains only a limited number of exceptions to the contract requirement (stipulations in favour of third parties, § 328, discussed in chapter 4, and *Auslobung* § 661, as to which see chapter 2, are examples).

Hence where parties have concluded a contract, a *relationship of obligation* arises. The parties will then find themselves under an obligation according to the terms of the contract they have concluded. This is the principle of *pacta sunt servanda*. The flexibility of this principle, together with the abundance of *general* rules applicable to contractual relationships of obligation, has allowed new types of contracts (such as factoring or leasing, unknown at the time of coming into force of the BGB) to be easily assimilated into the existing framework of the Code.

The provisions dealing with the conclusion of a contract reveal much about the style of the Code. The rule that a contract consists of two *corresponding* declarations of intention—offer and acceptance—was regarded as too trivial to deserve special mention in the text. And indeed it is much more interesting (and at the same time practically relevant) that the section on contract simply starts by laying down the rule as to the binding nature of an offer. (We will discuss the rationale of this approach in detail in the next chapter.) For it could be argued practitioners would show little interest in the sorts of things one learns in the first year of law school (eg, that correspondence of offer and acceptance are necessary) but will instantly take note when told until what moment in time an offer can be accepted (§ 147); or what the consequences of dissent are (§§ 154, 155, also discussed in the next chapter). This again demonstrates that the conceptualism of the BGB is not an end in itself. The fathers of the BGB took great care to ensure that the rules they laid down were capable of practical application; that they actually meant something and did not express superfluous doctrinal niceties. Neither of these features is often noticed by Anglo-American lawyers who tend to be quick to adopt the stereotypical image of German law and German professors. Yet, equally, it cannot be denied that the above way of thinking is not only abstract, but to a common lawyer also confusing. Yet it is included here since one cannot constantly 'depart' from the foreign model one is describing simply in order to please one's local audience! But, in the interests of a balanced presentation one might also add that on the wider observation we made about the abstract tendencies of German legal thought, examples can be given where the conceptualism was in fact carried further than was actually necessary. These however can wait for later since the present aim is to describe as clearly as possible the typical features of the BGB and not indulge oursleves by listing its oddities. So let us return to our main point.

The concept presupposed by § 311 I is that of a *legal transaction* (*Rechtsgeschäft*), which is accordingly more fundamental than a contractual relationship of obligation. The concept 'legal transaction' describes the power given to a person by law to determine his legal relationship with others through their mutual conduct. It can be easily seen that an abstract definition of this concept would serve no practical purpose and, consequently, no definition was included in the BGB. Likewise, a list of all such transactions would unduly hinder the further development of the law for it is impossible to describe at any given moment all conceivable acts which may affect the legal relationships of a person. Contract is thus but one incidence of a legal transaction. Accordingly, freedom of contract is only one aspect of personal autonomy in the field of private law. For other legal transactions reflect personal autonomy. They include, for instance, the making of a will (§ 1937), the transfer of property in chattels (§ 929) or in land (§§ 873, 925), and the giving of authority (§ 168). Yet, it would do injustice to the thoroughness of the BGB if the concept 'legal transaction,' as the nucleus of private autonomy, were not analysed further. And so it has.

Each legal transaction (*Rechtsgeschäft*) consists of at least one smaller 'incident' or 'event'—a *declaration of intention* (*Willenserklärung*). (Note that translation of these concepts is exceedingly difficult; for instance 'declaration of will' is equally useful and common. Since we are dealing with technical terms, consistency is of the greatest importance; all else is a matter of style.) Some *Rechtsgeschäfte* require one declaration of intention, others more.

Examples of *Rechtsgeschäfte* of the second kind, ie consisting of only one declaration of intention, include rescission of a contract affected by mistake (§ 143), termination of a contract for non-conformity of goods (§ 349), or the making of a will (§ 1937). It will be observed that these 'one-sided' legal transactions do not give rise to 'a relationship of obligation.' Such a relationship requires by virtue of § 311 I BGB a contract which is the paradigmatic example of a *Rechtsgeschäft* consisting of two declarations of intention: offer and acceptance (§§ 145 *et seq*). Finally, there are *Rechtsgeschäfte*, which consist of one or more declarations of intention *plus* some further act, which, because it need not be supported by a (qualified) intention when performed, is called *Realakt*. Thus the transfer of the property in a chattel requires, according to § 929 section 1, a contract to that effect *and* the transfer of actual possession of the chattel. Likewise, the transfer of title as to immovables requires the additional registration of that act in the land register (§ 873 I).

This overview is not comprehensive; but it illustrates how easily the entire private law can be analysed in these terms once such abstract basic concepts are introduced. In the next section, yet another fundamental set of concepts, determining the shape of many rules in the special parts of private law, will be discussed.

(c) The Principles of Separation and Abstraction

We now come to what is one of the most intriguing peculiarities of German contract law. Indeed, Zweigert and Kötz, in their treatise, *An Introduction to Comparative Law*, p 71, regard it as so distinctive as to argue that it gives the German legal system its characteristic style. (See also the first edition of their work (1977, translated by Weir), Vol 1, pp 177–89 a passage omitted from later editions.) Many common lawyers, and indeed French lawyers, might be tempted to describe it more than just 'distinctive'. 'Un-necessary' and 'excessively abstract' are words that have often been used; and not with some justification.

German law notionally distinguishes between the legal transaction that creates the relationship of obligation (*Verpflichtungsgeschäft*) from the legal transaction which transfers, alters, extinguishes, or encumbers rights (*Verfügungsgeschäft* = disposition contract). This distinction is accompanied by an important sub-rule: the validity of the second transaction is independent from the validity of the first. The first tenet is known as the 'principle of separation' (*Trennungsprinzip*), while the second is referred to as the 'principle of abstraction' (*Abstraktionsprinzip*). The justification for this theory is said to lie in the desire to promote certainty in the law and consequently enhance commercial convenience. (See, Medicus, *Allgemeiner Teil*, Rn. 226.) The

Commission on the BGB however was less motivated by such pragmatic considerations than one might be led to suspect. For it simply stated that the principle of abstraction represented the most accurate analysis of the intention of the parties. Any other approach would obscure the true nature of such transactions and, *therefore*, due to an analytical failure, create insecurity (uncertainty) in the law. (See *Motive* (the deliberations of the first commission of the BGB), vol III, Law of Property, pp 6–7 (1888)). This is a point worth stressing. For whether one shares such analysis or not it reveals, yet again, the conviction of the Commission that only a careful conceptual analysis could provide the system with solutions that worked satisfactorily *in practice*. In a strange sort of way therefore the worlds of theory and practice were not kept as separate as the stereotypical image of German attachment to dogma would have us believe.

The strict notional separation of *Verpflichtung* (which comes first as we saw) and *Verfügung* (which follows) would thus still prevent a German lawyer from giving a book on contract law (in the sense a common lawyer would understand it) the simple title: 'The Law of Contract.' The transfer of a right regularly requires a contract actually transferring the right (*Verfügung* = transaction of transfer or conveyance) *in addition* to a contract that stipulates the obligation to transfer the right (*Verpflichtung* = contract of obligation). Speaking of 'contract' would thus obscure which of the two legal transactions was actually meant. Contract law proper, contract law as part of the law of obligations, is denominated in German law by 'contractual relationships of obligation' (*Vertragliche Schuldverhältnisse*). This might seem cumbersome but, like much in the BGB, it is (for that system) both logically necessary and conceptually sensible to keep both these ideas in mind. When the BGB thus refers to *Vertrag* and not to a *vertragliche Schuldverhältnis*, the term includes both contract of obligation and contract of transfer.

It should be noted that the rules on offer and acceptance, found in §§ 145 *et seq*, apply equally to the contract by which ownership is transferred. Yet it is fair to say that the particulars of these rules (time of acceptance, etc) are almost exclusively relevant to the conclusion of a contract of obligation (the first step) and we shall, therefore, discuss them in the next chapter on formation. (The above observations will help us understand better the seemingly opaque wording of § 311 I, which is the opening paragraph of the law of contract: the creation of a relationship of obligation by legal transaction requires the parties to enter into a contract. The voluntary undertaking of an obligation is in German law defined, not as 'contract', but is a subcategory of the concept 'contract'.) So much then for terminology.

If one distinguishes between a contract of obligation and a contract of transfer, it is necessary to introduce rules governing the relationship between the two. One such rule is the principle of abstraction (the invalidity of the contract of obligation does not necessarily induce the invalidity of the contract of transfer), which we discuss later in the text. Another set of rules is invoked by the concepts of 'causal' and 'abstract' transactions to which we now turn our attention.

As a general rule all contracts of obligation are causal while contracts of transfer or *Verfügungen* (dispositions more generally) are abstract. For present purposes we may safely neglect exceptions to this rule (eg, § 780 BGB) and proceed on the assumption that any contract of obligation is self-sufficient and does not need a reason for its conclusion outside itself. A contract of obligation usually contains the motivation for its conclusion (*causa*) in itself: A sells a book to B in order to obtain the price, just as B pays the price in order to obtain the book. This reason to obtain the counter-performance is sufficient to found the transaction. The making of a gift is, unlike in English law, also regarded as a sufficient reason.

Contracts of transfer are legal transactions which actually transfer or alter a proprietary interest as opposed to stipulating an obligation to transfer or alter. Contracts of transfer, unlike contracts of obligations, do not contain the reason for their conclusion in them. This type of transaction does not, in itself, contain a reason why the proprietary interest is transferred or altered. This is logical consequence of the principle of separation, ie, of distinguishing between the (first) contract creating the promise to transfer and the (second) contract through which the transfer is actually achieved. The most common reason for a contract of transfer is thus that it fulfils an obligation to transfer; the transfer takes then place *solvendi causa*. Separating the actual transfer transaction from the transaction creating the obligation to transfer entails that the actual transfer is no longer self-explanatory. For instance a contract of transfer regarding a chattel (§ 929 BGB) may be concluded in order to fulfil an obligation arising from a contract of sale (§ 433 I BGB), or from making a gift (§ 516 BGB), or even pursuant to a relationship of obligation imposed by law (eg, delict). Hence, the abstract transfer transaction is 'neutral' as to the reasons why it is actually carried out. Again, there are qualifications to be made, which we need not discuss here in detail.

To summarise: the *principle of separation* means that one must distinguish conceptually between the relationship of obligation and the transfer transaction. The relationship of obligation (*Verpflichtungsgeschäft*) concerns the obligation to transfer or alter a proprietary interest but does not, of itself, achieve the transfer or alteration. The actual transfer occurs exclusively by virtue of the transfer transaction (*Verfügung*), which in the case of transferring ownership in chattels for instance requires another contract, namely the contract of transfer and in addition the passing of possession (§ 929 sentence 1 BGB). The transfer transaction is abstract, ie it does carry a reason for its conclusion in itself. Generally speaking the contract of obligation provides the reason for the transfer transaction.

Moving now to the *principle of abstraction* one notes the following. According to this principle, the validity of the contract of obligation and the validity of the contract of transfer are independent from each other. The practical consequence of the principle of abstraction is that where the contract of obligation is invalid, eg, where it is rescinded *ex tunc* or *ab initio*, the person who had transferred property in fulfilling the obligation arising under that contract has a personal remedy only against the other party. In the terms of the BGB, he cannot raise a *Vindikations* claim, requesting as owner the restoration of possession under § 985, but may only claim the transfer of ownership back to him according to the rules of unjustified enrichment (§ 812 I 1 Alt. 1). The principle of abstraction presupposes of course the principle of separation; yet it is not derived from it.

We can understand better now why the contract of obligation was rationalised as providing a reason (*causa*) for the contract of transfer. It ties in with the law of unjust enrichment. The idea of having causal and abstract transactions is able to explain (effortlessly) what happens if the contract of obligation is *void*. In this case, the transfer occurred *without reason* and has thus *unjustifiably* enriched the promisee. The latter is therefore required, according to the rules of unjustified enrichment (§ 812 I 1 Alt. 1, *Leistungskondiktion*), to return the proprietary interest.

The principle of abstraction does not exclude however the possibility that the same source of invalidity might affect *both* the contract of obligation and the contract of transfer. Lack of capacity (§ 104), for instance, will nullify both a contract of sale under § 433 and also any ensuing transfer of the property according to § 929. The same applies where the promise and the transfer were obtained as a result of threats, § 123 I. (In English law, see the result of the duress case of *Barton v Armstrong* [1976] AC 104.) It must be stressed once more: in these cases the contract of transfer is invalid because it suffers from a defect of its own. The invalidity does not follow from the fact that the contract of obligation is invalid.

If the contract of obligation is invalid while the contract of transfer does not suffer from a defect, the transferee is according to the rules of unjust enrichment required to restore the property to the transferor. One might wonder therefore whether the principle of abstraction is needed after all. Its importance becomes clear however if one considers *the position of third parties.*

The main effect of the principle of abstraction is that it acts like a 'filter': certain grounds of invalidity (notably mistake) of the contract of obligation do not also affect the passing of property. If the transferee remains owner by virtue of the principle of abstraction he may validly pass on the property to third party purchasers regardless whether the contract of obligation has been later rescinded for mistake by the original owner. The German adoption of the abstraction principle increases commercial certainty at the expense of the original owner's interest in retaining his title to the goods. This approach achieves consistency and clarity with regard to the position of the third party/acquirer of the mistakenly sold chattel. It effectively guarantees that he is always protected provided that the contract of transfer does not suffer from a defect of its own. No allowance is made for the possibility of the third party being 'less innocent' than the seller and victim of mistake. Flexibility is thus sacrificed to the value of certainty.

Adopting such a rule is, ultimately, a question of a value judgment. And German law, in tort as well as in contract, often declares its preference for certainty even if this brings rigidity in its wake. One cannot criticise this value judgment for, like all value judgments, it has pros and cons. Yet one is encouraged to discuss its merits and contrast it to the more flexible approach of the common law. Furthermore, the existence of the principle of abstraction may also explain why German law recognises more extensively mistake as a reason for setting a contract aside than is the case with English law. For in English law the fine-tuning of the rules on mistake directly affects the extent to which commercial certainty is threatened in dealings with third parties. This is not the case in German law where the abstraction principle effectively shields the contract of transfer from such defects. (We will return to this aspect in chapter 6.)

There is an important qualification to be made. Even if the contract of transfer is invalid and property did not pass, third parties may nevertheless be able to acquire property from the non-owner if they are in good faith and further conditions are met (this and exceptions to the English *nemo dat* rule are explained more fully below). Yet this solution favoured by the common law achieves less certainty precisely because it depends on further and often difficult to establish factors to allow property to pass down the line.

The system-building principle of abstraction was not an ad hoc 'discovery' of the Commission entrusted with the task of drafting the BGB. The principle of abstraction was the fruit of scholarly work, being developed mainly by Savigny (see his *Obligationenrecht*, vol 2 (1853) 256 *et seq*). Savigny observed that there were cases where the transfer of possession and a concordant intention of the parties transferred ownership without a prior obligation to do so: eg, when a spontaneous donation is made. If the contract creating the obligation were void, this also he argued should not make the transfer of the property invalid. The validity of a contract of obligation and that of a contract of transfer are to be assessed independently of each other.

Though the conceptualism described above is missing from English theory, the question that has to be addressed is: how does the latter system resolve the kinds of issues which the above-mentioned conceptualism was meant to address? (For a recent discussion providing interesting comments upon some of these issues, see Swadling, 'Rescission, Property and the Common Law' (2005) 121 *LQR* 123.) Looking at matters functionally, one (somewhat) tentatively would suggest the following.

In English law the principle of separation is not recognised. The passing of the property normally follows from the contract of obligation. Even if a further act is required, such as conveyance or delivery, this does not involve a separate 'contract of transfer.' The principle of abstraction in the narrow technical meaning of the term is thus also not known to English law. However, in some cases the passing of property is allowed to stand even if the contract turns out to be void or unenforceable. It suffices here to make two general observations: the first explores the complex relationship between the invalidity of the contract and the passing of property, and the second provides a brief outlook on the law of restitution.

First, in English law, *the precise ground that invalidates the contract has important implications* for the nature of the remedy and the party against whom it is available. Thus it is necessary to distinguish contracts that are void for illegality (which is usually the case only where so provided by statute) from those that are merely unenforceable in which case the transfer of property is not affected (as was the case in *Bowmakers Ltd v Barnet Instruments Ltd* [1945] KB 65; cf *Singh v Ali* [1960] AC 167 (Privy Council); Goode, *Commercial Law* (3rd edn, 2004), pp 130-5 on illegality; and see further, chapter 5, section 3, p 240 and the references cited therein). More complex is the situation where the contract is void. Here the effect on transfer of property depends on whether it is derived from the contract or from a subsequent separate act of conveyance. If derived from the contract, the transfer is rendered void by the invalidity of the contract. (See, however, Swadling (2005) 121 *LQR* 123, 152, who argues that English law should move in a different direction. In his view the question ought to be whether, in spite of the voidness of the contract, property nevertheless passed *by delivery*. Whether the courts will ascribe such a crucial role to the rules on delivery remains to be seen. Interestingly, Swadling derives at least some of his argument from the 'principle of abstraction' as recognised in German law.) If however the contract was followed by a separate conveyance (as is the case on the sale of land) the invalidity of the contract has no effect on the conveyance.

If a mistake made by the seller was sufficiently fundamental to render the contract void, then property does not pass to the buyer. (On this see *Cundy v Lindsay* (1878) 3 App Cas 459 and Treitel, *The Law of Contract* (11th edn, 2003), chapter 8, especially pp 286–304; also, see chapter 6, p 276 for fuller discussion of mistake.) The buyer cannot transfer a better title than he himself possesses: *nemo dat quod non habet*. However, exceptions to the *nemo dat* rule are recognised in English law, such as section 25 of the Sale of Goods Act 1979, where the buyer acquires possession with the consent of the seller and then transfers them to a bona fide third party who lacks notice of any rights of the original seller. (On this, see *Newtons of Wembley Ltd v Williams* [1965] 1 QB 560, which concerned the position under the similarly worded section 9 (*juncto* section 2(2)) of the Factors Act 1889, concerning mercantile agents. On *nemo dat* and bona fide purchase more generally, see Davies, 'Transferability and Sale of Goods' (1987) 7 *Leg St* 1 and Swadling, 'Restitution and *Bona Fide* Purchase' in Swadling (ed), *The Limits of Restitutionary Claims: A Comparative Analysis* (1997).) Yet such exceptions are not available where the mistake is so fundamental that it renders that contract void. In the absence of any *vindicatio*, English law deals with such property interests through the law of wrongs: in this case, via the tort of conversion. Thus, under a transfer of the chattel that was made subject to a fundamental mistake, the original seller can proceed in conversion against third parties who have subsequently acquired the chattel from the original buyer (*Cundy v Lindsay* (1878) 3 App Cas 459; and cf *Lewis v Averay* [1972] 1 QB 198, where the mistake was not fundamental and rescission of the contract had not been effected in time, so that a bona fide purchase by the third party (Averay) without notice of the interest of the owner (Lewis) prior to that attempt to rescind meant that the third party acquired good title to the car; and compare *Lewis v Averay* with *Car & Universal Finance Co Ltd v Caldwell* [1965] 1 QB 525, where rescission was effected in time). Such a claim in conversion is a personal claim for damages in which the claimant recovers the market value of the thing and any special loss that has resulted; and where such damages represent the whole of the claimant's interest, payment extinguishes the claimant's title and vests it in the defendant (by virtue of section 5 of the Torts (Interference with Goods) Act 1977).

Misrepresentation on the other hand makes the contract *voidable* by the representee but not void. Thus, if property in a chattel was intended to be, and has been, transferred to the representor then the representor holds it until such time as rescission occurs. That is to say, the representor acquires a voidable title, so that if the chattel is then transferred for value to an innocent third party then the representee's right to avoid the original contract is lost (see, eg, *Stevenson v Newnham* (1853) 13 CB 285; 138 ER 1208). This however is not the end of the matter.

Further complications may thus arise as a result of equitable proprietary analyses of the consequences of mistaken payments. In the case of *Chase Manhattan Bank v Israel-British Bank (London) Ltd* [1981] 1 Ch 105, a bank that had mistakenly duplicated a payment was held to have retained an equitable interest in the value of those funds. While it seems clear, as a result of the House of Lords' decision in *Westdeutsche Landesbank Girozentrale v Islington London Borough Council* [1996] AC 669, that payments made under a contract that was void (due to a lack of capacity on the part of the council) are not automatically subject to a resulting trust, fears remain that payments made due to a fundamental mistake may make such moneys subject to a resulting trust in favour of the payor (see, eg, Bridge, *Personal Property Law* (3rd edn, 2002), pp 111–14). The reader is referred to more specialist works on equity to delve more deeply into these complexities (see, eg, Goode, 'Proprietary Restitutionary Claims' in Cornish, Nolan, O'Sullivan and Virgo (eds), *Restitution: Past, Present and Future* (1998) and *Snell's Equity* (2005)).

Secondly, the approach of English law to restitution is markedly different from that of German law sketched out above. The defendant need not justify his acquisition from the plaintiff. Even if that acquisition was without legal basis the plaintiff still needs to establish a positive ground of restitution or a so-called 'unjust factor'. The German *Leistungskondiktion*, by contrast, does not require more than that the transaction lacked a justifiable legal basis. The difference between the two approaches in practice is not as great as it might seem at first sight, since the grounds of restitution recognised in English law are wide-ranging. They include mistake, necessity, failure of consideration, illegality etc. In most cases, therefore, the reason for setting the contract of obligation aside or declaring it void and the ground of restitution will be functionally equivalent, so that in the end it does not make a difference whether the claim is for unjustified enrichment or proceeds upon the basis of unjust factors. It is not the place here to go into details. (For useful comparative overviews and discussion, see Johnston and Zimmerman (eds), *Unjustified Enrichment—Key Issues in Comparative Perspective* (2002) and Beatson and Schrage (eds), *Cases, Materials and Texts on Unjustified Enrichment* (2003), pp 252 *et seq*, 343 *et seq*, and Birks's remarkable attempt to found the English law of restitution on the principle of unjust enrichment, *Unjust Enrichment* (2nd edn, 2005).)

The above remarks show that the result in individual cases, the results reached by German and English law, may well converge despite the very different conceptual starting points. To the extent that this is so, what then are the advantages, if any, of a strict notional separation of the contract of obligation and the transfer transaction in German law?

The principle of separation, independently of whether one also adopts the principle of abstraction, has—to German eyes—analytical advantages compared with systems which view the contract of obligation and the contract of transfer as being one and the same thing. The reason is simple. If contracts creating obligations and contracts transferring, altering, extinguishing, or encumbering rights are clearly distinguished, it becomes possible to subject each class to different rules as the subject matter requires. This does not mean that these requirements are necessarily absent if a system (such as the English) does not require a separate contract of transfer. In such a system, the criteria for the passing of property (eg, that delivery to the carrier is sufficient) are then merged into the discussion of the scope of the contractual obligations of the parties. In other words, it is generally easier to state in abstract terms and independently from the contract of obligation that the parties happen to conclude what the *conditions for the passing of property* are. This enhances legal certainty.

This may sometimes be the case in English law. In certain contexts, however, statutory criteria exist on when property passes or on what sorts of provision can be chosen by the parties for the passing of property—see, generally, the Sale of Goods Act 1979 (discussed by Brown, *Commercial Law* (2001), chapter 16, especially pp 302 *et seq*; see, generally, on the passing of property, Lawson, 'The Passing of Property and Risk in Sale of Goods—A Comparative Study' (1949) 65 *LQR* 352 and Smith, *Property Problems in Sale* (1978) chapters II and III).

In the following, we will focus on four particular features of *Verfügungen* which are *irrelevant* in relation to a contract of obligation. In the course of these observations we will venture beyond the realms of the law of obligation, but this is necessary to understand the operation of the principles of separation and abstraction.

First, legal transactions that directly affect rights are required to set out specifically which rights are affected. This is referred to as the *Bestimmtheitsgrundsatz*. For instance, it is not possible to transfer property in bulk commodities before such commodities have been specifically apportioned according to the contract.

English law experienced similar difficulties in this situation (due to section 16 of the Sale of Goods Act 1979, which prevents property from passing under a contract of sale where the goods are unascertained) as the case of *Re Goldcorp Exchange Ltd* [1995] 1 AC 74 (in the Privy Council) made clear: the seller's promise to hold an agreed quantity of gold bullion for the buyer did not specify any particular bullion, but was rather intended to be covered by whatever bullion the seller held in its possession as and when the buyer claimed the agreed quantity. This difficulty concerning unascertained goods was partly addressed by section 1(3) of the Sale of Goods (Amendment) Act 1995, which inserted section 20A into the Sale of Goods Act 1979. The effect of section 20A is to allow the buyer to become owner in common of the goods (to the extent that he has paid for them), provided that the bulk cargo in question is 'identified' (suggesting that the specific situation in *Goldcorp* would still not be covered, as there was no *identified* bulk held by the sellers in their possession). Likewise, in German law a contract that transfers the property in goods in a certain warehouse up to a certain value is invalid for lack of specificity: one would not know in which particular goods ownership was transferred. It should be noted that assignment (§ 398) is also categorised as *Verfügung*. As a result it must be possible to determine exactly which is the particular claim assigned.

A second requirement peculiar to *Verfügungen* is that the promisor has the legal power (*Verfügungsmacht*) to transfer, alter etc the right in question. (English law would rely upon the maxim *nemo dat quod non habet* here to achieve a similar result: for discussion, see, eg, Bridge, *Personal Property Law*, pp 117–36). A person is not able to transfer ownership in a chattel that is not owned by him. A person who is not the creditor in relation to a particular claim cannot validly assign it. In the interests of commercial convenience, there are certain limited exceptions to this rule. Thus, where the promisor has actual possession of a chattel and the owner did not lose possession involuntarily, the promisee, who did not know and could but for gross negligence not know of the lack of ownership, will become owner of the chattel to the detriment of the real owner, § 932 (*gutgläubiger Eigentumserwerb*). Similarly, such exceptions to the *nemo dat* rule exist in English law to facilitate commerce: thus, the transfer of coins or banknotes *as currency* to a recipient taking them in good faith and for valuable consideration will confer a good title to that currency upon the transferee (*Miller v Race* (1758) 1 Burr 452; 97 ER 398). Further exceptions are laid down by statute, either generally in relation to the sale of goods (see the Sale of Goods Act 1979: sections 21(1) (estoppel); 23 (sale under a voidable title); 24 (sale by a seller in possession); 25(1) (sale by a buyer in possession) and 62(2) (sale by a mercantile agent) or in relation to specific types of property (eg, a car subject to a hire-purchase agreement: Part III of the Hire Purchase Agreement Act 1964).

In relation to interests in land, the promisee to a *Verfügung* is protected in his reasonable reliance on the content of the land register (*Grundbuch*), § 892. No protection however is afforded to an assignee, even if he had reason to believe that the assignor was entitled to the purported claim. In the case of chattels and land, reasonable reliance is supported by general presumptions as to the entitlement to the right: the actual possessor is presumed to be the owner (§ 1006), the content of the land register is presumed to be correct (§ 891). No such presumptions can be made in relation to personal claims. In English land law, the register operates to fulfil this function in a very similar way (see the Land Registration Act 2002 and the regulations adopted thereunder; for discussion, see Harpum, *Megarry and Wade—The Law of Real Property* (6th edn, 2000), chapter 6).

Interrelated with this is the *third* requirement that, in relation to *Verfügungen* of property law the transfer must in some form be made 'public', *Publizitätsprinzip*: in the case of chattels by the *traditio* (transfer of possession) in the case of immovables the land register fulfils this purpose. (On the origins of *traditio* see, eg, Zimmermann, *The Law of Obligations*, pp 239, 240 and 271 ff.)

The transfer of chattels can operate in this way in English law (and is particularly important in the case of gifts not expressed in the form of a deed—see *Irons v Smallpiece* (1819) 2 B & Ald 551; 106 ER 467; effectively, this active demonstration of donative intent is seen to make up for the fact that the transaction is otherwise gratuitous, thus justifying the law in enforcing the transfer of property); however, the current statutory provisions start from the presumption that it is for the parties to determine the point at which property passes (section 17 Sale of Goods Act 1979). Nevertheless, it should not be forgotten that the legislation also contains a number of presumptive rules to cover situations where the parties have not made their intentions on this point clear. While the land register in England and Wales could also be said to fulfil this 'publicity' function, it should be noted that it was not open to public inspection until 3 December 1990 (see the Land Registration Act 1998 (Commencement) Order 1990, SI 1990/1359, which brought into force the new rules on public access, on payment of a fee and subject to certain conditions (for which see the Land Registration (Open Register) Rules 1991 SI 1992/122 (as amended)). Thus, it is difficult to argue that such a 'principle of publicity' was in any way behind the original adoption of the registration system back in 1925: indeed, the main aims appeared instead to have been to speed up conveyancing and to reduce the costs associated therewith, by obviating the need for costly and time-consuming duplications of effort in re-examining title to the same land (see Harpum, *Megarry and Wade—The Law of Real Property*, pp 201–3).

Finally, so far as the law of property is concerned, the parties are not free to deviate from the requirements as to *Verfügungen* laid down in the BGB; this is referred to as the so-called *Typenzwang*. For instance, an interest in land exists only within the framework provided by the law. The parties cannot set up a scheme outside the bounds of the rules of property law as contained in the Code and applied by the courts. Likewise, a proprietary interest can only be successfully transferred if the statutory requirements for such transactions are met, eg, the requirement of notification of the transfer in the land register. The difference with § 311 I BGB is striking. As far as contractual relationships are concerned the parties are in principle free to determine the content and form of their agreement.

Similarly, in English law there are formal requirements for effecting a transfer of freehold land (a simple statutory form of transfer and the land certificate must be lodged at the appropriate District Land Registry—see rules 74, 74A, 83, 98 and Schedule 1 of the Land Registration Rules 1925); however, it is the act of registration that confers the legal title, so that if registration is granted, any formal defects are cured (rule 322 of the Land Registration Rules 1925 and see *Morelle Ltd v Wakeling*

[1955] 2 QB 379). A consequence of this is that the *nemo dat* principle is not applied to real property: nevertheless, the fact that a disposition of land may have been fraudulent is likely to be relevant if rectification of the register is sought (see Harpum, *Megarry & Wade—The Law of Real Property*, pp 278–86).

The rationale of this strict approach to *Verfügungen* or transfer transactions is to achieve as much security in the law as is conceivable by the means of private law. While some of the strict rules as to the transfer of proprietary interests are self-evident and in the practical end result shared by the common law (for instance the *Bestimmtheitsgrundsatz*), others have been met with great scepticism by English lawyers. In particular, in relation to the land register (*Grundbuch*) there was a considerable debate as to whether a similar system ought to be introduced in England and Wales (see, (1897) 13 *LQR* 210; Burns, 'Land Transfer in Germany and Austria' (1897) 9 *The Juridical Review* 155; *Royal Commission on the Land Transfer Acts*, vol II, Cd 5483 (1911)) before the registration system eventually established itself in England and Wales in 1925. More recently, the debate surrounding overriding interests shows consideration of similar issues: see the Law Commission's Consultation Paper and Report on *Land Registration for the 21st Century* (Law Com Nos 254 and 271 respectively), considering why, in the face of the pursuit of certainty (in relying upon the contents of the register), certain interests should still override properly registered conveyances (eg, actual occupation under section. 70(1)(g) LRA 1925).

The strict rules applying to contracts of transfer do not prejudice the protection of the autonomy of a person. Indeed, it is one of the advantages of the principles of separation that freedom of contract must not be restricted: the needs of commercial convenience and security in the law can be met by subjecting the contract of transfer to strict rules. Thus, I am free to *undertake* to deliver goods which do not yet belong to me or which are still to be produced. It is only when it comes to the transfer of the proprietary interest that the requirements of specificity must be observed. But even as far as property law is concerned, the autonomy of the person is affected only marginally in the interest of the protection of the legal community (*Rechtsverkehr*). For, of course, I am free to decide whether or not, to whose benefit, for what reason and how much of a/my proprietary interest I transfer, extinguish, encumber or alter, provided only that the rules of Book Three of the BGB (as to the way in which it is done) are followed.

A drawback of forcing the parties to use pre-defined and mandatory models (*Typenzwang*) is the danger of the stagnation over time of such models (or the risk that, over time, such rules will not prove sufficiently malleable): the lack of flexibility to adapt to the changing demands of business. On the whole, however, the doctrine has not caused major problems in practice, mainly because the courts have seized every opportunity provided by the BGB to soften and adapt the strict rules of property law to fulfil the demands of modern commerce. Since this topic is best dealt with in a book on property law, it suffices here to give just one example for the creativity of the judiciary: this is the development of the so-called 'security ownership' (*Sicherungseigentum*). The rules of the BGB do not provide for a lien without actual possession (§ 1205). This can cause difficulties where banks insist on a security for a loan and at the same time the debtor has a vital interest in keeping possession of the said thing because, for instance, he is using the machine for production. It is sensible to provide a way to secure the loan by not transferring actual possession, for otherwise the debtor might not be able to generate the means to pay the loan back. In § 930 the BGB actually stipulates for the transfer of the ownership while actual possession remains with the transferor. The difficulty is that full ownership is more than the security interest which would suffice to secure the loan. The courts solved the dilemma by applying § 930 yet not attaching to it the full implications of 'ownership', hence developing what in effect is a 'possession-less' lien and, remaining faithful to the BGB, calling it 'security ownership'. (See, eg, BGHZ 72, 141, granting the possessor a right to object to an arrest by creditors of the 'security owner'; and BGHZ 28, 16, discussing the conditions of specificity.)

6. THE CONSTITUTIONALISATION OF PRIVATE LAW

The classic purpose of human rights (or *Grundrechte*) as they are laid down in Articles 1 to 19 of the German Constitution ('Basic Law', *Grundgesetz*) is to protect the citizen against intrusions of the state into the private sphere. Whether human rights also bind citizens in private law relationships is a matter of considerable debate.

The original position was that they did not, though already during the period of the Weimar Republic (1919–33) the signs of the first stirrings in the opposite direction can be found. (For instance, article 111 § 1, 2nd sentence, of the 1918 Constitution provided that free speech must not be hampered by any employment relationship and no one should be disadvantaged for exercising such rights.) The Basic Law of 1949 was to prove here, as in so many other respects, the catalyst for change. Academics moved first, Hans Nipperdey—a professor and later the first president of the Federal Labour Court—firing the first serious salvo with an important article published in 1950 ('Gleicher Lohn der Frau für gleiche Leistung. Ein Beitrag zur Auslegung der Grundrechte' in *Recht der Arbeit*, 1950, 121 *et seq*). His court followed by proclaiming that the Constitution had a 'direct effect' (*unmittelbare Drittwirkung*), only to be moderated a few years later by the famous *Lüth* decision (*The German Law of Torts*, case no 36, BVerfGE 7, 198).

There, the *Bundesverfassungsgericht* (the German Constitutional Court) stopped short of giving the constitution direct horizontal effect—ie allowing the direct invocation of human rights in disputes of private law—yet attributed to it what is usually referred to as 'indirect horizontal effect' (*mittelbare Drittwirkung*) which requires the courts, when interpreting the Civil Code, to give due regard to the Constitutional values. (In *The German Law of Torts*, pp 28 *et seq*, we discuss in detail this process of 'constitutionalisation' of private law. The present outline should be read in conjunction with those passages, as well as with the remarks as to the different functions of general clauses in the BGB, p 23, section 14.)

Regarding human rights as embodying an authoritative hierarchy of values seems at first a modest claim. Yet it forces one to attach indirect horizontal effect to these constitutional values through means of codal interpretation. When it came to developing private law remedies for the invasion of the right of privacy (which were deliberately not provided for in the Code), the Constitutional Court explained: 'Occasionally, the law can be found outside the positive legal rules erected by the state; this is law which emanates from the entire constitutional order and which has as its purpose the "correction" of written law.' (BVerfGE 34, 269.) Thus, occasionally, arguments deriving from the human rights provisions of the Constitution have enabled the courts to develop new private law remedies even where the text of the Code was not susceptible to interpretation.

Yet the weight of an argument derived from the Constitution is all the greater if the provisions of private law leave room for interpretation. General clauses, such as those found in §§ 138 and 242, contain open-textured principles with no clearly pre-defined content. 'Public policy' and 'good faith' were, applying the broad value-based approach of the Constitutional Court, bound to be interpreted in the light of the Constitution. Human rights as the supreme values of the *Grundgesetz* have thus acquired special weight in interpreting the general clauses of the Code. A classic statement of this approach can be found in the famous *Bürge* decision (BVerfG NJW 1994, 36, 38, case no 81 reproduced below):

> The Basic Law contains in its basic rights section fundamental decisions in constitutional law for all areas of the law. These fundamental decisions develop through the medium of those provisions which directly control the area of law in question, and above all have significance in the interpretation of general clauses in civil law (references). When § 138 and § 242 of the BGB refer quite generally to good morals, custom (*Verkehrsitte*) and good faith, they require concretisation by the courts by the standard of value concepts which are primarily determined by decisions of principle in the Constitution. Therefore the civil courts are constitutionally obliged to have regard to the basic rights as 'guidelines' in the interpretation and application of the general clauses. If they fail to recognise this, and therefore make a decision which is to the disadvantage of a party to the proceedings, they violate that party's basic rights . . .

Hence, soon after the adoption of the Constitution of 1949 the general clauses of the BGB came to be regarded as 'entrance points' for Constitutional values. Indeed, the *Bundesverfassungsgericht* regularly reminds the civil courts to give due consideration to human rights issues when applying general clauses and, where it thinks necessary, it has not hesitated to interfere in the resolution of private law disputes by imposing a specific interpretation of the constitution which in effect pre-determines the result of the litigation: eg, BVerfG NJW 1990, 1469; NJW 1994, 36, case no 81; NJW 1994, 2749; NJW 1996, 2021. (For a review of the case law in English, see Markesinis, *Always on the Same Path. Essays on Foreign Law and Comparative Methodology*, vol II, (2001), chapters 7 and 8.) It is thus mainly through the medium of general clauses that value-judgments regarding the protection of human dignity, the prohibition of discrimination, etc, find their way into the policing of contracts. It should be noted, however, that it is to a great extent 'accidental' which of the general clauses is used in justifying the indirect impact of the human rights arguments.

It is perhaps useful to give a few brief illustrations, which will be taken up later in the book.

The first is BAG NZA 1994, 1080, case no 42, discussed in chapter 3, section 2(d), p 123 where the dismissal of an employee was declared contrary to good faith because it was solely motivated by the employer's aversion to the homosexual orientation of the employee.

The second example concerns the line of succession in the Hohenzollern family. The great-grandchild of the German Emperor Wilhelm II claimed the estate that had been denied to him because he had married a woman of less than equal birth. His disqualification resulted out of a contract of inheritance and the question arose whether this contract was void as being contrary to public policy § 138 I (or contrary to good faith, § 242). The *Bundesgerichtshof* (NJW 1999, 566) came to the conclusion that the contract was not void under § 138 but the *Bundesverfassungsgericht*, NJW 2004, 2008, case no 78, quashed the decision because it did not give sufficient consideration to the right of the beneficiary freely to select his spouse (Article 6 I of the Basic Law, freedom of marriage) when interpreting the general clause and overvalued the testator's right to dispose of the estate as he saw fit (Article 14 I, *Testierfreiheit*).

The decision is an impressive illustration of how the content of general clauses changes over time. Initially, it was obviously the case that the law of succession of the Hohenzollern family was not *contra bonos mores*. During the period of the monarchy, these rules were part of the constitutional arrangements. Yet, as the court stressed, with the abolition of the monarchy on 11 August 1919, the laws of inheritance also had to be interpreted in a new light and balanced against the civilian liberty freely to choose a partner for marriage! (See, also, for a discussion in English of the inheritance cases and the BGH decision referred to above: Heldrich and Rehm, 'Importing Constitutional Values through Blanket Clauses' chapter 6 in Friedmann and Barak-Erez (eds), *Human Rights in Private Law* (2002), pp 113–28.)

Two further examples complete this survey of the constitutionalisation of private law by the means of interpretation of general clauses. The recent vintage of these lines of cases indicates that the tendency is rather towards increasing the importance of human rights in private law; and a growing number of British lawyers seem to share this belief so far as their own law is concerned.

The *Bundesverfassungsgericht* laid the foundations for a stricter judicial control of the fairness of contract terms in its famous *Bürge* decision (NJW 1994, 36, case no 81), a case concerning guarantees undertaken by close family members who were in no financial position to pay the loan. In this decision, the court stressed that where the terms of a contract were considerably imbalanced and 'unfair' to one party (*'ungewöhnlich belastend und als Interessenausgleich offensichtlich unangemessen'*) the civil courts should inquire whether this contract was the result of a systemic imbalance of bargaining power (*'strukturell ungleiche Verhandlungsstärke'*; the court also used the term distorted 'parity' of contract, *'gestörte Vertragsparität'*). If this were indeed the case, to have upheld the contract would have been to violate that party's constitutional right to self-determination in matters of private law. Contract as a means of achieving personal autonomy would here amount to heteronomy.

Above, by way of introduction (section 1) we already noted the influence of the *Sozialstaatsprinzip* on the court's reasoning in this case. It is necessary at this stage to explain the principle in more detail. (For an overview see, eg, Badura DÖV 1989, 491; Schnapp JuS 1998, 873.) The *Sozialstaatsprinzip* constitutes first and foremost an obligation addressed to the legislator. (BVerfGE 8, 274, 329: 'The details of what the social state requires are determined by the legislator.') Introduced for the first time in 1949, the principle attempts a modification of the classical (liberal) *Rechtsstaat* tradition and calls for a reduction of glaring social inequalities (BVerfGE 5, 85, 198), the protection of socially and economically weak parties (eg, employees, tenants, women and children, minorities), and a guarantee concerning the most basic preconditions of subsistence through the social security system. One can find judgments from such diverse areas of the law as social security, pension claims, landlord and tenant law, labour law, consumer protection and legal aid law, which contain references to the principle—passing and some times more detailed. (See, eg, BGH NJW 2002, 1269; NJW-RR 2003, 1441: maintenance claims; BGH FamRZ 2004, 1274: pension claims flowing from a life insurance dating back before German reunification in 1990; BGH NJW-RR 2004, 507: margin of subsistence under § 850f ZPO in enforcement proceedings of an alimony order; likewise BGH NJW 2003, 1457: limits of enforcement imposed by 'social' legislation; BGH NJW 2003, 2906: termination of employment contracts, *Leiharbeitnehmer*.)

It is however important to emphasise that unlike the *Rechtsstaatsprinzip*, which is reflected in many provisions of the Constitution and numerous decisions of the Constitutional Court, the *Sozialstaatsprinzip* has not been used as a directly applicable legal principle by German courts. Indeed, as indicated by its systematic position outside the catalogue of individual rights and freedoms (*Grundrechte*), the principle does not establish immediate and legally enforceable rights or obligations (BVerfGE 39, 302, 315). Yet, both the executive and the courts are, however, bound by the Basic Law. In conjunction with other principles, the *Sozialstaatsprinzip* thus appears to feature as an interpretative tool (*Auslegungshilfe*: BVerfGE 1, 97, 105). In the decision here under consideration, the *Bürge*-decision, BVerfGE NJW 1994, 36, case no 81, the principle was also deployed as an interpretative guideline, namely in concretising and fleshing out 'general clauses' of the BGB. A contract that places an unusually heavy burden on one of the parties involved in the transaction, and is the result of a 'structurally unbalanced distribution of bargaining power' is thus said not to be acceptable in the light of the principle of 'private autonomy' and ultimately the *Sozialstaatsprinzip*. A more prominent role of the latter principle had in fact been demanded previously for instance by the later President of the Court Jutta Limbach, JuS 1985, 10 (the article 'Das Rechtsverständnis der Vertragslehre' in which the author expresses the hope that the 'individualistic' perspective of private lawyers will be overcome, and is cited with approval in the decision at hand) and Raiser, 'Vertragsfreiheit heute' JZ 1958, 1, though the *Sozialstaatsprinzip* had rarely been used by a court in such a bold fashion in policing a contract. (Approving: Larenz and Wolf, *Allgemeiner Teil* (9th edn, 2004) § 42, 754 ff.) It comes as little surprise therefore that the *Bundesgerichtshof* follows only reluctantly the policy oriented stance of the Constitutional Court and many private lawyers strongly oppose the idea of constitutionally guaranteed 'equality of bargaining power.' (For an alternative explanation of the *Bürge*-decision and for a more detailed discussion, see chapter 5, p 256.)

From the vast literature on these topics see further: Adomeit, 'Die gestörte Vertragsparität—ein Trugbild' NJW 1994, 2467; Canaris, 'Grundrechte und Privatrecht' AcP 184 (1984), 201; AcP 185 (1985), 9 and *Grundrechte und Privatrecht* (1999); Cherednychenko, 'The Constitutionalization of Contract Law: Something New under the Sun?' (2004) 8(1) *Electronic Journal of Comparative Law* (available at: http://www.ejcl.org/81/art81-3.PDF); Hager, 'Grundrechte im Privatrecht' JZ 1994, 373; Hönn, *Kompensation gestörter Vertragsparität* (1982); Honsell, 'Bürgschaft und Mithaftung einkommens- und vermögensloser Familienmitglieder' NJW 1994, 565; Singer, 'Vertragsfreiheit, Grundrechte und der Schutz des Menschen vor sich selbst' JZ 1995, 1133.

A certain affinity between the court's blend of criteria for invalidating the contract and Lord Denning MR's (failed) formula of 'inequality of bargaining power' can readily be appreciated, although a good deal of this resemblance is owed to the vagueness of the respective 'tests'. Lord Denning remarked in *Lloyds Bank Ltd v Bundy* ([1975] QB 326, at 339) that this principle gives relief to someone who entered into a contract where consideration was 'grossly inadequate' and his 'bargaining power' was 'grievously impaired by reason of his or her own needs or desires, or by his own ignorance or infirmity.' (It should be noted that Lord Denning's formulation in *Bundy* has not commanded a strong following in the subsequent general English case law (see Treitel, *The Law of Contract* (11th edn, 2003), pp 420–3). Such inequality of bargaining power is however relevant under legislation which has granted discretion to the judges to supervise the terms of contracts (see, eg, the Unfair Contract Terms Act 1977, Schedule 2 para (a)) and also has a role in the judicial scrutiny of particular types of contract, such as covenants in restraint of trade (where only 'reasonable' covenants will be enforced by the courts: see, eg, *Shell UK Ltd v Lostock Garages Ltd* [1976] 1 WLR 1187 at 1197).

It is perhaps also worth noting that a parallel development has taken place in English law where the application of EC competition law renders a contract void as a result of Article 81(2) EC. While this EC Treaty rule is not, in the strict sense, traditionally a 'constitutional value', the application of the EC law doctrines of direct effect, supremacy of EC law and the need for an effective remedy for a breach of EC law grants this rule a status that is very similar to that of constitutional principles. In the case of *Courage Ltd v Crehan* (Case C-453/99 [2001] ECR I-6297), a brewery tie agreement was claimed to be contrary to Article 81 EC and the publican, Mr Crehan, sought to claim damages for the higher prices charged to the tied publicans for the beer supplied. Leaving aside the arguments concerning the proper approach in English law to the question of recovery in such circumstances (on which see, eg, Odudu and Edelman's case note: (2002) 27 *EL Rev* 327, 337–9), as a result of the Court of Justice's decision it could be argued that, *as a matter of EC law*, Article 81 EC can be the basis for such a claim (in this sense Mäsch, 'Private Ansprüche bei Verletzung des europäischen Kartellverbots—"Courage" und die Folgen' EuR 2003, 825; the issue is controversial). Further, national law cannot preclude recovery merely upon the ground that the claimant was a party to the contract that was found to restrict or distort competition. Instead, the court gave guidance as to the ways in which national law might and might not restrict the exercise of such a right to claim damages. 'In particular,' the court stated (at para 33), 'it is for the national court to ascertain whether the party who claims to have suffered loss through concluding a contract that is liable to restrict or distort competition found himself in a markedly weaker position than the other party, such as seriously to compromise or even eliminate his freedom to negotiate the terms of the contract . . .' Thus, for all EC Member States applying the EC competition rules, these factors will be of relevance in assessing the position of the parties to a contract held to violate Article 81 EC. Indeed, in the UK the existence of section 60 of the Competition Act 1998 may apply similar criteria to claims for breach of the analogous national competition law rules. This illustrates what we might term the impact of a 'quasi-constitutional value' (the economic goals of free and undistorted competition) upon the enforcement of contracts and upon the very content of national contract law. Certainly, the European Court of Justice has often been accused of reifying such economic goals to constitutional status in the past (see, eg, Coppel and O'Neill, 'The European Court of Justice: Taking

Rights Seriously?' (1992) 29 *Common Market Law Review* 669). An alternative analysis is that this case shows an interpretation of the EC (and, *a fortiori*, the new UK) competition rules as some measure of 'protection' for the weaker commercial party, so as to allow recovery of damages as otherwise the protective purpose of the superior rule (here, the EC Treaty) would be frustrated. (At the same time, it should be acknowledged that neither of these analyses would find favour with certain schools of economic thinking in the competition law context: see, eg, Bork, *The Antitrust Paradox: A Policy at War with Itself* (1993 edn).)

Returning now to developments in German law we note that the Constitutional Court subsequently extended its approach in *Bürge* to contracts between spouses (*Eheverträge*) regulating the economic consequences of divorce in advance (FamRZ 2001, 343; FamRZ 2001, 985). The *Bundesgerichtshof* was thus forced to reconsider its previous practice. (See BGH NJW 2004, 930, case no 83; and for an evaluation: Langenfeld, ZEV 2004, 311; Rauscher, DNotZ 2004, 524) We will return to this subject in chapter 5, section 4(c)(i), 259, where we will examine more closely the notion of (procedural or substantive?) justice put forward by the *Bundesverfassungsgericht*. However, it should be noted already at this stage that the jurisprudence—according to which general clauses are springboards for constitutional value-judgments—is not without its difficulties. Three such difficulties may be identified at this stage.

First, in private law disputes we are confronted with an exceedingly difficult balancing exercise. Invariably, both plaintiff and defendant are able to rely upon human rights arguments. Thus, in the succession cases we have, on the one hand, the right of the testator to dispose of his patrimony as he thinks fit (Article 14 I) and, on the other, the right of the prospective beneficiary freely to choose wife or husband (Article 6 I). In the *Bürge* decision all actors were said to be able to rely on the right to self-determination through private law acts (Article 2 I). In English law, the recent spate of privacy-related cases brought under the action for breach of confidence has showed a similar dilemma. Thus, at an early stage in the now famous *Douglas v Hello!* saga (*Douglas v Hello! Ltd* [2001] QB 967, at [136]), Sedley LJ made it clear that an appeal to Article 10 ECHR could necessarily include a competing Article 8 ECHR right, by virtue of the exceptions laid down in Article 10(2) ECHR (and of course vice versa) and that this was highly significant in interpreting private law in the light of the UK's Human Rights Act 1998. Further, in the *Theakston v MGN Ltd* ([2002] *EMLR* 22) and *Flitcroft* (*A v B Plc and another* [2003] QB 195) cases, it is clear that the courts approached the question of publication of the activities of celebrities from the perspective that those with whom Messrs Theakston and Flitcroft had chosen to dally also had a right freely to express their views and experiences under Article 10 ECHR. (On these cases see further, Deakin, Johnston and Markesinis, *Markesinis and Deakin's Tort Law* (5th edn, 2003), pp 713–20.)

This leads to the second difficulty. The human rights aspect of a private law dispute is impossible to ascertain in advance with any measure of accuracy. For even if the court takes the view that the basic rights of one of the parties are affected by the conduct of the other party, the balancing of the competing interests is difficult and its outcome difficult to predict. The great number of actions brought after the *Bürge* decision supports this argument. Indeed, it took the different Senates of the *Bundesgerichtshof* eight years to develop a consistent jurisprudence regarding the application of the principles ascribed to the *Bürge* decision (see, for the final episode of this saga, BGH NJW 2002, 2228). The 'guidelines' laid down by the English Court of Appeal in the *Flitcroft* case illustrate this point very well from an English perspective, as does their application by a subsequent Court of Appeal in the Naomi Campbell litigation (*Campbell v MGN Ltd* [2003] QB 633). Both cases concerned claims by very public figures to a private life under Article 8 ECHR. In the former, Lord Woolf CJ (giving the judgment of the Court of Appeal) gave great weight to the importance of the role of the press as a vital conduit for the dissemination of freely expressed views and information, even to the extent of justifying disclosure of Mr Flitcroft's extra-marital affairs to the world via the tabloid press, simply because 'the public have an understandable and so a legitimate interest in being told the information.' In the latter, however, their Lordships were at pains to point out that Lord Woolf had 'not [been] speaking of private facts which a fair-minded person would consider it offensive to disclose.' The House of Lords eventually upheld Miss Campbell's claim against *The Mirror* newspaper for breach of confidence ([2004] 2 WLR 1232), in spite of her celebrity status, which she had done much to cultivate. (Again see *Markesinis and Deakin's Tort Law*, pp 713–20 for further discussion.) And, lest the reader should think that this citation of tort cases suggests that the contractual law of confidential obligations is immune to such human rights-influenced reasoning, it should be noted that, in the recent contractual confidence cases of *Campbell v Frisbee* [2003] ICR 141 and *Lady Archer v Williams* [2003] EWHC 1670; [2003] *EMLR* 38, the courts made clear and explicit reference to the significance of the Human Rights Act 1998 in their reasoning. In the *Frisbee* case, it led the court to refuse to grant a summary judgment of breach of confidence as it raised an arguable issue for the trial ([23]ff, especially [33]–[34]); in the *Archer* case, the argument based upon Article 10 ECHR failed to convince the court that this was sufficient reason to override the contractual duty of confidentiality owed by a secretary and personal assistant to her employer relating to confidential information learned during the currency of that post (see, in particular, [64]–[67]).

Finally, from an institutional point of view, the controversial question arises as to what extent, if at all, the Constitutional Court is justified in interfering with private law disputes.

7. FREEDOM OF CONTRACT

Atiyah, *The Rise and Fall of Freedom of Contract* (1985); Canaris, *Die Bedeutung der iustitia distributiva im deutschen Vertragsrecht* (1997) and 'Wandlungen des Schuldvertragsrechts. Tendenzen zu seiner "Materialisierung"' AcP 200 (2000), 273; Drexl, *Die wirtschaftliche Selbstbestimmung des Verbrauchers* (1998); Fastrich, *Richterliche Inhaltskontrolle im Privatrecht* (1992); Hofer, *Freiheit ohne Grenzen? Privatrechtstheoretische Diskussionen im 19. Jahrhundert* (2001); Junker, 'Individualwille, Kollektivgewalt und Staatsintervention im Arbeitsrecht' NZA 1997, 1305; Kramer, *Die 'Krise' des liberalen Vertragsdenkens* (1974); Limbach, 'Das Rechtsverständnis der Vertragslehre' JuS 1985, 10; S Lorenz, *Der Schutz vor dem unerwünschten Vertrag* (1997); Mayer-Maly, 'Der liberale Gedanke und das Recht' in *Festschrift Merkl* (1970), 247; Medicus, 'Abschied von der Privatautonomie' in

Einheit und Vielfalt der Rechtsordnung (1996), 9; Neuner, *Privatrecht und Sozialstaat* (1999); Oechsler, *Gerechtigkeit im modernen Austauschvertrag* (1997); Pflug, *Kontrakt und Status im Recht der Allgemeinen Geschäftsbedingungen* (1986); L Raiser, 'Vertragsfreiheit heute' JZ 1958, 1; Rittner, 'Über das Verhältnis von Vertrag und Wettbewerb' AcP 188 (1988), 101; E Schmidt, 'Von der Privat- zur Sozialautonomie' JZ 1980, 153; Schmidt-Rimpler, 'Grundfragen einer Erneuerung des Vertragsrechts' AcP 147 (1941), Singer, *Selbstbestimmung und Verkehrsschutz im Recht der Willenserklärungen* (1995); Thüsing, 'Vertragsfreiheit, Persönlichkeitsschutz und Effizienz' ZGS 2005, 49; Trebilcock, *The Limits of Freedom of Contract* (1993); Weitemeyer, 'Das Gesetz zur Regelung der Miethöhe und die Vertragsfreiheit' NZM 2000, 313; HP Westermann, 'Sonderprivatrechtliche Sozialmodelle und allgemeines Privatrecht' AcP 178 (1978), 150; M Wolf, *Rechtsgeschäftliche Entscheidungsfreiheit und vertraglicher Interessenausgleich*, (1970).

(a) Preliminary Observations

It is to state the obvious that the importance one attaches to freedom of contract depends largely on the view one takes, explicitly or implicitly, on matters of political theory. This is as true in Germany as it is elsewhere. On the one hand, there are the more liberally inclined writers who favour the view that the parties to a contract are best left to their own devices, whereas on the other there are those who emphasise the 'social' function of private law and the need for the courts to step in and protect the 'weaker' party. To the reader of the previous section it will come as no surprise that, in German law, a further dimension is added to these aspects of freedom of contract, namely that provided by the wider constitutional context. It is not for us to put forward and defend a specific interpretation of freedom of contract. Rather, the task of this book is to determine the position of contemporary German law.

The history of freedom of contract is in many ways the history of its restrictions. It is more through the scope and nature of the restrictions and less by examining abstract pronouncements of principle that we get a glimpse of the current state of affairs. The reader will also recall Sir Henry Maine's classic analysis of the movement of progressive societies 'from Status to Contract':

> Starting, as from one terminus of history, from a condition of society in which all the relations of Persons are summed up in the relations of Family, we seem to have steadily moved towards a phase of social order in which all these relations arise from the free agreement of Individuals. In Western Europe the progress achieved in this direction has been considerable. (*Ancient Law* (1864), p 165.)

However, after the progressive dissolution of family ties, many other factors have, over time, weighed heavily on freedom of contract. Various restrictions have flowed from birth, guild, or social position in the feudal system of times past. Only slowly did freedom of contract come to be regarded as the crucial asset of nations built around manufacture and trade, Adam Smith's *An Enquiry into the Nature and Causes of the Wealth of Nations* (1776) representing the high-water mark of this faith in the forces of the market. (See, for a discussion of the impact of his ideas in the common law, Atiyah, *Essays on Contract* (1988), chapter 12, pp 355–85.) It is no coincidence that we begin this section on freedom of contract under the BGB with a reference to Adam Smith.

(b) The Initial Position

Initially, the number of restraints on freedom of contract in the BGB was very limited. The guiding principle, though nowhere expressly proclaimed in the text of the Code itself, was summarised by Flume thus: 'The idea behind contract is that what has been agreed is binding because in making the contract the parties have agreed that it should determine their rights and liabilities' (*Allgemeiner Teil*, vol 2, p 7, in the translation of Tony Weir in Zweigert and Kötz, *An Introduction to Comparative Law*, p 325). In the *Motive* (vol 1, p 126) this was reduced to the formula: 'A legal transaction is a private declaration of intention aiming at a legal consequence which the law sanctions because it is intended.' The advocates of a more paternalistic approach to private law, however, severely criticised the BGB for containing only a few 'drops of social oil' (Otto von Gierke, *Die soziale Aufgabe des Privatrechts* (1889), p 10). At the time these debates were taking place, the latter were bound to lose the argument.

It will be recalled that contract is but one instance of a legal transaction; freedom of contract is accordingly only one aspect of the more fundamental idea that a person in possession of legal capacity, not influenced by mistake or undue pressure, is fully capable of determining his fate as far as legal relationships of private law are concerned. This wider idea is referred to by the fathers of the BGB as the *principle of personal autonomy* (*Privatautonomie*), in *Motive*, vol 1, p 10. The importance of personal autonomy can be also seen from the fact that the concept of legal transaction is one of the three basic concepts of the General Part of the BGB (persons, things and legal transactions).

The only conditions for the validity of a 'legal transaction' contained in the General Part are, naturally, legal capacity (§§ 104–13), absence of mistake or vitiating factors (§§ 116–24), compliance with form (§§ 125–9), proper notification of the addressee of a declaration of intention *inter absentes* (§§ 130–2). To this list we must add the 'negative criteria' of absence of a statutory prohibition (§ 134), no violation of public policy (§ 138 I), or the creation of a grossly inadequate *and* unduly obtained bargain (§ 138 II). These are all conditions of validity of legal transactions envisaged by the fathers of the BGB—the wording of § 242 (good faith), being originally limited to the manner of performance. The very fact that nothing more is required gives credit to the liberal spirit in which the BGB was drafted. § 134 was meant mainly to ensure that the provisions of criminal law were also given effect in private law while, as already indicated above, the general clause of § 138 I was expected to be interpreted by the courts in a narrow fashion.

Of particular note is the absence of the requirement of a 'just' price which would have enabled the courts to police contracts much more extensively than under § 138 II, which demanded (in addition to a gross inadequacy of consideration) the presence of vitiating factors (which basically required there to have been some exploitation of the lack of judgement or grave weakness of will of the other party). The doctrine of *laesio enormis* (allowing a contract to be avoided if the disparity between the values of what was exchanged was beyond a certain multiplier—in Roman law, this was two to one or greater) was expressly rejected by the drafters of the BGB (*Motive*, vol 1 (1888), p 321), though it did make a limited appearance in the French Code in the context of transactions concerning land). (For the historical perspective, see Zweigert and Kötz, *An Introduction to Comparative Law*, p 329, and Zimmermann, *The Law of Obligations*, p 259.)

A number of other significant aspects must be mentioned in order to reveal the full scope of freedom of contract under the BGB.

Generally speaking, the parties can contract out of the rules of law contained in the first two books of the BGB concerning the law of obligations arising out of contracts. These rules constitute what is referred to as '*dispositives Recht*,'which means that these rules must be treated as 'default rules' to be applied *unless* the parties have stipulated otherwise. Similarly, the parties are free to define the scope and nature of their contractual obligations. § 311 I, in conjunction with § 241 I, merely emphasise the binding nature of the obligation but does not (unlike the law of property as explained above) force the parties down the path of pre-defined models of contracts. Finally, there are no prerequisites as to the acceptance of an offer; everyone is free to reject the conclusion of a contract (this aspect is referred to as *Abschlußfreiheit*).

The original position of the BGB can be thus summarised as follows. The content of a contract as such was (except for the violation of statutory provisions or *bonos mores*) not to be regarded as sufficient ground to justify the intervention of a court. In terms of substantive and procedural justice, the BGB proceeded on the footing that if the requirements of the latter were fulfilled the former would not be questioned. Thus, in accordance with traditional liberal theory, the parties were the best guarantors of their respective rights and the contractual process was the epitomy of fairness. In the words of the French philosopher Fouillé (a disciple of Kant) 'Qui dit contractual dit juste': He who says contractual is saying fair! (See, as to procedural and substantive fairness, inter alia, von Mehren, *IntEncCompLaw* vol VII, chapter 1 (1982), p 72; Atiyah, *Introduction to the Law of Contract* (5th edn, 1995), p 289.)

(c) Modern Constraints

The halcyon days envisaged by the Code were not destined to last long. The socio-economic developments that followed the First World War (and more so the Second) would gain momentum and encourage a marked tendency towards the establishment of a regime of substantive justice. In recent years, under the influence of EC law, the scope for avoiding contracts on procedural grounds has increased further providing yet another instance of the 'internationalisation' of what (since the emergence of the modern states) used to be a very 'national' based branch of the law. In some instances the freedom to enter into a contract has also been restricted (this so-called *Kontrahierungszwang* is discussed in chapter 2, p 70). Four of these developments, typical of the post-Wars period, and related to the general themes mentioned at the very beginning of this chapter, may be singled out in the remainder of this chapter. (They will be picked up in greater detail later in this book. See, also, for further discussion, eg, Canaris AcP 200 (2000) 273.)

First, we must mention the comprehensive judicial control exercised in relation to 'standard terms' or general conditions of business (*Allgemeine Geschäftsbedingungen*). Nearly a century after the adoption of the BGB, the Constitutional Court in the *Bürge* case was able to state that there was widespread consensus that the principle of good faith justified policing the content of a contract (*richterliche Inhaltskontrolle*) (in NJW 1994, 36, 39). The development referred to here is that of the emergence of a strict regime of rules concerning the conclusion and, crucially, the content of pre-formulated, standard term contracts. This was done first on the basis of § 242, later aided by a special statute and today is laid down in §§ 305–10 and Directive 93/13/EEC on Unfair Terms in Consumer Contracts (although it should be noted that the BGB rules are not, on the whole, limited to consumer transactions). The nature and scope of this intervention of the courts into contract law is discussed in detail in chapter 3, p 163 and represents one of the best examples of one of the most important developments of modern contract law: the appearance of the consumer as a litigating party. To borrow a metaphor used by Lord Denning MR in the case of *George Mitchell (Chesterhall) Ltd v Finney Lock Seeds Ltd* [1983] QB 284 (affirmed: [1983] 2 AC 803) (cited in full in chapter 3, section 5(a), p 166), German courts did not feel the need to conceal their 'weapon' and did not need to 'stab the idol in the back', but professed openly to control the fairness of exclusion clauses and indeed many other terms written 'in small print.' One of the consequences of policing standard terms has been that contracting out of the *'dispositive Recht'* of the Code has become more difficult. The default rules are the guiding principle in policing 'standard' terms and thereby indirectly acquire a quasi-'strict' character (see now § 307 II Nr. 1). It would seem that, to paraphrase the famous slogan of the French Revolution, *égalité* was destined to trump *liberté*.

The impact of the human rights of the Basic Law upon the BGB has already been pointed out in section 6, p 37. It provided the second (and, doctrinally, the most intriguing) development relevant to freedom of contract. Freedom of contract is protected as part of the general right to act freely (Article 2 I GG, *allgemeine Handlungsfreiheit*). The wider aspect of human dignity is also relevant since the ability of a person to determine his fate autonomously is a central element of dignity as envisaged and protected by Article 1 I. This conforms to traditional contract doctrine. But then we begin to find concessions to the alternative position. So the German courts (since the aforementioned *Lüth* decision) have come to regard general clauses as 'entrance points' for constitutional values. Thus, in some cases freedom of contract was balanced against some other basic right of the Constitution, for instance the right of free marriage or the right to one's personality or the right to freedom of expression. This leads to the most difficult aspect that has arisen following a number of highly controversial cases. The question is whether the Constitution is also relevant to defining the limits of freedom of contract, ie does it contain principles which determine the fairness of contract terms and the requirements as to the manner in which contracts are concluded? Here, *both* parties are said to be able to rely upon freedom of contract. One party invokes freedom of contract in the classic sense: the courts should not interfere with the contract. The other party's invocation of freedom of contract is less easy to sustain on orthodox analysis, for this party demands that the courts should police the contract because of its unfair terms and because there was no 'parity' of bargaining power. In the view of the Constitutional Court, freedom of contract, or personal autonomy more generally, does not entail unlimited power to enter into contracts on terms which are unfair; further, the conditions of the exercise of this freedom, the 'parity' of bargaining power, must also be secured. We will return to this topic in chapter three below. Here, suffice it briefly to make three points.

First, despite the far-reaching language of these judgments, the cases could also be rationalised in the terms of more traditional concepts of private law. After all, lawyers are, in most cases, able to find a 'justification' for most propositions they wish to advance. The time, however, may have come when one should treat these developments as prompted by a socio-economic environment which is different from that which gave rise to the classical law of contract.

Secondly, this debate can also be found in other systems which have borrowed the German thinking and even the language of some leading German judgments. (Israel offers an excellent illustration where Justice Barak has drawn largely on the German reasoning and, in a contractual context, has been challenged by Professor Shalev among others. See: 'Constitutionalisation of Contract Law' in A Gambaro and AM Rabello (eds), Towards a New European Ius Commune (1999), pp 205–35).

Thirdly, it could be argued that these results are not so different from those achieved by apparently more conservatively minded English courts in comparable situations, such as cases relating to the incorporation of contract terms in certain situations (discussed below in chapter 3, particularly p 163 ff), misrepresentations inducing contracts (see chapter 6, sections 4, p 302 ff) and the doctrine of undue influence (treated in chapter 5, particularly section 4(c), p 253 ff).

Another major topic which must be discussed in the present context and which reveals a considerable constraint upon freedom of contract is the emergence of *tightly regulated contracts* in certain fields of law which were once seen as dealing with 'specific' aspects of contract law but which, nowadays, represent the part of the law of contract which is closer to the average citizen than any other (except sale of goods). Here, we will allude briefly to the law of leases and labour law, areas of contract law which have witnessed radical departures from traditional doctrine.

In the case of *leases*, this trend is described by adding the adjective 'social': '*soziales Mietrecht*'. (Initially, these strict regimes of (new) rules were contained in statutes outside the BGB but a reform of 2001 incorporated them into the BGB. (§§ 549–577a comprise the special rules applicable to leases of accommodation for private living (*Mietverhältnisse über Wohnraum*). While the original norms contained only some 'drops' of social oil (like the strict liability of the landlord if the flat were defective from the outset: now § 536a I), the present regime can be more accurately described as a thicket of 'social' regulation designed to protect the tenant.

To achieve this new protective aim, a whole range of protective measures has been invented. Thus, we find special formal requirements (eg, §§ 550, 558a), measures prohibiting deviations to the detriment of the tenant (eg, § 551 IV, 553 III, 554 V), narrowing down the reasons for which the landlord may terminate the contract (normally a long-term contract concluded for an indefinite period can after notification in advance freely be terminated; § 573, however, requires a 'legitimate' interest of the landlord if he is to be allowed to terminate the contract), and even provisions introducing mechanisms which allow the courts to control the rent at least in certain respects (the 'just price' idea applies to any demand of a rent increase after the conclusion of the contract (for which the contract has not expressly provided: §§ 559, 557–61, setting the level at the local spot rate plus a certain margin forming a ceiling; and other costs in connection with the lease, § 556). As a result of all of this, it is no surprise that most German 'county' courts have set up special departments to deal with leases, alone. Again, as a general rule it could be said that this 'socially impregnated law' finds its counterparts in most continental European systems, with the US standing at the other end of this spectrum (though here, too, state legislation and regulations provide some evidence of traditional contract doctrine being challenged by the social realities of the twenty-first century).

English law also reveals characteristics similar to those found in German law, though the protection given to tenants had ebbed and flowed, followed political developments in the country during the last quarter of the twentieth century. Thus, the early legislation (the Increase of Rent and Mortgage Interest (War Restrictions) Act 1915 covered no more than six pages (in response to the wartime shortages) but this grew into a complex network of systems filling hundreds of pages and leading to thousands of cases interpreting the rules. Despite the fact that more recent English developments (see Part I of the Housing Act 1988 and also the Housing Act 1996) have seen a move back towards a lower level of regulation of the private lettings market, there still exist seven different systems of control (although Assured, Shorthold and Regulated Tenancies are the general regimes, while the other categories are either narrowly restricted or more concerned with granting a right to the tenant to acquire the freehold in the property: see, generally, Harpum, *Megarry & Wade—The Law of Real Property*, pp 1383 ff). Overall, however, the English system (within the various categories mentioned above) does provide a goodly measure of protection to tenants. For example, in assured tenancies under the Housing Act 1988, protection of tenure is provided to tenants by the imposition of a statutory periodic tenancy when the term of the tenancy expires. The landlord is then reduced to proving one of the statutory grounds for possession laid down in the Act (see Schedule 2 of the 1988 Act), if he is to recover possession of the property. Furthermore, on the death of the tenant of an assured tenancy, the relevant person untitled under the tenant's will can succeed to a fixed-term assured tenancy. Finally, rent increases in periodic assured tenancies are subject to rent assessment committees, if the tenant objects to the proposed new rent (although it should be pointed out that this can often operate as much to protect the landlord who has forgotten to include a rent review clause—if such a clause has been included then the statutory procedure will not apply (section 13(1) (b) of the 1988 Act)). Assured shorthold tenancies, however, are now the default tenancy (see sections 19A, 20 and 34 of the 1988 Act) and these provide much less security of tenure beyond the fixed term period as the landlord is then entitled to recover possession as of right by serving a notice in writing on the tenant (section 21(1) of the 1988 Act). Nevertheless, a measure of rent protection is also available here, even if the landlord and tenant have already reached agreement (section 22 of the 1988 Act), although the powers of the rent assessment committee are somewhat more limited (section 22(3) of the 1998 Act). The advent of the assured shorthold tenancy has significantly reduced the importance of regulated tenancies under the Rent Act 1977, but where this is still relevant (typically due to grandfathering provisions relating to existing regulated tenancies—see section 34(1) of the Housing Act 1988) the major benefit for the tenant is a system that imposes and enforces a maximum rent and also prohibits premiums (for grant, renewal, etc of the tenancy—see Part XI, Schedule 1, Part II of the Rent Act 1977), although this will only operate once the rent for the dwelling is registered (sections 44, 57, 66 and 67 of the Rent Act 1977). And this is all without detailed discussion of the position of long leaseholders and their security of tenure (Part I of the Landlord and Tenant Act 1954) and possibilities to 'enfranchise' themselves by acquiring the freehold interest in the relevant property (the Leasehold Reform Act 1967 and the Leasehold Reform, Housing and Urban Development Act 1993); and without coverage of secure tenancies where the landlord is a public body (particularly including the tenants' right to buy under Part V of the Housing Act 1985). (See generally, Harpum, *Megarry & Wade—The Law of Real Property*, chapter 22; *Megarry on The Rent Acts* (11th edn, 1988); Driscoll, *Residential Leasehold Property Law* (2004) and Smith, *The Law of Landlord and Tenant* (6th edn, 2002).)

This brief *tour d'horizon* should serve to convince the reader that there is a fair parallel in the 'social' law of leases in English law to those developments in Germany, even if the overlap is not complete, and the increased burden that these provisions place upon landlords and conveyancers in appreciating the lie of the land in this area is clear to see. This is not an insignificant conclusion since it shows that despite the fact that English variant of market economy is 'more liberal and less interventionist' than the German, the country and its system have not escaped the current political preoccupation to give rights and entitlements to those who for social, ethnic or religious reasons are deemed to belong to the weaker sections of society.

The contract of services (§ 611) also encompasses *relationships of labour law*. Except again for a 'drop' of social oil (§ 618, which establishes certain protective duties regarding the health of employees), few constraints were originally envisaged in the BGB. (In the UK, the relevant avenues are compensation funded by social security contributions (laid down by the (much amended) National Insurance (Industrial Injuries) Act 1946) and claims for damages against an employer for breach of the employer's statutory (eg, the Health and Safety at Work Act 1974) or tortious (such as negligence—see, eg, *Walker v Northumberland County Council* [1995] 1 All ER 737) duties.) The position of contemporary German law is thus characterised by a considerable number of (one-sided) significant restrictions of freedom of contract. Unlike in the case of the 'social law of leases,' however, these matters have been dealt with outside the Code. These specialised statutes include protective rules dealing with the right to a holiday (*Bundesurlaubsgesetz*—in the UK, see The Working Time Regulations 1998, SI 1998/1833, regulation 13), regulating the payment of loans in the case of illness (*Entgeltfortzahlungsgesetz*) and restricting the reasons for and setting out the procedure regarding dismissals (*Kündigungsschutzgesetz*).

Here, too, the law in the UK has, generally speaking, followed suit and contains an extensive set of legal rules regulating unfair dismissal. These were first developed at common law in the nineteenth century, where the increasing effectiveness of collective bargaining to set the terms of employment contracts led to adjudication by the courts upon those terms, their interpretation and application (see, eg, Collins, Ewing & McColgan, *Labour Law Text and Materials* (2001), pp 481–520; and see Deakin and Morris, *Labour Law* (4th edn, 2005)). It should be emphasised that, initially, these results were achieved using the ordinary rules of contract law in the relevant context (implication of terms, etc), although, eventually, the perceived limitations of this approach led to the introduction of statutory regulation of unfair dismissal (which are now consolidated in the Employment Rights Act 1996). This legislation provides mandatory standards (based upon 'fairness' as applied in the relevant context—see section 98 of the 1996 Act) for the control of the employer's discretionary power of dismissal (see Collins, Ewing & McColgan (above) 520ff.; and see Deakin and Morris, *Labour Law*), although a desire to support flexibility in the labour market has led to certain possibilities for the employee to contract out of the statutory rights (such as compromise agreements where termination of the contract of employment is the result—in such a case, there will be no 'dismissal' under the legislation). Needless to say, we are dealing here with mandatory and not dispositive law (on this point, in relation to English labour law and issues of status and contract, see Kahn-Freund, 'A Note on Status and Contract in British Labour Law' (1967) 30 *MLR* 635 and Deakin and Morris, *Labour Law*, section 4.2). The *Bundesarbeitsgericht* has also interpreted the applicable BGB provisions rather narrowly. For instance, the court has tightened the conditions for dismissal under § 626 for a breach of duty by the employee. It requires (though there is no indication of this in the wording of § 626) that, even for a gross violation of the employee's duties, dismissal is an *ultima ratio* measure which requires a negative prognosis as to the mutual trust of the parties (see, for criticism from a liberal perspective prompted by the current economic crises: Rüthers, 'Vom Sinn und Unsinn des geltenden Kündigungsschutzrechts' NJW 2002, 1601).

The alteration of the contractual background has come with an increase in litigation. As a result, special civil courts were set up in Germany to deal with matters of 'labour' law (*Arbeitsgerichtsbarkeit*). In the year 2000 alone 574,644 claims were brought before these courts (Rüthers, NJW 2002, 1601, 1602). It seems that the number of claims in the UK is smaller than in Germany (even allowing for the smaller UK economy). Nevertheless, litigation has grown rapidly throughout the 1980s and 1990s as the increase in individual (as opposed to collective) employment rights led to growing demands for their enforcement. This was a major motivation for the introduction of the Employment Act 2002, Part 2 of which creates restrictions upon the enforcement of the statutory rights by a reform of the tribunal system, while Part 3 introduces statutory dispute resolution procedures. It seems clear that the 2002 Act effects significant restrictions upon the exercise of employees' individual rights and the legislation has attracted much comment and concern. For discussion, as well as wide-ranging and trenchant criticism of the 2002 Act, see Hepple and Morris, 'The Employment Act 2002 and the Crisis of Individual Employment Rights' (2002) 31 *ILJ* 245. This 'un-noticed' rapprochement of English and German law must again be contrasted with the American notion of contract terminable at will which offers American employers unimaginable freedom to terminate employment contracts. Having said this however one must again remind the reader of the (wider) economic conditions and philosophies that may be associated with these rules of law.

These developments foreshadowed the broadly drafted and construed *consumer legislation* across the European Community commencing in the 1980s. This is the fourth and final type of constraint on freedom of contract which we discuss here (see also, chapter 3). We have already mentioned the growing influence of European Community law in this field and we refer to it again since it is a main theme of this book (and one which we feel is applicable even to English law) that the 'national' flavour of contract law has, in some areas, succumbed to this 'international' climate of regulation. Thus, on this topic see, the Consumer Credit Directive 87/102/EEC (implemented in §§ 488–507 of the BGB—in the UK, see the Consumer Credit Act 1974, which pre-dated the Directive: many of the regulations adopted thereunder served to implement those aspects of the Directive that had not already been covered by the 1974 legislation. Note that this Directive is currently under review with a view to its revision by further EC legislation); Directive 90/314/EEC on Package Travel (§§ 651a–651m and §§ 305–10 and The Package Travel, Package Holidays and Package Tours Regulations 1992, SI 1992/3288); the Timeshare Directive 94/47/EC (§§ 481–7 and the Timeshare Act 1992 (as amended by The Timeshare Regulations 1997, SI

1997/1081)); and Directive 1999/44/EC on Consumer Sales (inter alia §§ 474–9 and The Sale and Supply of Goods to Consumers Regulations 2002, SI 2002/3045 (amending the Supply of Goods (Implied Terms Act) 1973, the Sale of Goods Act 1979 and the Supply of Goods and Services Act 1982)).

The common element of these 'harmonisation' measures is that they introduce a regime of rules regarding 'business-to-consumer' transactions which is said to afford a minimum protection to the consumer: in other words they cannot be departed from to the detriment of the consumer. To give some examples, it is no longer possible to sell newly produced goods to a consumer at a price which was reduced in view of a shorter limitation period: reducing the limitation period will be held invalid (§ 475 II); and where the buyer is a consumer, the goods remain at the seller's risk until delivered to the consumer (section 20(4) of the Sale of Goods Act 1979, as inserted by SI 2002/3045 (above)).

The combined effect of this legislation upon the BGB has been considerable. Most Directives have been implemented in the text of the Code itself and, as we have already suggested, from a point of legislative style, the lengthy and verbose formulations of these provisions contrasts rather unfavourably with the abstract and succinct traditional BGB provisions.

English law has adopted a similarly wholesale incorporation of the terms of many of these Directives, typically by means of statutory instruments: this has left difficult questions of interpretation to be resolved, relating to the relative scope of pre-existing national law (such as the Consumer Credit Act 1974 and the Unfair Contract Terms Act 1977) and the new, EC Directive-inspired/required statutory instruments (such as the current Unfair Terms in Consumer Contracts Regulations 1999 (SI 1999/2083); and this is a further 'background' factor which accounts for what we have described as the 'un-noticed rapprochement' with German law. (For brief discussion of this methodological approach, see Weatherill (1998) *Amicus Curiae* 11; for discussion of proposals to combine the 1977 Act and the 1999 Regulations, see the Law Commission Consultation Paper No 166 and Scottish Law Commission Discussion Paper No 119, *Unfair Terms in Contracts—A Joint Consultation Paper* (2002). Equally, it should be noted that in English law many of the provisions of those EC consumer-related Directives that concern the sale and supply of goods have been accommodated by amendment of the overall regime under the 1979 and 1982 Acts (above), rather than added as extra layers whose relationship with pre-existing provisions must then be disentangled.) Overall, however, the clear impression in English law is that there has been a significant shift towards the provision of information to the consumer and the existence of compulsory statutory rules that seek to protect the position of the consumer in the contracting process.

The clearest sign of this emergence of a special private law for consumers in Germany is the insertion, into the General Part in the section on the basic concept of 'Person', of two definitions of a Dealer (*Unternehmer*, § 14) and Consumer (*Verbraucher*, § 13). Irrespective of whether one welcomes these relatively recent departures of European law, the restrictions on freedom of contract cannot be ignored. Consumers—ie persons acting outside their business or trade—are not regarded as fully capable of taking charge of their affairs: apparently, they need protection and EC law is prepared to afford it to them.

This tendency towards increasing the control over the content of a contract on grounds of substantive fairness is supplemented by protective measures which increase the range of reasons for avoiding the contract, which could be said to undermine the principle of *pacta sunt servanda*. The right of termination granted by Directive 85/577/EEC (implemented in § 312 of the BGB and in the UK by The Consumer Protection (Cancellation of Contracts Concluded away from Business Premises) Regulations 1987 (SI 1987/2117, as amended by SI 1988/958 and SI 1998/3050)), concerning the protection of consumers in respect of contracts negotiated away from business premises, is the paradigm case. The justification for the right is procedural: in certain situations, the conclusion of the contract might have been premature, the consumer perhaps feeling an awkward pressure when goods are merchandised at his private home. Yet, in effect, it amounts to saying that a contract concluded under those particular circumstances can be freely revoked and is not binding, for the consumer must not show that he was in fact exposed to undue pressure. He may avoid the contract simply because he has had second thoughts.

A corollary of this consumer legislation is the proliferation of duties to provide information to the consumer. These duties can be fairly complex and extensive, yet failure to fulfil them means that the consumer's rights are further increased. A good illustration of this point is provided by EC law in Case C-481/99 *Heininger v Bayerische Hypo- und Vereinsbank AG* [2001] ECR I-9945, NJW 2002, 281, concerning the application of Directive 85/577/EC: national law provided for a limitation period of one year within which the consumer had to bring his claim. However, the Court of Justice held that this period could not start to run unless and until the consumer had been properly informed of his right to avoid the contract, as required by the Directive. See now § 355 III sentence 2, the effect of which is that the right to terminate the contract never expires or lapses. This has prompted the German legislator to draft a special regulation, which contains 'model' information to be provided to consumers (*BGB-Informationspflichten-Verordnung*).

We may conclude this brief examination of some modern restrictions of freedom of contract with a few general remarks.

The constraints on freedom of contract appear considerable. Policing the content of a contract and a tight control of procedural fairness are closely related to transactions between dealers and consumers. The presumption here is that one party is weaker than the other and, faced with a dispute between the 'little man' and the 'big concern', it seems a foregone conclusion that the 'weaker' consumer or employee needs and deserves protection. However, this development that has seen the courts give up their neutrality towards the content of a contract is not limited to such relationships. It will be remembered that, for instance, the control of standard terms extends also to purely commercial transactions in German law. Conversely, in the law of leases it will often be persons acting outside their business or trade who let accommodation, yet they are still subject to the same strict requirements as any other 'commercial' landlord. These are the realities of contemporary private law systems and it would be misleading if in this book we were not to mention and discuss the considerable quantities of 'social oil' which have been poured over the BGB since its adoption in 1896 (although whether this has acted as a useful lubricant, as oil on otherwise 'troubled' waters or has added fuel to the fire is another matter). We will discuss specific aspects of these rules, as far as they can be regarded to affect general principles of German contract law, in the following chapters.

2

The Formation of a Contract

1. INTRODUCTORY REMARKS

Two observations of a general nature are called for before we go into the details of the material discussed in this chapter.

The first is that the German law of contract, from its birth (discussed in this chapter) to its death (considered in chapters 8 and 9), immediately reveals its basic 'theoretical' differences with English law. Their nature is so obvious at first sight that they may also conceal the equally interesting similarities so a special effort will also be made to make these apparent to the reader. But, theoretically, their significance cannot be underestimated, while also revealing the impact that history has had on the shaping of modern law. Two differences will be noted at this stage; others of a more specific nature will unfold as the reader progresses with the study of the text.

The first of these differences is the idea that in German (and indeed continental European law) the obligation arises out of the promise of the parties (with its almost religious connotations in the Middle Ages) and not, as in the common law, from the notion of a bargain or (in later times) the idea of detrimental reliance. The second is linked to the continental search for principle which contrasts with the common law attachment to casuistry. The principle is that of agreement; and as one has come to expect, it finds its simplest and purest expression in the laconic Article 114 of the French *Code civil*. But what we mean by agreement is another matter; and the importance attributed to the presence of this notion (objective or subjective determination etc) has given rise to much debate and the adoption of varying positions in different systems. Agreement or, to use the Latin expression *consensus at idem*, is just as important to English law; but here the requirement is satisfied through the examination of a very rich set of factual examples which have become rules of law in accordance with the common law tendency to harden fact into law. The point just made is worth stressing, not just because we find it repeated in other parts of the law of contracts (eg, the area of damages for bad performance), but because it often makes it difficult to find exact factual litigated parallels in other systems. This has, at times, made our task more difficult since we have striven, in this book and its companion volume to find factually analogous cases for the purposes of attempting the comparison of the two systems. The difficulty is due to the fact that the foreign system, the French in an even more pronounced way than the German, having declared that the presence of agreement is what is required in law to create the contractual bond, then leaves it the triers of fact—ie, the lower courts—to determine whether this has been satisfied in each concrete case.

Secondly, the first chapter has already stressed that the Pandectist structure of the German Code is particularly evident in the sections that deal with the law of obligations in general, the law of contracts in particular. As a result, special efforts have to be made by the comparatist to re-shape the material (without, of course, betraying the spirit of the system) in order to place it in some kind of logical juxtaposition with the English and American law and make it 'user-friendlier' to the common lawyer. This is not a task that is easily accomplished. And this general warning is, as we shall see, particularly appropriate for the topics that will be studied in chapters 5 (policing the contract), 9 and 10 (irregularities of performance). But it also has some bearing on the present chapter. Thus, reference has to be made in this chapter to the doctrine of *culpa in contrahendo*, which sets out the obligations of the parties during the phase of negotiations leading up to the conclusion of a contract, as well the German notion of representation (*Stellvertretung*). The latter is a notion approximately the equivalent of, but not identical (as we shall explain later) to, the English notion of agency, which deals with the question of how contracts can be formed through the participation of third parties in German law. These topics will also re-appear in later sections of this book (for instance, in chapters 3, section 2, and 6, section 4).

The preceding preliminary observations bring out a peculiarity of the German treatment of our topic, to which we have already alluded in chapter 1. This is that many questions related to contract law find, in the BGB, their treatment not only in the contract sections proper of the Code, but in its first book, which deals with matters of general (ie, wider) importance, and indeed even in other codes such as for instance the Commercial Code. This, for instance is the case with commercial agency which finds many of its rules not in the Civil but the Commercial Code.

It bears repeating that to the German systematically inclined mind, such a division of the material is obvious since both the offer (*Antrag* or *Angebot*) and the acceptance (*Annahme*) are declarations of a person's intention; and the treatment of such declarations (what form should they take; when do they become effective etc) may be of relevance not only to the specifically regulated types of contracts in the special part of the law of contract (Book Two of the Code) but other areas of the law as well. Contracts giving rise to obligations (*Verpflichtungsgeschäft*) as opposed to those transferring or altering rights directly (*Verfügungsgeschäft*) can be found not only in the special part of the law of contract, but in family law (Book Four)—eg, setting out obligations between spouses (§§ 1353 *et seq*)—and in the law of succession (§§ 2274, 2346). Furthermore, according to the principle of separation, discussed in chapter 1, p 27 ff, the transfer of ownership rights does occur through contract, yet under a different contract from the contract stipulating the obligation to transfer the right. Thus, the rules governing offer and acceptance in Book One, General Part, are also relevant to Book Three, ie, Property Law (§§ 929, 925, 873).

2. THE OFFER (*ANTRAG, ANGEBOT*)

Bailas, *Das Problem der Vertragschließung und der vertragsbegründende Akt* (1962); Bydlinsky, 'Kontrahierungszwang und Anwendung des allgemeinen Zivilrechts' JZ 1980, 378; Dieterich, 'Der Kauf im Selbstbedienungsladen' DB 1972, 957; Henrich, *Vorvertrag, Optionsvertrag, Vorrechtsvertrag* (1965); Hilger, 'Die verspätete Annahme' AcP 1985 (1985), 559; EA Kramer, *Grundfragen der vertraglichen Einigung*

(1972); Leenen, 'Abschluss, Zustandekommen und Wirksamkeit des Vertrages' AcP 188 (1988), 381; Lutter, *Der Letter of Intent* (1982); Lindacher, 'Die Bedeutung der Klausel „Angebot freibleibend"'DB 1992, 1813; Mayer-Maly, 'Vertrag und Einigung' in *Festschrift für Nipperdey* (1965), I, p 509; Mayer-Maly, 'Die Bedeutung des Konsenses in privatrechtsgeschichtlicher Sicht' in *Rechtsgeltung und Konsens* (1976); R Raiser, 'Schadenshaftung bei verstecktem Dissens' AcP 127, 1; M Wolf, *Rechtsgeschäftliche Entscheidungsfreiheit und vertraglicher Interessenausgleich* (1970). Ben Abderrahmane, *Le droit allemand des conditions générales dans les ventes commerciales francoallemandes* (1985); Horn, Kötz and Leser, *German Private and Commercial Law: An Introduction* (translated by Tony Weir) (1982), pp 76–80; Lorenz, 'German Report' in E Hondius (ed), *Precontractual Liability*, pp 159–77 (1991); Nussbaum, 'Comparative Aspects of the AngloAmerican Offer-and-Acceptance Doctrine' *36 Columbia LR.* 920 (1936); Pedamon, *Le contrat en droit allemand* (1993); Rabel, *Recht des Warenkaufs,* vol. 1 (1936), pp 69–93; Rieg, *Le rôle de la volonté dans l'acte juridique en droit civil français et allemand* (1961); Schlesinger et al, *Formation of Contracts. A study of the Common Core of Legal Systems,* 2 vols (1968); von Mehren, 'The Formation of Contracts' in *International Encyclopedia of Comparative Law,* vol VII, chapter 9 (1992); Winfield, 'Some Aspects of Offer and Acceptance' (1939) 55 *LQR* 499; Witz, *Droit privé allemand,* I, (1992); Zimmermann 'Vertrag und Versprechen' in *Festschrift für Andreas Heldrich* (2005), p 467.

(a) General Observations

A contract is an agreement, typically between two parties who wish to bring about certain legal consequences. (In modern conditions more than one party may be involved on one side: eg, a husband and wife take out a lease on a flat. Obviously, in commercial settings, the factual context can become more complex.) For these consequences to come about in law one of the parties must declare to the other his intention to enter with the other into a binding arrangement provided certain conditions are met, and the other must then assent to this proposal. A contract thus, essentially, involves two reciprocal, corresponding declarations of intention *(Willenserklärungen)* of the future contracting parties which subject each other to the contractual bond. Normally, this *vinculum iuris* does not affect third (ie other) parties; but, as we shall see in chapter 4, both the Code and case law of the German courts have expanded the contractual relationship (in some, at least, of its effects) to cover third parties. As a result of the Contact (Rights of Third Parties) Act 1999 English law has now moved closer to German law but (as will be noted) is not identical. Needless to say the law will ascribe legal consequences to such a reciprocal exchange of declarations only if the other conditions laid down by the BGB (eg, formality where this is required, capacity etc) have been observed and the contract does not offend against the legal and moral order. These will be discussed in chapter 5, p 227.

Though in theory the constituent elements of a contract, one declaration of intention of each party, can easily be distinguished the one from the other, in practice it may be exceedingly difficult to analyse the formation of contract in such simple terms. As von Mehren has pointed out: 'In real life, the contracting process is frequently more disorderly than the neat categories of negotiation, offer, and acceptance suggest.' (*Int Enc Comp Law* VII, para 9-112.) He continued as follows (9-113):

At one extreme, negotiation is absorbed by offer and acceptance; at the other, negotiation takes the form of a protracted exchange of information, a slow identification of party interests and differences followed by a series of compromises that may ultimately result in tentative agreement . . ., general agreement, when reached, may then be refined into a detailed contract.

To reflect this phenomenon, some more recent approaches have indeed departed from the concepts of offer and acceptance. (See, for instance, UNIDROIT Principles, Article 2.1: 'A contract may be concluded either by acceptance of an offer or by conduct of the parties that is sufficient to show agreement.' Cf Principles of European Contract Law, Article 2.211.)

But the German Code is already one hundred years old and thus proceeds on the basis of traditional thinking namely, that offer and acceptance can and should be notionally separated. This traditional approach fits best the exchange of sequential written declarations of intention *inter absentes*. However, identifying a declaration which embodies all elements of an 'offer' may sometimes involve a fiction, as has been noted also by German writers. Nevertheless, in practice this difficulty does not result in any major problems. (See: *MünchKomm*-Kramer, § 145 Rn. 2.)

Some rules attached to the traditional approach, as for instance the question whether an offer is binding, may have less significance when a contract is concluded by compromise negotiations at a conference table. Indeed, in such negotiating situations it is often difficult to establish precisely what was agreed and when, let alone which of the numerous statements and suggestions might be characterised as 'offer' or 'acceptance' in any formal sense. (For an excellent example of the English approach to these matters, see *G Percy Trentham Ltd v Archital Luxfer Ltd* [1993] 1 Lloyd's Rep 25, where work had already commenced before final terms had been agreed between the parties. The court was even prepared to give retroactive effect to the agreement to encompass the work already performed.) But even here the traditional terms can be relevant, as for instance if one party does not sign the document instantly then the rules as to the binding nature of an offer and the time for acceptance may come into play.

On the other hand, certain crucial problems in the formation of contracts cannot even be formulated if one does not assume that offer and acceptance are different legal concepts. This concerns the question (referred to above) of the binding nature of an offer, the problem of distinguishing offer and invitation to treat, the 'battle of the forms' etc. Thus, although we are fully aware of the limitations of this approach, in this exposition we follow the German pattern of distinguishing between offer and acceptance.

There is one aspect of the formation of contract, however, which cannot be squeezed into such a straitjacket. It concerns the much-debated issue of pre-contractual obligations. This topic raises intricate issues, such as whether the parties are required to act 'equitably' or in 'good faith' towards each other, or whether they are under an obligation not to endanger the other party, etc. German law has developed rules, separate from the concepts of offer and acceptance, which attempt to solve these issues. We will find some answers to the question when the relevant formation phase begins, whether the parties are free to break off contract negotiations, etc, in the section on *culpa in contrahendo*, below. It suffices here to point out that German law thus acknowledges the limitations of the concepts of 'offer' and 'acceptance' and provides a more flexible device in dealing with the obligations of the parties prior to the conclusion of a contract, or where the purported contract later turns out to be void. These problems are accommodated within the framework of pre-contractual liability.

(b) Necessary Content of an Offer

An offer must be precise and complete as to the essential elements of the proposed contract (*essentialia negotii*). The duties of the parties must be at least ascertainable. One often finds statements in German books to the effect that a declaration of intention is an offer if it can mature into a contract when its recipient can respond to it by a simple 'yes' or 'I accept'. (Cf RGZ 124, 81, case no 1, concerning a pre-contract to a contract of sale. Contrast OLG Hamm NJW 1976, 1212, case no 2, which however must be approached with extreme caution. For English law see Treitel, *The Law of Contract* (11th edn, 2003), pp 49–51.)

What is an essential element of the contract depends on the nature and type of the contract. The requirements of completeness and definiteness apply to the main obligations under the contract which, in turn, are usually spelled out in the very first paragraphs regulating the type of contract in question. For instance, an offer concerning a lease must state the beginning and the end of the term of the lease, the rent, and the specific property leased, corresponding to the obligations of the parties under § 535 BGB. (Cf *Harvey v Pratt* [1965] 1 WLR 1025, where failure to specify the commencement date rendered the agreement sufficiently incomplete as to be unenforceable. See further chapter 3, p 144 ff, for a discussion of the main features of the types of contract dealt with in the BGB.) In the sale of goods, it is essential that the goods sold and the purchase price agreed are determined by the parties to the agreement: see § 433 BGB.

This general rule as to completeness is subject to two exceptions.

First, German law (unlike other systems, for instance French law) accepts that, provided this is stated in the contract itself, the price or, indeed any other aspect of performance, may be fixed at a later stage. This can be done either by one of the parties themselves acting freely (*freies Ermessen*) or equitably (*billiges Ermessen*: see § 315 BGB), or by a third party acting freely or equitably (see §§ 317 *et seq* BGB). (For an English example concerning place of performance see *David T Boyd & Co v Louis Louca* [1973] 1 Lloyd's Rep 209: an agreement to sell goods for delivery 'free on board . . . good Danish port' was a good contract requiring the buyer to specify the port of shipment: see Treitel, *The Law of Contract*, p 50.) If the parties have stipulated for equity to be respected, which is presumed, the court is empowered to review the exercise of discretion of the contracting party (§ 315 III BGB) or of the third party (§ 319 BGB) and if necessary replace it with its own determination. (For illustrations see: BGHZ 41, 271, case no 3; BGHZ 55, 248.)

Secondly, one should also note that in some instances even if the parties do not specify a certain price and do not leave the determination of the price to one of the parties or a third party, the contract will not be void for the sake of incompleteness but the court may fix the remuneration. There are rules in the Code as to certain types of contract which imply that if no price is fixed, while at the same time the performance of the contract can be expected only in return for remuneration, the parties are presumed to have agreed that the compensation is to be set under existing statutory tariffs. (In the absence of such a tariff, the price is to be fixed at the level of 'customary' remuneration, provided it is discernable: § 612, contract for services; § 632, contract for work; § 653, brokerage contract. See also, OLG Hamm NJW 1976, 1212, case no 2, a decision which, arguably, in the absence of an equivalent rule in sales law, goes too far in supplementing the parties' intention in respect of the purchase price. Cf *Münchener Kommentar*-Kramer, § 154 Rn. 5.)

English law is also open to enforcing contracts where the price has not been stipulated expressly. Thus, section 8(2) of the Sale of Goods Act 1979 provides for a reasonable price to be paid where no price is specified in the contract, while section 15(1) of the Supply of Goods and Services Act 1982 covers the same situation with regard to the supply of services. However, as Treitel points out (*The Law of Contract*, p 51), the absence of an agreed price may be evidence that there is no contract between the parties because agreement on the price was to be fixed through further negotiations. (For an example, see *Russell Bros (Paddington) Ltd v John Elliott Management Ltd* (1992) 11 *Const LJ* 337.) In such a situation however any work completed without a contractual basis may still be recovered under the law of restitution where the work was done in anticipation of the conclusion of a contract between the parties at a later date (see *British Steel Corporation v Cleveland Bridge & Engineering Co Ltd* [1984] 1 All ER 504). This argument will not succeed however where the party performing the work has taken the risk that a contract might not eventually be concluded between the parties, eg, where the work was done with the intention of securing the contract (*Regalian Properties plc v London Docklands Development Corp* [1995] 1 WLR 212). (We return to this below in our discussion of *culpa in contrahendo* in section 5(c).)

It is necessary to emphasise that the requirements of specificity (*Bestimmtheit*) and completeness are applied much more strictly where a contract directly transfers property rights (which, it will be recalled, is to be distinguished from the contract establishing the obligation to transfer the property right, eg, contract for the sale of goods. On this see the discussion of the principle of abstraction in chapter 1, p 27 ff). Regarding such transactions immediately affecting rights *in rem*, it is required that the parties exhaustively determine the object of the contract at the time of contracting. They cannot, as far as the contract of transfer is concerned, leave this matter of specificity to be determined by a future appropriation of goods to a contract.

The offer to enter into a contract of obligation need not be (and hardly ever is) complete as to all the *detailed, auxiliary terms* which the parties themselves may be willing to leave for subsequent determination by the default rules contained in the Code and developed by the courts. It is a recurrent theme of this book that the net of default rules is wider in German than it is in English law and one practical consequence of this is that the parties need not attempt to anticipate in the contractual drafts all eventualities. The nature of codified law explains this phenomenon; but the increased significance of default rules can also be accounted for by the fact that German judges seem to be more willing to interfere with the contract than their English counterparts, as can be noticed in particular in relation to 'pre-formulated' and/or standard form contracts discussed in chapter 3, p 163 ff. For, although offers can run into many pages, in practice matters can be made quite simple due to the sophisticated system of default rules governing all aspects of the transaction. In such cases it is thus for the parties to decide whether, in addition to agreeing on the object of the transaction and the price, they wish to spell out the detailed terms of the contract or to rely on default rules (and save transaction costs).

When the most frequently used contracts are concluded (such as sale of goods, hire etc), in the absence of any contrary indication, it can be assumed that the parties are leaving the details of their contract to be regulated by the appropriate codal provisions. (For an overview, see the next chapter.) Thus, if I enter a general store and take an electrical appliance to the counter at the exit, the purchase price will be assumed to be the one mentioned on the label and all other related contractual obligations of the parties (eg, what will happen if the appliance does not work or if the purchaser is injured because the product's instructions are obscure) are regulated by the law of sales (§§ 433–79 BGB) without the parties having to say anything about these matters in the course of the transaction. The same is—in principle—true for contracts involving more complex transactions, such as the sale of a company, though in such cases the parties will no doubt seek to adapt the default rules to their needs where they prove unsatisfactory because they do not meet the demands of business in a particular situation.

From a comparative perspective, it should be noted that the English approach to implied terms can provide a degree of coverage in this field of 'default'-type rules. For example, some such terms are implied by operation of law in particular generic types of contract (see Treitel, *The Law of Contract*, pp 206–13). Such terms were frequently implied by the courts at common law (particularly relating to employment contracts: see, eg, *Hivac Ltd v Park Royal Scientific Instruments Ltd* [1946] Ch 169) though many have since been reduced to statutory form. Particularly important examples concern the sale of goods (sections 12 to 15 of the Sale of Goods Act 1979), the supply of services (sections 13 and 14 of the Supply of Goods and Services Act 1979), and hire-purchase agreements (Supply of Goods (Implied Terms) Act 1973, sections 8 to 11). While some such implied terms cannot be excluded (and are thus perhaps better viewed as terms *imposed* by law—see, eg, section 2(1)(b) of the Landlord and Tenant (Covenants) Act 1995), it is generally the case that such implied terms can be excluded by clear agreement to do so or if an express term is in conflict with the term claimed to be implied. The effect of the above is that many such terms amount to 'default rules' in a manner similar to those contained in the German Civil Code. Overall, however, the reach (in terms of areas covered) of such terms in English law is more limited.

In certain areas of German law, standard terms of business have to a considerable extent modified or replaced the rules of the Code. (The most famous example is perhaps the *Verdingungsordnung für Bauleistungen (VOB)*, which contains an optional body of rules and pre-formulated clauses adapting the rules in §§ 632 *et seq.* BGB (contracts for work) to the needs of the construction industry. On the sale of a company see Holzapfel and Pöllath, *Unternehmenskauf in Recht und Praxis* (11th edn, 2003) including tax aspects. A selection of model contracts in the various areas of private law can be found in: *Beck'sches Formularbuch Bürgerliches, Handels- und Wirtschaftsrecht*, (8th edn, 2003), and similar books.) This task of adjusting or replacing default rules and terms implied by law is more often than not a delicate one, as the extensive commentary on the individual clauses of these contracts proves (as we will see also in the section on pre-formulated contract terms in chapter 3, section 5). The reason is an interventionist attitude of the courts which are, in principle, prepared to step in and strike out clauses that in their view have gone too far in protecting one party at the expense of the other. As already stated, in practice, this can result in much shorter contractual documents compared with those found in comparable Anglo-American transactions where the lawyers of the parties vie with one another to anticipate every possibility and to insert them into the contractual document.

At the other extreme we find the consumer protection measures of Community (EC) law which, with its 'minimum harmonisation' policy increasingly establishes mandatory regimes of contract rules (as noted in chapter 1, p 43 ff). Thus, in some instances, the parties are restrained from determining the terms of the contract except for little more than the contractual object and the price. Directive 99/44/EC [1999] OJ L171/12, on certain aspects of the sale of consumer goods and associated guarantees, is a recent example of these ever-stronger inroads into freedom of contract (discussed in chapter 10, p 515).

(c) Offer and Invitation to Treat

A declaration to indeterminate persons (*ad incertas personas*) is possible. Offers made through vending machines come into this category. In such an instance the offer is binding so long as there are goods of the appropriate kind in the machine. The acceptance here does not need to be 'notified' to the offeror but is seen as an act of intent governed by § 151 BGB. Case law and academic opinion are also at one in treating newspaper advertisements, prospectuses, merchandise catalogues, displays in shop windows, as invitations to treat (*invitatio ad offerendum*) and not as offers. (Thus, see: RG JW 1919, 325; RGZ 133, 388, 391; BGH NJW 1980, 1388. For academic references see *Staudinger*-Bork, § 145 Rn. 3 ff; Flume, *Allgemeiner Teil*, vol II, para 35, I, 1.) But not all Germanic systems have taken this stance. Thus, Article 7(3) of the Swiss Code of Obligations has expressly stated that '[t]he display of goods along with an indication of price is deemed to be an offer.'

The basic German position is shared by English law (see *Partridge v Crittenden* [1968] 1 *WLR* 1204), although on particular facts the courts have been prepared to find such an advertisement to amount to an offer (see *Carlill v Carbolic Smoke Ball Company* [1893] 1 QB 256 and cf *Lefkowitz v Great Minneapolis Surplus Store* 251 Minn. 188; 86 NW 2d 689 (1957) for an American example of similar reasoning).

Whether the display of goods on shop shelves amounts to an offer or an invitation to treat does not appear to have been resolved by the German courts (see BGHZ 66, 51, 55), while academics seem divided on the subject. Thus, *Münchener Kommentar* (-Kramer, § 145 Rn. 10) favours the view that such displays should be treated as offers, while other writers (eg Dietrich, 'Der Kauf im Selbstbedienungsladen' DB 1972, 957) prefer the view (invitation to treat) which finds most favour in Anglo-American law (see, for instance, *Pharmaceutical Society of Great Britain v Boots Cash Chemists (Southern) Ltd* [1953] 1 QB 401) but seems to have been rejected by French and Italian courts. As in Anglo-American law however these are essentially policy decisions; and in the case of advertisements and the like they are often explained by the wish to avoid the kind of consequences that might follow if the opposite solution were adopted and the prospective vendor/offeror ran out of the goods he was proposing to sell (see, eg, *Esso Petroleum Co Ltd v Customs & Excise Commissioners* [1976] 1 *WLR* 1, at 5, 6 and 11). Yet in practice these awkward consequences could be avoided if these situations were construed as involving offers subject to a condition of continued existence of supplies. The best explanation therefore for the prevailing solution may be the willingness of the legal system to accept that in such cases the offeror typically wishes to retain the opportunity of deciding at a later stage whether and with whom he wishes to conclude a contract. Though the theoretical explanation for this solution may be debatable (see Treitel, *The Law of Contract*, pp 12-13), the end result generally is not. Thus, in German law (as indeed in Anglo-American law) it is the customer who makes the offer; and the contract is concluded only when the first person (typically the prospective vendor) indicates, by words or deeds, that he is prepared to conclude the transaction.

The same position is reached in those cases where the offeror declares his willingness to enter into a contract but expressly suspends its performance through the use of such expressions as 'subject to contract' or 'while stocks last' etc. (See, for a recent application of these principles to internet auctions and the distinction between offer and invitation to treat, BGH NJW 2002, 363, case no 4.)

(d) The Duration of the Offer

As in Anglo-American law, so too in German law an offer made to another person who is in the same place as the offeror (or is using means of instant communication such as a telephone: see § 147 I, sentence 2 BGB) must be accepted immediately and, if it is not, then it will normally lapse. (See § 147 I BGB.) But in cases of transactions *inter absentes* the offer normally remains binding until such time as it expires in accordance with § 146 BGB (referring to §§ 147–49 BGB) or is rejected by the offeree.

The period during which the offer should be kept open is determined by the offeror or by what is reasonable in the circumstances (see: § 147 II BGB. *Münchener Kommentar*-Kramer, § 147 BGB Rn. 7; cf *Ramsgate Victoria Hotel Co Ltd v Montefiore* (1866) *LR* 1 Ex 109 for a similar approach in the English case law). In deciding this one must take into account the offeror's expectations, the time needed for his offer to reach the offeree, the time necessary for the latter to accept (including, where appropriate, the need to make enquiries or test samples etc), and generally prepare an appropriate reply. Circumstances likely to delay a reply and known to the offeror (eg, the offeree's absence from his office, illness, strikes, etc) must also be taken into account in determining the period during which the offer remains 'open' (cf RGZ 142, 402, 404; and for more details, see: *Staudinger*-Bork, § 147 BGB Rn. 10–11).

In appropriate circumstances, the offeree may even be placed under a duty to make up for such initial delays by, for instance, sending his acceptance by express delivery rather than an ordinary letter. A telegram response is, in any event, normally expected from offers made in such form or, otherwise, indicating the need of a speedy reply. There are even occasions when the acceptance may be deemed to have arrived in time even if this did not actually occur. This is envisaged by § 149 BGB, which states that if an acceptance reaches the offeror late but was sent in such a way that it would have arrived within the ordinary forwarding time (and the offeror can see this, for instance from the postmark) then the offeror must, on receipt of the acceptance, notify the offeree of the delay. (See, for instance, RGZ 105, 255, 256, case no 5.) If such a notification is not made immediately, then the acceptance is deemed to have arrived in time. (For other cases dealing with problems of transmission of a declaration of intention, see: RGZ 144, 289, case no 6; BAG NJW 1963, 554, case no 7; RGZ 125, 68, case no 8, also discussed below.)

If the offer is accepted after it has lapsed then, according to § 150 I BGB, it will be deemed to be a new offer. The same, of course, would be true of Anglo-American law. German case law, however, has refined this situation even further where the lateness of the acceptance is minimal (a matter of fact). Such a (barely) late acceptance will, in principle, make the offeror's offer lapse according to the general rules; but it may also put him under an obligation to respond instantly if he does not wish to accept this counter-offer. Thus, contrary to the general rule that silence cannot normally amount to acceptance (see below), in such cases the original offeror's silence may thus end up by binding him to this slightly delayed acceptance which has now become a counter-offer (cf RGZ 103, 11, 13). This last-mentioned case, however, is regarded as exceptional, containing as it does what is, in essence, a kind of extension to the *ratio legis* of § 149 BGB. Moreover, it presupposes that the offeror has not set any time limit for the acceptance; and it also assumes that the offeree (ie, the new offeror) reacted immediately. In general, therefore, it must be stressed that the *Bundesgerichtshof* does not regard the silence of the offeror in response to the new offer as an acceptance. (See, for instance, BGHZ 18, 212; BGHZ 61, 282, 285. For further discussion, see: Schlesinger, *Formation of Contracts*, II, 1568 and note 18.)

A more interesting variation from English and French law can be found in § 153 BGB. Here German law provides that, in the absence of a contrary intention on the part of the offeror, his subsequent death (or incapacity) does not prevent the acceptance of his offer by the offeree. In such an event the acceptance must, of course, be directed to the heirs of the deceased or, in the event of legal incapacity, to his legal representative. Treitel (*The Law of Contract*, p 44) takes the view that in English law 'the death of either party should not of itself terminate the offer except in the case of such "personal" contracts as are discharged by the death of either party.' The operation of this area of the law will depend greatly on the precise construction of the offer made and how performance was to be rendered.

(e) The Irrevocability of the Offer

The binding effect of an unaccepted offer—inconceivable in systems such as the English, which take the doctrine of consideration very seriously—has a number of interesting consequences which will be discussed below (see sections 2(f) and (g) and 3(c), below). Here, suffice it to make two observations.

First, this binding effect can be avoided if the offeror expressly states this in the offer using, for instances, such words as 'offer subject to change' (*Angebot freibleibend*) or 'revocable offer' (*Angebot widerruflich*). It has been disputed whether such 'qualified' offers are real offers after all. In the past, the case law of the *Reichsgericht* on the whole treated them as non-offers (see RGZ 102, 227; 105, 8, 12; also: BGH NJW 1996, 919, 920). However, if an offer was subsequently made by the other party the offeree's silence is treated as an acceptance. The person making the 'revocable offer' is thus in the end compelled to revoke the initial 'offer' if he does not wish the contract to be concluded. The alternative view is that they are offers, though they are freely revocable before acceptance; or even that they are contractual clauses which allow the offeror to revoke the contract if he changes his mind, though such an option must be exercised promptly and in accordance with the requirements of good faith. (See Medicus, *Allgemeiner Teil*, Rn. 366; Flume, *Allgemeiner Teil*, vol II, § 35 I 3c.) In the end, it is safer to say that the precise effect of such qualifying statements depends on the facts of each case and is a matter of construction. (See, eg, BGH NJW 1984, 1885, where it was found that a revocable offer was intended.)

Secondly, such an approach is largely dictated by the belief that since the initiative for the contract has come from the offeror he can, normally, be expected to have made up his mind whether he wishes to be bound or not before externalising his intention to contract. As for the period during which the offer remains binding, one notes that this can either be stipulated expressly by the offeror himself (in which case the acceptance must take place during this stated period: § 148 BGB); or it can remain 'open' until such time as the offeror could expect to receive a reply under ordinary circumstances. (See § 147 II BGB.)

(f) The Rationale of the German Approach

A few further observations should be made about the way German law deals with the consequences of the rule that an offer may be irrevocable even before it has been accepted. Though this problem does not arise in the English common law, other systems, notably the American and the French, have had to address it once they were eventually forced to abandon their original positions and accept that commercial realities required (in some cases at least) that offers be irrevocable. The American courts achieved this result via the use of the doctrine of promissory estoppel alongside an offer to enter into a unilateral contract: the offeree's change of position in reliance on the original offer is reasonably foreseeable, thus giving a basis for an implied further promise from the offeror that the offer will not be revoked (see *Drennan v Star Paving Co* 51 Cal 2d 409, 333 P 2d 757 (1958)). This estoppel can be used as a cause of action by the offeree. Interestingly, this approach has not been applied to bilateral contracts in the US (see *James Baird Co v Gimbel Bros Inc* 64 F2d 344 (2d Cir 1933)); further, the English courts have recognised the detriment that could be suffered by an offeree under a unilateral contract and came to the conclusion that revocation is no longer possible in such contracts once the offeree has started to perform (see *Daulia Ltd v Four Millbank Nominees Ltd* [1978] Ch 231). This approach functions by identifying an implied promise not to revoke, which leaves the offeree free to accept the original offer by means of commencing performance (see, further, Treitel, *The Law of Contract*, pp 37–9).

This latter-day conversion, however, has not brought the French and American systems entirely into line with the German Code since, unlike the latter which treats such a premature revocation as being without effect, the former systems (*American Restatement (Second) Contracts*, para 90(1); France, Cass civ 17 dec. 1958, D1959, I, 33; Civ 10 mai 1968, Bull civ, III, no 209) regard such a revocation as effective, but require the offeror to pay to the disappointed offeree damages equal to his 'reliance interest': ie, damages that will restore him to the position he was before the offer was made. (For France see; Bordeaux 17 jan 1870, S 1870, 2, 219.) The German position was justified thus in the *Motive zu dem Entwurfe eines Bürgerlichen Gesetzbuches für das Deutsche Reich*, 165-6 (1888) (translation from von Mehren and Gordley, *The Civil Law System* (2nd edn, 1977), pp 877–8) and deserves to be quoted more fully:

The binding effect of the offer is a requirement of commerce. If someone receives an offer, he must be able to count on a contract arising when he on his side makes a timely acceptance of the offer. The recipient of the offer requires a sure point of departure for the decision that he is to make; he must in certain circumstances at once take the steps necessary if the contract is to be concluded; he will refuse and ignore other offers dealing with the subject matter in question, he will, for his part, make offers based on the offer made to him. If a recall of the offer that has reached the offeree were still permissible before the effectiveness of the acceptance, the offeree would feel himself severely injured. Likewise, the inclination to enter into contract negotiations would, in general, become less; commerce would be rendered more difficult and would decrease. The binding effect of the offer also corresponds to the rationally probable intention of the offeror himself. This is most apparent in the cases in which the offeror has set a certain time within which the declaration as to acceptance is to take place. The setting of such a period has, according to everyday conceptions, not only the meaning that the period within which the offer may be accepted is limited, but at the same time the meaning that the offeror binds his hands for this period . . . The impracticability of the doctrine of the revocable offer was also recognized by the Pandecten School [ie, before the adoption of the BGB]. One sought to correct the danger to which the offeree would be exposed by various theories [very similar to those advanced in France by authors such as Colin and Capitant, *Cours Elémentaire de Droit Civil français* (10th edn by J de la Morandière 1948) pp 35–6; Cf *Drennan v Star Paving Co* 333 P 2d 757 (1958)] which placed a duty on the revoker to compensate the other party for what he would have had if the possibility of the contract arising had not been presented to him. *Commerce is not, in view of the great practical importance of the question, adapted to such an action for damages. Commerce requires a smooth and rapid resolution of transaction, while limiting recourse to an action in damages leads to difficult suits whose chances of success are doubtful and hinders commerce.*

Four brief observations are called for in response to this interesting extract.

First, the general assumptions made at the beginning of this extract are correct and German law was, probably, the first to recognise the need to mitigate the rigours of the school of thought which, for whatever doctrinal reasons (consent, consideration), favours free revocability of offers.

Secondly, one must note the emphasis laid here (and repeated in many other contexts of German contract law) on the exigencies of commerce and the security of commercial transactions. This line of justification also resonates strongly throughout English contract law in general, yet it contrasts strongly with the French emphasis on 'consent' and 'autonomy of the will,' though in fairness to French law one must add that these starting positions have been considerably modified with the passage of time.

Thirdly, one must ponder over the two italicised sections. In particular, the validity of the first of these italicised sections seems dubious; and there is nothing in other systems which have taken a different view on this matter to suggest that the fears of the German legislator are justified.

The last italicised section poses difficulties of its own. To be sure, the German view (according to which a claim for damages is a cumbersome way of protecting the disappointed offeree who is best served by a rule which plainly proclaims that the revocation is without effect) may appear at first glance to be convincing. On closer inspection, however, one may be permitted to wonder about the validity of such an argument. For in the final analysis how can a frustrated offeree protect himself against an offeror who has revoked his offer and refuses to perform other than through an action for damages? The question thus seems to boil down to: what should the measure of damages be? And the German insistence on the irrevocability of the offer suggests that the frustrated offeree (whenever he cannot claim specific performance of the offeror's promise) will be able to claim a full, contractual measure of damages rather than the lesser 'reliance' loss, which the American and French systems allow. Whether this is a preferable solution, however, is one on which views may legitimately differ. The paucity of case law on the subject could be taken to suggest that these are academic squabbles which have not bothered the real world unduly. (See further, Zimmermann, *Festschrift Heldrich*, pp 476–7.)

Before closing this sub-section one should add that the practice in English law of requiring the withdrawal of an offer to be communicated to *and* received by the offeree (see section 3 on acceptance, below) often achieves some of the goals at which the German approach to the irrevocability of offers aims. The well known case of *Byrne & Co v Leon van Tienhoven* (1880) 5 CPD 344 illustrates this point clearly. There a postal offer had been received on 11 October and immediately accepted by telegram, yet the offeror had posted a withdrawal of the offer on 8 October: despite the absence of a consensus at the point in time when the offer was accepted, the court held that there was a contract in existence due to the failure to communicate the withdrawal of the offer before it had been accepted. As Treitel states (*The Law of Contract*, p 41), 'the rule is based on convenience; for no one could rely on a postal offer if it could be withdrawn by a letter already posted but not yet received.' Naturally, problems of this nature become less acute as the speed of communication of offers, acceptances and withdrawals gets ever closer to instantaneous.

(g) Communication of the Offer

For an offer to have binding effect it is necessary that it be communicated to the other party. An offer is a declaration of intention (*Willenserklärung*). Consequently, it is governed by the rules applicable to such declarations generally, which are contained in §§ 130–2 BGB. These provisions form part of the General Part of the Code and thus apply to all declarations of intention. Accordingly, from a German perspective declarations of intention are discussed in abstract and the application of these rules to 'offers' is only an incident of these rules. This must be kept in mind when reading the following remarks. Thus, the cases dealing with problems of transmission of a declaration of intention generally (see: RGZ 144, 289, case no 6; BAG NJW 1963, 554, case no 7; RGZ 125, 68, case no 8; BGHZ 67, 275, case no 9; RGZ 50, 191, case no 10) apply *mutatis mutandis* to offers just as much as to an acceptance letter. Since we present the material wherever possible from the point of view of a common lawyer, we will give here a general outline of these rules as applicable to offers and in the next section return to them to add considerations special to the acceptance of an offer.

The first distinction to make is that between declarations which are directed at an addressee (*empfangsbedürftig*) and those which do not have a particular addressee.

The latter category includes the making of a will (§§ 2229 *et seq* BGB) but also the 'public' promise of a reward for the performance of an act (*Auslobung*, §§ 657–61 BGB). They are examples of ordering one's private affairs through unilateral (as opposed to contractual) 'legal transactions' (*Rechtsgeschäfte*). Unlike offers (§ 145), promises of this kind are, generally speaking, freely revocable (§ 2254, § 658—until the act is performed).

It is worth pausing at this stage to consider the offer of a reward more closely. The general rule of the BGB is that in order to create a relationship of obligation the parties must enter into a contract (§ 311 I BGB, see also chapter 1, p 25 ff; see for a comparative historical discussion of the 'contract dogma' Zimmermann, *Festschrift Heldrich* (2005), p 467). The offer of a reward (*Auslobung*) is a textbook example for an exception to this rule. Such promises for reward do not require to be accepted and therefore do not constitute 'offers' in a strict sense of that term. In this context the following problem tends to arise. What if the 'offeree' has done what the 'offeror' would like him to do even though he is unaware of the promise? The problem has divided Anglo-American courts but, on the whole, tend to opt for the view that in such circumstances there is no contract, suggesting that the key element is the need to come to some agreement where the promise or conduct amounting to acceptance must be rendered in return for that which was offered. German law, on the other hand contains a specific regulation of the matter and, in its basic position (contained in § 657 BGB), it differs from the prevailing common law view, accepting that the reward has to be paid even if the other party who performed the act was unaware of the public promise, in other words the 'offer' need not be communicated to an 'offeree'. (For the US, see: *Vitty v Eley* 54 App Div 44, 64 NYS 397 (1900); *Glover v Jewish Veterans of US* 68 A 2d 233 (DC App 1949). For England, see Treitel, *The Law of Contract*, p 36 criticising *Gibbons v Proctor* (1891) 64 LT (NS) 594 and preferring the Australian judgment in *The Crown v Clarke* [1927] 40 CLR 227. In the famous case of *Carlill v Carbolic Smoke Ball Co* [1893] 1 QB 256 the plaintiff knew of the offer though it was presumably not the dominant motive for using the smoke ball: so long as knowledge of the offer played *some* part in motivating the conduct treated as acceptance, this will be sufficient; *Lark v Outhwaite* [1991] 2 Lloyd's Rep 132, at 140. But if the conduct were completely referable to another motive, then the courts have refused to find the offer to have been accepted; *The Crown v Clarke* (above), although cf Mitchell and Phillips, 'The Contractual Nexus: Is Reliance Essential?' (2002) 22 *OJLS* 115).

'Offers' in the technical sense, ie an offer to enter into a contract, are subject to acceptance and therefore in the end must reach a particular addressee (however, see the possibilities of offers *ad incertas personas*, above). This is true of all declarations of intention which affect the content or the validity of a contract (eg, rescission, § 143 BGB). The first condition for a declaration of intention is that the intention is declared externally. An offer, being a declaration with a particular addressee, must be communicated to that person. A number of specific requirements must be satisfied before the offer can be regarded as properly communicated to the offeree. This is of great importance, for unless the offer is communicated it does not have any of its desired legal effects (for instance it is not binding in the sense of § 145 BGB). Furthermore, the offer can be withdrawn according to § 130 I 2 BGB (*Widerruf*) provided that the withdrawal is communicated at the same time or before the offer itself is communicated. (As noted above in discussing the irrevocability of offers in German law, English law takes a rather different view: an offer may be withdrawn at any point in time, unless it has been accepted. Often, the apparent rigours of this approach are mitigated by the use by the offeror of specified time limits within which acceptance must be made, or by the conclusion that merely acting inconsistently with the offer (eg, by selling the item offered to a third party in the interim) does not, without more, amount to a withdrawal of the offer (*Adams v Lindsell* (1818) 1 B & Ald 681; 106 ER 250).)

The conditions for *communication* of an offer under German law are twofold.

First, the declaration containing the offer must be transmitted to the offeree (*Abgabe*). The initiation of the transmission must be supported by the intention of the offeror. This was self-evident to the drafters of the BGB (*Motive*, vol 1, p 157) but is controversial nowadays. The question can make a difference, for instance where the offer was posted accidentally by a third person (eg, a secretary; see for details, Medicus, *Allgemeiner Teil*, Rn. 266).

The second condition, which completes the process of communication, is referred to as *Zugang* (receipt). This concept is referred to but not defined in § 130 I 1 BGB. At least four answers are possible (see, *Motive*, vol 1, pp 156 *et seq*) moving, on the timescale, from the earliest possible point to the latest point in time at which a declaration of intention may come into existence: the declaration (or externalisation of the will) as such (*Äußerungstheorie*), the dispatch of the declaration in the direction of the addressee (*Entäußerungstheorie*), the receipt of the declaration in the sense of its arrival in the hands of the other party (*Empfangstheorie*), and the actual notification of the content of the declaration been received by the addressee (*Vernehmenstheorie*). Choosing the right moment depends on an evaluation of the competing interests between sender and recipient of a declaration of intention.

To this problem the BGB offers a compromise solution and regards it as sufficient that the addressee has the *possibility to take notice* of the content of the declaration and can *reasonably be expected* to do so (*Empfangstheorie*). As a result, the sender bears the risk of destruction or postponement during transport. This seems sensible for it is he who has chosen the method of communication. Furthermore, it would not be practicable to make communication dependent on the actual notice by the addressee, for it would be difficult to establish for the sender that the receiver had actually become aware of the declaration. Thus, the latter bears the risks that stem within 'his sphere of influence.' The full legal effect of a declaration, therefore, does not require that the other party actually knows of it. The communication of the declaration only requires that the addressee is reasonably able to learn of it.

The BGB deals only with declarations of intention *inter absentes* in § 130 BGB and two special provisions: §§ 131–2 BGB. § 130 I 1 BGB does not define the requirement of proper communication. § 130 I 2 BGB introduces the already explained right to withdraw an offer *before* it is communicated. § 130 II BGB clarifies that a declaration of intention will not be affected by the death or incapacity of the sender once it has been transmitted (*abgegeben*). A special qualification of this rule in relation to *offers* is contained in the already mentioned § 153 BGB: the offer remains valid if the offeror dies or loses capacity before the acceptance of the offer, unless the intention of the offeror was otherwise (this negative formulation indicates that it is presumed that the offeror intended that the offer remains valid).

An offer *inter absentes* is communicated in the sense of § 130 I 1 BGB as soon as the offer enters the sphere of influence (*Verfügungsgewalt, Machtbereich*) of the addressee (eg, letterbox) *and* under normal circumstances (eg, usual office hours) it can be expected that the letter will be opened and its content noted. (See, for useful illustrations of this principle, RGZ 144, 289, case no 6; BAG NJW 1963, 554, case no 7; RGZ 125, 68, case no 8; BGHZ 67, 275, case no 9; RGZ 50, 191, case no 10.) Whether the addressee actually read the letter is immaterial, but if the letter is read before it would or could reasonably have been expected this also seems sufficient (see Medicus, *Allgemeiner Teil*, Rn. 276).

Oral declarations of intention are not expressly dealt with in the BGB. Such declarations are deemed to have been communicated if the receiver was actually capable of understanding the declaration—whether he comprehended it correctly or not does not matter, provided that it could be reasonably expected that he would comprehend it.

Finally, a number of problems have arisen in connection with acts committed by the addressee that prejudice the communication of a declaration of intention. This problem arises because under German law the declaration of intention must come into the sphere of influence of the addressee. This approach faces difficulties when the addressee deliberately prevents this from happening (eg, refuses to accept the letter, which he suspects to be the notice of termination of his labour contract, his lease, etc and thus seeks to delay its coming into effect). These problems are usually dealt with under the heading of good faith (abuse of rights; as to which see chapter 3, p 123) and need not be covered in detail here, for they seldom if ever arise in connection with offers. (For details see, Brox, *Allgemeiner Teil*, Rn. 157 *et seq.*)

Given the revocable nature of an offer under English law, many of these situations for which German law has made provision have received far less attention. In the absence of valid consideration, there can be no 'binding contractual effect' of the offer in any case. Instead, the cases have focused more on the question of the acceptance of an offer since it is the event of this acceptance that constrains the offeror's freedom to change his mind in the great majority of cases (particularly if the acceptance can also be construed as sufficient consideration in itself). It is questions of acceptance to which we now turn.

3. THE ACCEPTANCE (*ANNAHME*)

The acceptance must be free and unreserved, corresponding to the offeror's declared intention. As a general rule, it must be communicated to the offeror.

(a) Free

Freedom of contracts is as essential a tenet of German contract law as it is of the common law of contract. As a result of this in the vast majority of cases, there is no obligation to accept an offer; indeed, in the case of unsolicited goods, there is no obligation to do anything whatsoever about them. (See however, § 362 of the Commercial Code discussed briefly under the sub-heading of 'silence', below. See also, Directive 97/7/EC [1997] OJ L144/19 on consumer protection in distance selling which has led to a presumption in English law that any goods sent without being requested in advance by their recipient may amount to a gift rather than an offer that might or might not be accepted: Consumer Protection (Distance Selling) Regulations 2000, SI 2000/2334, regs 22 and 24; and cf § 241a BGB.)

Modern conditions have created a number of exceptions where there is a duty to contract *(Kontrahierungszwang)*. The following are the two most important instances. (Note, also, that as will be explained below in the section on *culpa in contrahendo* the offeree may become liable in damages if he creates the impression that he will accept and subsequently does not communicate to the offeror that he has changed his mind.)

The first deals with public utilities such as electricity, gas, rail and aerial transportation and in these cases the consumer (or traveller) is, generally speaking, 'entitled' to have his offer to use these services accepted by the providers of these services.

The second exception to the rule that the offeree is, in principle, entitled to refuse an offer to enter into a contract can be found in § 20 II (previously: § 26 II) of the Law against Unfair Competition (*Gesetz gegen Wettbewerbsbeschränkungen*). This law, as the title suggests, prohibits certain discriminatory practices by enterprises that hold a dominant position in the market or operate restrictive price practices, thereby preventing smaller firms from having access to the market. (Similar considerations may arise in all EU Member States as a result of certain aspects of EC competition law, such as mandating access to facilities that are 'essential' to competition in downstream markets (eg, non-replicable infrastructure such as high voltage transmission lines: see Case C–7/97 *Oscar Bronner GmbH & Co KG v Mediaprint Zeitungs- und Zeitschriftenverlag* [1998] ECR I-7791) or in requiring 'non-abusive' licensing of intellectual property rights (see Joined Cases C–241 and 242/91 P *Radio Telefis Eireann (RTE) and Independent Television Publications (ITP) Ltd v Commission* [1995] ECR I-743 (also known as '*Magill*' or '*TV Guides*')).

This area of the law is quite technical; but its general aim and operation are well illustrated by the '*Rossignol skis*' litigation, which was resolved by the *Bundesgerichtshof* in 1976 (BGH NJW 1976, 801, case no 11). The action was brought by a sports shop in Bavaria against the sole German distributor of the said mark of skis who refused to supply the plaintiffs because they were selling them below the recommended price. This practice was deemed to be legally unjustifiable and the supplier was thus forced to resume contractual delivery of skis to the plaintiff. (It is disputed whether the right to force the other party to enter into a contract is based on the general rule contained in § 249 BGB which requires restoring the pre-existing state of affairs *in specie* or whether this right stems from § 20 II of the Unfair Competition Act; but the outcome itself is not in doubt.) Protection against monopolistic abuse may, in fact, go beyond the purely economic sphere. Thus a doctor or a pharmacist may be liable if he refuses his services without proper cause. (Compare, on this last point, *Hurley v Eddingfield* 156 Ind. 416, 59 N.E. 1058 (1901) and, for further details on the whole matter see: *Münchener Kommentar*-Kramer, Vor § 145 Rn. 15. For a discussion in French, see: Pedamon, 'De quelques traits essentiels du droit allemand de la concurrence' *Cah dr Entr* (1987) 28.)

(b) Unreserved Acceptance; Dissent

As in English law, the acceptance must be unreserved and it must not introduce new elements into the offer. (This is sometimes referred to as the 'mirror image' rule.) As § 150 II BGB states, 'an acceptance under extensions, limitations or other alterations is deemed a refusal combined with a new offer' (which, of course, can then be accepted by the original offeror). (For English law, see the discussion by the various members of the Court of Appeal in *Butler Machine Tool Co Ltd v Ex-Cell-O-Corporation (England) Ltd* [1979] 1 WLR 401.)

The German Code goes into the question of discord of offer and acceptance in greater detail than English law. This discord is often referred to as 'dissent' (*Dissens*) and, since it comes close to the notion of 'error' (*Irrtum*), it will be reviewed in the third chapter of this book. Here, suffice it to say that under the Pandectist regime of the nineteenth century, *Irrtum* and *Dissens* used to have the same consequence, ie, to make the transaction void. Nowadays, however, a transaction tainted by error ('mistake') is voidable whereas a transaction afflicted by dissent makes the transaction non-existent. A further distinction should, perhaps, be borne in mind. In the case of error there is a divergence between the real and declared will, whereas in the case of unconscious dissent, the parties erroneously believe that they have concluded a contract.

Dissent is best discussed if a distinction is drawn between disagreement concerning essential terms of the contract (*Hauptpunkte*) or merely subsidiary terms (*Nebenpunkte*). In the former case the contract usually fails, while in the latter case the gap left by the dissent may be more easily filled by means of interpretation. The guiding principle in all these cases is the intention of the parties so far as it discernable and the Code provides two rules of interpretation in §§ 154, 155 BGB. Somewhat unhappily, however, the Code distinguishes between open (or conscious) dissent (*offener Dissens*: § 154 BGB) and hidden (or unconscious) dissent (*versteckter Dissens*: § 155 BGB), which we follow here for the sake of convenience.

In the first case—open dissent—if the discord is over essential terms such as the price, generally speaking there is no contract. (Yet, see for instance BGH NJW 1997, 2671, amount of rent left open; BGH NJW 2002, 817, commission of a broker left open; where the court held that there was a contract and filled the gap by applying §§ 612 II, 632 II BGB by analogy. See, as to these provisions, the section on completeness of the offer, above, including the discussion of terms that can be supplied by looking to a reasonableness standard under legislation such as the Sale of Goods Act 1979.) If, on the other hand the open dissent refers to subsidiary terms—eg, who will bear the cost of delivery of sold goods—§ 154 I BGB establishes the harsh presumption that if one point has been left open which according to one of the parties was to be part of the contract, however insignificant its purpose, the contract is deemed to be void. The prevailing opinion nowadays seeks to limit this provision by emphasising that one must search for the true intention of the parties taking into account the type of contract they have concluded or by resorting to an analogical application of § 315 BGB (cf BGHZ 41, 271, 275; BGH NJW 1975, 1116, 1117). The contract may thus still be saved if this emerges to be the true intention of the parties. This conclusion may be helped by the fact that one of the parties has commenced delivery of the goods. Thus, if the parties have commenced performance, the chances are that the contract will be treated as having been validly concluded. If, on the other hand doubts remain as to whether the agreement was concluded then, according to § 154 I BGB, the contract will be deemed not to have come into existence. Thus, if performance has commenced, the clear inclination of the courts in both England and Germany has been to try to leave in place a sensible contractual structure between the parties. However, if sufficient consensus on key elements cannot be found, a restitutionary remedy in the form of payment of the cost of services rendered in anticipation of a contract being concluded may be available (see the discussion in section 2(b), above).

Where the parties are unaware of their discord, and this discord refers to an essential part of their agreement, then no contract is considered to have come into existence. The contrary presumption in § 155 I BGB is then disproved. This applies, for instance, where parties have bought and sold goods in dollars, the buyer thinking in terms of (the weaker) Canadian dollar and the seller in terms of (the stronger) US dollar (a standard example given by the German text books. See, for instance, Flume, *Allgemeiner Teil*, II, § 34, 4; Köhler, *Allgemeiner Teil*, § 8 Rn. 41.) See also, RGZ 104, 265 (case no 12), where each of the parties believed that the other intended to buy: no contract concluded (the case is discussed further in section 5 on *culpa in contrahendo*). But if the disagreement refers to a minor point in the contract, then one may fall back on § 155 BGB, which stipulates that that 'which is agreed on is valid if it may be assumed that the contract would have been concluded even without a settlement of this point.' This means that the judge has to search for the 'presumed intention' of the parties (*hypothetischer Parteiwille*), taking into account all relevant surrounding circumstances. For an illustration of these problems, see also the battle of forms cases discussed below.

English law's insistence on a sufficiently unqualified acceptance might seem to leave little or no room for manoeuvre in matters such as those referred to in the immediately preceding paragraphs. Indeed this is its basic position. Nevertheless, certain statements made alongside an acceptance of an offer may be treated as a sufficient acceptance to conclude the contract, while also making a further offer concerning the matters under that first contract: eg, a request for extra time to complete work or to pay a sum will not always prevent the contract being concluded on the original terms, so long as the offeree makes it clear that he does accept the original terms if his request is refused (Treitel, *The Law of Contract*, p 19, referring to *Global Tankers Inc v Amercoat Europa NV* [1975] 1 Lloyd's Rep 666, at 671). This will be a matter of careful interpretation of the terms of the offer and acceptance in every individual case.

(c) Communication of the Acceptance

The acceptance must, in principle, be in response to an offer made by the offeror. Hence, the general rules as discussed in the previous section (communication of the offer) apply. The offeree must not only accept the offer in his innermost mind; he must also communicate this to the offeror. This is also the general rule in English law (see, eg, *Allied Marine Transport Ltd v Vale do Rio Doce Navigacao SA ('The Leonidas D')* [1985] 1 WLR 925, at 937).

The acceptance is deemed to be complete, as explained in relation to the communication of the offer, when it reaches the sphere of influence of the offeror (*Empfangstheorie*) though, again, it is not necessary that he actually becomes aware of it, eg, by reading the offeree's letter. (RGZ 50, 191, case no 10, and settled law since. For English law see *Entores Ltd v Miles Far East Corp* [1955] 2 QB 327, at 322.) As a rule, actually bringing the acceptance to the notice of the offeror is required so that if, for instance, a passing aeroplane drowns the sound of the acceptance out, this would prevent a contract from having been concluded, although there are exceptions to this (eg, unilateral contracts (see above, section 2(f)), communication to the offeror's agent and the postal rule—see Treitel, *The Law of Contract*, p 23 ff).

The Common law 'postal rule' (that an offer is deemed to have been accepted when the letter of acceptance is posted: *Dunlop v Higgins* (1848) 1 HLC 381; 9 ER 805, *Henthorn v Fraser* [1892] 2 Ch 27 and *Holwell Securities v Hughes* [1974] 1 WLR 155;

Treitel, *The Law of Contract*, pp 24–9, McKendrick, *Contract Law* (2003), pp 117–24 and Gardner, 'Trashing with Trollope: A Deconstruction of the Postal Rules in Contract' (1992) 12 *OJLS* 170) is thus not adopted by German law, largely because the irrevocability of offers (made possible, as we have seen, by the absence of the doctrine of consideration) means that the offeree is sufficiently protected during a reasonable period after the offer has reached him. (Compare BGH NJW-RR 1989, 757 with *Byrne & Co v Leon van Tienhoven & Co* (1880) 5 CPD 344. However, see McKendrick, *Contract Law*, p 123, who criticises the English position, preferring instead the approach that the offer can no longer be withdrawn once the acceptance has been posted as providing sufficient protection for the offeree. This approach is also in line with the CISG and the Unidroit Principles.) Incidentally, one must note that offer and acceptance are both declarations of intention and thus treated identically: they produce their effect on reaching the other party's sphere of influence. Once again, however, the German Code provides for some exceptions.

The first of these exceptions has already been encountered above, when we discussed sales through vending machines. There we saw that, according to § 151 BGB, no communication of the acceptance need be made to the offeror: all that the offeree need do is externalise his intention through an appropriate form of conduct (*Willensbetätigung*). (As to the possibility of acceptance pursuant to § 151 BGB, see the illustration in BGH NJW 1957, 1105, case no 13.) § 152 BGB contains another such exception for contracts which have to be notarially authenticated and are concluded by parties who are not simultaneously present for the event. Here, in the absence of a contrary intention, the contract is concluded on authentication of the acceptance to the notary of the acceptor and no further communication to the offeror need take place.

From these simple cases others, far more complicated, have arisen which have prompted what must be seen as a typically Germanic theoretical debate (although cf the debate that Gilmore started in the US with his book *The Death of Contract* (1974)). Thus, a young child gets on a bus and travels without his parent's permission without a ticket or with an expired ticket; or a driver enters into an open air parking lot where he fervently believes he is allowed by ancient custom to park without paying the parking fee demanded from the attendant (BGHZ 21, 319); or, finally, a house owner takes electricity directly from the power lines, by-passing the company's meters (BGH JZ 1957, 275).

These cases, where no will has (apparently) been declared (indeed, in the parking lot case it was expressly withheld), were once treated as examples of what became known as a factual contract (*faktischer Vertrag*). The term came from Günter Haupt's inaugural lecture in 1941 and was subsequently reprinted (with some modifications) in the *Festschrift für Siber*, vol I, p 1. (For more details, see Spyros Simitis, *Die Faktischen Vertragsverhältnisse als Ausdruck der gewandelten sozialen Funktion der Rechtsinstitute des Privatrechts* (1957).) This view was subsequently justified by such eminent jurists as the late Professor Karl Larenz (*Allgemeiner Teil*, § 28, II) as involving a declaration of a will which is manifested simply by the use of the service provided *(Inanspruchnahme)*. According to Larenz, in such cases typical social conduct *(sozialtypisches Verhalten)* replaced the formal element of overt acceptance in the process of creating a contractual obligation. However, despite the authority of its academic patron, this view has now been abandoned both by scholars (among the strongest critics one finds Lehmann,

Medicus and Nipperdey) and the courts (see: BGH NJW 1965, 387, 388, case no 14; BGH MDR 1968, 406; although cf BGH FamRZ 1971, 247) on the double grounds that (a) it finds no support in the Code (a favourite argument of German jurists), but also (b) because it is often seen as being not necessary and indeed dangerous. This, for instance, would be the case as far as infants (or young children) are concerned to the extent that it may deprive them of the protection given to them by other provisions in the Code (eg, §§ 105 I, 107 BGB) which can be greater than that provided by English law. This school of thought, which has opposed the notion of factual contract, thus believes that most cases brought under the heading can also be seen as cases where there was *implicit* or tacit acceptance *(konkludente Annahme)*; and where this seems too far fetched—as in the case of the child getting a free ride on the tram or the driver parking his car in the parking lot without paying the required fee—the legal solution can be sought either in the law of tort or, even, unjust enrichment. (See Brox, *Allgemeiner Teil*, Rn. 194, and Medicus, *Allgemeiner Teil*, Rn. 245 ff. Cf, however, Wieacker, 'Willenserklärung und sozialtypisches Verhalten' in *Göttinger Festschrift für das Oberlandesgericht Celle* (1961), pp 263, 267–8 doubting the suitability of these other causes of action.)

Thus, for all intents and purposes, the *'faktischer Vertrag'* is now part of recent legal history. Yet in the area of partnership (*Personalgesellschaft*) and labour relations (*Arbeitsverhältnis*) we find some vestiges of this idea. For here relationships may have 'defectively' *(fehlerhaft)* been brought about but, because of their continuing nature (*Dauerschuldverhältnis*) cannot, pragmatically speaking, be ignored and are thus brought to a juristic end only *ex nunc*. (These cases are currently known as *fehlerhafte Gesellschaft* and *fehlerhaftes Arbeitsverhältnis*. See, for details: Maultzsch, 'Die fehlerhafte Gesellschaft: Rechtsnatur und Minderjährigenschutz' JuS 2003, 544; Goette, 'Fehlerhafte Personengesellschaftsverhältnisse in der jüngeren Rechtsprechung des Bundesgerichtshofs' DStR 1996, 266; Preis in *Erfurter Kommentar zum Arbeitsrecht* (4th edn, 2004), § 611 Rn. 170 *et seq*.)

(d) Waiver of Notification of Acceptance; Silence and Letters of Confirmation

Can the notification of the acceptance be waived? According to § 151 BGB the answer is positive if: (a) such a waiver is normal in the circumstances or (b) the offeror has waived the requirement. Little need be said about the second possibility. So far as the first is concerned, suffice it to say that such waiver of communication of the acceptance is commonly found in mail order businesses and in situations where the parties are in a continuing business relationship. One must note however that what can be waived is the notification of the acceptance and not the intention to accept. The result is that the intention to accept must have in some way been externalised and in some instances this could raise problems of proof (see: BGH NJW 1957, 1105, case no 13; Treitel, *The Law of Contract*, pp 18–19 on acceptance by conduct discusses some of these problems, pointing out that the requisite evidence of the intention to accept must be assessed on the facts of each case: sometimes, the conduct is clearly consistent only with the conclusion that there was no intention to accept—see, eg, *Beta Computers (Europe) v Adobe Systems (Europe)* 1996 SLT 604).

It follows from the preceding paragraph that, like English law (*Feldthouse v Bindley* (1862) 11 CB (NS) 869; 142 ER 1037, affirmed (1863) New Rep 401 (see Miller (1972) 35 *MLR* 489)—an unsatisfactory case since on its facts it may be that the offeree had done enough to indicate his acceptance to the offeror's proposal (see Treitel, *The Law of Contract*, p 32)) and French law (Cass Civ 25 mai 1870, D 1870.1.257, but with the important exception that silence may constitute an acceptance where the offer is to the exclusive interest of the offeree: see Cass Req 29 mars DP 1938.1.5; Cass Civ 1 dec, 1969, D 1970.422.), German law takes the view that silence cannot amount to an acceptance since contracts cannot be forced upon unwilling partners. Furthermore, silence is often equivocal as to the intentions of the offeree: inactivity could just as well evince an intention not to accept in many cases (see, eg, *Allied Marine Transport Ltd v Vale do Rio Doce Navegacao SA ('The Leonidas D')* [1985] 1 WLR 925). But this is only the position in principle; and one can find some exceptions created either by the Codes (Civil or Commercial) and the case law.

The BGB exceptions include the following.

The first can be found in § 455 BGB and deals with sales on approval or inspection. If the item offered for sale was delivered to the purchaser for the purposes of trial or inspection, the latter's silence after the lapse of the stated time (or, if no time was stated, a reasonable period) will be deemed as approval (whereby, strictly speaking, parties are considered to have concluded a contract which however is subject to this approval).

A second exception can be found in § 516 II BGB. If a donor offers to make a donation and sets a time limit within which the donee must express his willingness to take the gift, the offer is deemed to have been accepted through silence after the fixed period has expired (unless the donee has expressly declined it within the said period). Likewise, §§ 545, 581 II and 625 BGB allow for the tacit renewal of contracts of lease and a contract of services. § 177 II 2 BGB treats the principal as having denied ratification if the third party demanded a decision to that effect and two weeks lapsed since then (cf § 108 II 2 BGB concerning the ratification of acts by minors). More important in practice are §§ 346 and 362 of the Commercial Code (*Handelsgesetzbuch, HGB*). The former, § 346 HGB, states that acts or omissions will in general have the effects common usage and good faith attribute to them, and in practice this mean that in appropriate circumstances, commercial usage may ascribe legal consequences to silence (which aligns nicely with the position apparently accepted in English law relating to a course of dealing between the parties, where previous offers to buy have been accepted simply by sending the product ordered. See Treitel, *The Law of Contract*, p 33, who cites the American case of *Cole-McIntyre-Norfleet Co v Holloway* 141 Tenn 679; 214 SW 817 (1919)). The latter provision, § 362 HGB, deals with merchants whose 'business includes solicitation or conclusion of business transactions for others' in an independent manner and who are placed under a duty to reply without delay if they receive an offer concerning the performance of such services from a person with whom they maintain business relations. Thus, not every merchant is covered by this rule but only those who either have the kind of relationship with the client envisaged by this article or who have offered their services to such a client. Thus, this provision would typically cover brokers or other financial agents who pay, transfer, or otherwise in their professional capacity take care of the business affairs of others.

The German judge-made exception to the rule that silence cannot amount to an acceptance refers to so-called 'confirmation letters' and these play an even more significant role in everyday German life. A number of decisions dealing with this issue are reproduced below so here it suffices to state the topic in its barest outline. (See, for instance, BGH NJW 1965, 965, case no 15; OLG Köln RBRK 1980, 270, case no 16; BGHZ 54, 236, case no 17; BGH NJW 1974, 991, case no 18.)

Confirmation letters (*kaufmännische Bestätigungsschreiben*) are usually sent following oral negotiations for the conclusion of a contract. The party sending such a letter may in such cases add in that letter terms which may not have been envisaged or agreed on at the oral stage of negotiations but which the writer of the letter believes to have been part of the negotiations. When the 'co-contractor' receives such a letter of confirmation he must, according to consistent case law since the beginning of last century, inform the writer of the confirmation letter of his disapproval of any new terms; and if he does not, his silence will be taken as an acceptance of these terms. (See, for instance: BGH NJW 1974, 991, case no 18; NJW 1994, 1288.) In examining such letters the courts will not enquire whether, in fact, a contract has already been concluded, but only whether there were negotiations between the parties. Additionally, this judge-made rule is applied to merchants (and more recently has also come to be applied to professional people) who compose such letters and send them to the opposite side immediately after the negotiations asserting the validity of such terms— terms, one might add, which one might normally expect to find in the kind of contract that has allegedly been concluded.

But by far the clearest limitation to the possibility of introducing new terms into a contract comes from one of the most important general clauses of the Code—§ 242 BGB (discussed in greater detail in chapters 3 and 7). Thus, the 'deviation' by means of addenda or modifications must not be contrary to the principle of good faith—an exhortation which clearly allows plenty of room for judicial policing of the parties' behaviour. The burden of proof for the existence of a significant deviation rests on the addressee of such a confirmation letter, yet is for the sender to show that the letter was preceded by contract negotiations which the letter is meant to 'confirm'. (See, eg, BGH NJW-RR 2001, 680, which contains a useful summary of the applicable rules.)

The German position on confirmation letters contrasts with that which obtains in English law. As the case of *Jayaar Impex Ltd v Toaken Group Ltd* ([1992] 2 Lloyd's Rep 437: see Treitel, *The Law of Contract*, p 18) makes clear, any such attempt to use such a confirmation letter to incorporate written terms which are substantially different from those agreed in the original oral contract will not be treated as having been accepted by the recipient of that letter merely by his conduct in taking delivery of the goods (and his subsequent silence as to the 'new' terms). Any such conduct refers to the oral contract itself, not to the varied terms in the confirmation letter. The English courts ask whether a contract has been concluded and do not allow this subsequent communication to vary that contract, in the absence of acceptance and consideration for such a variation. At the same time, it should be pointed out that such cases concerning 'confirmations' can often bear strong factual similarities to cases involving a 'battle of the forms' between prospective contracting parties, particularly if no firm agreement can be established on which terms were actually agreed on orally and/or accepted by conduct. Sometimes, gaps left in the agreement will be filled by the courts using various methods of implication (see p 59, section 2(b)), but on other occasions the last shot fired in the battle may well prevail. We will return to 'the battle of the forms' below (see section 3(f), p 79).

(e) Pre-contracts; Option Contracts; and Letters of Intention

In German law, a pre-contract (*Vorvertrag*) allows one or both parties to make a legally binding agreement to enter at a later date into what is known as the principal contract (*Hauptvertrag*). (For English law, see Treitel, *The Law of Contract*, pp 51–66 for a discussion of issues of certainty and conditional agreements, with which some of this discussion overlaps.) This postponement of the principal contract may be due to technical reasons (prices may be fluctuating, the place of delivery may be undecided, etc) or legal reasons (the necessary licence has not yet been granted etc) though this assumes that the outstanding terms are either determined or determinable, if necessary through an equitable interpretation of the contract in accordance with § 157 BGB. Such a pre-contract must contain all the terms necessary for the main contract (see RGZ 124, 81, case no 1). This differs from the situation discussed in the well-known English case of *Walford v Miles* [1992] 2 AC 128, where the principal agreement was subject to contract and therefore not binding, while the attempt to imply a term into a collateral agreement that negotiations should continue in good faith was rejected by the House of Lords (see McKendrick, *Contract Law*, pp 535–43). Treitel (citing *Donwin Productions Ltd v EMI Films Ltd*, The Times, 9 March 1984) suggests (*The Law of Contract*, pp 61–2) that where all essential points have been resolved between the parties but some issues remain open, a term might be implied by the court that negotiation in good faith *was* required to resolve those other issues.

The pre-contract is also subject to the same formalities as the principal contract whenever the purpose of the formality is not merely probative but aims at protecting one of the parties against precipitous action. It is enforceable against the party who has bound himself to enter into the main contract (or indeed it is enforceable against either party if both have assumed such an obligation) by means of a declaratory judgment. It differs from the Option Contract (*Optionsvertrag*), which gives to one party the legal option (*Optionsrecht*) to force, by means of a unilateral declaration of his will, a contractual relationship on the other. Once again, the option contract is subject to the same formalities as the main or final contract; but it is not settled whether the exercise of the option itself also has to comply with the same requirements.

The weakest and least binding of the preliminary skirmishes in the process of concluding a binding contractual relationship is the letter of intent. Such an *Absichtserklärung,* though the Germans themselves use the term 'letter of intent,' is usually made by one of the parties as he is feeling his way towards a potential, future contract and, according to standard practice, has no binding legal effects (the standard work on this is Lutter, *Der Letter of Intent* (3rd edn, 1998); see also Treitel, *The Law of Contract*, pp 167–8).

It should be noted that such pre-contractual representations might have other consequences for the validity and enforceability of a contract finally entered into (eg, if they are misrepresentations that have induced the other party to accept the offer). We will discuss this issue in chapter 6, below. Otherwise, in English law the possibility of claims based on estoppel to bring an enforceable agreement into being will not be successful in the absence of pre-existing contractual relations between the parties (although cf *Thornton Springer v NEM Insurance Co Ltd* [2000] 2 All ER 489, at 519, criticised by Treitel, *The Law of Contract*, p 113 note 44). Further, a right founded on an estoppel cannot be used as a cause of action to pursue the offeror or hold him to

his word—rather, it acts as a shield to protect (typically) the reliance by the other contracting party on the statements or conduct of the offeror (see Treitel, *The Law of
Contract*, pp 105–24 and McKendrick, *Contract Law*, pp 231–67). (The only place
where in English law an estoppel is capable of founding a cause of action is in the
sphere of real property, where a right can be based on an assurance relating to the
ownership of real property, coupled with detrimental reliance on that assurance and
in circumstances where repudiation of that assurance would be unconscionable: see,
for a recent example, *Gillett v Holt* [2001] Ch 210. See generally, Treitel, *The Law of
Contract*, pp 134–49; Sparkes, *A New Land Law* (2nd edn, 2003), chapter 23 and
Harpum, *Megarry & Wade—The Law of Real Property* (6th edn, 1999), chapter 13.)

(f) The Battle of the Forms

We have already seen that an acceptance of an offer that departs from the contents of
the latter, typically by introducing different terms will, in the absence of a contrary
indication, mean that no contract has been concluded. The starting point of German
(and Anglo-American) law is that such an 'acceptance' should be treated instead as a
rejection of the original offer as a counteroffer. The use of standardised clauses and
the rapid exchange of documents as a result of improved communications brought a
change in the area of the law, especially since the parties themselves were not always
quick to pick up the differences that arose in the process of their communications. As
a result, the legal problem known as the 'battle of forms' became increasingly acute.
§ 150 II BGB suggests that any deviation, however minor, contained in the acceptance
constitutes a counter-offer. Silence is not, as such, capable of acquiring the meaning
of an acceptance of the counter-offer. What about the carrying out of the main purported contractual obligations? Does this amount in the absence of an express protest
to a 'tacit' acceptance of the counter-offer? If this were the case one would force the
parties to seek to take the last 'shot' before performance commences. This seems
somewhat arbitrary, yet the other extreme in concluding that the contract never came
into being for failure of complete and unreserved acceptance, does not seem satisfactory either.

Originally, German law took the position found in current English law (exemplified
by such cases as *British Road Services Ltd v Arthur V Crutchley Ltd* [1968] 1 All ER
811) and opted for the 'theory of the last word' which corresponds to the English 'last
shot' doctrine. In practice, this meant that the contract was concluded on the sellers'
terms since they tend to 'fire the last shot' and buyers do not object (because they want
the goods or services for which they have contracted). A defensive mechanism thus
became fashionable. Parties, usually buyers, started to include a defensive clause
(*Abwehrklausel*) which protected them against all contrary clauses of the other party
(present or future) to which they did not formally assent in writing. Initially, the
courts seemed favourably inclined towards such a device; in fact, they still pay much
attention to it. (See, for a similar defence strategy, *Butler Machine Tool Co Ltd v Ex-
Cell-O Corp Ltd* [1979] 1 WLR 401, where the seller signed a slip incorporating the
buyer's terms and returned it to them failing explicitly to refer once again to *all* terms
of his offer. Cf Treitel, *The Law of Contract*, p 21, suggesting that by careful drafting
one can avoid losing the battle of the forms but one cannot win it if the other party is
equally careful: no contract is then concluded.)

Overall, however, the approach of the *Bundesgerichtshof* has become more sophisticated, with much attention being paid not only to the intention of the parties, butto custom, usage in a particular trade and good faith (§§ 133, 157 and 242 BGB are frequently relied on to justify the final outcome). (For illustrations, see: OLG Cologne RBKR 1980, 270, case no 16; BGHZ 54, 236, case no 17; BGH NJW 1974, 991, case no 18.) The end result may thus vary. Different clauses may survive to the extent that they are compatible with those of the other party; alternatively, where they are irreconcilable with one another they may be removed and replaced by statutory rules, see § 306 II BGB, and finally, in certain circumstances, one set of clauses may prevail over the other. This, for instance, occurred in an important case decided in the mid-1980s (BGH NJW 1985, 1838, case no 19) where the seller's attempts to sell his goods subject to an extended property reservation clause *(verlängerter Eigentumsvorbehalt)* until the buyer had paid the purchase price failed, in particular because of the presence in the buyer's contract of one of the above-mentioned *Abwehrklausel.* (In BGH NJW 1995, 1671, for instance the buyer did not object in this qualified way and the extended retention clause survived the battle of the forms.) However, this was not the sole reason for this result. For in contracts containing conflicting provisions, where the issue is the validity of the seller's 'retention of title' clause, solutions are more nuanced (for discussion of such clauses in English law, see McCormack, *Reservation of Title* (1995) and Sealey and Hooley, *Cases and Materials on Commercial Law* (3rd edn, 2003), pp 428–46). For a rich, recent case law (see, for instance, BGH NJW 1982, 1749; BGH NJW 1982, 1751; BGH WM 1986, 643, BGH NJW-RR 2001, 484 etc) has distinguished between simple retention clauses and the extended kind *(verlängerter Eigentumsvorbehalt)* both of which actually serve to protect the seller's rights. In the first category of 'retention of title' clauses the sellers' claims tend to be upheld (at the expense of the buyers' contrary clauses) whereas in the case of the 'extended retention of title' clauses they tend to be set aside and the buyers' position seems to prevail. The 'simple' retention of title clause is stronger because it is rationalised in property law terms. The buyer cannot obtain by means of the contract for the transfer of the right (§ 929 BGB) more than the seller is willing to give up. The 'extended' retention clause is weaker because it is based not on a legal power of the seller, but on the buyer's consent to transfer to the seller as security the claims he acquires against his buyers. The seller is interested in such a security because by processing the goods sold the seller is likely to lose all his proprietary interest reserved by a 'simple' retention of title clause. This was, in fact, the case in the aforementioned decision of the BGH (NJW 1985, 1838, case no 19) where the seller's contract contained a clause according to which any claims that the buyer had against its customers for the sale of goods produced by the buyer using the goods supplied by the seller were automatically assigned to the seller. As already noted, the buyer's general objection to accepting any different terms prevailed in the end and the seller's contentions were rejected. The decision has been interpreted to signify a departure from the 'theory of the last word' derived from § 150 II BGB (noted by de Lousanoff NJW 1985, 2921). Instead, while taking the successful formation of the contract as such for granted, the court also focuses on the substance of the terms and how material the conflict of the terms is. The courts have, however, never openly questioned the approach of § 150 II BGB and prefer to solve the conflict at an earlier level by applying subtle reasoning as to what actually was the 'last word' of the parties and allowing a protest 'in advance'. It is tempting to say that the reasoning is typically Germanic, involving not only contract and property law reasoning, but having regard also to trade practice (the latter under §§ 157 and 242 BGB). Yet, the choice between the strictly formal reasoning and approaches which look more at the substance of the terms, has also occupied the minds of common lawyers, as the *Butler Machine Tool* case (referred to above) shows; Lord Denning's attempt to depart from the traditional formal approach and to replace conflicting terms by reasonable implication has remained the minority view. (See generally, McKendrick, *Contract Law*, pp 91–128; Treitel, *The Law of Contract*, pp 20–1.) It should also be noted that straining to find a concluded contract between the parties is not the only way to deal with the situation: a more relaxed approach to the English offer and acceptance rules might lead to a better treatment of the messier realities of the contracting process (albeit at the cost of a degree of certainty: there is not such a range of statutory default rules in English law to fill the 'non-material' gaps), but it is also possible to acknowledge that no contract has been concluded and then deal with the consequences through other legal doctrines (such as restitution, where work has commenced in anticipation of a contract being concluded and expenses have been incurred: see, eg, *British Steel Corporation v Cleveland Bridge & Engineering Co Ltd* [1984] 1 All ER 504).

4. FORM AND EVIDENCE OF SERIOUSNESS

(a) Formalities

Bernard, *Formbedürftige Rechtsgeschäfte* (1979); Boente/Riehm, 'Das BGB im Zeitalter digitaler Kommunikation—Neue Formvorschriften' Jura 2000, 793; Einsele, 'Formerfordernisse bei mehraktigen Rechtsgeschäften' DNotZ 1996, 835; Häsemeyer, *Die gesetzliche Form der Rechtsgeschäfte* (1971); Häsemeyer , 'Die Bedeutung der Form im Privatrecht' JuS 1980, 1; Holzhauer, *Die eigenhändige Unterschrift– Geschichte und Dogmatik des Schriftformerfordernisses im deutschen Recht* (1973); Köbl, 'Die Bedeutung der Form im heutigen Recht' DNotZ 1983, 207; W Lorenz, 'Das Problem der Aufrechterhaltung formnichtiger Schuldverträge' AcP 156, 381; Reimann, 'Formerfordernisse beim Abschluß von Gesellschaftsverträgen' DStR 1991, 154; Richardi/Annuß, 'Der neue § 623 BGB—Eine Falle im Arbeitsrecht?' NJW 2000, 1231.

German law, like most modern legal systems, is based on the principle of consensualism, which means that contracts (and unilateral juristic acts) in most cases require no formalities *(Formfreiheit* = freedom of form). Indeed, if anything this statement seems truer of German law than French, given the greater liberality of the rule allowing proof through witnesses and, effectively, leaving it to 'the free appreciation of the judge' *(freie Beweiswürdigung)* to decide whether a contract exists and what, in case of doubt, are its terms (see §§ 286, 373 *et seq*, ZPO). But this last point also serves as an excuse to make an important observation, namely that, on the whole, in German law the rules about formality are meant to protect the parties by ensuring that they enter legal transactions only after serious consideration of the consequences of their acts. As Zweigert and Kötz point out (*An Introduction to Comparative Law*, translated by Tony Weir (3rd edn, 1998), p 371), it is,

[o]nly against the background of this fundamentally different point of view [that] . . . the many peculiarities of the legal rules in the German legal family become comprehensible. Thus Germany and Switzerland put in the general part the rule that a legal transaction not in the form legally prescribed is in principle void or invalid (§ 125 BGB, Article 11 OR). The precise formal requirements are to be found here and there throughout the civil codes wherever the legislator specifies in relation to each type of transaction, whether simple writing is sufficient or whether notarial attestation is required, whether the declaration of one contractor or both must be in the proper form, whether formal invalidity may be cured by subsequent performance, and so on. Such ad hoc rules are needed in the German legal family because the need for protection from surprise varies from one kind of transaction to another. Problems of proof, on the other hand, are common to all transactions. So the Romanistic legal systems can develop general clauses like art. 1341 Code civil [which curtails the means of proof in all non-commercial transactions in excess of €800 if they did not take the form of private writing].

Thus, some transactions have to be in written form (*Schriftform*). In practice, this means that the maker of the document must sign it (or, if he cannot sign, his mark must be placed on the document and notarially authenticated (see § 126 I BGB)). Only the signature need be hand-written; and what must be used is the surname (or, in the case of a legal entity, the name of the firm: see RGZ 50, 51, 60). The use of the first name of a person will not suffice, though apparently a customary rule predating the German Code allows bishops and princes so to sign (cf Flume, *Allgemeiner Teil*, vol II, § 15, II, 1-a, where doubt is expressed about such a rule on the grounds that it conflicts with the equality clause (Article 3) of the Constitution).

Where a contract is concluded through the intervention of an agent, the latter must make it clear that he is acting as agent only, using such terms as *in Vertretung* or *im Auftrag*; the *Reichsgericht* has even allowed agents to sign such documents using the principal's name (RGZ 58, 387, 388).

In contracts both parties must sign the same document; and if several counterparts are drawn up, it is sufficient if each party signs the copy intended for the other. Such a document is, for instance, needed for a lease for a definite period exceeding one year (§ 550 BGB) or a contract of guarantee (§ 766 BGB), whereas, however, only the guarantor's declaration of intention needs to be in writing (a formal requirement which does not apply to merchants under § 350 of the Commercial Code). The Code contains further provisions where such signature is required. For examples from the law of obligations, see §§ 623, 761, 781 BGB.

More recently, a lesser formality has been introduced into the Code, the so-called 'textual' form (*Textform*, § 126b BGB). No signature is required, yet the statement must be in some form peremptorily incorporated (e-mail, for instance, is sufficient). This type of form is reserved for transactions which, while still perceived to be important enough to require form in the interest of security in the law, are less 'invasive' than the transactions requiring written form. Examples include a landlord demanding an increase in rent for a flat (§ 558a I BGB); the termination of a consumer transaction according to § 355 I 2 BGB; and the notification to the consumer of his consumer rights under § 355 II BGB.

A further new type of form is the so-called electronic form concerning electronic signatures (§ 126a BGB, § 292a ZPO), which, however, has thus far not played a significant role in practice.

A notarial (or public) certification (ie a stricter type of formality: *öffentliche Beglaubigung*), on the other hand, requires that the will of the (contracting) party be expressed in writing and the signature(s) notarially authenticated (§ 129 I BGB). § 403 BGB provides an illustration. The assignor shall on demand execute in favour of the assignee a publicly certified document of assignment. (For another illustration, see § 1154 BGB.) In practice, this means that the notary will demand that the signature is affixed on the document in his presence or, at least, recognised by the signatory in his presence.

There is, finally, a very austere type of form known as the notarial authentication (*notarielle Beurkundung*). This, according to § 17 of the *Beurkundungsgesetz* of 28 August 1969, requires the notary 'to ascertain the will of the parties, explain the content of the transaction, instruct the parties about the legal consequences of the transaction, and record their statements clearly and unequivocally' (translation from Zweigert and Kötz, *An Introduction to Comparative Law*, p 367).

An interesting parallel to this need for independent advice is provided by the complex and ever-expanding English case law on undue influence exerted on one party to enter into a contractual arrangement. One key element in allowing such a transaction to stand is that independent advice must have been provided to the 'influenced' party. (For further discussion see Treitel, *The Law of Contract*, pp 408–27 and Capper, 'Undue Influence and Unconscionability: A Rationalisation' (1998) 114 *LQR* 479.) This is part of a court-developed series of rules which, while not strictly 'formal' in nature, fulfil a somewhat similar protective function in this area in attempting to ensure that both parties were in a position to consider carefully the consequences of entering into the contract.

In such cases a number of duties of information and control are thus imposed on the notary in German law (*Prüfungs- und Belehrungspflichten*) and these include an obligation on the part of the notary to inform the parties that their transaction is subject to foreign law, even though clearly he is under no duty to advise them on this foreign law. (The preceding comments help underline a terminological point which is well known, namely that a German notary is a member of a highly skilled and regulated profession and should thus not be confused with the American or English 'notary public'.)

The following transactions are those that must be subjected to these rigid formalities.

First, the promise of a gift must take this form (see § 518 I BGB). It should be observed, however, that a promise lacking the required form is deemed valid retroactively if it is actually carried out (see § 518 II BGB).

Secondly, one must note § 311b BGB, which envisages a contract whereby one person promises to assign his present property (or a fraction of it) to another or to charge it with a usufruct. § 311b I BGB deals with a contract to transfer ownership of land and is most important in practice. This *contractual* obligation is, as already stated, known as the *Verpflichtung*, whereas the actual disposition of the right (by means of delivery (*traditio*) if it is a chattel, or transcription into the Land Register (*Grundbuch*) if it concerns land) is known as the *Verfügung*, which attracts a lesser degree of formality. § 925 BGB stipulates that the contract to transfer title must be declared in the simultaneous presence of both parties before a notary. (We remind the reader that the distinction between the two is known as the principle of abstraction (*Abstraktionsprinzip*) and has been discussed in chapter 1, p 27.) For other transactions requiring such notarial intervention, see §§ 1410, 2276, 2348, 2371 BGB.

Formal requirements are introduced on the basis of three policy considerations.

First, the form is meant to warn the parties (or one of the parties) that they are about to perform an important act; this is usually referred to as *Warnfunktion*. Accordingly, we find that normal requirements are usually associated with a potentially 'dangerous' transaction. Falling into this category are, for instance, guaranteeing the payment of a debt owed by another person, surety, § 766 BGB (exempting certain groups of persons who are deemed 'capable' of overseeing the consequences of such transactions, cf § 350 of the Commercial Code); or the sale of land (§ 311b I BGB).

Secondly, requiring form also serves to secure—usually written—evidence, which can later be used to establish the intention of the parties more easily (*Beweisfunktion*). This aspect is particularly obvious where the person uttering the statement is no longer around to explain it; hence, in relation to wills § 2247 I BGB demands even more than simple written form (signature): the whole text must be in the handwriting of the testator.

Finally, where notarial authentication is required, it is hoped that this will provide a basic level of legal advice before the agreement is concluded (*Beratungsfunktion*). The first two of these policy factors are well illustrated by BGH NJW 1996, 1467, case no 20, a case concerning the question whether a so-called 'blanc signature' (ie one which leaves the text to be completed) suffices to meet the requirements of § 766 BGB. (The decision is also noteworthy in a number of other respects. Involving the 'overruling' of previous decisions, it contains one of the rare statements of the *Bundesgerichtsshof* as to the 'binding' nature of its previous pronouncements and as to whether it is the task of the courts to discover the law or to make it. As a matter of general interest one observes that even though the doctrine of *stare decisis* (in the strict English sense) is unknown in German law, German courts do not easily depart from existing constant case law. Yet, as this decision indicates, sometimes even constant case law cannot be relied on.)

Where form is required, its absence will typically make the transaction void (§ 125 BGB). But the Code itself provides some derogations from this principle. This, for instance, is the case where the invalidity would harm that person whose interest the formal requirement is meant to protect or where it would be contrary to legal certainty (*Rechtssicherheit*) to hold certain transactions invalid even though they were actually carried through.

An instance of the first type is § 550 BGB mentioned above. Entering into a lease for a specific period over one year can be accomplished only in written form, but in the absence of the required form it will be valid but will be treated as a lease for an indeterminate time. In this category, the consequence of failing to comply with the required form is a valid contract yet with a content that is assumed to be in the best interest of the lessee. (For a possible English law parallel in questions of the statutory illegality of particular terms not operating to the detriment of the party to be protected by the statute, see *Kiriri Cotton v Dewani* [1960] AC 192, discussed in some detail in chapter 15, section 3(b), p 243.)

Examples of the second type take a different form. If the parties have carried the contract out then the defect in form is cured. As already noted, the defect of a promise of a gift made other than in notarial authentication is cured if the chattel which is the object of the gift is handed over to the donee (§ 518 II BGB). The same is true of an oral guarantee—once the guarantor has fulfilled the principal obligation, the defect of form is cured (§ 766 sentence 3 BGB)—and of a contract involving the obligation to transfer the title in land: once it is carried out (by entering into a separate contract transferring the title and entering the new owner in the register, §§ 873, 925 BGB) the contract is deemed to be valid, § 311b I BGB.

The above instances, where the effects of the lack of form are mitigated by the Code itself, are seen as exceptional derogations from the basic rule of nullity contained in § 125 BGB. Both the legislator and the case law have not departed from this position of principle though a considerable case law has developed since the inter-war years which has tried to mitigate the rigour of the basic rule in deserving cases.

This litigation has been mainly concerned with the absence of form in the context of § 311b I (ex-313) BGB where the vendor intentionally or, even negligently, induced the purchaser to believe that no form was needed. In such cases, to allow a vendor to reclaim the property, or conversely to deny the purchaser his claim to performance because of the lack of the written form, could be contrary to good faith. The older case law took this view fairly consistently, starting with the famous *Edelmann* decision of 1927 which allowed for the possibility of awarding damages to such a purchaser under the heading of *culpa in contrahendo* or § 826 BGB, *damages* for non-conveyance of the sold land (RGZ 117, 121, case no 21, though the claim failed on the facts of that case; see also, RG JW 1938, 1023 using the dangerous term '*allgemeines Volksempfinden*' which was abused during the Nazi years to justify some outrageous results in other contexts. See, for a confirmation of this line of reasoning: BGH NJW 1965, 812). Later decisions went a step further and even ordered specific performance of the contract despite the absence of form, where invalidity would lead to an 'extremely harsh' ('*schlechthin untragbar*') result. In BGHZ 48, 396, case no 22, the *Bundesgerichtshof* took the next step in a case which shows how and when § 242 BGB can successfully be invoked. In that case the defendant company sold the plaintiff a plot of land. The transaction was in writing; and it bore the signature of the managing director of the defendant who, at one time, had been the plaintiff's boss. When the plaintiff asked for the agreement to be properly notarised, the defendant brushed the request aside on the grounds that it was his 'habit to honour his obligations no matter whether they were made orally, in writing, or were in notarial form.' To the plaintiff's reply that they were both mortal and that the director's assurances, though convincing, might not bind the company, the latter replied that he had signed the document in the name of the company and that 'the contract was equivalent to a notarial act.' The *Bundesgerichtshof* took the view that insistence on formal requirements would be unduly 'harsh' where it could be shown that 'one party has assumed a new way of life or given up his own way of life in reliance to the promises made by the other party.' The contract was thus specifically enforced. The decision is remarkable because in this case the abuse of rights argument serves to justify a cause of action, initially for recovering the reliance interest, yet in BGHZ 48, 396, case no 22, the performance interest itself is protected and this, as we will see in the section on good faith in the next chapter, is not the way good faith arguments usually operate. While a reliance-based measure may be explained on the basis of the duty-creating aspect of good faith discussed also in conjunction with *culpa in contrahendo*, as a judicial parallel to provisions such as § 122 BGB in the context of a failed contract for lack of form, or alternatively be explained as liability in tort under § 826 BGB, it is more difficult to see why the *expectation* interest ought to be protected. Good faith is here used to create full contractual obligations where according to § 125 BGB there are none. (See, Medicus, *Bürgerliches Recht*, Rn. 181 *et seq*, objecting that these judgments have created significant insecurity in the law; and Flume, *Allgemeiner Teil*, vol 2, § 15 III 4c, bb; both however argue that where one party was deceived as to a formal requirement he may elect to have the contract enforced; this case has apparently not yet been decided.) However, such a solution would only be sanctioned where not to do so would create an 'absolutely unbearable result' (*ein schlechthin untragbares Ergebnis*) for the 'innocent' party and not merely a 'harsh' one (*nicht bloß ein hartes Ergebnis:* see BGHZ 85, 315, 319).

The facts of the later decision of the BGH NJW 1972, 1189, case no 23, give a good illustration of what the courts have in mind when making such pronouncements for in that case the plaintiff, an old man purchased (without observing the necessary formalities) what he intended to use as his retirement home. His advanced years, the purpose of the transaction, and the fact that an action for damages might be an inadequate remedy given the possibility of imminent death, all weighed heavily on the court which finally allowed him to insist on a conveyance of the property. These illustrations however also show that the new case law can give rise to difficult demarcation problems and thus, not surprisingly, it has not earned many supporters, at least among academic writers. (For further discussion, see the section on *culpa in contrahendo*, below, and on good faith in chapter 3; Medicus, *Allgemeiner Teil,* Rn. 630 *et seq* and W Lorenz, AcP 156, 381.)

A useful comparison can be drawn here with the English cases on estoppel. This nuanced case law only seems to allow the avoidance of strictly 'formal' requirements in the context of proprietary estoppel (where the court's order appears to provide sufficient formality to effect a transfer of real property, thus avoiding the formal strictures Law of Property (Miscellaneous Provisions) Act 1989, which requires such transfers to be in writing: see *Gillett v Holt* [2001] Ch 210 and the references in section 3(e), above). (Although cf *Shah v Shah* [2001] 4 All ER 138 at [31], where an estoppel by representation was held to prevent reliance on a small defect of form in the contract as a ground for avoiding the agreement.) Nevertheless, the broader run of the estoppel case law responds to very similar motivating factors to those discussed above in relation to the German law that derogates from formal requirements: the English case law gives great weight to *reliance* on conduct or representations by one of the parties, leading to a refusal to allow the other party to rely on his strict legal rights as against the relying party. While this does not typically relate to the stage of forming the first (contractual) link between the parties (again, except in the case of proprietary estoppel), the result is to vary the application to the relying party of otherwise binding terms, because to apply the original terms would not be appropriate in the circumstances (eg, the result would be 'unconscionable' or it would be 'inequitable' to allow the other party to go back on his promise). (See generally, Treitel, *The Law of Contract*, pp 105–24.)

(b) Evidence of Seriousness

Gehrlein, 'Vertragliche Haftung für Gefälligkeiten' VersR 2000, 415; Grundmann, 'Zur Dogmatik der unentgeltlichen Rechtsgeschäfte' AcP 198 (1998), 457; Hau,

Vertragsanpassung und Anpassungsvertrag (2003); Hirte and Heber, 'Haftung bei Gefälligkeitsfahrten im Straßenverkehr' JuS 2002, 241; Pallmann, *Rechtsfolgen aus Gefälligkeitsverhältnissen* (1971); Willoweit, 'Schuldverhältnis und Gefälligkeit' JuS 1984, 909 ff.; Willoweit, 'Die Rechtsprechung zum Gefälligkeitshandeln' JuS 1986, 96.

The question of deciding which promises are legally binding is one that has occupied all developed legal systems; and all agree on according greater attention to the promise that was 'bought' by some kind of counter-performance. Thus, gifts are enforceable in the common law only if they are under seal; and in both the Romanistic and Germanic families they are subject to special requirements of form, some of which have already been briefly noted. Where the systems differ is as to the criteria they use to determine the seriousness (and binding nature) of a declared human will. The common law's prime test is, of course, consideration; but, as Zweigert and Kötz correctly observe, '[b]y taking counterperformance as the sole indication of seriousness . . . the Common law renders it impossible to do justice in all cases.' Decisions such as *Stilk v Myrick* (1809) 2 Camp 317; 170 ER 1168), *Foakes v Beer* (1884) 9 App Cas 605 and *Brawn v Lyford* 103 Me 362; 69 A 544 (1907) thus represent to continental eyes the unfortunate side effects of the doctrine of consideration. (Yet perhaps the result of some of these decisions may also be sustained on different grounds—eg, duress, etc— in civil law systems. See, for an evaluation of these cases, Treitel, *Some Landmarks of Twentieth Century Contract Law* (2002), chapter 2; Hau, *Vertragsanpassung und Anpassungsvertrag,* pp 87 *et seq.*) The merits and demerits of the English doctrine of consideration (for in America the concept has been considerably weakened over the years) are still discussed in its country of origin, but happily we do not have to consider them in this work. Here, it is sufficient to say that in German law the seriousness of the parties is not determined by any doctrine even remotely akin to that of consideration. Nor is there any recourse to the notion of *causa*—a concept that only comes into its own in the context of the German law of unjust enrichment (§§ 812 *et seq* BGB.) § 118 BGB provides that a declaration that was not intended to be taken seriously is void; it should be noted that this is an exception applied narrowly by the courts. It is fair to say, however, that an agreement involving a counter-performance (eg, § 433 BGB, sale of goods) will hardly ever prompt an inquiry by the court into whether the declarations of intention were meant to be taken seriously and if on occasion one party actually raises such a defence he is very likely to be judged by the objective meaning of his declaration. (See chapter 1 for a discussion of this objective approach, which need not be repeated here. We will also return to the topic in the next chapter, section on interpretation.) One can safely conclude that, so far as promises supported by consideration are concerned, there is little difference between the common law and German law.

It has been argued that there is, or should be, no separate requirement in the common law to show an intention to create legal relations before a contract can be said to exist (see, eg, Williston, *Contracts* (1990), Section 21 and Furmston (ed), *Butterworths Common Law Series: The Law of Contract* (1999), para 2.165). Yet it seems clear that (in English law at least—see Treitel, *The Law of Contract*, chapter 4 and McKendrick, *Contract Law*, chapter 7) such an intention must still be found (see, for recent confirmation of this position, *Baird Textile Holdings Ltd v Marks & Spencer plc* [2002] 1 All ER (Comm) 737, at [30] and [59]). The variety of fact scenarios, situations and contexts in which no such intention can be shown is huge, but classic examples include arrangements relating to social or domestic occasions (a famous, and perhaps famously borderline, example being *Balfour v Balfour* [1919] 2 KB 571, at 627, where a husband's promise to pay a £30 per month allowance to his wife while he was working abroad was held to be unenforceable 'because the parties did not intend that [it] should be attended by legal consequences'), letters of intent and letters of comfort (such as stating a company policy on a particular matter: *Kleinwort Benson Ltd v Malaysia Mining Corpn Berhad* [1989] 1 WLR 379, where no binding promise was found that this was an undertaking not to change that policy at a later date).

It also seems clear that, while consideration and the intention to create legal relations are often closely linked—either on the facts used to prove their existence or in the language used in the reasoning of the judges—they nonetheless remain distinct. (On the latter point, see the judgment of Pollock CB in the case of *White v Bluett* (1853) 23 LJ Ex. 36 and the discussion in McKendrick, *Contract Law*, pp 299–300.) Similarly, common elements may be relevant to the decision whether an agreement has been reached between the parties at all and whether, even if such an agreement can be shown, it was intended to create legal relations (see *Baird Textile Holdings*, above, at [30]). All three elements must be present if a binding contract is to exist. In the requirement that there be shown an intention to create legal relations, English law clearly has a further means of assessing 'indications of seriousness' that can be quite subtle in its operation. It places a heavy burden on a party to a proved or admitted express agreement to demonstrate that there was no intention to create legal relations as a result of that agreement (*Edwards v Skyways Ltd* [1964] 1 WLR 349, at 355) while requiring strong evidence the other way if an attempt is being made to imply a contract in the circumstances (*Blackpool and Fylde Aero Club Ltd v Blackpool Borough Council* [1990] 1 WLR 1195, at 1202).

So far as promises not supported by consideration are concerned, the situation is more complex. Two observations are called for.

First, as has already been pointed out, most of these transactions are regarded as potentially 'dangerous' by German law and therefore subjected to strict requirements of form. It will be recalled that the making of a gift will not enable the promisee to claim the gift unless the contract was notarially authenticated. Thus, the general theoretical approach could not be more different. Yet at the level of application the results converge. At the same time, certain characteristics of the development and current state of English law should be borne in mind, which underline the similarities behind the reasons for such rules relating to 'seriousness of intention' and the need for apparently strict rules to be given flexible interpretation. The English legislature took the decision in 1677 to pass the Statute of Frauds, the broad policy of which 'was to require written evidence of important legal transactions as a prerequisite to their enforcement, to insist, that is, on a measure of formality in areas in which wholly informal transactions had come to be legally effective' (AWB Simpson, *A History of the Common Law of Contract—The Rise of the Action of Assumpsit* (1975, reprinted 1996), pp 599–600; see also, generally, chapter XIII). Sections 4 and 16 of the Statute gave the six categories of contract to be covered and, while many such formalities were later removed, some still remain today in particular areas (even outside the field of real property): eg, 'regulated consumer credit agreements' (under the Consumer Credit Act 1974—see Treitel, *The Law of Contract*, p 178), bills of sale (Bills of Sale

Act 1878 (Amendment) Act 1882) and promissory notes (sections 3(1) and 17(2) of the Bills of Exchange Act 1882)—the last two requiring a contract in writing.

Also, while many commentators (such as Zweigert and Kötz, cited above) have criticised the doctrine of consideration for its inflexibility and consequent inability to do justice in many cases, it should be noted that the English courts have proved creative on occasion in 'discovering' consideration by reinterpreting what counts as being of sufficient value in the eyes of the law to amount to valid consideration. The well-known case of *Williams v Roffey Bros & Nicholls (Contractors) Ltd* [1991] 1 QB 1 seems best interpreted as allowing a practical (or factual) benefit rendered by performing a *pre-existing* contractual obligation owed to the other party to amount to sufficient consideration to allow the enforcement of a promise to make extra payments in return for that performance. Such an analysis is understandable only when coupled with an appreciation that the courts are becoming more (although still not very) willing to consider separately any claims that such promises have been extracted by duress, rather than using the earlier requirement that a *legal* (rather than merely factual) benefit was required to prevent such duress. Further, the English courts have proved able to allow certain promises to suspend the enforcement of strict contractual rights against the promisee, even where that promise was not supported by consideration: as discussed above, this has been achieved through the doctrine of (promissory) estoppel (stemming from the leading case of *Hughes v Metropolitan Railway Co* (1877) 2 App. Cas 439). Indeed, such suspension of rights might become definitive where the course of events means that it would be highly inequitable to demand performance as per the original contract, even if reasonable notice of an intention to return to the original deal were given. (A similar argument concerning practical benefit could be applied in cases regarding the part-payment of a debt, but as yet this practical benefit approach has not been applied by the English courts to relax the rule that a creditor's agreement to accept part of a debt in satisfaction for the whole is not binding: see *Foakes v Beer* (1884) 9 App Cas 605 for the House of Lords' endorsement of the rule and *Re Selectmove Ltd* [1995] 1 WLR 474 for the Court of Appeal's refusal to use the *Williams v Roffey Bros* reasoning in such a situation. See Treitel, *The Law of Contract*, p 125 ff, where the application of estoppel principles to such part-payment questions is also discussed, particularly the (in)famous case of *Central London Property Trust Ltd v High Trees House Ltd* [1947] KB 130 (an extemporary judgment of Denning J, as he then was: see Denning, *The Discipline of the Law* (1979), Part 5—The *High Trees* case).)

Secondly, outside the reach of formal requirements, one finds the problem whether the performance of an act not supported by any counter-performance may give rise to liability. As far as gifts are concerned the problem is expressly dealt with in the Code. First, the lack of form is cured by the performance of the act promised (§ 518 II BGB). If, accordingly, the object presented as a gift causes damage to the donee then his liability is contractual; § 521 BGB reducing the standard of care of the donor.

In relation to liability for the performance of 'unpaid for' services the situation is more difficult to ascertain. German law distinguishes legally binding declarations of intentions (usually mandate, § 662 BGB) from mere acts of kindness or generosity (*Gefälligkeiten*) by trying to discover the true intention of the parties. 'This method of abandoning specific indicia of seriousness and leaving the matter in the hands of a qualified judge' is, according to some comparatists, 'the best way of dealing with the problem' (cf Zweigert and Kötz (2nd edn), p 427). On the whole, this seems a convincing comparative observation, but it should not conceal two further facts.

First, at the end of the day the solutions the different legal systems reach are, in many situations, similar even if the routes by which they are reached are different. Secondly, and this is the point that will detain us in this exposition, the German preference for construing the transaction in order to discover the true intention of the parties is not free of difficulties and ambiguities.

Thus, to say that the declared intention will prevail and, in its absence, the objective intention of the parties will form the basis of the determination of any disputes that may arise between them, is often a way of leaving it to the judge to determine the issue *after the conclusion of a trial*; raising interesting issues about the need to go to court to resolve such questions and the costs (both in time and money) of having to resort to this approach. The above, may also give courts the power to attribute intentions to the parties which *may* not have been there in the first place. Two decisions may help provide illustrations to these points without distracting from the basic merit of the German position, which is flexibility.

In the first of these cases (BGHZ 21, 102, case no 24) a transport company ('A') placed at the disposal of another company ('B') a chauffeur-driven car, without A having the intention to make a charge for this service or enter into a further contractual relationship with B. The chauffeur was inexperienced and injured his passengers. The court took the view in this leading case that, although there was no contractual obligation on A's part to provide the service, if it nevertheless did provide the service then it undertook a contractual obligation to select a dependable driver for the job. Judging by the objective significance of its actions and good faith, therefore, company A could be said to have assumed legal responsibility (*Rechtsbindungswille*) towards B leading to contractual liability in damages if it breached that obligation. It is not difficult to see why liability was rationalised in contractual terms. The tort route was essentially blocked because pure economic loss (in the form of liability loss) was at stake (an interest clearly not protected under § 823 I BGB: see *The German Law of Torts*, pp 52–69 and 203–356 for cases and discussion). Interestingly enough, the obligation identified by the court and purportedly 'assumed' by the defendant, the selection of a careful driver, mirrors in all other respects exactly the duty of care imposed by § 831 BGB. So it does not seem far-fetched to contend that we are dealing here, once more, with an exception to the rule that pure economic loss is not recoverable in German law outside the realm of contract. Indeed, some writers have raised the objection against the approach in this decision that the attribution of a legally relevant undertaking of responsibility is fictitious and thus amounts to imposing liability in law (see, in particular, Flume, *Allgemeiner Teil*, vol 2, § 7, 7, p 91: '*reine Fiktion*').

Despite this criticism, this formula of liability for carrying out non-obligatory acts used in that judgment has been repeated since by other cases and represents the present position of German law. The criteria applied in arriving at liability are frequently referred to in judgments. (See especially, BGHZ 21, 102, 106–8, case no 24, where the court emphasised, inter alia, the nature of the transaction, the prospective gains made by the parties and the economic value it represented for them, as well as the danger one party might be running by accepting the services of the other.) Apart from the question whether the parties intended to assume responsibility by carrying out the altruistic act, the court had also to consider whether the normal or a reduced standard of care applied. Though most writers favour an analogy to §§ 521, 599, 690 BGB (liability only for gross negligence), the case law on the whole is divided, much depending on the facts of the individual case (see, for references: Medicus, *Bürgerliches Recht*, Rn 369): in BGHZ 21, 102, we find a carefully reasoned illustration of this approach (in the end imposing liability even for 'slight' negligence).

A decision of the *Bundesgerichtshof* of 1974 (NJW 1974, 1705) further illustrates the interpretative powers of the German judge. In that case, the three plaintiffs and the defendant habitually placed bets of an equivalent of €25 each on the lottery, the defendant being left to sign all necessary forms on behalf of all of them. On the day when he omitted to do this, the numbers he had been asked to back won and the parties failed to collect the sum of €5000. The three plaintiffs sued the 'forgetful' defendant, but lost. The BGH took the view that the parties had, between them, a legally binding agreement to share the profits in the event of a win as well as the costs of placing the bets. But there was, according to the principle of good faith (§ 242 BGB), no legal obligation imposed on one of the parties to indemnify the others in the event that he omitted to place the bet. The economic consequences of such a solution could destroy financially the party held responsible; and, no doubt, if the parties had been asked in advance whether they agree to assume such a responsibility, they would have answered such a question in the negative. (See, for further illustrations: *Münchener Kommentar*-Kramer, vol 2a, Introduction to Book 2, Rn. 32 *et seq.*)

One should finally note that this case law has some bearing on liability for negligent misstatements. Though in this category of cases liability is all the more difficult to justify on the basis of imputed intentions given that § 675 II (previously 676) BGB declares that, unless the parties have entered into a contract to that effect, no liability arises from the giving of advice except in the law of delict or under other statutory provisions. To derive from this that the above 'near' contract-based approach fails would be to underestimate the eagerness of German courts to arrive at just solutions in deserving cases. Wanting other satisfactory explanations in these cases (usually involving incorrect statements made/provided by banks), the courts simply 'found' a contract even though the recipient of the information did not provide any consideration for it. (Cf BGH NJW 1979, 1595; NJW 1990, 513; NJW 1993, 3073; BGHZ 100, 117. See also, below, the section on *culpa in contrahendo* and negligent statements. Note, in particular, the parallelism of reasoning between imposing liability in relation to carrying out such non-obligatory acts and the *Hedley Byrne*-type of liability as expressed by Lord Goff's 'assumption of responsibility' approach: see *The German Law of Torts*, p 337.)

5. *CULPA IN CONTRAHENDO*: FAULT IN CONTRACTING

Ballerstedt, 'Zur Haftung für c.i.c. bei Geschäftsabschluß durch Stellvertreter' AcP 151 (1950/51), 501; von Bar, *Verkehrspflichten* (1980); von Bar, 'Vertragliche Schadensersatzpflichten ohne Vertrag?' JuS 1982, 637; BMJ (ed), *Abschlußbericht der Kommission zur Überarbeitung des Schuldrechts* (1992), p 142; von Caemmerer, *Festschrift für den DJT*, vol 2 (1960), p 479; Canaris, *Festgabe 50 Jahre BGH*, vol 1 (2000), p 129; Canaris, *Die Vertrauenshaftung im deutschen Privatrecht* (1971);

Fleischer, *Informationsasymmetrie im Vertragsrecht* (2001); Fleischer, 'Vertragsschlussbezogene Informationspflichten im Gemeinschaftsprivatrecht' ZEuP 2000, 772; Ebke, *Wirtschaftsprüfer und Dritthaftung*, 1983; Friedl, 'Haftung bei Abbruch von Vertragsverhandlungen im deutschen und anglo-australischem Recht' ZVglRWiss 97 (1997) 161; Grigoleit, *Vorvertragliche Informationshaftung* (1997); Grunewald, 'Das Scheitern von Vertragsverhandlungen ohne triftigen Grund' JZ 1984, 708; J. Hager, 'Die culpa in contrahendo in den Unidroit-Prinzipien und den Prinzipien des Europäischen Vertragsrechts' in Basedow (ed), *Europäisches Rechtsvereinheitlichung und deutsches Recht* (2000), p 72; R von Jhering, *Culpa in contrahendo*, JherJb. 4 (1861), p 1; D Kaiser, 'Schadensersatz aus c.i.c. bei Abbruch von Verhandlungen über formbedürftige Verträge' JZ 1997, 448; Kessler and Fine, 'Culpa in Contrahendo, Bargaining in Good Faith, and Freedom of Contract: A Comparative Study' (1964) 77 *Harvard LR.* 401; Larenz, 'Bemerkungen zur Haftung für "c.i.c."' in *Festschrift für Ballerstedt* (1975), p 397; S Lorenz, *Der Schutz vor dem unerwünschten Vertrag* (1997); S Lorenz, 'Die culpa in contrahendo im französischen Recht' ZEuP 1994, 218; Medicus, *Gutachten zur Überarbeitung des Schuldrechts*, vol 1 (1981), p 479; Stoll, *Festschrift für von Caemmmerer* (1978), p 435; Neuner, 'Der Schutz und die Haftung Dritter nach vertraglichen Grundsätzen' JZ 1999, 126; Nirk, 'Rechtsvergleichendes zur Haftung für c.i.c.' RabelsZ 18 (1953) 319; Oertmann, 'Bemerkungen zur Haftung bei einem wegen Mißverständnis nicht zustande gekommenen Vertrage' AcP 121 (1923) 122; Ulmer, 'Volle Haftung des Gesellschafter/Geschäftsführers einer GmbH für Gläubigerschäden aus fahrlässiger Konkursverschleppung?' NJW 1983, 1577.

(a) General Observations

Culpa in contrahendo is a peculiarity of German law (and, with variations, of its derivative systems). It is a concept *sui generis*, floating freely between contract and tort, sometimes acquiring the characteristics of one and sometimes of the other classic category of obligations. It is, in contemporary English parlance (ironically formulated over forty years ago by Professor Canaris of the University of Munich), 'the third way' ('die dritte Spur'). It was, in fact, Rudolph von Jhering who firmly established the idea of pre-contractual liability imposed by law in his 'Culpa in Contrahendo oder Schadensersatz bei nichtigen oder nicht zur Perfection gelangten Verträgen' (1861), though earlier traces can be found. His main concern was the protection of the parties to a void contract. Even though the Code of 1900 to a certain extent assimilated the idea of liability arising in the pre-contractual phase, namely in the specific situations that Jhering placed in the foreground of his treatment of the subject, the perceived need for this cause of action did not end there. Since then, an immense body of case law applying the doctrine has developed outside the Code, something which speaks for itself. Today, the idea of pre-contractual liability imposed by law is rationalised as a reliance-based relationship of 'obligation imposed by law' (*gesetzliches Schuldverhältnis*). It is only the most recent 'modernisation' of the Civil Code (BGBl. 2001 I, 3183) that finally brought the doctrine into the Code (§ 311 II, III), which goes to show that this institution has been one of the main 'corrective' devices developed by the courts outside the Code. No fewer than five major fields of application can be distinguished, ranging from establishing duties of care not to damage physically one's customers at the pre-contractual phase, to expert liability for advice, valuations, and the like. No doubt other categorisations are possible. Indeed, the extent of the treatment accorded by the commentaries to the subject equals that of good faith. (*Münchener Kommentar*-Emmerich, § 311 Rn. 59 *et seq*).

From the above it will be obvious that the device fulfils a whole range of different and diverging purposes. It is virtually impossible to identify one single common element among them except that liability is derived from the conduct of a person occurring *before* the formation of the contract. Reliance is said to be crucial in some cases while in others it is present only in the weakest sense of that term: one person 'relying' on the other to refrain from harming him. While we attempt to give an overview of this topic in this chapter, it would be misleading to discuss all of its aspects in the context of the formation of the contract. Instead, we discuss that tenet of this doctrine concerned with getting out of a contract in chapter 6 and refer the reader to *The German Law of Torts* for other aspects of this doctrine which a common lawyer would be accustomed to find in a book on tort law.

The recent codification of the concept itself is utterly vague which, in one sense, is to be regretted since it will give German academic writers the opportunity to claim that the new Code has adopted his own particular understanding of the topic. Be that as it may, we do not learn much more than that there exists an obligation not to harm the interest of another and that this obligation may arise in a pre-contractual situation (§§ 311 II, 241 II BGB). In so far as third parties to a contract are concerned, reliance comes into play (§ 311 III BGB). The merit of distinguishing subtly, as § 311 II BGB does, between the commencement of contract negotiations (Nr. 1), the preparation of a contract where it enables one party to affect the interests of the other (Nr. 2), and 'other similar' business relationships (Nr. 3) has yet to be demonstrated. The obligation not to harm the 'interests' of others is expressed in § 241 II BGB, a provision, it must be stressed, which (despite its appearance) is *not* the general rule of German tort law but intended as a general principle of contract law. § 311 II BGB extends this obligation into the pre-contractual realm. It should be noted that these provisions were not drafted in order to change the law. It is thus safe to extrapolate the reasoning behind *culpa in contrahendo* from the existing case law and await further clarification of the codal text by future cases.

Before we look at the specific instances of *culpa in contrahendo* and their treatment in contemporary German law, it is useful to gain some understanding of the reasons for resorting to this hybrid type of obligation. Jhering's train of thought ('Culpa in Contrahendo') is highly interesting in this respect (see in particular von Mehren's analysis in *International Encyclopedia of Comparative Law*, vol VII, chapter 9 (1992), para 9-23 ff). The starting point was the (by no means self-evident) observation that a party that has entered into contract negotiations should not need to protect itself against the other party's fault in the formation phase of a contract. The law, Jhering suggested, should impose on the parties a fault-based obligation not to prejudice the interests of the other party during the formation of a contract, if the parties did not take the precaution to enter into a (collateral) contract stipulating for liability for fault in negotiating the (main) contract. The breach of this obligation would give rise to liability in damages based on a reliance measure. Since a delict/tort solution would have meant establishing liability for pure economic loss in tort law, it was not seriously considered. (See his famous rejection of this idea quoted in *The German Law of*

Torts, p 52, where the underpinnings and also the shortcomings of the German approach are expounded in detail. It suffices to note that the strong influence of this narrow view of tort law was later to become law in § 823 I BGB.) As a result neither contract nor tort reasoning was available to support liability. This, inevitably, led to the creation of an obligation imposed by law (yet outside the ambit of tort liability) not to harm the (economic) interests of parties involved in negotiating the contract and the right to claim damages based on a reliance measure if the obligation is breached. The only remaining question was whether this liability ought to be strict or based on fault. To Jhering the answer was, as already indicated, obvious, no doubt under the influence of the then dominant Pandectist fault principle, the reflection of which nowadays is found in § 276 I BGB. (The recent major reform incorporated, as explained, this approach to *culpa in contrahendo* into the Code: see § 311 II in conjunction with §§ 241 II, 280 I BGB.)

The fathers of the BGB then took up the idea of a legal obligation to compensate the other party's reliance interest in the case of a failed contract (both in the sense of a failure to validly conclude a contract and in the sense of a validly concluded contract that is later avoided. Interestingly enough in some instances this introduced strict liability. The common denominator of these instances is that the 'guilty' party is in a certain respect 'responsible' for the failure of the contract because the reason for the failure occurred within his sphere of influence, even if this did not amount to negligence in the technical sense of § 276 II BGB. (See, for a similar concept of responsibility, Honoré, *Responsibility and Fault* (2002).)

The first illustration of the above is found in § 122 BGB. The rules as to mistake will be discussed in detail in chapter 6. Here, suffice it to say that under the BGB contracts affected by a mistake relating to the content of a declaration of will (§ 119 BGB) are, as a general rule, not void but voidable (§ 142 II BGB). If the mistaken party rescinds the contract and thus renders it void *ex tunc*, can the other party claim his reliance interest? The answer given by § 122 I BGB is 'yes'. Liability is strict: this is the 'price' to be paid for having the contract set aside. It is the responsibility of the 'guilty' party to make sure that his declarations of intention are capable of being understood in their true sense also by objective standards. If the contract fails for this reason, the innocent party (that could not have known of the mistake—§ 122 II BGB) is entitled to claim damages up to the ceiling of the hypothetical expectation loss. (The innocent party should not be in a better position than if the contract had remained valid.) The same applies where a declaration of intention is wrongly transmitted (§ 122 BGB) or a contract is void because a declaration of intention was not intended to be perceived as such (§ 118 BGB).

The second illustration comes from the law of agency, examined in the last section of this chapter. Under § 179 II BGB if a *falsus procurator* did not know of the lack of authority he is strictly liable for the third party's reliance loss.

The third example, this time of a fault-based claim in § 307 (old version) BGB, has vanished with the recent reform of the BGB. A promise to perform an impossible act is no longer deemed void—see § 306 before the reform and now § 311a BGB—ie this is no longer an example of pre-contractual liability. The valid contract gives rise to liability in damages based on the expectation interest (this is discussed further in chapter 9, p 456. Yet, it is important to note this example in passing for it shows that the fault principle was not completely absent in the context of failed contracts.

Indeed, when the *Reichsgericht* in 1922 (RGZ 104, 265, case no 12) faced the question whether in situations outside the narrow limits of § 122 BGB a claim for damages was available where a party relied on a failed contract, the guiding principle was once again fault. This can to some extent be explained by the peculiarity of the situation the parties were in and to some extent must be credited to the fact that the Code in § 276 BGB laid down fault as the basis of liability in the law of obligations generally. The parties sent each other offers to sell, but each assumed that the other intended to buy. The contract was void because there was no 'meeting of the minds' as to an essential term (*Dissens*, discussed above, section 3(b)). Unlike in the situation of § 119 BGB discussed in the previous paragraph (setting the contract aside for an agreement mistake), where by definition one party is the ultimate 'cause' of the failure of the contract, in the case at hand both parties were to blame for the lack of consensus. Neither of them articulated the offer as clearly as they should have done. The simple fact that one party took the first step by opening negotiations was not regarded as sufficient to found strict liability. In the end result the reliance losses suffered where thus shared by the parties—certainly a reasonable outcome. As a result of that case, the fault-based explanation of *culpa in contrahendo* came generally to be accepted in the context of failed contracts. Somewhat oddly, however, liability under the heading of *culpa in contrahendo* was derived from an 'analogy' to § 122 BGB and the other instances of reliance-based damages discussed above. The claim based on *culpa in contrahendo* claim was eventually granted even alongside § 122 BGB, in order to get round the expectation interest ceiling in § 122 I BGB. Thus, soon after the entry into force of the Code, *culpa in contrahendo* was leading a life of its own, being established by the courts as a general fault-based remedy for loss occurring in the context of contract negotiations.

There is another and quite independent strand of *culpa in contrahendo* reasoning. It is of more recent origin than Jhering's initial theory, but equally forceful. It was first deployed in 1911 in the famous *Linoleum* case of the *Reichsgericht*, RGZ 78, 239, case no 25 (see later, BGH NJW 1962, 31). In this case, a linoleum roll fell on a customer who was being served by a sales clerk and injured him. A sales contract was, perhaps as a result of the incident, never concluded. The question was whether the customer could recover the loss caused by sales clerk's negligence from the shopkeeper. An English lawyer would no doubt look to the law of tort/delict in such a situation. German tort law, however, arguably fails to provide an entirely satisfactory solution to the problem because § 831 BGB allows the shopkeeper to exonerate himself by showing that he carefully selected and supervised the clerk. § 278 BGB, on the other hand, imputes the clerk's negligence to the shopkeeper *if the claim is contractual* and in addition § 280 I 2 BGB shifts the burden of proof in respect of the presence of fault to the defendant. For *culpa in contrahendo* is governed by § 278 BGB and not by the special tort provision § 831 BGB and thus the 'employer' of the 'guilty' servant was deprived of this right of exoneration. Indeed, this 'advantage' turned out to be a strong incentive to frame claims in the terms of *culpa in contrahendo*. In a remarkable extension of the initial theory of *culpa in contrahendo* (that was limited to failed contracts and pure economic loss) the *Reichsgericht* held that the potential seller in the *Linoleum* case owed a pre-contractual duty of care to the potential buyer not to harm his body or health. Quite apart from the general observation that it may be questionable to correct defects in one area of the law by expanding exceptions to general principle in another (on which see discussions relating to concurrent liability in contract and tort (eg, *Henderson v Merrett Syndicates* [1995] 2 AC 145) or at law and in equity (*Westdeutsche Landesbank Girozentrale v Islington London Borough Council* [1996] AC 669), where the need to decide the issue depended on distinctions in incidental rules applicable to each area (limitation periods and the availability of compound interest, respectively), the explanation of a pre-contractual duty of care as derived from an obligation in law has its own difficulties. (For example, when does the relevant pre-contractual obligation arise? Is this liability still reliance-based? How does one define a 'potential' customer? Are family members of the 'potential' customer also covered?)

The last question was answered in the affirmative by the *Bundesgerichtshof* in a famous decision in BGHZ 66, 51, case no 26. There the daughter of the customer slipped on a vegetable leaf in the shop. The Court held that she could sue the shopkeeper because she was there to help her mother do her shopping. (Note that in that case the plaintiff also benefited from what was at the time the longer limitation period applicable to a claim in *culpa in contrahendo*, thirty years, compared with a claim in delict, three years. Today, the period is three years in both cases, § 195 BGB.) The absence of true vicarious liability in tort law has thus not only put pressure on German contract law, but on the notion of *culpa in contrahendo*. In our context of the formation of contracts, the details of this development are not of prime concern for these problems are intimately connected to the law of delict. They are discussed in detail in chapter 3 of *The German Law of Torts* (see in addition, von Mehren, *International Encyclopedia of Comparative Law*, pp 9–28 *et seq*).

Finally, it should be noted that some writers suggest extending these pre-contractual protective duties (*Schutzpflichten*) to cover pure economic loss. The example given is this. In the course of preparing a sale of a company, the potential buyer obtains sensitive information which, after the deal fails, he uses to the detriment of the company. (Canaris, JZ 2001, 499, 519.) Liability is said to flow here from § 311 II Nr. 2 BGB. This is in fact a problem dealt with in tort law by § 826 BGB, though the *culpa in contrahendo* explanation is, of course, attractive for plaintiffs seeking to avoid the stricter requirement of intentional conduct which, in addition, is *contra bonos mores*: § 826 BGB. (For this new and as yet uncertain category of liability for pure economic loss outside contract, see *The German Law of Torts*, pp 888 *et seq*.) In English law, this type of situation concerning confidential information would be treated as an actionable breach of confidence where the subsequent use of the information was for a purpose other than that for which it was originally disclosed (see, eg, *Seager v Copydex Ltd (No 1)* [1967] 1 WLR 923 and *Satnam Investments Ltd v Dunlop Heywood & Co.* [1999] 3 All ER 652 (noted by Freedman [2000] *IPQ* 208). The conduct of the party using the information need not include an intention to act in a reprehensible manner (although bad faith may be relevant to the availability of certain remedies, such as an account of profits). Indeed, so long as the defendant was objectively aware of the confidence, then that duty can be breached unconsciously (see *Seager v Copydex (No 1)* where the source of the information had been forgotten), with good intentions or by error or oversight. (See generally, Cornish & Llewelyn, *Intellectual Property: Patents, Copyright, Trade Marks and Allied Rights* (5th edn, 2003), chapter 8 and Bently and Sherman, *Intellectual Property Law* (2nd edn, 2004), chapters 44–6.)

We may conclude our general observations by turning our attention to the latest sweeping reform of contemporary law, which one could say brought about the ultimate triumph of *culpa in contrahendo* by incorporating the concept as a *general* principle into the Code in § 311 II BGB and to some extent in § 241 II BGB. Yet it is the logical end-result since both the exclusion of pure economic loss in § 823 I BGB and the approach to liability for others of § 831 BGB have been maintained by the reform. One might be inclined to observe that the greater the number of (well entrenched) ways of getting around a problem, the less the need to deal with the source of the problem head on. In any event, the lack of reform of these aspects of liability in delict cannot be explained by lack of adequate proposals for law reform. (See, for instance, von Bar's report in *Gutachten zur Überarbeitung des Schuldrechts*, vol 2 (1981), p 1681 *et seq.*)

(b) Situations Covered

The connection between the intended contract and the duty of care not to cause (physical) damage is fairly loose—indeed almost at random in the group of cases discussed in the previous section. Thus, even 'conservative' German jurists would agree that these cases really belong to the law of delict, not the law of contract. All other groups of cases however show a more genuine connection between the damages sought and the intended or actual contract, for in a very real sense they are all dependent in some way on the terms of an actual or intended contract. The cases can be conveniently classified by looking at the complaint of the plaintiff viz the defendant's pre-contractual conduct. Looking at matters in this way we can thus distinguish three types of situation.

In the first, the plaintiff claims that he is worse off because a contract was not concluded. In the second, he claims that the defendant induced him to enter into an unfavourable contract with a third party. In the third, he complains that the contract was concluded on unfavourable terms.

It can immediately be seen that the type of harm in question in all three groups of cases is pure economic loss which (in principle) can be compensated, if at all, only through the law of contract. Yet the existence of liability for *culpa in contrahendo* can only be partially attributed to the fact that in German law there is no general liability for negligently inflicted pure economic loss in tort. If this is indeed one reason for the development of the doctrine, it only applies to the first two of the situation mentioned in the previous paragraph. Thus, in order to disentangle the different strands of reasoning, it is necessary to refine our assessment of the function of pre-contractual 'liability'.

In the first situation, the plaintiff relied on the coming into being of a valid contract which, due to the defendant's fault, did not happen. As already indicated, the Code itself provides two examples of this: agreement formed through mistake (§ 122 BGB) and the liability of a *falsus procurator* (§ 179 II BGB). *Culpa in contrahendo* serves here to generalise this approach to a general fault-based principle. Thus, the concept is deployed in this situation for the purpose of deciding in what circumstances there is a duty of care not to cause purely economic loss to a person that relied on a contract that failed to materialise. The particulars of the formation phase of a contract are skilfully used by German jurists to build further sub-categories of liability and to (seek to) make the application of the principle predictable.

It is in this area of the law where one can observe substantial differences between German law and the common law, especially the English common law, which is rather more cautious in affording protection to parties disappointed by contract negotiations. This may be the case in English law even where express agreements have been concluded concerning the negotiation phase itself: a mere agreement to negotiate is not a contract 'because it is too uncertain to have any binding force' (*Courtney & Fairbairn Ltd v Tolaini Bros (Hotels) Ltd* [1975] 1 WLR 297, at 301). The same appears to be true of an agreement to use 'best endeavours' to agree on the terms of a contract (*London & Regional Investments Ltd v TBI plc, Belfast International Airport Ltd* [2002] EWCA Civ 355, [38]–[40]). However, the outcome of *Walford v Miles* [1992] 2 AC 128 suggests that the use of misrepresentation leading to reliance damages (even in the absence of an enforceable primary contract or collateral 'lock-out' agreement not to negotiate with third parties) may in some cases produce results not dissimilar from those achieved under *culpa in contrahendo*. At the same time, it must be conceded that these possibilities have, in English law, a rather limited scope. (On this, see again the decision of the Court of Appeal in *Walford v Miles* (1991) 62 P & CR 410, where it was noted that on the facts of that case it would have been hard to show that Mr Miles had knowingly made a false representation.)

The second situation is essentially concerned with the personal liability of intermediaries involved in negotiating the contract and the liability of experts for (negligent) statements. These situations can take very different forms, ranging from the director of a 'limited company' (*GmbH*) becoming personally liable for having induced special reliance by the creditor of the (by then usually insolvent) company or by misleading investors in a brochure into investing in a bad company, to situations in which a report or some other evaluation is circulated and creates incentives for investment (which subsequently turns out to be less than sound). Again the central question is whether liability, independently of contract, for pure economic loss attaches to the negligent preparation of reports and other conduct which is likely to induce the 'innocent' parties to enter into unfavourable contracts with third parties. There is no need to labour this point here, since for the common lawyer it is self-evident that at least some of these problems can be rationalised in terms of duties of care in tort law. The different nomenclature, and the apparently different approach suggested by §§ 823 I, 826 BGB, need not concern him, once the conceptual skeleton has been exposed.

The third situation is best analysed independently of the protection of pure economic interests outside contract law (ie to the English mind: tort law); indeed its very inclusion under the present heading alongside the other groups of cases is a source of constant confusion.

When a party complains that the very terms of the contract are unfavourable and he thereby relies on *culpa in contrahendo*, this is invariably by claiming that he feels in some way deceived or at least misled by the other party during the negotiation of the contract as to the true nature of the object of the contract. In this group of cases, the purpose of *culpa in contrahendo* is to supplement the rules on rescission of the contract (for instance based on deceit, § 123 BGB) and also to provide a way out of unfavourable contracts in cases not explicitly dealt with in the Code, for instance in cases of negligent misrepresentation.

It suffices here to point out, first, that these questions *are* questions of contract law. Every imaginable model of contract law has to deal with them and provide answers to these points in some way. Secondly, using *culpa in contrahendo* for this purpose brings in its wake specific conceptual difficulties which are peculiar to German law and need not concern us here. To put it in simple terms, the problem is that the usual legal consequence flowing from fulfilling the conditions of application is liability in damages (§§ 249 *et seq* BGB), which does not always fit the legal consequence desired in this particular group of cases, namely rescission or at least varying the terms of the contract.

We will return to this subject in more detail in at p 311. It remains here briefly to illustrate the other two main fields of application of the doctrine: failed contracts and negligent misrepresentation. As in the *Linoleum* case discussed above, in these cases obligations are imposed in law during the formation phase of a contract. This is enough, to the German eye, to bring them under the general heading of *culpa in contrahendo*.

(c) Failed Contracts

Freedom of contract demands that each party is allowed to act in his own interest and, of course, is not required to further the interest of the 'opponent' in contract negotiations. (See, eg, *Walford v Miles* [1992] 2 AC 128, at 138, where the House of Lords refused to impose a duty to negotiate in good faith as that would have been 'inherently inconsistent with the position of a negotiating party,' free to look after his own interests during the negotiations (Treitel, *The Law of Contract*, p 60 ff).) Therefore, it may seem somewhat odd to impose liability in damages for having relied on the valid conclusion of a contract. Such liability for the failure of a contract is derived in German law from the duties of the parties to act in good faith towards each other. We will discuss good faith in relation to the content of a contract (see chapter 3), which is most extensively affected by the principle. Yet, as this section demonstrates, it applies also to the pre-contractual stage.

Founding liability on good faith—the famous general clause § 242 BGB—also means that on the whole we are confronted here by judge-made law. Liability is confined to the reliance measure, ie loss caused by relying on the contract—and amounts to recovery of pure economic loss outside contract. There is also the tort provision of § 826 BGB (see, *The German Law of Torts*, chapter 4, p 888), which imposes liability also for pure economic loss provided that such loss was caused *intentionally* and *contra bonos mores*. In the cases discussed in this sub-section, however, liability is imposed under much less onerous conditions. Fault in the form of negligence suffices. The tension between the two approaches is occasionally noted (eg, BGHZ 99, 101 = NJW 1987, 639, 640, case 27). Yet, apart for stating the difference between the two, we learn nothing more from case no 27 and one might suspect that any more explanation would make the boldness of such judicial creativity all too obvious. There is a distinction to be made between liability for the responsibility of having concluded an invalid contract and liability for the manner in which negotiations were conducted where no contract was formally concluded.

There are but two instances in the Code, itself, where liability is derived from the flawed conclusion of a contract leading to its invalidity. Thus, as we have already explained above, § 122 BGB imposes liability if a party nullifies the contract because he made an agreement mistake whereas § 179 II BGB holds the agent liable who did not know of a lack of authority when concluding the contract. As also noted, the courts quickly expanded this approach to cover the case of *Dissens* and imposed liability where one party was at fault in expressing himself in ambiguous terms. (See above, RGZ 104, 265, case no 12.) In these instances it does not seem that freedom of contract is seriously threatened. The question is whether one considers it a deserving case where one party relies on the valid conclusion of a contract and as a result incurs loss (for instance by letting another contract possibility pass).

We need not reiterate the already extrapolated rationale of this approach. The courts have generalised this pre-contractual liability to virtually all cases where one party is responsible (normally, fault is required) for the failure of a formally concluded contract. In the following situations, in addition to those already discussed, the courts have found pre-contractual liability. First, where the contract was subject to a licence (*Genehmigung*) or the like and one of the parties failed to draw to the attention of the other party that the grant of the licence was in fact still outstanding or needed in the first place (eg, BGHZ 6, 330, case no 28; BGHZ 18, 248; BGHZ 142, 51). Secondly, where the contract is void under § 134 BGB (illegality) for failure to meet other mandatory statutory requirements (OLG Düsseldorf BB 1975, 201) or because the contract is contrary to *bonos mores*, § 138 BGB (eg, BGH NJW 1987, 639, case no 27).

To this general category we can also add those cases in which the courts have awarded damages where a contract did not comply with formal requirements (eg, BGH NJW 1965, 812, discussed in the section on formalities, above). While the underlying idea of founding liability in these cases may indeed be similar, each line of cases poses characteristic challenges. Thus, why is one party to blame rather than the other for failing to observe legal requirements? Is sharing the loss a better option? How is the blame then to be apportioned? In the case of requirements as to form, is it not the very object of these provisions that one should not rely on a contract that lacks the required form?

The second and more problematic sub-group of cases concerns liability in cases where no final agreement was reached and nevertheless one of the parties relied on the conclusion of a contract on certain terms. In general, the parties are free to break off contract negotiations when they think fit. If they were not free to do so, the law would implicitly impose on them (or at least on one of them) an obligation to enter into a contract. This would undermine a central aspect of freedom of contract, namely to be free to enter into a contract. In very exceptional circumstances the law indeed imposes an obligation to contract (*Kontrahierungszwang*), as we have seen above in the section on the acceptance. However, in the cases under consideration here no such obligation has ever been considered. The basis of liability can thus never be the breaking off of the contract negotiations as such. Some further 'blameworthy' act must occur if the party backing out of the negotiations is to face liability in damages. While the danger to freedom of contract is in principle acknowledged, German law still requires the parties to take special care in the way they conduct the negotiations.

The *Bundesgerichtshof* decided early on that, under certain conditions, the breaking off of negotiations or withholding of the final acceptance after reaching agreement seemed certain may give rise to liability for the expenditure the other party incurred in relying on the eventual conclusion of the contact. Three conditions must be satisfied. (See, eg, BGH WM 1969, 595; NJW 1975, 1774, case no 29; NJW-RR 1989, 627). First, one party must have led the other to believe that conclusion of the contract was certain. Secondly, that expense was incurred in view of the contract. Finally, that subsequently the other party broke off the negotiations without good reason ('*ohne triftigen Grund*').

This case law has not escaped criticism; but it is also fair to say that there are also a good number of academics that have supported it. (Cf von Bar, JuS 1982, 639; von Mehren, *International Encyclopedia of Comparative Law*, vol VII, chapter 9, para 9-122). Three observations spring to mind.

First, while it is clear that it is the *manner* in which the negotiations are conducted (and not the decision to break them off) that is the basis of liability, one still wonders whether the 'guilty' party is *de facto* forced to accept the contract. This is particularly obvious where carrying out the contract is less burdensome financially than covering the 'innocent' party's expenses. One might answer that in these cases the 'guilty' party has manoeuvred himself into a position where the exercise of his freedom 'to' contract will cost him dearly.

The second observation adds to the above the concern that the limits of freedom of contract are not easy to predict. For when has one party *wrongfully* aroused the belief/faith that a contract will be concluded? (For example, BGH NJW-RR 2001, 381: nearly concluded lengthy negotiations are not sufficient; it is also disputed whether fault in the technical sense is necessary, see BGH NJW-RR 1989, 627; *Münchener Kommentar*-Emmerich, § 311 Rn. 184, with references.) Is it not a paradox to require reliance on the formation of a contract when at the same time the parties are free to break off contract negotiations? The binding nature of an offer is expressly regulated in § 145 BGB, as explained above (section 2(e)). Does it not follow from this that, before an offer becomes 'binding', parties should not be considered bound by negotiations? What can be considered to amount to a good (enough) reason for abandoning negotiations?

Finally, and critically, is it sufficient if the economic prospects of the deal have worsened? The courts have failed to clarify this last point entirely, yet it seems that even if there *is* a good reason for abandoning the contract, the 'guilty' party is still under an obligation to 'warn' the other party that he no longer intends to continue with the negotiations if he has led the other party to believe that he will conclude the deal and knows that the other party will rely on that and incur expense accordingly (BGH NJW 1996, 1884, case no 30).

This latter decision concerned the sale of land, which involves the further complication that such a contract is subject to strict formal requirements (§ 311b I BGB, see above. As a result, it is even more difficult to maintain that one party can rely on the conclusion of the contract). A tenant negotiated for the purchase of the leased property. The landlord apparently agreed and allowed the commencement of building works. Conclusion of the contract was postponed for tax reasons, was not in the end achieved and the lease was terminated. The former lessee claimed the (considerable) cost of the building works. The court readily conceded: imposing liability in such a situation indirectly forces one party to enter into the contract and this is not easy to reconcile with the purpose of the form requirement. Even a perfectly valid agreement has no binding force before notarial authentication; how can liability then attach simply to the breaking off of negotiations? The Court sought to solve the problem by referring to that line of cases where good faith was used to do away with formal requirements (see section 4, above). Liability will only arise if breaking off negotiations can be regarded as a particularly grave breach of the other party's 'trust': at the very least, this presupposes intentional conduct. Because the lower court did not consider this possibility, the case was remitted for decision on this issue.

English legal scholarship has recently placed under close scrutiny its case law on work done in anticipation of a contract that does not come about. The attempt has been to analyse the fact situation as involving issues of unjust enrichment and a restitutionary response to that enrichment. (See, particularly, McKendrick, 'Work Done in Anticipation of a Contract which does not Materialise' chapter 11 in Cornish, Nolan, O'Sullivan and Virgo (eds), *Restitution Past, Present and Future* (1998); see also the response by Hedley in chapter 12). Contractual analyses of such situations *are* possible. Thus in *Way v Latilla* ([1937] 3 All ER 759), the House of Lords appeared to conclude that (either expressly or by implication) a contract of employment did exist between the parties but that a rate of remuneration for the plaintiff's services had not been agreed. As a result, an implied promise to pay on a *quantum meruit* basis was held to have been made. This analysis will obviously be heavily dependent on the facts of the case; and it overlaps substantially with what level of agreement must be found between the parties before a court is prepared to find a contract to exist. (See, eg, Atiyah, *An Introduction to the Law of Contract* (5th edn, 1995), p 154). Equally, there are some cases where no contract can be found and other analyses are employed such as restitution. (Although cf Hedley in *Restitution Past, Present and Future*, chapter 12, at 197, discussing the case of *Regalian Properties Plc v London Docklands Development Corporation* [1995] 1 WLR 212: just because a grander, overarching contractual scheme has not been concluded, does not exclude the possibility that, construing the circumstances, the parties have in fact concluded a 'rather more modest' contractual arrangement.)

A restitutionary analysis based on unjust enrichment can provide a sensible explanation of cases where a clear benefit has been conferred by the plaintiff on the defendant by his anticipatory work, eg where delivery of a product of that work has been made to the defendant (*British Steel Corporation v Cleveland Bridge Engineering Co Ltd* [1984] 1 All ER 504). At the same time, preparatory work may often produce no clear benefit to the defendant. In this situation, McKendrick has suggested that it is performance *at the request* of the defendant that could show enrichment (see, eg, *William Lacey (Hounslow) v Davis* [1957] 1 WLR 932). Further problems relate to whether or not such enrichment (if it can be found) is *unjust* in the sense used in *Lipkin Gorman v Karpnale Ltd* [1991] 2 AC 548 (see McKendrick's 'Work Done in Anticipation of a Contract which does not Materialise' at 181–6 for discussion). Intriguingly for comparative purposes, some of the cases focus on the reasons for the collapse of the negotiations in deciding whether or not the plaintiff can recover: see, eg, *Jennings and Chapman Ltd v Woodman, Matthews & Co* [1952] 2 TLR 409. Similarly, an estoppel-based approach (which is problematic in English law due to the general inability to use estoppel as a 'sword' to found positive rights against a defendant (see the discussion above, section 2(e)) would also look carefully at the quality of the defendant's conduct and would also avoid needing to tangle with knotty issues of enrichment (see Jones, 'Claims Arising out of Anticipated Contracts Which Do Not Materialize' (1980) 18 *Univ of W Ontario LR* 447, at 457 and Carter, 'Contract, Restitution and Promissory Estoppel' (1989) 12 *Univ of NSW LJ* 30: the latter discusses the Australian position, freed from the 'no sword' restriction by *Waltons Stores (Interstate) Ltd v Maher* (1988) 164 CLR 387).

(d) Negligent Misrepresentation

The cases on negligent misrepresentation cannot easily be brought under one heading in German law. Leaving the dangers of over-simplification on one side, the following features are typical for all groups of cases. First, we usually face the problem of liability in a triangular situation where at least two corners of the triangle are connected by a contract. Secondly, the claim is for pure economic loss. Thirdly, and related to the previous point, tort solutions are not easily available in German law: pure economic loss is not usually recoverable in tort actions. Finally, the loss can be related to the conduct of an 'expert', ie a person who professes certain skills or information on which the 'innocent' party relied. (Since *Hedley Byrne*, in English law the problem of negligent misrepresentation is normally associated with the tort claim in negligence. Accordingly, we have dealt with expert liability for statements in some depth in *The German Law of Torts*, pp 52 *et seq*, 291 *et seq* and 332 *et seq*.) It suffices here to note that, apart from *culpa in contrahendo*, two other mechanisms are available to a German court in establishing liability for the statement whichever form, memo, report, valuation etc, it takes. In some cases (eg, *The German Law of Torts*, case nos 20, 22, 23 and 24), the party employing the expert was said to enter into a contract 'with protective effects' towards the third party. For example, A employs B to survey a building; C relies on B's report and incurs loss. Thus, in this group of cases liability is derived from a contract concluded between the expert and another person, yet it is clear that such inference owes little to the actual intention of the parties (see also, the section on interpretation in chapter 3, as well as the sections on privity). In other cases, where there was no express contract of employment, the court nevertheless found a contractual relationship to arise, this time directly between the supplier of the information (eg, a bank making statements as to the creditworthiness of one of its clients) and potential recipients or investors (see eg, *The German Law of Torts*, case nos 19 and 21). For example, B issues a statement as to the financial status of A; C relies on that statement, invests in A and suffers loss. There is a fragility in imputing corresponding intentions to the parties—the fictitious nature of the contract approach—yet the similarity of this line of argument to that used in the English tort cases has been noted (for a more recent example considering the various routes of recovery, see: BGH NJW-RR 2003, 1035). Indeed, we have observed elsewhere that it is unclear whether the courts will in future acknowledge more openly that the reliance-based liability is imposed by law. One way of achieving that result would be to apply the doctrine of *culpa in contrahendo* and impose liability for reliance on statements uttered in a pre-contractual context (see *The German Law of Torts*, pp 703–5).

(e) Liability of Intermediaries

We must briefly point to another related group of cases, in which *culpa in contrahendo* reasoning has *traditionally* been deployed and is now expressly set out by the Code in § 311 III BGB. The first sentence of that provision states that a relationship of obligation as defined in § 241 II BGB may also arise with persons who are not themselves intended to become privy to the contract. The second sentence specifies that this is the case in particular where the third party influences the contract negotiations or the formation of the contract by inducing/encouraging special reliance on his skills and abilities/experience. This provision is meant to reflect the approach of the case law decided prior to the latest amendment of the Code and we will here illustrate the problem by reference to that case law. We are concerned with the liability of agents or other persons who, without being agents or privy to the contract, are nevertheless involved in negotiating a contract (*Verhandlungsgehilfen*). For example, C enters into a contract with A; after A becomes insolvent, C seeks to recover from A's agent, B. In this category of cases, the mechanisms to which we alluded previously do not work. The main contract is between the principal and the plaintiff; by definition, if the principal is named and authority is present there is no contract with the agent himself. This would contravene first principles of representation, as to which see the next section, below. Likewise, if the director of a company is involved it would run contrary to his acting as a mere organ of that company to hold him personally liable on the contract. On similar grounds, it cannot be said that the contract with the principal has 'protective' effects towards the plaintiff: this again would illegitimately cut across the framework set up by the agency. If the agent or any other person 'breaking the deal' is to be held personally liable in addition to the principal, this must be on the basis of tort duties of care or 'pre-'contractual liability, ie *culpa in contrahendo*. The proposition that the agent should be held liable in tort will usually be given short shrift by the German courts, if it is considered at all, for the simple reason that pure economic loss is involved and the complained-of conduct is unlikely to have reached the level of recklessness required by § 826 BGB.

Culpa in contrahendo thus provides the only conceivable basis for liability in German law. Clearly, if it was not to erode the contract/agency principles, on the one hand, and the exclusion of pure economic loss, on the other, this type of liability had to be limited to special cases. The courts are at pains to emphasise that any liability of the agent under *culpa in contrahendo* principles is the exception. Two criteria have emerged which may, each independently of the other, give rise to liability, although the two elements of liability are not easy to distinguish and are often considered alongside each other. (See eg, BGHZ 56, 81, case no 31; BGHZ 88, 67; BGH NJW-RR 1991, 1241 case no 32; NJW-RR 1992, 605; NJW-RR 2002, 1309; NJW 1990, 1907. BGH, NJW-RR 2004, 308, is particularly interesting because the court considered German and English law in parallel.

Three main points from this case deserve to be stressed.

First, the court stated that, on the facts of the case, the result would be the same in both jurisdictions. Secondly, the court commented that the parallel to a *culpa in contrahendo* liability of the agent would be the *Hedley Byrne*-type of liability. Thirdly, it is worth noting that this exercise in comparative reasoning was prompted by conflict of laws rules and, regrettably, not by a desire to secure the result from a comparative angle!

The first criterion of liability under this sub-heading is mentioned in § 311 III 2 BGB: it concerns the special reliance induced by the agent in respect of his own person (*besonderes Vertrauen in Anspruch nehmen* (note that this can also be translated as nourishing the trust of the other party, or inducing special trustworthiness; yet these translations import the notion of ethical duties, whereas what the courts have in mind is more akin to the 'reasonable reliance' known from English negligence cases). It is said that the agent must have caused the other party to rely on the agent beyond what is customary in contract negotiations. Other factors are also relevant: drawing attention to extraordinary skills, his special expertise concerning the subject matter of the contract, his profession (*Sachwalter*) and, by 'guaranteeing' the 'seriousness' or the 'flawless execution' of the deal. The last two factors seem to be the most important (see: BGHZ 56, 81, case no 31). The difficulty with this approach is its vagueness. The test depends entirely on the circumstances of the individual case and, taken together with the reluctance of German courts to distinguish earlier case law, can create considerable uncertainty. (See, however, BGH NJW-RR 1991, 1241, case no 32, for a useful summary of the case law; the court is at pains to explain and limit previous rulings, thus showing the exceptional nature of this type liability.) For instance, the presence of special knowledge is not as such regarded as sufficient (BGH NJW 1990, 506). But who is to define the 'normal' standard of trust or reliance placed on persons involved in negotiating a contract? Is trust/reliance (*Vertrauen*) a *legally* relevant category or is not the contract itself, with its enforcement mechanisms, the sole source of legal obligations? Does this approach serve to circumvent the limits of contractual liability and do justice on an arbitrary case-by-case basis? The answer is not immediately obvious, but it seems that this approach has not caused major problems in practice and that this must be due to its sensible handling in individual cases (something which is not of course easily conveyed in an abstract treatment of the subject). While the element of special reliance is thus difficult to define in the abstract and its purpose ambiguous, it is clearly a very flexible control factor of liability.

The criterion has been watered down on occasion to include trust typically associated with certain acts preparing the formation of a contract and which do not need to be invoked in face-to-face negotiations: indeed, the agent may never personally have dealt with the third party. This concerns the liability flowing from statements made in brochures directed at potential investors in companies, which although initially derived from *culpa in contrahendo* has increasingly become an independent category of liability (*Prospekthaftung*). This liability becomes essential when the company itself becomes insolvent and concerns those who initiated, modelled or founded the company (*Initiatoren, Gestalter, Gründer*). (See BGHZ 71, 284; BGHZ 77, 172; BGHZ 111, 314; BGH NJW 2001, 436.) See also the specific statutory liability in these situations—as to which see *Palandt*-Heinrichs, § 311 Rn. 30—which affords additional protection.

In these circumstances, English law provides a range of options for the recipient of untrue or misleading information in such prospectuses relating to *public offers* to pursue the responsible *company* (see Davies, *Gower and Davies' Principles of Modern Company Law* (7th edn, 2003), pp 670–9). The key possibilities are compensation for breach of various statutory duties laid down in section 90 (prospectuses, which forms a separate head of liability in its own right) and Schedule 10 (listing particulars) of the Companies Act 1985 in conjunction with regs 13–15 of the Public Offers of Securities Regulations 1995 (SI 1995 No 1537), damages for misrepresentation (including fraudulent misrepresentation (*Derry v Peek* (1889) 14 App Cas 337) and the remedy under section 2(1) of the Misrepresentation Act 1967 (which is subject to certain limitations, however: see Cartwright, *Misrepresentation* (2002) for detailed discussion) and damages for negligent misstatement (stemming from the *Hedley Byrne & Co Ltd* (above) line of cases and focusing on assumption of responsibility and the *purpose* of the statement embodied in the prospectus: see *Caparo v Dickman* [1990] 2 AC 605 and the subsequent cases of *Al-Nakib Investments (Jersey) Ltd v Longcroft* [1990] 1 WLR

1390 and *Possfund Custodian Trustees Ltd v Diamond* [1996] 1 WLR 1351; 2 BCLC 665).

However, whether it is possible to pursue an individual officer or agent of the company in respect of any tort so committed depends on the basis by which the company is made liable for that act by the individual. (Note that, in general terms, what follows here also applies to agents more generally.) If the company is held vicariously liable for the tortious act of the individual then the individual remains personally liable in tort (on vicarious liability generally, see *Lister v Hesley Hall Ltd* [2001] 2 All ER 769 and Deakin, Johnston and Markesinis, *Markesinis & Deakin's Tort Law* (5th edn, 2003), pp 571–603): this will be true of most torts, including fraudulent misrepresentation (although cf in Canada the dissenting judgment of La Forest J in *London Drugs Ltd v Kuehne & Nagel International Ltd* (1992) 97 DLR (4th) 261, with the subsequent case of *Edgeworth Construction Ltd v N D Lea & Associates Ltd* [1993] 3 SCR 206). Difficult questions arise, however, when applying the tort case law on assumption of responsibility (on this, see Deakin, Johnston and Markesinis, p 114 ff). It might be argued that to hold the individual responsible in tort for such a personal assumption of responsibility would effectively deprive the company of the protection of limited liability status, and that in a situation where it is entirely possible that a contractual claim might also lie and yet only against the company due to agency principles (on the latter point, see Campbell and Armour, 'Demystifying the Civil Liability of Corporate Agents' [2003] *CLJ* 290, especially pp 300–3). This could be particularly deleterious for the one-man company (Davies, *Principles of Modern Company Law*, p 167, although cf Armour, 'Corporate personality and assumption of responsibility' [1999] *LMCLQ* 246, especially pp 252–4). Alternatively, assumption of responsibility could be analysed as a tort *sui generis*, for which the attribution rules are more akin to contract; there would then be no question of vicarious liability and, instead, the 'relationship of responsibility' created by the individual would operate more like that of an agent negotiating a contract for his principal (in this case, the company). The House of Lords (in *Williams v Natural Life Health Foods* [1998] 1 WLR 830) declined to take the *personal* assumption of responsibility as the starting position, instead holding that responsibility is usually to be treated as assumed by the company, which renders the company's liability in tort direct, rather than vicarious. We will return to the *Williams* case below when discussing the nature of intermediary liability. (See generally, Glick, *Attribution of Liability*, a research document submitted to the *Company Law Review* run by the UK's Department of Trade and Industry (available at http://www.dti.govuk/cld/glick.pdf) for a helpful discussion; see also Davies at 165 ff.)

The second criterion in German law, which (as explained above) may of itself found liability under this heading, is somewhat easier to apply in a predictable manner. The courts require that the agent (or other person involved in negotiation the contract) had a financial interest of his own in the bargain. This condition easily excludes 'simple' employees who negotiate contracts because they are paid to do so (eg, BGHZ 88, 67: yet, only as a 'general rule'). Furthermore, the payment of commission does not suffice to make an agent liable under this heading (eg, BGHZ 56, 81, case no 31; BGH NJW 1990, 506). This requirement will only be satisfied where the agent acts as though he were the principal (*procurator in rem suam*). (See eg, BGHZ 56, 81, case no 31; BGH NJW-RR 2002, 1309, where the contract was concluded exclusively in the financial interest of the agent.) Only a strict application of this criterion ensures that the personal liability does not undermine basic principles of company law (especially that of the limited company: *GmbH*). Thus, directors of such companies who naturally negotiate contracts on behalf of the company (this being their very task as 'organs' of the company) are as a general rule not liable under *culpa in contrahendo*. The same applies in principle to stakeholders in the company: the general interest in the success of one's own company is not sufficient to found liability. After a period of uncertainty and strong criticism from academics (eg, Ballerstedt, AcP 151 (1950/51), 505; K Schmidt, NJW 1993, 2935), the *Bundesgerichtshof* now stresses that such liability must be limited to exceptional cases. (BGHZ 126, 181: in the case at hand it was held that providing a security for claims against the company was not sufficient to establish the director's own financial interest in concluding the contract.) It is thus not sufficient that the director of the limited company is the sole owner of it: additional circumstances must be present which show that the director acted in her personal interest ('*in eigener Sache*') or that he meets the other condition mentioned above, namely of inducing 'special reliance' (eg, BGH ZIP 1986, 26; ZIP 1988, 1543). This clarification was overdue, for the extended liability of the director-owner of a limited company was not easy to square with the liability regime of a 'limited' company: as a general rule the director is not personally liable (see § 13 II of the *Gesetz betreffend die Gesellschaften mit beschränkter Haftung*). (See the discussion above of the *Williams* case, (*Williams v Natural Life Health Foods* [1998] 1 WLR 830)) suggesting that similar concerns over the 'one-man band' and limited liability have actuated the English case law.)

A further established line of cases concerns car dealers who as agents of their customers sell second hand cars. In this category of cases both requirements of liability are usually fulfilled. Such a dealer is deemed to be personally liable if he acts as if he were the principal, inducing special reliance by the third party and having the financial interest in selling it (other, eg, tax, reasons account for the agency). (An example of *Sachwalter*-liability: eg, BGHZ 87, 302; BGHZ 79, 281; BGHZ 63, 382.)

What, then, is the thrust of this case law on the liability of agents and other 'intermediaries'? To some extent it makes up for the absence of liability for pure economic loss in tort law, yet the picture is complex. For here the law of contract and company law are supplemented and the basic rules against the personal liability of the intermediary are undermined: English law provides an excellent illustration of this difficulty in the *Williams* case, although the result of the case would seem to supplement contract law with tort law and then to reify company law's limited liability principle to *prevent* personal liability of the intermediary where this would otherwise have obtained. Had the analysis in *Williams* been on a contractual basis, then the status of the individual as an agent contracting for his principal (the company) would have led to the company being held responsible (see Reynolds, 'Personal Liability of an Agent' (1969) 85 *LQR* 92)—ie, the same result as achieved by holding that the company was taken to have assumed responsibility to the plaintiff. As Armour suggests ([1999] *LMCLQ* 246, 249), this leads us to think that the 'purpose of *Hedley Byrne* . . . focuses on the compensation of those whose economic interests are harmed by reliance upon the (in)actions of those who have assumed responsibility for the performance of a task. The relationship between the two parties is basically voluntary, more akin to contract than the non-consensual paradigm of tort.' The result in this English case, therefore, might appear to use a kind of analogy with the contractual situation to justify *not* imposing a personal tortious liability on the individual intermediary, in the interests of defending the company law principle of limited liability and its influence on the way in which such businesses are structured. (Whether this is always a desirable outcome is another matter: see eg, Halpern, Trebilcock and Turnbull, 'An Economic Analysis of Limited Liability in Corporation Law' (1980) 30 *Univ of Toronto LJ* 117, especially at 148, for discussion. An alternative analysis of the *Williams* reasoning could be that it turns much more on the nature of liability for assumption of responsibility than any kind of analogical reasoning, although the result reached would be much the same.)

In the German cases however one could be led to speculate whether, beneath the surface, the cases are contractual in nature and merely serve the different purpose of procuring a further contractual debtor where diffuse good faith considerations 'demand' as much. Looking at the damages awarded in a number of the German cases reinforces the plausibility of this suggestion. Liability in *culpa in contrahendo* entails a reliance measure. However, in many cases the damages awarded are equivalent to the expectation interest of the third party. Had the third party not relied on the intermediary who 'guaranteed' the perfect execution of the contract, he would not have entered into that contract or would not have performed his obligation. As a result, the intermediary is under an obligation to put the third party into the position he would have occupied had the contract been fulfilled. This can mean, for instance, that where the third party fulfilled its obligations but received no remuneration then the intermediary becomes liable for the outstanding payments as damages (eg, BGHZ 56, 81, case no 31). Or, in the cases concerning car dealers where the car does not measure up to the description in the contract, the car dealer becomes liable for the refund of the price (eg, BGHZ 87, 302). Yet, as explained, it is impossible to derive liability in these cases from the contract; this would be incompatible with the contractual framework. Hence, this type of liability also fulfils the role usually played by tort law. This means that the principles described here can be rationalised in terms of a duty of care of the agent not to harm the financial interest of the third party. The fact that this liability indirectly protects the expectation interest is only the result of the particular duty of care not to 'guarantee' the performance of the contract and thereby induce the reliance of the third party who is subsequently disappointed. The case law can be criticised for being vague and introducing insecurity into the law. Yet, despite its flexible control mechanisms, this jurisprudence does not seem to have severely prejudiced contract law principles or to have led to unbearable insecurity in the law. The reason for this must surely lie in a measured application of the test in deserving cases (see eg, BGH NJW-RR 1992, 605, emphasising that, except in the car dealer and the *Prospekthaftung*- cases referred to above, liability is imposed in truly exceptional circumstances only). It seems, thus, and this can also be said in relation to the negligent misrepresentation cases discussed in the previous section, that if liability for pure economic loss outside contract is established in more or less defined categories of cases, the floodgates can be kept shut.

6. AGENCY

Beuthien, 'Gibt es eine organschaftliche Stellvertretung?' NJW 1999, 1142; Beuthien, 'Zur Theorie der Stellvertretung im Bürgerlichen Recht' in *Festschrift für Medicus* (1999) 1; Drexl, 'Wissenszurechnung im Konzern' ZHR 161 (1997) 491; Einsele, 'Inhalt, Schranken und Bedeutung des Offenkundigkeitsprinzips' JZ 1990, 1005; Fikentscher, 'Scheinvollmacht und Vertreterbegriff' AcP 154 (1955) 1; Hager, 'Die Prinzipien der mittelbaren Stellvertretung' AcP 180 (1980), 239; Joussen, 'Die Generalvollmacht im Handels- und Gesellschaftsrecht' WM 1994, 273; McMeel, 'Philosophical Foundations of the Law of Agency' (2000) 116 *LQR.* 387; Markesinis and Munday, *An Outline of the Law of Agency* (4th edn, 1998); Müller-Freienfels, *Stellvertretungsregelungen, in Einheit und Vielfalt, Rechtsvergleichende Studien zur Stellvertretung* (1982); Müller-Freienfels, *Die Vertretung beim Rechtsgeschäft* (1955); Pawlowski, 'Die gewillkürte Stellvertretung' JZ 1996, 125; Prölss, 'Vertretung ohne Vertretungsmacht' JuS 1985, 577; Prölss, 'Haftung bei der Vertretung ohne Vertretungsmacht' JuS 1986, 169; Reynolds, *Bowstead and Reynolds on Agency* (17th edn, 2001); Treitel, *The Law of Contract* (11th edn, 2003), chapter 17.

(a) General Observations

In common law books, this topic would receive a short treatment in general books on contract law and the greater attention it deserves in specialized monographs. The same is true of German law (Müller-Freienfels, *Die Vertretung beim Rechtsgeschäft* (1955) is, despite its age, still regarded as an important work), so what follows here, of necessity, does little credit to the attention the subject has received from German lawyers. Yet even this warning is not sufficient to alert the common law reader to the dangers and difficulties which lurk in the summary treatment that follows—hence the need for these introductory comments.

First, we must consider the translation of the German term *Stellvertretung* as 'agency'. To the common lawyer, this immediately conjures up a triangular relationship in which all three sides of the triangle (principal/third party, agent/third party and principal/agent) are interrelated in a close manner. Leaving ratification aside, the relationship between principal and agent is constituted by agreement between principal and agent creating internal rights and duties between agent and principal and giving the agent external authority to affect the principal's legal relations with third parties (see *Bowstead and Reynolds on Agency*, 17th edn, Article 3, para 2-001). In German law, on the other hand, since Laband's famous theory was first presented in the 1860s (*Die Stellvertretung bei dem Abschluß von Rechtsgeschäften nach dem Allgemeinen Deutschen Handelsgesetzbuch,* ZHR 10 (1866), 183) a strict separation has been made between the agent's authority (*Vollmacht*) to bind his principal and the underlying relationship that links the principal and the agent. The latter may be based on mandate (*Auftrag*) (regulated by §§ 662 *et seq* BGB) or *negotiorum gestio* (regulated by §§ 677 *et seq* BGB) or even some rule of family law (eg, a parent representing his child, § 1626 BGB). Yet the differences seem to be largely conceptual. For English law also differentiates between internal rights between principal and agent (for instance an agent's fiduciary duties (on which see, Reynolds, *Bowstead and Reynolds on Agency*, chapter 6; Millett, 'Equity's Place in the Law of Commerce' (1998) 114 *LQR* 214 and Brown, *Commercial Law* (2001), chapter 8)) and the agent's external authority to create privity of contract between principal and third party. Furthermore, the authority of the agent may not stem from the contract between principal and agent but from a unilateral act of granting authority which may be wholly independent of any contract between agent and principal (see Reynolds, chapter 6, para 1-005). It should also be noted, looking now at the civil law side, that the separation of the external aspect of agency in German law does not entail a general principle that agency is unlimited. This *can* be the case, as with the famous *Prokura*—a general authority in the commercial context which is highly formalised—but it is not the paradigm case. As a general rule, as in English law, it is the voluntary act of the principal that defines the scope of the authority. The practical significance of this so-called abstraction doctrine (*Abstraktheit der Vollmacht*) is thus restricted and may be limited to the conclusion that the nullity of the underlying transaction (between principal and agent) will not affect the agent's authority to bind the principal. To take an example: A instructs B, a minor, to purchase a motorcycle on A's behalf. B's authority to bind A is, in this case, valid (§ 165 BGB) even though the underlying mandate is void because of B's minority (see §§ 107, 108 BGB). See, however, § 168 BGB (discussed below), which stipulates that the end of the underlying contract also terminates the agent's authority. The emphasis of German law on the agent's power to bind the principal would thus make it better to talk of representation (even though, subject to the caveat just expressed, it remains linguistically more attractive to continue to use the terms 'principal' and 'agent', instead of 'representee' and 'representor' respectively). As we shall see, the same terminological differences arise with other words encountered in this area of the law such as *Anscheinsvollmacht* which is probably best rendered into English as 'pretended' authority (see the comments on this subject, below). Terms of art must thus be used with great caution in this area of the law.

Secondly, the German Civil Code only regulates 'direct representation' (*unmittelbare Stellvertretung*) ie, the situation where the agent acts on behalf of his principal. The agent is required to declare that he is acting for a principal (*Offenkundigkeitsprinzip*), § 164 I 2 BGB (see for an illustration, BGHZ 36, 30, case no 33). German law does not recognise indirect representation (*mittelbare*, or *verdeckte Stellvertretung*) ie, the case where the agent contracts personally or, as it is usually put by German lawyers, acts in his own name, as an incident of agency. This is what the common law would in many cases regard as an undisclosed agency, which in common with most civil law systems, German law does not recognise. The result—that in these cases there is only a commercial/contractual legal relationship between third party and agent—raises two difficult questions. (For an illustration of the consequences of this approach, see also the brief exposition of the law of the commission agent, below (section 6(f)) p 117.)

First, how can an agent who has sold goods for an 'undisclosed' principal transfer the property of the goods (which do not belong to him) to the purchaser and, conversely, how can the agent, who bought goods for an 'undisclosed' principal, ensure that the property of the bought goods vests in his principal when the seller intended it to vest in the agent? The second, related problem, is how one can minimise the intervention of the agent's creditors in this case at the expense of one of the parties (principal or third party). German law has had to resort to some complicated ways of reducing these inconveniences, for instance by allowing an advance assignment of the agent's contractual rights to the principal or the anticipated transfer of the title to the principal which occurs at the very moment that the title is vested in the agent. In such cases, however, German law must also ensure (and indeed does so) that the debtor/third party does not end up with a creditor (principal) he does not wish. In the end, therefore, a special rule (§ 399 BGB) had to be provided preventing the assignment in almost precisely those kinds of cases where the common law allows the third party to oppose the appearance on the scene of the undisclosed principal (see eg, Reynolds, *Bowstead and Reynolds on Agency*, chapter 8 and Brown, *Commercial Law* (2001), pp 168–78). Thus, in both systems it is possible expressly to exclude the intervention of an undisclosed 'principal'. Likewise, §§ 404, 406 and 407 BGB ensure that the assignee/principal, suing under the contract made between the agent/third party, may be faced with the defences that the third party may have against the agent. We have, in short, an institution (undisclosed agency) which on the surface is known to one legal system but not to another; but we also have an intricate set of mechanisms which make up for the lack of such an institution and which operate in a more indirect way. It is a well-known paradox that English lawyers regard the undisclosed principal doctrine as anomalously creating privity of contract without the consent of the third party, while comparative lawyers admire the pragmatic English solution on the ground that it achieves the results of complex continental reasoning with less effort. There is one aspect of the undisclosed principal doctrine, however, that cannot be accounted for in the civil law model: this is the right to sue the (initially) undisclosed principal. For further details, see: Müller-Freienfels, 'Die "Anomalie" der verdeckten Stellvertretung (undisclosed agency) des englischen Rechts' *RabelsZ* 17 (1952) 578; 18 (1953) 12 and (in English) 'Comparative Aspects of Undisclosed Agency' (1955) 18 *MLR* 33; 'Law of Agency' 6 *AJCL* 165 (1955). (Incidentally, in some limited circumstances an 'undisclosed agency' of sorts has been recognised by German courts. This happens in transactions involving what is commonly known as 'business for whom it may concern' (*Geschäft für den, den es angeht*). Every day, cash transactions take place in which the third party is not concerned with the identity of his co-contractor. But in these instances the difficulties associated with undisclosed agency rarely arise in practice; and, in any event, this exception is narrowly construed and thus does not represent a significant derogation from the principle that 'undisclosed agency' is unknown to the German civil law.)

This brief excursus into the realm of undisclosed agency provides an opportunity to make our third general observation about this subject. For here, as indeed elsewhere in German law, one is forced to leave the Civil Code and search for supplementary regulation of the topic under discussion in other enactments, mainly the Commercial Code, which contains some provisions on indirect agency for three categories of agents: commission agents, forwarding agents and agents who enter into insurance arrangements on behalf of third parties. More importantly, in its §§ 48 to 53 the Commercial Code deals with the agent's authority (*Prokura*) to deal extensively in a commercial setting, with his principal's business. Thus, the understanding of this subject involves an intricate inter-relationship of the provisions of different enactments, something which makes the exposition of the subject in a summary way even more prone to be misleading.

(b) The Giving of Authority—*Bevollmächtigung*

The first thing to make clear is that in what follows we shall be discussing what is known as 'contractual representation'. However, German law also recognises another kind of representation, which is called 'legal representation' because its source is the law, itself, rather than the will of the parties (*gesetzliche Vertretungsmacht*). Examples include the authority of parents to represent their children (§ 1629 BGB); the authority of 'guardians' to administer the affairs of their charges (§§ 1789, 1793 BGB); the authority of trustees in bankruptcy (*Insolvenzverwalter*) to represent the estate in bankruptcy and so on. These institutions can provoke some interesting comparative observations largely by raising the question 'how are these matters handled by the Common law?' (On this matter see, briefly, Zweigert and Kötz's insights in *An Introduction to Comparative Law*, (English translation by Tony Weir, 3rd edn, 1998), especially pp 431 *et seq*.)

Authority (*Vollmacht*) is conferred on the agent by the principal by means of a unilateral juridical act known as the *Bevollmächtigung*. This declaration will determine the external relationships of the principal and the third party (*Außenverhältnis*), whereas the underlying contract between principal and agent will determine the 'inner' or 'internal' relationship between principal and agent (*Innenverhältnis*) which will deal with such matters as, for instance, whether the agent will be entitled to be paid for his services. (As a result of Directive 86/653/EEC [1986] OJ L382/17 (31 December 1986) on Self-Employed Commercial Agents, certain incidents of the relationship between a principal and a self-employed commercial agent are now provided for by legislation: for the UK implementation, see the Commercial Agents (Council Directive) Regulations 1993 (SI 1993 No 3053) (as amended by SI 1993 No 3173).) According to § 167 I BGB, such a grant of authority can take place by means of a declaration (express or implied) of the principal which is made to (a) the agent; (b) the third party; or (c) more generally, the public at large (*öffentliche Bekanntmachung*). Such authority can, so far as the civil law is concerned, be given informally, even when it concerns the accomplishment of a transaction that requires form (see § 167 II BGB). But exceptions to this rule may be specified by legislation. Thus, § 135 of the *Aktiengesetz* states that authority given to a bank to exercise a shareholder's voting rights at the company's general meetings must be complete and documented (although it need not include the shareholder's signature). Likewise, the grant of authority to represent a client before a court must be made in writing (see § 80 of the *Zivilprozeßordnung*).

As § 167 I BGB makes clear, the authority can be created by the principal making a declaration to the third party. This is similar to the English notion of apparent authority (see generally, *Freeman & Lockyer v Buckhurst Park Properties (Mangal) Ltd* [1964] 2 QB 480, at 503 (*per* Diplock LJ) and Brown, *Commercial Law* (2001), chapter 4) and is regulated by § 171 I BGB, sub-paragraph (2) of the same paragraph, declaring the obvious rule that in such cases the power of representation remains in force until the notice is revoked in the same manner as it was given. (Although see § 173 BGB, which excludes the effects of authority if the third party knew or could have known that the authority was revoked as between agent and principal.) English law reaches a similar result via applying doctrines of actual notice of lack of authority (see eg, *Overbrooke Estates Ltd v Glencombe Properties Ltd* [1974] 1 WLR 1335) and of the third party having been 'put on enquiry' by circumstances where the court would deem that the third party should have known (or at least been suspicious) that the agent was not in fact so authorised (see *Lloyds Bank Ltd v Chartered Bank of India, Australia and China* [1929] 1 KB 40). The key point is that the third party must reasonably have relied on the principal's representation of authority (see the judgment of Diplock LJ in *Freeman & Lockyer* (above)). Clearly, whether the third party is put on enquiry will depend on a careful assessment of all the facts of the case (*Feuer Leather Corpn v Frank Johnstone & Sons Ltd* [1981] Com LR 251).)

As in English law, apparent authority thus differs from implied authority, the latter being largely discovered through interpreting the principal's will as declared to the agent. In practice, however, the distinction is not as clear as it appears in theory; and it is made that much more difficult by the fact that German law recognises two other types of situation where the agent can actually bind his principal even though the latter has given neither him nor the third party any real indication of his willingness to grant such authority to the agent.

The first of these cases is called tolerated authority (*Duldungsvollmacht*) and it involves a 'principal' who knows that another person is pretending to act as his agent but takes no steps to correct this impression. The other kind of authority, known as 'pretended' authority (*Anscheinsvollmacht*) involves analogous facts, except that the so-called principal is negligently unaware of the acts of the so-called agent (see BGHZ 5, 111, case no 34). It is, however, not sufficient that the agent merely pretends to have authority. The principal must have negligently permitted the agent to appear to have authority. In both these instances, the case law attaches the usual incidents of representation; but the theoretical explanation for this result has divided academic writers who, on the whole, do not seem to favour it. Especially in the case of 'pretended' authority, it is difficult to see why the third party should be entitled to anything more than his reliance loss (see, for instance, Flume, *Allgemeiner Teil*, vol II, § 49. 4.; others, like Medicus, *Allgemeiner Teil*, Rn. 971, 972, prefer to limit the effect of these notions of 'tolerated' and 'pretended' authority to the commercial field).

(c) The Extent of the Authority

If the agent declares that he is acting for a principal (*Offenkundigkeitsprinzip*), and has acted within the scope of his authority, then he will create contractual privity between his principal and the third party.

But what if he did not declare that he was acting on behalf of another person or had no authority (or, which amounts to the same thing, exceeded his authority)? In the former case we are faced with an indirect agency (which we have already discussed briefly in the preceding paragraphs), while in the latter situations (and subject to the exceptional rules to be discussed below) the agent and not the principal will be liable towards the third party. (See below (section 6(d)(ii)) for a brief discussion of how English law deals with this issue.)

As in English law, so in German law, determining the exact scope of the agent's authority is thus a matter of some considerable importance. This, of course, is ultimately a question of interpretation of the *Bevollmächtigung* and not of the underlying contract between principal and agent, though the latter may help to provide interpretative clues; and in cases of apparent authority, the creation of authority and its exact scope will become totally blurred. (Cf BGHZ 6, 330, case no 34.) But often the law, itself, will provide some help by defining the limits of authority. This is particularly true of commercial law where special rules are supplied for the so-called 'limited commercial authority' (*Handlungsvollmacht*), regulated by § 54 HGB; the authority of commercial representatives (*Handelsvertreter*), regulated by § 84 HGB; and the authority of sales assistants (*Ladenvollmacht*), regulated by § 56 HGB, and others.

However, by far the most important of these special provisions are those found in §§ 48–53 HGB, which deal with full commercial authority (*Prokura*). Such authority can only be given by 'full' businessmen (*Vollkaufmann*) which essentially means that it is not available to small tradesmen. It can only be given by the businessman personally; and it must be in writing and duly entered in the Commercial Register (§ 53 I HGB). The purpose of this provision is to protect third parties who rely on such authority, so registration and publication do not affect the grant of the authority itself. Such authority is of the most comprehensive kind, allowing the third party to assume that the agent can enter into all transactions which the principal himself can undertake in connection with his business affairs. § 50 I HGB makes it clear that any 'internal' limitations of this authority will have no effect as against third parties. § 49 HGB contains the only restrictions that can be placed on such authority. Thus, the agent cannot undertake transactions that affect his principal's private affairs; he cannot sell or otherwise wind up the principal's business; and he may not mortgage or sell land that belongs to his principal, though he has unlimited borrowing powers and can bind his principal personally to repay such loans. Such full commercial authority survives the death of the principal (§ 52 III HGB) and is in practice more commonly terminated when revoked (§ 52 I HGB). Third parties are bound by such revocation once it has been duly published in the Commercial Register (§ 53 III HGB). Thus, third parties dealing in good faith with the agent subsequent to revocation of his authority but prior to its publication will be protected (§ 15 I HGB).

In the interest of commercial certainty, this unlimited authority extends to all matters of commercial nature relating to the particular business. It is, however, subject to the general principle of good faith, which in individual cases of evident misuse of the agent's powers may not give rise to liability of the principal. Generally speaking, an agent has power to bind the principal within the scope of the authority even if his acts run contrary to some purely internal obligation owed to the principal. In BGHZ 50, 112, a case concerning a *Prokura*, however, the court stated that this broad principle is subject to qualifications of good faith. If it is evident to the third party that the agent is misusing his authority and acts against the obvious best interest of the principal, the agent will not according to the principle of good faith create an obligation that is binding on the principal. The principal is allowed to invoke the agent's abuse of his rights as against the third party. See, for a more recent application of these principles: BGH NJW 1999, 2883, case no 35, spelling out the obligation of a bank in relation to its clients. (See further, the sections on good faith and abuse of rights in the next chapter, p 123.)

(d) Lack of Authority

Three topics must be discussed briefly under this heading, namely: (i) the possibility of ratification; (ii) the liability of the *falsus procurator* and (iii) some exceptional rules devised to protect third parties dealing with an agent who has acted without authority.

(i) Ratification

Lord Sterndale MR's statement in *Koenigsblatt v Sweet* ([1923] 2 Ch 314, at 325) that 'Ratification . . . is equivalent to an antecedent authority . . . and when there has been ratification the act that is done is put in the same position as if it had been antecedently authorized' is echoed in § 177 I BGB; and § 184 BGB likewise contains a rule similar to that stated by Harman J in *Boston Deep Sea Fishing and Ice Co Ltd v Farnham (Inspector of Taxes)* ([1957] 1 WLR 1051), to the effect that ratification has a retroactive effect. Ratification requires no formality; and according to § 182 I BGB, it may be done by the principal expressing his willingness to ratify either to the agent or the third party—unless the third party asks the principal for ratification, in which case the relevant intention must be directed to him (§ 177 II BGB). § 178 BGB contains, however, an important proviso by enabling the third party (who did not know of the lack of authority) to withdraw from the transaction before the principal purports to ratify it. This proviso does not exist in English law, which takes the retroactive effect of the principal's ratification so seriously that a prior attempt to withdraw is rendered invalid by the subsequent act of ratification (see the well known case of *Bolton Partners v Lambert* (1889) 41 Ch D 295). It should be noted that this approach has been subjected to criticism (see *Fleming v Bank of New Zealand* [1900] AC 577 (where the Privy Council reserved the right to reconsider *Bolton*) and Seavey, 'The Rationale of Agency' (1920) 29 *Yale LJ* 859, 886–92), although the English rule also has its supporters (eg, as it safeguards certainty in business transactions—see Brown, *Commercial Law*, pp 36–7 and Stoljar, *The Law of Agency* (1961), p 191). The American approach started from the opposite end of the spectrum, taking the view that the principal's ratification only became effective if the third party had consented to it (*Dodge v Hopkins* 14 Wis 630 (1861)). Now, however, the Second Restatement on Agency (§ 88) permits the third party to withdraw prior to ratification, aligning the American approach more closely with that available in German law under § 178 BGB.

(ii) The Liability of the Falsus Procurator

If no ratification takes place, § 179 BGB prescribes the legal consequences that will follow. Broadly speaking, these are three. First, if the third party knew or ought to have known of the lack of authority then he has no rights against the agent (§ 179 III BGB). Secondly, if the third party and the agent were ignorant of the lack of authority (or the exceeding of the true bounds of the authority) then the agent is responsible to the third party only for the damage that the third party has suffered by relying on the authority: ie, the third party is put in the position he would have occupied if the contract had never come into existence (the so-called negative interest, implying a reliance-based measure: § 179 II BGB). Finally, in the most serious of cases where the third party was ignorant of the lack of authority, but the agent acted in full knowledge of this fact, then the latter is liable to the former either to carry out the contract or to compensate him for the full expectation interest (§ 179 I BGB).

In English law, the case of lack or excess of authority is dealt with by finding that the agent has breached his warranty that he had authority from the principal to contract with the third party: see *Collen v Wright* (1857) 7 El & Bl 301; 119 ER 1259, affd 8 El & Bl 647; 120 ER 241 (although if the agent has acted fraudulently, then the tort of deceit can clearly render him liable: *Polhill v Walter* (1832) 3 B & Ad 114; 110 ER 43). This liability is strict and is (thus) seen as contractual, amounting to a contract collateral to the 'main' contract and unilateral in nature (accepted by the third party's entry into the contract with the principal). It is acknowledged however that in certain fact situations there will actually have been no breach of this warranty: thus, as in German law, where the third party is aware of the agent's lack of authority, it cannot be said that the third party was misled by the breach into acting as he did and so the agent will not be liable (*Lilly, Wilson & Co v Smales, Eeles & Co* [1892] 1 QB 456). (See further, Brown, *Commercial* Law, pp 204–13 and Reynolds, 'Personal Liability of an Agent' (1969) 85 *LQR* 92.)

Interesting questions arise where the principal is insolvent, as the measure of damages is a contractual one: so, if the principal repudiates the contract arranged by the agent, the measure of damages is what the principal would have had to pay had he refused to perform a properly authorised contract. In such cases, one might argue that a claim based on negligent misstatement (and the *Hedley Byrne* line of authority, discussed briefly above (sections 5(d) and (e), p 103 ff) is the only chance that the third party has to recover his loss, although there appears to be no case law on this possibility at present.

(iii) Exceptional Rules

This heading covers a number of miscellaneous situations (in addition to the instances of commercial agency already discussed) where rules have been devised to protect the third party who acted in good faith when dealing with the agent. §§ 170, 171 II, 172 III BGB provide such limited exceptions to the general rule. Here, suffice it to mention the first: if the principal revokes his authority by so informing the agent, the latter's authority comes to an end. But if the authority was granted in the first place by a declaration to the third party, then such a revocation (made only to the agent) will not affect the third party.

(e) Termination of Authority

There are various ways this can happen, and these can be found either in provisions expressly dealing with agency or in the general law. An example of the former can be found in § 168 sent. 1 BGB, where the Code states that the agency is terminated when the legal relationship on which it is based comes to an end. Likewise, the death of the principal will bring the agency to an end except in those cases where the contrary has been provided. Likewise, the authority will, in principle, be terminated by revocation (§ 168 sent. 2 BGB, although where the authority also serves the interests of the agent it may be made irrevocable; on this point in English law, see *Gaussen v Morton* (1830) 10 B & C 731, especially. at 734; 109 ER 622 and generally, Reynolds, 'When is an Agent's Authority Irrevocable?' chapter 10 in Cranston (ed), *Making Commercial Law—Essays in Honour of Roy Goode* (1997): the authority must granted *explicitly* to secure a particular interest of the agent, so that a more general interest (such as a salary or commission) in performing that authority will not suffice). Alternatively, authority may be terminated as a result of the operation of ordinary legal principles. Thus, this will be the case where the agent dies or is deprived of his legal capacity.

(f) The Commission Agent

Indirect representation, as to which see already the preliminary observations above, is to a great extent unnecessary in English law, since the latter recognises undisclosed agency (although see the discussion of the limits of that doctrine in Unberath, *Transferred Loss* (2003), p 178 *et seq*; see also Reynolds, 'Practical Problems of the Undisclosed Principal Doctrine' [1983] *CLP* 119), yet it is not expressly dealt with in the BGB (in particular, not as part of the agency provisions). The paradigm case of *mittelbare Stellvertretung* ('indirect representation') is the contract of commission (*Kommissionsgeschäft*). It should be noted that those rules apply in other contexts as well, for instance in the area of carriage of goods or construction. The common denominator of these situations is that a person—the intermediary—who contracts personally, acts in the interest and on the account of another.

The closest analogy to this role in English legal history appears to be that played by the old 'factors' who acted as mercantile agents for a principal, who contracted personally with third parties and deducted their commission from the sale price received before accounting for the remainder to the principal. Out of this role (and its difficulties, particularly in the event of the factor's bankruptcy prior to accounting to his principal) developed the doctrine of the undisclosed principal: see Stoljar, *The Law of Agency* (1961), pp 204–11 for an account of this development). Today, however, as Goode describes (*Commercial Law* (3rd edn, 2004), p 164), 'a purely internal mandate by which P instructs or authorizes A to enter into a commitment with a third party not only in A's own name but without involving P even as undisclosed principal does not fall within the English notion of agency.'

A commission agent is someone who sells or buys goods the property of another (§ 383 I HGB). The commission agent (*Kommissionär*) acts in his own name but on the account of the 'indirect' principal (*Kommittent*). The contract between intermediary and 'indirect' principal is usually a contract for managing the affairs of another for consideration (§ 675 BGB, discussed in the next chapter). The agent is not answerable in respect of negligence on the part of the third party, but only in respect of his own negligence in selecting an unreliable third party or because he did not follow the instructions of the principal (§ 384 HGB). The agent is entitled to commission (*Provision*) and the principal has an obligation to indemnify the agent for all expenses connected with the transaction (§§ 670, 675 BGB, § 396 II HGB). For example, the principal has a duty to refund the price paid to the third party in respect of the goods bought on commission.

Since the doctrine of the undisclosed principal is not recognised in German law, the contract of sale creates rights and liabilities only between the commission agent and the third party, § 392 I HGB. However, the economic interests involved (loss suffered by principal) and the legal position of the parties (right to recover damages in the agent) do not match. The function of the doctrine of *mittelbare Stellvertretung* is to redress this imbalance so far as the law of obligations is concerned: the intermediary is allowed to recover damages in respect of the principal's loss (on the basis of *Drittschadensliquidation*). The principal has a contractual right against the agent to require the agent to assign his damages claim to the principal (§ 384 II HGB). The third party will then, however, be able to raise all defences available in relation to the commission agent also against the indirect principal (§§ 404, 407 BGB). As far as property rights are concerned, it is impossible completely to avoid the agent's transitory ownership of the goods. The agent becomes owner at least for a so-called 'logical' second (or *scintilla temporis*) before he can pass on the money or the goods to his principal. These, however, are all details which are best left to specialised works on agency, and the reader must therefore seek further enlightenment in such works (references to which have been provided at the start of this section).

3

The Content of a Contract

1. INTRODUCTORY REMARKS

In chapter 2, we examined the obligations of the parties during the phase of formation of a contract and explored the formation process itself. We noted that in German law the parties are said to be bound by a 'relationship of obligation' imposed by law (*gesetzliches Schuldverhältnis*) once the formation of a contract commences. This notion of 'pre-contractual' obligations facilitates the bringing of claims by the parties for physical damages and, crucially, for pure economic loss caused by conduct preceding the conclusion of the intended contract. In this chapter we leave the phase of formation behind and turn to methods of determining the content of a contract. Two fundamental issues must be addressed by each legal system. First, to what extent are the subjective intentions of the parties relevant in determining the terms of a contract? Secondly, to what extent are the courts entitled to supplement the actual terms of the contract by implying terms in law? We will begin with an exposition of the principle of good faith, which sets the scene against which these two questions are to be answered in German law. While it should be noted from the outset that this principle transcends contract law, the principle is also relevant to the formation of contracts and most of its functions are directed at the terms of a contract. It serves as a foundation for many collateral obligations of the parties and is regarded as an 'inherent' limit on the exercise of contractual rights. Most importantly, perhaps, the objective method of interpretation in German law is founded on this very same principle. In the remainder of this chapter, we then provide an outline of the legally implied content of typical contracts. Finally, the special issues raised by 'pre-formulated' contract clauses are considered, though some of the issues discussed there relate back to the formation of a contract while others introduce the notion of assessing the substantive fairness of contract terms, which will be one of the central themes of chapter 4.

2. THE PRINCIPLE OF GOOD FAITH

Baumgärtel, 'Treu und Glauben im Zivilprozess' ZZP 86 (1973), 353; Baumgärtner, *Rechtsformübergreifende Aspekte der gesellschaftsrechtlichen Treuepflicht im deutschen und angloamerikanischen Recht* (1990); Canaris, 'Voraussetzungen und Inhalt des Anspruchs auf Freigabe von Globalsicherheiten gem. § 242 BGB, ZIP 1997, 813; Coester-Waltjen, 'Die Inhaltskontrolle von Verträgen außerhalb des AGBG' AcP 190, 1; Collins, 'Good Faith in European Contract Law' (1994) 14 *OJLS* 229;

Ebke and Steinhauer, 'The Doctrine of Good Faith in German Contract Law' in Beatson and Friedmann (eds), *Good Faith and Fault in Contract Law* (1995) 171; Esser, '§ 242 BGB und die Privatautonomie' JZ 1956, 555; Gernhuber, '§ 242 BGB-Funktion und Tatbestände' JuS 1983, 764; Honsell, 'Teleologische Reduktion vs Rechtsmißbrauch' *Festschrift für Mayer-Maly* (1996), 369; Immenga, 'Bindung von Rechtsmacht durch Treuepflichten' in *Festschrift 100 Jahre GmbH-Gesetz* (1992), 189; Mader, *Rechtsmißbrauch und unzulässige Rechtsausübung* (1994); R Singer, *Das Verbot widersprüchlichen Verhaltens* (1993); R Weber, 'Entwicklung und Ausdehnung des § 242 BGB zum königlichen Paragraphen' JuS 1992, 631; Wieacker, *Zur rechts-theoretischen Präzisierung des § 242 BGB* (1956) (a seminal work: see especially, pp 20–44); Wiedemann, 'Zu den Treuepflichten im Gesellschaftsrecht' in *Festschrift für Theodor Heinsius* (1991), 949; Zimmermann and Whittaker (eds), *Good faith in European Contract Law* (2000).

(a) Preliminary Observations

Mention good faith to a German lawyer and his mind will dart to the twenty words of § 242 BGB and next, perhaps, to the voluminous tome in *Staudingers Kommentar* which dedicates over five hundred pages exclusively to the topic. If you push an Anglo-American down that path, a number of thoughts will start to cross his mind. Here are some, which we cannot pursue in detail, but which can serve as a general introduction to what follows.

The wording of the text of § 242—'The debtor is obliged to perform in such a manner as good faith requires, regard being had to general practice'—gives no clue as to why such a general and somewhat bland statement could have been of such importance to German law, justifying a voluminous tome. (To ascribe it to the assumed characteristics of the German character and legal mind would be too facile.) Certainly, in drafting terms, it is neither as elegant as some of the staccato aphorisms one finds in the French Code civil (eg, *en fait des meubles la possession vaut titre* = Article 2279 CC); nor is it as detailed and exhaustive as so many other important paragraphs of the BGB which have made their mark for their concise thoroughness. Indeed, in one sense, reading the text may even give a misleading impression insofar as its wording suggests that it only regulates the conduct of the debtor (though it has always been assumed that it also applies to the creditor as well). At first glance, therefore this paradigm of BGB provisions is not at all German!

Yet, strangely, it is in this generality that we find the first clue of the importance of the paragraph. For its blandness allowed it to become the peg on which numerous value judgments of German courts could be hung, thus acquiring legitimacy in the eyes of jurists who are accustomed to justifying their decisions by reference to a written legal text.

This thought leads to a second one and it is related to the question: 'how do Codes keep up to date?' The BGB offers many examples of how this has been done. In some cases, new sections have been added to the Code (see, for instance, the new paragraphs on the travel contract, §§ 651a–651m, below, p 157). In others, the addition is found outside the Code, perhaps because pragmatic considerations suggested that it would be too slow and controversial to incorporate the new provisions into the codal text. The reform of the law of obligations of 2001 (BGBl. I, 3138) was seen as an opportunity to (re-)integrate many of these special statutes concerning isolated aspects of contract law into the Code. (This happened, for instance, in the case of the 'standard conditions of business,' *Allgemeine Geschäftsbedingungen*, §§ 305–10, discussed below in section 5.) A third way is through interpretation of the text of the Code (which 'interpretation' often can amount to judicial legislation). In *The German Law of Torts*, we saw how this happened in the context of §§ 253 and 823 I BGB and the new personality right created by the *Bundesgerichtshof* in 1953 (on which see p 74 *et seq* of that work). Exceptionally, sections of the Code have been systematically re-drafted by the legislator (which occurred mainly in the area of family law after the courts in the 1950s and 1960s un-picked, one by one, those of its provisions which proved incompatible with the (newer) Constitution). But in many other areas, and this is particularly true of the law of contract, the codal regime has been modified, amplified and even revolutionized by the courts themselves, having recourse to the so-called general clauses of which § 242 BGB is, arguably, the most famous (§ 826 is another; see, *The German Law of Torts*, chapter 4). Judicial reliance on a grand, 'ethical rule' can thus justify all sorts of things, though the Nazi period showed that by no means all of these were welcome or justifiable. Thus, for instance, Palandt's *Kommentar* on the BGB (6th edn (1944), § 242, 6, c, mentions that during this period the 'basis of the transaction' came to be understood as including the 'existence and continuation of those circumstances which are required to make the transaction appear *as a useful order of things which is appropriate within the total complex of the racial system*' (translated by Cohn, emphasis added). Relying on such definitions courts were thus able to 'dissolve' contracts, especially pension agreements, made with Jewish and other anti-Nazi individuals. (For further details, see Gernhuber, *Festschrift Kern* (1968), p 168.)

We obviously cannot elaborate on this last and disturbing historical event; but, as chapter seven will show, much of the law of 'frustration' was developed in the post-First World War era when Germany was plunged into an unprecedented socio-economic chaos, much of which was brought about by the understandable but short-sighted wish of its victorious opponents to exact their pound of flesh (there was also significant inflation even during the war). When this was added to the resources lost by the hand-over of German territories under the Versailles Treaty to the 'victors' to meet the debt incurred in financing the war effort and the cost of paying reparations, it was clear that the economic measures needed to deal with the situation were vastly more complex than any previous government anywhere in the world had had to face. Furthermore, alleviation of the reparations burden required international co-operation and agreement, which fluctuated from the depths of the re-occupation of the Ruhr by France and Belgium in January 1923 (the passive resistance to which cost the German economy still more overall), through the Dawes Plan (from 1 September 1924) to the positive impact of aid and loans to Germany and German business in the later 1920s. For discussion, see Hiden, *The Weimar Republic* (1974); Kolb, *The Weimar Republic* (1993) and Nicholls, *Weimar and the Rise of Hitler* (4th edn, 2000). The case law of the 1920s can only be properly understood if this socio-economic background is held firmly in mind. But although one hopes such upheavals are largely things of the past (though not entirely, as the reunification of Germany has shown), one aspect of this crisis is still with us today. Indeed, in England it may only now be revealing more of its full significance (in the light of the advent of the Human Rights

Act 1998 and the recent and intense debate surrounding the UK government's constitutional reform proposals, including the creation of a Supreme Court). The issue relates to the powers of the judiciary and its ability to ignore, or strike down, the acts of an elected government or to act when the government remains inactive. Much of this German socio-economic background is, nowadays, available to the reader in various books and articles (many written in the English language: see, eg, Bessel, *Germany after the First World War* (1995)) so it need not be repeated here in any detail. But when trying to understand the rich and varied case law—here and in chapter 7—these wider issues must not be allowed to drop entirely out of sight. This then is a third theme, indirect to the main aim of this chapter but one which nevertheless teachers with a constitutional or historical bent may wish to develop further by relying on the cases given in this book.

A fourth theme can be said to spring from our observation that German jurists have bracketed everything that pertains to good faith in one paragraph and one volume of their standard treatise. Yet for us, trying as we have repeatedly said to Anglicise this material, such an arrangement makes little sense, not least because good faith has been relied on to justify very different legal institutions of the law of contract. No other principle of German law has given rise to such diverse, complex and at the same time subtle developments as the principle of good faith. There is a further complication, namely the tendency that prevails in all the decisions relying on § 242 BGB to insist that the ruling need not be taken further than the facts of each case require (RGZ 131, 274, case no 36 is a good example). In other words, there is something in this rich case law that reminds one of the English case law techniques and, perhaps, of the equitable jurisdiction of the courts, although with one notable exception: little attempt is made to reconcile the rich decisional law. (Summers has argued that the US concept of good faith operates in a similar way: 'The General Duty of Good Faith: Its Recognition and Conceptualization' 67 *Cornell L Rev* 810 (1982) 821–4. His position is that the concept of good faith allows judges to develop law according to no fixed principle. This also is the position of the Restatement, Second, of Contracts § 205, comment (d): 'A complete catalogue of types of bad faith is impossible.')

Even experienced German academics admit that any attempt to present this seamless web systematically, following every twist and turn, must fail (Gernhuber, JuS 1983 765). (One should note of course that there are occasions when the English approach, and its obvious focus on achieving such reconciliation also fails to make the mass of case law cohere successfully.) We are thus left with the need to generalise. The most promising way of organising the material is by reference to the different (well established) functions which the concept fulfils: in what follows, sub-section (b) covers sanctioning an 'abuse' of rights; (c) treats implying obligations into the contract; and (d) deals with policing contract terms. (In US law, the concept of unconscionability covers the last of these functions, while good faith deals with those covered in (b) and (c), below.) This, in accordance with our declared interest to avoid putting the emphasis on 'differences' rather than 'similarities', will illustrate to the common lawyer that many a concept that in German law follows from good faith has a parallel (of sorts) in the common law, albeit operating under a less ambitious name.

(b) Abuse of Rights

Perhaps the most characteristic feature of good faith relates to the limits it imposes on the exercise of one's rights (*unzulässige Rechtsausübung, Rechtsmißbrauch*). It is of general importance insofar as every right is subject to the requirement of being exercised in a manner consistent with good faith (often referred to as the 'internal' limit of rights or *Schrankenfunktion*). Yet it is incapable of abstract definition as, once more, the application of the good faith principle depends on the facts of the individual case. While good faith as a foundation of collateral duties (see (c), below) serves as an obligation-creating tool, in this first function it operates in a negative way. It limits the enforcement of existing rights. One could thus compare it to the *English* principle of estoppel which, as is well known, acts (or is said to act) as a shield and not a sword (see the discussion of the estoppel concept in chapter 2, pp 64, 86). (Note that, so far as promissory estoppel is concerned, it is said typically only to operate with suspensory effect, ie the enforcement of existing rights is delayed until such time as it becomes equitable to insist on their enforcement again, although it is possible that, due to a change of circumstances, it may never be equitable so to insist.)

Some cases (eg, BGHZ 25, 47, 51 and 52) show that reliance placed by a debtor on the creditor's behaviour will be protected, while yet others (eg, RGZ 153, 59) clearly suggest that the law will not allow parties to contracts to blow hot and cold. If the creditor is under an obligation to return the very object of his claim against the debtor, then he forfeits the right. (*Dolo agit, qui petit, quod statim redditurus est*: see, eg, BGH NJW 1990, 1289.) Likewise, the person exercising a right must not thereby contradict his own previous conduct provided that he induced reliance by the debtor, referred to as the prohibition of *venire contra factum proprium*. Examples can be found in a wide variety of contexts. (BGHZ 18, 340 (lawyer not entitled to charge more than he suggested on earlier occasion); BGHZ 34, 355 (exposing oneself to a dangerous situation); BGHZ 50, 191 (person invoking arbitration clause before ordinary court after having previously opposed arbitration on grounds of jurisdiction); BGHZ 63, 140 (participation in dangerous sports); BGHZ 127, 378 (employer himself inducing the mistake in a surveyor's report); BGHZ 143, 362 (state liability). For further details see Dette, *Venire contra factum proprium nulli conceditur* (1985); Singer, *Das Verbot widersprüchlichen Verhaltens* (1993).) A similar argument applies in a related category of cases, where the lapse of time accompanied by the creation of an impression that the creditor waives his right actually leads to the premature extinction of the right through laches (*Verwirkung*). BGHZ 21, 66, case no 37, provides an illustration of this aspect of good faith. English law on this point has two main strands. At law and in the absence of a valid and new contract of waiver, what Treitel terms 'forbearance' (Treitel, *The Law of Contract*, p 103) may apply to limit some of the rights ordinarily held under the contract. The application of such forbearance to the party who grants it can prove difficult: compare *Plevins v Downing* (1876) 1 CPD 220 (where the party granting forbearance in extending the due delivery date was not held liable in damages for refusal to accept delivery) with *Hartley v Hymans* [1920] 3 KB 475 (where refusal to take delivery in similar circumstances did sound in damages). The second strand is promissory estoppel, which operates in equity and has been discussed above (chapter 2, sections 3(e), p 78, 4(b) p 86). BGHZ 43, 289, case no 38 shows how § 242 BGB also applies to procedural matters, including proceedings in non-contentious litigation:

thus, for instance, the late lodging of an appeal may make it inadmissible through *Verwirkung*. Yet other decisions show how § 242 BGB has been applied to easements, which may also have to be adjusted in the light of changed circumstances (RGZ 169, 180), or agreements to discontinue legal actions, which then give rise to a valid defence (RGZ 159, 186, 189) etc.

Bolder are the judicial interventions which, also by reference to abuse of rights, have set aside rules concerning necessary formalities. Some of these were discussed in chapter 2 in the section on formalities (p 81 ff). We thus said that varying degrees of formality are (for different reasons which need not concern us here) required for specific transactions. And we also noted in chapter 2 that in some cases, eg, the creation of rights over land, the absence of the requisite form may be fatal to the validity of the transaction. The *Edelmann* case, there cited (RGZ 117, 121, case no 21), showed how the courts were willing, in appropriate circumstances, to condemn promisors to pay damages on the basis of a reliance measure for transactions which were not specifically enforceable because of absence of form (though on the facts the claim failed) and in later judgments the *Bundesgerichshof* even went so far as to order specific performance of such agreements lacking the required form under the heading of good faith (BGHZ 48, 396, case no 22). This line of cases must also briefly be recalled in the present context, for here, somewhat anomalously, the abuse of rights argument serves to justify a cause of action, initially for recovering the reliance interest and in some cases even to protect the performance interest itself. The general parallel here to arguments based on proprietary estoppel in English law (which can create rights in land even in the absence of the usual formalities: see, eg, *ER Ives Investments Ltd v High* [1967] 2 QB 379) is clear. This has been discussed briefly in chapter 2, section 4(a). (See also, Treitel, *The Law of Contract*, pp 134–49.)

There are other less controversial instances of abuse of rights which cannot be explained as either instances of the *dolo petit* objection or the *venire contra factum proprium* rule. They are derived from a more general, if vague, idea of fairness. Again, only examples help to flesh out the principle. It may constitute an abuse of rights if the right was acquired through unfair (*unredlich*) conduct. For example, BGHZ 57, 108, concerned a case where a creditor allegedly secured his superior right in insolvency proceedings by unfair means. Other creditors, the court stated *obiter*, would in such a situation have been allowed to intervene and prevent him from enforcing his right. Furthermore, as we have seen in the previous chapter in the section on agency (chapter 2, p 114), an abuse of right may limit the power of an agent to bind the principal. It will recalled that such an 'abuse of authority' (*Mißbrauch der Vertretungsmacht*) is said to depend on whether it is 'evident' to the third party that the agent, while formally empowered to conclude the contract, is seriously harming the interests of the principal (see BGH NJW 1999, 2883, case no 35).

Many other examples of abuse of rights cases can be found. Some of them are based on the idea that a right-holder may not enforce his right where he does not pursue a legitimate motive, though again the courts will only intervene in extreme cases. Thus, in BGHZ 90, 198, case no 39, the court held that it was contrary to good faith if a buyer rejected the goods because of the breach of a condition if the breach ceased to exist at the time of the rejection. Other cases also suggest that a breach of contract with only slight consequences may not always give rise to (the full range of) secondary rights. (Eg, BGHZ 21, 122, 136, *obiter*: late payment of a minuscule debt of insurance premium. Likewise, slight delay may not be treated as bad performance: RGZ 92, 208; 117, 354; or, good faith may justify a change of the place of performance: *OLG Düsseldorf, Dt. RZ* 1948, 307.) However, the number of cases where such a defence has failed is great and the courts are keen to emphasise that ordinarily even a merely technical breach leads to liability (eg, BGH NJW 1981, 2686; BGHZ 88, 91). (Contrast the approach in *Arcos Ltd v EA Ronaasen & Son* [1933] AC 470, where the buyer was allowed to get out of a bad bargain on the grounds of what seemed to be a mere 'technical' breach, although the decision has not met with general approval (cf *Reardon Smith Line Ltd v Yngvar Hansen-Tangen ('The Diana Prosperity')* [1976] 1 WLR 989, 998 and Treitel, pp 793 and 825. The reforms made by the Sale and Supply of Goods Act 1994 (see what is now section 15A of the Sale of Goods Act 1979, which applies only where the buyer does not deal as a consumer) seem to have failed to redress the position reached in the *Arcos* case: the right to rescind the contract can only be removed in the face of a breach 'so slight that it would be unreasonable' for the buyer to reject the goods. (See Treitel, *The Law of Contract*, pp 801–2.) In the US, James J White & Robert S Summers, *Uniform Commercial Code* (3rd edn, 1988), pp 355–7, have concluded that 'relatively little is left' of the UCC perfect tender rule because courts have used a variety of devices to prevent sellers from rejecting goods in bad faith to escape a disadvantageous bargain.)

Finally, the wording of § 242 BGB itself refers to a special form of abuse of rights, namely as to the manner in which the debtor performs. As already mentioned, the narrow confines of the exact wording of § 242 BGB have from the very outset been ignored. The manner of performance of the debtor was taken as a mere illustration of a much broader principle of good faith. Ironically, the case envisaged by § 242 BGB itself plays only a minor role in German law. We may refer the reader also to chapter 8 concerning the manner of performance, below. § 723 II BGB illustrates a similar point: a partnership may not be terminated without good reason at an inappropriate time. If this rule is not obeyed, the relevant partner will be liable for the resulting loss. This shows that in some instances not only the manner of the performance by the debtor may be questionable, but the enforcement of a right by the creditor may be objectionable. The right as such is not contested but merely the manner in which its enforcement is attempted. (For a further example, see BGHZ 27, 220, which suggests that when a contract of services is terminated with immediate effect, the employer of a sales representative may be limited to the relying on reasons indicated in the note of termination and may not change or add to them subsequently.)

(c) Implying Collateral Obligations

Courts regularly invoke good faith when they establish collateral obligations owed between contracting parties or when fleshing out the (main or collateral) obligations of the parties. This is referred to as the *Ergänzungsfunktion* of good faith, its 'supplementing' function. The interventions taken separately appear to be relatively minor, though of no less significance to the parties concerned and, considering their added effect, quite remarkable. At times, the intervention of the court can plausibly be brought under the heading of 'interpretation' or contractual 'construction'. Indeed, the courts sometimes quote both relevant codal provisions simultaneously.

Paragraph 157 BGB is, in fact, the provision which deals with contractual inter-pretation, requiring that this is undertaken in accordance with good faith, due regard being had to general practice. At first sight this seems to overlap with § 242 BGB; and in some cases the result achieved through § 242 could arguably also have been based on § 157 BGB. This in part explains the huge importance that good faith has in German law. It is a vehicle for the courts to specify the obligations owed by the parties in the absence of express provisions in the contract. The Code will spell out the main obligations of the parties regarding most types of contract and, although less often, expressly stipulate collateral obligations (for illustrations, see section 4, p 144, on individual types of contract). Yet it goes without saying that not all possibly relevant obligations can be specified in a code. This is where good faith comes in. This abstract concept enables the courts to fashion new obligations by implying into the contract appropriate terms in law, even where they are not sup-ported by the actual intentions of the parties. New institutions, such as that of con-tracts with protective effects towards third parties, also owe their justification to the same, cardinal notion.

There is one type of obligation that can be singled out for special treatment. It is the so-called *protective* duty (*Schutzpflicht*). In abstract terms, it states that one party should not violate the interests of the other party. Broadly speaking, it is derived from the principle of *neminem laedere*. This obligation may arise also in a pre-contractual context, as was explained in the section on *culpa in contrahendo* in the previous chap-ter (see, RGZ 78, 239, case no 25, customer injured by linoleum roll; BGHZ 66, 51, case no 26, daughter of customer slips on vegetable leaf; discussed in chapter 2, p 96). It constitutes a breach of this obligation, for instance, when a seller supplies a defec-tive object thereby causing physical damage to other property of the buyer or to his health. From this it can be immediately seen that these obligations will often be con-tractual obligations that mirror duties of care that belong (in the common law) to tort law. Such obligations exist in most legal systems; the peculiarity of German law is that these duties of care are rationalised also in terms of collateral *contractual* obligations. The German preference for contract, noted on many occasions in *The German Law of Torts* (eg, p 703), manifests itself here, motivated once more by arguable 'structural weaknesses' of German tort law, referred to throughout this book. (See also, the discussion in BGHZ 66, 51, case no 26.)

Yet, as can be seen from English cases, collateral contract duties resembling duties of care in tort are known also to the common law. An excellent example of this phenomenon is provided by the case of *Esso Petroleum Co Ltd v Mardon* [1976] QB 801, where the representation made by Esso's local manager concerning the likely throughput of petrol at the Eastbank Service Station induced Mr Mardon to take a lease of the petrol station from Esso. Under the *Hedley Byrne* principle allowing recovery of economic loss occasioned by a negligent misstatement, the Court of Appeal held Esso liable in the tort of negligence. However, their Lordships also ruled that the representation as to throughput amounted to a contractual warranty (the warranty being that Esso had made the assessment of throughput with reason-able care and skill) that had induced Mr Mardon to enter the contract, so that breach of that warranty sounded in damages. The Court was at pains to emphasise that Esso had special knowledge and skill—as Lord Denning MR pointed out (at 818):

It was the yardstick [the estimate as to throughput] by which they measured the worth of a filling station. They knew the facts. They knew the traffic in the town. They knew the throughput of comparable stations. They had much experience and expertise at their disposal. They were in a much better position than Mr Mardon to make a forecast. It seems to me that if such a person makes a forecast, intending that the other should act on it—and he does act on it, it can well be interpreted as a warranty that the forecast is sound and reliable in the sense that they made it with reasonable care and skill.

Shaw LJ stressed the need to examine the context in which any such representation was made (at 831):

What is clear . . . is that the answer to the question warranty or no warranty cannot be given by looking simply at the words which are used. How must the respective parties have regarded the representation when it was made? How were they then related respectively to the subject matter? What was the purpose of making the representation and might it influence the outcome of what was in negotiation between the parties? The answers to these questions will provide the touchstone for answering the ultimate and critical question, did the representation made found a warranty by the party making it?

All this makes clear that, while the English courts have referred to the incidence of such collateral contracts as 'rare' (see Lord Moulton in *Heilbut, Symons & Co v Buckleton* [1913] AC 30, at 47), they are prepared to examine the circumstances carefully and to come to an objective assessment as to whether such a representation was intended to operate as a contractual warranty. Equally, it should be noted that the relevant facts referred to by Lord Denning also play a key role in deciding on *Hedley Byrne* liability. This suggests a tolerance, not only for contractual duties of care that resemble those in tort, but for the concurrent operation of such duties. (See further, *Henderson v Merrett Syndicates* [1995] 2 AC 145; *Barclays Bank plc v Fairclough Building Ltd (No 2)* [1995] IRLR 605 and the discussion in *The German Law of Torts*, pp 336–8 and 348–56. Note also the famous American case of *Hoffman v Red Owl*, 133 NW 2d 267 (Wis 1965), which was decided on promissory estoppel grounds. It seems likely that the *Esso Petroleum Co Ltd v Mardon* case could also sound in negligent misrepresentation in the US.)

The reform of 2001 (BGBl. I, 3138) of the German law of obligations endorsed this contractual approach to 'protective' obligations. The opening paragraph of the law of obligations, § 241 BGB, now introduces two sets of obligations flowing from a 'relationship of obligation' (*Schuldverhältnis*): the obligation to perform an act in § 241 I and the obligation not to prejudice the interests of another in § 241 II.

The first type (representing the original position of the BGB, § 241 I BGB) relates to the performance of an obligation, where performance (ie, the commission of a positive act) was promised (*Leistungspflicht*): one party may demand performance of the obligation of performance from the other party. A great number of such performance obligations are set out in more specific terms in the special part of the law of obligations (and in chapters 9 and 10 we will discuss the consequences of a failure to perform). For example, the obligation of a seller to supply the thing sold: § 433 I 1 BGB. Paragraph 241 I BGB articulates the expectation interest of a party and, interestingly (although this is secondary in the present context—see chapter 9, below, for fuller discussion), entitles the creditor to (specific) performance and not merely damages.

In § 241 II BGB, the Code itself for the first time expressly provides for an abstract, general obligation mutually owed between the parties to respect the rights and interests of the other party depending 'on the content of the relationship of obligation.' This new section validates the previous and well-established practice of the courts of implying 'protective' obligations (*Schutzpflichten*) into contracts. The abstract formulation of the principle does not aid the inference of more specific obligations in the individual case. Hence, while good faith, the previous foundation of this jurisprudence, has been given a more distinct shape, nothing has changed so far as practical application is concerned. It should be stressed that this section does not, despite appearances, establish the broad principle of *neminem laedere* in relation to tort law. Tort law is governed by the more specific 'general clause' of § 823 I BGB, which limits the duty of care to the protection of certain 'absolute' rights: property, health, etc and excluding pure economic loss (see *The German Law of Torts*, chapter 2).

While these 'protective' obligations (*Schutzpflichten*) may be slotted into a special category due to their resemblance of duties of care in tort law, there is a plethora of other collateral contractual duties which cannot be traced back to one single principle (*Neben-Leistungspflichten*). In general, it can be said that their implication is often necessary to make the contract work out as it was originally intended, or rather when the courts think it reasonable to impose a certain obligation. This phenomenon confirms two observations often made in relation to good faith.

First, it cannot be doubted that it creates insecurity in the law. Yet one must not forget that the courts are aware of this danger and seek to alleviate it by proceeding incrementally, on a case-by-case basis, and at the same time trying to limit their intervention by attaching great weight to the actual intentions of the parties in the individual case. This however cannot make up for the second aspect of the deployment of good faith to justify interferences with the contract, namely that it does serve to regulate and police rather than simply enforce contracts (this is the very characteristic of the third dimension of good faith discussed in the next sub-section). We can only give a few examples here of typical implied obligations before returning to this theme of implying terms into a contract in the next section on interpretation. Note, however, that they cannot be easily equated with one particular concept or singular technique in English law (eg, some of the ground may be covered by terms implied in fact by the courts, others may find expression in specific statutory rules, etc). The development of the numerous, secondary obligations referred to, for instance, in the section on breach of contract, offers good examples and we refer the reader to the law discussed in chapter 9. The remaining obligations may tentatively be further sub-divided along the following lines. The reader is referred to specialised treatises on the subject for further details (see further, GH Roth's account in the *Münchener Kommentar* § 242 Rn. 141–337).

The common denominator of these collateral obligations is that they relate to the *performance* of the *main* obligations owed by the parties. The parties are under an obligation to assist each other in respect of the performance of the contract where good faith requires it. Such an obligation is likely to arise where it is necessary to secure the effectiveness of that performance. Again, the precise scope of this obligation can only be determined by looking at individual cases. Such a duty of co-operation may arise in a purely commercial context, as RGZ 101, 47, case no 40, illustrates. One party may be under an obligation to provide documentation where this is necessary in dealing with tax authorities (eg, BGH NJW 1992, 1695) or where it is needed to procure a loan (eg, BGH NJW 1973, 1793). Similarly, where the performance of the contract hinges on some act by the other party, the other party is required to co-operate, for instance where the required authorities' approval of the transaction depends on it (eg, BGH NJW 1989, 1607). In company law the general obligation flowing from good faith to facilitate the performance of the contract and abstain from acts which may endanger performance, has more specifically led to the creation of a number of 'equitable' obligations (*Treuepflichten*) between shareholders or partners (see, eg, BGHZ 129, 136. We must leave a comparison with fiduciary obligations to more specialised work). To give another important example, in the law of contract governing labour relations many such duties of 'equitable' character (*Treue-, Fürsorgepflicht*) are said to be vital considering the long-term character of such contracts and the resulting trust relationship between the parties (see for details, Preis in *Erfurter Kommentar zum Arbeitsrecht* (4th edn, 2004) § 611 Rn. 754 *et seq* and compare the English position as discussed in Deakin and Morris, *Labour Law* (4th edn, 2005)).

Even though there is no general obligation to disclose information in support of claims of the contracting parties, such an obligation may be derived from good faith in the individual case. These obligations are referred to as *Auskunftspflichten*. If a plaintiff is excusably ignorant of his rights—for instance, if his trademark rights are violated but he does not possess enough information to quantify his claim—then the defendant may be under a duty to supply it to him (RGZ 108, 1, 7; case no 41; an alternative way of achieving a similar result is to delay the start of the period of limitation until the claimant knew or should have been aware of his claim—in English law see, eg, section 32 of the Limitation Act 1980). As the court put it: 'In such cases in which a right to information by the debtor greatly facilitates the prosecution of rights and often is the only means of making the latter possible, the principle of good faith . . . requires that a claimant, who is excusably unaware of the existence and extent of his right, be given that information from the debtor who has easy access to it.' (See now also, § 19 *Markengesetz*.) This example is interesting in a number of respects.

Good faith serves here to achieve some of the results of the English approach to pre-trial discovery (since the Woolf reforms of English Civil Procedure, known simply as 'disclosure' (see Civil Procedure Rules, Part 31). For detailed discussion, see Andrews, *English Civil Procedure* (2003) chapter 26.) It should be noted that the key point here is how far a legal system is prepared to facilitate and enforce pre-action disclosure. The further a system goes in this regard, the more strongly it will rely on 'access to justice' arguments (see, eg, the position in the US); the UK has been more reluctant to sanction such disclosure, although there is a fairly wide power in the Civil Procedure Rules to achieve this, and it has been granted quite commonly by the courts in personal injury claims (again, see Andrews, *English Civil Procedure*, chapter 26).) The German law of civil procedure does not facilitate the acquisition of information by one of the parties from their opponent (quite narrow exceptions relating to documents have recently been introduced, eg, § 425 ZPO). Together with a strict handling of the substantive burden of proof rules, this absence of pre-trial discovery sometimes gives plaintiffs severe difficulties of proof. However, where the plaintiff is excusably ignorant of the relevant information and at the same time it is easy for the defendant to supply the information, the courts are prepared to impose an obligation on the latter to disclose the information (see in addition, BGHZ 10, 385). This is of great practical value, for instance in calculating the amount of maintenance owed according to the provisions of the family law section of the Code (eg, BGH NJW 1988, 1906; claim by one parent against the other for the supply of information needed to calculate the amount of maintenance owed towards the child).

Duties of disclosure of a different kind form the next category. While the obligation to supply information discussed so far (*Auskunftspflicht*) is geared towards the information necessary in order to carry out the obligations provided for in the contract (to calculate the amount of maintenance owed to the other party or to prepare a law suit), the duties here under consideration, the so-called *Aufklärungspflichten* ('duties to inform'), arise before the formation of the contract and affect the motivation for entering into the contract. In German law, as indeed in English law, it is presumed that when negotiating a contract each party may pursue its own interest, especially when dealing at arm's length. While it is not permitted actively to misrepresent facts, one party is as a general rule allowed to keep certain facts to himself even if they are known to be vital to the other party (see, in English law, *Norwich Union Life Insurance Co Ltd v Qureshi* [1999] 2 All ER (Comm) 707, at 717 for a similar starting point). However, German courts have in some circumstances imposed an obligation to reveal certain crucial information before the contract is concluded. It suffices here to note that these duties are derived from good faith. (For the English position, see Treitel, *The Law of Contract*, pp 392–9. A particularly good example is a contract *uberrimae fidei* (or of 'utmost good faith')—particularly important in the insurance industry. In US law, these matters are treated as incidents of the duty to disclose, which extends into both contract law (eg, as a basis for avoiding a contract) and tort law (as a basis on which to sue for damages).) Since these issues relate to the question as to when a contract may be set aside, this line of cases will be considered in more detail in chapter 6.

(d) Policing the Contract

One must bear in mind that the rulings in the cases discussed under the heading of abuse of rights (above, section 2(b)) are not to be generalised. They are but mere examples of certain types of conduct which may in extreme cases justify the intervention of the court and disallow the enforcement of an otherwise perfectly valid right. What these examples have in common is that they relate to an overall assessment of the conduct of one of the parties that appears grossly unfair, either because it is self-contradictory, or in no way appropriate in the circumstances. One may object to this by saying that the judge should not interfere at all and it is for the parties alone to determine the limits of contractual rights. What should be noted, however, is that the courts in these cases do not look (or at least do not purport to look) at the terms of the contract in order to decide whether they are just. In this respect, one could explain the approach in the cases discussed in the previous section on the basis of procedural fairness. (Indeed, in American law this would be the province of UCC § 2-302 and the concept of procedural unconscionability.)

In relation to the creation of collateral duties (sub-section (c), above) we noted that the courts have resorted to good faith a great deal in order to imply terms in law into contracts and create or 'discover' all sorts of collateral duties. This, again, is not directed against the terms of the parties' agreement but aims to complete them in the absence of express provisions in the parties' contract. Creating default rules in the absence of express terms is a task which, in principle, is also performed by the common law judge, although perhaps with less frequency. Operating with the presumed intention of the parties, however, often conceals the fact that the court is, in reality, 'policing the contract.'

So finally, the question arises whether the concept of good faith enables the courts openly to police the express terms of a contract as such, ie to modify or annul them in accordance with the court's view of substantive justice. Generally speaking, this is not the case. Good faith in German law, it should be stressed, does not *as a general rule* empower the judge to look at the terms of the contract and decide whether they are substantively fair, ie, whether the price agreed is 'just' or whether the bargain evinces a significant imbalance in the parties' rights. (This is in fact the test laid down in Article 3 of Directive 93/13/EEC concerning the use of standard terms.) Nevertheless, there are three major lines of cases, each raising special considerations, in which German courts have been bold in using good faith in interfering with the content of a contract, the third of which is a direct result of the effect of the constitutional values on private law relationships and is interlinked with the development in German law of a theory of the indirect horizontal effect of the constitution (a topic discussed in some detail in *The German Law of Torts*, pp 28–32, 406–12, 472–84 and 499–505).

The *first* line of cases is discussed in chapter 7—which deals with what we call 'frustration' in Anglo-American law—involved some very bold judicial constructions, and indeed re-constructions of contractual obligations (referred to as the so-called *Korrekturfunktion* of good faith). The reason for this judicial boldness is, as we shall see, the fact that the Civil Code, drafted during an era of stability, implicit optimism, and legal positivism, omitted all treatment of this subject. This, too, should be borne in mind by teachers using this book. For French civil law is, likewise, guilty of such an omission; yet it failed to develop a private law doctrine of frustration.

The *second* line of cases, by now almost completely transmuted into statutory law, concerns the policing of 'pre-formulated' contract terms, 'standard terms of business,' and exclusion clauses in particular. Even before a specialised statute regulating standard terms was passed (*Gesetz zur Regelung des Rechts der Allgemeinen Geschäftsbedingungen* of 1 April 1977, now repealed), the German courts had assumed the power to strike out specific standard terms if they thought them grossly unjust (according to the requirements of good faith in § 242 BGB; note that in American law this function is the main work of unconscionability, although under insurance law the doctrine of 'reasonable expectations' would also play an important role). In fact, they still do, even outside the scope of that statute. The role of good faith in this development must be understood in terms of rules of state organisation rather than contract law. It brings us back to the general point, raised by way of introduction, on how one keeps a code up-to-date. Good faith was a means for the courts to achieve the results later provided for by specialised legislation. How successful this judicial 'reform' of the law can be is illustrated by the very fact that the legislator subsequently endorsed the judicial rulings. With the latest reform of the BGB of the year 2001 (BGBl. I, 3138), one has come full circle: the legislator, while abolishing the special standard terms statute, incorporated the respective provisions in §§ 305 *et seq* into the Code itself. We will return to these provisions in more detail below.

One final note may be added. Perhaps somewhat ironically, it is now an EC Directive (93/13/EC) that has introduced the notion of good faith, a concept that in German law served as the basis on which to police standard term contracts, into English law as well.

Finally, turning to the *third* line of cases, in chapter 1 we have already pointed out the crucial role that general clauses have played in the process of the constitutionalisation of private law. Its main tenet can be put thus: general clauses and the inherently vague notions imported into the BGB by them are to be interpreted in the light of the constitution. Human rights thus acquire an indirect horizontal influence on private law relationships (the so-called *mittelbare Drittwirkung*). The principle of good faith is such an 'entrance point' for constitutional values. As was explained in chapter 1, this approach is not without its difficulties. It will be recalled that the outcome of the balancing act required between the competing constitutional values is difficult to predict. It should also be noted that it is on the whole arbitrary which of the general clauses is used in justifying the indirect impact of the human rights arguments (which contrasts with similar developments in English law where, since the advent of the Human Rights Act 1998, the vast majority of references has been to the role of the courts as a public authority under section 6 of the 1998 Act (although reference might also be made to sections 3 and 12 in certain contexts: see Deakin, Johnston and Markesinis, *Markesinis & Deakin's Tort Law* (5th edn, 2003), pp 68–71 and the references cited therein)). This is quite natural given the inherent vagueness of concepts such as public policy or good faith. On the whole, however, the discussion tends to focus on § 138 BGB rather than § 242 BGB (possibly because the legal consequence of § 138 I, invalidity, is more suitable to human rights violations) and it is for this reason—and the more adequate thematic context of chapter 5—that we postpone further deliberations to that part of this book.

We are thus lucky to be able to provide an illustration for the impact of constitutional values on § 242 BGB (though note that the court indicated that the result derived from § 242 BGB could also have been achieved by applying § 138 BGB). (The decision must be read in conjunction with the other decisions referred to in chapter 1 on the impact of human rights on general clauses.)

In BAG NZA 1994, 1080, case no 42, an employee whose task it was to promote certain packaging products was given notice during the trial period despite his good performance, apparently because he was homosexual. The court held that the dismissal constituted a violation of his right of personality guaranteed by Article 2 I in conjunction with Article 1 of the Basic Law (*Grundgesetz*) and therefore was contrary to good faith (§ 242 BGB) and hence void. The case contains all of the typical ingredients of a human rights dispute in a private law context. Both parties could rely on human rights considerations. The employer could invoke the right guaranteed by Article 2 I of private autonomy in the sphere of private law freely to dismiss an employee during the trial period. Indeed, the very purpose of the trial period was to enable the employer to dismiss an employee without having to justify the termination of a long-term contract. This was to be weighed against the right of personality of the employee freely to determine his sexual orientation. The court came down in favour of the employee on the ground that the private life of the employee was no concern of the employer and the employee's sexual orientation did not affect in any way the performance of the employee's obligations under the labour contract. While these arguments seem plausible, it cannot be denied that the interference with the contract was quite substantial. For if the employer is normally entitled to dismiss the employee without having to justify his decision it seems somewhat far-fetched to declare a dismissal void because its presumed motivation was contrary to human rights. (In American law, note that such a claim would clearly not be entertained under contract law: instead, it would fall under the tort of 'wrongful discharge' (also known as the 'public policy tort').)

3. THE SOURCES OF CONTRACTUAL TERMS: INTERPRETATION AND BEYOND

Bickel, *Die Methoden der Auslegung rechtsgeschäftlicher Erklärungen* (1976); Coing, *Die juristischen Auslegungsmethoden und die Lehren von der allgemeinen Hermeneutik* (1959); Hager, *Gesetzes- und sittenkonforme Auslegung und Aufrechterhaltung von Rechtsgeschäften* (1983); Kötz, 'Vertragsauslegung' in *Festschrift Zeuner* (1994) 219; Kramer, *Grundlagen der vertraglichen Einigung* (1972); Leonhard, 'Die Auslegung der Rechtsgeschäfte' AcP 120 (1922) 14; Lewison, *The Interpretation of Contracts* (3rd edn, 2004); Lüderitz, *Auslegung von Rechtsgeschäften* (1966); Mangold, 'Eigentliche und ergänzende Vertragsauslegung' NJW 1961, 2284; Mayer-Maly, 'Die Bedeutung des tatsächlichen Parteiwillens für den hypothetischen' in Festschrift Flume (1978) 629; Scherer, *Andeutungsformel und falsa demonstratio in der Rechtsprechung des BGH* (1987); Singer, *Selbstbestimmung und Verkehrsschutz im Recht der Willenserklärungen* (1995); Smith, *Contract Theory* (2004), chapter 8; Ulmer, 'Teilunwirksamkeit von teilweise unangemessenen AGB-Klauseln?—Zum Verhältnis von geltungserhaltender Reduktion und ergänzender Vertragsauslegung' NJW 1981, 2025; Wieacker, 'Die Methode der Auslegung des Rechtsgeschäfts' JZ1967, 385.

(a) General Observations

Generally speaking, in interpreting contract terms one can adopt one of two approaches: a subjective or an objective approach. Contracts bring on the parties obligations that they themselves intend to incur. It therefore seems natural to contend that the prime purpose of interpretation is to seek to identify the true, subjective and shared intentions of the parties. This was indeed the main claim of the will theory advocated for instance by Friedrich Karl von Savigny (see his *System des heutigen Römischen Rechts*, vol 3 (1840), especially § 130) and Bernhard Windscheid (see his *Lehrbuch des Pandektenrechts*, vol I (6th edn, 1887). Windscheid emphasised (§ 69, at pp 186–7):

> *Es wird der Wille erklärt, daß eine rechtliche Wirkung eintreten solle, und die Rechtsordnung läßt diese rechtliche Wirkung deswegen eintreten, weil sie vom Urheber des Rechtsgeschäftes gewollt ist.* (The will declared is directed at a legal consequence, and the legal order gives effect to this legal consequence because it is intended by the author of the declaration.)

Here, the parties' subjective intention is regarded as the guiding principle and not as a factor among others. § 133 BGB is a clear manifestation of this theory, no doubt arousing, at first sight, some suspicion in the mind of a common lawyer. A declaration of intention is to be interpreted by seeking the 'true intention' without regard to the declaration's literal meaning. A contract consists of two declarations of intention—offer and acceptance. Hence, is one to infer that contracts are to be interpreted subjectively in German law? The answer is, on the whole, negative. The will theory was watered down considerably in the final draft of the BGB, despite Windscheid's views as an academic.

An objective approach to interpretation (*Auslegung*) is presupposed by the rules as to mistake contained in § 142 and §§ 119 *et seq* BGB (to be discussed in detail in chapter 6). The contract, as derived from the objective meaning of the declaration of the parties' intentions, is valid unless rescinded on the basis of a deviation of the objective meaning from the subjective intention. In addition, § 122 BGB entitles the other party, who relied on the contract as construed objectively, to claim the loss flowing from rescission. Accordingly, the courts have from the very outset applied to this matter an objective test.

Apart from drawing on the rules found in the section on mistake, the courts could more broadly base this approach on § 157 BGB (discussed above) which stipulates that contracts are to be interpreted according to the requirements of good faith, giving consideration to common usage. Indeed, the reader of the previous section will recall that 'good faith' has some bearing on the interpretation of contracts. The principle of good faith often serves to correct a result reached on a different ground. Good faith in the context of interpretation thus enabled the courts to give prevalence to the objective meaning of the terms of a contract.

It is perhaps no coincidence that the practice in common law jurisdictions is analogous. Pragmatic reasons weigh heavily in favour of an objective approach when considering the merits of the rivalling approaches. If contracts, which on their face display perfect agreement, are in fact void because there was no meeting of the innermost minds of the parties, one could never be sure whether a contract is valid. There are no means to determine the hidden, subjective (and from an objective point of view, mistaken) intentions of the parties. Thus, to rely on the judicial or other divination of such intentions, would create insecurity and endanger the administrability of the law. Commercial certainty, and therefore commercial convenience, are furthered if contracts based on objective agreement are prima facie valid (even if they may afterwards be rescinded by one of the parties). Another difficulty with the will theory is establishing the loss flowing from the reliance on the objective meaning of a declaration of will. It is easier to determine the financial position of the promisee if he had known that the contract (as objectively construed) would have been rescinded.

A famous illustration of the objective approach is found in BGHZ 91, 324, case no 43. In this seminal case the court held that an objective approach applies not only in relation to the content of a contract, but also in respect of the intention to enter into the contract in the first place. There, the promisor was not aware that he was 'promising' anything; yet the other party's reliance on the objective appearance of his conduct was protected. The question is controversial, as the court also acknowledged. For, while there is consensus that a declaration of intention must be interpreted objectively, many consider it necessary (in order to preserve the autonomy of the party in question) that the very act of making this declaration must be supported by an intention to utter a legally relevant declaration. (See eg, Wieacker, JZ 1967, 385; Thiele, JZ

1969, 405; the case is also discussed in chapter 6. For brief discussion of the English approach to intentions to create legal relations, see above, chapter 2, p 86). As a basic matter however in the common law this reliance on the objective appearance of the other party's conduct is entirely uncontroversial.)

It is necessary to add five important glosses or qualifications to the general rule that what prevails is the objective meaning of an offer (or an acceptance).

First, the objective meaning is determined from the perspective of the addressee of the declaration (*objektive Empfängerhorizont*) by taking into account the special circumstances of the position of the person making the declaration as far as they were (or should have been known) to the addressee. The method of interpretation is thus objective, taking account not only of the (written) statement of intention itself, but of the other (known) circumstances and the context in which the statement was made.

Secondly, one notes a certain tension between subjective and objective tests within the general part of the BGB. This is the result of the battles between the different schools of thought alluded to at the beginning of this section. How the objective test embodied in § 157 BGB can be reconciled with § 133 BGB (which refers to the true intention of the parties) has remained controversial. Yet, nowadays, the issue is of only theoretical (if indeed any) importance.

Thirdly, there is consensus that where the true intention of *both* parties coincides but deviates from the objective meaning of their declarations, good faith does not require that the literal meaning prevails. Where the parties' *shared* subjective understanding deviates from the objective understanding the subjective understanding prevails. This was held in the famous *Haakjöringsköd* case (RGZ 99, 147, case no 44). In the Norwegian language *Haakjöringsköd* refers to shark meat. Somehow, the parties to the transaction mistakenly believed the word referred to whale meat. What was actually delivered was *Haakjöringsköd*. In the court's view, the delivery of shark meat constituted a breach of contract. (This is also the position of the US Second Restatement.)

Fourthly, it is important to note that the objective approach is not confined to offer and acceptance but applies to all declarations of intention that bear on the contractual obligations of the parties, such as rescission, ratification etc. Since § 157 BGB only mentions the 'contract' itself, this section is applied by analogy to any other such declaration of intention.

Fifthly and finally, although the true scope of application of § 133 BGB is much diminished, it should be noted that it embodies the exclusive test when it comes to the interpretation of unilateral legal transactions independent of contract, such as wills (§ 1937 BGB): in such situations, a subjective test is applied.

(b) Comparative Observations

Comparing the German approach with the common law, it immediately springs to mind that the parties' 'true intentions' are given more weight in the civil law. The common law lays great emphasis on commercial certainty and thus on the administrability of the law. How else can one explain such apparently harsh concepts as the parol evidence rule? It should be noted that there are a number of important exceptions and qualifications to the parol evidence rule, notably including situations where the written terms do not cover the whole agreement (*Allen v Pink* (1838) 4 M & W 140), as an aid to construction where terms in the contract are ambiguous (*Prenn v*

Simmonds [1971] 1 WLR 1381) and (although not strictly an exception *per se*) to prove that a oral contract had been agreed that was collateral to the written contract (*Mann v Nunn* (1874) 30 LT 526; and see (and cf) *City and Westminster Properties (1934) Ltd v Mudd* [1959] Ch 129: an oral collateral contract was found by the court, even though it contradicted the written contract), provided that there was an intention to create such legal relations and consideration to support that contract (Treitel, *The Law of Contract*, p 200). Nevertheless, it is the case that the parol evidence rule can operate to cause injustice while performing its function of promoting certainty: see *Hutton v Watling* [1948] Ch 398, especially at 404. Finally, note the vital procedural role that the parol evidence rule plays in the US, since it allows contract interpretation to be kept out of the hands of civil juries. (On English law see generally, McKendrick, *Contract Law*, chapter 2 and Vorster, 'A Comment on the Meaning of Objectivity in Contract' (1987) 103 *LQR* 274. On the parol evidence rule, see Law Commission, *Law of Contract: The Parol Evidence Rule* (Law Com No 154 Cm 9700, 1986)).

Yet the difference may not be as great as it seems and first appearances may be deceptive. The importance of the written text in establishing the meaning of a contract and the exclusion of evidence to prove the text wrong, enhance certainty at a high price where it can be determined objectively from the context of the declaration that the parties' intentions were otherwise. The sole reliance on the written words has also become questionable against the insights of philosophy of language emerging in the last century. It is thus interesting to note that, at least so far as commercial contracts are concerned, the House of Lords in recent times seems to be prepared to apply a more flexible approach, focusing on the *context* in which the words were used (see *Investors Compensation Scheme Ltd* v *West Bromwich Building Society (No 1)* [1998] 1 WLR 896. See, for a discussion of the *ICS* case, Kramer, 'Common Sense Principles of Contract Interpretation' (2003) 23 *OJLS* 173. Note also, the Californian case *Pacific Gas & Elec Co v GW Thomas Drayage & Rigging Co* 442 P 2d 641 (Cal 1968), which is on very similar lines, and compare the trenchant criticism of that case in *Trident Center v Connecticut General Life Ins Co* 847 F 2d 564 (9th Cir 1988). See also the approach taken by Article 8(3) CISG, which allows all circumstances to be taken into account in the interpretation of a contract). How far and how much of this approach (so far) has moved substantially beyond the previous position is a matter of some debate. Staughton LJ has summarised the position as follows (*Youell and Others v Bland Welch & Co Ltd and Others* [1992] 2 Lloyd's Rep 127, 133–4):

> It is now, in my view, somewhat old-fashioned to approach such a problem armed with the parol evidence rule, that evidence is not admissible to vary or contradict the words of a written contract. The modern approach of the House of Lords is that, on the positive side, evidence should be admitted of the background to the contract, the surrounding circumstances, the matrix, the genesis and aim. Almost every day in these Courts there is a contest as to what comes within that description. As Lord Wilberforce said in *Reardon Smith Line Ltd v Hansen-Tangen* [1976] 2 Lloyd's Rep 621, at p 624 col 2; [1976] 1 WLR 989 at p 995, the expression 'surrounding circumstances' is imprecise. But so to some extent is 'matrix', if I may say so, although it is a picturesque metaphor. It may well be that no greater precision is possible. The notion is what the parties had in mind, and the Court is entitled to know, what was going on around them at the time when they were making the contract. This applies to circumstances which were known to both parties. And to what each might reasonably have expected the other to know.

> The negative aspect of the modern doctrine is that evidence of negotiations is not admissible as an aid to interpretation, at all events unless they show an agreed meaning for the language used.

Smith ('Making sense of contracts' [1999] *SLT* 307) has argued that the extent of the use of *context* is significantly greater, tending towards the *implication* (rather than merely interpretation) of terms. See eg, *Phillips v Syndicate 992 Gunner* [2003] EWHC 1084; [2004] Lloyd's Rep IR 426, at [23], where Eady J cited the 'old' approach of *The Moorcock* ((1889) LR 14 PD. 64; [1886–90] All ER Rep 530) and the 'modern' approach of Lord Hoffmann in *ICS* to the implication of terms. There is also the further, potentially difficult, issue of how far the context (or 'factual matrix'—see *Prenn v Simmonds*, above) extends and what it includes. (See Smith, 'Making sense of contracts' 311–12 and recent cases on the point, such as *BP plc v GE Frankona Reinsurance Ltd* [2003] 1 Lloyd's Rep 537, at [80], point 5: 'the background knowledge which would reasonably have been available to the parties at the time of the contract.' From this formulation, it seems that this context could extend beyond what the parties actually knew at the time. Where a literal interpretation entailed a ridiculous commercial result—or in the words of Lord Hoffmann 'commercial nonsense'—then the court could depart from the text. However, it seems that this still is the exception rather than the rule (see, for an illustration of the rule, *Centrovincial Estates plc v Merchant Investors Assurance Company Ltd* [1983] Com LR 158; The Times, 8 March 1983 and *Benjamin Developments Ltd v Robert Jones (Pacific) Ltd* [1994] 3 NZLR 189, at 202–3 (*per* Henry J (in the New Zealand CA)); see generally, Staughton, 'How do Courts Interpret Commercial Contracts?' [1999] *CLJ* 303.) The exception is available only where either the falsity of the text is obvious or the text leads to obviously unreasonable results.

On the other hand, it cannot be denied that the text of an agreement also attracts considerable weight when the meaning of contract terms is disputed before a German court. The starting point of interpretation will invariably be the wording of the contract. A party claiming that an unequivocal statement was meant in a different way bears the burden of proof for this contention (BGH NJW 1995, 3258; in BGHZ 21, 109 it was held that the party who seeks to derive a benefit from the text bears the burden of proof for any evidence outside the text; likewise, BGH NJW 1984, 721). Those circumstances in which such a claim (or an attempt) may succeed may also justify a departure from the parol evidence rule—hence, the difference may not be so great after all. German courts make a basic assumption that is very similar to that underlying the outcome and much of the reasoning in the *ICS* case, referred to above. It is to be assumed that—in the case of doubt, ie, where the wording is ambiguous—the parties intended what is reasonable/sensible (*das Vernünftige*) in the circumstances. Thus, a particular construction of a term which would mean that the parties agreed on something that makes no sense is to be avoided as contrary to the reasonable interests of the parties (eg, BGH NJW 1999, 3704, case no 45). That interpretation is to be preferred which ensures coherence in the contract as a whole and is compatible with the nature of the contract and the requirements of the law (illustrations of this can be found in: BGH NJW 1997, 1003; NJW 1981, 816. *Münchener Kommentar*- Mayer-Maly and Busche, § 133 Rn. 56, give further references). Of course, what is reasonable is often far from clear and may be a vehicle for the covert importation of policy considerations. The point we wish to make here, however, is that the overall approach of the German and English courts is (despite different starting points) remarkably similar.

In legal transactions subject to formal requirements, the courts attach greater significance to the wording of the contract, which again can be taken as an instance of convergence. When a contract is subject to certain formal requirements—eg, in writing, notarial authentification etc—the parties' intention must be properly articulated in the text itself (see eg, the judgment of Lord Hoffmann in *Mannai Investments Co Ltd v Eagle Star Life Insurance Co Ltd* [1997] 2 WLR 945, at 969C-D, where his Lordship acknowledged the need to respect compliance with any strict formalities laid down by the contract). In establishing the meaning of the text, resort to circumstances outside the text can then only be had if the text at least can be taken 'somehow' to allude to them (the so-called *Andeutungstheorie*; eg, BGH NJW 2000, 1569: § 766 BGB; BGH NJW 1983, 672: interpretation of a will). The courts are at pains to emphasise that the test does not preclude an inquiry as to the real intentions of the parties; it is only when it comes to the assessment of whether requirements regarding formalities have been met that some evidence may have to be disregarded. It should be noted, however, that the test is vague and has given rise to artificial constructions of the text. Many reject it for this reason. (Eg, Flume, *Allgemeiner Teil*, vol II, § 16, 2a; *Münchener Kommentar*- Mayer-Maly and Busche, § 133 Rn. 53.)

We may conclude our more general observations on the choice between objective and subjective approaches by quoting Judge Learned Hand's well-known formulation of the objective approach (in *Hotchkiss v National City Bank of New York*, 200 F 287, 293 (SDNY 1911)):

> A contract has, strictly speaking, nothing to do with personal, or individual, intent of the parties. A contract is an obligation attached by the mere force of law to certain acts of the parties, usually words, which ordinarily accompany and represent a known intent. If, however, it were proved by twenty bishops that either party, when he used the words, intended something else than the usual meaning which the law imposes on them, he would still be held, unless there were some mutual mistake, or something else of the sort.

The reminiscence of the will theory is too strong in a German judge's mind to allow him to agree with the first line of this bold statement. In his eyes, contract has everything to do with the personal intent of the parties. But he will go on and immediately qualify his starting point by adding that good faith requires that the word of twenty bishops has no weight if it is deployed to disprove the objective meaning of a declaration of intention.

(c) Express Terms, Terms Implied in Fact and in Law

While the approach used by the English and German courts to determine the meaning of express terms of the contract may be said to be surprisingly similar, at least in certain important respects, it cannot be ignored that interesting differences start to appear if one looks at the determination of terms implied in fact and in law. The reason why we call them 'interesting' is because they reveal the predilection of German judges to interfere with the contract rather more often than their English counterparts. The section on good faith, above, has suggested that German courts imply a term more easily where they think fit than their English counterparts and this tendency is much aided by the broad approach to interpretation already explained. The interpretation of the contract, by applying § 157 BGB, extends beyond the bare text of the agreement. It includes also the context of the contracting process, peripheral circumstances, and an analysis of the parties' interests. This is why in German law interpretation can be a powerful tool for the implication of terms. However, it would be an exaggeration to contend that the overall approach is—if contrasted to the English judge's neutrality or 'diffidence'—*inherently* paternalistic. Though exaggerated reactions must be avoided, overall there can be little doubt that German courts are more readily prepared to imply terms into a contract.

It should be noted from the outset that the distinction between express terms, terms implied in fact, and terms implied in law, should be made only with extreme caution in German law. The German concept of 'completive' contract interpretation (*ergänzende Vertragsauslegung*) is not an exact equivalent of terms implied in fact. In German law, the parties can agree 'tacitly' to a term even though it was not expressly articulated. In this case, the courts will infer the agreement as to the term from the actual intention of the parties as 'expressed' by their conduct. By contrast, it seems that in English law this case would be regarded as an application of the rules on terms implied in fact (see *Shirlaw v Southern Foundries (1926) Ltd* [1939] 2 KB 206). Completive interpretation is in German law to be distinguished from such 'tacitly' agreed 'express' terms.

Regarding completive contract interpretation, it is said that this applies where it is not possible to determine the (tacit or express) *actual* intention of the parties even if the context of the text is taken into account. If the contract contains a 'gap', the filling of this gap by means of interpretation is then based on a *hypothetical* intention of the parties. It can be easily seen that in German law the preferred way of distinguishing contract terms is by focusing on the method used in establishing them, and less on whether they are articulated in the text of the agreement or orally.

We may illustrate this by giving a few examples. In RGZ 117, 176, 180, case no 46, it was held that a merchant, who promised to a vendor who sold him his business and its good will that the vendor would get a share in the profits for ten years following the sale, was entitled to expect from the vendor that he would not set up a competing business for at least that period of time. The court found that the parties 'tacitly' agreed on the term. This, the court derived from the context of the agreement, the interests of the parties, and the general scheme of the contract. It was thus not necessary to resort to the narrower notion of completive interpretation in justifying the term. The next two cases, however, represent the first step along the path from interpretation to creative construction.

In RGZ 131, 274, case no 36, a tenant of leased premises was allowed to stop the landlord from letting adjoining premises to a businessman who carried out the same trade as he did. The court—which used both codal provisions, § 157 and § 242, to reach its conclusion—accepted that normally there is no such implied term in contracts of lease. 'The statutory duty to afford the tenant the use of the leased property does not, of itself, embrace an obligation to protect him from competition,' reasoned the court. Given all the facts of this case, however, such a term was in the end implied by the court.

One also finds decisions which, for instance, say that a defendant/developer/vendor of land may not build on land adjoining that he sold to the plaintiff, if such building would destroy the view that could be enjoyed from the plaintiff's land. (See RGZ 161, 330, case no 47.) Again, such a result will not normally be sanctioned, especially if there is no such covenant in the relevant contract. Yet such a conclusion may follow where the price charged for the first sale was high because of the exceptional view available to the land. 'Accordingly,' reasoned the court 'it was a feature of the purchased land [known to both contracting parties] that it should provide an unimpeded view of the wooded slopes of the neighbouring mountain and that this view could not be curtailed by the erection of building on the intermediate strip.' (English law would treat this issue as a question of the law of restrictive covenants relating to freehold land: see Harpum, *Megarry & Wade—The Law of Real Property* (6th edn, 2000), chapter 16, particularly p 1017, note 73. It is not possible to acquire an easement for insufficiently precisely defined rights, such as 'a view': see the venerable *William Aldred's Case* (1610) 9 Co Rep 57b, at 58b; 77 ER 816—'for prospect [ie a view], which is a matter only of delight, and not of necessity, no action lies for stopping thereof . . . the law does not give any action for such things of delight' (*per* Wray CJ). However, this area has mainly focused on the enforcement of express covenants as against subsequent owners of adjoining land, rather than the implication of such obligations in the original contract of transfer. If any such representation that no building would take place on the adjoining land were made during the contract negotiations, then it is possible that proprietary estoppel could operate to achieve a result similar to that in RGZ 161, 330, case no 47, although there is a remedial discretion in the court, so that the remedy given may not exactly mirror that of an express restrictive covenant: see Harpum, chapter 13, and the discussion in chapter 2, p 81 ff.)

Finally, terms implied in law are not commonly referred to as '*implied terms*'. German law does not make much use of the concept of 'terms' implied in law. Rather, German law speaks in terms of the 'obligations' of the parties to the contract imposed by the Code. Accordingly, they are better referred to as 'default rules', rather than 'terms implied in law' into, the contract. As was explained in the previous section, one of the main functions of good faith is taken to be to empower the courts to imply into the contract a wide range of collateral obligations, all flowing from the presumed intentions of parties assumed to be 'acting in good faith.' We must return to this issue here since it also helps to explain the relationship between interpretation and judicial 'law reform' in German law.

(d) 'Completive' Interpretation (*ergänzende Vertragsauslegung*)

English courts adhere to the essentially sound principle that, in implying a term in fact, it must be asked whether the parties would have agreed to it and not simply whether it would have been reasonable to do so. Whether German courts also subscribe to this principle is open to doubt. On a conceptual level, however, there are similarities.

Supplementing the contract requires first that there is a gap in the contract, ie a certain situation is not covered by an express term of the contract and it cannot be said that the parties 'tacitly' agreed on a solution.

In filling the gap (which, as indicated, may be wider in English law), English courts sometimes apply the officious bystander test (*Shirlaw v Southern Foundries (1926) Ltd* [1939] 2 KB 206, 227: a term so obvious that it goes without saying) and sometimes a 'business efficacy' test (*Luxor (Eastbourne) Ltd v Cooper* [1941] AC 108, 137: a term that is necessary to give the transaction business efficacy). As to the relationship between the two, see Treitel, *The Law of Contract*, pp 202–3, who describes the position as 'not entirely clear.' If the key point is to give effect to (some formulation of) 'the intentions of the parties' (*Luxor* (above), at 137 (*per* Lord Wright)), then it would seem that either of the two tests is a sufficient condition for the implication of a term in fact, so long as the evidence of the parties' intentions does not run contrary to such an implication (see, eg, *Clarion Ltd v National Provident Institution* [2000] 1 WLR 1888, 1896–7).

Similarly, in German law it is said that it is of first importance that the judge in filling the gap spells out the logical or normative implications of the contractual framework set out by the parties. The metaphor of a 'gap' imports this very idea: only where a term is necessary to ensure the purpose of the contract can it be said that the contract is *incomplete*. (See, for illustrations of this approach, BGHZ 16, 71, 76 and BGHZ 23, 282, case no 48.) The task of the court is not to interfere with the terms of the contract as it thinks just, but merely to complete the contract by inserting a term on which the parties would have agreed had they actually considered the unforeseen situation. (The so-called 'hypothetical intention of the parties,' *hypothetischer Parteiwille*. BGHZ 9, 273, 278; BGHZ 23, 282, case no 48.)

The difficulties start to emerge when, in addition to the actual intentions, concepts such as reasonableness or (in German law) 'good faith' are utilised in determining the hypothetical intention(s) of the parties. Good faith is indeed routinely referred to as a yardstick against which to test whether the parties would have agreed to a term if they had considered the situation. (For example, BGHZ 23, 282, case no 48; BGH NJW 1981, 2241; NJW 1998, 1219.) German academics are at pains, however, to emphasise that completive interpretation does not give the judge a 'free mandate' to draw up contract clauses as he pleases and ascribe them to the 'reasonable' intentions of the parties. In filling the gap, one ought not to apply a general standard of reasonableness, but draw reasonable conclusions from the parties' actual intentions. (See eg, Ulmer, NJW 1981, 2025; *Münchener Kommentar*- Mayer-Maly and Busche, § 157 Rn. 38). This is also the position of the English courts, which have repeatedly stated that they would not imply a term simply because it is reasonable to do so, but would insist that it was necessary to give the agreement 'business efficacy' (see eg, *Reigate v Union Manufacturing Co (Ramsbottom) Ltd* [1918] 1 KB 592, at 605 (*per* Scrutton LJ). Further, the courts seem to take the view that express evidence of the parties holding intentions contrary to the proposed implication will prevent any such implication. (See the *Clarion* case, referred to above). In a similar vein, the *Bundesgerichtshof* stressed that, in such gap-filling, creative interpretation (even though based on good faith) cannot justify a result that is incompatible with the actual intention of the parties or which would unduly alter the object of the contract (BGHZ 9, 273; NJW 1984, 1177). The purpose of completive interpretation may thus be likened to terms implied in fact, although note how far the method was carried in relation to contracts for the benefit of third parties, discussed in the next sub-section.

(e) Default Rules and Terms Implied in Law

The Code contains what we referred to as 'default rules', ie a great number of, if not always the most crucial, terms implied in law. They will take effect unless the contract stipulates otherwise. The reader will also recall the section on completeness of the offer in the previous chapter. These default rules are referred to in German law as *dispositives Recht*, ie rules that can be departed from by agreement, as opposed to *zwingendes Recht*, ie strict (imperative or mandatory) law out of which the parties cannot contract.

Thus, the sections on sale of goods imply terms as to the required quality of the goods sold (§ 434 BGB, cf section 14 of the Sale of Goods Act 1979). Likewise, the provisions concerning leases determine when the rent is due (at the beginning of the relevant time interval covered by the lease, § 556b I BGB) and thus imply in law such a term into the contract. § 618 BGB applies to a contract for services and imposes a duty of care on the employer, in particular to ensure that the employee is not endangered by the condition of the rooms in which he is working or the tools with which he is provided. Examples such as these abound in the Code. Thus, each section of the Code dealing with a specific kind of contract contains numerous provisions setting out the obligations of the parties and in this way indirectly specifies the terms that will be implied in law (for details, see the next section). This does not mean that if there is a default rule in the Code covering the case at hand there is no room for completive interpretation. In particular, if the contract comprehensively regulates complex issues (such as the relationship between the parties in a partnership) the parties cannot be easily presumed to have relied on default rules if the contract contains a gap (an illustration is provided by BGH NJW 1993, 3193).

One must, of course, point out the obvious, namely that the Code does not contain all terms implied in law and all essential default rules. 'Even' in a civil law system, it remains for the courts to discover new terms imposed by law and refine or adapt existing ones which are not satisfactory. On certain occasions, the German legislator expressly has left it to the courts to develop the law further, sometimes eventually incorporating the rules developed by the courts into the Code. This happened in the case of *culpa in contrahendo* and the concept of the foundation of the transaction (now found in §§ 311 II and 313 BGB respectively, discussed in detail in chapter 2, section 5, and chapter 7 respectively).

In a codified system, however, such judicial activism is bound to be seen as (more) suspicious and in need of justification. The *primary* task of the judiciary in a civil law system is not to create law but to apply it. For these essentially institutional reasons, a German court is not entirely free to imply terms in law outside the ambit of the existing default rules. It is from this perspective that the function of § 242 BGB becomes fully apparent. It enables the courts to imply terms in law where the default rules of the Code are not regarded as sufficient or adequate. This is a delicate task, for the courts may not overstep the limits set by the Code and create default rules *contra legem*. Any assessment of what these legal limits actually are may well be controversial. The reference to good faith mainly serves to impose a number of collateral obligations on the parties, which we discussed in the previous section of this chapter in the context of § 242 BGB. As we will see also in chapter 9, p 469 ff, numerous such duties of care, warning, supervision and advice have been introduced into contracts and can also remain alive, even after the termination of the contract. (Thus, see the *obiter dicta* contained in RGZ 161, 330, 338, to the effect that after the termination of a lease, the landlord may still be under a duty to display for a reasonable period of time the new address of his former tenant. See, also, RGZ 117, 176, 180, case no 46, discussed above.)

A common law judge, on the other hand, is much less impeded by (obvious) institutional considerations in implying terms in law. (On the debate about institutional
constraints on English judges in carrying out their interpretive, legal development and
enforcement functions, see Lord Reid, 'The Judge as Law Maker' (1972–73) 12
JSPTL (NS) 22 and Sir Stephen Sedley, 'The Sound of Silence: Constitutional Law
without a Constitution' (1994) 110 *LQR* 270.) The hesitation on the part of common
law judges over the introduction of terms implied in law is, rather, dictated by doctrinal reasons rooted in the protection of freedom of contract. Nevertheless, it is clear
that English courts *do* imply terms in law: the Sale of Goods Act 1979 is itself a
codification of previous case law. See also, for a more recent example: *Re Charge Card
Services* [1989] Ch 497, 513, implying a term on the ground of fairness (although
Treitel (*The Law of Contract*, p 211) would prefer to see such use of terms like
'fairness' and 'reasonableness' understood within the context of the particular type of
contractual relationship in question (see eg, Lord Radcliffe's observation (in the context of frustrated contracts) in *Davis Contractors Ltd v Fareham Urban District
Council* [1956] AC 696 at 728, that '[b]y this time it might seem that the parties themselves have become so far disembodied spirits that their actual persons should be
allowed to rest in peace. In their place there rises the figure of the fair and reasonable
man. And the spokesman of the fair and reasonable man, who represents after all
no more than the anthropomorphic conception of justice, is and must be the court
itself.')

The policy arguments in favour of implying terms or in favour of a rule of law or
'default rule' can be more easily identified if a term is implied in law than if, in an
attempt to conceal judicial creativity, the term is ascribed to the fictitious 'intentions'
of the parties. A symptom of this latter, doubtful technique is that the courts imply a
term as an incident of every contract of that kind, ie on the basis of abstract criteria
and not on the basis of the actual intentions of the parties. Sometimes the distinction
between terms implied in law and in fact is less clear than it arguably should be in
German law. The good faith element in *ergänzende Vertragsauslegung*, implying terms
in fact, enabled the courts to transcend the actual intentions of the parties and imply
terms, not which the parties would have included, but which they *should* have included
in the contract. One famous example of this approach is the development of the contract with protective effects towards third parties. This concept is based on § 157 BGB
and completive interpretation, though there can be little doubt that we are confronted
here by rules and terms imposed by law. Since the concept mainly serves to get around
the absence of true vicarious liability in tort law, and furthermore to solve certain
cases of negligent misrepresentation, it is dealt with in some detail in *The German Law
of Torts*, pp 59 *et seq* and 291 *et seq* and also in the privity chapter of this book (chapter 4, section 3, p 204). It should be emphasised however that this tendency runs contrary to what also in German law is considered as the gist of completive
interpretation, namely giving effect to the intention of the parties not modifying it.
German courts are reluctant to acknowledge that in these lines of cases they are not
implying terms in law, because this would require them to discuss the rationale of
these rules more openly. The upshot of this is not, it should be stressed, that German
courts are not able properly to apply the concept of terms implied in fact, but that
sometimes they (mis-)use the concept in order to avoid objections directed against
developing default rules outside the strictures of the Code.

4. SPECIFIC TYPES OF CONTRACT

Selected reading (with rich references to specialised monographs): Oechsler, *Schuldrecht Besonderer Teil– Vertragsrecht* (2003); Oetker and Maultzsch, *Vertragliche Schuldverhältnisse* (2nd edn, 2004); for a compact exposition: Brox and Walker, *Besonderes Schuldrecht* (29th edn, 2004), §§ 1–31.

(a) Preliminary Observations

The 'special part' of the Code's Book on the law of obligations includes provisions that regulate particular types of contract. The contract of sale is the paradigm among them. However, it should be recalled from our discussion in the first chapter that the Code also contains many rules relating to contract in different sections or parts of the Code. If one considers how much of German contract law is, in fact, common to all types of contract, it makes sense to speak of a German law of 'contract' rather than of a German law of 'contracts'. Thus, in German law, most major issues are subject to general rules. So, the formation of a contract is dealt with, as has been explained in chapter 2, in the general part of the BGB, which also contains the general rules on mistake and those relating to standard terms, but also rules as to the performance and discharge of an obligation. To give a final example, the general rules relating to irregularities of performance are contained in the 'general part' of the law of obligations (§§ 280 *et seq* and 320 *et seq*). It is against this background that the rules contained in the 'special part' of Book Two of the BGB must be understood. Seen in this way, the often-claimed difference in approach between German and English law turns out to be less significant. For English law, too, consists of a body of shared general rules and special regimes of rules differentiated along the lines of particular kinds of contracts. Indeed, readers of *Chitty on Contracts* will notice a division between a general and a special part and this illustrates our point very well.

The rules of contract law regulating specific types of contract fulfil two main purposes. The first is to set out the requirements as to the performance of the parties which are to be met in the absence of express stipulations. Some of them have already been discussed in the section on the completeness of the offer in chapter 2. These provisions describe what is expected from a promisor in relation to certain kinds of promises. They define the presumed intention of the parties in relation to particular and rather typical transactions of everyday life. In English law, we would speak of terms implied in law and sections 13–15 of the Sale of Goods Act 1979 are an example in point (compare the German law equivalent, § 434 BGB).

The second main purpose of this special part of the law of obligations is to introduce variations to the general rules contained in the other parts of the BGB. Thus, to give another example from the sale of goods, § 437 BGB refers to the general rules as to irregularities of performance but subjects them to certain modifications. (Compare sections 51 and 53 of the Sale of Goods Act 1979.) Sometimes, these special rules provide an idiosyncratic system of remedies, as is the case in relation to the law of leases (eg, § 536a BGB). This interplay between rules of general and special nature can give rise to (technical) difficulties and constitutes one of the challenges of establishing a complex system of rules such as that of the BGB. Generally speaking, these special rules are not strict (in the sense of obligatory law) for in their turn they can be varied by agreement between the parties. Note, however, that the rules concerning standard terms (discussed in the next section) have made it more difficult to deviate from default rules in 'pre-formulated' contracts (§ 307 II Nr. 1 BGB, discussed below). Consumer protection lies behind introducing strict rules; and it has sanctioned significant intrusions into the notion of freedom of contract. (For example, § 475 BGB: consumer sales.) While some of the special incidents of particular types of contract are discussed in those parts of this book dealing with irregularities of performance, it may be useful to give at this stage a brief overview of the different types of contract which have received special attention by the BGB. They are, as explained, an important source of the terms of such contracts. (Note that certain types of contract are regulated outside the BGB, for instance the contract of insurance. See *Gesetz über den Versicherungsvertrag* of 30 May 1908 as amended.)

Several ways of dividing these different types of contract could be devised. One can thus conveniently distinguish (cf Brox and Walker, *Besonderes Schuldrecht*) between contracts involving the permanent 'transfer' of a right or corporeal thing (eg, sale, barter, donation), contracts enabling the other party to make a particular 'use' of a right or thing for a limited or unspecified period of time (eg, lease, rent, loan, lending, leasing) and contracts for the provision of 'services' (eg, contracts for work, services, labour contract, mandate, surety). Another way of distinguishing these transactions would be to differentiate them on the basis whether one party promised a counter-performance in return of performance (eg, price of a corporeal thing, rent) or not (eg, 'lending', mandate), which does not necessarily mean that the contract is 'gratuitous' (eg, surety). Roman law, while moulding many features of contemporary German law, put the different types of contracts in yet another different order. For instance, Roman lawyers classified the letting and hiring of things, services and work under one single contract (namely *locatio conductio*. See, Zimmermann, *The Law of Obligations* (1990), p 338). Yet again, Kant's table of contracts (in his *Metaphysik der Sitten* (1797) § 31) claimed to be comprehensive, including all conceivable contracts. It rationalises all contracts as contracts of 'acquisition' (gratuitous, onerous and contracts for security)—the provision of services, for instance, is said to involve the transfer of the right to use one's talents (see Byrd, 'Kant's Theory of Contract' in Timmons (ed), *Kant's Metaphysics of Morals* (2002), p 121 *et seq*). These distinctions are of theoretical importance, but to some extent also pragmatic, depending on which particular element is stressed, and we need not pause too long in discussing them here. (In US law, for example, the principal distinction is usually drawn between sales law (which is codified) and the rest of contract law (which is not), although certain other more specialised bodies of law seem to have 'outgrown' any place in the simple 'contract' canon (eg, oil, gas and mineral leases).)

Though these divisions take up large amounts of space in student text books, they are not of the same system-building 'quality' or importance as the divisions discussed in chapter 1, p 27 ff, between the 'contract of obligation' and the 'contract of transfer' (principles of separation and abstraction) and between 'causal' and 'abstract' legal transactions. The significance of these cornerstones of German private law must be recalled, however, before the individual types of contract are approached in what follows.

The principle of separation has important consequences for the regime of duties incumbent on the parties. Thus, contracts which involve the permanent transfer of an object (right or corporeal thing) from one party to the other will not, according to the principle of separation, automatically transfer the object itself. A separate, so-called 'abstract' legal transaction is necessary in order to achieve that transfer (eg, assignment, § 398, or contract of transfer of property in chattels plus *traditio*, § 929). Consequently, such contracts 'of acquisition' (*Veräußerung*)—sale (§ 433, *Kaufvertrag*), barter (§ 480, *Tausch*) and donation (§ 516, *Schenkung*)—necessarily contain (as one of the main obligations of the promisor) the duty of the promisor to transfer the object of the contract to the promisee. Systems of private law (such as the French), to which the principle of separation is not known and where consequently the transfer occurs pursuant to the contract of sale, do not need to stipulate for such an obligation on the part of the promisor.

Unlike these contracts of acquisition, leases, loans and similar contracts do not involve the permanent transfer of an object but merely the granting of a right to make a particular use of an object for a definite or indefinite period of time (*Gebrauchsüberlassung*). Normally, this entails that the promisor is not required to transfer any proprietary rights as to the subject matter of the contract: transfer of possession suffices. To this category belong the contract of rent of movables and immovables (§ 535, *Mietvertrag*, note the extended form in § 581, *Pachtvertrag*) and the 'lending' contract (§ 598, *Leihe*). There are however special forms of such 'transfer of use' contracts, which do involve the transfer of property in the object of the contract. These are the loan of money (§ 488, *Gelddarlehen*) and the loan of movables (§ 607, *Sachdarlehen*). Here, the property in the subject matter is transferred. At the end of the loan period, the promisee is under an obligation merely to return the same sum of money or, in the case of chattels, objects of the same kind, quantity, and quality.

Another group of contracts which share important features are contracts of employment (§ 611, *Dienstvertrag*), contracts for work (§ 631, *Werkvertrag*) and travel contracts (§ 651a, *Reisevertrag*). They all involve the 'use' of the promisor's skills and labour. The difference lies in whether, in addition to the performance of the particular act, the achievement of a specific result is also promised.

From a wider perspective, if one regards the performance of a service in its widest meaning as the guiding principle, the following contracts can also be included here, though no doubt due to their different categorisation in Roman law they are usually treated separately.

Services, in a wide sense, also encompass mandate (§ 662, *Auftrag*, which as explained in chapter 2 must be strictly distinguished from agency, § 164), the management of affairs for remuneration (§ 675, *Geschäftsbesorgung*), brokerage contracts (§ 652, *Maklervertrag*), contracts for the keeping of chattels (§ 688, *Verwahrung* (which basically equates to the common law concept of bailment)), and surety (§ 765, *Bürgschaft*). Surety, unlike the other contracts in this list, must be singled out as a transaction of personal security (as opposed to a security *in rem*, such as retention of title: § 499, *Eigentumsvorbehalt*).

(b) Contract of Sale

The contract of sale (*Kaufvertrag*) is regulated in the BGB in §§ 433–73 which have been considerably modified by the recent reform of the law of obligations (BGBl 2001 I, 3183). These general rules apply irrespective of the person entering into the contract and represent therefore the core of German sales law. However, special rules were recently introduced for consumer sales in §§ 474–9 as a result of EC legislation (see Directive 99/44/EC). (For the UK implementation, see the Sale and Supply of Goods to Consumers Regulations 2002, SI 2002 No 3045, which made various amendments and additions to existing legislation, in particular the Sale of Goods Act 1979, eg, the new Part 5A on 'Additional Rights of buyer in Consumer Cases'. The impact of the 2002 Regulations is discussed by Willet, Morgan-Taylor and Naidoo in [2004] *JBL* 94 (and the references cited therein).) Paragraphs 358–9 contain special rules concerning sale contracts financed by consumer credit. § 449 II regulates hire-purchase agreements. And §§ 481 *et seq* implement the time-share Directive 94/47/EC (in the UK, see the Timeshare Regulations 1997 (SI 1997 No 1081), which make various amendments to the Timeshare Act 1992.) The Commercial Code (HGB) also contains a number of deviations as to the remedial regime in contracts of sale concluded between merchants (§§ 373–82 HGB). This includes, for instance, the buyer's duties of inspection. Finally, Germany is a party to the 1980 United Nations Vienna Convention on the International Sale of Goods (CISG). This Convention may apply (as provided in its Articles 1–6) to international contracts of sale (see Schlechtriem and Schwenzer (eds), *Commentary on the UN Convention on the International Sale of Goods* (2nd edn, 2005)). Note that barter (*Tausch*) is governed by one provision only, § 480, which declares sale of goods law applicable to such contracts. The above clearly display the growing importance of the international background on national law, alluded to at the beginning of the first chapter of this book. (English law has not escaped from these influences yet they are less clearly reflected in English textbooks, which still tend to downplay the growing internationalisation of modern contract law.)

The main duties of the seller are to hand the thing over to the purchaser, to provide the property in the thing and to provide the thing to the purchaser free from physical and legal defects (§ 433 I). As explained above (and in chapter 1) the contract of sale does not transfer ownership; hence it stipulates for an obligation to transfer title. Whether or not property passes is thus subject to the rules of property law (§§ 929 *et seq* concerning movables and §§ 873 and 925 concerning immovables). § 449 does in one respect bridge this gap between the 'contract of obligation' and the 'contract of transfer' for it contains the default rules as to retention of title as security for the payment of the price. The seller may be under a number of collateral obligations regarding the protection of the integrity of the buyer (§ 241 II, see the section on good faith for details; one purpose of implying such duties is to circumvent certain 'weaknesses' of German tort law). The main duty of the buyer is to pay the price, § 433 II. The BGB contains a number of further collateral duties of the buyer. Thus, he is obliged to take over the thing sold (also § 433 II), bear the cost of shipping the goods to another place than the place of performance (§ 448 I) or, if land was sold, the cost of notarial authentication and land registration (§ 448 II). A special regime of limitation periods for claims arising out of a defect of the thing sold is set up by § 438. (Note that the special regime of liability of the seller is discussed in chapter 10, p 494, and irregularities of performance more generally in chapter 9.)

The rules on sale of goods apply in principle also to the sale of a right (§ 453 I). This means that the seller has the duty to transfer the right, which normally occurs through assignment (§ 398; land law contains special provisions for mortgages and the like, eg, §§ 873, 1154). Note, that factoring in German law may involve the sale of a right (so-called *echtes Factoring*, where the assignee bears the risk of insolvency of the debtor; BGHZ 69, 257; contrast: BGHZ 58, 367). § 453 I stipulates further that the law of sale of goods also applies to objects 'akin to rights.' An important example is the sale of a company, which is thus, presupposing that the company as a whole was the object of the transaction, subjected to the rules on sale of goods (eg, BGH NJW 2002, 1042). Finally, certain specific sale contracts are dealt with in § 454 (sale by sample), § 456 (option of buying back the thing sold) and § 463 (option to interpose into a contract of sale). Note that irregularities of performance and the remedies available to seller and buyer (including the issue of passing of risk) are discussed in chapter 9, below.

(c) Donation

The rules on the making of gifts—donation (*Schenkung* = §§ 516–24)—have been touched on in chapter 2 in the context of formal requirements and signs of seriousness. From a comparative perspective this also constitutes the most intriguing aspect. Consideration is not required for the valid agreement by which one person from his assets enriches another person and both agree that the transaction is gratuitous (§ 516 I). The '*causa*' for the donation is the agreement between the parties that one party enriches the other. However, such one-sided obligations are regarded as potentially dangerous by German law. To protect and warn the donor, his promise to make the donation is subjected to strict formal requirements in § 518 I (notarial authentication). No such form is necessary, however, for an instantaneous donation carried out on the spot (ie, which is not preceded by a contract of donation). This so-called *Handschenkung*, § 516, is informally valid. Also, where a prior promise of donation is effected, which means that the donated object is transferred according to the rules of property law, the defect in form is cured, § 518 II. This is an example where the contract of transfer serves as an indication of the seriousness and is therefore taken to 'validate' the contract of obligation (see on this, chapter 1, principle of separation and abstract legal transactions).

An account, however brief, of the German law of donation would not be complete without a reference in passing to the following three rules. First, there is § 530, which entitles the donor to revoke the contract on the ground that the donee has been ungrateful. Secondly, there is § 528, which allows the donor to re-claim the donation according to the rules on unjustified enrichment (§§ 818 *et seq*) if he becomes poverty stricken. (See, on this and other points of comparative interest in this area, Dawson, *Gifts and Promises: Continental and American Law Compared* (1980).) Modern practice has it that this right will often be exercised by the State via subrogation, where it seeks to recoup social welfare payments (eg, BGH NJW 2004, 1341). Thirdly, § 521 contains a rule typical for gratuitous transactions, namely the standard of liability of the promisor is restricted to intent and *gross* negligence.

It should be noted that donation does not cover all gratuitous transactions. The rules as to lending (§ 598) and mandate (§ 662) regulate important special cases which follow distinct rules. Finally, a line of cases has emerged in German law in which, although no 'counter-performance' in the strict sense was agreed, the transaction was nevertheless not treated as gratuitous in the sense of § 516 (or for this purpose, § 662). The problem arises mostly in relation to 'gifts' between spouses which are claimed back after divorce. The BGH explains these transaction as being founded on the marital community and not a 'gratuitous' transaction in the technical sense. Instead, the court developed a relationship of obligation *sui generis*, the basis of which may collapse with an ensuing divorce and thus may give rise to claims according to the rules on a change in the foundation/basis of the transaction (§ 313, discussed in chapter 7, below. See eg, BGHZ 84, 361; 129, 259.)

(d) Contract of Rent

The contract of rent or tenancy, *Mietvertrag* (§ 535) covers the use of corporeal things, both movables (eg, renting a car) and immovables (eg, 'leases'), for remuneration. If the right to use the object includes the right to the product or fruits of this object (defined in § 99; quite literally, eg, the fruits of an orchard; or in the case of a right, the dividends of shares for instance), then §§ 581 *et seq* contain special rules for these contracts (so called *Pachtverträge*). As a general rule the regime of rules of the contract of rent applies by analogy (§ 581 II; unless the subject matter is land).

The main obligation of the promisor of the promise to rent (*Vermieter*, the landlord in the case of immovables) is to enable the promisee to use the corporeal thing which is the object of the contract for a certain amount of time (§ 535 I), while the tenant owes as his principal obligation the payment of the agreed rent (§ 535 II). The tenant must further return the object at the end of the contract (§ 546 I), though this obligation is not part of the *Synallagma* (ie, not a counter-performance). The promisee must keep the object in good repair (§ 535 I 2); but it is possible (and common) to impose on the tenant of premises an obligation to carry out the repairs which have become necessary as a result of normal wear and tear (*Schönheitsreparaturen*, eg, BGHZ 92, 363). Again, the parties owe each other the collateral obligations not to cause physical damage to the other party (§ 241 II).

With regard to this type of contract the BGB contains fairly detailed rules, especially since a major reform of this part of the law in the year 2001 (BGBl. I, 1149), which has included in the Code matters that were previously dealt with by special statutes. It suffices to here to mention two of their features. (Irregularities of performance are, as with the other contracts, discussed in the respective chapter.)

First, special attention is paid to the termination of the contract (*Kündigung*, see, §§ 541–5, 568–74c, 575a, 576a, 577a, 580 and 580a). Generally speaking, if the contract was entered into for a specified period of time, then the contract comes to an end at the stipulated end of that period (§ 542 II). The parties have 'exceptionally' (*außerordentliche Kündigung*) a right to terminate the contract for an important reason (*wichtiger Grund*): § 543. The main example of a sufficient reason is where one of the parties has committed a clear breach of the contract, eg, the tenant fails to pay rent. (Normally, two months' missed rent is sufficient to justify termination, cf § 543 II Nr. 3; note however § 569 III as to the residential leases). If the contract was entered into for an indeterminate period of time (*unbestimmte Zeit*), then the parties have, in addition to the 'exceptional' right of termination, the 'ordinary' right of termination which requires notice to be given in advance (§ 542 I). But this does not call for special justification (see, however, § 573, referred to below). The notice of termination must be communicated by the tenant in the case of private accommodation roughly three months in advance of the envisaged end of the lease (§ 573c I 1).

The *second* characteristic is that, unlike the original position of the BGB, the present regime of rules distinguishes quite strictly between the rent of movables and the rent of premises (especially residential leases, *Wohnraummiete*). Accordingly, §§ 535 *et seq* consist of a general part applicable to all contracts of rent (§§ 535–48), a special part containing rules directed at leases of premises used for private accommodation (§§ 549–77a), and rules governing the rent of other premises, land, and ships (§§ 578–80a).

The main impetus for setting up a special regime for private accommodation has been to protect the tenant who is deemed to be the weaker party. Indeed, if the lease could be terminated by the landlord without prior notice and for whatever reason, this could cause hardship to the tenant and to his family. After all, the residential space forms the centre of his private life. To this consideration, we must add the phenomenon of a fragile market. After the Second World War, for instance, there was in a Germany a severe shortage of accommodation. Accordingly, freedom of contract was much restricted in the interest of coping with this problem. A similar phenomenon of statutory protection for tenants (including businesses and agricultural holdings, as well as dwellings) can be observed in the UK (and, indeed, in the US) throughout the twentieth century, although more recent developments have moved back towards allowing greater freedom of contract and less statutory regulation of landlords. (For further details see Harpum, *Megarry and Wade—The Law of Real Property*, chapter 22, especially 1383 ff.) Nowadays, the market in Germany can be regarded as relatively stable so the regime of legal rules has become less strict, although important restrictions remain in place and new ones have been added. For instance, the reasons given for the termination of a contract by the landlord (§ 573, reasonable motive required) are still subject to close judicial control, as is the level of rent itself (§§ 556 *et seq*). Likewise, a sale of the premises does not terminate the lease: the purchaser is deemed to enter into the contract with the tenant (§ 566). (English law achieves this result by treating the lease (in appropriate circumstances) as an estate in land, and hence a proprietary interest that endures as against subsequent purchaser of the freehold. Nevertheless, it should more generally be noted that the 'contractual' (rather than proprietary) view of leases has gained strength in English law in recent years (by applying contractual reasoning such as the doctrine of frustration, seeing the rent as a contractually agreed sum rather than flowing from the land, etc.), although it is clear that a lease is still a legal estate in land. On this see Bright, 'Repudiating a Lease—Contract Rules' [1993] *Conv* 71 (discussing the case of *Hussein v Mehlman* [1992] 32 EG 59) and, for a useful summary, Harpum, *Megarry and Wade—The Law of Real Property*, pp 753–4 and the references therein). If the tenant dies, his family has the right to enter into the contract and continue it (§ 563). Other illustrations of norms belonging to what has been coined 'social tenancy law' (*soziales Mietrecht*) could be given. The reader is referred to the discussion of these issues in chapter 1, p 43, on freedom of contract and in chapter 10, p 533, on the contract of rent (see also, Cohen, *Manual of German Law*, vol 1 (2nd edn, 1968), pp 139–41 for a brief historical outline).

Modern forms of leases of chattels have emerged, which cannot be exclusively accommodated within the framework of the contract of rent as defined in § 535 (confusingly, the term, 'leasing', is used in German law). The so-called 'Operating Leasing', however, where the object is simply rented to the tenant, causes no difficulties and constitutes mostly a straightforward contract in the sense of § 535. Other forms of leasing have been more difficult to categorise. This problem concerns the so-called *Finanzierungsleasing* in particular, see also below, § 500, where the promisee in effect assumes the role of financing the 'purchase' price, here the 'lease' can be likened to a hire purchase agreement. These cases usually involve a triangular relationship between the seller, the lessor (*Leasinggeber*), and the lessee (*Leasingnehmer*). The interplay between the contract of sale between the seller and the lessor and the 'Leasing' contract between the lessor and the lessee is complex. The rights of the lessor against the seller are assigned to the lessee in return for a total exclusion of the liability of the lessor vis-à-vis the lessee; however, on termination of the contract of sale the foundation of the 'Leasing' contract is said to collapse (§ 313); see eg, BGH NJW 1985, 796, enabling the lessee to terminate the contract also with the lessor. (For a very helpful discussion of the finance lease in English law, see Goode, *Commercial Law*, chapter 28.)

(e) Lending

Lending, *Leihe* (§ 598) is the agreement to allow the use of a chattel or an immovable for a certain period of time *gratuitously* (thus distinguishing itself from 'rent', above; in the common law, this situation would usually be covered by a form of gratuitous bailment). The obligation of the lender is to grant the use of the object, while the borrower is obliged to return possession at the end of the lending period (§ 604). As is typical in gratuitous contracts, the standard of care of the lender is reduced to intent and gross negligence (§ 599). The contract can be immediately terminated as soon as the lender requires the object himself: § 605 Nr. 1. The contract does not play a crucial rule in practice though, and at first blush this might seem to be another situation where in German law a promise not supported by consideration is fully effective even in the absence of 'consideration' in the common law sense. However, it can be argued that a common law court would indeed find consideration under this fact scenario, on the basis that the bailee gets the use of the property in return for whatever promise he makes (while the bailor has effectively made a conditional gift). Sometimes, the distinction between such gratuitous contracts (where for instance § 599 would be available as a defence) and purely amicable acts (*Gefälligkeiten*) not governed by the rules of contract law, has caused difficulties. (See the discussion above in chapter 2, p 86 ff, on indications of seriousness.) In practical terms, this is not an important transaction.

(f) Loan and Other Forms of Credit

Since the reform of 2001 (BGBl. I, 3183) the loan of money is regulated by §§ 488–90 and the loan of chattels by § 607–9. In this contract, the creditor transfers full property in the subject matter and the debtor is under an obligation to return at the end of the loan objects of similar kind and quantity. The loan of money is important in practice and thus an outline is called for.

Paragraph 488 I BGB now clarifies that the contract of loan, like other contracts, requires two corresponding declarations of intention (*Konsensualvertrag*). The main obligation of the creditor is to provide the loan (§ 488 I 1). The counter-obligation of the debtor usually is to pay the agreed amount of interest (§ 488 I 2). Other bargains are possible, for instance a deduction from the loan (*Disagio*). It should be noted that the loan can also take the form of a gratuitous contract, where no interest or other counter-performance is agreed (§ 488 III 3). Another duty of the debtor is to pay back the loan (§ 488 I 2) which is however not part of the *Synallagma*, ie it is not the reason (*causa*) for the performance (the loan) but merely a necessary incident of every loan.

The termination of the contract follows the principles applicable to contracts running over a certain period of time and is accordingly referred to as *Kündigung*. Where no time for the repayment has been fixed, the parties are 'ordinarily' entitled to terminate the contract within three months. (§ 488 III 1, 2.) In practice however such a time is stipulated by the parties. In such cases only the debtor is entitled to terminate 'ordinarily' under certain conditions which depend on the nature of the loan and the nature of the interest agreed. (The details are stated in § 489.) § 490 provides an 'extra-ordinary' right of termination available to both parties. Thus, the creditor may terminate the contract where the financial position of the debtor deteriorates (§ 490 I).

Paragraphs 491–8 contain special rules for consumer credit transactions, implementing EC Directives 87/102/EEC and 98/7/EC. (For the English law on consumer credit and hire see the Consumer Credit Act 1974 ('CCA 1974'), as amended to implement the above-mentioned Directives. For details see Brown, *Commercial Law* (2001) Part III (chapters 30–8). Interestingly for comparative purposes, the UK legislation requires careful *classification* of the nature of such agreements ('regulated agreements', as defined by section 189(1) CCA 1974) and of the types of credit that are available to would-be debtors. The notion of a 'regulated agreement' is 'the key to an understanding of the scope of the Act' (Goode, *Consumer Credit Law and Practice* (looseleaf) vol 1, para [23.3]), since the agreement, itself, is regulated by the Act, as are many ancillary activities connected to the agreement. The question of licensing by the Office of Fair Trading is closely linked to the scope of such agreements.)

The means of consumer protection include special requirements as to form. (For example, § 492 I 1, 494; cf sections 55, 60 and 61 CCA 1974 and the Consumer Credit (Agreements) Regulations 1983 (SI 1983, No 1553), as amended. The Regulations are extremely detailed in their provisions of requirements of form, content, etc of regulated agreements.) There is a right to avoid the contract *ab initio* during the first two weeks after its conclusion (*Widerruf*, revocation) § 495; cf sections 57 (withdrawal); 67 and 68 (cancellation) CCA 1974, although these rights are subject to conditions: see Brown, *Commercial Law*, chapter 33.) One also finds a special protection of the debtor in the case of assignment (§ 496); special rules as to interest for late payment (§ 497) and so forth.

Paragraphs 499–504 regulate consumer contracts which do not involve a loan of money but which nevertheless serve the purpose of financing a transaction (*Finanzierungshilfen*). In part, these provisions refer back to the rules on consumer credit (§ 499 I) and in addition contain special provisions. The most important examples are the *Finanzierungsleasing* (§ 500, referred to above) and the payment of the contract price in instalments: *Teilzahlungsgeschäft* (§ 501).

Finally, § 505 (*Ratenlieferungsverträge*) deals with special consumer transactions which do not involve the financing of a transaction but which create similar dangers as they establish regularly recurring obligations to pay for the delivery of corporeal things (such as newspaper subscriptions). Again, the consumer is afforded special protection by inserting formal requirements, a qualified right of revocation, etc.

A common denominator of these special regimes of rules for credit contracts and similar contracts is that they impose as a general rule a minimum protection of the consumer, which means that they cannot be departed from to the detriment of the consumer (§ 506). To the extent that they give rights to one party to the contract, and indeed favour, the one considered to be weaker, they represent examples of the modern tendency to question if not overturn some traditional principles of contract law. On the whole, these are also provisions found in most so-called Western legal systems (America providing the most frequent exception) and can thus also be seen as providing evidence of the internationalisation of modern contract law.

(g) Contracts for Services

The contract for services or contract of employment (*Dienstvertrag*) is regulated in §§ 611–30. The main obligation of the employee is to provide the service as laid down in the contract. The counter-obligation of the employer is to pay the remuneration (§ 611 I). As § 611 II clarifies, the nature of the service can be of any nature whatsoever, although one should note that some specific types of service have been subjected to special rules (eg, *Makler*, § 652; *Geschäftsbesorgung*, § 675). (See on irregularities of performance chapter 9 and chapter 10, p 528.)

The main difference between the contract for services and the contract for work (*Werkvertrag*, § 632) which must be explained at the very outset, is that a contract for services does not stipulate an obligation to achieve a specific result. The employee merely promises to perform the act required of him in the contract. This becomes obvious if typical examples of contracts for services are analysed. § 611 covers what has been called the 'free' contract for services (in the sense of being less closely regulated) and also 'labour contracts' (*Arbeitsverträge*). The first category includes, for instance, a contract with a solicitor or a contract for treatment concluded with a medical doctor (*Arztvertrag*). In both these cases, the person 'hired' to provide the services is, generally speaking, only required to perform the service *lege artis* but does not (and usually cannot) promise a particular outcome (eg, that the disputed litigation is won or that the patient regains his health). This does not mean that contracts with such professionals may never come under § 632. Occasionally, they do involve the promise of a result (what French lawyers refer to as an *obligation de resultat*): for instance, the promise of a solicitor to draft contract terms.

Turning to the second main class of contracts of employment—labour contracts—it is equally clear that, for instance, a worker in a factory is required to show up at the factory gates at a certain hour and follow the instructions of his foreman but does not promise anything more, for instance a 'successful' end-result in the production process.

In the earlier discussion concerning the completeness of the offer (above, chapter 2, p 59 ff) we noted § 612. This stipulates that where a service is usually provided only for remuneration the law will presume that, in the absence of express stipulation, the remuneration will be fixed by reference to the 'usual' rates.

Like all contracts involving the use of a particular thing or service over a period of time, the right to termination of the contract (*Kündigung*, notice) acquires special importance. § 620 follows the already familiar pattern of distinguishing between contracts entered into for a specified period of time and those entered into for an indefinite period of time. In the latter case, the parties may terminate the contract by 'ordinary' notice (*ordentliche Kündigung*), which must be given a specified period in advance (see § 621 for 'free' contracts, and § 622 for labour contracts. On these matters, US law operates in a very different manner due to the presumption of employment at-will). All contracts of employment may be terminated 'extra-ordinarily' and without notice in advance for an 'important reason' (§ 626, *außerordentliche Kündigung*). This usually refers to when a gross violation of the duties of the other party is required. (For irregularities of performance, see chapter 9, below.)

The liability of the medical and legal professions plays an immense role in practice. They are obliged to take out liability insurance and are subjected to strict confidentiality requirements (sanctioned by criminal law, § 203 of the *Strafgesetzbuch*). The remuneration of lawyers is highly regulated so far as the cost of litigation is concerned (*Rechtsanwaltsvergütungsgesetz*); and a number of professional duties are set out by statute. More particularly, the contractual relationship between medical practitioner and patient is governed by the complex system of the statutory health insurance (*Gesetzliche Krankenversicherung*, regulated in: *Sozialgesetzbuch V*). This means, for instance, that the claim for remuneration arises not against the patient, but against a professional association of medical practitioners in charge of administering the health insurance scheme. This in turn is funded by particular public bodies that ultimately charge the patient, not on the basis of insurance premiums but on the basis of social criteria (ie, a fixed percentage of a patient's income). A less regulated contractual relationship arises with the smaller group of privately insured patients. Contracts involving treatment in hospital also comprise elements of other contracts (rent of the bed; contracts for work in respect of the meals, etc). (See, from the extensive literature: Katzenmeier, *Arzthaftungsrecht* (2002); Deutsch and Spickhoff, *Medizinrecht* (5th edn, 2003); Vollkommer and Heinemann, *Anwalthaftungsrecht* (2nd edn, 2003).)

It would be misleading to suggest that 'free' contracts of employment and 'labour contracts' share more than a number of abstract, formal characteristics, some of which have been discussed here. 'Labour contracts' are part of a special branch of law, the distinctiveness of which can hardly be gleaned from the few provisions in the BGB, although they too have started to distinguish as to the nature of the contract. Most of the regulations are contained in special statutes which do govern not only the content of the contract (eg, the extent of holiday, *Urlaubsgesetz*), but also a range of other important matters. These include the internal organisation of a company and the participation of employees in the internal affairs of the company (eg, *Betriebsverfassungsgesetz*), the status of trade unions and their power to determine working conditions, salary levels etc, by negotiations with representatives of the employers ('collective labour law' eg, *Tarifvertragsgesetz*), regulation of the 'end' of the contract—ie, restricting the reasons for dismissals (eg, *Kündigungsschutzgesetz*) and so forth. The power of the courts to control the terms of the contract and to evaluate the circumstances of the termination of the contract is also extensive. It cannot come as a surprise, therefore, to note that a special branch of the judiciary had to be set up to deal with labour law matters (now regulated in *Arbeitsgerichtsgesetz*).

Naturally, if the labour contract is heavily regulated it is of great importance to establish a clear demarcation line between free and regulated contracts. The courts have over the years developed a whole range of criteria for identifying true 'labour contracts.' The issue is complex, for not only is the concept differently defined in the various pieces of specific legislation, but the concept also does not have definite limits: all of the criteria involve questions of degree. The 'typical' contract of labour usually exhibits the following features: the employee is subject to the directions of the employer in all material respects; he receives a 'salary' (*Arbeitslohn*) on a regular basis; his working place, time and conditions are determined by the employer. A detailed treatment must be reserved to specialised work. (See, for an introduction, Junker, *Grundkurs Arbeitsrecht* (3rd edn, 2004) and in English, chapter 11 in Ebke and Finkin (eds), *Introduction to German Law* (1996), p 305.) It should also be noted that, for the purposes of EC law, there is a Community law definition of a 'worker' which must be respected by national courts where claims to exercise EC law rights (such as to non-discrimination on grounds of nationality and to ancillary rights such as those laid down in reg 1612/68/EEC) are in issue (see eg, Case 66/85 *Lawrie-Blum v Land Baden-Württemberg* [1986] ECR 2121, para 17: 'the essential feature of an employment relationship . . . is that for a certain period of time a person performs services for and under the direction of another person in return for which he receives remuneration.' This definition bears a striking resemblance to the German criteria discussed above, which is perhaps unsurprising, given that the reference that gave rise to the ECJ's ruling in *Lawrie-Blum* was sent from the *Bundesverwaltungsgericht*). The reader is also referred to chapter 1 (the section on freedom of contract), where some of the protective measures are discussed. Finally, see also *The German Law of Torts*, pp 705 *et seq* (liability regimes in labour law), and pp 910 *et seq* (insurance for accidents at work). European law also has an influence in this protective field: Directive 76/207/EEC has been implemented in §§ 611a, 611b, 612 III which all seek to prevent discrimination based on gender (see, in the UK, the Sex Discrimination Act 1975 and the Equal Pay Act 1976, discussed in McColgan, *Discrimination Law: Text, Cases and Materials* (2000)); Directive 77/187/EEC concerning the safeguarding of employees' rights in the event of transfers of undertakings, businesses or parts of businesses was implemented in § 613a (for the UK position, see SI 2003 No 131 and the discussion in Deakin and Morris, *Labour Law* (4th edn, 2005)). Both Directives have given rise to prolonged and intense disputes between the national legislator, the national courts and the ECJ, though the position of the law now seems (more) settled. (See generally, Sciarra (ed), *Labour Law and the National Courts* (2001) and Barnard, *EC Employment Law* (2nd edn, 2000) for discussion of these dynamics, covering both EC and national law perspectives.)

(h) Contract for Work

Like the contract of sale, the contract for work (*Werkvertrag*, § 631) has been affected by the recent reforms of the law of obligations (BGBl 2001 I, 3183). The central element of the contract for work has already been mentioned above: it is the obligation of the contractor (*Unternehmer*) owed to the employer (*Besteller*) to achieve a certain result (§ 631 II). (See on the consequences of a failure of performance, chapter 9 and chapter 10, p 520.) A corollary of this is that until completion of the work the contractor bears the risk of destruction of the asset, materials etc which are to be worked on or used (§ 644 I 1).

Distinguishing this type of contract from the contract of sale (§ 433) has become less difficult after the reform of § 651 (concerning the so-called *Werklieferungsvertrag*). The law of the sale of goods applies to a contract which has as its subject matter the delivery of movable things *to be manufactured or to be produced*. In the case of non-fungible things, certain provisions of the contract for work apply in addition to the provisions of sales law (§§ 642, 643, 645, 649, 650). In short, in respect of the production of movable things § 651 declares the law of the contract of sale to be applicable. This includes the available remedies but also, for example, imposes on the contractor the obligation to transfer property in the produced thing under § 433 I 1.

As a consequence, the main fields of application of the contract for work are works on land such as the construction of buildings, the repair of movable things (as opposed to their production) and the production of non-corporeal works (for instance the drafting of an expert opinion, the services of an architect). The law of construction contracts is of great practical importance and forms another special branch of private law dealt with in specialised monographs (eg, Pause, *Bauträgerkauf und Baumodelle* (4th edn, 2004); Uff, *Construction Law* (8th edn, 2002)). It is interwoven with the law of the contract of sale and raises a number of issues relating to the position of inter-mediaries (trustees, agents etc), which cannot be examined here. It should be observed, however, that in this area of construction law standard terms of business have to a considerable extent modified or replaced the rules of the Code. The *Verdingungsordnung für Bauleistungen (VOB) Teil B* (introduced 1926 by the Ministry of Finance but nowadays evaluated and adapted by a private body consisting of representatives of both employers and contractors) contains an optional body of contract clauses which adapts the rules in §§ 631 *et seq* BGB, to the needs of the construction industry. Furthermore, particular contracts for work have been subjected to special regimes of rules. This concerns, for instance, certain contracts for the transport of goods dealt with in the Commercial Code (forwarding agents, § 453 HGB, *Spedition*; contract of transport of goods, § 497 HGB, *Frachtvertrag*) and or publishing contracts (regulated in the *Verlagsgesetz* of 19 June 1901).

The system of remedies available for irregularities of performance is discussed in detail in chapter 9. Here, suffice it to name a few further characteristics of the contract for work. As explained, the main obligation of the contractor is to produce the work (§ 631 I). The main obligation of the employer is to pay the remuneration (*Werklohn*) of the contractor (§ 631 I). As with the contract of employment, it is presumed that (in the absence of express provision) the remuneration is to be fixed at the usual rate where the work is usually performed in return for remuneration, § 632. A deviation from a cost estimate (*Kostenvoranschlag*, §§ 632 III, 650) may entitle the employer to terminate the contract. As a general rule, payment is due after the acceptance of the work as complying in all material respects with the requirements of the contract, (§ 640). Acceptance (*Abnahme*), which is the second main obligation of the employer, can be replaced by supplying an expert opinion that the work is in conformity with the contract (§ 641a). § 632a clarifies that the parties may agree to part payments as soon as certain parts of the work have been completed. As far as the completion of a work requires the co-operation of the employer, the latter cannot compel the employer to do so, but if the employer fails to co-operate then the contractor is entitled to adequate compensation (§ 642) and may terminate the contract (§ 643). § 647 creates by law on behalf of the contractor a 'lien' (over chattels belonging to the employer which have passed into his possession) to secure his (future) claim of remuneration (in English law, this result is achieved via the possessory lien, the classic example being the garage that fixes a car having a lien over the car until the bill is settled. As in German law, such a right is not consensual, but is created by law and seems to be confined to cases where past practice has established such a right (Bridge, *Personal Property Law* (3rd edn, 2002), p 170 and, generally 170–5), although statutes can also create a similar relationship (see the case of *Bristol Airport Plc v Powdrill* [1990] Ch 744, construing section 88 of the Civil Aviation Act 1982 (which allows an airport to detain an aircraft until airport charges, etc have been paid) as a lien (in the insolvency context). It should be noted that, in the absence of a statutory or contractual provision to the contrary, a lien confers no power of sale at common law: it operates as a possessory security only and is in this respect different from a pledge); § 648 entitles the contractor to demand the grant of a mortgage for the purposes of securing the remuneration for the construction of a building. Finally, § 634a provides for special limitation periods for claims in respect of defects of the work. (Note here that the common law may provide protection for the contractor in such situations of default after partially performing the contract by means of the law of restitution: these matters are discussed further in chapter 9, below.)

(i) Travel Contract

The BGB did not initially contain special provisions for the contract of travel (*Reisevertrag*). §§ 651a–651m are the result of the wish of the legislator to increase consumer protection in this very common type of contract. We are consequently dealing with (on the whole) obligatory and not dispositive law (§ 651m). These paragraphs also serve to implement Directive 90/314/EEC but are in fact of older origin (BGBl. 1979 I, 509). (For the UK implementation, see the Package Travel, Package Holidays and Package Tours Regulations 1992 (SI 1992, No 3288) and the discussion in Grant and Urbanowicz, 'Tour operators, package holiday contracts and strict liability' [2001] *JBL* 253 and Mason, 'Package holiday claims—"the short but tortured history of tour operator liability"' (2001) 4 *JPIL* 296. More generally, see the Commission's Report on the Implementation of the Directive: SEC (1999) 1800.)

The main duty of the service provider (*Reiseveranstalter*) is to provide the travel and holiday services as promised (§ 651a I 1) while the traveller's (*Reisende*) principal obligation is to pay the price (§ 651a I 2). The obligation is, like the contract for work, directed at achieving a specific result (see eg, BGHZ 130, 128). It suffices here to point out the obligation of the service provider to take out insurance which will secure fulfilment of the contract in the case of insolvency (§ 651 k); and that § 651f II entitles the traveller, in the case of a breach of the main obligation of the provider, to compensation 'for lost holiday.' (This head of damage, loss of amenity, was (prior to the reform of the law of damages (BGBl 2002 I, 2674)) the only situation where German law afforded protection to non-pecuniary interests in the law of contract. For English law, see the well-known cases of *Jarvis v Swan Tours Ltd* [1973] QB 233 and *Jackson v Horizon Holidays Ltd* [1975] 1 WLR 1468 on exactly the same point. More generally, see Treitel, *The Law of Contract*, pp 987–91). Nowadays, § 253 II makes damages for pain and suffering (but not for loss of an amenity) more widely available.

(j) Mandate and the Management of Affairs for Others

Mandate (*Auftrag*, §§ 662–674) is, following the tradition of Roman law (see, Zimmermann, *The Law of Obligations*, p 415), a gratuitous contract, by which one party undertakes to do something on behalf of another (which in US law would be a part of the law of agency, covering as it does both paid and unpaid agents). This contract, unlike donation, is not subject to special requirements of form. It can be distinguished from contracts of employment or contracts for work, for only mandate is a contract where the service (in its wider meaning) is not performed in return for remuneration. It is important to note that in German law, unlike in other civil law systems, mandate and the giving of authority (§ 167) are strictly separated from and independent of each other. (The experience in systems such as the American suggest the wisdom of this careful distinction, not least due to the fact that if it is found that authority has been given then this creates a fiduciary obligation, the breach of which can amount to a tort attracting punitive damages.) Agency may be accompanied by a relationship of mandate, but the granting of authority may occur in an entirely different contractual context; indeed, most agents are (as commercial agents) not employed on the basis of a gratuitous contract (see, for instance, §§ 84 *et seq* of the Commercial Code dealing with self-employed commercial agents, *Handelsvertreter,* implementing Directive 86/653/EEC. (For the UK implementation of this Directive, see the Commercial Agents (Council Directive) Regulations 1993 (SI 1993 No 3053) (as amended by SI 1993 No 3173).)

The main duty of the mandatary is to carry out the mandate (§ 662). While the contract is not performed for reward, the mandatary ought not be left out of pocket due to the mandate. Accordingly, § 670 gives him the right to recoup expenses which he reasonably incurred in connection with the performance of the mandate. This provision has been interpreted by the courts to include the right to claim damages (irrespective of fault) for losses which are intimately connected with the carrying out of the mandate (eg, BGHZ 38, 270; the legislator had left the question open, *Motive*, vol II, p 541). The mandatary, on the other hand, is under an obligation to hand over to the employer everything which he acquires in the course of the mandate (§ 667). He is also under a duty to inform the employer about progress and give him an account of his performance of the mandate (§ 666). The standard of liability, unlike other gratuitous contracts, is not lowered in the typical way but is governed by the general rule found in § 276 (fault in the sense of intent and negligence). It is presumed that the promisor is not allowed to instruct a third person to carry out the mandate. However, if this is possible then he is liable only in respect of the selection of that person (§ 664 I).This rule is peculiar to the rules on mandate.

Mandate, as a gratuitous contract, does not play a major role in practice. Indeed, the principal difficulty in its application is to distinguish mandate from simple amicable acts which do not convey an intention of the parties to be bound by their conduct (discussed in chapter 2, p 86 ff). The main reason why a brief account of the principal rules on mandate has nevertheless been included here is that these rules serve as a model for the regulation of other types of contracts supported by consideration which are concerned with the management of the affairs of another. (It should also be noted that the law of *negotiorum gestio* (§§ 677 *et seq*) also refers to some of the provisions on mandate. But since managing the affairs of another without mandate is an example of a relationship of obligation implied by law—*gesetzliches Schuldverhältnis*—it will not be discussed here in detail.)

Paragraph 675, which concerns the managing of affairs of others in return for remuneration (*entgeltliche Geschäftsbesorgung*), stipulates that contracts of employment (§ 611) and contracts for work (§ 631) are subject to some of the rules on mandate (§§ 663, 665–70, 672–4, under certain conditions: 671 II) insofar as the contract involves 'managing of the affairs of another' (*Geschäftsbesorgung*). The meaning of this technical term has not been defined in the BGB and has remained controversial. The *Bundesgerichtshof* requires that the activity in question be of an 'economic' nature (eg, the managing of financial affairs; not for instance giving piano lessons), which is carried out independently (ie, not as part of a labour contract) in the interest of another (see, *Palandt*-Sprau, § 675 Rn. 1–4, for references). The main field of application is the contractual relationship between banks and their customers. Some of these contracts are now (BGBl 1999 I, 1642, implementing Directive 97/5/EC [1997] OJ L43/25) specially provided for in the Code. Thus, we have contracts of transfer of money between bank accounts (*Überweisungsauftrag*, §§ 676a–c), concerning the relationship between the customer transferring the money and his bank; the so-called 'payment' contract (*Zahlungsvertrag*, § 676d–676e), governing the relationship between the banks involved in the transfer; and the contract between bank and customer concerning the keeping of a bank account (*Girovertrag*, § 676f–h). (For the UK implementation of Directive 97/5/EC, see the Cross-Border Credit Transfers Regulations 1999 (SI 1999 No 1876). See generally, Ellinger, Lomnicka & Hooley, *Modern Banking Law* (3rd edn, 2002).)

Apart from banking law, the other main fields of operation of § 675 are construction law, where one party (*Baubetreuer*) undertakes the responsibility for carrying out the construction project. Likewise, the drafting of expert opinions often involves the managing of the affairs of another within the meaning of § 675. Despite the stipulation in § 675 II that the giving of advice does not as a general rule lead to liability, German law has developed quite strict rules of liability for this type of professional negligence (as to which see, chapter 2, p 86 ff); some of this field is covered by the law of trusts and questions of fiduciary duties in the UK and the US—see, eg, McGhee (ed), *Snell's Equity* (31st edn, 2005), chapter 7 on fiduciaries and 27 (on the duties and discretion of trustees).

A special form of managing the affairs of another person constitutes the contract of brokerage (*Mäklervertrag*, § 652–5) which is however subject to a special regime of rules independent of mandate. In German law, this regime denominates a contract whereby one party undertakes to facilitate the conclusion of a contract with a third person (for instance by bringing the two parties of the contract together). One comes across this type of contract mostly in the property market and in the market for leases. The most striking feature of this contract is that it does not entitle the employer to demand the performance of the contract. However, if the broker carries out the service provided for in the contract, then an obligation of remuneration on the part of the employer arises, provided only that the conclusion of the contract was at least to some extent brought about by the interposition of the broker (§ 652 I). Special protection is afforded to consumers in relation to the procurement of consumer loans by brokers (§§ 655a—e).

Finally, the keeping of movable corporeal things for another is also a specially regulated contract (*Verwahrung*, §§ 688–700) which, broadly speaking, involves the managing of affairs of another but follows its own rules. If it is performed gratuitously, the standard of liability of the keeper is reduced to *diligentia quam in suis* (§§ 690, 277). Note that the liability of an innkeeper, who accommodates guests as part of his trade, for damage to things that a customer brought into the premises (as provided for in §§ 701–4) is independent of contract (*gesetzliches Schuldverhältnis*).

In English law, this area shows a considerable overlap with the law on bailment, which at base is a question of the possessory/proprietary relationship (as laid down by the general law, including the law of tort) between bailor and bailee of a chattel, but can be added to and expanded on by the parties if the bailment is executed pursuant to a contract. Once a fairly coherent, separate body of law, the common law's treatment of bailment is now scattered over a range of areas (contract, tort, property, restitution, agency, etc). An interesting case to examine for historical and comparative purposes is the well-known decision of Lord Holt CJ in *Coggs v Bernard* (1703) 2 Ld Raym 909; 92 ER 107, which summarised bailment law and its consequences using significant insights from the Roman law principles and categories (such as *commodatum*, *depositum* and *pignus*) (see Zimmermann, *The Law of Obligations*, p 204 and the references cited therein, and generally, Bridge, *Personal Property Law* (3rd edn, 2002), pp 33–43). Nevertheless, it should be remembered that the current English approach focuses more on the particular circumstances of the bailment, including issues such as the skill which the bailee held himself out as possessing, any consideration which has moved from the bailor, bailee or from both, and the terms of the agreement. These are the relevant questions in any assessment of what amounts to reasonable care on the part of the bailee in performing the obligation in question and illustrate the tendency of English law in the twentieth century to view most tortious duties as ones of reasonable care (see, eg, Bridge, *Personal Property Law*, p 37). This expansion means that great care needs to be taken in examining the older authorities as accurate statements of the current approach (eg, *Coggs* (above) comes from a time when such duties of care required a specific undertaking to have been made or a very specific fact scenario to have been in issue).

(k) Surety

The contract of surety is regulated in §§ 765–78. Surety involves a triangular relationship between the creditor (*Gläubiger*), the principal debtor (*Hauptschuldner*), and the surety (*Bürge*). It is important to note from the outset that 'contract of surety' (*Bürgschaftsvertrag*) denominates only the relationship between surety and creditor, namely the undertaking of an obligation towards the creditor to guarantee the performance of the principal debt (*Hauptschuld*: see § 765 I). Thus, special care must be taken not to identify too hastily the German concepts with those of the contract of guarantee or suretyship in English law. (On the English law on these topics, see Moss and Marks, *Rowlatt on Principal and Surety* (5th edn, 1998); Phillips & O'Donovan, *The Modern Contract of Guarantee* (English edn, 2003) and Beale (ed), *Chitty on Contracts* (29th edn, 2004), chapter 42.)

The promise of the surety must be in writing (§ 766), except where given by a merchant when it is part of his trade to do so (§ 350 HGB). (In English law, a binding guarantee must be made by deed or be supported by consideration *and* be evidenced by a written memorandum signed by the guarantor (section 4 Statute of Frauds 1677; if a regulated agreement under the CCA 1974 (see above, section 4(f)) is to be secured, then the guarantee itself must be in writing: section 105(1) CCA 1974.) This formal requirement is supposed to 'warn' the surety. See also, chapter 2 on the purpose of formal requirements). The contract is implicitly regarded as a potentially dangerous transaction, for the surety does not obtain a counter-performance for undertaking the guarantee. Hence, it is not surprising that consideration proved difficult to establish for the English courts, though these problems are nowadays of mostly theoretical nature. (See Goode, *Commercial Law*, p 813: either guarantees are given by deed or consideration is found in the conclusion of the primary transaction by making the advance of funds to the prospective debtor.) This 'dangerous' nature of the transaction also explains the great number of cases in which the courts have been tempted to intervene and declare void any contracts of guarantee which seemed procedurally or substantively 'unfair' and which will be discussed in the next chapter.

Surety is accessory in nature, which means that the extent of the principal debt determines the extent of the surety. (For English law see *Bechervaise v Lewis* (1872) LR 7 CP 372.) This general principle is more specifically spelt out in §§ 767, 768, 770. In particular, the surety is entitled to avail himself of all defences of the principal debtor against the creditor (§ 768 I) even if the principal debtor waived them (§ 768 II). While this accessory nature is well known to English law, the rule that the creditor must sue and attempt to enforce the judgment against the principal debtor first (*Einrede der Vorausklage*, § 771) is not a part of the English regime. However, in German law it is also possible that the surety may waive this right in the contract with the creditor. (§ 773 I Nr. 1, the so-called *selbstschuldnerische Bürgschaft*.) Also, where the surety is given by a merchant as part of his trade, the defence of § 771 is not available (§ 349 HGB).

Another special form of surety is the 'first demand guarantee' (*Bürgschaft auf erstes Anfordern*), which was developed by the courts. Its main purpose is to exclude defences of the surety derived from § 768, ie the relationship between creditor and principal debtor. This exclusion enables the creditor to obtain from the surety immediately the sum promised, while the disputes as to defences are postponed to the claim for restitution of the surety against the creditor under § 812 I 1 alt. 1. (See eg, BGH NJW 1992, 1446; NJW 2001, 1857; in pre-formulated contracts, as to which see next section, the courts are very reluctant to recognise this form of surety.)

The relationship between surety and principal debtor can take different forms which are not directly covered by §§ 765 *et seq* (although see § 775, which refers to mandate and *negotiurum gestio*). The participation of the principal debtor is not required for the contract of guarantee to come into existence. He need not even know of it, in which case the relationship between him and the creditor is likely to be one of *negotiorum gestio* (§ 677). There may be a contract in which the surety promises against consideration to the debtor to undertake the guarantee vis-à-vis the creditor; this contract will normally be considered as *entgeltliche Geschäftsbesorgung* in the sense of § 675. Outside family relationships this will be often the case. (For example, of banks providing guarantees for their customers.)

The contractual relationship between surety and principal debtor may entitle the former to recoup the payments made to the creditor (for instance § 670, discussed in the section on mandate, would entitle the surety to claim the amount paid to the creditor). The law of suretyship entitles the surety to rights of contribution against the principal debtor irrespective of a contract between those parties. § 774 stipulates for the right of subrogation of the surety (*cessio legis*). The surety may enforce after fulfilment of the guarantee the rights of the creditor against the principal debtor. In English law, this result is achieved either by the surety suing on his implied contractual right to be indemnified by the principal debtor (*Re a Debtor (No 627 of 1936)* [1937] 1 All ER 1) or by becoming subrogated to the creditor's claim(s) against the principal debtor (having discharged the full debt owed to the creditor) (*Yonge v Reynell* (1852) 9 Hare 809; 68 ER 744 and *Forbes v Jackson* (1882) 19 Ch D 6 15).

The contract of guarantee (ie, the contract between surety and creditor) is regarded as a 'causal' contract (see the explanation of the principle of abstraction in chapter 1, p 27 ff), which means that it contains a reason—*causa*—in itself and does not require another contract of obligation to found it (examples to the contrary are §§ 780, 781, also discussed in chapter 1). Whether the surety was undertaken as a result of an obligation owed to the main principal is irrelevant; as a general rule, the invalidity of such a contract would not mean that the contract of surety lacks a *causa* and the surety could be reclaimed under unjustified enrichment principles. (Note that the position of German law is presented in a necessarily simplified manner here; see, for an illustration, BGH NJW 2001, 1857, referred to above.)

It should be noted that surety is but an example of personal security. There are other obligations resulting out of a contract which also serve to secure a debt. The main examples are: '*Garantie*' where the promisor undertakes an indemnity for the fulfilment of a debt of another; and the contract (again similar to an indemnity) whereby one party undertakes to be liable in the same way as the principal debtor (the so-called '*Schuldbeitritt*.' See eg, BGH NJW 1996, 2165). (Both these types of transaction would be treated as a form of indemnity, rather than guarantee/surety. See Goode, *Commercial Law*, pp 816–17.) Since these contracts are not subject to the formal requirement of § 766, and the defences available to a surety are not available here, the courts are at pains to emphasise that a clear intention of the parties is required to infer that the parties did not intend a surety. Other forms of security include the security transactions of property law (eg, the different forms of mortgage, *Hypothek*, § 1113, *Grundschuld*, § 1191; retention of title, *Eigentumsvorbehalt*, § 449, and *Sicherungseirgentum*, as to which see chapter 1, section 3(c) on the principle of abstraction, in particular the lien based on possession, § 1205). (See, for an introduction to credit security instruments, Rimmelspacher, *Kreditsicherungsrecht* (2nd edn, 1987) and Goode, *Legal Problems of Credit and Security* (3rd edn, 2003).)

(l) Mixed and New Types of Contract

The parties are free to structure their contractual relationship of obligation in a way which does not fit the special types of contract for which the BGB has introduced detailed rules (§ 311 I). The types of contract contained in the BGB should be regarded as merely representing an attempt to regulate the most commonly encountered sorts of contracts. The list is neither comprehensive, nor does it attempt to be. This is the only way to give full effect to freedom of contract. Three kinds of modification of the types of contract can be observed.

The first need not be discussed here. It concerns the deviation from particular rules by agreement of the parties. The default rules governing particular types of contracts are *ius dispositivum*—the parties can contract out of them, should they so wish. Strict or obligatory rules are the exception, eg, rules protecting the weaker party, formal requirements (although, as we noted, in the field of consumer law the exception has become the rule). One particular way of contracting out of the Codal provisions—by using standard terms—will be discussed in the next section.

The second deviation cuts across the division of individual types of contracts. The parties promise a performance and counter-performance which cannot be accommodated in the framework of one of the types of contract provided for in the BGB but which instead assume the features of several of these contracts. These contracts are usually referred to as 'mixed contracts' (*gemischte Verträge*). For instance, a stay in a hotel often comprises the performance of several obligations which belong to several different types of contract: lease (the hotel room), contract for work (preparing meals) and services (laundry). The treatment of mixed contracts gives rise to difficulties, but a pragmatic approach seems most sensible, which evaluates the particular contractual obligation in question and determines in the individual circumstances which regime of rules is most appropriate.

The third deviation is the most fundamental. Here, the mutual promises of the parties cannot be linked to the types of contract of the BGB—they are atypical. This concerns in particular the emergence of new kinds of contracts such as 'Factoring', 'Leasing', and 'Franchising'. (The fact that they figure under their English names in German law shows the strong recent influence of Anglo-American law and business practices). The rules applicable to these contracts are to a great extent shaped by case law, but the courts seek to draw on their resemblance to known types of contracts and apply the traditional BGB rules by analogy. We have come across this phenomenon above in the context of 'Factoring' (which may involve the sale of a right) and 'Leasing' (which raises the difficulty of reconciling rules of sales law and the law of leases). The reader is referred to specialised works for further details (see eg, Oetker and Maultzsch, *Vertragliche Schuldverhältnisse*, § 16)

5. STANDARD TERMS AND EXCLUSION CLAUSES

Basedow, 'Eine Deponie wird geschlossen–Ein Rückblick auf die Karriere des AGBG' ZEuP 2001, 433; Basedow, 'Handelsbräuche und AGB-Gesetz' ZHR 150 (1986) 469; Coester-Waltjen, 'Die Inhaltskontrolle von Verträgen außerhalb des AGBG' AcP 190 (1990) 1; Fastrich, *Richterliche Inhaltskontrolle im Vertragsrecht* (1992); Jaeger, 'Einfluss der Rechtsprechung auf die Entwicklung von Allgemeinen Geschäftsbedingungen am Beispiel von Haftungsausschlußklauseln' VersR 1990, 455; Kötz, 'Der Schutzzweck der AGB-Kontrolle–eine rechtsökonomische Skizze' JuS 2003, 209; Lindacher, 'Kenntnisnahmemöglichkeit und Kenntnisnahmeobliegenheit bei Allgemeinen Geschäftsbedingungen' JZ 1981, 131; Pfeiffer, 'Vom kaufmännischen Verkehr zum Unternehmensverkehr' NJW 1999, 169; Rabe, 'Die Auswirkungen des AGB-Gesetzes auf den kaufmännischen Verkehr' NJW 1987, 1978; Raiser, 'Vertragsfreiheit heute' JZ 1958, 1; Stoffels, *AGB-Recht* (2003); Remien, 'AGB-Gesetz und Richtlinie über missbräuchliche Verbrauchervertragsklauseln in ihrem europäischen Umfeld' ZEuP 1994, 34; Roussos, 'Die Anwendungsgrenzen der Inhaltskontrolle und die Auslegung von § 9 AGBG' JZ 1988, 1003; Tonner, 'Die Rolle des Verbraucherrechts bei der Entwicklung des europäischen Zivilrechts' JZ 1996, 533; Ulmer, Brandner and Hensen, *AGB-Gesetz* (9th edn, 2001); Wackerbarth, 'Unternehmer, Verbraucher und die Rechtfertigung der Inhaltskontrolle vorformulierter Verträge' AcP 200 (2000) 45; Wolf, Horn and Lindacher, *AGBG*, 3. Aufl. 1994; M Wolf, 'Die Vorformulierung als Voraussetzung der Inhaltskontrolle, in *Festschrift Brandner* (1996), 299.

(a) Preliminary Observations

Towards the end of the nineteenth century, the industrialisation of the production process led to an increased standardisation of contract terms in Germany. Standard terms are nowadays invariably used in the commercial context in virtually all dealings between sellers/suppliers and consumers and sometimes also between parties acting outside their business or trade. The vital importance of standard terms should thus not be underestimated. It is no coincidence that the Unfair Terms in Consumer Contracts Directive (93/13/EEC [1993] OJ L95/29) is regarded by many as the most important measure of harmonisation in the area of contract law, even though as a consumer protection measure it covers only one type of the relationships mentioned above. The German approach to the control of standard terms is not limited in this way. The reason for this is interesting in itself, as it is linked to the purpose of the control of standard terms. But first let us consider how German law reached the present sophisticated position of policing standard term contracts.

As early as 1958, Raiser could, in his discussion of inroads into freedom of contract, refer to a solid body of case law that openly professed to evaluate standard terms on their merits (JZ 1958, 1, 7). He was not alone in welcoming this development; indeed, he claimed that the abandonment of 'neutrality' towards contractual bargains should be seen as an heroic deed of the German courts (*'Ruhmesblatt der deutschen Rechtsprechung'*). At the time, the Code itself did not provide for the control of standard terms. There were, however, the general clauses of good faith (§ 242 BGB), contracts contravening *bonos mores* (§ 138 BGB), and a provision which stipulated that courts could exercise their equitable discretion if one party was empowered to determine the content of a core term unilaterally (§ 315 III BGB). All of these devices were used by the courts to justify their intervention and strike out clauses which they regarded as unjust. It was good faith which was to prove the most flexible and the most reliable basis for the growing stream of cases on policing standard terms.

Having a complex system of codified default rules proved to be an invaluable asset in performing this self-assumed task. The courts never went so far as to invalidate a term merely because it deviated from the default rules in the Code. Yet the Code itself turned out to be a useful tool in assessing the fairness of terms. Assuming that its rules constituted a fair distribution of risk, the degree of deviation from the rules was taken by the courts as an indication (though not the only one) of the fairness of a standard term. The user of the term could still show that it operated reasonably in the circumstances of the particular trade. This approach is well illustrated by BGHZ 41, 151. One should also note that not all the rules in the Code were taken to embody 'ethical' values, but those laying down the 'cardinal' obligations of the parties were at the top of this value hierarchy.

Good faith was said to be relevant and standard terms unfair if and when they showed that one party had abused his dominant position by pursuing his interest recklessly and selfishly (eg, BGHZ 54, 106, 109). This rationalisation, using the concept of the abuse of a superior position, has had a remarkable influence in its heyday and is still strong today. Raiser was a particularly outspoken proponent of this approach. The conflicting values in policing standard terms were, he explained, freedom of contract and 'social' justice. He conceded that it was not always economic power that enabled one party to impose standard terms but rather the 'intellectual inferiority' of the other party (who would not be able to assess fully the implications of standard terms) that justified the intervention of a court. The difficulty with this explanation (quite apart from the fact that in effect it stigmatises the party who seeks to set aside a standard term) has always been that the courts never actually inquired in individual cases into whether the party successfully incorporating standard terms was in a dominant position, or whether the other party was in some respect incapable of either understanding the terms or bargaining out of them. Indeed, many cases concerned the use of standard terms outside the consumer sphere (see, for instance, BGHZ 41, 151). So when the legislature finally decided to implement legislation in this field, turning many judicially developed rules into statutory form, it did not limit the *Gesetz zur Regelung des Rechts der Allgemeinen Geschäftsbedingungen* of 1977 (now repealed) to *consumer* transactions, though some provisions differentiated along these lines and the idea of unduly imposing standard terms on the 'weaker' party was clearly present at the back of the minds of the promoters and draftsmen of the new legislation.

More recently, a different explanation has been gaining ground. The reason for interfering with the contract in the case of standard terms is said not to be an abuse of any kind in imposing them—not a question of the 'little man' versus the 'big concern'—but rather that the parties are not likely to negotiate the details of standard terms in each and every case. Indeed, this would contradict the very purpose of using standard terms. Thus, saving transaction costs is a strong incentive, even for a customer in a strong market position, to accept standard terms whatever their content. (Others have argued that so long as some consumers are prepared to meet the costs of such complaints and bargaining over standard terms, others will then be able to free-ride on their efforts). Since the market mechanisms will not ensure that the terms adequately protect both parties, the courts are justified in policing standard terms. (See, with references, *Münchener Kommentar*- Basedow, Vor § 305 Rn. 5; Kötz, JuS 2003, 209.) This modern explanation provides a reason for policing standard terms quite apart from the arguments from inferiority and abuse. Happily, we need not decide here which policy reason is to be preferred. Nonetheless, a few tentative remarks may be of use.

While it is clear that the latter approach explains better the fact that standard terms are controlled whatever the respective position or power of the parties, it cannot be doubted that in some situations the customer is in a weak position and may have no choice except to take or leave the offer as it is. This may be particularly true in consumer transactions. Yet, again, if the parties are dealing at arm's length and nego-tiate a complex deal such as the sale of a company, is it then really justified to inter-vene and control the terms insofar as they represent standard terms, ie, insofar as they have not been individually negotiated? Is the modern explanation not another way of saying that the parties need not worry about the precise terms of their agreement, because the (paternalistic) court will in the end ensure that it is a 'fair' deal?

In England, the overall situation as to standard terms is not easy to ascertain, as dif-ferent overlapping layers of rules come into play. First, the Unfair Contract Terms Act 1977 is not limited to standard terms but applies to exclusion clauses whatever form they take. Secondly, the Unfair Terms in Consumer Contract Regulations 1999 (SI 1999 No 2083 ('UTCCR 1999'), as amended by the Unfair Terms in Consumer Contracts (Amendment) Regulations 2001 (SI 2001 No 1186), superseding the Regulations of 1994) implement Directive 93/13/EEC (see Treitel, *The Law of Contract*, 267 ff and McKendrick, *Contract Law*, chapter 14). Finally, there are the common law rules of offer and acceptance with which the parties must comply in order successfully to incorporate standard terms (see Treitel, *The Law of Contract*, pp 216–21), as well as the question of the proper construction of such terms if validly incorporated (at 221 ff). English courts have been reluctant to implement a regime like that developed by German courts on the basis of § 242 BGB. Indeed, it is difficult to imagine in England statements such as the above—encouraging the courts to aban-don their 'neutrality' towards contract terms. Yet even in England, standard terms have been the subject of a regime that was sometimes rather strict, and subject to closer scrutiny by the courts than is noticeable from the (sometimes superficially) tough (freedom of contract-respecting) language of their judgments. For even before the Unfair Contract Terms Act 1977 ('UCTA 1977') enabled the courts openly to police exclusion and limitation clauses, the courts used various techniques in order to get around unfair exclusion clauses. One of them was the (ultimately failed) attempt to claim that certain breaches of contract were so 'fundamental' that they extin-guished the contract containing the exclusion clause (see *Photo Production Ltd v Securicor Transport Ltd* [1980] AC 827). A much more effective device was to apply rules of interpretation to this purpose. Lord Denning MR gave an elegant account of these developments in the Court of Appeal decision in *George Mitchell (Chesterhall) Ltd v Finney Lock Seeds Ltd* [1983] QB 284 (affirmed: [1983] 2 AC 803) and we quote in full the respective passage. Though it is certainly to be approached with caution, it reveals much about the attitude of the English courts, and also parallels to a surpris-ing (or perhaps not so surprising?) extent the policy reasons which are discussed in German law:

> The heyday of freedom of contract. None of you nowadays will remember the trou-ble we had—when I was called to the Bar—with exemption clauses. They were printed in small print on the back of tickets and order forms and invoices. They were contained in catalogues or timetables. They were held to be binding on any person who took them without objection. No one ever did object. He never read them or knew what was in them. No matter how unreasonable they were, he was bound. All this was done in the name of 'freedom of contract.' But the freedom was all on the side of the big concern which had the use of the printing press. No free-dom for the little man who took the ticket or order form or invoice. The big concern

said, 'Take it or leave it.' The little man had no option but to take it. The big concern could and did exempt itself from liability in its own interest without regard to the little man. It got away with it time after time. When the courts said to the big concern, 'You must put it in clear words,' the big concern had no hesitation in doing so. It knew well that the little man would never read the exemption clauses or understand them. It was a bleak winter for our law of contract. . . .

The secret weapon. Faced with this abuse of power—by the strong against the weak—by the use of the small print of the conditions—the judges did what they could to put a curb on it. They still had before them the idol, 'freedom of contract.' They still knelt down and worshipped it, but they concealed under their cloaks a secret weapon. They used it to stab the idol in the back. This weapon was called 'the true construction of the contract.' They used it with great skill and ingenuity. They used it so as to depart from the natural meaning of the words of the exemption clause and to put on them a strained and unnatural construction. In case after case, they said that the words were not strong enough to give the big concern exemption from liability; or that in the circumstances the big concern was not entitled to rely on the exemption clause. If a ship deviated from the contractual voyage, the owner could not rely on the exemption clause. If a warehouseman stored the goods in the wrong warehouse, he could not pray in aid the limitation clause. . . . But when the clause was itself reasonable and gave rise to a reasonable result, the judges upheld it; at any rate, when the clause did not exclude liability entirely but only limited it to a reasonable amount. So where goods were deposited in a cloakroom or sent to a laundry for cleaning, it was quite reasonable for the company to limit their liability to a reasonable amount, having regard to the small charge made for the service. . . .

It seems clear that Lord Denning would have welcomed Directive 93/13/EEC. Indeed, his statement could easily figure as one of Directive's recitals (consumers 'should be protected against the abuse of power by the seller or supplier, in particular against one-sided standard contracts and the unfair exclusion of essential rights in contracts.') The Directive is thus clearly based on the argument from an abuse of market position. It aims at minimum harmonisation between the Member States and thereby at reducing 'distortions' of competition between Member States and sellers operating therein. Its central provision is contained in Article 3(1):

> A contractual term which has not been individually negotiated shall be regarded as unfair if, contrary to the requirement of good faith, it causes a significant imbalance in the parties' rights and obligations arising under the contract, to the detriment of the consumer.

This rather abstract test is accompanied by an 'indicative' list of prohibited terms in the Annex (Article 3(3): the list in the Annex runs from (a) to (q) in providing such 'indications'). Since the inclusion of a term in the list does not necessarily mean that it is unfair, the list is often referred to as a 'grey' list (in the UK, see Schedule 2 UCTTR 1999). (See generally, Beale, 'Legislative Control of Unfairness: the Directive on Unfair Terms in Consumer Contracts' chapter 9 in Beatson & Friedmann (eds), *Good Faith and Fault in Contract Law* (1995).)

The level of harmonisation actually achieved by the Directive is difficult to ascertain for two reasons.

First, the Directive was implemented in very different ways in the Member States so that it is difficult to state to what extent national practice actually hinges on the Directive. (See, on the implementation process: COM (2000) 248 final (27 April 2000), especially Annex I; *MünchKomm*-Basedow, Vor § 305 Rn. 22 *et seq.*) Germany has taken the view that only minimal changes to the existing law were required, while in England instead of amending previous legislation to produce a consolidated version of the statutory law on exclusion clauses, a 'carbon copy' of the Directive in a statutory instrument was regarded as the best way of implementing it (UTCCR 1999 (SI 1999 No 2083), as amended by SI 2001 No 1186).

Further, by far the most significant role with regard to the UK application of the Directive has so far been played by the Office of Fair Trading and its Unfair Contract Terms Unit (see regs 10–15 UTCCR 1999; this topic is discussed by Bright, 'Winning the Battle Against Unfair Terms' (2000) 20 *Leg St* 331), rather than through private enforcement of the regulations in the courts. The European Commission has developed a database of case law (available in the original language and French and English translations) on unfair consumer contract terms in the EEA (known as CLAB: see the Commission's consumer protection website for details), which may facilitate the cross-fertilisation of ideas and experience on the application of the Directive throughout Europe.

Secondly, and this brings us to a deeper concern, achieving harmonisation is difficult because the control of standard terms is interwoven with the function of the specific term within the framework of national law. So while 'good faith' may now (in some respects) be part of English law, it is not impossible that the concept means (or will be taken to mean) something quite different to a common lawyer when it comes to be applied to individual cases. This may also be true on a more abstract level. The test of fairness is embedded in the context of the rules of national law; it is difficult to flesh out the test without a careful appreciation of the context of the regime of the relevant particular default rules. In Germany, this approach to standard terms is expressly formulated in § 307 II BGB (which was, as explained, the guiding principle from the outset): a term will be more likely to be deemed unfair the more it departs from the central default rules of the Code. These default rules may, in turn, be (and frequently are) different from, for instance, the rules applicable in common law jurisdictions. (See also, Whittaker, ZEuP 2004, 75, discussing *Director General of Fair Trading v First National Bank plc* [2002] 1 AC 481; see further, Elvin, 'The application of the Unfair Terms in Consumer Contracts Regulations 1999' (2003) 14 *KCLJ* 39; Dean, 'Defining Unfair Terms in Consumer Contracts—Crystal Ball Gazing?' (2002) 65 *MLR* 773 and MacMillan, 'Evolution or Revolution? Unfair Terms in Consumer Contracts' [2002] *CLJ* 22. For a useful survey of the relevant case law on the regulations to date see Ervine, 'The Unfair Terms in Consumer Contracts Regulations in the Courts' [2004] *SLT* 127). The *First National Bank* decision is itself an example of this phenomenon: it concerned a term on post-judgment interest on a loan, which in German law would be a matter expressly dealt within the Code, § 291 BGB, while in England it depends on the agreement of the parties.

Nevertheless, or perhaps for this very reason, it is interesting to explore the German approach to standard terms, of which the reader can find an outline in what follows. Within the scope of application of the Directive, one can understand §§ 305 *et seq.* BGB as a comment on and possible interpretation of the Directive itself and this may add to a common understanding of such abstract concepts as good faith on the European level. (See further, Zimmermann and Whittaker (eds), *Good faith in European contract law* (2000), for a useful collection of materials, commentary and analysis.) Furthermore, quite independently of the European legislation, the recent decision of the House of Lords in *The Starsin* [2004] 1 AC 715, has shown that comparative law also has something to contribute in this area of the law. The problem in that case was—much simplified—whether the contract of carriage was between buyer and ship-owner, as a clause in the standard form suggested, or between buyer and charterer, as the signature and some other circumstances indicated. One central aspect of this case thus concerned the relationship between a standard term and an individually agreed term. The majority attributed an overriding effect to the latter. Interestingly, Lord Millett (at p 185) quoted and relied in support of his view on § 305b BGB, according to which specific stipulations of the parties override clauses contained in standard form contracts. He also referred to BGH VersR 1990, 503, a decision to the same effect concerning similar circumstances.

Finally, we must note that the English and Scottish Law Commissions recently produced a Joint Report (Law Com No 292, Scot Law Com No 199 (Cm 6464, 24 February 2005)) in which they proposed the creation of a unified and UK-wide regime for the regulation of unfair terms in contracts. While this is not the place to enter into a detailed assessment of this latest development, and it remains to be seen whether such legislation will be introduced, a brief summary of those elements of the Law Commissions' proposals which are remarkable also from a comparative perspective may prove useful. The report clarifies that the burden of proof should fall on the business to show that the relevant term is fair and reasonable where a consumer has raised this issue (paras 3.124–3.130). Further, terms that are currently of no effect as a result of UCTA should remain so (paras 3.14–3.15), while other non-core (on which see paras 3.56–3.72) terms in *consumer contracts* should be subjected to an assessment of their 'fairness and reasonableness,' these being tested *even* where they had been individually negotiated (paras 3.50–3.55). The report also recommends the removal of any express reference to 'good faith' and concludes that 'we consider that our proposed test does meet the requirements of the Directive. It will be easier for UK lawyers to apply than a more 'European' test which makes express reference to good faith' (see para 3.89). The report proposes that the protection afforded by UCTA to contracts between businesses should be retained, with some minor exceptions (see Part 4 of the report). Most significant in this area however are the proposals in Part 5 of the report to include a general clause to allow *small businesses* (those with nine or fewer employees) to challenge any non-core and 'standard' (ie, non-individually negotiated) contract term under a 'fair and reasonable' test (paras 5.27–5.30). The report makes the case that in many respects small businesses find themselves in a similar position to that of consumers when negotiating with larger and powerful commercial entities (paras 5.12–5.24), although the regime ultimately suggested does not differentiate between contracts on the basis of the size of the other business party to the contract with the claimant small business (para 5.32). However, the proposals do not go so far as to release the small business from the burden of proving that the relevant term is unfair (para 5.31).

(b) Structure and Scope of Application

The relevant provisions governing 'standard terms' (*Allgemeine Geschäftsbedingungen*) can now be found in §§ 305–10 BGB. § 310 BGB defines the scope of application of this sub-section of the Code and of the specific rules contained therein. One should note that, outside §§ 305 *et seq* BGB, standard terms may be evaluated by the courts on the basis of good faith, which the courts used initially for all types of contract. Here, it suffices to point to § 310 IV BGB, which excludes the control of standard terms as laid down in §§ 305–9 BGB in the law of succession, family law, and company law, as well as 'collective labour' agreements (ie, agreements between trade unions and employers). Contracts in 'individual labour' law, ie contracts between employers and employees, are not exempt but instead are subject to a rather vague compatibility test ('due regard' must be given to the special nature of such contracts).

Once this test concerning the scope of application has been passed, one must then proceed by asking the following questions. Is the relevant term a *standard term* in the first place (*Allgemeine Geschäftsbedingung*)? Has the relevant term been successfully incorporated into the contract? How is the term to be understood (construction)? Can the term as interpreted withstand the test of substantive fairness? If not, what rules apply instead and are there any implications as to the validity of the remaining terms? We will take each in turn.

The rules at every level are not to be unduly avoided by agreement between the parties, as § 306a BGB clarifies (the most obvious candidate for manipulation being the scope of application, as discussed). (See section 10 of the UK's Unfair Contract Terms Act 1977, which provides measures to prevent circumvention of the protection it offers: see Treitel, *The Law of Contract*, p 261 ff for discussion.) Finally, it must be emphasised that at *no* stage of the inquiry is it necessary to ask whether the party whose offer includes the standard terms in any way unfairly imposed the terms on a 'weaker' party. Since the German approach is not limited to consumers, there is no general presumption of a 'weaker' party. We must qualify this in one respect: some rules are—or appear to be—stricter if standard terms are used in a 'b-to-c' (ie, 'business-to-consumer') as opposed to 'b-to-b' ('business-to-business) situation.

The approach in UCTA 1977 in the UK (though note the changes proposed by Law Com No 292, above section 4(a)) is closer to this overall position than it might appear at first sight. It is possible for a business to be 'dealing as a consumer' when entering into a contract (see section 12(a) and (b) UCTA 1977), so long as the business does not make the contract *in the course* of a business and the other party does do so. Also, section 3 of UCTA 1977 applies to a contract where anyone deals with a business on its 'written standard terms of business' (section 3(1)). This makes the terms subject to a reasonableness test, even if the other party was not dealing as a consumer (see also, section 2(2) on attempts to exclude liability for harm other than death or personal injury). In this context, it seems tolerably clear that the courts, when applying the reasonableness test under UCTA 1977 (and the guidelines thereon—see sections 11(2) and (4)) to contracts on standard terms or for the supply of goods (see sections 3(1) and 6(3) and 7(3) respectively), will be unlikely to strike down terms where the parties were of equal bargaining power. (On this point see eg, *Watford Electronics Ltd v Sanderson CFL Ltd* [2001] EWCA Civ 317; [2001] 1 All ER (Comm) 696, noted by Peel (2001) 117 *LQR* 545.) Thus, although there is some focus on the notion of a 'consumer', the test is a more fact-sensitive one and there are also situations where b-to-b relations are explicitly covered. Further, it seems that b-to-c relations are likely to receive more careful attention under this scheme for testing the reasonableness of terms. Finally however it should be noted that Lord Bridge of Harwich (in his judgment in the House of Lords in *George Mitchell (Chesterhall) Ltd v Finney Lock Seeds Ltd* [1983] 2 AC 803, at 815F–816C) has warned subsequent appellate courts that,

> a decision under any of the provisions referred to will have this in common with the exercise of a discretion, that, in having regard to the various matters to which . . . section 11 of the Act of 1977 direct[s] attention, the court must entertain a whole range of considerations, put them in the scales on one side or the other, and decide at the end of the day on which side the balance comes down. There will sometimes be room for a legitimate difference of judicial opinion as to what the answer should be, where it will be impossible to say that one view is demonstrably wrong and the other demonstrably right. It must follow, in my view, that, when asked to review such a decision on appeal, the appellate court should treat the original decisions with the utmost respect and refrain from interference with it unless satisfied that it proceeded on some erroneous principle or was plainly and obviously wrong.

This tends to suggest that the appellate courts, at least, should be wary of disturbing the view formed by the trial judge on the question of reasonableness, which may provide a brake on any interventionist tendencies of the courts in regulating the reasonableness of such contractual arrangements.

(c) Standard Terms, their Incorporation and Construction

According to § 305 I BGB, standard terms are those terms which have been devised for use in a multitude of contracts, have been suggested by one of the parties (as opposed to a third person), and crucially which have not been individually negotiated. This last point is also reflected in the English case law relating to section 3 of UCTA 1977 (though note that Law Com No 292, see above, section 4(a), recommends extending the control of the fairness of non-core terms in consumer contracts to individually negotiated terms). See *Flammar Interocran Ltd v Denmac Ltd (formerly Denholm Maclay Co Ltd) ('The Flammar Pride')* [1990] 1 Lloyd's Rep 434, at 438 (specially negotiated contracts are not caught within the 'standard terms' net) and cf *St Albans City & District Council v International Computers Ltd* [1996] 4 All ER 481 (where section 3 could still bite where such negotiations had left those terms 'essentially untouched'). Further, where a trade association drafts such terms and its members proceed to use them, section 3 is highly likely to catch those terms, so long as the party 'invariably or at least usually' entered into contracts on those terms (*British Fermentation Products Ltd v Compair Reavell Ltd* [1999] 2 All ER (Comm) 389, at 401). Under German law, the intended use of a term in three different contracts is sufficient to characterise it as not being individually negotiated (thus, BGH NJW 2002, 138). (Note that US law does not treat 'standard terms' as a formally separate category of contract terms, thus leading to greater contortions to reach many of the (sometimes rather similar) practical results discussed above and below.)

It is more difficult to determine when a term has been individually negotiated, yet on this turns whether the term is a standard term in the first place. (Note that the Directive contains the same rule in Article 3(2).) This 'easy' way out has, however, been much narrowed down by a consistent jurisprudence of the *Bundesgerichtshof* (eg,

BGH NJW 1992, 2759; NJW-RR 1987, 144, case no 49). It does not suffice if one party orally explains the nature of the term in question and the other party agrees. More is required. That aspect of the term which embodies the deviation from the provisions of the Code must 'seriously' be made the object of negotiations and it must be clear that the other party has a 'real' chance of influencing the result of the negotiation (compare the *St Albans City & District Council* case, above). The test is a strict one, especially because the burden of proof rests on the person claiming that a term was individually negotiated (*'ausgehandelt'*). For when can it be, retrospectively, firmly established whether or not one party had a chance to change the outcome of negotiations? There are but few examples where pre-formulated clauses were used and such a defence succeeded. Where the other party is confronted with a form which offers a free choice between different options (eg, as to the method of payment, BGH NJW 1998, 1067; or the duration of a contract for services, BGH NJW 2003, 1313) such a clause will not be considered a standard term. This does not hold true, however, if the addition merely concerns formalities which do not affect the substance of the term (BGH NJW 1988, 558).

While this test (of individual negotiation) for determining whether we face a standard term can be found also in the Directive, in other respects the latter takes a broader approach to the definition of standard terms. § 305 I BGB thus had to be supplemented by special provisions in § 310 III Nr. 1 and 2 BGB as far as contracts between dealers and consumers are concerned. All standard terms are attributed to the dealer if the consumer did not put them forward. This means that terms of a third party (eg, a notary) are imputed to the dealer.

Terms are also deemed to be standard terms even if they are (or are intended to be) used only once, so long as the consumer was not able to influence the drafting of such terms (note however that §§ 305 II, 305b, 305c I BGB are not applicable). (For the implementation in the UK of these points, see reg 5 UTCCR 1999.)

Paragraph 305 II BGB modifies the rules as to offer and acceptance in the context of standard terms. § 310 I 1 BGB exempts such contracts from these requirements where standard terms are used as against a dealer (or a body governed by public law). Hence, these further requirements apply only if standard terms are to be incorporated into a contract where the other party is a consumer. (There is no general statement to this effect in US law, although the run of the case law generally does reach this result (albeit via a rather convoluted process of reasoning).)

First, § 305 II Nr. 1 BGB demands from the user of the standard terms that he ought to draw the attention of the other party to them expressly, or if such notification is too burdensome, by a clearly visible display at the place of contracting. (In US insurance law, this result is reached via the doctrine of 'reasonable expectations,' but this approach is not generalised throughout US contract law.) In addition, according to § 305 II Nr.2 BGB, the user of the terms must enable the other party to take notice of the exact content of the standard terms. Special cases are dealt with in §§ 305 III, 305a BGB.

Paragraph 305c I BGB adds a further qualification to the general rules of offer and acceptance. If a clause is regarded as so surprising, especially giving consideration to the appearance of the contract, that the other party would be entitled not to expect it to be included, then it is not part of the contract. (Again, this approach is mirrored in the doctrine of 'reasonable expectations' in US insurance law.) It is exceedingly difficult to draw a clear line between this test and the test to be discussed in the next sub-section, which is directed at the substantive fairness of a clause. This is because the surprising effect of a clause depends on the degree to which it deviates from the default rules of the Code, which define the legitimate horizon of expectation of the other party. § 305c I BGB merely shifts the emphasis to the appearance of the contract. Thus, even where the clause can be upheld on other grounds it may still not become part of the contract simply because it was somewhat 'hidden', in too small print etc, in the contract document. The relevant perspective is that of an average customer. These principles are usefully illustrated in BGHZ 130, 19, case no 50, to which we will return in the next sub-section. (See also, eg, BGH NJW 1995, 2637; NJW 1988, 558.)

The developments in the English case law on the question of the incorporation into the contract of standard terms have shown a marked similarity to the issues considered in the BGB, as discussed in the preceding paragraphs. The provision of notice of the term is crucial. (See generally, Clarke, 'Notice of Contractual Terms' [1976] *CLJ* 51.) Any document in which the term was contained must have been intended to have contractual force (see eg, *Harling v Eddy* [1951] 2 KB 739, especially at 746) and the party relying on the term must have taken at least reasonable steps to bring it to the attention of the other party (*Parker v South Eastern Railway Co* (1877) 2 CPD 416, and it is not sufficient to argue that the other party should have discovered or read the term if they had taken reasonable care). This preserves the principle that the incorporation of a term by reference to another document or source remains possible under English law which is a practical and pragmatically useful stance to avoid contractual documentation becoming unwieldy in the extreme. (See, for a modern example, *O'Brien v MGN Ltd* [2001] EWCA Civ 1279; [2002] CLC 33, where competition rules relating to a scratchcard had been printed in the newspaper that had issued the cards: these rules were held to have been incorporated into the contract, even though the competitor had never read them.) Such notice must also be provided before or, at the latest, at the time that the contract was made (see *Olley v Marlborough Court Ltd* [1949] 1 KB 532, where a notice in a hotel room concerning the hotel's liability for articles that were lost or stolen was not part of the contract, since the deal had been struck before those terms had even been seen by the guest). This can raise difficult issues as to the precise timing of such notice (eg, terms in a brochure prior to conclusion of the contract, raising the question of when the contract was actually concluded (see eg, *Hood v Anchor Line (Henderson Brothers) Ltd* [1918] AC 837, at 847, etc) (although many of the terms that led to such contortions would now be regulated by UCTA 1977 in any case). See eg, *Hollingworth v Southern Ferries Ltd ('The Eagle')* [1977] 2 Lloyd's Rep 257 (affd, without reference to this issue [1981] 1 WLR 120) and the note by Clarke [1978] *CLJ* 21.

English law, however (in the absence of other, statutory controls) does not go so far as § 305c I BGB in its treatment of unexpected or unusual terms: instead, these are treated as subject to the general rules on notice, but the level of notice required will increase as the term in question becomes more unusual or unexpected. To quote Denning LJ (*J Spurling Ltd v Bradshaw* [1956] 1 WLR 461, at 466):

> I quite agree that the more unreasonable a clause is, the greater the notice which must be given of it. Some clauses I have seen would need to be printed in red ink on the face of the document with a red hand pointing to it before the notice could be held to be sufficient.

While, in that case, the clause in question was not found to require that treatment, Lord Denning MR's later judgment in *Thornton v Shoe Lane Parking Ltd* [1971] 2 QB 163 illustrated the potential force of this consideration. In the days prior to UCTA 1977, it was possible to exclude liability for personal injury (while today, if this is caused by negligence, this is no longer possible: section 2(1) UCTA 1977) and this is what the Shoe Lane Parking garage attempted to do. For the ticket issued at the automatic machine referred to a list of conditions, displayed on a pillar opposite the machine, to which the issue of the ticket was said to be subject. Referring to the clause, Lord Denning commented (at 170):

> All I say is that it is so wide and so destructive of rights that the court should not hold any man bound by it unless it is drawn to his attention in the most explicit way. It is an instance of what I had in mind in *J Spurling Ltd v Bradshaw* [1956] 1 WLR 461, 466.

Megaw LJ took a similar view (at 173) and emphasised:

> I think it is a highly relevant factor in considering whether proper steps were taken fairly to bring that matter to the notice of the plaintiff that the first attempt to bring to his notice the intended inclusion of those conditions was at a time when as a matter of hard reality it would have been practically impossible for him to withdraw from his intended entry on the premises for the purpose of leaving his car there.

Thus, the Court of Appeal held that the clause could not be treated as part of the contract, so that Mr Thornton would be compensated for the injury he had suffered (an injury due in part to Shoe Lane Parking's negligence—the trial judge had held them and Mr Thornton equally to blame).

Likewise, the general rule as to interpretation, as explained above, is altered. § 305c II BGB stipulates (cf Article 5, second sentence of the Directive) that any doubt in interpreting standard terms is to be resolved against the user of such terms (see eg, *Houghton v Trafalgar Insurance Co Ltd* [1954] 1 QB 247). This rule of interpretation *contra proferentem*, also one of the rules initially developed by the courts, is derived from the argument that it is in the hands of the user of standard terms to phrase them in plain and unambiguous language. This rule does not apply, however, (cf also Article 5, third sentence of the Directive) if consumer organisations bring an action as to whether contractual terms drawn up for general use are unfair: in such a situation, the most unfavourable interpretation prevails (in the UK, see regs 7(2) and 12 UCTTR 1999. Note that Article 5, second sentence and reg 7(2) aim to avoid the paradoxical result that a more narrowly construed exclusion clause then is treated as 'reasonable' and thus, ultimately, operates to the detriment of the consumer: cf, for example, the *Watford Electronics* case [2001] EWCA Civ 317; [2001] 1 All ER (Comm) 696). It is important to stress that German courts insist on the presence of a genuine ambiguity as to the true meaning of a term. It does not suffice that the meaning is disputed between the parties (see eg, BGH NJW 2002, 3232). Nevertheless, the law reports contain a considerable number of cases in which the court found that a term was not sufficiently clearly drafted and allowed for more than one interpretation, even on objective standards (eg, BGH NJW-RR 2003, 1247; NJW-RR 2002, 1257; NJW 1998, 2207. In English law, see *Ailsa Craig Fishing Co Ltd v Malvern Fishing Co* [1983] 1 WLR 964, at 966F (*per* Lord Wilberforce) and *BHP Petroleum Ltd v British Steel plc* [2000] 2 Lloyd's Rep 277, [47] (*per* Evans L.J.)). English law operates a similar interpretive scheme, although it has been noted

(Treitel, *The Law of Contract*, p 222) that the courts seem less hostile to clauses that aim to limit liability than those that attempt to exclude it altogether (see eg, the *Ailsa Craig Fishing* case (above), at 970 (*per* Lord Fraser of Tullybelton) and the *BHP Petroleum* case (above) (from which compare [46]—[47] (*per* Evans L.J.) and [71]—[72] and [76]—[77] (*per* May L.J.)).

(d) Assessing the Fairness of Standard Terms

We come now to what lies at the heart of policing (or 'regulating') standard terms, namely assessing their fairness. The German approach resembles that of the Directive by combining a general clause with a non-exhaustive list of prohibited terms. It is also in this respect that the text of the Code differentiates between the commercial and the consumer context. We say 'the text of the Code', since in reality the difference is not as great as it seems. A number of subtle explanations are called for to shed some light on this complex framework of substantive control.

The first step of the inquiry is to determine whether the term in question contains a deviation from or a qualification to any rule of law; if this is not the case, the term is subject to one requirement only, namely that it must be phrased in unambiguous, plain language: § 307 III BGB. This provision has two situations in mind: the first is where standard terms conform to rules of law (eg, repeating them; see BGH NJW 2002, 1950; cf BGH NJW 2001, 2014).

The second, which is much more important, and which is expressed more clearly in Article 4(2) of the Directive: '[a]ssessment of the unfair nature of the terms shall relate neither to the definition of the main subject matter of the contract nor to the adequacy of the price and remuneration, on the one hand, as against the services or goods supplies in exchange, on the other, in so far as these terms are in plain intelligible language.' The 'adequacy of the price' as against 'the services or goods or supplies' received in return is exempt from the fairness test (see, for the same point in English law, Treitel, *The Law of Contract*, p 271: 'the Regulations are not intended to operate as a mechanism of quality or price control' (although see also *The Law of Contract*, p 271, note 77 and the reference to *Director General of Fair Trading v First National Bank* [2002] 1 AC 481)). Thus, whether the deal is a good or bad one is no concern of the courts when assessing standard terms under the Directive or § 307 BGB. Accordingly, both descriptions of the performance and the determination of the price are outside the reach of the fairness test. However, the general rule is subject to so many exceptions that it is doubtful whether this exemption effectively closes the door to substantive control (or, indeed, was intended to do so).

Descriptions of the exact nature of the performance are exempt, but only if they concern a matter which belongs to the *essentialia negotii* of the contract in question: that is, if they were missing the contract could not be regarded as concluded—offer and acceptance would be incomplete in a vital respect (eg, BGH NJW 1993, 2369; see reg 6(2)(a) ('definition of the main subject matter' and (b) ('adequacy of the price or remuneration') UTCCR 1999). The *Bundesgerichtshof*, in a somewhat circular piece of reasoning, held that clauses that in any way alter the main, 'promised' performance are subject to full control. This was said in relation to a clause stating that the account on a pre-paid telephone card expired after a fixed period: BGH NJW 2001, 2635. A clause containing information as to the price to be paid is not subject to control—

unless the price is regulated by statute (this concerns, for instance, lawyer's fees and those of medics, eg, BGH NJW 1998, 1786; see reg 4(2)(a) UTCCR 1999, where the use of the phrase 'mandatory' (as opposed to 'default') rules could give rise to certain difficulties—see McKendrick, *Contract Law*, pp 497–8). Likewise, clauses which 'indirectly' influence the price but which if struck out could easily be replaced by default rules in the Code are also not exempt from the scrutiny of the courts (sometimes referred to as *Preisnebenabreden*). (See, for instance: BGH NJW 1999, 2276: clause setting up a charge for the client of a bank for services rendered to the creditors of the client in fulfilling arrest orders; BGH NJW 2001, 751: term that purported to exclude liability of bank if their online services fail out of technical reasons. In BGH NJW 1998, 383, however, a clause was said to be exempt from control where it charged the client of a bank for using his credit card aboard.) A further exception is made for services the performance of which is not related to the main performance and is not in the interest of the customer (eg, BGH NJW 2002, 2386: in this case a fee charged by a telecommunications company for shutting down an account was not regarded as exempt). Clauses only 'indirectly' influencing the price include, for instance, terms fixing the time when payment is due, stating whether one party is under a duty to perform first, whether a tenant is to bear the cost of refurbishing the flat, and so on. (See for details: Palandt-*Heinrichs* § 307 Rn. 60 *et seq.*) The result is not always easy to predict: Treitel comments (*The Law of Contract*, p 272) that one should not forget that the benefit of protecting the core subject matter of the bargain from scrutiny only operates where the term in question is 'expressed in plain, intelligible language' (reg 6(2) UTCCR 1999), so that ambiguously or obscurely phrased pricing terms could still be subject to scrutiny. (On this point, see *Bankers Insurance Co Ltd v South* [2003] EWHC 380; [2003] PIQR 28; [2004] Lloyd's Rep IR 1.) How these different decisions are to be reconciled is thus not an easy task for legal advisers. We have dwelt on this issue as it illustrates the potential difficulties flowing from Article 4(2) of the Directive and the narrow limits it arguably imposes. (Cf also the discussion in: *Director General of Fair Trading v First National Bank* [2002] 1 AC 481, especially at [12], [20] and [34]: the House of Lords was concerned not to interpret these provisions too narrowly, lest the object of the regulations be 'plainly frustrated' (at [12], *per* Lord Bingham of Cornhill) and held that the 'ancillary' obligation on the debtor under a consumer credit agreement to pay interest on sums still outstanding (even after a the principal sum had been the subject of a judgment against him) was not a term that related to the 'adequacy of the price or remuneration' (reg 6(2)) *above*. In the final analysis, however, their Lordships refused to find this term unfair or contrary to good faith, since it should have been clear to both parties that the lender would not deny his claim to interest and the principal sum ([20]).)

The test of fairness as laid down in §§ 307–9 BGB is highly differentiated and thus aims to further security in the law; something all the more to be welcomed in view of the strict consequences flowing from failing the test. The approach of the BGB consists of a combination of a general clause in § 307 BGB and two lists of specific questionable terms in § 308 and § 309 BGB. Before we turn to the core of the test we must address a peculiarity of German law which, judging by the bare text of the Code, may give rise to misunderstandings. It concerns the application of the test of fairness to standard terms used as against a dealer (as defined in § 14 BGB). As was already stressed, German law extends the policing of standard terms beyond the consumer context (as noted above, English law also makes such an extension, although on more strictly specified and limited grounds: s. 3 UCTA 1977 and note that sections 2(1), 5(1), 11(3) and 11(4) UCTA 1977 explicitly also apply to limitation and exclusion notices that do not form a part of any contract). This general rule is apparently heavily qualified in § 310 I 1 BGB, which prescribes that the two provisions containing the list of prohibited specific terms is not to be applied to standard terms used as against a dealer. However, § 310 I 2 BGB then qualifies this qualification considerably. It states that a term listed in §§ 308 or 309 BGB can be treated as unreasonable under the general clause in § 307 BGB provided that regard is had to trade usage. The courts have interpreted this power in a broad way. If a term contravenes either §§ 308 or 309 BGB this is taken as an indication of its unfairness (see eg, BGHZ 90, 273; BGH NJW 1996, 389). Upholding such a term is thus technically, as well as in reality, the exception rather than the rule (see eg, BGH NJW 2003, 1447, term justified). A useful illustration is provided by BGHZ 130, 19 = NJW 1995, 2553, case no 50 (see, also, BGH NJW 2000, 2675; NJW 2002, 3167): in this case, a surety undertook a guarantee that extended beyond the loan to be secured and which initially was the sole reason given by the bank for demanding the guarantee (the so-called *Anlassrechtsprechung*). It was held that such a guarantee could be surprising (§ 305c I BGB) and might constitute an unreasonable deviation (in the sense of § 307 II BGB) from the rule in § 767 I 3 BGB. The case is noteworthy for a number of reasons. Not only does it display the courts' full arsenal for the control of standard terms even in a commercial context, the decision also leads one to speculate that courts will be more readily inclined to intervene if the transaction in question is dangerous for the promisor: in this line of cases, so-called 'global guarantees' (*Globalbürgschaften*) were at stake, ie, guarantees covering all present and future debts of the company.

For the sake of completeness, the reader should note that § 310 III Nr. 3 BGB (cf Article 4(1) of the Directive) tightens the applicable standard in consumer transactions: in addition, the surrounding circumstances peculiar to the individual case may be relevant in determining the fairness of a term (normally, fairness is assessed on the basis of an abstract evaluation of the contract terms; see reg 6(1) UTCCR 1999 on the same point, although the case law discussed above (section 5(c)) suggests that the English courts have always relied heavily on the context in assessing the incorporation of terms).

The 'general clause' in § 307 BGB is subdivided into several principles. § 307 I 2 BGB stresses the transparency requirement (Articles 4(2) and 5 of the Directive), yet it is doubtful whether this adds anything beyond the relevance of clear wording in relation to the incorporation and the construction as discussed above (section 5(c)).

More relevant is § 307 I 1 BGB, which invalidates terms that—contrary to good faith—operate unreasonably to the detriment of the other party (contrast Article 3(1) of the Directive referring to good faith, an imbalance of the rights and duties and a detriment to the consumer; see reg 5(1) UTCCR 1999, which reproduces Article 3(1)). This abstract formula is fleshed out in § 307 II BGB. Nr. 1 of this provision embodies what hitherto has already been identified as the essential feature of the German approach: in case of doubt, a term is unreasonable if it deviates from a central purpose of the statutory rule (eg, the default rules contained in the Code). Nr. 2 adds that this is also the case when the term interferes with the essential rights and duties of the parties (the so-called *Kardinalpflichten*) and thereby endangers the purpose of the contract. Since this presupposes a concept of contractual duties and rights distinct from the contract to be assessed, and since this concept is in virtually all cases derived from the Code, there is little need to differentiate between Nr. 1 and Nr. 2. This general clause is, as explained, the main basis on which the control of standard terms in a commercial context is exercised. Furthermore, the general clause will be applied to contract clauses which are not included in §§ 308, 309 BGB; so far as the English statutory material is concerned, the position is clearly different (although note that the general rules of the common law apply to all contracts and can lead to *some* results that would overlap with the use of the general clause in German law, as discussed above).

The combined effect of these provisions is that the law of contract as contained in the Code is, to a certain degree, strict. Freedom of contract is the basic notion in German law, and the default rules in the Code are accordingly called *dispositives Recht*. Yet by using standard terms (pre-formulated contracts) it is quite difficult to derogate from or contract out of those provisions of the Code which are regarded as essential by the courts. This basic stance, once explained, is clearly some way from the default position in English law, as discussed above.

The scope of direct application of the list of terms in §§ 308, 309 BGB has already been pointed out: consumer transactions. It remains to be said that there are two lists, because the list in the former section is deemed to be indicative only, whereas the list in the latter section is said to be applied strictly. Not much depends on this difference, however, since the indication of the first list is quite strong and the second list contains a great number of abstract terms ('reasonable', etc), which by their very nature do not lend themselves to application in a 'technical' manner. For reasons of space we give only two examples of each.

Thus, § 308 Nr. 6 BGB invalidates terms which deem certain 'important' declarations of intention of the user of the term to have come to the notice of the other party (no equivalent can be found in Annex I of the Directive). Thus, a clause which treats the other party as having been notified if a declaration was sent to the last known address is not valid (see for details as to this clause which via § 307 BGB also applies in a commercial context, the annotation of *MünchKomm*-Basedow, § 308 Nr. 6).

Paragraph 309 Nr. 7 BGB contains an important example of prohibited terms in relation to exclusion clauses, which should be compared with para 1 of the Annex to the Directive. Generally speaking, § 309 Nr. 7 lit. a BGB provides that, as far as dangers to life, health and bodily integrity are concerned, a term may not exclude or limit liability for negligent or intentional conduct. The UK's implementation of the Directive by simply adopting the regime in a separate statutory instrument has left some difficulties of consistency and interpretation in relation to para 1(a) of the Annex to the Directive: Schedule 2, para 1(a) UTCCR 1999 overlaps substantially with s. 2(1) UCTA 1977, yet the consequences of each are different. Under UCTA 1977, such a term is void, while it is only indicatively unfair under UTCCR 1999—this raises questions of implied repeal and is at the very least a messy way of achieving an uncontroversial result (see Reynolds' discussion of the predecessor 1994 Regulations: (1994) 110 *L.QR* 1 and the proposals of the Law Commission Consultation Paper No 166 and Scottish Law Commission Discussion Paper No 119, *Unfair Terms in Contracts—A Joint Consultation Paper* (2002) developed and finalised in their Joint Report of 24 February 2005 (Law Com. No 292, Scot. Law Com. No 199 (Cm 6464)). § 309 Nr. 7 lit. b BGB allows an exclusion of liability in the case of 'simple' negligence (as opposed to gross negligence as a form of fault, *Verschulden*, see generally, § 276 II BGB) in all other cases. There seems to be consensus that, based on § 307 BGB, a term purporting to exclude liability for gross negligence and intention also cannot be sustained in the commercial context (BGHZ 95, 170); the same applies where liability is excluded for gross negligence and the duty breached is of central importance to the parties (BGHZ 89, 363). Whether exclusion in the case of 'simple' negligence is possible as against a dealer has not yet been authoritatively determined. Note also that in the commercial context limitations may be easier to justify where the sum awarded covers typical risks (BGH NJW 1993, 335).

(e) Consequences of Invalidity

The Directive stipulates that unfair terms shall not be binding on the consumer and that the remainder of the contract shall continue to be binding (in Article 6(1); see reg 6(1) UTCCR 1999). This leaves it to the Member States to determine how the gap left by the invalid term is to be filled, if indeed, any such gap exists: one could argue that, if too much needs to be added to the contract to replace the now non-binding term, then the contract is not 'capable of continuing in existence without the unfair term' (reg 8(2) UTCCR 1999). As McKendrick has pointed out (*Contract Law*, p 503), the 'regulation does not . . . confer on the court a power to re-write the term of the contract in order to make it conform with the requirements of fairness.' § 306 I BGB contains a similar provision to Article 6(1), further qualified in § 306 III BGB. It is particularly interesting to note, from a comparative perspective, that § 306 II BGB provides that the gap left by the unfair term is to be filled by applying the rules contained in the Code or other statutory source. This is taken by the courts to mean that the unfair term in question cannot be replaced with a term which contains the possible maximum tolerated by the test of fairness (*Verbot der geltungserhaltenden Reduktion*, consistent jurisprudence, see eg, BGHZ 84, 109; also in the commercial context: BGH NJW 2000, 1110). The courts stress that it is not their task to design a clause which, while giving effect as far as possible to the unfair clause, at the same time respects the limits flowing from the law. Furthermore, this would encourage the use of unfair standard terms because one could rely on the courts to cut such terms down to a legally sound level of fairness. Hence, the purpose of controlling standard terms in setting incentives for the use of fair terms would be undermined. Others argue that in some cases the courts have in fact filled the gap left by an unfair term by constructing a new term which corresponded best with the purpose of the term which was struck out. In any case, these writers suggest, it is more appropriate that the gap should be filled in the first place by determining the hypothetical intentions of the parties (term implied in fact) and only failing this by applying the rule contained in § 306 II BGB seeeg, *Münchener Kommentar-* Basedow, § 306 Rn. 12 *et seq*.) For reasons of space, we cannot discuss this intriguing argument, but the reader should be aware of the fact that the courts for the time being are clearly not prepared to depart openly from the principle that gaps are to be filled by having recourse to the rules contained in the Code. Treitel suggests (*The Law of Contract*, p 281) that, in such a 'gap' situation in English law in relation to para 1(l) of the Annex to the Directive (concerning a price of goods to be determined at the time of delivery, held to be unfair because the consumer was given no right to cancel if 'the final price is too high in relation to the price agreed when the contract was concluded'), three possibilities exist. First, the contract as a whole is not binding in the absence of the term as to price; secondly, the remainder of the contract still binds the parties and a reasonable price must then be paid (see section 8(2) of the Sale of Goods Act 1979); or, thirdly, the contract as a whole remains in place, only the price term is the one originally agreed, rather than subject to the variation clause. There is no suggestion in English law that the courts are empowered to supply alternative terms to fill such gaps, although there is no case law to date to test this proposition. However, it should be pointed out that at least in some instances the courts have limited the effect of their ruling, thus cutting back to a reasonable extent the scope of the standard term in question. See, for an example of this approach, BGHZ 130, 19, case no 50, discussed above.

4

Relaxations to Contractual Privity

1. INTRODUCTORY REMARKS

This topic offers a fertile ground for comparative study since the problem it addresses has occupied all the systems of the industrialised world and has received a wide variety of answers. Also, it presents a particular interest to English lawyers since they have (fairly) recently adjusted their law on this matter in a way that while it has not pleased everyone it has brought English law closer to continental European law.

The starting point is not of course in dispute. Generally speaking, persons who enter into a contract intend to create rights and obligations that will affect them, alone, and no one else. Occasionally, however, it makes commercial sense to allow third parties, who are not parties to the transaction, to claim the promised performance directly from the promisor. This chapter will deal with the main situations where this is allowed by German law. In what follows we shall continue to use the English terms promisor, promisee, and third party, but they should be taken to refer respectively to the German *Versprechender* (the French *promettant*), *Versprechensempfänger* (the French *stipulant*) and *Begünstigter* (the French *bénéficiaire*). Incidentally, the French terms are also given here for occasional references to French law may be necessary. The reason for this is that these two great systems—French and German— have adopted slightly varying approaches to some aspects of this problem. Thus, English lawyers who seem keener than ever to adapt their law may thus be well advised to bear both variants in mind when weighing the pros and cons of the options they have chosen to favour. It is interesting however to note that other systems that have chosen to modernise their law—the Israeli for instance—have chosen to be influenced by the German model. On the whole, we shall see that this may have been a wise decision since the German approach to this problem has proved flexible and, on the whole, very carefully thought out.

The utility of the foreign material for the English lawyer becomes obvious at two levels. The comparative method can be utilised to clarify the basic approach to privity problems a legal system chooses to adopt, but is equally invaluable when it comes to deciding individual cases.

At the first and most *abstract* it should make him question the influential but dogmatic assertion of Lord Haldane in *Dunlop Pneumatic Tyre Co Ltd v Selfridge & Co Ltd* ([1915] AC 847, 853) that the common law recognises no *ius quaesitum tertio* on the double grounds of consideration and the doctrine of privity.

The first prong of the argument is easily rebutted For if it is formulated to read that the third party's rights are prevented by the idea that 'consideration must move from the promisee,' it falls flat once one realises that consideration has, in fact, moved from the promisee (who is always the co-contracting party and not the third party/plaintiff). And if the consideration argument is put in the form that 'only the person who has given consideration can enforce the contract' then, though it can frustrate the rights of third parties, it raises the question why does the performance of the promise to the third party undermine the true aim of consideration (which, as we have seen, is to distinguish between serious binding promises and those which are not binding)? For, as Zweigert and Kötz have remarked (in a passage from the second edition of their *Introduction to Comparative Law* (1992), p 498): 'if a person has made a promise in return for consideration provided by the other contractor, the seriousness of his promise to contract is established, and it should not be reckoned any weaker simply because the agreement provides that what was promised should be capable of being demanded not only by the other contracting party but by the beneficiary as well.'

As for Lord Haldane's second objection, that third party rights run counter to the doctrine of privity, the answer must surely be that this objection is not unknown to the modern civil law as well but has been overcome easily and painlessly by these systems in their desire to accommodate commercial realities which, in many instances, do require the possibility of exceptions. If hardship to the creditors of the promisee can be avoided (often the key but unexpressed objection to granting third party rights), then what remains of the doctrine of privity may be little more than a mental block against allowing third parties to enter such arrangements.

The House of Lords nevertheless refused to change its approach to privity (see *Midland Silicones Ltd v Scruttons Ltd* [1962] AC 446) despite several attempts by Lord Denning to allow rights of suit by third party beneficiaries and despite the fact that judicial and academic criticism of the third party rule continued over the years, culminating in Steyn LJ's strong attack on the privity doctrine in *Darlington BC v Wiltshier Northern Ltd* ([1995] 1 WLR 68, 76):

> The case for recognising a contract for the benefit of a third party is simple and straight-forward. The autonomy of the will of the parties should be respected. The law of contract should give effect to the reasonable expectations of contracting parties. Principle certainly requires that a burden should not be imposed on a third party without his consent. But there is no doctrinal, logical, or policy reason why the law should deny effectiveness to a contract for the benefit of a third party where that is the expressed intention of the parties. Moreover, often the parties, and particularly third parties, organise their affairs on the faith of the contract. They rely on the contract. It is therefore unjust to deny effectiveness to such a contract. I will not struggle with the point further since nobody seriously asserts the contrary.

One reason for the judicial reluctance for reform may have been that the number of exceptions to the doctrine was so great that it could be doubted whether it could be still regarded as a 'general' rule. In any event, it could be argued with some justification, in most cases practical justice could be done. A good example is *Beswick v Beswick* [1968] AC 58, also discussed in section 2, p 188. Specific performance was granted at the suit of the promisee, who was in fact dead but was represented by the third party beneficiary as his administratrix. But where specific performance is not available the result becomes questionable. One drawback of this pragmatic approach to privity clearly was that the law became increasingly complex and therefore was not regarded as being in a satisfactory condition. The English agonising on this point is well revealed in The Law Commission's Consultation Paper No 121 entitled *Privity of*

Contract; Contracts for the Benefit of Third Parties (which was published in 1992; see also, eg, para 3.6 of the Report no 242 (1996), discussed in what follows).

The pursuant Report No 242 (1996) of the Law Commission with the same title and subject came out in favour of abolishing the traditional third party rule and was accompanied by clearly phrased corresponding recommendations and a draft Bill. (See for comments on the Report: Adams, Beyleveld and Brownsword, 'Privity of Contract' (1997) 60 *MLR* 238; Burrows, 'Reforming Privity of Contract' [1996] *LMCLQ* 467 and Tettenborn, 'Third Party Contracts' [1996] *JBL* 602.) This report, and in the face of judicial reluctance to tackle the problem, finally paved the way for introducing *by legislation* the concept of a contract for the benefit of a third party into English law. It suffices here to point out that one of the main arguments for reform of the Law Commission was that the 'legal systems of most of the member states of the European Union recognise and enforce the rights of third party beneficiaries under contracts' (Law Com No 242 (1996), para 3.8).

The intended reform followed just a few years later with the passing of the Contracts (Rights of Third Parties) Act 1999 (or 'the 1999 Act'). (On which see Burrows, 'The Contracts (Rights of Third Parties) Act 1999 and its Implications for Commercial Contracts' [2000] *LMCLQ* 540; Dean, 'Removing a Blot on the Landscape' [2000] *JBL* 143; Kincaid (ed), *Privity—Private Justice or Public Regulation* (2001); Macaulay, 'Warranting Third Party Rights' [2000] *Constr LJ* 265; Merkin (ed), *Privity of Contract—The Impact of the Contracts (Rights of Third Parties) Act 1999* (2000); Roe, 'Contractual Intention under Section 1(1)(b) and 1(2) of the Contracts (Rights of Third Parties) Act 1999' (2000) 63 *MLR* 887; and Stevens, 'The Contracts (Rights of Third Parties) Act 1999' (2004) 120 *LQR* 292.) For the first case on the 1999 Act, see *Nisshin Shipping Co Ltd v Cleaves & Company Ltd and Others* [2003] EWHC 2602 (Comm), [2004] 1 Lloyd's Rep 38 (discussed by Stevens, 'The Contracts (Rights of Third Parties) Act 1999' 309–10 and McKnight, 'A Review of Developments in English Law during 2003—Part II' (2004) 19 *JIBLR* 151, 169–71). But the change has not left everyone happy; rarely does reform have such an effect. Thus one author (Stevens (2004) 120 *LQR* 292, 322), after discussing the reasons given for the reform, concluded that:

> The illness diagnosed was not as serious as it was thought and the operation may have caused more problems than it solved. Developments in the remedies available to the promisee meant that by the time of the passing of the Act the need for surgery had largely disappeared. If the third party has no right to compel the promisee to seek a remedy on his behalf, for example under a contract or trust, the robust response is tough luck. In addition to the uncertainty generated by the Act the fear is that the unwary will be caught out by conferring enforceable rights on third parties when they do not intend to do so. This appears to be behind the widespread exclusion of the operation of the Act.

It should be clear from the outset, and is self-evident from a comparative perspective, what are *not* the implications of the 1999 Act. The acceptance of the notion of a contract for the benefit of a third party does not bring in its wake the abolition of the general rule that a third party cannot derive rights from a contract. The Act merely adds a wide-ranging exception to the privity doctrine but does not replace it with a different general rule (see Law Com No 242 (1996), paras 5.16 and 13.2). The doctrine of privity or, to use the German term, of 'relativity of contract' continues to apply to prevent strangers from enforcing a contract. The effect of importing the concept of a contract for the benefit of a third party into English law is to allow enforcement by a third party whom the original parties intended should receive a benefit and be able to claim it.

Under the Act the third party has a direct remedy in contract against the promisor. The central provision of the English Act is its test of enforceability contained in section 1(1). According to this section, a contract is for the benefit of a third party if it purports to confer a benefit on an expressly identified (including identifiable by class) third party: section 1(3). Under the first limb of the test, section 1(1)(a), the parties expressly declare the contract to be one in favour of a third party. The more difficult to apply is, obviously, the second limb, section 1(1)(b). It is interesting to note that the English Act opted for a presumption in favour of such a contract if the contract confers a benefit on a third party, a solution which was rejected by the fathers of the BGB as being too sweeping (see § 328 BGB; see for discussion, Kötz, *International Encyclopedia of Comparative Law*, chapter 13 (1992), p 22). One might be tempted, therefore, to conclude that the scope of application of the Act is extremely wide. However, on closer analysis one can see that this might not be the case. For the presumption is founded on a specific preconception of a classic contract for the benefit of a third party, which is very similar to that presupposed by § 328 BGB. The wording is meant to convey this even if the restriction envisaged by the Commission is not an easy one. The distinction relevant to the second limb is that between 'to confer' a benefit and merely being (incidentally) 'of' benefit. The first situation triggers the presumption and corresponds to the classic contract for the benefit of a third party. The special feature of this situation is that the third party is *meant* to be able to enforce the contract as a whole, section 1(5), including for instance the right to rescind a contract or, where available, to seek specific performance.

Applying such a test to the *Hedley Byrne*-type situations (*Hedley Byrne & Co v Heller & Partners* [1964] AC 465 and the subsequent English negligent misstatement cases) means excluding them from the scope of the Act (as also suggested in *The German Law of Torts*, p 302). This result also derives support from a comparative perspective. The insight that the third party must have an interest in the performance of the contract as such lies at the heart of the contract with protective effects towards third parties (to be discussed in section 3, p 204), which is recognised alongside § 328 BGB (the classic contract for the benefit of a third party) and serves a function similar to that of the English tort of negligence. Ironically, the Law Commission stressed that the intention test did not embrace the wider German concept of a contract with protective effects towards third parties (reference to Markesinis, 'An Expanding Tort Law—the Price of a Rigid Contract Law' (1987) 103 *LQR* 354; see para 7.25, note 22, of the report). This is yet another indication that the Commission regarded the second limb of the test to be confined to cases where the parties intended to grant the third party 'primary enforcement'. (Accordingly, an exclusion clause operating for the benefit of a third party was analysed in German law as an instance of the contract with protective effects towards third parties. See *The German Law of Torts*, p 540; BGH JZ 1962, 570 and 333. By contrast, the Law Commission regards the 1999 Act to be applicable to such a situation: see para 7.43 of the report.)

Overall, however, the presumption contained in section 1(1)(b) of the 1999 Act is limited in a very similar way to the German (classic) contract for the benefit of a third party defined in § 328 BGB. Hence, if the second limb of the enforceability test is construed by the courts in the way that the Law Commission suggests, comparative law could thus provide invaluable assistance in deciding in which circumstances a contract 'confers a benefit' in a third party, ie in which situations the presumption is raised. (See for examples, Unberath, *Transferred Loss* (2003), pp 26–33.)

In imposing a change of paradigms, the English legislator used comparative material on the first and most abstract level as an argument for reform. This change in the basic attitude towards third party rights also altered the practical purpose of the comparative method. Henceforth, foreign material is of use to the English lawyer primarily at a *secondary* and more *specific* level. For here the foreign solutions not only reveal which of a possible range of technical answers may be most desirable to a given problem, they also suggest the best technical way of achieving these results. It is thus intriguing to note that it is in this area of 'detail' that English law, arguably, stands to gain most from the study of the modern civil law.

Consider also the following illustration that further underlines the point just made. It is, of course, a truism to state that the validity of the life insurance contract paved the way for the recognition of an important area of exception to the starting point about contractual privity. How this was achieved in three major systems—the English, the French and the German—is instructive. For, to begin with, we note that in England, a case law country, it took a statute—the *Married Women's Property Act* 1882—to create a right in favour of the spouse or children of the insured, whereas in France, a country with a codified system, it required the intervention of the Court of Cassation (D1885.1.150; D1934.1.141.) to establish, unequivocally, such a right. But the paradox, in itself, though interesting is not that important. What is important is to note is that in England the exception to the rule is defined in a very narrow way, with the result that those persons who are not the spouse or the children of the insured will not be allowed to recover under the policy unless a trust has been expressly constituted in their favour under the policy. The injustice of this result has been noted both by writers on the subject (eg, Colinvaux, *The Law of Insurance* (1984) 361) and by courts which have striven, sometimes through fictions, to avoid it. (Cf *In Re A Policy No 6402 of the Scottish Equitable Life Assurance Society* [1902] 1 Ch 282; *In re Schebsman* [1944] 1 Ch 83.)

The (wider) result favoured by French law is also achieved by § 330 BGB which stipulates that, in case of doubt, the third party (beneficiary of the policy) acquires the right directly against the insurer to demand payment of the insurance monies (the word 'directly', incidentally, having been interpreted to mean that the monies do not go through the deceased's estate, thus avoiding potential clashes between the interests of the beneficiary and the deceased's creditors. (See RGZ 128, 187; BGH NJW 1965, 1913.) The German example thus shows that legislation not only can provide an answer to these problems, but that it can do so with suitable flexibility. Indeed, one could argue with Professor Werner Lorenz that one reason why the German Code has withstood the passage of time is because it (and its practitioners) managed so skilfully to combine the phrasing of a sufficiently general rule with a precise regulation of the triangular relationship. (See 'Contract and Third Party Rights in German and English Law' in Markesinis (ed), *The Gradual Convergence* (1994), p 65). The discussion that follows reveals other areas where particular problems are susceptible to different answers and that the ones given by the German legislator have much to commend them to the impartial observer.

One final general observation should be made by way of introduction. So far, we have been speaking of the English common law and contrasting its basic premises with those of German and French law. Such differences however do not exist (or at any rate, become diminished) once we change the focus and begin comparing German and American common law. The same is now true, as we have already intimated, of the English 1999 Act. Indeed, here one is faced with quite a remarkable degree of similarity. Thus, three important areas of convergence must be stressed.

First, the right of the beneficiary to claim directly from the promisor depends on the intentions of the promisor and the promise. (See eg, sections 302 and 304 of the Restament (Second) Contracts; section 1(2) of the 1999 Act.) It may be different, however, when we come to discuss contracts with protective effects towards third parties (especially in the 'defective' wills cases) where it is arguable that the intention that matters is that of the promisee and not the promisor (see below).

Secondly, unlike French law, German and American law take the view that the beneficiary need not assent to the contract in order to take the benefit from it, though he has the right to reject it within a reasonable period of time. (Cf § 333 BGB with 306 Restatement. See also, Farnsworth, *Contracts* (1990), p 769 *et seq* and section 1 (1) of the 1999 Act). In relation to the third party the contract between the main parties contains thus a unilateral stipulation.

Thirdly, as § 334 BGB states with admirable terseness, '[d]efences arising from the contract are available to the promisor even as against the third party'. (Cf the more verbose formulations of section 309 of the Restatement (Second) Contracts and section 3 of the 1999 Act).

The richness of German law is once more demonstrated by the fact that not only does it recognise the classic contract for the benefit of a third party, but the related idea of a contract with protective effects towards third parties and the doctrine of transferred loss, which have no *exact* equivalent in the other legal systems. However, only the former is regulated in the Code, namely in §§ 328–35 BGB, while the other two concepts are the results of judicial law-making on a case-by-case basis. These latter relaxations to contractual privity can at least in part be explained as a counter-reaction to the limitations imposed by the BGB on tort actions in § 823 and § 831 BGB. They are to some extent an illustration of the phenomenon of a rigid tort law provoking an expansive contract law. In the following, we will deal with the classic and relatively straightforward *Vertrag zugunsten Dritter* and in the remainder of the chapter seek to shed some light on the more complex and subtle mechanisms of the *Vertrag mit Schutzwirkung für Dritte* and *Drittschadensliquidation*.

2. CONTRACTS IN FAVOUR OF THIRD PARTIES
(*VERTRÄGE ZUGUNSTEN DRITTER*)

Bayer, 'Vertraglicher Drittschutz' JuS 1996, 473; Bühler, 'Die Rechtsprechung des BGH zur Drittbegünstigung im Todesfall' NJW 1976, 1727; v Caemmerer, 'Verträge zugunsten Dritter' in *Festschrift für Wieacker* (1978) 311; Gernhuber, *Das Schuldverhältnis. Begründung und Änderung, Pflichten und Strukturen, Drittwirkungen* (1989); Gernhuber, 'Gläubiger, Schuldner und Dritte' JZ 1962, 553; Kaduk, 'Fragen zur Zulässigkeit von Verfügung zugunsten eines Dritten' in *Festschrift für K. Larenz* (1983) 303; Kötz, 'Rights of Third Parties' in *International Encyclopedia of Comparative Law*, chapter 13 (1992); Kötz, 'The Doctrine of Privity of Contract' (1990) 10 *Tel Aviv Univ Studies in Law*, 195; Kortmann and Faber, 'Contract and Third Parties' in *Towards a European Civil Code* (1994) 237; W Lorenz, 'Contract and Third Party Rights in German and English Law' in Markesinis (ed), *The Gradual Convergence* (1994) 65; W Lorenz, 'Some Thoughts about Contract and Tort' in *Essays in Memory of Professor FH Lawson* (1986); W Lorenz, 'Die Einbeziehung Dritter in vertragliche Schuldverhältnisse' JZ 1960, 108; Markesinis, 'An Expanding Tort Law the Price of a Rigid Contract Law' (1987) 103 *LQR* 354; Martens, 'Rechtsgeschäft und Drittinteressen' AcP 177, 113; Millner, '*Ius quaesitum tertio*: Comparison and Synthesis' (1967) 16 *ICLQ* 446; Papanikolaou, *Schlechterfüllung beim Vertrag zugunsten Dritter* (1977).

(a) Typical Factual Situations where such Contracts are Discovered by the Courts

When the BGB provisions were being drafted, the German legislator mainly had insurance and anuity contracts in mind—the so-called contracts for the care of third persons (*Versorgungsverträge*); but the flexibility of the main provision—§ 328 BGB— allowed the courts to apply the new notion to new situations that called for this treatment. It is customary for German books to group the relevant case law under different headings; and it may serve our purpose to start our treatment of the subject in the same way so as to show how similar (or different) are the various solutions reached by the English Common law. The following list of headings is thus indicative of the factual situations where contracts in favour of third parties have been discovered:

(i) widows' insurance schemes and workers' retirement benefit schemes;
(ii) parent contracting with doctors for the treatment of their child;
(iii) savings accounts; third parties as account holders;
(iv) carriage of persons in connection with the services of travel agencies;
(v) insurance contracts stipulating performance to third parties;
(vi) carriage of goods where the consignee is treated as a third party beneficiary;
(vii) contracts of lease. Family members of the lessee regarded as contract beneficiaries of the contract with the lessor;
(viii) sales of land and restrictive covenants in favour of owners of adjoining land;
(ix) certain dealings between a trustee in bankruptcy or a reciever in favour of the creditor;
(x) maintenance and separation agreements providing for the financial support of a child living with one of the spouses;
(xi) sale of goods; warranty of the manufacturer running with the goods.

Contractual privity is also relaxed, and third parties are again brought under the protective umbrella of the contract in other situations covered by the akin concepts of contract 'with protective effects' towards a third party and the theory of 'transferred loss'. But these, for reasons which will soon become obvious, are best discussed under separate headings (see below, sections 3, and 4). Here, because of lack of space, we shall limit our comments to the first six categories of cases. (For category (vii), see: BGHZ 77, 116, 124 and cf *Jackson* v *Horizon Holidays Ltd* [1975] 3 All ER 92 and

Law Com No 242 (1996), para 7.40. See also: BGHZ 3, 385; BGHZ 49, 350; BGHZ 61, 227, 233, case no 59; BGHZ 70, 327, 329, 330 (concerning a sub-lessee), case no 60. For category (viii) see: BGH NJW 1975, 344. For category (ix) see: RGZ 117, 143, 149. For category (x) see: BGHZ 5, 302 but contrast BGH NJW 1983, 684, 685.)

(i) Retirement Benefits and Widows' Pensions under Private Law Agreements

For the sake of comparison, it may be helpful to begin with a factual situation which presents the problem that confronted the House of Lords in *Beswick v Beswick* ([1968] AC 58). It will be recalled that in that case a coal merchant had assigned to his nephew the assets of his business, and the nephew undertook first to pay the uncle a certain sum of money per week for the remainder of his life and then to pay the uncle's wife an annuity in the event of his death. After the husband's death, which occurred a mere year later, the nephew made just one weekly payment to the widow, and then refused to make any further payments. The widow's action succeeded because she had a right, as administratix of her husband's estate, to require her husband's nephew to perform his obligation under the agreement. As a mere contract beneficiary however she would not have been successful since the contract made by her husband with his nephew did not confer on her a direct right of action. (After having quoted from the recommendation of the Law Revision Committee (1937—Cmnd 5449, 31), which would have enabled the widow to enforce the nephew's promise in her own name, Lord Reid (*Beswick v Beswick* at 72) expressed his disappointment with what he called 'Parliamentary procrastination'. The foreign observer may wonder why the House of Lords did not make use of the freedom given to it by the 'Practice Statement' of 1966 to deal with the 'privity problem'. Be that as it may, however, the solution, once again, came from the legislator. Thus, under section 1 of the 1999 Act, someone in the position of Mrs Beswick would now have a right to enforce the contract as a third party beneficiary. In the view of the Law Commission, the presumption of a contract for the benefit of a third party would apply. The nephew would be unlikely to be able to prove that he and old Mr Beswick had no intention at the time of contracting that Mrs Beswick should have the right to enforce the provision. (See Law Com No 242 (1996), para 7.46.)

In German law plaintiffs like Mrs Beswick have long had the right to sue the promisor in their *own* right by relying on § 328 I BGB. The *Bundesarbeitsgericht* repeatedly accepted this, the labour courts exercising jurisdiction whenever the claim originates from labour relations. It must be emphasised however that this approach has not been limited to labour law alone. The decision would not have been different if—in a fact situation like *Beswick v Beswick*—the *Bundesgerichtshof* had been the court of last instance because the dispute was not related to labour relations. Thus, since 1966 it has been clearly established that the contract of employment between employer (promisor) and employee (promisee) is to be regarded as a contract in favour of a third party if it contains a stipulation to the effect that a widow's pension will be paid after the employee's death. (BAG NJW 1967, 173, case no 51; see also BAG NJW 1973, 963.) In another case, decided by the *Bundesarbeitsgericht*, concerning retirement payments, the employer had founded a registered association for the sole purpose of paying extra pensions to employees, the amount of which varied according to the period of their employment. (BAG NJW 1973, 1946. This association

(*Unterstützungskasse*) was a legal entity under § 55 *et seq* BGB.) On his retirement, an employee brought an action against this association claiming a certain amount believed to be due to him under the articles of association. In the opinion of the court, this claim was based on a contract between the employer and the association in favour of retiring employees (§ 328 I BGB). (For the sake of clarity, it should be pointed out that these cases have nothing to do with pensions payable under the general social insurance legislation. The money paid in accordance with these private agreements is in addition to social insurance.)

(ii) Parents Contracting with Physicians for the Treatment of their Child

In a fairly recent decision of the Federal Supreme Court concerning medical malpractice, a four-month old girl had been in urgent need of a kidney operation. (BGHZ 89, 263.) Her parents consulted a university hospital. Leaving aside the details of the somewhat complicated legal relations that exist in some cases of admission to state-owned hospitals, it is important to realise that directors and chief surgeons of such public institutions are allowed, within certain limits, to make contracts for the private treatment of patients. In the instant case, the parents of the child had made such a contract with the director of the urology clinic. The operation was successful, but due to a negligent omission in the phase of post-operative care, the child suffered serious and lasting injuries. The case is complicated, not least by the fact that two different departments of the hospital were involved: the urology clinic and the paediatric clinic. Here, suffice it to say that the urologist, who had carried out the operation, was also held responsible for providing the proper post-operative care.

The child's action succeeded because the contract for medical treatment concluded by the parents in their own name with the director of the urology clinic was regarded as a contract in favour of the child. In German law, it is well established that a minor whose parents arrange for his medical treatment is a contract beneficiary within the meaning of § 328 I BGB. (See also, BGHZ 2, 94, case no 52, contract with husband for the treatment of his wife, also stressing the limits of the contractual bond; and, for details, *Münchener Kommentar*- Gottwald, § 328 Rn. 39 *et seq*, a distinction is drawn between a '*Privatpatient*', where such effects in favour of third parties are more easily implied, and a '*Kassenpatient*' where they are not.) However, the present case deserves special attention insofar as in this action the parents had joined personal claims for their *own* costs of looking after the disabled child. This action too was successful. This solution is not as obvious as might seem at first sight. Whether a contract in favour of a third party includes the protection of the promisee's interests as well is ultimately a question of construction to be determined according to the facts of each case.

In such a contract English law would imply a term that the doctor will perform his duties with reasonable care and skill. (See *Eyre v Measday* [1986] 1 All ER 488 and *Thake v Maurice* [1986] 1 All ER 497.) But such a duty will also exist in tort where there has been a sufficient undertaking by the doctor to take care. (See *Barnett v Chelsea and Kensington Hospital Management Committee* [1969] 1 QB 428.) Thus, the result reached in classical English law would be similar, albeit that the child would most likely recover in tort for the physical injury suffered, while the parents could sue under the contract. After the 1999 Act, it would seem that the contract between the doctor and the parents could also be said to be one containing a term conferring a benefit on a third party (ie, the child). However, the enforceability of the contract at the suit of the child (or, in practice, the child's 'next friend') will depend on section 1(2): no such right will exist 'if on a proper construction of the contract it appears that [the parents and the doctor] did not intend the term to be enforceable by [the child].' (See, on this, Colman J's judgment in the recent case of *Nisshin Shipping Co Ltd v Cleaves & Company Ltd and Others* [2003] EWHC 2602 (Comm), [2004] 1 Lloyd's Rep. 38, [23]–[24], treating the issue as a rebuttable presumption in favour of an intention to benefit, unless proved otherwise (citing Burrows [2000] *LMCLQ* 540, at 544). See further, Stevens (2004) 120 *LQR* 292, 306–10.) If recovery were available under the contract for both the parents and the child, then section 5 of the 1999 Act would come into operation, to ensure that double recovery was avoided (eg, if the damages award to the child were to include expenses relating to care, etc).

(iii) Savings Accounts: Third Parties as Account Holders

Legal problems arising in connection with bank savings books and third parties are not peculiar to German law. In *Birch v Treasury Solicitor* [1951] Ch 258, the Court of Appeal was confronted with a situation which is typical of the kinds of problems with which German courts have to deal from time to time. What makes these cases so difficult is the interaction of the law of obligations with the law of succession. The *donatio mortis causa* raises its formidable head.

In the English case, an elderly lady who had been injured in a road accident was staying in hospital. Her husband had already died and she was without relatives. When the nephew of her husband and his wife visited her in hospital she told them to go to her flat in order to get a black bag containing several savings bank books. She allowed them to take these books home and to keep them, saying 'If anything happens to me I want you and Frank to have the money in the banks.' These were the decisive words on which the judgment proceeded. Lord Evershed, MR, delivering the opinion of the court, raised three questions (at least two of which would have been relevant if the case had to be decided by a German court). First, whether there was a sufficient 'delivery' to the two plaintiffs of the bank savings books to constitute a gift. Secondly, whether there was the requisite *animus donandi*. Thirdly, whether it was sufficient to hand over the indicia of title, choses in action being incapable themselves of delivery. (See also *Sen v Headley* [1990] 1 Ch 728. The deceased, who formerly had lived with the plaintiff for ten years, had tried to make an informal gift of land: 'The house is yours, Margaret. You have the keys. They are in your bag. The deeds are in the steel box.' It was held by Mummery J that mere delivery of title deeds to land could not establish a legal or equitable title in the donee, because the donor had failed to part with dominion over the subject matter of the gift. An informal gift of land does not comply with the Law of Property Act 1925 or the Wills Act 1837. It is different where a savings bank book is handed over *donandi causa*. This amounts to a transfer so that the possessor is entitled to the money. However, this decision was overturned by the Court of Appeal ([1991] Ch 425), Nourse LJ pointing out (in the judgment of the court) that the doctrine of *donatio mortis causa* was developed as an exception to the Wills Act and that the court saw no reason to refuse to enforce such informal dealings with land in the same way. Indeed, to maintain an exception to the *donatio mortis causa* rules would fail to take proper notice of the development of the law on the courts' acceptance and enforcement of certain informal dealings with land under section 53(2) of the Law of Property Act 1925 (439–40). Further, the objection that up to his death the donor could still deal with the property inconsistently with his stated intention to give it to the donee could also be made against accepted cases of choses in action (at 438). (See the discussion of the Court of Appeal judgment in notes by Halliwell [1991] *Conv* 307 and Martin [1992] *Conv* 53, the latter of which also considers the decision of the Court of Appeal in *Woodard v Woodard* [1995] 3 All ER 980.) All these questions having been answered in the affirmative, the plaintiff's action succeeded against the Treasury Solicitor acting as administrator *ad colligenda bona* of the deceased's estate.

Turning now to German law, it is necessary to distinguish between *donatio mortis causa* (§ 2301 BGB) and performance in favour of a third party to be made on the death of the promisee (§ 331 BGB). Under § 2301 I BGB, the promise of a gift—which is made subject to the condition that the donee shall survive the donor—is valid only if it satisfies the formal requirements of the law of succession on death. What is needed therefore is a contract of inheritance (*Erbvertrag*) which must be authenticated by a notary (§ 2276 BGB). However, § 2301 II BGB makes an important exception to this rule: 'If the donor executes the gift by delivery of the object given, the provisions relating to gifts inter vivos apply.' This is a reference to § 518 BGB concerning the form of a promise of a gift. For such promises to be legally valid, they must also be authenticated by a notary. But any defect of form is cured by the performance of the promise. Therefore, delivery of the subject matter of the gift, if made *animo donandi*, would create a valid gift *inter vivos*. However, in the present case the subject matter of the gift is a chose in action not being capable of 'delivery' and therefore the decisive question is whether there had been an assignment (see §§ 398 *et seq* BGB). A chose in action may, by contract with another person, be assigned by the creditor to him. On the conclusion of the contract the assignee takes the place of the assignor. The debtor need not be notified of the assignment, but if he did not know of the assignment he is entitled to assume that the creditor has not changed (§§ 407, 408 BGB). For this reason, an assignee is well advised to notify the debtor forthwith. However, in the case of a savings account, possession of the savings account book is both necessary and sufficient for withdrawing money from the account (§ 808 BGB). Since the bank savings book is a mere document of debt within the meaning of § 952 BGB, ownership of the book belongs to the creditor, ie the assignee. In other words, delivery of the savings bank book is merely of evidentiary significance because it serves as an indication of an assignment. The position of both English and German law may, perhaps, be stated thus: *donatio mortis causa* of personal property, tangible as well as intangible, is not subject to the formalities of the law of wills if it is executed by delivery (in case of movables) or by assignment (in case of a chose in action).

In German law however difficult questions have arisen in cases where somebody nominating a third person as beneficiary had opened savings accounts. In 1966 the *Bundesgerichtshof* had to deal with such a case (BGHZ 46, 198, case no 53). A grandmother had paid a substantial amount into two savings bank accounts nominating her grandchild as account holder. The bank savings books were still in her possession when she died. Moreover, she had not told her grandchild of the savings intended for her benefit. Did the money belong to the grandchild or was it still part of the estate of her grandmother? In the latter case it would have been the common property of three daughters of the deceased in their capacity as statutory co-heirs. When the defendant, one of the daughters, took possession of the savings bank books, the grandchild brought an action against her demanding their delivery. This action would have been successful if the plaintiff had been the account holder (§§ 985, 952 BGB. Paragraph 985 BGB replicates the Roman *rei vindicatio*: the owner can demand the delivery of the thing from its current possessor. This presupposes, of course, that the possessor cannot raise any objections within the meaning of § 986 BGB. But in the present case, there was no ground for finding a right to the possession of the savings bank book which could be opposed against the owner. Paragraph 952 BGB, already mentioned in the text above, states that ownership of a written acknowledgment of debt drawn up for a claim belongs to the creditor.)

The case raises the difficult question whether this was a *donatio mortis causa* (§ 2301 BGB) or a contract in favour of a third party, stipulating performance on the death of the promisee (§ 331 BGB). If § 2301 BGB were to be applied to a case of this type, the grandchild would not be entitled to the money in the bank because neither the provisions relating to the form of dispositions *mortis causa* were satisfied, nor had the gift been executed *inter vivos* by assignment evidenced by delivery of the savings bank books. But the grandchild might be in a more favourable legal position if § 331 BGB were to apply, because the courts are inclined to give priority to this provision in case of conflict with § 2301 BGB. This case law development began in 1923 when the former *Reichsgericht* held that the regular forms of wills need not be observed if there was an agreement between the customer and the savings bank to the effect that, on the death of the payor, the money he had paid into his account should become the property of a third party (RGZ 106, 1, case no 54). The deceased had reserved the right to withdraw the money at any time and without the consent of the named beneficiary. But it is important to note that the deceased had handed over the savings bank book to the beneficiary before she died. This means that the beneficiary acquired the right to the performance on the death of the promisee. The law of succession on death was thereby ousted. The *Bundesgerichtshof* has continued along these lines. (See also, BGHZ 41, 95, case no 55.) But, returning to the case of the grandchild (BGHZ 46, 198, case no 53), the court was confronted with a difficult question of construction because the savings bank books had always been in the possession of the deceased. Moreover, she had not told the beneficiary of the money she had deposited for her. Therefore, the case had to be sent back to the court below for further fact-finding, the decisive question being whether the deceased had the intention to stipulate performance for the benefit of her grandchild within the meaning of § 331 BGB when she made the contract with the savings bank.

It is not surprising that this tendency to give priority to § 331 BGB and to neglect § 2301 BGB has met with severe criticism in German legal literature. Although this discussion cannot be repeated here in detail, at least two points which have emerged in this controversy should be mentioned briefly.

First, the result of this case law is that the formal requirements of the law of wills are by-passed at the expense of certainty in the law. The case of the savings bank books, nominating the grandchild as account holder, shows the evidentiary difficulties inherent in § 331 BGB, since the person on whose intention the case turns is no longer alive. Secondly, serious problems will arise with regard to the distribution of assets if creditors of the estate must be satisfied. This leads to the strange consequence that the third-party beneficiary may be in a better position than close relatives who are, by law, entitled to compulsory portions (*Pflichtteilsberechtigte*) of the estate. In a case like this, the compulsory portion may be supplemented by demanding the surrender of the gift by the recipient. This claim is based on a theory of unjust enrichment (cf §§ 2325, 2329 BGB). Other creditors of the estate are in an even worse position, for they must try to contest the disposition in favour of the third party by special proceedings aiming at the attachment of the gift of money (*nemo liberalis nisi liberatus*). Such proceedings may be initiated if the debtor has acted to the disadvantage of his creditors, especially where he has made gifts to third persons. The *Anfechtungsgesetz* as well as the *Insolvenzordnung* have laid down exact time limits within which creditors may contest such dispositions of the debtor.

(iv) Carriage of Persons in Connection with the Services of Travel Agencies

It is very often the case that travel agents, who are obliged by the travel contract (*Reisevertrag*) to provide a number of travel services for the traveller (§ 651a I BGB), enter into a contract with an airline for the carriage of their customers. In a contract such as this, the airline company places a fixed number of seats for a certain flight at the disposal of the travel agent (charterer). The charterer, who issues air tickets to the travellers, does not necessarily act as an agent of the airline. Nevertheless, the traveller acquires a right to demand performance from the airline. This follows from a construction of the contract between the airline and the travel agency. In view of the object of the contract, the airline (which has promised the charterer to transport the travellers to their destination) is deemed to have stipulated that the travellers acquire the direct right to demand performance, ie they are regarded as contract beneficiaries within the meaning of § 328 BGB. (For this proposition see BGHZ 52, 194 (201–2), case no 56, where this construction seems to have been applied for the first time.)

In 1985 the *Bundesgerichtshof* had to deal with a case which deserves special attention, partly because it provides an example of what we are considering here, but because it offers an illustration of the extent to which the defences that the promisor has against the promisee are also available against the third party. (BGHZ 93, 271, case no 57.) In view of the clear wording of § 334 BGB this last point seems to be obvious. Since the beneficiary's right is based on the contract between the promisor and the promisee, it is generally subject to all defences arising out of that contract that the promisor may have against the promise. For English law, see now section 3(2) of the 1999 Act for confirmation of this basic principle, while acknowledging that the contract can exclude (or, indeed, extend) such defences expressly. For further details, Treitel, *The Law of Contract*, pp 660–1.

For present purposes, the somewhat complicated situation in the case may conveniently be simplified without fear of distortion. A travel agency had chartered a number of seats for a flight from Frankfurt am Main to Santa Lucia in the Caribbean. When two travellers, who had made a contract with this travel agency, checked in for their flight back to Germany, employees of the airline refused to accept them as passengers because in the meantime the travel agency had become insolvent and was unable to pay for the tickets which had already been paid for by the travellers. The travellers were thus obliged to buy tickets from another airline for their return journey to Frankfurt. They were reimbursed by an insurance company, which in turn brought an action against the airline based on *cessio legis*. The action succeeded.

The travellers were regarded as third-party beneficiaries of the contract made between the airline and the travel agency. Under this analysis, it did not matter whether the tickets were issued by the travel bureau as agents for the airline. Since the contract between the airline and the travel agency is made in the interest of the travellers, the parties must be presumed to have conferred on them the right to demand direct performance (§ 328 II BGB). In construing this contract, the court took a bold step further by holding that the provision of § 334 BGB (which is not mandatory) did not apply in this case. As a result of this the promisor could not plead failure of performance on the part of the promisee. Again, this is based on a construction of the particular contract. An airline contracting with a travel agency must be aware of the fact that travellers usually have to pay in advance. They are not required to understand the somewhat complicated legal relations existing between the airline and the travel agencies. Therefore, they are entitled to expect that the airline will not plead failure of performance because it did not receive payment from the travel agency. 'It is within its sphere of risk to see to it that payments made by travellers for their flight are received in time,' is the sentence concluding the reasoning of the court. (See now § 651k BGB implementing Directive 90/314/EEC on package travel, package holidays and package tours ([1990] OJ L158/59) that stipulates for an obligation of the travel agent to take out insurance that covers the expense of the traveller should the travel agent become insolvent. In the UK, see reg 16 *et seq* of The Package Travel, Package Holidays and Package Tours Regulations 1992, SI 1992 No 3288.)

(v) Insurance Contracts Stipulating Performance to a Third Party

Even a brief look at §§ 328 *et seq* BGB will suffice to show that insurance contracts in favour of third parties are the paradigm of contracts for the benefit of third parties as conceived by the German legislature. Thus, § 330 BGB expressly mentions the contract for life insurance (*Lebensversicherungsvertrag*) in which payment of the sum insured is stipulated for the benefit of a third party. In this type of contract it is to be presumed, in case of doubt, that the third party acquires the right directly to demand payment. This rule of construction is supplemented by § 331 I BGB: if the performance in favour of the third party is to be made after the death of the person to whom it was promised, then for the avoidance of doubt, the third party acquires the right to the performance on the death of the promisee.

Shortly after the entry into force of the Civil Code, the *Reichsgericht* was given an opportunity to decide a typical case which reveals the social conflict inherent in these provisions. In 1900 a merchant entered into a life insurance contract in favour of his wife. After his death, which occurred in 1901, bankruptcy proceedings were instituted against his estate. The trustee in bankruptcy claimed the sum insured for the estate, but the widow insisted that it should be paid to her (RGZ 51, 403, case no 58). It was held that she was entitled to the money. The creditors of the deceased, for whom the trustee in bankruptcy had claimed the sum insured, were left empty-handed. The court arrived at this conclusion by combining § 330 BGB with § 331 I BGB. Such an insurance contract grants the third party a direct right of action (*unmittelbares Klagerecht*). However, the right to the performance is not acquired until the promisee has died. Until that moment, the intended beneficiary has nothing but the hope of getting the sum insured, which is less than a right subject to a condition. What is at the outset but a mere chance ripens into a right on the death of the promisee who had regulated this property in such a way that it did not become part of his estate. The beneficiary thus has no claim against the estate of the deceased. The third party (beneficiary) acquires the right to the performance directly by reason of the contract between the insurance company and the policy-holder. This construction of provisions of the Code makes good sense and seems to be in keeping with the intention of the legislature. Contracts for life insurance for the benefit of a third party—usually a family member—are 'maintenance contracts' (*Versorgungsverträge*). This being so, it is sound legal policy to make the beneficiary's right to such maintenance independent of the distribution of the assets of the deceased, for otherwise, or so experience suggests, there may be unpleasant disputes or even litigation among heirs. All this is avoided if the beneficiary receives the money directly and without any delay.

The decisions of the *Bundesgerichtshof* have not departed from these lines. (BHZ 13, 226, 232; BGHZ 32, 44, 47.) These rules of construction laid down in §§ 330 and 331 I BGB apply to all types of contracts for life insurance (lump sum or annuity), but if no beneficiary is nominated in the contract, then the sum insured becomes part of the estate of the deceased.

It may happen however that the promisee has designated his heirs as beneficiaries without mentioning their names. In such circumstances, does the sum insured belong to the estate of the deceased? The question is by no means otiose. Suppose the estate turns out to be insolvent? In such a case, the heirs must be careful not to be held liable for the debts incurred by the deceased and other obligations imposed on the heirs as such. The easiest way to get rid of all liability would be to exercise the right to disclaim the inheritance (§§ 1942 *et seq* BGB: *Ausschlagung der Erbschaft*). But what will be the effect on their claim to the sum insured? The first case in which the promisee had made such a contract for life insurance 'in favour of my heirs' (*zugunsten meiner Erben*) came before the *Reichsgericht* in 1906. It was held that this was clear enough and equivalent to mentioning the beneficiaries by their names. (RGZ 62, 259.) This result was reached after careful consideration of its merits and demerits. The court took great pains in order to show that a previous decision of another division of the court did not stand in the way of such a conclusion, because it was a judgment which had been handed down several years before the Civil Code came into force and which had been based on the Prussian Code of 1794 (RGZ 32, 162). The decision of 1906 anticipated a rule which was incorporated a few years later in § 167 II of the Law relating to Insurance Contracts: the promisee may stipulate payment of the sum insured 'to the heirs' without further explanation. A disclaimer of inheritance does not negate their right to the performance (*Versicherungsvertragsgesetz*—henceforth'VVG'–, first promulgated 30 May 1908, Reichsgesetzblatt I 1908, 263). This law also introduced a special rule with regard to the nomination of the beneficiary under a lump sum insurance contract. The promisee may at any time substitute another person for the party named in the contract without the consent of the promisor (ie, the insurance company) (§ 166 I VVG). It goes almost without saying that no consent of the third party is required for such a change, even though he was named in the contract (§ 166 II VVG). Compare this special rule with the general rule in § 332 BGB: if the promisee has reserved to himself the right of substituting another person for the party named in the contract without the consent of the named third party, this may also be done, in case of doubt, by disposition *mortis causa*. As long as the promisee is alive the third party has a mere chance—but no right—to receive the sum insured (RGZ 51,403, 404 called it a 'mere hope': *nur eine Hoffnung*).

The foreign observer of English law notices—again with amazement if he has been brought up to believe that this is a case-law based system—that in the area of insurance law the rigour of the common law doctrine was modified successively by many Acts of Parliament. So see, for instance, the Married Women's Property Act 1882; the Third Parties (Rights Against Insurers) Act 1930; the Law of Property Act 1925 section 47; the Road Traffic Act 1988 section 148(7); and the Marine Insurance Act 1906 section 1(1), all of which introduced limited statutory exceptions to the third party rule. The 1882 Act is an outstanding example of this special legislation. The policy taken out by a husband in favour of his wife is regarded as a trust for her benefit. The legal effect of section 11 is comparable to §§ 330 and 331 I BGB; the moneys payable under such policy do not form part of the estate of the insured. Without such statutory intervention there would be no trust, for the insured could have changed the destination of the money at any time (see the remarks of Lord Esher in *Cleaver v Mutual Reserve Fund Life Association* [1892] 1 QB 147, 152). This piecemeal approach however did not cover all types of insurance contracts. The courts reacted by extending the notion of the 'insurable interest' of the insured to cover the interest of third parties and allow the insured to recover on behalf of the third party in cases in which this proved commercially convenient (eg, *Waters v Monarch Fire and Life Assurance Co* (1865) 5 El & Bl 879). Yet this line of cases also had its limitations, as it was confined to bailees. In particular, personal accident or liability insurance policies posed special difficulties and, more often than not, the English courts stressed that third parties to such an insurance policy did not have a right to payment of the benefits. (See eg, *Green v Russell* [1959] 2 QB 226.) It comes as no surprise therefore that insurance contracts for the benefit of third parties formed a substantial part of the Law Commission's argument for reform (see in particular, Law Com No 242 (1996), paras 7.31–7.34 and 7.50–7.51).

(vi) Carriage of Goods where the Consignee is Treated as a Third Party Beneficiary

The carriage of goods by land and by air is regulated in Book 4 Part 4, §§ 407–475h, of the Commercial Code (HGB). The contract of carriage is traditionally regarded as a contract for the benefit of a third party (see for details but also comparative analysis: Basedow, *Der Transportvertrag* (1987) especially p 322). It should be noted, however, that as soon as the consignee demands the goods he becomes liable for the price of carriage: § 421 II 1 HGB. The contract is thus not a 'pure' contract for the benefit of the third party (§ 328 BGB). The consignor enters into the contract as principal and the consignee is a third party beneficiary. Thus both consignor and consignee are entitled to bring an action for loss of or damage to the goods against the carrier.

In effect, this doubles the risk of litigation for the carrier. The dual entitlement of consignor and consignee does not give rise to problems of double liability because the fulfilment of the obligation owed to either consignor or consignee discharges the other (§ 428 BGB. For Example, RGZ 75, 169, 172; BGH NJW 1979, 2472, 2473). In addition to this dual entitlement, German courts have also allowed recovery of damages in respect of a third party's loss. They founded recovery of such damages on the consideration that the passing of risk under the sales contract is immaterial: the carrier cannot rely on the incidence of loss (eg, RGZ 62, 331, 335; BGH VersR 1972, 1138, 1139; VersR 1976, 168, 169). As a result, the carrier cannot object that the plaintiff did not suffer a loss as a result of the breach of contract of carriage, provided that the loss that would ordinarily have been suffered by the cargo-owner is suffered instead by a third party. The reason for this flexible approach is that the carrier should not derive a benefit from the fact that the wrong nominal plaintiff brought the action, while the correct plaintiff becomes time-barred or does not sue for some other reason.

The question of who suffers the loss is determined by reference to the contract of sale between consignor and consignee and is often difficult to establish in advance. This uncertainty should not determine the outcome of the litigation against the carrier. As can be seen from *The Albazero* [1977] AC 774, this concern is legitimate. In that case, the wrong nominal plaintiff brought the action while the 'correct' plaintiff became time-barred shortly after the proceedings were brought against the carrier. The reason why the consignor was not the correct plaintiff was that Brandon J at first instance had found that, due to exceptional circumstances, property in the goods passed early. In the view of the Court of Appeal, the consignor's claim failed on the 'merest of technicalities.'

It should be noted that this approach, initially introduced by the German courts, has now been incorporated into the HGB. According to § 421 I 2 and 3 HGB, it makes no difference whether the plaintiff is claiming damages for loss suffered by him or by a third party (see for details: Herber, NJW 1999, 3297, 3302).

German courts have applied the approach developed in relation to domestic contracts of carriage and to contracts of carriage under the CMR (the Convention on the Contract for the International Carriage of Goods by Road 1956) (eg, BGH NJW 1989, 3099). But not all contracts of carriage are analysed as contracts for the benefit of a third party. A different regime applies to freight forwarders. Carriage by sea also follows special rules. Both are discussed below in section 4, below, on *Drittschadensliquidation*.

(b) How is the Right Acquired?

In German law, it is generally agreed (but not expressly stated) that the acquisition of a right by the third party depends on the intention of *the promisor* and *the promisee*. This is deduced from § 328 II BGB, which states that 'the object of the contract' and 'the surrounding circumstances' of the transaction will determine whether the third party acquires a right, but only in the 'absence of express stipulation.'

The position in English law under the 1999 Act would appear to be very similar: see section 1(1)(a)—where express provision in the contract that the third party can enforce it will suffice—and section 1(1)(b) in conjunction with section 1(2)—where a term that purports to confer a benefit on a third party is enforceable by that third party, provided that it cannot be shown that the parties to the contract did not intend the third party to be able to enforce it. (Note that the result of section 1(2) has, so far, been to prompt law firms drawing up contracts to include as a matter of course a clause that expressly denies any intention to grant such rights to third parties: McKnight (2004) 19 *JIBLR* 151, 170 and see eg, the agreement at issue in

P C Partitions Ltd v Canary Wharf Ltd [2004] EWHC 1766, at [10] (clause 12 of the agreement).)

The intention of the parties thus assumes primary importance in this matter (see eg, *Münchener Kommentar*- Gottwald, § 328 Rn. 19 *et seq*). In the absence of specific provision, it will become a matter of objective interpretation which, in practice, probably means the judge deciding what is fair and reasonable in the circumstances. It is then a matter of inference from all the circumstances, especially the purpose of the contract, whether the third party is to have a direct right to claim performance. (Cf the judgment of Colman J in the *Nisshin Shipping* case [2004] 1 Lloyd's Rep 38, where great care was taken in construing the contract, its clauses and purposes). The fact that the promisee was acting in the exclusive interest of the promisor is probably not enough to create such a right for the third party (see Kötz, *Encyclopedia*, p. 21, citing Enneccerus and Lehmann, *Recht der Schuldverhältnisse* (1954), p 144); and according to § 329 BGB, if one party (the promisor) contractually assumes to satisfy the creditor of another party (promisee) without assuming the debt then, in case of doubt, it must not be assumed that the creditor (third party) has acquired a direct right to demand satisfaction from the first party (promisor). See, for a useful illustration of the application of § 328 II and § 329 BGB in the context of banking law: RGZ 102, 65, case no 61.

To assist in the search for the true intention of the parties, the BGB has opted for a *series* of rebuttable presumptions which correspond to situations commonly encountered in everyday life. One such presumption—against the existence of a direct right—has been mentioned already (§ 329 BGB); but the case law also shows that it is rebuttable. (See: RGZ 65, 164, 167; RGZ 114, 298, 301.) On the other hand, § 330 BGB contains presumptions in favour of a direct right of action been given to the third party. One such case is the old Roman law rule of *donatio sub modo*—a gift accompanied by a condition to perform an act requested by the transferor of the property. Another such instance can be found where a person (transferor) transfers all his property or goods to another person (transferee) in exchange for the latter promising to settle the former's debts to third parties. (There is a long history of this rule going back to the Prussian Code of 1794 (and before) concerning the sale of agricultural estates from a father to one of his children in exchange for part of the purchase price being payable to another.) Finally, and most importantly, § 330 BGB contains the significant presumption that in the case of an insurance or annuity policy, payments meant to be made to a third party confer on him the right to demand direct performance.

By contrast, in the 1999 Act England has opted for a *general* presumption in favour of a third party's right to enforce the contract where 'the term purports to confer a benefit on him' (section 1(1)(b)), albeit subject to rebuttal where it can be shown 'on a proper construction of the contract . . . that [the parties to the contract] did not intend the term to be enforceable by' the third party (section 1(2)) (discussed in *Nisshin Shipping* (above) [21]-[24]). It is however likely to assume that the approach to this general presumption will be developed by the case law into various categories concerning commercial (and other) situations where third party rights are regularly encountered. Thus, one could predict fairly confidently that a set of case law categories may develop (although whether those categories will bear any strong resemblance to those of German law remains to be seen).

We shall return to the topic of this sub-paragraph in the next major section (on contracts with protective effect towards third parties, section 3, below) for we shall see that it is in this context that most disputes have arisen, even though to a common lawyer the factual situations discussed here are tortious rather than contractual. In the meantime however the reader would be well advised to read the section 3 in conjunction with the previous sub-paragraph (section 2(a), p 187) which, using an easily recognisable typology of cases, together show how the courts have used these provisions of the Code in practice.

(c) When does the Third Party's Right Vest?

This question can also be posed in an alternative way, namely, can the promisor and the promisee, acting together or separately, revoke or modify the third party's right? If the answer is in the affirmative, until what time does this right persist? These questions can, in principle, be resolved in three different ways. For one can say that either: (a) rescission or modification of the third party's right can take place up until the moment the third party has somehow relied on it and would suffer harm if it was then removed. Alternatively (b), it can be made to depend on the intention of the parties and the surrounding circumstances. Finally (c), a legal system can attempt in a more or less detailed way to supplement one of these basic rules with some more detailed regulation of specific instances. France (and the Romanistic systems) come, on the whole, under the first category. Germany and the US (Second Restatement on Contracts), broadly speaking, fall under the third. So now does the UK, insofar as the 1999 Act provides such third party rights (see section 2(1) of the 1999 Act). Indeed, English law starts from the general proposition that once the third party has acquired the right to enforce a contract term under section 1 of the Act, then the original contracting parties may not 'extinguish or alter' that right without the third party's consent, *provided* that the third party has *either* by words or conduct (section 2(2)(a)) assented to the term and communicated that assent to the party against whom the term can be enforced (section 2(1)(a)) *or* has relied on it to the knowledge of that same other party (section 2(1)(b)) or where that other party could reasonably have foreseen such reliance (section 2(1)(c)). (See generally, Treitel, *The Law of Contract*, pp 657–8.) For discussion of these requirements in the context of third party reliance on a clause excluding liability to the first party, see the recent case of *Precis (521) plc v William M Mercer Ltd* [2004] EWHC 838 (judgment of HH Judge John Behrens) (see [102] for the clause and [309]–[320] for discussion of the operation of section 2(1)(a) of the 1999 Act). The judge took the view that there was no requirement that assent be communicated before performance of the act in respect of which liability is then sought to be excluded: in his view, '[p]roviding the assent under section 2(1)(a) is communicated before the rescission is effected the parties cannot rescind without the consent of the third party' (at [318]). This had the interesting result in the case that Mercer were allowed to rely on the exclusion clause, even though they had been unaware of it at the time that they had provided their (admittedly negligent) advice and had only discovered the existence of the exclusion clause during disclosure in the course of the court proceedings. Fortunately for them, their solicitors managed to send a letter relying on it before a deed of variation of the original agreement was executed that expressly excluded Mercer from relying on the exclusion clause.

But let us return to German law. As one would expect, it starts with the intention of the parties, supplemented by all the surrounding circumstances. Paragraph 328 II BGB states (as does § 302 (1) of the US Restatement (Second) Contracts) that *both promisor and promisee* must agree in the creation, modification, and extinction of the third party's right. But everything depends on the contract. So the right to alter or rescind the third party's right may be left to one of the contracting parties in which case it is exercised like all unilateral declarations of will and becomes effective the moment it reaches the other co-contracting party. Such a unilateral alteration of the third party's rights is inferred from the wording of § 332 BGB which states that 'if the promisee has reserved to himself the right of substituting another for the party named in the contract without the consent of the named third party, this may also be done, in case of doubt, by disposition mortis causa.' Likewise, the third party's rights may unilaterally be altered or rescinded by the promisee (insured) in the life insurance contract, though in this case the change must also be indicated to the insurer (promisor) in writing (see § 166 VVG).

Note also, the point carefully allowed for in the UK's 1999 Act, as discussed by Treitel (*The Law of Contract*, p 659): in the situation 'where A promises B to perform in favour of C *or as B shall direct*' and B then directs A to perform in favour of (say) D, this does not amount to a variation of the original contract but rather the performance of that contract according to its original terms. In other words, on a proper construction of the contract there was no intention in A and B to confer an 'indefeasible right' on C. This is an example that does not require specific treatment in the 1999 Act, but any express terms of the contract that run contrary to the requirement that the third party's consent must be obtained can displace that requirement (section 2(3)(a)). This holds *even* if a right has arisen under section 1(1) *and* the third party has fulfilled the communication or reliance requirements of section 2(1). Similarly, a specification of a time period within which the third party's consent is required, or a form that such consent must take, can also be set down in the express terms of the contract and will operate in place of the general rules of section 2(1) (see section 2(3)(b)).

More difficult than the question of who can alter or revoke the third party's right is the question until what *time* can such alteration or revocation take place. It will be clear from the discussion above that this is the basis on which the English system under the 1999 Act seeks to balance the interest acquired by the third party with the ability of the original contracting parties to vary their agreement by mutual consent. We have already indicated that the German law leaves the answer to this question to the parties, themselves. This is different from the French position which extinguishes such a right once the third party beneficiary has declared to the promisor, by words or deeds, his willingness to take the conferred benefit; and it is certainly harsher on the third party where the latter's interests are paid lesser attention than the interests of the parties to the contract who have expressly reserved their right to alter or rescind the conferment of intended benefits. But there are two reasons that the difference may be less pronounced than it appears to be at first sight.

First, in the absence of an express agreement, the intention of the contracting parties to retain a right to alter or revoke the intended benefits will be judged by the purpose of the contract and all relevant surrounding circumstances. A German judge would thus be well advised to take into account any action on the part of the beneficiary indicating that he had altered his position as a result of the promise to confer on him a benefit. And if this had occurred, it could be argued that the contracting party's right to annul or modify the beneficiary's rights had been lost. This is certainly the position taken in a more overt manner by § 311 of the American Restatement (Second) Contracts; and the introduction of such specific rules into German law has been urged by at least one learned comparatist (Kötz, *Encyclopedia*, p. 47). It seems, by contrast, that the English position does require an express statement in the contract to reserve to the contracting parties a right to alter or rescind the contract term in question (section 2(3) of the 1999 Act). The provisions that allow for judicial discretion to dispense with the third party's consent do not provide a wide range of further options to the original contracting parties: section 2(4)(a) concerns the situation where the third party's 'whereabouts cannot reasonably be ascertained,' section 2(4)(b) where the third party is not mentally capable of consenting and section 2(5) where it cannot reasonably be ascertained whether the third party has in fact relied on the right in question.

Secondly, the Code itself contains an important provision which applies to a group of significant cases where the rights of the third party—always in the absence of a contrary express agreement—vest at the time of the death of the promisee. (See § 331 BGB.) These are the life insurance contract, savings accounts, and partnership agreements in favour of third parties (usually partners' widows). In these cases, it is often said that the third party's 'rights' do not amount to more than a *nuda spes*, though this characterisation may be partly misleading since German courts and academics have held that the expectancy of a revocable insurance beneficiary is both assignable and garnishable (*Staudinger*-Kaduk, § 331 Rn. 9). The same is true of the promisee's rights during this period of limbo when his creditors might, in the case of an insurance policy, claim its cash surrender value. But one must never forget that most of this part of the law is *ius dispositivum* and will thus yield to the parties' contrary and expressly declared intention. Thus, German law accepts that it is possible (subject to observing specific requirements laid down by the law—usually the law of insurance contracts) to create irrevocable rights for the beneficiary, including the right of the promisee to waive his right to change the beneficiary. In such cases, the insured money still is payable on the death of the promisee (insured); in the meantime, however, the beneficiary's irrevocable 'right' to claim the insurance money once the promisee has died forms part of the former's assets and can be assigned by him, seized by his creditors or inherited by his heirs if he (the third party) dies before the promisee.

(d) Defences against the Beneficiary

These can be grouped into three categories. First are the defences which the promisor himself has against the third party (the *Vollzugsverhältnis* relationship). Then we have the defences that the promisor has against the promisee stemming from the underlying contract between them (the *Deckungsverhältnis* relationship). And, finally, one must consider the possibility of the promisor invoking the defences that the promisee has against the third party (the *Zuwendungsverhältnis* or *Valuta* relationship).

The answer to the first group of cases is an easy one. Though the German Code (unlike § 309 (4) of the US Restatement (Second) Contracts) contains no specific provision on this point, it is generally accepted that the promisor can oppose against the third party whatever defences he may have against him that arise from whatever relationship they may have (typically, this will be a set-off claim). We must not, however, forget that this area of the law contains rules that can be displaced by the contrary agreement of the parties, so the main (or underlying) contract between promisor and promisee could envisage a situation where the promisor had to make payment to the third party and was prevented from using any set-off claims he might have against him from their own relationship (cf Lange in NJW 1965, 657, 661 *et seq*).

The same basic position obtains in English law under the 1999 Act: section 3(4) allows the promisor to rely on defences such as misrepresentation or a set-off of a debt incurred under another transaction between them, so long as the promisor could have used such defences had the third party actually been a party to the contract. (Note that express provisions in the contract can modify the application of these default rules: section 3(5).)

In practice, much more important is the second group of cases which deal with the defences that the promisor has in his contract against the promisee (see *Münchener Kommentar*- Gottwald, § 328 Rn. 26, § 334 Rn. 1). The general rule here is that they can be opposed against the third party (§ 334 BGB; section 3(2) of the 1999 Act adopts a similar general rule). This includes claims that this contract is void, voidable, affected by lack of capacity, is contrary to the law or public morals, etc. Defences that become available to the promisor after the conclusion of the contract with the promisee (for instance, the promisee is not performing his part of the bargain) are also available to the promisor and can be opposed against the third party (RGZ 66, 97, 101. This seems similar to §§ 267 and 268 BGB).

In the UK, the 1999 Act allows the availability of such defences to be excluded or extended by express terms of the contract (section 3(3)) (although, as Treitel notes (*The Law of Contract*, p 660), if the contract between promisor and promisee were to be held void, such terms would presumably have no effect vis-à-vis the third party). It is apparently open to the third party to offer, himself, to perform the obligation of the promisee and then demand the performance of the promisor's obligation towards him. But the promisor cannot oppose against the third party defences which he has against the promisee which arise from a transaction other than the one that creates the rights of the third party (the *Deckungsverhältnis*): Article 1413 of the Italian Civil Code in fact makes this point explicitly. The English position under the 1999 Act on this last point would appear to be different, by virtue of section 3(3), so long as this is expressly provided for in the contract and would have been available to the promisor had proceedings been brought by the promisee.

Finally, we come to defences that may possibly exist in the relationship between promisee and third party (*Zuwendungsverhältnis*). Such defences cannot be opposed by the promisor against the third party. This point has not always been grasped by common law jurisdictions that allow a tortious action by the third party against the promisor but allow it to be shaped by the underlying contract between the promisor and promisee (see eg, *Henderson v Merret Syndicates Ltd* [1995] 2 AC 145). This, as we have seen, is what the German law also does (though in a contractual way) by allowing the promisor to use defences existing in the *Deckungverhältnis* against the third party. But the use of defences existing in the relationship between promisee and third party is not allowed and, in any event, is alien to the purposes that the institution of contracts *in favorem tertii* is trying to achieve. (For further details with references to English cases see, *The German Law of Torts*, p 333 *et seq*.)

(e) Unjust Enrichment of the Beneficiary

In one sense, this is really a sub-heading of the issues discussed in the previous paragraph; and it is best introduced by elaborating on the point just made, namely that the relationship that is really crucial in these cases is that between promisor and promisee. There may, however, be instances where the relationship between promisee and beneficiary may have some bearing on the law on this topic. This relationship (promisee/beneficiary) may, in the terminology of the old Restatement, be one of 'creditor beneficiary' or 'donee beneficiary.' To put it differently, the reason why the promisee is asking the promisor to do something for the beneficiary may be because his owes the beneficiary a debt or simply wishes to make him a gift. The nature of this relationship could have some significance in the context of defences discussed in the previous paragraph. The following example serves to illustrate this point.

Suppose that the promisor pays the beneficiary (the wife of the insured/promisee) an amount of money under an insurance policy, which is voidable on the grounds of fraud (§ 123 BGB) committed by the insured husband (eg, he concealed a material fact about his health). If the contract is rescinded by the insurance company (promisor), it disappears retrospectively and that means, in theory, that the insurance company should have a restitutionary right under § 812 I BGB against the beneficiary. (Of course, this is subject to the requirement that the third party has been enriched; and he would not be enriched if he had already spent the money in good faith (§ 818 III BGB), but he would be liable if he spent the money after he has learnt that he had obtained it in the absence of a legal cause (§ 819 I BGB).

English law would reach a similar conclusion on this last point by treating such later expenditure as not in sufficient good faith to allow the third party to take advantage of the defence of change of position: see *Lipkin Gorman (a firm) v Karpnale Ltd* [1991] 2 AC 548 and *South Tyneside MBC v Svenska International plc* [1995] 1 All ER 545. According to the BGH however (BGHZ 58, 184, 188–9, case no 62, *obiter*) such a rule should probably not apply to cases where the relationship between the promisee and beneficiary was one that was determined by a bargain ('creditor beneficiary relationship' in the American terminology). As Professor Werner Lorenz has observed, 'where the legal relationship between the promisee and the third party is an exchange contract it is not to be presumed that the promisor and the promisee wished to expose the third party to restitution if the contract with the promisor should prove to be void. Therefore the party liable to make restitution (to the promisor) should be the promisee who has been unjustly enriched at the expense of the promisor whose performance has extinguished the promisee's obligation vis-à-vis the third party. Against this restitutionary claim the promisee may, of course, set off the money already paid to the promisor' (*The Gradual Convergence*, p 95. Cf Virgo, *The Principles of the Law of Restitution* (1999), pp. 40–3 and *The Trident Beauty* [1994] 1 WLR 161 (where the plaintiff's right to restitution as against the defendant was held to be excluded in a contract between the plaintiff and a third party, even though the defendant was not a party to that contract)).

3. CONTRACTS WITH PROTECTIVE EFFECTS TOWARDS THIRD PARTIES

von Bar, 'Liability for Information and Opinions Causing Economic Loss to Third Parties' in Markesinis (ed), *The Gradual Convergence* (1994) 98; Canaris, 'Die Reichweite der Expertenhaftung gegenüber Dritten' ZHR 163 (1999) 206; Ebke, 'Die Haftung des gesetzlichen Abschlussprüfers in der Europäischen Union' ZVglRWiss 100, 2001, 62; Martiny, 'Pflichtenorientierter Drittschutz beim Vertrag mit Schutzwirkung für Dritte' JZ 1996, 19; Musielak, 'Die Haftung der Banken für falsche Kreditauskünfte' VersR 1977, 973; Puhle, *Vertrag mit Schutzwirkung zugunsten Dritter und Drittschadensliquidation* (1982); Schlechtriem, 'Schutzpflichten und geschützte Personen' in *Festschrift für Dieter Medicus* (1999) 529; Schneider, 'Die Reichweite der Expertenhaftung gegenüber Dritten' ZHR 163 (1999) 246; Sonnenschein, 'Der Vertrag mit Schutzwirkung für Dritte—und immer neue Fragen' JA 1979, 225.

(a) Preliminary Observations

The somewhat cumbersome term '*Verträge mit Schutzwirkung für Dritte*' or 'contracts with protective effects towards third parties' was chosen to distinguish this type of contract from the classic contract for the benefit of a third party. We are here concerned with a new institution created by the courts, more often than not in close co-operation with academic writers in order to overcome two narrow (some might say defective) provisions in the tort section of the Code. The first is § 823 I BGB, which is one of the main tort provisions of the BGB and which does not allow recovery in tort for negligently inflicted pure economic loss. The second is § 831 BGB, which establishes a weak rule of vicarious liability allowing the master to avoid liability for the torts committed by his servants whenever he can prove that he selected them and supervised carefully. (For details in English see *The German Law of Torts*, chapter 3, p 693 *et seq.*) In one sense this development, having been prompted by 'defects' in the German Code itself may hold little interest for the common lawyer. As we shall note in the paragraphs that follow, this is not necessarily true since the German reasoning (rather than the German conceptualism) does contain interesting ideas even for the common lawyer. But even if this development were of purely Germanic interest, we would have to deal with it in a book which aims at providing common lawyers with an introduction to the German law of contract. (See also, *The German Law of Torts*, pp 58–64; 301 *et seq.*)

(b) Cases Involving Personal Injury or Physical Damage

The problem that gave rise to this jurisprudential development has already been alluded to. What made its solution possible was the realisation that in each contract one finds a cluster of obligations. Some of them are primary obligations (*primäre Leistungsansprüche*); others are secondary or collateral obligations which often take the form of duties of protection (*Schutzpflichten*). The old English decision of *Cavalier v Pope* ([1906] AC 428) neatly illustrates the difference.

In that case the husband took out a lease in a property but it was his wife who was injured due to its defective state. She had no contract with the lessor and, as the law then stood, the courts took the view that she could not succeed in tort either. In such a case, German lawyers would have given the injured woman a remedy (see RGZ 127, 218). Their reasoning proceeds along the lines we have indicated. In the absence of specific circumstances to the contrary, the woman might not be seen as a third party beneficiary of the contract of lease, in the sense of being allowed to bring a claim demanding the specific performance of the *primary* obligation of the lessor to deliver the leased premises. Nor would she in turn be liable to perform the *primary* obligation of the promisee/lessee, ie paying the agreed rent. She would however be brought under the 'protective umbrella' of the contract in such a way as to make the lessor liable to her for any breach of his *secondary* obligations to keep the premises in a safe condition.

A similar construction can apply to the contract of sale. Here too the distinction is between primary and secondary obligations. The primary obligations include the duty to deliver the sold item and to pay the purchase price. But if the item is dangerous, if the warnings are inadequate, or if the area where the sale takes place is unsafe, then the vendor may incur additional liability; and not only towards the purchaser, but other parties that are with him (how the range of persons is kept under control is explained below). The 'vegetable leaf' case (BGHZ 66, 51, reproduced in *The German Law of Torts*, case no 112, p 789) offers a well-known illustration.

In that case the fourteen year-old plaintiff accompanied his mother when she went to do her shopping in her local supermarket. While she was queuing to pay, he went round the counter to help pack the goods and slipped on a vegetable leaf that was lying on the floor and injured himself. Though no money had yet exchanged hands and thus, technically speaking, no contract had yet been concluded between the mother and the shop, the court took the view that (a) the doctrine of *culpa in contrahendo* afforded the mother contractual protection and (b) this extended to include her accompanying child in accordance with the doctrine that we are here examining. The judgment was clear about the advantages that this contractual approach offered to the plaintiffs; but it was also clear that it would not be extended to all persons who entered into the shop and slipped on such debris. The potential customer would thus have to be distinguished from the potential thief, although how each future case would be decided the court—quite properly—refused to speculate.

Likewise, if a manufacturer of a dangerous chemical enters into a contract with a haulage firm to transport the chemical and fails to give proper warnings about how it should be handled, he may be liable to the carrier's employees who are injured while handling the dangerous substance (BGH NJW 1959, 1676). Such reasoning has been extended to numerous situations involving liability to injured workers in the context of building contracts (BGHZ 33, 247, case no 63); leases (RGZ 102, 231; RGZ 91, 21, case no 64); contracts for medical services (see: BGHZ 2, 94, case no 52; OLG Düsseldorf NJW 1975, 596, case no 65); carriage contracts (RGZ 87, 64) and many more. One situation, almost anticipated by the Code, deserves to be mentioned and to serve as the last illustration of the points made so far.

Its origin lies in § 618 BGB, which gives employees some of the advantages of the contract and tort regimes. This basically obliges the employer 'to fit up and maintain rooms, equipment and apparatus which he has to provide for the performance of the service' he expects from his employee and 'so to regulate matters' to ensure that the employee is protected against danger to life and health 'as far as the nature of the service permits'(§ 618 I BGB). Sub-paragraph 3 of § 618 BGB then states that §§ 842–846 BGB (taken from the law of tort) apply *mutatis mutandis*, thus extending some of the advantages of the law of tort to the contractual action. (In the UK, see the Health and Safety at Work Act 1974, especially sections 2 and 33 for the regulatory system, although note that this does not give rise to a general action for breach of statutory duty (section 47(1)(a)). Instead, breaches of specific duties imposed by the health and safety regulations can be a ground for an action for breach of statutory duty (again, section 47(1)(a) of the 1974 Act). See generally, Markesinis, Deakin & Johnston, *Markesinis and Deakin's Tort Law* (5th edn, 2003), pp 559–71, for coverage of the common law and an introduction to the statutory duties. For detailed coverage of the latter, see Redgrave, Hendy and Ford, *Health and Safety* (3rd edn, 1998).) These protective duties, which the Code imposes on the employer for the benefit of his employee, have thus been extended to the situation where a tenant entered into a contract with a plumber to do some work to her gas system. The work was defectively done and the tenant's daily help was injured. The Court took the view that her daily help was also included in the list of protected persons envisaged by § 618 BGB and that these persons must have been within the contemplation of the defendant firm, which was thus liable for the injuries sustained by the daily help (see also, BGHZ 33, 247, case no 63).

Even this summary account of the case law is sufficient to show the success with which this new notion met in practice. At the academic level, however, it was met by two concerns. First, how should one explain this new institution doctrinally, and secondly, how should one set out workable parameters that would not allow the expansion of liability to undermine the notion of contract. On the first score, the ingenuity of German academics was considerable.

Thus first, the *Reichsgericht* tried to base this outcome on a broad interpretation of the contract, the implied intentions of the parties or, even, the ultimate aim of the transaction (see RGZ 87, 289, 292; 98, 210, 213; 106, 120, 126; 127, 218), and for a time this practice was continued by the *Bundesgerichtshof* (BGHZ 1, 383, 385–6, case no 66; 5, 378, 384; BGH NJW 1956, 1193). Under the influence of the late Professor Larenz (*Schuldrecht*, I (1st edn, 1953), p 16, III; *Larenz*, in NJW 1956, 1193) the new notion was increasingly separated from the traditional *Vertrag zugunsten Dritter* (regulated by the BGB) and based on the more amorphous idea of good faith contained in § 242 BGB. For the courts however this was a non-problem. What they were concerned with was doing justice to each case, leaving the theoretical justification of their result either undecided (BGHZ 56, 269, 273) or even treating it as irrelevant (BGH NJW 1977, 2073, 2074, case no 67). Somewhat unusually then we encounter here a judicial attitude which many outside observers often detect in the judgments of state courts in the US.

The second concern—how to define workable parameters for the new notion in a way that would not totally destroy the notion of contract as a *vinculum iuris* between two persons—proved more difficult to satisfy. Once again, we shall see that these academic concerns have not been totally shared by the courts, which have proceeded to create a substantial and fairly bold case law. In this domain academics have, with rather greater consistency than the courts, insisted that three requirements be satisfied before the contractual umbrella can be opened to include the plaintiff/third party. (For rich references, see Sonnenschein, 'Der Vertrag mit Schutzwirkung für Dritte— und immer neue Fragen' JA 1979, 225 and Martiny, 'Pflichtenorientierter Drittschutz beim Vertrag mit Schutzwirkung für Dritte' JZ 1996, 19.) We must look at them in turn.

First, there must be an especially close relationship between the third party/plaintiff and the promisee (contractual creditor), usually referred to as 'proximity of performance' (*Leistungsnähe*).

Secondly—and this is a requirement that has been loosely construed by the courts—the promisee (contractual creditor) must have some interest in protecting the third party/plaintiff. (The usual jargon states that the creditor must be responsible for the third party for better or for worse: *Wohl und Wehe*.)

Finally, the promisor (contractual debtor) must have been able to foresee that the third party/plaintiff would suffer damage in the event that he—the contractual creditor/promisor—performed his obligation badly.

A useful illustration of this approach is provided by BGH NJW 1964, 33, case no 69. Here the court held that a contract of lease had protective effects towards fellow tenants only where the tenant was responsible for the well being of the third person. Such a close personal relationship existed, for instance, in RGZ 102, 232, case no 69, where the plaintiff was the husband of the tenant. Note that in that case the protective effect of the duty of care is founded on a direct application of § 328 BGB; the full emancipation of the contract with protective effects was still to come. The decision also highlights the scope of § 278 BGB and thus one of the main reasons for framing the action in contract rather than tort (§ 831 BGB). BGH NJW 1964, 33, case no 69, contains a summary of the position of the *Bundesgerichtshof* in cases involving physical damage. The Court stated:

> It accords with the sense and purpose of the contract and the principle of good faith that the only persons to whom the debtor owes his contractual duty of care and protection are those who are brought into contact with his performance by the creditor and in whose welfare the creditor has an interest because he himself is bound to take care and protect them, like the members of a man's family or the employees of an entrepreneur. To extend the contractual debtor's responsibility in this way is justified because he must know that the safety of the limited and compact group of persons to whom the contractual protection ensures is of as much concern to the creditor as his own.

See, for a further illustration for the desire of the courts to emphasise the narrow limits of the doctrine: OLG Düsseldorf NJW 1975, 596, case no 65, where once again the protective ambit of the contract is limited by using the criterion of the personal responsibility of the creditor for the third party. BGH NJW 1968, 1929, case no 70, likewise, is a decision which utilises the criterion of close personal ties to keep the floodgates shut. In this case a 'sub-buyer' contended that good faith required that he ought to be included in the protective scope of the contract between buyer and seller. The court stated that commercial certainty would be endangered if the contract with protective effects were to be applied in the commercial sphere between tradesmen:

> Still, this court has frequently emphasised that it is only within narrow limits that contractual duties of care are to be extended outside the circle of the actual parties to the contract . . . The distinction between direct and indirect victims should be maintained. The general rule is that

contractual liability is annexed to the tie that binds the creditor to his contractual partner. If these principles are forgotten, a contractor will be unable to tell, and so calculate, what risk he is undertaking, and it will be difficult to justify holding him liable. Thus it is by no means enough that third parties 'come into contact' with the performance of the debtor through the creditor. In modern commercial transactions involving long chains of dealers this is almost always the case. The concept of 'contract with protective effect for third parties' must be restricted not only as regards the subjects, ie, those third parties who are drawn into the protected area, but also as regards its objects, ie, the terms of the contract from which it is sought to draw such protective duties. The meaning and purpose of a contract, once it is construed in accordance with the principle of good faith (§ 157 BGB), will only justify the extension of the duties of care and protection to third parties if the principal creditor himself owes them protection and care and is in some sense responsible for their weal and woe (see BGHZ NJW 1964, 33 [= case no 69]). This will normally be so only in rather personal situations, such as exist in the family or in employment or in tenancy. An especially strict test must be applied if the protective effect is to apply to property damage and economic loss. . . . Doubtless tradesmen do think it important to take care of their customers' interests, but not in the sense of owing them 'protection and care'. . . .

(c) Economic Loss Cases

The above mentioned controlling device 'of a close personal relationship' has not always been interpreted so strictly. This has been the case where the concept of contracts with protective effects towards third parties has been considered in situations involving pure economic loss. It is to this development, therefore, that we must now turn our attention. The attentive reader will, of course, have noticed by now that the cases that supported the new notion of contracts with protective effects towards third parties initially dealt with physical damage and, as stated repeatedly, aimed at overcoming the limitations of § 831 BGB. In the mid-1960s however a new development started with the well-known *Testamentfall* decision (BGH NJW 1965, 1955; JZ 1966, 141, with an important note by Professor Werner Lorenz. The facts of the case have become too well known and thus do not deserve to be repeated.) The importance of the decision lay perhaps less in the fact that it made a negligent and inactive notary liable to the testator's frustrated beneficiary, but more significantly because it chose to do so in terms which, in effect, extended the notion of *Verträge mit Schutzwirkung für Dritte* to cases involving pure economic loss. The genie was out of the bottle and, arguably, about to become mischievous.

Three reasons lay behind this decision. First was the fact that pure economic loss is not recoverable in a tort action (§ 823 I BGB). Secondly, the defendant notary must have known that the timely performance of his obligation was of essence both to the deceased testator and to his daughter (the plaintiff who, as a result of the notary's negligence did not become the sole heiress of her father's estate but took it jointly with her niece according to the rules of 'community of heirs': *Erbengemeinschaft*). Finally, and just as crucially, the daughter was the only person likely to suffer damage because of the defendant's non-performance of his obligation. (The same of course applies to cases of negligent acts on behalf of notaries or attorneys. See: OLG Bremen NJW 1977, 638.)

Once the dam was thus breached and economic loss could be recovered through a tort claim dressed up in contract clothes, the question was where would the new development stop. In Professor Kötz's words ((1990) 10 *Tel Aviv Univ Studies in Law* 195, 202) for economic loss 'the signs are on the wall. The distinction between harm to protected interests and mere pecuniary harm, while still fundamental, begins to wear thin at times.' The law concerning the liability of sub-contractors to building owners, the law concerning the liability of suppliers of negligent certifications or valuations and the law concerning tort recovery for damage caused to defective but not dangerous products would seem to support this assertion. Here we shall only look at the first two factual situations; and to these one must also add the types of economic loss recoverable under the related notion of *Drittschadensliquidation*, which will be discussed below (section 4).

In *construction contracts* the major participants are linked by a chain of contracts; and the question that often has to be asked by the courts is the one that confronted the House of Lords in *Junior Books v Veitchi* ([1983] 1 AC 520) and the Supreme Court of California in *J'Aire Corporation v Gregory* (598 P 2d 60 (1979)): can the sub-contractor be made liable to a party other than the contractor (with whom he is in privity of contract) for economic losses caused by his shoddy work? The tortious solution reached by the common law courts would probably be reached in Germany by applying the notion of *Vertrag mit Schutzwirkung für Dritte*. The reason why one qualifies this answer with the word 'probably' is only due to the fact of the dearth of German case law. For Professor Kötz (at 206), the reason for this (fortunate) result may be the fact that 'it is common practice in the German construction industry to include in the contract between owner and the main contractor a provision by which the main contractor's warranty claims against the sub-contractor are assigned to the owner.' The advantage of such an approach—as indeed of all contractually-flavoured solutions—is that the plaintiffs take the claim subject to equities so that the sub-contractor can set up all defences against the owner that would have been available to him in a suit brought by the main contractor. (For German law, see §§ 334 and 404 BGB and cf the discussion of some confusing English decisions in *The German Law of Torts*, p 333 *et seq*. See also, the complicated saga of sub-contractors, defences of contributory negligence and the existence of (concurrent) duties of care in contract and tort in *Barclays Bank plc v Fairclough Building Ltd (No 1)* [1995] QB 214 (concerning the claim by the building owner against the head contractor) and *(No 2)* [1995] IRLR 605; [1995] PIQR P152 (concerning the action by the first sub-contractor against its own sub-contractor). This case illustrates a need for careful thinking about the nature of such claims and how defences thereto should properly be analysed.)

The situation with *negligent certifications* is both more intriguing and more controversial; and it is here that the German courts have arguably over-stretched the notion of contract with protective effect towards third parties as a result of abandoning the *Wohl und Wehe* requirement and replacing it with a much more open-ended question. ('. . . in what circumstances the objective interests involved permit the inference that the parties [debtor/creditor] have [even] implicitly stipulated a duty of care towards third parties.' (BGH NJW 1984, 355, 356, reproduced in *The German Law of Torts*, case no 22, p 275.) Since the case from which this statement comes offers a good illustration of this trend, its facts should be looked at in some detail.

The defendant, a professional valuer of land, was asked by S to advise him on the value and rental income of a particular building. The instructions were given at a meeting attended by a banker, S, and the plaintiff who subsequently bought the premises. The defendant did not know whether S and the plaintiff were intending to purchase the building jointly. In a subsequent letter (addressed to another party but placed before the court) he accepted that he believed that S had probably made the inquiry on behalf of a consortium interested in purchasing the premises. The defendant's valuation concerning the rental income proved greatly exaggerated, due to the fact that he had failed to realise that some of the apartments in the building were subject to rent control restrictions. When the error was discovered the contract of sale was rescinded by entry into a new contract; but the purchaser/plaintiff, in trying to effect the unfortunate transaction, had also incurred considerable expenses which he now claimed as damages from the defendant/valuer. The BGH first agreed with the Court of Appeal that there was no question here of a contract in favour of third parties in the sense of § 328 BGB, since only S had a right to demand the performance of the primary obligation to supply the expert valuation. The Court then continued:

> [However] this consideration alone does not exclude the locus standi of the plaintiff to pursue his claim for damages since it is necessary, in addition, to consider whether the plaintiff is included in the area protected by the contract. For it is recognized today . . . that the contractual obligation may create duties of care towards third parties who themselves are not entitled to demand performance of the principal obligation. As this Senate has stated (. . . [references] . . .) this consideration applies also to contracts with officially appointed and sworn experts . . . Duties of care can also be created in favour of those persons who are not mentioned by name to the other contracting party [debtor]. Nor is it necessary that the contracting party [debtor] should know the exact number of persons to whom a duty of care is owed. The Federal Court has recognized in its case law a duty of care towards third parties even if the [debtor] owing the duty of care was ignorant of the number and the names of the persons to whom the duty was owed (. . . [references] . . .). It is essential, however, that the group to whom the duty of care is owed should be capable of being determined objectively . . .

The judgment contains many interesting insights into the abandonment of the *Wohl und Wehe* requirement and for that reason it is reproduced below; but it is not the only one that has opted for such a broadening of the contractual protection. Just as indicative of this trend is the so-called *Danish Consul* case (BGH NJW 1982, 2431, reproduced in *The German Law of Torts*, case no 21, p 273), which can serve as the last of our examples. There an expert valuer of land supplied the Danish Consul in Munich with inaccurate information concerning the commercial value of a certain area of land. The Consul passed this information on to a Danish bank, which, in reliance thereon, invested money in a building project to be carried out on this land. Even though the loan was secured by a land charge, the bank suffered considerable loss due to the incorrect expert valuation. In the opinion of the *Bundesgerichtshof*, the bank was in the position of a third party beneficiary of a contract that had come into existence between the expert valuer and the Danish Consul. For this purpose, it was not necessary to spell out an express or implied agreement between the promisor (the valuer) and the promisee (the Danish Consul) as to the inclusion of the third party (the bank) within the sphere of protection of this contract, for the expert could have foreseen that his statement would serve as basis for an investment decision. (Comparing this reasoning with the English cases discussed below, it is strongly arguable that the supply of that information on to the bank would have meant that, even if a duty had been owed to the Consul, it would have been highly unlikely to have been held to be owed to the bank as well (by analogy with *Caparo Industries plc v Dickman* [1990] 2 AC 58 and the purpose of the advice or statement given (below).)

In the abstract, the decisive question may be reduced to the following formula: 'is the group of persons to be contractually protected capable of description by objective standards?' ('. . . *sofern die zu schützende Personengruppe objektiv abgrenzbar ist.*') It goes without saying that such criteria are more easily stated than applied to concrete situations. It also makes no difference to reassure German lawyers that they have not been alone in dealing with such difficult demarcation questions. *Caparo Industries plc v Dickman* demonstrates that this is not so. German lawyers, however, are unique in having placed what are essentially tort problems into contractual settings in order to overcome structural deficiencies of their Code. Methodologically, this result is not very neat; but to the extent that it shows that the promisor/defendant is not more extensively liable towards the plaintiff/third party than he is towards his co-contractor/debtor, they may have something to teach to the common lawyer. (For a thorough discussion of the banking cases in English see: von Bar, 'Liability for Information and Opinions Causing Pure Economic Loss to Third Parties: A Comparison of English and German case law' chapter 3 in Markesinis (ed), *The Gradual Convergence*. See also, *The German Law of Torts*, p 295 *et seq*.)

The concerns about indeterminate liability noted in the foregoing exposition of the German cases have also marked the development of English tort law in the field of negligent misstatements. Various control devices have been discussed by the courts in a wide variety of contexts and a brief summary will be given here (see generally, Markesinis, Deakin & Johnston, *Markesinis and Deakin's Tort Law* (5th edn, 2003, pp 114–131 (especially 114–24)). Thus, in *Hedley Byrne & Co v Heller & Partners* [1964] AC 465 some of their Lordships spoke of the voluntary assumption of responsibility by the defendant bank, on which the claimants relied (sein particular, the judgment of Lord Morris of Both-y-Gest at 503). Thus, in *Hedley Byrne* itself, the fact that the statement had explicitly been made 'without responsibility' allowed the defendant to escape liability (such exclusions would today be subject to section 2(2) of the Unfair Contract Terms Act 1977 and would have to satisfy a 'reasonableness' test). However, as has subsequently been pointed out by Lord Oliver in *Caparo* (above at 607), the phrase 'voluntary assumption of responsibility' 'was not intended to be a test for the existence of the duty for, on analysis, it means no more than that the act of the defendant in making the statement or tendering the advice was voluntary and that the law attributes to it an assumption of responsibility . . . [but] it tells us nothing about the circumstances from which such attribution arises.'

Thus, subsequent efforts have focused more carefully on a contextual analysis: in what circumstances has the advice been offered or the service been rendered? To put the matter another way, was there a 'special relationship' between the parties, such as to give rise to a duty of care? This language bears distinct similarities to the approach of the German cases discussed above. Many of the successful claims in this area have related to situations where the category of recipients of the relevant statement or advice was small and obvious to the defendant: see *Esso Petroleum Co Ltd v Mardon* [1976] QB 801 (concerning pre-contractual representations as to likely business generated by a petrol station) and *Smith v Eric S Bush*; *Harris v Wyre Forest DC* [1990] 1 AC 831 (where surveyor's valuation reports were prepared under a contract with a third party but would clearly be relied on by the prospective purchaser). By contrast, the *Caparo* case (above*)* illustrates that a different definition of the purpose of the exercise carried out in giving the advice can lead to the opposite result: thus, by describing the purpose of the annual audit of a publicly listed company's accounts as the protection of the collective interest of the shareholders in ensuring the effective management of the company, a claim by a successful purchaser of the company that the audit had been negligent failed. This was because such reliance on a 'statement ... put into more or less general circulation and [which] may foreseeably be relied on by strangers to the maker of the statement for any one of a variety of purposes which the maker of the statement has no specific reason to contemplate' fell outside the duty as defined by the purpose of auditing the accounts (*per* Lord Bridge, at 620–1).

This raises the spectre of open-ended liability, but the interpretation adopted by the House of Lords has been criticised strongly (see eg, Percival, 'After *Caparo*: Liability in Business Transactions Revisited' (1991) 54 *MLR* 739): after all, it is only the party engaged in the take-over that ended up over-bidding that lost out as a result of such advice (while the other shareholders who sold to that other party were bought out at a premium)—this hardly resembles indeterminate liability concerns. Perhaps Hoffmann J provides the best rationalisation of the case law in *Morgan Crucible v Hill Samuel* [1991] Ch 295, at 305, where he emphasised the different economic relationships between the parties. Typically, the English cases have not been sympathetic to parties claiming to have relied on negligent misstatements made during arm's length commercial negotiations (unless they amount to misrepresentations, on which see chapter 6, sections 3 and 4, p 302) and the *Caparo* situation could be said to fall within this category. However, when the nature of the market is one where the party relying on the advice or statement is at a disadvantage in obtaining the relevant information (such as in *Esso v Mardon* (above) or in the surveyor cases such as *Smith v Eric S Bush*), then the relationship between the parties is such that a duty to take care will be held to exist.

Finally, similar control device difficulties can be seen in the cases that have expanded the *Hedley Byrne* principle into the field of the negligent performance of a service (begun with *Henderson v Merrett Syndicates Ltd* [1995] 2 AC 145). Cases such as *White v Jones* [1995] 2 AC 207 raise the difficult question of determining the extent of such a tortious duty, which Lord Goff stressed is shaped by the underlying contract between (in *White v Jones*) the testator and the defendant solicitor. In so doing, a key question is the identification of the intended beneficiaries of the performance of such services, which again is strongly redolent of the notion developed in German law that 'the group of persons to be contractually protected [must be] capable of description by objective standards': compare *Goodwill v British Pregnancy Advisory Service* [1996] 1 WLR 1397; *MacFarlane v Tayside Health Board* [2000] 2 AC 59 and *Rees v Darlington Memorial Hospital NHS Trust* [2002] 2 WLR 1483 (all concerning failed vasectomies or sterilisation operations, yet receiving different answers as to who counted as the 'intended' or only 'incidental' beneficiaries of the performance of the (contractual) service). (On the sterilisation cases, see the comparative discussion in *The German Law of Torts*, pp 178–91 and 194–8.)

One thing that emerges clearly from this summary of the English position is that the English courts, while prepared to broaden the application of this area of the law, remain concerned to keep such liability within fairly strict boundaries and still insist on a strong nexus between the provider of the advice or the service and the recipient who relies thereon. In this respect, while the moves towards the appropriate control criteria do seem similar to those used in the German cases, it would appear that the English approach remains somewhat more restrictive.

The trend of lessening the requirement of the creditor's interest in the protection of the third party has been continued in many decisions confirming BGH NJW 1984, 355. We may briefly discuss BGHZ 127, 378, reproduced in *The German Law of Torts*, p 280, case no 23, annotated at 293 *et seq*. The decision deals with the problem whether and to what extent the co-responsibility of the contractual partner of the surveyor should be taken into account in an action by the third party/purchaser of the land. In this instance the site owner, who intended to sell the property, commissioned a report from a surveyor to estimate the value of the house. The surveyor over-valued the house. This was because he negligently relied on the misleading information given to him by the site owner. The third party/purchaser relied on the surveyor's report and bought the house at an unrealistic price. The court allowed the action of the third party. The actual result of the decision surely appears reasonable. In the final analysis, however, the BGH took another step in the direction of an extra-contractual liability for certain cases of economic loss. The court sought to derive this result from the intention of the parties to the contract of employment of the surveyor which was given protective effect towards the third party/purchaser. The BGH resorted to two fictions to achieve the 'desired' result on the basis of contract.

The first was that the site owner had a real interest in including the buyer in the protective scope of the contract. In fact he had not, since he and the purchaser were on opposite sides of the bargain, and as a result the survey gave rise to a conflict of interests. (While the site owner is clearly interested in a favourable valuation, the purchaser/plaintiff is interested in a valuation at the lower end of the scale). It is therefore difficult to argue that the site owner wished to benefit the third party/plaintiff. Such an intention could be 'discovered' only if one could show that, had the parties openly discussed the issue, they would have agreed that good faith required that the site-owner also contracted for the benefit of the purchaser. Such a construction, however, is so unconvincing that in reality it shows that it is the law that is imposing on the surveyor such a duty towards the purchaser and not the will of the parties.

The second fiction is even more striking. It is inherent in the derivative nature of the third party's cause of action that the promisor/surveyor can rely, vis-à-vis the third party, on any defences available to him against the promisee (§ 334 BGB, which in the UK corresponds to section 3(2) of the Contracts (Rights of Third Parties Act) 1999). In an action by the site owner, the surveyor could have objected that the promisee/site owner who commissioned the report had acted contrary to good faith in concealing a crucial defect of the property. The BGH held that the promisor could not avail himself of this defence as against the third party/purchaser. The court relied on a device—which is not always available—to solve this problem, namely implied term reasoning. Thus, it assumed that in the contract that created the 'duty of care' towards certain third parties, the surveyor tacitly waived his right to avail himself of any defence against the plaintiff/potential purchaser which he, the contractual debtor, had against his contractual partner (the person commissioning the report). This waiver, the BGH stated, was justified by the fact that the expert knew that his performance was intended to form the basis of the financial calculations of the purchaser of the land (who, one might add will—reasonably—rely on the report). It goes without saying that these considerations might also justify imposing liability in these circumstances under the *Hedley Byrne* principle (eg, as in *Smith v Eric S Bush*, above). However, it is more difficult to see how this result, imposing liability, can be derived from applying the concept of a contract in favour of the third party. For not only is this result incompatible with the traditional model of a contract in favour of third parties; it is also doubtful that the surveyor would have accepted such a waiver had it been discussed before entering into the contract. Once again, such analysis indicates that the duty is imposed by law and does not flow from the will of the contracting parties (*quaere* what the result would be if an attempt were made by the surveyor expressly to exclude liability by stating this clearly in his report: this device failed in *Smith v Eric S Bush* as a result of section 2(2) of UCTA 1977—in the context of a business-consumer relationship, where the consumer had no opportunity to renegotiate terms, etc. See especially, the judgment of Lord Griffiths [1990] 1 AC 831, 857–60). It also casts new doubt on the whole construction of a contract with protective effects towards the purchaser (see Ebke, JZ 1998, 991, 993, who suggests that 'implied term' reasoning is in such cases used to make up for the exclusion of pure economic loss from the list of protected interests in § 823 I BGB).

In the light of the above, it comes as no surprise to discover that some academic commentators have argued in favour of abandoning the contract with protective effects as theoretical basis of the decisions of the court—at least in cases such as the present one. But the BGH remains to be convinced and has yet to give any signs that it is about to change its present stance (see eg, Canaris, ZHR 163 (1999) 206, and JZ 1995, 441). Professor Canaris submits that at least in situations like the present one, the theoretical basis of the liability of the 'expert' for negligent misstatements in German law ought to be *culpa in contrahendo* (now § 311 II and III BGB). Such an analysis would entail a number of advantages, such as a better explanation of the independence of the action from the contract between the person who commissioned the statement and the expert. It would also cater for the need to limit liability in relation to third parties by disclaimers etc. One is reminded here of the reasoning in *Smith v Eric S Bush* (as discussed above).

However, as Professor Schlechtriem remarked it is not so much the theoretical basis that counts. What really matters is that the specific criteria for imposing liability receive attention and are developed rationally on a case-by-case basis. (See his 'Schutzpflichten und geschützte Personen' in *Festschrift für Dieter Medicus* (1999), p 529.) Against this background, the comparative study of each other's systems can provide useful insights to both of them and make the lawyer—student or practitioner—understand better what he is trying to achieve. Another and perhaps more important lesson that can be drawn from comparing liability for negligent misstatements is that, in this field of 'professional negligence,' the traditional compartmentalisation of obligations into contractual and tortious bases very often lacks explanatory power. (See further Coester and Markesinis, 'Liability of Financial Experts in German and American Law: An exercise in Comparative Methodology'(2003) *Amer J Comp L* 275–309.)

(d) Summary and Comparative Epilogue

To summarise, it can be stated that German courts have deployed the concept of a contract with protective effects in two quite different groups of cases.

In the first category, the function of the *Vertrag mit Schutzwirkung* is to frame certain protective duties of care as collateral obligations under the contract (or in pre-contractual situations as *culpa in contrahendo*) in order to avoid the weak vicarious liability rule contained in § 831 BGB. The well-known decision in *Cavalier v Pope* provides an excellent English illustration of the problem that has to be solved. These cases involve physical damage to property or to the person, and clearly this aspect of the concept is of less interest to English lawyers.

The second type of situation in which the notion of *Vertrag mit Schutzwirkung* has been used is however much more interesting and it concerns the so-called 'liability of experts.' Here the absence (in Germany) of a tortious exception to the rule that pure economic loss is not recoverable in tort (such as the *Hedley Byrne* principle) has prompted German courts to extend contractual reasoning. It suffices here to point out that this category of liability causes great *conceptual* difficulties in both systems but the control mechanisms applied by the courts are quite similar from a pragmatic point of view. (For a more detailed account, see notes to cases 19–24, p 265 *et seq*, and case 27, p 328 *et seq* in *The German Law of Torts*.)

The contents of this chapter should reveal both the strengths and weaknesses of German law. To the common law observer, it is really little short of amazing to see the lengths German lawyers have gone to in order to overcome some defective provisions in their Code. Common law students repeatedly ask the question 'why did not German law abrogate the unfortunate provision of § 831 BGB and choose instead to go to such lengths to by-pass its unwanted consequences?' Such a question of course ignores the special force that the Codes have and the dangers of amending them in a piecemeal manner, but it nevertheless adequately expresses the perplexity experienced by foreign observers. Another concern that common lawyers tend to voice is however less easy to answer. Do we really need all these variations of the contract *in favorem tertii*, and in particular, is it still really necessary to retain both the institution of *Vertrag mit Schutzwirkung für Dritte* and *Drittschadensliquidation* (to be discussed next), especially now that the former institution has been extended to cover economic loss as well? The German writings leave the foreign observer impressed with their ingenuity; but they also fail to convince entirely that the *Vertrag mit Schutzwirkung für Dritte* is giving effect to the intentions of the parties rather than imposing obligations in law on the parties, which are perhaps more easily explained on an extra-contractual basis. More importantly, perhaps, the relaxation of the conditions necessary in order to discover contracts with protective effects towards third parties has not only caused concern within German academic circles; it has led some English observers of the German scene to dismiss it rather more summarily than it deserves (see Beatson, 'Reforming the Law of Contracts for the Benefit of Third Parties? A Second Bite at the Cherry (1992) 45 *CLP* 1, and Barker, 'Are we up to Expectations? Solicitors, Beneficiaries and the Tort/Contract Divide' (1994) 14 *OJLS* 137). For, despite its propensity towards theoretical constructions, German law in this area has some interesting lessons to offer to those who are willing to look behind the different conceptualism. Here are two examples; and others were noted in the preceding pages, especially whenever the German solutions were compared to those adopted by French law.

The first point has already been noted in passing when we talked about defences available to the promisor/debtor. In daily life the problem that confronts the courts is not only how to make one of the contracting parties liable to a stranger. Just as important is another question: how to ensure that the contractual debtor is liable towards the third party in exactly the same way as he would be liable towards his co-contractor, the promisee. If the liability is different in nature, all manner of issues will be affected: jurisdiction (internal and international), standard of care, period of limitation, exemption clauses, etc. To impose liability *simpliciter* could mean that one side of the triangle (debtor/third party) was subject to one set of rules while the other (creditor/debtor) was subject to another. The contractual solutions of German law ensure that this does not happen (§ 334 BGB). But even where they are not available (or not attractive) to common lawyers, more accustomed to handling problems through tort law and the notion of duty of care, they should still be of use to them in so far as they suggest that the fashioning of the tort duties must be determined by the underlying contract (see eg, *White v Jones*, above, for this very point). Equally, it is important to remember which contract is the one that matters for these purposes; and as we saw in the relevant section of the German law, the contract that should matter is the one between promisor and promisee (and not, as some English decisions have implied, the relationship between promisor and third party). On this point, the general rule of German law seems clear and convincing. Yet, as the discussion of the baffling decision BGHZ 127, 378 (reproduced in *The German Law of Torts*, case no 23) shows, there may be cases where the third party may be entitled to recover more than the promisee.

Secondly, German lawyers have also rendered service to legal science by analysing the contractual link thoroughly and distinguishing between primary and secondary obligations. The importance of this can be seen when comparing the Germanic approach with the French in the context of the well-known '*blood transfusion*' case. (Civ GP 1955.1.54.) In that case, the *Centre National de Transfusion Sanguine* entered into a contract with a hospital to supply it with blood to be transfused to its patients. Some of the blood so provided was infected by syphilis and one of the patients who received it sued the Centre and was allowed to claim damages on the ground that he was a third party beneficiary of the contract concluded between the *Centre* and the hospital. This *stipulation pour autrui* is analogous to the German *Vertrag zugunsten Dritter*. In theory, it means that the promisor (the *Centre*) is liable to the third party for the performance of the primary obligation in such a way that he could be sued by the patient for non-delivery of the blood. Clearly, this was not intended by the parties; and if such an action were brought it would have failed. This, in reality, was a tort situation, and should have been solved through Article 1382 CC. Why the contractual approach was preferred can only be matter of speculation. Often, in French law contractual solutions offer procedural advantages to plaintiffs. But if a contractual solution were needed, the Germanic *Vertrag mit Schutzwirkung für Dritte* offers a neater approach.

4. *SCHADENSVERLAGERUNG* AND TRANSFERRED LOSS

Büdenbender, 'Wechselwirkungen zwischen Vorteilsausgleichung und Drittschadens-liquidation' JZ 1995, 920; von Caemmerer, 'Das Problem des Drittschadensersatzes' ZHR 127 (1965) 241; Oetker, 'Versendungskauf, Frachtrecht und Drittschadensliquidation' JuS 2001, 833; Peters, 'Zum Problem der Drittschadensliquidation' AcP 180 (1980) 329; Ries, 'Grundprobleme der Drittschadensliquidation und des Vertrags mit Schutzwirkung für Dritte' JA 1982, 453; von Schröter, 'Die Haftung für Drittschäden' Jura 1997, 343; Tägert, *Die Geltendmachung des Drittschadens* (1938).

(a) Preliminary Observations

The doctrine of transferred loss is meant to ensure that the defaulting party in the contract does not benefit from his fault in those cases where the loss has been shifted from the creditor to a third party. If this exception to the notion of relativity of contracts had not been accepted, the defaulting party would not be liable to his creditor since the latter has suffered no loss; nor would he be liable to the third party in contract in the absence of any contractual link between them. Likewise, since the harm involved is pure economic loss, in German law there would be no chance of an action in tort. Thus, what makes it necessary to create a new mechanism is the fact that in some cases the party who has suffered the loss has no right to claim and the party who has the right to claim has suffered no loss. From this situation emerged the notion of *Drittschadens-liquidation*, which allows the contractual creditor to claim (liquidate) the loss suffered by the third party as a result of the non-execution or faulty execution of the contract by the contractual debtor. This theoretical analysis is best understood through some concrete examples, although perhaps one can state that what all these cases have in common are two factors. First, there is a 'fortuitous' shift of liability as the loss is transferred from the contractual creditor to the third party. Secondly, the fear of opening of the floodgates (the 'shop-soiled argument of the timorous' as Professor John Fleming has called it in his *Introduction to the Law of Torts* (2nd edn, 1985), p 3) does not arise here precisely because only one person can suffer loss in these cases.

The case law probably goes back to a decision of the Court of Appeal of Lübeck, which allowed an agent to claim damages for loss suffered by his 'undisclosed' principal (Seufferts Archiv, II (1857) 36, 37). It will of course be remembered from chapter 2 that German law does not recognise the concept of undisclosed agency, so in such a situation the principal who suffered the loss had no right to claim for its compensation. Allowing the agent to claim for the third party's loss accounts for the name of the device: *Drittschadensliquidation*) (see for details: von Caemmerer, ZHR 127 (1965) 241).

Recovery of third party loss is not governed by any provision of the BGB. Some commissioners had proposed a general rule as to when third party loss is recoverable, but it was not in the end included (see Mugdan, *Die gesamten Materialien zum Bürgerlichen Gesetzbuch*, II (1899), pp 517–18). The majority was of the opinion that the problem was too controversial. Like the English Law Commission in 1996 (Report No 242), the BGB Commission one hundred years earlier decided to leave the question unanswered and expressed the conviction that the courts would be able to develop a solution outside the code. It is important to note from the outset that recovery of third party loss is possible only in special cases. Like English law, the BGB proceeds on the assumption that every party to a contract may only recover his own loss. This is usually referred to as the 'doctrine of the creditor's interest' (*Dogma des Gläubigerinteresses*)—an equivalent to the English notion of the compensatory nature of damages. The concept of *Drittschadensliquidation* is thus an exception to the doctrine of the creditor's interest.

(b) Theoretical Basis

The theoretical basis of *Drittschadensliquidation* has remained somewhat controversial. It should not be concealed that some academics doubt whether the concept is needed at all. They prefer to explain the cases discussed under this heading on an alternative basis. Usually the loss is said to be suffered not by the third party but by the promisee himself. Yet this analysis is not that far removed from the transferred loss explanation. For, in a second step, these writers argue that damages are nevertheless recovered on behalf of the third party. Accordingly, either the third party has a right to have the right assigned or a right to claim the proceeds of the action by the promisee (see eg, Büdenbender, 'Wechselwirkungen zwischen Vorteilsausgleichung und Drittschadensliquidation'). The difference in practice is not very great and we may thus safely concentrate on the development of the doctrine by the courts.

There was a time when German judges also thought that the theoretical basis of awarding third party damages was agreement. The peak of this (not always consistent) line of argument was the decision of the RG in RGZ 170, 246, where construction of the contract was employed in order to hold that the defendant (who had contracted to repair a cold store) had granted the plaintiff (a city council which owned it) the right to sue for any loss suffered by third parties (the butchers whose meat in the cold store was spoiled as a result of careless repair work). The BGH endorsed the intention-based reasoning of the RG in BGHZ 15, 224. In this case a carrier had contracted with a forwarding agent. Owing to the fault of the latter, the authorities in the Soviet zone of Germany had confiscated a lorry, which belonged to the carrier's wife. The court held that the contract between the carrier and the forwarding agent contained an implied term allowing the carrier to claim damages on behalf of the owner of the lorry. Yet in this decision the implied term reasoning already seems open to question. The general rule is that if there is a gap in the contract, the respective term must be a compelling and self-evident conclusion from the agreement as a whole such that, unless the term is implied, the result would be in conflict with what was in fact agreed (see chapter 3 for a fuller explanation). In this early decision, the BGH did not even attempt to show why the actual contract necessitated the third party term. On the contrary, the court proceeded on the basis that the promisor need not have contemplated that the truck belonged to a third party. The reason for implying the term was simply that any solution other than allowing recovery of third party loss would unduly benefit the promisor, who would escape liability for the breach of the contract. The use of such a policy argument surely cast doubts on the intention test.

The drawbacks of an implied term test were openly admitted only a few years later in BGHZ 40, 91, case no 71. The plaintiff bought leather from the defendant and made it into belts. Most of the belts were sold to the firm KF. The leather was defective and produced stains where the belt met with other material. KF had as a result suffered loss, but it was common ground that KF had made no claim for this sum against the plaintiff and the plaintiff did not contend that it was liable to KF. The plaintiff nevertheless claimed to be entitled to sue for the loss suffered by its purchasers. The Court of Appeal based its decision on an implied term and held that the plaintiff was entitled to sue for any loss suffered by KF. The BGH, on the other hand, held that such an approach amounted to a fiction. Nothing of what the parties said justified the finding of a term that the plaintiff should be able to sue for damage

suffered by its purchasers. The express terms of the contract were not obviously inadequate. Experience showed that, in reality, businessmen are principally interested in
protecting themselves. Moreover, claims on behalf of sub-buyers are 'unpredictable in
their extent and incapable of being covered in an economically satisfactory manner by
increasing the sales price or taking out insurance.' (A similar conclusion was reached
in *Bence Graphics International Ltd v Fasson UK Ltd* [1998] QB 87.) There was therefore no reason to deviate from the general rule. As a consequence, the claim of the
contractor on behalf of his purchasers was rejected.

The decision was reaffirmed in 1968 in a seminal case that established a stricter
(though not strict) regime of tortious product liability, the '*chicken pest case*' (BGHZ
51, 91, reproduced in *The German Law of Torts*, case no 61, p 555 *et seq*). It was held
that *Drittschadensliquidation* could not be extended to cover product liability situations. The veterinarian could not demand from the pharmaceutical company (which
had sold him defective vaccine) the loss suffered by the owner of chickens (which died
as a result of inoculation).

What is apparent from this development is a gradual departure from pinning liability
on (an often strained, and sometimes downright fictitious,) interpretation of the parties'
intention(s). Instead, the BGH now focuses on objective requirements for claims in
respect of a third party's loss. The aforementioned BGHZ 40, 91, case no 71, contains a
useful summary of the underlying rationale. A claim may be available only 'where all
the damage due to the harmful conduct of the obligor is suffered by a third party rather
than by the person with title to sue.' Thus, 'there must be only one damage, one which
the claimant would have suffered if the protected interest had been vested in him.' The
doctrine was not triggered by the mere fact that, in addition to the person with title to
sue, a third party has suffered harm: 'allowing a person to sue for damage to a third
party must not be permitted to bring about any extension of liability founded in law or
contract by duplicating the victims whom the person causing the harm must satisfy.' In
the '*chicken pest case*' the BGH confirmed this analysis once again and added that:
'Only in special cases have the courts admitted exceptions, namely where special legal
relations between the creditor under the contract and the beneficiary of the protected
interest cause the interest to be 'shifted' on to the third party, so that as a matter of law
the damage is done to him, and not to the creditor.' This was denied, for instance, in the
famous 'cable cases' (BGH NJW 1977, 2208, case no 72; reproduced also in *The German
Law of Torts*, case no 13, p 211; cf *Spartan Steel & Alloys Ltd v Martin & Co
(Contractors) Ltd* [1973] 1 QB 27 and see also *Martindale v Duncan* [1973] 1 WLR 574).

We can see now more clearly why it was necessary to develop the notion of *Vertrag
mit Schutzwirkung* examined in the previous sub-section. For in these situations the
risk of liability of the promisor is increased. To put it simply, the range of plaintiffs
who can rely on a contract and who can sue the promisor directly is potentially indeterminate. The delicate balance between imposing contractual liability and the danger
of blurring the boundaries between contract and tort is achieved by confining
Drittschadensliquidation to cases where there is one loss, one interest at stake and the
third party did not sustain loss 'in addition to' the promisee. This means that loss
resulting from a breach of contract typically suffered by the promisee is actually suffered by a third party; or to put it differently: the promisee would have been harmed
in the very same interest had it not been shifted to the third party. In this sense, the
concept of *Drittschadensliquidation* is indeed one of 'transferred' loss.

Two consequences follow from this. First, it is irrelevant whether the third party is entitled to a tortious claim that covers the loss (BGH NJW 1985, 2411, reproduced in *The German Law of Torts*, case no 25, p 289). The second is of equal practical importance. The courts do not allow enrichment of the promisee at the expense of the third party. The courts are keen to emphasise that damages are recovered on behalf of the third party. Therefore, the BGH is willing to 'create' contractual remedies for the third party against the promisee; for instance, to imply a duty on the promisee to assign the right of action to the third party or to account for the damages recovered. The court has said recently that it would be difficult to imagine a *Drittschadensliquidation* case where such a right to assignment would not exist (BGH ZIP 1998, 511, 512). Usually the legal basis remains open. One possibility is an implied term, the other an analogy with § 285 BGB. Moreover, if the third party does not wish to claim for its loss, the basis of the promisee's claim in respect of that loss collapses (eg, RGZ 115, 419, 426; BGH WM 1987, 581, 582). The concept of *Drittschadensliquidation* governs not only the relationship between the contracting parties, but the rights of the third party against the promisee.

However, despite several attempts at further rationalisation, the law has grown in a patchy way. The judicial exceptions to the doctrine of the creditor's interest gathered more or less loosely under the heading of *Drittschadensliquidation* are to a certain extent founded on an abstract concept, as explained, but they have been specifically developed in particular types of contractual situations. There are three principal lines of cases in which such claims have been successful. An overview of the case law is given in the BGHZ 40, 91, case no 71, already mentioned. Ironically, all types of situations had been part of the original proposal to include the idea of awarding damages for a third party's loss in the BGB. Cases falling outside these main groups are controversial; the courts are reluctant to subject the doctrine of the creditor's interest to further exceptions (eg, BGHZ 133, 36).

(c) Risk Cases

In this line of cases, there is a 'transfer of risk' from the promisee to a third party. The promisee is allowed to recover damages in respect of that party's loss. The new doctrine was to find a wider application in the context of the law of sales whenever risk and property do not pass at the same time. Paragraph 447 BGB regulates one such case. If the buyer has requested the seller to dispatch the goods sold to a place other than the place of performance, the risk passes to the buyer as soon as the seller has delivered the goods to the forwarder, freighter etc, even though the property in the goods is not normally transferred to the buyer until delivery. Thus, the seller still has a claim against the person who damaged the goods during transit, even though he has suffered no loss. The buyer, on the other hand, has suffered a loss, but has no valid claim. In German law, as we have already seen above, it is well established that the seller can recover from the carrier in order to pay the money over to the buyer. Alternatively, if the seller does not co-operate in this, the buyer can have this right assigned to him by operation of law (§ 285 BGB). (See: RGZ 62, 331; BGH VersR 1972, 1138; BGH VersR 1976, 168.) It is interesting to note that the reasoning would also found a tort action by the owner on behalf of the purchaser who is on risk but has not yet acquired ownership of the goods when the damage occurred (BGHZ 49, 357, case no 73). In this case, the purchaser brought an action in tort *as assignee* of the rights of the owner against the carrier. Therefore, the court did not need to decide whether the damages awarded compensated the loss of the owner, the vendor or that of a third party, ie, the party at risk, namely the purchaser. This would only make a difference, the court indicated, where the loss of the third party would be idiosyncratic, ie, exceed that of the vendor. In the case at hand this was not the situation.

This case law, incidentally, would be applicable not only to terrestrial transport, but to carriage of goods by sea so that it would neatly solve the problem that perplexed the English courts in *The Aliakmon* ([1986] AC 785) which in the end had to be solved by means of legislation (see the discussion of this case, below). Indeed, the Germanic approach may offer one advantage over the attempted English tort solution. Being a contractually-flavoured action, it ensures that the defences available to the debtor/carrier against the creditor/seller are also available against the third party/plaintiff; and this may be a neater way of achieving this desirable result than by trying to fashion a tort duty (towards the third party) in accordance with the underlying contract between seller and carrier. (See on this, Kötz (1990) 10 *Tel Aviv Univ Studies in Law* 195, 211; Markesinis (1987) 103 *LQR* 354 and 'Doctrinal Clarity in Tort Litigation' in (1991) 25 *The International Lawyer* 953.)

Parties to contracts of carriage of goods by sea regularly use bills of lading (*Konnossement*). In such cases, the Hague-Visby Rules may govern the contract of carriage. The relevant provisions of the HGB are mostly contained in Book 5 ('Sea Trade'), §§ 476–905. The lawful holder of a bill of lading is entitled to the rights under the bill of lading: § 364 I HGB. (For English law in this area see, generally, Treitel and Reynolds, *Carver on Bills of Lading* (2001).) Although the problem does not seem to have generated much litigation, recovery of damages in respect of a third party's loss in actions against carriers is regarded as both desirable and possible.

This was held by the BGH as early as 1957 in a seminal case concerning a ship named '*Aspirator*'. (BGHZ 25, 250.) The action was by the consignor against the shipowner. The shipowner had issued bills of lading in respect of the cargo. When the goods were delivered at the port of destination, their weight was considerably less than what was stated in the bill of lading. In the meantime, the consignor had sold the goods and his buyer had in turn endorsed the bill of lading to a forwarder, company D. However, the buyer bought (and paid for) the actual quantity delivered and not that stated in the bill of lading. The consignor claimed for the difference. The BGH held that the consignor could recover in principle. First, it was confirmed that, generally speaking, the correct nominal plaintiff would have been the company D in its capacity as lawful holder of the bill of lading. However, the breach of contract by the carrier caused loss to the original holder of the bill of lading, the plaintiff consignor, and not to the present holder of the bill of lading. Hence, the latter's right to recover damages for breach of contract was of no avail unless he were allowed to recover damages on behalf of the original holder of the bill of lading. The BGH clarified that this was indeed the case. The present holder of the bill of lading, the company D, could have claimed damages on behalf of the plaintiff according to the doctrine of *Drittschadensliquidation*; ie, the company D could have recovered damages in respect of the consignor's loss (BGHZ 25, 250, 258).

Overall it can be stated that German courts are 'generous' in allowing recovery of damages in respect of a third party's loss and hostile to technical defences such as that

that the wrong nominal plaintiff brought the action or that the claimant was not the party who sustained the loss. (See eg, *Münchener Kommentar HGB-* Basedow, vol 7 (1997), § 429 HGB Rn. 52. See also, the line of cases concerning carriage by land, discussed above, section 2(a)(vi): here the contract of carriage is analysed as one for the benefit of a third party and in addition the promisor is not allowed to object that the loss arising from damage to or loss of the goods has been shifted to a third party.)

By contrast, carriage of goods by sea has given rise to formidable difficulties in English law and we may briefly allude to one line of cases in which the problem of third party loss became acute. *The Aliakmon* [1985] QB 350 (CA); [1986] AC 785 (HL) concerned an action by the consignee buyers (who were on risk) against the shipowner for damage to goods caused by bad stowage. The sale contract was not performed as contemplated. The buyers had problems in paying the price. The Court of Appeal held that, by reason of section 19(1) of the Sale of Goods Act 1979, the true inference from the negotiations between the parties was that the seller had retained the ownership of the goods notwithstanding the delivery of the bill of lading to the buyers; and consequently that section 1 of the 1855 Act did not transfer to the buyers any rights of suit under the bills of lading contract.

The buyers, however, had failed to have the sellers' right against the carrier assigned to them. Therefore, the rule developed in *The Albazero* case ([1977] AC 774) could not be applied. In this case Lord Diplock stated in a famous passage of his speech (at 847):

> The only way in which I find it possible to rationalise the rule in *Dunlop v Lambert* so that it may fit into the pattern of English law is to treat it as an application of the principle, accepted also in relation to policies of insurance on goods, that in a commercial contract concerning goods where it is in the contemplation of the parties that the proprietary interests in the goods may be transferred from one owner to another after the contract has been entered into and before the breach which causes loss or damage to the goods, an original party to the contract, if such be the intention of them both, is to be treated in law as having entered into the contract for the benefit of all persons who have or may acquire an interest in the goods before they are lost or damaged, and is entitled to recover by way of damages for breach of contract the actual loss sustained by those for whose benefit the contract is entered into.

In *The Aliakmon*, Robert Goff LJ (as he then was) remarked that the rule in *The Albazero* was of no value where the promisee was not willing to co-operate and sue on behalf of the consignee or assign his right of suit ([1985] QB 350, 396–7). The Court of Appeal concluded that all contractual claims against the shipowners failed.

The focus was thus on the buyers' claim in tort. It was held by the House of Lords that, since the buyers were not the owners of the goods nor had an immediate right to possession in the whole course of the carriage on the defendant's ship, they had no right to sue in tort. Robert Goff LJ, on the other hand, submitted that there was no good reason in principle why the buyers should not have a direct cause of action against the shipowner in tort; but on the facts, the shipowners were not liable for bad stowage (at 398–401).

It is not the place here to discuss whether a direct tort action based on the 'principle of transferred loss' is a satisfactory solution to the problem encountered in such triangular cases, or whether the law of contract ought to provide efficient remedies to the parties to the contract of carriage contained in the bill of lading. (See, for further discussion: Unberath, *Transferred Loss* (2003) 117 *et seq.*) It suffices here to point out that a flexible approach in relation to the rights arising under the contract of carriage, as described in this sub-section, seems to have created few problems in German law.

In the end, English law also sought the solution in the law of contract and not in the law of tort. The Bills of Lading Act 1855 transferred the contractual rights to the consignee or endorsee provided that property in the goods passed to him on or by reason of the consignment or endorsement. There remained gaps, however, for instance where property did not pass by reason of the endorsement, as in some odd cases like *The Aliakmon* or in the more common cases of bulk cargoes, which was the main source of difficulties (see Reynolds. 'The Significance of Tort Claims in Respect of Carriage by Sea' [1986] *LMCLQ* 97, 108 and 110). The most significant change for our purposes is that the transfer of the rights under the contract of carriage contained in or evidenced in the bill of lading depends not on the passing of property, but on the claimant becoming the lawful holder of the bill of lading. In *The Aliakmon*, the sellers retained the right of disposal of the goods and the buyers could therefore not rely on the bill of lading. Under section 2(1) of the 1992 Act, they could now have recovered as holders of the bill of lading. This was regarded as highly desirable, especially by Lord Goff of Chieveley, who welcomed the result of *The Aliakmon* being reversed by statute. (*White v Jones* [1995] 2 AC 207, 265. Lord Goff introduced the Bill himself as a private peer's measure in the House of Lords.) Furthermore, section 2(4) of the Carriage of Goods by Sea Act 1992 (which repealed the Bills of Lading Act 1855) is remarkable because it is the only statutory provision in which a (limited) right to recover a third party's loss in a contractual action is expressly confirmed.

Finally, it should be noted that cases such as *The Aliakmon* are not covered by the Contracts (Rights of Third Parties) Act 1999. Section 6(5) excludes from the application of the Act contracts of carriage of goods by sea covered by the Carriage of Goods by Sea Act 1992.

(c) Indirect Representation

A second line of cases (historically, as explained, the origin of the doctrine) involves what has in chapter 2 been called 'indirect' representation. A party concludes a contract in his own name but at the instance and on the account of a third party. The person executing the order can sue for loss suffered by the person giving it. The commission agent is the paradigmatic case, discussed in detail in chapter 2, section 6(f), p 117. It will be recalled that German law does not accept undisclosed agency. But there are other examples. Freight forwarders, regulated by Book 4, part 5 of the HGB, are also normally allowed to recover substantial damages from the carrier employed by him 'on behalf of' (though not as agent of (within the meaning of § 164 BGB)) the consignor or the consignee respectively (eg, RGZ 75, 169; 115, 419). A forwarder undertakes to organise the transport while sub-contractors carry out the actual transport. The forwarder enters into the sub-contracts as 'indirect agent' of the consignor. The consignor is entitled to sue only after the forwarder's rights have been assigned to him: § 392 I HGB. (See also, BGH VersR 1972, 274, reproduced in *The German Law of Torts*, case no 26, p 290, annotated at p 305, where indirect representation prompted the application of the doctrine in a construction context.)

The issue has arisen in English law in the cases of *St Martins Property Corporation Ltd v Sir Robert McAlpine Ltd* [1994] 1 AC 85; *Darlington BC v Wiltshier Northern Ltd* [1995] 1 WLR 68, and *Alfred McAlpine Construction Ltd v Panatown Ltd* [2001] 1

AC 518. In this controversial line of construction cases, the defendant sought to rely on the fact that the employer did not have a proprietary interest in the subject matter of the contract at the time of the breach and did not incur any financial loss. The courts held that this 'no-loss' point could not in itself prevent the employer from recovering substantial damages. Otherwise the contractor would in effect enjoy an undesirable immunity in respect of breaches of contract (thus giving rise to a 'legal black hole'). However, these cases are not easily reconciled with each other and the reasoning is not always easy to follow. As a result, the right to recover damages on behalf of a third party remains somewhat uncertain. For instance, according to the majority in the *Panatown* case it is not available if the third party has a right of his own (even if it is only a limited right) against the promisee. Furthermore, while Lord Clyde in that important case expressly adopted a 'transferred loss' approach to solve the problem of the 'legal black hole,' Lord Goff —who had previously favoured such a principle in the Court of Appeal in *The Aliakmon*, referred to above—now preferred to solve the case on the basis of a far-reaching 'performance interest' theory. A detailed treatment of these cases must be reserved to more specialised works. (See for a brief annotation, *The German Law of Torts*, p 304 *et seq*, and more detailed examination: Unberath, *Transferred Loss* (2003), chapters 2 and 8; Goode, *Commercial Law* (3rd edn, 2004), p 117, and McKendrick, 'The Common Law at Work: The Saga of *Alfred McAlpine Construction Ltd v Panatown Ltd*' Oxford U Commonwealth LJ [2003] 145.)

It suffices here to note that this line of cases reopens important contractual avenues in the area of construction law, after the decision of the House of Lords in *Murphy v Brentwood DC* [1991] 1 AC 398 made it all the more difficult to recover pure economic loss in the tort of negligence in relation to latent defects in buildings. The reasoning clearly reminds one of the approach of the German courts in *Drittschadensliquidation* cases. One could venture the thought that comparative law might be of assistance in developing the law further. The right of the third party to have the promisee's right assigned or to be able to claim the proceeds of an action by the promisee is an example in point. The German courts achieved such a neat solution with little effort, whereas the English courts have had considerable difficulties in solving cases where promisee and third party were not willing to co-operate.

(d) Taking Care of Another's Goods

A third class of cases is that where a person is looking after the goods of another. Consider the following example: BGH NJW 1985, 2411 reproduced in *The German Law of Torts*, case no 25, p 289. The first plaintiff had a continuous business relationship with the defendant, a forwarding agent, and stored goods in one of his warehouses. The second plaintiff owned the goods. The first plaintiff was the parent company of the second plaintiff. Some of the goods were stolen. Both plaintiffs sought to obtain declaratory judgments to the effect that the defendant was liable in damages for the loss of the goods. The second plaintiff's claim was exclusively founded on the law of delict. It was held that this direct right of action of the second plaintiff did not prevent the first plaintiff from pursuing his contractual claim based on *Drittschadensliquidation* against the defendant. The BGH held that the fact that the second plaintiff suffered the loss and not the first plaintiff was not a bar to that right of action: '[i]n cases like the present, where a bailor enters into a contract with a bailee whereunder the bailee undertakes to store and guard the goods the promisee or bailor is entitled to recover damages in respect of the loss suffered by the third party owner of the goods.' The second context in which *Drittschadensliquidation* has been applied resembles the situation in *The Winkfield* [1902] P 42. The bailee takes possession of another's goods and owes certain duties of protection regarding them. If a third party contractually linked to the bailee (for instance a carrier) damages the goods, the person who suffers the loss is the owner. Contractually linked to the person responsible for the damage is, however, the person who has agreed to take care of the goods. The bailee may claim damages on behalf of the bailor (BGHZ 15, 224, 229; BGH NJW 1969, 789, 790, case no 74). A typical example arises where a person who rented a chattel enters into a contract to have it repaired. If the chattel is damaged or lost by the contracting party, then the promisee will not normally be liable to the owner of the goods and as a result will not suffer loss. However, he may claim damages on behalf of the owner. While this situation is parallel to that in *The Winkfield*, in German law the emphasis is on the contractual remedy. Overall, the German cases relating to contracts to take care of chattels give rise to very similar problems to those experienced in the English bailment cases. This is remarkable if one remembers that bailment is a peculiarity of English law that does not have an exact equivalent in German law.

5

Validity

1. INTRODUCTORY REMARKS

So far we have explored the manner in which a contract is concluded and the various methods used in determining its content. We will concentrate in the following two chapters on the validity of a contract and the possible grounds on which to set a contract aside at the request of one of the parties. It should be stressed that in this (and the next) chapter we are concerned only with the invalidity of the contract as a whole. So far as individual terms of a contract are concerned, German law provides a range of subtle mechanisms for policing the content of a contract. One example of this was given earlier (in chapter 3) in relation to standard terms of business. Furthermore, good faith has provided a springboard for the courts to imply in certain circumstances terms into a contract beyond the actual intentions of the parties for no better reason that they are regarded as 'just' by the courts. Generally speaking, the rules and principles discussed here presuppose that the process of formation of the contract has been completed and that the content of the contract has been determined in accordance with the rules explained in chapter 3. For instance, as we have already seen, the courts will seek to avoid a construction of the contract that would lead to its illegality. Only if all mechanisms discussed in the previous chapter fail will the court step in and, as a measure of last resort, declare the contract void for being contrary to 'good morals'. Also, the objective method of interpretation must be applied first before one can establish a difference between (objective) declaration and (subjective) will which may justify rescission for mistake.

The reader should be aware that the grounds for invalidity could be presented in various ways. One way of analysing the material is from the perspective of 'procedural' versus 'substantive' *contractual justice*. This would not however allow for clear lines of demarcation and would produce a kaleidoscopic image of German law, as the following remarks readily illustrate.

Defects in the contracting process are commonly referred to as problems of 'procedural' contractual justice. Accordingly a number of 'procedural' standards have been set up to which the parties must adhere in addition to reaching agreement through offer and acceptance. 'Substantive' contractual justice is—on a theoretical level—independent from issues raised by the contracting process; this sort of argument attempts to measure the fairness of the end result of that process. If one were to apply an exchange standard of justice one could for instance claim that the terms of a contract are unfair for one party if that party receives less than the equivalent value of what he gives up. (See, for a useful exposition of these basic concepts of contractual justice, von Mehren, *International Encyclopedia of Comparative Law* Vol. VII chapter

1, p 64 *et seq*.) While German law provides a confusing variety of mechanisms to deal with 'procedural' contractual justice, it does not recognise a general exchange standard as a sufficient reason for setting a contract aside. And yet, in combination with procedural defects, onerous terms of the contract may well lead to the invalidity of the contract as a whole.

The rules relating to incapacity, mistake, deception, other forms of 'misrepresentation' and coercion are centred on procedural justice. A new form of procedural standard is set up by the rules of consumer protection. These rules, however, border on substantive justice. Likewise, some cases of 'misrepresentation' are more concerned with the fairness of terms of the contract than with any deficiency of consent. Aspects of substantive justice become the focus of attention when it comes to contracts void under § 138 II BGB, a provision which presupposes a violation of the exchange standard, but crucially in addition also requires the existence of grave procedural flaws.

There is, finally, another category of reasons for declaring a contract void which is independent of what has been said so far. These reasons are directed at the content of the contract, but unlike 'substantive' contractual justice are largely independent of the fairness of the exchange of values. These are external, ie extra-contractual, reasons and therefore not to be confused with the exchange standard of justice. In German law contracts contrary to statutory prohibitions, eg, § 134 BGB, fall under this heading. Contracts contrary to 'good morals', § 138 I BGB, seem to imply an external standard, but in some cases (as we shall see) it is the contracting process as well as the exchange standard that forms the basis of the intervention of the court in much the same way as they form the basis for judicial interference under § 138 II BGB (usury).

Another more obvious way to organise the material is by differentiating according to the *consequences* of the deficiency of the contract, ie according to whether the contract is void or can merely be set aside at the request of one party, which in effect gives that party a choice whether to back out of the contract or to accept it. Thus, the contract is void according to rules of capacity, illegality, and public policy, but only voidable (ie, may be set aside if the aggrieved party exercises a right to set the contract aside), under the rules of consumer protection, mistake, the removal or disappearance of the foundation of the transaction, fraud, and duress. This way of proceeding seems most convenient and is adopted here. Issues of validity are discussed in the present chapter; and the various rights to set a contract aside are examined in chapter 6.

It should be stressed from the outset however that once again the picture is more complex than is apparent at first sight. The rules of capacity declare contracts void but in some cases keep the contract in 'suspended animation' to allow the legal representative to decide whether to give his consent and 'validate' the contract. Consumer rights, if they are exercised, do not make the contract void retroactively, yet the effects of performance are to be reversed under § 346 BGB. A contract affected by (unilateral) mistake becomes, if rescinded, void retroactively and this leads to the application of § 812 BGB (on unjustified enrichment). The doctrine of the foundation of the transaction requires an adjustment of the contract and only where this is not possible does it allow for the termination of the contract according to principles similar to those applicable in consumer protection cases. Illegal contracts, or contracts contrary to public policy, finally, are void *ab initio* and thus lead (like rescission for mistake) to the application of the rules of unjust enrichment.

2. CAPACITY

Beitzke, 'Mündigkeit und Minderjährigenschutz' AcP 172 (1972) 240: Coester-Waltjen, Überblick über die Probleme der Geschäftsfähigkeit' Jura 1994, 331; Hartwig, '"Infants"Contracts in English Law: with Commonwealth and European Comparisons' (1966) 15 *ICLQ* 780; Petersen, 'Die Geschäftsfähigkeit' Jura 2003, 97; Stürner, 'Der lediglich rechtliche Vorteil' AcP 173 (1973) 402; Treitel, *The Law of Contract* (11th edn, 2003), chapter 13; W Zimmermann and J Damrau, 'Das neue Betreuungs- und Unterbringungsrecht' NJW 1991, 538.

(a) Preliminary Observations

Every contractual relationship of obligation consists of at least two declarations of intention: offer and acceptance (as to which see chapter 2). The declaration of intention is the nucleus of self-determination and as such presupposes the capacity for uninhibited rational decision-making. The starting point of the BGB is the presumption that every person possesses the required quality for entering into contractual relationships. This general principle is qualified in three respects.

First, the BGB stipulates for different degrees of capacity for different brackets of age; only children younger than seven years are regarded as lacking such contractual capacity altogether. Children between the age of seven and eighteen are at least for some respects treated as capable of forming a free will (§§ 106–13, 165 BGB), while after reaching the age of eighteen no restrictions apply whatsoever. As with all rules that generalise in such a sweeping fashion, drawing a line at a certain age, will necessarily be arbitrary. The justification for this approach is nevertheless strong. Security of legal transactions would be seriously endangered if, in individual cases involving children of more than average maturity, the rules could be questioned. The rules are thus strict.

In English law, the clear starting point is that in general a minor is not bound by his contracts. While also adhering to the age of eighteen as the end of a child's 'minority' (following section 1 of the Family Law Reform Act 1969), English law does not differentiate within minority by reference to age brackets, but instead by reference to the nature of the contract entered into and/or the basis on which liability may be incurred by children towards adults. The relevant rules are drawn from the common law, as modified by the Minors Contracts Act 1987 (implementing the Law Commission's report, *Minors' Contracts*, Law Com No 134, 1984). It should be appreciated that a very large proportion of the English cases that developed the law on minors' contracts concerned young people between the ages of 18 and 21. Thus, the change in the age of majority in 1969 removed much of the practical importance of the rules relating to the contractual capacity of minors, Although some key issues still remain, eg, contracts for young professional sportsmen or entertainers, as well as employment contracts more generally for those leaving school before the age of 18.

Secondly and thirdly, the BGB distinguishes between persons who due to mental illness that is of a certain duration, are incompetent to exercise a free will (§ 104 Nr. 2 BGB) and persons who lack capacity because of a more temporary mental disturbance or due to unconsciousness (§ 105 Nr. 2 BGB). In all these cases however the declaration of intention is void under § 105 BGB. The English law on mental incapacity grants broad powers to the court where the property of the incapacitated person is subject to the control of the court under Part VII (particularly section 94) of the Mental Health Act 1983 (see Fridman (1963) 79 LQR 502 and (1964) 80 LQR 84). Otherwise, contracts concluded with those suffering from mental incapacity are generally subject to the rules of the common law.

The rules on capacity are all contained in the General Part of the BGB. This is sensible for they concern one of the basic preconditions of every declaration of intention, not only contractual relationships of obligation. They are supplemented by special rules of representation from the family law part of the Code. It is essential to read the rules on capacity in conjunction with the family law rules. In order to avoid a legal 'vacuum' the law must provide a mechanism of representation for those who are deemed incapable of articulating or forming their will and nominate persons who act on their behalf or provide for procedures which lead to the appointment of such persons.

(b) Age-related Distinctions—Minors

Persons up to the age of seven are deemed to be incompetent: § 104 Nr. 1 BGB. Their declarations of intention are void: § 105 I BGB. Legal representation is entrusted to those person(s) who are legally in charge of the welfare of the child and its upbringing, ie normally the parents of the child (*elterliche Sorge*): §§ 1629, 1626 BGB. If the parents are not legally responsible for the child, the so-called '*Vormundschaftsgericht*' (guardianship court), a special division of the *Amtsgericht*, appoints a *Vormund* or guardian for the child, who will then act as its legal representative: §§ 1773–95 BGB. From the number of provisions it can immediately be seen that the BGB devotes special care to the definition of the duties of the *Vormund* in the interest of the child. It suffices here to point out that certain legal transactions require the express permission of the court for their validity (eg, § 1821 I Nr. 1 BGB: the disposition of land belonging to the child must be sanctioned by a court order of the guardianship court). Some of these restrictions also apply in relation to the parents of the child. Certain legal transactions, which include the example of the disposal of land belonging to the child, are subject to the assent of the guardianship court, § 1643 BGB.

English law has long been prepared to enforce what is known as a 'contract for necessaries' even against children of this age. Indeed, at common law, such contracts were the only type to which the status of minority did not afford the child some defence. The old common law position (for which see eg, *Peters v Fleming* (1840) 6 M & W 42; 151 ER 314 and *Nash v Inman* [1908] 2 KB 1) has now been placed on a statutory footing by section 3 of the Sale of Goods Act 1979. In section 3(2) it is provided that '[w]here necessaries are sold and delivered to a minor or to a person who by reason of mental incapacity or drunkenness is incompetent to contract, he must pay a reasonable price for them.' 'Necessaries' are 'goods suitable to the condition in life of the minor or other person concerned and to his actual requirements at the time of sale and delivery.' (Section 3(3) of the 1979 Act.) These terms reproduce those developed in the case law (see *Peters* and *Nash*, cited above) and show that 'necessaries' are not synonymous with 'necessities' (see Law Com No 134, paras 5.4–5.6). These cases also illustrate that the courts will not be quick to hold extravagant or frivolous articles to be 'necessaries' for this purpose. (See for instance, the purchases of crystal, ruby, and diamond solitaires and an antique goblet in silver gilt, by a minor who 'moved in the highest society' (*Ryder v Wombwell* (1868) LR 3 Ex 90, affd (1869) LR 4 Ex. 32) were not covered by the term 'necessaries'.) This underlines that fact even here a strong protective function is at work vis-à-vis the minor; and the same is indicated by the rule that the minor will only be liable to pay a 'reasonable price' for such necessaries. (This may not necessarily be the same as the contract price.) Finally, it should be noted that modern legislation relating to parental duties to maintain a child even when the parent is absent (section 1(1) of the Child Support Act 1991), or allowing the courts to make orders against parents to provide financial support for their children (section 15 and Schedule 5 of the Children Act 1989), may have the result that the child is well provided. Such a finding would mean that the later supply of goods and services may not be able to be characterised as a supply of 'necessaries' in the sense given, above. (Treitel, *The Law of Contract*, p 543.) Contracts other than those discussed here fall under the general rules and will be discussed alongside the German law that covers the next age bracket.

In German law, from the age of seven to the age of eighteen (§§ 2, 106 BGB), children are subjected to the rules relating to minors (*Minderjährige*). As is the case with children below that age, the parents are legally empowered to represent the child and enter into contracts as 'agent' on behalf of the minor. Likewise, a *Vormund* or guardian may be appointed.

German law however also recognises a partial capacity of minors to exercise a free will. Thus, minors may under certain circumstances validly conclude contracts. This guiding principle seems evidently sensible—at any rate if the legal transaction in question does not entail any *legal* disadvantage. In such a case it is valid: § 107 BGB. On closer inspection, however, the concept of 'legal (dis-)advantage' raises doubts, and indeed has given rise to many controversies in German law. It seems easy to apply if equated with whether the minor incurred an obligation by entering into the legal transaction. Yet difficulties start to emerge once one starts to differentiate between immediate legal disadvantage and more remote disadvantages. For instance, the making of a gift entails only legal benefits. However, if the gift consists of a piece of land, then the transaction may entail a number of consequential 'public' duties such as the payment of tax. Is this still a legal advantage? The answer of German law tends to be formalistic in the interest of certainty. Thus, the transaction may indeed be commercially disadvantageous—so long as it does not impose any 'immediate' duty on the minor it is valid under § 107 BGB. (See for details, Medicus, *Allgemeiner Teil*, § 39 II.)

There are also so-called 'neutral' transactions, which are treated as valid. An example is provided by § 165 BGB in the context of agency. The minor may act as agent as this provision expressly stipulates. No obligation is incurred, for in the case of a valid authorisation the contract is between principal and third party. Further, if the minor is a *falsus procurator* he is nevertheless not personally liable in damages. For in this case § 179 III 2 BGB makes an exception to the general rule in the interest of the minor. This rule is in fact typical of the desire of the BGB to provide comprehensive protection to minors in the sphere of private law. Reliance on legal transactions performed by minors is consequently deemed not to be justified. A contracting party that contracts with a minor without the consent of his representative thus runs a considerable risk that the contract is invalid and no damages can be claimed.

In English law, an employment or training contract can also be binding on a minor, provided that it operates on the whole to the minor's benefit (see eg, *Clements v London & North Western Railway Co* [1894] 2 QB 482), although it must be remembered that certain statutory provisions now also cover such contracts entered into by children. (Thus, see the Employment of Children Act 1973, as amended by the Employment Act 1989 and the Children Act 1989.) If however such a contract is more onerous than beneficial to the minor, then it will not impose liability on the minor: see *De Francesco v Barnum* (1890) 45 Ch D 430. It is also clear that 'if the contract as a whole is beneficial, the infant cannot pick and choose and adopt those terms which are clearly beneficial while rejecting those terms which are not beneficial or not clearly beneficial.' (*per* McNair J in *Slade v Metrodent Ltd* [1953] 2 QB 112.) Such an assessment of the contract must be undertaken by the court looking 'at the whole contract, having regard to the circumstances of the case.' (*De Francesco*, cited above, at 439.) Again, contracts for necessaries will be valid and enforceable against minors in this age bracket and the case law shows that it is not just goods that are covered. Medical assistance may fall within this definition at common law (*Dale v Copping* (1610) 1 Bulst 39; 80 ER 743 and see *Gillick v West Norfolk and Wisbech Area Health Authority* [1986] 1 AC 112, at 166–7, 183 and 195). However, this category does not include trading contracts, even though they may be of benefit to the minor in the sense that they allow him to carry out his business (*Cowern v Nield* [1912] 2 KB 419). In difficult borderline cases, this distinction between exercising a profession and earning a living as a trader can be difficult to justify (indeed, some authors see cases such as *Chaplin v Leslie Frewin* (below) as blurring the distinction still further. (See Beatson, *Anson's Law of Contract* (28th edn, 2002), pp 219–20, and generally, Treitel, *The Law of Contract*, p 545.)

As in German law, the decision whether a contract is, on the whole, to the benefit of the minor can create many difficult problems of assessment (particularly given the result, noted above in conjunction with the *Slade v Metrodent Ltd* case, that if the contract as a whole is beneficial then it is also enforceable as a whole, including the detrimental elements). The case of *Chaplin v Leslie Frewin (Publishers) Ltd* [1966] Ch 71 provides an excellent example of the problem and (along with other decisions such as the *Clements* case, above) also illustrates nicely that the approach taken by the English courts in assessing benefit or detriment in such cases is very far from formalistic. The plaintiff, who was the son of the famous silent film star Charlie Chaplin, was a minor and he sought to repudiate his assignment to the defendant of the exclusive right to publish the plaintiff's autobiography when the completed work showed him (so he alleged) to be a 'depraved creature.' He had received considerable advance royalties for the assignment. The Court of Appeal split on whether this contract could be said to have been beneficial to the plaintiff. While Lord Denning MR felt that it could hardly be beneficial for the minor 'that he should exploit his discreditable conduct for money' (at 88), Winn and Danckwerts LJJ preferred the view that the contract gave him a start as an author and '[t]he mud may cling but the profits will be secured' (*per* Danckwerts LJ at 95). As Treitel points out (*The Law of Contract*, p 544, note 62) in that case it may have been significant that royalties had already been paid in advance and that it was difficult to see how in practice the defendant would have been able to recover them had the plaintiff been allowed to repudiate the assignment.

Beyond these cases relating to necessaries and beneficial contracts relating either to issues analogous to necessaries or to employment or training, the basic approach of the common law was that all minors' contracts were voidable at the option of the minor, either before or after reaching majority. Some such contracts were binding until the minor disclaimed them. (They were christened 'positive voidable contracts' in *Anson's Law of Contract* (28th edn, 2002), p 216.) This category of contracts relates to the acquisition by the minor of an interest of a continuous or permanent nature, such as an interest in land. All other contracts were not binding unless ratified by the minor within a reasonable time after reaching majority. (Known in *Anson* as 'negative voidable contracts,' albeit recognising that to use the term 'voidable' here will offend some, since 'the essence of a voidable contract is that it is binding unless it is repudiated whereas these contracts were not binding unless affirmed. However, the terminology is a convenient one, and it would be inadvisable to reject it merely on purist grounds'. See, p 216, note 58 and cf Treitel, *The Law of Contract*, p 549.) We will return to the operation of this approach below.

In German law, if the legal transaction is neither solely legally advantageous nor at least neutral to the position of the minor, § 107 BGB stipulates that the consent of the legal representative is necessary. If the consent was declared beforehand the BGB speaks of *Einwilligung* (§ 183 BGB). In this case the declaration of intention of the minor is perfectly valid. If the consent was not actually obtained prior to the contract entered into by a minor, then the contract is neither (immediately) void nor valid. This strikes one as odd, but the BGB defines some middle ground between the seemingly exclusive pair of values. The best way to translate the respective term of '*schwebende Unwirksamkeit*' is perhaps 'suspended invalidity.' As § 108 I BGB stipulates, the validity depends on the subsequent consent (*Genehmigung*, § 184 BGB) of the legal representative. If the consent is denied, the declaration is invalid; if it is granted it is (retroactively) valid. Under certain conditions, the other party is given by § 109 BGB a right to terminate the period of suspension by revoking his declaration of intention. It should be noted that in the interest of security in the law unilateral legal transactions require *prior* consent for their validity: § 111 BGB.

The English approach to negative voidable contracts creates a similar 'suspended invalidity,' in that failure to ratify the contract on reaching majority would operate as a repudiation of the contract by the minor. Such contracts generally concerned isolated acts that were not continuous in nature and this category operates as the default rule, in the absence of any of the other categories covering the situation. During his minority, although the minor is not bound by such contracts, the other party is bound (*Bruce v Warwick* (1815) 6 Taunt 118; 128 ER 978). The minor cannot secure the specific performance of such a contract, since the court will not order this if it is not available to both parties (see eg, *Lumley v Ravenscroft* [1895] 1 QB 683 and Treitel, p 1037), but damages for breach of contract will be available. Thus, the consent that can perfect the transaction is that of the minor himself; but it can only be given on reaching majority. This raises the difficult question of the position of the other party in the interim period, but here it seems that the law on personal property can fill much of the gap. It would seem that property passes to the minor on delivery (*Stocks v Wilson* [1913] 2 KB 235 at 246) and also that the minor can validly pass property to the other party by delivery (see the *Chaplin* case, above). As Treitel points out (p 550), this analysis has the beneficial effect of protecting innocent third parties who later acquire the property thus passed.

A number of typical situations of consent have been specifically dealt with in the German Civil Code. Thus, § 110 BGB declares such contracts valid which have been fulfilled with the financial means provided to the infant for this purpose or for his free disposition ('pocket money'). § 112 BGB provides that if the minor is authorised by his legal representative and the guardianship court to carry out a gainful occupation, he may perform all acts within the scope of that occupation. Similarly, § 113 BGB provides that the minor may perform legal transactions in connection with a contract of employment entered into with the consent of the legal representative. Finally, the consent of a legal representative is not sufficient in those cases in which the representative is not legally authorised to act on behalf of the minor without the support of the guardianship court. A good example of this situation is if the minor seeks to become a partner in a company that is run as a profit-making enterprise. Under § 1822 Nr. 3 BGB, the minor needs both the consent of the legal representative and of the guardianship court. (See, as to problems resulting from a lack of consent: Maultzsch, 'Die "fehlerhafte Gesellschaft": Rechtsnatur und Minderjährigenschutz' JuS 2003, 544.)

In English law, it is clear that a minor may become a partner during his minority and, while bound by the partnership agreement, cannot be made liable during his minority for any debts that the partnership incurs. Such liability can accrue only once he reaches majority and fails to repudiate his partnership (see *Goode v Harrison* (1821) 5 B & Ald 147; 106 ER 1147), thus making this an example of a positive voidable contract: ie a definite act of repudiation is required for the minor to avoid being bound once he reaches majority.

In the light of the above, one could say that the essence of the German provisions is to enable the minor to participate in the legal community by entering into contracts. However, the law is at pains to ensure that the minor does not enter into dangerous contracts without proper control by his parents and occasionally a neutral institution solely concerned with the best interests of the child. By contrast, the English approach has been to provide the minor with an opportunity to repudiate contracts entered into during his minority (subject to the exceptions already discussed relating to necessaries and the like) in certain cases. Outside those categories, the minor is not bound by the contract at all, unless he later ratifies the contract on reaching his majority (*Williams v Moor* (1843) 11 M & W 256; 152 ER 798).

The problems raised by this approach are usefully illustrated by BGHZ 78, 28 = case no 75. In this case the parents intended gratuitously to transfer residential property, a flat (*Wohnungseigentum*) to their child. The contract of obligation containing the gift was legally advantageous as it did not impose any obligations on the minor (§ 107 BGB). However, the court stated that the contract of transfer in the case at hand entailed legal obligations which would not be compatible with the purpose of § 107 BGB to protect the child. By the entry of the minor into the community of the owners of flats in the building the transferee minor implicitly accepted a number of obligations which went beyond what was imposed by law. As a result the valid conclusion of the contract of transfer required the consent of the legal representative. The parents gave this consent. However, the parents now acted on both sides of the bargain: as transferors and as legal representatives of the transferee. § 181 BGB prohibits this form of representation because of the potential conflict of interest. Unfortunately this is not the end of the story. For § 181 BGB also makes an exception in relation to contracts of transfer. Here, a so-called 'internal transaction' (*Insichgeschäft*), is allowed. This would have meant that since the contract of obligation (gift) was valid the parents could validly transfer property, even though this constituted a legal disadvantage for the minor. The court argued that such a result would not comply with the purpose of § 107 BGB and therefore, exceptionally, the contract of transfer and the contract of obligation were to be construed together. This approach has attracted harsh criticism as it involves a relaxation of the principle of separation (discussed in chapter 1; see Medicus, *Allgemeiner Teil*, Rn. 565; Bork, *Allgemeiner Teil*, Rn. 1002). As a result, since the parents themselves may not legally represent the minor on this occasion, to effect the valid transfer of the property there is a need to obtain the consent of a so called *Ergänzungspfleger*, ie a neutral person appointed for this particular occasion by the guardianship court, § 1909 BGB.

In English law, the subject matter of the fact scenario in BGHZ 78, 28 = case no 75 would fall under the heading of positive voidable contracts since it related to the transfer of an interest in land. Thus, unless he repudiates a lease, a minor is liable to pay the rent due: *Keteley's Case* (1613) 1 Brownl 120; 123 ER 704 and *Davies v Beynon-Harris* (1931) 47 TLR 424. The latter case makes clear that, although the minor cannot hold a legal estate in land (as a result of sections 1(6) and 19 of the Law of Property Act 1925), he can still hold an equitable interest and so be bound in exactly the same way. This is as a result of section 26(6) of the Settled Land Act 1925 for land acquired prior to 1997, and section 2(6) and Schedule 1, para 1 of the Trusts of Land and Appointment of Trustees Act 1996 for land acquired after 1996. Under the latter statute, any such attempted conveyance of the legal freehold or leasehold estate operates as a declaration that the transferor holds the property in trust for the minor. (On these matters see, generally, Harpum, *Megarry and Wade: The Law of Real Property* (6th edn, 2000), pp 1289–96.)

The other major example of this category of minors' contracts is the acquisition of shares in a company. So long as the shares are held, the minor remains liable for any calls on the shares unless he expressly repudiates that holding. (*North Western Railway Co v M'Michael* (1850) 5 Ex. 114; 155 ER 49.)

Finally, despite these highly detailed rules for the protection of the minor, not all aspects of the law relating to minors have been laid down in the BGB and it may be appropriate to illustrate one of these regulatory gaps of the BGB—namely the absence of rules protecting minors in the law of restitution. In particular, the legal consequences of the provision of luxury services to minors have raised a number of interesting questions, which are well illustrated by the so-called 'Travel-by-air decision' (*Flugreisefall*): BGHZ 55, 128. In this case a minor, who had flown from Munich to Hamburg with a valid ticket, managed to step on board a flight to New York without this time having a valid ticket. On arrival he was denied entry into the US and the airline flew him back. The airline claimed the market price for such a return flight. The airline recovered the price for the *return* flight under *negotiorum gestio* rules (as to which see chapter 3) for it was in the interests of the child and the parents for him to be transported back to Germany.

More interesting is the reasoning for allowing recovery of the price for the flight *to* New York. The question was what the airline was entitled to by way of unjustified enrichment? Generally speaking, § 818 II BGB provides that where the object cannot be returned, as was the case here with the service provided by the airline, the debtor is obliged to return the value of the service. There is considerable controversy as to what exactly the enrichment of the minor is in such a case. Let us, however, assume that he was at least no longer enriched because he did not save the expense for the service; he would not have flown to New York anyway.

It is generally accepted that such a change of position under § 818 III BGB cannot be invoked if the debtor knew that he was not entitled to the service. This is derived from § 819 I BGB. A similar result is achieved in the English law of restitution by requiring that the party claiming to have changed his position must have done so in good faith (see *Lipkin Gorman (a firm) v Karpnale Ltd* [1991] 2 AC 548, at 558, 568 and 578) and not running the risk that he might not have been entitled to receive the benefit conferred (*South Tyneside Metropolitan Borough Council v Svenska International Plc* [1995] 1 All ER 545, at 569). (See generally, Nolan, 'Change of Position' in Birks (ed), *Laundering and Tracing* (1995) and Virgo, *The Principles of the Law of Restitution* (1999), p 709 ff. and the references cited therein.) In other words, if the debtor is aware of the fact that he is being enriched without any 'justification' he cannot raise the defence of change of position. He is treated as remaining enriched.

In the case of minors however the situation is slightly more complex. For §§ 107 *et seq* BGB require the consent of the legal representative for incurring an obligation. If consent is absent the minor ought to be free of liability. This principle also ought to prevail in relation to unjust enrichment claims. It is therefore the knowledge of the legal representative that should determine whether the minor becomes liable. This reasoning applies in relation to void contracts. For other claims of unjust enrichment not pursuant to a failed contract the delictual capacity (§§ 827, 828 BGB) may be the appropriate yardstick for holding the minor liable. In the *Flugreisefall*, the court regarded the minor as enriched and liable for returning the value of the service because he acquired it through an intentional tort. (See, for a critical discussion of the case, eg, Medicus, *Bürgerliches Recht*, Rn. 176 with references.)

The English material relating to awards of restitution against minors is complex due to a number of overlapping possible bases of claim for the other party. Restitution may be possible at common law, in equity (where the minor has acted fraudulently), or under section 3 of the Minors Contracts Act 1987—indeed, section 3(2) of the 1987 Act explicitly preserves other remedies available to the claimant. Interestingly for comparative purposes, it seems that much of the case law on this subject has provided a significant level of protection for minors from restitutionary claims (although whether this has always been justifiable in the various circumstances is a matter of some contention among commentators).

For example, the common law rules on fraud prevented the other party to a contract induced by the minor's fraud from suing the minor on that contract (see eg, *Bartlett v Wells* (1862) 1 B & S 836; 121 ER 63). Equity did step in to offer relief to plaintiffs against fraudulent minors, typically (and perhaps only—see Treitel, *The Law of Contract*, p 554) relating to a misrepresentation by the minor of his true age. (See the cases of *Stocks v Wilson* [1913] 2 KB 235 and *R Leslie Ltd v Sheill* [1914] 3 KB 607 and their discussion in Beatson, *Anson's Law of Contract*, pp 226–7; McKendrick, *Contract Law*, p 792; Virgo, *The Principles of the Law of Restitution* (1999), pp 759–61 and Jones, *Goff & Jones: The Law of Restitution* (6th edn, 2002), paras 25-002–25-011 (especially 25-010)), although this case law is difficult to reconcile in an internally consistent manner. For Treitel, in such fraud cases, 'the purpose of the equitable . . .

remed[y] is to ensure that the minor is not enriched as a result of the transaction which is not binding on him; but the remedy should not diminish such general resources as he had apart from the transaction' (*The Law of Contract*, p 555). Thus, for Treitel, decisions such as *R Leslie Ltd v Sheill* are supportable because the money lent (or any asset representing it) was no longer identifiable in the hands of the minor: as a result, the Court of Appeal refused to order the minor to repay the sum borrowed. This would seem to operate as a kind of relaxed change of position defence (see, in apparent agreement, Virgo, *The Principles of the Law of Restitution*, p 760) for the minor, interpreted in the light of the purpose of protecting the minor's general assets. A similar construction can be placed on section 3 of the Minors Contracts Act 1987: 'the court may, if it is just and equitable to do so, require the defendant to transfer to the plaintiff any property acquired by the defendant under the contract, or any property representing it' (section 3(1)). Both the equitable and the statutory remedies are available only at the discretion of the court and not for the claimant as of right, although there is no need to show fraud to rely on section 3(1). (On the 1987 Act, see Treitel, *The Law of Contact*, pp 551–4.)

The other example of the common law operating in a protective manner towards minors in the sphere of restitution is the care taken by the courts to ensure that the grant of a restitutionary remedy would not amount to the indirect enforcement of a contract made void by the policy of the law of protecting minors. Where restitution is available at common law, it is available to the claimant as of right, but not if this would effectively allow the claimant to circumvent the lack of contractual capacity of the minor by simply framing the action as one for restitution (see the alternative ground of claim for money had and received in the *R Leslie Ltd v Sheill* case, cited above, at 621). However, some of the older cases (such as *Cowern v Nield* [1912] 2 KB 419) seem in their reasoning to turn on the court's refusal to imply a contract for the minor to repay the purchase price, on the basis that this would amount to indirect enforcement of the original contract that (due to the protective policy relating to minors' contracts) could not be enforced. Insofar as English law has since turned its back on the 'implied contract theory' of restitution and instead bases liability on 'unjust enrichment' (*United Australia Ltd v Barclays Bank Ltd* [1941] AC 1 and *Lipkin Gorman*, above), an action for the recovery of the purchase price should in principle be available against the minor, subject to the defence of change of position (as discussed above).

Overall, therefore, it seems that the common law developed some fairly strong protective tendencies towards awards of restitution against minors. While the 1987 Act has extended the equitable discretion to order the return of property acquired under the transaction to cover cases where no fraud is present, this remains subject to the condition that the property thus transferred has not been consumed or lost. This restriction exists to avoid the effective enforcement of the contract against the minor, which is the very thing that the protective policy seeks to avoid (see Law Com No 134, para 4.23). Arguably, viewing these issues from the relatively unified perspective of unjust enrichment theory will allow current English law to develop a more consistent approach to the situations where such returns of property are to be required, whether the basis for the claim is at law, in equity or under statute (although there are those who might question this unified approach on other grounds).

(c) Individual Lack of Capacity

As explained, the BGB distinguishes between transitory lack of judgment (§ 105 Nr. 2 BGB) and lasting impairments of the capacity to exercise a free will (§§ 105 Nr. 1, 104 Nr. 2 BGB). While the former category of temporary 'blackouts' does not pose many problems of general importance, the second category is worth discussing in more detail.

Some features, however, apply to both categories. It is not necessary that the other party could in some way know that the promisor was not acting with full responsibility. Thus, the interest of legal certainty is sacrificed and the objective approach abandoned in order to protect those who are not capable of exercising a free will. This is a prerequisite of the will theory, but one should bear in mind that the defect must be truly considerable to hold the acts of a certain person void for lack of capacity. It must negate fully the capacity for autonomous decision making. This is not only in the interest of legal certainty, but also—and foremost—in the interest of the person concerned. Treating them as incompetent, means denying them the ability to be responsible for their own self-determination. This harsh verdict must be reserved for clear and extreme cases. In practice, this will rarely if ever occur without the hearing of an expert opinion before a court in which the validity of the legal transaction in question is contested.

This approach in German law accords with that of Scots law where the mental incapacity of a party can, in itself, give rise to a claim in restitution. (See *John Loudon & Co v Elder's Curator Bonis* 1923 SLT 226). At English common law however it is clear that two conditions must be satisfied. First, the party relying on mental incapacity must show that this prevented him from comprehending the nature and effect of the transaction in question (see eg, *Re K* [1988] Ch 310). Secondly, it must also be shown that the other party to the transaction was aware of that incapacity. (See *Imperial Loan Co Ltd v Stone* [1892] 1 QB 599, at 601, affirmed by the Privy Council in *Hart v O'Connor* [1985] AC 1000.) This second requirement could be said to leave those suffering from mental incapacity in a rather vulnerable position and has (arguably) led the courts to stretch the facts in trying to find some indications of the other party's knowledge of that incapacity (see eg, the unreported case of *Ayres v Hazelgrove*, 9 February 1984, discussed in Birks, *Restitution—The Future* (1992), pp 50–1). Further, McKendrick has suggested (*Contract Law*, p 802) that this desire to preserve the contractual capacity of the elderly and infirm may have the paradoxical effect of encouraging their relatives to seek a power of attorney so as to protect them from exploitation. This could be seen as just as serious an incursion into their self-determination as a more protective policy in the general legal regime. In all events, where the other party is unaware of that incapacity then the only possible grounds for avoiding the contract are those that are available to persons of normal capacity, such as undue influence or unconscionable bargains. (See *Hart v O'Connor*, above, and *Irvani v Irvani* [2000] 1 Lloyd's Rep 412, at 420, and Treitel, *The Law of Contract*, pp 408–23.) Only in these senses can the 'unfairness' of the bargain be challenged under English law (cf the views of McMullin J in *Archer v Cutler* [1980] 1 NZLR 386 (noted by Hudson [1984] *Conv* 32) and in *O'Connor v Hart* [1983] NZLR 280 (on which see Hudson, 'Mental Incapacity Revisited' [1986] *Conv* 178, which also discusses the decision of the Privy Council on the appeal in *Hart v O'Connor*).

The exception to this basic position is that, as with minors, contracts for 'necessaries' those concluded with someone suffering from mental incapacity lead to that person being required to pay a reasonable price for them. (Section 3(2) of the Sale of Goods Act 1979—see p 230 above, section 2(b), for discussion of this general point, and Treitel, *The Law of Contract*, pp 558–9.) Of course, if the recipient of such necessaries would be bound by the contract in any case (eg, if the provider did not know of their incapacity), then the contract governs the situation (*Baxter v Portsmouth* (1826) 5 B & C 170; 108 ER 63). But even if the provider of such necessaries was aware of that incapacity, section 3(2) allows the recovery of a reasonable price.

Incapacity need not be total. It may be limited to certain types of transactions, so-called 'partial' incapacity, such as for instance in relation to marriage/divorce in the case of 'abnormal' jealousy (BGHZ 18, 184). The issue whether the incapacity can be limited not only as to the type of contract, but also within one category of contract as to the complexity of the transaction is controversial. The great majority of German courts does not recognise such 'relative' incapacity, for it would 'destroy' legal certainty. (See *Palandt*-Heinrichs, § 104 Rn. 6; Larenz and Wolf, *Allgemeiner Teil*, § 6 Rn. 25 with references.) § 105a BGB declares transactions of trivial nature (necessaries) to be valid. This poorly drafted provision has sparked controversy, which need not concern us here being of little practical significance. (See, Larenz and Wolf, *Allgemeiner Teil*, § 25 Rn. 8 for details.) Arguably, the approach in English law that requires proof of an inability to understand the nature and effect of the relevant transaction could operate so as to allow this kind of 'partial' incapacity, although whether this is the case will obviously depend on the facts of each individual case and contract.

In relation to persons with lasting disabilities that affect rational thinking, a need arises to provide for legal representation. Originally, there existed a procedure by which a person could be formally declared 'incompetent', known as *Entmündigung*, and another person could be declared his guardian (*Vormund*). This procedure was (in relation to adult persons, guardianship still exists in relation to children, see above) abolished by the *Betreuungsgesetz* (BGBl 1990 I, 2002; in force since 1 January 1992) and replaced by another legal instrument regarded as more flexible and at the same time less 'discriminatory' towards those inhibited in their capacity to act rationally. Since this reform took effect the legal representation of adults (called *Betreuung*, a special form of guardianship, regulated in §§ 1896–1908k BGB) and individual lack of capacity do not necessarily coincide. The reason for this separation was to preserve as much of the autonomy of the individual as possible. Thus, where a person needs assistance, it is now possible to provide that without necessarily declaring that person to be incompetent. As a matter of fact, persons in need of a guardian may also lack capacity and once a lack of capacity has been acknowledged, this will invariably prompt the guardianship court to appoint the so-called *Betreuer*. For in such a case the criteria laid down in § 1896 BGB would then be fulfilled. Where an adult cannot take care of his affairs totally or partially due to being disabled, the court appoints a 'guardian' at his request or *ex officio*. The scope of the guardianship is strictly limited to those affairs where there is a clear need for assistance and it is only to this extent that the guardian also acts as the legal representative, § 1902 BGB. Again, a court order is required for certain far-reaching legal transactions (§§ 1904 et seq BGB). The person for whom a guardianship has been ordered remains capable of entering into contracts unless the conditions of § 104 Nr. 2 BGB are met, namely if a lack of capacity is present. The court may also order that the person may need the consent of the guardian for certain legal transactions: § 1903 BGB. In this case the rules as explained in relation to minors between the ages of 7 and 18, above, apply.

In specific cases under Part VII of the Mental Health Act 1983, the property of a mental patient is placed under the control of the court, which then has broad powers over that person's property: any attempt by the patient to dispose of property will not be binding on him, for to hold thus would be to oust the jurisdiction of the court under the statute. (See, by analogy, the cases of *Re Walker* [1905] 1 Ch 160 and *Re Marshall* [1920] 1 Ch 284.) Powers of attorney can operate to allow another to act as legal representative within their terms and statutory developments—the Powers of Attorney Act 1971 and the Enduring Powers of Attorney Act 1985—have sought to smooth their operation to provide greater security for third parties (Treitel, *The Law of Contract*, pp 751–2 and see Cretney and Lush, *Enduring Powers of Attorney* (5th edn, 2001)). The 1985 Act is particularly significant in this context, for so long as the power of attorney is executed in the form prescribed by the statute (see the Enduring Powers of Attorney (Prescribed Form) Regulations 1990, SI 1990 No 1376) then it can endure even beyond the mentally incapacity of the donor of the power (section 2), which reversed the position at common law (see the Law Commission's Report, *The Incapacitated Principal* (Law Com No 12, 1983), para 3.2). The Act provides certain safeguards, which aim to ensure that this enduring power is not acquired inappropriately: eg, on incapacity, under section 2 the donee of the power must apply to the Court of Protection to register the power.

3. ILLEGALITY

Buckley, 'Illegality in Contract and Conceptual Reasoning' (1983) 12 *Anglo-Am LR* 280; Buckley, *Illegality and Public Policy* (2002); Canaris, *Gesetzliches Verbot und Rechtsgeschäft* (1983); Enonchong, *Illegal Transactions* (1998); Furmston, 'The Analysis of Illegal Contracts' (1966) 16 *Uni Toronto LJ* 267; Hager, *Gesetzes- und sittenkonforme Auslegung und Aufrechterhaltung von Rechtsgeschäften* (1989); Kötz, 'Die Ungültigkeit von Verträgen wegen Gesetzes- und Sittenwidrigkeit', RabelsZ 58 (1994) 209; Law Commission, *Illegal Transactions: The Effect of Illegality on Contracts and Trusts* (Law Com Consultation Paper No 154, 1999), especially Parts II and VII; Teichmann, *Die Gesetzesumgehung* (1962).

(a) Preliminary Observations

Paragraph 134 BGB refers to legal transactions as such, a concept which (as we have seen in chapter 1) is all-embracing. It is commonly agreed however that the main field of application of § 134 BGB is the law of contract or, more specifically, contractual relationships of obligation, and it is in this context that the provision is of interest here. § 134 BGB declares any contract violating a statutory prohibition void unless a contrary intention appears from the statute. The concept of 'statutory prohibition' (*Verbotsgesetz*) is thus central to the approach to 'illegal' contracts adopted in German law.

The first observation to make is that 'statutory prohibition' must not be confused with 'strict law' in the sense of *ius cogens* (*zwingendes Recht*). (See, for instance, Larenz and Wolf, *Allgemeiner Teil*, § 40 Rn. 2.) Strict laws are, for instance, most rules of consumer protection. (Some have been briefly discussed in chapters 1 and 3 (consumer sales) and others will be explored in the next chapter, eg, right of cancellation of 'doorstep selling' contracts.) These rules imply in law certain terms into the contract or determine the obligations of the parties. The strictness of their character stems from the fact that, within their scope of application, the parties are not free to contract out of them, and for instance abolish the right of cancellation of a doorstep selling contract. It is common therefore to contrast these laws, sometimes referred as *ius cogens* with dispositive rules or otherwise known as *ius dispositivium*. Such strict provisions restrict freedom of contract in a direct and paternalistic way. If parties to a contract enter into contracts of the type envisaged by the statutory provisions they have to follow the rules stipulated therein. (In fact, the consumer rules are sometimes referred to as 'semi'-strict because it remains possible to *increase* further (but not decrease) the protection of the consumer by contract.)

Another strict statutory provision is § 276 III BGB: a debtor may not be released beforehand from responsibility for willful conduct. Although this provision operates exclusively in a negative way it is not, nevertheless, seen as a 'statutory prohibition' under § 134 BGB.

These provisions of 'strict law' restrict private autonomy directly. The invalidity of any contrary contract term results automatically from the infringement of that provision. It is not necessary however as § 134 BGB would demand, to inquire whether the invalidity was the purpose of the statutory prohibition. Statutory prohibitions in the sense of § 134 BGB often do not expressly concern the validity of contract. Generally speaking, they are not aimed at restricting freedom of contract as such but at banning a certain type of conduct irrespective of the legal form that it takes. The invalidity of the contract is thus merely a reflection, an indirect consequence, of the wish of the legislator that certain incidents do not occur. This distinction may appear artificial and may often be of only theoretical importance. Nevertheless, it is helpful in understanding the function of § 134 BGB.

This provision serves to import 'external'—in the sense of extra-contractual— standards of justice, ie, which are as a general rule independent of procedural or substantive contractual justice. § 134 BGB in a sense establishes consistency between the law of contract and the rest of the legal order. It ensures that the political will of Parliament cannot be called into question by the means of contract law. This insight determines the conditions of application of § 134 BGB: it must be established that it is the will of the legislator that demands that the contract is void and this is something which is not always easy to ascertain.

One point to make concerning the English law on illegality is that it is not limited to statutory illegality. Although this is undoubtedly the most significant source of rules that may render contracts illegal, the principles of the common law have also been held to have this effect in certain circumstances.

One of the most significant common law regimes is that which refuses to enforce contracts in restraint of trade. For the 'public have an interest in ever person's carrying on his trade freely: so has the individual. All interference with individual libery of action in trading, and all restraints of trade themselves, if there is nothing more, are contrary to public policy and therefore void' (*Nordenfelt v Maxim Nordenfelt Guns and Ammunition Co Ltd* [1894] AC 535, at 565 (*per* Lord Macnaghten). See further, Treitel, *The Law of Contract*, p 453 ff; Heydon, *The Restraint of Trade Doctrine* (1972) and Trebilcock, *The Common Law of Restraint of Trade: A Legal and Economic Analysis* (1987)).

Another example is agreements to commit a crime (for a modern example, see *Bigos v Bousted* [1951] 1 All ER 92) or civil wrong (such as agreeing to publish a deceit: *Brown Jenkinson & Co Ltd v Percy DAlt.on (London) Ltd* [1957] 2 QB 621) will not be enforced by the courts. Further discussion of these and other such grounds will be deferred to section 4 of this chapter, in parallel with the examination of the German law on public policy issues in this context.

One further introductory comment on English law is called for. 'The single word "illegal" may embrace varying degrees of impropriety, and it should not be supposed that the effect of illegality is always identical' (Beatson, *Anson's Law of Contract*, p 395; see also *Phoenix General Insurance Co of Greece SA v Adminstratia Asigurarilor de Stat* [1987] 2 All ER 152, at 176 (*per* Kerr LJ)). This will become clear from the comments that follow.

(b) Statutory Prohibition—General Principles

Paragraph 134 BGB presupposes that a statutory prohibition has been violated and that, if properly construed, the provision demands that the contract be declared void. These two elements are not necessarily the same thing. As explained above, the aim of the statutory prohibition is not directly to ban certain types of contract, but rather to ban certain types of behaviour or prevent the occurrence of certain incidents. It is not necessarily the case that the nullity of the contract is required; sometimes another sanction might suffice (eg, a fine). To give one example: in Germany selling in shops during certain hours (after 8pm) or on Sundays is prohibited (*Ladenschlußgesetz*). A contract of sale concluded during the prohibited periods of time violates the statute. However, the statute does not require the invalidity of such contracts. This consequence would clearly be excessive (see already, RGZ 60, 276; 103, 264).

Every application of § 134 BGB is thus preceded by an interpretation of the statutory prohibition. English law adopts a similar approach, including the possibility of implied illegality stemming from the construction of a statute. (See Buckley, 'Implied Statutory Prohibition of Contracts' (1975) 38 *MLR* 535 and generally, Bennion, *Statutory Interpretation* (4th edn, 2002) and *Understanding Common Law Legislation* (2001).) Equally, it should be noted that, as a general starting point in English law, in the absence of an express statutory provision making a contract void for illegality, the contract will generally merely be unenforceable (see eg, Beatson, *Anson's Law of Contract*, pp 349–50).

The method of interpretation used by the German courts is that used more generally for interpreting statutes and which, in a nutshell, proceeds in four steps. First, the wording of the statute is analysed (grammatical or semantic interpretation). Secondly, the position of the norm in question within the entire legal order is considered (systematic interpretation: eg, is it a norm of private law? How is the term in question used elsewhere in the statute?). Thirdly, an enquiry is made to discover what was the historic intention of the legislator (historic or subjective interpretation; an examination of the preparatory works is essential for this task). Finally, one asks what is the objective purpose or aim of the provision in question (teleological interpretation)? The nomenclature varies but these four criteria of interpretation (the influence of Savigny in establishing these criteria of interpretation should be noted) figure in most if not all theories of interpretation. (Thus see, eg, Larenz and Canaris, *Methodenlehre* (3rd edn, 1995) 141 *et seq.*) In attempting the above, the courts proceed in an eclectic manner and do not recognise a fixed hierarchy of criteria. Instead, they weigh the arguments depending on the particular context and their respective force in the individual case.

A first indication that the provision in question is a statutory prohibition requiring the nullity of the contract is the language used. However, the use of 'must not' or 'may not' ('*darf nicht*') is not regarded as conclusive since it is inherent in every prohibition and does not have a specific contractual meaning (BGH NJW 1992, 2022). Only if the statute states that certain acts are illegitimate ('*unzulässig*') or that they cannot be exercised ('*kann nicht*') might this suggest that § 134 BGB is applicable. Sometimes, the provision expressly declares that any legal transaction contravening the statute shall be void. This for instance is the case in relation to insider trading: § 14 of the *Wertpapierhandelsgesetz*. However, the consequence of a violation of a statute cannot normally be derived from the wording of the statute. In that case the subjective and objective purpose of that provision becomes of central importance. Before we examine typical fields of application of § 134 BGB three more general points should made briefly.

First, the purpose of the statute is also relevant to the decision whether the contract is void as a whole or merely in certain respects. If, as in most cases, the contract as a whole is void then the obligations between the parties are determined by law. This can be the law of delict (§§ 823 *et seq* BGB), the law of unjust enrichment (§§ 812 *et seq* BGB), or that of *negotiorum gestio* (§§ 677 *et seq* BGB). In some cases declaring the contract void would not be compatible with the aim of the statute to protect one of the parties. If, for instance, certain maximum prices are laid down by statute, then the contract remains valid and in place of the excessive contract price the maximum statutory price takes effect. (BGH NJW 1989, 2471, lease; BGH NJW-RR 1990, 276, lawyer's fees.)

An excellent parallel to this consideration can be found in the English cases where the protective purpose of the statute was key in formulating the consequences of the relevant illegality. For example, in *Kiriri Cotton Co Ltd v Dewani* [1960] AC 192 a landlord had charged a premium in consideration for granting a sub-lease of a flat in Kampala (Uganda), but charging such 'key-money' was in contravention of section 3(2) of the Uganda Rent Restriction Ordinance 1949. Unlike the English legislation on this issue, the 1949 Ordinance made no provision for the repayment of such money if it was unlawfully charged, although a penalty was imposed on any landlord for breach of the Ordinance. It was clear that neither party was aware that any illegality had transpired and the judgment of Lord Denning in the Privy Council centred on the question of whether the parties were *in pari delicto* with regard to the illegality. However, in making this assessment, he placed great weight on the context provided by the Ordinance and the purpose that it sought to achieve: the Ordinance was designed to protect tenants from exploitation by landlords in times of housing shortage. 'The duty of observing the law is firmly placed by the Ordinance on the shoulders of the landlord for the protection of the tenant: and if the law is broken, the landlord must take the primary responsibility' (at 205). Thus, the parties were not *in pari delicto* and the tenant could recover the money at common law under the action for money had and received, while retaining his right to the sub-lease. Further, the reference (at 206) to the case of *Green v Portsmouth Stadium Ltd* [1953] 2 QB 190 (Parker J), overruled by the Court of Appeal at [1953] 2 WLR 1206, serves to underline the centrality of this approach. The first instance judgment was overruled because the Court of Appeal took the view that the nature of the statute was to regulate racecourses, rather than to protect bookmakers from the demands of racecourse owners. Thus, no protective purpose was involved that could show that the parties there were not *in pari delicto*.

This purposive interpretation is also relevant to the application of the rules of competition law to various contracts, both in European Community and national competition law. Thus, under Article 81 EC, an agreement that restricts competition is prohibited (Article 81(1) and section 2(1) of the UK's Competition Act 1998) and the consequence of that prohibition is to render the agreement void (Article 81(2) and section 2(4) of the 1998 Act). Nevertheless, there are indications in the case law (concerning restrictions on competition held to be justifiable for achieving a legitimate purpose—such as the promotion of inter-brand competition via a selective distribution system that prioritised service levels and customer advice (see eg, Case 26/76 *Metro v Commission (No 1)* [1977] ECR 1875)) and in the implementing legislation (concerning the severability of certain restrictive clauses in vertical agreements (see Regulation 2790/99/EC [2000] OJ L336/21, Article 5)—such clauses are not exempted, but the remainder of the agreement can benefit from the exemption, so long as the agreement can stand and function without the severed clauses) that only certain aspects of such contracts will be adjudged void for breach of Article 81 EC. (On the notion of severance in general English contract law, see Beatson, *Anson's Law of Contract*, pp 413–18 and the references cited therein.) So far as EC law is concerned, the prohibition in Article 81 EC has direct effect and must be enforced by all national courts in the Member States (see our brief discussion of the consequences of this for English law in the *Courage Ltd v Crehan* case, in chapter 1, section 6, p 37)) and so may of itself effect a degree of harmonisation among national legal systems in this area.

Another difficulty as to the consequences of invalidity arises in German law in relation to illegal labour contracts. As will be explained in the next section, such contracts are void under § 134 BGB. In principle, this would mean that the performance of the invalid contract may be reversed according to § 812 BGB. However, § 817 S. 2 BGB excludes restitution where both parties have violated the statute. This would have meant in the case of the so-called 'black labour market' that an illegal state of affairs would have been perpetuated. The *Bundesgerichtshof* held that this consequence could not be squared with the purpose of the statutory prohibition. The court used good faith (§ 242 BGB) in order to disregard § 817 S. 2 BGB. For a typical example of the complex reasoning involved in ascertaining the legal consequences of statutory prohibitions see BGHZ 111, 308, case no 76. From these examples, one can appreciate the overarching importance that a purposive interpretation of the statutory prohibition has acquired in the jurisprudence of the *Bundesgerichtshof*.

The second general observation is this. Paragraph 134 BGB does not of itself contain a subjective element. However, the prohibition in question may presuppose a subjective element (thus, intention is required by most prohibitions of criminal law: some refer to recklessness, others to 'simple' negligence, etc). In such cases, the subjective element must be present, otherwise there would be no violation of the prohibition in the first place.

Thirdly, as a general rule the prohibition must be present at the time of entry into the contract. Yet, in the case of long term contracts a subsequent prohibition may lead to invalidity for the future (eg, BGH NJW 2003, 3055).

(c) Statutory Prohibition—Fields of Application

In analysing the purpose of a statutory prohibition it is convenient to differentiate as to whether the prohibition bans a certain conduct because of the content of the legal transaction in question, its purpose, or merely the manner in which it was carried out. (See Larenz and Wolf, *Allgemeiner Teil*, § 40 Rn. 11 *et seq*.) It would serve no practical purpose to give a comprehensive overview of the case law for which the reader is advised to consult the larger commentaries. (Compare Treitel (*The Law of Contract*, chapter 11), who discusses 22 different types of illegal contracts and apologises for the brevity and relative simplicity of his coverage of such a complex subject. See further, Treitel, chapter 12 on statutory invalidity, with particular emphasis on gaming and wagering contracts.) Yet, it may be worth pointing out typical groups of cases.

Prohibitions that concern the *content of the obligations* arising under a contract normally imply that the contract is void if the statute is violated. Thus, if the contract concerns for instance the preparation of a crime, the contract is void (eg, BGHZ 115, 123, a case concerning the assignment of claims for medical fees which was executed without the consent of the patient: violation of the duty to maintain confidentiality. § 203 Abs. 1 Nr. 1 Criminal Code; see also, BGHZ 132, 313). Since both parties contravene the prohibitions of criminal law, the statutory prohibition is directed at both parties to the contract (eg, hiring a contract killer: § 211 Criminal Code—murder; § 28 Criminal Code-instigation). As noted, p 242 (in section 3(a)), English law achieves this result via the application of common law principles, but the relevant policy is clearly the same.

Likewise, if the *purpose of a contract* violates a statutory prohibition, the contract will in most cases be treated as void. For instance, in the case of illegal labour (*Schwarzarbeit*), the content of the contract is not illegitimate but neutral, eg, the erection of a building. However, the purpose of the contract, namely to avoid tax and/or social security contributions, makes it illegal and this violation of a number of statutes, including provisions of criminal law, is considered to be so grave that the invalidity of the labour contracts or contracts for work and material is an inevitable consequence. (BGHZ 85, 39; BGHZ 111, 308, case no 76).

Similarly, in English law the courts have been prepared to hold that the purpose of the statutory prohibition is sufficiently achieved by the imposition of a penalty on the 'guilty' party, rather than making the contract completely unenforceable. Again, this will depend on the careful interpretation of the purpose to be achieved by the prohibition. Thus, in *St John Shipping Corporation v Joseph Rank Ltd* [1957] 1 QB 267, the prosecution and fining of the master of the ship for breaching the statutory rules on overloading merchant vessels did not prevent the shipping company from claiming the full freight due for the full cargo. Indeed, the court allowed the 'guilty' company to sue on the contract when the defendant withheld the proportion of the freight that related to the overloading. The criticism by Buckley (see (1983) 12 *Anglo-Am LR* 280, 281–2) of the unnecessarily lengthy analysis by the Court of Appeal of the illegality argument in *Archbolds (Freightage) Ltd v S Spanglett Ltd* [1961] 1 QB 374 underlines the point that great care should be taken to establish the purpose and reach of the relevant statutory regime. Even where the statutory purpose clearly intends to cover the contract in question and is held to render it unenforceable due to its illegality, sometimes English courts have been prepared to find a warranty collateral to that contract to give an innocent party a remedy in damages. On this point, see the judgment of Devlin LJ in the *Archbolds* case (above), at 392 and *Strongman (1945) Ltd v Sincock* [1955] 2 QB 525.

The purpose of the contract may also justify declaring contracts void in German law in which only one of the parties violated a statute, for instance because the person promising the performance of the service is not authorised to perform it. The provision of legal counsel is restricted to lawyers admitted to the Bar by the *Rechtsberatungsgesetz*. Contracts which contravene this statute are treated as void (BGHZ 37, 262). The case law in this area of the law cannot however be easily generalised. For instance, contracts with workmen or craftsmen who are not properly registered in the *Handwerksrolle* are valid (BGHZ 88, 240 = NJW 1984, 230, case no 77). The requirement of registration on the craftsmen's roll serves the interest of the public at large (one could perhaps also say that these regulations are the last vestiges of the mediaeval guild order). Yet, the requirement that only acknowledged qualified professionals are hired to perform certain services could also be said to protect individual customers. This was said, for instance, in relation to the statute prohibiting non-lawyers from giving legal advice. Unlike in that case, the court in our case no 77 came down in favour of the validity of the contract. Obviously, the court regarded the performance without authorisation of one activity (the provision of legal advice) as more dangerous than the other (the services of a craftsman) for the individual customer.

A parallel to this type of case is provided by the English decisions relating to a contract rendered illegal due to the manner in which it has been performed (eg, through some failure to complete formal statutory requirements or to observe statutory limits). In these cases, the innocent party can still seek to enforce the contract because he has no need to rely on the illegality to make out his claim (see eg, *Marles v Philip Trant & Sons Ltd* [1954] 1 QB 29 and *Archbolds (Freightage) Ltd v S Spanglett Ltd* [1961] 1 QB 374). However, if the other party has agreed to the illegal performance or has participated therein, then he will be unable to rely on the contract (*Ashmore, Benson, Pease & Co Ltd v A V Dawson Ltd* [1973] 1 WLR 828, concerning the loading of a lorry exceeding its lawful maximum load, where the loading had been observed by the plaintiff's transport manager: the plaintiff's subsequent claim for damage to the load when the lorry overbalanced was rejected).

The third group of cases concerns contracts which violate a statute merely because of *corollary circumstances* (eg, because of the time at which they were concluded). These contracts are generally regarded as valid. We have already given the example of disregarding statutory shop closing hours.

Finally, § 134 BGB is also said to apply to so-called '*Umgehungsgeschäfte*' ('evasive' legal transactions). This is certainly the most controversial field of application of § 134

BGB. Such a bypassing contract is said to be present where the purpose of a prohibited legal transaction is sought to be achieved by entering into another legal transaction which as such is not expressly prohibited. The contract is void provided that the statutory prohibition aims, not only to prevent a certain type of conduct, but to prevent the economic or other effect or result of the prohibited conduct (eg, BGH NJW-RR 2003, 1116). Some statutes (for instance § 42 of the *Abgabenordnung* in the context of tax evasion) even expressly prohibit 'bypassing transactions'.

This category of 'evasive' contracts must be distinguished from 'sham transactions.' The latter are governed by § 117 BGB. According to § 117 I BGB a declaration of will that is made with the consent of the other party only *in pretence* is void: sham transaction (*Scheingeschäft*). If, however, the parties intend to cover up a different legal transaction which they in fact intend then the actually intended legal transaction is valid and the rules applicable in respect of that particular transaction apply.

A common example is indicating a fictitious price of land in the contract document to cover up the higher price that was actually agreed on and as a result to avoid the accrual of tax and notarial fees on the difference between the nominal and the intended price (eg, BGHZ 54, 62). Here, according to § 117 BGB, the contract at the indicated price is invalid; the contract at the actually intended price is in principle valid subject to further conditions. Since the requirement of proper notarial authentification (§ 311b I BGB) in respect of this contract price is not met, the contract as a whole is invalid (§ 125 S 1 BGB). The lack of form however is cured if the property is effectively transferred to the purchaser (§ 311b I 2 BGB); formal requirements are discussed in detail in chapter 2, section 4(a), p 81.

A comparable series of cases in English law relates to the distinction between leases and licences and attempts by landlords to use 'sham devices and artificial transactions' and 'pretences' to disguise a tenancy as a mere contractual licence and thus avoid the protective legislation designed to safeguard the position of agricultural, business and residential tenants (see *Street v Mountford* [1985] AC 809 and *AG Securities v Vaughan; Antoniades v Villiers* [1990] 1 AC 417). The result of this scrutiny will be that the court aims to ascertain the true nature of the bargain and will then enforce it as such (see *Aslan v Murphy (Nos 1 and 2); Duke v Wynne* [1990] 1 WLR 766, at 770–1), rather than rendering the transaction void. Here again it could be argued that the motivating factor is to ensure that sham devices do not frustrate the protective purpose of the surrounding legislation. (See generally, Harpum, Harpum, *Megarry and Wade: The Law of Real Property*, chapter 14 (and especially pp 765–6).)

4. PUBLIC POLICY (*SITTENWIDRIGKEIT*)

Becker, *Die Lehre von der laesio enormis in der Sicht der heutigen Wucherproblematik* (1993); Bezzenberger, 'Ethnische Diskriminierung, Gleichheit und Sittenordnung im bürgerlichen Recht' AcP 196 (1996) 395; Canaris, *Grundrechte und Privatrecht* (1999); Eckert, 'Sittenwidrigkeit und Wertungswandel' AcP 199 (1999) 337; Habersack, *Vertragsfreiheit und Drittinteressen* (1992); Haberstumpf, *Die Formel vom Anstandsgefühl aller billig und gerecht Denkenden in der Rechtsprechung des BGH* (1976); Hager, 'Grundrechte im Privatrecht' JZ 1994, 373; Hönn, *Kompensation gestörter Vertragsparität* (1982); Honsell, 'Die zivilrechtliche Sanktion der Sittenwidrigkeit' JZ 1975, 439; Kötz, 'Die Ungültigkeit von Verträgen wegen Gesetz- und Sittenwidrigkeit' RabelsZ 58 (1994) 209; Mayer-Maly, 'Was leisten die guten Sitten?' AcP 194 (1994) 105; Sack, 'Das Anstandsgefühl aller billig und gerecht Denkenden und die Moral als Bestimmungsfaktoren der guten Sitten' NJW 1985, 761.

(a) Preliminary Observations

Unlike § 134 BGB, which appears as a necessary device to ensure that the will of the *legislator* is applied also in relation to social ordering by contract, the rationale of § 138 I BGB is much less self-evident. Declaring contracts which are contrary to public policy or good morals (*gute Sitten*) to be void, seems not only to create the danger of uncertainty in the law, but to transfer to the *judiciary* a considerable power to police the content of contracts (and that according to very vaguely defined standards). A number of important questions are raised by this provision. Is it desirable in the first place that a codified system of private law should include such a provision? Any attempt to answer this question must start from the observation that § 138 I BGB declares void contracts which do not violate any particular statutory provision but which are nevertheless deemed to be illegitimate on the basis of a vague, open-textured notion of public policy.

We have already introduced some important aspects of this 'general clause' in chapter 1, section 4, p 19. There, we noted that the drafters of the BGB were aware of these dangers but inserted the blanket clause nevertheless because they were confident that the judiciary would apply the provision in the 'right spirit' and show self-restraint. We also remarked that this did not always prove to be the case. One can thus easily observe that the term 'good morals' has served quite different purposes over time. Its content changes just as much opinions as to what is regarded as important and valuable in society change. This has proved both a good and a bad thing.

A significant (and one would argue welcome) change was prompted by the Constitution of 1949. It was initiated mainly by the jurisprudence of the *Bundesverfassungsgericht* and the emergence of the doctrine of indirect (horizontal) effect of constitutional values, especially those embodied in the human rights section of the Basic Law (*Grundgesetz*). General clauses are thus nowadays regarded as 'entrance points' for arguments derived from the constitution. (For a discussion of this aspect of the constitutionalisation of private law, see chapter 1, section 6, p 37. Consider the example given there concerning the line of succession in the Hohenzollern family: BVerfG NJW 2004, 2008, case no 78. That decision is itself a telling example how values change over time, at least during the turbulent times of the last one hundred years of German history. For further discussion in English see, Basil Markesinis, *Always on the Same Path. Essays on Foreign Law and Comparative Methodology*, vol II (2001), chapters 7 and 8.)

The English development of public policy (or the policy of the common law) in refusing to enforce a contract, even where the contract is not prohibited by statute, has had an uneven history. The nineteenth-century combination of unease with the ill-defined situations when public policy could lead to such results (called 'a very unruly horse,' in *Richardson v Mellish* (1824) 2 Bing 229, at 252; 130 ER 294 (*per* Burrough

J), along with the emphasis placed on the idea of freedom of contract, generated considerable reluctance on the part of the courts to use public policy in the way the Germans have. (See in particular, *Printing and Numerical Registering Co v Sampson* (1875) LR 19 Eq 462, at 465 (*per* Jessel MR). For an interesting historical account see Winfield, 'Public Policy in the English Common Law' (1928–9) 42 *Harvard LR* 79 and the references cited therein.) Matters, however, change during the twentieth century when there was a greater recognition of the utility of public policy as a control device. The need for flexibility was, in particular, noted, since public policy could not remain fixed while social conditions changed at an unprecedented rate. (See *Nagle v Feilden* [1966] 2 QB 633, at 650 (*per* Danckwerts LJ).) This new spirit was captured by Lord Denning MR in his usual felicitous manner by transforming the older saying in *Enderby Town Football Club Ltd v Football Association Ltd* [1971] Ch 591 (at 606) where he stated: '[w]ith a good man in the saddle, the unruly horse can be kept in control. It can jump over obstacles.' (See further, Treitel, *The Law of Contract*, pp 439–53 and 477–80 and Beatson, *Anson's Law of Contract*, pp 352–65. Both cover the control of contracts in restraint of trade separately, while acknowledging their position as another public policy ground for the regulation of contracts.)

Public policy thus serves as a springboard for extra-contractual standards of justice in both systems. Just as § 134 BGB imports the values laid down by the legislator, § 138 I BGB serves to import judge-made standards of extra-contractual justice. While some of these standards may be founded on the human rights section of the Constitution, the balancing exercise necessary to arrive at the solution of an individual case is, at the end of the day, carried out by judges—be they the ordinary or the constitutional judges—who thus determine the standards to be applied.

Matters however are not devoid of difficulties given the fact that some of the constitutional values are used to affect notions of contractual justice. In this group of cases, to be discussed below, the Constitutional Court purported to act as a guardian of contractual standards of justice embodied in the Constitution. Whether this intervention of the Constitutional Court was justified or not is a matter of debate. The reasoning used is meant to impose contractual standards of justice. The same is true of § 138 II BGB, which for this reason must be carefully distinguished from § 138 I BGB.

It would be wrong, however, to restrict the concept of 'public policy' to the impact of human rights in the sphere of private law. As we will see when we discuss recognised typical situations where the verdict of 'social illegitimacy' is regularly used by the courts, quite a range of policies not founded on the Constitution are pursued by the courts when assessing the merits of contracts.

Paragraph 138 II BGB introduces usury (*Wucher*) as an example of a contract being *contra bonos mores*. This provision is a cornerstone of German private law and clearly an expression of contractual conceptions of justice. As we explained in chapter 1 (in the section on freedom of contract (p 45), it represents the deliberate decision of the drafters of the BGB to reject the idea that contracts can be policed on the basis of a 'just' price, as the advocates of the doctrine of *laesio enormis* had claimed. As a result, in German law contracts cannot be declared void solely by applying an exchange standard of justice. § 138 II BGB demands, in addition to a gross inadequacy of consideration, the presence of vitiating factors (which basically means the exploitation of the lack of judgment or grave weakness of will of the other party). This also has consequences for the interpretation of § 138 I BGB and means that an element of procedural unfairness must be present in addition to an inadequacy of the terms of the contract. It is therefore convenient to deal with usury first.

Another general remark should be made at this stage. The principles of separation and abstraction also serve to increase the certainty of commercial transactions in this area of the law. For the contract of transfer, or the disposition (*Verfügung*) more generally, is as a general rule regarded as a neutral transaction (eg, the transfer of property in chattels) and as a result § 138 BGB does not apply to it. Since the transaction remains valid, third parties who subsequently acquire property are, generally speaking, not affected by the invalidity of the contract of obligation. However, exceptions are many and the case law is not always consistent. An exception is made where the disposition itself prompts the intervention of the court, as for instance in the conflict of securities cases (to be discussed in the third subsection of this passage section 4(c)(iii), p 261). In such situations, § 138 I BGB affects both the contract of obligation and the contract of transfer. (See for details, *Palandt*-Heinrichs, § 138 Rn. 19.)

(b) Usury (*Wucher*)

§ 138 II BGB stipulates that two conditions must be met for the contract to be void. First, the terms of the contract must show an evident disadvantage for one party to the contract because the values of performance and counter-performance are manifestly disproportionate to each other (*auffälliges Mißverhältnis*). Here, an exchange standard of justice is applied (substantive justice). Secondly, in concluding the contract the party benefited by the contract must have taken advantage of a predicament of the other party (*Zwangslage*), his inexperience (*Unerfahrenheit*), his lack of judgment (*Mangel an Urteilsvermögen*) or considerable weakness of will (*erhebliche Willensschwäche*). This second criterion refers to deficiencies in the contracting process (procedural justice): ie, the formation of will must have been significantly impeded.

As to the exchange standard, no abstract definition is possible. In particular, the courts have refused to introduce certain fixed rates at which the contract is deemed substantively unfair. Generally speaking, the measure for the appropriateness of the consideration is the market price. A price that exceeds more than 100 per cent of the market value will, as a general rule, be regarded by the courts as a manifest disadvantage. (See eg, BGH NJW-RR 1989, 1068; NJW 1992, 899; NJW 2000, 1254, 1255; NJW 2003, 1860, case no 79.) It should be emphasised, however, that the standard is a flexible one and depends on a variety of factors. In cases of loan sharking, for example, relevant issues include whether loans are easy to obtain in the market, the securities provided by the debtor, and more generally the risk that the creditor may not recover the loan (see eg, BGHZ 99, 333; BGH NJW-RR 2000, 1431; NJW-RR 1990, 1199). The standard also varies according to the particular type of contract. So far as leases of residential housing are concerned, a rent that exceeds more than 50 per cent of the market rent may constitute usury (see BGH NJW 1997, 1845, 1846; in relation to commercial leases the 100 per cent rule applies, eg, KG NJW-RR 2001, 1092).

It should be noted that leases are not simply declared void, but rather the excessive price is instead replaced by the market rent. In relation to § 134 BGB a slightly different solution applies. The rent at the top limit of what is allowed is applied there (see above). If no market measure is available, then the fairness of the price depends on an evaluation of the contract terms as a whole (eg, OLG Hamm NJW-RR 1993, 629).

The crux of § 138 II BGB however is that it further requires that the contract be affected by a significant defect of procedural nature. The process of self-autonomous decision-making must also have been prejudiced. The outrageous deal must not merely be the result of foolishness but of an abuse of a superior position by the party that is benefited by the terms of the contract.

'Predicament' (*Zwangslage*) is defined as the existence of an urgent need for money or goods (eg, BGH NJW 1994, 1275, 1276, a decision which also clarified that the need must be acute and not merely concern future plans). See also, BGH NJW 2003, 1860, case no 79, which contains important clarifications as to the interpretation of the subjective elements of § 138 II BGB. On the whole, these subjective elements are interpreted in a narrow fashion. In the case at hand (our case no 79) the desire to live together with a foreign partner who is about to be deported was not regarded as amounting to a predicament and as a consequence the legal transaction resting on this motive did not constitute usury. From this perspective the decision of *AG Langenfeld* (NJW-RR 1999, 1354) seems questionable (ie, too generous in establishing the presence of a predicament). In this case it was suggested that the calamity might even be of only a temporary nature, such as a shortage of electricity on a Saturday afternoon. The contract with the workman hired in order to repair the electricity supply and who charged nearly three times the ordinary rate was thus declared void. It must be admitted that in systems reflecting more strongly market oriented ideology (such as in America), such interferences may seem odd to say the least.

The 'inexperience' (*Unerfahrenheit*) must be related to commercial matters more generally. It does not suffice that the contracting party is inexperienced only in relation to the particular transaction in question (eg, OLG Hamm NJW-RR 1993, 629). This severely restricts the scope of application of this criterion and means that it overlaps with the other two criteria of a 'lack of judgment' and 'considerable weakness of will.' These concepts denominate quite serious personal defects which border on a lack of capacity (as discussed in the previous section, § 104 Nr. 2 BGB). Even though the presence of a pathological condition in a technical sense is not required, the number of cases is quite limited (see eg, BGH NJW-RR 1988, 763).

As a consequence, in many cases it will not be possible to establish the subjective element of usury (ie, the requirement of procedural justice). This it goes without saying has put considerable pressure on § 138 I BGB, and as we will see in the next section the courts have been quite willing to apply § 138 I BGB to many of the cases which fall through the net of § 138 II BGB (BGH NJW 2003, 1860, case no 79 is also an example of this way of proceeding). The practical upshot of this is that the subjective criteria of § 138 II BGB resurface in a considerably watered down version under the label of 'public policy' in § 138 I BGB.

The legal consequence of a finding of usury is the invalidity of the contract. The obligations between the parties are those imposed by law. If performance has already commenced then it is to be reversed according to the rules of unjust enrichment: § 812 I 1 Alt. 1 BGB. § 817 S. 2 BGB stipulates that the performance may not be claimed back if both parties have acted *contra bonos mores*. This is commonly understood also to apply only if the creditor acted wrongfully (which suggests a parallel with the

English idea that recovery may be possible, so long as no reliance on the relevant illegality or wrongdoing is required: see the discussion in section 3(c), p 245). It would not be consistent to exclude restitution if both parties acted wrongfully but to allow restitution where the creditor alone acted wrongfully. This means that in the case of loan sharking, for instance, the creditor is generally prevented from claiming back the value of the performance. § 817 S. 2 BGB however is not understood by the courts to exclude the right to claim back the value of the loan, but merely to claim the money back before the date fixed in the invalid contract. (For example, BGHZ 99, 338; BGH NJW 1983, 1422.) In effect this allows the debtor to keep the loan interest free. Protecting the innocent party and in effect punishing the creditor may also serve as a deterrent against loan sharking.

The exact analogue of the German usury provisions in English law relating to the provision of moneylending services has been subject to a variety of specific statutory interventions which have altered over time (see Treitel, *The Law of Contract*, p 427). The current rules are contained in the Consumer Credit Act 1974, which grants the court the power to 'reopen' any 'extortionate credit bargain' (section 137(1) of the 1974 Act). To be extortionate, section 138(1) provides that the bargain had to be 'grossly exorbitant' or must otherwise 'grossly contravene ordinary principles of fair dealing.' These matters are to be assessed at the time of contracting (*Paragon Finance plc v Staunton* [2001] 2 All ER (Comm) 1025, at [66]). These strictures clearly go beyond merely 'unreasonable' bargains and, in making this assessment, various factors bearing a strong similarity to both limbs of § 138 II BGB must be taken into account (see section 138(2), (3) and (4)). Thus, the prevailing level of interest rates must be considered, as must the age and business capacity of the debtor and the degree to which the debtor was under financial pressure when entering into the agreement. However, the statute specifically reminds the court that the degree of risk accepted by the creditor is also important and this factor has been significant in some of the cases. (See *Ketley (A) Ltd v Scott* [1981] ICR 241, where very little security was taken for the loan and a 48 per cent annual rate of interest was thus not considered 'extortionate'.) Should the court rule the bargain to have been extortionate, the 'reopening' of the bargain allows the court a wide discretion 'to do justice between the parties' (section 137(1) of the 1974 Act). Relief from payment of sums 'in excess of that fairly due and reasonable' may be granted (section 139(2)) and repayment of excessive sums already paid can be ordered. (Note that the 1974 Act is due to be revised on this issue: see the Consumer Credit Bill 2004, clauses 19 ff. The Bill was scheduled to have its second reading in early 2005.)

Outside this limited sphere, the closest English comparator to the German rules is provided by the category of unconscionable bargains (see eg, Treitel, *The Law of Contract*, pp 420–3 and Capper, 'Undue Influence and Unconscionability: A Rationalisation' (1998) 114 *LQR* 479). These cases relate to a situation of potential exploitation of particular weaknesses of one party by another. The key protective element of this case law is that the burden of justifying the enforceability of the agreement is placed on the party that would benefit under the contract (*Earl of Aylesford v Morris* (1873) LR 8 Ch App 484). The classic example of this category is that of so-called 'catching bargains,' which are agreements with an heir in anticipation of the receipt of his expected inheritance (see Dawson, 'Economic Duress—An Essay in Perspective' (1947) 45 *Mich LR* 253, 267–79).

However, a better general comparison with the German law on *Wucher* is provided by the cases where relief is given 'when unfair advantage is taken of a person who is poor, ignorant or weak-minded, or is for some other reason in need of special protection' (Treitel, *The Law of Contract*, p 421). While these cases are not great in number, their focus on the unconscientious conduct of the benefiting party *and* their refusal to intervene merely because the deal was unfair, improvident or for inadequate consideration show effectively the same twin conditions as those required under the German law on usury (albeit taking what seems a slightly more relaxed approach to the question of a 'procedural defect,' as discussed above. See further, section 4(c)(i), p 254). (For recent restatements of these principles and their continuing validity in the modern context, see the cases of *Boustany v Pigott* (1995) 69 P & CR 298; *Irvani v Irvani* [2000] 1 Lloyd's Rep 412, at 425 and *Kalsep Ltd v X-Flow BV*, The Times, 3 May 2001. It should also be noted that, very often, the relevant fact scenarios overlap with cases concerning presumed undue influence, which will be encountered briefly in the following paragraphs. For an example that could have been reasoned on either ground, see the unfortunate case of *Credit Lyonnais Bank Nederland NV v Burch* [1997] 1 All ER 144, especially at 151.)

(c) Contracts Contrary to *Bonos Mores*

§ 138 I BGB is, as we have already stressed, a blanket clause through which the courts may import policy considerations into private law. The evident ambiguity of the term '*gute Sitten*' is not at all reduced by the common definition as the 'common decency of reasonable persons' ('*Anstandsgefühl aller billig und gerecht Denkenden*' Motive, vol II, p 125, BGHZ 10, 232). Little is gained by defining the term in this way as Heinrichs in *Palandt*, § 138 Rn. 2, drily remarks.

It is generally agreed that it is not the task of the courts to impose their view of morality on society at large, but rather to apply recognised and widely held value-judgments. If anything, however, the definition begs the question as to who is to define what is regarded as decent by a reasonable person, which confirms our initial thesis that § 138 I BGB provides the judge with the opportunity to impose his conception of justice in policing contracts. (On this thesis in a more philosophical vein, see generally Dworkin, *Law's Empire* (1986).) As we have explained previously (in chapter 1, section 4) however, one should not forget that this also enables the courts to adapt a Code to the (perceived) needs of modern society or business and thus to develop the law further or to correct rules which are commonly regarded as unsatisfactory.

As already stated, the influence of constitutional law has in more recent times helped to promote the cause of public policy in contract law. For general clauses, such as § 138 I BGB, have proved important gateways for the entry of constitutional arguments into contract law analysis. At the same time, as we shall see in the next section, this influence has created new challenges for the law of contract and it is not yet clear how far the intervention of the Constitutional Court will go.

As a general guideline one must concede that it is impossible to explain the scope of application of § 138 I BGB in an abstract way. Public policy extends so far as the courts are willing to enforce it in individual cases. It is thus necessary to concentrate on the case law. It is convenient to group the cases along the following lines (following in this respect *Palandt*-Heinrichs, § 138 Rn. 24–64, with comprehensive references to the jurisprudence; noting, however, that various others categorisations have been made; eg, Bork, *Allgemeiner Teil*, Rn. 1184). Thus we note: illegitimate behaviour towards the contracting party, illegitimate behaviour towards the community at large and illegitimate behaviour towards third parties. In the following we will give examples for each of these three categories.

(i) Contracts Violating the Interests of One of the Parties to the Contract

The protection of one of the parties to the contract may prompt the courts to declare a contract void for failing the public policy test embodied in § 138 I BGB. Yet this is in fact the prime object of § 138 II BGB. As we already explained however the rather strict subjective requirements of § 138 II BGB have increased the incentive for plaintiffs to seek to rely on § 138 I BGB rather than to invoke the rules on usury contained in § 138 II BGB. Although cases in this area must be approached with extreme caution, one can with some measure of justification say that this attempt to get around the strict subjective requirements of § 138 II BGB has been successful. The clear and express decision of the drafters of the BGB not to introduce an exchange standard as the sole test of validity had however to be respected by the courts. Consequently, for § 138 I BGB to apply, the courts also require, in addition to proof of a manifest disadvantage (ie, the element of substantive fairness), the presence of certain vitiating factors which cast doubt as to whether the decision of entering into a contract was the result of the exercise of a free will. However, these elements of procedural fairness have been watered down considerably by comparison with § 138 II BGB and in some cases amount to little more than fiction. For specific aspects of this jurisprudence as to usury-like contracts (*wucherähnliche Rechtsgeschäfte*) it is best to start with the cases on credit agreements, which are its origin. (For the relevant English law on this specific matter, the reader is referred to the discussion in section 4(b), p 252.)

So far as the substantive fairness assessment of loans is concerned, the courts apply the exchange standard laid down in § 138 II BGB (*auffälliges Missverhältniss*; evident disproportionality). The remarks made above in this respect also apply in relation to § 138 I BGB. In relation to loans, the courts generally regard the charging of interest at a rate higher than 100 per cent of the market rate or 12 percentage points above the market rate as constituting a manifest disadvantage (BGHZ 110, 336, 338, case no 80). Nevertheless, as already explained, this evaluation turns on the facts of each individual case, so these are mere guidelines. The key requirement, however, concerns the subjective element of such contracts. The courts regard it as sufficient that the creditor has taken advantage of the 'weaker' position of the debtor and 'imposed' the unfavourable terms on him or has carelessly ignored that the debtor accepted the terms because of his 'weak' position (eg, BGHZ 128, 255, 257). While this approach only appears to require that the contract was *actually* the result of a defect in the contracting process, this is not the whole story. For, in a second step, the courts reversed the burden of proof. In other words, it is presumed that once there is a manifest disadvantage the creditor has abused his superior position if the debtor is a consumer (BGHZ 98, 178; BGH NJW 1995, 1019, 1022). The presumption does not apply, however, if *the debtor* required the loan for the exercise of his profession (BGH NJW 1991, 1810). Likewise, if *the creditor* is not offering loans on a professional and consistent basis (*gewerbsmäßig*), the presumption does not apply (BGH NJW-RR

1990, 1199). The presumption is thus confined to business to consumer (b-to-c) situations. While the English law on unconscionable bargains discussed above (section 4(b)) does not express this presumption to be confined to such b-to-c situations, the cases often relate to situations of employment (eg, the *Burch* case, cited above) or family scenarios or similar (eg, *Cresswell v Potter* (1968) [1978] 1 WLR 255, where the transfer took place during divorce proceedings) and the courts are reluctant to find any such exploitation where businesses have dealt at arm's length (see *Kalsep Ltd v X-Flow BV*, above).

This reasoning was soon applied also in relation to other types of contracts. The courts emphasise, on the one hand, that the existence of a manifest disadvantage alone does not justify the intervention of the court. However, they are quick to point out that in contracts between professionals and consumers it may be presumed that the unfavourable terms are the result of a deficiency in the contracting process, ie the abuse of a superior bargaining position (eg, BGH NJW 2001, 1127; NJW 2002, 3165; NJW 2003, 2230).

On this point, it should be noted that the notion of inequality of bargaining power should be a further general ground of relief in English law (perhaps as a generalisation of a number of heads of recovery, such as unconscionable bargains, undue influence, and duress) has not met been adopted by the courts, despite Lord Denning MR's efforts in cases such as *Lloyds Bank Ltd v Bundy* [1975] QB 326. It is relevant as a factor motivating the supervision of contracts in restraint of trade, but has not (in the absence of the grounds to make out a more specific head of claim) reached the status of raising a presumption of sufficient 'exploitation' or taking advantage. (See Treitel, *The Law of Contract*, pp 421–3; Thal, 'The Inequality of Bargaining Power Doctrine: The Problem of Defining Contractual Unfairness' (1988) 8 *OJLS* 17 and Cartwright, *Unequal Bargaining* (1991), pp 214–20 and 230–1.)

In the case of a sale of *residential property* or building *land* (also a common subject-matter in the English case law), § 138 I BGB has frequently been applied where the price was more than double the market value. (BGH NJW 1992, 899; NJW 2001, 1127; NJW 2003, 1860, case no 79.) This case law is not limited to the sale of land: eg, BGH NJW-RR 2003, 558, relating to the sale of a horse.

An exchange standard of justice is more difficult to apply where the contract constitutes a unilateral obligation. This has given rise to considerable difficulties in policing contracts of *guarantees*. (Surety, *Bürgschaft*, §§ 765 *et seq* BGB; see, as to some crucial features of this type of contract, chapter 3 p 160 *et seq*. The human rights aspect of this line of cases was introduced in chapter 1 p 37 *et seq*, on the constitutionalisation of private law.) The *Bundesgerichtshof* was at first reluctant to apply § 138 I BGB to such contracts. The *Bundesverfassungsgericht* laid the foundations for stricter judicial control in its famous *Bürge* decision (BVerfGE 89, 214 = NJW 1994, 36, case no 81), a case concerning guarantees undertaken by close family members who were in no financial position to pay the loan. In this decision, the court stressed that where the terms of a contract were considerably disadvantageous for one party ('*ungewöhnlich belastend und als Interessenausgleich offensichtlich unangemessen*') the civil courts should inquire whether this contract was the result of a systemic imbalance of bargaining power ('*strukturell ungleiche Verhandlungsstärke.*' The court also used the term of 'disparity' of contract, '*gestörte Vertragsparität*'). In such circumstances, to uphold the contract would have been to violate that party's constitutional right to self-determination in matters of private law. Contract as a means of achieving personal autonomy would here amount to heteronomy.

This justification for intervention does not seem so far removed from the general reason for intervention given by Lord Nicholls in *Royal Bank of Scotland Plc v Etridge (No 2)* [2002] 2 AC 773, at [7]—if a contract has been procured by undue influence then it cannot 'fairly be treated as the expression of a person's free will'—although the English courts do not treat this value as having constitutional force.

On the other hand, relief in equity under undue influence principles can be available even where the other party to the contract did not gain any (much less very significant) personal benefit or advantage from the transaction (see eg, *Allcard v Skinner* (1887) 36 Ch D 145) (although it should be conceded that most cases do involve just such benefits being obtained and often entirely gratuitously!). Nevertheless, the one thing that is clear after *Etridge (No 2)* is that it is not sufficient simply to raise factors showing that the allegedly exploited party has actually reposed trust and confidence in the other. The transaction must also be one that 'calls for explanation' (at [14]; see also [104] and [158]). The application of this criterion in *Etridge (No 2)* itself shows that it has the scope significantly to reduce the potential for undue influence claims to assist wives who have acted as surety for their husbands: 'there is nothing unusual or strange in a wife, from motives of affection or for other reasons, conferring substantial financial benefits on her husband' (at [19], *per* Lord Nicholls). Nevertheless, there may still be cases where no plausible explanation exists other than the procurement of the transaction by undue influence: see eg, the colourful and yet tragic case of *Tate v Williamson* (1866) LR 2 Ch App 55.

Finally, in the absence of proof of actual undue influence, it is still open to the other party to attempt to rebut a presumption that such influence existed by showing that the transaction was in fact 'the free exercise of independent will' by the allegedly influenced party (*Inche Noriah v Shaik Allie bin Omar* [1929] AC 127, at 136 and see also *Etridge (No 2)*, above, at [7]). The result of rebuttal would thus be to show that (in the terms of *Bürge*) personal autonomy had indeed been respected

The intervention of the Constitutional Court in the aforementioned *Bürge* case has met with approval (eg, Larenz and Wolf, *Allgmeiner Teil*, § 42) but has also provoked harsh criticism (eg, Adomeit, 'Die gestörte Vertragsparität–ein Trugbild' *NJW* 1994, 2467). A recurrent objection is directed at whether it was necessary that the Constitutional Court introduced the vague notion of 'disparity of contract.' For this apparently new approach embedded in human rights reasoning remained utterly vague. Arguably, the pre-existing control mechanisms of traditional contract law would, if properly applied by the *Bundesgerichtshof*, have solved the problem in most if not all cases. Thus, in the *Bürge* decision the agent of the bank trivialised the risk of the transaction by pointing out that the guarantee was merely a formality needed 'for the file.' This outrageous distortion of the truth should easily have justified the application of *culpa in contrahendo* principles, which will be explained in more detail in the next chapter, p 302, and under English law would surely have amounted to a material misrepresentation inducing entry into the contract, which prima facie could have been raised by the guarantors as a defence to the bank's action to enforce the guarantee. (See, for a *culpa in contrahendo*-based explanation of these cases with extensive borrowings from the English undue influence jurisprudence, S Lorenz, *Der Schutz vor dem unerwünschten Vertrag* (1997), pp 445 *et seq*, 520).

However, this is not how events developed. The Constitutional Court did not pre-determine the means by which the ordinary courts were to implement its potentially far-reaching directives. The *Bundesgerichtshof* subsequently utilised § 138 I BGB to tighten its grip on guarantees undertaken by family members. The difficulty of this approach lies in the legal consequence of § 138 I BGB: the contract is void. In effect, within the scope of application of this line of cases, this destroyed the contract of guarantee as a means of security for loans (hence, at the same time making it more difficult to get a loan; indeed, it could be argued that the recent limitations in English law on the apparent scope of the doctrine of presumed undue influence are a response to that very concern). And as we shall see the scope of application of this jurisprudence is considerable.

We already pointed out in chapter 1 a weakness of the argument for the stricter control of contracts as derived from the constitution. The human rights aspect of a private law dispute is impossible to ascertain in advance. The outcome of the *balancing* process of the different values is difficult to predict and is extremely fact-sensitive. The great number of actions brought after the *Bürge* decision indicates just that; it took the different *Senate* of the *Bundesgerichtshof* eight years to develop a consistent jurisprudence regarding the application of the principles ascribed to the *Bürge* decision (see, for the final episode of this saga: BGH NJW 2002, 2228, case no 82, containing a review of the case law).

The following criteria are applied in order to determine whether a guarantee is contrary to § 138 I BGB. As a general rule, it is the responsibility of the surety to ascertain whether or not he is capable of paying back the loan and interest, should the principal debtor become insolvent. However, where the contract of guarantee considerably overstretches the financial means of the surety ('*krasse Überforderung*') and the surety is a close family member of the principal debtor it is presumed that the surety has undertaken the guarantee due to the emotional ties ('*emotionale Verbundenheit*'), see BGH NJW 2002, 2228, case no 82.

A financial overburdening is said to accrue where the surety is not even capable of paying the interest of the loan. The relevant time is the time of entry into the contract—this is thus a prognosis. Such evidence would seem likely to fulfil the requirement in English law post-*Etridge (No 2)* that the transaction must 'call for explanation,' but whether or not the nature of the relationship between the parties would be sufficient to show trust and confidence reposed in the other party would depend on the facts. Thus, in *Irvani v Irvani* [2000] 1 Lloyd's Rep 412 the ties of 'family loyalty' between brothers running a partnership were not sufficient to raise the presumption (at 425).

The presumption that the guarantee, which is financially overburdening the surety, was undertaken as a result of emotional ties may be rebutted, for instance, where the surety derives a 'direct' benefit from the granting of the loan to the principal debtor, eg, by acquiring a share in the land financed with the loan. (For example, BGH WM 2003, 1563; NJW 1999, 2584.) A merely 'indirect' benefit however does not suffice to rebut the presumption. The details depend on the facts of the individual case. (See eg, BGH NJW 2002, 2705.) The interest of the creditor in preventing the debtor from transferring material values to his spouse and thereby avoiding the enforcement of the obligation to pay the loan back needs to be made an express term of the contract in order to be recognised by the courts. (For example, BGH NJW 2002, 2228.)

In the English cases, the major method employed to rebut the presumption of undue influence is the provision of competent and independent advice that was based on the knowledge of all of the relevant facts (see the cases of *Allcard* and *Inche Noriah*, cited above), although it is not always vital to ensure that such advice was received to allow the transaction to be enforced (see *Re Brocklehurst* [1978] Ch 14). Where the transaction is entered into by the influenced party with a third party (rather than the party (presumed to be) exercising that influence), then the question is whether that third party (almost inevitably a bank or building society in the cases) is 'put on inquiry' about the risk that the consent of the influenced party has been obtained improperly (*Etridge (No 2)*, above, [39] ff). This will occur if it appears that the transaction is prima facie disadvantageous to the influenced party (eg, a wife guaranteeing a husband's business debts) and where the nature of the relationship between the (say) surety and the benefited party is a 'non-commercial' one (*Etridge (No 2)*, at [82]). If the third party is indeed put on inquiry, then a duty will arise to take reasonable care to protect the surety against the risk of undue influence, so generally the confirmation from an independent solicitor to the third party that the effect of the transaction has been explained to the surety will suffice (see *Etridge (No 2)*, [56]—[63] and [79]). Note that this duty exists even where (after *Etridge (No 2)*) it will not be possible for a wife to establish a presumption of undue influence, since the factors putting the third party on inquiry can be satisfied even without such a finding. However, it is also clear that a mere failure by the third party to fulfil this duty will not, in and of itself, allow the wife to avoid the transaction. Only if the presumption *was* raised does the failure to fulfil this duty become important, because that will mean there has been a failure to rebut the presumption so that undue influence may then be relied on.

This approach (that requires a financial overburdening and the presence of emotional ties between surety and principal debtor) is applied in relation to children (eg, BGH NJW 2000, 1182; see *Bullock v Lloyds Bank Ltd* [1955] Ch 317) or parents (eg, BGH ZIP 2001, 1190) of the principal debtor, spouses (who are specifically *not* covered by the irrebuttable presumption of undue influence under the English case law: see eg, *Kingsnorth Trust Ltd v Bell* [1986] 1 WLR 119 (noted by Andrews [1986] *CLJ* 194)), fiancé(e)s (who are covered by the irrebuttable presumption in English law in certain circumstances: see eg, *Ellis v* Barker (1871) LR 7 Ch App 104) and unmarried couples (eg, BGH NJW 2002, 744).

The *Bundesgerichtshof* is reluctant to extend this jurisprudence any further; in particular, in relation to partners or (more generally) shareholders of a company the Court has repeatedly emphasised that the presumption does not apply (eg, BGH NJW 2003, 967; NJW 2002, 1337). Taking account of the drastic consequences of applying the presumption—any guarantee is void if the person in question is financially weak—this reluctance cannot come as a surprise. Yet, only time will tell whether the *Bundesverfassungsgericht* will accept the present limitations of the application of § 138 I BGB.

In fact, the Constitutional Court did subsequently extend the reasoning of the *Bürge* decision to cover other types of contract. The court argued in favour of a stricter control of the terms of contracts between spouses (*Eheverträge*) regulating in advance the economic consequences of divorce (NJW 2001, 957; NJW 2001, 2248). In the first of these cases, a pregnant woman entered into a contract regulating the consequences of divorce in which she waived her right to claim maintenance payments from the future husband and father of her child. The court regarded this situation as a 'predicament' (*Zwangslage*) which justified an intervention of the court and called for a more paternalistic approach from the ordinary courts. The *Bundesgerichtshof* was thus once more compelled to reconsider its previous practice. (See also, BGH NJW 2004, 930, case no 83, for a useful summary of the jurisprudence of the *Bundesverfassungsgericht*; cf the annotations by Langenfeld, 'Die Ehevertragsgestaltung auf dem Prüfstand der richterlichen Inhaltskontrolle' ZEV 2004, 311; and Rauscher, 'Ehevereinbarungen: Die Rückkehr der Rechtssicherheit' DNotZ 2004, 524.) This decision, case no 83, is noteworthy in three respects.

First, it emphasises the importance of the principle of freedom of contract (and an appreciation of what this is understood to entail). While the Constitutional Court stressed that freedom of contract requires that each party is *actually able* to exercise a free will, the *Bundesgerichtshof* seems to adopt the traditional (and orthodox) view that freedom of contract means that the parties are left alone to determine their relationship of obligation.

Secondly, the criteria set up to justify interference by the judge are limited to extreme cases. Not every exclusion of the rights granted by the Civil Code prompts an in-depth review of the merits of the terms of the contract. However, the more extensive the exclusion then the more pressing the need becomes to inquire whether the disadvantaged party entered into the contract as a result of a significant predicament. This clearly reminds one of the approach to usury-like transactions (*wucherähnliche Rechtsgeschäfte*). However, unlike in relation to that line of cases, it seems that the court is not prepared to apply a sweeping assumption as to the existence of a defect in the contracting process. In the case at hand, the wife was academically trained and neither pregnant nor in financial difficulties when the contract was concluded. Indeed, it would appear odd if in such circumstances one were to conclude that her decision to enter into the contract showed that she was not able to exercise a free will (and this point finds a nice parallel in the discussion of *Etridge (No 2)*, above, concerning the reasons why a wife may stand surety for her husband). Freedom of contract would then be no more than a sham (however, it should be noted that the Court of Appeal felt compelled to declare the contract void as a result of the jurisprudence of the Constitutional Court).

The third remarkable aspect of the decision concerns the willingness of the court to move away from § 138 I BGB and to apply the more flexible § 242 BGB. This means that if a contract entails manifest disadvantages for one party and was concluded as a result of a predicament, the voidness of the contract is not the automatic consequence. Rather, the judge may strike out only certain terms of the contract or adjust it under § 242 BGB, good faith. This more flexible approach, however, does little to ensure certainty and predictability in the law. Finally, one should note that contracts concluded on the occasion of marriage may also violate the interest of the community at large, discussed in the next section.

Another major line of cases concerning the protection of one of the parties to the contract concerns contracts which diminish the capacity of one of the parties to exercise a free will (*Knebelungsverträge*). As an extreme example, one might think of a contract to become a slave. The difficulty, of course, is to draw a line and to decide which contracts restrict the freedom of self-determination excessively. The *Bundesgerichtshof* has applied § 138 I BGB on the basis of this type of reasoning mainly in relation to *long-term contracts* where one of the parties was in a position to impose the terms of the contract virtually unchecked. (See eg, certain incidents of contracts between persons running a restaurant and breweries for the supply of beer. BGHZ 74, 293; BGH NJW 1992, 2145: such contracts may not run for longer than twenty years. Under EC competition law principles (Article 81(1) and (2) EC), such agreements may be void if they are part of a saturating network of agreements creating a significant barrier to entry to the market: see eg, case C–234/89 *Delimitis v Henninger Bräu* [1991] ECR I-935 on the very issue of tied house agreements.)

(ii) Contracts Violating the Interests of the Community at Large

The cases belonging to this group do not form a homogeneous mass. In part they concern the protection of the society against the commission of crimes (eg, BGH NJW-RR 1990, 1521, dealing with stolen goods; NJW 1985, 2405, bribery of a foreign official; in English law this is covered by the policy of the common law: see eg, *Bigos v Bousted* [1951] 1 All ER 92). In these cases, the result could often also by achieved by applying § 134 BGB; in any event they can be characterised as attempts to enforce extra-contractual values of significant weight and incorporated in the legal order by means of legislation.

Another group of cases concerns the protection of the financial interest of the state and seek to prevent contracts which transfer financial burdens from individuals to the tax-paying community. In the previous section, we discussed cases where a contract regulating the economic consequences of marriage and divorce was reviewed because it harmed the interest of one of the parties to the contract for taking advantage of a predicament. Waiving the right to maintenance on the occasion of a divorce may also violate the interests of the community at large. This has been held to be the case where one of the parties renounces the right in a contract concluded during divorce proceedings and it is evident that, as a result, the person entitled to maintenance will be dependent on social benefit payments (eg, BGH NJW 1983, 1851; NJW 1992, 3164). Since the parties thus conclude a contract at the expense of the taxpayer, the contract may be struck down as contrary to § 138 I BGB.

The most controversial cases of this category concern the protection of certain moral views believed to be widely held in society. This is also the area where notable changes have taken place, for instance in relation to the evaluation of sexuality. The opinion that all extra-marital sexual conduct is contrary to public policy (BGHZ 20, 72; see similar English cases, such as *Walker v Perkins* (1764) 1 W Bl 517, refusing to enforce a promise by a man to pay money to a woman if she would become his mistress) has long been given up. § 138 I BGB, for example, does not apply to a lease entered into with a non-married couple: BGHZ 84, 36; 92, 213, 219; the old English approach, exemplified by *Upfill v Wright* [1911] 1 KB 506, is unlikely to obtain today: see eg, *Eves v Eves* [1975] 1 WLR 1338, section 62 of the Family Law Act 1996 (defining 'cohabitants') and Dwyer, 'Immoral Contracts' (1977) 93 *LQR* 386). Outside the scope of § 180a Criminal Code, even the contract of lease for a brothel may not be contrary to § 138 I BGB; BGHZ 63, 365. (See also, the *Prostitutionsgesetz*, BGBl. 2001 I, 3983, which seeks to protect the claim for remuneration of the prostitute but does not reverse the verdict of § 138 I BGB that the promise to perform sexual acts cannot be binding.) It is likely that English law may still not be so lenient so far as contracts involving prostitution are concerned (see the discussion in *Coral Leisure Group Ltd v Barnett* [1981] ICR 503, and see generally, Beatson, *Anson's Law of Contract*, p 362 and Treitel, *The Law of Contract*, pp 443–4), although the Court of Appeal has been prepared to enforce a contract for the advertisement of telephone sex lines (see *Armhouse Lee Ltd v Chappell*, The Times, 7 August 1996, although the Court was also of the view (*obiter*) that a contract to promote 'sex dating' would probably have been illegal and unenforceable). Also, included in this category are cases in which the courts held that it would be objectionable that a certain activity was carried out against remuneration; to give just a few examples: OLG Hamm NJW 1985, 679, contract to acquire patients against commission; KG NJW 1989, 2893, clients of an attorney; OLG Koblenz NJW 1999, 2904, buying an academic title. (For comparable English cases, see *Parkinson v College of Ambulance Ltd* [1925] 2 KB 1 (charitable donation in return for securing a knighthood) and *Osborne v Amalgamated Society of Railway Servants* [1910] AC 87 (salary paid to an MP in return for his vote in the House of Commons as directed by the Society).)

(iii) Contracts Violating the Interests of a Third Party

The general rule is that persons who are not bound by the terms of a contract may pursue their interest, even if it runs contrary to the purpose of the contract: this is part of the relativity of contractual obligation. However, where the interposition of the third party in the contractual relationship is particularly reckless and abusive, the contract between the third party and one of the contracting parties may be void under § 138 I BGB. This is the case in particular where the third party attempts to incite the contracting party to forego the contractual obligation to the detriment of his contractual partner (eg, BGH NJW 1981, 2184, 2185, where the stranger to the contract offered to indemnify the promisor against any claims for damages for breach of contract of the promisee). In addition to the sanction of § 138 I BGB, which concerns the relationship between promisor and the person inciting the breach of contract, the latter may become liable under § 826 BGB for recklessly causing the promisee economic loss (see *The German Law of Torts*, p 891 and Weir, *Economic Torts* (1998) for a comparative discussion of these cases). In general, the case law requires a collusive collaboration which aims at prejudicing the interests of the promisee, thus limiting the application of § 138 I BGB to extreme cases. (For example, BGH NJW-RR 1996, 869; NJW 1988, 902.)

However, some of the cases in which the courts have had recourse to § 138 I BGB are perhaps best explained on an alternative basis. The problem has arisen in the law of securities. Banks often seek to obtain an assignment of all future claims of a commercial enterprise as security for loans (the so-called '*Globalzession*'), which they may enforce as assignees in the bankruptcy of the lender. However, suppliers of the client of the bank (we may refer to him as 'the debtor') may also have a legitimate interest in securing their claims against the debtor. This is usually achieved by reservation of title clauses (see also chapter 2, p 79, on the battle of the forms). The reservation of title however does not sufficiently protect the supplier in some circumstances: for instance, where the debtor will sell the goods on. Therefore, the debtor assigns in advance his claims arising from the sale of the goods to the supplier as security for the claims the latter may have against the former. According to general principle, the conflict between the first assignment to the bank and the second assignment to the supplier is to be decided in favour of the bank because, chronologically, this assignment came first (*Prioritätsprinzip*). This means that the supplier would lose his security, and also that the debtor would not fulfil his promise to procure the security for the supplier (since he is insolvent, this breach of contract matters little for the relationship between supplier and debtor but it is more significant for the relationship between bank and supplier as we shall see in the following). The *Bundesgerichtshof* did not regard this result as satisfactory (since BGHZ 30, 149; for a more recent illustration see: BGH NJW 1999, 940; NJW 1999, 2588). In order to protect the supplier it declared the first, 'global', assignment void according to § 138 I BGB as far it extended to the claims also covered by the second assignment. The bank was said to incite the breach of contract of the debtor towards his supplier: the bank knows that the supplier will not be supplied goods unless he provides security and therefore he will assign the claims a second time even though he had already assigned them to the bank. This reasoning strikes one as artificial and to reproach the bank for 'blameworthy' conduct seems somewhat far-fetched. Is it really the task of the bank to prevent its clients from committing breaches of contract? Or could not one also say that the dealer ought to inquire whether there had been a prior assignment? (See, Medicus, *Bürgerliches Recht*, Rn. 527.) The issue is rather which security ought to prevail and thus whether the principle of priority should be qualified in this line of cases. Indeed, there may be sensible reasons for protecting the security of the supplier (and thus enabling him rather than the bank to finance the transactions of the debtor in relation to the goods supplied), but this concerns the question whether the rules of assignment generate satisfactory results and not whether the bank acted recklessly. (See, for an economic analysis of these cases: Eidenmüller and Engert, 'Prioritätsgrundsatz, Vertragsbruchtheorie und die richtige Zuordnung von Kreditsicherheiten' in Bork, Hoeren and Pohlmann (eds), *Festschrift für Helmut Kollhosser* (2004) 103 *et seq.*) This line of cases, however, demonstrates what we have highlighted as one of the main functions of general clauses: on occasion they are deployed by the courts to develop (covertly) the rules of the Code further and to adapt them to the demands of modern commerce.

6

Setting the Contract Aside

1. INTRODUCTORY REMARKS

The doctrine of *pacta sunt servanda* requires that, once an agreement is found to exist, the parties are henceforth bound by its terms and may not back out of their contract simply because they have had second thoughts. If one party does not perform his obligations under a validly concluded contract, he is bound to become liable in damages or (especially in civil law systems) the contract may be subjected to specific performance. However, in the civil law as well as the common law the existence of formal agreement as such is not sufficient to generate the binding force associated with the doctrine of *pacta sunt servanda*. The theory that is adopted to justify the binding nature of an obligation also determines the reasons for denying binding force to the agreement.

As was alluded to in previous chapters, what has become known as the 'will theory' had a strong influence in the nineteenth century, having been advocated by such great jurists as Friedrich Karl von Savigny, and later Bernhard Windscheid. The will theory founds the binding nature of contract on personal autonomy. (See for Savigny's theory his *System des heutigen Römischen Rechts*, vol 3 (1840), § 130.) Contractual obligations are self-imposed and therefore require that the 'will' of the respective contracting party be accurately reflected by the obligation undertaken. Defects in the contracting process that distort the subjective intention of the promisor are thus reasons for setting the contract aside. It would be wrong, however, to assume that the will theory did not take account of the interests of commercial certainty and the principle of *pacta sunt servanda*. As we will see in the section on mistake, these elements serve as arguments for limiting the relevance of mistake.

Conversely, self-determination is also the starting point for the reasoning of the rival approach, traditionally labelled as the 'declaration theory'. (See for an overview Flume, *Das Rechtsgeschäft*, p 55; Windscheid, *Lehrbuch des Pandektenrechts* (8th edn by Theodor Kipp, 1900), § 75 note 1a.) This theory merely emphasises to a much greater extent the argument that contract, as a two-sided social ordering, must take into account the reliance of the promisee on the validity of the promise. Reliance will be reasonable if it is directed at the objective meaning of the declaration of the promisor. In other words, self-determination through the means of contract takes place in a social context, and therefore carries with it the idea of responsibility for one's own conduct. If the promisor, who fails effectively to express his intention, was allowed to back out of the agreement without even being held liable in damages there would be no responsibility for making declarations of will. Yet such declarations of the will form the basis on which the promisee will reasonably rely. The insight behind the objective approach in contract law, as we have already noted above (in chapter 3, sections 1, 2(c) and 3, p 133) in relation to interpretation, is that reliability increases security in the law and this in turn is essential for the institution of contract as such. The parties ought to be able to assume that the contract will be enforced as (objectively) agreed.

From a comparative perspective it is interesting to observe how German law balances the need to enforce contracts 'objectively' agreed on against the need to allow an 'innocent' party to back out of agreements which were not 'subjectively' intended. When examining the approach to mistake one should also keep in mind the fundamental importance which the principle of abstraction has for German law. As stated in the first chapter (p 27) this requires that the invalidity of the contract of obligation does not induce the invalidity of the transfer transaction. There we also suggested that as a result of this principle, commercial certainty (and, more precisely, the position of third parties) is best safeguarded as a result of the above. All of this may help explain not only the enduring influence of the will theory in German law but also the fact that German law, unlike English law, is more willing to recognise 'unilateral' mistake as a reason for setting aside contracts affected by mistake.

The rules of the BGB regulating deficiencies in consent cannot be attributed to one or the other 'theory': most of its provisions embody a pragmatic compromise. Nevertheless, the impact of the will theory can still be noted. The law of mistake in particular reveals important differences from the position in English law, which itself, if any such categorisation is appropriate, could be characterised as an emanation of the 'declaration theory.' (Though English law can in practice be more nuanced given the impact that equity has had on the common law.)

In the light of earlier, general comments about the way modern trends are affecting the development of modern law, the reader will not be surprised to be told that in more recent times a new and significant qualification of the doctrine of *pacta sunt servanda* has been established in the context of contracts between dealers and consumers. These rules, most of them in force in national law as a result of developments in harmonising legislation on the European Community level, introduce new procedural requirements in order to safeguard the uninhibited self-determination of the consumer. Seen in this light, they could be argued to be giving effect to the will theory. Yet, as we shall see, the element of generalisation inherent in these rules makes them difficult to square not only with commercial certainty, but with the will theory itself.

2. CONSUMER RIGHTS

Adomeit, 'Herbert Marcuse, der Verbraucherschutz und das BGB' NJW 2004, 579; Artz, 'Die Neuregelung des Widerrufsrechts bei Verbraucherverträgen' BKR 2002, 603; Boente/Riehm, 'Besondere Vertriebsformen im BGB' Jura 2002, 222; Drexl, *Die wirtschaftliche Selbstbestimmung des Verbrauchers* (1998); Fischer, 'Das verbraucherschützende Widerrufsrecht und die Schuldrechtsreform' DB 2002, 253; Grigoleit, 'Besondere Vertriebsformen im BGB' NJW 2002, 1151; Meller-Hannich, 'Vertragslösungsrechte des Verbrauchers aus dem BGB—Geschichte und Gegenwart' Jura 2003, 369; Reiner, 'Der verbraucherschützende Widerruf im Recht der

Willenserklärungen' AcP 203 (2003) 1; Riesenhuber, *System und Prinzipien des Europäischen Vertragsrechts* (2003).

(a) Preliminary Observations

In the absence of personal ties characteristic of family relationships or friendship, the parties to a contract rely on the courts to enforce the promise embodied in the agreement. If the parties could simply withdraw from the contract at will, the whole idea of enforcing a contractual promise would be belittled and the basis on which contract law is founded would collapse. The doctrine of *pacta sunt servanda* can thus be seen as a cornerstone of private law because it is a pre-condition for the functioning of contract as a means of social ordering between strangers. The doctrine however does not apply with full force, and often not even at all, to contracts that are the result of a defective contracting process. The doctrine presupposes that the parties to the contract can have these declarations of will imputed to them. Otherwise, it would not be justifiable for the law to hold the parties to their promise(s). The parties' responsibility for promising ends where the promise is not the result of the exercise of a free will.

The key question, of course, is which defects prevent the law from attributing the declaration of intention to the promisor?

Certain procedural standards can be regarded as classic, such as mistake, fraud or duress. In the second half of the twentieth century, new types of procedural standards have emerged. They seek to redress a (perceived) imbalance in the negotiating process in transactions between dealers and consumers. In Germany, this development started in 1969 with the introduction of a right of cancellation or revocation of contracts (*Widerrufsrecht*) where German consumers purchased foreign investment shares away from the business premises of the trader (now contained in § 126 *Investmentgesetz*, BGBl. 2003-I, 2676). A number of specialised statutes, some as a result of the implementation of EC Directives, were subsequently passed, all of which afford the consumer considerable protection within the scope of their application. With the recent major reform of the BGB of 2002, most of these special statutes have found their way into the Civil Code. Directive 85/577/EEC, intended to protect the consumer in respect of contracts negotiated away from business premises ([1985] OJ L372/31) was the first measure of this kind on the European level and others have followed since and will be discussed in more detail in the following sections, below.

A brief comment as to terminology: while in German law the term '*Widerruf*' (revocation) is consistently used (see also § 130 I 2 BGB discussed in chapter two, section 2(g) p 67), Directive 85/577/EEC uses the term 'right of cancellation' and newer Directives prefer the term 'right to withdraw' (eg, Directive 94/47/EC on timeshares). The UK implementation of Directive 85/577/EEC (in the The Consumer Protection (Cancellation of Contracts Concluded away from Business Premises) Regulations 1987, SI 1987 No 2117 (as amended by SI 1998 No 3050), on which see Brown, *Commercial Law* (2001), pp 249–53) follows the 'cancellation' terminology of the Directive, while the implementation of Directive 94/47/EC (in The Timeshare Regulations 1997, SI 1997 No 1081) retains the language of 'cancellation' (which is consistent with the earlier Timeshare Act 1992) in preference to that of 'withdrawal' as used in Article 5 of the Directive. See also, The Consumer Protection (Distance Selling) Regulations 2000, SI 2000 No 2334 and their reference to a 'right to cancel' (reg 10(1)) as opposed to 'the right to withdraw' in Article 6 of Directive 97/7/EC [1997] OJ L144/19, etc.

Special consumer rights to set the contract aside independently from the substantive fairness of the actual terms of the contract have been introduced for two main reasons. The first could be because the negotiating technique is particularly aggressive, eg, door-to-door selling by specially trained salesmen. Alternatively, the subject matter of the contract is deemed difficult for the consumer to assess, eg, as in the case of so-called distance contracts. Finally, the two reasons may be combined (eg, in the sale of time-share properties). These means, provided to strengthen the position of the consumer, exist to ensure that he has carefully considered his decision to enter into the contract. This cautionary purpose is served by affording the consumer a *right to withdraw* from the contract within a limited amount of time, usually one or two weeks, by requiring special *form* (usually written form), and finally by introducing a number of *duties to inform* the consumer.

The right of cancellation deeply affects the binding nature of contract and it is this right on which we focus here. The declaration of intention of a consumer is not binding until the cancellation period has lapsed. The cancellation period is relatively short (seven days minimum in various EC Directives; two weeks in German law; seven days in the UK's 1987 Regulations (reg 4(5)) and fourteen days in sections 2(2)(a), 5 and 6 of the Timeshare Act 1992 (comparing favourably with the ten day minimum in Article 5 of the Timeshare Directive)), which may explain why suspending the binding nature of a promise in this way has not created intolerable uncertainty in the law. Another factor that increased commercial certainty was that the right of cancellation is granted in certain typical situations regardless of whether or not a procedural defect actually occurred in the individual case. In effect, the consumer is given a short trial period during which he may reconsider the contract and during which the trader cannot rely on the contract. However, the introduction of this new procedural standard is not without its difficulties. Three of them may be addressed here. First, is the generalisation inherent in the consumer protection legislation. Secondly, the question whether a right of cancellation is after all the appropriate means of redress. Finally, the complex interplay between formal requirements, duties to inform, and the right of cancellation which create uncertainty in the law.

The first set of problems arises because the consumer legislation on national as well as European level does not inquire whether there actually was a procedural defect in the individual case but presumes that, in certain formally defined kinds of transactions, there is typically a defect in the contracting process that needs to be corrected. Furthermore, the presumption cannot be rebutted. As Professor Stephan Lorenz has shown in his survey of the right of the consumer to set the contract aside, this formalised approach *inevitably* leads to excessive protection of consumers while at the same time leaving considerable gaps of protection in deserving cases which fall through the net of strict formal criteria. (*Der Schutz vor dem unerwünschten Vertrag*, 1997, p 200 *et seq*; but see also Riesenhuber, *System und Prinzipien des Europäischen Vertragsrechts*, p 348 *et seq*, and Mankowski, *Beseitigungsrechte* (2003), p 222 *et seq* (especially pp 268–74), who come to a more favourable conclusion.) Invariably, cancelling the contract does not presuppose that the exercise of the free will of the consumer was actually impaired. Furthermore, exercising this right does not require a causal link between the reason for the right of cancellation—the imbalance in the negotiation process—and the conclusion of the contract. Accordingly, the consumer may set the contract aside even though he had made a perfectly reasonable and well-informed decision when entering into it, simply because he had second thoughts after the conclusion of the contract. Moreover, the presumption that a consumer is typically not in a position to make a well-informed decision in the situations covered by the new legislation, the number of which is growing by the day, sits uncomfortably with the very idea of a free and self-responsible individual. One is tempted to conclude that the consumer is denied capacity in a manner that is similarly sweeping as that found in the case of minors. It cannot be the purpose of books such as the present one to question the decision to introduce consumer rights on such a broad scale but merely to point out the limits of the approach chosen to achieve the protection.

Restricting the right to cancellation to consumers and to particular situations also means that in cases falling outside this pattern no relief is available, even if it is abundantly clear that the contracting process in fact suffered from a defect of a similar nature. An inexperienced dealer, for instance, will never be able to rely on such 'consumer' rights even though he was exposed to an inappropriate, aggressive negotiating technique. One way of solving this dilemma *de lege ferenda* would be the introduction of an individual procedural standard irrespective of the particular type of contract aimed at the protection from aggressive selling techniques (*Schutz gegen Überrumpelung*). However, the legislator has not taken up such recommendations in the past. (See eg, Professor Medicus' commendable draft provision in his report for the reform commission of the BGB which was published in 1981: 'Verschulden bei Vertragsverhandlungen' in: *Gutachten zur Überarbeitung des Schuldrechts*, vol 1, 534.)

Professor Medicus has also pointed out what is, arguably, the *second* weakness of introducing the right of cancellation indiscriminately as a standard measure of consumer protection (above, p 523). Granting the consumer a period during which he may reconsider his decision is sensible where the decision to enter into the contract was unduly manipulated, for instance by contracting at an inappropriate place or time. Here, introducing a short 'cooling off' period seems to be a satisfactory solution to the defect in the contracting process. However, in the majority of cases the right of cancellation is granted, not because of the manner in which the negotiations were conducted, but because it is assumed that the nature of the subject matter cannot properly be assessed until after the conclusion of the contract. Examples are time-share contracts, insurance, distance contracts, contracts for distance learning and consumer credit agreements. (In the last two examples, the right of cancellation is peculiar to German law, in the other the right of cancellation is provided for on the EC level.)

In the case of so-called distance contracts (eg, contracts concluded over the internet), it is difficult to see why a contract of sale ought to be cancelled at will simply because the consumer did not have the possibility to inspect the sold goods before the conclusion of the contract. If the goods are not in conformity with the (exaggerated or otherwise misleading) description in the contract the traditional remedies in respect of a breach of contract seem to afford adequate protection; yet Directive 97/7/EC takes a different view. In effect, this transforms such a sale into a sale on approval. (For English law, see The Consumer Protection (Distance Selling) Regulations 2000, SI 2000 No 2334: note that its reg 13(1)(b) makes clear that the right to cancel does not extend to contracts 'for the supply of goods or services the price of which is dependent on fluctuations in the financial market which cannot be controlled by the supplier.')

In the case of consumer credit, where German law grants a right to cancellation in § 495 BGB (in English law, see section 67 of the Consumer Credit Act 1974 ('CCA 1974')), it is said that the consumer needs to be able to reconsider his decision and evaluate alternative offers once he has received the contract documents (preparatory works, BT-Drucks. 11/5462, 12). One wonders however whether it is not customary and indeed essential that such comparison and evaluation takes place before the contract is concluded. The duties to inform the other party in the offer of credit before the conclusion of the contract are clearly spelled out in German law as well as in Directive 87/102/EEC. Is it realistic to assume that the consumer will rethink his decision *shortly* after he has signed the contract? This is not likely to happen in the ordinary run of the mill case. The dangerous characteristic of such contracts, namely that they overstretch the financial capabilities of the consumer, will typically manifest itself at a time when the cancellation period has long since expired. Overall, thus one could with some justification classify these rules more as examples of the exchange standard of contractual justice rather than as purely procedural standards.

In the UK, this consideration of financial overstretching as a result of high-pressure sales techniques, coupled with the danger that such doorstep sellers may lack a permanent business address where a consumer might go to complain (etc), had already led in the Hire-Purchase Acts of 1964 and 1965 to a right for the consumer to cancel concluded credit agreements within four days of the receipt of that agreement. The position is now regulated by the CCA 1974, which provides an extensive control regime to which we will refer by way of comparison in what follows. (More generally see: Goode, *Consumer Credit Law and Practice* (looseleaf) and Brown, *Commercial Law* (2001), chapter 33).

Thirdly, the interplay between, on the one hand, the duty to inform and the requirements as to form, and on the other, the right to cancellation is complex and thus not without its pitfalls which in turn may create uncertainty. Failing to inform the consumer comprehensively about the right of cancellation in the required form will not trigger the cancellation period, § 355 II BGB. This requirement is further complicated by additional duties in relation to special transactions, such as for instance e-commerce, § 312e III 2 BGB (see Directive 2000/31/EC [2000] OJ L178/1 and, for the UK implementation, The Electronic Commerce (EC Directive) Regulations 2002, SI No 2002/2013), or distance contracts, § 312d II BGB (see The Consumer Protection (Distance Selling) Regulations 2000, SI 2000 No 2334, discussed in Brown, *Commercial Law* (2001), pp 253–5). For the UK regime on consumer credit, see sections 62–4 CCA 1974 and The Consumer Credit (Cancellation Notices and Copies of Documents) Regulations 1983, SI 1983 No 1557 (as amended): failure to observe, eg, the requirement to send a notice in the relevant form concerning the right to cancel means that the agreement is not properly executed (section 64(5) CCA 1974)—in such a situation, section 127(4)(b) CCA 1974 makes clear that the court will then not make an enforcement order relating to the agreement under section 65(1) CCCA 1974.

Paragraph 355 III 3 BGB, a provision which became necessary after the *Heininger* decision of the ECJ (case C–481/99, [2001] ECR I-9945; NJW 2002, 281), clarifies that the right of cancellation never ceases if the consumer has not been properly informed of the right. This means that in such a case, even after a considerable lapse of time, the contract can be cancelled if the 'defect' in the contracting process, which may well-be technical and of little real significance, is discovered subsequently. Even in the case of fraud, surely a 'defect' of a far more serious quality, the fathers of the BGB regarded the period of one year after the discovery as sufficient and this is extended to ten years if the fraud remained hidden (§ 124 BGB). Again, one wonders whether this brand of consumer protection has not rather overstepped the mark. (This point has not been explicitly considered in the UK, either by the various statutory instruments or by case law. On the CCA 1974 see: Brown, *Commercial Law*, p 807, suggesting the same solution reached by the ECJ in *Heininger*. It should be noted however that the discussion in the previous paragraph concerning sections 64(5), 65(1) and 127(4)(b) CCA 1974 suggests that in such circumstances a court may not make an enforcement order in relation to such an agreement in any case, even if the agreement has not been cancelled.)

Furthermore, the duty to inform is not such a straightforward requirement with which to comply and mistakes may easily occur. An indirect confirmation of this danger, although it is itself a piece of legislation adopted to reduce it, is the existence of the *BGB-Informationspflichtenverordnung* (BGBl. 2002-I, 342), a regulation passed to aid dealers to perform the intricate task of informing the consumer correctly (it contains a model written notice of the right of cancellation, running to more than a whole page of text and including six footnotes). A similar provision exists in UK law as a result of The Consumer Credit (Cancellation Notices and Copies of Documents) Regulations 1983, SI 1983 No 1557 (as amended).

Before turning to the specific requirements, we may state by way of conclusion that during the last few decades the level of consumer protection has certainly increased considerably. As is typical of EC legislation, the measures are sector specific and German law in some cases provides an even more effective and far-reaching protection of the consumer than do the 'foreign' measures. Similarly, the UK had adopted the Consumer Credit Act 1974 long before any EC legislative activity in the field (although it has been amended subsequently to conform to the provisions of relevant EC Directives). A certain consolidation of the new procedural standards cannot be denied. However, the right of cancellation with which we are here concerned in particular does seem to be a somewhat indiscriminate instrument, which may not always be readily justified and which allows the consumer to escape the responsibility for his actions on what would very often appear to be 'mere technicalities.' One systemic point of comparative interest that is worth noting here is that the UK regime on consumer credit vests quite significant discretion in the courts (under section 127(1) CCA 1974) when enforcement orders are sought, where only minor infringements of the requirements of the Act have occurred. So, section 127(2) empowers the court, if it appears just to do so, to reduce or even discharge a sum payable by the debtor if this would be appropriate compensation for prejudice as a result of the infringement. See for example, *National Guardian Mortgage Corpn v Wilkes* [1993] CCLR 1 (where failure to supply a copy of the agreement prior to contract, as required under section 58 CCA 1974, led to a significant reduction of the interest payable) and *Rank Xerox Finance Ltd v Hepple and Fennymore* [1994] CCLR 1 (in which a failure to provide information concerning accelerated payments in the event of default, so that the agreement had not been properly executed under section 61, resulted in those default payments being reduced by over 90 per cent to just £500). Equally, where no such prejudice has been suffered, then the agreement may be enforced *in toto*: *Nissan Finance UK v Lockhart* [1993] CCLR 39.

Finally, it is also worthy of note that the general run of EC case law on the application of the provisions on free movement of goods (Article 28 EC) has had to face up to a dilemma relating to the capacity of consumers to remain sufficiently well informed to take purchasing decisions. These cases relate to national laws aimed at protecting consumers, when ranged against the imperative of the EC Treaty that goods must be allowed to move freely across the whole EU market. The issue is raised where a national rule is prima facie contrary to Article 28 EC and yet may escape if it exists for a reason considered justifiable (and proportionate to the goal to be achieved) by the Court of Justice. One such ground of justification for national rules is 'consumer protection' and the Court has generally approached this question from the starting point of the 'reasonably circumspect' consumer. If he would not be confused or misled by the practice in question, then a national provision seeking to prevent that confusion could not be upheld (see eg, case C–470/93 *Verein gegen Unwesen in Handel und Gewerbe Köln e V v Mars GmbH* [1995] ECR I-1923). It is in the application of this standard that matters become very difficult, particularly because these cases deal with so-called 'negative harmonisation' at EC level (by means of the basic Treaty and its case law, rather than by positive legislative provisions, such as the various consumer protection Directives discussed above). Sensitive issues about national regulatory competence are raised by this case law and are not apposite to our discussion here. (See generally, eg, Poiares Maduro, *We the Court: The European Court of Justice and the European Economic Constitution* (1998), chapter 3.) Nevertheless, even in the absence of specific consumer legislation at EC level, insofar as the free movement case law is involved, it is clear that EC case law has a contribution to make in deciding how far national notions of consumer protection can be allowed to restrict the achievement of the internal market. (On this, see Micklitz, 'Perspektiven eines Europäischen Privatrechts' ZEuP 1998, 253, 257–62; Mortelmans and Wilson, 'The Notion of Consumer in Community Law: A Lottery?' in Lonbay (ed), *Enhancing the Legal Position of the European Consumer* (1996), pp 36–57; Weatherill, *EC Consumer Law and Policy* (1997) and, 'Recent Case Law Concerning the Free Movement of Goods: Mapping the Frontiers of Market Deregulation' (1999) 36 *CML Rev* 51.)

(b) Right of Cancellation (*Widerrufsrecht*)

It would serve no practical purpose to repeat the lengthy provisions dealing with the technical details of the right to cancellation and which are reproduced in translated form in Appendix 2 below. A number of points are, nevertheless, worth mentioning, especially since the manner of implementation of the EC Directives in Germany may be of particular comparative interest.

The right of cancellation is now regulated in §§ 355–9 BGB which, to name but the most important aspects, concern the period of cancellation, the manner in which the right is exercised, and the consequences for the restitution of the performance of the contract. These provisions also contain rules for contracts for the supply of goods or services where these are interlinked with consumer credit contracts (see § 358 BGB). This 'general part' of the consumer's right of cancellation is supplemented by special regimes of rules dealing with specific types of contracts or specific types of negotiating procedures. These special rules usually partially qualify or depart from the rules found in the general part, which can result in highly complex lines of reasoning. In the UK, the implementation of these rights of cancellation has been effected in specific statutory instruments relating to the particular areas of consumer protection in question (see the references above for these regulations). There has yet to be any legislative attempt to combine these rights in any generalised terms.

It is common to all rights of cancellation (except in the case of insurance contracts, as to which see below) that the relevant contract is concluded between a dealer (as defined in § 14 BGB)—ie, a person acting for the transaction in question in his commercial or professional capacity—and a consumer (§ 13 BGB)—ie, a natural person acting outside his trade or profession. Some controversy has been sparked by the question whether the objective quality of the person as consumer is decisive or whether instead the objective appearance of that person should be the criterion. The second solution appears more consistent with the objective approach to interpretation, as explained in the previous chapter, and is therefore desirable. (See *Münchener Kommentar*- Basedow, § 310 Rn. 48 with references.)

Another problem is how to solve so called 'dual-use' cases, in which the subject matter of the contract serves both private and professional purposes. Again, a pragmatic approach seems preferable: the *prevailing* use is decisive (in this sense eg, Wendehorst, DStR 2000, 1311).

The standard/normal period of cancellation is two weeks: § 355 II 2 BGB. In the UK however the period in which cancellation may be made varies according to the relevant, sector-specific rules. Thus, the CCA 1974 provides for five days after the receipt of the copy of the executed agreement, while the period seven days is found in the UK's 1987 Regulations on contracts concluded away from business premises (CCA 1974, reg 4(5)) and fourteen days in the Timeshare Act 1992 (sections 2(2)(a), 5 and 6).

According to § 355 I 2 BGB, the notice of cancellation does not need to indicate any reasons though it must be in text form (ie, writing or similar means but not signed, § 126b BGB). (See, eg, sections 69 and 189(1) CCA 1974 and sections 5 and 12(6) of the Timeshare Act 1992: in these statutes, 'notice' is taken to mean 'notice in writing.' Further, section 69(1) CCA 1974 does not require any specific form or content, so long as the intention to cancel is clear). This is a direct consequence of the fact that there does not need to be a causal nexus between the reason for granting the right—ie, the defect in the contracting process—and the decision to enter into the contract.

The period of cancellation commences with the fulfilment of the duty to notify the consumer about the right, § 355 II 1 BGB, and is extended to one month if the notification took place after the conclusion of the contract, § 355 II 2 BGB. By way of a UK comparison in the field of consumer credit, in the CCA 1974 the cancellation period starts to run from the moment the debtor signs the unexecuted agreement (section 68) and runs until five days after the copy of the agreement has actually been received by him *or* after the notice informing of the right to cancellation has been received. This copy must reach him within seven days of the making of the agreement (section 63(2)), which is usually when the creditor posts the executed agreement to the debtor. Meanwhile, the notice that informs the debtor of his right to cancel the agreement must be sent separately from the agreement itself, and must again arrive within seven days of the making of the agreement (section 64(1)(b)). Thus, whichever of the copy and the notice arrives later then forms the starting point for the five-day period to run.

It has already been explained (and indeed criticised) that if the consumer is not properly notified of his right, then the right of cancellation continues indefinitely (§ 355 III 3 BGB). If other duties to inform have been violated, the right of cancellation ceases after six months (§ 355 III 1 BGB). The general requirements as to notification are also laid down in § 355 II BGB and have been explored above. They are, like all other requirements of the general part, subject to significant modifications in the 'special parts' of the consumer legislation incorporated into the BGB.

The cancellation of the contract is analysed in German law as a declaration of intention and as such is subject to the general rules applicable to such acts. Thus, it is necessary that the trader be properly notified, as to which see chapter 2 (particularly sections 2(g) p 67). Unlike the requirements of § 130 BGB, however, a punctual dispatch suffices to satisfy the time requirements of the period of cancellation: § 355 I 2 BGB. (See, similarly, section 69(7) CCA 1974).

The consequences of cancellation are laid down in § 357 BGB. § 357 I 1 BGB declares—with modifications—that the rules on termination of the contract under §§ 346 *et seq* BGB apply. Hence, the parties are under an obligation to return the performance of the contract to the other party (§ 346 I BGB), and if they are not able to do so in principle they are under an obligation to compensate the other party for the value of the performance that cannot be returned (§ 346 II BGB). (For details, see chapter 9, below.) To continue the comparison with the UK's CCA 1974, the basic position is that cancellation has the effect of treating the agreement 'as if it had never been entered into' (section 69(4)). Thus, section 70 provides that any sums that had been payable will, on cancellation, cease to be payable and any sums that were paid before the cancellation must be repaid. Further, under section 72 there is a duty to return any goods received to the other party once cancellation has taken place. The Act contains detailed provisions on how these general principles are to be put into practice. An attempt has been made to cover all possible situations (including linked transactions, credit card purchases, perishable or consumable goods and the duty to take reasonable care of goods during the pre-cancellation period). (For fuller discussion, see Brown, *Commercial Law*, pp 808–18.)

The reference to the law of termination of contract § 357 I 1 BGB is important for it excludes the applicability of the law of unjust enrichment and opts for a model of restitution *ex nunc* rather than *ex tunc*. (Similarly, the provision of a specific regime in the CCA 1974 will be treated as excluding the general law of restitution in the English context.) The rules applicable are thus similar to those where the contract is terminated due a breach of contract, eg, for the delivery of defective goods. This is somewhat odd from a theoretical point of view, since defects in the contracting process—the application of a procedural standard—usually entail invalidity *ab initio* and, accordingly, the application of the rules contained in §§ 812 *et seq* BGB; see as to the law of mistake, below. Yet, § 346 BGB may be more appropriate since its starting point is a valid contract and a pragmatic reversal of the exchange of performance and counter-performance rather than treating the contract as being void retroactively. (It should be noted that, despite the reference to § 346 BGB, Larenz and Wolf, *Allgemeiner Teil,* § 39 Rn. 30, suggest that the contract should be treated as void *ab initio*. Otherwise, the consumer could be held liable for breaches of contract. This is difficult to follow since imposing liability in damages would also be possible in the pre-contractual stage under *culpa in contrahendo* rules: see chapter 2, section 5.) In any event, Directive 85/577/EEC (see Article 7 thereof) does not in our view pre-determine which model of restitution the national legislator may adopt. On this point, the only restriction may be the case law of the ECJ relating to the adequacy and effectiveness of national remedies for the enforcement of EC rights. This requires both that such remedies are the equivalent of any that are available for the enforcement of sufficiently comparable national rights *and* that the remedies do not render it impossible or excessively difficult to enforce the EC law right. (See, generally, case 14/83 *Von Colson and Kamann v Land Nordrhein-Westfalen* [1984] ECR 1891; case C–271/91 *Marshall v Southampton and South West Area HeAlt.h Authority (No 2)* [1993] ECR I-4367; case C–261/95 *Palmisani v Istituto Nazionale della Previdenza Sociale* [1997] ECR I-4025; Prechal, 'Community Law in National Courts: the Lessons from *Van Schijndel*' (1998) 35 *CML Rev* 681 and Craig & de Búrca, *EU Law: Text, Cases and Materials* (3rd edn, 2003), pp 230–57.) Setting the contract aside *ex nunc*, therefore, appears to be the best explanation of the right of cancellation in German law.

(c) Scope of Application

§§ 355 *et seq* BGB govern the conditions for exercising the right of cancellation and its consequences but do not stipulate the situations in which it arises. These are defined in the special sections of the BGB, which will then refer back to § 355 BGB for the conditions of the exercise of the right. There are a good number of instances in which a right of (free) revocation for a short period after the conclusion of the contract is granted to a consumer. Yet, as explained, there is no single general principle according to which a declaration of will may be 'revoked' or *widerrufen*.

The most prominent and also, as was explained above, the most deserving field of application of the right to free cancellation are contracts negotiated away from business premises such as 'doorstep transactions': §§ 312 and 312a BGB (which seek to implement Directive 85/577/EEC; in the UK, see The Consumer Protection (Cancellation of Contracts Concluded away from Business Premises) Regulations 1987, SI 1987 No 2117 (as amended by SI 1998 No 3050)).

The justifying reason for the right of revocation is the protection of the consumer against aggressive negotiating tactics or unfair commercial practices by granting him a 'cooling off' period in which he may reconsider his decision. Such inappropriate or potentially dangerous situations are defined in § 312 I BGB (cf Article 1 of the Directive and reg 3(1) of the 1987 Regulations). The most important is, as already stated, the door-to-door canvassing, ie oral negotiations or in the area of a private dwelling or at the workplace of the consumer. The assumption is that in these situations the trader may apply psychological pressure on an unprepared consumer and take advantage of the reluctance to say 'no'. The surprise element (*Überrumpelungsgefahr*) is aggravated by the fact that where the contract is negotiated away from business premises, the consumer is not able to compare the offer with other offers.

The only requirement for the right to arise is that the decision of the consumer to enter into the contract was determined (*bestimmt*) in such a situation. It is immaterial therefore if (for instance) the contract is in fact concluded subsequently to the negotiations at the doorstep so long as the doorstep situation was decisive for the decision process of the consumer. (See, BGH NJW 1994, 262; reg 3(1)(c) of the 1987

Regulations, although this includes no criterion of the 'decisive' role played by the offer made while door stepping (and there is no case law on this as yet)).

If the contract was concluded on the spot or shortly after the negotiations the right of cancellation arises. As alluded to above, no further causal element is necessary. In particular it is not necessary that the dealer did in fact apply undue pressure or that the consumer was particularly easy to influence, etc. Accordingly, the exercise of the right of cancellation itself does not need to be motivated.

Perhaps the most intriguing issues have arisen in relation to the involvement of third parties in the negotiation process. The problem arises if a third person carries out the negotiations on behalf of the dealer at the private dwelling of the consumer. Is this a doorstep situation within the meaning of § 312 I BGB or the Directive? (In the UK, see reg 2(1), where 'trader' means 'a person who, in making a contract to which these Regulations apply, is acting for the purposes of his business, *and anyone acting in the name or on behalf of such a person*' (emphasis added).)The *Bundesgerichtshof* applies § 123 II BGB, discussed in detail below, by analogy in such situations (see eg, BGH NJW 2003, 424). This means that it is decisive whether the dealer knew or could have known that the negotiations took place in such a situation. Moreover, where the third person acted as agent or in a similar capacity for the dealer, then the doorstep situation may be attributed to the principal. In all other cases however the influence of the third person does not warrant the grant of a right of cancellation. The dealer cannot be held responsible for the defect in the contracting process. This makes sense, for it would not appear appropriate to apply stricter standards than is the case with the manipulation of the exercise of a rational choice through fraud.

A useful discussion of the rationale of the right of cancellation can be found in BAG NZA 2004, 597, case No 84. The decision concerns the question whether an employee is entitled to a right of cancellation according to § 312 BGB if he enters at his 'place of work' (cf Article 1 of the Directive) into an agreement with the employer to terminate the contract of labour. The incentive to set the agreement of termination aside is considerable because the rules as to termination of the contract unilaterally by giving notice are quite strict (as noted previously), and crucially may also entitle the employee to a down payment (*Abfindung*). The issue had been controversial and the *Bundesarbeitsgericht* concluded in a well-reasoned judgment that the employee did not have such a right. (However, the Court did not decide whether an employee was a 'consumer' at all, yet this point is also controversial: see eg, Hromadka, NJW 2002, 2523; Singer, RdA 2003, 194).

First, the existence of such a right was rejected because a literal interpretation of these provisions did not support it; more importantly, the court also held that the purpose of granting the right of cancellation does not apply to the situation of an employee entering into a contract with his employer at the workplace. The decision also provides an ideal example of the method of interpretation of a statutory provision. The court discussed not only the systematic context of the new consumer legislation and the historic intention of the legislator, but its reasoning also revealed important dogmatic foundations of the right of cancellation in contracts with consumers, which we likewise have attempted to explore in the present section. (See also case C–45/96 *Bayerische Hypotheken- und Wechselbank AG v Dietzinger* [1998] ECR I-1199, which provides another interesting perspective on when someone is acting as a consumer vis-à-vis the trader when entering an agreement. Thus, a son standing guarantor for his father's business was held by the ECJ to have created a unilateral obligation, with no goods or services being supplied directly to him, when signing the agreement on a visit by the trader to his father's house. A further issue was that his father was not a consumer and Article 1(1), second indent, point (i) of the Directive refers only to a visit to the consumer's home or that of another consumer. Compare this restriction with the wording of reg 3(1) of the 1987 UK Regulations, which cover a visit to 'the consumer's home or to the home of another person.')

Directive 97/7/EC [1997] OJ L144/19 on the protection of consumers in respect of distance contracts, implemented in § 312b and § 312c BGB (and in the UK in The Consumer Protection (Distance Selling) Regulations 2000, SI 2000 No 2334), similarly focuses on a particular contracting process. Yet there is nothing obviously questionable about the negotiating technique of concluding contracts under an organised distance sales or service-provision scheme run by the supplier (cf Article 2 of the Directive). The reason for granting the right of cancellation (or right of withdrawal as it is called in this Directive) is rather, as the preamble of the Directive clarifies, that the consumer is not actually able to see the product or ascertain the nature of the service. (Note that Brown, *Commercial Law*, has commented (at 253) that a 'principal target of the Regulations is those mail order companies which take payment from the consumer and then fail to deliver the goods for an unconscionable period of time.')

In fact, a model for this sort of argument already existed in Germany, namely the right of cancellation in relation to contracts for 'distance learning,' merely a special type of 'distance contracts' (§ 4 of the *Fernunterrichtsschutzgesetz* of 1976). As we remarked above, the right of cancellation transforms the contract into a 'sale on approval' or 'service on approval.' It may be doubted whether this is strictly necessary in addition to imposing comprehensive obligations to provide information (cf Articles 4 and 5 of the Directive; regs 7 (on content) and 8 (in a durable medium) of the 2000 Regulations). It is difficult to detect a *procedural* defect in the conclusion of the contract; the Directive seems rather to aim at shaping the terms of the contract and thus is an example of the desire to increase substantive justice.

In the remaining areas, the right of cancellation has been introduced because the (usually long-term) contract is regarded as potentially dangerous and the contractual framework difficult for lay persons to understand. The cautionary purpose of warning the contracting party is traditionally served by formal requirements and duties to inform. The right to withdraw is less apt to serve this purpose because it is restricted to a short period after the conclusion of the contract, yet the consumer may realise at a much later point that he did not need in fact the service or that it over burdens him financially.

Directive 94/47/EC [1994] OJ L280/83 concerning contracts relating to the purchase of the right to use immovable properties on a timeshare basis was implemented in §§ 481 *et seq* BGB (in the UK, see the Timeshare Act 1992, as amended by The Timeshare Regulations 1997, SI 1997, No 1081). The reason for introducing the right to withdraw within a short period after the conclusion of the contract (Article 5 of the Directive provides for ten days, while both § 485 BGB and sections 2(2)(a), 5 and 6 of the Timeshare Act 1992 allow for two weeks) is the complexity of time-sharing contracts, as the preamble to the Directive states: to give the purchaser the chance to realize more fully what his obligations and rights under the contract are (11th recital to Directive 94/47/EC).

For similar reasons, § 495 BGB (see also, § 505 BGB for contracts for delivery by instalments of goods) allows the consumer who entered into a consumer credit agreement to back out of the contract. In fact Directive 87/102/EEC does not require the introduction of such a right. For the English law on this topic, see section 67 of the CCA 1974: the right to cancel is only available if certain conditions are met. Thus, the 'antecedent negotiations' that led to the agreement must have 'included oral representations made in the presence of the debtor . . . by an individual acting as, or on behalf of, the negotiator.' (On this, see *Moorgate Property Services v Kabir* [1995] CCLR 74.) Even then, there will be no right to cancel if the agreement is signed at the business premises of the creditor, a party linked to the transaction or a negotiator in any antecedent negotiations. (See generally, Brown, *Commercial Law*, pp 802–7.)

Finally, the right to withdraw from a long-term insurance contract is laid down in § 8 IV and in relation to life insurance in § 8 V of the *Versicherungsvertragsgesetz*. Interestingly, the personal scope of application is not limited to consumers, although § 5a of the *Versicherungsvertragsgesetz* broadens the right to withdraw where it is claimed for the benefit of consumers.

3. MISTAKE

Atiyah, 'Judicial Techniques and the Law of Contract' Essay 9 in his *Essays on Contract* (1986); Brox, *Die Einschränkung der Irrtumsanfechtung* (1960); Bydlinski, *Privatautonomie und objektive Grundlagen des verpflichtenden Rechtsgeschäftes* (1967); Bydlinski, 'Erklärungsbewußtsein und Rechtsgeschäft' JZ 1975, 1; Canaris, *Die Vertrauenshaftung im deutschen Privatrecht* (1971); Cartwright, '*Sole v Butcher* and the Doctrine of Mistake in Contract' (1987) 103 *LQR* 594; Cheshire, 'Mistake as Affecting Contractual Consent' (1944) 60 *LQR* 175; Fleischer, 'Der Kalkulationsirrtum' RabelsZ 65 (2001) 264; Flume, *Eigenschaftsirrtum und Kauf,* (1948); Grigoleit, 'Abstraktion und Willensmängel' AcP 199 (1999) 379; Kötz and Flessner, *European Contract Law*, vol 1 (1998) § 10; Kramer, *Grundfragen der vertraglichen Einigung,* (1972); Kötz and Flessner, 'Mistake' in *Int Enc Comp Law*, Vol VII, Ch 11 (2001); S Lorenz, *Der Schutz vor dem unerwünschten Vertrag* (1997); Mankowski, *Beseitigungsrechte* (2003); Mayer-Maly, 'Rechtsirrtum und Rechtsunkenntnis als Probleme des Privatrechts' AcP 170 (1970) 133; Mayer-Maly, 'Bemerkungen zum Irrtum über den Wert', *FS Pedrazzini* (1990) 343; Mayer-Maly, 'Bemerkungen zum Kalkulationsirrtum' *FS Ostheim* (1990) 189; Schermaier, 'Europäische Geistesgeschichte am Beispiel des Irrtumsrechts' ZEuP 1998, 60; Singer, 'Geltungsgrund und Rechtsfolgen der fehlerhaften Willenserklärung, JZ 1989, 1030; Singer, 'Der 'Kalkulationsirrtum—ein Fall für Treu und Glauben' JZ 1999, 342; JC Smith, 'Mistake, Frustration and Implied Terms' (1994) 110 *LQR* 400; Treitel, *The Law of Contract* (11th edn, 2003), chapter 8; Wieacker, 'Gemeinschaftlicher Irrtum der Vertragspartner und clausula rebus sic stantibus' *FS Wilburg* (1965) 229; Wieser, 'Zurechenbarkeit des Erklärungsinhalts' AcP 184 (1984) 40; Wieser, 'Wille und Verständnis bei der Willenserklärung' AcP 189 (1989) 112; Wolf, *Rechtsgeschäftliche Entscheidungsfreiheit und vertraglicher Interessenausgleich* (1970); Zweigert, 'Irrtümer über den Irrtum' ZfRV 1966, 12.

(a) Preliminary Observations

The law of mistake presents formidable difficulties in all legal systems. In any event this is true for German (Stephan Lorenz, *Der Schutz vor dem unerwünschten Vertrag* (1997), p 260: 'one of the most controversially discussed' areas of the law) and English law (an 'extremely difficult area of the law,' McKendrick, *Contract Law*, p 69). However, it should be observed from the outset that the position of German law as reflected by the practice of the courts can be stated with a relatively high degree of certainty. There are two reasons for this. The codal provisions dealing with mistake are clearly drafted and, at least in the interpretation given to them by the courts, leave little room for argument. Secondly, applying the rules that were developed by a roughly consistent case law quickly filled the gaps left by the Code. The law of mistake in §§ 119–24 BGB is thus supplemented by the principles of the foundation of the transaction and *culpa in contrahendo*. In the meantime, since the recent reform of the BGB, these rules can even be found in the Code itself (§ 313 and § 311 II respectively). Instead, the controversy is rooted in theoretical disagreements as to what constitutes valid consent. This becomes evident, for instance, if one recalls the conflict of nineteenth century academic debate between the will theory, which emphasised subjective elements, and its antithesis—the declaration theory—which stressed the responsibility for one's actions in a social context. (See, for illuminating expositions of past theories and their lasting influence, Flume, *Das Rechstgeschäft* (3rd edn, 1979), p 435 ff; von Mehren and Gordley, *The Civil Law System* (1977), p 854 *et seq*; Zimmermann, *The Law of Obligations* (1990), chapter 19.)

The (second) Commission of the BGB did not embrace wholeheartedly one or the other approach, neither of which would—in the view of the Commission—work in practice if adopted in a 'pure' form (*Protokolle*, vol I, 223). The position of the BGB, which has survived unchanged until the present day, is thus commonly characterised as a 'compromise' between the two models, although (as we will see) the will theory gained the upper hand. Central features were shaped after Friedrich Karl von Savigny's exposition of the law of mistake (in vol 3 of his *System des heutigen römischen Rechts*, 1840). Savigny's remarkable influence is less attributable to the originality of his writings, for most of his ideas had been discussed before, than to his elegant combination of two strands of reasoning: that of the natural law and of the Roman law tradition. From the natural law school, Savigny took the principle that the foundation of contract was the will of the parties. Accordingly, if the declaration of the will and the will itself did not coincide then the basis for enforcing the contract collapsed. Without declaration of will there could, as a consequence, also be no contractual obligation (*System des heutigen römischen Rechts*, p 264). In this respect, he departed radically from the traditional interpretation of Roman law that in cases of mistake there was no meeting of the minds; ic, the lack of consensus justified the invalidity (cf Flume, *Das Rechtsgeschäft*, p 441).

The contradiction between declaration and will in the case of error meant that there was only the appearance of a declaration but no valid act of self-determination (Savigny, *System des heutigen römischen Rechts*, § 135). The following statement, stressing the fundamental importance of the (subjective) will, captures the essence of Savigny's reasoning and that of the will theory more generally (*System des heutigen römischen Rechts*, p 258):

Denn eigentlich muß der Wille an sich als das einzig Wichtige und Wirksame gedacht werden und nur weil er ein inneres, unsichtbares Ereignis ist, bedürfen wir ein Zeichen, woran er von Anderen erkannt werden könne, und dieses Zeichen, wodurch sich der Wille offenbart ist eben die Erklärung. (For the will is ultimately the only thing that matters and only because it is an internal, invisible occurrence, we need a sign for it, if others are to learn of it, and this sign by which the will reveals itself is the declaration.)

How does one determine the range of relevant mistakes? The analysis of contract as consisting of two declarations of will, where each declaration of will contains the elements of 'declaration' and 'will' proved very useful in limiting the types of relevant errors. For an error was only conceivable where the 'declaration' was part of the agreement. This approach narrowed mistake down to expression mistakes. The promisor was only required to be conscious of what he was declaring. The motives for entering into the contract did not directly affect his 'will' as transparent from the 'declaration'. Therefore, Savigny regarded it as irrelevant that the motives for entering into a contract (*Irrtum in den Beweggründen*) turned out to be wrong; as a general rule this 'error' did not invalidate the declaration of will. (This approach was subsequently endorsed and refined by Bernhard Windscheid, see his *Lehrbuch des Pandektenrechts*, I, (6th edn, 1887), § 78, p 233 *et seq*.) This distinction between an error in declaring the will and operating on the basis of mistaken motives was later (alongside the concept of 'declaration of will') to become the mark, the cardinal notion or key feature of the law of mistake in the BGB. (We will return to it in the next section.)

Since Savigny's treatise was not purely theoretical, but aimed at providing a foundation for Roman law as it was in force qua *ius commune*, he adopted the traditional categories of mistake of Roman law—*error in negotio, error in persona, error in corpore* and *error in substantia*—and thus limited the range of relevant mistakes further. The last of these categories of error proved difficult to square with his theory, for the error as to the quality of the subject matter of the contract was not an example where declaration and will deviated but concerned the motives for entering into the contract. A variant of this type of error has survived in the BGB in § 119 II BGB and limiting the scope of this provision has been a constant concern of the courts ever since.

Savigny shaped the BGB in three ways. First, unilateral mistakes are relevant. Secondly, they are relevant only insofar as they affect the process of transforming an internal will into an external meaning and irrelevant insofar as they concern the motivation for entering into the contract. Thirdly, factors other than the mismatch of declaration and will are irrelevant. This last aspect cannot be overestimated. It excludes a number of criteria which play a decisive role in other models of mistake. For instance, it is entirely irrelevant for the application of § 119 BGB whether the other party was able to detect the mistake (such an approach was expressly rejected by the Commission: *Prot*, vol I, p 223). Likewise, it is irrelevant whether the mistake was self-induced or induced by some 'misrepresentation' of the other party.

Other aspects of Savigny's theory were not adopted by the BGB-Commission. Thus, mistakes do not render the contract void but according to § 142 BGB merely voidable (though note that rescission operates *ex tunc*, ie retroactively). Clearly, this was a concession to the declaration theory while preserving the basic prevalence of the will. Moreover, the mistaken party was to pay a 'price' for rescinding the contract for mistake. The BGB introduced in § 122 BGB the liability of the mistaken party for the reliance interest. This was, as explained in more detail in chapter two, a materialisation of Jhering's theory of *culpa in contrahendo* and again the declaration theory was influential in making this liability independent of fault. Finally, the piecemeal approach of Roman law to mistake was abandoned and the deviation between will and declaration considered relevant regardless of whether the mistake could be slotted into one of the traditional categories of mistake (*error in persona*, etc). However, the basic thesis of the 'declaration theory'—that mistake does not affect the validity of the con-tract–(which had prevailed in the Austrian Civil Code of 1811, for instance) was clearly rejected.

The presentation of English law by way of comparison with the German position is not straightforward. The comparison is difficult, indeed nigh on impossible, not only because the former seems to lack the extent of theoretical discussion one finds in the latter (though there was a time that almost every English contract lawyer felt almost obliged to write something about the topic), but because the common law position was modified by occasional equitable intervention. Beatson, in *Anson's Law of Contract*, pp 308–9), captures this duality of problems when he writes,

> [m]istake . . . principles have never been precisely settled, the decided cases are open to a number of varying interpretations and the position is further complicated by two factors. First, there has been a distinct change in the attitude of judges towards the question of mis-take during the last hundred years [moving away from a consensus theory of contract towards great reluctance to intervene: see Lando and Beale, *Principles of European Contract Law* (2000), p 235]. . . . [Second, there is the] separate development of common law and equi-table doctrine before the Judicature Act 1873.

The difficulties caused by the second point, especially confusing to non-common lawyers, have been substantially eased by the recent decision in *Great Peace Shipping Ltd v Tsavliris Salvage (International) Ltd ('The Great Peace')* [2003] QB 679 (on which see the notes by Phang [2003] *Conv* 247; Hare [2003] *CLJ* 29; Reynolds (2003) 119 *LQR* 177 and Midwinter (2003) 119 *LQR* 180; see further, Chandler, Devenney and Poole, 'Common Mistake: Theoretical Justification and Remedial Flexibility' [2004] *JBL* 34), but problems still remain that can only be touched on by our brief excursus here and there. At this point however a few preliminary remarks may not be out of place. The basic position of English law on this topic is thus as follows (see, gen-erally, Treitel, *The Law of Contract*, chapter 8).

First, it is clear that a common fundamental mistake of fact (where the parties share the relevant error) nullifies consent and renders the contract void. This category includes a mistake as to the existence of the subject-matter of the contract (such as an annuity being purchased where the annuitant had pre-deceased the purchase: *Strickland v Turner* (1852) 7 Ex 208; 155 ER 919) or as to the identity of the subject-matter (see *Bell v Lever Brothers Ltd* [1932] AC 161 at 225 as applied in *Grains & Fourrages SA v Huyton* [1997] 1 Lloyd's Rep 628: both parties agreed to rectify a con-tract to correct a perceived error, but both were mistaken as to the actual nature of the error) or as to the possibility of performing the contract (eg, *Sheikh Bros Ltd v Ochsner* [1957] AC 136, where the agreement to deliver 50 tons of sisal fibre per month was held to be void because the land in question simply could not produce that much, even though both parties had assumed that it could). Common mistakes as to the quality of the subject-matter form a difficult section of the case law. The famous case of *Bell v Lever Brothers* (cited above) adopted strict requirements for such mistakes to render the contract void. The mistake must be made by both parties and must relate to 'something which both must necessarily have accepted in their minds as an essential and integral element of the subject-matter' (*per* Lord Thankerton, at 256). As Lord Atkin put it, the quality must be something 'which makes the thing without the quality essentially different from the thing it was believed to be' (at 218). The cases before and after *Bell v Lever Brothers Ltd* are difficult to interpret consistently (for judicial discussion, see Steyn J's judgment in *Associated Japanese Bank (International) Ltd v Crédit du Nord SA* [1989] 1 WLR 255 and *The Great Peace*, above), but Treitel's formulation seems to capture their essence (*The Law of Contract*, p 292):

> A thing has many qualities. . . . For any particular purpose one or more of these qualities may be uppermost in the minds of the persons dealing with the thing. Some particular quality may be so important to them that they actually use it to *identify* the thing. If the thing lacks that quality, . . . the parties have made a fundamental mistake, even though they have not mistaken one thing for another, or made a mistake as to the existence of the thing.

The main caveat to this proposition is where, on a proper construction of the contract, one or other of the parties has accepted the risk of such uncertainties of existence, identity, impossibility and quality. The normal principle of *caveat emptor* will usually throw this risk on the buyer, but the seller can also take on such a risk if there is some express or implied warranty in the contract relating to the existence, quality or description of the subject matter. On these matters, compare the cases of *Couturier v Hastie* (1856) 5 HLC 673; 10 ER 1065 and *McCrae v Commonwealth Disposals Commission* (1951) 84 CLR 377 (and see the discussion by Atiyah, '*Couturier v Hastie* and the sale of non-existent goods' (1957) 73 *LQR* 340 and Atiyah and Bennion, 'Mistake in the Construction of Contracts' (1961) 24 *MLR* 421). See also, section 6 of the Sale of Goods Act 1979: 'where there is a contract for the sale of specific goods, and the goods without the knowledge of the seller have perished at the time when the contract is made, the contract is void' (discussed in Treitel, pp 296–7).

Another caveat is that the party claiming to rely on the fundamental mistake must have had reasonable grounds for having held the belief that led to the mistake (see the *McCrae* case, cited above, at 408 and the *Associated Japanese Bank* case, above, at 268).

A mistake can cause the parties to be severely at cross-purposes, resulting in any expression of consent being negatived and the parties not reaching a genuine agreement. As a result, this heading of mistake is heavily influenced by the rules on the interpretation of expressions of contractual intention (discussed above in chapter 3, p 133). An objective test of inferring the parties' intentions from their words and conduct will usually exclude any reliance on the argument that a mistake caused them not to reach agreement (see eg, *Smith v Hughes* (1871) LR 6 QB 597 (especially at 601)). From the perspective of the party relying on such a mistake, the mistake will usually have been a unilateral one (in the sense that the other party has his own belief as to the correct position, against which the claim of mistake is being ranged). In other situations, each is mistaken (ie, mutually—each misunderstanding the other's proposals) but the mistake is not common to both parties. (See eg, *Raffles v Wichelhaus* (1864) 2 H & C 906; 159 ER 375 and the debate surrounding the ground for the decision: Treitel, *The Law of Contract*, p 303). The types of mistake relevant in these circumstances include:

— a mistake as to the *identity* of the person with whom the contract is concluded (but not mere attributes: see *Cundy v Lindsay* (1878) 3 App Cas 459; *King's Norton Metal Co Ltd v Edridge, Merrett & Co Ltd* (1897) 14 TLR 98 and *Lewis v Averay* [1972] 1 QB 198 (and compare the latter with *Ingram v Little* [1961] 1 QB 31, itself recently disapproved by the House of Lords in *Shogun Finance Ltd v Hudson* [2004] 1 AC 919—this case is discussed further in section 3(e), p 299));

— a mistake as to the subject-matter of the contract—(eg, where the parties intend to deal about different things: *Falck v Williams* [1900] AC 176, where two charterparties were under negotiation and ambiguity in a communication was misunderstood to refer to a different charterparty from the one understood by the recipient); and

— a mistake as to the terms of the contract (see *Hartog v Colin & Shields* [1939] 3 All ER 566, where one party intended to sell rabbit skins at a certain price per piece, while the other intended to buy at the same price per pound, and there were roughly three pieces to the pound).

For such a mistake to render the contract void, it must be of a *fundamental* nature, it must induce the contract and it must be operative. It is the satisfaction of this last point that the objective interpretation principles will usually scupper.

Inducement requires that the relevant party did not simply take the risk that the facts might be otherwise (*Wales v Wadham* [1977] 1 WLR 199, at 220; cf *Boulton v Jones* (1857) 2 H & N 564; LJ Ex 117; 6 WR 107; 157 E.R. 232), but that the mistake must have been key in the decision to contract. Thus, in *Boulton v Jones* it was important for the defendant to contract with the previous owner of the shop (who owed him money, against which the defendant intended to set-off the purchase) rather than the new owner (the plaintiff). Normally, in such retail situations it makes very little difference to the purchaser who the seller is, so long as the required product can be supplied. (See Pothier, *Traité des Obligations* (1821 edn), Article 19, a passage that has often been quoted by the English courts, but perhaps not always accurately. See Treitel, *The Law of Contract*, p 305.) A mistake may be operative where the other party knows of the mistake (see *Boulton v Jones*, above) or where that other party has negligently induced that mistake (*Scriven Bros & Co v Hindley & Co* [1913] 3 KB 564).

Clearly, the common law of fundamental mistake operates very restrictively indeed and shows a strong preference for the enforcement of what appear to be contracts between the parties, facilitating commercial certainty that a bargain struck can be enforced and respecting the sanctity of contract. However, this would present an incomplete picture, as English law also has a highly developed and nuanced law of misrepresentation, which is capable of covering many situations that might be treated under the heading of 'mistake' in other jurisdictions. We will return to this point in what follows.

Finally, and as already hinted, in English law there is the added complication of the situations where equity plays a role in refusing to order specific performance or allowing contracts to be avoided or rectified on mistake grounds. (See Treitel, *The Law of Contract*, pp 310–26.)

So far as avoiding the contract is concerned (rescission on terms), the case law aimed at mitigating the harshness of the strict definition of what counts as a 'fundamental' mistake at common law. See the (in)famous case of *Solle v Butcher* [1950] 1 KB 671, where a lease was rescinded due to a mistaken belief that the flat in question was not subject to rent control, which would not have satisfied the fundamentality test at law (as the subject-matter received was still the same flat). A number of cases applied this approach in subsequent years (see, most recently, *West Sussex Properties Ltd v Chichester DC* 28 June, 2000 (Court of Appeal, unreported), but the decision in *The Great Peace* [2003] QB 689 has closed off this avenue to rescission, holding that *Solle v Butcher* could not be reconciled with *Bell v Lever Brothers Ltd* and intending that 'coherence . . . be restored to this area of our law' (*The Great Peace*, at [157]), while suggesting that there is 'scope for legislation to give greater flexibility to our law of mistake than the common law allows' (at [161]). It should be noted however that the strict result of *The Great Peace* is only to prevent equity from using such mistakes to achieve rescission of the contract. Presumably, rectification will still be available provided that the mistake was of both parties (eg, *Thomas Witter Ltd v TBP Industries Ltd* [1996] 2 All ER 573, at 601) or that the mistake was due to the other party's fraud or was known to the other party (see eg, *Commission for the New Towns v Cooper (Great Britain) Ltd* [1995] Ch 259, at 280). (Cf also the Canadian case of *McMaster University v Wilchar Construction Ltd* (1971) 22 DLR (3d) 9 (affd (1973) 69 DLR (3d) 400n, where Canadian law would allow rectification if the mistake should have been known to the other party.)

The final key point to note about the continued existence of the equitable jurisdiction is that the remedies available differ from those on offer at common law and that those remedies are within the discretion of the court: even after the Judicature Acts, it may still be very significant to identify whether the mistake rules at issue are those at law or those in equity.

As stated, the above bird's eye view of English law hardly does justice to such a complex subject nor does it really bring into relief the similarities and differences between the two systems. So, in the presentation of German law that follows, we will attempt to raise points of comparison with the English law as and where appropriate, to illustrate how similar scenarios and issues would be treated in both systems.

(b) The Distinction between Declaration Mistakes and Errors in the Motivation

The key to understanding the basic position of the BGB is the distinction between errors affecting the declaration itself and errors affecting the reasons for entering into a contract (as was already explained by way of introduction in section (a)). In the law of contract the latter type of error is not relevant. There are however other areas of the law where even errors in the motivation can lead to rescission. In the law of succession, for instance, the subjective intention of the testator is of prime importance. Accordingly, the subjective meaning of a declaration prevails (§ 133 BGB, as explained in chapter 3). Where the subjective intention can nevertheless not be brought to bear, for instance because the formal requirements would not be met, the will may be rescinded for mistake in the motivation. § 2078 II BGB contains an abstract definition of the error in motivation. It is defined as an erroneous assumption that a particular circumstance will or will not occur which influenced the will. For the sake of completeness, it should be added that a testator's right to rescind is not necessary so long as the declaration is freely revocable (§ 2254 BGB). Only where it becomes binding, is the right to rescind granted to the testator himself (§ 2281 BGB). In all other cases, the right to rescind vests in potential beneficiaries and accrues with the death of the testator (§ 2080 BGB).

It is a recurrent criticism of the approach of the BGB that it proceeds on the basis of a 'psychological' theory of mistake which cannot be justified by legal considerations and, as a result, gives rise to serious inconsistencies. (See, for instance, the trenchant criticism of Professor Kramer in the *Int Enc Comp Law*, paras 11–24; also, his annotation of § 119 BGB in the *Münchener Kommentar* (4th edn, 2001); but also Zweigert, 'Irrtümer über den Irrtum' ZfRV 1966, 12; and previously, Titze, 'Vom sogenannten Motivirrtum' *Festschrift Heymann* (1940), vol 2, p 72.) The example often given (eg, by Kramer, above) is that of the so-called 'calculation-mistake'. If the contract price is misspelled when making an offer, this technical mistake will allow the promisor to rescind the contract. However, if 'the same' error occurs during the phase of preparation of the offer, and the mistake is merely not detected when making the offer, then the contract cannot be avoided. This 'hair-splitting distinction,' it is claimed, is 'of questionable intrinsic merit.' Hence, the critics argue, the 'psychological' approach of the BGB should be abandoned in favour of a more flexible model, based on the assumption of risk. The question ought not to be when the mistake occurred but rather whether the promisor assumed the risk that the price was calculated correctly or whether it would be contrary to good faith to allow the other party to enforce the contract. There is little doubt that such an approach cannot be reconciled with § 119 BGB in a methodically satisfactory way. (See Stephan Lorenz, *Der Schutz vor dem unerwünschten Vertrag* (1997), p 284 *et seq*. For an English case on somewhat similar facts where the common fundamental mistake was sufficient to avoid the contract, see *Grains & Fourrages SA v Huyton* [1997] 1 Lloyd's Rep 628.)

For a similarly broad approach, see Article 4.103 of the Principles of European Contract Law:

(1) A party may avoid a contract for mistake of fact or law existing when the contract was concluded if:
  (a) (i)   the mistake was caused by information given by the other party; or
      (ii) the other party knew or ought to have known of the mistake and it was contrary to good faith and fair dealing to leave the mistaken party in error; or
      (iii) the other party made the same mistake,
  and
  (b) the other party knew or ought to have known that the mistaken party, had it known the truth, would not have entered the contract or would have done so only on fundamentally different terms.
(2) However a party may not avoid the contract if:
  (a) in the circumstances its mistake was inexcusable, or
  (b) the risk of the mistake was assumed, or in the circumstances should be borne, by it.

Article 4.103 also applies to declaration mistakes: Article 4.104. This provision does not differentiate as to the type of mistake, but makes the right to avoid the contract for mistake dependent on a number of factors: the actions of the other party, his imputed knowledge of the mistake or his causing the mistake and whether the error was excusable or the risk of making the mistake was assumed by the innocent party. As appears from our brief discussion of English law above, most of the points raised by these Principles are evident in the English approach. Even the points about good faith and fair dealing do put in an appearance in equity when assessing whether to allow the relevant party to rely on the mistake. The key potential difference would appear to be the strictness with which English law adheres to the fundamentality requirement to allow a contract to be avoided.

The distinction between declaration mistakes, which are *per se* treated as relevant, and erroneous motives, which are *per se* irrelevant, is too deeply rooted in the BGB to be easily discarded. The question then is whether it can still be defended from today's perspective. The answer is a qualified 'yes'.

The 'yes' is qualified because it is true that the original approach of the BGB has been subsequently supplemented with additional rules, without which perhaps the exclusion of motivation mistakes may have resulted in somewhat harsh results in hard cases. In any event, the exclusion as a general rule of the unilateral error in motive from the range of relevant mistakes rests on an insight that is not only correct from a phenomenological point of view, but is also derived from an essentially sound principle of corrective justice. The hopes and expectations associated with the performance of the contract are of no concern to the other party so long as they are not agreed on. The unilateral motive for entering into a contract may be readily disappointed. A buyer, for instance, may have misjudged his need for the purchased goods or may have speculated that the market will fall whereas in fact it rose. In such cases the promisor knows exactly what he is doing. It is only that he is mistaken as to the value of the contract for him, personally. All this is his responsibility alone if he has not succeeded in including a term in the contract that protects the particular expectation in question. For Savigny, this was all too obvious. Indeed, for him the irrelevance of this type of mistake was decisive for protecting the very institution of contract, ie the only salvation of the legal community against unlimited insecurity and arbitrariness ('*grenzenlose Unsicherheit und Willkür,*' *System des heutigen römischen Rechts* vol 3 (1840), p 355). It is worth observing at this point that the English approach achieves much of this by reliance on the objective principle in interpreting the words and conduct of each of the parties and by its willingness to examine the nature and construction of the bargain reached to see where the risks have been allocated. Further, where the mistake is a unilateral one, the criteria that require a mistake to have induced the contract and to be operative change the mistake from a purely unilateral one, internal to the thinking of the first party, to one that has (or really should have) come to the attention of the other party.

The situation is different if the *declaration* of intention suffers from a defect. For here the promisor does not know what he is doing. He has declared something different from what he had intended to declare. This may justify allowing the promisor to withdraw the flawed declaration. The fact that the promisor did not know what he did is a strong reason for not imputing the declaration to him, just as (for instance) an unconscious act would not be imputed to him. The distinction between declaration mistakes and motivation mistakes is thus more than just a factual observation. There may be reasons for denying the promisor the right to withdraw his declaration at all in the interest of certainty in the law (a criterion to which the English common law (as opposed to equity) has attributed great weight since *Bell v Lever Brothers Ltd*: see *The Great Peace*, etc) by emphasising the social aspect of the transaction etc. Yet the solution of the BGB does appear as a consistent model of mistake rules with the exception perhaps of § 119 II BGB, mistake as to quality, as to which see below.

But let us return to the example of an error in the calculation of the contract price. If, in relation to one of the constituent elements of the agreement, the promisor did not know what he was doing, then this declaration cannot be imputed to him. However, if the promisor knew what he was declaring but erred in respect of the correctness of his preparatory calculations, then there is no reason for not imputing the declaration. For the motives that the promisor had for entering into the contract are his own sole responsibility. This error is of the same kind as a misapprehension of the market price. In this latter situation, the objective principle of interpretation in English contract law would achieve the same result.

It is of first importance to stress from the outset that the approach of the BGB is much more flexible than the above analysis suggests. In fact many, if not all, the factors contained in Article 4.103 of the European Principles of Contract Law also play a significant role in German law. However, they come into play only in relation to mistakes other than declaration mistakes. They are thus available, for instance, to solve the problem of a wrongful calculation of the contract price in deserving cases. § 119 I BGB is just the first layer of mistake rules in German law. The principle of the irrelevance of a mistake in the motivation is subject to a crucial qualification. Where the error in the motivation is *imputable to the other party* the contract may (under certain further conditions) be rescinded (which provides a nice parallel to the English case law discussed above concerning fault in inducing the mistake (*McCrae*) and negligence in inducing the mistake (*Scriven Bros v Hindley & Co*)). Apart from declaration mistakes, the BGB thus provides three other categories of reasons for allowing a contract to be rescinded for mistake—they will be discussed in detail in sections 4 and 5, p 302 (and see also section 3(e), p 297). It suffices here to make three observations.

First, if the will of the innocent party is manipulated by the other party, ie the other party committed a fraud, the contract may be rescinded: § 123 BGB. (In English law, see *Car and Universal Finance Co Ltd v Caldwell* [1961] 1 QB 525. Note that the tort of deceit may also provide a damages remedy for losses suffered, so long as this does not lead to double recovery: see *Derry v Peek* (1889) 14 App Cas 337.) Here, the reason for rescinding the contract is not a mismatch of will and declaration. The innocent party knows what he is declaring, but a wrongful act of the other party manipulates the motivation for entering into the contract. The error in motivation is exceptionally relevant in such circumstances.

Secondly, so far as acts of a quality below that of a (deliberate) fraud are concerned, the mistake model is abandoned and a 'delictual' explanation adopted for the right of rescission. Of course, as was remarked previously (see chapter 2, p 91), since we are not dealing with physical damage this means that delict principles in the narrow German sense are not applicable. Instead, the doctrine of *culpa in contrahendo* comes into play (now § 311 II BGB). Thus, where a (negligent) misrepresentation by the other party caused the innocent party to enter into the contract for the wrong motive, the contract itself is treated as a harm which is remedied by granting the innocent party a right of rescission. This is however the most difficult area of the German law of mistake since it is not expressly regulated in the BGB. Details will be discussed below. (English law treats such situations under a complex and overlapping series of possible claims, including the tort of negligent misrepresentation and the various provisions of the Misrepresentation Act 1967.)

Thirdly, where both parties have proceeded on the basis of mistaken motives, the contract may be adjusted or even avoided under the rules as to the *foundation of the transaction*, also explained in detail below (see chapter 7).

One final general remark may be appropriate, especially with the English lawyer in mind. One reason militating against allowing contracts to be rescinded for mistake is the need to protect third parties in good faith. For instance, if the rescission of a contract of sale would mean that property in the goods did not pass and none of the subsequent buyers acquired ownership of the goods, this could seriously undermine commercial certainty. German law has two mechanisms which prevent this from happening (see for a more detailed analysis, chapter 1, section 5(c), p 27).

First, according to the principles of separation and abstraction (as to which see chapter 1, section 5(c)), rescinding the contract of obligation does not affect the contract of transfer. The transfer of the interest in the goods remains valid. There arises only a personal obligation in unjust enrichment that the other party to the contract must return the value of the property in the goods, for the rescission (*ex tunc*) of the contract of obligation also caused the *causa* for the transfer of the proprietary interest to vanish. There are exceptions to this rule where the defect affected both contracts. Yet in the typical cases of declaration mistakes, the contract of transfer is not affected: when the promisor offered to transfer ownership he knew what he was declaring. Declaration and will coincide, the contract of transfer is not voidable and the third party may thus retain the property acquired.

Secondly, in German property law it is possible for a third party acting in good faith to acquire property from a non-owner to the detriment of the owner. In the case of chattels, this will occur where the transferee did not know and but for gross negligence could not have known that the person having actual possession of the goods was not the owner (see § 932 BGB). In the case of immovable property, it can operate where the transferee did not positively know that the entry on the land register listing the transferor as holder of the proprietary interest was false (§ 892 BGB). Thus, even if—exceptionally—the contract of transfer is voidable, subsequent buyers are sufficiently protected. The principle of *nemo dat quod non habet* operates in English personal property law to prevent good title in chattels being passed (see section 21(1) of the Sale of Goods Act 1979). If rescission is held effectively to have occurred before the transfer to the third party, then rescission revests title in the claimant and the third party's claim will be defeated (*Car and Universal Finance v Caldwell* [1961] 1 QB 525). There are specific statutory exceptions to this basic rule as, for instance, the case of sale by a mercantile agent. (See eg, *Newtons of Wembley Ltd v Williams* [1965] 1 QB 560—this good faith purchase operated under sections 2 and 9 of the Factors Act 1889; see now, section 62(1) of the Sale of Goods Act 1979.) Other relevant sections include sections 23 (sale under a voidable title), 24 (sale by a seller in possession) and 25(1) (sale by a buyer in possession) of the 1979 Act.

(c) Right to Rescind

At the outset of this section, it should be noted that one must take great care in the use of terminology when seeking to compare the German and English law on the consequences of a suitable mistake. The English use of the term 'rescission' (in both case law and statute) is notorious for the variety of different situations in which it has been utilised. (See for instance, Bowen LJ in *Mersey Steel & Iron Co v Naylor Benzon & Co* (1882) 9 QBD 648, at 671 and the use of the term 'rescission' throughout the Misrepresentation Act 1967 without any attempt to define it. For further details see Treitel, *The Law of Contract*, pp 370–1.)

The second key preliminary point to remember is the availability under English law of different remedies at law and in equity. (See the brief discussion in section 3(a), p 277). Thus, great care must be taken to identify the ground on which a mistake claim is based.

To return to German law. If the declaration of will of one party suffers from a defect and this defect is relevant according to §§ 119, 120 or 123 BGB, then the declaration may be annulled and as a consequence the contract is void *ab initio* or *ex tunc*: § 142 I BGB. (The same basic result applies under the English system at law relating to fundamental mistakes. See the *Associated Japanese Bank* case, cited above, at 268. Nevertheless, the common law would treat the contract as having no legal effect whatever: 'it is axiomatic that there is no room for rescission of a contract which is void' (*The Great Peace*, above, at [96]). A key consequence of this is that no property in goods passes under a void contract.) This concerns declaration mistakes (§ 119 I BGB), mistakes as to quality (under § 119 II BGB), mistakes in the transfer of the declaration (§ 120 BGB), fraud and illegitimate coercion (§ 123 BGB). In accordance with the starting point of Savigny's theory, it is the declaration of will itself which may be annulled and it is merely an inevitable consequence that the contract becomes void retroactively.

The exercise of the right of rescission, itself a new declaration of will, is regulated by § 143 BGB. This provision differentiates as to whether the legal transaction was unilateral or not, so in the case of contract the declaration must be directed to the other contracting party, § 143 II BGB. In other words, the other party must be notified within the meaning of § 130 BGB (as to which see chapter 2). The declaration does not need expressly to use the term 'rescission' or '*Anfechtung*', but the reason for avoiding the contract must be apparent from it. This means that the mistaken party must make it clear that he wishes to set the contract aside *for mistake*. The reason for this requirement is that the other party should be put into a position to be able to assess whether the claim to exercise the right of rescission complies with the legal requirements. This will only possible if he knows why the contract is being set aside. This condition can, on occasion, prove to be a pitfall—see eg, BGHZ 91, 324, case no 43—but overall it has not been applied in a formalistic manner by the courts.

If the contract is not rescinded at all, or not rescinded in time, or the contract was affirmed (§ 144 BGB), then the contract remains valid. The mere voidability of the contract (instead of invalidity) serves not only the interest of commercial certainty. It also leaves the party acting under mistake the choice whether after all to accept the contract as objectively construed and disregard the mistake. Such affirmation is also possible in English law, as may be the rectification of the agreement to embody what the parties had actually intended to agree (see eg, *Thomas Witter Ltd v TBP Industries Ltd*, above).

Rescission, if exercised, operates in a negative way: it pre-empts consent but it does not create new agreement. The only exception occurs where the other party agrees to the terms of the subjectively intended declaration—in this case it is said that it would be contrary to good faith (§ 242 BGB) to allow the mistaken party to escape the contract as it was in fact intended by him. The agreement is then upheld as it was subjectively intended. (See eg, Bork, *Allgemeiner Teil*, Rn. 954.)

This technique, contract voidable for mistake (*anfechtbar*), is a corollary of the basic approach the German legal system adopts towards *interpretation* (explained in chapter 3). Declaration and will can only differ from each other if the significance of the declaration is not determined subjectively. Under § 157 BGB contracts are to be interpreted objectively. A declaration of intention that is part of a contract is construed in the way a reasonable addressee of that declaration would understand it in the circumstances. This is coined as the doctrine of (the prevalence of) the 'objective horizon' of the recipient of the declaration (*Empfängerhorizont*). Since the contract is merely voidable and not void, the objective meaning of the declaration of will prevails. An exception to this rule is made when the parties share the misconception as to the objective meaning of a term. This principle of *falsa demonstration non nocet* was illustrated in the section on interpretation in chapter 3 (p 135) with the *Shark-meat* case, RGZ 99, 147, case no 44 (both parties misunderstood the term 'Harkjöringssköd' in the same way, so the shared subjective meaning prevailed). Hence, in German law the first step in assessing consent is to clarify the objective meaning of a declaration of will. Once that has been determined and offer and acceptance actually match each other, objective agreement is established and a contract is concluded on those terms. In a second step, the subjective intentions (even if they have remained concealed) may become relevant according to mistake rules (if one party invokes them). (In English law, this is the situation where rectification of the agreement in equity is commonly sought, so as to represent the subjectively shared view.) However, the range of mistakes which are legally relevant is limited. In particular, as we have seen, an erroneous motive for entering into the contract does not as a general rule make the contract voidable. In the absence of wrongful conduct on the part of one of the parties, only a defective act of declaration will entitle the party operating under mistake to rescind the contract.

Rescission, as was already intimated, comes at a price. If the contract is rescinded the other party is entitled to *damages based on the reliance interest* under § 122 BGB (as explained in chapter 2, p 94), independently of fault. This in itself is remarkable as it deviates from the fundamental fault principle of German law. It goes to show that, besides the objective principle of interpretation, German contract law takes account of the interest of commercial convenience and is not solely concerned with protecting subjective intention. The right to damages is founded on the idea that one is responsible for the act of declaring a legally relevant intention. English law knows no such basic principle, although in such situations its more limited doctrine of mistake may lead to the party being held to the contract (and liable to pay damages for its breach). (Note however that there may be restitutionary consequences of such a void contract in English law: see eg, the discussion in Treitel of *Cooper v Phibbs* (1867) LR 2 HL 149, where one party had to pay the other for improvements made to the relevant land and to pay a reasonable rent for other land, even where the contract (it seems) was held to be void at law for mistake.) The liability of the mistaken promisor does not arise where the mistake or the defect of the declaration of will is imputable to the other party, as in the case of fraud or coercion, § 123 BGB. Again, this is sensible for if the other party is responsible for the defect in the contracting process it does not seem appropriate to protect his reliance on the conclusion of a valid contract.

A typical head of damage that may be claimed according to § 122 I BGB is having foregone another opportunity to sell or buy goods. If this alternative contract was not entered into because the other party relied on the validity of the rescinded contract, the other party may claim the lost profit under the alternative, hypothetical deal. This right is limited in only two ways. The amount of damages must not exceed the expectation interest (the other party should not be put in a better position than if the contract had been valid); and according to § 122 II BGB, the right is excluded where the other party knew of the reason for rescission or negligently did not know of it. Since it is no business each of the contracting parties to concern themselves with the innermost intentions of the other, the standard is relatively high. It must have been obvious that there was something wrong. Because of these limitations, a claim on the basis of *culpa in contrahendo* principles is sometimes attractive but it requires that the party rescinding the contract was at fault when making the mistake. For the sake of completeness, it should be mentioned that the right under § 122 BGB also arises in the case of § 118 BGB. This concerns the case where someone merely pretended to make a declaration of will and expected the other party to notice that the declaration was not intended seriously. Consistently with the will theory, such a declaration is void (not voidable); yet the right to damages under § 122 BGB still arises.

The right to rescind is subject to time limits, which vary according to the type of defect. If an error in expression is at stake (and similar defects), §§ 119–120 BGB, rescission must take place without undue delay ('*ohne schuldhaftes Zögern*') once the party becomes aware of the error, § 121 BGB. (See, for an illustration, BAG NZA 2004, 597, case no 84; BGH NJW 1995, 190, case no 86.) This permits, for instance, the taking of advice in appropriate cases. As in the case of the consumer legislation, § 355 I 2 BGB, the punctual dispatch of the notice of rescission suffices, § 121 I 2 BGB. The right of rescission is extinguished ten years after the declaration, § 122 II BGB. In the case of § 123 BGB (fraud and coercion), the innocent party is allowed one year to consider rescission of the contract: in the case of fraud, one year after its discovery. And in the case of threats, the period commences once the danger from the threats subsides, see § 124 BGB. Ten years is also the maximum period here, § 124 III BGB. The generous time limit is due to the wrongful conduct of the other party, which is lacking in the case of § 121 BGB.

One final remark must be made as to the consequences of rescission. If a contract has been entered into by mistake that is relevant according to § 119 BGB, the contracting party whose declaration of intention was defective may rescind the legal transaction with retrospective effect (§ 142 I BGB). It will also be recalled that rescission of the contract of obligation does not induce the invalidity of the transaction of transfer that has been carried out in fulfilment of the contract of obligation. (See chapter 1, section 5(c).) In situations like these, the parties are bound to return the benefits received because the performance was made without any legal ground (§ 812 I 1 Alt. 1 BGB, ie the so-called *Leistungskondiktion*). However, an innocent party is only obliged to restore the benefits retained: the obligation to return or to make good the value is excluded where the recipient is no longer enriched (§ 818 III BGB). It is different only if the recipient knew of the absence of a legal ground at the time of receipt, or if he subsequently became aware of it (§ 819 I BGB). In the present context however only the basic principle of restoration of benefits according to the rules governing unjust enrichment needs mentioning. The difficult problems which arise in synallagmatic contracts (*gegenseitiger Vertrag*), where the performances of the two parties are to be exchanged for each other, cannot be dealt with here. (See for details, Larenz and Canaris, *Schuldrecht Besonderer Teil II/2*, p 145 *et seq* and p 321 *et seq*; and for an overview, Beatson and Schrage (eds), *Unjustified Enrichment* (2003), p 179 *et seq* and 343 *et seq.*) Suffice it merely to say that certain adjustments may become necessary if one of the parties is no longer in a position to return a benefit received from the other party. The situation may be compared with the English leading case of *Erlanger v New Sombrero Phosphate Co* (1878) 3 App Cas 1218 where equity could order an account of profits and make necessary allowances for deterioration of property transferred under the contract. It should also be noted that the same basic rules of restitution apply if a contract has been induced by fraud (§ 123 BGB), or dissent, ie where the parties believe to have made a valid contract, but in reality there had been no true meeting of the minds (§ 155 BGB).

We are now in a position to understand another major restriction on the right of rescission for mistake that must be mentioned here. It does not concern the time period in which it may be exercised but the period of time for which rescission may take effect. The paradigmatic case of the BGB rules is that of a contract of obligation consisting of obligations that arise only once. In such a case it may be justified to treat the contract as void *retroactively* ('*ex tunc*') after rescission has been declared. The effect of this is that, as we have seen, the performance of the contract may be reclaimed under principles of unjust enrichment (§ 812 BGB). This model of restitution leads to a reversal of all acts committed in pursuance of the avoided contract. This approach would cause considerable difficulties if it were also to be applied in relation to contracts that give rise to what Flume calls 'status relationships' (*Rechtsgeschäft*, above, p. 426) and also to some long-term contracts. For here the reversal of the execution of the contract will be exceedingly difficult. The status contract forms the basis for innumerable other decisions and actions taken in reliance on the contract. Despite the two mechanisms mentioned above (abstraction and good faith acquisition of property), third parties could not be adequately protected, and more generally commercial certainty would be seriously undermined if such contracts could be avoided retroactively. The legislator has expressly dealt with this issue only in relation to marriage (§§ 1313–14 BGB: it is dissolved *ex nunc* only). It is however common practice today that the founding acts as well as subsequent membership of financial corporations (*Kapitalgesllschaften*)—like the *Aktiengesellschaft (AG)* and *Gesellschaft mit beschränkter Haftung (GmbH)*—cannot be rescinded on mistake grounds once they have been listed in the commercial register (*Handelsregister*). (See eg, Larenz and Wolf, *Allgemeiner Teil*, § 36 Rn. 100 *et seq* with references.) Likewise, the contract founding the basis of partnerships (*Personengesellschaften*) cannot be rescinded *ex tunc* once the company has commenced trade. A right to terminate the partnership *ex nunc* may however be available. Finally, the right to rescind a contract of labour (for details, see chapter 3, p 153) retroactively ceases once and so long as the contract is performed by the employee. The contract may, in such circumstances, be avoided for mistake only with effects for the future.

(d) Declaration Mistakes

(i) 'Expression' and 'Meaning' Mistake

According to § 119 I BGB, the right to declare void one's declaration of will arises when one is in error as to its content or did not intend to make such a declaration at all. These are commonly explained as two different categories of mistake: *Erklärungsirrtum* or 'expression mistake' and *Inhaltsirrtum* or 'meaning mistake'. In both cases the (unilateral) error is relevant. Distinguishing between the two is not essential though it helps accurately describe the instances of declaration mistake. In the former instance, *Erklärungsirrtum,* the party does not know what he is declaring, ie, he is using the wrong word by mistake and without noticing it; in the latter instance, *Inhaltsirrtum,* the party knows what he is declaring but is mistaken as to the meaning of the word used. Typical examples of expression mistakes are typographical errors that affect the meaning of what has been said. For instance, if in the offer machine 'ABC' was ordered where in fact the customer intended to say 'ACB' he will be entitled to rescind the contract, although of course at the price of compensating the supplier for his reliance loss. Likewise, if A intends to contract with Smith but sends the offer to the wrong Smith he may rescind the contract if the confusion as to the identity of the person has been cleared up.

A useful illustration of meaning mistake is provided by LG Hanau NJW 1979, 721, case no 85. Here, a teacher ordered toilet paper on behalf of the school. She was under the impression that the expression 'Gros' signified double packs whereas the objective meaning of this term is the amount of '12 x 12' (ie, a 'gross' in English). Her order of '25 Gros' thus objectively meant 3600 packs of toilet paper instead of 50. The action of the supplier for the price of 3600 packs of toilet paper failed because the teacher was allowed to declare her declaration of will to be void for meaning mistake. (As a result, she would have been strictly liable under § 122 BGB in damages but the decision does not suggest that any such (reliance) damages were sought. Whether the error was to be blamed on the teacher is entirely irrelevant for the right to rescind the contract in German law; but it may found liability of the mistaken party over and above § 122 BGB under *culpa in contrahendo* principles.)

This case can usefully be compared with the result of the English case of *Centrovincial Estates plc v Merchant Investors Assurance Co Ltd* [1983] Com LR 158, where an offer assessed the current market rental value of the premises as £65,000, but this was later claimed to have been included in error in place of the intended figure of £126,000. Slade LJ explained (*obiter*), that 'it is contrary to the well established principles of contract law to suggest that the offeror under a bilateral contract can withdraw an unambiguous offer, after it has been accepted in the manner contemplated by the offer, merely because he has made a mistake which the offeree neither knew nor could reasonably have known at the time when he accepted it.' Rectification may be available in such circumstances, but *only* where it would give the document the meaning that *both* parties had originally understood or where the other party knew that that rectified meaning was what the first party had really meant (see *Thomas Bates & Sons Ltd v Wyndham's (Lingerie) Ltd* [1981] 1 WLR 505).

Another example is provided by BGH NJW 1995, 190, case no 86. In this case, the contracting party signed a contract of guarantee, but since she did not understand

German, she did not actually know what the document contained. As it turned out the declaration of guarantee as signed deviated considerably from what the intended surety thought it would mean and that the surety would not have signed the document had she known the real meaning. The Court held that this constituted a 'meaning mistake', § 119 I first alternative BGB. However, it should be noted that as the court also indicated, signing a document without having a definite conception of its content does not entitle the signatory to rescission for mistake. (See, for further discussion, Medicus, *Allgemeiner Teil*, Rn. 752 *et seq.*)

On this fact scenario, the English use of the doctrine '*scriptum predictum non est factum suum*' (or *non est factum*, as it is usually abbreviated) provides perhaps the closest comparator. In English law however this defence is construed very narrowly due to the fear that much 'confusion and uncertainty would result in the field of contract and elsewhere if a man where permitted to try to disown his signature simply by asserting that he did not understand that which he signed' (*per* Donovan LJ in *Muskham Finance Ltd v Howard* [1963] 1 QB 904, at 914). Thus, the party relying on the defence must show that there is a 'radical', 'fundamental', 'essential' or 'serious' difference between the document signed and what they had intended. (*Saunders v Anglia Building Society* [1971] AC 1004.) This difference will be assessed in the light of the purpose to be achieved by the transaction. Thus, in the *Saunders* case, what had been intended as a gift of a house to the owner's nephew to allow him to use it as security to raise money was in fact turned into a sale of the house to the nephew's friend on the owner's signature of the document. While no money was in fact paid to the nephew, it was conceivable that this was the way that the nephew intended to raise the funds, so the House of Lords refused to find the transaction to be of a fundamentally different nature from the document that the owner had believed she was signing. A further requirement is that the signatory must show that reasonable care was exercised in signing the document. Unsurprisingly, few cases have succeeded on *non est factum* grounds. (See *Foster v Mackinnon* (1869) LR 4 CP 704 and *Lewis v Clay* (1898) 67 LJQB 224: for a more recent judicial discussion of the area, see *Lloyds Bank Plc v Waterhouse* [1993] 2 FLR 97.)

(ii) Transmission Mistake

Paragraph 120 BGB treats mistakes in the transmission of a declaration in the same way as § 119 I BGB. Once again the person declaring does not know what he is declaring. This type of mistake occurs, for instance, where the party transmits his declaration through a messenger who alters the declaration. The provision does not apply however where the declaration was deliberately falsified or where it did not exist in the first place. In these cases the declaration of will is not imputed to the alleged maker. Likewise, this provision does not apply in those cases where the messenger was appointed by the addressee of the declaration.

(iii) Causality

A prerequisite for the right of rescission under § 119 I BGB is that the mistake has been the cause for the conclusion of the contract (see eg, BGH NJW 1995, 190, case no 86). It is not sufficient however to claim that the party would not have entered into the contract had he been aware of the mistake. In addition, it must be shown that in the circumstances it would have been reasonable not to enter into the contract. This caveat clearly serves the need to increase certainty in the law and to ensure that only objectively significant mistakes affect the validity of consent. Trivial misconceptions that are objectively irrelevant should thus not provide a pretext for backing out of an agreement. In this way, German courts are further empowered to limit the range of relevant mistakes by having recourse to causative reasoning.

Generally speaking, where the mistake concerns the subject matter of the contract or the identity of the contracting person, the mistake will be regarded as (reasonably) relevant for the decision to enter into the contract. The criteria in English law relating to mutual and unilateral mistakes include one of inducing entry into the contract (see the discussion in section 3(a), above). It is worth noting here that a similar requirement exists in the law on misrepresentations; there must have been *reliance* on the misrepresentation. (See eg, *Pan Atlantic Insurance Co Ltd v Pine Top Insurance Co Ltd* [1995] 1 AC 501, and generally, Cartwright, *Misrepresentation* (2002).)

Even though the typical cases of declaration mistakes do not pose any particular problems, it cannot be denied that there are hard cases in which the solution is more controversial. These are briefly explored in what follows.

(iv) Intention to Create Legal Relations?

Much ink has been spilt on the issue of whether the acts of a person which appear to be declarations of will, but are not intended as such, can be assimilated to the category of declaration mistakes. One aspect of this problem is dealt with by the already mentioned § 118 BGB. Where the person expected that the declaration would be recognised as not intended, the declaration is void. The situation where a person does not know that his acts are understood as signifying a declaration of intention has not been expressly regulated. The crucial question here is not whether there is a relevant mistake, but rather whether there is consent in the first place, ie whether this case should be likened to § 118 BGB (contract void) or § 119 BGB (contract voidable). The classic example is that of the wine auction in the city of Trier, located in the Mosel vineyard area. If a person raises his hand to greet a friend who is also attending the auction and this gesture appears to contain a declaration of intention, namely to buy at the price announced, is a contract concluded? In order to answer this question, it is useful to recall the threefold nature of declarations of will.

On a first level, each declaration of this kind consists of the intention to act as such (*Handlungswille*). It is absent when the person is unconscious or in (some) cases of *vis absoluta*, eg, where his hand is literally forced to sign a document. In such a case, the position of German law is clear: the declaration cannot be imputed.

On a second level, a declaration of will presupposes the intention to act in a legally relevant sense (*Erklärungsbewußtsein*). In other words, the person must be conscious of the fact that he is making a declaration which will have legal consequences, ie an intention to create legal relations.

On a third level, the declaration is directed at specific legal consequences (*Geschäftswille*), eg, to buy a specific object from a specific person at a specific price.

Paragraph 119 BGB is said to cover mistakes on the third level only, ie the person making the declaration errs as to the specific legal consequences of his declaration while knowing that the declaration has legal relevance. Yet, from the perspective of a third party, the two cases appear the same. It thus seems plausible that in BGHZ 91, 324, case no 43 (discussed in chapter 3, section 3(a), p 134), the Court—in the interest of commercial certainty and in order to leave the mistaken party the choice as to whether to avoid the contract—applied § 119 I BGB by analogy. (For a different view see, Singer, *Selbstbestimmung und Verkehrsschutz im Recht der Willenserklärungen* (1995), p 128, who argues that in the absence of subjective intention the declaration ought not to found consent. Yet, extra-contractual liability may be established for the reliance interest.)

In this case, a bank issued a statement meant to be of merely informal character and assuming that it had *already* given a guarantee. In fact it had not, and the statement thus appeared to an objective bystander as the giving of a guarantee. The court imputed the declaration of intention but granted the bank in principle a right of rescission under § 119 I BGB. On the somewhat ambiguous facts of the case, the bank was ultimately denied the benefit of exercising this right of rescission, because the court found that the rescission was not declared on time (§ 121 BGB).

Somewhat confusingly, the Court did not apply the same (objective) standard for imputing a declaration of intention as that of § 119 I BGB. If a person errs as to the specific legal consequences (declaration mistake), the declaration of will is imputed to him whether or not the mistake was excusable. The Court, following the writings of Larenz and others, held that if a person was not aware that his acts had legal significance, the declaration could be imputed to that person only if the error was inexcusable. (See, for a criticism of this position, Stephan Lorenz, *Der Schutz vor dem unerwünschten Vertrag* (1997), p 220 *et seq.*)

The difference between the two approaches is not dramatic. If consent is said not to be present, then liability for the reliance interest arises under *culpa in contrahendo* rules, while if consent is affirmed the contract may be rescinded with the consequence of liability for the reliance loss (this time, however, irrespective of fault: § 122 BGB). The objective approach seems in the end more convincing as it promotes commercial certainty (one need just think of the time limits for rescission) and leaves the mistaken party the choice as to whether to treat the contract as valid.

It has been suggested (by Beale, Hartkamp, Kötz and Tallon, *Cases Materials and Text on Contract Law—Ius Commune Casebooks for the Common Law of Europe* (2002), p 354) that English law would deal with the Trier wine auction scenario by holding the person to the contract apparently concluded, so long as the auctioneer reasonably believed him to be bidding for the wine. The above authors see this as an application of the objective principle (as discussed above, in chapter 2 and chapter 3, p 133). It should be noted however that an absence of an intention to create legal relations might prevent a contract coming into being in such circumstances. This will depend on the context in which the apparent agreement is reached (see Treitel, *The Law of Contract*, pp 169–70 and the cases there discussed).

(v) 'Calculation Error'

We have already discussed the so-called 'calculation error' which is said by the critics of the BGB to illustrate the drawbacks of § 119 BGB. A relevant declaration mistake is present where the price of the offer is wrongly expressed, but no rescission is possible under § 119 I BGB where the error occurred in the preparatory phase preceding the conclusion of the contract. The rationale of this distinction, it will be recalled, is that in the former case the party does not know what he is declaring and therefore may withdraw the declaration, while in the latter case the error merely affects the motivation for entering into the contract.

Where the 'calculation error' does not occur in relation to the declaration of will but precedes it, the error is not relevant under § 119 I BGB. However, other rules may be applied to aid the mistaken party. (For a useful overview see, Medicus, *Allgemeiner Teil*, Rn. 757 *et seq.*) One exception is that an error in the motivation is relevant where it is due either to a wrongful act of the other party (see section 4 on fraud and misrepresentation, p 302) or where the other party shares the error. In the latter case, interpretation may yield a satisfactory solution if the misunderstanding is shared (*falsa demonstratio non nocet*: 'false description does not vitiate if the thing is sufficiently described'; cf *Münchener Kommentar*- Kramer § 119 BGB, Rn. 49). But this approach is only available where the error concerns the declaration itself. Where this is not the case, it is still possible that the common error may affect the foundation for the transaction (as to which see below, chapter 7).

The error however must then concern an issue which according to the intention of both parties was essential for concluding the contract (which formulation shows an interesting similarity to that used in English law for assessing the fundamentality of a common mistake: see the discussion in section 3(a), p 280). It is not sufficient simply to make the basis of the calculation known to the other party. For as a general rule it is no concern of the customer to agree to, or even to follow the motivation of the supplier for concluding the contract. Furthermore, it would not be justified to increase the protection of the 'talkative' party (as Professor Medicus has put it, *Allgemeiner Teil*, Rn. 758; see also, Flume, *Rechtsgeschäft*, § 25). Instead of relying on such incidental circumstances, the decisive element ought to be whether the basis of the calculation is part of a shared assumption of risk of the parties. However, if one party's claim reveals a decision-making process that is in open contradiction to the declaration of will, then the contract may not be concluded because the declaration of will itself is inconsistent and thus null and void. The approach of German law is thus a flexible one and depends to a large extent on the facts of the individual case.

An illustration is provided by BGH NJW 2002, 2312, case no 87, which reveals the typical approach adopted by the German courts in relation to mistakes in the 'calculation' of the contract price. In that case the plaintiff was mistaken as to the tax which would have to be paid for the transaction, believing that the price agreed was the price without tax ('netto') while objectively the price agreed included tax ('brutto'). The Court stated that the unilateral error in his motivation was irrelevant and that, since the misconception was not shared by the other party, there was no room to apply the rules of completive interpretation or the doctrine of the foundation of the transaction (for which see chapter 7, below).

(vi) Mistakes of Law

Mistakes of law are not easily subsumed under § 119 I BGB and raise special difficulties. German law has not been alone in facing such problems. For in English law, as well, mistakes of law have caused difficulties, both in distinguishing between what counts as 'fact' and what as 'law', but also as to whether such mistakes should be a ground for avoiding a contract at all.

The question is whether the party erred as to the meaning of the words used (*Inhaltsirrtum*). Meaning refers here to the legal consequences the law attaches to certain human conduct. The prevailing opinion differentiates between mistakes of law directed at the immediate consequences and those mistakes that relate to auxiliary or more distant 'reflex' consequences. Needless to say, this distinction leaves ample room for the employment of policy considerations; and there is a clear tendency on the part of the courts to limit the relevance of the mistake of law in the interest of commercial certainty.

Mistakes as to the type of the agreement concluded, eg, confusing donation with loan, are relevant because they concern the very nature of the promise undertaken (eg, RGZ 89, 33). They are treated in the same way as an error concerning the non-legal meaning of a word. Beyond that, it is difficult to state the position of the courts with any measure of certainty.

There is however consensus as to the other extreme, namely as far as irrelevant errors. Where a party did not have a positive preconception of the legal consequences he is not entitled to rescind. Furthermore, even if he did have a misconception of the legal consequences, it is still questionable whether this would have been causal according to the reasonableness test. A reasonable person would be expected to enter a contract on those terms which the law imposes as adequate. For instance, a seller who is of the opinion that he does not need to cure defects of sold goods ought not to be allowed to invoke § 119 I BGB. (For example, BGH NJW 2002, 3100, 3103; OLG Karlsruhe NJW 1989, 907. See, for a detailed discussion of this group of cases, Stephan Lorenz, *Der Schutz vor dem unerwünschten Vertrag*, p 268 *et seq*.)

The English position concerning mistakes of law is, nowadays, perhaps more satisfactory than say ten years ago, though the precise parameters of the subject are still being worked out following the decision of the House of Lords in *Kleinwort Benson Ltd v Lincoln City Council* [1999] 2 AC 349. Traditionally, mistakes of law did not affect the validity of a contract, whether the claim was brought at law or in equity (see *British Homophone Ltd v Kunz & Crystallate Gramophone Record Manufacturing Co Ltd* [1935] All ER Rep 627, at 633; (1932) 152 LT 589, at 593 and *Midland Great Western Railway of Ireland v Johnson* (1858) 6 HLC 798, at 810–11; 10 ER 1509), although the wisdom of making this distinction (which also exists in the law on misrepresentation) has been questioned. (See particularly, *Woolwich Equitable Building Society v Inland Revenue Commissioners (No 2)* [1993] AC 70, at 154 and 199.) The *Kleinwort Benson v Lincoln CC* case decided that there was a right to recover money paid under a mistake of law. The mistake there was that the contract was thought to be valid, but had in fact been entered into by the local authority beyond its statutory powers (and was thus void). Most commentators (eg, Beatson, *Anson's Law of Contract*, p 311; Treitel, *The Law of Contract*, p 314) seem to take the view that this will lead to the extension of the principle into general contract law. *Dicta* in other cases however (eg, in *S v S* [2002] NLJ 398) suggest that *Kleinwort Benson* was 'specific to the law of restitution and was not intended to apply across the board to every branch of law.'

(vii) Electronic Declarations of Will

Modern means of communication have created new challenges for the law of mistake. (For an overview, Köhler, AcP 182 (1982), 126.) One of the difficulties concerns the question whether technical mistakes in entering data into computer processes which lead to computer-generated declarations of will can be treated as declaration mistakes within the meaning of § 119 I BGB. The case resembles the problems raised by the calculation error. The question is where the preparatory phase ends and where the conclusion of the contract commences. Mistakes will be relevant only if they affect the declaration of will itself.

Some courts have come down in favour of a generous attitude towards allowing rescission and have held that if the technical mistake is merely perpetuated by the machine, then the mistake is relevant even if strictly speaking it occurred in the preparation of the declaration. The mistake is relevant if the *last* human act of the process of producing the declaration of will has been affected by a (technical) mistake as envisaged by § 119 I first alternative BGB ('expression mistake'). In this sense: OLG Hamm NJW 1993, 2321, case no 88; eg, Larenz and Wolf, *Allgemeiner Teil*, § 36 Rn. 19; Medicus, *Allgemeiner Teil*, Rn. 256, agree.)

Others object that this approach would privilege the user of computer-generated declarations by unduly extending the meaning of 'declaration of will' (eg, Stephan Lorenz, *Der Schutz vor dem unerwünschten Vertrag*, p 276 *et seq*). On this view, rescission should be limited to those cases where the user of the computer actually checked the final outcome of the computing process and actually had a false conception of its significance (compare the situation concerning the signing of a legal document, discussed above); only this type of error would then constitute a meaning mistake, whereas any other error during the preparation of the declaration of will ought to be treated in the same way as any other 'calculation mistake' (also discussed above).

(e) Mistake as to the Quality of the Subject-matter or the Person

According to § 119 II BGB, an error as to the characteristics of a person or thing is a ground for rescission where the error relates to characteristics which are regarded in business as essential (again showing a strong similarity to the criteria for testing for a fundamental mistake in English law: see the discussion in section 3(a), p 280). This provision, which is a faint echo of the category of *error in substantia* of Roman law (though note that the modern emanation is much wider than the Roman rule: see Zimmermann, *The Law of Obligations* (1990), pp 592–5, 616) has been repeatedly criticised. Perhaps the first Commission on the BGB was right when it concluded that such a provision, which was nevertheless eventually introduced by the second Commission, is not needed because the innocent party is sufficiently protected by other devices, mainly liability for breach of contract. (*Motive*, vol 1, p 199.) In any event, the categorisation and delimitation of this error as to quality ('*Eigenschaftsirrtum*') has remained controversial. The prevailing view is that this provision contains an exception to the rule that an error in motive is immaterial.

The problematic aspect of § 119 II BGB is that assumptions as to quality may remain hidden to the other party and thus may entitle a party to a contract to back out of an agreement, even if the motive in question has not become/been agreed on as a term of contract. In this context, it is important that § 119 II BGB restricts the right to rescind to qualities which are *objectively* essential. This includes all factual or legal relationships of a person or thing that are of such nature and duration that they influence the usability and the value (BGHZ 34, 32, 41). Such qualities may also give rise to liability for breach of contract. As a result, the range of unilateral mistakes as to the quality will overlap considerably with the remedies for breach of contract. The group of cases falling under § 119 II BGB which could not also be analysed on the basis of a different concept (breach/foundation of the transaction) is small and concerns purely unilateral motives. However, a right to rescind for such mistakes, in the absence of factors that are imputable to the other party (knowledge of the error, misrepresentation etc), seems questionable. The objective assessment of the relevance of the quality for business leaves ample room for the courts to restrict the provision and, since the courts have taken this opportunity, the provision has not caused major distortions in German law. Three restrictions must be discussed here.

The first qualification that was introduced at an early stage is that the *price* itself of a thing does not constitute a quality within the meaning of § 119 II BGB (BGHZ 16, 54, 57). Only those qualities which determine the (market) value of an object are relevant. The rationale of this caveat is evident. It is the sole responsibility of each party to the contract to decide whether the price is adequate. In other words, each party assumes the risk that its evaluation of the price is correct. Otherwise, any party could back out of a 'bad bargain' by claiming that he misjudged the market price. This would undermine the doctrine of *pacta sunt servanda*, damage commercial certainty and distort the price-building mechanisms of the market.

The second restriction of the scope of application is of equal importance and concerns the (partial) exclusion of § 119 II BGB by remedies in respect of breach of contract. Qualities which are essential in business will often also determine the expectation interest. Thus, if a thing sold does not function properly this may disappoint the buyer in two ways. First, he may be mistaken as to the motive for entering into the contract, § 119 II BGB; the usability of the thing is certainly an essential quality. Secondly, he may under the terms of the contract be entitled to expect that the thing worked properly. The latter would found liability for breach of contract. This raises the question: which set of rules is applicable?

The legal consequences vary significantly. It is irrelevant for § 119 II BGB whether the error was self-induced. § 442 I 2 BGB, by contrast, excludes the remedies of the buyer if he was grossly negligent in failing to detect the defect. The right of the seller to cure the defect before the buyer may terminate the contract (§ 439 BGB, see chapter 9, below) is unknown under mistake rules. The period of limitation may also be different: it is a maximum of ten years under § 121 II BGB, but only two years under § 438 I Nr. 3 BGB. Furthermore, in the case of rescission under § 119 II BGB, the contract is void retroactively (*ex tunc*) and the performance is reversed under the rules of unjust enrichment (§ 812 BGB). The buyer's remedies against the seller for breach of contract are more differentiated and arguably also more appropriate than the rules on rescission for mistake. The contract can be terminated only for a considerable defect (§ 323 V 2 BGB); and termination takes effect only for the future (*ex nunc*). One can easily see here that § 119 II BGB could also create inconsistencies with the regime of remedies for breach of contract and would give rise to considerable difficulties.

Since § 119 II BGB is regarded with scepticism, it comes as little surprise to note that the courts have excluded its application where the quality in question also entails liability for the seller's breach of contract. (See, for instance, BGH NJW 1988, 2597, case no 89).

There is no reason for restricting this approach to contracts of sale. The exclusion of § 119 II BGB is also sensible in contracts for work and services, or leases, the latter however being controversial. (See eg, *Palandt*-Heinrichs § 119 Rn. 28, disapproving of the views of Larenz and Wolf, *Allgemeiner Teil*, § 36 Rn. 50.) Note however that the right of the seller to rescind the contract is only excluded by the rules applicable in relation to defects of the object sold (§ 437 BGB) if this would prejudice the interests of the buyer. (BGH NJW 1988, 2597, case no 89.) In this case, the seller was mistaken in relation to the identity of the painter of the sold painting. He was allowed to rescind the contract because of his mistake as to the quality of the painting (§ 119 II BGB).

This fact scenario was discussed by Lord Atkin in *Bell v Lever Brothers Ltd* (cited above at 224) and was treated under the law on misrepresentation in *Leaf v International Galleries* [1950] 2 KB 86. While there Lord Atkin suggested that a common mistake of both parties that the painting was an old master (rather than the modern copy it turned out to be) would not render the contract void (in the absence of a representation or warranty), Treitel has taken a different view (*The Law of Contract*, p 293). Thus, the latter argues that the subject-matter should not be seen simply as 'a picture', so that the quality of the thing is not fundamentally mistaken by the parties, but rather as (say) 'a Rembrandt'. This would be a sufficiently *identifying* quality to render the mistake fundamental, which test then also applies to a mistake as to the subject-matter made by only one party, so long as such a mistake induces entry into the contract and is operative. Thus, English law would ask further questions (if presented with a case such as no 89), concerning the facts surrounding the purchase of the painting: eg, was the seller's mistake known to, or negligently induced by the other party? It is this extra inquiry that illustrates the narrowness of the English approach, although this is mitigated if misrepresentations are involved.

Thirdly, the criterion of *business relevance* found in § 119 II BGB helps to ensure that the provision does not distort the contractual allocation of risk. Thus, although financial difficulties are in principle possible characteristic of a person, a surety is not allowed to invoke an error as to the creditworthiness of the principal debtor, for it is the very risk he is assuming when entering into a contract of guarantee. One can conclude that a unilateral mistaken assumption as to quality does not, without important further conditions being met, entitle a party to a contract to back out of the agreement—a general statement that could also be made of English law. (The difference is that those conditions are generally even more restricted in the English than German system.) Identifying those further conditions however is a task which § 119 II BGB does more to obscures than to clarify.

For a recent discussion of the English position on fundamental mistakes as to the identity of the other contracting party one must consult the decision of the House of Lords in *Shogun Finance Ltd v Hudson* [2004] 1 AC 919. There, by a bare 3 to 2 majority, their Lordships declined to overturn the case of *Cundy v Lindsay* ((1878) 3 App Cas 459), so that the fraudster who had entered into a car hire-purchase agreement by using an unlawfully procured driving licence (in another's name) to establish his (false) identity never became a debtor under section 27 of the Hire Purchase Act 1964.

Thus, property did not pass to the defendant and the car finance company could assert its ownership of the vehicle. It was important to establish that the hire-purchase agreement was vitiated by a fundamental mistake, rather than by fraud alone, as the consequence of the former is to render the contract void (while the latter renders it only voidable).

For comparative purposes, a number of points should be noted about this case.

First, the key issue here (as in *Ingram v Little* [1961] 1 QB 31) was the checks of the creditworthiness of the buyer, albeit that the assessment of that status was made only as against the false name given, rather than the fraudster's true details. These checks were undertaken by the claimant finance company after the car dealer had faxed through a copy of the forged driving licence and the draft agreement (including the forged signature). In the *King's Norton Metal Co Ltd* case ((1897) 14 TLR 98), in the absence of any other mistake, such a mis-assessment of creditworthiness did not suffice to render the contract void: there the fraudulent recipient had actually been the sole proprietor of 'Hallam & Co' with whom the plaintiffs had contracted and sent goods on credit. This illustrates the difficulty of distinguishing between those 'attributes' that *identify* a contracting party and those that do not (see Treitel, *The Law of Contract*, pp 301–2).

Secondly, the consequences of section 27 of the Hire Purchase Act 1964 operate to provide a defence for the subsequent bona fide private purchaser of a motor vehicle subject to a hire purchase agreement, provided that that purchaser had no notice of the hire purchase agreement. In *Shogun Finance Ltd v Hudson*, Lord Millett's dissenting judgment noted that this basic result parallels the position under § 932 BGB in protecting the bona fide purchaser and he declared himself to be in agreement with Atiyah's view (in *An Introduction to the Law of Contract* (5th edn, 1995), p 86) that 'a person who hands goods over to a stranger in return for a cheque is obviously taking a major risk, and it does not seem fair that he should be able to shift the burden of this risk on to the innocent third party' ([84]—[86]). But as a result of the reasoning of the majority, where a fundamental mistake as to identity is established, then this statutory protection falls away and English law is left with its strict application of the maxim *nemo dat quod non habet*. For Lord Millett, 'it would be unfortunate if our conclusion proved to be different [from that of German law]. Quite apart from anything else, it would make the contemplated harmonisation of the general principles of European contract law very difficult to achieve' (at [86]).

Finally, the result of the *Shogun Finance Ltd v Hudson* decision has led to calls for the reform of the law in this area by Parliament. Thus, Lord Nicholls of Birkenhead remarked in the case itself that 'Sedley LJ said the law has tied itself into a Gordian knot. Brooke LJ said the law is in a "sorry condition" which only Parliament or your Lordships' House can remedy: see [2002] QB 834, 847, 855, paras 23, 51.' The Law Reform Committee, in its Twelfth Report on *Transfer of Title to Chattels* (Cmnd 2958, 1966) examined the issue and suggested that such mistakes should render the contract *voidable* only, rather than void (paras 9, 12 and 15 of the report; cf also, section 2–403 of the US Uniform Commercial Code, which was mentioned in the judgment in *Shogun Finance Ltd v Hudson* at [35] and [84]). This was also the suggestion of Lord Denning MR in *Lewis v Averay* [1972] 1 QB 198 and of Lords Nicholls of Birkenhead and Millett of the minority in *Shogun Finance Ltd v Hudson*, although this has been criticised as too favourable to the position of the third party (see eg, Phang,

Lee and Koh's case note on the latter case [2004] *CLJ* 24, at 26). If the only viable solution is some form of loss apportionment between the innocent third party and the original owner (see Devlin LJ in *Ingram v Little*, cited above, at 73–4), then it seems that legislation vesting such discretion in the courts in a manner similar to the position under the Law Reform (Frustrated Contracts) Act 1943 would be the better approach. For those advocates of voidability however the decision in *Shogun Finance Ltd v Hudson* is a blow to hopes that such a reform could have been achieved judicially (although note how close their Lordships came: see eg, *per* Lord Phillips of Worth Matravers at [170]). (For further discussion of this intriguing case, see McKnight (2004) 19 *JIBLR* 97, 211–12 and the case notes by Phang *et al* ([2004] *CLJ* 24, at 26); MacMillan (2004) 120 *LQR* 369; Elliott [2004] *JBL* 381 and Hare (2004) 67 *MLR* 993.)

(f) Common Error

The rules on mistake as contained in §§ 119–20 BGB do not require that the mistake be shared by the other party, nor even that the recipient of the declaration of will could have noticed that the other party had operated under a mistake. In accordance with the will theory, it is the unilateral mistake of one party—the divergence of will and declaration—which justifies an exception from the principle of *pacta sunt servanda*. Therefore, the BGB does not and need not contain any specific rules dealing with 'common' mistake. Indeed, the technical term 'common mistake' is reserved in German law for a specific incident of the broader notion of a shared misapprehension or misconception, namely a shared mistaken motivation for entering into the contract. The question then is how German law solves those cases in which both parties share a misconception in relation to the contract. There is no single answer and a number of techniques are used to deal with this kind of common mistake.

A possible answer to a common error problem lies in applying rules of interpretation. We have already discussed (in section 3(c), above, and in chapter 3, p 135) the case that both parties misunderstand the objective meaning of a term in the same way (the famous *Shark-meat* case was given as an illustration). Here, the subjective meaning prevails in establishing true consent, or 'meeting of the minds' to use the English term. There is no room for mistake rules here. If the shared assumption does not concern the meaning of the terms of the contract but goes deeper, and for instance affects the basis of the calculation of the contract price, we are faced with a shared mistake in the motivation of the parties for entering into the contract. This kind of mistake does not, as we have seen, entitle the contracting parties to set the contract aside. However, if the common error affects the foundation of the transaction it may entitle one party to have the contract adjusted and, failing that, to a right to terminate the contract (see § 313 II BGB).

This incidence of common error is referred to in German law as 'common mistake' and will be discussed in more detail in the section on the doctrine of the foundation of the transaction, chapter 7 p 346. It can already be said at this stage that the approach of the German courts is a flexible one and depends largely on whether the risk that the shared assumption turns out to be wrong is also shared by the parties. (See also the *Roubles* case, RGZ 105, 406, case no 98, discussed in chapter 7, p 347) A similar point on common fundamental mistake, the construction of the contract and taking care to respect the allocation of risk therein has been made above (in section 3(a)) in relation to English law: see the discussion of *Couturier v Hastie* (1856) 5 HLC 673 and *McCrae v Commonwealth Disposals Commission* (1951) 84 CLR 377.

4. DECEPTION AND OTHER FORMS OF 'MISREPRESENTATION'

Cartwright, *Misrepresentation* (2002); Fleischer, *Informationsasymmetrie im Vertragsrecht* (2001); Fleischer, 'Konkurrenzprobleme um die culpa in contrahendo' AcP 200 (2000) 91; Grigoleit, 'Irrtum, Täuschung und Informationspflichten in den European Principles und in den Unidroit-Principles' in Schulze, Ebers and Grigoleit (eds), *Informationspflichten und Vertragsschluss im Acquis communautaire* (2003), p 201; Kötz and Flessner, *European Contract Law* (1998), vol. 1, chapter 11; Grigoleit, *Vorvertragliche Informationspflichten* (1997); S Lorenz, *Der Schutz vor dem unerwünschten Vertrag* (1997); Mankowski, *Beseitigungsrechte* (2003); Rehm, *Aufklärungspflichten im Vertragsrecht* (2003); Probst, 'Deception' in *Int En cComp Law*, Vol VII, Ch 11 (2001); Schuster, 'Unredliches Verhalten Dritter beim Vertragsabschluß' AcP 168 (1968) 470; Windel, 'Welche Willenserklärungen unterliegen der Einschränkung der Täuschungsanfechtung gem. § 123 Abs. 2 BGB?' AcP 199 (1999) 421.

(a) Preliminary Observations

The BGB expressly recognises two main reasons for setting a contract aside for mistake. The first, as we have seen in the previous section, is that the promisor does not know what he is doing. The second is that the promisor knows what he is doing (ie, he is aware of the objective meaning of his declaration of will) but he has been deceived and therefore errs in relation to the motives for entering into the contract: § 123 I first alternative BGB. This error in the motivation, which as a general rule is irrelevant, becomes crucial when the process of formation of the will has been manipulated by the other party.

Parties to a contract ought not to lie to each other when negotiating the contract. If, nevertheless, this occurs, then the aggrieved party is allowed to withdraw his declaration of will by rescinding the contract. Since the cause of the defect of the consent is imputable to the recipient, his reliance on the validity of the contract is not deemed worthy of protection. As a consequence, the BGB lowers the hurdle for obtaining rescission in comparison with the rescission for declaration mistake. (This, it will be recalled, does not presuppose any 'wrongful' act of the other party.) Thus, it is sufficient for § 123 I BGB that as a matter of fact, the deception caused the innocent party to conclude the contract and it is not necessary to show also that the causal nexus is reasonable. Furthermore, the innocent party is not liable in damages for the reliance interest of the other party. So, § 122 BGB does not apply. Finally, the exercise of this right of rescission is subject to more generous time limits compared with those available under § 121 BGB. § 124 BGB states that rescission is possible for one year after the deception has been discovered, with ten years after the declaration of will came into existence serving as the maximum objective time limit. Moreover, the decision whether to treat the contract as void retroactively (*ex tunc* or *ab initio*) rests with the innocent party, who may have reasons (for instance, because the surrounding circumstances have changed and an originally bad deal has turned out to be positively advantageous), to enforce the contract as agreed. Given the strong justification of the right of rescission, at least in the paradigmatic case of fraud, it is no surprise that the remedies in respect of breach of contract do not exclude the right to rescind the contract for deception. If the conditions of both sets of right are met, the aggrieved party has a further choice which of them to pursue. (For example, BGH NJW 1997, 254; NJW-RR 1998, 904.)

It should also be recalled as to the consequences of rescission that the retroactive nullity of the contract brings in its wake the rules of unjustified enrichment. As also explained in section 3(c), p 289, in situations like these the parties are bound to return the benefits received because the performance was made without any legal ground (§ 812 I 1 Alt. 1 BGB, ie the so-called *Leistungskondiktion*).

Notwithstanding the above, §§ 119–44 BGB leave a gap that is quite obvious to the common lawyer. These provisions do not cover the middle ground between the two extremes marked by § 119 I BGB and § 123 BGB. What if the conduct of one of the parties is misleading but does not amount to deception? Neither the will theory nor the declaration theory demands that the contract remain valid. The process of the formation of the will is disturbed and the party who induced the contract through a 'misrepresentation' cannot be said reasonably to rely on the contract, at least if the representation is imputable to him (ie, he is deemed responsible for it). One could speculate whether in these circumstances the courts would be reluctant to grant relief to the innocent party because the BGB remained silent on this point. The issue is indeed controversial, with strongly held (academic) views at both ends of the spectrum. Yet the courts have in such cases cautiously, and not always consistently, allowed the right of rescission for mistake. We shall return to this point later. Here, however, it should be pointed out by way of introduction that this is an example where the courts have in effect altered the position of the BGB and supplemented it with flexible rules so as to meet the demands of business.

(b) Deception

Paragraph 123 I BGB uses the term deceit or deception ('*Täuschung*') rather than fraud ('*Betrug*'), which is in common use in criminal law (§ 263 Criminal Code) and there has a different connotation. To this term of 'deceit', the BGB adds the adjective '*arglistig*' or 'malicious'. This criterion however is not taken to mean anything more than 'fraudulent' or 'wilful', despite the fact that this is already implied by the term 'deceit'. Deceit is thus defined as the deliberate misrepresentation of facts with the intention to arouse or sustain an error. (Compare the definition of fraud in the tort of deceit in the case of *Derry v Peek* (1889) 14 App Cas 337: a statement is fraudulent if made with knowledge of its falsity, without belief in its truth or recklessly. See, also, *Car and Universal Finance Co Ltd v Caldwell* [1961] 1 QB 525 and see generally, Treitel, *The Law of Contract*, pp 343–4 and Markesinis, Deakin and Johnston, *Markesinis and Deakin's Tort Law* (5th edn, 2003), pp 501–5 for further discussion.)

If the parties to a contract make statements during the negotiation of the contract, they must speak the truth. The induced error must have been relevant for the decision of the deceived party. The *Bundesgerichtshof* has extended the concept of 'deceit' in important ways, while the case law of the labour courts has restricted the scope of application of § 123 I (first alternative) BGB in an important respect.

An intriguing point is whether the deceit must be unlawful. § 123 I BGB expressly requires unlawfulness only for coercion. The assumption seems to be that every deceit is *qua* being deceit unlawful and cannot be justified. This radical position, famously advocated by Immanuel Kant (eg, in his *Grundlegung zur Metaphysik der Sitten*, Akademie-Ausgabe vol IV (1911), p 402: English edition under the title *Groundwork of the Metaphysics of Morals* (CUP edn, 1998)), has not prevailed. Exceptionally, German courts do recognise reasons which justify lying during the process of entering into the contract.

It is no coincidence that the *Bundesarbeitsgericht* was first called on to decide whether there was a 'right to lie' (*Recht zur Lüge*) in exceptional circumstances. Long-term contracts such as the contract of labour are normally preceded by an interview in which the employer will, by means of specific questions, try to discover all that he regards as essential for the post his wishes to fill. Because, as noted above, (chapter 3, p 153 ff) the right to terminate a contract of labour by giving notice is considerably restricted in German law, rescission under the rules of mistake is an attractive way out of the contract if one of the answers in the interview turns out to be false. Nevertheless, the labour courts have consistently taken the view that the questions put by the employer must be reasonable and if they are not, then the prospective employee is entitled intentionally to give a false answer. (Eg, BAG NJW 1958, 516.)

The incentive to rely on § 123 BGB is particularly high in the typical case in which a right to lie is regularly invoked: is a female applicant for a post entitled to lie about her possible pregnancy? If the contract cannot be rescinded, the *Mutterschutzgesetz* and other statutes will exclude the right to terminate the contract for at least six weeks around the date of the birth and for the period during which parental leave is taken. The question as to pregnancy has been held not to be justifiable because it discriminates against women. (BAG NJW 1993, 1154; this is also a requirement of European law: see Directive 76/207/EEC and case C–421/92 *Habermann-Beltermann v Arbeiterwohlfahrt, Bezirksverband Ndb./Opf. eV* [1994] ECR I-1657; NJW 1994, 2077; for a case originating in the UK, with issues along somewhat similar lines, see case C–32/93 *Webb v EMO Air Cargo (UK) Ltd* [1994] ECR I-3567).

There is no abstract criterion for assessing the reasonableness of questions. At first, the employer was allowed to ask questions directed at such qualities which are essential for the actual performance of the contract. Thus, the question as to pregnancy had been considered reasonable if the employer is required by statute not to employ pregnant women to carry out the job in question. (BAG NJW 1994, 148; in the *Webb v EMO Air Cargo (UK) Ltd* the issue was whether dismissal could take place on grounds of unavailability for work where the pregnant employee had been employed specifically to cover the maternity leave of another pregnant employee.) However, the ruling made in this decision has now been abandoned. (BAG NZA 2003, 848, case no 90, which also contains a useful summary of the case law of the ECJ and declares that the question on pregnancy is illegitimate, even if the contract of labour has been entered into on a long-term basis.) The main argument of the court is that even if the employer is not able to provide an adequate working place during the pregnancy, the pregnancy is only of temporary nature. Other examples of controversial questions include questions as to membership of a trade union or religious sect, financial difficulties, previous salary etc. (See for details: *Münchener Kommentar*- Kramer (4th edn, 2001), § 123 Rn. 10.) The upshot of this is that giving false answers may sometimes be justifiable in German law.

The most important clarification of the *Bundesgerichtshof* as to the scope of application of § 123 I BGB was that deceit can be committed not only by actively lying to the other party, but by withholding information which is crucial to the other party. A deceit by omission (*Täuschung durch Unterlassen*) presupposes that the party withholding the information was under an obligation to reveal it (*Aufklärungspflicht*). The courts recognise however that as a general rule the parties to a contract do not owe each other wide-ranging duties of disclosure because every party is responsible for acquiring for himself the information which he regards as relevant to the decision to enter into the contract.

German courts soon introduced important exceptions to this general principle on the basis of good faith (discussed in detail in chapter 3, section 2, p 119). Since the issue is of paramount importance for the scope not only of § 123 BGB, but for liability under *culpa in contrahendo* rules, we explore this topic in more detail in the next sub-section. At this juncture however it is useful to note that English law also denies any general duty of disclosure of material facts. (See, for a recent confirmation of this principle, *Norwich Union Life Insurance Co Ltd v Quereshi* [1999] 2 All ER (Comm) 707, at 717). Thus, in a deceit claim the court refused to hold a landlord liable where he had failed to divulge that the house being let was in a ruinous condition: *Keates v Cadogan* (1851) 10 CB 591; 138 ER 234.

So far as the subjective elements of deceit are concerned, the *Bundesgerichtshof* has adopted a broad approach. § 123 I BGB requires '*Arglist*', ie fraudulent or wilful behaviour. The Court developed the rule that *dolus eventualis* (*bedingter Vorsatz*) suffices to establish 'wilful' deceit. Thus, statements made without certain knowledge that the facts are as claimed, and to the contrary the statement is known potentially to be false, are also classified as deceit ('*Angaben ins Blaue hinein*'): eg, BGHZ 63, 282, 286; BGH NJW 1998, 302.

Finally, it is worth considering the significance of acts of third parties.

As we have seen, the rationale of the right of rescission for deceit is that the other contracting party manipulated the formation of the will of the aggrieved party. A fraudulent statement of a third party does not therefore entitle the aggrieved party to rescission unless that statement can be imputed to the other contracting party. § 123 II 1 BGB lays down the relevant rules of imputation. The deception is imputable when the party to the contract actually knew or ought to have known of it. (It will be recalled that the same standard is applied for imputing a situation which gives rise to a right of cancellation under § 312 BGB—'doorstep-selling', see p 274.)

While this seems to be a sensible approach it did not go far enough to satisfy the *Bundesgerichtshof*. The Court argued that where a person is 'on the side' of the contracting party and contributes considerably to the conclusion of the contract, then the deception ought to be imputed regardless of whether the party to the contract could have known of the deception. It brushed aside the wording of § 123 BGB and simply claimed that such persons are not 'third parties' within the meaning of that provision. This was certainly a bold move and an indication of how willingly the Court modifies the rules of the BGB where it thinks fit. Paradigmatically, the agent is thus not 'a third party' to the contract (BGHZ 20, 36, 39) and neither are such persons who, without having full authority, nevertheless take an active part in the negotiations (a so-called 'Verhandlungsgehilfe'): eg, BGH NJW 1989, 2879.

The English case law on the position of agents in this situation is nuanced, but would seem to achieve a similar level of coverage. Thus, an agent acting within the scope of his authority who makes a statement that he knows to be false will render his principal liable for that fraud (*S Pearson & Son Ltd v Dublin Corporation* [1907] AC 351 and *Briess v Woolley* [1954] AC 333). However, if the agent was unaware of the falsity of his statement and the principal was so aware, this will not suffice as neither party satisfies the state of mind necessary to show fraud (*Standard Chartered Bank v Pakistan National Shipping Co* [2003] 1 AC 959 and *Niru Battery Manufacturing Co v Milestone Trading Ltd* [2002] All ER (Comm) 701, at [53]). But if the principal stood by and failed to correct such a false impression created by the agent when the principal knew of its falsity, then the principal would be liable for the fraud thus perpetrated (*London County Freehold & Leasehold Properties Ltd v Berkeley Property and Investment Co Ltd* [1936] 2 All ER 1039). (See generally, Treitel, *The Law of Contract*, pp 343–4.)

In English law, if a fraudulent misrepresentation is proved, a range of different possible remedies is available. The contract may be affirmed and the aggrieved party may sue for damages in the tort of deceit. Alternatively, the contract may be rescinded and an action may be brought for any loss suffered. The fraud can be set up as a defence against an action for specific performance of the contract, and if the contract has yet to be executed the aggrieved party can repudiate it and claim to recover any money paid under it. On this last possibility see *Kettlewell v Refuge Assurance Co* [1908] 1 KB 545, and on appeal, *Refuge Assurance Co v Kettlewell* [1909] AC 243.

(c) Duties to Inform (*Aufklärungspflichten*)

As was explained earlier, § 123 BGB applies not only where one party makes a false statement, but where one party withholds information despite being under an obligation to disclose it. Crucial for establishing a right to rescind is accordingly the precise scope and nature of the duty of disclosure or duty to inform (so called 'Aufklärungspflicht'). Here, it should be stressed, we are not talking of cases where providing the information is required under a previously undertaken *contractual* obligation of the party. Such a duty to advise may exist for instance between a bank and its customers (eg, BGHZ 72, 92; cf also BGH NJW 1981, 1440; NJW 1982, 2815). The violation of such an obligation may constitute deceit or indeed lead to liability for breach of contract. The question however is whether the courts may *in law* impose on the parties to a contract an obligation to disclose information that would prevent the other party from entering into it. In effect this often amounts to requiring the party to act against his own commercial interest. Can there really be a duty to warn that the 'opponent' is about to enter into a bad bargain or committing a foolish act?

In the common law, which traditionally stresses the responsibility of the individual for his decision to enter into the contract, the answer is clear. English courts have been extremely reluctant to recognise general duties to inform. Thus, there is no general duty of disclosure of material facts before entry into a contract (see Lord Atkin in *Bell v Lever Brothers Ltd* [1932] AC 161, at 227); and silence will not normally amount to a representation. (*Keates v Cadgoan* (1851) 10 CB 591.) However, it should be noted that failure to disclose certain important facts might amount to a misrepresentation in English law (as touched on briefly in the discussion of the position of agents in section 4(b), above). Thus, in *Dimmock v Hallett* (1866) LR 2 Ch App 21, it was strictly true to say that all the farms on the vendor's land were fully let, but it amounted to a misrepresentation not to have disclosed that the tenants had given notice to quit. Further, if a representation had been true when it was made, but the representor is aware that subsequent developments have made that statement false, then the representor must reveal that change in circumstances to the representee, otherwise this will be treated as an actionable misrepresentation. (See *With v O'Flanagan* [1936] Ch 575 and *Dietz v Lennig Chemicals Ltd* [1969] 1 AC 170; see also section 2(1) of the Misrepresentation Act 1967, under which the representor can avoid liability only 'he proves that he had reasonable ground to believe and did believe up to the time the contract was made the facts represented were true.')

Further, it should be noted that there are exceptions to the basic rules on non-disclosure where certain types of contract are involved: eg, contracts *uberrimae fidei*, contracts of insurance (on which see, eg, Clarke, *Policies and Perceptions of Insurance* (1997) 80–108) and a number of other examples (discussed helpfully in Beatson, *Anson's Law of* Contract, pp 263–75), including the regulatory regime of the Financial Markets and Services Act 2000 for those conducting investment business. Finally, it should be noted that the English approach to implied terms (eg, that the goods should be of a satisfactory quality—section 14 of the Sale of Goods Act 1979) may protect some interests similar to those covered by duties of disclosure in civil law systems. (See, for instance, Zimmermann and Whittaker, *Good Faith in European Contract Law* (2000), pp 194–5.)

German courts, by contrast, have also given a typical answer, already alluded to in chapter 3. If it is contrary to good faith (§ 242 BGB) to withhold the information then a duty to inform can be established. Failing to inform then amounts to deceit and it entitles the other party to rescind the contract *ex tunc*. It is quite obvious that no abstract hard and fast rules have emerged as to when good faith requires disclosure. The law is developed here on a case-by-case basis, with much turning on the facts of the individual case. Thus, we can only indicate guidelines and point out groups of cases where such duties were established. (For an overview see, *Palandt*-Heinrichs § 123 Rn. 5–9; and for detailed discussion: Stephen Lorenz, *Der Schutz vor dem unerwünschten Vertra*g, p 416 *et seq*.)

First, a duty to inform arises where one party specifically requests the information by asking questions (BGHZ 74, 383, 392).

Secondly, and this is the area where most of the controversies arise, circumstances which are of *evident and overwhelming importance* for the other party must be disclosed. This applies in particular if certain circumstances are essential for achieving *the purpose of the contract* (eg, BGH NJW 1980, 2460). A person who undertakes a considerable debt is under an obligation to disclose financial difficulties if bankruptcy is imminent (eg, BGH NJW 1974, 1505). In the case of a contract of sale, the seller may not withhold information as to grave defects of the sold goods (eg, BGH NJW 1990, 975; compare this with the various terms implied by law under the Sale of Goods Act 1979, especially sections 12, 13 and 14). In the case of particularly substantial defects, even the mere danger of them occurring in the future must be made known (see BGH NJW 1993, 1323).

Many of these cases concern the sale of used cars by professional car dealers or the sale of land. In this particular group of cases the courts tend to impose quite extensive duties to inform. For instance, a previous accident must be disclosed even if the car has been repaired (eg, BGH NJW 1982, 1386). Likewise, in the case of land, any major defect must be brought to the attention of the potential purchaser. For instance, if the building suffered damage from humidity and it is not clear whether an attempt to rectify the defect will be successful, then this must be disclosed. (BGH NJW 1993, 1703.) Similarly, if the land was contaminated the seller must inform the potential buyer of this fact. (BGH NJW 1995, 1549: land used as waste dump. But no duty, for instance, exists where a gas company previously operated on the land: BGH NJW 1994, 253.)

In English land law there are, in effect, some limited duties of disclosure relating to misdescriptions of the nature of the seller's right or interest in the land (see eg, *Charles Hunt Ltd v Palmer* [1931] 2 Ch 287 and *William Sindall Plc v Cambridgeshire County Council* [1994] 1 WLR 1016. See generally, Harpum, 'Selling Without Title: a Vendor's Duty of Disclosure' (1992) 108 *LQR* 280, 320–33 and Beatson, *Anson's Law of Contract*, pp 272–4).

It is not only physical defects or the danger thereof that may trigger a duty to inform. The duty may also arise in the absence of a permission, authorisation, or licence required to achieve the purpose of the contract (quite apart from the question whether the seller would not also be liable under breach of contract rules, as to the concurrence of these different sets of rights, see above). If, for example, it is prohibited to build on land sold for development and the seller knew that but did not inform the purchaser, then this entitles the latter to rescind the contract under § 123 BGB, eg, BGH NJW 2003, 2381. The same applies if a particular use is prohibited or where that use is essential for the intended utilisation of the land. (BGH NJW-RR 1988, 394.) Likewise, if the land is included in a particular 'nature protection district' (*Landschaftsschutzgebiet*), which prohibits a number of common uses of the land, this gives rise to a duty to inform (OLG Oldenburg NJW-RR 2003, 448).

In the case of the sale of a company, it is clear that false statements by one party entitle the other party to rescission. (BGH NJW-RR 1989, 306, 307: profit and revenues.) Even though normally the parties are here dealing at arm's length, the courts have in individual cases imposed duties to inform. For instance, significant unpaid debts (in particular tax burdens) must be disclosed. (For example, OLG Köln NJW-RR 1994, 1064.) Also, the catastrophic financial condition of the company must be revealed. (BGH NJW 2001, 2163.) Or a sudden dramatic fall in revenues shortly before the conclusion of the contract must also be notified. (BGH NJW-RR 1996, 429, case no 91.) It should be emphasised once more however that decisions in this area of the law must be approached with extreme caution. For each rests on its special facts and for many of these examples one can, if one digs deep enough, unearth counter-examples.

In these situations English law would in principle deal with the fact scenario by way of a misrepresentation claim (see eg, *Redgrave v Hurd* (1881) 20 Ch D 1), which would allow, *inter alia*, rescission of the contract. However, in practice it is far more likely that the issue would turn on the comprehensive schedule of warranties agreed between the parties to the transaction. Any breach of such a warranty would then sound in damages and a further clause would usually be included stating that anything not covered in the warranties is at the buyer's risk (thus precluding the possibility of any claim for misrepresentation).

The third and vaguest factor that serves to establish duties to inform is the existence of a relationship of *trust* (in a broad sense). This is typical of family relationships or close personal ties (BGH NJW 1992, 300, 302) but also the particular position of a professional in his trade (as we have already seen in chapter 2 in the section on *culpa in contrahendo*: eg, car dealers are regarded as falling under this category).

In English law, the closest parallel can be found in contracts between those in a fiduciary relationship. Here, the parties are under a duty fully to disclose all material facts that are likely to affect any transaction with those to whom the duty is owed. The key element of such relationships is the duty to act in the interests of another. (*Bristol and West Building Society v Mothew* [1998] Ch 1, at 8.) Such relationships may arise in a number of specific status-based situations (eg, principal and agent, trustee and beneficiary) and fact-based circumstances (eg, employment relationships: *Nottingham University v Fishel* [2000] ICR 1462, at 1491, although note that the context of the relevant contract is critical here).

The following considerations may be relevant for an assessment of the advantages and disadvantages of the approach of the German courts.

It is essential for the negotiation phase that each party knows in advance to which kind of information one is entitled. A buyer or customer will rest assured if he knows that the courts will step in and allow him to rescind the contract if the other party withheld crucial information. On the other hand, if he cannot expect that the sort of information he needs will be provided by the opponent, then he must procure it independently and at his own expense. Conversely, for the seller of an object or provider of a service, it is essential to know which information he must provide and which he may withhold so as to not make the contract voidable.

From this perspective, the jurisprudence of the German courts can be criticised for its occasional paternalistic overtones (ie, imposing excessive duties to inform) and for creating uncertainty in the law. The major criterion, namely that the information is of manifest and crucial importance to the other party, is just like the concept of 'good faith': utterly vague. Hence, it is difficult to determine the result in each individual case. Moreover, the apodictic reasoning typical of the application of the test (cf the reasoning in BGH NJW-RR 1996, 429, case no 91) does little to reduce the uncertainty.

However, this 'good faith' approach to duties of inform should not be dismissed categorically. For, among other things, it allows the courts to decide each case on its merits. Imposing obligations may after all yield economically sensible results—at least in some cases. A duty to inform may be appropriate, as Professor Kötz suggests, where the information that is of evident interest to the other party was obtained with no cost (eg, the information the vendor of land acquired conerning the characteristics of the land or the building), or where the information is shortly going to be made public (eg, the outbreak of war) (Kötz and Schäfer, *Judex Oeconomicus* (2003), p 173 *et seq*). Likewise, if the cost of obtaining the information is much higher for the buyer than for the seller (eg, as is the case with the sale of second hand cars), an 'information asymmetry' arises. In such a situation, the buyer will prefer to pay the seller for the extra cost of obtaining the information (ie, an increased price), rather than bear the much higher cost of finding it out for himself. This may, accordingly, justify the courts in imposing higher standards of disclosure on the seller. (See, for a comprehensive economic explanation of these cases: Fleischer, *Informationsasymmetrie im*

Vertragsrecht (2001). See also, Stephan Lorenz, *Der Schutz vor dem unerwünschten Vertra*g, p 421, who stresses that the difficulties faced by the contracting party in obtaining the information in question ought to play a central role; it is not the task of a party to a contract to inform the other party of circumstances which that party could find out for himself.)

The correct evaluation of market movements or the value of the subject-matter of the contract is an asset which is the basis for making profit out of market activities. This concerns the motivation for concluding the contract, which (as we have seen in the previous section) is the sole responsibility of each party. Imposing excessive duties of disclosure would therefore undermine the institution of contract. However, the distinction between those facts which determine the value of an object and the personal appreciation of market conditions is a fine one. Some of the decisions of the *Bundesgerichtshof* may be criticised for going too far in demanding disclosure. Consider the following example.

In BGH LM § 123 BGB Nr. 52, case no 92 (the '*Daktari*' case), the defendant transferred the right of exploitation of film rights (one concerning the serial 'Daktari') to the plaintiff. However, the defendant was to receive half of the earnings if a German TV company was granted a licence. Later the defendant offered to waive this right of participation in the profits for the sum of US $10,000. The plaintiffs agreed. Shortly before however and unknown to the defendant, the plaintiffs were offered 8.3 million Deutschmarks (more than €4 million) by a major German broadcasting corporation for the broadcasting of films from the package. The BGH, unlike the lower courts, held that the plaintiffs should have disclosed this information. (See, for a critical discussion of this case: Kötz and Schäfer, *Judex Oeconomicus*, p 178; Fleischer, *Informationsasymmetrie im Vertragsrecht*, p 322 *et seq.*) The risk that the estimation of the value of the film rights is correct is—according to the analysis suggested above—to be borne by each party. Hence, the fact that the defendant made a bad bargain is his bad luck. The *Bundesgerichsthof* seems to have been aware of this objection, however. For it based its decision on the peculiar facts of this case. The Court derived the duty from a special relationship of trust. Apparently, the parties had been in a long-term business relationship. The court spoke of their relationship as being one of friendship; and the less well-informed defendant had obviously relied on the market assessment of the plaintiffs. Yet one wonders whether these considerations should be left to a court of law or whether good faith is used here as an excuse to evaluate the (purely) moral value of the behaviour of the parties. It may be that the plaintiffs may have betrayed their friendship with the defendant. Yet friendship is not the basis for the doctrine of *pacta sunt servanda*. This doctrine would have required the courts to enforce the contract as agreed. While it is possible that some common law courts might infer such a special relationship of trust and confidence between business parties that a fiduciary duty existed between them (thus requiring disclosure of certain facts in certain circumstances)—see *Lac Minerals Ltd v International Corona Resources Ltd* [1989] 2 SCR 574 (Sup Ct of Canada) (noted by Hayhurst [1990] *EIPR* 30)—it seems tolerably clear that the English courts are much less willing to do so. (On this see the helpful discussion by Millett LJ (as he then was) in *Bristol and West Building Society v Mothew* [1998] Ch 1, at 16ff and Millett, 'Equity's Place in the Law of Commerce' (1998) 111 *LQR* 214, especially at 221.)

(d) Other Forms of 'Misrepresentation'

The subjective element of deception as defined by § 123 I first alternative BGB requires at least *dolus eventualis*. In many cases this test will not be fulfilled. It suffices, for instance, to misjudge the subjective relevance of a circumstance for the other party to exclude wilful conduct. In this case, the party did not know all facts which the application of § 123 BGB presupposes (namely that the circumstance as to which one party was misled was actually relevant for her decision). As a result, the subjective element of deception is missing.

In German private law, wilful conduct further requires that the person acting was aware that he violated a duty (*Vorsatztheorie*). This means that a party who has knowledge of all relevant facts but evaluates them wrongly does not act wilfully in the sense required by § 123 I first alternative BGB (see Stephan Lorenz, *Der Schutz vor dem unerwünschten Vertra*g, p 438). This restrictive view of intention further increases the need for a regime of rules governing 'negligent' deception.

The question already raised by way of introduction is thus whether German law simply disregards other forms of 'misrepresentation' and proceeds on the basis of *pacta sunt servanda*. The first half of the answer is that, so far as mistake rules are concerned, such less 'wrongful' conduct does not entitle the aggrieved party to rescission. Unless the declaration itself is affected and the contracting party does not know what he is declaring, a less than deliberate misrepresentation does not entitle him rescission for mistake under § 119 or § 123 BGB. However, and this is the important second half of the answer, other rules are used to achieve the same result. The courts deploy the principle of *culpa in contrahendo* (as to which see chapter 2, p 91 ff: this principle is now laid down in § 311 II BGB) in order to afford the innocent party adequate protection. This is somewhat ironic for, as will be remembered, the device was initially developed by Jhering in order to establish liability for failed contracts, while in the present context it is used to get out of an otherwise perfectly valid contract. The practical significance of this development cannot be underestimated, however, if one recalls the relatively strict subjective element required for § 123 I (first alternative) BGB. In many of the cases discussed in the previous section on duties to inform, it would not have been possible to recognise a right to set the contract aside if *culpa in contrahendo* were not a recognised way to invoke negligent 'deception'. (For example, BGH NJW-RR 1996, 429, case no 91; BGHZ 69, 53, case no 93.)

If a party enters into a contract on the basis of false information which is imputable to the other party to the contract, then being bound by the contract (or, in other words, the very existence of the contract) may be regarded as a loss. The right of rescission is accordingly granted in order to restore the innocent party to the position in which he would have been had he not been provided with the wrong information (§ 249 I 1 BGB); eg, BGH NJW 1985, 1769; NJW 1993, 2107. The mis-statement must have caused him to enter into the contract. If a duty to inform was violated (ie, an omission is at stake), then the other party needs to show that he would not have entered into the contract if he had possessed knowledge of the respective circumstance (eg, BGH NJW 1985, 1769).

In some cases, the courts have even allowed the 'innocent' party to claim that he would have entered into the contract on different terms from those actually agreed. They accordingly awarded him damages, which are measured by the difference between the price actually agreed and the hypothetical price. To take a pair of examples, in BGH NJW 1989, 1793 and BGHZ 69, 53, case no 93, the court simply assumed that the other party would have agreed to a price that reflected the market value. This assumption amounts to a fiction that is impossible to justify on the basis of freedom of contract. (For example, see for this argument, Stephan Lorenz, NJW 1999, 1001.) In BGH NJW 1998, 302 however the Court required the other party to prove that the other party was actually willing to contract on the alternative terms. However, even though this holding was in clear contrast with previous case law, the court did not attempt to reconcile the decisions (see Lorenz, NJW 1999, 1001). It will not be easy to prove that the other party would have agreed to enter into the contract on different terms (see also, BGHZ 69, 53, case no 93, 'factually almost impossible'). In any event, this line of cases is better explained as an attempt to get round the deficiencies of the 'old' law of irregularities of performance, which since the recent reform of 2002 have to a great extent been rectified. It will have to be seen whether they will play a role in future. It should be emphasised however that if a party to a contract shows that he would not have entered into the contract *at all*, then the above objection does not apply and a right to set the contract aside arises under *culpa in contrahendo* principles. One is tempted to conclude that here it is not the financial loss measured by the reliance interest that is made recoverable. Rather, the rules of *culpa in contrahendo* are applied to safeguard the autonomy of the decision to enter into a contract just as in the case of § 119 and § 123 BGB.

At first sight, this damages-based explanation of the right to back out of a contract appears ingenious. On closer analysis, it is not as new as one might have thought, if one remembers that likewise in the natural law tradition 'relief for fraud was viewed in delictual terms as relief for harm caused by wrongful conduct, the harm in this case being the contract itself' (von Mehren and Gordley, *The Civil Law System*, p. 858—the reference is to Grotius, *De iure belli ac pacis libri tres*, vol II). Once more, the thesis is confirmed that the principle of *culpa in contrahendo* is an emanation of the idea of *neminem laedere* and a way to get round the restriction of tort law to *physical* damage.

In any case, the approach of the BGH to establish outside the scope of § 123 and § 119 BGB a right to set a contract aside for 'negligent misrepresentation' or *fahrlässige Täuschung* on the basis of *culpa in contrahendo* was an ingenious way of filling the gap (arguably) left by the Code in respect of the middle ground between mistake and deception. Note however that jurisprudence has attracted support as well as criticism. (This in itself is not surprising since the courts departed from the original strictures of the Code. Approving, though with different emphasis in respect of the foundations of this line of cases: Stephan Lorenz, *Der Schutz vor dem unerwünschten Vertrag* (1997), p 392 *et seq*; W Schur, *Leistung und Sorgfalt* (2001), p 328 *et seq*; *Palandt*-Heinrichs, § 311 Rn. 42; Larenz and Wolf, *Allgemeiner Teil*, § 37 Rn. 22. Contrast eg, Lieb, 'Culpa in contrahendo und rechtsgeschäftliche Entscheidungsfreiheit' in *Festschrift Dieter Medicus* (1999), p 553; see also: Mankowski, *Beseitigungsrechte* (2003), pp 221, 342–6, and Grigoleit, *Vertragliche Informationshaftung* (1997), p 75 ff who prefer an analogous application of § 123 BGB to the *culpa in contrahendo* approach.)

Before we conclude this section, it is necessary to point out two of the conditions that must be satisfied to exercise this right to get out of an unwanted bargain.

First, the misrepresentation must be at least negligent: ie, the party should and could have known that the information was misleading. This was also the position of

German law before *culpa in contrahendo* was regulated in the Code, yet now the fault standard is expressly established in the BGB. The right follows from a joint consideration of §§ 311 II and 280 I BGB which, in turn, presupposes that the requirements of § 276 BGB are met (ie, fault). However, it is for the party making the false statement to prove that he was not at fault (§ 280 I 2 BGB is formulated as an exception). As a result, there is no right to back out of an agreement in German law for 'innocent' representation, unless—in exceptional cases—the misrepresentation affects the foundation of the transaction. (This is discussed in detail in chapter 7.)

By contrast, English law (via equity) has long provided a right of rescission on the ground of innocent misrepresentation (although note that, prior to modern developments in the law of tort and in statute, all non-fraudulent misrepresentations were classified as 'innocent': see eg, *Heilbut Symons & Co v Buckleton* [1913] AC 30, at 48). The importance of the distinction was that damages were only available in the event of fraud. However, since the Misrepresentation Act 1967 it has been possible to claim damages in lieu of rescission (section 2(2)) for an innocent misrepresentation. The court is granted a discretionary power to declare that the contract still subsists and instead award damages in place of the rescission claim. In exercising this discretion, the court may so rule only 'if it would be equitable to do so, having regard to the nature of the misrepresentation and the loss that would be caused by it if the contract were upheld, as well as to the loss that rescission would cause to the other party' (section 2(2)). (On this topic, see Treitel, pp 358–60.)

Since *Hedley Byrne & Co Ltd v Heller & Partners Ltd* [1964] AC 465, a duty of care in tort has existed not to make negligent misstatements where there was an assumption of responsibility such as to create a 'special relationship' between the maker and recipient of the statement. This duty can exist concurrently with a contract between the parties (*Henderson v Merrett Syndicates Ltd* [1995] 2 AC 145, especially at 186–91) and is not restricted to statements that induce a contract (*Williams v Natural Life Health Foods Ltd* [1998] 1 WLR 830, at 834–5). A key consideration is the context in which the representation is made. This will lead to variations in the extent of the duty of care in negligence. (For further treatment of the situation in tort, see Deakin, Johnston & Markesinis, *Markesinis and Deakin's Tort Law* (5th edn, 2003), pp 114–24.)

Further coverage for negligent pre-contractual statements is now provided by statute. Thus, section 2(1) of the Misrepresentation Act 1967 provides:

> Where a person has entered into a contract after a misrepresentation has been made to him by another party thereto and as a result thereof he has suffered loss, then, if the person making the misrepresentation would be liable to damages in respect thereof had the misrepresentation been made fraudulently, that person shall also be so liable, notwithstanding that the misrepresentation was not made fraudulently, unless he proves that he had reasonable grounds to believe and did believe up to the time the contract was made that the facts represented were true.

Clearly, section 2(1) is both broader and narrower than the tort principle. It is broader in not requiring special relationships or skills, etc and thus placing the burden on the representor not to state facts that he could not prove he had reasonable grounds to believe were true. It is narrower because it only applies where a contract has been concluded as a result of the misrepresentation *and* where another party to the contract was the representor (although this does include agents). The measure of damages under section 2(1) seems to be the tortious measure for fraud (rather than for negligence) (*Royscot Trust Ltd v Rogerson* [1991] 2 QB 297), although the defence of contributory negligence would appear to be available (*Gran Gelato Ltd v Richcliff (Group) Ltd* [1992] Ch 560, at 574) and the choice of the fraud measure has been criticised (see, eg, Beatson, *Anson's Law of Contract*, pp 249–50 and Treitel, *The Law of Contract*, pp 351–2).

Finally, it should be noted that in English law if the misrepresentation has become a term of the contract then its breach will entitle the aggrieved party to damages or, possibly, even to rescind for breach. (See section 1(a) (and indeed section 2(2)) of the Misrepresentation Act 1967 and Treitel, *The Law of Contract*, pp 375–7).

A second important limitation stems from the fact that, at least according to the prevailing view, the application of *culpa in contrahendo* is not possible where the information in question concerns a characteristic of the subject-matter of the contract that may give rise to liability for breach of contract under the special regimes of rules of the respective type of contract (cf the result reached in *Henderson v Merrett Syndicates Ltd*, cited above, at 186–91). For instance, in relation to a sale of a company the only such features of the enterprise that may give rise to liability under *culpa in contrahendo* are those which do not fall under § 434 BGB, ie which do not constitute a defect of the object of sale. For instance, in relation to the law before the 2002 reform of the BGB (which as we will see extended the notion of defect), the courts applied *culpa in contrahendo* in relation to the revenue and profit of a company (BGH NJW-RR 1989, 306, 307). In a nutshell: a wilful false statement in relation to those figures would give rise to a right to rescind under § 123 BGB; a merely negligent false representation would entitle the innocent party to get out of the contract under *culpa in contrahendo* rules.

5. COERCION

Benecke, 'Der verständige Arbeitgeber- Anfechtung arbeitsrechtlicher Aufhebungsverträge wegen widerrechtlicher Drohung' RdA 2004, 147; Karakatsanes, *Die Widerrechtlichkeit in § 123 BGB* (1974); Mankowski, *Beseitigungsrechte* (2003); Probst, 'Coercion' in *Int Enc Comp Law*, Vol. VII, Ch 11 (2001); Kötz and Flessner, *European Contract Law* (1998), chapter 11.

(a) Preliminary Observations

As we explained in the section on mistake, above, it is a necessary condition of a declaration of will that it is carried out with the intention to act (*Handlungswille*). Hence, if a person is forced with *vis absoluta* to carry out an act then this particular conduct is not imputable and therefore does not constitute a declaration of will. (In English law, it is arguable that such a situation of *vis absoluta* might come within the doctrine of *non est factum*, outlined in section 3(d), p 292, and thus render the contract void.) This was self-evident for the drafters of the BGB (see, *Motive*, vol I, 204). If the person intends to perform the act but was motivated by the fear that certain threats will be carried out, the act in question is nevertheless regarded as a prima facie valid declaration of will. However, § 123 I second alternative BGB entitles the party aggrieved to have the contract set aside 'where a person has been induced by . . . illegitimate threat to make a declaration of intent . . .'. This type of defect may be conveniently called 'coercion' in order to avoid confusion with the technical term 'duress' of English law. (See also, Probst, 'Coercion', para 11-362 with a comparative overview.) It is usually explained as an incidence of *vis compulsiva* (eg, Larenz and Wolf, *Allgemeiner Teil*, § 37 Rn. 27); note however that physical violence may well play a role in extracting the declaration of will desired, for instance where a person is kept incarcerated for as long as he does not sign the contract document. Treating the contract as prima facie valid leaves the aggrieved party the choice whether to accept the contract (*Motive*, vol 1). § 124 BGB allows a full year after the danger ceased for considering whether to rescind the contract (while ten years is again the maximum period after the coming into existence of the declaration of will). Note further, that English common law for many years refused to acknowledge that any duress other than those to the person of the other contracting party was relevant. (See eg, *Cumming v Ince* (1847) 11 QB 112; 116 ER 418.) The result of showing such threats rendered the contract voidable at law. (See eg, *Universe Tankships Inc of Monroviva v International Transport Workers' Federation ('The Universe Sentinel')* [1983] 1 AC 366, at 383.)

By way of introduction, three further points should be made.

First, the BGB regards this type of defect in the contracting process as so grave that it grants the right of rescission irrespective of the person who exerted the pressure to make the declaration of will. Unlike with deception (§ 123 II BGB discussed above), coercion need not be imputable to the other contracting party but may be committed by a total stranger without the knowledge of the contracting party. It would not be reasonable to require that the innocent party must prove that the other party knew of the coercion. (*Motive*, vol 1, 206; sceptical, eg, Lorenz, *Der Schutz vor dem unerwünschten Vertrag* (1997), p 348.)

Secondly, the coercion must have been causal for the declaration of will. Yet it does not matter whether it was reasonable that the coercion influenced the motivation for entering into the contract (contrast § 119 BGB). The requirement of illegitimate pressure, discussed below, offers an adequate control mechanism to exclude trivial threats. Some of the English cases suggest a similar approach. See *Hennessy v Craigmyle & Co* [1986] ICR 461: if it would have been reasonable to have resisted the pressure by, for example, issuing legal proceedings or some other course of lawful action then there no duress will be found. (See further, Lord Goff of Chieveley's view in *The Evia Luck* [1992] 2 AC 152, at 165 that the economic pressure need only have been 'a significant cause.') However, in *Barton v Armstrong* [1976] AC 104, the threats only needed to have been 'a reason' for entering into the contract; further, it was for the party that had made the threats to prove that they had 'contributed nothing' to the other party's decision to sign.

Thirdly, the reliance of the contracting party on the validity of the contract is not protected. § 122 BGB does not apply.

(b) Elements of Coercion

Coercion is defined in § 123 I second alternative BGB as the presence of (unlawful or) illegitimate threats (*widerrechtliche Drohung*). A threat is defined as the announcement of certain future events constituting a wrong and which at least appear to be in the power of the person expressing the threat (eg, BGHZ 2, 287, 295). Anything that restricts a person's ability to act or is otherwise undesirable may be classified as a wrong so long as it is not entirely trivial. (See for instance, BGH NJW 1997, 1980, 1981: the threat of a bank to cancel a line of credit to a company if no further security for the loan were offered may constitute an evil from the point of view of the director of the company, although in the case at hand the threat was regarded legitimate. Likewise, the threat of an employer to dismiss an employee amounts to an evil from the perspective of the latter: eg, BAGE 32, 194; see also the examples discussed below.) It is essential that it at least appears that the occurrence of the event lies in the power of the person uttering the threat (eg, BGH NJW 1988, 2599, 2601). Otherwise we are not dealing with a threat but a simple warning, which does not constitute coercion (eg, BGHZ 6, 348).

In English law, ever since the doctrine of duress was broadened somewhat to include forms of compulsion beyond (threats of) physical violence, the key question has been whether there has been 'compulsion or coercion' (*Occidental Worldwide Investment Corpn v Skibs A/S Avanti ('The Siboen and The Sibotre')* [1976] 1 Lloyd's Rep 293, *per* Kerr J; noted by Beatson (1977) 92 *LQR* 496 and see further, Beatson, 'Duress, Restitution, and Contract Renegotiation' chapter 5 in his *The Use and Abuse of Unjust Enrichment* (1991)). If so, it is then asked whether the effect of the threat was to bring about a 'coercion of the will, which vitiates consent' (*Pao On v Lau Yiu Long* [1980] AC 614, at 636; see the note by Coote [1980] *CLJ* 40). This has recently been held to mean, not that the consent has been negatived (cf Atiyah, 'Economic Duress and the 'Overborne Will'' (1982) 98 *LQR* 197) but rather that it has been improperly obtained– a 'deflection' of the will (*Huyton SA v Peter Cremer GmbH* [1999] 1 Lloyd's Rep 620, at 638). Thus, the focus in English law has shifted from *what* was threatened to the *effect* of the threat. (See generally, Treitel, *The Law of Contract*, pp 405–8 and Beatson, *Anson's Law of Contract*, pp 276–84.)

The subjective element of coercion is somewhat controversial. It seems generally accepted that the person threatening must wilfully seek to influence the conduct of the other person (*dolus eventualis* suffices). Also, the former does not need to be aware of the unlawfulness of the threat. It is controversial however whether he needs to know the facts which make the threat unlawful. See, in this sense, BGHZ 25, 217 where it is further required that in addition the person making the threat(s) is at least negligent in relation to the evaluation of those facts as unlawful. (For sceptical commentary on this requirement see Medicus, *Allgemeiner Teil* Rn. 820 and *Münchener Kommentar*-Kramer, § 123 Rn. 51, who do not require that the person threatening is aware of the facts which make the threat unlawful, let alone of the evaluation of those facts as unlawful.) For the inhibition of the will of the innocent party it does not matter whether the other party acted in bad faith.

(c) Illegitimacy of Threats in Particular

The concept of the illegality or illegitimacy of the threat (*Widerrechtlichkeit*) is of fundamental importance for the model of coercion in German law. It is this open-textured and flexible notion that not only imports uncertainty, but allows the courts to mark off the large area of activity that—though potentially or actually harmful to other persons—is nevertheless legitimate. One must only think of the fact that economy is based on (fair) competition to accept the need for powerful control mechanisms for policing threats. A range of policy factors is taken into account in assessing the legitimacy of threats and evaluating the behaviour of the parties. In English law too (and particularly following the relative liberalisation of the duress rules from *The Siboen and the Sibotre* onwards) unlawful or illegitimate pressure must be shown to render a contract voidable and mere 'commercial pressure' (at 336) will not suffice.

Three categories of cases are recognised. A threat is unlawful if first, the means of threatening is illegitimate, or secondly the end (the desired result) is objectionable, or thirdly, the particular connection between means and end makes the threat appear unlawful.

First, the threat is unlawful if the means (*Mittel*) of threatening, ie, that which is threatened, are unlawful. The paradigmatic case is threatening to commit an act that the legal order classifies as a crime (eg, threatening physically to hurt a person, assault, § 123 Criminal Code etc) and English law would clearly take the same view (see eg, *Scott v Sebright* (1887) 12 PD 21 and *Barton v Armstrong* [1976] AC 104). The means of the threat, that what is threatened, are by definition not unlawful if they represent a procedure which was put into place to achieve the end desired. Thus, 'threatening' to pursue a claim in court or pursuing the applicable remedies of administrative law is obviously an adequate means of exerting pressure (eg, BGHZ 79, 131, 143–4). (Compare the equitable rule in English law that a threat by one party to prosecute the other for a criminal offence could amount to duress and allow the contract to be set aside: see *Williams v Bayley* (1866) LR 1 HL 200 and *Mutual Finance Co Ltd v John Wetton & Sons Ltd* [1937] 2 KB 389. These cases may perhaps, as with the German ones, be better explained under the third heading, below.) Likewise, reporting a fact to the police does not as such constitute illegitimate behaviour, but may in connection with the desired result constitute unlawful pressure (discussed below).

The second criterion of illegitimate pressure does not play any major role in practice. If the desired result or end (*Zweck*) is unlawful the contract will invariably be void under § 134 or § 138 BGB, discussed in the previous chapter.

The most difficult to apply is the third category of coercion. Here, the illegitimacy is said to result from the connection between the means of the threat and the end or desired effect of the threat: *Mittel-Zweck-Relation* (eg, BGHZ 25, 217, 220). The application of this test depends to a great extent on the facts of the individual case. The general rule is that where the means of the threat and the end are intimately connected, the pressure is lawful; and where they are not related to each other, the pressure may be unlawful. It suffices here to give two illustrations taken from labour law, which provides numerous examples for the application of § 123 I second alternative BGB. (See for further illustrations, *Münchener Kommentar-* Kramer, § 123 Rn. 48 *et seq*, and Mankowski, *Beseitigungsrechte* (2003), pp 355–68.)

Thus, A threatens B, who is suspected of having committed a crime, to report him to the police if he does not pay him a certain sum of money. Reporting someone to the police is legitimate, at least if the person raised suspicion. Likewise, entering into a contract whereby someone promises to pay money to another is not unlawful. Hence, neither means nor end is unlawful. The legitimacy of the threat will depend on whether the alleged criminal behaviour and the desired result are intimately connected. This may be the case, for instance, if they concern the same event. A useful illustration is provided in BAG NJW 1999, 2059, case no 94. In this case, a cashier was suspected of harming the employer by omitting to charge relatives for the goods bought at the market where she worked. Her employer confronted her and faced her with the decision to sign a contract in which she would undertake to make good the damage caused or be reported to the authorities. This, the court held, did not constitute coercion. (See already, RGZ 110, 382, 385.)

In cases in which the dismissal of an employee is threatened, the *Bundesarbeitsgericht* has developed the rule that the threat is legitimate if a 'reasonable' employer had considered dismissal; eg, BAG NZA 2002, 731. If that were the case, then the employee is not entitled to rescind a contract of termination (*Aufhebungsvertrag*) entered into under the influence of the threat for coercion. While it is not necessary that the dismissal would have been upheld by a court *ex post* (eg, BAG NJW 1997, 676), overall, the test applied is strict and, crucially, difficult to predict; for criticism, see eg, Hromadka, EWiR 1998, 251, 252 and Benecke, RdA 2004, 147, who object that this test creates insecurity. (See also, for a summary of the case law, BAG NZA 2004, 597, case no 84, discussed in section 2 on consumer rights, p 274.)

English law, likewise, recognises a category of 'illegitimate' threats, which fall short of threats to act unlawfully and yet are threats to do something 'wrongful' (such as blackmail) or threats which are held to be contrary to public policy (eg, the practice of 'blacking' ships by trade unions: compare the situation at the time of *The Universe Sentinel* [1983] 1 AC 366 with that when the series of cases on *The Evia Luck* was decided: see *Dimskal Shipping Co SA v International Transport Workers' Federation ('The Evia Luck (No 1)')* [1986] 2 Lloyd's Rep 165 and *Dimskal Shipping Co SA v International Transport Workers' Federation ('The Evia Luck (No 2)')* [1989] 1 Lloyd's Rep 166; [1990] 1 Lloyd's Rep 319 and [1992] 2 AC 152). For example, in *The Universe Sentinel* (cited above) Lord Scarman made it clear that '[d]uress can, of course, exist even if the threat is one of lawful action: whether it does so depends on the nature of the demand. Blackmail is often a demand supported by a threat to do what is lawful, eg, to report criminal conduct to the police' (at 401. See, also, Lord Diplock, at 385). The key question will thus be whether or not the relevant demand is 'unwarranted' and given the basic position discussed in the next paragraph, it seems that this will rarely be held to be the case. A possible example is the case of *Norreys v Zeffert* [1939] 2 All ER 187, where a threat was made to notify trade protection societies and the defendant's social club of his default on moneys owed under certain bets. Atkinson J (*obiter*, having ruled that there was no agreement in any case) drew a distinction (in assessing whether there as consideration for an agreement to pay off those debts) between threats carried out in the lawful furtherance of the creditor's business and those that merely intended to injure the debtor in order to induce payment of money. Thus, one might characterise the threat to inform his social club and the trade protection societies as illegitimate and the demand is not one to enforce a legal debt, as the gaming contract is illegal and unenforceable in a court (unless a new promise to pay can be extracted and supported by valid consideration).

Nevertheless, it must be remembered that the basic position is that it will not normally be duress to threaten to do something that one has the right to do. For a recent discussion, see the case of *CTN Cash & Carry Ltd v Gallagher Ltd* [1994] 4 All ER 714, especially at pp 718–19: to quote Beatson's summary, 'as a general rule the determination of when socially objectionable conduct which is not itself unlawful should be penalized is for the legislature rather than the judiciary' (*Anson's Law of Contract*, p 283).

7

The Doctrine of the Foundation of the Transaction

1. INTRODUCTORY REMARKS

This German term of *Wegfall der Geschäftsgrundlage* or, more accurately, of *Störung der Geschäftsgrundlage* includes three main types of situations: (a) cases where the purpose of the contract cannot be fulfilled because of the occurrence of subsequent unforeseen events; (b) cases where the performance, though strictly possible, has become 'impracticable' or where the value of the counter-performance has significantly changed; and (c) mistake in shared basic assumptions. The foundation may never have existed; it may have been shattered; or it may have totally collapsed. Though different terms are used for these situations, it is by no means obvious that they should entail different consequences. Indeed, they are treated in the same way in German law. This marks a fundamental difference from the position under English law, which proceeds on the assumption that mistake rules apply if a common misapprehension is present at the day of entry into the contract, while the doctrine of frustration takes effect where events have occurred *after* the conclusion of the contract which make performance illegal, impossible, or radically different from what the parties contemplated when making the contract. In German law both cases are discussed under the common name of a 'disturbance of the foundation of the transaction' (*Störung der Geschäftsgrundlage*). Note however that cases where the performance has strictly and literally become impossible are (and have traditionally been) expressly dealt with in the Code under the heading of impossibility (§ 275 I BGB). Moreover, certain cases of 'practical' or 'personal' impossibility, which had previously been discussed as examples of frustration, are now assimilated to the law of impossibility in § 275 II and III BGB respectively. Likewise, illegality is—traditionally—governed by a special rule in § 134 BGB (discussed in chapter 5, p 240). The term 'frustration' thus has a different breadth from that of the doctrine of the foundation of the transaction and should therefore be avoided when discussing German law.

The concept of the foundation of the transaction occupies middle ground between interpretation, setting the contract aside on the basis of mistaken assumptions and irregularities of performance. Indeed, the concept assumes characteristics of each of these three devices. This is why we have devoted a separate chapter to it in this book.

2. THEORETICAL EXPLANATIONS

Cohn, 'Frustration of Contract in German Law' (1946) 28 *J Comp Leg & Int L* 15; Dawson, 'The Effects of Inflation on Private Contracts: Germany' 33 (1934) *Michigan L Rev* 171–238; Dawson, 'Judicial Revision of Frustrated Contracts' (1982) *Juridical Review*; Dawson, 'Judicial Revision of Frustrated Contracts: Germany' (1983) 63 *Boston University L Rev* 1039; Ebke, 'Legal Implications of Germany's Reunification' (1990) 24 *Int Lawyer* 1130; Hay, 'Frustration and its Solution in German Law' 10 *The Amer J Comp L* 345 (1961); Kegel, 'Empfiehlt es sich, den Einfluß grundlegender Veränderungen des Wirtschaftslebens auf Verträge gesetzlich zu regeln und in welchem Sinn? (Geschäftsgrundlage, Vertragshilfe, Leistungsverweigerungsrecht)' *Gutachten für den 40. Deutschen Juristentag*, I (1953) 135 (a comparative study which also reproduces summaries of the forty-two decisions published after the end of the Second World War); Kegel, Rupp and Zweigert, *Die Einwirkung des Krieges auf Verträge* (1941); Köhler, 'Die Lehre von der Geschäftsgrundlage als Lehre von der Riskiobefreiung' in *50 Jahre Bundesgerichtshof* (2000) vol 1, 295; Larenz, *Geschäftsgrundlage und Vertragserfüllung* (3rd edn, 1963); von Mehren and Gordley, *The Civil Law System* (2nd edn, 1976), pp 1038 *et seq*; Oertmann, *Die Geschäftsgrundlage* (1921); Philippe, *Changement de circonstances et boulversement de l'economie contractuelle* (1986); Nussbaum, *Money in the Law* (revised edn, 1950) (excellent on the socio-economic background of the post-First World War period); Schmidt-Rimpler, 'Zum Problem der Geschäftsgrundlage' *Festschrift für H.C. Nipperdey zum 60 Geburstag* (1955) 1; Simon, *Der Wegfall der Lehre von der Geschäftsgrundlage* (1988); Treitel, *Unmöglichkeit, Impracticability und Frustration im Anglo-Amerikanischen Recht* (1991); Zimmermann, *The Law of Obligations: Roman Foundations of the Civilian Tradition* (1990), especially pp 579–82. Special emphasis must be given to: W Lorenz, 'Contract Modifications as a Result of Change of Circumstances' in Beatson and Friedmann (eds), *Good Faith and Fault in Contract Law* (1995), p 357 (on which we have drawn freely).

If the circumstances in which a contract was concluded change after its conclusion, the ensuing legal difficulties bring into relief a clash between important contract values. The first is the principle of *pacta sunt servanda* and the certainty which this brings to legal transactions. Against this may stand the vaguer idea of fairness, often advanced behind the opaque Latin motto: *clausula rebus sic stantibus* (the historical, but not theological, foundations of which—which go back to Thomas Aquinas's *Summa Theologica*—are fully discussed by Pfaff, 'Die Clausel Rebus Sic Stantibus in der Doctrine und der Osterreichischen Gesetzgebung' in *Festschrift Unger*, pp 223–354 (1898). See also, Voirin, *De l'imprevision dans les rapports de droit prive* (1922)).

Throughout the nineteenth century, German states and jurists were divided as to which of these ideas deserved to take precedence. (For a comparative summary, see Schmitz, '*Clausula rebus sic stantibus*' in *Rechtsvergleichendes Handwörterbuch* I (1929), p 634.) For instance, the 1863 Civil Code of Saxony, in its § 864, took the view which had then come to prevail in Germany and ruled out any one-sided withdrawal from the contract because 'the circumstances under which the contract was made [had] changed or performance or counter performance [had] become disproportionate.' The earlier Prussian Code of 1794 had, on the other hand, provided a more detailed regulation (as was in keeping with its massive size) as well as a general provision—§ 378 I, 5—which stated that if '. . .an unforeseen change [of circumstances] makes it impossible to achieve the final aim pursued by the parties as expressed in the contract or inferable from the nature of the transaction, then each of them may withdraw from the unperformed contract.' (Likewise, see the *Codex Maximilaneus Bavaricus* of 1756, part 4, chapter 15.)

At first the importance of personalities played the decisive role in this area; later events of broader historical significance also played their part in influencing the development of the law. The personality to whom we refer was that of Bernhard Windscheid, arguably the most influential of the Pandectists of the nineteenth century and chief draftsman of the first version of the Civil Code. Now Windscheid had, as far back as 1850, written a monograph entitled '*Die Lehre des römischen Rechts von der Voraussetzung*'; and much of that thinking later found its way into his influential treatise on civil law (*Pandekten*, II (8th edn by Kipp, 1900)). Not surprisingly therefore the thesis came to the fore when Windscheid had his chance to draft the Code.

At its simplest, the theory posited that promisors usually assume that the intended legal consequences will occur only in certain circumstances. This assumption however about the continued existence of a certain state of affairs, has not been made a term of the contract. If the promisee had been in a position to realise that this 'presupposition' (*Voraussetzung*) had crucially influenced the will of the promisor, then the latter should not be held to his promise if this basic assumption (presupposition) was subsequently falsified. This comes close to saying that the contract itself was concluded under a condition (*Bedingung*) that the assumed state of affairs would remain unaltered for the period of the contract; and that is why Windscheid described this assumption as an 'inchoate condition' (*unentwickelte Bedingung*). The theory thus became known as the 'theory of presupposition' (*Lehre von der Voraussetzung*).

Those who were concerned with the security of commercial dealings struck back against this theory. The unilateral motives of one party, even if recognised by the other, could not be treated like conditions unless they had been incorporated into the contract. To do otherwise would allow one party to pass on his contractual risks to the other; and both legal certainty and commercial dealings would be impaired. Anyway, it was thought that the courts had other means at their disposal to cope with such cases since they could, where this seemed just and equitable for them to do so, imply a reservation of a right to terminate (*Vorbehalt eines Rücktrittsrechts*).

Doubts of this kind won the day, especially since Windscheid was not re-appointed as a member of the Second Commission that (partly) re-drafted the projected Code. But in an article published in volume 78 of the *Archiv für die civilistische Praxis* ((1892) 161, 197), he replied to Lenel's earlier objections (published in AcP 74, 213 *et seq* (1888)), retorting that the problem could not be brushed aside. 'The theory of tacit presupposition,' he argued, 'will, time and again, claim recognition. Thrown out by the door, it will always re-enter through the window.' He was right about the need to deal with the problem; less right about the fate of his theory. (Though Lenel returned to the fray again in AcP, 79, pp 49–107 (1899) with an article entitled 'Nochmals die Lehre von der Voraussetzung'.)

The 'Economic Consequences of the Peace' treaty (to borrow the title from John Maynard Keynes's famous book), signed at Versailles in 1919, led to the case law of the 1920s, described in the next section. The problem was thus back, the calm confidence of the nineteenth century having been shattered by a war that put an end to three empires—the Russian, the Austrian and the Ottoman—besides ruining Germany. Inevitably, the courts were forced to solve the new problem in a pragmatic way; but they needed a theory with which to justify their work. Oertmann obliged with a book entitled *Die Geschäftsgrundlage; Ein neuer Rechtsbegriff* ('The Basis of the Transaction: A new Legal Concept') but not before having had one last attempt to redefine the notion of impossibility (see his 'Der Einfluß von Herstellungsverteurungen auf die Lieferpflicht' JW 1920, 476). The new theory appeared just as inflation was about to take off and enter its last and deadliest phase. Oertmann thus looked as if he was going to be luckier than his father in law (Windscheid).

The basis of the transaction, according to this theory, is the 'assumption made by one party which has become obvious to and acquiesced in by the other' that certain circumstances which they regard as important are either extant or will come about, even though this assumption was not expressed in their declarations exchanged when making the contract. (Oertmann, *Die Geschäftsgrundlage; Ein neuer Rechtsbegriff*, at 37.) This distinguishes Oertmann's theory from Windscheid's doctrine, for it is not sufficient that the assumption belied by the future course of events was privately entertained by the party to whose disadvantage things have worked out; it must have been manifested by him 'during the process of the formation of the contract' and 'acquiesced in by the other party.' Thus, in essence, Oertmann had shifted from the hopes and expectations of the parties (stressed by his father in law) to the obvious effects which the changed circumstances had had on the transaction. (For a detailed comparison of Oertmann's theory with that of Windscheid (as well as the older doctrine of *clausula rebus sic stantibus*), see: Locher, 'Geschäftsgrundlage und Geschäftszweck' in 121 AcP, 1 (1923).)

Oertmann's theory, though an improvement on Windscheid's, is not without its difficulties. A typical, if somewhat outdated example given in German books, talks of the father of the bride who buys furniture for his daughter's new household. Disaster then strikes in the form of the cancellation of the wedding. Everyone, including Oertmann, agrees that it would be absurd to argue that the contract of sale disappears with the cancelled wedding. But why is this not so? The better answer is because this is not within the sphere of the seller's contractual risk. Oertmann's theory also fails to provide an answer to all those cases where, at the time when the contract was made, the parties did not foresee the alteration of circumstances. The most that can be said here is that the parties regarded the continuation of the present circumstances as self-evident. This however means that the theory excludes any assumptions about the future course of events; and this means that, in the end, we are back to the old theory of *clausula rebus sic stantibus* and the view that what matters is that the situation remains as it was at the time of conclusion of the contract.

A theory which has had the express or tacit support of scores of decisions of the *Bundesgerichtshof* cannot easily be brushed aside, even if the criticisms levelled against it are weighty. Yet as Werner Lorenz (among others) has argued, 'a perusal of these cases leaves the reader with the impression that these citations are mere ornaments' ('Contract Modifications as a Result of Change of Circumstances' at 370). Every result thus seems, on closer analysis, to turn on the facts of each case (as we shall try to show in the next sub-section). Moreover, the weight to be attached to such supervening events is not the same in all types of contract. The allocation of risk, inherent in each type of contract, seems to be the most important element in these crucial cases, turning on the 'collapse of the underlying element of the transaction.' It is also worth noting that in English law in the closely related area of 'failure of consideration' as a ground for restitution, this point concerning the allocation of risk as between the parties has been a key element in deciding exactly what was the basis of the transfer and whether this has failed sufficiently to entitle one party to claim restitution of any benefits already conferred. (For further details, see Virgo, *The Principles of the Law of Restitution* (1999), chapter 12.) Fuller discussion of this area does not seem appropriate in this context although one should note that the restitutionary principles can only come into play once any contract has been set aside. This leads to issues of electing between suing for breach of contract and rescinding the contract and then claiming a restitutionary remedy. This should not obscure the fact that, even once set aside, the contract, its terms and context, may be vital in assessing the availability and extent of any restitutionary claim (see *The Principles of the Law of Restitution*, pp 323–4).

This point concerning risk allocation will be found in most of the cases reproduced in translated form; and, according to Schmidt, it has become the common denominator of the case law since the decision of the *Bundesgerichtshof* of 1978 (BGH JZ 1978, 235, consolidating a trend which started with BGH NJW 1958, 297: *Staudinger-Schmidt*, § 242, Rn. 946). In this context it is perhaps also interesting to note that Treitel, who has written extensively on the subject both from the point of view of English and comparative law, shows equal scepticism about the utility of the search for the 'so-called theoretical or juristic basis of the doctrine of frustration' (*The Law of Contract*, p 920). To say, in a book on German law, that too much attention should thus not be wasted on theories, may sound heretical (especially since the post-Second World War period has seen no abatement to the Germanic ability (and predilection) to theorise; but with such powerful (and Anglo-German) authority backing such scepticism, the common lawyer may contemplate the thought, albeit with bated breath.

3. THE INITIAL APPROACH AND THE PRESENT POSITION OF THE BGB

There are (or used to be) a number of areas which the BGB left unregulated. One of them is the topic Anglo-American lawyers call frustration (subject to the reservations noted about this term, above). Yet it would be wrong to say that the Code (initially) totally ignored the problems raised by an unexpected change in circumstances. We thus find individual provisions, scattered in both the general and special part of the law of obligations, which deal with precisely such problems. We thus already referred to the rules of impossibility (§ 275 BGB) and illegality (§ 134 BGB) which would cover such cases as *Taylor v Caldwell* (1863) 3 B & S 826, ie the case of subsequent impossibility for which neither party is responsible, or *The Fibrosa* case [1943] AC 32. Here, then are two important English cases the facts of which have found an answer in the original text of the BGB. But there are other provisions which are narrower in scope, though the drafting commissioners of the Code made it clear that these exceptions were *not* meant to reflect the existence of a general principle. (See *Motive*, vol I, pp 248–9; *Protokolle*, vol II, pp 690–1.)

Further, § 321 BGB provides an important right to the contractor who has to perform his obligation first. For such a person is entitled to refuse such performance until an appropriate security is given if, after the conclusion of the contract, there has been a significant deterioration in the financial position of his co-contractor which endangers the claim for counter-performance. Likewise, § 490 BGB allows the person who has promised to make a loan to revoke his promise if a serious deterioration in the financial position of the borrower endangers the repayment of the loan. § 779 BGB deals with a slightly different factual situation, namely one in which the agreeing parties have entered into a compromise (*Vergleich*) on the basis of a commonly believed state of affairs which turns out to be wrong. Analogous situations in English law would, probably, be handled as cases of common mistake (see the recent case of *Grains & Fourrages SA v Huyton* [1997] 1 Lloyd's Rep 628 (above, chapter 6, p 279), concerning a common and fundamental mistake as to the basis on which the contract terms were rectified). Finally, even though § 138 BGB conceives of usury in broad terms (which in some respects bring the German notion close to the English treatment of undue influence), its utility in the kind of cases we are considering in this chapter is limited since it can only alleviate hardships which arose before the making of the contract. It is readily observable that these isolated rules did not cover the bulk of cases discussed by Oertmann. Despite this cautious attitude of the BGB, the courts have—in what could be called a 'revolution'—developed their own general principles as to when a change of circumstances is relevant and based them on the general clause of good faith in § 242 BGB. This function of general clauses in allowing reform of the law through judicial decision-making has been highlighted in chapter 1.

The major reform of the German Code of 2002 eventually supplied an all-encompassing statutory basis for the doctrine of the foundation of the transaction in § 313 BGB. (For a short but useful treatment of this aspect of the reform, see Lorenz/Riehm, *Lehrbuch zum neuen Schuldrecht* (2002), Rn. 388 *et seq*.) This provision attempts to capture the basic tenets of the doctrine as developed by academics and applied by the courts in an abstract yet flexible way. It was thus not the intention of the legislator to change the previous (case) law. (See preparatory works, *BT-Drucks.* 14/6040, pp 374–5.)

It is important to stress from the outset that § 313 BGB is open-textured and does not pre-determine the result of the application of the doctrine to individual cases. Its importance is of more symbolic nature and lies, first, in validating the introduction of the doctrine into German law by the courts, and secondly, in empowering the courts to step in and change the terms of the contract where they think it necessary to correct a 'disturbance' of the foundation of the contract. On closer examination, the provision leaves ample room for policy considerations when allocating the risk of the occurrence of unforeseen circumstances. In order to understand the field of application of this provision, it is therefore necessary to review the landmarks of the development of the doctrine of the foundation of the transaction. In the following we will give a brief conceptual outline of the doctrine and subsequently illustrate how this position of German law was developed step-by-step by the courts.

Paragraph 313 BGB differentiates conceptually but not as to the legal consequences between the so-called 'objective' and the 'subjective' foundation of the transaction.

§ 313 I BGB defines the *objective* foundation of a contract thus: 'If the circumstances which have become the foundation of the contract have seriously altered after the conclusion of the contract and if the parties would not have concluded the contract, or would have concluded it with a different content if they had foreseen this alteration, then adaptation of the contract can be demanded in so far as adherence to the unaltered contract cannot be expected of one party taking into consideration all the circumstances of the individual case and in particular the contractual or statutory division of risk.' Whether the objective foundation of the contract needs to be in the contemplation of the parties, at least insofar as they have regarded it as self-evident (eg, BGHZ 131, 209, 215), is subject to some controversy. The issue may be left open here since the courts do not actually inquire whether the parties did regard the circumstance in question as self-evident.

In § 313 II BGB, the *subjective* foundation of the transaction is treated in exactly the same way as the objective basis of the transaction. It is derived from the horizon of expectations of the parties and concerns the case that essential assumptions of the parties which have become the foundation of the contract turn out to be wrong.

The *legal consequences* of a disturbance of the foundation of the transaction are laid down in § 313 III BGB. In the first place, an adaptation of the contract is required. Only where such a 'gap-filling' exercise is not possible, may the disadvantaged party withdraw from the contract. The disadvantaged party is thus granted a right to have the contract terms adapted or, in exceptional cases, a right to terminate the contract. Long-term contracts are terminated with consequences only for the future; in respect of all other contracts a reversal of any performance of the contract hitherto also takes place (under § 346 BGB).

The *contractual distribution of risk* is central to the application of the provision. The contractual risk-allocation is determined by reference, first, to the contract terms themselves and, second, in the absence of an express stipulation, by reference to general contract law principles. Ultimately this is a decision taken on the basis of policy considerations. It is difficult to state many general principles used in defining what is seen as the foundation of a transaction. The application of the doctrine depends on the facts of the individual case. As a result, it is even more important to understand the historical development of this area.

There is one insight, however, which underpins the doctrine of the foundation of the transaction and which should be emphasised at this stage. The doctrine of *pacta sunt servanda* requires that a subsequent change of the terms of a contract must be restricted to extreme cases. Only where it cannot reasonably be asked of one party (*unzumutbar*) to bear the risk of a subsequent change of events, or to bear the risk of certain assumptions as to the state of affairs when entering into the contract, does the doctrine of the foundation of the transaction come into play.

As a general rule, in all three major lines of cases which have emerged over the years the debtor is required to stick to the terms of the contract. The three *main* groups of cases are: an imbalance between performance and counter-performance, the frustration of the purpose of the contract and common mistake.

First, the mere fact that performance has become more burdensome than anticipated does not as a general rule entitle the promisor to back out of the contract. (This is also the basic starting point in the English law of frustration: see eg, *Davis Contractors Ltd* v *Fareham Urban District Council* [1956] AC 696, especially at 729.)

However, if the value of the counter-performance consisting in the payment of a sum of money has changed, the courts tend to show more sympathy with the debtor and adapt the contract to the value at the time of entry into the contract.

Turning to the second main group of cases, likewise, it is only in exceptional cases that courts will step in and allow the debtor to invoke a change of circumstance in relation to the intended use of the object of the contract. Generally speaking, every party to a contract is taken to assume the risk that he will be able to make a profitable or otherwise satisfactory use of the object of the contract.

Thirdly, in relation to the subjective basis of the transaction, it does not suffice that, for instance, the basis of the calculation of the price has been made known to the other party. Other circumstances are required to justify transferring the risk of an erroneous calculation of the price to the other party. In the subsections below we will give illustrations for all three of these lines of cases. It may be useful first, however, to explore the origins of the doctrine.

4. THE CAUSE OF THE REVOLUTION

The origins of the courts' preoccupation with the effects of a change of circumstances, but not yet the cause of the revolution, can be found in those cases which attempted (often successfully) to enlarge the notion of impossibility regulated by the Code. The illustrations here show the courts starting with a notion found in the Code (objective, subsequent impossibility), to which the debtor's subsequent 'inability' is assimilated and extending it to economic impossibility (sometimes with the help of § 242 BGB) on the grounds that to decide otherwise would be 'asking too much of the debtor' (*dem Schuldner unzumutbar*). This has, with the latest major reform, become law in § 275 II and III BGB. These groups of cases thus form a convenient bridge to the more adventurous case law we shall encounter in the next subsection.

The first of these cases dealt with subsequent impossibility concerning generic goods. Here, the governing rule used to be found in § 279 BGB, which stated that 'if a debt described by class is owed, and so long as delivery of this class of object is possible, the debtor is responsible for his inability to deliver, even though no fault may be imputed to him.' The same rule is now contained in § 276 I 1 BGB (under the heading of '*Beschaffungsrisiko*'). In RGZ 57,116, the defendant had agreed to sell the plaintiff flour produced in accordance with his own mill's secret recipe. Before the goods could be delivered, the mill was destroyed by fire but not before 2000 tons of this flour had left the mill, destined for another customer. In the light of this last-mentioned fact, it was not possible to maintain that such merchandise of this kind was no longer available. If § 276 I 1 (ex § 279) BGB were to be applied literally, the seller could always re-purchase this flour from his other customer or, arguably, find similar flour in a distant market. Nevertheless, *aided* by § 242 BGB, the *Reichsgericht* took the view that the debtor is relieved where the fortuitous event has rendered performance so difficult that commercial men would regard such extraordinary difficulty as amounting to 'impossibility'. (Some earlier decisions, dealing with almost identical facts, had also absolved such 'innocent' debtors on the grounds that the accidental destruction of their mills made the performance of their contractual obligations 'essentially different.' Their inability to deliver the promised flour, while their mill was being re-built, was thus seen as amounting to 'impossibility' and not as 'delay'. See, for instance, RGZ 42, 114, 115.) On this point, compare the discussion of the well known English case of *Taylor v Caldwell* by Fuller and Eisenberg (*Basic Contract Law*, 3rd edn, p 801): the music hall could have been rebuilt in time to perform the contract, but it would have been so expensive that no reasonable businessman could be expected to pay out such sums in those circumstances. This reasoning is a nice parallel with the flour mill case discussed above (albeit not concerning bulk sales of generic goods), showing that 'impossibility' is a more relative term than it might appear at first sight (see further, Treitel, *The Law of Contract*, pp 880–1).

However, subsequent case law on bulk sales of generic goods showed that the courts were not automatically going to consider price increases, even when they exceeded 100 per cent of the originally agreed price, as constituting 'economic impossibility' leading to the absolution of the debtor. RGZ 88, 172, is one of a number of cases involving the sale of tin just before the First World War. The subsequent outbreak of hostilities sent the price of tin shooting up by some 200–300 per cent, but the *availability* of the goods was otherwise unaffected. In refusing to release the sellers (defendants) from their contractual duties, the courts took various factors into account, including the fact that these sellers were experienced wholesalers accustomed to price fluctuations. In the case in question, the court also felt that if the seller were released, the effect on retailers, who were more cautious in calculating resale prices, would have been disastrous because the percentage of price increases in their resale contracts would be much lower. The result might then be that such retailers would not have been able to plead 'economic impossibility'. The court thus held (at 177) that '. . . for such transactions the principle holds good that the seller will never be released as long as such goods are still being sold and bought on the market and are available in sufficient quantity for the performance of the contract. What the situation would be if only a few parcels of goods could be obtained by a fantastic offer or from a single supplier at an exorbitant price need not now be decided.' The final result was thus that the plaintiff (buyer) of the tin was allowed to claim the difference between the contract price of the tin and the amount he had to pay to another seller in order to obtain a substitute delivery. (For another 'tin' case, see RGZ 92, 322 and 95, 41.)

After the First World War, the case law shifted its ground somewhat on the basis of a new distinction. Were the generic goods in the wholesale contract in question available on a world market or was the debtor unable to choose between different suppliers? In the second situation, there could be cases where it would be 'utterly ruinous' (*geradezu ruinös*) to the seller to insist that he must perform at the originally stipulated price. For a time the idea of economic ruination held out some appeal and led to the so-called 'defence of ruination' (*Einrede der Existenzvernichtung*) being successfully pleaded in a number of cases. Thus, in RGZ 100, 134, the *Reichsgericht* was faced with an action brought against the sole distributor of Opel motorcars in Southern Germany who had entered into contracts to sell cars on the basis of the 1919 price list. Because of the hyperinflation that affected Germany after the end of the War (see next section), the price of the cars had increased very considerably when the contract had to be performed. The court stressed that sellers should carry the risk of price increases just as buyers should carry the risk of a fall in prices. In this case, however, the court took the view that the supplier had entered into a large number of such contracts and that their fulfilment at the originally stipulated price would be totally ruinous to him. (For further illustrations, see RGZ 101, 79; 102, 98; 102, 272.) By now, however, inflation was here to stay, and indeed the signs were that matters were going to get worse; and the defence of ruination was also increasingly criticised as failing to provide sure guidance for courts when deciding whether to intervene in cases concerning such contracts. Another Division of the *Reichsgericht* thus wondered whether this defence led to an unfair distinction between wealthy and impecunious or badly organised debtors, the latter categories too easily attracting the sympathy of the courts (RGZ 103, 177, 178); and by the end of 1921, when the movement of prices had become even more pronounced, this theory was abandoned (RGZ 103, 177; and for criticisms, see: Locher, 'Geschäftsgrundlage und Geschäftszweck' 121 AcP, 93 (1923)).

By this time jurists had also come to realise that all attempts to 'enlarge' the codal notion of impossibility suffered from two major flaws. The first, obvious to the reader from what has already been said, stemmed from the vagueness of the notion of 'economic impossibility', however one tried to define it. The second was linked to the fact that the pleas of impossibility, if accepted by the courts, resulted in the contract in question automatically being discharged; and a number of disputes soon made it clear that in many instances this was not the wish of either party to the affected contract! The search thus started for another theory which would make the answer turn more openly on the disproportionality between performance and counter-performance brought about by the unexpected turn of events, and which would also allow the parties to keep the contractual bond alive through mutually advantageous adjustments. The theories of Oertmann and Krückmann (enunciated in an important article published in 1918 in 116 *Archiv für civilistische Praxis*, 157 and based on the idea that proportionality between performances is of the essence in synallagmatic contracts) were to perform this function. These theoretical underpinnings arrived not a moment too soon. For the type of case that was now coming before the courts was different; and the economic imbalance, resulting from the galloping inflation, much larger (while in some instances also posing a direct challenge to statutory law). So we must turn our attention to this aspect of the case law and then look at the casuistry of the courts.

When Windscheid predicted in 1892 that the drafters of the Code were too optimistic in their belief that they could make do without a legal theory for changed circumstances he was right; but he could not have foreseen the events which brought this topic to the fore just after the end of the First World War.

The political events are well known. The victors of the war, largely under pressure from the French (on whose soil much of the war had been fought), demanded severe economic reparations from the defeated Germany, coupled with the 'occupation' of the German industrial zone in the Ruhr as a guarantee that these huge sums of economic atonement would be paid. In human terms, the demand was understandable; in economic and political ones, it proved a disaster. A disaster in social and economic terms for Germany, but ultimately for the rest of Europe as well. For the internal dislocation in Germany provided, eventually, the ideal conditions for the rise of the National Socialist movement which capitalised on the frustration induced in the German people, first by the hyperinflation of the 1920s and then the American-led deflation of the 1930s. If this appears easy to assert with the benefit of hindsight, one must not forget the handful of brilliant individuals (such as John Maynard Keynes) who foresaw much of this at the time but were unable to stem the tide of events.

These catastrophic consequences followed, indeed with a ferocity and a rapidity that may well be unique in world history. They certainly give the German law of 'frustration' a sense of uniqueness which contrasts sharply with the more 'commercial crises' that provided the staple diet of the English courts. (It is interesting, for instance, to note that we have been unable to find a German Suez case: for the English cases see eg, *Tsakiroglou & Co Ltd v Noblee Thorl GmbH* [1962] AC 93 and Treitel, *The Law of Contract*, pp 879–80.) Certainly, England never experienced inflation of this kind; and one may be permitted to speculate that if it ever did, its attachment to nominalism would fall by the wayside as it did in Germany. (Lord Denning's views in *Staffordshire Area Health Authority v South Staffordshire Waterworks Co* [1978] 1 WLR 1387, accord with this hypothesis; and their force is not diminished by the fact that in his country the great judge's views have, often, met with suspicion or rejection.)

Be that as it may, in Germany, at the beginning of the First World War, one gold mark had an internal purchasing power of RM1.05. By the end of the war, the figure was RM2.62 (somewhat higher than the rise that occurred in the US but lower than that found in France); and it had risen to 36.7 RM by 1922. But one year later— 1923—the rise became steep: 2,785 RM had the purchasing power of 1 RM of 1914. Then in May of that year prices literally went berserk, so that by the end of that year the mark had a trillionth of its 1914 value (1,200,400,000,000 RM equalled one 1914 RM). One can look at these figures in a different way. At the beginning of the war 4.2 RM bought one US dollar. By the end of the war, the mark stood at 7.43 to the dollar; and by the early Autumn of 1923 98,860,000 marks in order to purchase one US dollar. After that date, quotations were in billions of marks to the dollar.

In the light of the above economic developments, the calls for legislative intervention were very loud; but the problem was not easily soluble. Influential financiers, among them Schacht in an important book entitled *The Stabilization of the Mark* (1927), expressed serious doubts about the economic advisability of these revalorisation moves. Others thought that the social inequities of this situation required urgent action whatever the merits of purely financial arguments. Foreign creditors were also proving intransigent, thwarting the Reichsbank's attempts to stabilise the mark. (The financial aspects of the crisis are thoroughly discussed by Elster, *Von der Mark zur Reichsmark* (1928) who provides many interesting figures about the collapse of the German currency. For a discussion in English see: Graham, *Exchange, Prices, and Production in Hyper Inflation: Germany, 1920–1923* (1930).)

To this financial debate another one of a political/legal nature was soon to be added. Could the courts take matters into their hands when the legislator was unable and or unwilling to act? The outcry that followed in some quarters after the *Reichsgericht's* decision of 1923 (discussed in this section) was published, led the President of the Association of Judges of the *Reichsgericht* to issue a stern statement to the press. Some extracts deserve to be quoted in full since they give an idea of how extreme the tone of the debate had become:

No one will criticize the Reichsgericht for having too quickly and without mature reflection given up the principle that mark equals mark . . . the cautious way in which the decision [of 1923] is reasoned shows how fully the senate was aware of its responsibility in view of the significance of the decision. When the highest court of the Reich, after careful consideration of the arguments for and against, has come to such a decision, it believes that it can expect that the government will not set aside the view taken by the court by fiat (*Machtspruch*) of the legislator. The decision is grounded on the great concept of good faith which rules our legal life, and supported by the recognition that to continue to hold to the notion that mark equals mark would lead to a great deal of injustice, unbearable in a State based on justice (*Rechtsstaat*) . . . the concept of good faith stands outside of individual statutes, outside of particular provisions of the positive law. No legal order that deserves this honourable name can exist without this fundamental principle. Consequently, the legislator cannot by his fiat frustrate a result that good faith imperatively requires. (Statement of 8 January 1924, translated by von Mehren and Gordley, pp 1090–1.)

(For a fuller discussion see Kübler, 'Der deutsche Richter und das demokratische Gesetz' in AcP 162 (1963), pp 114–5.)

The statement elicited a prompt response from the Reich's Minister of Justice. Overall, it was more restrained in tone. In it he first claimed that the judge's reaction was based on newspaper reports about contemplated government action which had not yet been decided. But he then took particular objection to the judge's notion that the court's decision could not be altered by legislative action. He concluded thus,

. . . it would lead to a dissolution of the legal order and to a fatal dislocation of the governmental framework if a court claimed the right not to apply a law that had been enacted by the constitutionally required procedures because a majority of [the court's] members believe that the law is not in accord with the general moral law. . . .

In constitutional terms this must have surely been right.

Yet the courts were also right to take note of the fact that by this time the collapse of the mark in the foreign exchanges was largely the result of foreign perceptions and attitudes, something which gave them the opportunity to adopt a different optic towards the problems confronting them. The most important consequences followed from this realisation that the problem was no longer one of rising prices but of depreciation in the value of money. For, as Professor Dawson observed (33 *Michigan Law Rev* 171 at 190 (1934)):

A gross inadequacy of price could then be ascribed, not to the general disruption of economic life from which all Germans suffered alike, but to a change in the standard of value selected by the parties in the particular case. The creditor in a money obligation might fairly be required to forego the substance of his claim for the sake of the national interest or to preserve the sanctity and certainty of contract. It was quite another thing to require that he bear the risk of blind and capricious changes in the purchasing power of money.

Seen in this light, the 1923 decision acquires a certain aura of inevitability.

Two years later the dispute was brought to an end by the enactment of a statute (the *Aufwertungsgesetz*—Law of Revalorisation of 15 July 1925, superseding temporary legislation enacted on 14 February 1924) which adopted the court's ratio and allowed owners of land to extinguish their mortgages by paying a sum amounting to 25 per cent of the value of the mortgage in gold marks.

Yet the 1925 Act only applied to some transactions—mainly mortgages of land and negotiable bonds; and it allowed fixed adjustments to be made which varied according to their type or nature. (For instance, 25 per cent for debts secured by mortgage; 15 per cent for negotiable bonds; for most banks and insurance companies, partial receiverships were employed; bonds of government agencies received nothing etc. Clearly, these percentages meant that claims were, in large part, wiped out.) This approach did not please everyone (cf, for instance, Oertmann's views in *Die Aufwertungsfrage* (1924), pp 72–4); but the contrary decision to leave every possible transaction to be adjusted by the courts would have entailed huge delays and prolonged uncertainty. The Act (and a number of hotly contested government decrees) further excluded from the courts all public obligations of the Reich—a decision which obviously had an important effect on the country's public debt. Additionally, and perhaps most importantly from the point of view of private law, §§ 10 and 63 of the Act listed the bulk of the transactions (which included all synallagmatic contracts, payments for maintenance and support, etc) for which the adjustment and revalorisation was to be made 'according to general provisions of law.' So the 1923 decision retained a large area of application; it also ushered in a host of other problems. In what follows we discuss some of these difficulties. The precise way that each was solved must be sought in more specialised works, since it would be of little use to go into them in a book of this kind. (For a brief account in English see 'The Effects of Inflation on Private Contracts: Germany' 33 *Michigan L Rev* 171, 213–38 (1934).)

First, in effect the decision declared a 1909 Act of the German legislature (which had made the *Reichsmark* legal tender) no longer to be in force. Writing in 1934, Professor Dawson suggested '[t]hat a court of law could do so much [as was done by the Decision of 1923] is proof of the courage and imaginative insight of the German judiciary.' And he continued (33 *Michigan L Rev* 171, 238 (1934)):

> Seldom in history has there been a revolution in judicial thinking so complete, in the short space of four or five years. In retrospect it seems plain that every available resource of legal science was applied to relieve the mounting burden of intolerable injustice, to preserve what was left of order in the midst of universal collapse, and finally to reconstruct those values that the wreck had not wholly destroyed.

That the decision showed courage is beyond doubt; but Professor Dawson also might well have been right to add (as he did in an article written in 1983 (93 *Boston University L Rev* 1085) that the judges, who by that time were increasingly recruited from the middle classes which 'had suffered severely during the inflation,' might have been showing through their decisions their growing impatience with the 'political leadership that the Weimar Republic had installed—popularly elected, leftist in tendencies, and more and more helpless to cope with the array of interconnected and insoluble problems that piled up after the war.'

Secondly, the revalorisation that was proposed came to cover not only contracts not yet executed, but those—going back to 1922—which had been 'closed' through performance, compromise, litigation or otherwise. Coupled with the next point, this meant that a huge number of cases had to be resolved by trial judges and other administrative officials who were charged with the task of adjusting all such contracts. Professor Nussbaum, among others, has described the effects of this measure. He wrote:

> In his budget of 1926, the Prussian Minister of Finance mentioned that it had been necessary as a result of revaluation to appoint more than three thousand officials, permanent and auxiliary, to the Prussian courts. A figure of five thousand for all of Germany is probably not an exaggeration. Litigation, as if to imitate the scale of depreciation, rose to millions of cases.

Three reporter systems were created for evaluation cases alone; the *Reichsgericht* itself rendered considerably more than two thousand judgments on revaluation during a period of about ten years. Nearly half of them reversed the decision of the lower appellate courts, thus evidencing the bewilderment of the judiciary (Nussbaum, *Money in the Law*, pp 206–11).

The above was largely the result of the third consequence of the 1923 decision; and here again it deviated (for reasons which are not entirely clear) from the firmly-held principle expressed by the *Reichsgericht* only eight years earlier (RGZ 86, 397, 398, case no 95, cited with approval two years later by RGZ 90, 374, 375) that '[b]y the provisions of positive law the power is not conferred on the judge to re-adjust contracts for the purpose of alleviating the hardships of war.' Thus the possibility of merely discharging the parties (and ordering restitution where this was necessary) was ignored, the German courts moving increasingly (and with strengthened conviction since the second World War period) towards the position that contracts whose foundations were destroyed by unexpected events or discoveries would be revised and not terminated since 'in law it is a basic premise that contracts should be performed.' (BGH JZ 1952, 145, 146. Many other cases adopted this stance. For instance: BGH NJW 1953, 1585; NJW 1958, 785; NJW 1969, 233; BGHZ 58, 355; BGH NJW 1984, 1746, case no 106.) The 'claim for adjustment' (*Ausgleichsanspruch* on which see Hedemann, *Reichsgericht und Wirtschaftsrecht* (1929), especially 312 *et seq*) thus became an essential feature of this litigation.

How burdensome if not impossible was this task, which was now placed on the shoulders of the trial judge, can be seen from the 1923 decision itself, which allowed the owner mortgagor to pay off his loan (and remove the mortgage) by ordering him to pay the mortgagee/lender a supplementary amount. The instructions to the trial judge as to how this supplement should be calculated included the order 'to take into account not only the increase in the value of the land—measured according to paper marks . . . but also the other circumstances of the case such as the economic strength of the debtor and the nature of the land (ie, whether it was agricultural, industrial or urban). Also the charges, especially of a public character which burden the land must be taken into account.' And if that seems a Sisyphean task, consider the trial judge who had to comply with the instructions of the *Bundesgerichtshof* in the Volkswagen case decided in 1952.

The facts of this strange decision can be abridged as follows. Just before the beginning of the second World War the two plaintiffs, along with a further 336,000 other potential purchasers, made small payments to the DAF (*Deutsche Arbeitsfront*, an entity set up by the Nazi regime as a substitute for all former labour trade unions). The DAF acted as a sort of 'trustee' for the defendant, which was a car manufacturer that had the full backing of the Nazi apparatus in its effort to produce 'the people's car'. The money, prepaid through savings books made available for this purpose, was deposited by the DAF in a Berlin bank. The potential purchaser, known as a *Volkswagensparer*, would typically purchase stamps which would be stuck in a book and, when the requisite amount had been gathered, he could exchange the book for a car. When war broke out, the car factory was first turned to military purposes, and subsequently was largely (but not entirely) destroyed by Allied bombing. The series of disasters was then completed by the Russians entering Berlin before the Americans and confiscating the said DAF account. After the war had come to an end, and the dust—literally—had began to settle, the plaintiffs sought the delivery of their cars (and were willing to pay for them whatever price was assessed by the court). Their action was dismissed on the ground that the foundations of their contracts had been totally destroyed by the aforementioned events.

The *Bundesgerichtshof* disagreed, starting from the premise (mentioned above) that contracts once entered into must be enforced. The *Bundesgerichtshof* thus ordered the trial judge to find out how many of the other 336,000 prospective purchasers wished (and were able) to proceed with the purchase of their cars, as well as answers to a host of other questions. And, as if all this were not enough, the defendant firm was to be instructed to produce the maximum possible number of cars in order to ensure that this performance was not pushed too much into the future while ensuring that all new customers were also fully satisfied. Professor Dawson has observed that 'the trial judge to whom the case was returned must have had the sensation that he was wandering lonely as a cloud among the daffodils as he set about performing these multifarious tasks' (93 *Boston University L Rev*, 1085 (1983)). Professor Larenz, more Germanically and prosaically, wondered whether such an order required of the judge resources which he simply did not have at his disposal. No wonder then that in recent times academics, relying on judicial hints, have encouraged the idea of the parties being placed under a duty to renegotiate their dispute and only if they fail to reach an agreement to be allowed to have recourse to a court of law. (See, for instance, Eidenmüller, 'Neuverhandlungspflichten bei Wegfall der Geschäftsgrundlage' ZIP 1995, 1063 *et seq*, essentially reviewing Nelle's more wide-ranging *Neuverhandlungspflichten* (1993/4).)

But such attempts failed in the early 1920s, when the courts came increasingly under very heavy pressure of litigation, not least because the interests of the parties can be so diametrically opposed. One wonders, therefore, what might make such attempts succeed today, especially when the case law under this heading has, if anything, decreased in volume compared with the 1920s. In any event, rather than invent new duties to negotiate and, *faute de mieux*, hang them on the peg of § 242, one might well try to abandon the whole predilection for 'adjustment' and try to shift the judges towards the idea of termination (plus rights under the rules of unjustified enrichment). Professor Dawson was thus at his most convincing when he asked 'why should such a monumental, unmanageable task be undertaken at all?' (93 *Boston University L Rev*, 1086 (1983)) This preference to 'reconstruct' the contract rather than to 'dismantle' it rested in the first instance on the premise (established in the 1920s) that, since a contingency had occurred for which the contract had not provided, a court must step in and fill the gap. Few persons, even among the more sceptical authors, have been willing to admit that the conclusion had no connection whatever with the premise.

In comparative terms, the result of the above was that, at least in this respect, the German doctrine of 'frustration' is closer to the English equitable doctrine to order rectification in the case of a contract entered into by mistake than to the English law of frustration. For in the latter case the contract comes to an end automatically and without the court having any powers to adjust the parties' obligations except for certain restitutionary consequences. (See *Fibrosa Spolka Akcyjna v Fairbairn Lawson Combe Barbour Ltd* [1943] AC 32, and now the extended rights given by the Law Reform (Frustrated Contracts) Act 1943. On this see: *BP Exploration (Libya) Ltd* v *Hunt* [1979] 1 WLR 783, affd [1983] 2 AC 352.) Contrary attempts, made by Lord Denning in *British Movietonews Ltd v London and District Cinemas* [1951] 1 KB 190, were emphatically turned down on appeal by the House of Lords in [1952] AC 166;

and the same position seems to prevail in the US, even though one does find the odd case where judges have displayed the Germanic tendency to redraw the contract for the parties. (Thus see, the inconclusive case of *Aluminum Co of America v Essex Group Inc* 499 FSupp 53, 1980.) It should also be noted that, in English law, the relatively restrictive approach to the frustration of contracts has led to the development of an extensive and sophisticated practice of including *force majeure* clauses, particularly in standard form contracts. These clauses have a number of benefits for the parties: they can be triggered off even where the relevant event would not have amounted to frustration in the strict sense and the remedies provided under such clauses can be made more flexible than the total discharge of the contract (eg, suspending performance until the effect of the event has subsided, granting extra time to perform or providing further remuneration for performance that has become more onerous). (See generally, Treitel, *Frustration and Force Majeure* (1994) and McKendrick, *Force Majeure and Frustration of Contract* (1994).)

If the English story is much less dramatic than the German, it is not without its difficulties. Major adjustment of the strict English approach to the consequences of the frustration of a contract came in the form of legislative intervention in 1943 in the form of the Law Reform (Frustrated Contracts) Act. At common law, the result of frustration was to bring the contract to an end automatically and immediately (*Hirji Mulji v Cheong Yue Steamship Co Ltd* [1926] AC 497), with the result that all future obligations were discharged (*Appleby v Myers* (1867) LR 2 CP 651: obligation to pay for the partial erection of machinery was discharged when the premises and the machinery were destroyed by fire, because payment was to be made on completion of the work). Equally, obligations already accrued prior to the frustrating event remained in place (*Chandler v Webster* [1904] 1 KB 493), although the development of the law of restitution since the *Fibrosa* case (*cited above*) has allowed recovery of moneys paid over where there has been a 'total failure of consideration' (in the sense that none of the performance, for which the payment had been made, has actually been received). Even this last common law development left certain difficulties unanswered. For the requirement that such a failure of consideration be 'total' meant that receipt of any part of the performance could render the *Fibrosa* type of claim inapplicable. Further, the party that was thus forced to return such payments might have incurred preparatory expenses or left with goods now worthless due to the failure of the contract, neither of which it could claim against that sum to be repaid. It was such problems that the 1943 Act aimed to resolve and we provide a brief summary of the Act here.

Section 1(2) of the Act concerns the restitution of money paid. It basically embodies the *Fibrosa* position, but makes clear that the requirement of 'total' failure of consideration need not be satisfied to recover any payments made. The proviso to section 1(2) goes further, however, allowing any expenses incurred 'in, or for the purpose of, performing the contract' to be set off against any such repayments 'if [the court] considers it just to do so having regard to all the circumstances of the case.' Indeed, a claim can be made for such expenses under section 1(2) *even if no payments were made the other way* under the contract, *so long as* some payment was due to be paid in advance. Meanwhile, section 1(3) concerns the restitution of any 'valuable benefit' in kind, which again can be set off against any repayments to be made if the court considers that it is just to do so in the circumstances. The application of section 1(3) requires that the relevant benefit first be identified and valued and then the court must assess how much the party providing that benefit should be awarded (*per* Robert Goff J (as he then was) in *BP Exploration (Libya) Ltd v Hunt* [1979] 1 WLR 783). For analysis of the detailed operation of these provisions, see Beatson, *Anson's Law of Contract*, pp 558–62; Treitel, *The Law of Contract*, pp 913–17; Burrows, *The Law of Restitution* (2nd edn, 2002), pp 361–72 and Virgo, *The Principles of the Law of Restitution* (1999), pp 376–88.

A detailed analysis of the Act cannot be undertaken here; rather we wish to highlight certain issues raised by the operation of the Act.

First, we must note that the Act does not apply where a provision of the contract excludes it: section 2(3). This is consistent with the point made above concerning the allocation of risks by the parties: where this has been made explicitly, the courts will not intervene simply if one party has made a bad bargain.

Secondly, and interestingly from a comparative perspective in the light of the foregoing discussion, it may be asked whether the Act aims at a general apportionment of the loss suffered by the parties as a result of the frustrating event. In the first major case on the matter, the court held that the 'fundamental principle underlying the Act . . . is prevention of the unjust enrichment of either party to the contract at the other's expense' and not more general loss apportionment (*per* Robert Goff J in *BP Exploration (Libya) Ltd v Hunt* [1979] 1 WLR 783, at 799–800). This approach has been criticised by some. See, for example, McKendrick, 'Frustration, Restitution and Loss Apportionment' in Burrows (ed), *Essays on the Law of Restitution* (1991), p 147, on the basis that it is particularly difficult to distinguish between those actions in reliance on the contract that create a benefit and those that do not. Others, however, point out that the part-performer can more easily assess the risks involved and obtain insurance (Posner and Rosenfield, 'Impossibility and Related Doctrines in Contract Law: An Economic Analysis' (1977) 6 *Jo Leg Stud* 83, 112 ff) or suggest that such an approach would be contrary to 'the basic individualistic tradition of contract law whereby contracting parties are viewed as pursuing their own self interest and taking their own risk.' (Burrows, *The Law of Restitution*, p 365. More generally see Virgo, *The Principles of the Law of Restitution*, pp 373–90 (especially 388–90).)

The most recent case on the matter engaged in a detailed discussion of section 1(2) of the Act and in particular of the proviso thereto. (See *Gamerco SA v ICM/Fair Warning Agency Ltd* [1995] 1 WLR 1226 (noted by Clark [1996] *LMCLQ* 170)). In that case, Garland J concluded that section 1(2) was not merely a statutory formulation of the defence of change of position (on which see *Lipkin Gorman Ltd v Karpnale* [1991] 2 AC 548) but rather encompassed a broad discretion for the court to do what was just in all the circumstances, which could include some measure of loss apportionment (subject to the conditions of section 1(2)). It seems that it is accepted that some level of loss apportionment is thus possible under section 1(2), (thus Burrows, *The Law of Restitution*, pp 363–5), alongside a limited change of position defence. This is however a far cry from the legislation adopted in other Commonwealth jurisdictions which allows full loss apportionment to deal with frustrated contracts. (See, for instance, the Frustrated Contracts Act 1974 (British Columbia), the Frustrated Contracts Act 1978 (New South Wales) and the Frustrated Contracts Act 1988 (South Australia), helpfully discussed by Stewart and Carter, 'Frustrated Contracts and Statutory Adjustment: The Case for a Reappraisal' [1992] *CLJ* 66 (especially 79ff).

This is not the place to attempt to resolve this involved debate. Nevertheless, these points are highlighted to show that the effects of the common law and the various statutory interventions that have sought to improve the position have not been blind to arguments based on loss apportionment, although how far these interventions have dealt successfully with the issues raised is another matter, particularly when discussing the UK's 1943 Act.

5. ADJUSTING PERFORMANCE AND COUNTER-PERFORMANCE: A CLOSER LOOK

Outside the area of bulk sales where, as we have noted, some experiments were carried out with the notion of economic ruination, the attitude of the German courts remained reserved, initially at any rate. After all, the oracles of the law came from a background that had taught them that important legal changes come from the legislature, guided by the informed mind of trained jurists. Not surprisingly, therefore, the first rumblings of discontent with the economic consequences of a prolonged war fell on unsympathetic ears.

RGZ 86, 397, case no 95, is as good an example as any. There the defendant gave the plaintiff in 1913 the option to hire his circus. Because of the war, the takings at the gate were diminished; and the plaintiff tried to get out of his agreement. The court replied sternly that according to the law 'the judge is not empowered to adjust the relations between the parties . . . in order to mitigate the hardships of war.'

Five years later, in RGZ 100, 129, case no 96, the first signs of weakening appeared. The plaintiff, who in 1915 had let industrial premises to the defendant, was also expected to supply steam for the purposes of the business. By 1920, the cost for this had gone up considerably; and the plaintiff sought extra money, or at least a declaration that he had to supply steam only at a reasonable price. The *Reichsgericht* first referred to its earlier, harsher law (of which RGZ 99, 258, is particularly noteworthy since it (a) dealt with very similar facts and (b) was decided a mere three months before the present case) and then trumpeted the retreat from the positivistic positions of earlier years. 'The first and noblest task of the judge,' said the court, 'is to satisfy in his decisions the imperative demands of life and to allow himself in this respect to be guided by the experiences of life.' The case must be read carefully, not only for its disregard for strict legal analysis in favour of 'fairness', but because it contains the seeds of the new approach (criticised above), namely that the courts will not only terminate the contractual relationship, but will adjust it provided that three conditions are satisfied: first, both parties must wish to continue with the contractual relationship; secondly, an adjustment for both parties must be possible; and thirdly, such an endeavour will be undertaken only in the case of a 'very exceptional transformation of circumstances.' As repeatedly stated so far, the first of these features was, in one sense at least, the most important since both parties were unwilling to accept the one remedy (discharge of the contract), which the hitherto favoured theory of 'impossibility' would allow.

The new approach did not find immediate favour with all the divisions of the *Reichsgericht*. (At that time there were seven, though two years later that had risen to thirteen. For a disapproving decision see, for instance, RGZ 103, 170, 177.) Yet the dam was breached; and RGZ 103, 328, case no 97, unequivocally confirmed the new trend, for the first time also alluding to Oertmann's theory rather than using the more emotional language of the earlier decision. The court at least made the pretence that it was applying a scientific theory emanating from a professor of the University of Göttingen, a comforting refuge for most German judges. But as we have already noted and Kegel has pointed out, the decision ultimately hinges on the court's distribution of risk on the basis of policy considerations: the risk of currency depreciation, following a lost war, is not one which can be allocated to one party or the other but must be born by both, ie the population at large. The road for the revalorisation (*Aufwertung*) decisions was now wide open; and not a moment too soon, for by the Spring of 1923 inflation had entered its most virulent stage.

The facts of that landmark case (RGZ 107, 78, case no 99) were simple; and the policy question it had to answer was how could one achieve an equitable distribution of the currency risks in a currency market which found itself in great turmoil. But it also had to confront two difficulties which had not figured so prominently in the earlier case law. The first was the language of the private bargain which left no room for judicial intervention; the second the unequivocal and forbidding wording of the statute which adopted the principle of nominalism. The litigation arose because the owner of land (mortgagor) tried to pay off his lender (mortgagee) with old marks. The mortgagee refused to surrender the mortgage unless and until he was paid a properly revalued sum. The language of the Supreme Court has none of the emotive tone of the earlier case (RGZ 100, 129, case no 96); nor does it show any traces of the politically provocative stance found in the subsequent press announcement of the presiding judge—no doubt because it was conscious of the significance of its decision. But the opinion did contain a number of very important points, which had been foreshadowed in the earlier cases and have been maintained intact ever since (in addition, of course, to invoking the Oertmann theory).

The first point was that such interventions would only be undertaken in cases involving the most serious of disruptions. The 1920 decision had thus ruled that 'only very special and quite exceptional transformation and change of circumstances . . . can bring about the result outlined above [revalorisation]. The fact alone that a subsequent change in the conditions is not foreseeable and could not be foreseen does not suffice.' The 1923 decision justified its abandonment of 'nominalism' by stressing the fact that 'this principle must be disregarded . . . if as a result of an especially heavy depreciation of legal tender, not foreseen at the time when the currency regulation was passed [ie,1 June (1909)], it would lead to results which can no longer be reconciled with § 242 BGB.'

This point was well made in a post-Second World War case (the facts of which can be found below: BGH NJW 1959, 2203–4, case no 102). There the *Bundesgerichtshof* stated:

One of the stated requirements for the application of the theory of the collapse of the basis of the transaction . . . is that the intervening change be of critical nature and affect the interest of the parties to a significant degree. Not every adverse modification of the prior relationship of equivalence, unforeseen by the parties at the time of the contract, justifies a departure from the principle that contracts must be adhered to (*pacta sunt servanda*). What is really required is such a fundamental and radical change in the relevant circumstances that it would be an intolerable result, quite inconsistent with law and justice, to hold the party to the contract.

The 1923 case, RGZ 107, 78, case no 99, also re-emphasised a point that we made earlier, namely that these cases do not purport to lay down a general rule which will be applied mechanically in each subsequent decision. Thus the court stressed that 'it will be necessary to determine in each case and in accordance with the principle of good faith what degree of monetary depreciation is necessary before a creditor's claim must be revalued.' Indeed, earlier in its opinion the court had expressly stated that no general principles can be established requiring the revalorisation of every mortgage claim as such, nor that they must all be revalorised to the same extent.' (This last point, however, was abandoned by the 1925 legislation which set fixed amount of revalorisation for the various typed of transaction for which it provided.)

The third point implicitly confirmed by this landmark case was that adjustment, and not termination of the contract, was the logical reaction to this crisis. This pre-ferred option seemed to follow from the principle enunciated many times since that 'in law one must start from the premise that contracts are to be performed'; and a number of subsequent decisions have stressed their belief that they do not regard themselves as intervening in these cases but merely helping bring about the natural result of the contract. (See, for instance, BGH JZ 1952, 145 and note by Kegel.) That this, however, does not necessarily follow from abstract contractual logic can be seen by looking at other legal systems which have not followed the German approach. A number of cases, which are noted below, make one wonder whether this approach is in many cases at least preferable to a simple termination of the contract followed by an application of the rules of unjust enrichment, if any. But whatever the merits of the 'adjust' rather than 'dissolve' approach, let us stay with it for a moment and see what forms this adjustment took in practice.

More often than not, the adjustment took the form of increasing the amount of the performance in order to provide the equivalent of the counter-performance which had already been rendered. One thus assumes that in the 1923 case the mortgagor would have been made to pay a higher amount in exchange for the removal of the mortgage from the *Grundbuch* (the German equivalent of the Land Registry.) (See, for instance, BGH DB 1958, 1325.) Indeed, as already stated, the Revalorisation Act made this equal 25 per cent of the mortgage in gold marks. Even with the sum of revalorisation fixed (from 1925 onwards) to 25 per cent of the mortgage, other difficulties arose in practice. Here are two of the variations that confronted the courts.

In the first variant, cases arose in which the *vendor* (mortgagor) of land undertook, as part of his obligations of sale, to extinguish any mortgages which existed on the sold land. If he did this before the transfer to the purchaser, but the lender/mortgagee had been paid with worthless money, he could demand the reinstatement of the mort-gage in the Land Registry. This revival of the mortgage, however, had the conse-quence that the vendor could no longer be said to have transferred the land to his purchaser, free of all encumbrances (*lastenfrei*), as he is obliged to do under § 439 II (now § 442 II) BGB. This meant that he thus had to pay off the mortgage for a second time and, what is more, in hard currency—a sum which invariably exceeded the pur-chase money. The *Reichsgericht* held that in such cases good faith required that the vendor of the land be granted a contribution claim (*Ausgleichsanspruch*) against the purchaser, so that the purchaser was thus obliged to contribute to the cost of paying off the mortgage. The size of this contribution, invariably left to the lower courts to assess, was determined by a variety of circumstances, though it must be added that a purchaser unwilling to go along with such an arrangement was allowed to terminate the contract of sale.

The second variation on this theme involved the reverse situation. Here the purchasers of land were again asked to make increased payment to the vendors in cases where, as a result of altered circumstances, *they* (and not the vendors as in the preceding example), were relieved of obligations under the contract of sale. This situation was, for instance, brought about where the purchase price was less than it would otherwise have been because the purchaser had expressly undertaken to pay any mortgages that burdened the land.

This factual variant was litigated after the Second World War as a result of a series of crucial economic decisions taken in the summer of 1948 by the German civilian leadership (of the 'Allied-occupied' Germany). The decision of 23 June 1948 in particular gave rise to this problem by introducing new currency legislation which allowed Reichsmarks already in circulation to be exchanged for the new DM at a rate of 10 RM for DM1. The measure (and the freeing of price controls, also taken at the time) put Germany on the path of its astonishing post-war economic recovery. But it also meant that purchasers, in cases like the one just described, ended up with a windfall at the expense, one could say, of vendors for they were able to pay off mortgage-secured debts at one tenth of their value. Once again therefore a judicial order was thus made that the amount 'saved' by the purchasers should be paid to the vendor. (See BGH MDR 1959, 564. Purchasers might make other such savings, for instance when they assumed tax obligations related to the land which turned out to have been grossly over-estimated by the parties.) Overall, the amazing—to an outsider at least—feature of this case law is not only its volume, but more the fact that 'adjustments' were ordered where the purchasers had made benefits of something in the order of 10 per cent of their total obligations. (See on this, Rothe, 'Lastenausgleichskslauseln im Grundstücksverkehr' DB 1963, 1527.)

In the cases just mentioned, the adjustment took the form of an added or *increased* amount which had to be paid by one of the parties to another. Alternatively, the value of the contractual performance could be *decreased* or scaled down, or the time of performance altered, eg, extended. (BGH MDR 1953, 282, case no 101; BGH NJW 1958, 785.) The sugar beet case offers the best-known example.

There, two major landowners in post-Second World War East Germany (before it was defeated by the Russians) dealt in sugar beets. One—the seller/plaintiff—grew them on his land; the other—the defendant—extracted the sugar from them and then sold it. On one occasion, and after the extraction had taken place, the plaintiff demanded the sale price but before the case could be decided, the defendant's land was confiscated by the Russians. At first instance, the action for the price was dismissed, the lower court in effect taking the view that the defendant had lost enough and should not be asked to pay damages in the circumstances. The *Bundesgerichtshof* took a different view. Good faith applied to this case; and it required that the defendant pay something—the lower court would have to determine the amount—though not the entire contract price.

The possibility of *substituting* a different subject matter (rather than increasing or decreasing the obligations) was, on the other hand, very rarely ordered. Thus, in 1971 the Court of Appeal of Karlsruhe decided (JZ 1972, 120) that a contract to deliver over a long period of time coal from certain mines which were closed down (because of their high costs) could not be substituted by an offer by the seller to deliver coal of similar quality but coming from other mines. Yet in another case, the promise to supply alternating electrical current was substituted without hesitation by an obligation to provide direct current. (BGH NJW 1954, 1323.)

The decision of the Court of Appeal of Karlsruhe looks decidedly odd in the light of a decision handed down by the *Bundesgerichtshof* some ten years earlier. The facts of this unusual case were as follows.

A city dweller, who wished to live in the country, was offered the possibility of a lease on which the defendant/builder was to erect for him a pre-fabricated house. When, to the surprise of both contracting parties, the local authority declined to give building permission, the plaintiff sought to recover his down-payment to the builder. The latter however was able to offer to build the house on another plot of land, located nearby, which had the same characteristics as the first plot (view, clean air etc) but belonged to another landowner who however was willing to lease it to the plaintiff for the same rent. The BGH was of the view that if these assertions could be proved, then the substitute performance should be allowed to go ahead.

Cases where the contract has been entirely terminated seem rare, though on many occasions the courts have not denied the fact that 'good faith may also require the total release from contractual liabilities' (see, for instance, BGH MDR 1953, 282, 283, case no 101). One case where this happened, since no other solution was available to the court, is the case discussed below concerning the transfer of a football player who, prior to the transfer and unbeknown to the selling and buying clubs, had accepted a bribe to lose a game (BGH NJW 1976, 565, case no 105). Surprisingly however the highest court failed to reach this result—termination—in the so-called *Volkswagen* case, discussed above, which would appear to have offered the ideal kind of facts for such an answer. There, termination coupled with restitution of the sum paid—perhaps adjusted to take into account of the effects of war—would have been the most practicable solution given that the basis of that particular transaction had been so dramatically destroyed by the intervening war and the subsequent Russian occupation of Berlin.

No exclusive list of the types of cases that have been caught by § 242 BGB can be given here; even the large German treatises content themselves with giving illustrations. So we shall mention only two more.

The first concerned contracts which had linked payment to the gold standard or to currencies such as the English pound which were tied to gold. Through this device, they had found salvation from the ravages of the inflation of the 1920s. Yet the American-led deflation of 1930 led to the abandonment of the gold standard and a new round of decisions, often provoked by sellers asking for an increment (*Ausgleichsanspruch*) toward the loss attributable to devaluation (usually in the order of 20 or 30 per cent). Where the claims were accepted, they were accompanied by the usual request to the trial judge to investigate a number of relevant points (eg, had the seller in his capacity as importer of the merchandise taken advantage of the devalued pound? Was the buyer an exporter, and if so did he suffer any losses from the diminished value of the foreign currency? See, RGZ 112, 329, 333–4. See also, RGZ 119, 133 (sale of land); RGZ 147, 286 (sale of cotton) pegged to the American dollar leading to a loss of 13 cents to a dollar).

The second group of cases present a somewhat unique feature, namely that the hardship was solely one-sided. These were obligations to make periodic payments of money for another's support, typically concerning pensions. In such cases, the person entitled to be paid could not be expected to pay anything more. This type of case really called for only one type of reaction: upward adjustment. This indeed happened in the 1920s; but in the post-Second World War period, the *Bundesgerichtshof* showed itself to be remarkably slow in taking the same steps. The fact that living costs had not experienced catastrophic increases was at best a partial reason, since we have noted that in other contexts the courts had been willing to intervene in circumstances where the change in the situation was anything but enormous. It is more likely that judges— like everyone else—had become aware that by the mid-1960s the total cost of pensions ran into billions of marks and that thus a decision in one pension case, though limited (in the light of what we have already said) 'to its particular facts' would, inevitably, extend over a very wide range of similar transactions the features of which would be 'virtually indistinguishable' (Stötter, 'Der Wegfall der Geschäftsgrundlage wegen Kaufkraftminderung bei Gehalts-und Ruhegeldvereinbarungen' DB 1966, 809). But in 1973 the *Bundesgerichtshof* decided to bite the bullet and authorise an upward adjustment to prevent 'unbearable' injustice (BGHZ 61, 31, case no 104). The decision was controversial at the time; but it also contains interesting *dicta* and it thus deserves a closer look.

The action in that case was brought by the plaintiff who became the defendant company's director in 1935. He was employed at a very high salary and that salary formed the basis for generous calculations for his retirement pension, which he took in 1951. During the next decade the cost of living in the Federal Republic of Germany rose by approximately 1per cent per annum but then, from 1960 onwards, it started a steep rise so that by 1971 it had reached approximately 54 per cent (which amounted to an internal devaluation of about 35 per cent). The plaintiff's demand for an adjustment was accepted by the *Bundesgerichtshof*, which referred to its earlier reluctance to take such a step but also to some recent decisions of the Federal Labour Court which had, more recently, blazed the trail in this respect. Such an adjustment of the pension would be made out of the profits of the enterprise, which the pensioner had helped create; and would also represent an appropriate reward for his long loyalty towards the company. The Federal Labour Court had added that,

> [t]hese services had been rendered by the pensioner in advance, trusting that he could plan the later stages of his life on the basis of a maintenance promised to him. If this expectation should be disappointed as a result of the depreciation of the currency, a pensioner would have no longer the means of bargaining for an adjustment, contrary to the sections of the population whose income would have kept up with the increase in prices.

Naturally, the court repeated the usual ritual of sending the case down to the trial judge to do all the hard work; and for good measure added the standard statement that every case turned on its facts. Nevertheless, it also contained two very interesting strands of thought, which must be mentioned briefly.

First, the court stated that in future cases one should not rush to the courts but first try to explore the possibility of a negotiated agreement between the parties concerned. (A view which, as we have seen, has since gained some support among certain academics and also accords with the current trend in the UK to encourage negotiation, alternative dispute resolution and settlement out of court: see the recent reforms of English Civil Procedure, treated in Andrews, *English Civil Procedure* (2003).) If that failed, then the employer should be expected to put forward his own, reasonable proposals; and only if they failed to meet with the agreement of the pensioner should the possibility of a court action be entertained. In this respect, the court noted that such a practice had indeed become fairly widespread in the world of business.

The court then stressed in various forms that the plaintiff's high earnings should in no way be held against him in this process. 'The extent of the rise in prices should be the standard for fixing the extent of the adjustment,' reasoned the court and 'no attention should be given in principle to any other aspects of the pensioner's assets or income, except, perhaps possibly to any increase in income arising from any statutory insurance.' On the other hand, the profitability of the enterprise and the 'principle of equality of treatment' might well be relevant considerations for the calculations of the trial judge.

6. FRUSTRATION OF PURPOSE

We have stressed from the outset of this chapter that the German term *Störung der Geschäftsgrundlage* covers a variety of legal problems which in other systems—eg, English law-would be handled by a variety of different concepts. So far we have concentrated on altered circumstances which have destroyed (*Erschütterung*) the balance between the performances of the parties or made the foundation disappear (*Wegfall*). In this section we shall concentrate briefly in the remaining two major headings: the 'frustration' of the common purpose of the contract and mistake as to basic assumptions (*Fehlen der Geschäftsgrundlage*). Cases of literal or physical impossibility (*Unmöglichkeit*) will, of course, be discussed in greater detail in chapter 9, section 3, p 406. Three preliminary notes of warning are however necessary.

First, as Palmer has observed about American law (but which, we believe, also holds some truth for German and English law as well) '[t]here is a marked similarity between mistake in basic assumptions, impossibility, and frustration of purpose' (*Treatise on Restitution*, II, § 7.2 (1978)). This leads us to the second warning. Differentiations may be possible at a theoretical level; but in practice, the results may well be very similar whichever road one chooses to go down. Finally, and in view of the above, it does not really matter where one treats this last subject of mistake as to present facts: under the heading of mistake (which is what common lawyers would prefer to do) or 'changed circumstances' which currently is the preferred approach in Germany.

Turning then to our first kind of problem, we note that debtors are not, normally, excused if the occurrence of events has frustrated their assumptions about the profitability of their transaction (see, eg, *Davis Contractors Ltd v Fareham Urban District Council* [1956] AC 696). In such cases the normal rule is that the risk falls on them. This fundamental principle is not expressly laid down in the BGB but presupposed by a number of more specific provisions. Thus, § 537 I BGB states that the lessee is not exempt from paying the rent if he is for a personal reason unable to use the rented object. Likewise, § 649 BGB entitles the employer under a contract for work and materials to terminate the contract if he no longer requires its performance; however, the contractor remains entitled to the counter-performance subject to any savings he made because he did not actually carry out the contract. The case law confirms the validity of this risk-allocation but occasionally distributes the risk of being able to use the object of the contract otherwise.

Thus, in one case, the *Bundesgerichtshof* stated that 'the risk of being unable to dispose of the [purchased] goods normally falls within the purchaser's area of risk' (BGH NJW 1984, 1746, 1747, case no 106); and in another case it added that,

> in a contract for the production and sale of goods, the intention of the person placing the order to forward the . . . products to a particular client does not render this purpose of concluding the contract a basis of the transaction which affects both parties. Reasons of contractual certainty require that in principle each party must bear the risk that the purposes intended by him in concluding the contract cannot be achieved (BGH MDR 1953, 282, 283, case no 101).

In appropriate circumstances, however, both parties may understand the purpose for which the contract was concluded; and future failure of this purpose may make the contract worthless for the party now seeking relief. Four cases illustrate this; and their similarity with the *Krell v Henry* type of situation [1903] 2 KB 740 has been discussed *ad nauseam* by German jurists (eg, Larenz, *Schuldrecht I* (14th edn, 1987), § 21 II 1). If they have one thing in common, it is that they show that the German courts seem if anything more willing than the English to intervene and adjust the contract. The cases also show a strong preference for doing this through the notion of 'frustration' rather than impossibility or mistake, perhaps because this gives them more room to manoeuvre and fine-tune the contractual obligations. Whether they should be doing this is, as we have seen, another matter.

In the first case (OLG Bremen NJW 1953, 1393, case no 100), the plaintiff hired a sports hall from the defendant for a special appearance of a well-known singer. The rent was to be 15 per cent of the profit but not less than DM1500, this last amount to be paid at the time of conclusion of the contract. When the singer fell ill and the performance was cancelled, the plaintiff demanded the return of the money paid. The Court of Appeal of Bremen held that he was entitled to it. For this was not a simple hiring of a hall, but a hiring of a hall for a specific purpose which was known to the other party and had become the foundation of the transaction.

A year later the *Bundesgerichtshof* itself had occasion to confirm this approach in another case (BGH MDR 1953, 282; '*Bohrhammerfall*' or pneumatic drill case, case no 101). The case has been criticised, mainly on the grounds that it paid too much attention to vague ideas of equity rather than looking at the proper distribution of risks; but for present purposes it provides an illustration of how 'frustration of purposes' can work in practice.

In that case the defendant, who did business in West Berlin, ordered six hundred drill hammers, which the plaintiff knew were destined to be used in mines in East Germany. By the time the plaintiff accepted the order and started production, the (first) Berlin blockade had already been brought into effect. The plaintiff asked for payment of the contract price. The defendant refused, pleading that (at that time) he could no longer dispose of them in the East (and, apparently, not easily even in the West since the drills were of an out-dated type). Though the court took the view that neither the defendant's order nor the plaintiff's letter of acceptance stated that the validity of the order depended on the possibility of delivery in the eastern zone, such delivery had nevertheless become the basis of the transaction 'since both parties shared the assumption that delivery of the drills to the east zone would become possible in the foreseeable future.' In the court's view it was immaterial whether the basis of the transaction had disappeared after the conclusion of the contract, or whether it did not exist at the time when the contract was concluded, since the legal consequences were in both cases, the same: the transaction was not invalid; but had to be adapted to the actual situation in accordance with the dictates of § 242 BGB. The defendant thus had to pay for the drills which had already been completed (even though he could not ship them to the East) but was relieved of all liability for the remainder.

The third (and chronologically most recent) case on this kind of 'frustration' related to the performance of a music band at a carnival event which was cancelled as a result of the Gulf War. The Oberlandesgericht of Karlsruhe (NJW 1992, 3176) did not even discuss impossibility, but relied on the doctrine of *Wegfall der Geschäftsgrundlage* in order to relieve the music band from liability.

Arguably, the fourth case is the most important in this series. It arose out of the fall of the Shah and the advent of the regime of the ayatollahs in Iran. The full and complicated facts can be found in the translation reproduced below. (See BGH NJW 1984, 1746, case no 106.) Here suffice it to say that the dispute concerned the shipping of German beer to Iran, some of which arrived in a damaged state. A compromise was then reached by the parties which provided, inter alia, that the plaintiff would (a) be allowed to get his next consignment of beer at two-thirds of the original price per case and (b) would be paid the sum of DM20,000 as compensation for the damaged beer when he put in his next order for beer. However, the advent of the fundamentalist regime in Iran made such further orders impossible; and without them the amount promised as damages also failed to reach the plaintiff. His attempt to secure a new compromise having failed, he then tried to claim the full loss originally sustained by him as a result of the defective consignment.

The *Bundesgerichtshof* started with the by now customary dictum that a 'change in circumstances does not make contracts disappear *in toto* [but that, on the contrary,] the general rule is that they should be maintained.' It then addressed the crux of the matter with the following statement:

> It is true that in commercial matters the risk of being unable to dispose of the goods normally falls within the purchaser's area of the risk; but the court below was right to point out that this was not a contract of sale but a transaction by which the defendant was to compensate the plaintiff for its losses. There is nothing to suggest that if the compensation envisaged by the compromise failed to materialise, the parties intended the loss to be borne by the plaintiff alone.

The court thus accepted that the best way out of this impasse was to order the defendant to pay half of the profit which the plaintiff would have made if the compromise agreement had not been disturbed by the events in Iran.

This case, unlike the previous one, not only offers a good illustration of 'frustrated purpose' litigation, it also represents a good example of a decision applying the more legalistic approach which currently prevails among German courts. This, as already stated at the beginning of this section, pays more attention to the allocation of risk which the contract and the surrounding circumstances dictate than to the vaguer, equitable grounds which figured so prominently in the earlier case law. Indeed, this approach which was confirmed by the *Bundesgerichtshof* in its decision of 8 February 1978 (BGH JZ 1978, 235), has provided constant guidance ever since. In 1972 the defendant, an oil importer, agreed to supply the plaintiff oil by instalments at an agreed price. At the time when the contract was made the price of oil was approximately DM100 per ton. After the Yom Kippur War in October 1973, the price of oil, which had been steadily rising during the preceding months, rose further and reached DM600 per ton. At this stage, the defendant informed the plaintiff that he would only supply him with further oil at an adjusted price. The plaintiff refused to consent to this proposal and, on the contrary, warned him that he would treat any interruption in supply as amounting to a breach of contract. This indeed occurred, and the plaintiff claimed from the defendant the amount he had to pay to obtain his oil from another source.

The *Bundesgerichtshof* accepted the claim as well founded. True, it admitted that in synallagmatic contracts the starting assumption was that performance and counter-performance were of equivalent value. Yet the contract and its surrounding circumstances might indicate how the parties intended to delimit their respective spheres of risk. The fact that this was a fixed price term indicated that the defendant was willing to assume the risk of price fluctuations. To the argument that, even if this were so, the assumption was limited to 'normal' fluctuations and not to increases of the kind experienced here, the court's view was that the defendant should have realised that further price increases were imminent and could have absorbed their effect by stockpiling oil while its price was still at manageable levels. In view of the paramount importance of the principle *pacta sunt servanda*, the defence of the collapse of the underlying basis of the transaction would not be permitted; and it should be limited to those cases where it was 'indispensable for avoiding intolerable results, irreconcilable with law and justice.'

This disinclination to be easily carried away by the *Geschäftsgrundlage* theory has been confirmed repeatedly since 1978, the emphasis having shifted to the objectively ascertained 'allocation of risks.' BGH NJW 1977, 2262 brings this point out clearly.

There builders who sold family homes also offered to supply them with direct heating produced by their own power station nearby. The prices would be determined by tariffs charged by the public utility of this community. Soon after the contract was concluded, the builders discovered that they had made a bad bargain since the public utility in question did not shift the full burden of the price increase of coal and oil on to its customers (since it was able to make up for these rising costs in another way). The *Bundesgerichtshof* insisted that the builders could not escape their contractual undertakings even though they were losing nearly DM60,000 per annum. This was a bad bargain, and it could not be pleaded as being due to changed circumstances because the circumstances causing these losses were clearly within the builder's sphere of risk. Besides, reasoned the court, the enterprise was large enough to absorb such losses! (In the same vein, see: BGH NJW 1978, 2390; BGHZ 74, 370.)

Yet it would be wrong to pronounce the traditional 'equitable' approach to intervention to be dead in the German courts. On the contrary, given the slightest sign of a return to a genuinely unusual and abnormal situation, the courts will revive the old theory. This indeed occurred after the reunification of Germany when the old West swallowed up a bankrupt East. The planned economy regime which prevailed in the latter thus meant that, in appropriate circumstances, the contractual allocation of risk approach which had come to prevail in the West, had to be modified when litigation emanating from the East reached the courts. The decision of the *Bundesgerichtshof* of 14 October 1992 (NJW 1993, 259, case no 107) shows this. Its reading should cause no difficulties to the reader; but what the translated extracts do not do is reproduce the economic adjustment engineered by the court. Since it is not without interest, nor indeed is it beyond criticism, a few words on this aspect of the case alone may not be out of place.

The case involved a buyer (defendant) and a seller (plaintiff), of a machine originally acquired from Austria, both parties operating in the state-controlled economy of communist (former) East Germany. The two Germanys agreed to unite in 1989 and the currency of East Germany ceased to exist in July 1990. East German marks (for brevity: EDM) were converted into West German marks (WDM) at a rate of 2:1. The purchase price of the sold object was 1.3 EDM; and before the disappearance of the EDM, the plaintiff had paid (through state credits) 400,000 EDM. The BGH took the view that the two parties should share the cost; and here is how it worked it out.

1.7 EDM (purchase price) minus 400,000 EDM (deposit) left 1.3 EDM unpaid. Exchanged for WDM, this meant 650,000 WDM, half of which– ie, 325,000 WDM— should be paid by the defendant (buyer). This may sound as very much less that the originally agreed purchase price of 1.7 EDM, but in fact it may have been too generous to the plaintiff (seller). For the 1.7 EDM were based on an unrealistically inflated price of EDM and the Austrian Schilling (from where, it will be remembered, the sold object was originally acquired). If one used the WDM /Schilling market exchange rate, the purchase price would have been 380,000 WDM.

Now, it will be recalled that the plaintiff was allowed to claim 325,000 WDM; and he was allowed to keep the deposit already received (which was 400,000 EDM or, at a 2:1 exchange rate, 200,000 WDM.) This means that the plaintiff (seller) ended up with a total of 525,000 WDM for a machine which, realistically priced, was worth 380,000 WDM. That 525,000 WDM sum covered the plaintiff's costs and left a profit of about 40 per cent. That the court should have used its 'adjusting' powers under § 242 BGB is understandable, and arguably fair; that it should have been so generous to the plaintiff is more open to doubt. But then such injustices are bound to occur when one expects judges to act not only as judges, but also as businessmen and accountants!

7. COMMON MISTAKE

In this group of cases we are faced with a mistake as to an extant fact which is shared by both parties at the inception of the contract. (The English case of *Griffith v Brymer* (1903) 19 TLR 434, illustrates the kind of factual problem with which we are here concerned. In that case, it will be remembered, a room was hired to watch the coronation parade of King Edward VII at a time when, unbeknown to both parties, the parade had already been cancelled. Thus, in one case the parties expressly assumed that the stipulated rent of land would equal the peacetime rent, but it did not.) Since the German § 119 BGB does not apply to this kind of mistake, any insistence to pay the stipulated rent would have to be determined by good faith, which in turn could be invoked only if the common assumption of the parties had become the foundation of the contract. (See, OLG München, MDR 1950, 672. See, also, BGHZ 25, 390, 392.) Cases 103 and 105 provide two further interesting illustrations.

In the first case (BGHZ 37, 44, case no 103) the plaintiff agreed in 1959 to sell land to the defendant in exchange for a series of 'building' obligations assumed by the latter. Both parties were aware of planning difficulties since the plots in question had not yet been subjected to building regulations, but believed that these difficulties could, in part at least, be overcome soon. This however had not happened by the time of the trial (1967); and the prognosis was uncertain. The plaintiff thus asked for the plots to be reconveyed to him and for a declaration to be made that the arrangement was invalid. The court agreed, adding that 'where the contacting parties know of the existence of an impediment but assumed mistakenly that it could be removed . . . a mutual mistake has occurred, the legal consequences of which are not to be determined by § 306 BGB. Instead, they must be considered from the aspect as to whether the basis of the transaction has disappeared (§ 242 BGB). It is thus necessary to examine whether and to what extent, as a result of unforeseen delay in fixing the date of performance, the situation as seen originally by he contracting parties has been changed so fundamentally that according to good faith the contract can no longer be executed in the manner envisaged at the beginning.'

The next case (BGH NJW 1976, 565, case no 105) is, in fact, more interesting since here we find one of the rare examples in which 'adjustment' meant termination of the contractual bond. Here the dispute arose as a result of one football club 'transferring to another one of its players who, unbeknown to both parties had, before the transaction was agreed, accepted bribes to 'lose' a game. The *Bundesgerichtshof* agreed with the lower courts that,

> not every disturbance of the basis of the transaction is significant. In view of the paramount importance in the law of contracts of the principle that they must be carried out, reliance on the fundamental disturbance of the basis of a transaction is only admissible in exceptional cases and only if it appears imperative in order to avoid an unbearable result which cannot be reconciled with the demands of law and justice.

Bribery in cases such as this was a very serious matter which had clearly falsified the common assumptions of the parties. This clearly was also not one of the cases where one could say that the plaintiff buyer club had assumed the risk of an event such as this occurring. (For good measure, the *Bundesgerichtshof* also pointed out that the defendant club had to bear the risk which originated in its sphere of influence.) The event had further made the player 'worthless' for both parties to the contract and so, in the instant case, no modification was possible other than to order the complete rescission of the transaction followed by the return of the transfer fee.

See also, the famous 'Roubles case', RGZ 105, 406, case no 98. In this case the plaintiff lent the defendant 30,000 Russian roubles in return for two promissory notes whereby the defendant undertook to pay the plaintiff 7500 marks. It was found that the parties assumed that a rouble was equivalent to 25 pfennigs and neither party was aware that the value of the rouble was much lower at the time. The court solved the case on the basis of § 119 I BGB. However, the assumption of a declaration mistake seems artificial. There are better, alternative explanations of this case. See for instance, Medicus, *Allgemeiner Teil*, Rn. 758, who suggests that the case should have been solved on the basis of interpretation: the correct exchange rate was agreed by the parties. In any event, the case can be solved on the basis of the doctrine of the foundation of the transaction; in this sense: Larenz and Wolf, *Allgemeiner Teil*, Rn. 64. The *Reichsgericht* however must have felt unease in applying this newly developed doctrine and preferred to (over-) stretch existing rules.

8

The Performance of a Contract

1. INTRODUCTORY REMARKS

The section of the BGB dealing with the 'extinction of obligations' (*Erlöschen der Schuldverhältnisse*) enumerates four different ways of extinguishing a debt, 'performance' (*Erfüllung*) being the normal way in which this result is achieved (§§ 362–71). Paragraph 362 I BGB states the general rule that an obligation owed to the creditor comes to an end if the debtor performs it. The remaining three ways are substitutes for performance (*Erfüllungssurogate*). They are: deposit (*Hinterlegung*, §§ 372–86), set-off (*Aufrechnung*, §§ 387–96) and release (*Erlaß*, § 397). The manner in which an obligation is performed raises a number of questions. In this chapter we will limit our observations to three main points: the relationship between performance and counterperformance (below, section 2); time and place of performance (below, section 3); and performance through third parties (below, section 4). In actual legal practice the most important among the 'substitutes' for performance is set-off which will be discussed in the remainder of the chapter (below, section 5). At the same time, the conditions of performance determine the background against which irregularities of performance must be understood, so these conditions form a key thread that runs through this and the next two chapters.

2. PLEA OF UNPERFORMED CONTRACT (*EINREDE DES NICHTERFÜLLTEN VERTRAGES*)

Brox, *Die Einrede des nichterfüllten Vertrages beim Kauf* (1948); Bydlinski, 'Die Einrede des nichterfüllten Vertrages in Dauerschuldverhältnissen' in *Festschrift für Steinwenter* (1958) 140; Jahr, 'Die Einrede des bürgerlichen Rechts' JuS 1964, 125, 218, 293; Keller, 'Das Zurückbehaltungsrecht nach § 273 BGB' JuS 1982, 665; Kirn, 'Leistungspflichten im gegenseitigen Vertrag' JZ 1969, 325.

(a) Classification of Contracts

Before discussing the problems which in German law are regulated by §§ 320–2 BGB, it may be helpful to recall briefly the classification of contracts.

In common law systems the most significant classification is that which distinguishes between, on the one hand, offers in which the offeror seeks to obtain a promise, ie an obligation of the offeree in exchange for his own promise (bilateral or synallagmatic contract) and, on the other hand, offers in which the offeror does not seek a promise, but merely an act or result on which his own promise is conditioned, ie a promise in return for what common lawyers would call executed consideration (unilateral contract). In German law almost all offers, including those calling for an act, are capable of acceptance by any expression of assent on the part of the offeree. Therefore, when A has made an offer to B, and such offer is one calling for an act, B's act of performance will normally be regarded as expression of assent to the offer as well as performance of the contract concluded by such assent. (See also, § 151 BGB: acceptance without declaration to the offeror.) However, the classical example of a unilateral contract in common law systems, the offer to the public of a reward for the doing of some act, is treated as a 'one-sided legal transaction' (*einseitiges Rechtsgeschäft*). (For more details see our discussion of this topic in chapter 2, section 2(g), p 67). It is distinguished from a contract because no agreement is necessary. Therefore, the actor is entitled to the reward even though he had no knowledge of the promise (§ 657 BGB: *Auslobung*). This avoids the difficulty, if not impossibility, of explaining that, in a situation like this, a contract has come about. It follows from what has been said that unilateral contracts, as understood in the common law, have no parallel in German law. All contracts are 'bilateral' in the sense that they are conceived of as 'bilateral legal transactions' (*zweiseitige Rechtsgeschäfte*). But this broad category is subdivided into two main groups of 'bilateral' contracts. Thus, we can have (a) contracts obliging one party only (*einseitig verpflichtende Verträge*) such as a promise to make a gift, here only the promisor incurs an obligation (§ 516 BGB) (other examples would be a gratuitous loan (§ 607 BGB) and a gratuitous deposit for safekeeping (§ 688 BGB)). Alternatively, (b) we have synallagmatic (from the Greek word 'synallagma', which means exchange) contracts where the performance promised by one party is to be exchanged for that of another (*gegenseitiger Vertrag* or *synallagmatischer Vertrag*). For the sake of clarity, however we must hasten to add that this classification is not yet complete.

First, the German concept of gratuitous agency or mandate (*Auftrag*) does not fit into these two main categories of contract. 'By the acceptance of a mandate the mandatary binds himself gratuitously to take care of some matter for the mandator entrusted to him by the latter' (§ 662 BGB). But the mandator is under an obligation to reimburse the mandatary if he incurs expenditure which he may regard as necessary under the circumstances (§ 670 BGB). This being so, mandate is neither a purely gratuitous transaction nor can it be regarded as a synallagmatic contract, for the mere reimbursement of outlays is no counter-performance. Therefore mandate is classified as 'imperfectly bilateral' (*unvollkommen zweiseitig*).

Secondly, the brokerage contract (*Mäklervertrag*) yields a close analogy to the unilateral contract as defined in common law systems. In the normal case of a simple brokerage contract, a fee is promised for an act, the requested act being the supply of information concerning the opportunity to make a contract (§ 652 BGB). The broker is under no obligation to perform the requested act and the promisor may withdraw his promise. Thus, at least at the outset, the situation is comparable to the typical fact-situations giving rise to a unilateral contract in common law systems. However, it must be borne in mind that supplying the information does not make the promise binding at that point because the promisor still remains entirely free to enter or not to enter into the contract the conclusion of which is suggested by the broker's information. The broker is not entitled to his fee if the principal's decision is negative. Freedom of contracting does of course permit a contrary stipulation. Where this has been done, the contract is synallagmatic (so-called *Maklerdienstvertrag* or *Maklerwerkvertrag*, as the case may be). But the simple brokerage contract would thus have an even less binding effect than a unilateral contract in common law systems. Nevertheless, the brokerage contract must be regarded as a contract which is concluded at the moment when the parties agree on its terms. The consideration doctrine being unknown in German law, there is no conceptual barrier to the recognition of a 'contract' that creates obligations only on a condition the occurrence of which depends on the will of the promisor. (In the common law systems the estate agency contract is another type of unilateral contract; but some of its unusual features are best studied in specialist works.)

Thirdly, the mandate to grant a credit (*Kreditauftrag*) is functionally related to the common law concept of unilateral contract. The relevant Code provision deals with the case where A asks B to grant a credit to C. If B grants the credit in his own name and on his own account, the mandator (A) becomes liable to the mandatary (B) as a guarantor for the obligation of the third party (C) arising from the giving of credit (§ 778 BGB). Again, the similarity between German law and common law systems is limited, for A's promise of guarantee may be accepted by B's counter-promise, ie his promise to grant the requested credit to C. In spite of the power to revoke vested in each party (§ 671 I BGB), a consensual contract has come about by B's acceptance. (For more details of these types of obligations with a close affinity to the unilateral contract of the common law systems, see W Lorenz, 'Acceptance by Performance' in: R B Schlesinger (ed), *Formation of Contract II* (1968), pp 1256–64.)

(b) Plea of Unperformed Contract (*Einrede des nicht erfüllten Vertrages*)

The aim of this brief introduction to the classification of contracts in German law has been to show that those sections of the BGB which deal with the *exceptio non adimpleti contractus* (§§ 320–2) are applicable only if the obligation which the claimant has failed to perform is synallagmatically related to the obligation that he seeks to enforce. In other words, these provisions are concerned with the fulfilment of the main obligations embodied in a synallagmatic contract. In a wider sense, the *exceptio* may be regarded as granting a right of retention (*Zurückbehaltungsrecht*), though a warning must be added not to confuse the *exceptio* with the general right of retention (the so-called *allgemeines Zurückbehaltungsrecht*) laid down in § 273 BGB, which is in the nature of a lien. It will be necessary to come back to this legal institution at a later stage of this discussion (below, section 2(c)).

Unless the parties to a synallagmatic contract, for instance a contract of sale, have agreed that one of them has to render performance before that of the other, the rule laid down in § 320 I 1 BGB is that performances must be exchanged contemporaneously or concurrently. Leaving aside the dogmatic differences existing in this area of the law between common law systems and the civil law, this statement is, at least in its essentials, in conformity with the formulation used in section 28 of the Sale of Goods Act 1979, which says that delivery of the goods and payment of the price are concurrent conditions and which presupposes that the seller must be ready and willing to give possession of the goods to the buyer in exchange for the price, and the buyer must be ready and willing to pay the price in exchange for possession of the goods. The policies behind these two rules are the same, that is to say, to protect the party from whom performance is claimed against the risk of having to make performance without being sure that the agreed counter-performance will be forthcoming. The claimant, on the other hand, must be 'willing and capable to render the performance incumbent on him,' for otherwise the other party cannot be considered to be in default in performing his obligation (see RGZ 126, 280, 285).

This being so, one would have thought that synallagmatically-related obligations are subject to the restriction that each party must frame his action so as to demand only *Erfüllung Zug um Zug* (contemporaneous performance). However, the BGB has adopted a different method, for it merely speaks of a 'right' of the defendant to refuse to perform his part until the plaintiff has performed his part (§ 320 I 1 BGB). This countervailing right (*Gegenrecht*) provides the basis for his defence (*Einrede*); but this defence must be pleaded by the defendant. Therefore the judge will not take notice of it *ex officio* nor will he ask the plaintiff whether he has performed his part of the bargain. The practical consequence of this so-called 'defence theory' (*Einredetheorie*) may be tested by looking at the case where the defendant has failed to appear in court. In such an event, the plaintiff need not allege that he has performed his obligation and a judgment by default will be entered against the defendant (*Versäumnisurteil*, see § 331 Code of Civil Procedure, ZPO) provided of course that the plaintiff has convincingly established his claim.

English law can be contrasted with the position under § 320 I 1 BGB: except where legislation specifically provides otherwise (and even section 28 of the Sale of Goods Act 1979 is 'only' *ius dispositivum*), the question of the accepted order in which the parties are to perform their synallagmatically related obligations is dependent on the construction of the contract and the nature of the promise that each has made to the other. Express provision in the contract that one party's performance is a condition precedent to that of the other is a relatively straightforward case, although even here the interpretive question may arise whether such a condition is one on which the existence of the contract is itself contingent or whether A has promised B that A will bring about that stipulated event: see *Trans Trust SPRL v Danubian Trading Co* [1952] 2 QB 297 and the discussion in Treitel, *The Law of Contract*, pp 762. Equally, the contract could be construed to require concurrent (or simultaneous) performance: indeed, in the absence of express contractual provision to the contrary, this would appear to be the default position for the delivery of goods and payment of freight (respectively) under a charterparty (see *Paynter v James* (1867) LR 2 CP 348, at 355). (See further, *China Offshore Oil (Singapore) International Pte Ltd v Giant Shipping Ltd ('The Posidon')* [2001] 1 Lloyd's Rep 697, especially at 701–2.) If however the parties' promises are construed as operating independently each of the other, then each can enforce the other's promise even if he has yet to perform his own: in this circumstance, the other party must then bring a counterclaim to enforce the performance of the first party's promise. (On this, see *Leiston Gas Co v Leiston-cum-Sizewell Urban District Council* [1916] 2 KB 428, at 434, *Aegnoussiotis Shipping Corporation of Monrovia v A/s Kristian Jebsens Rederi of Bergen, ('The Aegnoussiotis')* [1977] 1 Lloyd's Rep 268, at 276 and Treitel, *The Law of Contract*, pp 763–6.)

If the defendant raises the defence under § 320 I 1 BGB, it is up to the plaintiff to show that he has either performed his part or that the contract imposes on the defendant a duty to perform first (*Vorleistungspflicht*). Such a duty may result from a term in the contract or it may be imposed on that party by law. In contracts where the performance of one party extends over a period of time, the BGB lays down a duty to perform in advance; but it must be emphasised that these rules are not mandatory (but *ius dispositivum*). In practice, stipulations to the contrary are regularly made.

The Code contains many illustrations of this rule. Thus, according to § 579 I BGB, the rent is payable at the end of the term of lease of an object other than residential property (for which see § 556 b I BGB: rent is due at the beginning of the respective period of time). If the rent is measured in periods of time, it is payable after the expiry of each of the periods. In contracts for service (§ 611 BGB) the remuneration is payable after the performance of the service (§ 614 sentence 1 BGB). Again, if the remuneration is measured in periods of time, it is payable at the end of the periods (§ 614 sentence 2 BGB). In contracts for work on goods and building contacts (§ 631 BGB) the remuneration is payable at the time of acceptance of the work; but if the work is to be accepted in parts then the remuneration for each part is payable at the time of its acceptance (see § 641 I BGB). 'Acceptance' of the work is usually defined as 'the act of physical reception of the contractor's performance by the customer, accompanied by the express or tacit declaration of the customer that, in substance, he acknowledges the work as a performance conforming with the contract' (RGZ 110, 404, 406–7). Where the nature of the work is such that 'acceptance' is impossible, the completion of the work takes the place of acceptance (§ 646 BGB). It should however be borne in mind that the general conditions of building contracts most widely used in Germany contain detailed rules governing the acceptance of the work (*Verdingungsordnung für Bauleistungen* = VOB [B] § 12 and § 13 no 4). In this context, the German VOB (B) provides that acceptance of construction work is to take place in stages and the remuneration is usually apportioned to each stage (BGH NJW 1982, 2494, case no 108, concerning the retention of a certain percentage of the remuneration as security).

Since the party who has to perform in advance is, in essence, giving unsecured credit to the other party, he runs the risk of not receiving the agreed counter-performance. The legislator has alleviated this risk by granting a special defence which is based ultimately on the idea underlying the *clausula rebus sic stantibus*, ie, that a contract ceases to be binding because 'matters did not remain the same as they were at the time of contracting.' Thus, the BGB provides that a person obliged by a synallagmatic contract to perform his part first may refuse to perform it if, after the conclusion of the contract, a significant deterioration in the financial position of the other party occurs which, thereby, endangers the claim for the counter-performance. In such cases, the other party is faced with two alternatives: either he can offer the counter-performance or he can give adequate security for it (§ 321 BGB). In his analysis of English law, Treitel (*The Law of Contract*) pp 764–6, notes this risk of requiring performance without security for the performance of the other party: if classified as independent promises, each party bears this risk with respect to the other's performance and this consequence has led the courts to show great reluctance to construe promises as independent (see eg, *Jones v Barkley* (1781) 2 Dougl 648, at 689; 99 ER 434). This risk is further mitigated in the consumer context by the Unfair Terms in Consumer Contracts Regulations 1999: see its reg 5(5) and Schedule 2, para 1(o), which renders prima facie unfair any term which has not been individually negotiated and which makes the consumer's promise independent of the other party's obligations. The risk run by the party who is required to perform first (as a condition precedent to the accrual of the other party's liability to perform) is acknowledged by the US Restatement 2d, *Contracts* in its § 234(1), by adopting simultaneous performance as the default position where there is any doubt as to the interpretation of the contract. Treitel takes the view that English law should typically adopt the same approach (*The Law of* Contract, p 764; although cf his subsequent discussion (pp 764–5) of cases where construction of the contract as involving independent obligations would be appropriate).

There are further situations in which a party who is obliged to perform in advance will be relieved of this duty. Suppose the other party is in default of acceptance (*mora creditoris*) or he refuses to make the counter-performance. This would entitle the party who has to perform first to bring an action for performance after receipt of the counter-performance (§ 322 II BGB). Yet, this is not the only choice open for this party. For he may also decide to treat this as a repudiation of the contract and take the steps provided in § 323 BGB leading to the termination of the contract. Similarly, under English law it is highly likely that such refusal to accept (see Treitel, *The Law of Contract*, pp 766–8) or to perform would amount to a repudiatory breach of the contract and would entitle the first party to rescind the contract and thus refuse to perform. More generally, at any stage where the other party's non-performance amounts to a substantial failure to perform (on which see Treitel, *The Law of Contract*, p 769 ff for detailed discussion), this will usually entitle the first party to rescind the contract and thus refuse (or cease) to render performance himself.

Since clauses stipulating for the advance performance of one party derogate from the principle that performance and counter-performance are concurrent conditions, the legislator takes a critical view of such clauses if they are contained in the general conditions of contract (*Allgemeine Geschäftsbedingungen* = AGB). Therefore it is laid down in § 309 Nr. 2 (a) BGB that the plea of non-performance (§ 320 BGB) may not be excluded or restricted in such standard form contracts. (See, as to judicial control of standard terms and the scope of application of § 309 BGB, chapter 3, section 5, p 163.) However, so far as clauses stipulating a *Vorleistungspflicht* are concerned the courts have adopted a flexible attitude because there are numerous situations in everyday life where advance payments are indispensable (BGHZ 100, 158, 161 concerning the general conditions of a travel agency; the relevant case law is listed by *Münchener Kommentar*- Basedow, § 309 Nr. 2 Rn. 7 *et seq*).

(c) General Right of Retention (*allgemeines Zurückbehaltungsrecht*)

As already indicated above (section 2(b)), the legislator has also made provision for a general right of retention which operates in situations where the duties of the parties are not synallagmatically related to each other. If the debtor has a matured claim (*einen fälligen Anspruch*) against the creditor arising 'from the same legal relationship' (*aus demselben rechtlichen Verhältnis*) on which his own obligation is based, he may, unless a contrary intention appears from the obligation, refuse to render the performance due from him until the performance due to him is effected (§ 273 I BGB). The effect of this right of retention is comparable with the effect of the plea of unperformed contract (§ 322 I BGB), ie the court may order the other party to perform on receipt of the performance due to him (§ 274 I BGB: contemporaneous performance).

But the similarity does not extend any further, because here we are not dealing with synallagmatic contracts.

A good example is provided by mandate (*Auftrag*), ie gratuitous agency, which is classified as an imperfectly bilateral contract (see above, section 2(a)). The mandatary is bound to hand over to his mandator all that he receives for the execution of the mandate and all that he obtains from his charge of the matter (§ 667 BGB). On the other hand, he may claim reimbursement of any outlay which was necessary for the purpose of the execution of the mandate (§ 670 BGB). Both of these claims arise independently of each other, even though they originate in 'the same legal relationship' within the meaning of § 273 I BGB. It is this real connection (*Konnexität*) which justifies the right of retention with its legal effect of contemporaneous performance.

Another example of this right of retention is supplied by § 273 II BGB, which provides that a person who is obliged to hand over a particular thing to its owner can refuse to do so if he has incurred expenses in connection with the thing or if it has caused any damage to him. In commercial relations among merchants the right to retain specific things is a genuine lien combined with the right to sell the things retained and so to obtain satisfaction of the claim (§§ 369, 371 BGB; broadly analogous to the so-called 'workman's lien' under English law, discussed in chapter 3, section 4(h), p 155).

3. TIME AND PLACE OF PERFORMANCE

Christiansen, *Forderungsrecht und Leistungszeit* (1998); Gernhuber, *Die Erfüllung und ihre Surrogate* (2nd edn, 1994); U Huber, 'Zur Konzentration beim Gattungskauf' in *Festschrift Ballerstedt* (1975) 327; S Lorenz, 'Leistungsgefahr, Gegenleistungsgefahr und Erfüllungsort beim Verbrauchsgüterkauf' JuS 2004, 105; Medicus, 'Die konkretisierte Gattungsschuld' JuS 1966, 297; K Schmidt, 'Geld und Geldschuld im Privatrecht' JuS 1984, 737; Wieacker, 'Zum Verhältnis von Leistungshandlung und Leistungserfolg' in *Festschrift Nipperdey* (1965) 783.

(a) Time of Performance

The general part of the law of obligations starts with the rule that the creditor may demand performance at once, and the debtor may perform his part at once, provided the time for performance is neither fixed nor can be deduced from the circumstances (§ 271 I BGB). (Compare the general position in English law, as stated by Treitel (*The Law of Contract*, p 753): 'performance is due without demand: a debtor must seek his creditor,' citing *Walton v Mascall* (1844) 13 M & W 452; 153 ER 188.) However, in German law this rule is not mandatory nor, indeed, does this represent the basic position of English law. Moreover, the BGB contains numerous special provisions dealing with the time for performance. In the present context we will only mention those provisions which may be found in the special part of the law of obligations dealing with specific contracts such as, for instance, § 556b I BGB (payment of rent in contracts of lease); § 604 BGB (time for returning a thing gratuitously borrowed for use); §§ 608, 609 BGB (time for repayment of a loan and time for payment of interest on a loan);

§ 614 BGB (due date for remuneration payable under a contract of service); § 641 BGB (due date for remuneration payable under a contract for work and labour), etc. It must be emphasised again however that these special provisions are not mandatory either. Indeed, the consistent (opposite) practice of the parties in many spheres of activity has made some of them quite obsolete.

This used to apply with particular force to the payment of rent in contracts for lease of residential property. Thus, § 551 BGB now repealed, stated that the rent is payable after the expiry of each of the periods if the rent is measured by periods of time. This was hardly ever applied in practice. The standard form contracts, which are in daily use in Germany in cases of residential leases, have always contained contrary stipulations. These state that the rent must be paid in advance of each of the periods of time. The reform of the contract for lease of 2001 has adapted the rule to actual practice. According to § 556b I BGB, the rent is thus due at the beginning of the period. (Compare the position in English law under section 166 of the Commonhold and Leasehold Reform Act 2002, which provides that a tenant who holds a long lease of a dwelling owes no duty to make payment of rent under that lease unless and until the landlord has served a notice on him that relates to that payment.)

The BGB makes a distinction between the date when an obligation is due (*Fälligkeit der Forderung*) and the date at which the debtor may tender performance (*Erfüllbarkeit der Forderung*). This distinction is inherent in § 271 II BGB: if a time is fixed it is to be presumed, in case of doubt, that the creditor may not demand the performance before that time, but the debtor may perform earlier. However, a debtor who pays a non-interest-bearing debt before it is due is not entitled to any reduction on account of interim interest (§ 272 BGB: *kein Abzug von Zwischenzinsen*). This is confirmed by another provision laid down in the context of unjust enrichment: if an obligation due on a certain date is fulfilled in advance, the right to demand return is barred and a discount of interim interest may not be demanded (§ 813 II BGB). Payment of a debt before it falls due can be attractive to a debtor of an interest-bearing debt. But there is authority for the proposition that the creditor need not accept such a premature performance which would deprive him of part of the interest (BGHZ 64, 278, 284). The position is different only under § 504 BGB, which states that a consumer who has bought goods or has received other benefits against payment of the price by instalments may pay the remaining debt before it falls due. In this case the instalment price is reduced by the amount of interest which would have to be paid if the credit had been used for the full length of the stipulated period.

Occasionally, no date will have been fixed for the performance of the obligation. In such a case, its maturity depends on the giving of notice (*Kündigung*) by the creditor or the debtor. Thus, if the time for repayment of a loan is not fixed, notice must be given either by the creditor or the debtor (§ 488 III 1 BGB). The term of notice is three months (§ 488 III 2 BGB), although the parties remain free to agree a different period. If interest is not stipulated for, the debtor is entitled to make repayment even without notice (§ 488 III 3 BGB). In this context, the so-called 'requirement' contract—where a party has agreed to deliver certain quantities of goods 'on call' (*auf Abruf*)—should be noted. In a situation like this, both *Fälligkeit* and *Erfüllbarkeit* are postponed, *viz,* the debtor must not tender performance until the creditor has requested delivery of the goods. It goes without saying that the creditor must do so within the period of time which the parties had in mind when making such a contract.

If the debtor does not tender performance at the stipulated time, or at the time to be deduced from the circumstances, he has violated his main obligation under the contract. The creditor may, of course, insist on performance by the defaulting debtor whose primary obligation is not extinguished by the delay. This does not however apply to the case where the contract states a time which is regarded as of essence to the transaction ('*mit der zeitgerechten Leistung soll das Geschäft stehen und fallen*': eg, BGHZ 110, 96). Thus, § 323 II Nr. 2 BGB lays down that in a situation like this the creditor shall be entitled to terminate the contract if performance is not made at the fixed time or within the fixed period (so-called *relatives Fixgeschäft*). The Commercial Code contains a rule to essentially the same effect (§ 376 HGB, *Fixhandelskauf*). This may be compared with those cases which in English law entitle the aggrieved party to terminate the contract because performance at the stipulated time goes to 'the essence of the contract' (see the following charterparty cases: *Glaholm v Hays* (1841) 2 Man & G 257 = 133 ER 743; *The Mihalis Angelos* [1971] 1 QB 164 and *Universal Cargo Carriers v Citati* [1957] 2 QB 401).

German law also recognises what is referred to as *absolutes Fixgeschäft*. In this case, performance beyond a certain date no longer constitutes performance of the obligation. With the passage of time, the performance becomes impossible in the sense of § 275 I BGB. For instance, if a taxi is ordered to carry a passenger at a certain time to the airport, punctual arrival is so important that a delay will result in the *ex lege* extinction of the obligation. The same applies to the obligation of the employee in a contract of labour (eg, BAG NJW 1986, 1832). If it is not performed during the stipulated time it cannot be repeated at a later time. It has become impossible. Thus, unlike the simple *Fixgeschäft* (discussed previously), in this case no notice of termination is necessary.

Leaving aside such special fact-situations, the consequences of the debtor's default are dealt with in § 286 BGB *et seq* in conjunction with § 280 II BGB. This requires fault on the part of the debtor (§ 287 BGB), and generally speaking a warning of the debtor that performance is due (§ 286 I BGB). (Delay by the debtor is considered in more detail in chapter 9 below. For a comparable situation in English law, see *Behzadi v Shaftesbury Hotels Ltd* [1992] Ch 1: where one party has failed to perform by the date fixed by the contract, the other party can immediately serve a notice making time of the essence. But the time limited by the notice must be reasonable.)

(b) Place of Performance

In German law, the place of performance (*Erfüllungsort*) is the place at which the debtor ultimately acts in order to bring about the result which he owes to the creditor. Suppose the seller of goods, at the request of the buyer, dispatches the goods sold to a place other than his place of business. In such a case, he has performed the last act owed (*Leistungshandlung*) as soon as he delivers the goods to the forwarder, freighter or other person designated to carry out the consignment. However, since property in the goods has yet to pass to the buyer by virtue of the contract, the desired result of this act of performance is not achieved until the goods are handed over to the buyer at their destination. While the goods are *in transitu*, they travel at the buyer's risk (§ 447 BGB; the rule does not apply to consumer sales, see § 474 II BGB). Strictly speaking, in our case *Erfüllung*, in the sense of extinction of the obligation by performance (§ 362

BGB), is achieved at the moment when the buyer acquires possession and ownership of the goods. Nevertheless, when speaking of the *Erfüllungsort*, this usually designates the place at which the debtor takes the last and decisive step in order to bring about this result. For all practical purposes, therefore, the *Erfüllungsort* means the *Leistungsort*. It is this last-mentioned place with which the BGB deals in § 269 and in § 270 IV. This also applies to § 447 BGB (referred to above), even though this provision uses the term *Erfüllungsort*.

Since sale of goods is the 'paradigmatic contract,' it might be helpful to use this type of contract as a model for explaining the possible places of performance and the legal consequences connected therewith. Two types of risk must be distinguished. (See BGH NJW 2003, 3341, case no 109, discussed below, and also in chapter 9, section 3(e)(ii), p 410.)

First, if the goods are accidentally destroyed before the buyer has obtained possession and ownership, the question then arises whether the seller has to make a second attempt at delivery. The answer to this question depends on whether the seller bears the so-called *Sachgefahr* (risk of the thing: *risque de la chose*).

Secondly, if the seller is relieved from his obligation to deliver, the further and independent question arises whether the buyer is equally relieved of his obligation to pay the price. This would be the case if, at the moment of destruction of the goods, he bears the 'risk of counter-performance' (*Preisgefahr* or *Gegenleistungsgefahr*). The general rule, contained in § 326 I 1 BGB, is that he does not bear this risk. But there are exceptions to this rule. (See, for instance, § 447 BGB.)

The concept of 'risk of the thing' needs to be explored further. The content and nature of the seller's promise determines whether the seller is under an obligation to make a second attempt of delivery. If a specific thing has been sold (*Stückschuld*), its destruction will automatically relieve the promisor of the obligation to deliver (impossibility, § 275 I BGB: this is irrespective of the responsibility for the destruction or when the impossibility to deliver occurred). If generic goods have been sold, ie, objects that are described by class (§ 243 I BGB: *Gattungsschuld*), the destruction of one object of this class does not render performance impossible in the sense of § 275 I BGB. The seller remains liable to deliver an object of the respective class. (*Beschaffungsrisiko*, § 276 I BGB, previously § 279 BGB.) The obligation becomes impossible to perform only if it has been reduced to an obligation to deliver the particular object that perished. This is referred to as *Konkretisierung* and, according to § 243 II BGB, this depends on whether the seller had already complied with his duties under the contract when the destruction occurred. The duties of the seller depend in turn on whether his obligation is a *Holschuld*, *Bringschuld* or *Schickschuld*, as explained in the following paragraphs.

So far as the seller's main obligation is concerned, the following three 'delivery points' (§ 269 BGB) may be distinguished.

The minimum obligation of the seller would be merely to hold the goods available for collection by the buyer (*Holschuld*). Apart from keeping the goods available for collection during normal business hours, the seller may be under an *additional* obligation to notify the buyer that the goods are ready for collection. This is important in cases where no exact time for delivery has been fixed by the contract. The last and 'maximum' obligation of the seller would be to deliver the goods to the buyer's own premises or to those of a third party such as, for instance, a warehouseman or a sub-buyer (*Bringschuld*). Between these two extremes lies the case already dealt with above: the seller, on the request of the buyer, delivers the goods to a carrier for onward transmission to the buyer (*Schickschuld*). The degree of movement for which the seller is responsible determines the point at which the risk passes to the buyer.

In the case of a *Holschuld*, this would mean that the goods were ready for collection and, if necessary, the buyer had been notified accordingly. Speaking in terms of risk (*Gefahrtragung*), this means that the goods are no longer at the seller's risk. This type of risk is called *Sachgefahr* (risk of the thing—*risque de la chose*). Therefore the seller need not deliver substitute goods, for he is relieved of his obligation (§ 275 I BGB). But it is an entirely different question whether, in a case like this, the seller could still insist on payment of the price. This aspect of the risk involved is the aforementioned *Preisgefahr*. Always provided that the buyer had not been in default of acceptance (*Gläubigerverzug*) when the accidental destruction of the goods occurred (§ 326 II 1 BGB), this question must also be answered in the negative (§ 326 I 1 BGB). In other words, the risk of being obliged to pay the purchase price without receiving anything had not yet passed to the buyer.

The case may be contrasted with the *Schickschuld* (where, it will be remembered, the seller delivers the goods to a carrier for onward transmission to the buyer). If the goods perish during transmission, both the *Sachgefahr* (regulated by §§ 269, 243 II BGB) and the *Preisgefahr* (regulated by § 447 BGB) are risks that have been transferred to the buyer. This means that the buyer has to pay for the price even though he does not receive the goods, while the seller's obligation has been extinguished (§ 275 I BGB). The buyer may, however, be able to recover for the loss of the goods from the carrier, or compel the seller to assign his rights against the carrier. (The intriguing third party loss issues raised by this tripartite situation have been discussed in chapter 4, p 220.)

In the case of a *Bringschuld* (seller obliged to deliver the goods to the buyer's own premises or to those of a third party), then both risks will still have to be borne by the seller. This means that the seller is not discharged according to § 275 I BGB from his obligation under § 433 I 1 BGB to deliver the goods. The seller's attempt at performance fails if a *Bringschuld* was agreed and the goods are destroyed before they reach the destination agreed in the contract.

The above lead us to a critical question: how, in each case, is the *Leistungsort* to be determined?

German law is in basic agreement with section 29(1) of the Sale of Goods Act 1979. The answer to the question whether it is for the buyer to take possession of the goods, (*Holschuld*) or for the seller to send them to the buyer (*Schickschuld*), or to deliver them to the buyer's own premises (*Bringschuld*) must, in each case, depend on the express or implied terms of the contract concluded by the parties. In the absence of an express stipulation, the courts will look at the circumstances of the particular case, having regard to the nature of the obligation. In German law the Code is explicit: if no clear answer can be found as a result of applying these criteria, 'performance shall be effected in the place where the debtor had his residence at the time the obligation arose' (§ 269 I BGB). In the normal case where the obligation arose in the course of the debtor's business, and if the debtor's business is located in another place, that place is substituted for the residence (§ 269 II BGB). It may be derived from this provision that, in case of doubt, there is no *Bringschuld*. This is confirmed by § 269 III

BGB, The mere fact that the debtor has assumed the cost of delivery does not mean that the place to which delivery is required to be made is the *Leistungsort*. In a case like this, it must be presumed that the parties have agreed on a *Schickschuld*. In all other cases we are dealing with a *Holschuld* which may, therefore, be regarded as the normal content of the obligation.

A useful illustration of these principles can be found in BGH NJW 2003, 3341, case no 109; a case which, since the lower courts erroneously applied the new version of the BGB instead of the version in force until end of December 2001, contains a first and authoritative commentary on the new law. (See for an annotation of this decision S Lorenz, JuS 2004, 105, and also chapter 9, section 3(e)(ii), p 410.)

In that case the plaintiff ordered a video camera from the defendant. The goods were dispatched by courier to the buyer, who, however, contended that he did not receive the goods. He accordingly demanded the delivery of a (new) camera by way of specific performance. His claim failed.

A correct analysis of this case must start with a meticulous classification of the nature of the obligation of the seller. Such contracts between a consumer and a dealer who maintains a system of distance selling (*Versandhandel*) are commonly treated as involving merely an obligation to dispatch (*Schickschuld*). In other words, the place of performance (*Leistungsort,* § 269 I BGB) is the seller's place of business. It follows that the seller's obligation is fulfilled once he has handed over the goods to the carrier provided that he has apportioned the goods to the respective contract (§ 243 II BGB). The risk of having to deliver the goods afresh (*Sachgefahr*) passes at this very moment. If the goods perish subsequently, the seller is according to § 275 I BGB relieved from his obligation under § 433 I 1 BGB to transfer ownership in the goods and hand them over to the buyer. As a result the buyer has no claim for specific performance of that obligation. So far the—correct—reasoning of the BGH.

The lower courts arrived at the 'correct' result (ie, rejected the claim) but for the wrong reason. They applied § 447 BGB. This was wrong because this provision concerns the question whether the buyer must pay the price even though he has not received the goods (*Preisgefahr*). The seller's claim for the price, however, was not the object of the actual proceedings. The court thus confused the two types of risk which must be strictly separated in German law. This fundamental misconception of the issue of risk obviously irritated the judges of the BGH who did not spare the lower court their harsh criticism.

Nevertheless, it is worth considering—hypothetically—whether the seller would have been able to claim the price even though the goods were destroyed during transport. According to § 447 BGB this would indeed be the case. However, this provision is, according to § 474 II BGB, excluded if the contract of sale is a 'consumer sale'. Instead, the general rule of § 326 I 1 BGB applies: since the seller is relieved from his obligation to perform under § 275 I BGB he loses his right to demand the counterperformance from the buyer. In a nutshell: the buyer (provided he is a consumer) does not have to pay the price for the perished goods nor does the seller have to deliver afresh. We shall return to many of these points in chapter 9, below where we shall analyse the consequences of irregularities in performance.

So far we have concentrated on the obligation of the seller to deliver the goods sold. It is now necessary to add a few words about the buyer's obligation to pay or, generally speaking, about the place of payment of a money debt (*Geldschuld*). In § 270 I and

II BGB it is stated that, in case of doubt, the debtor shall remit money at his own risk and expense to the residence or place of business of the creditor. At first sight, this provision gives the impression that money debts must, as a rule, be regarded as *Bringschulden*. This would be in keeping with the rule prevailing in English law (see Goode, *Commercial Law* (3rd edn, 2004), p 393). However, this provision concludes with a last paragraph which destroys this illusion: 'The provisions relating to the place of performance (*Leistungsort*) remain unaffected' (§ 270 IV BGB). Therefore, in German law money debts are *Schickschulden* of a special kind. The debtor takes the risk that the money will get into the hands of the creditor. If it is lost due in the post or through a failure of the bank engaged in the process of transmission, the debtor must make another effort to fulfil his payment obligation. However, a mere delay in the transmission of the money could not be blamed on the debtor, provided always that the cheque was posted in time, or the transfer order was made in due course (RGZ 78, 137, 140; RGZ 99, 257–8).

The practical upshot of the German rules contained in § 270 IV BGB is this: an unpaid creditor must bring his action against the defaulting debtor at the debtor's place of residence or, as the case may be, at the debtor's place of business (§§ 12, 13, 29 of the Code of Civil Procedure, ZPO). However, in cases containing foreign elements the reasoning is more complicated. Thus, Article 5(1)(b) of the Council Regulation 44/2001/EC on jurisdiction and the recognition and enforcement of judgments in civil and commercial matters (replacing the 1968 Brussels Convention on Jurisdiction and Recognition of Judgments, and applying directly in the national legal systems of all Member States to determine such jurisdictional questions) states that, in the case of the sale of goods, the place of performance of the obligation in question is the place in a Member State where, under the contract, the goods were delivered or should have been delivered. In the case of the provision of services the place of performance is the place in a Member State where, under the contract, the services were provided or should have been provided. This also applies to the obligation to pay the price of the goods or for the service; ie a single forum is established for all the (main) obligations arising under a contract. (The previous practice of the ECJ relating to the Brussels Convention, namely that the court seised of the case would have to determine the place of performance according to the *lex causae* (case 12/76, *Industrie Tessili Italiania Como v Dunlop AG* [1976] ECR 1473) no longer applies.)

4. PERFORMANCE THROUGH THIRD PARTIES

Von Caemmerer, 'Verschulden von Erfüllungsgehilfen' in *Festschrift Hauß* (1978) 33; von Caemmerer, 'Bereicherungsansprüche und Drittbeziehungen' JZ 1962, 385; Canaris, 'Der Bereicherungsansgleich im Dreipersonenverhältnis' *Festschrift für Karl Larenz* (1973) 799; W Lorenz, 'Gläubiger, Schuldner, Dritte und Bereicherungsausgleich' AcP 168 (1968) 286; W Lorenz, 'Work on Goods and Building Contracts' in *International Encyclopedia of Comparative Law*, VIII (1980) chapter 8, 30 *et seq* (concerning sub-contracting in the building industry); S Lorenz, 'Bereicherungsrechtliche Drittbeziehungen' JuS 2003, 729, 839; Metzler, 'Zur Substitution, insbesondere zu ihre Abgrenzung von der Erfüllungsgehilfenschaft' AcP

159 (1961) 143; E Schmidt, 'Zur Dogmatik des § 278 BGB' AcP 170 (1970) 502; Thomä, 'Tilgung fremder Schuld durch irrtümliche Eigenleistung?' JZ 1962, 623.

(a) Preliminary Observations

The basic rule is that a third partly may also make performance if the debtor does not have to perform in person. The approval of the debtor is not necessary, but the creditor can refuse the performance if the debtor objects (§ 267 BGB). Before going on to explain the operation of this rule, it is necessary to say a word about its exceptions and to draw attention to certain fact-situations and legal institutions which must be distinguished from § 267 BGB.

Whether or not the debtor has to perform 'in person' depends on the nature of his obligation or on the intention of the parties. Several provisions in the special part of the law of obligations contain examples of such contracts which, as a rule, are concluded *intuitu personae*. Thus, in contracts for service, the employee must in case of doubt perform his service in person; and the claim for service is in case of doubt not transferable (§ 613 BGB). (The position in English law on contracts of service is very similar: see eg, *John McCann & Co v Pow* [1974] 1 WLR 1643 at 1647 (an estate agent instructed to find a buyer for a house) and generally, Treitel, *The Law of Contract*, pp 756–7.)

It is different in the neighbouring field of contracts for work and labour where no analogous provision exists in the Code. Therefore, it is permissible to conclude that this restriction does not apply there. This means that a contractor may employ servants in order to execute the work, but it is necessary to distinguish such employment of servants from the further question whether and to what extent the contractor may be allowed to delegate performance to a sub-contractor. However, even in contracts for work and labour, there are of course situations in which personal performance is required *stricto sensu* although the parties did not make an express stipulation to this effect. Thus, a contract with an artist to paint a portrait or to model a bust will normally be concluded *intuitu personae*. (Compare the perhaps extreme English case of *Robson v Drummond* (1831) 2 B & Ad 303; 109 ER 1156, where the defendant's promise to paint and keep in repair a carriage for a five-year period was held not to be one the performance of which could be delegated to his partner.)

Other similar cases where the BGB has laid down rules of construction to the effect that a personal obligation exists can be found in the contract of mandate (§ 664 BGB), the contract of deposit (§ 691 BGB), and the obligations of the managing partner in a partnership which are determined by reference to the provisions applicable to mandate, unless a contrary intention appears from the contract of partnership (§§ 713, 664 BGB).

(b) Vicarious Performance: Sub-contracting and Substitution

So far as sub-contracting is concerned, English law essentially adopts principles similar to those found in the BGB. The leading case of *British Waggon Co v Lea & Co* ((1880) 5 QBD 149) may serve as an example for this proposition.

In that case the plaintiff, a wagon company, had let to the defendant a number of railway wagons for a term of years at an annual rent, the agreement providing that the plaintiffs should during the term keep the wagons in repair. When the plaintiff company was wound up, the liquidators entered into a contract with another company who took over the repairing stations of the plaintiffs and henceforth executed all necessary repairs to the wagons. The plaintiffs' action for the full rent succeeded, for repair of the wagons by the company with whom the sub-contract had been made was a sufficient performance by the plaintiffs of their agreement to repair. The judgment turns on a careful construction of the contract. If it can be inferred that the contractor was selected with reference to his individual skill, competence or other personal qualifications, sub-contracting is not permissible. But in the present case Cockburn CJ reached a different result, because it appeared extremely unlikely that in stipulating for the repair of these wagons the defendants attached any importance to the identity of the party who would do the repairs (ie, whether the repairs were done by the company, or by anyone with whom the company might enter into a subsidiary contract to do the work).

In this context, it is necessary to add a warning against terminological confusion which may be caused by an indiscriminate use of the word 'assignment'. Vicarious performance is clearly distinguishable from assignment. Therefore, it must be emphasised that the delegation of the obligation to perform by way of sub-contracting does not relieve the original contractor of his own obligation to achieve the promised result. There is no 'assignment of contract,' but the contractor has merely chosen vicarious performance by a sub-contractor. It follows that no direct contractual relationship between the employer and the sub-contractor comes into existence. Express or implied authority to employ a sub-contractor and the assignment of the contractual obligation, like the assumption of debt (*Schuldübernahme*, §§ 414–419 BGB) are therefore distinguishable. Such an assignment of liabilities would require the employer's special consent, which is not normally implied in the permission to employ a sub-contractor. (On the general position in English law, which is very similar, see Treitel, *The Law of Contract*, p 758.)

One final warning must be added with respect to the special rules prevailing in civil law systems which are unhampered by the common law doctrine of consideration and which, therefore, recognise a gratuitous contract by which one party undertakes to do something on behalf of the other without receiving a *quid pro quo*, ie mandate (*Auftrag*, §§ 662–76 BGB). The mandatary may then either expressly or impliedly be permitted to substitute another person for himself (§ 664 BGB). There are two possibilities of bringing about such 'substitution'. Either the mandatary acts in the name of the mandator when transferring the execution of the mandate to a third party (ie, the substitute), or he does so in his own name. In the first case a direct contractual relationship between the mandator and the substitute comes about. This means that the substitute may become liable vis-à-vis the mandator for breach of contract. In the latter case the situation is somewhat complicated. In the absence of a contract between the mandator and the substitute, the mandatary would be entitled to claim damages on behalf of the mandator under the principles governing *Drittschadensliquidation* (discussed in chapter 4, section 4, p 216). As for the liability of the mandatary, the BGB states that he is responsible only for fault imputable to him in making such transfer (§ 664 I 2 BGB: liability for *culpa in eligendo*). This clearly shows the difference between sub-contracting and substitution.

The normal consequence of sub-contracting is that the main contractor remains fully liable for the workmanlike performance of his contractual obligation and he cannot exculpate himself from this liability by pleading lack of fault in selecting a particular sub-contractor, a plea usually open to the mandatary if substitution was allowed (RGZ 161, 68 dealing with the different effects of substitution and sub-contracting with respect to liability). By contrast, § 278 BGB states that a contractual 'debtor' is responsible for the fault of persons whom he employs in fulfilling his obligation, 'to the same extent as for his own fault.' It thus imposes on the debtor 'strict' vicarious liability for faults of the persons he uses in the course of fulfilling his contractual obligations. The possibility of exoneration, which can be found in § 831 BGB or if substitution is allowed, is absent in this case. Moreover, the terms used in § 278 BGB, namely 'contractual assistant' (*Erfüllungsgehilfe*), suggest that the debtor's liability may cover the faults of persons whom he uses in the performance of these obligations, but who may not, strictly speaking, be his 'servants' (in the sense of § 831 BGB, *Verrichtungsgehilfe*). Sub-contractors employed for the purpose of fulfilling the obligation that the main contractor owes towards his employer typically are 'contractual assistants' in the sense presupposed by § 278 BGB. (See for a commentary on § 278 BGB also, *The German Law of Torts*, pp 703–5.)

An illustration is provided by RGZ 87, 64, case no 110. In this case, passengers in a taxi were injured in a collision between the taxi and a tram. The contract of carriage was concluded not with the taxi driver but his employer (incidentally, the contract was construed as a contract in favour also of the wife and the daughter of the contracting party, § 328 BGB). The employer was held responsible for the fault of the driver according to § 278 BGB. Note that the actual claim was brought by the tram company, which had indemnified the passengers against their loss, by way of subrogation. In this case, the 'sub-contractor' was employed to carry out the very task which constituted performance of the main contract. The principle of vicarious liability applies with full force to this situation. For the sake of completeness it should be noted, however, that where the 'sub-'contract was concluded merely in preparation of the performance the principle does not generally apply. Thus, for instance, the producer is not regarded as the 'contractual assistant' of the seller of the product (eg, BGHZ 48, 118, 120).

(c) Sub-contracting in the Building Industry

In the building industry, the steady growth of specialisation has led to the widespread use of sub-contracts involving not merely the supply of materials, but the doing of substantial work. Although the Roman *locatio conductio operis* did not merely cover work on goods, but comprised also the erection of buildings, the codifications in the civil law countries, while following the Roman law model, largely ignore the special conditions under which construction work on land is carried out in modern times. Therefore, only a very few specific rules dealing with this subject matter are to be found in the BGB.

The gap thus left by the legislator has been filled by the parties. Since most of the provisions on contracts for work and labour are not mandatory, professional groups and other associations in the building industry were free to introduce what has aptly been called the 'self-made law of industry' (*selbstgeschaffenes Recht der Wirtschaft*). Certainly this is not 'law' in terms of a theory of sources of the law, but the term describes a sociological fact of considerable importance. Of course this does not mean that there is unlimited freedom of contracting in this area of the law, for the courts have become increasingly aware of the necessity to control general conditions of contract emanating from powerful groups of society. (See, more generally, the discussion in chapter 3, p 163.)

This applies with particular force to the law of liability for defective construction work. In this context it should, however, not be overlooked that the state and other financially potent corporate bodies are also in a position to make use of contractual freedom. Since their power as employers may easily supersede the power of competing contractors, there is also the phenomenon of the employer who 'dictates' general conditions for construction and building contracts. In Germany, the General Conditions for Construction Works (*Verdingungsordnung für Bauleistungen* = VOB) is a typical example of a private codification which is not infrequently used where the state or a municipal corporation is the employer. It was drawn up by the *Deutscher Normenausschuß* (Standards Association of German Industry) and has constantly been adapted to modern needs and the relevant case law during the past seventy years of its existence. Compared with the standard conditions issued by various organisations in other branches of industry, which tend to make an excessive use of freedom of contracting to their own advantage, the draftsmen of the German VOB have tried to strike a balance between the diverging interests of contractors and employers. The guiding motives were promotion of competition and prevention of acts in restraint of trade.

The first question to be answered in the context of sub-contracting in the building industry concerns the extent to which it is regarded as permissible. If specialisation in the building industry were the only legitimate reason for concluding sub-contracts, it would follow that a contractor might employ a sub-contractor only for such parts of the work for which he himself was not sufficiently qualified. Indeed, this is also the principle on which the German VOB is based: the contractor has to perform the works in his own enterprise. This means that he must not sublet the contract works as a whole. Moreover, even parts of the works may only be sublet on two alternative conditions.

First, the contractor needs the written authorisation of the employer (§ 4 No 8 para1 sentence 2 VOB/B). The main reason underlying this provision is that the employer must be protected against the risk that the contractor selects an incompetent or inefficient sub-contractor.

Secondly, sub-contracting is permissible without the consent of the employer if it concerns such special works which are outside the field of works normally executed by such a contractor (§ 4 No 8 para 1 sentence 3 VOB/B). There is however an agreement that this exception must be narrowly construed, because a contractor should in principle undertake only such works for which his enterprise is suited both as regards quality and quantity (see *Staudinger*-Peters, § 633 Rn. 151). Since the employment of such a sub-contractor amounts to vicarious performance of the contractor's obligation vis-à-vis the employer, the contractor remains fully liable for the workmanlike performance of the work carried out by his sub-contractor (§ 278 BGB). This problem has already been dealt with in the more general context of sub-contracting (above (b)) and the situation is the same in the area of building contracts.

(d) Payment of Another's Debt

The basic rule laid down in § 267 BGB has already been introduced (above (a)). This rule has no parallel in English law because in German law a debt can be discharged by the payment of a third party even though the debtor had not authorised such payment. (For English law see eg, Birks and Beatson, 'Unrequested Payment of Another's Debt' (1976) 92 *LQR* 188; Friedmann, 'Payment of Another's Debt' (1983) 99 *LQR* 534; Goode, *Commercial Law* (2nd edn, 1995), pp 564–5; Goode, 'The Bank's Right to Recover Money Paid on a Stopped Cheque' (1981) 97 *LQR* 254; Beatson, 'Unrequested Payment of Another's Debt' chapter 7 in *The Use and Abuse of Unjust Enrichment* (1991) and Treitel, *The Law of Contract*, pp 755–6. These last two references suggest that it is an open question whether payment without the debtor's knowledge or consent can discharge the debt.) Moreover, the creditor's consent is not required. This means that he—the creditor—would be in default if he did not accept this payment. (*Mora creditoris = Gläubigerverzug*, § 293 BGB. For the consequences of this, see chapter 9, p 411.) The creditor can refuse the performance only if the debtor objects (§ 267 II BGB)—a case which is not likely to occur.

Where the third party has a special interest in paying another's debt however not even the joint objection of the creditor and the debtor can prevent the third party from intervening (§ 268 BGB). Suppose the creditor levies compulsory execution on an object belonging to the debtor, but as a result of the execution a third party incurs the danger of losing a right in the object. This entitles the third party to satisfy the creditor. The same right is granted to the possessor of a thing if he incurs danger of losing possession through the execution. Satisfaction entails assignment by operation of law of the creditor's claim to the payer, who thus becomes entitled also to securities and priorities of the original debt (*cessio legis*, §§ 268 III, 412, 401 BGB).

Before discussing the practical operation of the basic rule (§ 267 BGB) with its possible restitutionary consequences, it is necessary to draw attention to a number of neighbouring legal institutions which cannot be ignored in the present context even though they are distinguishable from § 267 BGB both as regards their dogmatic structure and their scope of application.

First, there is the so-called *Erfüllungsübernahme* (§ 329 BGB). If, in a contract between P and D, one party (P) binds himself to satisfy the creditor (C) of the other party (D) without assuming the debt (cf §§ 414 *et seq* BGB), it is not to be presumed, in case of doubt, that the creditor (C) shall acquire a direct right to demand satisfaction from him (P). This provision is one of the rules of construction laid down in the context of contracts for the benefit of third parties (§§ 328 *et seq* BGB, discussed in chapter 4, section 2, p 186). The legislator points out that such a promise by P vis-à-vis D does not, without more, amount to a genuine contract for the benefit of a third party (*echter Vertrag zugunsten Dritter*). The affinity with the situation underlying § 267 BGB is obvious: payment by P discharges D's debt; but there remains the difference that this payment was not requested by C from P.

This may be relevant when it comes to a problem of restitution which arises if it turns out that C had no valid claim against D. Can P claim the money back from C because the payment failed to achieve its purpose, *viz* the discharge of a debt owed by D? If this were denied the alternative would be that C is unjustly enriched at the expense of D who, in turn, would be obliged to compensate P. The present authors favour the first solution in German law (while noting that it would also seem to be achievable in England on the ground of mistake under the law of restitution). Nonetheless, it must be admitted that in the German legal literature there is some controversy about the correct solution. The *Bundesgerichtshof* seems to prefer the second solution, but so far there is only an *obiter dictum* to this effect (BGHZ 72, 246, 249. For details see *Staudinger*-Werner Lorenz, § 812 Rn. 45 with further references).

Secondly, a debt may be assumed by a third party (P) by agreement with the creditor (C) in such manner that the third party takes the place of D, the former debtor (*Schuldübernahme*, §§ 414 *et seq* BGB). If the assumption of the debt is agreed on between P and D, the validity of the transfer depends on the ratification of C (§ 415 I 1 BGB; see also, in English law, *Walter v James* (1871) LR 6 Ex 124, at 127). This legal institution has its main function in the context of mortgage debts. Thus, if the purchaser of a piece of land, by agreement with the vendor, assumes a debt which is secured by a mortgage on the land, the creditor may ratify the assumption of the debt provided the vendor informs him. However, if six months have elapsed since receipt of the communication, ratification is deemed to have been given, unless the creditor has refused it to the vendor within such period (§ 416 BGB). This is one of the rare cases where silence amounts to approval.

Assumption of another's debt is, of course, distinguishable from § 267 BGB because P now pays a debt which, strictly speaking, has become a debt of his own. Nevertheless, when it comes to the defences of P and their restitutionary consequences there is a large area of agreement between the two cases. Therefore, the person assuming the debt (P) may raise against the creditor (C) all defences arising from the legal relationship between C and the former debtor (D). On the other hand, it is clear that P may not raise any defences against C originating in the legal relationship between himself and D on which the assumption of debt is founded (§ 417 BGB). It follows that C would be unjustly enriched at the expense of P if it turned out that C had no valid claim against D. But it does not concern C if the internal legal relationship between P and D was ineffective because this is *causa remota* in regard to C who has rightfully received what was owed to him. Therefore, it is a matter which must be resolved by P and D.

Thirdly, where a person (P) has guaranteed the debt owed by another (D) by a contract of guarantee made with D's creditor (C), we are again confronted with a triangular relationship the ultimate purpose of which is, broadly speaking, the payment of another's debt. This may even be an unrequested payment because the contract of guarantee (*Bürgschaftsvertrag* §§ 765 *et seq* BGB) is concluded between the guarantor (*Bürge*) and the creditor, no consent of the debtor being required, although in actual practice it is mostly the debtor who has to find a guarantor. As for the legal consequences regarding the extent of guarantor liability and the defences of the guarantor, the following points deserve special mention because they have some bearing on the law of restitution. The principal obligation of D vis-à-vis C determines the obligation of the guarantor (P) at any time. This applies also in particular where the principal obligation is altered by the fault or default of D (§ 767 I 1 and 2 BGB). Moreover, the guarantor may raise all defences available to the debtor (§ 768 I 1 BGB). The guarantor may also as a rule refuse to satisfy the creditor so long as the creditor has not attempted compulsory execution against the debtor without success (the so-called *Einrede der Vorausklage* = claim for prior execution against the debtor, § 771 BGB).

Suppose a guarantor has lost this defence, and therefore satisfies the creditor. The effect of this payment is not the extinction of the debt, but the claim of the creditor against the debtor is transferred to the guarantor by operation of law (*cessio legis*, § 774 I 1 BGB), operating in a similar fashion to the law of subrogation in England. (On which see *Banque Financière de la Cité v Parc (Battersea) Ltd* [1999] AC 221, and generally, Mitchell, *The Law of Subrogation* (1994).)

Problems of restitution may arise if it turns out that C had no valid claim against D. In this case, P has a direct restitutionary claim against C because the chief purpose of his payment, the *causa solvendi*, has not been attained. The same result must follow if the contract of guarantee between P and C was void. It does not then matter that C had a good claim against D. In view of what has already been said in connection with the *Schuldübernahme*, it goes without saying that P cannot set up any defences originating in his legal relationship with D. If this transaction were found to be ineffective, it may only have restitutionary consequences *inter se*.

The three legal institutions just described may still be regarded, in a broader sense, as belonging to the category of 'payment of another's debt.' However, it will increase the clarity of our subsequent discussion to mention briefly two more fact-situations which must be distinguished because they have nothing in common with such payments.

There is thus, firstly, the case where several persons are liable for the same debt (so-called *Gesamtschuld*, §§ 421 *et seq* BGB). If several persons owe one performance in such manner that each is bound to effect the whole performance, but the creditor is entitled to demand the performance only once, the creditor has an option: he may demand the performance from any one of the debtors, in whole or in part. Until the whole performance has been effected, all the debtors remain bound (§ 421 BGB). Such liability *in solidum* is not confined to the law of torts (cf §§ 830, 840 BGB) but cuts across the entire field of private law. In all these cases, payment by one of the joint debtors means that he has paid a debt which has always been a debt of his own.

The right of contribution, which arises if a joint debtor satisfies more than his proper share of the common debt, is not classified as a matter pertaining to the law of unjustified enrichment. The rule is that, as between themselves, joint debtors are liable in equal shares, unless it is otherwise provided. If one joint debtor satisfies the creditor and can demand that the other debtors make up the difference, the claim of the creditor against the other debtors is assigned to him by operation of law (§ 426 II BGB). (On the issue of contribution and joint liability in this context in English law, see Mitchell, 'The Civil Liability (Contribution) Act 1978' [1997] *Restitution LR* 27; Virgo, *The Principles of the Law of Restitution* (1999), pp 23–45 and Burrows, *The Law of Restitution* (2nd edn, 2002), pp 291–3.)

The second multi-party situation which must be distinguished from payment of another's debt concerns payment orders (*Zahlungsanweisungen*).

Suppose one party (D) instructs another party (P), usually a bank, to transfer a certain sum of money from his account to a third person (C). In a case like this, two sets of legal relations must be distinguished: that between the party who gives the instruction (D) and the party who acts in accordance with this instruction (P), and that between D and the third party (C) who is to receive the benefit of the performance. The relation D/P is called the 'cover relation' (*Deckungsbeziehung*) and the relation of D/C is described as the 'value relation' (*Valutaverhältnis*). Although there is a direct transfer of the money from P to C, P merely performs an obligation under his contract with D, whereas D, through the medium of P (the so-called *Leistungsmittler*), makes performance to C. It is important to note that P, in transferring the amount to C's bank account, has no intention of paying another's debt or, expressing the same idea in technical language, the payment is not accompanied by a 'discharge designation' (*Tilgungsbestimmung*) specifying a certain debt originating in the 'value relation' D/C. This is only natural because a bank (P) neither knows nor is interested in knowing why D had given this instruction to transfer money from his account to C's account. This three-party system of performance also determines who may claim restitution against whom if either the 'cover relation' or the 'value relation' turns out to have been void or otherwise legally ineffective. The answer must necessarily be that restitution can only be had within the respective 'performance relation' (*Leistungsverhältnis*), *viz*, the claims are to be by P against D, and by D against C. Although C received the payment from P so that, at first blush, one might think he is enriched at P's expense (if, for example, P's contract with D was void), there is, as a common lawyer would prefer to say, no privity between them. However, there is an important exception to this rule. It concerns cases where there had been no valid instruction by D with regard to the payment made by P. Thus, the German courts had to deal repeatedly with cases where a bank erroneously transmitted money to the wrong recipient (BGHZ 66, 372) or where such transfer was mistakenly carried out twice (BGH NJW 1987, 185). In the absence of an instruction by D, the bank (P) is not entitled to debit his account. Therefore, P is granted a direct action against the recipient of the payment (C). The same must apply to the case where D had revoked his instruction, but P inadvertently made payment to C (eg, payment by a bank of a stopped cheque).

Basically, this is the fact-situation underlying the English case of *Barclays Bank Ltd v WJ Simms (Southern) Ltd* [1980] QB 677, where the problem arose directly for the first time. The bank had made payment to the defendant company in liquidation, overlooking the fact that its customer, the drawer of the cheque, had countermanded payment. Robert Goff J (as he then was) held that the bank could recover the payment. The payment was made without the customer's mandate who had not subsequently ratified the payment. Therefore, the bank could not debit its customer's account, nor could this payment be effective to discharge the obligation (if any) of the customer on the cheque, because the bank had no authority to discharge such obligation. The relevant German decisions have taken the same approach to this type of cases. There is, however, an important difference when it comes to the question whether the payee's (=C) reliance should be protected. If, at the time of the payment, C had no knowledge of the customer's (=D) revocation of the mandate, the action of the bank (=P) must fail, always provided that the payment has effectively discharged the drawer's (=D) liability on the cheque (see, eg, BGHZ 87, 246; BGHZ 87, 393 with special emphasis on the distribution of the burden of proof; BGHZ 89, 376). In this latter case, the bank may recover the amount paid from its customer (D) for whom the discharge, even though unrequested, means enrichment (so-called *Rückgriffskondiktion*). But this claim by the bank would have to be denied if such payment had deprived D of a defence to C's claim (*Staudinger-Werner Lorenz*, § 812 Rn. 53 with further references).

The English case of *Barclays Bank v Simms* gets around such consequences. However, the question remains: what would have happened if the bank's claim against the payee had failed because there had been evidence of an actual change of position? (On change of position in the common law, see *Lipkin Gorman v Karpnale Ltd* [1991] 2 AC 548; *National Bank of New Zealand Ltd v Waitaki International Processing (NI) Ltd* [1999] 2 NZLR 211 (NZCA); *Dextra Bank & Trust Co Ltd v Bank of Jamaica* [2002] 1 All ER (Comm) 193 and Burrows, *The Law of Restitution*, pp 510–29.)

Having sorted out a number of three-party relations that have some affinity with payment of another's debt, we may now concentrate on the basic rule as laid down in § 267 BGB. Two illustrations will serve to show how it operates in actual practice.

Suppose C has agreed to sell D a certain movable, the purchase price to be paid by instalments. In a case like this, possession is transferred to the buyer immediately though the seller is well advised to retain title until the moment when the last instalment is paid. The relevant provision of the Code is § 449 BGB. According to this paragraph, in case of doubt, it is to be presumed that the transfer of title takes place subject to the condition precedent of payment in full of the purchase price, and that the seller is entitled to rescind the contract if the buyer is in default with payment. In this context, it should be remembered that German private law neatly distinguishes between the *obligation* entitling each party to such a synallagmatic contract to claim performance from the other party (§§ 241, 433 BGB) and the *transfer* of ownership in a movable thing (§ 929 BGB). (See the discussion in chapter 1, p 27 ff.) These are separated legal transactions and, so far as the transfer of ownership is concerned, it is necessary that the owner of the thing deliver it to the acquirer and that both agree that ownership is transferred thereby. It is this agreement (*Einigung*), within the meaning of § 929 BGB, which is subject to the condition precedent (*aufschiebende Bedingung*) referred to in § 449 BGB, the key provision for *Eigentumsvorbehalt* (reservation of title).

Returning now to the illustration introduced above, it is of the utmost importance to realise that D, even though he has not yet paid all instalments of the purchase price, has already gained a legal position which may be described as ownership *in statu nascendi*, ie, a property right in the nature of an expectancy of ownership (*Eigentumsanwartschaft*). This expectancy (*Anwartschaft*) may already be used as a security, the value of which depends on the object to which it pertains and the amount of instalments paid by the buyer. Thus D, if in need of a loan, could transfer his *Anwartschaft* to the lender (P) as a security in return for credit.

Let us further assume that D is both unable to pay C the last instalments of the purchase price and to repay the loan granted by P. In a situation like this P could intervene in the legal relation of C/D and pay the last instalment(s). The effect of this payment, made in accordance with § 267 BGB, would be that P's *Anwartschaft* immediately ripens into ownership (BGHZ 75, 221, 228, case no 111, referring to an earlier decision of the same court BGH NJW 1954, 1325, 1328). For this reason, P can demand from the possessor (D) the delivery of the thing (§ 985 = *rei vindicatio*).

The second illustration which can help to explain the function of § 267 BGB concerns third party insurance (*Haftpflichtversicherung* = liability insurance). Obviously, an insurer (P), who satisfies the claim of an aggrieved party (C), cannot be regarded as an 'officious intermeddler,' for he pays because his contract with the insured (D) obliges him to do so. Therefore it could perhaps be maintained that P's payment is not unrequested, and as a consequence, § 267 BGB cannot apply to this fact-situation. Indeed, this is a matter of some controversy in German legal literature. The alternative would be to regard D as a party who has 'instructed' (*angewiesen*) the insurer to pay a certain sum of money to C as compensation for the damage suffered. It must be emphasised that this controversy is by no means otiose. Its practical consequences can immediately be seen when it comes to the following problem of restitution.

Suppose that in our previous example C had no valid claim against D (the tort was committed by somebody else). Certainly C is obliged to return the money received because he is unjustly enriched. But to whom must he return this sum or, using the terminology of § 812 BGB, at whose expense is he unjustifiably enriched? If the insurer (P) were regarded as a third party within the meaning of § 267 BGB, he could claim repayment from C. But if the other approach were deemed correct, only the insured (D) could succeed with an action against C. However, this would not yet end the case, because now it is obvious that D has acquired something at the expense of his insurer (P). Those who advocate this circuitous method of restitution argue that the insurer is not a payer who acts on his own initiative. But this is a specious argument which ignores the essential fact that an insurer does not act on an 'instruction' (*Anweisung*) of the insured, for he will of course examine the facts allegedly giving rise to his obligation. The decision to pay or not to pay is made on these findings. If payment is eventually made, its declared purpose is the satisfaction of an existing claim C/D. It is accompanied by a 'discharge designation' (*Tilgungsbestimmung*) to this effect or, as a Romanist would prefer to say, the payment is made *solvendi causa* in regard to this claim. This is distinguishable from the payment made by a third party (eg, a bank), who merely acts on the instruction of his customer (D), and need not care about the effect of this payment on D's relation with the recipient (C). These reasons militate in favour of a solution treating the insurer as a third party payer (*Drittzahler*) within the meaning of § 267 BGB (BGHZ 113, 62, 68–70, case no 112; but see also the critical review of this decision by Canaris, NJW 1992, 868; for a full discussion of this controversy, see *Staudinger*-Werner Lorenz, § 812 Rn. 44. The decision was confirmed in BGH NJW 2000, 1718).

This survey of the problems surrounding 'payment of another's debt' would be incomplete if it did not mention the English case of *Owen v Tate* [1976] 1 QB 402 (CA), which calls for a short comparative observation.

It will be remembered that in that case the defendants had received a loan of £350 from a bank which was secured by a mortgage on the property of Miss Lightfoot, a former employee of the plaintiff. She wanted to be released from this mortgage and to recover her title deeds. The plaintiff, who was in no way concerned with the transaction, without consulting the defendants deposited an amount equivalent to the loan with the bank and signed a form of guarantee to pay money due from the defendants to the bank, limited to the amount he had deposited, in return for the release of Miss Lightfoot of her title deeds. The plaintiff's motive was to help her. The defendants protested when they learnt of the plaintiff's action. Nevertheless, although the plaintiff's action was contrary to their wishes, they requested the bank, when pressed for payment of their debt, to have recourse to the money deposited with the bank by the plaintiff. The plaintiff subsequently sought an indemnity from the defendants for the debt paid. This action failed because the plaintiff was regarded as a mere volunteer. In the leading judgment delivered by Scarman, LJ, the principle on which this decision rests was stated as follows ([1976] 1 QB 402, 411–12):

If without an antecedent request a person assumes an obligation or makes a benefit for another, the law will, as a general rule, refuse him a right of indemnity. But if he can show that in the particular circumstances of the case there was some necessity for the obligation to be assumed, the law will grant him a right of reimbursement if in all the circumstances it is just and reasonable to do so. In the present case the evidence is that the plaintiff acted not only behind the backs of the defendants initially, but in the interest of another, and despite their protest. When the moment came for him to honour the obligation thus assumed, the defendants are not to be criticised, in my judgment, for having accepted the benefit of a transaction which they neither wanted not sought.

In view of what has already been said, it will be obvious that a German court, had it been called on to decide such a case, would decide it in favour of the plaintiff. Although in actual practice it will rarely happen that someone guarantees the debt of another without having been asked to do so, such request is no legal requirement. As has already been pointed out above, the contract of guarantee (*Bürgschaftsvertrag*) is concluded between the guarantor and the creditor, no consent of the principal debtor being required. It may perhaps be added that this is no peculiarity of German law, for the same follows from Article 2028 para1 of the French Code civil: '*La caution qui a payé, a son recours contre le debiteur principal, soit que le cautionnement ait été donné au su ou à l'insu du débiteur.*' The guarantor who satisfies the creditor is subrogated to the creditor's claim against the principal debtor whose defences remain unaffected (§ 774 I BGB). This applies not merely to his legal relationship with creditor, but holds good also for his relation with the guarantor which, in a case like *Owen v Tate*, would be governed by the rules pertaining to *negotiorum gestio* (§§ 677 *et seq* BGB; on which see generally, Dawson, 'Negotiorum Gestio: the Altruistic Intermeddler' (1960–1) 74 *Harvard LR* 817, 1073 and Stoljar, 'Restitution—Unjust Enrichment and Negotiorum Gestio' (1984) *Int Enc Comp L* vol 10, c 17.). Assuming that the plaintiff's undertaking of the 'management of the matter' (*Geschäftsführung*) had not been 'in accordance with the interest and actual or presumptive wishes of the principal' (§§ 683 and 684 BGB), the question arises whether the subsequent request of the defendants must be regarded as ratification (*Genehmigung*). The effect of such ratification would be that the plaintiff, apart from possible benefits resulting from subrogation (cf §§ 774, 412, 401 BGB), could demand reimbursement of his outlays as if he had acted as a mandatary (§§ 684 sentence 2, 683, 670 BGB). If the defendant's request did not amount to ratification, the BGB refers the plaintiff to the provisions relating to the return of unjustified enrichment (§ 684 sentence 1 BGB).

In the light of the above, the German approach to the problems suggested by *Owen v Tate* calls a careful examination of the question whether the defendants must really be regarded as having been unjustly enriched by the plaintiff's unrequested payment of their debt. This would have to be denied where the period of prescription had already expired and probably also where the expiry of this period had been imminent. The same would apply if the creditor went bankrupt and the principal debtor had a good counterclaim against him which he could have used for a set-off. Generally speaking, a third party who makes an unrequested payment of another's debt, thus depriving the debtor of his right to set off a counterclaim, will not be able to recover from the debtor. The simple explanation for this is that in a case like this, the debtor is not unjustifiably enriched.

This shows that German law, too, might be confronted with undesirable consequences of 'officious intermeddling' which English law tries to brush aside at the earliest possible stage. (See also, *Esso Petroleum Co Ltd v Hall Russell & Co Ltd and Shetland Islands Council ('The Esso Bernicia')* [1989] AC 643). However, if subrogation is denied as a matter of principle, several burning questions must be answered: does the unauthorised payment by a third party discharge the debt? If the debt is discharged then the debtor received an incontrovertible benefit. If, on the other hand, this were denied the question remains whether the creditor has retained his claim, and if so whether the payer can recover the payment from him on the ground that there had been a total failure of consideration or, as a German lawyer would express it, because the payment did not achieve its purpose (*condictio causa data, causa non secuta = Kondiktion wegen Zweckverfehlung*). In the opinion of Goff and Jones, the plaintiff in *Owen v Tate* would have succeeded with his action if the bank had expressly assigned its claim against the defendants to the plaintiff. It is therefore strongly arguable that the plaintiff should be subrogated to the creditor who has accepted his suretyship and his payment (Goff and Jones, *The Law of Restitution* (6th edn, 2002), paras 3-016 and 15-010–15-011 and see also Watts, 'Guarantees undertaken without the Request of the Debtor' [1989] *LMCLQ* 7. Indeed, neither the common law authorities on subrogation nor the statutory adoption of the right in section 5 of the Mercantile Law Amendment Act 1856 was mentioned in the judgments of their Lordships in *Owen v Tate*; but see also Birks, *An Introduction to the Law of Restitution* (1989), pp 191–2 who maintained that this is not essentially different from a restitutionary right directly available to the surety against the defendant). There is also something to be said against generalisations from *Owen v Tate*, the facts of which are exceptional. This is why Ormrod LJ, even though concurring in the result with Scarman LJ, remarked that he would prefer to reserve any opinion about guarantors who enter into guarantees without the request of the principal debtor (at 414). (On the restitutionary analysis of *Owen v Tate*, see further Burrows, *The Law of Restitution*, pp 282–6 and the references cited therein.)

5. SET-OFF (*AUFRECHNUNG*)

A Blomeyer, 'Außerprozessuale Aufrechnung und Prozeßaufrechnung' ZZP 88 (1975) 439; Bötticher, 'Die 'Selbstexekution' im Wege der Aufrechnung und die Sicherungsfunktion des Aufrechnungsrechts' in *Festschrift für Schima* (1969) 95; Coester-Waltjen, 'Die Aufrechnung im Prozess' Jura 1990, 27; Derham, *The Law of Set-off* (3rd edn, 2003); Kegel, *Probleme der Aufrechnung* (1938); Gernhuber, *Die Erfüllung und ihre Surrogate* (2nd cdn, 1994) §§ 12–14; Goode, *Legal Problems of Credit and Security* (3rd edn, 2003) chapter 7; Goode, *Principles of Corporate Insolvency Law* (2nd edn, 1997) chapter 8; Lüke and Huppert, 'Die Aufrechnung' JuS 1971, 165; McCracken, *The Banker's Remedy of Set-Off* (1993); Meagher, Heydon and Leeming, *Meagher, Gummow and Lehane's Equity—Doctrines and Remedies* (4th edn, 2002) chapter 37; Musielak, 'Die Aufrechnung des Beklagten im Zivilprozeß' JuS 1994, 817; Tiedtke, 'Zur Aufrechnung mit verjährten Schadensersatzforderungen gegen den Anspruch des Verkäufers auf Zahlung des Kaufpreises' JZ 1988, 233;

Wood, *English and International Set-Off* (1989); Wood, *Law and Practice of International Finance: Title Finance, Derivatives, Securitisations, Set-Off and Netting* (1995) Part III; Zimmermann, *Comparative Foundations of a European Law of Set-Off and Prescription* (2002).

(a) Preliminary Observations

As was explained earlier in the text, set-off (*Aufrechnung*, §§ 387–96) is treated by the BGB as a substitute for performance. Its effect is to extinguish the relevant obligation. It follows that the civil law rules on set-off are of a substantive character. Traditionally, English courts regarded this form of relief as a matter of *procedure* (see eg, the discussion in Derham, *The Law of Set-off* (3rd edn, 2003), chapter 1), since the substantive effect—the extinction of both claims—can be produced only by the courts, that is to say by a judgment which allows the set-off and therefore dismisses the plaintiff's claim. This approach to set-off remains true of the common law rules on the subject: see *Stein v Blake* [1996] AC 243, 251 (*per* Lord Hoffmann). More recent developments in equity however have confirmed that certain types of equitable set-off do have a *substantive* character: see *BICC plc v Burndy Corpn* [1985] Ch 232 and *Pacific Rim Investments Ltd v Lan Seng Tiong* [1995] 3 SLR 1 (see Goode, *Legal Problems of Credit and Security* (3rd edn, 2003), paras 7-05 and 7-48). The judgment of the House of Lords in *Bank of Boston Connecticut v European Grain & Shipping Ltd* [1989] 1 AC 1056 confirmed this position, the area often being known as 'transaction set-off.' '[T]he party seeking the benefit of [the set-off must] show some equitable ground for being protected against his adversary's demand' (*Rawson v Samuel* (1841) Cr & Ph 161, 178; 41 Eng Rep 451, 458, *per* Lord Cottenham LC). To show this, there must be a cross-claim 'flowing out and inseparably connected with the dealings and transactions which also give rise' to the claim (*Bank of Boston Connecticut*, 1102–3; cf the discussion in *Meagher, Gummow and Lehane's Equity* (cited above), para 37-050, criticising the loose language used by a number of English courts in defining this connecting requirement in equity). Note also that express contractual set-off can operate as a substantive defence under English law: where the parties specify a particular event or act that is to trigger the netting out of mutual obligations, then on the occurrence of that event the contractual set-off takes on a substantive character that can be ranged against claims to the debt due. In civil law systems, the extinction of debts is effected not by the court but by an informal unilateral, extra-judicial declaration by one of the parties or, under certain circumstances, even by operation of law, ie, by the mere fact that the creditor owes his debtor the same amount as he is entitled to claim (*ipso iure compensatur*; see Article 1290 *Code civil* which, however contrary to its categorical wording, operates only if one of the parties relies on it).

The key differences between common law and equity when dealing with set-off are as follows: first, equitable set-off allows an equitable claim to be set-off against another equitable claim or against a common law claim. Secondly, the common law requires a liquidated claim to ground a set-off, while equity does not insist on this requirement. Thirdly, equity does not require that there be precise mutuality if set-off is to be available: at common law, the two claims had to be between the same parties, owed in the same capacity and relating to the same right. However, equity does require a sufficient ground be shown for protecting the defendant against the claimant's demand (ie, the defendant's claim must 'impeach' the claimant's claim in some way: '[t]he mere existence of cross-demands is not sufficient' (*Rawson v Samuel* (1841) Cr & Ph 161 at p 178–9; 41 Eng Rep 451 at p 458). (See generally, Spry, 'Equiatble Set-Offs' (1969) 43 *ALJ* 265 and the judgment of Woodward J in *D Galambos & Son Pty Ltd v McIntyre* (1974) 5 ACTR 10.) Note also that in the English case law concerning substantive set-off in equity, it remains an open question whether such a set-off must be asserted by notification to the other party before it can take effect: compare the judgments of Dillon and Ackner LJJ (finding that set-off was self-executing in those circumstances) with that of Kerr LJ (assertion by notification to the other party is required) in *BICC plc v Burndy Corp* [1985] 1 All ER 417. Goode has supported Kerr LJ's view as according better with the expectations of the other party, at least where the obligation appears prima facie independent of the obligation claimed to be set-off (*Legal Problems of Credit and Security* (3rd edn, 2003), para. 7-52). (See also *Re Palmer's Decoration and Furnishing Co* [1904] 2 Ch 743; *Stewart v Latec Investments Ltd* [1968] 1 NSWR 432 and *Stehar Knitting Mills Pty Ltd v Southern Textile Converters Pty Ltd* [1980] 2 NSWLR 514, at 518.)

The difference in classification which exists between English law and the continental rules can be of particular importance in disputes containing foreign elements (although insofar as the substantive version of equitable set-off is applicable, the classification difference may be so small as to be insignificant). Hence English courts apply the *lex fori*, while continental courts apply the proper law of contract in which the debt arose. This difference of classification does not however prevent the application of foreign substantive rules on set-off in an English court if, for instance, the proper law of the contract is German and the defendant's plea is that the plaintiff's claim has been extinguished according to the rules governing the contract in which the claim originates. In a case like this, the defendant who pleads a set-off against a German debt in an English court does not ask for a ruling of the court to set one claim off against another (*compensatio debiti per iudicem*), for his plea is that the plaintiff's claim has been extinguished under the applicable German law. (For further examples, see Martin Wolff, *Private International Law* (2nd edn, 1950), pp 233–4 and 456–7. Cf *Staudinger*-Magnus, Article 32 EGBGB, Rn. 61 *et seq.*)

In German law, to which we now turn, the set-off is made by declaration to the other party. Such a declaration will be ineffective if it is made subject to any condition or limitation of time (§ 388 BGB). A valid set-off has retrospective effect: insofar as the two claims cover each other, they are deemed to have expired at the moment at which, being suitable for set-off, they are ranged against each other (§ 389 BGB). All the conditions for set-off are laid down in § 387 BGB, which requires careful reading. It states: 'If two persons mutually owe acts of performance which are of the same kind, either party may set off his claim against the claim of the other party as soon as he can demand the performance due to him and effect the performance due by him.' The criteria for set-off contained in this provision must now be considered *seriatim*.

(b) Mutuality of Claims

The creditor of the one claim must be the debtor of the other claim and vice versa, which is also the basic position in English law (both at law and in equity: see eg, *Stein v Blake* (cited above) and *Clark v Cort* (1840) Cr & Ph 154; 41 ER 449). As a matter of principle therefore third parties may not intervene. For a common lawyer this may not be worth mentioning; but in German law § 267 BGB permits performance by third parties, the approval of the debtor not being necessary. This covers all cases where a debtor need not perform in person, especially money debts. Only in the extremely rare case that both the creditor and the debtor object will performance by a third party not be allowed (§ 267 II BGB). However, the rule against intervention by a third party by way of set-off is subject to exceptions in cases where such third party has a right to substitute performance. Suffice it here to mention only the basic fact situation which is directly in point: if the creditor levies compulsory execution on an object belonging to the debtor, any person who through that execution incurs the danger of losing a right in the object is entitled to satisfy the creditor. This includes satisfaction by set-off (§ 268 BGB; see also §§ 1142 II, 1150 and 1249 BGB concerning analogous cases in the law of mortgages and rights of pledge on movable things).

(c) Claims of the Same Kind

The performances mutually owed must be of the same kind. This refers, in the first place, to money debts, always provided that they are expressed in the same currency; but it is different in the case envisaged in § 244 BGB: in Germany money debts expressed in a foreign currency are payable in German currency, unless payment in the foreign currency is expressly stipulated.

The English common law approach is similar, insisting that the 'debts . . . [be] either liquidated or in sums capable of ascertainment without valuation or estimation' (*Stein v Blake* (cited above) at 251). Thus, a claim to property by the first party will be of the 'same' kind where the second party is authorised to dispose of that property and convert it into money. Equally, if such claims are ascertainable only by litigation, then they will not be sufficiently ascertainable to qualify (see *Hanak v Green* [1958] 2 QB 9, at 14 (*per* Morris LJ)). In equity, however, the courts have not imposed such strict requirements that the claim must be liquidated: see eg, *Lord Cawdor v Lewis* (1835) 1 Y & C Ex 427; 160 Eng Rep 174 and *Pigott v Williams* (1821) 6 Madd 94; 56 Eng Rep 1027.

(d) Validity, Maturity and Enforceability of the Claim Set Off

It goes almost without saying that the claim actively used for set-off (*Aktivforderung*) must be enforceable, because the party setting off his claim against the claim of the other party thereby forces on this party the fulfilment of an obligation which otherwise could be achieved only with the aid of a court. Since set-off under German law is nothing but a form of self-help, this can only be tolerated if all the conditions, which a court would require, are met when ordering the enforcement of a claim. This is supplemented by § 390 BGB: a claim against which there is a defence (*Einrede*) may not be set off. This provision has in mind claims, the performance of which is deferred by agreement of the parties (*Stundung*) or situations where the person bound is temporarily entitled on any other ground to refuse to make performance. (A similar basic position is reached at common law by the insistence that the debt be due and enforceable, and that where ascertainment of the debt is only possible through litigation this would not be sufficient: see the discussion in *Hanak v Green* and *Stein v Blake* (cited above).) However, in German law there is an important exception to this rule. Prescription (*Verjährung*) does not exclude set-off if the claim barred by prescription had not prescribed the time at which, being suitable for set-off (see § 389 BGB), it could have been set off against the other claim (§ 215 BGB). For the sake of clarity, it should be added that this does not apply if the claim has already been extinguished because a period of time absolutely limiting the exercise of a right has elapsed (so-called *Ausschlußfrist*; English law would take the same view, since in such cases a time bar would render the debt unenforceable). In such cases, the BGB does not speak of 'prescription' but states categorically that action must be taken within a certain period of time (see, eg, §§ 121, 124, 214 BGB). A good illustration of the present problem is provided by a leading case decided by the Federal Labour Court (BAG NJW 1968, 813).

In that case, an employee wished to set off a claim against a claim of his employer, but when he made this declaration to the employer his claim had already been barred absolutely by a clause contained in the collective agreement (*Tarifvertrag*) made between the employers' union and the trade union. The court distinguished this case from the case envisaged in § 215 (previously § 390 sentence 2) BGB and denied the analogous application of that provision to the present fact-situation (*contra* BGHZ 26, 304, 308–10 which however has since then come round to the view of the *Bundesarbeitsgericht*; see the cases listed by *Palandt*-Heinrichs, § 215 Rn. 2).

(e) Existence of the Claim of the Other Party

The existence of the other party's claim seems to be an obvious requirement of set-off, because otherwise the party who wishes to set off his claim would not be the debtor of the other party. However, this statement should be received with some caution. In German law, gaming or betting creates no obligation; but what has been given by reason of gaming or betting may not be demanded back on the ground that no legally enforceable obligation existed in the first place (§ 762 BGB). The policy behind this rule need not be analysed at this juncture. One thing, however, is clear: the loser of the game or bet, who has paid his 'debt' in cash, cannot afterwards rely on a claim for the return of an unjust enrichment. In other words, gaming or betting is a sufficient *causa acquirendi* or *naturalis obligatio* (*Naturalobligation*). The solution can hardly be different if the loser has set off his claim against the 'claim' of the winner. The loser's claim is extinguished thereby and the winner is relieved from a debt. So much then for the 'basics' of set-off in German law.

The BGB supplements these rules by some special provisions (§§ 391–6), which need not be explained in detail because their wording is clear beyond all doubt. The policy pursued by the legislator is also easily recognisable. Thus, § 393 BGB forbids any set-off against a claim arising from a delict wilfully committed. Special mention however should be made of §§ 94 *et seq* of the Bankruptcy Act (*Insolvenzordnung*) for the effect of set-off. For these provisions put a creditor, who is able to set off his claim against a claim of the debtor, in a privileged position when compared with the other creditors of the insolvent estate. For, unlike the latter (who must content themselves with the dividend, if any, at the end of the bankruptcy proceedings), the former's claims receive full satisfaction. Similarly, in English law this basic result is achieved by the mandatory operation of rule 4.90 of the Insolvency Rules 1986: see Goode, *Legal Problems of Credit and Security*, para 7-76 ff for discussion of this complex area. Indeed, great care must be taken in the drafting of multilateral netting regimes to ensure that they do not fall foul of mandatory rules of insolvency set-off and *pari passu* distribution on the liquidation of one of the parties. For an especially tricky example, see *British Eagle International Air Lines Ltd v Compagnie Nationale Air France* [1975] 1 WLR 758 (where the involvement of the International Air Transport Association (IATA) as a clearing house for payments from and credits to member airlines raised difficult issues of netting payments among different airlines when British Eagle went into liquidation, while still holding a claim against Air France. See Goode (above), para 7-76 ff for discussion and critique).

Finally, BGHZ 24, 97, case no 113, provides an interesting illustration of the complex interplay between the rules of civil procedure, set-off and the right of retention. In this case, a surety sought to rely on a set-off declared by the principal debtor. If the set-off had served to extinguish the debt, the surety would (following the accessory nature of the guarantee: § 767 BGB) likewise have been relieved from liability. Furthermore, § 770 II BGB entitles the surety to a defence if the principal debtor could declare a set-off. However, in the case at hand the set-off was invalid under the rules of civil procedure. This was because the principal debtor had not raised the defence of set-off before the conclusion of the legal proceedings against him (§ 767 II ZPO; see also, BGH NJW 1994, 2769). Thus, the surety could not invoke the set-off either. However, since the principal debtor could in respect of the counterclaim have invoked the general right of retention under § 273 BGB (discussed above, section 2), the surety could rely on this defence (§ 768 I BGB).

9

Breach of Contract: General Principles

1. INTRODUCTORY REMARKS

Irregularities of performance or *Leistungsstörungen* are the theme of this and the following chapter. The term 'irregularities' of performance however is not a technical term but a 'collective term' (as Ulrich Huber calls it: *Leistungsstörungen* (vol 1, 1999), p 2) comprising all possible variations on the theme of non-fulfilment of an obligation, much in the same way as the term 'breach of contract' (commonly used in the common law systems) covers all known and imaginable deviations from the regime of contractual obligations. Indeed, with the recent adoption by German law of a unitary notion of 'breach of duty' or *Pflichtverletzung* in § 280 and § 323 BGB as the basis of all irregularities of performance it has become possible to present German law from a remedy-focused (and more Anglicised) perspective without distorting its dogmatic structure. Prior to the reform, which is so fundamental that we need to discuss its ramifications in a separate section below, the approach to irregularities of performance was highly fragmented. (For further details in English, see the first edition of this work.)

The first reason for the abundance of rules for breach was the line of demarcation between the general part of the law of obligations and the special part. Impossibility and delay were clearly given special attention by the drafters of the BGB in the general part, while according to the 'orthodox view' there was no general principle of liability in damages for the breach of a contractual obligation in the Code itself. This, it was said, had to be developed outside the Code under the heading of '*positive Vertragsverletzung*'. In practice however the bulk of the cases was not covered by these rules but was solved by resorting to the 'special part' of the law of obligations dealing with specific types of contract. Thus, the Code established idiosyncratic rules for the phenomenon of non-conforming performance or *Schlechtleistung*. The influence of the *actio*-based Roman law tradition was particularly noticeable in this area of the law. The rules governing the contract of sale, for instance, not only determined the requirements of conformity, but included a special and exclusive regime of remedies such as price reduction or a highly peculiar right to demand termination called '*Wandelung*'. All this has dramatically changed with the new law. The rules in the special part of the BGB no longer lead a life of their own. At least as far as the two important types of contract—the contract of sale and contract for work and materials—are concerned, the remedies available for non-conformity of performance are in essence derived from the general part of the law of obligations (§ 437 and § 634 BGB bring this out very clearly). §§ 280 and 323 BGB thus become the true cornerstones of the German approach to 'breach of contract.' Since most cases in practice concern non-conforming performance, it seems worthwhile also to discuss the rules contained in the special parts of the law of obligations. Therefore, by way of illustration, in the next chapter certain types of contract are examined in more detail in order to complement the account given here of German law.

The second and closely intertwined reason for the fragmentation of German law in this field was that the remedies for each type of irregularity were largely independent from one another. It was thus necessary to adapt the presentation of German law accordingly and choose as a starting point not the remedy but the irregularity of performance. For instance, under the old law subsequent impossibility for which the debtor was responsible gave rise to not less than seven possible remedies, some of them mutually exclusive. Objective initial impossibility induced the invalidity of the contract. As a result the promisee could recover only his reliance interest. Delay of performance not only made recovery dependent on different requirements but included its own system of legal consequences. It would serve no practical purpose to continue the list of headings appropriate to the old regime. The 'new' BGB no longer proceeds in this way. The desired legal consequence is placed at the forefront of the new approach to breach. Thus, § 323 and § 324 BGB determine the conditions for termination of the contract in the case of a breach (note that § 314 BGB governs the—equivalent—right to give notice in 'continuous' contracts), while § 280 BGB is the general clause for the right to recover damages for a breach of contract. The preconditions for receiving these remedies still depend on the form of the irregularity in question. Here, the traditional categories—impossibility, delay, other breaches—resurface. However, there is nothing surprising about that, as we will show in this chapter. The differentiation at the level of the conditions for recovery or termination is a natural consequence of the preference (in theory at least) in German law for primary performance, ie the performance *in specie* of the contractual obligation.

Before we discuss the rules in more detail, it is necessary to add a few caveats at the outset. The term '*Pflichtverletzung*' in § 280 BGB covers both legal and contractual obligations ('*gesetzliches*' and '*vertragliches Schuldverhältnis*'). This was the reason why the term 'breach of duty' rather than 'breach of contract' (*Vertragsverletzung*) was chosen as the core concept of the reformed law (see Medicus, NJW 1992, 2384). (Note however that duties that sound in tort (regulated in § 823 BGB) are not covered by the term breach of duty in § 280 BGB.) In this work however we are concerned only with the breach of a contractual obligation (although we have previously discussed the breach of a special type of extra—namely pre-contractual—obligation in the context of *culpa in contrahendo*; see chapter 2, p 91 ff). We therefore use the term 'breach of contract' as shorthand for 'breach of (contractual) duty.'

This terminology may suggest a misleading familiarity to the Anglo-American jurist. The reader should be aware from the very beginning that vital differences from the common law idea of liability for breach of contract still remain. It suffices here to mention two.

First is the important difference found in the insistence of German law to find fault as a precondition for liability *in damages*—the 'fault principle' or *Verschuldensprinzip*. History combined with conceptualism account for this. For, unlike 'The Common law [which] treats any failure to perform a duty imposed by a contractual relationship as presumptively a breach of contract and then considers the question whether, under the circumstances, the failure to perform should be excused' (von Mehren), the civil law systems do not in general regard a failure to perform *simpliciter* as a breach of contract. For contractual liability to ensue, fault on the part of the obligor must also be shown to exist (see §§ 276, 278 BGB). This different approach, described in a masterly way by Rheinstein, *Die Struktur des vertraglichen Schuldverhältnisses im anglo-amerikanischen Recht* (1932); and Rabel, *Das Recht des Warenkaufs*, vol 1 (1936), stems from the different optic historically adopted by the common law and civil law systems towards the concept of contractual bond. For the former systems see contracts essentially in terms of 'guarantees' which result in liability when the guaranteed result is not brought about, while the latter see in the promisor a person who has promised to bring about a certain state of affairs and who thus should not be made liable if the promised result has not come about despite the fact that he has done all he could to conform with his promise.

The second difference with far-reaching implications is the mandatory regime of enforced performance. If, in the words of McKendrick, the rationale of many a rule in English law is that the parties to a contract should in case of breach 'walk away from the deal and seek satisfaction elsewhere' ('Sale of Goods' in Birks (ed), *English Private Law*, vol 2 (2000), para 10.45), the idea behind the German approach may be best encapsulated in this way: before the parties seek satisfaction elsewhere they should at least make one attempt to keep the contract alive. Hence, granting the debtor a period of grace (*Nachfrist*) becomes a *Leitmotiv* of the German approach to 'breach'. This also ties in well with the German (indeed continental European) predilection to protect the debtor.

Before closing this section we should also note that the doctrine of the foundation of the transaction (§ 313 BGB) or 'change of circumstance,' as it is sometimes called, can also be—and frequently is—discussed under the heading of *Leistungsstörung*. The doctrine concerns a number of situations where performance of one contractual obligation is or has become more onerous than anticipated. We have discussed the doctrine (in chapter 7, p 319) separately for two reasons. First, if a change of circumstance occurs in a relevant sense of the concept then the debtor is not in breach of a contractual duty. Rather, the contract terms are adjusted and only if that cannot be achieved may the contract be terminated. Secondly, the doctrine is closely interrelated with the rules on interpretation and mistake. However, this should not detract from the possibility that certain impediments to performance may, although not amounting to 'impossibility' in the strict sense, nevertheless release the debtor from his obligation. We will return to this particular aspect in the section on enforced performance (section 3, below).

2. THE REFORMED SYSTEM OF REMEDIES FOR BREACH OF CONTRACT

Canaris, 'Die Neuregelung des Leistungsstörungs- und des Kaufrechts' in Egon Lorenz (ed), *Karlsruher Forum 2002*, (2003) 5; Canaris (ed), *Schuldrechtsmodernisierung* (2002), (a collection of the preparatory works); Canaris, 'Die Reform des Rechts der Leistungstörungen' JZ 2001, 499; Dauner-Lieb, Konzen and K Schmidt (eds), *Das neue Schuldrecht in der Praxis* (2003); Dauner-Lieb, Heidel and Lepa (eds), *Das neue*

Schuldrecht (2002); Ehmann and Sutschet, *Modernisiertes Schuldrecht* (2002); Ernst and Zimmermann (eds), *Zivilrechtswissenschaft und Schuldrechtsreform* (2001); Haas, Medicus, Rolland, Schäfer and Wendtland (eds), *Das neue Schuldrecht* (2002); Peter Huber and Faust, *Schuldrechtsmodernisierung* (2002); Kohte, Micklitz, Rott, Tonner and Willingmann, *Das neue Schuldrecht* (2003); Stephan Lorenz and Riehm, *Lehrbuch zum neuen Schuldrecht* (2002); Schlechtriem, 'The German Act to Modernize the Law of Obligations in the Context of Common Principles and Structures of the Law of Obligations in Europe' (2002) *Oxford Univ Comparative L Forum* 2; Schmidt-Räntsch, *Das neue Schuldrecht* (2002); Schulze and Schulte-Nölke (eds), *Die Schuldrechtsreform vor dem Hintergrund des Gemeinschaftsrechts* (2001); Westermann (ed.), *Das Schuldrecht 2002* (2002); Zimmer, 'Das neue Recht der Leistungsstörungen' NJW 2002, 1; Zimmermann, *Breach of Contract and Remedies under the New German Law of Obligations* (Sapienza, Rome, 2002). See for more recent overviews that discuss the problems that have occured so far: Stephan Lorenz, *Neues Leistungsstörungs- und Kaufrecht: Eine Zwischenbilanz* (Juristische Gesellschaft Berlin, 2004); Stephan Lorenz, 'Schuldrechtsmodernisierung'—*Karlsruher Forum 2005* (forthcoming); and Schulze and Ebers, 'Streitfragen im neuen Schuldrecht' JuS 2004, 265, 366 and 462. See, for an excellent historical and comparative account though now outdated in parts, Rheinstein, *Die Struktur des vertraglichen Schuldverhältnisses im anglo-amerikanischen Recht* (1932); Treitel, *Remedies for Breach of Contract: A Comparative Account* (1988) based on his contribution 'Remedies for Breach of Contract' to the *International Encyclopedia of Comparative Law*, vol VII, chapter 16 (1976); and Zimmermann, *The Law of Obligations* (1990) chapter 25, p 783 *et seq*. A voluminous collection of essays under the general title *Les Sanctions de l' inexécution des obligations contractulles. Etudes de droit comparé*, edited by Marcel Fontaine and Geneviève Viney was published by Bruylant and the LGDJ in 2001. They cover mainly French and Belgian law but also other legal systems. The account of German law is that of the old regime so the essays will be mainly of interest to those who would like to compare the German law (as expounded in this chapter) with French and Belgian law.

(a) History of the Reform and Main Objectives

The recent reform of the law of obligations is the most fundamental reform of the first two books of the BGB since its adoption. The *Gesetz zur Modernisierung des Schuldrechts* of 26 November 2001 (BGBl I-3138) came into force on 1 January 2002. While the impetus for reform stemmed from European (Community) law, the scope of the reform reaches far beyond the narrow field of application of the 1999 Consumer Sales and Guarantees Directive. Five main objectives can be identified.

The first reason for the reform, and for the reform now, was the implementation of the aforementioned Directive 1999/44/EC ([1999] OJ L171/12) on certain aspects of the sale of consumer goods and associated guarantees. (Directives 2000/31/EC ([2000] OJ L178/1) and 2000/35/EC ([2000] OJ L200/35) were also implemented on this occasion; however, both may be neglected for present purposes.) There was no strict necessity to establish more than limited special rules for consumer sales. Indeed, this is how the Directive was implemented in England: see the Sale and Supply of Goods to Consumers Regulations 2002 (SI 2002, No 3045), which have been in force since 31 March 2003. In Germany, this was not regarded as satisfactory as it would have increased the fragmentary nature of the old law (alluded to above) still further. For, in practice, it would have resulted in yet another layer of rules been added to an already complex regime (sketched out above). (In this sense, the 'official' motivation of the reform: *Bundestags-Drucksache* 14/6040, p 2. Incidentally, the 'isolated' implementation in England can be criticised for this very reason: increasing the complexity of the law and creating uncertainty. Cf Arnold and Unberath, ZEuP 2004, 366.)

There is little doubt however that the sole argument that an isolated implementation would have added another set of rules to an already over-saturated system would not of itself have warranted such a wholesale revision of the law of obligations. A fundamental revision was on the agenda long before the European Community discovered the contract of sale as a target of harmonisation measures. This leads us to the second and third purposes of the reform: improving and simplifying the system of remedies for irregularities of performance and the corresponding periods of limitation (prescription). The remaining two objectives can be classified as being mostly of a 'cosmetic' nature. By this, we mean that in most cases and with very few exceptions, the intention was to change the *form* of the law, while leaving much of its substance intact.

Thus, the aim of the reform was, fourthly, to codify a number of rules already developed by the courts outside the Code. We have already referred to this phenomenon in relation to the existence of contractual 'protective duties' (under § 241 II BGB), the principle of *culpa in contrahendo* (under § 311 II and III BGB) and the doctrine of the foundation of the transaction (§ 313 BGB). Additionally, and fifthly, the legislator integrated into the Code special statutes dealing with certain aspects of contract law. We have already come across this transposition of the legal basis in relation, for example, to: §§ 305–10 BGB, the rules on standard terms of contract; consumer credit, § 491 BGB; dealings away from business premises, § 312 and § 355 BGB; and 'time-share' contracts, § 481 BGB. Most of these provisions aim to protect the consumer and, insofar as they have this aim, they all correspond to a European Community blueprint. They must be read together with the definition of 'consumer' and 'dealer' in the General Part of the BGB in the section on 'Persons' (§§ 13 and 14, included in the year 2000). Thus, roughly one hundred years after the entry into force of the BGB, the consumerist spirit (so often alluded to in various parts of this book) has left its mark on the BGB in an indelible manner. To reiterate the well-known polemic of von Gierke directed against the original version of the Code: the few 'drops of social oil' have been transformed into veritable streams. Thus, sooner or later, any law is forced to catch up with changing societal needs and values.

In the present context, only the first three objectives of the reform will be explored—these are all to some extent related to the simplification of the system of remedies for irregularities of performance (although 'simplification' in German legal literature is something that outsiders will find is a relative term). As suggested, the reform had in fact been long in the making.

The story begins in the late 1970s when the Ministry of Justice commissioned academic reports on the desirability of a reform of the law of obligations. These were published in 1981 and 1983 in three volumes as *Gutachten und Vorschläge zur Überarbeitung des Schuldrechts* and dealt with various aspects of the law of obligations (see for irregularities of performance, Ulrich Huber's report in vol 1, p 647). As a result of the recommendations, a Law Reform Commission composed of academics and practitioners was appointed in 1984, which in turn presented a final report with detailed recommendations and draft provisions in 1992. (*Abschlußbericht der Kommission zur Überarbeitung des Schuldrechts*; for a summary of the draft concerning irregularities of performance see Medicus's account in NJW 1992, 2384.) The ambitious reform project met with little enthusiasm. It was locked away until the Ministry of Justice somewhat unexpectedly unearthed the draft in 2000 and re-launched the discussion when presenting a so-called 'discussion draft' on the basis of the aforementioned *Abschlußbericht*.

The reason for the sudden interest in the reform was the need to implement the consumer sales Directive. How this could have been the triggering event, ie, the connection between the two projects is not immediately obvious. It turned out that if the system of irregularities of performance as contained in the draft were to be adopted, only a few and marginal further additions were necessary in order to encompass the requirements of the Directive regarding consumer sales. This is not a coincidence. For both drafts were modelled to a considerable extent on the United Nations Convention on the International Sale of Goods (henceforth CISG, in force in Germany since 1 January 1991; its predecessor was the Convention relating to a Uniform Law on the International Sale of Goods of 1973). (On all this see: *Abschlußbericht*, p 19; and for the Directive see, for example, Grundmann, 'Verbraucherrecht, Unternehmensrecht, Privatrecht—warum sind sich UN-Kaufrecht und EU-Kaufrechts-Richtlinie so ähnlich?' AcP 202 (2002) 40. It is perhaps worth recalling that the efforts to develop a uniform sales law go back to an initiative of Ernst Rabel, also regarded as the 'mastermind behind the draft Uniform International Sales Law': see, Schlechtriem, *Internationales UN-Kaufrecht* (2nd edn, 2003), p 2. Rabel's comprehensive comparative studies of the contract of sale as submitted to the International Institute for the Unification of Private Law were published in 1936: *Das Recht des Warenkaufs*, vol 1; vol 2 published posthumously in 1958.)

As already stated, the Directive itself did not warrant such a fundamental revision of the law of obligations. But it did provide a welcome opportunity for the Ministry of Justice to resurrect the draft provisions produced under its auspices eight years earlier, only this time purportedly also furthering the 'Europeanisation' of German law. The rather loose connection between the Directive and the core of German law of obligations gave rise to frequent and strongly voiced objections against combining a fundamental reform of the law of obligations with the need to implement the Directive. The reform project, as embodied in the 'discussion draft' of 2000, came under attack from very different directions. For reasons of space we cannot here reproduce the full 'back and forth' of the discussion (though see, especially, the contributions to Ernst and Zimmermann (cited above)).

The storm of criticism did not leave the Ministry of Justice unaffected. It quickly resurrected the Law Reform Commission, entrusting it with the task of rectifying the perceived or real 'defects' of the 'discussion draft'. One of the working groups dealt with irregularities of performance and also included, along with members of the original Commission (eg, Professors Medicus and Schlechtriem) some of the most prominent critics of the discussion draft. (Notably, Professors Ernst and Canaris, the latter, arguably becoming the most influential member. Much of his account of the deliberations as published in JZ 2001, 499 made it into the 'official' motivation of the government draft of May 2001.) At this late stage, the concept of impossibility was reintroduced and with it much of the dogmatic structure of the old law.

Another working group introduced last minute changes to the system of limitation periods, which will also be discussed in more detail (see section 6, below). The outcome of this second commission was published as the so-called '*Regierungsentwurf*' of May 2001 (published as *Bundestags-Drucksache* 14/6040). During the legislative process, over one hundred more minor corrections were made before the law was finally adopted as late as November 2001 and came into force on 1 January 2002. The speed of the last phase of the reform process was quite remarkable: the legal community was given little more than a month to get acquainted with the final version of the sweeping reform.

Much of the debate surrounding the reform is now only of historical interest. Two objections however deserve to be mentioned briefly here.

One of its fiercest critics was Ulrich Huber. Ironically, he had initially recommended a far-reaching reform of irregularities of performance in his aforementioned report of 1981, but in the intervening years he had changed his position. In his monumental treatise *Leistungsstörungen* (2 vols, 1999) he had 're-discovered' the 'beauty' of the solutions of the BGB as originally intended. There he laid out how the BGB had been intended to be applied and how it was in fact subsequently misunderstood. Only this 'misconstrued', 'distorted' version of the rules of the BGB (which however it is fair to say represented the firmly established view both in academic writings and court decisions) merited criticism, while the 'original' was both elegant and adequate. Reform was not needed if the BGB were applied as initially intended. (See eg, 'Die Unmöglichkeit der Leistung im Diskussionsentwurf eines Schuldrechtsmodernisierungsgesetzes' ZIP 2000, 2137, and 'Die Pflichtverletzung als Grundtatbestand der Leistungsstörung im Diskussionsentwurf eines Schuldrechtsmodernisierungsgesetzes' ZIP 2000, 2273.) This complex and fascinating argument however came too late to have any significant impact on the final shape of the reform.

Others, including Professor Zimmermann (eg, his *Breach of Contract and Remedies under the New German Law of Obligations* (Sapienza, Rome, 2002), p 8) objected that, despite emphatic assertions that the new law would bring German law in line with 'modern' European standards, by taking up the recommendations of 1992 the draft 'missed out' on significant developments on the European level since then, especially the Dutch *Burgerlijk Wetboek*, the *Principles of European Contract Law* by the Lando Commission (published 1995 and 2003, henceforth PECL) and the *Unidroit Principles of International Commercial Contracts* (1994 and 2004, henceforth PICC). The final draft of the reform proposal attempted to meet this objection by inserting occasional references to those aforementioned Principles. One gets the impression however that these references are somewhat random and the convergence of solutions accidental (eg, *Bundestags-Drucksache* 14/6040, 129). The similarity of solutions is particularly noticeable in those areas in which the CISG has influenced the position of the new law (as it also served as a model for many provisions of the Principles). We will return to some of these aspects in the sections dealing with particular remedies. Lando, who also published a provisional evaluation of the new law, came to the (perhaps unsurprising) conclusion that the PECL were far superior to the 'maze' ('*Irrgarten*') of old and new created by the reform ('Das neue Schuldrecht des Bürgerlichen Gesetzbuchs und die Grundregeln des europäischen Vertragsrechts' RabelsZ 67 (2003), 230, 244).

It is certainly too early to dismiss the reform in this wholesale fashion. At the very least, it strikes one as odd that the high level of abstraction of the new law is criticised, when one could argue that the Principles are even more abstract. As we will attempt to show, the reformed system of irregularities of performance is consistent and draws together the advantages of a unified notion of breach and the finer achievements of the traditional approach, ie, of over one hundred years of experience with specific types of irregularities of performance.

(b) Outline of the Reform

What then are the key features of the new system of remedies for irregularities of performance?

Three main types of *'remedy'* are recognised: enforced performance (§ 241 I BGB and numerous other provisions); termination (§§ 314, 323–5, 326 V, 346–54 BGB); and damages (§§ 249–55, 276–8, 280–4 BGB). Only as far as the specific requirements are concerned do the traditional categories of irregularities of performance resurface. The reason for maintaining them (although in a modified form) was not to perpetuate historical coincidence, but rather the insight that, if the protection of the interest in the performance of the contract is the guiding principle, then the traditional categorisation becomes a logical necessity. To give just one example: the central notion of *Nachfrist*, ie an additional period of grace for performance, would amount to a meaningless formality if performance were impossible. It is therefore sensible to waive this requirement in cases of impossibility (eg, § 283 BGB).

Three main types of *irregularity of performance* are acknowledged in German law. The first two types concern the duty of performance or *Leistungspflicht*, ie, the duty of the debtor to do what he promised to do or refrain from doing in the contract. The corresponding right to demand performance is laid down in § 241 I BGB. The first type of failure of performance is this: the debtor does not perform on time although he is capable of performing—ie, performance is delayed (§§ 280 II, 281, 286–92, 323 BGB). The second type arises in the following situation: the debtor does not perform because he cannot perform—ie, performance is impossible (§§ 275, 283, 311a, 326 BGB).

The third category of irregularities of performance involves a duty of a different kind, namely the so-called 'protective duties' or *Schutzpflichten*. Here, the debtor does perform but he also violates an auxiliary protective duty (for instance not to physically injure the promisee while carrying out performance). These duties are collateral, in fact entirely auxiliary, because they never provide a reason in themselves to enter into the contract. From a comparative perspective this is a peculiar category. In order to understand it, it must be recalled that in German law most delictual duties of care tend to be transposed into contract law (mainly because of structural deficiencies or limitations of the tort provisions of the Code). This was established by consistent case law before the new reform came into force and has now been codified in § 241 II BGB. The contractual explanation of these protective duties not to harm another person (in this case the other contracting party) is particularly attractive in German law because of the existence of vicarious liability in contract law absent from tort law (contrast § 278 with § 831 BGB: liability in delict only if servant was negligently selected or supervised). From a comparative perspective, most of these breaches are not interesting because they do not give rise to genuine contract law problems. However, in some cases the breach of such a collateral duty may affect the performance of the contract itself. This is where German law provides some interesting answers (§§ 282, 324 BGB). (For a fuller discussion of some of these issues from the angle of tort law, see *The German Law of Torts*, chapters 2 and 3.)

As already pointed out in the introduction, one of the major goals of the reform was to dissolve the special regime of remedies concerning *non-conformity of performance*. This was achieved (as far as the contract of sale is concerned) by applying the analysis of delay and impossibility to the seller's duty to perform. The seller promised to deliver conforming goods. If he delivers non-conforming goods, he is given a second chance to perform. If he fails to do so, this is either because he did not bring the goods into conformity with the contract even though he could have done so (this is a case of partial delay of performance) *or* he was unable to cure the defect or deliver substitutes (this is a case of partial impossibility of performance). It accordingly becomes possible to define the remedies of the buyer by simply referring back to the rules of the general part of the law of obligations with only a few qualifications (§ 437 BGB). The same approach was adopted in relation to the contract for work (§ 634 BGB). The economising effect of this way of proceeding is considerable. It suffices here to note further that the scope of reform was limited to these two types of contract. The contract of services (§ 611 BGB) was however already traditionally governed by the rules of the general part of the law of obligations. Only leases are still subject to a special— and complex—regime of liability (§ 535 BGB). Nevertheless, the general part of the law of obligations is now treated as a basic 'model' for the special parts of the law of contract, to which we will turn in the next chapter.

As a result, the present system of irregularities of performance is much leaner than before the reform. The fragmentation of the old law has been diminished considerably (even though an outside observer can often only understand the new law by knowing something of the old). This is also reflected by the adoption of a *unitary notion of breach*. Delay, impossibility and non-conformity of performance are all rationalised as a breach of duty (*Pflichtverletzung*) or, more precisely, as breach of a contractual duty of performance—in short, as breach of contract.

It is worth pausing to consider some of the implications of this concept, as well as to add a few words of caution. In particular, it is important to distinguish 'breach' from 'liability for breach.' A unitary notion of breach does not imply a unitary approach to liability. Once a breach is identified, the debtor may still be able to raise defences against liability. The defence will depend on the type of remedy to which the claimant has resorted. 'Breach of contract' in German law is defined as the absence of due performance or part thereof. If performance has not been effected then the defaulting promisor (or guilty party) has breached the contract. As a result, the promisee (or innocent party) may resort to the three main remedies already mentioned.

First, he may demand performance *in specie*. The 'guilty' party may by way of defence prove that performance is impossible. As a result, he is released from the primary duty of performance *regardless* of whether he is responsible for the impossibility (§ 275 I-III BGB). This does *not* however prejudice the innocent party's other rights (§ 275 IV BGB, *cf* Article 9:103 PECL). Even if the performance is impossible due to an Act of God this still constitutes a breach of duty. However, whether liability in damages follows from this 'breach' is a different matter. This is referred to as the 'dualistic' approach of the new law (Ernst in *Münchener Kommentar*, vol 2a, § 275 Rn. 1). The exclusion of the *duty* of performance and the exclusion of *liability* for non-performance of that duty are not the same. There are breaches of contract giving rise to liability in damages even though the duty of performance is excluded. It must be admitted that it is somewhat peculiar that a duty of performance is 'breached' even though at the same time § 275 BGB releases the debtor from that duty. (Huber even regards this as 'illogical', ZIP 2000, 2276.) The obvious answer to this criticism is that the rights arising from a breach must be distinguished from the breach as such. § 275 BGB releases the debtor not from the breach as such, but only in respect of the duty to performance *in specie*, as sub-section 4 of that provision expressly clarifies. (The problem of initial impossibility regulated in § 311a BGB raises special considerations, discussed below in section 5(d).) In the common law the issue is simply non-existent due to the fact that specific performance as a remedy is very much the exception rather than the rule. An order of specific performance is difficult to imagine where the performance is impossible. A court will not order specific performance if an order is difficult to enforce or if performance entails an undue burden (see for a discussion of the approach of the common law section 3(a) below). However, other systems recognising primary enforcement of the contract do not exclude the duty of performance in cases of impossibility (see eg, Article 79(5) CISG, but cf also Article 28 CISG). An alternative solution would be retain the right to the performance but limit the actual enforcement of the judgment requesting performance (some of these rules are examined below, section 3(d)).

Secondly, the innocent party may seek to *terminate* the contract. The (old) incompatibility between termination of contract and damages is removed (§ 325 BGB). However, while liability in damages is (as we shall see shortly) still fault-dependent, *fault is not a pre-requisite to a claim to terminate the contract* (this was a requirement under Directive 1999/44/EC but had already been part of the *Abschlußbericht* of 1992). Furthermore, according to § 326 V BGB the right to termination is also available where the right to performance is excluded under § 275 BGB. The CISG excuses the debtor for a failure to perform under certain circumstances. However, this does not affect the right to terminate the contract (Article 79(5) CISG and the analogous Article 7.1.7(4) PICC; contrast Article 9:303(4) PECL: contract comes to an end *ex lege*). Unlike French law but like the common law, German law does not require that the termination be pronounced by a court of law but will be effected by the innocent party—provided that (in most cases) additional time has been given to the guilty party to perform (§ 323 I BGB). If the breach committed by the guilty party concerns non-conformity of performance, it must be (when objectively measured) a serious one (or, in the words of the original text in § 323 V 2 BGB, it must not be *unerheblich*—ie, not insignificant, negligible or slight). It should be noted that the right to a reduction in the price payable will normally follow the same pattern as the right to terminate the contract, except that the breach must not be serious or fundamental (§§ 441 I 2, 638 I 2 BGB; Article 50 CISG).

This insistence that the guilty party be given 'one more chance'—which we will also encounter in relation to the right to recover damages—is in keeping with the Germanic preference (where possible) for *specific performance* and the desire to keep the contract alive. (Interestingly, American law seems to be moving in the same direction. This is analogous to the concept of cure in American sales law, UCC 2-508. Restatement Second of Contracts §§ 241 and 242 make the likelihood a defaulter will cure a relevant factor in determining if a breach is total and so grounds for discharge.) The CISG, by contrast, while in principle allowing the debtor to remedy any failure of performance of his obligations, grants the innocent party a right to *immediate* termination if the breach is 'fundamental', see Article 25, 49 (cf Article 7.3.1 PICC and Article 9:301 PECL). It should be noted that § 323 BGB does not require (as however Article 25 CISG *does*) that the detriment substantially deprives the innocent party of what he is entitled to expect; a much lesser breach suffices, provided that as explained the debtor has been accorded 'a second chance.' According to Article 3 of Directive 1999/44/EC, the seller is likewise granted a second chance to bring the goods into conformity with the contract before the consumer may exercise any further rights. In this regard, the implementation of the Directive thus presented a much greater challenge for English law than for German law. The challenge was in fact avoided by the 2002 Regulations, by granting the rights of the Directive alongside the traditional right of a buyer to immediate termination if a 'condition' has been breached (this is discussed further in chapter 10, p 494 ff).

The reform also dealt with the *effects* of termination through *Rücktritt* (§ 346 BGB). *Rücktritt*, as understood in German law, will be discussed in greater detail below (p 419 ff), so here we shall only mention the outline of the reform. Restitution for termination aims to achieve, as far as humanly possible, the principle of *restitutio in integrum*. The parties are thus expected to return to each other whatever they may have already received from the other (§ 346 I BGB); and this rule also applies to all cases of statutory termination (*gesetzliches Rücktrittsrecht*) and those cases where one of the parties has reserved the right of termination (*vertragliches Rücktrittsrecht*). Difficulties arise however where it has become impossible to return the performance received. According to § 346 II BGB, the debtor must compensate the creditor for the value of the performance. Certain exceptions to this general rule are laid down in § 346 III BGB. In practice, the greatest difficulty arises where goods delivered to the buyer are destroyed while in his possession, even though the buyer has exercised normal care (*diligentia quam in suis*). The new § 346 III Nr. 3 BGB excludes the duty to compensate. It cannot be doubted that the new law has simplified the effects of termination. Whether one agrees with the actual results thus effected is a different matter. (Cf Lorenz, *Zwischenbilanz*, above, p 14.) (American law is more liberal on this point. Restatement, Third, Restitution and Unjust Enrichment § 37 requires restoring value received but doesn't require return of performance in kind or specie.)

The third remedy that may be available is the right to claim substitute compensation, in short, *damages*. The first central aspect of the right to claim damages for breach of contract is that as a general rule the guilty party is once again given a second chance to perform, § 281 I BGB. The second aspect concerns the standard of liability. 'Breach of duty' or 'breach of contract' used to have the connotation in German law of a fault-based standard of liability. This is no longer the case. Breach of duty is defined objectively as the absence of performance or a part thereof. However, a fault-based standard of liability is retained in relation to the remedy damages. Breach of duty will lead to liability in damages if the debtor is at fault (§ 280 I in conjunction with § 276 BGB). In practice however the fault principle is considerably attenuated by four countervailing factors, which will be discussed in more detail below (p 444; and to this extent minimising the differences in practice with the common law). First, fault is presumed. This is expressed by the negative formulation of § 280 I 2 BGB. The debtor will have to rebut the presumption of fault if he wishes to avoid liability. Secondly, the standard of fault is an objective one. Thirdly, the emphasis on enforced performance further tightens liability. This point will be examined more fully below. Finally, certain categories of 'strict' liability are recognised, such as the promise to deliver generic goods.

Paradigmatically, the common law does not associate fault with liability for 'breach of contract.' However, a variety of doctrines excuse non-performance in the face of mistake, impracticability, impossibility, frustration of purpose, or failure of a condition. The approach of the CISG is analogous. One notes that 'breach of contract' does not presuppose the existence of fault to give rise to liability (Articles 74, 45(1) and 61(1) CISG use the term 'failure of performance' synonymously). Liability (in damages), however, is excluded where an impediment to performance is beyond the control of the debtor: Article 79(1) CISG. (For competing views as to the differences between the 'guarantee' liability of the common law and the fault principle of German law, compare: Stoll, in Schlechtriem (ed), *Kommentar zum Einheitlichen UN-Kaufrecht-CISG* (4th edn, 2004), Article 79 CISG, Rn. 9; and Tallon, in Bianca-Bonell (ed), *Commentary on the International Sales Law* (1987), 572.) Article 7.1.1 PICC and Article 8:101 PECL use 'non-performance' as the basic concept covering all irregularities of performance. Both proceed on the assumption that fault is not required to establish liability, but both also exclude liability for certain events beyond the control of the debtor (cf Article 7.1.7 PICC, which refers to this as *'force majeure'*; and Article 8:108 PECL). Ulrich Huber, in his recommendations of 1981, also followed the CISG model of liability. (He there preferred the term 'non-performance' or *Nichterfüllung* to 'breach'. In any event, the difference between the two terms is negligible. What matters is whether liability for 'breach' or 'non-performance' depends on fault or is strict.)

If one were to reduce the difference between the reformed remedy of damages in German law and the approach of the CISG (and the Principles) to a simple pattern, one could conclude that in German law liability requires that the promisor can be held responsible for the breach of contract (§ 276 BGB), while according to the CISG a breach entails liability unless the promisor cannot be held responsible for it (Article 79 CISG). The difference is not only one in drafting technique since the conditions for establishing respectively excluding responsibility are not the same.

Our brief overview of the system of remedies for breach has shown that a unitary notion of 'breach of contract' does not pre-determine the conditions for liability. Breach of contract in all systems must be distinguished from liability for that breach. A 'breach' may be excused in relation to the duty of primary performance but may not be excused so far as secondary rights are concerned. The right to terminate the contract is independent of fault but (unlike price reduction) presupposes a certain objective quality of the breach. The right to recover damages (liability for breach in a stricter sense) depends in German law on whether fault can be imputed to the guilty party in relation to the breach. The difference between the new German approach and the model of the CISG (excuse for certain impediments 'beyond the control' of the guilty party) does not seem dramatic and is further attenuated by other factors.

This introduction to the new system of remedies for failure of performance would be incomplete without a brief coverage of the reformed *periods of limitation*.

The law prior to the reform was highly unsatisfactory (see *Bundestags-Drucksache* 14/6040, 90–1). Prescription was perhaps the area of the law where the pressure for reform was most obvious. The great variety of periods of prescription had led to discrepancies in some areas of private law, particularly with regard to the special rules governing warranties in the fields of sales law and contracts for work and labour. A good example is provided by former § 477 BGB, dealing with the prescription of claims on sales warranties. There the claims of the buyer were barred by prescription six months after delivery if the object of sale was a movable thing. By contrast, the normal period of prescription used to be 30 years. There was widespread agreement among lawyers in Germany that, while six months was too short a time, the 30-year period was too long. A promisee who had discovered the non-conformity of performance after the six-month period had expired invariably sought to rely on the remedies of the general part of the law of obligations and to avoid the special regime of rules dealing with non-conformity. The courts were thus frequently forced to differentiate between the scope of application of the General and Special Parts of the law of obligations. The outrageous difference in length between these periods of limitation applicable to actions for breach of contract led to artificial distinctions being drawn in cases which lacked any real differences in substance.

This observation forms a neat parallel to those cases in English law where the incidental rules in one area of the law led to pressure to expand other related areas to accommodate what were perceived to be deserving cases by developing concurrent liability on different and overlapping grounds. See eg, the expansion of tort law to deal with various three-party situations that many systems would treat as problems of contract law (such as *Henderson v Merrett Syndicates (No 1)* [1995] 2 AC 145, especially at 174 (*per* Lord Goff of Chieveley): more favourable limitation rules would apply if a tort duty could be shown, which their Lordships held that it could) and the complex discussions in the law of restitution concerning liability under common law rules on failure (or indeed absence) of consideration and equitable principles relating to resulting trusts (in *Westdeutsche Landesbank Girozentrale v Islington LBC* [1996] AC 669, especially at 684 (*per* Lord Goff of Chievely) and 700–2 (*per* Lord Browne-Wilkinson: more favourable rules as to the availability of compound interest applied if the claim could be made out in equity (which their Lordships held that it could not)).

To abolish these inconsistencies in German law and to remove the pressure on the rules of substantive law, the reform project initially favoured a uniform period of prescription for all claims based on contract, which was to be three years. In the case of sale of movables this period would have begun to run from the moment of delivery (see *Abschlußbericht* (1992) 283). (A uniform regime of prescription is now adopted by Article 14:201 *et seq* PECL.)

The final draft moved away from the idea of a single rule for all contractual claims. Instead, it adopted a two-stage approach. The general period of limitation is three years and commences at the end of the year in which the creditor had or could have had knowledge of the claim and the person of the debtor (§§ 195, 199 I BGB). The general rule however is supplemented by a number of special periods of limitation in respect of claims for non-conforming performance. These were regarded to be necessary in the interest of commercial convenience. They commence irrespective of whether the debtor could have had knowledge of the claim. For instance, the remedies of the buyer in respect of non-conforming goods are subject to an objective period of limitation of two years commencing with the delivery of the thing (§ 438 I Nr. 3 BGB; this was also the minimum period under Article 5 of Directive 1999/44/EC). Despite the move away from a single rule for all claims, the reform has considerably simplified the previous proliferation of limitation periods, and by adjusting the length of the two sets of periods, has minimised (although unfortunately not completely removed) the incentive to bring oneself within the application of the general rules of breach of contract. The details of this aspect of the reforms are discussed below (p 486).

3. ENFORCED PERFORMANCE

Canaris, 'Die Behandlung nicht zu vertretender Leistungshindernisse nach § 275 Abs. 2 BGB beim Stückkauf' JZ 2004, 214; Canaris, 'Die Reform des Rechts der Leistungsstörungen' JZ 2001, 499; Canaris, 'Schadensersatz wegen Pflichtverletzung, anfängliche Unmöglichkeit und Aufwendungsersatz im Entwurf des Schuldrechtsmodernisierungsgesetzes' DB 2001, 1815; Canaris, 'Grundlagen und Rechtsfolgen der Haftung für anfängliche Unmöglichkeit nach § 311a Abs. 2 BGB' in *Festschrift für Andreas Heldrich* (2005) 11; Emmerich, *Recht der Leistungsstörungen* (5th edn, 2003); Grunewald, 'Neuregelung der anfänglichen Unmöglichkeit' JZ 2001, 433; P Huber, 'Der Nacherfüllungsanspruch im neuen Kaufrecht' NJW 2002, 1004; U Huber, 'Die Schadensersatzhaftung des Verkäufers wegen Nichterfüllung der Nacherfüllungspflicht und die Haftungsbegrenzung des § 275 Abs. 2 BGB neuer Fassung' in *Festschrift für Peter Schlechtriem* (2003), p 521; Jones and Goodhart, *Specific Performance* (2nd edn, 1996); Jones and Schlechtriem, 'Breach of Contract' in *International Encyclopedia of Comparative Law*, vol VII, chapter 15 (1999), para 157 *et seq*; McGhee (ed), *Snell's Equity* (31st edn, 2004), chapter 15; Meagher, Heydon and Leeming, *Meagher, Gummow and Lehane's Equity: Doctrines and Remedies* (4th edn, 2002), chapter 20; Medicus, 'Die Leistungsstörungen im neuen Schuldrecht' JuS 2003, 521; S Meier, 'Neues Leistungsstörungsrecht' Jura 2002, 118 and 187; Neufang, *Erfüllungszwang als ‚remedy' bei Nichterfüllung* (1998); Picker, 'Schuldrechtsreform und Privatautonomie' JZ 2003, 1035; Schwarze, 'Unmöglichkeit, Unvermögen und ähnliche Leistungshindernisse im neuen Leistungsstörungsrecht' Jura 2002, 73; Spry, *Equitable Remedies* (6th edn, 2001), chapter 3; Treitel, 'Remedies for Breach of Contract' in *International Encyclopedia of Comparative Law*, vol VII, chapter 16 (1976), para 7 *et seq*.

(a) Preliminary Observations

The idea of specific enforcement of an obligation is much narrower in the common law than in the civil law. In accordance with its equitable origins, the remedy is discretionary in nature. Its enforcement presupposes a court decree, which is directed at the defendant personally. The use of specific performance has traditionally not been regarded as generally desirable because it places a strain on the machinery of law and interferes with the personal freedom of the contractual debtor (or defendant). In English law, the remedy has thus been confined to exceptional cases in which an award of damages would not afford sufficient protection to the contractual creditor (or claimant): in the classic terminology, where damages are not an 'adequate' remedy. (See the various references in the bibliography above, particularly: *Snell's Equity*, chapter 15; Jones and Goodhart, *Specific Performance*; see also, Treitel, *The Law of Contract*, p 1019 ff; McKendrick, *Contract Law*, chapter 26; and as to the law in the US, Dobbs, *Law of Remedies* (2nd edn, 1993), § 12.8.) Where it concerns an obligation to forbear from doing something, the order is known as a prohibitory injunction. An important exception to the rule that the obligation of performance is not enforced *in specie* arises in relation to an obligation to pay a certain amount of money, which even the common law (as opposed to equity) was prepared to enforce. Here, an action 'for an agreed sum' is available that is neither a suit for specific performance nor damages.

In providing a basis from which to make a comparative assessment of the German law on enforced performance, it is necessary to consider an outline of the English law of specific performance. First, when will an award of specific performance be made—what are the major relevant factors in the exercise of the court's discretion to make such an order? Secondly, are there signs that English law is moving towards a more liberal interpretation of the availability of the use of this remedy? In dealing with these questions, we must also consider the impact of the significant recent decision of the House of Lords in the *Co-operative Insurance Society Ltd v Argyll Stores (Holdings) Ltd* [1998] AC 1, which is the leading modern authority on specific performance in English law.

As noted above, a key element in the court's analysis in this area is whether damages would provide an adequate remedy for the breach suffered by the claimant. Thus, in the typical case, where the subject matter of the contract is readily available on the market (ie, its specificity is not of the essence of the contract), damages *will* be an adequate remedy. Indeed, for the claimant to fulfil his 'duty' to mitigate his loss, it will usually be necessary for him to attempt to procure just such a substitute (on which see below, p 475 ff): to order specific performance would cut across this 'duty' (see eg, *Buxton v Lister* (1746) 3 Atk 383 at 384) and in such cases there is a clear and ready means of assessing the measure of damages for breach. By contrast, where the contract is for the sale of a specific thing with unique characteristics, it is clear that such an order is likely to be made (see the reasoning of Sir Richard Kindersley V-C in *Falcke v Gray* (1859) 4 Drew 651 and the similar position under section 52 of the Sale of Goods Act 1979 ('the 1979 Act'); the latter is discussed in Treitel, *The Law of Contract,* pp 1022–5). Whether this includes what McKendrick has termed 'commercial uniqueness' (in the sense of market availability at the relevant time) is dependent on the possibility of alternative performance and a claim for damages to cover the extra cost of that alternative: compare *Behnke v Bede Shipping Co Ltd* [1927] 1 KB 649 with *Société des Industries Metallurgiques SA v The Bronx Engineering Co Ltd* [1975] 1 Lloyd's Rep 465. In the former, Wright J held that the ship's characteristics (cheap, yet recently refitted to satisfy German regulations) meant that she was 'of peculiar and practically unique value to the plaintiff' (at 661), while in the latter the mere fact that the plaintiffs would have had to wait a further nine to twelve months for delivery of replacement machinery was not such as to 'remove . . . this case from the ordinary run of cases arising out of commercial contracts where damages are claimed' (*per* Lord Edmund Davies, at 468). In the *Bronx Engineering* case, it was clear that the defendants could have met any subsequent damages claim brought by the plaintiffs and the court assumed that such machinery was readily available in the market and so refused specific performance. Another aspect of this analysis is whether damages would be capable of sufficiently precise and accurate assessment (and recovery) (see again, the *Bronx Engineering* case for discussion).

This criterion (of damages not being an adequate remedy) was often described as a precondition of any award of specific performance; however, this was strongly challenged in the famous case of *Beswick v Beswick* [1968] AC 58 (discussed in chapter 4 p 188, concerning contractual privity). See in particular, the speech of Lord Pearce, who preferred to focus (at 88) on the question of whether the more 'appropriate' remedy was that of specific performance. This language reflects that found in section 52 of the 1979 Act when describing the possible exercise of the court's discretion to order specific performance. This suggests that, while the inadequacy of a damages remedy remains an (and indeed probably the most) important factor in the exercise of the court's discretion here, it is only one factor among a number of others that may be taken into account. In this sense, it seems that the courts are moving towards a less restrictive approach to the availability of specific performance: courts have become more willing to order specific performance. (See eg, Laycock, *The Death of the Irreparable Injury Rule* (1991).) A huge range of potentially relevant other factors has been identified by various writers (see eg, Treitel, *The Law of Contract*, pp 1026–9 and 1037–8 on factors affecting the court's discretion and 1029–37 on cases where an order of specific performance will not be made; and cf Burrows, *Remedies for Torts and Breach of Contract* (2nd edn, 1994), pp 337–81 for a slightly different categorisation): this is not the place to engage in an exhaustive analysis of these factors. One deserves a certain emphasis here however due to its centrality to the speech of Lord Hoffmann in the *Co-operative Insurance Society* case. It is the oft-stated refusal of the courts to make an order for specific performance where the result would be to require constant supervision by the court (see eg, *Powell Duffryn Steam Coal Co v Taff Vale Rly* (1874) LR 9 Ch 331: no specific performance of an obligation to operate railway signals). However, note that where such supervision would not be too difficult to secure, the courts have not been unwilling to order specific performance: see, eg, cases on building work such as the recent *Rainbow Estates Ltd v Tokenhold Ltd* [1999] Ch 64 (where Lawrence Collins J emphasised that careful drafting could satisfactorily define what work needed to be completed to satisfy the court's order (eg, at 73)).

In the light of this background, we are now in a position to consider the significance of Lord Hoffmann's speech in *Co-operative Insurance Society v Argyll Stores (Holding) Ltd* [1998] AC 1. In that case, the defendants ('Argyll') decided to close their supermarket, which was the 'anchor tenant' in the Hillsborough Shopping Centre of which the plaintiffs ('CIS') were the landlords. This action was in breach of a covenant in their lease to 'keep the demised premises open for retail trade during the usual hours of business in the locality . . .' (clause 4(19) of the lease; see [1998] AC 1, at 10). This closure was announced in early April 1995, to take effect from 6 May 1995; in spite of CIS's protests in a letter of 12 April 1995, no reply was forthcoming, the shop closed as planned and within two weeks its fittings had been stripped out of the premises. CIS claimed specific performance of the covenant to remain open and damages for breach. The case reached the House of Lords after the Court of Appeal, overturning the first instance judge's ruling, ordered that Argyll specifically perform the covenant.

Lord Hoffmann analysed the basis of the previous practice of the courts and advisers, under which received wisdom held that mandatory injunctions would not be awarded to require a business to be carried on, on the basis that such an order would require the constant supervision of the court. His Lordship also sought more precise analysis of the reasons why this consideration was thought to be so problematic: he emphasised, first that the key concern of the courts in this area is 'the possibility of the court having to give an indefinite series of . . . rulings [on compliance with an order for specific performance] in order to ensure the execution of the order' (12). This is because of the very heavy consequences of the breach of any such order: ie, a finding that the defendant is in contempt of court, which is a quasi-criminal procedure. Secondly, he was keen to draw the distinction (adverted to above) between orders requiring that an activity be carried on and orders requiring a result to be achieved. This flowed from the concern about constant court visits to rule on continuing compliance: '[e]ven if the achievement of the result is a complicated matter which will take some time, the court, if called on to rule, only has to examine the finished work and say whether it complies with the order' (13). Thirdly, he drew attention to the need for precision in the definition of what it is that must specifically be performed by the defendant, which point again followed from his basic concern about 'wasteful litigation over compliance' (13–14). This concern was also evident in his treatment of the argument that an order for specific performance may have the effect of permitting the enrichment of the plaintiff at the defendant's expense, since the loss suffered by the defendant in complying with the order may exceed any loss to the plaintiff from the breach of contract (at 15, citing Sharpe, 'Specific Relief for Contract Breach' in Reiter and Swan (eds), *Studies in Contract Law* (1980), chapter 5 at 129). For Lord Hoffmann (15–6):

> From a wider perspective, it cannot be in the public interest for the courts to require someone to carry on business at a loss if there is any plausible alternative by which the other party can be given compensation. It is not only a waste of resources but yokes the parties together in a continuing hostile relationship. The order for specific performance prolongs the battle. If the defendant is ordered to run a business, its conduct becomes the subject of a flow of complaints, solicitors' letters and affidavits. This is wasteful for both parties and the legal system. An award of damages, on the other hand, brings the litigation to an end. The defendant pays damages, the forensic link between them is severed, they go their separate ways and the wounds of conflict can heal.

Taking all these factors into account, Lord Hoffmann was of the view that the terms of the obligation in clause 4(19) were not sufficiently precise to allow an order for specific performance, since it said 'nothing about the level of trade, the areas of the premises within which trade is to be conducted, or even the kind of trade . . . [which] seems to me to provide ample room for argument over whether the tenant is doing enough to comply with the covenant' (16–17). Finally, his Lordship took a less condemnatory view of the conduct of Argyll than had the Court of Appeal, holding that while failure to reply to the letter from CIS had been 'no doubt discourteous,' both parties were 'large sophisticated commercial organisations. . . . The interests of both were purely financial [and] there was no element of personal breach of faith. . . . No doubt there was an effect on the business of other traders in the centre, but Argyll had made no promises to them and it is not suggested that CIS warranted to other tenants that Argyll would remain' (18). Thus, the appeal was allowed and the original order of the judge, refusing specific performance, was restored.

A number of aspects of Lord Hoffmann's speech are worthy of comment.

First, while acknowledging that it was a matter of the court's discretion whether to grant specific performance, Lord Hoffmann stressed that there were 'well-established principles which govern the exercise of the discretion,' even though he ultimately retained great flexibility for the court to assess the relevant factors in each individual case. This balance between certain and reliable principles and the need for the courts to assess all the facts and factors in the context of each case might be thought to undermine the ability to provide clear legal advice to parties entering into such obligations in the future. However, Lord Hoffmann's emphasis on the 'settled practice' (and the 'sound reasons' for it) seems to indicate that the parties should both have been 'perfectly aware that the remedy for breach of the covenant was likely to be limited to an award of damages' (18): this would seem to suggest that, at least in clearly commercial situations, the focus is likely to remain on damages as the typical remedy. However, it might be argued that such a focus here did not take into account the difficulty of assessing any damages that CIS might claim. As McKendrick suggests (*Contract* Law, pp 1132–3), '[s]uppose that the departure of the defendants led to such a loss of trade that other tenants were forced to close? Would the plaintiffs have been entitled to recover the loss of rent from such tenants from the defendants?' (Equally, it might be suggested that such considerations are more relevant to a consideration of the remoteness of any damages claimed, on which see section 5(f)(ii), below.) Perhaps therefore the practical application of the *Co-operative Insurance Society* approach (especially given Lord Hoffmann's reformulation of the underlying reasons of principle) may yet lead to more frequent awards of specific performance in such cases: although the early case law is not promising, neither is it conclusive either way (see, eg, *North East Lincolnshire BC v Millennium Park (Grimsby) Ltd* [2002] EWCA Civ 1719).

A second interesting element in Lord Hoffmann's speech is its reference (both explicitly—eg, to Sharpe's piece ('Specific Relief for Contract Breach')—and implicitly) to considerations drawn from the 'law and economics' literature. While this is not the place to attempt to summarise the details of the debate on the desirability of the wide(r) availability of the remedy of specific performance, Lord Hoffmann's references to wasteful and repeated litigation show a concern for the costs of enforcement, both for the parties themselves and through the provision of court infrastructure, time and resources (see eg, at 13). Meanwhile, his discussion of the likely impact on the respective subsequent positions of the plaintiff and defendant once operating under an order for specific performance (see 12–13 and 15) illustrates the impact that such an order can have on the incentives of each party to act in a certain way. To put the matter simply, one concern of economists in such a situation relates to whether or not this effectively provides an incentive to performance by the defendant that is more costly than the value placed by the claimant on that performance (at 15). This is a distributional concern related to the ex-post *distribution* of the costs of requiring specific performance. This insight accords with the approach of the English courts to deny specific performance where it would cause 'severe hardship' to the defendant (see *Denne v Light* (1857) 8 DM & G 774; Treitel, *The Law of* Contract, pp 1026–7). A particularly good parallel to the point raised here is the recognised 'hardship' situation where the cost of performance by the defendant is out of all proportion to the benefit that such performance would render to the claimant (*Tito v Waddell (No 2)* [1977] Ch 106, at 326, although this standard is a rather blunt one in economic terms). However, these references in the speech do not cover explicitly the more central concern of the economic analysis of contract remedies: *viz*, the *ex ante* impact of such rules on the subsequent process of entering into contractual obligations (including the terms to be included, etc). Also it misses the crucial argument that the parties will renegotiate in face of an order to render performance that costs more than it is worth. (For further detailed analysis on this aspect, see the classic articles of Kronman, 'Specific Performance' (1978) 45 *Univ Chicago L Rev* 351 and Schwartz, 'The Case for Specific Performance' (1979) 89 *Yale LJ* 271; and see the summary of McKendrick, *Contract Law*, pp 1133–5.)

Finally in this vein, note that prior to the House of Lords' delivery of its judgment, Argyll had managed to assign the lease to another tenant—indeed, the Court of Appeal had suspended its order for specific performance for a three-month period, so that this could be completed (see [1998] AC 1, at 9). This point may be seen to be analogous to the position where the contract does not require *personal* performance by the defendant, where the courts have been prepared to order the defendant to enter into a contract with a third party, so as to ensure that those acts are performed (albeit by the third party instead of the defendant himself): *Posner v Scott-Lewis* [1987] Ch 25. One can only speculate whether future cases may involve an argument by claimants that a court order should be granted requiring the assignment of the contract within an appropriate period (plus a residual damages claim for any resulting and unmitigated loss), with the default position then being a claim in damages for the full loss suffered (rather than specific performance, as under the approach of the Court of Appeal in the *Co-operative Insurance Society* case).

The following paragraph of Lord Hoffmann's judgment in the *Co-operative Insurance Society* case ([1998] AC 1, at 11–12) is also of particular interest to the comparative lawyer:

> Specific performance is traditionally regarded in English law as an exceptional remedy, as opposed to the common law damages to which a successful plaintiff is entitled as of right. There may have been some element of later rationalisation of an untidier history, but by the 19th century it was orthodox doctrine that the power to decree specific performance was part of the discretionary jurisdiction of the Court of Chancery to do justice in cases in which the remedies available at common law were inadequate. This is the basis of the general principle that specific performance will not be ordered when damages are an adequate remedy. By contrast, in countries with legal systems based on civil law, such as France, Germany and Scotland, the plaintiff is *prima facie* entitled to specific performance. The cases in which he is confined to a claim for damages are regarded as the exceptions. In practice, however, there is less difference between common law and civilian systems than these general statements might lead one to suppose. The principles on which English judges exercise the discretion to grant specific performance are reasonably well settled and depend on a number of considerations, mostly of a practical nature, which are of very general application. I have made no investigation of civilian systems, but *a priori* I would expect that judges take much the same matters into account in deciding whether specific performance would be inappropriate in a particular case.

From what follows in our discussion of the German law, the reader can judge for him- or herself how far this similarity actually holds true. Equally however simply to state that such similarities are 'expected' to exist without any (even cursory) examination of the relevant civilian systems is perhaps somewhat presumptuous.

Indeed, it is interesting to note that Lord Clyde's judgment, while agreeing with Lord Hoffmann's reasons for allowing the appeal (as did the rest of their Lordships), specifically stated that 'I should wish to reserve my opinion on the approach which might be adopted by civilian systems' (above, at 19). This proved a prescient (and well-informed) statement, in the light of the judgment of the Inner House of the Court of Session in *Highland and Universal Properties Ltd v Safeway Properties Ltd* 2000 SLT 414, where an extremely similar covenant *was* held to be specifically enforceable under Scots law. The position of German law seems to be controversial: see for instance OLG Celle NJW-RR 1996, 585, where the court had little difficulty in ordering the enforcement of a judgment for the actual running of a business by a commercial tenant, discussed further in section 3(d), p 405, contra eg, OLG Naumburg NJW-RR 1998, 873. See also, *City Stores Co v Ammerman*, 266 F Supp 766 (DDC 1967), aff'd, 394 F.2d 950 (DC Cir 1968), ordering specific performance of developer's promise to make plaintiff anchor tenant in new mall. (Dobbs, *Law of Remedies*, § 12.8(3) collects similar cases.)

The key difference in starting points may sometimes be resolved where the burdens of proof (whether to establish a case *for* specific performance, in English law, or one *against* enforced performance, in civilian systems) result in a similar balance being struck, but the extent to which these matters are also ones of substance is underlined by the different formulations of international instruments dealing with these issues (see McKendrick, *Contract Law*, pp 1135–6): compare Article 28 CISG and Article 9:102 PECL—the former simply allows domestic law to govern such orders, while the latter starts from the civilian premise (of entitlement in principle to specific performance) and then balances this with some of the concerns that feature in the common law, as discussed above. These factors (Article 9:102(2) PECL) will require analysis on a case-by-case basis.

Indeed, the one thing that is abundantly clear from this brief survey of the English law of specific performance is that the availability of this remedy is heavily dependent on a careful analysis of the facts in each given case and a weighing up of the effect on both parties of a court order that the contract be specifically performed.

By contrast to the starting point of the common law however German law entitles the promisee in principle to enforce *in specie* the obligation of performance, whether or not it is a monetary obligation. The right to demand performance of the promise undertaken by the promisor in the contract is laid down in § 241 I BGB. It is referred to as the *Primäranspruch* (primary right) as opposed to *Sekundäranspruch* (secondary right) concerning substitutes for performance (eg, damages). In order to avoid terminological confusion, it is thus best to avoid the technical term of specific performance in relation to the civil law. Following Treitel in this respect, we prefer the concept of enforced performance. 'By enforced performance is meant, in its broadest sense, a process whereby the creditor obtains as nearly as possible the actual subject matter of his bargain, as opposed to compensation for money for failing to obtain it' (*International Encyclopaedia of Comparative Law*, cited above, para 16-7). Enforced performance is of first importance in cases of a total lack of performance but is also appropriate and of great practical significance in cases of partial non-performance. For instance, a seller who promised to deliver goods of a certain quality and has failed to do so is required by a regime of enforced performance to cure the defect or deliver conforming goods (see § 439 BGB, Article 3 of Directive 1999/44/EC and Article 46 CISG).

(b) The Primary Duty of Performance

Demanding the performance is the primary right of the promisee. Performing the contract is the primary duty of the promisor. Making enforced performance the 'primary' remedy implies that the promisee ought to be able to get exactly what he bargained for. The availability of enforced performance makes it all the more difficult to commit successfully what (mainly American) writers have come to refer to as an 'efficient breach of contract.' (See however Restatement, Third, Restitution and Unjust Enrichment § 39, that permits a claim for the breacher's profits if the breach is opportunistic.) A breach may be regarded as efficient in economic terms if it entails an advantage to the guilty party that is greater than the pecuniary detriment to the innocent party. In such a case, compensating the innocent party would still leave the guilty party better off than if the contract were required to be fulfilled *in specie*. While German law does not completely preclude the idea of an 'efficient' breach in relation to certain types of contract such as the contract of services, it is clearly hostile towards allowing the promisor to avoid the promise to perform and pay damages instead. Thus, the question whether breaching the contract is appropriate does not arise in the first place. After all, the promisee is entitled to enforce the promise specifically. (See, for a criticism of the 'efficient breach' doctrine from the perspective of German law, Huber, *Leistungsstörungen*, vol 1 (1999), p 49, and from an Anglo-American perspective, Friedmann, 'The Efficient Breach Fallacy' (1989) 18 *J Leg Stud* 1.)

The actual importance of enforced performance is often doubted in works of comparative law. See for instance, Zweigert and Kötz, *Comparative Law* (3rd edn, 1998), p 484: 'actual contrast not quite so sharp'; 'commercial men prefer to claim damages rather than risk wasting time and money for a claim for performance whose execution may not produce satisfactory results.' (See also, Lord Hoffmann's statement in the *Co-operative Insurance Society* case discussed in the previous section.) It will be different in times of scarcity of goods and other sudden changes of economic circumstances. The buyer will then be interested in specific performance because damages will not be sufficient compensation. The petrol crisis in the early 1970s offers a good illustration for this proposition (see *Sky Petroleum Ltd v VIP Petroleum Ltd*, [1974] 1 WLR 576, Chancery Division, *per Goulding* J). Yet in the vast majority of cases, commercial men will prefer to hold the defaulting promisor liable in damages.

The significance of enforced performance should nevertheless not be underestimated. It is not to be found in the actual numbers of claims but is derived from the idea of *pacta sunt servanda*, of ascribing binding force to the promise of performance. The regime of enforced performance as such may place a heavy burden on the promisor in civil law systems. In particular, where the debtor regrets having entered into the contract, forcing him to perform may be more attractive to the promisee than relying on the remedy of damages which, as we shall see below, is subject to a whole range of further limiting principles and rules such as the fault principle, causation, mitigation and so forth. Compared with these numerous principles restricting the recovery of damages, here the creditor is entitled to an almost unconditional right to get what he is entitled to expect under the contract. In fact, the only major limitation on this right is when to carry out that performance would be impossible or unreasonably burdensome.

If the regime of enforced performance is taken into account, the 'fault principle' of German law applicable to claims for damages appears in a new light. The interest in the performance of a contract is already *significantly* protected by enforced performance. Damages may more easily be limited as a result. The 'guarantee'-type of liability of the common law contrasts favourably with the fault-based approach of many civil law systems that appear to protect the debtor at the expense of the creditor. However, if the focus is extended to the primary rights, the regime of strict liability no longer appears generous, but rather as a necessary substitute for performance. This function of an award of damages is stressed by more recent attempts to increase the protection of the 'performance interest' in English law. (See Friedmann, 'The Performance Interest in Contractual Damages' (1995) 111 *LQR* 628; Lord Goff of Chieveley in *Alfred McAlpine Construction Ltd v Panatown Ltd* [2001] 1 AC 518, 549; and McKendrick, 'The Common Law at Work: The Saga of *Alfred McAlpine Construction Ltd v Panatown Ltd*' [2003] *Oxford Univ Commonwealth LJ* 145, 173: 'While recognition of the principle that the aim of an award of damages is to provide the claimant with a substitute for the performance for which she contracted will reflect more clearly the values of our society, it will not bring an end to all of our problems.' See, for further discussion, Unberath, *Transferred Loss* (2003), pp 35–82. It is not the place here to justify one or the other approach to liability, but the role of enforced performance in the civil law must be viewed in this broader context. These brief comments show how in comparative law, the mere changing of the optic from which a particular system is looked at can help minimise differences with other systems which otherwise look formidable.

(c) Requesting Performance—Relation to Secondary Rights

We turn now to a related matter, which is a central theme of the reformed law. The emphasis on the enforcement of the primary duty is further increased by compelling the creditor/promisee to grant the debtor/promisor a period of grace or *Nachfrist* before allowing him to rely on secondary rights, ie to terminate and/or to recover damages. Thus, § 281 I BGB requires the expiry (without result) of an additional period of performance before *damages* for non-performance (or, as the original states, '*instead of*' performance) may be claimed. The same applies to the right of *termination* or *Rücktritt* according to § 323 I BGB and also by analogy to the remedies for *non-conforming* performance (eg, §§ 437, 634 BGB).

It is important to observe at the outset that the creditor may continue to demand the performance of the contract after the expiry of the fixed period for performance or *Nachfrist*. The primary duty of the promisor only comes to an end once the promisee makes a claim for damages 'instead of' performance (*Schadensersatz statt der Leistung*, § 281 IV BGB) and/or terminates the contract (*Rücktritt*, § 346 BGB). This may leave the debtor in an awkward position, since he may not know whether he is allowed to perform or whether the promisee will in fact choose compensation in monetary terms. Of course, the promisor can reduce this uncertainty himself by performing within the period of performance (*Bundestags-Drucksache* 14/6040, p 140). It is to be expected that the abuse of rights aspect of good faith (§ 242 BGB) will enable the courts to deal with hard cases.

It should also be noted that the period of performance set must be of a 'reasonable' (*angemessen*) length. The creditor is not however required to set this period so as to assist the debtor to commence performance. Instead, its length may be shorter than the period for delivery fixed in the contract. The purpose of the period of grace is merely to give the debtor a last chance to complete performance. The interest of the creditor in timely performance may also be taken into account. (See, for an example of the application of these criteria: BGH NJW 1985, 320, 323, dealing with the old § 326 BGB which in so far served as a model for § 323 I BGB.) Since most secondary rights depend on the proper fixing of a period of grace, and considering the open-natured requirement of reasonableness, it is evident that judicial control of the length of the grace period is a potential source of uncertainty. To avoid this, German courts simply extend *ex post* any period that is too short to a reasonable length. (See Ernst in *Münchener Kommentar*, vol 2a, § 323 Rn. 77.) §§ 323 III and 281 III BGB further provide that, where appropriate, the setting of a period of performance may be replaced by a simple warning to the debtor. (The usefulness of this rule is questionable, see Ernst, *Münchener Kommentar*, § 323 Rn. 79: no field of application.)

Since the debtor is given a second chance, the idea of *Nachfrist* is sometimes said to protect the debtor. However, this is only superficially the case. It forces both parties to the contract first to attempt to keep the contract alive before putting an end to it and seeking satisfaction elsewhere or in monetary terms. Hence, even if the creditor is no longer interested in receiving performance *in specie* but would prefer to make a claim for damages, he cannot do so unless he grants the promisor a second chance. The argument that a second chance to perform (over-)protects the debtor is misconceived if the comparison is with the common law. This is because, as explained above, the regime of enforced performance as such may impose a considerable burden on the debtor.

There are situations in which there is no need to fix a *Nachfrist*. (See for an overview Looschelders, *Schuldrecht Allgemeiner Teil*, Rn. 619, 704.) The first and perhaps most obvious situation in which a period for performance would not make sense arises if performance is impossible (§ 275 BGB). If this is the case, the creditor may be entitled to immediate termination (§ 326 V BGB) and damages instead of performance (§ 311a II and § 283 BGB). §§ 281 II and 323 II BGB contain a comprehensive list of further situations in which the setting of a period for performance is not necessary. Thus, if the debtor unequivocally refuses to make performance (*endgültige und ernsthafte Erfüllungsverweigerung*) or 'repudiates', the setting of a period of performance would amount to a meaningless formality and is dispensed with. (Note that this also applies in the case of anticipatory breach, § 323 IV BGB.) Likewise, if according to the contract the time of performance is of the essence, then late performance may *per se* entitle the creditor to secondary rights. We have come across this so-called *relative Fixgeschäft* in chapter 8, p 357 (when discussing the time of performance). Note also, that performance after a certain date may amount to impossibility (*absolutes Fixgeschäft*, also discussed there). A third exception is defined in a catch-all manner. Where a balancing of the interests of creditor and debtor justifies immediate relief, then the parties may also dispense with the setting of a grace period.

The importance of the request of performance, and of the setting of a period for performance as a *pre-condition* to the exercise of secondary rights—ie, the prevalence of enforced performance—is illustrated by Figure 1 (always provided that performance is not impossible in the sense of § 275 BGB, for which see Figure 2, discussed below, p 408).

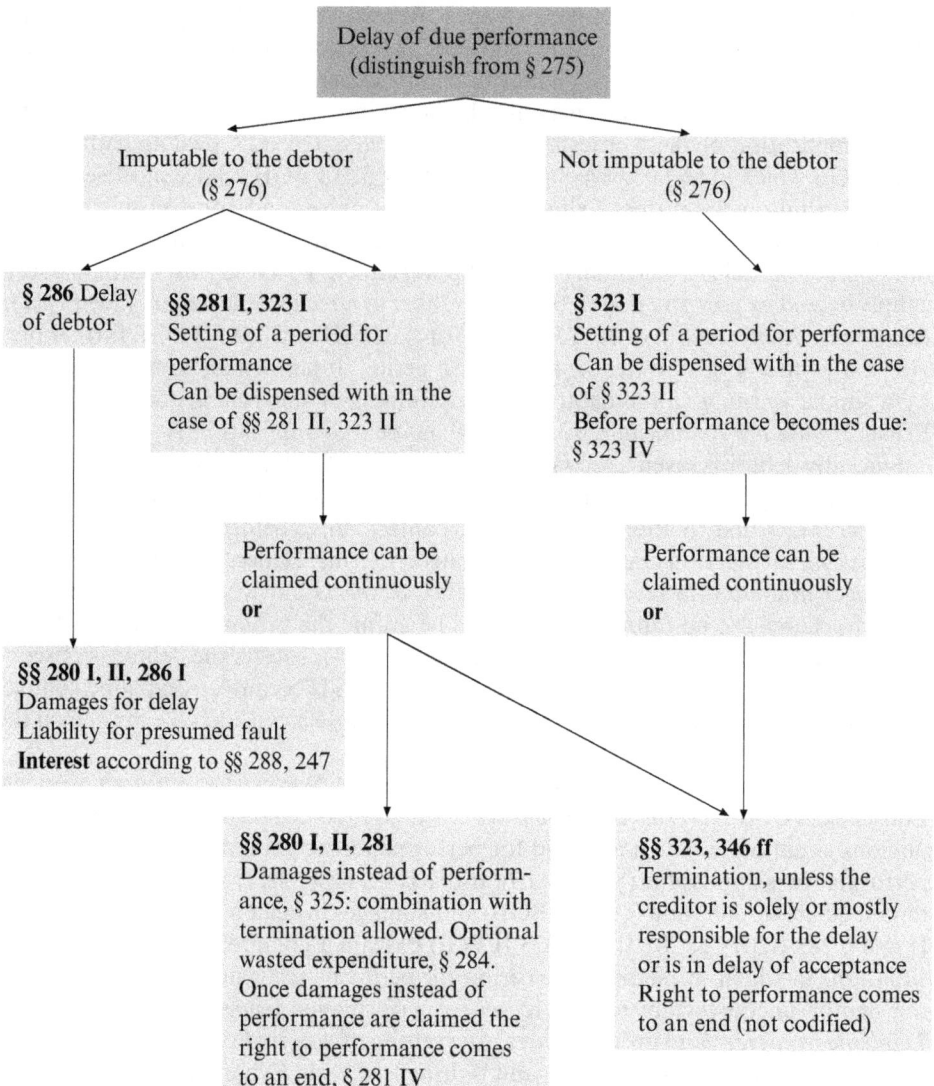

* Reproduced with kind permission of Professor Stephan Lorenz.

FIG 1: Late performance*

Finally, as a general rule *damages for delay* (§ 280 II BGB) may only be awarded from the moment that the debtor has been requested to perform. An award of interest is another consequence of delay, although it is not explained as damages: § 288 BGB. This special request or *Mahnung* (§ 286 I BGB) serves as a warning to the debtor, that from that moment on he is liable in damages. Hence, unlike the *Nachfrist*, a *Mahnung* does not grant the debtor a period of grace. However, requiring that the creditor reminds the debtor that performance is due serves to motivate the debtor to perform. The regime of enforced performance may to some extent also account for what is, from a common law perspective, the somewhat peculiar requirement of a warning. For the sake of completeness, it should be pointed out that the request of performance or *Mahnung* may also be dispensed with in a number of situations, some of which are analogous to those already described (eg, refusal to perform). Delay will also commence irrespective of a warning if a time for performance has been fixed with reference to the calendar (§ 286 II Nr. 1 BGB). (Details on these points are discussed in the following sub-sections, below.) In English law, it is clear that (as a general rule) performance is due without demand: for a relatively recent example, see *Carne v De Bono* [1988] 1 WLR 1107 (see Treitel, *The Law of Contract*, p 753: 'a debtor must seek his creditor.') Of course, this general rule can be varied by the express terms of the contract or by statute.

(d) Methods of Enforcement

The situations in which enforced performance may be particularly attractive cannot be analysed independently of the methods by which a right to enforced performance can actually be *enforced* (the discussion of the *Co-operative Insurance Society* case [1998] AC 1 in the previous section showed as much). The pertinent procedural remedy is an action for performance (*Leistungsklage*), which the Code of Civil Procedure (ZPO) prescribes for all cases in which a plaintiff asks the court for a judgment ordering the defendant to do or not to do a particular thing (this is also the definition of the corresponding notion of substantive law: *Anspruch*, § 194 I BGB).

The procedural means of enforcement of a judgment are regulated in Book Eight of the ZPO. First of all, taking steps to enforce a contract specifically presupposes as a general rule obtaining an enforceable judgment for performance from a court of law (§ 704 I ZPO, *vollstreckbares Endurteil*). The particular method of enforcement then depends on the nature of the claim. The main divide is between the enforcement of a judgment ordering the defendant to pay money (*Zwangsvollstreckung wegen Geldforderungen*, §§ 803 *et seq* ZPO) and one ordering him to hand over things or perform another act or abstain from performing (*Erwirkung der Herausgabe von Sachen und zur Erwirkung von Handlungen und Unterlassungen*, §§ 883 *et seq* ZPO).

The first limb (*Geldforderungen*) covers what in English law would be regarded as an action for an agreed sum (eg, the seller claims the price), but it also includes all claims for compensation in monetary terms (ie, it also concerns the enforcement of the secondary rights, damages, of the promisee). Execution of the judgment is against property in its widest sense and either depends on further court decisions (of the *Vollstreckungsgericht*) ordering enforcement or requires the involvement of a court 'official' or bailiff (*Gerichtsvollzieher*) actually carrying out the confiscation of movable property of the debtor. Self-help is not permitted (compare the self-help remedy of distress for rent under English land law: see Harpum, *Megarry & Wade: The Law of Real Property* (6th edn, 2000), paras 14-253–14-258). The Code of Civil Procedure provides detailed rules for the sequestration of movable property (distraint of chattels, §§ 808 *et seq* ZPO, and garnishment of claims, §§ 828 *et seq*) and the seizure of immovable property (§§ 864 *et seq* ZPO).

The second limb concerns all non-monetary obligations. This is the area where German law differs from Anglo-American law in allowing the promisee to avail himself of the machinery of the law so as enforce such obligations as a matter of principle.

The first set of rules regulates the enforcement of the obligation to hand over a thing, the second concerns obligations that can be vicariously performed, the third those which cannot, the fourth category is formed by obligations to forbear from doing something or to suffer something, and the final category concerns the enforcement of obligations to make a declaration of will.

First, the obligation to hand over a thing has been specifically dealt with in the Code of Civil Procedure. The execution of such an order is carried out by an officer of the court. If the obligation concerns chattels, the object is taken from the debtor and handed over to the creditor, § 883 ZPO. § 893 ZPO clarifies that the rules of execution do not preclude the creditor from demanding compensation in monetary terms, ie, damages instead of executing the judgment of enforced performance. Whether the creditor is actually entitled to damages (remembering the fault principle!) depends entirely on the conditions set out by the substantive law (§ 281 BGB). In the case of immovables, the debtor is forced to vacate the property and the creditor is enabled to take possession of the object, § 885 ZPO. In the case of residential property, the tenant is granted special protection under §§ 721, 794a ZPO, eg, stipulating for a certain period of grace (*Räumungsfrist*). (See for details, Brox and Walker, *Zwangsvollstreckungsrecht* (7th edn, 2003), § 34.)

Secondly, if the obligation to perform an act can be performed vicariously, the execution consists of expressly allowing the creditor to have the act done at the expense of the debtor (§ 887 I ZPO, *Ersatzvornahme* ordered in a so-called *Ermächtigungsbeschluß*). If the costs are considerable, the court may also order the debtor to pay an advance on those costs (§ 887 II ZPO). Generally speaking, activities that do not require the special skill of the debtor can be performed vicariously. For instance, effecting repairs on building work can, of course, be performed by a third party, whereas the painting of the portrait of the creditor cannot be vicariously performed. (See Brox and Walker, *Zwangsvollstreckungsrecht*, Rn. 1066, for further illustrations.) The common law and American law are different. The plaintiff will only have a claim for damages as they are an adequate remedy. There is no rule requiring the debtor to pay in advance.

The effect of this method of enforcement is to transform the obligation *in specie* into a corresponding monetary obligation that will then be enforced through the less invasive means of enforcement of monetary obligations under the first limb (§ 788 ZPO; ie execution against property. However, where the debtor opposes the measures taken in accordance with § 887 ZPO, his resistance may be overcome with physical violence, § 892 ZPO). This method of enforcement comes very close to awarding the creditor damages protecting his expectation interest on the basis of a 'guarantee' type of liability. For instance, the duty to effect repairs can be specifically enforced independent of fault. Provided that the court allows vicarious performance according to § 887 I ZPO, the execution of the resulting judgment would in the end consist in enforcing a claim for the cost of cure vicariously performed. The execution of this monetary claim is directed against the property of the debtor. It is interesting to note that § 637 BGB actually entitles the creditor to the cost of the cure independent of fault if the debtor fails to effectuate the repairs. The contract of sale does not contain such a provision. Here, at the level of the law of procedure, § 887 ZPO tightens the grip on the debtor by making recovery of cost of cure independent of fault.

Thirdly, it is obvious that acts that can only be performed by the debtor personally cannot be transformed into monetary obligations in this manner. Execution is by means of fines and imprisonment imposed by court order (*Zwangsmittel*, § 888 I ZPO). Examples include the disclosure of information (an interesting illustration is provided by: OLG Bremen JZ 2000, 314: illegitimate child seeking to learn the name of the father from the mother) and the actual running of a business by a commercial tenant (OLG Celle NJW-RR 1996, 585; cf OLG Düsseldorf NJW-RR 1997, 648; *contra* OLG Naumburg NJW-RR 1998, 873; contrast also the *Co-operative Insurance Society* case [1998] AC 1, discussed in section (a), p 394). In such cases however the proportionality of means and result must be respected. Thus, imprisonment is a measure of last resort (Brox and Walker *Zwangsvollstreckungsrecht*, Rn. 1087). Fines are limited to a maximum of €25000 (§ 888 I 2 ZPO) and are handed over to the State. All of which goes to show that they are not intended to serve the expectation interest of the promisee but merely to compel the debtor to do what he promised.

There are a number of important rules excluding the execution of such an order. According to § 888 I ZPO, execution is not possible where the act in question in the individual case does not depend exclusively on the will of the debtor (eg, this was the argument in OLG Naumburg NJW-RR 1998, 873, against enforcing a judgment for the running of a shop). Equally important is § 888 III ZPO, which expressly excludes specific performance for certain personal obligations. These include promises involved in marriage and significantly, the promise to perform services under a contract of services: § 611 BGB (see chapter 10, section 4, p 529 for further discussion). The principle underlying this provision is that it would be contrary to the human dignity of employees to force them to labour. This is one of the few examples in German law where an 'efficient breach' is to a certain extent 'tolerated' (Huber, *Leistungsstörungsrecht*, vol 1 (1999), p 53). § 888 III ZPO does not exclude the possibility that the obligation to provide a service can be vicariously performed, and therefore that the debtor may become liable for the costs of such vicarious performance according to § 887 ZPO. (In this sense Brox and Walker, *Zwangsvollstreckungsrecht*, Rn. 1066; the issue is controversial.)

The fourth sub-category of the enforcement of non-monetary obligations concerns judgments that order the debtor to forbear or suffer something. According to § 890 I ZPO, execution is by court decree issuing fines or ordering the imprisonment of the debtor. Obligations to refrain from doing something giving rise to 'injunctions' are common in the law of intellectual property, competition law and regarding the protection of certain 'absolute' (in the German sense, ie, in contradistinction to relative (= contractual rights): eg, the right of privacy). An obligation to forbear may arise, for instance, where a landlord is entitled to effectuate certain construction works on the residential property and the tenant must suffer them accordingly (§ 554 BGB).

In contract law, the fifth and final sub-category of enforcing an obligation to perform an act is particularly interesting. It involves a judgment ordering the debtor to utter a certain declaration of will (for a discussion of this basic concept of German contract law see chapter 1, p 25 ff). In fact, this would be a duty of performance that clearly cannot be vicariously performed. Compelling the debtor to make the declaration by means of force would be cumbersome and unnecessarily restrictive. This is also not the solution of the ZPO. Instead, § 894 ZPO adopts a pragmatic approach. The *judgment* ordering the debtor to make the declaration is simply ascribed the effect of that very declaration. This fiction is needed more often in German law than one would expect from the perspective of other civil law systems or the common law. The reason is the principles of separation and abstraction, discussed in chapter 1. If the subject matter of the claim is the transfer of property, German law requires a declaration of will in addition to the promise to transfer property contained in the contract of obligation. Consider the enforcement of the main obligation of the seller under a contract of sale of a chattel (§ 433 I 1 BGB). As explained, the transfer of property is not implied in the contract of sale but is regarded as a separate contract of transfer (*dinglicher Vertrag*), which must be distinguished from the underlying obligation. According to § 929 sentence 1 BGB, it is necessary that the seller of the chattel delivers it to the buyer and both agree that the ownership is transferred thereby. At this point, three provisions of the ZPO fill the gap which arises if the seller is unwilling to co-operate: the judgment ordering specific performance is treated as a substitute for the 'agreement' (*Einigung*) to transfer the ownership (§ 894 ZPO), and the 'delivery' (*Übergabe*) of the chattel is enforced by the bailiff, who takes it from the seller and hands it over to the buyer (§§ 883, 897 ZPO).

Considering these subtle and highly differentiated methods of enforcement, it is no exaggeration to suggest that enforced performance to a considerable extent serves to protect the promisee's interest in the performance of the promise. This is achieved, so far as monetary obligations are concerned, without the use of physical force or the imposition of fines against the debtor personally. Execution is against property, and although we cannot deal with the details of enforcement in this work, it should be noted that the machinery of the law is capable of dealing with these requests in an efficient manner. The same applies to those obligations that can be vicariously performed. They are, ultimately, transformed into monetary obligations and follow the rules set out above. Allowing force is inevitable as a last resort in order to enforce the obligation to hand over a corporeal thing or to take possession of immoveable property. The most difficult judgments to enforce are those that order the debtor to forbear or suffer something, or that require the performance of an act that cannot be vicariously performed. Using indirect means or threats entails the danger that the personality rights of the debtor are violated. The law therefore imposes several limitations on the enforcement of performance.

(e) Limits of Enforced Performance—Impossibility

Considering the various and serious consequences of enforced performance discussed in the previous section, the reasons for excluding it acquire special importance.

Impossibility is the most important limit on performance, although the defence is less obvious than commonly assumed (eg, 'obviously' performance may not be claimed where it is impossible: Treitel, *International Encyclopaedia of Comparative Law*, para 16-11). Indeed, under the old law, according to the intention of the drafters of the BGB, the action for performance was also available if performance was impossible, provided that the debtor was responsible for the impossibility (Huber ZIP 2000, 2141, *contra* the traditional interpretation of the BGB. Likewise, Article 79 CISG excludes the duty of performance only in relation to impediments beyond the control of the debtor and only as far as the right to claim damages is concerned; it will be recalled that according to Article 28 CISG it is for the applicable domestic law to decide whether a judicial order for enforced performance is available. By contrast, Article 7.2.2 PICC and Article 9:102 PECL expressly exclude the obligation of performance if performance is impossible). Of course, the debtor cannot be forced to do something that he cannot do (ought implies can, or: *impossibilium nulla est obligatio*). But the impossibility of performing the promised act may be taken into account at the level of execution of the judgment for performance. This is mainly a question of style. A more relevant matter is how impossibility is defined, and correspondingly, how much is asked of the debtor. The precise nature of the promise must first be examined, ie, the content of the obligation must be determined before the impossibility of performance can be assessed.

The question as to the extent to which impossibility releases the debtor from the obligation of performance does not arise directly in Anglo-American law. Since specific performance is the exception, it is not necessary to deal with impossibility as a defence to a claim for performance. Rather, the issue is whether damages cannot be claimed because the contract is void for common mistake (eg, sale of non-existent goods) or frustrated for subsequent impossibility (for the English law on both of which see our brief summary in chapter 7, sections 4 and 7 respectively).

It is important to stress at the outset that in the reformed German law, the questions (a) whether the duty of performance is excluded and (b) whether a claim for damages arises are *conceptually* independent from each other. This is stated expressly in § 275 IV BGB, which clarifies that a claim for damages is not affected by the defence of impossibility (embodying the 'dualistic' approach of the new law, to which we have already adverted, p 388). Furthermore, the right to terminate the contract is granted to the creditor regardless of the nature of the impossibility and whether the debtor is in any way responsible for the impediment. The only precondition is that the (objectively assessed) breach is serious (ie, *erheblich* in the sense of § 323 V 2 BGB). For obvious reasons, § 326 V BGB dispenses with the requirement of fixing an additional period for performance: the right to terminate accrues as soon as the impossibility occurs. Finally, in all cases of impossibility, and irrespective of fault, the creditor may claim any surrogate that the debtor received from a third party for the destroyed object (so called *stellvertretendes commodum*, § 285 BGB). This means that each of the main remedies available—enforced performance, termination and damages—has different pre-requisites. The duty of performance may be excluded under § 275 BGB but the innocent party may still be able to terminate the contract, recover damages, or claim the surrogate.

The various consequences of impossibility, and its highly differentiated effects on the remedies available to the promisee, are illustrated by Figure 2.

It has been objected that it is logically inconsistent to hold the debtor liable for a breach of the duty of performance if that duty is excluded by § 275 BGB (Huber ZIP 2000, 2276). This apparent contradiction only exists in a terminological sense. It disappears if impossibility is regarded as a defence against a claim for enforced performance but does not eliminate other rights in respect of a breach of the duty of performance. The breach of the duty of performance consists in the simple absence of performance, whether or not the duty can be specifically enforced. The binding nature of the promise is not completely removed. It is merely protected by other means, such as a claim for damages or the right to terminate the contract. In any event, so far as the substance of the new law is concerned, there can be little doubt as to how the rules were intended to operate. (See Stephan Lorenz, *Karlsruher Forum 2005*, sections II4.a), III1.c))(2).)

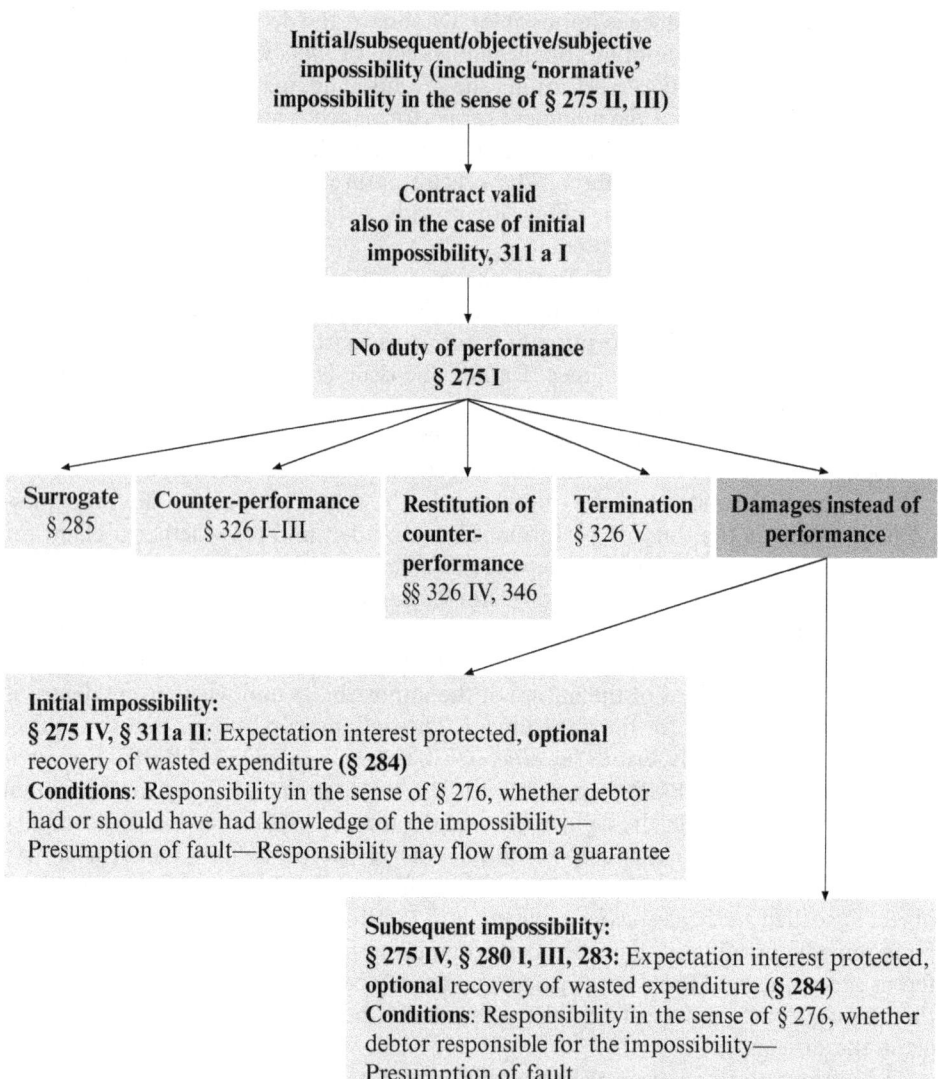

* Reproduced with kind permission of Professor Stephan Lorenz.

FIG 2: Impossibility of performance*

(i) Impossibility in the Sense of § 275 I BGB

According to § 275 I BGB, the debtor is released from his obligation of performance (ie, the right to demand enforced performance is excluded) whether the impossibility accrued before or after the conclusion of the contract, whether the debtor was responsible for it, and whether the impossibility was subjective or objective.

Compared with the old law, two changes are noteworthy. First, following the wording of the old § 275, the debtor was only to be released if he was not responsible for the impossibility. As suggested, while this may have been the original intention of the drafters of the BGB, the courts ignored the literal meaning of the provision and the debtor was released in all cases. Therefore, no change in substance has actually occurred here: the new wording reflects the substance of the position already reached by the courts. Secondly, in relation to the treatment of objective initial impossibility the new § 275 I BGB represents a significant change. The contract is no longer regarded as void (as under the old § 306) but remains valid. This is made clear by the express wording of the new § 311a I BGB. Only enforced performance of the contract is excluded by § 275 I BGB. Objective impossibility arises where nobody can perform the contract. For instance, where I promise to deliver a specific painting by Picasso and the respective painting does not exist, is a forgery, or has been destroyed, performance is objectively impossible. However, if the painting does in fact exist, but the present owner is not willing to sell it, performance of the contract is (subjectively) impossible in the sense that it is the seller only who cannot perform.

The law Commission understood objective and subjective impossibility in a narrow sense (see Canaris, JZ 2001, 499; *Bundestags-Drucksache* 14/6040, p 129). Objective impossibility does not cover impediments to performance that can be overcome by the debtor, even if the expense is considerable. For instance, if the car being sold is stolen after the conclusion of the contract of sale, but can be retrieved at a certain cost, performance is not impossible within the meaning of § 275 I BGB. Performance may have become more onerous, but this fact alone does not exclude the duty of performance according to § 275 I BGB. The same approach applies to obstacles that make it more onerous for the particular debtor to perform the contract. If the object sold belongs to a third party who is willing to sell it to the seller, this is not regarded as an instance of subjective impossibility regardless of the price the seller would have to pay to acquire the object. Impediments that are not total are thus not intended to be covered by § 275 I BGB, and it is to be expected that the courts will follow this approach.

Cases, however, in which performance requires 'unreasonable' efforts may constitute impossibility according to § 275 II BGB. Hence, we will return to the issue of how much is expected from a promisee to fulfil his promise of performance in that context below. Nevertheless, it is useful first to examine the consequences that impossibility entails for counter-performance.

(ii) Consequences of Impossibility for the Counter-performance

In chapter 8, p 357 ff, we introduced the notion of risk of performance (*Leistungsgefahr*) as opposed to the risk of counter-performance (*Preisgefahr*). The risk of performance is on the debtor so long as he is not released from the obligation to perform the contract *in specie*. It passes to the creditor as soon as the debtor is so released. The risk of the counter-performance concerns the question whether the promisor retains the right to claim the counter-performance, *even though* he has been released from the obligation to perform *in specie*, ie, the primary obligation. The promisee bears this risk for instance if he is required to pay the price despite the fact that the object sold perished during transport. Paragraph 275 BGB concerns the first aspect of risk: the risk of performance. (It should be noted once more that since the common law does not have to deal with impossibility as a defence to a claim for performance this aspect of risk is also unknown to it: the issue of risk is usually associated with the consequences for the counter-performance only.)

If the conditions of § 275 BGB are satisfied, the debtor does not need to perform: he is released from the obligation to fulfil the contract *in specie*. Naturally, this depends on the exact content of the obligation of performance. A seller of generic goods (goods defined by abstract characteristic, § 243 I BGB, *Gattungsschuld*) is not released from his obligation of performance unless all objects belonging to the class defined by the contract become extinct. However, under certain conditions the obligation may be reduced to an obligation to deliver a specific object. This occurs where the object has been singled out, appropriated to the contract, and the seller has delivered the object at the agreed place of performance: § 243 II BGB (*Konkretisierung*).

In chapter 8, when we discussed the duties of the seller of goods, we noted that they would vary depending on where performance was to take place (§ 269 BGB) which, in turn, depend on whether his obligation was a *Holschuld*, *Bringschuld* or *Schickschuld* (as the terms were explained in section 3(b), p 358 ff). Assuming that the seller does not have to do more than hand the goods over to a carrier (*Schickschuld*), the risk of performance passes at this very moment. This means that even if the goods perish before they are actually handed over to the buyer and property passes (§ 433 I 1 BGB), the seller does not need to attempt to perform a second time even though he has not yet fulfilled his obligation within the meaning of § 362 BGB (see for an illustration case no 109, BGH NJW 2003, 3341). He is released from his primary obligation according to § 275 I BGB. The same rule applies to the sale of specific goods (*Stückschuld*). If the seller promised to deliver a specific thing only, and this very thing is destroyed or it never existed, then the seller is as a general rule released from his obligation to perform according to § 275 I BGB.

The reciprocal nature of contracts supported by what common lawyers would call consideration (ie, consisting of performance and counter-performance) would be undermined if the release of the promisor/debtor did not have any consequences for the obligation to pay the price. Having said this one must add the obvious, namely that the obligation of the buyer to pay the price does not become impossible if the goods perish. (Contrary dicta in *Taylor v Caldwell* (1863) 3 B&S 826 are to this extent misleading since in law, apart from bankruptcy, there can never be an impossibility to pay money.) Accordingly, § 275 BGB does not operate to release the promisee/creditor from his obligation to pay the price. A special rule is thus necessary to regulate the consequences of impossibility on the fate of the counter-performance.

In relation to reciprocal contractual obligations this rule is found in § 326 I 1 BGB which provides that the promisee is also released from his obligation to pay the price if the promisor is released from his obligation to perform the contract according to § 275 BGB. The rationale is this: it would not be fair to shift the risk of impediments to performance to the creditor if he is not responsible for the impediment. In such a case, the debtor does not need to perform and the creditor does not need to pay the price either. Further, any amount already paid can be claimed back according to the rules of termination (§ 326 IV in conjunction with §§ 346–8 BGB).

An exception to this general provision is provided in § 326 I 2 BGB. It refers to cases of non-conformity of performance (*Schlechtleistung*) and in these cases the obligation to pay the price is not excluded *ex lege*. The reason is that the special rules covering non-conformity frequently provide the creditor with an option to choose either termination of the contract (§ 326 V BGB) or a reduction of the price (for which a special calculation is provided, eg, §§ 441, 638 BGB). Applying § 326 I 1 BGB would mean that the creditor would be denied this choice, hence § 326 I 2 BGB excludes that rule in cases of non-conformity. (See Lorenz and Riehm, *Lehrbuch zum neuen Schuldrecht* (2002) Rn. 327.) Note also, that if the creditor claims the surrogate according to § 285 BGB, then the obligation to pay the price is not extinguished (§ 326 III BGB).

This rationale of the general rule of symmetrical release (in *Taylor v Caldwell*, cited above, Blackburn J used the less felicitous words 'parity of reasoning'), namely that it would not be fair to shift the risk of impediments to performance to the creditor, does not apply where the creditor is responsible for the impediment. § 326 II 1 BGB accordingly makes an exception and preserves the right of the debtor to the counter-performance even though the debtor is released from his obligation. § 326 II 1 BGB also makes an exception for the situation in which the creditor is in delay of acceptance of the performance (*mora creditoris*, §§ 293 *et seq* BGB, see section 4 below). Again, the risk of counter-performance is shifted to the creditor of the performance that has become impossible. Note however that the debtor must deduct, from any claim to receive counter-performance, any expenditure saved as a result of being released from the obligation to perform: § 326 II 2 BGB. (Clearly however the value of the impossible performance cannot be deducted.) The same rule applies in relation to benefits that the defendant acquired (or that he wilfully refrained from acquiring) by some other use of his power to work. (See further, Looschelders, *Schuldrecht Allgemeiner Teil* Rn. 718 *et seq.*)

The special parts of contract law contain further exceptions to the rule that both parties are released in cases of impossibility. It suffices here to mention two such cases, to illustrate the types of reason for making an exception as provided for in the BGB.

In sale of goods cases, the risk of counter-performance passes once the goods are handed over to a carrier if the seller did not undertake to do anything more than hand them over to a carrier (*Schickschuld*, § 447 BGB). Note that the rule does not apply to consumer sales (§ 474 II BGB: in case no 109, BGH NJW 2003, 3341, the question was whether the debtor/seller was released from his obligation of performance and not whether he was entitled to claim the price).

In contracts for work (*Werkverträge*, § 631 BGB), the contractor promises to achieve a certain result. It is therefore consistent that the contractor is not released from his obligation to perform before the employer accepted the performance: the contractor bears the risk of performance according to § 644 I 1 BGB. The right to claim the price is 'earned' only once the employer has accepted the performance as being in conformity with the contract (*Abnahme*, § 640 BGB). If however the work is destroyed during a delay in the acceptance of the work by the employer, or because of the material supplied by the employer, then the risk passes, § 645 I 1 BGB. In such circumstances, the creditor cannot claim performance of the contract and the debtor is entitled to the price (on a pro-rata basis).

(iii) Excursus: Delay of the Creditor

The performance of a contract very often presupposes the co-operation of both contracting parties. In practice, the 'delay of the creditor' takes the form of non-cooperation on his part with the debtor. This problem is addressed by §§ 293–304 BGB.

As we have already seen (for instance in relation to § 326 II BGB), the delay of the creditor is sanctioned indirectly by the Code. If during the delay of acceptance of the performance it becomes impossible to perform, then the creditor is not released from his obligation of counter-performance (provided of course that the debtor is not himself responsible for the impossibility). This means that the creditor bears the risk of counter-performance. He has to pay according to § 326 II 1 BGB, but receives nothing in return. Another such indirect consequence attached to a delay of the creditor is § 323 VI BGB, which will be discussed in section 4, below. Suffice it to say here that if the breach of contract that justifies termination occurred during a delay of the creditor, then the latter loses the right of termination. Furthermore, § 300 I BGB reduces the standard of care owed by the debtor to the avoidance of gross negligence. However, the delay of the creditor also entails consequences that do not exclude rights that the creditor might otherwise have, but concern his liability towards the debtor. To give an example, the extra expense caused by the delay may be claimed by the debtor according to § 304 BGB. Although, strictly speaking, these different aspects of delay belong to a discussion of the remedy in question, it is useful to bring together the main conditions and consequences of *mora creditoris* at this stage.

For the creditor to find himself in 'delay' the following *conditions* must be satisfied.

First, the debtor must be under a duty to perform and be able to do so (the claim must be *erfüllbar*) (§ 271 II BGB). This of course assumes that performance is possible.

Secondly, the debtor must be able and willing to perform in the precise manner agreed (as to both time and place of performance and corresponding to the requirements of good faith (*tatsächliches Angebot*: § 294 BGB)). Generally speaking, the offer must be in such a form that 'all that is left for the creditor to do is to accept' (RGZ 85, 415, 416). However, a mere verbal offer by the debtor to perform (*wörtliches Angebot*: § 295 BGB) will suffice whenever the creditor has either (a) already declared that he will *not* accept performance or (b) his co-operation (*Mitwirkung*) is essential for the performance of the debtor's obligations.

Thirdly, the creditor must refuse the performance, or refuse to co-operate where co-operation is necessary for the fulfilment of the contract, or finally, in the case of synallagmatic contracts, refuse to perform *simultaneously* his part of the bargain.

One thing is beyond doubt: delay on the part of the creditor does *not* give the debtor the right to demand damages from the creditor, although the debtor does have a claim to all expenses reasonably incurred to conserve the subject matter of the contract (since, as we shall see, he remains liable to perform his obligations: § 304 BGB). Otherwise, the *consequences* of the creditor's delay are as follows.

First, the debtor remains responsible for rendering his promised performance.

Secondly, if the subject matter of the contract is destroyed subsequent to the creditor's unwillingness to accept performance, the debtor is only liable for damage caused through his intentional or grossly negligent conduct but is no longer liable for consequences arising from his 'light negligence' (§ 300 I BGB). The risk for generic goods is also transferred to the creditor 'in delay' (§ 300 II BGB).

Finally, in a synallagmatic contract the debtor retains the right to demand the creditor's counter-performance, even if the debtor's own performance has (by now, ie, *after* the creditor's delay) become impossible, § 326 II 1 BGB (cf § 645 I 1 BGB). See also, § 323 VI BGB which excludes the right of termination if the circumstance justifying termination occurred during a delay of the creditor.

(iv) Impossibility in the Sense of § 275 II BGB

The interplay between the duty of performance and defence of impossibility pre-determines in crucial respects the regime of liability that applies to the debtor. These indirect consequences of enforced performance for the liability of the debtor must be considered carefully in order to understand the scope and significance of having a regime of enforced performance. As we have seen, § 275 I BGB releases the debtor only in cases of impossibility in a strict sense. All other cases (ie, where performance has become onerous because of some impediment but is, technically speaking, still possible) are covered by § 275 II and § 313 BGB. The crucial question addressed by these provisions is *how much* is expected of the debtor before he is released from the obligation to perform *in specie*. Somewhat unfortunately, the precise limits of enforced performance have sparked controversy following the recent reform, although it seems to us that there is little doubt how the new law was intended to be applied. To be sure, the approach that the courts will adopt remains to be seen; yet it is unlikely that they will change their approach in substance. The most likely outcome is therefore a relatively strict notion of impossibility and significant reluctance on the part of the courts to release the debtor if the impediment to performance is not total but may be overcome.

Paragraph 275 II BGB was intended to cover what has been coined 'practical' impossibility, although it should be pointed out at the outset that the term is misleading. It is not meant to convey that performance is practically difficult to achieve, but rather that it would require a financial effort that cannot reasonably be expected from the debtor. § 275 II BGB entitles the debtor to invoke impossibility as a defence/plea (*Einrede*) in such a situation, though he is of course free to perform nevertheless.

The hypothetical often discussed in law works (*Bundestags-Drucksache* 14/6040, pp 129–30) is that of a contract of sale regarding a ring which, after the conclusion of the contract, has fallen into a lake. The assumption is that it would technically be possible to retrieve the ring, but that it would involve an excessive amount of money which would be wholly disproportionate to the value of the ring. The expenditure required would be in gross disproportion to the creditor's interest in the performance, having regard to the content of the relationship of obligation and the requirement of good faith (§ 275 II 1 BGB). § 275 II 2 BGB therefore states that, when determining the efforts to be expected of the debtor, consideration must also be given to whether the debtor is responsible for hindering the performance. This would mean that, in the example of the ring, it would entail a difference in what is expected of the debtor if the ring was dropped deliberately into the lake or not. Overall, § 275 II BGB is intended to exclude the duty of performance only in 'extreme cases' (Canaris, JZ 2001, 502).

Paragraph 275 II BGB must be distinguished from § 313 BGB, ie the doctrine of the foundation of the transaction (sometimes confusingly referred to as 'economic impossibility'). Both deal with the problem that performance has become more onerous. The decisive difference is said to lie in the fact that the starting point for § 275 II BGB is the creditor's interest in obtaining performance, while § 313 BGB focuses on the debtor's interest in refusing performance. (See Canaris, *Karlsruher Forum 2002*, p 14; Zimmermann, *Breach of Contract and Remedies under the New German Law of Obligations* (Sapienza, Rome, 2002), p 13.) In the aforementioned example of the ring on the bed of the lake, the interest of the creditor in obtaining the ring is (primarily at least) represented by the value of the ring. The value of the ring, it is assumed, does not change because it is at the bottom of the lake. By contrast, if performance has become more onerous because of a rising market, the interest of the creditor does not remain the same but grows symmetrically. This is because the purported impediment to performance also makes the performance more attractive to the creditor. It is not the case therefore that the interest of the creditor and the effort in obtaining the performance are in any way disproportionate in the sense of § 275 II BGB. In exceptional cases, the impediment to performance may be said to affect the foundation of the transaction and as a result necessitate an adjustment of the contract (see chapter 7 for more detailed discussion of this area).

Paragraph 275 II BGB was not meant to change the law but rather to encapsulate the *rationes* of two decisions of the BGH dealing with the exclusion of the main obligation of performance due to disproportionate outlays. (Note that Article 9:102(2)(b) PECL and Article 7.2.2(b) PICC also contain a caveat to the right to demand enforced performance: *viz*, that performance cannot be required if it causes unreasonable effort or expense.)

In the first case (BGHZ 62, 388), the defendant sold residential property to the plaintiffs. The flats were erected on a plot of land, part of which was to be transferred to the purchasers. On the remaining land the defendant built an underground car park. By mistake, the parking space extended to cover about 20 square metres of the land of the plaintiffs, who demanded the removal of the interference. This removal however would have entailed considerable costs (in particular rebuilding the entrance to the car park) and the Court concluded that taking the interests of the creditor into account it could not be reasonably expected that the debtor be forced to remove the interference.

In the second case (BGH NJW 1988, 799), the defendant acquired land that he held on trust (*treuhänderisch*) for the plaintiff. The defendant sold part of the land on his own account to a third party. The third party had not yet acquired full title but was granted a quasi-proprietary interest in the land (*Vormerkung*), which interest prevailed over any rights of the plaintiff. (Under English law the basic result on these facts would probably not be dissimilar; though trust reasoning would be used; for details, see Harpum, *Megarry & Wade: The Law of Real Property* (6th edn, 2000), para 4-029ff and chapter 6.) The third party was willing to renounce the right, provided that the defendant bought it back at thirty times the estimated value of the land. The plaintiff claimed that the defendant should hand the land over to him (§ 667 BGB, from the rules on mandate (discussed in chapters 3 and 8) applies. The court once again had recourse to good faith and concluded that it could not reasonably be expected that the defendant/debtor should be forced to buy the land back. Therefore, he was released from his obligation to hand over the land to the plaintiff.

The importance of enforced performance becomes apparent once we examine the consequences of denying the debtor the defence of § 275 II BGB. If the debtor is released according to § 275 II BGB, then § 326 I 1 BGB provides that as a general rule he also loses his right to the counter-performance. If he is not released, he retains the right to claim the price but he is required to undertake all necessary efforts to perform *in specie*. These efforts may completely outgrow the expected profit. The debtor is not able to escape the effects of the rule. First of all, the creditor may enforce the primary obligation specifically (as discussed above). Secondly, the degree of liability in damages is also pre-determined by the scope of the duty to perform. If the debtor is released according to § 275 BGB he may still be liable in damages as a substitute for performance. However, following the fault principle, liability depends on whether he can be imputed knowledge of an initial impediment (§ 311a II BGB) or whether he is at fault in causing the subsequent impossibility (§ 283 BGB). If the debtor is not released from his obligation of performance, liability in damages as a substitute for performance still depends on fault (§ 281 BGB). However, there is a crucial difference in the case where the debtor's obligation of performance subsists. If the debtor is required to perform, he is unlikely to be able to exculpate himself if he fails to do so. He cannot invoke the impediment to performance, since it is expected that he must overcome it. He cannot argue that he lacks the financial means to effect performance, for this defence (as will be explained below) is not recognised in German law. Hence, the only imaginable defence would be an error in law, but the courts are reluctant to accept that the error could not be avoided. As a result, this regime of liability comes quite close to the 'guarantee'-type of liability of Anglo-American law, even though on its face the German approach is, as we have said, fault-based.

The question that has caused some disagreement following the reform is the extent to which the *nature* of the obligation influences the outcome of the balancing exercise required by § 275 II BGB. There is widespread agreement that in certain groups of cases the nature of the obligation is consistent with a strict approach to the duty to render primary performance, ie, a narrow interpretation of § 275 II BGB. This concerns, for instance, the contract for work (*Werkvertrag*, § 631 BGB: see Huber's contribution in the *Festschrift Schlechtriem*, p 553). Here the promisor undertook to achieve a certain result; he bears the risk of performance and will not succeed in making the plea that performance is now more onerous than anticipated. Similarly, the sale of generic goods involves the promise to achieve a certain result (see, Huber, above, p 530). If for instance acquiring the goods on the market has become more onerous than expected, this normally is the 'risk' of the seller.

The treatment of the sale of a specific thing (*Stückkauf*) is more controversial however. How is subjective impossibility to be distinguished from § 275 II BGB? How much is required of a seller who is not responsible for the impediment to performance? Some writers argue that the seller's duty of primary performance ought to be excluded in situations in which an impediment to performance occurred that would entail that the seller has to spend more than the contract price to perform the contract (Ackermann, JZ 2002, 383; Huber, p 566; Picker, JZ 2003, 1035 goes even further in watering down the primary obligation of the seller in contracts for the sale of specific goods). It will be recalled that if the thing sold is destroyed, then according to § 275 I BGB the seller is released from the obligation to perform (contained in § 433 I 1 BGB). It will also be remembered that in such a case the seller also loses the right to claim the counter-performance (§ 326 I 1 BGB): both parties are released. The same principle, these writers suggest, should apply if performance is not factually impossible but merely more onerous: the seller should not lose more than the contract price (in this sense, Ackermann and Huber). The following example may illustrate the problem (it is taken from Picker, JZ 2003, 1035; see already, Schlechtriem (2002) *Oxford U Comparative L Forum* 2).

A sells B a secondhand car for €10,000 that is subsequently stolen and later reappears in Murmansk. The cost of retrieving the car is €10,000. B has sold on the car for

€20,000. If the car were destroyed, the seller A would lose the right to claim the price (§ 326 I 1 BGB) but would be released from the obligation to perform (§ 275 I BGB). Unless he was responsible for the destruction, he would not be liable for the loss of profits of the buyer B (§ 283 BGB). According to Huber's view, the seller does not need to spend more than the contract price to retrieve the car. In the example, A would not need to spend more than the actual €10,000 to retrieve the car. He loses €10,000 but of course retains the right to claim the price (also €10,000). Hence, it does not make a difference to the seller whether he retrieves the car or not. For the buyer it does make a difference, for only if the seller is obliged to retrieve the car will he be able to make the profit of €10,000 (either by selling the car on or by claiming damages from the seller if the seller fails to retrieve it).

Let us assume now that the cost of retrieving the car is €12,000. If the seller is under an obligation to retrieve the car he will lose more than if the car had perished. That the seller is bound to recover the car nevertheless is the view adopted by (for instance) Canaris (an influential member of the Second Law Reform Commission). This approach has important consequences for the regime of liability of the seller (JZ 2004, 214, 223–4):

> If the seller does not fulfil his obligation of performance (*Leistungspflicht*) even though he has not been released from it according to § 275 II BGB . . . he is in principle liable to the buyer for damages instead of performance according to §§ 281, 280 I BGB, be it because he deliberately breaches the duty of performance or because he acts negligently in this respect, for instance because he was mistaken. He is burdened with this liability despite the fact that he is not responsible for the impediment to performance.

This means in our example that if the seller fails to retrieve the car he will be liable to the buyer in damages and will not only lose the right to the price, but will have to compensate the buyer for his lost profit. The total loss of the seller adds up to €20,000. If he retrieves the car he is better off; for his loss of €12,000 must be balanced against the right to obtain the price of €10,000. The strict approach to enforced performance, unsurprisingly, provides an incentive to perform the contract.

Subjective impossibility, ie, impediments derived from a lack of legal power of the debtor as opposed to factual impediments, raises very similar issues in applying § 275 II BGB. Consider once again the sale of a specific thing, a painting for instance, by A to B. A subsequently sells the painting and transfers it to X. Provided that the sale to X does not constitute fault in relation to B, and provided that X is willing to transfer the painting back, how much is A expected to pay in order to be able to honour his promise to B? (See the example given by Zimmermann, *Breach of Contract*, p 15 and Meier, Jura 2002, 128.) The answer again depends on whether the contract price forms the threshold for releasing the debtor or not.

It remains to be seen which view will convince the courts. The strict approach to performance is consistent with the principle of *pacta sunt servanda*, while the rival approach—by alleviating the burden of performance for impediments to performance for which the seller is not responsible—emphasises the need to protect the debtor. It seems fair to say, however, that the protection of the performance interest stands at the forefront of how § 275 II BGB was intended to operate (cf Canaris, JZ 2004, 214, 221). It is a natural consequence of this overriding importance of enforced performance that the debtor may incur a greater burden if the contract can still be performed, even though this entails greater expense than if the contract cannot be performed.

In any event, it is of the first importance to realise that the problem of reasonableness cannot be discussed in isolation from other limitations on the principle of enforced performance. This is emphasised by the advocates of both views. (Huber and Canaris in particular.) As explained above, enforced performance is also available in relation to non-conforming performance. The two most important examples are first, a seller is under an obligation to bring the goods into conformity with the contract according to § 439 I BGB (cf Article 46 CISG and Article 3 of Directive 1999/44/EC), and secondly, the same principle applies to the contract of work (§ 635 I BGB, cf *Ruxley Electronics and Construction Ltd v Forsyth* [1996] AC 344, where the issue of bringing the dimensions of the swimming pool into conformity with the contract specifications arose only in an attempt to quantify the damages recoverable). It should be noted that while the buyer may choose the manner in which this is done, the contractor is given the choice whether to cure the defect by repair or to perform afresh. Both rights are however subject to the limitation that the cost of cure must not be unreasonable (§ 439 III and § 635 III BGB; again, in *Ruxley*, this issue of reasonableness (or proportionality) related to whether the award of damages should be for the cost of cure or the loss of amenity value (a substantially lesser sum on the facts) to the buyer: see Treitel, *The Law of Contract*, pp 947–8). Unlike the position under § 275 II BGB, the disproportionality between cost of cure and the interest in obtaining the performance need not be grave. The intention was clearly that it should be easier to invoke unreasonable expense against the claim to cure the defect. It would not be consistent to release the debtor in the case of non-conforming performance more easily than in the case of the total non-fulfilment of the primary obligation of performance.

The sale of *generic goods* and the *contract for work* entail a strict duty of performance on the part of the debtor, as already explained in relation to § 275 II BGB, and therefore it is commonly agreed that the contract price cannot be taken as a benchmark for the reasonableness test: this much is common ground among commentators.

However, if in the case of the contract of *sale of a specific thing* the contract price forms the ceiling for the unreasonableness within the meaning of § 275 II BGB (ie, as to whether there is performance in the first place), likewise the seller cannot be required to spend more than the contract price to cure the defect (§ 439 III BGB; ie in the case of non-conforming performance). This is indeed the—consistent—position of Huber, above, p. 545, and Ackermann, JZ 2002, 383). Canaris, on the other hand, equally consistently does not regard the contract price as an appropriate yardstick to determine reasonableness, neither in § 275 II BGB nor in § 439 III BGB. In his view (JZ 2004, 214, 217), it would be contrary to the requirements of Article 3 of Directive 1999/44/EC to treat the contract price as the benchmark for the cost that a seller is reasonably expected to bear in order to cure the defect of the goods or deliver conforming goods. If the Directive indeed requires more of the seller in respect of non-conforming performance than to spend the contract price, it would be inconsistent to release the seller in the context of § 275 II BGB under less stringent conditions. It follows that here too the seller is required to bear the cost of securing performance even if it exceeds the contract price. This latter argument is not to be underestimated. If it applies it would demonstrate the far-reaching effect that a seemingly minor intervention by an EC harmonisation measure may have on the system of remedies for irregularities of performance. (We will return to the issues raised by §§ 439 and 635 BGB in the next chapter (sections 2(d) and 3(d) pp 502, 524).)

The foregoing considerations should not be (dis-)regarded as an example of Germanic obsession with abstract concepts. What we have been trying to show is that the differences of approach can be traced back to different conceptions about the nature of the performance interest. In addition, the dispute has significant practical implications. The sale of a specific thing illustrates the wider issues raised by the availability of enforced performance in German (and also now European Community) law. If anything, the discussion shows that enforced performance is not only relevant as a remedy, but also that the scope of the primary duty of performance predetermines the liability in damages of the debtor. The view that is adopted in the motivation of the new law approximates the Germanic fault principle to the 'guarantee'-type of liability of the common law.

That performance entails an undue burden is a ground for denying specific performance also in American law. *Van Wagner Adverstising Corp v SM Enterprises*, 67 NY 2d 186, 501 NYS 2d 628, 492 NE 2d 756 (1986), is a familiar illustration. The plaintiff had a lease to a billboard space facing the Lincoln Tunnel on a building the defendant proposed to tear down to build a much larger building. The court denied specific performance. This issue also comes up in the measurement of damages when the plaintiff seeks the cost of obtaining substitute performance when that is grossly disproportionate to his loss from the non-conformity. *Peevyhouse v Garland Goal & Mining Co*, 382 P 2d 109 (Okl 1962), is a famous case denying the cost of restoring stripmined land (estimated to $29,000), which the defendant had promised to do, when the loss in market value from not restoring was only $300. *Groves v John Wunder Co*, 205 Minn 163, 286 NW 235 (1939), comes out the other way. Carol Chomsky, Of Spoil Pits and Swimming Pools: Reconsidering the Measure of Damages for Construction Contracts, 75 *Minn L Rev* 1445, 1451–60 (1991), reviews many similar cases and concludes that the primary focus is avoiding economic waste. (Cf also Restatement (Second) of Contracts, § 348.)

(v) Impossibility in the Sense of § 275 III BGB

The third category of impossibility of the new law can be referred to as 'moral impossibility' (Zimmermann, *Breach of Contract*, p 16). Again, performance is not strictly speaking 'impossible', but it cannot reasonably be expected that the promisor should perform his obligation. Consequently, § 275 III BGB merely entitles the debtor to raise the defence of impossibility as a plea (*Einrede*), but does not exclude the duty of performance *ex lege*. The provision is confined to contractual obligations that must be performed in person. It does not, therefore, have a wide application. The paradigmatic case (*Bundestags-Drucksache* 14/6040, p 130) is that of an opera singer who refuses to sing at the performance because her child has been taken seriously ill. Another illustration given in the motivation of the 'government draft' is the case of BAG NJW 1983, 2782: a Turkish national did not appear at work in Germany because he had been required to perform his national service in Turkey and faced the death penalty if he failed to honour his duty towards the State. The provision also solves many situations of conflict in daily life, at least according to the motivation of the new law: necessary visits to the doctor, the duty to appear in court and so forth are said to fall under this provision.

4. TERMINATION

Gaier, 'Das Rücktritts(folgen)recht nach dem Schuldrechtsmodernisierungsgesetz' WM 2002, 1; Gsell, 'Das Verhältnis von Rücktritt und Schadensersatz' JZ 2004, 643; Jaensch, 'Der Gleichlauf von Rücktritt und Schadensersatz' NJW 2003, 3613; Kaiser, 'Die Rechtsfolgen des Rücktritts in der Schuldrechtsreform' JZ 2001, 1057; Kamanabrou, 'Haftung des Rücktrittsberechtigten bei Untergang der empfangenen Leistung' NJW 2003, 30; Kohler, 'Rücktrittsausschluß im Gewährleistungsrecht bei nachträglicher Nacherfüllungsmöglichkeit—Wiederkehr der §§ 350, 351 BGB a.F.?' AcP 203 (2003) 539; Perkams, 'Die Haftung des Rücktrittsberechtigten im neuen Schuldrecht' Jura 2003, 250; Treitel, 'Remedies for Breach of Contract' in *International Encyclopedia of Comparative Law*, vol VII, chapter 16 (1976) para 143 *et seq.*

(a) Preliminary Observations

Termination of the contract must be distinguished from what we referred to as 'rescission' of the contract. Rescission or *Anfechtung* (§ 142 BGB) operates to negative retroactively (*ex tunc* or *ab initio*) the validity of the contract (see chapter 6, p 286 ff). As a result, the parties are treated as if there never had been an agreement between them. Consequently, in the absence of a *causa*, any performance that has been exchanged must be reversed according to the rules of unjustified enrichment (*Leistungskondiktion*: § 812 I 1 Alt. 1 BGB). The rationale of this drastic consequence is that the agreement between the parties was flawed, ie, affected by a defect in the contracting process that the law recognises as a 'vitiating' factor. That is not the issue now under consideration; and this is best reflected if a distinct term is used for the right to avoid the contract. 'Termination', in the sense in which we use the term here, presupposes that there has been a perfectly valid agreement. (In German two terms are used depending on whether the contract is a 'continuing contract' or not; in the first *Kündigung* is the relevant term, in the second *Rücktritt* is used.) A clearly different reason justifies 'termination' and introduces yet another exception to the principle of *pacta sunt servanda*, releasing the parties from the obligation undertaken in the contract. In the words of Treitel (*Encyclopaedia*, para 16-143):

> A party who is aggrieved as a result of not obtaining the performance for which he bargained may wish, in a general sense, to put an end to further performance of the contract and also as far as possible to put matters back into the position in which they were before performance on either side was begun.

The *main aim* of termination is to allow the innocent party to withdraw from the contract if the guilty party committed a breach of contract. The objection of the innocent party against hanging on to the contract is not that the contract is flawed but that the performance is not forthcoming and that the creditor ought therefore to be released from the obligation of counter-performance. (See Ernst in *Münchener Kommentar*, vol 2a, § 323 Rn. 13.) Since the purpose of termination concerns the effect of a breach of contract on the obligation of counter-performance, the central provisions (§§ 323, 324 BGB) on termination are confined to reciprocal contracts (*gegenseitige Verträge*) or, in the terminology of the common law, contracts supported by consideration. While the obligation breached must not be the main obligation, it must as a general rule be synallagmatic, ie concern the promise of something that constitutes the reason for entering into the bargain.

The *reason* for termination is the breach of contract. Termination is a remedy for breach of contract. Termination is (and always has been in German law) *effected* by a declaration of will by the innocent party (§ 349 BGB). Termination is therefore a power (*Gestaltungsrecht*) of the innocent party to change, by a unilateral act, the content of the contractual obligations.

Once the contract is terminated, the parties may—as a *consequence* of termination—refuse any further performance and claim any performance back that may already have been rendered according to the rules of restitution laid down in § 346 *et seq* BGB. Termination does not therefore negative consent. Indeed, there would be no reason to do so. Nor does termination have any retroactive effects so far as the validity of the contract is concerned: it operates *ex nunc*. The rules of unjustified enrichment (§ 812 BGB) do not apply. Rather, the effect of termination is to bring the obligations of the parties to an end from the moment that the innocent party terminates the contract. If performance has not yet commenced, the only necessary rule is one that releases the parties from their reciprocal obligations. However, in most cases the parties will have already effected part of the performance. In order to restore the position of the parties before performance was begun, it is necessary to attribute 'restitutionary' consequences to termination (discussed in detail below). This is achieved in German law by actually reversing the contractual obligations and transforming the contract into a 'relationship of obligation for restitution' or *Rückgewährschuldverhältnis*. Any performance already effected must be returned, according to § 346 *et seq* BGB. Since this sweeping regime of restitution would cause difficulties if applied to long-term or 'continuing' contracts, a different approach to termination is adopted in relation to these contracts (§ 314 BGB, discussed below).

Note that the right of cancellation of certain consumer transactions (*Widerruf*, § 357 BGB, discussed in chapter 6, p 270) is—for entirely pragmatic reasons—also ascribed the effect of termination as laid down in § 346 BGB. This should not give rise to the misunderstanding that in those cases the 'guilty party' also breached the contract: that is not the case. The right of cancellation is derived from the contracting process and operates irrespective of performance.

It would serve no practical purpose to explain the approach of the old law to termination (for which the previous edition of this book may be consulted). It suffices here to say that it was highly complex and almost impossible to understand fully without reading a few hundred pages of Enneccerus, Larenz or Medicus. As already suggested, the new law is much easier to apply. The reform simplified the law in respect of the conditions of termination as well as the consequences of termination. § 323 BGB is the central provision that establishes a clearly phrased uniform approach to termination and does away with the fragmented previous rules of restitution.

So far as the substance of the new law is concerned two points should be emphasised. Termination is independent of the fault of the 'guilty party'—another important inroad into the fault principle. This has made it possible to incorporate the various rights of termination in relation to non-conforming performance, which previously had led a life of their own. Termination and damages may be combined (§ 325 BGB).

This brings German law closer to Anglo-American law, though it should be observed that even before the reform of 2001 the courts had in effect allowed the innocent party to claim the counter-performance back *and* claim damages at the same time. As a result of the reforms, it has now become much easier to justify this result. It should also be noted that the right to claim damages instead of performance is modelled after the same principles underlying § 323 BGB (except of course for the rule that liability in damages is fault-dependent). This way of proceeding was intended to achieve consistency among the secondary rights and to simplify as much as possible the remedies available in respect of a failure of performance.

Before we examine the right of termination in more detail it is necessary briefly to draw the attention of the reader to two legal instruments which, to varying degrees, play a role similar to the right of termination.

First, under certain conditions, a party may retain the counter-performance on the ground that (and so long as) he has not yet received the performance. However, this plea of an unperformed contract (§ 320 BGB) is not a remedy for breach of contract for the simple reason that it does not presuppose a breach. Rather, it translates the reciprocal nature of the contract into procedural terms and allows a party who is not required to perform first to insist on a reciprocal or concurrent (*Zum um Zug*) fulfilment of the obligations of performance. (We therefore discussed this principle in the context of chapter 8, p 349. However, it is readily conceded that the plea may also operate provisionally to protect an innocent party in relation to a claim by a party in breach.)

Secondly, in section 3(e)(ii) on impossibility, p 409, we discussed the rule that if performance is impossible within the meaning of § 275 BGB, the other party is automatically released from the obligation of counter-performance. (§ 326 I 1 BGB; the rule does not apply to non-conforming performance.) This rule, it should be stressed at the outset, has the same purpose as the right to terminate. We will need to return to this rule in the present section (see section 4(b)(iv), below).

(b) Duties of Performance (*Leistungspflichten*)

The central provision on *Rücktritt* or termination is § 323 BGB. It entitles the innocent party to terminate the contract if the guilty party failed to perform a reciprocal obligation of performance (*Leistungspflicht*, § 241 I BGB). This is by far the most important instance of the right to terminate. It is useful to give an overview of the main rules.

Any failure of performance constitutes an (objectively) assessed breach of contract. The right to terminate originates in this breach. It does not presuppose that the 'guilty' party was answerable (under the fault principle) for the breach. The objective nature of the breach is relevant, however, for the conditions on which the right can be exercised. If the breach consists in the total absence of (due) performance, the conditions are derived from § 323 I BGB. As a general rule, the debtor is given a second chance to perform. The innocent party is required to set a (reasonable) period for performance and only after the fruitless lapse of that period does the right to terminate arise. § 323 II BGB contains exceptions to this requirement. § 326 V BGB equally dispenses with this requirement if the breach of contract consists in the impossibility of performance. If the breach consists of a partial absence of performance, § 323 V 1

BGB requires that if the contract as a whole is terminated, the innocent party must not have an interest in the partial performance: ie, it must be reasonable to extend termination to the whole obligation. If the breach consists of a non-conforming performance (*Schlechtleistung*, literally 'bad performance'), the further condition of § 323 V 2 BGB must be met for the right of termination to arise: the breach must be serious (*erheblich*). The problem of anticipatory breach is dealt with in § 323 IV BGB. § 323 VI BGB excludes the right to terminate if the 'innocent' party is solely or overwhelmingly responsible for the breach or if the breach occurred while the creditor was in delay of acceptance and the debtor is not answerable for the breach. Finally, the effects of termination are regulated by § 346 BGB (considered separately below, section 4(d)).

It is already apparent from a first reading of the provisions of the BGB that German law (unlike French law) does not put too many obstacles in the way of an innocent party seeking release from the obligation of counter-performance. Generally speaking, so long as performance is still possible the innocent party must give the guilty party a second chance to perform (*Nachfrist* approach). The breach of contract must not, however, be trivial. This condition is obviously satisfied in the case of a total absence of performance. Where only part of the performance is absent, the innocent party must show that he does not have an interest in partial performance, while in the case of non-conforming performance the breach must be 'serious'. The same approach is adopted in Directive 1999/44/EC: the innocent party must first require that the goods are brought into conformity with the contract (Article 3(3)) and termination is not available in relation to 'minor' defects (Article 3(6)).

The CISG adopts a different approach. It makes it considerably more difficult to 'avoid' the contract (referred to in German as *Vertragsaufhebung*). Accordingly, the right to claim damages plays a more central role. Under the CISG, the innocent party has a right of termination only if the breach is 'fundamental'. The right to avoid the contract arises on the occurrence of the breach. No further period of grace needs to be fixed. A breach is fundamental if it substantially deprives the other party of what he is entitled to expect under the contract (see Articles 25, 49(1)(a) and 51 (2) CISG). Non-delivery of the goods without more is not regarded as a fundamental breach (see eg, Schlechtriem, *UN-Kaufrecht* (2nd edn, 2003), Rn. 189). Yet in order to avoid possible argument over whether the non-delivery is a fundamental breach, a period for performance may be fixed. If the seller has still not performed by the end of this period, the buyer is also entitled to avoid the contract (Article 49(1)(b)). This is not possible however in the case of non-conforming goods. The setting of period of performance does not turn a non-fundamental breach into a fundamental breach. (Once more, the *Principles* follow the lead of the CISG, see Article 9:301 PECL, Article 7.3.1 PICC.)

The approach of English law can hardly be called a 'model' approach. It has become rather fragmented and its current state clearly betrays the various concerns of its development throughout its history. (See Treitel's succinct discussion of the relevant policy considerations concerning the interests of each side in seeking and resisting 'rescission', in the sense of the termination of the contract while leaving intact the claimant's right to seek damages for breach, *The Law of Contract*, pp 760–1; and more generally, McKendrick, *Contract Law*, chapter 24 for useful source materials and discussion.) The basic starting point is that a defect in performance must amount to a 'substantial failure' in that performance to entitle the innocent party to rescind. Even the operation of this test is open to a considerable degree of uncertainty, although Treitel suggests that the overriding consideration of the courts is to ensure that the availability of rescission corresponds to the practicalities of the situation in the case at bar (*The Law of Contract*, pp 770–1). Thus, let us look at two examples. First, where the claimant has received a benefit from the other party's performance (however defective or incomplete) and refuses to (or cannot) return that benefit, then the courts seem unlikely to grant rescission. Secondly, and by contrast, where damages would not adequately compensate the claimant this is often a ground on which the courts rely to justify allowing rescission (compare *Vigers v Cook* [1919] 2 KB 475 (rescission granted since the loss—of not being able to get the coffin into the church for the funeral, due to the coffin's negligent construction—was not one that could be measured in money) with *Decro-Wall International SA v Practitioners in Marketing Ltd* [1971] 1 WLR 361 (where small delays in payments by the defendants under an ongoing contract that led to small interest payments by the claimant caused a loss that was easily quantifiable and recoverable in damages from the defendants, so rescission was refused).

The unpredictability of the operation of these principles on substantial failure of performance led both the courts and the legislature to take steps to secure greater certainty in the application of the law on termination of contracts. While this area cannot be developed in detail here, some of its basic elements should be noted.

First, where the contract expressly provides for the availability of rescission after some particular and specified failure to perform by the defendant, then as a general rule the courts will enforce that provision. (See eg, *The Laconia* [1977] AC 850 and *Union Eagle Ltd v Golden Achievement Ltd* [1997] AC 514—in the latter, the contract was declared to be rescinded a mere one minute after the specified time had passed, so that an attempt to enforce the contract by tendering the purchase price ten minutes late was rejected: 'the parties should know with certainty that the terms of the contract will be enforced' (at 519).) However, this may be subject to exceptions where the assumption that the parties bargained on equal terms to agree the contract is displaced: such cases commonly concern stringent forfeiture clauses in leases (eg, breach of *any* covenant entitling the landlord to forfeit) and normally only amount to the provision of extra time to perform. (See eg, *Nutting v Baldwin* [1995] 1 WLR 201.) Similar bargaining considerations apply in the consumer sphere under the Unfair Terms in Consumer Contracts Regulations 1999 (see regs 5(5) and 8(1) and Schedule 2, para 1(g)). See however the broader statements of the House of Lords on this area in *The Scaptrade* [1983] 2 AC 694, suggesting that these exceptions might apply in any case where the literal enforcement of the contract would deprive the defendant of 'proprietary or possessory rights' (at 702). This possibility was taken to quite an extreme in the case of *On Demand Information plc v Michael Gerson (Finance) plc* [2003] 1 AC 368 and has been criticised by Treitel as contrary to commercial certainty, since 'the *policy* stated . . . of giving effect to commercial agreements between parties bargaining on equal terms . . . has in effect been subordinated to the *legal technique* used . . . to give effect to that policy' (ie, the distinction between 'proprietary/possessory' and 'merely contractual' rights) (emphasis in the original).

Secondly, if an obligation can be characterised as an 'entire obligation', then failure to perform it in its entirety can entitle the claimant to refuse to pay and can treat the contract as terminated. For (in)famous examples see *Cutter v Powell* (1795) 6 TR 320 and *Sumpter v Hedges* [1898] 1 QB 673, which raise the spectre of the unjust enrichment of the claimant, if he is to be permitted to rescind and not be forced to pay the defendant some reasonable remuneration for the performance that has been tendered. This problem can be avoided where the contract and the facts allow a different interpretation to be placed on the nature of the obligation entered into. Thus, *Hoenig v Isaacs* [1952] 2 All ER 176, where finishing the furnishing job could be characterised as an entire obligation, while the *quality* of that performance fell to be assessed under the basic rules on substantial failure—this allowed the claimant to recover the full contract price for the furnishings, less the cost of making good the defects identified. However, it will not always be possible to analyse the case at hand in this fashion, suggesting that the doubts about the restitutionary consequences of this area are well founded. (See Treitel, *The Law of Contract*, pp 782–7 and 825–6, Law Commission, *Pecuniary Restitution on Breach of Contract* (Law Com No 121, 1983) and McFarlane and Stevens, 'In Defence of *Sumpter v Hedges*' (2002) 118 *LQR* 569. *Jacob and Youngs v Kent* 230 NY 239, 129 NE 889 (1921), is the classic American counter-example. The contract specified Redding pipe. The builder used Cohoes, which was precisely the same as Redding. The court over-looked language of condition to hold the contractor was entitled to be paid. More generally, a party who substantially performs is entitled to be paid the contract price. *Plante v Jacobs* 10 Wis 2d 567, 103 NW 2d 296 (1960) (holding misplaced living room wall is substantial performance).)

Thirdly, and most importantly, as a further exception from the requirement to show substantial failure of performance, English law has long recognised a classification of contract terms into 'conditions' and 'warranties'. While the former entitles the innocent party to immediate termination regardless of the severity and/or relevance of the breach (alongside which termination he may also sue for damages), a breach of the latter only gives rise to a claim for damages (see section 61(1) of the Sale of Goods Act 1979). The difficulty with this analysis is that it enables the innocent party to avoid the contract for what appears to be a mere technicality because he regrets the contract. (See the well known case of *Arcos Ltd v Ronaasen* [1933] AC 470: timber bought to make cement barrels was said to be 'half an inch thick' in the contract, but on delivery most of it was in fact 9/16 of an inch thick. It could still be used to make perfectly satisfactory cement barrels, but since the half inch stipulation was held to be a condition, the buyers were entitled to reject the timber delivered, even though the actual motivation appeared to be to avoid paying more for the timber since the market price for the timber had fallen by the time of delivery.) This 'all-or-nothing' solution could at least be said to have had the merit of certainty, by relieving the innocent party of the often dificult task of establishing whether the breach was sufficiently serious to amount to a substantial failure of performance. However, the extent to which this approach could also cause serious hardship to the party in breach prompted the courts to adopt a less restrictive attitude to the classification of terms. One device has been the courts' reluctance to categorise terms as conditions; but the perhaps better known approach has been the recognition of what have been called 'intermediate or innominate terms,' the breach of which will give rise to a right to terminate the contract only if the consequences are sufficiently serious.

The basic distinction between a condition and a warranty was that a condition was said to go 'to the very root of the contract' (and thus failure to fulfil it would amount to a 'serious failure in performance'), whereas a warranty related to less important or subsidiary elements of the contract: ie, requiring the claimant to accept something seriously different from that expected under the contract, would not be acceptable, but more minor defects in performance could be satisfied in the form of money (ie, damages). This approach to defining a condition would seem to cohere with the basic starting point discussed above. However, the House of Lords made clear in *Bunge Corp v Tradax Export SA* [1981] 1 WLR 711 that some terms have been held to be conditions, even where such substantial deprivation of the benefit expected by the innocent party had not occurred. Further, the parties may expressly classify terms as conditions and the courts will give effect to such intentions, subject to certain limitations that may be derived from the context of the use of the term 'condition'. See the important case of *Wickman Ltd v Schuler AG* [1974] AC 235, where the House of Lords held that the parties probably intended 'condition' in a non-technical sense, especially since breach of the term was possible in a very minor way causing little or no loss at all. For a further restriction on the literal approach to the construction of such contract terms, see also *Reardon Smith Line Ltd v Hansen Tangen* [1976] 1 WLR 989. In that case, Lord Wilberforce focused on the key elements of the 'description' of the tanker to be delivered and this approach allowed the House of Lords to rule that a tanker built elsewhere than 'Yard No 354 at Osaka' (as stated in the contract) was not a breach of condition, while still acknowledging the force of the implied condition that the goods delivered must conform with their (now more narrowly drawn) contractual description. Finally, statutes may classify a particular term as a condition rather than a warranty: see sections 12–15 of the Sale of Goods Act 1979, which are mainly concerned with implied conditions (rather than warranties) in contracts for the sale of goods. (Note also that the right to rescind for breach of these conditions is subject to specific statutory defences in the 1979 Act: see sections 15A and 48A–48C (the latter implementing Directive 1999/44/EC).)

As suggested above, the other device used by the courts to restrict the potentially harsh consequences of strict adherence to the classification of contract terms as either conditions or warranties has been to acknowledge that there are other terms that fall into *neither* of these categories—known as 'intermediate or innominate terms'. (For example, *Bunge Corp v Tradax Export SA*, cited above, at 714.) For the claimant to be able to assert a right to rescind for a breach of such a term, he must show that a substantial failure of performance has occurred (see, for a good illustration, *The Hansa Nord* [1976] QB 44, helpfully noted by Reynolds (1976) 92 LQR 17 and Weir [1976] CLJ 33). The identification of this category raises the key question: which terms fall into which of the three categories? Once again, the competing policy considerations (of restricting the right to rescind to cases of serious injury to the claimant's rights and of securing sufficient commercial certainty) pull in different directions and the cases reflect this balance. Thus, in the *Bunge Corp* case (above), their Lordships were careful to stress that 'the courts should not be too ready to construe terms as conditions unless the contract clearly requires the court to do so' (*per* Lord Wilberforce at 715), yet on the facts applied the commercial certainty standard to allow rescission when notice was given 5 days after the final date specified in the contract. The general position would appear to be that stipulations as to time are likelier to be classified as conditions if the commercial context of the contract seems to require this approach; similarly, other terms seen as commercially vital or as clearly intended by the parties to have effect as conditions will be enforced as such. Nevertheless, while it can be argued that these developments have moved in an appropriately ameliorating direction, it cannot be said that their application on a case-by-case basis is a matter of the greatest certainty in the current state of the authorities. (For discussion, see Treitel, *The Law of Contract*, pp 797–800.)

It is suggested that in developing the law, English courts now have—with the new and improved German *Nachfrist*-model and the 'fundamental breach' model of the CISG—two consistent theories of the right to terminate a contract that may provide some guidance, at the very least as to the viability of alternative ways of balancing the competing interests at stake. (See eg, McKendrick, *Contract Law*, pp 970–5. See also, Robert A Hillman, 'Keeping the Deal Together After Material Breach—Common Law Mitigation Rules, The UCC, and the Restatement (Second) of Contracts' 47 *Colo L Rev* 553 (1976), for a good but now dated review of the law on the general topic.)

(i) Late Performance

Paragraph 323 I BGB is the starting point for the right of termination, which is then qualified by the other sub-sections of the same paragraph and a special rule for impossibility in § 326 V BGB. Its scope of application is overarching. It includes all kinds of non-performance. The provision encapsulates the basic principle of German law that a failure of performance as such does not entitle the creditor to exercise any secondary rights unless the creditor has demanded performance, fixed a period of grace, and notwithstanding this the debtor has not performed during the period set by the creditor (the *Nachfrist* requirement.) So let us assume a contract for the sale of goods. If the seller fails to deliver the goods, the buyer needs to set a period for performance and only if the seller fails to perform within that period can the buyer withdraw from the contract. Likewise, if the seller delivers non-conforming goods, the buyer must first set a period for performance, which may consist of curing the defect or delivering conforming goods. As already explained, the right to claim damages instead of performance follows the same pattern (§ 281 I BGB).

We have already discussed the specific requirements as to the setting of a period for performance, above. It suffices here to reiterate the main points. The setting of a period for performance does not make sense if performance is impossible. Consequently, § 326 V BGB dispenses with this requirement. (See § 283 BGB for the right to claim damages instead of performance.) We are dealing here, therefore, first and foremost with cases of *late performance*. (The reader is once again referred to Figure 1 p 402 for an overview of the consequences and remedies in relation to late performance.) The period for performance must be of reasonable length; however, if it is too short it is not invalid but will be extended *ex post* by the court. In cases of late performance there are certain further situations in which the creditor may dispense with setting a period for performance. These exceptions are laid down in § 323 II BGB, also discussed above. This duty to give further time to the debtor does not apply where the debtor refuses performance seriously (§ 323 II Nr. 1 BGB), where the contract stipulates that performance must take place by a date determined in the contract and where it is clear that the creditor no longer retains an interest in the performance of the debtor's performance after that date (§ 323 II Nr. 2 BGB), and where finally, special reasons and the interests of both parties, if balanced against each other, justify the immediate termination of the contract (§ 323 II Nr. 3 BGB).

(ii) Non-conforming Performance

Paragraph 323 V 2 BGB makes the *Erheblichkeit* of the breach of duty the prerequisite of the right to terminate in cases of non-conforming performance (*Schlechtleistung* or *nicht vertragsgemäße Leistung*). Hence, a minimum degree of seriousness is required for the right to terminate the contract for non-conforming performance. Of course, since seriousness is a question of degree, it is difficult to define in abstract terms. Judicial discretion thus plays a role in determining the fulfilment of this requirement in each individual case. In this sense, the presentation of English law (above) shows some similarities in that the courts have often been rather creative in exercising their interpretive power over the construction of contractual terms. (See in particular the case of *Wickman Ltd v Schuler AG* [1974] AC 235, discussed by McKendrick, *Contract Law*, pp 926–33).

Non-conforming performance is an instance of partial performance. One could therefore conceive a right of 'partial' termination. It is important to realise that a partial 'termination' is not available in relation to non-conforming performance. The interest of the creditor in being partially released from his obligation of counter-performance is protected by other means. He is granted a right to price-reduction in the special parts of the law of contract (eg, § 441 BGB, contract of sale; cf Article 3(5) of Directive 1999/44/EC and section 48C of the Sale of Goods Act 1979), which if exercised reduces the obligation to pay the price in relation to the extent of the non-conformity. (Further details on this are given in chapter 10.) If the price has already been paid, the creditor is entitled to partial restitution of the counter-performance (§ 441 IV BGB). However, restitution does not extend beyond that. In particular, the performance is not restored to the debtor. This right to price reduction fulfils the same purpose as a right to a partial termination. It accordingly follows the same requirements as the right to termination, except of course that the breach need not be serious. This is expressed in the respective provision by the words: the creditor may 'instead of termination' effect a price reduction and the proviso that § 323 V 2 BGB does not apply (eg, § 441 I BGB). It follows that where the breach is serious, the aggrieved party may elect between price reduction and termination.

When, therefore, is the breach sufficiently 'serious'? Under the old law, the threshold of seriousness affected *all* rights in respect of the non-conformity. Unsurprisingly, only the most trivial breaches were slotted into this category and did not play any role in actual practice. The present approach is different, for it entitles the creditor to price reduction in cases of minor breaches and to price reduction or termination in cases of serious breaches. The question therefore is whether the distinction is made, between those breaches that entitle the creditor to terminate and those that do not, by following the old criteria. This is a matter of some controversy. (In favour of retaining the old standard, see Faust in Bamberger and Roth (eds), *BGB*, (2003), § 437 Rn. 25 *et seq* with references, *Bundestags-Drucksache* 14/6040, pp 187, 231; preferring the new approach, Ernst in *Münchener Kommentar*, § 323 Rn. 243; *Staudinger*-Löwisch, § 323 Rn. C30.) It is interesting to observe that the ECJ will also have something to contribute in this respect. For Article 3(6) of Directive 1999/44/EC entrusts the court with the task of defining a 'European' threshold for the right of termination ('minor breaches' do not entail a right of termination). It was the intention of the legislator, so far as it can be discerned from the preparatory works, that the Directive's approach to the question of the 'seriousness' of the breach was also adopted in § 323 V 2 BGB (*Bundestags-Drucksache* 14/6040, p 231: '*geringfügige Vertragswidrigkeit*'). This clearly excludes a threshold such as that contained in Article 25 CISG (*contra* Ernst, cited above). For a breach that substantially deprives the aggrieved party of what he was entitled to expect under the contract cannot be regarded as 'minor'—indeed, such a breach is rightly termed 'fundamental'. It therefore seems likely that only trivial breaches will be covered ('*Bagatellfälle*'), although where exactly one draws the line will depend on the facts of the individual case.

'Minor breaches' may arise if, for instance, defects of goods can be put right without any delay and great effort (see the example provided by Faust, cited above: a car is delivered that has a defective bulb), insignificant diminutions in value, or defects that do not prejudice the utility of the performance for the creditor. If these guidelines were to be adopted, the discretion of the court would be much reduced. Of course, this comes at the price: 'escaping' the contract for ulterior motives becomes easier, athough it should be noted that termination would still not be available for purely 'technical' breaches, ie, breaches that are insignificant from an overall evaluation of the parties' obligations. This remains an advantage over the 'condition'-based approach of English law, although when this is analysed in the light of sections 48A–48C of the Sale of Goods Act 1979 and of the case law discussed above, the English approach is perhaps less consistently wedded to this starting point than it might appear at first sight. Nevertheless, it is certainly the case that where the wording and context of the contract are clear and commercial, the *Arcos Ltd v Ronaasen* (cited above) result is indeed still the basic position.

(iii) Partial Failure of Performance

Paragraph 323 V 1 BGB deals with partial performance. Partial performance must first be distinguished from non-conforming performance. It is clear from the foregoing section that non-conforming performance is regulated separately by § 323 V 2 BGB, and it is therefore not covered by § 323 V 1 BGB. Generally speaking, this is common ground. At the fringes however differentiation between the two becomes controversial. (For instance, § 434 III BGB treats the delivery of a lesser quantity than promised as a case of non-conforming performance. It is controversial whether (as one would assume at first sight) the application of § 434 III BGB to quantitative part-performance implies the criteria of sentence two of § 323 V BGB; see *Münchener Kommentar*- Ernst, § 323 Rn. 213 *et seq*, for a discussion of the different views.)

Partial performance must be further distinguished from total non-performance. This may seem obvious, but the distinction sometimes involves subtle reasoning. In the case of total non-performance, the right of termination of the whole contract follows exclusively from § 323 I BGB, whereas in the case of partial non-performance the innocent party must in addition prove a lack of interest in partial performance. (§ 323 V 1 BGB)

Partial non-performance presupposes, first, that performance can be divided and that dividing performance into several parts does not violate the will of the parties (see

Ernst in *Münchener Kommentar*, § 323 Rn. 201 for references). This means that even if a separation of different parts is possible on the facts, it still depends on the intention of the parties whether the performance can be so divided. Compare here the English cases on severable obligations, typically where payment is due from time to time, in return for performance of particular and specified parts of the contract: eg, employment contracts where a periodic wage is paid or building contracts involving progress or stage payments. See Treitel, *The Law of Contract*, pp 784–7 and note that a claim for breach for failure to render the remainder of the performance may still lie, even though the debtor may claim payment for those parts of performance properly completed: *Ritchie v Atkinson* (1808) 10 East 295 (re the debtor's claim) and 530 (*sub nom Atkinson v Ritchie*, re the creditor's claim in damages). See also, and Restatement, Second, of Contracts § 240 (Part Performance as Agreed Equivalents). UCC 2-612 has a liberal rule for instalment requirements that says non-conformity of one instalment is grounds for cancelling the whole if the noncomformity substantially impairs the value of the whole. The *Bundesgerichtshof* applies the criterion of whether the different parts of performance were meant according to the purpose of the contract to have the same fate ('*zusammen stehen und fallen sollen*'—literally, 'shall stand and fall together'). For instance, the delivery of computer software and hardware cannot normally be separated if the contractor promised a unitary solution and the customer sought to avoid having to deal with separate suppliers (eg, BGH NJW 1990, 3011, 3012, the same problem arose under the old § 326 BGB). If that is the case, performance in parts does not constitute 'partial performance' in the sense of § 323 V 1 BGB. The creditor does not need to show that he has no interest in partial performance to terminate the whole contract.

Secondly if performance is severable in the sense just indicated, the creditor may reject any part performance, in which case the failure of performance becomes total and § 323 I BGB applies. § 266 BGB stipulates that the debtor is not entitled to perform in part. If part-performance is rejected, then § 323 V 1 BGB does not apply. However, where the creditor has accepted a part performance, he can only withdraw from the contract as a whole if he shows that he has no interest in the partial performance.

When, therefore, does the creditor lack an interest in partial performance?

The test is whether the detriment to the creditor is greater than the outstanding performance. (In this sense eg, BGH NJW 1990, 2549, 2550; Ernst in *Münchener Kommentar*, § 323 Rn. 203 BGB.) The reason is this. In the case of partial performance, the creditor may declare partial termination. (In the case of non-conforming performance the right to price reduction assumes this role.) The creditor is therefore entitled to be released from the duty of counter-performance insofar as performance is still outstanding. § 323 V 1 BGB clarifies that if the creditor wishes to release himself from the whole obligation of counter-performance, he must show that the right to partial termination would not adequately protect his expectation interest. Hence, the detriment must be more than just the fact that performance is outstanding.

(iv) Performance being Impossible

If performance is impossible, the interest of the creditor (of the obligation to perform) in being released from his obligation of counter-performance is normally adequately protected by § 326 I 1 BGB (as to which see above in the section on impossibility (section 3(e)), p 408, see also Figure 2 reproduced there). Any part of the performance already effected may be claimed according to the rules of termination (§ 326 IV BGB). The creditor is automatically released from the obligation to pay the price if performance is impossible in the sense of § 275 BGB and, generally speaking, the creditor is not responsible for the impossibility. This is the old and new general rule of the BGB. Since, as explained, the main purpose of termination is to achieve just that, namely to extinguish the obligation to pay the price and to demand restitution, the question arises whether it is necessary to grant the creditor a right to termination where performance is impossible. The answer of the BGB is 'yes' and the relevant right is codified in § 326 V BGB. Sensibly, the provision releases the creditor from the requirement to set a period for performance. The reasons for this approach are threefold (see, eg, Huber and Faust, *Schuldrechtsmodernisierung* (2002), § 5 Rn. 63 *et seq*).

First, the right of termination fulfils a necessary and vital role in relation to non-conforming performance. It will be recalled that § 326 I 2 BGB excludes the application of § 326 I 1 BGB to non-conforming performance, ie, here the creditor is not automatically released from the obligation to pay the price. This concerns, for instance, the situation in sale of goods that a defect of the delivered goods cannot be cured because of impossibility. As we have seen, the debtor has a right to elect between price reduction and termination if the defect is sufficiently serious. It is in order not to prejudice this choice that § 326 I 2 BGB was introduced. As a consequence, it became necessary to grant the innocent party a right to terminate in cases of non-conforming performance where remedying the defect is impossible.

Secondly, where only part of the performance is impossible then only the right of termination in respect of the contract as a whole (§ 323 V 1 in conjunction with § 326 V BGB) ensures that the creditor is released from the obligation to pay the price as a whole.

However, the right of termination in § 326 V BGB is not limited to non-conforming and partial performance. Hence there must be a third reason for granting the right to justify this broader coverage of the right of termination. It is of a pragmatic nature. The provision enables the creditor in cases of doubt—ie, if it is not certain that impossibility releases the creditor according to § 326 I 1 BGB—to eliminate the obligation of counter-performance by setting a period for performance; if the debtor's failure to perform persists, the right of termination arises in any case. This strategy does not, however allow the creditor to make use of the exception to the requirement to set a period for performance. To be on the safe side, he must nevertheless set a period of grace. If performance turns out to have been impossible, the period of grace was superfluous but the right to terminate follows from § 326 V BGB. If performance was not impossible, the period of grace was essential and the right of termination follows from § 323 I BGB. The broad scope of the right of termination thus ensures that the remedies of the innocent party are, as far as possible, the same regardless of the reason for the absence of performance.

(v) Anticipatory Breach

Anticipatory breach is now expressly regulated in § 323 IV BGB. It entitles the creditor to terminate the contract if it is obvious that a breach of contract will occur that would entitle him to termination. The prognosis of breach must be derived from objective factors. (This is dealt with by UCC 2-609.) It is to be expected that the courts will adopt a similar approach to the prognosis as under Article 72 CISG; as to which see, Schlechtriem, *UN-Kaufrecht* (2nd edn, 2003), Rn. 269 *et seq*. Unlike the CISG, the anticipatory breach of the BGB need not be fundamental; if a partial non-performance is to be expected, then the criteria of § 323 V BGB apply.)

The paradigmatic case is a serious and final refusal to perform. This is not to be confused with § 323 II BGB. This provision exempts the creditor from the requirement of setting a period of grace if the debtor refuses to perform. It presupposes however that performance is due. In the case of anticipatory breach, the contract may be terminated before performance is due. (See, also, chapter 8, section 3(a), p 355, on the time of performance.)

On the English law on anticipatory breach, see Treitel, *The Law of Contract*, pp 857–65 and McKendrick, *Contract Law*, pp 975–85: rescission is available for anticipatory breach, but must fulfil the criteria for allowing such rescission as discussed above (although apparently not extending to the exception relating to the parties' express provision for determination in the contract: see *The Afovos* [1983] 1 WLR 195, at 203: 'it is to fundamental breaches alone that the doctrine of anticipatory breach is applicable' (*per* Lord Diplock). See Treitel's doubts, p 861). The more striking aspect of the English case law on anticipatory breach, stemming from the well known decision of *Hochster v De la Tour* (1853) 2 E & B 678, is that the creditor's acceptance of the anticipatory breach will entitle him to sue for damages immediately, even though the stipulated time for performance has yet to expire. This position has been criticised (for running the risk of an inaccurate quantification of damages and of bringing forward the debtor's obligation), but also defended. (Eg, for protecting the interest of the creditor who may lack the resources to procure replacement performance in time, in the absence of some compensation for the debtor's anticipatory breach—see Treitel, *The Law of Contract*, pp 859–60 and the references therein.)

(vi) Exclusion of the Right of Termination

Finally, § 323 VI BGB excludes the right of termination if the creditor is broadly speaking responsible for the failure of performance. The conditions are parallel to those provided for an automatic release of the obligation to pay the price in cases of impossibility of performance (§ 326 II BGB, see p 409 section 3(e)(ii)). The desire to achieve as much conformity as possible within the remedies available to the innocent party becomes once again apparent.

The first alternative concerns the situation that the creditor/innocent party is answerable or overwhelmingly responsible for the breach of contract by the debtor. This appears contradictory, but it is not if one remembers that breach is defined objectively as the absence or failure of performance. Consider, for instance, the duty of performance to cure defective goods and assume that the buyer has made it impossible to effect such cure (for instance, because he effected the cure himself). The failure to cure the defect constitutes a breach which would in principle entitle the buyer to terminate the contract (irrespective of fault of the seller), but since the creditor is responsible for the breach the right is excluded by § 323 VI BGB. The second alternative concerns the situation that the breach of contract occurred while the creditor was in delay of acceptance (*mora creditoris*, §§ 293 *et seq* BGB, discussed also above in the context of the effects of impossibility on the counter-performance). The prevailing view recognises a third qualification of the right of termination derived from good faith, § 242 BGB: the right to terminate the contract presupposes that the creditor has himself been on the whole faithful to the contract (*vertragtreu*). (See *Palandt*-Heinrichs, § 323 Rn. 29, and *Staudinger*-Löwisch, § 323 Rn. E11, for details.)

A possible English parallel to the first and/or the third alternatives discussed here may be the case where the creditor wrongfully refuses to allow the debtor to complete performance of the contract: in such situations, it seems that the debtor can claim a *quantum meruit* for the value of the work he has completed, which is founded not on the creditor's receipt of any benefit but on the creditor's wrongful refusal to allow the debtor to complete performance. See the much-discussed case of *Planché v Colburn* (1831) 8 Bing 14 (and cf *Whitaker v Dunn* (1887) 3 TLR 602, where very shoddily conducted building work was so bad that the creditor's refusal to allow the builder to complete was entirely justified and thus not wrongful in the circumstances. And see Restatement, Second, of Contracts 230(2)(a)(excusing non-occurrence of a condition when non-occurrence is a result of obligor's breach of duty of good faith and fair dealing).

(c) Duties of Protection (*Schutzpflichten*)

Paragraph 324 BGB entitles the creditor to terminate the contract even though the contract has been adhered to so far as the duties of performance (§ 241 I BGB) are concerned. In exceptional circumstances, the violation of protective duties (*Schutzpflichten*, § 241 II BGB) not to harm the interest of the other contracting parties may justify termination, provided that it cannot reasonably be expected that the creditor should abide by the contract. It is common ground that this must be limited to truly exceptional cases (eg, *Münchener Kommentar*- Ernst § 323 Rn. 7). The preparatory works (*Bundestags-Drucksache* 14/6040, p 141) give the example of a contractor who, while painting a flat as required, constantly and recklessly damaged other objects of the employer. Likewise, persistent or serious defamation of the creditor may also justify the termination of the contract.

(d) Consequences of Termination (*Rücktritt*)

Termination has two main purposes: to release the innocent party from the obligation to pay the price, and to put as far as possible matters back into the position in which they were before performance on both sides was begun. Accordingly, the effects of termination are twofold.

First, the duties of performance of the parties come to an end *ex nunc* (which is the same as the basic position under English law; cf *The Dominique* [1989] AC 1056 and, for a recent and interesting example, *Hurst v Bryk* [2002] 1 AC 185). This is not expressly stipulated, but is seen as obvious and clearly implicit in the German termination regime.

Secondly, the duties of performance are transformed or reversed into duties of restitution of performance. A so-called 'restitutionary relationship of obligation' arises

(*Rückgewährschuldverhältnis*). This regime of restitution makes it unnecessary (and indeed wrong) to fall back on the rules on unjustified enrichment. (§§ 812 *et seq* BGB do not apply. Note that the validity of the contract is not retroactively affected by termination, thus any performance already effectuated does not lack *causa*.) As also stated in the outline of the reform above, the effects of termination have been considerably simplified and 'streamlined' (Zimmermann, *Breach of Contract and Remedies* (Sapienza, Rome, 2002), p 42). Restitution is achieved in three steps, each of which corresponds roughly to one of the first three sub-paragraphs of § 346 BGB. In a nutshell: restoration of the performance is owed according to § 346 I BGB; if this is not possible, monetary compensation takes its place according to § 346 II BGB, which is itself excluded under certain conditions, § 346 III BGB.

The obligations of the parties pursuing termination to restore performance as far as possible are regulated in §§ 346–8 BGB, which apply to the statutory right of termination (ie, for breach of contract, § 323 BGB) and also to any expressly reserved right of termination. The synallagmatic character of the contract is also retained as far as the restitution of the performance is concerned. § 348 BGB declares the plea of an unperformed contract (§ 320 BGB, see chapter eight) applicable by analogy. According to § 346 I BGB, the general rule is that the parties are under a duty to return *in specie* whatever they may have already received from the other. For instance, if the seller of a car transferred property in the car and possession of it to the buyer, the latter must re-transfer property and hand over the car to the former. The obligations of § 433 I 1 BGB are thereby reversed.

In addition, the parties must hand over any benefits that they may have derived from the performance in the meantime (§ 346 BGB). What constitutes a relevant benefit is regulated by § 100 BGB. The paradigm case is the benefit of actually using or being able to use the subject matter of performance. § 347 BGB deals with the case where the innocent party failed to derive any of the benefits that a reasonable recipient of the performance would have derived. If the innocent party terminated the contract because of a breach of contract, the standard of liability applied is that of care that he usually uses in his own affairs (*diligentia quam in suis*, § 277 BGB).

If restitution *in specie* of the performance is not possible, § 346 II BGB stipulates that the party who cannot fulfil the obligation under § 346 I BGB is to compensate the other party in monetary terms for the value of the performance. The return may be excluded because of the very nature of what has been obtained (§ 346 II 1 Nr. 1 BGB). In our example, the *use* of a car cannot be returned *in specie*. Hence, the buyer must compensate the seller for the value of being able to use the car (the seller must do likewise in relation to having been able to use the money paid; ie, he will have to pay interest). The normal method of measuring the use of an object is by applying a linear measure and not by inquiring what the usual rental rate would be. The normal period of use is estimated and the price is then divided by that period (which price may be reduced to take account of a diminution in value of the object in question). The resulting figure is multiplied with the actual time of use of the object. (See for illustrations: BGH NJW 1991, 2484; NJW-RR 1995, 364; NJW 1996, 250.) If, for instance, an electrical appliance normally lasts for five years and the buyer actually used it for one year, he is under an obligation to the seller for one fifth of the contract price (subject to a reduction of that price due to a defect of the appliance). In the end the buyer can claim back only four-fifths of the contract price. However, in relation to the use of cars the relevant factor is not the time of being able to use the car, but the actual distance travelled with it. (See *Palandt*-Heinrichs, § 346 Rn. 10: the courts estimate as the value of the use of a car between 0.4 per cent and 1 per cent of the purchase price per 1000 km.)

Likewise, if the performance has been consumed or transferred (§ 346 II 1 Nr. 2 BGB), has deteriorated or has been destroyed (§ 346 II 1 Nr. 3 BGB), the obligation to compensate for the value of the performance arises. This constitutes a major change of approach by comparison with the old law. The destruction of the subject matter of the contract no longer hinders the exercise of the right of termination. The innocent party may terminate the contract even if in our example the buyer wilfully destroyed the purchased car. However, the buyer may be under a duty to compensate the seller for the value of the car. The price is to be taken into account in measuring the value of the car (§ 346 II 2 BGB; again the diminution in value due to a defect of the object must also be considered). Just as § 346 I BGB entitles the parties to restitution regardless of who committed the breach of contract, or of whether one of the parties was at fault in this respect, § 346 II BGB also imposes the obligation to compensate for the value of the performance regardless of whether the party obliged to return the performance was at fault or otherwise responsible for the deterioration or otherwise of performance. This is because the obligations under § 346 BGB simply represent a reversal of the duties of performance.

§ 346 III BGB contains a number of exceptions from the duty to compensate for the value of performance. The wording of the provision is quite clear. § 346 III 1 Nr. 1 BGB excludes the duty to compensate if the defect founding the right of termination showed itself for the first time while the object was transformed. § 346 III 1 Nr. 2 BGB excludes the duty if the creditor is responsible for the deterioration or if the harm would also have occurred in his hands. Finally, according to § 346 III 1 Nr. 3 BGB in the case of a statutory right of termination (ie, for breach of contract, § 323 BGB), there is no such duty where the deterioration or destruction occurred in the hands of the innocent party but he had observed that care that he usually applied in his own affairs (*diligentia quam in suis*, defined in § 277 BGB). Any remaining enrichment must be returned notwithstanding, § 346 III 2 BGB.

Nevertheless, § 346 III 1 Nr. 3 BGB has given rise to controversy following the recent reform. The focus of the controversy is whether it is in fact satisfactory that the innocent party is released from the obligation to compensate. The risk of accidental destruction of the object is thus not, as one would expect, on the owner, but on the 'guilty' party. Since it is commonly assumed that with the handing over of the subject matter of the contract to the promisee the risk of accidental destruction is borne by the promisee or owner of the thing, the risk is said 'to jump back' to the promisor. In our example, if the buyer terminated the contract for breach by the seller (the so-called 'statutory' ground for termination as opposed to an expressly reserved right of termination), the buyer could claim back the purchase price even though the car had been destroyed by accident (fire, lightning etc). On closer analysis, the promisee is privileged even further. For even if he destroyed the car negligently, he may be released if the standard of care shown was that of 'light' negligence as occurs also in relation to his own affairs (§ 277 BGB). To come back to our example, if the buyer clumsily, only 'lightly' negligently, damaged the car, then he is even released from the obligation to compensate for the deterioration of the car. The ordinary use of the object as such does never constitute gross negligence. If on the occasion of such use it is destroyed without fault of the innocent party the privilege of § 346 III 1 Nr. 3 BGB applies with full force (cf eg, *Palandt*-Heinrichs, § 346 Rn. 13).

The obvious objection to this approach is that the object is in the 'sphere of influence' of the innocent party who has complete control over it. (See, for criticism of the rule, eg, Gaier WM 2002, 11; Kaiser JZ 2001, 1057; Kohler AcP 203 (2003) 539. Article 1647 of the French Civil Code, for instance, also establishes a rule different from § 346 III 1 Nr. 3 BGB.) The justification of the approach adopted *de lege lata* is however easily discerned. After all, the 'innocent' party terminated the contract because of a breach of contract of the 'guilty' party. This means in our example that the seller has not fully performed his obligations. Therefore, it is considered appropriate that the risk of accidental destruction is to be borne by the 'guilty' party rather than the actual possessor of the object. (See Zimmermann, *The Law of Obligations* (1990), p 330 *et seq* for the origins in Roman law of this so-called *mortuus redhibetur* rule.)

Article 82 CISG opts for a more nuanced solution. In a first step, the right of avoidance is excluded if it is impossible for the buyer to make restitution of the goods substantially in the condition in which he received them. However, this exclusionary rule does not apply (ie, avoidance is possible despite the fact that restitution is not possible) if the buyer has not by his own conduct increased the risk of destruction: Article 82(2). Thus, in our example an accidental destruction by lightning would not exclude the right to avoid the contract. (See for details: Schlechtriem, *UN-Kaufrecht*, Rn. 326 *et seq*.) This approach was expressly rejected in the preparatory works as it would give rise to difficult distinctions (see *Bundestags-Drucksache* 14/6040, p 196): provided that the buyer was not at 'fault', it was not easy to see why it should matter whether the destruction of the car in our example was due to a traffic accident or a fire in the garage. Applying Article 82 CISG, it appears that in the first case the destruction was due to an act of the buyer while in the latter it was not. § 346 III 1 Nr. 3 BGB was phrased such that the two examples are to be treated in the same way.

An important caveat must be added at this stage. Once the innocent party actually terminates the contract, the situation is different. From the moment termination is declared, the innocent party is bound by the obligation to restitution of § 346 I BGB. If this duty is violated, the innocent party becomes liable in damages according to § 346 IV in conjunction with §§ 280 I, 283 BGB. In our example, if the buyer, after he has declared termination, damages the car negligently in a traffic accident, he is liable in damages to the seller for failing to return the car in the original condition. The standard of care implied by § 280 I 2 BGB is that of the general rule in § 276 BGB. 'Light negligence' suffices. Yet, the risk of accidental destruction remains, according to the wording of § 346 III 1 Nr. 3 BGB, on the 'guilty party.'

It should not be concealed that the rules just described have not escaped criticism and proposals have been made to restrict the scope of application of these provisions. Most of them suggest that once the innocent party knows of the right of termination or could have known of it, the privilege is not appropriate. From then on, the exclusion of the duty to compensate should not apply (eg, Gaier in *Münchener Kommentar*, § 346 Rn. 59). Hence, the controversies surrounding the *mortuus redhibetur* rule, which had rendered the previous position of German law so very uncertain, unfortunately, seem to resurface in relation to the new law. This is somewhat surprising given the clear wording and unequivocal intention of the legislator. (Such attempts to restrict § 346 III BGB are opposed on this ground by, among others, Lorenz and Riehm, *Lehrbuch zum neuen Schuldrecht* (2002) Rn. 434; *Palandt*-Heinrichs, § 346 Rn. 13.)

The English regime that follows rescission does bear some similarities to the German approach set out above. Thus, if the innocent buyer wishes to claim the return of his purchase price, he must return what he has acquired under the contract so as to effect a total failure of consideration and make good his restitutionary claim (see eg, *Baldry v Marshall* [1925] 1 QB 260; and generally, Treitel, *The Law of Contract*, pp 1049–57). Further, if it proves impossible to return the benefit received due to the defect that gave rise to the right to rescind (eg, non-conforming goods or goods to which the seller did not have title to sell: see *Rowland v Divall* [1923] 2 KB 500) or due to a cause beyond the control of either party (*Head v Tattersall* (1871) LR 7 Ex 7) then there is no duty to return that which was acquired as a precondition for the recovery of the purchase price. However, the major difference is that the basic remedy even on termination is a claim for damages; although it should be noted that the innocent party can elect not to rescind the contract and can instead continue to press for performance, this will most commonly end up in a subsequent action for damages for breach in any case. See generally, Treitel, *The Law of Contract*, pp 850–5 and chapter 21, section one on 'Damages'; the instructive judgments of Lord Diplock in both *Lep Air Services v Rolloswin Investments Ltd* [1973] AC 331 (especially 350–5) and *Photo Production Ltd v Securicor Transport Ltd* [1980] AC 827 will repay careful reading on these matters. Such damages liability can cover both loss suffered due to breaches prior to rescission and due to the repudiation of subsequent primary obligations, even though those primary obligations of performance are no longer due once rescission has been effected by the innocent party. (An interesting problem that has risen in America is whether an insured may recover premiums on breach (failure to pay a claim) by the insurer without a deduction for the value of insurance coverage received; cf *Bollenback v Continental Cas*, 243 Or 498, 414 P 2d 806 (1966). The Restatement, Third, Restitution and Unjust Enrichment § 37 permits a restitution claim when performance cannot be returned in kind and even if there is a benefit of inestimable value that cannot be restored.)

(e) Continuing Contracts (*Dauerschuldverhältnisse*)

A final word must be said regarding so-called 'continuing contracts' (*Dauerschuldverhältnisse*), ie contracts which are not fulfilled by single acts of performance on each side, but which require continuing acts of performance over a period of time, such as leases (*Miete*), usufructuary leases (*Pacht*), contracts of partnership (*Gesellschaft*) and contracts of labour (*Dienstvertrag*). It is important to observe that these contracts are not subjected to the regime of restitution described in the previous section.

Such long-term relationships may run for a stipulated period of time or for an indeterminate period of time. In the latter case, both parties may terminate the contract with effects for the future by giving notice, provided that certain time limits are observed in providing notice in advance. These time periods for advance notice vary according to the nature of the contract and the party seeking termination. Thus, for instance, employer and employee must respect different time limits (cf § 622 BGB, the postponement of the effect of the termination by the employer depends on for how many years the employee was employed). This right to give notice is commonly referred to as the ordinary right to terminate such continuing contracts (*ordentliche Kündigung*). It does not presuppose a breach of contract by the other party.

Termination however is also a remedy for breach in relation to this type of contract. A special right of termination may arise because of a breach of contract in relation to continuing contracts. It is referred to as an 'extra-ordinary right to give notice' (*außerordentliche Kündigung*). In these legal relationships, the legislator in § 314 I BGB has envisaged situations in which, for serious cause, notice may be given to terminate the contract without observing any term of notice. The pre-requisite of the right to give notice is a serious breach of contract (*wichtiger Grund*). It should be noted that this is more difficult to establish than meeting the requirement of seriousness in relation to non-conforming performance under § 323 V 2 BGB. According to § 314 I 2 BGB, all the circumstances of the individual case must be taken into consideration and, in balancing the interests of both sides, the continuation of the contractual relationship until the agreed termination date or until the expiry of a notice period cannot be expected of the party giving notice. The general right to give notice in § 314 BGB is supplemented and to a considerable extent replaced by special rules in relation to specific instances of continuing contracts: eg, §§ 543, 569, 581 II, 626, 723–4 BGB (some of which have been discussed in chapter 3). (See as to the remaining scope of application, Looschelders, *Schuldrecht Allgemeiner Teil*, Rn. 794 *et seq.*)

In these cases of 'termination by notice' (*Kündigung*), the legal relationship ends when notice is received by the other party (§ 130 BGB; see chapter 2 for the problem of when a declaration of will takes effect). It operates only in respect of performances not yet due at the time of termination (Larenz, *Schuldrecht I, Allgemeiner Teil*, 415–17). It follows that performance which was due, but had not yet been rendered, must still be made (as under English law: see the comments in section 4(d), above). The reason why *Kündigung* of a continuing contract has no retrospective effect must be sought in the fact that, for all practical purposes, the many acts of performance on each side which have taken place in the past cannot be ignored because this has happened within the framework of a functioning legal relationship. The termination of such continuing contract, therefore, does not as a general rule lead to restitution of past performance. It simply brings to an end the duties of performance from the moment of termination onwards.

5. DAMAGES

Altmeppen, 'Schadensersatz wegen Pflichtverletzung- Ein Beispiel für die Überhastung der Schuldrechtsreform' DB 2001, 1131; Canaris, 'Begriff und Tatbestand des Verzögerungsschadens im neuen Leistungsstörungsrecht' ZIP 2003, 321; Deutsch, 'Die Fahrlässigkeit im neuen Schuldrecht' AcP 202 (2002) 889; Gsell, 'Aufwendungsersatz nach § 284 BGB' in Dauner-Lieb, Konzen and Karsten Schmidt (eds), *Das neue Schuldrecht in der Praxis* (2003) 312; Grigoleit and Riehm, 'Die

Kategorien des Schadensersatzes im Leistungsstörungsrecht' AcP 203 (2003) 727; Hirsch, 'Schadensersatz statt der Leistung' Jura 2003, 289; Honsell, 'Herkunft und Kritik des Interessebegriffs im Schadensersatzrecht' JuS 1973, 69; U Huber, 'Die Pflichtverletzung als Grundtatbestand der Leistungsstörung im Diskussionsentwurf eines Schuldrechtsmodernisierungsgesetzes' ZIP 2000, 2273; U Huber, 'Normzwecktheorie und Adäquanztheorie' JZ 1969, 677; Jones and Schlechtriem, 'Breach of Contract' in *International Encyclopedia of Comparative Law*, vol VII, chapter 15 (1999), para 203 *et seq*; Kohler, 'Das Vertretenmüssen beim verzugsrechtlichen Schadensersatz' JZ 2004, 961; Lange and Schiemann, *Schadensersatz* (2nd edn, 2003); Larenz, 'Die Prinzipien der Schadenszurechnung' JuS 1965, 373; Looschelders, *Die Mitverantwortlichkeit des Geschädigten im Privatrecht* (1999); S Lorenz, 'Schadensersatz statt der Leistung, Rentabilitätsvermutung und Aufwendungsersatz im Gewährleistungsrecht' NJW 2004, 26; E Lorenz, 'Die Haftung für Erfüllungsgehilfen' in *50 Jahre Bundesgerichtshof*, vol I (2000) 329; Medicus, 'Normativer Schaden' JuS 1979, 233; Medicus, 'Naturalrestitution und Geldersatz' JuS 1969, 449; Medicus, 'Geld muß man haben. Unvermögen und Schuldnerverzug beim Geldmangel' AcP 188 (1988) 489; Schlechtriem, 'Schadensersatz und Schadensbegriff' ZEuP 1997, 322; Stoppel, 'Der Ersatz frustrierter Aufwendungen nach § 284 BGB' AcP 204 (2004) 81; Treitel, 'Remedies for Breach of Contract' in *International Encyclopedia of Comparative Law*, vol VII, chapter 16 (1976) para 40 *et seq*; Wagner, 'Das Zweite Schadensersatzrechtsänderungsgesetz' NJW 2002, 2049.

(a) Preliminary Observations

The recent reform has completely reshaped the right of a promisee to recover damages. Whatever may have been the merits of the previous fragmented approach, the present system is concise and reduces the number of rules needed considerably. This has been achieved by adopting a general rule with a limited number of qualifications in the general part of the law of contract, which also applies in relation to non-conforming performance. In order to enhance consistency between the remedies for breach of contract, the conditions for the application of the right to claim damages have been adjusted—with one notable exception (namely fault)—to align them with those of the remedies of termination and price reduction. The result can, with some measure of justification, now be regarded as a model approach for a legal system that adheres to the fault principle in respect of liability in damages and at the same time recognises the primacy of the right to demand performance *in specie*.

From a theoretical perspective, the combination of these two elements places German law in a diametrically opposed position to Anglo-American law. However, this different starting position may make comparison with the common law interesting and perhaps instructive. Given these differences in 'starting points,' the discovery of convergences between the systems may prove particularly rewarding, reinforcing a point often made in this book, namely that things are not always what they appear to be at first sight. But, where they persist, differences of structure, result or methodology also have the merit of challenging the outside observer to understand their rational and compare it to his own.

A few words may be appropriate to explain the unsatisfactory state of affairs *before the reform*. The Code as it was originally conceived devoted special attention to two types of irregularities of performance—namely, delay by the debtor and impossibility—and arguably neglected other types of irregularity of performance. This had already given rise, just a few years after the enactment of the Code, to a misunderstanding of far-reaching effects. The misconception was that other types of irregularities of performance were not provided for in the Code, or at least not in a principled fashion. The Code was said to have a 'gap' (Staub first made this contention in his highly influential *Die positiven Vertragsverletzungen* in 1902 (2nd edn, 1904). The courts responded to this academic criticism of the BGB and recognised a third category, purportedly not regulated in the Code, usually referred to as 'positive breach of contract.' The hypothesis that the drafters of the BGB had overlooked the irregularity of performance, later to be coined *positive Vertragsverletzung*, was peculiar, considering the dimensions of the apparent gap. Is it realistic to claim that the drafters of the BGB did not cater for instance for the possibility that a contract of service is badly performed? It is therefore somewhat surprising that it was not until Ulrich Huber's treatise *Leistungsstörungen* in 1999 that a fully fledged attempt was made to show that the BGB did indeed include rules for dealing with other categories of irregularity of performance (see chapter 3 of vol 1). His central thesis was that the old § 276 included not only the fault principle, but the general rule that a breach of contract entailed liability *in damages* (now codified in § 280). Huber claimed (at p 80) that this was self-evident to the drafters of the BGB and therefore they did not consider it necessary to use express words to that effect in the final version. There is something of a Gothic drama in this story of a collective and massive misunderstanding put right by an erudite academic just as the whole world of yesterday was brought to a close. But to most common law readers it will, at most, bring a wry smile to their lips. If it proves anything, it is that much though legal rules may converge, national temperaments remain solidly immutable!

It may be useful to give at this stage a brief overview of the central aspects of the *new* approach to liability (see Figure 3).

Paragraph 280 I BGB now contains the general rule that a breach of duty gives rise to liability in damages if the guilty party was answerable for it (fault principle). As already emphasised, the provision is of wider application than breach of contract, since it also covers non-contractual breaches of duty. For instance, it applies to liability derived from *culpa in contrahendo* (§ 311 II BGB, on which see chapter 2, p 91 ff) and it also comes into play if the obligations resulting from *negotiorum gesto* (§ 677 BGB) are breached. (On *negotiorum gestio*, see Dawson, 'Negotiorum Gestio: The Altruistic Intermeddler' (1960–61) 74 *Harvard LR* 817 and 1073; Stoljar, 'Unjust Enrichment and Negotiorum Gestio' in *International Encyclopedia of Comparative Law*, vol X, chapter 17 (1984) and Muir, 'Unjust Sacrifice and the Officious Intervener' 297 ff in Finn (ed), *Essays on Restitution* (1990).) Note however that tort liability is regulated separately in §§ 823 *et seq* BGB. In this chapter, we will focus on liability for breach of contract.

The general principle of liability in damages in § 280 I BGB is qualified in six respects:

(1) If damages instead of performance are sought, the innocent party must set a period for performance and only if the guilty party fails to perform by the end of that period, ie, the breach persists, does the guilty part become liable, §§ 280 III, 281 BGB.

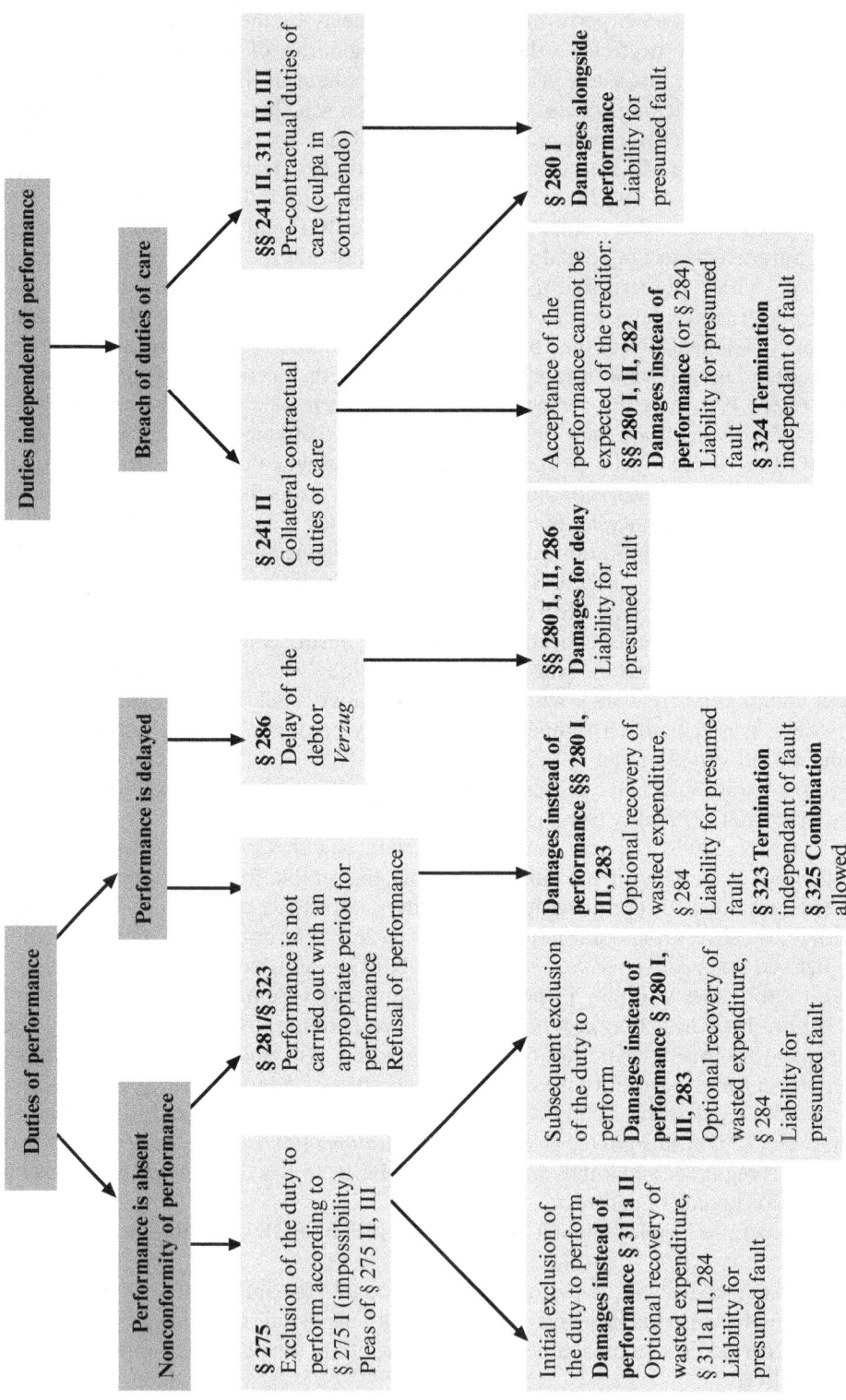

Fig. 3: Liability for breach of duty (*Pflichtverletzung*) (§ 280)*

* Reproduced with kind permission of Professor Stephan Lorenz.

(2) Any damages flowing from the delay of performance may be claimed separately according to §§ 280 II and 286 BGB once the debtor is in default (*mora debitoris*).

(3) If performance is impossible, to request it would be futile. So, the combined effect of §§ 280 III and 283 BGB, grants the innocent party an immediate right to recover damages calculated on his expectation interest.

(4) §§ 280 III, in conjunction with 282 BGB, extends this right to cases in which certain ancillary duties of protection have been infringed.

(5) § 311a II BGB contains a separate set of rules dealing with liability for initial impossibility.

(6) Finally, alternatively to damages instead of performance any expenditure made in reliance on the contract may be recovered: § 284 BGB.

It is already apparent from this brief survey that the right to recover damages is to the fore and the different categories of irregularities of performance only affect the conditions of recovery in order to maintain the prevalence of enforced performance. As a result, the Code now recognises three main different types of damages, namely: damages *instead* of performance in § 280 III, damages for *delay* in § 280 II and damages *alongside* performance or 'simple' damages according to § 280 I. (For an overview, see eg, *Staudinger*-Otto, (2004), § 280 Rn. E1 *et seq.*) Understanding the differences between these different heads of damages is also 'the key' to the new system of liability (Zimmermann, *Breach of Contract and Remedies* (Sapienza, Rome, 2002), p 20; Grigoleit and Riehm, AcP 203 (2003) 730, who rightly warn against interpreting the new in the light of the old).

Before we turn to the specific requirements of liability it is necessary to make two further preliminary observations in order to avoid misunderstandings.

First, the question must be addressed whether the German idea of *Schadensersatz* with which we are here concerned is in fact an equivalent of the Anglo-American notion of 'damages', ie, *monetary compensation* for breach of contract. §§ 280 *et seq.* BGB simply state that the creditor may claim *Schadensersatz* but they do not define the term. What the concept of damages in German law signifies can be discovered by looking at §§ 249–54 BGB.

The starting point and general rule is the principle of *Naturalherstellung*, now contained in § 249 I BGB. According to this principle, the debtor is under an obligation to bring about the state of affairs that would have existed had the circumstance giving rise to liability not occurred. (See, eg, Treitel, *Encyclopedia*, para 12, who discusses the principle in the context of enforced performance.) Three exceptions are made. First, if a person has been injured or physical damage to things has occurred § 249 II BGB entitles the aggrieved party to a substitutionary relief in money. Apart from that, it seems that the Code grants the right to claim *Schadensersatz in Geld* ('monetary compensation') only and in an exceptional fashion if a period for actual restoration has been set in vain (§ 250 BGB) or if actual restoration is impossible or insufficient (§ 251 BGB).

At first sight this could give the impression that 'damages' in German law are not primarily monetary relief, but rather are another variant of specific performance. In relation to breach of contract, this impression would be entirely wrong. It must be conceded, however, that the expression *Schadensersatz* in German law covers more than monetary compensation and if an exact equivalent of the English technical term 'damages' is sought, the term *Schadensersatz in Geld* is to be preferred. However, damages awarded for a failure of performance and as a substitute for performance are to all intents and purposes *Schadensersatz in Geld*. The apparent exception is the general rule so far as breach of contract is concerned. We have therefore used the term 'damages' throughout, although the reader should be aware that differences as to the actual consequences of the remedy damages in English law might exist in particular circumstances.

It is not difficult to see why monetary compensation is the form of relief for breach of contract so far as the right to claim *Schadensersatz* is concerned. If the principle of *Naturalrestitution* were to be applied to breach of contract, this would mean that the regime of enforced performance (the 'primary' right or *Leistungsanspruch*, § 241 I BGB) examined above would be duplicated. This would be contrary to the very essence of the remedy of damages. A claim for damages is the exercise of a 'secondary' right, which awards the aggrieved party a *substitute* for performance. It is therefore common ground that the remedy of damages in place of performance (*Schadensersatz statt der Leistung*; previously called *Schadensersatz wegen Nichterfüllung*) as well as damages for delay (*Verzögerungsschaden*) entitles the claimant to the protection of his expectation interest in monetary terms. (See Treitel, *Encylopedia*, para 12; Lorenz and Riehm, *Lehrbuch zum neuen Schuldrecht* (2002), Rn. 206. See however Lange and Schiemann, *Schadensersatz* (3rd edn, 2003), p 220; *Staudinger*-Otto, § 280 Rn. E81, who wish to retain exceptions to the general rule. In the past, these exceptions concerned primarily the interest of the creditor to be actually provided with what he bargained for during periods of crises in which goods were in short supply. Whether it is still necessary to retain this exception in addition to the remedy of enforced performance is doubtful.) If one were to pin this self-evident result on a provision in the Code, one could in cases of impossibility derive it from § 275 BGB and in all other cases from § 281 IV BGB: claiming damages instead of performance excludes the right to claim performance. In other words, if the promisee claims the performance and not monetary compensation he is not enforcing the remedy of damages.

We can therefore conclude that the aim of the remedy of damages for breach of contract is to protect the expectation interest (*Erfüllungsinteresse*) by the means of a substitutionary relief in money; that is 'to put the aggrieved party into as good a *financial* position as that in which he would have been if the contract had been duly performed' (Treitel, *Encyclopedia*, para 49, emphasis added; for details, see below). In this sense, the positions of German law and of the common law converge: 'the rule of the common law is, that where a party sustains a loss by reason of a breach of contract, he is, in so far as money can do it, to be placed in the same position, with respect to damages, as if the contract had been performed' (*Robinson v Harman* (1848) 1 Ex 850, 855 *per* Parke, B).

Insofar as a breach of contract causes damage to interests or rights other than the expectation interest (referred to as the interest in the integrity of these rights and interests, *Integritätsinteresse*), § 249 II BGB will often apply and this will also result in monetary compensation (see section 5(h)(iii), p 471, for details).

This situation must be distinguished from others in which a disappointed party may only recover wasted expenditure (*negatives Interesse* or *Vertrauensschaden*). Where such 'reliance loss' may be claimed, generally speaking the plaintiff is put into the position in which he would have been if the intended contract had never been concluded. In German law, as we have seen in chapter 6, the *Vertrauensschaden* may be remedied by a right to set the contract aside (*culpa in contrahendo*, explained on the basis of *Naturalrestitution*). However, insofar as wasted expenditure for breach of contract is claimed, the award will invariably take the form of monetary compensation (§ 284 BGB: *Aufwendungsersatz*). It should be observed at the outset, however, that § 284 BGB protects not the reliance on the contract, but reliance on its *performance*—it is therefore not to be equated with the protection of the reliance interest (details below). (In English law see, eg, *Cullinane v British 'REMA' Manufacturing Co Ltd* [1954] 1 QB 292, 303, *per* Lord Evershed MR. In *Anglia Television Ltd. v Reed* [1972] 1 QB 60, the damages awarded were the expense lost as a result of the breach. Thus they included pre-contractual expenditures made worthless by the breach.)

The second general comment concerns the *nature and purpose* of a monetary award.

Damages are first and foremost compensatory (Lange and Schiemann, *Schadensersatz* , p 9: '*Ausgleichsprinzip*'; the same is true for English law; see Treitel, *Encylopedia*, para 42 *et seq*). Damages are based on the loss of the promisee and do not exceed that loss. This excludes, firstly, damages calculated by reference to the loss of a third party. (There is a limited exception to this rule, which has been discussed in chapter 4, section 4, p 216; whether a similar principle of 'transferred loss' operates in English law is uncertain: see Unberath, *Transferred Loss* (2003).)

Secondly, damages are calculated by reference to the loss of the promisee and not by looking at what the promisor gained from the breach. In other words, damages are not awarded on a *restitutionary* basis. 'Restitution' aims at depriving the defendant of a benefit obtained at the expense of the plaintiff (although some would distinguish between 'restitution' and 'disgorgement', with the former covering subtraction of wealth from the claimant, but only the latter depriving the recipient of the benefit of profits made: see LD Smith, 'The Province of the Law of Restitution' [1992] *Canadian Bar Rev* 672; see further McInnes, " 'At the Plaintiff's Expense": Quantifying Restitutionary Relief' [1998] *CLJ* 472 and Burrows, *The Law of Restitution* (2nd edn, 2002), pp 25–31; Restatement, Third, Restitution and Unjust Enrichment draws this distinction in §§ 37 and 38 (restoration remedy) and § 39 (disgorgement of profits from opportunistic breach).) English contract law has not generally recognised this restitutionary purpose of an award of damages either (see eg, *Surrey CC and Mole DC v Bredero Homes Ltd* [1993] 1 WLR 1361), but has shown some (albeit limited and guarded) signs of change in recent times (see *Jaggard v Sawyer* [1995] 1 WLR 269, and in particular, *Attorney-General v Blake* [2001] 1 AC 268. The last of these has recently been considered and applied in *Experience Hendrix LLC v PPX Enterprises Inc* [2003] Fleet Street Reports 46; EWCA Civ 323 (noted by Graham (2004) 120 LQR 26) and *Severn Trent Water Ltd v Barnes* [2004] 2 EGLR 95; EWCA Civ 570). For discussion, see generally, Treitel, *The Law of Contract*, pp 928–32 and Edelman, *Gain-Based Damages* (2002). If the breach occasioned a profit to the guilty party, this profit will not be considered in calculating damages. It should be noted, however, that the *commodum ex negotiatione* may be recoverable under § 285 BGB (see p 407). If performance is impossible due to a transaction with a third party the price paid by that party to the promisor may then be claimed by the promisee. (The issue is controversial, see *Münchener Kommentar* § 285 Rn. 19.)

Finally, damages are not awarded to *penalise* the contract breaker (cf *Motive*, vol 2, at p 17 ff). Punitive or exemplary damages are not awarded. (German courts are remarkably hostile even towards the mere *execution* of *foreign* (typically US) judgments containing an award of punitive damages, eg, BGHZ 118, 312 = JZ 1993, 261.) It should be noted however that German law has no difficulty in giving full effect to *penalty clauses*. §§ 336–345 BGB contain the applicable rules. Particularly noteworthy in this regard is § 343 BGB, which entitles the guilty party to have the penalty reduced by the court to a 'reasonable' amount if it is found to be disproportionate. Penalty clauses in standard term contracts between dealer and consumer must meet the further requirements of § 309 Nr. 6 BGB (see the general discussion on assessing the fairness of standard terms in chapter 3, section 5(d), p 175. On this particular issue, see the UK's Unfair Terms in Consumer Contracts Regulations 1999, reg 5(2) and Schedule 2, para 1(e): a clause is prima facie unfair if it requires 'any consumer who fails to fulfil his obligation to pay a disproportionately high sum in compensation'). The common law has in principle been wary of so-called 'penalty clauses' that allow recovery by the claimant of a sum far in excess of his actual loss: the courts will not tolerate a clause providing for 'a payment of money stipulated as *in terrorem* of the offending party' (*Dunlop Pneumatic Tyre Co Ltd v New Garage & Motor Co Ltd* [1915] AC 79, at 86). However, clauses that have made a genuine advance attempt to estimate the loss that breach might cause will be enforced, even if the actual loss that has eventuated does not correspond exactly to the value thus estimated (see eg, *Robophone Facilities Ltd v Blank* [1966] 1 WLR 1428). Further, the courts have made it clear that they are reluctant to second-guess agreements reached by the parties on this issue: the burden of showing the penal nature of such a clause agreeing a sum to be paid on breach is most definitely on the party seeking to avoid the application of that clause, and where the parties are of equal bargaining power that burden will not be easy to discharge (*Philips Hong Kong Ltd v Attorney General of Hong Kong* (1993) 61 BLR 41 (especially at 55 and 61, *per* Lord Woolf)). Thus, once these caveats in English law are borne in mind, and once the proportionality criterion of German law is applied, it may well be that the apparently substantial difference in starting points between English and German law is in practice significantly reduced. (For further discussion of this issue, see Treitel, *The Law of Contract*, pp 999–1007; McKendrick, *Contract Law*, pp 1096–1104 and the Law Commission, *Penalty Clauses and Forfeiture of Monies Paid* (Working Paper No 61, 1975).)

(b) The 'Fault Principle'

Paragraph 280 I 2 BGB presupposes that, for the right to claim damages to be exercised by the creditor, the debtor is *answerable* for the breach (see also § 311a II 2 BGB for initial impossibility and § 286 IV BGB for damages for delay). The fault principle is of axiomatic character for German law. Its codal ramification is § 276 BGB. The debtor is answerable for *intention* and *negligence*, provided that no stricter or more lenient liability is either expressly determined or to be inferred from the content of the obligation, in particular from the adoption of a guarantee or the assumption of a risk of procurement. In a nutshell: in the absence of any provision to the contrary, in the individual case liability in damages is fault-dependent. As noted previously in this chapter, the main difference between the conditions for the application of the remedy of termination (and price reduction) and that of damages is that the latter presupposes fault—ie, that the debtor is answerable for the breach—whereas the former does not require that the 'guilty' party is answerable for the breach.

There are other significant inroads into the fault principle, but neither the first (*Abschlußbericht* (1992), p 123) nor the second Law Reform Commission (*Bundestags-Drucksache* 14/6040, p 131) went so far as to recommend abolishing it altogether. Yet both commissions stressed that the differences from the common law 'guarantee'-type of liability were 'not great' (making reference to Zweigert and Kötz, *Comparative Law* (3rd edn, 1998, translated by Weir), p 510). An influential member of the second commission subsequently emphasised repeatedly the 'obvious ethical superiority' of the fault principle (Canaris, eg, *Festschrift* (2005), 1, 22; similarly: *Bundestags-Drucksache* 14/6040, p 165). It would be self-evident that a promisor could be held liable for a breach for which he was 'responsible', whereas it would require justification holding him (strictly) liable for a guarantee. Huber also argued that the 'principle of fairness' requires that the promisor does not undertake a guarantee for performance whatever the nature of the impediment; hence the fault principle was the better approach (*Leistungsstörungen*, vol 1 (1999), p 31; though in his original report of 1981 he had suggested departing from it: *Gutachten*, p 673). With all respect, this argument proceeds on a very narrow view of the common law type of 'guarantee' liability. The days where, in the interest of the protection of the public against fraud, the liability of certain promisors (like 'common carriers') was considered to be absolute are long gone. (See, for the early approaches, Ibbetson, 'Absolute Liability in Contract' in Rose (ed), *Essays in the Honour of Guenter Treitel* (1996), p 1.) 'Strict' or 'guarantee' liability does not impose liability on the promisor whatever the circumstances of the breach. A variety of 'excuses' are recognised (for instance, frustration). Article 79 CISG is a paradigm example of this approach, which allows the debtor to object to liability because an impediment to performance occurred which was beyond his control. The common law thus also presupposes that the guilty party is 'responsible' for the breach (see generally, Treitel, *The Law of Contract*, pp 838–42). The difference merely lies in the definition of 'those impediments to performance for which the obligor will be held legally responsible and those for which he will be excused,' while in practical terms it is immaterial whether the prerequisites for liability are part of the content of the promisor's obligation or as a negative condition of liability (Jones and Schlechtriem, *Encyclopaedia*, para 203).

Further, there are many instances where liability for breach of contract under the common law requires a measure of fault: these occur where the nature of the contract itself presupposes that a standard of reasonable care must be met. Thus, under section 13 of the Sale and Supply of Goods Act 1982 it is provided that in 'a contract for the supply of a service where the supplier is acting in the course of business, there is an implied term that the supplier will carry out the service with reasonable care and skill.' However, section 16(3)(a) of the same Act makes clear that the Act does not exclude 'any rule of law which imposes on a supplier a stricter duty.' Thus, the final standard of care to be satisfied will depend on whether any pre-existing and stricter common law duty might apply to the provision of such services: hence, section 13 provides a default standard. See Treitel, *The Law of Contract*, pp 840–2 and Powell and Stewart (gen eds), *Jackson & Powell on Professional Negligence* (5th edn, 2001), paras 2-116–2-124 for further details. According to *Jackson & Powell*, the test of the standard of 'reasonable care and skill' (whether expressed under the law tort, the law of contract or under statute) is: 'that degree of skill and care which is ordinarily exercised by reasonably competent members of the profession, who have the same rank and profess the same specialisation (if any) as the defendant' (para. 2-120 (footnote omitted)). Clearly (para. 2-124), this standard will change over time as advances in skills, techniques, equipment and knowledge are made. (See chapter 10, section 4, p 528, for discussion of some of these aspects in their specific context.) Given the generality of section 13 of the 1982 Act, combined with the willingness of the courts at common law to conduct a similar exercise of implication of such terms in appropriate circumstances, it can be seen that a significant field of English contract law involves the application of a fault standard before breach can be shown.

It is generally agreed in the civil law systems, and is at least the majority opinion in the common law systems, that contract law ought to protect the expectation interest (though attempts to rationalise contract on the basis of reliance are frequent: see, eg, the influential article of Fuller and Perdue, 'The Reliance Interest in Contract Damages' (1936) 46 *Yale LJ* 52). The principle of *pacta sunt servanda* requires as much. There are many quite different ways to achieve this protection. It is difficult to derive a specific rule, *a priori*, with logical necessity, from the principle, as Huber (*Leistungsstörungsrecht*, vol 1, p 27) also concedes; obviously, history and coincidence also play a role. In particular, it would be wrong to discuss the fault principle solely against the background of the damages remedy. The civil law recognises other (in the eyes of a common lawyer quite drastic) methods of protecting the expectation of the promisee to get what he bargained for. The regime of enforced performance, as well as the remedies of termination and price reduction, are all independent of fault and are geared towards this aim. The common law does not—with the exception of termination—fully recognise these remedies. (See also the discussion in section 3, p 399.)

Hence, if one adds to this the many qualifications of the fault principle in the civil law and contrasts them with the limitations of the common law regime of strict liability, it becomes increasingly difficult to claim that one or the other approach is in the end 'ethically superior' over the other. Important differences remain, of course, and the precise degree of convergence is a matter of some speculation. The thesis seems plausible that the civil law can more easily 'afford' to expand the range of excuses available to a promisor because it gives efficacy to a strict regime of enforced performance and entitles the aggrieved party to the remedy of termination (and, in cases of non-conforming performance, to price reduction) irrespective of fault.

In what follows, we need to clarify the nature and ambit of the fault principle, the variations of this principle in the BGB and the exceptions from it.

(i) Elements of Fault

The first point to make is that according to § 276 I BGB fault covers intentional conduct as well as negligence. The relevance of fault is lessened by the rules as to the discharge of the burden of proof. The negative wording of § 280 I 2 BGB indicates that it is presumed that the debtor is answerable for the breach (the same is true for § 311 II 2 and § 286 IV BGB). German law thus imposes liability for presumed fault; ie it is for the debtor to show that he has not been at fault if he wishes to escape liability. (See BGHZ 8, 239, case no 117 for an illustration. The case further shows that in certain situations a 'prima facie proof' may be available which makes it easier to establish fault.)

Intention requires knowledge of all relevant factual circumstances as well as knowledge of the obligations of the promisor. The first source of a relevant defence is thus ignorance of, or wrongful assumptions as to, the real state of affairs. The debtor can be mistaken in law or in fact. Intention is excluded but the debtor will be held liable if he was negligent in making the mistake.

If the debtor errs in respect of his obligation—ie, makes a *mistake of law*—he does not act intentionally in the sense of § 276 I BGB, even if he has knowledge of all other relevant facts (*Vorsatztheorie*). His liability will depend on whether his mistaken evaluation of those facts is excusable. The courts are quite reluctant to allow the defence (see Huber, *Leistungsstörungsrecht*, vol 1, p 705 *et seq*). The underlying consideration is that legal opinions are held at one's own risk and one must take into account that a court of law might hold otherwise. If the promisor refuses to perform because in his view he is not under an obligation to perform, he assumes a considerable risk, which ought to be preceded by a careful evaluation of his chances of prevailing in legal proceedings. The defence might, for instance, be successful if the court wishes to depart from a clear and consistent jurisprudence. (See, for an illustration, BGH NJW 1972, 1045, case no 115.)

Mistakes of fact also exclude intentional conduct. Again, whether the debtor will be held liable depends on whether the mistake can be excused. The standard applied in this respect is less strict than in relation to mistakes of law (see Huber, *Leistungsstörungsrecht*, vol 1, p 694 *et seq*). Consider the following examples. A landlord who does not know that the residential property suffers from a defect cannot be liable for a delay in remedying it, unless and until the tenant notifies him of the defect or he failed to inspect the property although he was required to do so at certain intervals. This duty of inspection however is limited to defects that can easily be discerned (see eg, BGH NJW-RR 1993, 521). Likewise, a beneficiary who has no knowledge of the death of the testator and thus of his succession will normally be excused, until he acquires knowledge of the facts giving rise to his obligation (see Huber, *Leistungsstörungsrecht*, p 697; Meier, Jura 2002, 128 *et seq*).

Another important source of exoneration concerning breach of duties of performance is derived from *impediments to performance* for which the debtor is not answerable or, in other words, which are beyond the control of the promisor. If the impediment cannot be surmounted, the question is whether the impossibility of performance was due to the negligent conduct of the debtor; and if it is surmountable the question is whether the debtor was excused in postponing or refusing compliance with the obligation. (Initial impossibility raises special considerations, which are discussed in section 5(d), p 455.)

Finally, and this is the third main element of 'fault', the debtor may have acted negligently in violating *duties of care* that serve to protect the other party (*Schutzpflichten*; in German law these duties can also acquire a contractual flavour, § 241 II BGB).

(ii) Raising the Standard of Care

Apart from the reversed burden of proof (already discussed: § 280 I 2 BGB), there are no less than seven other main qualifications to the general rule, which evidently push liability for breach of contract in the direction of a 'guarantee' liability. Equally, it is clear that they do not completely abolish the fault principle.

First, it is common ground that negligence is determined objectively in private law, at any rate in relation to a breach of contract. (See Deutsch AcP 202 (2002) 889; Jones and Schlechtriem, *Encyclopdia*, para 235; Treitel, *The German Law of Torts*, p 83 *et seq* for the tort context; and for an attempt to deploy the 'Learned Hand formula' of liability in the context of § 276 BGB, see Grundmann in *Münchener Kommentar*, vol 2a, § 276 Rn. 62.) § 276 II BGB defines the relevant standard by reference to what is objectively required of the debtor. The test is not whether the individual debtor was subjectively capable of complying with the contract, but whether the standard of care observed met the standard that the promisee was entitled to expect from a member of his trade or profession, ie, the standard that generally prevails in the particular trade. This objective standard of care for breach of contract brings German law closer to the common law.

The rationale of this approach is that the promisor implicitly 'guarantees' that he has all of the skills necessary to effectuate performance (see Huber, *Leistungsstörungsrecht*, vol 1, p 670): if, for instance, a contractor promises to build a house in six months, it is inherent in this promise that he is capable of building a house in six months. The debtor cannot escape liability by contending that he personally was not able to perform the contract as promised because he lacked the required special skills. However, the debtor might be able to excuse himself on the ground that he has fallen ill if he can also show that he could not ensure the vicarious performance of the contract or instruct an agent to act on his behalf.

A useful illustration is provided by BGH NJW 2000, 2812. In this case, a dentist entered into a contract for the supply of computer equipment and software for his medical practice. At some stage, the hard disk containing information necessary for accounting purposes became defunct. The contractor was not able to retrieve the data from the disk as requested and contended that this was objectively impossible (which in fact it was not, as was subsequently discovered). As a result, the relevant data were entered by hand onto another computer and the cost of doing so was claimed as damages. In establishing whether the contractor was at fault, the *Bundesgerichtshof* emphasised that compliance with the standard of care prevailing in the respective trade was required. Since the contractor operated in this trade he should have known that not all possibilities of retrieving the data were exhausted. Whether the contractor personally was not able to perform the task or did not know of these further possibilities was entirely irrelevant. (See, for an illustration of this approach in the field of medical negligence, BGH NJW 2001, 1786: objective standard as to medical treatment must be adhered to, subjective factors are no defence. See, for further references: *Staudinger*-Löwisch, § 276 Rn. 60–91, with an overview of the case law involving contract claims.)

German law recognises strict liability in relation to certain categories of breach. We may view the next three instances as further inroads into the fault principle.

The second exception to the fault principle occurs in relation to money debts (*Geldschulden*). If the obligation concerns the payment of money, the debtor cannot invoke financial difficulties, which accords with the position in English law (see, eg, *Universal Corp v Five Ways Properties Ltd* [1979] 1 All ER 552 and Treitel, *The Law of Contract*, p 838). This is not expressly regulated by German law, but flows from the nature of the obligation: 'one has to have money' as the famous title of a paper by Medicus (in AcP 188 (1988), 449) dryly states. (Apparently, one of the reasons why words to that effect were not included in § 276 I BGB is that the government did not consider it opportune to introduce wording that would have 'sounded' harsh (!), cf

Canaris, JZ 2001, 519.) (See further, the coverage of the special rules relating to the place of performance of money payments and risk issues in chapter 8, p 361.)

Thirdly, the principle that financial difficulties do not serve as an excuse is also applied in relation to other non-monetary obligations and thus acquires a universal character. Any impediment of performance resulting from a financial problem of the debtor will not be taken into account (for the same point in English law, see, eg, *Francis v Cowcliffe* (1977) 33 P & CR 368). The courts will not entertain a plea by the debtor that he did not have the necessary financial recourses (see, eg, Huber, *Leistungsstörungsrecht*, vol 1, p 640; *Staudinger*-Otto, § 280 Rn. D28). In entering into the contract, the promisor is thus taken to have assumed the responsibility for having the objective skills and the financial resources to carry out the contract. It is important to realise that the 'fault principle' and 'strict liability' are in these respects very similar.

Strict liability is also entailed by the promise to deliver generic goods, the fourth countervailing rule. This is another important instance of 'guarantee' liability in German law (see also Jones and Schlechtriem, *Encyclopedia*, para 207 *et seq*). It is referred to in § 276 I BGB as the assumption of the risk of procurement (*Beschaffungsrisiko*). (Much the same position obtains under English law: thus, the seller cannot avoid liability by arguing that his supplier failed to provide him with the generic goods (*Barnett v Javeri & Co* [1916] 2 KB 390).) The content of the obligation determines the scope of this 'guarantee' liability. The courts have recognised several versions of the procurement guarantee, depending on the circumstance of the individual case. If the promise is market-orientated, the seller will not be able to escape liability so long as there are things of the promised class on the market. In many instances, the seller will restrict the obligation to a certain stock or a specific production line. In such cases, he is liable independently of fault for the procurement of objects belonging to that category only. (See, for other implications of *Gattungsschulden*, chapter 8, p 357 ff, and section 3 of this chapter.) The guarantee does not extend beyond procurement. If the delivered goods are defective, liability in damages still depends on whether the seller was at fault in relation to the defect. (On this point, English law retains its strict liability approach, by virtue of the various implied terms under section 14 of the Sale of Goods Act 1979 and analogous legislation (see Treitel, *The Law of Contract*, pp 838–9); however, note that section 14(2E)(a) of the 1979 Act does move towards some recognition of the need to show fault on the part of the seller—this arises due to the Sale and Supply of Goods to Consumers Regulations 2002 (SI 2002, No 3045), implementing Directive 1999/44/EC, see regs 3, 7, 10 and 13 for details.)

Fifthly, it is always open to the parties to raise the standard of care to one of strict liability by including a contractual term to that effect. This possibility is expressly provided for in § 276 I BGB ('*Übernahme einer Garantie*'). In that case, whether liability is strict depends on the construction of the guarantee clause contained in the contract. (See chapter 3, p 133 ff, for coverage of the objective method of interpretation, § 157 BGB. For an illustration in relation to sale of goods, see BGH NJW 1968, 2238, case no 116.)

Sixthly, if the impediment to performance accrued at a time at which the debtor was in default (*mora debitoris*), then he is also responsible for an impediment that is accidental, unless the impediment would also have accrued if performance had not been delayed: § 287, sentence 2 BGB. The debtor is in default if he has not performed, even though performance was due and a special warning (*Mahnung*, which generally speaking is required) had been issued. This is another instance of strict liability, although default is excluded if at the time of the warning the failure to perform is excused, § 286 IV BGB. To give an example: after the issue of the *Mahnung*, a seller who does not perform when requested bears the risk of an accidental destruction of the subject matter of the contract.

Finally, German law recognises strict *vicarious* liability for the fault of any person employed to carry out a contractual obligation. This is not an instance of strict liability, for § 278 sentence 1 BGB merely imputes the 'fault' of the person employed to perform the contract vicariously (*Erfüllungsgehilfe*) to the promisor. Yet it is only when contrasted with the rule of § 831 BGB applicable to delict claims that the true significance of § 278 BGB becomes apparent. Unlike under § 831 BGB, in contract law the debtor cannot exonerate himself by showing that he has carefully selected or supervised the person employed to perform the obligation owed to the creditor. Indeed, the 'strictness' of this rule of vicarious liability for the vicarious performance of a contract is one of the main incentives for plaintiffs in German law to bring themselves within the ambit of contract law. (See, for further discussion, *The German Law of Torts*, p 703 *et seq.* We have discussed the conditions of application of § 278 BGB in chapter 8, p 364.) § 278 BGB contains a rule of imputation only in relation to fault of the servant. If the promisor is strictly liable, no special rule of imputation is needed. The debtor will then be liable *per se* for a failure of performance.

From this survey, it is clear that there are large areas of contract law in which there is little or no disagreement between the common law and the approach adopted in § 276 BGB and where the solutions approximate well to each other. This is particularly true in relation to those aspects of liability in German law that clearly evince 'guarantee' elements and conversely in relation to those aspects of liability in the common law which do require fault for the right to claim damages to arise. Those areas of English law that are fault-based have both statutory (eg, section 13 of the Supply of Goods and Services Act 1982, where the service provider undertakes to 'carry out the service with reasonable care and skill' when he does this in the course of a business) and common law foundations. Many contracts for the supply of services alone are treated as imposing only duties of care on the supplier: typically, these are situations where no guarantee is offered as to the result or outcome—eg, the provision of legal services in the conduct of litigation or medical services (on the latter, see *Thake v Maurice* [1986] QB 644, where tort liability was made out for failure to warn that the operation might not effect permanent sterility, but no guarantee as to the success of the operation was held to have been made). (Compare, however, the position of architects where errors of design are made, where the courts have been prepared to hold that the design amounted to a guarantee that the resulting building would be suitable for the client's needs: *Greaves & Co (Contractors) Ltd v Baynham Meikle & Partners* [1975] 1 WLR 1095 (especially at 1101); and see generally, Treitel, *The Law of Contract*, pp 840–2.)

(iii) Alleviating the Standard of Care

Up to this point, we have examined instances in which the standard of care was similar to what one would expect from a 'guarantee'-type of liability. It remains to be observed that German law also provides for a standard of care that is even less strict than § 276 I BGB (intention and negligence). Sometimes the debtor is responsible only for a qualified 'fault'. This situation arises in three different lines of cases.

First, the parties may themselves insert an exclusion clause into the contract that alleviates the standard of care; similarly, clauses in a contract under English law that provide for certain excuses for what would otherwise be a breach may operate in similar fashion (see, eg, *The Angelia* [1973] 1 WLR 210 and Treitel, *The Law of Contract*, pp 238 and 835–6). § 276 III BGB however prohibits any prospective exclusion for liability for intentional breach. In standard form contracts, § 309 Nr. 7 BGB contains further conditions that must be satisfied for the exclusion to be effective (especially in a contract between dealer and consumer: this problem has been discussed in chapter 3, p 178). It is somewhat uncertain to what extent an amelioration of the standard of care can be derived from the fact that services are rendered on an amicable basis (*Gefälligkeitsverhältnis*, discussed in chapter 2). The labour courts also recognise quite far-reaching exemptions from the liability of an employee towards his employer, which are derived in the end from an objective interpretation of the contract of labour. (We have dealt with this complex issue elsewhere: see *The German Law of Torts*, pp 705–9. On the similar question whether or not participation in industrial action amounts to a breach of an employment contract under English law, see Treitel, p 843 and the references cited therein.)

Secondly, the BGB itself contains provisions for certain types of contract that reduce the standard of care. We have come across some of them in chapter 3. Their common denominator is that in contracts not supported by consideration the promisor should not be subjected to liability for 'light' negligence (donation, § 521 BGB, gratuitous loan, § 599 BGB). Where the parties to the contract are in great proximity to each other the standard of care is sometimes reduced to that of *diligentia quam in suis* as defined in § 277 BGB (eg, partners § 708 BGB, spouses § 1359 BGB, parents in relation to their children, § 1664 I BGB). Liability for 'light' negligence is excluded, provided that the debtor shows the same lack of care also in relation to his own affairs. Hence, a more subjective approach to 'fault' is applied here. As we noted in the previous section, the regime of restitution for breach of contract also refers to § 277 BGB, thereby affording a privilege to the innocent party in reversing the performance, § 346 III 1 Nr. 3 BGB.

Thirdly, the standard of care required can be lessened as a result of the conduct of the creditor. As we have seen, if the creditor is in delay of acceptance the debtor is not answerable for light negligence (§ 300 I BGB, discussed above, p 412).

(c) Damages instead of Performance—Late Performance (§ 281 BGB)

Damages 'instead of performance' (*Schadensersatz statt der Leistung*) serve to protect the expectation interest (*Erfüllungsinteresse* or *positives Interesse*). The purpose of an award of 'damages instead of performance' is to afford the promisee a monetary equivalent or substitute for performance (Canaris, JZ 2001 512). § 281 I 1 BGB entitles the promisee to damages for breach of obligations of performance in relation to which also enforced performance may be claimed (§ 241 I BGB). Apart from this, the nature of the obligation, whether main or ancillary, whether reciprocal or not, is immaterial.

(i) The 'Ultimate' Failure of Performance

It may not immediately be apparent why a separate provision for this category of damages is needed, in addition to the general rule in § 280 I BGB that the promisor is liable for loss negligently caused. The reason however will be clear to the reader of the two previous sections. In German law, the aggrieved party generally does not have a choice whether specifically to enforce the contract or to rely on a secondary right (termination, damages, etc). First, he is required to resort to enforced performance. It is clear from our discussion above of course that this does not mean that he must obtain title as against the guilty party. The setting of a reasonable period for performance suffices (§ 281 I 1 BGB). If the breach persists up to and beyond the end of that period, the innocent party may rely on secondary rights. He may also continue to demand performance. However, as soon as he requests damages instead of performance, the duty of performance is extinguished (§ 281 IV BGB; to this extent, this position coincides with the effect of termination; for the fate of the counter-obligation, see below).

While English law does not *require* that the aggrieved party must first seek performance, it is nevertheless clear that he may elect not to accept the breach and may instead continue to press for performance (see *Tate & Lyle Ltd v Hain Steamship Co Ltd* [1936] 2 All ER 597; *The Simona* [1989] AC 788, at 800 and cf the discussion by Thompson in his note in (1975) 38 *MLR* 346 and 'The Effect of a Repudiatory Breach' (1978) 41 *MLR* 137). (US law is different. A party may await and demand performance only for a commercially reasonable time: UCC 2-610(a).) Further, once rescission (ie, here, termination) has been effected, the promisor is released from his obligation to perform (see Treitel, p 850). If in German law we look at termination (and also, in the case of non-conforming performance, at price reduction), on the one hand, and damages instead of performance, on the other, the only significant difference as to the conditions for their application is the fault principle. Specific issues regarding these conditions, such as the circumstances in which the setting of a period for performance can be dispensed with (§ 281 II and III BGB), have been discussed above and need not be repeated here.

The *Nachfrist*-requirement is also central to the understanding of the type of loss that can be recovered under the heading of *Schadensersatz statt der Leistung*. (See in particular, Ulrich Huber's contribution to the *Festschrift Schlechtriem* (2003), at p 525 *et seq*; Canaris, *Karlsruher Forum 2002*, at p 32 *et seq*.) The remedy aims at procuring for the promisee a substitute for performance if the promisor has failed to perform after the setting of a *Nachfrist*. It follows that loss that would not have been avoided by timely performance cannot be recovered as damages instead of performance. In relation to this type of loss it would be futile to demand the setting of a *Nachfrist*. Any loss that has already irreversibly accrued while performance is still possible is excluded from § 281 I 1 BGB. The reason for this qualification is the *Nachfrist*-requirement. If enforced performance is accorded preference, then it is necessary to restrict the scope of application of § 281 BGB. Because of the requirement of the setting of a period for performance, it would not make sense to include loss in this category that could not be avoided by subsequent performance.

As a consequence, the loss recoverable under § 281 I 1 BGB as 'damages instead of performance' is the loss resulting from the *ultimate* failure of performance ('*endgültiges Ausbleiben der Leistung*'). Performance ultimately fails if the promisor is no longer allowed to perform against the will of the promisee because the latter claims damages instead of performance, § 281 IV BGB. If performance is impossible (§ 275 BGB), it also ultimately fails, but damages instead of performance are awarded on the basis of § 283 and § 311a II BGB, discussed below. (See for this approach in particular Stephan Lorenz, NJW 2002, 2497, 2500 and, more extensively, *Karlsruher Forum 2005*, section III.1.b); cf *Staudinger*-Otto, § 280 Rn. E7.)

While § 281 I 1 BGB is clearly a case of late performance, it is not to be confused with claiming damages *for delay*, which is subject to different conditions, discussed below. This latter head of damages concerns any loss resulting from a delay in performance, whether or not the performance is in the end forthcoming.

Whether a particular head of damages is covered depends on whether it would serve any practical purpose to demand subsequent performance. To come back to our example of non-conforming performance of a contract of sale (for which § 437 BGB is the starting point, details in the next chapter), concerning the delivery of infected fodder: if the horses perish this cannot be reversed by delivering conforming goods. Setting a period for performance would not have been helpful in preventing the loss from arising. It would therefore not be appropriate to include this type of loss in § 281 I 1 BGB. The loss is recovered 'alongside' performance under § 280 I BGB. By contrast, if the goods are not delivered and the loss in question consists in the extra-expense in procuring the goods from a third party, the buyer must first set a period for performance. Performance would avoid the loss. This approach is essentially pragmatic. Sometimes a head of damages may be recoverable under § 281 I 1 BGB and sometimes the same loss falls under § 280 I BGB. Consider, for instance, an opportunity to sell on the goods to turn a profit: the setting of a period for performance only makes sense if this opportunity still exists. A period of grace must be set for the loss to be recoverable (§ 281 I 1 BGB). If the opportunity were short-lived, the *Nachfrist* would be in vain and is therefore not required. The loss can then be recovered directly under § 280 I BGB; if applicable, the requirements of § 280 II BGB must also be met (*Verzögerungsschaden*), that is a special request of performance (*Mahnung*) must be made.

Accordingly, if performance is still possible, the promisee must first set a period for performance and *only* if the promisor still fails to perform may the promisee claim the value of that performance. If A bought from B a painting valued at € 100 for the price of € 90, he must proceed according to § 281 I 1 BGB and first give B a second chance to deliver before he claims € 10 as the value of the performance. It must be borne in mind however that the requirement to set a period of grace is essentially pragmatic. The question is whether the loss in question would be avoided by subsequent performance. Thus (to pick up the example given above), where A had the opportunity to sell the painting for € 110 to C and this opportunity is short-lived, a subsequent performance would not eliminate this particular loss. The loss has arisen and is irreversible. A may therefore recover € 10 (the difference between €110 and €100) as damages alongside performance, § 280 I BGB, although this represents part of the *value of performance*. (See, also, Ulrich Huber in *Festschrift Schlechtriem* (2003), pp 524–6.) Since the loss arises out of the fact that performance was late, it is possible that a special warning must be given the debtor (*Verzögerungsschaden*, § 280 II BGB, discussed below). In any event, the difference between €100 and the price of €90 must be claimed on the basis of § 281 I 1 BGB as damages instead of performance, since subsequent performance would avoid this loss.

(ii) Damages instead of the 'Whole' Performance

As is also the case with termination, the remedy of damages instead of performance gives rise to special considerations if the breach consists in partial or non-conforming performance. Again, the conditions for the exercise of the two secondary rights are parallel (for details the reader is referred to the respective passages above). In the case of part performance, claiming damages for the whole positive interest depends on whether the innocent party has an (objectively assessed) interest in partial performance, § 281 I 2 BGB. In relation to non-conforming performance or *Schlechtleistung*, recovering damages instead of the 'whole' performance (*statt der ganzen Leistung*) depends on whether the breach of contract was sufficiently serious (that is not 'minor', or *nicht unerheblich*), § 281 I 3 BGB. Recovering damages instead of the whole performance is referred to as '*großer Schadensersatz*'. If damages are limited to the actual extent of the breach, the innocent party may of course recover what is termed '*kleiner Schadensersatz*' irrespective of the conditions set out in § 281 I 2 and 3 BGB. If '*großer Schadensersatz*' is claimed, any performance rendered by the party in breach is to be restored according to § 281 V in conjunction with §§ 346–8 BGB. This is sensible, since the award of damages instead of the whole performance is a substitute for the performance. To summarise, if the failure of performance is not total then the right to claim damages instead of the whole performance depends, in the case of partial performance, on whether the innocent party has an interest in partial performance and, in the case of non-conforming performance, on whether the breach is not minor.

(iii) Effect on Counter-performance

An intriguing issue is the effect that a claim for 'damages instead of performance' has on the counter-performance. This problem obviously arises only in relation to reciprocal, synallagmatic obligations. The interest in being released from the counter-performance on the event of breach is, as we have seen above, protected by the right to termination (§ 323 BGB) and, in cases of impossibility, is also protected by the automatic release of the innocent party according to § 326 I 1 BGB.

Prior to the reform, the difficulty was that a combination of termination and damages was not allowed. This was unfortunate where the innocent party suffered loss above and beyond the value of the counter-performance. It would serve no practical purpose to discuss this issue and its critique in any detail here (for comment, see the previous edition of this book, at 635). (This was also a point of confusion in the common law. Happily, UCC 2-703 and 2-711 make it clear that a party may 'cancel', which frees him from a further performance obligation, and also recover damages for breach.) It suffices to state that, nevertheless, prior to the reform this combination of claims to terminate the contract and to claim damages *was* sometimes possible. On occasion, the courts allowed the restitution of the counter-performance as damages (the counter-performance was said to be the 'minimum amount of damages,' eg, BGH NJW 1982, 1279, 1280). The problem with this approach is that the counter-performance would also have been paid even if there had been no breach, ie, the breach was not causally linked to the payment of the contract price. Whether this approach will be continued due to the inertia of 'old habits dying hard' remains to be seen. However, it is no longer necessary to maintain these contortions under the new system.

Since the reform, the combination of the remedies is expressly allowed: § 325 BGB. Being released from the obligation of counter-performance (and the right to claim it back) can now effortlessly be explained on the basis of termination. Hence, if the innocent party seeks release from the counter-performance and claims the loss of profit consisting of the difference between the value of the promised performance and the saved counter-performance, this is a combination of termination and damages. (This point is forcefully made by Ernst in *Münchener Kommentar*, § 325 Rn. 4 *et seq*, but note that the issue is controversial; *contra*, eg, *Staudinger*-Otto, § 325 Rn. 36. See also Faust in Bamberger and Roth (eds), *BGB* (2003), § 437 Rn. 163.) For instance, if A buys an antique chair valued at €100 from B for the price of €90 and the seller B refuses to deliver, A is entitled to be released from the obligation to pay €90 (termination) and to the loss of profit of €10 (damages instead of performance). Damages instead of performance are, of course, limited to € 10 since in obtaining the performance (value €100) the buyer would have had to pay €90 (contract price). (See however as to abstract and concrete methods of assessment of damages, p 480, section 5(k)(i).) Under the old law this was referred to as claiming damages on the basis of the *Differenzmethode*.

In some cases, the innocent party may not have an interest in bringing the obligation of counter-performance to an end, namely if the counter-obligation does not consist of the payment of a sum of money (it would serve no practical purpose in the example above to require the buyer to pay € 90 and entitle him to the full value of €100 as damages). He may then claim damages on the basis of the *Surrogationsmethode* or *Austauschtheorie*. (In this sense, eg, Ernst, *Münchener Komment*, § 325 Rn. 11; Lorenz and Riehm, *Lehrbuch zum neuen Schuldrecht*, Rn. 214.) In this case the innocent party must perform the obligation of counter-performance and the 'guilty' party must compensate for the value of the performance promised to him. To give an example: A has agreed to *exchange* his piano for B's horse and B fails to deliver the horse. According to the *Austauschmethode*, A is entitled to compensation for the full value of the horse, but he must fulfil his part of the bargain concurrently. He will proceed in this way if he wishes to get rid of the piano.

(d) Damages instead of Performance—Impossibility (§§ 283 and 311a II BGB)

If performance is impossible, the promisor is automatically released from the obligation of performance according to § 275 I BGB (the debtor may under certain conditions raise a plea that performance cannot be asked of him according to § 275 II and III BGB, the effect is the same). The exclusion of the duty of performance (*in specie*) does not negative the breach of contract (or breach of duty). The breach is made out due to the failure of performance. This definition of breach is crucial to the understanding of the system of remedies for breach of contract in German law. Whether secondary rights arise is not predetermined by the release of the debtor from his duty of performance. In relation to the right to claim damages instead of performance, this is expressly stated in § 275 IV BGB. (We have already discussed this dualistic approach in relation to termination; on the concept of breach, see also section 3, p 388.)

It is equally clear however that the *Nachfrist*-approach adopted in § 281 I 1 BGB is not adequate if performance is impossible. Setting a period for performance would be futile. Therefore, special rules have become necessary to spell out the conditions for the recovery of damages instead of performance in such cases. This ties in with the thesis, articulated above, that the reason why the traditional categories of irregularities of performance also figure in the new law is the prevalence accorded to enforced performance. The gist of the right to claim damages instead of performance in cases of impossibility is accordingly that it is not necessary to set a period of grace for performance. The right to claim damages arises immediately on the event of breach. For reasons that will shortly become apparent, it was regarded as necessary to differentiate, so far as the right to recover damages was concerned, between initial and subsequent impossibility. It will be recalled that no such distinction is made, either in relation to enforced performance (§ 275 BGB) or to the fate of the counter-performance (§ 326 BGB).

(i) Subsequent Impossibility

The case for holding the guilty party liable for the subsequent impossibility of performance is straightforward: if he is answerable for the impossibility, he is liable for damages instead of the (impossible) performance: § 283 sentence 1 BGB. The fault principles incorporated in § 276 BGB apply, but again fault is presumed under § 280 I 2 BGB. The question in the much discussed case of *Taylor v Caldwell* (1863) 3 B & S 826; 122 Eng Rep 309, was whether the subsequent destruction of a music hall that rendered performance impossible gave rise to liability. In German law, the answer would depend on § 283 BGB and thus ultimately on whether the promisor was able to show that he was not at fault in relation to the destruction (unless of course he was taken to have provided a guarantee in that respect). It will be recalled that Blackburn J held that the contract of hire of the music hall contained an implied condition to the effect that the parties shall be excused where 'performance becomes impossible from the perishing of the thing without the default of the contractor.' If one were to adopt this implied terms terminology, one could say that § 283 BGB implies by law a term to that effect into *every* contract, not only contracts where the parties assumed the 'continued existence' of some specific thing. (See generally, Treitel, *The Law of Contract*, chapter 20 and JC Smith, 'Mistake, Frustration and Implied Terms' (1994) 110 *LQR* 400.) The parties remain free to raise the standard of liability as § 276 I BGB expressly provides.

Paragraph 283, sentence 2 BGB declares § 281 I 2 and 3, V BGB to apply to such claims for damages. See the discussion in the previous subsection regarding the conditions for claiming damages instead of the whole performance. For the sake of completeness, it should be pointed out that the fate of the counter-performance is determined by § 326 BGB (discussed above). Also, as in relation to § 281 I 1 BGB, damages can be claimed on the basis of the *Differenzmethode* or the *Austauschmethode*, discussed above.

(ii) Initial Impossibility

Initial impossibility poses special difficulties, as a comparative survey of English law and the approach in the PECL and PICC also suggests. Two issues were controversial in German law prior to the reform. If performance was impossible at the time of the contract, ought the reliance interest or the expectation interest be protected? In the latter case, should liability be construed as 'guarantee'-type liability or should the fault principle apply? The BGB used to differentiate. In the case of objective initial impossibility, the contract was deemed void *ab initio* (under the old § 306 BGB: this goes back to Friedrich Mommsen's influential treatise 'Die Unmöglichkeit der Leistung in ihrem Einfluß auf obligatorische Verhältnisse' in *Beiträge zum Obligationenrecht* I (1853). Whether the Roman principle of *impossibilium nulla obligation est* entailed the invalidity of the contract is controversial: see Zimmermann, *Breach of Contract* (Sapienza, Rome, 2002), at p 31, *contra* Huber, *Leistungsstörungen*, vol 1, p 115). The old § 307 BGB however entitled the promisee to claim damages based on the reliance interest if the promisor knew or ought to have known of the impossibility (applying the fault principle. This was one of the instances of *culpa in contrahendo* for which Jhering sought to establish liability: see chapter 2, p 91 ff). If the impossibility was subjective, the contract was not invalid and the courts imposed a 'guarantee'-type of liability on the promisor (no express provision to that effect was contained in the Code however). It was assumed that the promisor guaranteed that, at the time of entering into the contract, he was able to perform the contract (see Huber, *Leistungsstörungen*, vol 1, p 530).

English law tends to analyse these problems as instances of mistake nullifying consent (see eg, Treitel, *The Law of Contract*, p 295). Thus, in *Couturier v Hastie* (1856) 5 HLC 673 the buyer was absolved from his liability to pay the price for goods which no longer existed as a commercial entity. (Whether the contract is treated as void in such circumstances is subject to some controversy at common law. In any event, section 6 of the Sale of Goods Act 1979 gives effect to this view: 'Where there is a contract for the sale of specific goods, and the goods without the knowledge of the seller have perished at the time when the contract is made, the contract is void.') UCC 2-613 (casualty to identified goods) is in accord. It applies only if the goods 'continued existence is presupposed by the agreement' and they are destroyed 'without fault of either party' (Official Comment 1). The High Court of Australia, in the famous case of *McRae v Commonwealth Disposals Commission* (1951) 84 CLR 377, had no difficulties in imposing guarantee liability in a situation of initial objective impossibility. The seller sold the wreck of 'an oil tanker lying on the Journaund Reef . . . said to contain oil.' The buyer's salvage expedition however discovered that there never had been any such a tanker. The defendants were held liable for breach of an implied undertaking that there was a tanker there. (See, for a more recent attempt to reconcile these decisions: *The Great Peace* [2003] QB 679; EWCA Civ 1407, on which see our coverage of mistake in English law in chapter 6, p 279.)

The position of the Principles differs somewhat and a brief outline of their approach is useful at this stage (see also eg, Zimmermann, *Breach of Contract,* p 35; Huber *Leistungsstörungen*, vol 1, 116). The contract is valid in the case of initial impossibility (Article 3.3 PICC and Article 4:102 PECL). However, it may be rescinded for mistake if the promisor could not have known of the impediment (Article 4:103 (2)(b) PECL; Article 3.5 (2)(a) PICC excludes the right only if the mistake was made with gross negligence). In all cases in which rescission is excluded, the promisor is liable under the general rules: in these circumstances, he cannot then escape liability for the expectation interest (Article 9:501 PECL and Article 7.4.1 PICC).

The present position of German law is substantially different yet again, both from the traditional approach of the BGB and from that of English law. According to § 311a I BGB, the contract is also valid in the case of initial objective impossibility. Regardless of whether the impossibility is subjective or objective, the promisor is liable in damages based on the expectation interest: § 311a II 1 BGB. Liability is fault-dependent, but fault is presumed (§ 311a II 2 BGB). § 311a II 3 BGB declares § 281 I 2 and 3, V BGB to be applicable (see above as to damages instead of the whole performance). The intention of the legislator was to remove as far as possible any differences in liability between objective and subjective impossibility. Furthermore, it should not matter whether the impossibility occurred before or after the conclusion of the contract. The, at first sight, tempting solution of adopting a unitary approach to liability in damages for initial and subsequent impossibility was not regarded as satisfactory for two reasons.

First, § 283 in conjunction with § 280 I BGB presupposed a breach of duty. In the view of Canaris (JZ 2001, 507), who as an influential member of the Second Commission also shaped the reasoning in the preparatory works (*Bundestags-Drucksache* 14/6040, p 165), liability for initial impossibility could not be rationalised on the basis of a breach of duty. Due to § 275 BGB, the duty of performance never came into existence. In the absence of a duty, one could not speak of 'breach of duty'. Liability flowed directly from the undertaking, ie, the promise of performance. This argument begs the question what the basis of liability then is in cases of subsequent impossibility, for there too the promisor is released from the duty of performance (§ 275 BGB). Canaris argues that in cases of subsequent impossibility the duty existed before the actual breach of contract and thus could be 'breached', while in the case of initial impossibility there never was a duty that could be breached. Whether this explanation is in the end convincing and conclusive is doubtful. If breach is defined as the mere failure of performance, then the contract was also breached in the case of initial impossibility. The distinction between a breach (or lack of fulfilment) of the 'promise of performance' (initial impossibility) and a breach of 'duty' or 'contract' (subsequent impossibility) seems artificial. In any event, this conceptual difficulty does not affect the outcome and the conditions of liability.

The second reason is of more substantial nature. It concerns the conditions of liability. In the case of subsequent impossibility, fault is determined in relation to whether the promisor is responsible for the impediment to performance. This inquiry is not appropriate in relation to initial impossibility. The duty incumbent on the promisor is fundamentally different before and after the conclusion of the contract (Canaris JZ 2001, 507; Canaris, *Karlsruher Forum 2002*, 51; Grunewald, JZ 2001, 435; *Bundestags-Drucksache* 14/6040, pp 165–6). Before the conclusion of the contract, the prospective promisor is not under an obligation to procure or to maintain whatever later will become the subject matter of the contract. The only obligation conceivable is to request that he inquire whether he is actually capable of performing the contract before he enters into it. In the example of the oil tanker in the *McRae* case (cited above), this would require him to inquire whether the wreck actually lay on the bottom of the reef. In cases of initial impossibility, fault is accordingly determined in relation to whether the promisor knew or ought to have known (§ 276 BGB) of the initial impediment to performance: § 311a II BGB. This is an inquiry of a different nature from that presupposed by § 283 BGB (there the question is whether the debtor is responsible for the impediment and not whether he had learned of it). Therefore, it was necessary to differentiate between the two categories.

This approach to liability for an initial impediment has provoked harsh criticism (see eg, Meier, Jura 2002, 188; Altmeppen, DB 2001, 1400—see the reply by Canaris at p 1815; Lobinger, *Die Grenzen rechtsgeschäftlicher Leistungspflichten* (2004) 365 *et seq*). The main objection is that it was not consistent to derive liability for the expectation interest from the fact that the debtor knew or ought to have known of the impediment. The breach of this pre-contractual duty should only justify reliance damages (Huber, *Leistungsstörungen*, vol 1, p 117). It should be observed however that the present approach is not fundamentally different from that adopted in the PECL, even though different terminology is used. In both systems, the debtor can escape liability for the expectation interest if he could not have known of the impossibility. Whether one explains this on the basis of mistake or allows the debtor to exculpate himself does not seem material. Against this background, it is unsurprising that Canaris argues in favour of applying § 122 BGB by analogy and awarding the innocent party damages based on the reliance interest (though note that his view did not prevail in the deliberations of the Second Commission, see JZ 2001, 508). Escaping liability in the case of § 311a II 2 BGB functionally approximates, he argues, the right of setting the contract aside for mistake and the 'price' for this right according to § 122 BGB is strict liability for the reliance interest. (For § 122 BGB, see our discussion in chapter 2, section 5 and chapter 6, section 3, esp. p 288.)

A more recent attempt to explain the rule in § 311a II BGB in dogmatic terms is to rationalise this provision along the lines of a 'guarantee', despite the fact that fault is admittedly a prerequisite of liability for initial impossibility (Canaris, *Festschrift Heldrich*, (2005), p 31). The use of the term 'guarantee' is bound to give rise to misunderstandings. Of course, every promise contains the 'undertaking' that the promise will be fulfilled. This is the foundation of liability whichever form it takes. Canaris seems to use the word 'guarantee' in this sense. The essence of 'guarantee' liability however is that liability is not fault-dependent. This is the strong sense of the term and that in which it is used, for instance to distinguish the common law 'guarantee'-type liability from the fault principle. (See, for this understanding of 'guarantee': Huber, *Leistungsstörungen*, vol 1, p 528; Rabel, *Das Recht des Warenkaufs*, vol 1 (1936), p 275 *et seq*, 338.)

(e) Damages instead of Performance—Protective Duties (§ 282 BGB)

Claiming damages instead of performance for the violation of protective duties is not of central importance in contract law. It must nevertheless be discussed here. The ultimate reason is the German preference for explaining 'duties of care' (*Sorgfaltspflichten*)—also called 'duties of protection' (*Schutzpflichten*)—as auxiliary contractual duties (§ 241 II BGB). This has to do with certain weaknesses of German tort law, which we have discussed elsewhere (see eg, chapter 3, section 2(c), and section 4(c) of this chapter, p 432). These duties aim to protect the interest of the creditor in the integrity of his rights and interests. The remedy is parallel to the right to terminate in § 324 BGB, except for the need to show fault, which only the present remedy presupposes. In our discussion above (in section 4(c)), we gave the example of a painter who does his painting job well but repeatedly damages other things belonging to the employer. In relation to the damage to those other things, a contractual claim for 'simple' damages is available according to §§ 280 I, 241 II, 249 BGB (as well as the possibility of a claim in delict). It is also clear that neither § 281 nor § 283 BGB entitles the employer to damages instead of performance, because the performance obligation is not breached. § 282 BGB grants the right to claim damages instead of performance on the different ground that the creditor can no longer reasonably be expected to be bound by the contract. The creditor can, if the conditions are satisfied, claim a substitute for performance. The right is limited to exceptional, extreme cases (for details see section 4, above, in the context of § 324 BGB).

(f) Recovery of Wasted Expenditure (§ 284 BGB)

§ 284 BGB provides an alternative basis of recovery to the promisee. Instead of claiming damages as a substitute for performance, the promisee may recover any expenses (made in reliance on the obligation of performance) that are frustrated as a result of a failure of performance. The conditions for recovery are identical to the right to claim damages instead of performance and need not be repeated here. The main requirements are: non- or bad performance of an obligation in respect of which enforced performance is available, § 241 I BGB; fault of the promisor; and where appropriate, the setting of a period for performance which was to no avail.

English law, too, is no stranger to the possibility that such expenditure may form the loss to be compensated where the contract has been breached (Treitel, *The Law of Contract*, p 940 and McKendrick, *Contract Law*, p 1034 ff). The direct analogy with § 284 BGB is provided by those situations relating to expenditure that had to be made if the promisee was to fulfil his side of the bargain, which expenditure becomes wasted where the other party does not perform (see eg, *Robinson v Harman* (1848) 1 Ex 850, at 855 and *Lloyd v Stanbury* [1971] 1 WLR 535). However, it is clear that English law extends its conception of wasted expenditure into a somewhat wider notion of the reliance interest. (Note however that this notion does not stretch *so* far: the courts are extremely reluctant to allow such claims for reliance loss to rescue one of the parties from what was simply a bad bargain: see eg, *C & P Haulage v Middleton* [1983] 1 WLR 1461.) Thus, in the *McRae* case (cited above), the expenditure incurred in sending a salvage vessel to look for the (in fact non-existent) tanker could be recovered, even though the contract in no way *required* that such action be taken. Further, in the case of *Anglian Television Ltd v Reed* [1972] 1 QB 60 (discussed by Ogus in 'Damages for Pre-Contract Expenditure' (1972) 35 *MLR* 423), the television company's expenditure on preparing the production of the TV drama—in which the defendant had agreed to star before breaching his contract to do so only a few days after having signed it—was recoverable, even though it had been expended *prior* to the defendant signing the contract. Here, the explanation for recovery is that the 'pre-contract expenditure . . . leads to a loss which, after breach, can no longer be avoided' (Treitel, *The Law of Contract*, p 840, citing *CCC Films (London) Ltd v Impact Quadrant Films Ltd* [1985] QB 16 (noted by Owen [1985] *CLJ* 24 and Burrows (1984) 100 *LQR* 27); note that the *CCC Films* case also provides helpful guidance on the cumulation of claims for both performance and reliance interests and the avoidance of double recovery—see further, *Cullinane v British 'REMA' Manufacturing Co Ltd* [1954] 1 QB 292, especially at 303 (*per* Evershed MR) and *George Mitchell (Chesterhall) Ltd v Finney Lock Seeds Ltd* [1983] 3 WLR 163).

American law is quite clear. Reliance damages are a surrogate for expectation and may not put the plaintiff in a better position than performance. The effect of the rule is to shift the burden of proving the plaintiff would have lost money to the defendant. (See Restatement, Second, Contracts § 349: '. . . the injured party has a right to damages based on his reliance interest . . . less any loss that the party in breach can prove with reasonable certainty the injured party would have suffered had the contract been performed.' *L Albert & Son v Armstrong Rubber Co* 178 F 2d 182 (2nd Cir 1949), is a classic case in point with an opinion by Judge Learned Hand.)

(i) Reliance or Expectation?

The nature of this right to recover for wasted expenditure is not easy to determine. At first sight, one is reminded of the right to claim for the reliance interest in the common law. Indeed, some writers interpret § 284 BGB as an instance of the protection of the reliance interest (eg, *Staudinger*-Otto, § 284 Rn. 10). It may be useful to recall the influential definition of the 'reliance interest' by Fuller and Perdue ('The Reliance Interest in Contract Damages' (1936) 46 *Yale LJ* 52) 53):

> . . . the plaintiff has in reliance on the promise of the defendant changed his position. For example, the buyer under a contract for the sale of land has incurred expense in the investigation of the seller's title, or has neglected the opportunity to enter other contracts. We may award damages to the plaintiff for the purpose of undoing the harm which his reliance on the defendant's promise has caused him. Our object is to put him in as good a position as he was in before the promise was made.

A number of qualifications are necessary in order to rationalise § 284 BGB as reliance-based. Reliance damages normally seek to put the aggrieved party in the position in which he would have been, had there been no contract. By contrast, according to § 284 BGB the change of position of the creditor must be due to his reliance on receiving performance and the provision covers *only* that expenditure made in order to be able to use the performance. Consider the following example (Canaris, JZ 2001, 517): a buyer acquires a frame from a third party especially to fit a purchased painting, but the painting is never delivered. The cost of the frame was incurred in relying on the performance. The damages sought are explicable on the basis of protecting the reliance interest: had there been no contract, the aggrieved party would likewise not have changed position and ordered the frame.

The protection afforded by § 284 BGB is narrower than the protection normally associated with the reliance interest. A clear example for reliance damages is § 122 BGB, discussed in various sections of chapter 6: the creditor is compensated for loss incurred by relying on the contract. As we have seen in relation to § 122 BGB, one of the main heads of damages based on the reliance interest is the loss resulting from the foregoing of an opportunity to enter into other contracts. The wording of § 284 BGB was intended to exclude this type of loss. If the buyer did not avail himself of an opportunity to buy goods at a lower price because he relied on the promise of the seller, this clearly is reliance loss. However, it is not 'an expense' incurred (*Aufwendung*) in reliance on receiving the performance in the sense of § 284 BGB. To exclude recovery for this type of loss, the Second Commission chose to protect the reliance, not on the contract, but on receiving performance and further limited the provision to the recoverability of 'expenses incurred'. (*Bundestags-Drucksache* 14/6040, p 144; previously Canaris, JZ 2001, 517, who argued that awarding reliance damages in the aforementioned example would amount to an 'undeserved windfall'.) The terminology in § 284 BGB of *Aufwendungsersatz* is peculiar, for in all other instances the 'recovery of expenses' is not fault-dependent (eg, §§ 637, 670 BGB); however, it was chosen deliberately to emphasise that § 284 BGB does not entitle the claimant to recover reliance damages.

The recommendation of the First Commission (*Abschlußbericht* (1992), p 173) that the reform should introduce the right to recover reliance damages (or *Vertrauensschaden*) in the broader sense was expressly rejected (*Bundestags-Drucksache* 14/6040, p 144). Hence, § 284 BGB regulates a fault-dependent right to recover expenses incurred in reliance on the performance. The provision can be explained on the basis of the reliance interest, but not all instances of reliance loss are covered by it.

It is due to these limitations of the right to recover loss incurred as a result of reliance that some writers (although somewhat hesitantly, eg, Ernst in *Münchener Kommentar*, § 284 Rn. 6) regard § 284 BGB as an instance of the protection of the 'expectation interest'. For a definition that is, if not generally accepted, at least highly useful, we may again quote Fuller and Perdue ('The Reliance Interest in Contract Damages' (1936) 46 *Yale LJ* 52), at 53:

> ... we may seek to give the promisee the value of the expectancy which the promise created. We may in a suit for specific performance actually compel the defendant to render the promised performance to the plaintiff, or, in a suit for damages, we may make the defendant pay the money value of this performance. Here our object is to put the plaintiff in as good a position as he would have occupied had the defendant performed his promise.

Quite clearly, § 284 BGB (unlike § 281 BGB) calculates 'damages', not by looking at what the promisee was entitled to expect under the contract, but what he reasonably spent in reliance on the performance of the contract. The reason why German writers have developed an expectation-based explanation of § 284 BGB only becomes apparent if the previous practice of German courts is analysed. The only way to award damages for breach of contract on the basis of reliance was to rationalise the loss incurred as covered by the expectation interest. The expense incurred in relying on receiving the performance was used as an approximation of the 'expectation interest' (referred to as the *Rentabilitätsvermutung*, see eg, BGH NJW 2000, 2342). It was presumed that the investment would have resulted in a profit (of the same amount!) if the contract had been carried out. If the contract were not performed, this sum would also be 'profit' that was lost and therefore the promisee could recover 'damages' based on the 'expectation interest'.

This ingenious explanation enabled the German courts to get around the exclusion of awarding reliance damages for breach of contract in the BGB. (Note also that in American law reliance is a good approximation for expectation when the latter is speculative: Restatement, Second, of Contracts § 349 comment a.) If this explanation is adopted, compensating for expenses incurred also serves the protection of the expectation interest. § 284 BGB was meant to codify this case law and to extend it in one important respect. The approach of the courts did not assist the promisee if he did not intend to make a profit out of the contract and the contract was entered into for consumptive or other non-pecuniary interests (which, according to the general rule in

§ 253 I BGB, do not entail monetary compensation: see, eg, BGHZ 99, 182, 198). This was regarded as unsatisfactory (*Bundestags-Drucksache* 14/6040, p 143) and ultimately provided the reason for the introduction of the current § 284 BGB. The 'expectation'-based explanation of § 284 BGB is thus rooted in this weakness of the original approach of the BGB. Whether it is persuasive need not concern us further here.

(ii) Conditions of Recovery

§ 284 BGB now expressly provides for a right to recover wasted expenditure. The theoretical explanation of the equivalence between expense and profit is no longer necessary to found liability, although it is unclear whether the previous approach will be continued by the courts. (The relationship of exclusivity between, on the one hand, § 281–§ 283, and on the other, § 284 may well provide plaintiffs with an incentive to claim recovery for wasted expenditure as 'damages' rather than under § 284.) § 284 BGB makes recovery dependent on five requirements (see *Staudinger*-Otto, § 284 Rn. 12).

First of all, as already remarked, the conditions of the right to claim damages instead of performance must be met.

Secondly, the promisee must have incurred expenditure (*Aufwendungen*). This is, as explained, not the case in relation to the opportunity to enter into contracts. (Cf Dobbs, *Law of Remedies*, § 12.3(1) p 54.)

Thirdly, the expenses must be incurred 'in reliance' on receiving performance. To come back to our example of ordering a frame for a painting: if the buyer needed such a frame anyhow, for another painting of the same size, that expense was not incurred in reliance on receiving performance.

Fourthly, the expenses must have been reasonably incurred ('*billigerweise*'). The meaning of this restriction on recovery is controversial. Some interpret it in a narrow fashion in order to protect the right of self-determination of the promisee. They take the view that it would be illegitimate to make the appropriateness or the proportionality of the expense a condition of recovery (eg, Canaris JZ 2001, 517): in the example of the frame, the expense would be unreasonably incurred if the frame was ordered in spite of the fact that there were already signs that the contract would not be properly fulfilled by the seller of the painting. By contrast, it would be irrelevant whether the frame was outrageously expensive in relation to the value or objective significance of the painting. Others stress that the foreseeability of the expense was the appropriate yardstick (cf § 254 II 1 BGB; Leonhard AcP 199 (1999), 675; Ernst in *Münchener Kommentar*, § 284 Rn. 20; Lorenz and Riehm, *Lehrbuch zum neuen Schuldrecht* (2002), Rn. 228). This seems plausible. The promisee remains free to incur unreasonably high expenses should he so wish, but it would be unfair to impose liability on the promisor for unforeseeable changes of position by the promisee. Lorenz and Riehm, give the example of incurring the travelling cost of € 2000 to attend a series of operas in Milan (worth € 800). Since the expense was foreseeable, it was reasonably incurred and can be recovered. According to Huber and Faust, *Schuldrechtsmodernisierung* (2002), p 170, it may be asked of the promisee that he makes an alternative use of the investment: for instance, in the opera example, to use the visit to Milan for a different purpose in order to minimise 'loss'. The exact requirements of 'reasonableness' remain to be determined by the courts on a case-by-case basis. In so doing, it is worth pointing out that the English courts' approach to the remoteness of damage, stemming from the well-known case of *Hadley v Baxendale* (1854) 9 Exch 341 (on which see eg, Simpson (1975) 91 *LQR* 272 and Barton (1987) 7 *OJLS* 40) may provide useful comparative material. In that case, Alderson B explained that the damages should be such as may fairly and reasonably be considered *either* arising naturally, ie according to the usual course of things, from such breach of contract itself, *or* such as may reasonable be supposed to have been in the contemplation of both parties at the time they made the contract as the probable result of the breach (at 354). While, as Treitel states (at 965), the precise application of this test 'gives rise to many problems,' it is true to say that there is a wealth of case law on the topic that may yield helpful comparative insights. (See in particular, *C Czarnikow Ltd v Koufos ('The Heron II')* [1969] 1 AC 350; *Parsons (Livestock) v Uttley Ingham & Co Ltd* [1978] QB 791 and generally, Treitel, *The Law of Contract*, pp 965–74; McKendrick, *Contract Law*, pp 1057–74 and Article 9:503 PECL.)

Finally, recovery is excluded if the expenses would have failed to achieve their purpose even if the promisee had received the performance. This requirement excludes recovery if the expenses are frustrated for a reason independent of the failure of performance. The burden of proof is on the debtor. In the context of investments to make profit, the debtor may show that the investment would not have been profitable. In the context of transactions that serve a non-pecuniary aim, whether or not the expenses are profitable is immaterial.

(g) Damages for Delay (§ 280 II BGB)

Delay by the debtor or *Verzug* (*mora debitoris*) is a special form of late performance. According to § 286 BGB, it presupposes (in addition to the fact that the debtor is in default of performance) that the debtor is responsible for the delay (fault principle) and normally that a special warning (*Mahnung*) has been issued. The right to claim damages for delay follows from § 280 I, in conjunction with § 280 II and § 286 BGB. Damages for delay aim to compensate the promisee for the loss occasioned by late performance (moratory damages or *Verzögerungsschaden*). Claiming damages for delay therefore does not exclude the right to demand performance. Damages are claimed alongside performance. On the contrary, if the right to the performance comes to an end (either because the promisee claims damages instead of performance (§ 281 IV BGB) or because performance is impossible (§ 275 BGB)), the delay also ceases. Claiming damages for delay is therefore limited to the period during which performance was possible and not excluded.

Claiming interest also presupposes delay, but this element is specially regulated in §§ 288 *et seq* BGB (discussed below).

(i) Delay of Performance (Verzug)

The conditions for establishing a 'delay' by the debtor largely follow the traditional approach of the BGB. Four of them need to be discussed here, namely: the absence of impossibility; performance that is due and can be demanded; the debtor being on notice; and the fault of the debtor.

First, 'delay' (in the legal sense) presupposes that performance is still possible. Requesting performance would serve no practical purpose if performance were impossible and § 275 BGB, as discussed above, automatically releases the debtor from the obligation of performance. Liability in damages depends on whether the conditions of § 283 or § 311a II BGB are satisfied.

Secondly, delay can only occur if the performance of the contractual obligation is 'due' (*fällig*) and 'demandable' (*durchsetzbar*). When the performance is due depends on the intentions of the parties but, in the absence of a clearly indicated intention, the performance is due immediately (§ 271 I BGB). The details of this matter have been discussed in chapter 8, p 355 ff. 'Demandable' here means that the performance must not, although due, be suspended by the existence of some defence. The satisfaction of the first of these requirements (ie, that performance is 'due') will therefore not suffice on its own. In synallagmatic contracts, as explained in chapter 8, the general rule is that the two performances must take place simultaneously (*Zug um Zug*: see § 320 I BGB); in the present context, this means that the creditor must offer the counter-performance for the 'delay' by the debtor to arise (eg, BGH NJW 1982, 2242; see for a further illustration, BGH NJW 1971, 421, case no 114). But the rule in § 320 BGB may be excluded either by an agreement between the parties or by the Code. It should be noted that in relation to the plea of prescription (on which see section 6, p 486), it suffices that the period of limitation lapsed: it is not regarded as necessary that the debtor actually raised the defence (eg, BGH NJW 1971, 1747).

Thirdly, according to § 286 I 1 BGB the debtor must be put on notice by means of a warning (*Mahnung*). The *Mahnung* needs no special form but, nevertheless, must be made and must be specific and not conditional, unambiguous and serious (eg, BGH NJW 1998, 2132; OLG Düsseldorf NJW-RR 1998, 1749). This requirement was put to a test in LG Frankfurt NJW 1982, 650. Here, the defendant argued that the notice given by the plaintiff could not be a warning because it was written in rhyming verse. Not only did the court allow the action, but it also did so in delivering its judgment to be written entirely in the form of a poem. Likewise, a warning along the lines we have not checked whether you owe us anything but if you do please consider yourself to have been warned will not do. From a legal point of view, the warning is little more than a unilateral declaration, which is made by the creditor and must be received by the debtor, and generally must comply with all the rules we described in chapter 2. A warning is also subject to all the rules which apply to legal acts (BGHZ 47, 352, 357), and this for instance means that whereas a minor can give a warning under § 107 BGB (since he only derives an advantage from this act), a warning delivered to a debtor who is a minor must be served on his statutory representative (§ 131 I BGB). (See for further details of the concept of *Mahnung*, eg, *Staudinger*-Löwisch, § 286 Rn. 28 *et seq.*)

A warning need not only be made but, most importantly, it must if disputed subsequently be proved in court before the relevant legal consequences can ensue—a potential legal trap here for those lawyers who come from systems like the common law, which knows no such requirement.

This request of performance is not to be confused with the requirement that a period for performance must be set. If a period of grace is to be set (§ 281 I 1 BGB) liability will ensue only if the promisor fails to perform by the end of that period. This is entirely different from § 286 I BGB. The legal consequences of delay commence once

466 BREACH OF CONTRACT: GENERAL PRINCIPLES

the warning takes effect. The purpose of the *Mahnung* is twofold: first to make clear beyond all doubt that the creditor retains an interest in the performance of the contract and more importantly that from the moment in which the debtor has been put on notice he may be hold liable in damages for delay (see eg, Canarais, ZIP 2003, 322). The requirement of *Mahnung* is a practical manifestation of 'the principle of favouring the debtor' which is recognised by most continental legal systems.

It is possible for the claimant to dispense with making a request of performance or a *Mahnung*. First, the issuing of legal proceedings is treated as an equivalent (§ 286 I 2 BGB). The requirement may be dispensed with even before legal action is pursued in a number of situations of great relevance in practice. The circumstances in which it is not necessary especially to request performance are regulated in § 286 II and III BGB. A *Mahnung* is not necessary where a fixed date for performance was agreed by the parties (§ 286 II Nr. 1 and 2 BGB), where the debtor seriously and finally refuses to perform (§ 286 II Nr. 3 BGB) or when it is clear from nature of the transaction that after a certain date the creditor no longer retains an interest in the performance (§ 286 I Nr. 4 BGB). (See for an illustration of this point, BGH NJW 1963, 1823, case no 115. Note however that if time is of the essence, in some cases late performance may constitute impossibility: for details, see chapter 8, p 357; eg, a contract to deliver Christmas trees to a flower shop.) Moreover, if the obligation consists of a reciprocal money debt, the debtor is liable for damages for delay irrespective of a warning once thirty days have passed since payment fell due (§ 286 III BGB implementing Directive 2000/35/EC on late payments. For details, see Looschelders, *Schuldrecht Allgemeiner Teil*, Rn. 591 *et seq*).

Finally, the debtor must be answerable for the delay, which as a general rule means that it must be due to the debtor's fault (see § 280 I 2 and § 276 BGB). (See for an illustration of the fault aspect, BGH NJW 1972, 1045, case no 115.) This has already been mentioned, as has the fact that the law presumes fault. It is thus for the debtor to disprove the existence of any such fault. The exceptions to the fault principle (as discussed above) apply here as well. This is of particular relevance in relation to money debts for which, as will be recalled, the courts impose a 'guarantee'-type of liability. The same applies with regard to the obligation to deliver generic goods. It is not entirely clear whether the additional mention of this requirement in § 286 IV BGB acquires any relevance of its own (in this sense, eg, Kohler, JZ 2004, 961, who argues that § 286 IV BGB determines the moment in time at which fault must be present, namely at the moment of the warning). At least in relation to legal consequences other than the right to recover damages, discussed below, it fulfils a necessary role (on this point, see eg, Ernst in *Münchener Kommentar*, § 286 Rn. 102).

(ii) Consequences of Delay

Three main consequences of delay must be distinguished, namely liability in damages for delay, the award of interest and an enhancement of the responsibility of the debtor.

First, the right to recover damages for delay covers loss that is caused by the delay (*Verzögerungsschaden*). The right to the performance is not affected by recovering damages for delay. A typical head of damages is the loss that consists of extra expenses incurred as a result of the delay. If for instance a seller delays delivering a car on time, the buyer may need to rent a replacement car until the car is eventually delivered. The same applies in relation to the inability to put machinery to its intended use during the delay of performance of the obligation to deliver: if the production of the buyer is temporarily halted due to the delayed delivery by the seller, the loss will be recoverable from the seller only if the conditions set out above (*Verzug*) are met, in particular only after the date at which the seller was put on notice (unless of course a special date for delivery was fixed: then delay commences from that date, § 286 II Nr. 1 BGB).

'Damages for delay' must be distinguished from 'damages instead of performance' and from 'simple' damages. Damages instead of performance (§ 281 BGB) exclude the obligation of performance and aim to provide a substitute for the ultimate failure of performance. Damages for delay, by contrast, do not extinguish the duty of performance and are not awarded as a substitute for performance. Under § 286 BGB, the plaintiff can recover only that loss that is attributable to the fact that performance is late. (In this respect, the position of the law has changed; prior to the reform, a promisee who sought damages for delay could (under certain conditions laid out in the old §§ 286 II old 326) shift to a claim for damages for non-performance. This is no longer possible. Damages for delay and damages instead of performance are now regulated independently of each other.)

More controversial is the delimitation between 'damages for delay' and 'damages alongside performance' or 'simple' damages (which are awarded on the basis of § 280 I BGB alone). The distinction is crucial in respect of the conditions of recovery. If 'simple' damages are sought, it suffices that the debtor is answerable for the breach of contract. If damages for delay are claimed, the creditor is entitled to recovery only from the moment at which the debtor has been put on notice (*Mahnung*, § 286 I BGB). If, in the aforementioned example, production in the factory needed to be halted, not because the debtor failed to comply with his obligation to deliver, but because he delivered defective goods which required repair before being put to use, this question of categorisation arises. This type of loss is usually referred to as '*Betriebsausfallschaden*' and the issue of categorisation is controversial. If one slots the loss into the category of loss caused by delay, the requirement of *Mahnung* must be satisfied. This view assumes that it should not make any difference whether the seller failed to comply with his duty to deliver the goods (§ 433 I 1 BGB, see above, a warning is necessary) or whether he delivered defective goods that are in need of repair (§ 433 I 2 BGB). On closer examination, the two cases are not to be treated in the same way (see eg, Canaris, ZIP 2003, 326). If no goods are delivered, the loss caused by the disruption to production is exclusively due to the lateness of performance. In the case of non-conforming goods, the loss is primarily due to the fact that the seller delivered defective goods. In this respect, 'warning' the debtor would serve no practical purpose. The justification of the *Mahnung* approach is not particularly strong anyway (since the protection of the debtor may be achieved through other means). Therefore, the better view seems to be that no warning needs to be issued. (However, note that the theoretical explanation is controversial: Canaris, ZIP 2003, 326 and, eg, *Staudinger*-Otto (2004), § 280 Rn. E30, argue that in this case 'simple' damages may be awarded (§ 280 I BGB), while others suggest that requirement of a warning is dispensed with but damages are awarded on the basis of § 280 II BGB, eg, Grigoleit and Riehm, AcP 203 (2003), 755.)

The second consequence of delay arises in relation to money debts. § 288 I BGB stipulates that during 'delay' in the technical sense of the word (*Verzug*), the debtor of a money debt is required to pay interest. This is not phrased as a right to claim damages, thus the creditor does not need to show that he incurred a loss as a result of late payments and the debtor is not entitled to object that the creditor did not suffer loss (see eg, Looschelders, *Schuldrecht Allgemeiner Teil*, Rn. 597). However, § 288 IV BGB clarifies that the creditor is not precluded from recovering damages for delay under § 280 II BGB, provided that he shows that he has suffered a loss that exceeds the interest that can be claimed under § 288 I BGB (for instance, because he was compelled to take a loan and his creditor charges interest beyond the level stipulated for in § 288 BGB: for details, see *Staudinger*-Löwisch, § 288 Rn. 31 *et seq*). The right to recover interest under § 288 BGB is fault-dependent (this follows from § 286 IV BGB). However, it will be recalled that in relation to money debts generally speaking the law imposes what could be regarded as 'guarantee liability': 'one has to have money' (Medicus, AcP 188 (1988), 449). The amount of interest depends on whether a consumer was involved. If a consumer was involved on either side, then according to § 288 I 2 BGB the interest awarded is five per cent per annum above the 'basic level of interest' as defined in § 247 BGB (which fluctuates, since it is determined by reference to the interest rates set by the European Central Bank). In all other cases, the rate is eight per cent above the basic rate (§ 288 II BGB). The parties are free to set a higher rate in the contract (§ 288 II BGB). It should also be noted that, independently of 'delay', a money debt is subject to interest once legal proceedings are commenced (§ 291 BGB: *Prozeßzinsen*).

Under English law, one general analogy to this issue is likely to be found in express contractual provisions that lay down 'penalty' (in the non-technical sense) payments for every day (or other period of time) after the stipulated deadline that performance is not forthcoming (or completed, depending on the nature of the contract and its terms). Such payments can operate in a functionally similar way to a demand under German law for interest for delay. Further, under the Late Payments of Commercial Debts (Interest) Act 1998, where the parties are both acting in the course of a business and enter into a contract for the supply of goods and services (thus excluding a wide range of contracts, eg, consumer credit agreements: section 2(5)), there is a statutory right to interest by means of implying a term into the contract (section 1(1) and (2)). This interest starts to run (section 4) from the agreed payment date or (if not provided for in the contract) 30 days after *either* the promisee has supplied the goods or services *or* after the promisee has given notice of the debt to the promisor. The parties may contract out of the Act to an extent: once the debt has been created, the Act does not restrict the parties' power to make their own provisions as to interest (sections 7(2) and 8(5)). However, prior to the creation of the debt, the Act's implied term can be ousted only if the parties provide for a 'substantial remedy' for late payment of the debt (sections 8(1), (3) and (4), and 9) and, of course, the 'reasonableness' requirement of section 3(2)(b) of the Unfair Contract Terms Act 1977 must also be satisfied (see section 14 of the 1998 Act). Equally, if failure to perform led the promisee to decide to accept the breach of contract and sue for damages, then such questions of interest can also be taken into account in the assessment of damages for breach (although the statutory provisions only provide for a discretionary power of the court to award interest: see now, section 35A of the Supreme Court Act 1981). (On the topic of interest generally, see Treitel, *The Law of Contract*, pp 994–8.)

Finally, and this is the third consequence of *Verzug*, the debtor who has formally been placed 'in delay' will find himself in a position of enhanced responsibility (*Haftungsverschärfung*). According to § 287 BGB, this means that he is liable even for slight negligence (*jede Fahrlässigkeit*), even if normally he would have only been liable for a more severe form of carelessness; and it also means that he will assume, during the period of the delay, the risk that the performance due will become impossible—ie, he is answerable for the impossibility even if the impossibility is accidental. (We have already discussed this consequence of delay (see section 5(b), p 450) in the context of the fault principle.)

(h) Damages Alongside Performance, 'Simple' Damages (§ 280 I 1 BGB)

'Damages alongside performance' (*Schadensersatz neben der Leistung*) or 'simple' damages are awarded on the basis of § 280 I BGB. Liability in damages is imposed if the debtor was answerable for the breach of duty that caused the loss. The fault principle, including all of the qualifications to it, applies (§ 276 BGB); fault is presumed (§ 280 I 2 BGB). No further conditions must be met. In our context, we may safely replace the term 'breach of duty' with that of 'breach of contract,' although note that the rule in § 280 BGB also applies to certain statutory relationships of obligation. 'Simple' damages fulfil a residuary purpose and must be distinguished from 'damages instead of performance' and 'damages for delay.' The theoretical explanation of 'simple' damages is somewhat uncertain. It may therefore be useful to clarify the meaning of some basic principles of liability in which they are used here (noting, of course, that other definitions are conceivable).

(i) Theoretical Explanations

Imposing liability in damages may serve the protection of the 'negative' or 'reliance' interest (*Vertrauensschaden*). The aggrieved party is put in as good a position as he was in before the promise was made. Alternatively, the object of liability may be to put the promisee in as good a position as he would have occupied had the defendant performed his promise. This is the 'positive' or 'expectation' interest (*Erfüllungsinteresse*). Finally, awarding damages may aim to protect the interest of one of the parties in the integrity of his other rights and interests: in this scenario, the aggrieved party is put into a position in which he would now have been had the violation of the interest not occurred (*Integritätsinteresse*). We may neglect the restitution interest for it is not protected in German law by an award of damages (see however, the rules on termination, discussed in section 4, above).

The reliance interest cannot be recovered as damages for breach of contract under § 280 I BGB. The situation is fundamentally different outside the ambit of contract law and here § 280 I BGB regularly serves to protect reliance. For instance, a claim based on *culpa in contrahendo* (§ 311 II BGB) may entitle the creditor to recover any loss that he has made in relying on an invalid contract (as explained in chapter 2, this was the origin of the doctrine). So far as liability for breach of contract is concerned, the Second Commission rejected the idea of awarding the negative interest as an alternative to protecting the positive interest and came down in favour of an 'amputated' version of the right to claim for the negative interest in § 284 BGB.

It is important to emphasise that § 280 BGB cannot be restricted to the protection of either of the two remaining basic elements of liability (expectation and integrity). § 280 I BGB is a fallback provision, which applies if the special requirements of § 280 II BGB (delay) and § 280 III BGB (damages instead of performance) are not appropriate. Damages instead of performance (§§ 280 I, III, 281–283 BGB) cover loss that results out of the ultimate failure of performance. Performance ultimately fails if it is impossible (§ 275 BGB) or if the promisor is no longer allowed to perform against the will of the promisee (that is when the latter actually claims damages instead of performance, § 281 IV BGB). Loss that has arisen before that point falls outside this category. If the loss is due to delay, the special requirements of § 280 II BGB must be met (in particular, a *Mahnung* must be given) in addition to those of § 280 I BGB. If the loss is not due to delay, the basis of recovery is exclusively § 280 I BGB. This will normally be the case with any violation of the *Integritätsinteresse*, but may also include what can be regarded as the protection of the expectation interest. (For this approach, see Stephan Lorenz, NJW 2002, 2497, 2500 and *Karlsruher Forum 2005*, section III.1.b); Ernst in *Münchener Kommentar*, vol 2a, § 280 Rn. 67.)

It should not be concealed however that some writers argue in favour of limiting 'simple' damages to the protection of the interest in the 'integrity' of the promisee's sphere (eg, Grigoleit and Riehm, AcP 203 (2003), 751; *Staudinger*-Otto, § 280 Rn. E11). The difference of approach should not be overemphasised, however. What is important is whether the additional requirements of § 280 II (*Mahnung*) and § 280 III BGB (period of grace) are considered necessary preconditions for the imposition of liability: there is widespread agreement on this practical question, whatever the arguments concerning the 'correct' legal basis. The advantage of the approach followed here is that it becomes possible to focus on the *purpose* of the additional requirements, without having to rely on vague and abstract delimitations of the different interests protected. In what follows, we will endeavour to illustrate the main areas of application of 'simple' damages under § 280 I BGB.

(ii) 'Expectation Interest' (Erfüllungsinteresse)

The expectation interest is as a general rule protected by §§ 281–3 BGB, that is the right to claim damages instead of performance. As explained, the rationale of these provisions is to afford priority to enforced performance.

One aspect of the expectation interest is the interest in being able to put the subject matter of the contract to a *certain use*. As we have seen in the previous section, a temporary halt in production caused by the failure to deliver a piece of machinery may give rise to liability if the promisor has been put on notice (moratory damages for *Verzug*, § 280 II BGB). However, where the halt in production is due to the non-conformity of the (delivered) goods, liability does not depend on whether the promisor has been put on notice, as the requirement of *Mahnung* would serve no real purpose (we discussed this point in section 5(g)(ii), p 467, when examining *Betriebsausfallschaden*). At the same time, subsequent performance would not eliminate the loss caused by having to bring production to a stop. The loss has accrued irreversibly. Hence, the loss can be claimed on the basis of 'simple' damages. It follows that § 280 I BGB may on occasion serve to protect the expectation interest. This will be the case if the particular head of damages can be claimed alongside the performance or where subsequent performance would extinguish the loss (then § 281 BGB is to be applied).

(iii) Interest in the Integrity (Integritätsinteresse)

Finally, non-conforming performance may cause loss to the promisee over and above the loss of the value of the performance or the loss of the use he intends to make of it. This type of loss is an obvious candidate for § 280 I BGB. For instance, defective goods may explode and cause injury to the promisor. Or the contractor may do a bad job of repairing a roof, after which rain leaks through the roof and causes considerable damage to furniture and carpets on the upper floor(s) of the building. Since the interest in the integrity of the promisee's other rights and interests is affected (other than his expectation under the contract), the interest protected is also referred to as the *Integritätsinteresse*. We have stated on previous occasions (both in this book and in *The German Law of Torts*) that the contractual explanation of liability is due to certain advantages of framing a claim in contract in German law. Equally, a tort explanation would be both possible and plausible. This type of loss is usually referred to as 'consequential loss' in German law. The loss is a consequence of the non-conforming performance. This is important for the regime of prescription applicable (see section 6, p 486). This type of loss cannot be reversed by subsequent performance. Hence, it is invariably recovered alongside performance as 'simple' damages under § 280 I BGB. (See, for an illustration of a claim that now would be based on §§ 437 Nr. 3, 280 I BGB and in which such consequential loss was at stake: BGH NJW 1968, 2238, case no 116. The claim failed because the seller was not regarded as answerable for the defect in the goods (§§ 280 I 2, 276 BGB).) (See for a useful discussion of the concept in American law *Reynolds Metal Co v Westinghouse Elec Corp*, 758 F 2d 1073 (5th Cir 1985).)

'Simple' damages may further be awarded to compensate the promisee for any violation of auxiliary duties of protection (*Schutzpflichten*, § 241 II BGB). If the performance of the contract is not causally linked to the loss, but merely affords the promisor an opportunity to enter the sphere of the promisee, the promisee may recover any loss thereby caused as 'simple' damages. If for instance the contractor who was supposed to repair the roof, negligently drops a roof tile on the employer's car parked nearby, he violates a duty of protection and can be held liable in damages on the basis of § 280 I BGB (as also § 823 I BGB: delict). This loss at the occasion of performance clearly arises independently from the fact of performance. (See, for an overview of such collateral contractual duties of care and protection: *Münchener Kommentar*- Ernst § 280 Rn. 89 *et seq*; for an illustration see BGHZ 8, 239, case no 117.)

(i) Limiting Damages

A breach of contract may cause loss that is far greater than the value of performance. While the value of performance can normally be claimed, so far as other or 'consequential' losses are concerned further limiting factors often come into play. Civil and common law systems share the view the right to recover damages must be subjected to further limitations as regards the amount of loss recoverable. They disagree to some extent as to the methods of limiting damages. Several methods of limiting damages are conceivable and most legal systems combine a number of factors. (For an overview, see Treitel, *Encyclopedia*, para 77.)

A civil lawyer would probably not discuss the fault requirement in the present context of determining the amount of damages recoverable. We too examined it above as a condition of liability. As is already clear, fault is not a method of determining the *extent* of the loss recoverable. Fault needs to be established if liability is to arise. Once it has been established, it is not taken into account when assessing the damages awarded. (See Lange and Schiemann, *Schadensersatz* (2003), p 13. The fault of the debtor may be relevant in relation to an award of damages for pain and suffering (§ 253 II BGB) and in order to evaluate contributory negligence (§ 254 BGB), but these are exceptions.) Only with extreme caution can one maintain that the fault principle operates as a method of 'limiting' damages in German law (for this perspective on fault, see Treitel, *Encyclopedia*, para 78 *et seq*). Sometimes, in determining whether the debtor was at fault, the foreseeability of loss will be taken into account when defining the standard of (objective) care required. For instance, if the debtor has been engaged to perform a particularly dangerous activity, under § 241 II BGB he will be required to take a number of precautions to avoid causing physical damage. It should be noted however that the fault principle does not serve to limit the loss to that which is not too 'remote', but merely applies to determine whether the conditions of liability have been met. If so, then the debtor is in principle liable for all loss caused by the breach. Hence, it is not the primary aim of the fault principle to limit the extent of the damages recoverable. (It will also be remembered that the fault principle must be viewed in connection with the remedies of enforced performance, termination and price reduction, which are independent of fault and are more easily available than in common law systems.)

The common law, on the other hand, does not as a general rule require fault as a precondition for showing a breach of contract that sounds in damages. It is a sufficient condition of liability that there was a breach of contract. However, the common law limits the extent of the damages recoverable (and that more strictly than it seems at first sight) by asking whether they are too 'remote'. The formula usually applied in common law countries is that of *Hadley v Baxendale* (1854) 9 Exch 341; 156 Eng Rep 145: losses are not too remote if they are seen as 'arising naturally, ie, according to the usual course of things, from such breach of contract itself' *or* if they were 'such as may reasonably be supposed to have been in the contemplation of both parties at the time they made the contract as the probable result of the breach' ((1854) 9 Exch 341, at 354 (*per* Alderson B)). Any other loss will be treated as too remote. Subsequent case law has attempted to clarify the operation of this test, most important among which are *Victoria Laundry (Windsor) Ltd v Newman Industries Ltd* [1949] 2 KB 528, *Koufos v C Czarnikov Ltd ('The Heron II')* [1969] 1 AC 350 and *H Parsons (Livestock) Ltd v Uttley Ingham & Co* [1978] QB 791. Their precise interrelationship has caused some confusion and much debate (see eg, Cartwright, 'Remoteness of Damage in Contract and Tort: A Reconsideration' [1996] *CLJ* 488), largely stemming from the potentially confusing and overlapping terminology in tort and contract actions after Asquith LJ's judgment in the *Victoria Laundry* case. There, he asked (at p 539) whether the loss was 'reasonably foreseeable as liable to result from the breach'. The House of Lords in *The Heron II* however rejected the suggestion that this rendered the remoteness tests in tort and contract identical and instead insisted on a higher threshold for losses to be recoverable: phrases such as a 'very substantial' probability, a 'real danger' and a 'serious possibility' of loss were used in relation to the contractual test (at p 388, 425 and 414–15 respectively). The reasoning in the subsequent case of *Parsons* is difficult to reconcile precisely with either of the previous judgments (on which see Treitel, *Encyclopedia*, pp 967–8), but would seem to retain a stricter remoteness rule in contract than in tort. The justification for this difference was said by Lord Reid in *The Heron II* to result from the fact that when two parties enter into a contract, one 'who wishes to protect himself against a risk which to the other party would appear to be unusual, . . . can direct the other party's attention to it before the contract is made.' Even if the test itself can be agreed on, however, there remains the tricky task of deciding into which category (too remote or not) any given loss claimed actually falls. Atiyah has suggested (in *An Introduction to the Law of Contract* (5th edn, 1995), pp 467–8) that '[t]here does seem to be an air of unreality about the foreseeability test . . . virtually anything is foreseeable as possible from a base which supposes knowledge of the initial breach of contract.' Instead, he would prefer the courts to ask whether the loss in question was part of the risks inherent in the performance of the contract by the promisor or in the activity conducted by the promisee. Certainly, it seems that the courts continue to struggle with the classification of such losses: compare, eg, *Brown v MMR Services Ltd* [1995] 4 All ER 598 with *Balfour Beatty Construction (Scotland) Ltd v Scottish Power plc* 1994 SLT 807. (See generally, Treitel, *The Law of Contract*, pp 965–74; McKendrick, *Contract Law*, pp 1057–74 and Burrows, *Remedies in Contract and Tort*, pp 50–1. See as to the way in which the computation of damages is affected by the innocent party's decision to terminate or affirm: Goode *Commercial Law*, pp 118–19.)

(See further, UCC § 2-715(2): 'Consequential damages resulting from the seller's breach include . . . any loss resulting from general or particular requirements of which the seller at the time of contracting had reason to know . . .,' and, also, Restatement, Second, of Contracts § 351.)

The principal method of limiting damages in German law is causation. We have discussed the doctrine of causation in detail elsewhere (see *The German Law of Torts*, pp 103–44 and 687–91). It suffices here to recall some of the main points. Whether a causal connection exists depends first and foremost on whether the breach was a *conditio sine qua non* for the loss (*Äquivalenztheorie*). This is known as the 'but for' test in English law. (For the English law on this point, see Treitel, *The Law of Contract*, pp 974–6.) In many cases, this is no more than a first indication of whether or not a causal nexus exists. Secondly, once the breach has been identified as the cause or condition of the loss, it is necessary to establish in addition that the breach was also the 'legal cause'. There are two rival theories as to how the loss is to be attributed to the breach. The courts on the whole inquire whether the loss was adequately caused (that is they prefer what is known as the *Adäquanztheorie*). The standard applied is that of a reasonable person in the position of the 'guilty' party at the time of breach. This person is attributed with the knowledge that a reasonable person would be expected to have in that position. Academic opinion weighs heavily in favour of another approach that seeks to give effect to the purpose of the contract (and is therefore called the *Schutzzwecklehre*: in the tort context, the purpose of the duty of care must be determined).

The implications of the 'adequate cause' approach become fully apparent in the seminal decision of BGHZ 3, 261, reproduced in *The German Law of Torts*, case no 80 (at p 633). The decision is in fact a tort case and the factual circumstances are thus less relevant in the present context. However, the decision clarified a number of important points of principle that are also relevant for damages claims in contract law. First, the court stated that the theory of 'adequate causation' was not really a theory of causation but one of fixing the limits 'within which the originator of a condition can equitably be presumed liable for its consequences.' Secondly, a condition was an 'adequate condition' if it enhanced the objective possibility of a consequence of the kind that occurred. In making this assessment, account could be taken of all the circumstances recognisable by an 'optimal' observer at the time the event occurred and the additional circumstances known to the originator of the condition. The courts impute knowledge to the 'optimal' observer (*optimale Beobachter*) covering 'the whole human experience available at the time the decision is made.' In directing the lower court, whose decision imposing full liability was quashed, the BGH said: 'it should have been examined whether the coincidence of these manifold conditions, in part possibly accidental, were not unusual and outside the scope of normal risks.' It is true that the theory of adequate causation does on its face not ask whether the loss was foreseeable, rather whether the breach increased the risk that such a consequence may occur. The difference however appears to be one of terminology rather than substance. (The similarity between this approach to determining adequate cause and the test of reasonable foreseeability is stressed by Treitel, *Encyclopaedia*, para 93.)

The objection to this approach is that the 'optimal observer' test will hardly ever actually serve to limit liability and that the likelihood of a certain consequence is seldom of itself sufficient to found or deny liability (see Lange and Schiemann, *Schadensersatz*, p 91 *et seq*). Thus, at an early stage other rules of imputation were developed, which sought to complement or to replace the theory of adequate causation. Although the courts initially declined to adopt rivalling theories, one nevertheless finds many decisions in which the 'theory' of the *Schutzzweck der Norm* is applied. Thus, for instance, in BGH NJW 2001, 514, a case concerning liability for the report of a property surveyor, the court pointed out that the theory of adequate cause merely serves to eliminate highly unlikely consequences. The court applied the theory of the purpose of the contract alongside 'adequate cause': ie, it sought to limit liability to what is justified in the light of the violated contractual duty. Other areas of the law in which this approach is frequently applied are, eg, medical negligence (eg, BGHZ 106, 391) and legal malpractice (eg, BGH NJW 1997, 250). (See Lange and Schiemann, *Schadensersatz*, p 104 *et seq* for further references.)

The *Schutzzweck* theory focuses on the purpose of the contract in order to determine the extent of liability. It asks: what is the purpose of the rule that imposes liability? In relation to liability for breach, the nature of the obligation of the parties and the purpose of the undertakings in the contract become of central importance. Rabel was certainly one of the first writers who gave a prominent role to the purposive approach to liability for breach of contract (*Recht des Warenkaufs*, vol 1 (1936), p 495 *et seq*; according to Oetker in *Münchener Kommentar*, vol 2a, § 349 Rn. 118, Rabel was the first to advocate it). It is therefore highly interesting that not only did he suggest that this approach was compatible with the Anglo-American doctrine of remoteness, but that civil lawyers could derive great benefit from studying the decisions post-*Hadley v Baxendale*. For Rabel, the interpretation of the contract was decisive, and this he continued was the basis for foreseeability. The *source* of Rabel's 'theory', namely a comparative argument, is nowadays not given much attention. Indeed, on occasion the impression is created that German law is fundamentally different from the approach of foreseeability of the Common law. (See Canaris, JZ 2001, 517: whether the loss is 'foreseeable' in the Anglo-American sense of the term was 'alien' to German law. Contrast Treitel, *Encyclopedia*, para 94, who states that this approach comes 'very close indeed' to common rule of foreseeability. See also, *The German Law of Torts*, p 295. Cf Lord Hoffmann's approach in *South Australian Asset Management Corp v York Montague Ltd* [1997] AC 191, discussed in Deakin, Johnston and Markesinis, *Markesinis and Deakin's Tort Law* (5th edn, 2003), pp 211–13, 750 and 844–5.)

A further important limiting factor is derived from the actions of the aggrieved party. Since it is of special interest it will be discussed in a separate section below, but insofar as its function is one of limiting damages, it must also be emphasised at this juncture.

(j) Mitigation and Contributory Negligence

Mitigation is sometimes said to involve three main aspects (Treitel, *Encyclopedia*, para 100): first, the plaintiff cannot recover damages which he ought to have avoided; secondly, any 'contributory fault' or 'negligence' of the aggrieved party may be taken into account and the amount recoverable reduced accordingly; finally, any benefit gained by the promisee as a result of the breach of contract may have to be balanced against the loss arising out of the same breach. The first two aspects are governed in German law by an express provision in the Code: § 254 BGB. The third aspect is dealt with in German law under the heading of assessing the plaintiff's loss and we will therefore also discuss it in that context (section 5(k), p 479).

For present purposes, we will focus on § 254 BGB, which contains three rules of mitigation: an award of damages may be reduced on account of the plaintiff's contributory fault, on account of the loss being unusually high or because the plaintiff failed to minimise the loss.

First, in cases where the loss is partly caused by the plaintiff's fault, the defendant's obligation to make compensation and the extent of such compensation will depend on the circumstances, especially on how far the loss has been caused predominantly by the one or the other party. This principle is laid down in § 254 I BGB. To the extent that the aggrieved party has caused the loss, the award of compensation is reduced accordingly. This involves a balancing evaluation of the parties' contribution to the loss.

In § 254 II 1 BGB, the reduction of the award of damages is extended to two further situations.

Secondly, if the fault of the plaintiff consisted only of an omission to warn the defendant of the danger of unusually high damage of which the defendant neither knew nor ought to have known, the award will be reduced accordingly. This clearly reminds one of the rules in the *Victoria Laundry* case (rationalised in *The Heron II*, as discussed above), though it should be noted that this provision has not been often applied in practice in German law.

The third rule is also contained in § 254 II 1 BGB. It is of far greater importance in actual practice. If the plaintiff has omitted to avert or mitigate the loss, the award of damages is also reduced accordingly. (Examples are given below. See, for a further illustration, BGHZ 49, 56, case no 118; which has an English parallel in *Joyner v Weeks* [1891] 2 QB 31; and see further, Treitel, *The Law of Contract*, pp 976–82 and McKendrick, *Contract Law*, pp 1074–6.)

The wording of § 254 BGB, as well as its position in the general part of the law of obligations, shows that it applies to contracts and torts alike, although it appears that this defence is mostly raised in pure tort cases, particularly in cases involving traffic accidents. Equally important are cases of breach of a contractual duty of protection (§ 241 II BGB). The function of § 254 BGB in pure tort cases has been dealt with elsewhere (eg, *The German Law of Torts*, p 110). Moreover, it should be remembered that reduction of damages on account of contributory fault might also be relevant in the context of *culpa in contrahendo*. (Two typical cases concerning defects in the formation of contracts have already been mentioned in chapter 2: RGZ 97, 336, 339; RGZ 104, 265).

Before discussing briefly the nature of the injured party's 'fault' and his 'duty' to avoid or mitigate the loss, one last, preliminary point must be made about § 254 BGB. When speaking of contributory 'fault' or 'duty' it is obvious that in the present context these concepts convey a meaning that is different from their usual function as parts of a cause of action. The only effect of neglecting this 'duty' is that the victim's claim for damages may be reduced. There is no sanction for 'breach' of that 'duty' except for the reduction of the amount recovered from the defendant (Treitel, *Encyclopedia*, para 100). Similarly, 'fault' as used here is not a constitutive element of an actionable wrong. There is widespread agreement in German legal science that these concepts merely denote a failure on the part of the victim to take appropriate measures to safeguard his or her interests. Hence, the suggestion has been made that this should be called an *Obliegenheit*, rather than a duty owed to the person claimed to be liable (see Reimer Schmidt, *Die Obliegenheiten* (1953), p 105 *et seq* and Larenz, *Schuldrecht I, Allgemeiner Teil*, 540, 543 with further references).

Two cases decided by the *Reichsgericht* and the *Bundesgerichtshof* may serve as illustrations of the two special situations envisaged by § 254 II BGB (for further illustrations, see: Lange and Schiemann, *Schadensersatz*, pp 549 and 577 *et seq*). In both cases, the plaintiffs had been in contractual relations with the defendants, but in at least one of these cases the defendant's negligent breach of contract also amounted to a tort under § 823 I BGB.

In the first case (RGZ 83, 15), the plaintiff, a craftsman, had suffered an injury to the little finger of the right hand. He went to the defendant for medical treatment, which was not merely unsuccessful, but resulted in a so-called carbolic gangrene that required prolonged medical attention. The situation worsened to the point that the plaintiff's earning capacity could only have been restored if he had the finger amputated. The decisive question therefore in this medical malpractice case was whether the plaintiff was obliged to mitigate the harmful consequences of this injury by submitting to this operation. He refused to do so because, quite apart from the pain, he feared that it might lead to the whole hand becoming stiff. In the courts below the plaintiff was successful, but on the defendant's further appeal to the *Reichsgericht*, the decision of the court below was vacated and the case remitted for a new trial and judgment.

In the opinion of the *Reichsgericht*, certain requirements had to be fulfilled before the plaintiff's failure to undergo an operation of this kind could constitute a defence according to the second alternative of § 254 II 1 BGB: first, the operation must, in the view of experts, be free from danger, that is, it must be safe in the absence of unforeseen circumstances. In 1913 when this case was before the court, operations calling for a general anaesthetic with chloroform, as opposed to a purely local anaesthetic, were regarded as involving the risk of death even if a preliminary physical examination of the patient was carried out with utmost care. Secondly, the operation must be one that does not involve any significant pain, for the principle of *Treu und Glauben* (good faith) does not require the plaintiff to suffer significant pain for the defendant's benefit. Thirdly, the operation must, on the evidence of experts, be sure to bring about a major improvement in the victim's earning capacity. Finally, the defendant must assure the victim that he is willing to arrange for the operation to be carried out at his expense in an appropriate hospital and by professional doctors. Alternatively, he must pay the cost of the operation in advance and let the victim arrange it himself (RGZ 83, 15, 19–20).

The second case (BGH NJW 1969, 789), which turns on the first alternative of § 254 II 1 BGB, concerned a collateral contract of deposit concluded between the owner of a hotel and one of his guests, a general agent of a jeweller, who had made use of a special service offered in a notice in his hotel room which read as follows: 'Contract garaging. Day and Night. Cars Fetched and Returned.' On returning to the hotel in the evening he gave the night porter the keys of the car, including the key of the boot, and told him to have the car garaged. The garage was nearby but was not part of the hotel. It belonged to a firm that serviced and rented cars. If a guest wished his car to be garaged, this was the garage used by the hotel. In the present case, one of the employees of the garage collected the car and the porter gave him the keys of the car and its boot. The car was returned next morning by a different employee and left in front of the hotel. In the afternoon, the jeweller's travelling agent visited a customer. When he opened the boot in order to collect the jewellery he realised that a number of wristwatches had been stolen from this collection. The lock of the boot was undamaged. The jeweller claimed compensation from the company that owned the hotel, both in his own right and as assignee of the rights of his travelling agent. In the first place, this action was based on breach of a collateral contract of deposit. The courts below had dismissed the claim, but on the plaintiff's appeal the judgment of the *Oberlandesgericht Frankfurt* was reversed and the case remitted.

The reasons guiding the decision of the *Bundesgerichtshof* may be summarised as follows. It is immaterial that the car and its contents did not belong to the contractual guest in the defendant's hotel, for the principle of *Schadensliquidation im Drittinteresse* enables the owner of the car to bring this action based on the contract of deposit, concluded by his employee in his own name but in the interest of the car owner. This contract also covered the content of the boot. Given the findings made by the court below, that the watches were stolen while the car was in the garage, the defendant had the burden of proving that its inability to return the property was not due to its fault (§ 280 I 2 BGB). In the opinion of the court, the defendant had not discharged this burden of proof, which included all persons for which it was 'vicariously' responsible under § 278 BGB). However, this did not end the case, the final outcome of which depended on the defendant's plea of contributory fault on the part of the plaintiff's employee. Since the fact-finding of the court below in regard to this aspect of the case was manifestly incomplete, the *Bundesgerichtshof* had to send the case back with further instructions to be taken into consideration. More precisely, the *Oberlandesgericht* was instructed to find out whether fault on the part of the plaintiff or his travelling agent contributed to the loss of the watches, so as to reduce, perhaps to nothing, the damages payable by the defendant (§ 254 BGB). The first factor to be considered in apportioning responsibility for the plaintiff's loss was that his agent left the jewellery in the boot of the car without telling the porter or anyone else on the defendant's staff that it was valuable and that the risk of loss was consequently very high (§ 254 II 1 BGB). In the opinion of the court, this behaviour of the agent must be regarded as grossly negligent of his own interests. This might, without more, reduce the plaintiff's claim perhaps to nothing. However, certain circumstances, inferable from the plaintiff's evidence, militated against this conclusion, because the agent had been a frequent guest in the defendant's hotel in recent years and it was known to the hotel staff that he carried valuable collections of jewellery with him in the car. Moreover, it was not clear from the evidence whether he knew where his car was garaged or how it was secured, so he could perhaps have inferred from the information provided in the hotel that his car would be looked after carefully. In view of these and other circumstances still to be investigated, 'the causal potency of the conduct of both parties' (*die ursächliche Wirksamkeit des beiderseitigen Verhaltens*) could not yet be finally appreciated so as to apportion the responsibility between them.

In English law, it is submitted, this last-mentioned case would probably not have turned on 'contributory negligence'. Rather, the plaintiff's failure to notify the defendant would make the loss too remote, that is to say it could not have been in the contemplation of the defendant; for under the second branch of the rule in *Hadley v Baxendale* (1854) 9 Ex 341, the defendant would only be liable for the loss that he could reasonably have foreseen on the basis of facts which he knew. Therefore, it is likely that an English court would reach the same result as the German court, even though the reasoning would be guided primarily by considerations of causation and remoteness. (The same result would seem to follow from UCC 2-715(2) which includes in the requirement that the damages be foreseeable a requirement that the loss 'not reasonably be prevented by cover or otherwise.')

More generally, the common law doctrine of contributory negligence seems to have applied only where the relevant breach of contract also amounted to a tort; and even when it did apply, it was sometimes used to bar the claim altogether, while in other cases the effect of such contributory negligence was effectively ignored by the courts (see eg, Williams, *Joint Torts and Contributory Negligence* (1951)). Since the Law Reform (Contributory Negligence) Act 1945 however damages may be reduced by a proportion that reflects the level of the claimant's responsibility, but here again care must be taken to check that the 1945 Act applies to the relevant breach of contract. Its section 1(1) provides that the damage must be suffered 'as the result partly of his own fault and partly of any other person or persons,' while section 4 defines 'fault' to mean 'negligence, breach of statutory duty or other act or omission which gives rise to a liability in tort or would, apart from this Act, give rise to the defence of contributory negligence.' The Court of Appeal in *Forsikringsaktieselskapet Vesta v Butcher* [1989] AC 852 held that this definition meant that 'negligence' here had to be read in the tortious sense. Nevertheless, where a breach of contract is negligent (NB in the sense that a contractual duty of *care* has been breached, and not that a strict duty just happened to have been breached in a negligent fashion) it seems that the Act may apply (*Quinn v Burch Bros (Builders) Ltd* [1966] 2 QB 370, especially at 378–9). Further, where a breach of contract also amounts to a tort and the content of the concurrent duties is essentially the same (which after *Henderson v Merrett Syndicates Ltd* [1995] 2 AC 145, is clearly a possibility in many professional fields), it is clear that the Act can apply so as to reduce the extent of the claimant's recovery. (See for discussion, Treitel, *The Law of Contract*, pp 982–7 and McKendrick, *Contract Law*, pp 1076–82. US law is similar: comparative fault principles apply only in tort and so apply to some forms of malpractice. See Ronald M Mallen and Jeffrey M Smith, *Legal Malpractice* (5th edn, 2000), § 21.2 note 2.)

(k) Assessment of Damages

The rules that govern computation of damages are contained in §§ 249–53 BGB; § 254 BGB, which is also a damages provision, has been discussed in the previous section. The starting principle is § 249 I BGB. The general rule is that the debtor must restore the creditor to the position he would have been had there been no breach. This is referred to as restitution in kind (*Naturalrestitution*). When it comes to cases of injury to a person or damage to a thing, the creditor has the choice between restitution in kind (§ 249 I BGB) or a sum of money that is necessary for such restitution (§ 249 II BGB). Compensation in money may also be claimed in certain other situations: where restitution in kind may be impossible or insufficient to compensate the creditor (§ 251 I BGB); where restitution in kind would require disproportionate outlays (§ 251 II BGB); and where the creditor has fixed a reasonable period for the restitution to be made by the person claimed to be liable, but restitution is not effected in due time (§ 250 BGB).

Another important exception to restitution in kind as envisaged by § 249 I BGB (that is restoration by the debtor) was discussed above. It would be contrary to the very nature of the right to recover damages on the basis of the expectation interest if the creditor who is entitled to claim damages were to be granted a right to the performance *in specie*. This is expressly stated in § 281 IV BGB and also follows from the nature of such an award (for details, see section 5(a), p 442). Rather, the award of damages as a substitute for performance is aimed at compensating the creditor financially: thus, a monetary award is made.

So far as the protection of the expectation interest is concerned, the most important provision for calculating damages is § 252 BGB, which must be discussed in some detail at this stage. As we have seen in the section on 'simple' damages, a contractual action for damages may also concern physical damage to the person or property. It is for this reason that some of the issues raised by compensating this interest in the 'integrity' of one's sphere need to be discussed here. For a more comprehensive account of the approach of the BGB to assessing damages, the reader is referred to *The German Law of Torts*, pp 901–41. It suffices here to highlight some of the main points that arise in connection with §§ 249–53 BGB from the perspective of contract law.

(i) 'Expectation Interest'

The expectation interest (*Erfüllungsinteresse*) protects the expectation of the promisee to get that for which he bargained. The remedy of enforced performance aims at actually procuring the subject matter of the contract. The remedy of damages, if available, affords the promisee a substitutionary relief in money (referred to as *positives Interesse*). The plaintiff may make the defendant pay the money value of this performance. The object of an award of damages is to put the promisee in as good a financial position as that in which he would have been had the promisor performed his promise. The point of reference in time for calculating the hypothetical financial situation of the promisee without the breach is the position in which he would have been in now (that is in legal proceedings at their end). (See Emmerich in *Münchener Kommentar*, vol 2a, Vor § 281 Rn. 7.) The relief consists of a monetary award, while the principle of restitution in kind in the sense of § 249 I BGB applies if at all only in exceptional cases.

English law employs the same basic rule: 'the rule of the common law is, that where a party sustains a loss by reason of a breach of contract, he is, in so far as money can do it, to be placed in the same position, with respect to damages, as if the contract had been performed' (*Robinson v Harman* (1848) 1 Ex 850, 855, *per* Parke, B). Naturally, this formulation raises a key question of definition and interpretation of the scope of the bargain: without this, it is not possible to conclude what that 'position' would have been—ie, for what had the claimant bargained? This requires careful assessment of the nature of the duty owed to the promisee by the promisor under the contract, the breach of which forms the basis for the claim in damages. (See, for discussion, *South Australia Asset Management Corp v York Montague Ltd* [1997] AC 191 (usually known as the *SAAMCO* case) and Treitel, *The Law of Contract*, pp 937–40.)

Two provisions provide at least a starting-point for quantifying the expectation interest. Thus, § 252 BGB dealing with 'lost profit' (*entgangener Gewinn*) states: 'The compensation shall also include lost profits. Profit is deemed to have been lost which could probably have been expected in the ordinary course of events, or according to the special circumstances, especially in the light of the preparations and arrangements made.' This is supplemented by § 376 II of the Commercial Code (= 'HGB') concerning commercial sales with fixed delivery dates (*Fixhandelskauf*), which states that in cases of non-performance the creditor may demand the difference between the contract price and the market price of the goods at the time and place when they ought to have been delivered. This method of assessing damages for non-performance adopted by § 376 II HGB is known as *abstrakte Schadensberechnung*, ie the abstract method. This method is deemed to be embodied also in § 252 BGB, cited above. Thus, in the case of a bank whose customer is in default there is a presumption that the amount due would have been gainfully used in the course of the bank's 'active business' (BGHZ 62, 103, 107 permitting the 'abstract' assessment of damages according to § 252 BGB, but distinguishing *obiter* between various types of banks). As can be seen from § 376 II HGB, and the decision of the *Bundesgerichtshof*, the abstract method of assessment of damages may be used where profit would have been made 'in the ordinary course of events' (*nach dem gewöhnlichen Lauf der Dinge*). There is a presumption, derived from § 252 sentence 2 BGB, that merchants buy and resell goods at the market price if there is an available market in the goods in question. From this procedural perspective, § 252 BGB makes it easier to prove loss of profit.

For the sake of clarity, but also in order to understand how this works in practice, two typical fact-situations must be briefly examined.

Let us first take the example of a merchant who has agreed to buy certain goods, but the seller is in breach of contract because he has failed to make timely delivery. There exist numerous decisions by German courts allowing the buyer in such circumstances to recover damages according to the abstract method, which means the difference between the contract price and the market price at the time when delivery ought to have been made under the contract (see eg, RGZ 101, 217, 218–219; RGZ 101, 421, 423; RGZ 105, 293, 294). These decisions, however, have met with well-founded criticism on the ground that, normally, a merchant will obtain the goods elsewhere and resell them. In such a typical situation, the damage suffered by the merchant will be the difference between the price of the 'cover purchase' (*Deckungskauf*) and the contract price, provided that the former exceeds the latter. In some cases this sum may be increased by certain additional heads of damage, eg, expenses involved in the making of the contract that has been aborted by reason of the seller's default. (See *Robert Stewart & Sons Ltd v Carapanayoti & Co Ltd* [1962] 1 WLR 34, 39 *per* McNair J where such heads of damage, in addition to the loss of bargain, were considered.) Moreover, § 252 sentence 2 BGB does not lay down an irrebuttable presumption. Therefore, it is admissible to prove that in a concrete case there was no such possibility of a gainful resale.

The second example can be found in a decision of the *Bundesgerichtshof* concerning a wine dealer who had sold certain wines, but the buyer was in default of taking delivery and paying for the merchandise (BGH JZ 1961, 27). In a case like this, the difference between the contract price and the market price or current price would normally be the amount payable as damages for non-performance. In the instant case, the plaintiff had been able to sell the wine reserved for the defendant to other customers at the same price. Therefore, the defendant argued, the plaintiff had suffered no loss. However, this plea was defeated by the plaintiff, who maintained that these customers would have probably bought other wines of similar quality that he had in store or could easily have obtained from winegrowers with whom he had business contacts. But the court expressly admitted that the defendant could have disproved this 'ordinary course of events' (within the meaning of § 252 senence 2 BGB) on which the presumption of lost profit rests (see BGH JZ 1961, 27). The decision shows that the 'concrete method of assessment of damages' (*konkrete Schadensberechnung*) provides the starting-point, particularly in non-commercial sales.

In English law, the Sale of Goods Act (1979) favours the abstract method of assessing damages, both for non-acceptance of the goods by the buyer and for non-delivery for the goods by the seller if there is an available market. This follows from sections 50(3) and 51(3). In these cases, the aggrieved party can claim the difference between the contract price and the market or current price at the time when the goods ought to have been delivered. It does not matter whether the seller has resold at a price different from the market price or whether the buyer has made a cover purchase. (So too in the US under UCC 2-708(1) (buyer's right to contract-market differential) and 2-713 (sellers right to contract-market differential).) The concrete method is adopted only in cases in which there is no available market. This can be seen from sections 50(2) and 51(2) Sale of Goods Act (1979): the measure of damages is the estimated loss directly and naturally resulting, in the ordinary course of events, from the buyer's or seller's breach of contract. (See generally, Guest (gen ed), *Benjamin's Sale of Goods* (6th edn, 2002) and Bridge, *The Sale of Goods* (1998), chapter 10 for detailed discussion.)

Ultimately therefore it can be argued that in practice the difference between German and English law is yet again not as great as it appears to be at first sight. (See also, Treitel, *Remedies for Breach of Contract* (1988), p 114, who arrives at the same conclusion.)

(ii) Personal Injury

For obvious reasons, § 249 II 1 BGB leaves it to the injured person to decide whether the person claimed to be liable should have a determining influence on the restoration of his health. Under this provision, the injured person may demand 'the sum necessary for such restitution.' In the typical cases that have given rise to litigation, the injured person has already incurred medical expenses, and he (or the insurer by way of *cessio legis*), demands their reimbursement. In cases of serious injury, it may be that a costly medical treatment was not, or was only partially, successful. The defendant may then be tempted to question the necessity of the plaintiff's expenses. However, the courts will look at the chances of restoring health from an *ex ante* position when deciding whether this particular medical treatment was still in keeping with the *lex artis*.

As will be shown below, the *Bundesgerichtshof* has held repeatedly that in cases of damage to property, the owner or possessor is entitled to a sum of money necessary for repair, but need not use this money for carrying out such repair. In a case like this, it is entirely at the claimant's discretion how this money will be spent. This explains why the same question has been raised with respect to personal injury. May the injured person claim a 'fictitious' sum of money as compensation for the injury, even though the money will not be spent for the restoration of his health?

The problem has arisen in connection with personal injury sustained in a traffic accident. (See BGHZ 97, 14, reproduced as case no 142 in *The German Law of Torts*, p 994, discussed there at p 908.) The claimant had to undergo a bowel operation, which was the immediate consequence of the accident caused by the defendant. The operation was successful, but some scars remained on the skin of the abdomen. The defendant's insurer was willing to pay the estimated costs of this operation in advance and without being sure that this money would really be used for the removal of the scars. The *Bundesgerichtshof* dismissed the plaintiff's action for such 'fictitious' damages. The court took great pains to distinguish this case from previous cases concerning damage to property. While it is axiomatic that an owner may freely dispose of his movables, which necessarily includes the decision not to have the damaged chattel repaired and to buy something else instead, the same considerations cannot apply to the restoration of the bodily integrity (*Herstellung der körperlichen Integrität*) because this is essentially a non-pecuniary damage (*Nichtvermögensschaden*). Therefore, the decision of the injured person to continue to live with those scars, rather than submitting to a course of medical treatment with no guaranteed success, is made on an entirely different footing. Damage of this kind is not within the scope of § 253 BGB; and the point has been reached when § 253 I BGB becomes relevant. Compensation for non-material damage may thus only be demanded as provided by law. But in the instant case, the prerequisites of § 847 BGB (repealed, see now § 253 II BGB) granting damages for pain and suffering were absent.

It remains to be remarked that damages for pain and suffering are now also available in a contractual action for damages, see § 253 II BGB. (See *The German Law of*

Torts, pp 915–25, on possible effects of this extension of liability for the contract/tort divide and for a comprehensive account of the nature and extent of awards for pain and suffering of German courts.) In English law, the availability of such damages is restricted by the decision of the House of Lords in *Addis v Gramophone Co Ltd* [1909] AC 488, where the 'harsh and humiliating' manner of the defendant's dismissal of its manager, the plaintiff, did not attract a head of damages that covered his mental distress and humiliation as a result (although cf the Law Commission's report *Aggravated, Exemplary and Restitutionary Damages* (Law Com No 247, 1997), para 6.1(2), recommending that contractual damages should be able to cover the mental distress caused by the defendant's conduct). Against this unpromising backdrop however certain exceptions may actually cover much of the ground of such claims: thus, if a breach of contract causes personal injury then the claimant may recover for pain and suffering as well (*Godley v Perry* [1960] 1 WLR 9). Further, where one of the 'major and important' aims of the contract was to provide some form of enjoyment (etc– eg, holiday contracts) then here too damages seem to be available for distress or vexation caused by breach (see, eg, *Jarvis v Swan Tours Ltd* [1973] QB 233). (See, most recently, the interesting case of *Farley v Skinner* [2002] 2 AC 732 (concerning the duties and liability of a surveyor who had specifically been instructed to report on aircraft noise at a property (located only 15 miles from Gatwick Airport) that the claimant intended to be as his retirement home) and the discussion in Treitel, *The Law of Contract*, pp 987–94 and McKendrick, *Contract Law*, pp 1043–57.) The general rule in the US is that mental distress damages may be recovered for breach of contract only if the primary purpose of the contract is to secure personal and not economic interests. Thus, they are not recoverable for breach of an employment contract (*Valentine v General American Credit, Inc*, 420 Mich 256, 362 NW 2d 628 (1984)).

(iii) Damage to Property

Experience suggests that in the vast majority of cases, damage to property is caused by tortious acts or omissions. Such claims are based on the delict provisions of the BGB (§ 823 *et seq*). These provisions must however be supplemented by §§ 249–52 BGB, which contain the general rules of the law of damages that are also applicable to contractual relations. (For illustrations, see: BGH WM 1967, 749 concerning damage done to an apartment; liability of the lessee for the loss suffered by the lessor after the end of the contract period because the rooms were uninhabitable while under repair; BGHZ 96, 124 concerning the inconvenience caused by the defects of a car-park in the basement of a house for which the contractor was responsible to the building owner who could not garage his car. See also, BGH NJW 1968, 2238, case no 116: engines of plaintiff's vehicles suffered damage allegedly due to noxious qualities in the delivered diesel fuel.) Attention here will thus be drawn only to some exceptions from the principle of *Naturalherstellung* that may also have some bearing on the law of contract.

A crucial type of case that has come before German courts has turned on the question whether it may still be regarded as 'damage to property' if a person who, as a result of an accident caused by the defendant, is deprived to the possibility of use (*Nutzungsmöglichkeit*) of a chattel. It all started with actions brought by motor car owners whose vehicles were damaged in accidents for which the defendants were held responsible. While the car is undergoing necessary repair its owner cannot use it. It is settled law that the owner may make up for this loss by hiring a similar car at the expense of the tortfeasor. But may he also claim a corresponding sum of money if he abstains from hiring a substitute vehicle? Astonishingly enough, the *Bundesgerichtshof* has repeatedly held that this is a recognisable head of damage: the 'temporary loss of the possibility of using a car' is regarded as forming part of the damage to property that must be made good (see BGHZ 40, 345 and BGHZ 45, 212 applying § 251 BGB). These decisions have met with strong criticism in German legal literature. The fear was expressed that this new case law might open the floodgates and lead to the 'commercialisation' of all sorts of losses of amenities of life connected with the use of one's property. It thus became foreseeable that, henceforth, the courts would have to decide whether or not this *ratio decidendi* also holds good for such items as fur coats, motor-boats, swimming-pools and the like. Unsurprisingly perhaps, in most of these cases the actions failed; but the reasoning of the courts bristles with distinctions that are not really convincing. So eventually, the point was reached at which the Great Senate for Civil Matters (*Großer Senat für Zivilsachen*) had to be convened in order to secure the necessary uniformity of interpretation and approach in this area of the law.

In this case (BGHZ 98, 212, reproduced as case no 148 in *The German Law of Torts*, p 1019, further discussed there at p 939), a 'luxury residential building' had become uninhabitable for five weeks because construction work carried out on a steep slope below had endangered the safety of its foundations. Since the owner of his house was forbidden to live there, she used a nearby camping bus as an emergency shelter. There was no dispute about the amount necessary for the repair of the building. The controversy concerned DM3000, which the owner demanded from the defendant contractor in addition, for the 'loss of the possibility of using her house.' The *Bundesgerichtshof* reached the conclusion that this may be regarded as recoverable property damage under the compensatory principle of the BGB, even though the owner of the house did not incur expenses or lose any income thereby. The essential point in the elaborate reasoning of the court is this: there is no substantial difference between the use of one's property for gainful professional activities and the use of such property for maintaining one's typical lifestyle. However, beyond this limit no compensation can be awarded because this would violate § 253 I BGB, which allows compensation in money for non-material damage only as provided by law.

The reader will probably be inclined to ask whether this decision of the full court has brought about the final clarification of a difficult problem. The answer to this question can hardly be in the affirmative. More recently, the Court again had to deal with a case in which the owner of a house was prevented from using an apartment situated in the basement (BGHZ 117, 260). Owing to the insufficient outer insulation of the basement, humidity had penetrated the walls, making the apartment uninhabitable. The plaintiff had bought this house from the defendants four years previously. The contract contained a clause disclaiming all liability for defects in the building. In the instant case, this disclaimer was invalid because the vendors had fraudulently concealed this defect. The plaintiff was awarded a sum of money needed to carry out the repair of the building, but the court was not prepared to give judgment for an additional amount of DM7800. This head of damage had been claimed as compensation for not having been able to use the apartment in the basement. However, the plaintiff had to admit that it was used only occasionally by her son who was living elsewhere. Therefore, the Court was of the opinion that this apartment was not part of that property that the plaintiff had to have permanently at her disposal for maintaining her lifestyle. It would have been different had the apartment been used by a person belonging to her household (see BGHZ 117, 260 applying the *ratio decidendi* of BGHZ 98, 212).

As has been shown above (in section 5(k)(ii)), the *Bundesgerichtshof* does not recognise 'fictitious' damages in regard to personal injury. The decisive point is that non-material damage can only be compensated in money if the law expressly allows it (§ 253 I BGB). In cases of personal injury, § 253 II BGB is the relevant provision that grants money compensation for pain and suffering (*Schmerzensgeld*). Obviously, such considerations cannot apply to property that is at the owner's disposal. Let us suppose a car was damaged in an accident caused by the defendant. The owner of the damaged car may of course claim compensation covering the cost of repair, but he is free to decide whether to have the car repaired. If the owner of the car happens to be a motor mechanic by profession who has himself repaired the damage by using spare parts that he bought himself, he may also demand compensation in money. The amount will be the same as if this repair had been carried out in a garage. The *Bundesgerichtshof* in deciding such a case even held that the VAT sum which a garage would have added to its bill could be claimed (see BGHZ 61, 56); however, in this respect a recent reform reversed the holding of this decision: see now § 249 II 2 BGB, which at the same time confirms the right to claim fictitious damages for damage to property. (See, for further details, *The German Law of Torts*, p 931 *et seq*; and in relation to the cost of hiring a replacement car: Unberath, 'Ersatz "überhöhter" Mietwagenkosten nach einem Unfall?—Unfallersatztarife in Deutschland und England' NZV 2003, 497.)

Obviously the general rule that the person claimed to be liable owes *Naturalherstellung* (§ 249 I BGB) does not operate when reparation in kind is impossible or insufficient to compensate the claimant. Yet this does not yet bring our enquiry to an end. The person liable must compensate the creditor in money (§ 251 I BGB). The same applies 'if restitution in kind is possible only through disproportionate outlays' (§ 251 II BGB). In this context a very special problem may arise. Suppose that specific restoration is possible, but the result of so acting would leave the creditor with a more valuable object than he had before. The problem must be solved by applying the general rule (§ 249 BGB); but regard must be had to the 'compensatory principle' that permeates the law of liability and forbids any enrichment of the plaintiff. This is corroborated by another general principle known as *Vorteilsausgleichung*, ie compensating advantages resulting from the damaging event will be taken into account. It must however be emphasised that the present problem, usually expressed with the catchphrase 'new for old' (*neu für alt*), has nothing to do with *Vorteilsausgleichung stricto sensu* because this 'advantage' is not the immediate result of an injury inflicted on a person or on property, but accrues to the claimant at a later stage when the damage must be made good. Nevertheless, the tendency in German law is for the courts to make allowance for improvements in the claimant's position. In English law, there seems only to be the case of *Harbutts 'Plasticine' Ltd v Wayne Tank and Pump Co Ltd* [1970] 1 QB 447, decided by the Court of Appeal but subsequently overruled by the House of Lords ten years later, but not on the point presently under consideration (see *Photo Production Ltd v Securicor Transport Ltd* [1980] AC

827). In the case before the Court of Appeal, a factory was burned down due to the negligence of the defendant contractor. Lord Denning MR, who gave the leading judgment of the court, pointed out that the destruction of a building is different from the destruction of a chattel, as for instance where a second-hand car is destroyed. In this case the owner gets its value because he can go to the market and replace it. He cannot charge the defendant with the cost of a new car. But when the plaintiffs' mill was destroyed they had no choice: 'They were bound to replace it as soon as they could, not only to keep their business going, but also to mitigate the loss of profit for which they would be able to charge the defendants' (per Lord Denning, MR, cited above, at 468). The result was an improved, more modern, building. The plaintiffs got 'new for old', without giving credit under the heading of 'betterment'. (See also, the cases often discussed under the heading of 'mitigation in fact', especially where the claimant's performance of his duty to mitigate may cause him to benefit, which benefits may then be taken into account in assessing his damages claim against the defendant. For example, taking another job after wrongful dismissal from previous employment: *Cereberus Software Ltd v Rowley* [2001] ICR 376; EWCA Civ 78. Functionally, this approach might sometimes lead to similar results to the German cases discussed in the next paragraph.)

The *Bundesgerichtshof* has had to deal with comparable fact-situations at least twice. In both cases buildings were burnt down. In the first case, decided in 1959 (BGHZ 30, 29, case no 119), the defendants had set fire to an agricultural building and in the more recent case of 1987, a residential building was badly damaged in a fire negligently caused by the defendant. In both cases, there was no question about the existence of liability on the part of the defendants, but the extent of their liability was in doubt. Applying § 249 *et seq* BGB, the Court was confronted with the following alternative: if *Naturalherstellung* were deemed possible, the sum of money which the owner may claim under § 249 II BGB for the purpose of reconstructing the building would not cover the total amount necessary for all materials, work and labour. The Court will hear an expert in order to find out the market value of the former building and will then strike a balance between this value and the increased value of a new building of the same type. In the end, this will result in a deduction of 'new for old' under the heading of 'betterment'. This corresponds with the solution that would have been reached in cases falling under § 251 II BGB, ie where restitution in kind is possible only through disproportionate outlays. In other words: the sum of money which may be claimed for *Naturalherstellung* under § 249 II BGB is the same as the compensation in money under § 251 II BGB (see BGHZ 30, 29, case no 119, and BGHZ 102, 322).

6. PRESCRIPTION

Leenen, 'Die Neuregelung der Verjährung' JZ 2001, 552; Mansel, 'Die Neuregelung des Verjährungsrechts' NJW 2002, 89; Eidenmüller, 'Zur Effizienz der Verjährungsregeln im geplanten Schuldrechtsmodernisierungsgesetz' JZ 2001, 283; Law Commission, *Limitation of Actions* (Consultation Paper No 151, 1998); Law Commission, *Limitation of Actions* (Law Com No 270, 2001); McGee, *McGee on*

Limitation (4th edn, 2002), especially chapters 2 and 10; Prime & Scanlan, *The Law of Limitation* (2nd edn, 2001), chapter 4; Wagner, 'Die Verjährung gewährleistungsrechtlicher Rechtsbehelfe nach neuem Schuldrecht' ZIP 2002, 789; Wagner, 'Mangel- und Mangelfolgeschäden im neuen Schuldrecht' JZ 2002, 475; Zimmermann, Leenen, Mansel and Ernst, 'Finis Litium? Zum Verjährungsrecht nach dem Regierungsentwurf eines Schuldrechtsmodernisierungsgesetzes' JZ 2001, 684 *et seq*; Zimmermann, *Comparative Foundations of a European Law of Set-Off and Prescription* (2002).

(a) Preliminary Observations

Rights of action arising from breaches of obligations are not enforceable forever, and after a certain period of time has lapsed, the pursuit of legal remedies is barred. The BGB contains detailed rules on prescription (*Verjährung*) in its first book, ie the General Part (*Allgemeiner Teil*): §§ 194–218 BGB. These rules are no longer mandatory; prescription can be made more onerous by agreement of the parties (although it cannot extend beyond thirty years). Also, prescription may not be facilitated by advance agreement for intentional breach (§ 202 BGB). However, the provisions in the first book do not exhaust this subject. Numerous special provisions dealing with prescription may be found in the four books of the BGB that follow the general part as well as in other statutes dealing with matters of private law. Only the most important among them can be mentioned in the short survey of this area that follows here.

The recent reform has completely changed the law. Before we discuss some key aspects of the new system of prescription, it may be useful briefly to illustrate some of the reasons why reform was regarded as desirable (see, for an overview of the 'defects' of the old law: *Bundestags-Drucksache* 14/6040, p 87 *et seq*). As already stated in our general introduction to the reform (sections 1 and 2, p 391), this was an area of the law where the need for reform was perhaps most obvious.

The great variety of periods of prescription had led to discrepancies in some areas of private law, particularly with regard to the special rules governing warranties in the fields of sales law (under the old § 477 BGB, six months) and contracts for work and labour (under the old § 638 BGB). The short length of these periods provided an incentive for plaintiffs to avoid wherever possible the special rules on non-conforming performance and recover for this type of breach under a different head of claim, in order to avail themselves of a longer period of prescription. The interaction of these rules with the general rules of prescription applicable to actions for breach of contract led to artificial distinctions and forced the courts to bend the law in order to avoid unsatisfactory consequences in individual cases. Since, furthermore, the rules on periods of prescription used to be mandatory, the courts were not in a position to correct inconsistencies. Suggestions aimed at manipulating the beginning of prescription periods (so as to prolong this period in cases where the law has laid down extremely short periods) were regarded as *contra legem*. The regular period of prescription was thirty years (the former § 195 BGB). There was widespread agreement among lawyers in Germany that this period was too long. Even the draftsmen of the BGB had realised that in a large number of everyday transactions, practical justice requires much shorter periods of prescription. As a result, the former § 196 BGB contained a long list of claims to which a prescription period of two years applied (which list, however, became increasingly out-of-date). It covered the claims of merchants, manufacturers, artisans and those who engage in handicrafts, for the delivery of goods, performance of work and care of others' affairs, and it extended to public carriers, innkeepers, lawyers, notaries, medical practitioners, etc.

It therefore came as little surprise that the Ministry of Justice, in preparation of a more general reform of the law of obligations, also commissioned a report in relation to prescription periods. In their pursuant report of 1981, Peters and Zimmermann (*Gutachten und Vorschläge zur Überarbeitung des Schuldrechts*) suggested that a unitary approach to prescription should be adopted. The regular period of prescription was to be two years and it would cease to run if the creditor did not know of the claim or the person of the debtor. This is referred to as a 'subjective' approach, because the period of limitation depends on the knowledge of the creditor, both of the fact that the claim has arisen and of the person of the debtor. The First Commission in their *Abschlußbericht* of 1992 did not follow this approach but preferred an objective approach. An 'objective' approach determines prescription by events in the outside world, which operate independently of the (imputed) knowledge of the creditor. Eventually, the Second Commission switched back to a subjective approach to prescription as general rule and supplemented it with objective periods of limitations in relation to specific contracts. This has become the present position of German law. By contrast, the PECL adopt a uniform approach (see Article 14:201). The argument is straightforward: the simpler the regime of prescription, the more effectively it avoids litigation on whether or not prescription has occurred in the individual case (cf comment on Article 14:201 in Lando, Clive, Prüm and Zimmermann, *PECL*, vol 3 (2003), p 162). The reason for maintaining special objective periods for nonconforming performance is also easy to make out. It enables the promisee (usually a dealer, professional contractor or merchant) to 'close the books' after a certain date, which thus enhances commercial certainty and convenience. A unitary subjective approach cannot ensure this, for prescription will not easily take effect in relation to hidden or latent defects.

Before we examine the rules of the BGB in more detail, it is useful to add a few comparative remarks. In English law, consolidating legislation—in the form of the Limitation Act 1980—sets out the basic rules. Thus, the limitation period for a claim arising from a *simple* contract is six years from the date at which the cause of action accrues (section 5), and where the action is founded on a *specialty* contract, the period is twelve years from the date at which the cause of action arises (section 8; on 'specialty', see Prime & Scanlon, *The Law of Limitation* (2nd edn, 2001), pp 106–8 for a useful summary). A cause of action arises at the time of breach and not when the contract is concluded (see *Gibbs v Guild* (1881) 8 QBD 296, at 302 and note that the Latent Damage Act 1986 does not apply to claims for breach of contract). Until 1984, the year when the Foreign Limitation Periods Act came into force, English law was committed to the view that statutes of limitation, if they merely specified a certain time after which rights could no longer be enforced by action, were procedural and not substantive. This led to serious conflicts in disputes containing foreign elements, in particular in cases where the proper law of contract was the law of a country where limitation of actions or, for that matter, prescription (*Verjährung*) was regarded as a matter of substantive law (*materiellrechtlich*). Since procedure is governed by the *lex fori,* English courts ignored any classification of the foreign rule as substantive and applied the limitation statutes of the forum. This conflict of classification has its basis in the distinction between (substantive) right and (procedural) remedy. The terminology used in English law—that is to say, of 'limitation of actions'—is evidence of the procedural approach to the problem. It is the 'remedy' that is barred after a certain period of time. However, if seen in an international context, the emphasis on the remedy is very often artificial, because the decisive question must necessarily be whether a right has been created, and it is only fair to leave the decision whether this right is still enforceable to the legal system under which this right has arise. The Foreign Limitation Periods Act 1984 has abandoned the common law approach, which favoured the application of the domestic law of limitation. Instead, an English court is now expected to apply the proper law of contract that governs the substantive issue according to the English choice of law rules (see Cheshire & North's, *Private International Law* (13th edn, 1999), p 73).

(b) Periods of Limitation

The BGB now provides for certain special periods of limitation and a general period of limitation. The standard limitation period is three years: § 195 BGB. According to § 199 I BGB, this period commences from the end of the year in which the claim arises and the creditor acquires knowledge of the circumstances forming the basis of the claim and the identity of the debtor, or would have done so had he not been grossly negligent. Further, § 199 II, III and IV BGB stipulate for certain objective maximum periods of limitation. It would serve no practical purpose to repeat the lengthy wording of these provisions. Their object is to make sure that even if the creditor does not have imputed knowledge of the claim, or at least the debtor cannot prove this, the debtor is able to invoke prescription after the lapse of relatively long periods of time (thirty years after the event giving rise to liability or ten years after the accrual of the claim, depending on the nature of the claim); this provision aims to increase certainty in the law.

The legislator supplemented this general period with special objective periods of limitations for non-conforming performance (§§ 438, 548, 634a, 651g II BGB). They begin to run independently of the imputed knowledge of the promisee: for instance, in relation to sale of goods the period commences with the delivery of the thing (§ 438 II BGB). However, these special objective periods are considerably longer than they used to be. The shortest period under the old law has been raised from six months to two years (eg, § 438 I Nr. 3 BGB; § 548 BGB being the only exception retaining the six-month period). In relation to the law of consumer sales, this was also required for the implementation of Article 5 of Directive 1999/44/EC (which caused no specific implementation problems in the UK, since the applicable limitation period was already over the two-year minimum laid down by Article 5). Moreover, in relation to certain claims concerning land § 438 I Nr. 1 BGB extends prescription to a thirty-year period; § 438 I Nr. 2 BGB provides for a period of five years in relation to building works.

As was explained in the section on damages, p 469 (section 5(h)), the promisee may recover in contract what was there referred to as 'simple' damages (§ 280 I BGB) for any 'consequential' loss caused by the non-conforming performance. To give an example: suppose a chair supplied is defective and collapses, injuring the buyer who sat on it, he may (in addition to a claim in tort under § 823 I BGB) also recover damages in contract law in respect of the personal injury (§§ 437 Nr. 3, 280 I, 249 BGB, see above). The tort claim is subject to the (essentially subjective) general period of limitation in § 195 BGB (at least if the previous approach of the courts is continued in relation to the new law: BGH NJW-RR 1993, 1113). According to the wording of § 438 I Nr. 3 BGB, the contract claim, which may be advantageous in relation to vicarious liability (§ 278 BGB), is subject to the objective limitation period of limitation of two years. In relation to this so-called *Mangelfolgeschaden*, it is controversial whether the short period of limitation is appropriate: some argue in favour of restricting the scope of application of § 438 BGB for any violation of the interest in the integrity of one's other rights or interest (*Integritätsinteresse*, cf Canaris, *Karlsruher Forum 2002*, at p 98; Wagner, JZ 2002, 475, 479). This 'correction' of the legislative intention once more in effect attempts to remedy deficiencies of the law of tort by the means of contract law. (See, further, Beale, Hartkamp, Kötz and Tallon, *Ius Commune Casebooks on the Common Law of Europe—Cases, Materials and Text on Contract Law* (2002) 70–2.) Whether the courts will follow this suggestion to disapply a newly introduced law remains to be seen (opposing the view aforementioned on this ground: eg, Faust, in Bamberger and Roth (eds), *BGB*, (2003), § 438 Rn. 9; Mansel NJW 2002, 89, 95).

Paragraph 196 BGB contains yet another special period of limitation of ten years for claims in relation to a proprietary interest in land (when they begin is determined objectively, § 200 BGB). Finally, § 197 BGB subjects certain specific claims to a period of prescription of thirty years. This concerns, eg, claims that have been confirmed in legal proceedings (§ 197 I Nr. 3 BGB) as well as claims from the field of family law and the law of succession (§ 197 I Nr. 2 BGB). The commencement of these periods is objective (regulated in § 200 and § 201 BGB and depends on the nature of the claim).

(c) Suspension, Restart and Effects of Prescription

The beginning of the period of prescription was described in the previous section. Here we are concerned with any action or measure that the creditor may take that prevents the period from lapsing. The BGB recognises three types of measures.

First, the 'suspension' of the period of prescription (*Hemmung der Verjährung*) is possible. This means that the period during which prescription is suspended is not reckoned in the period of prescription (§ 209 BGB). Thus, prescription is suspended for so long as the injured party and the person claimed to be liable are engaged in negotiations with each other aimed at achieving a settlement (§ 203 BGB). Suspension also takes effect for the sake of keeping the 'family peace': prescription of claims between spouses is suspended as long as the marriage continues (§ 207 I 1 BGB). The same applies, for instance, to claims between parents and children during the minority of the children (§ 207 I 2 Nr. 2 BGB). The most important instance of suspension now is the commencement of legal proceedings (§ 204 BGB). The paradigm case is that of bringing an action for the enforcement of the obligation (§ 204 I Nr. 1 BGB), although note that the same effect is attributed to a number of other procedural techniques.

Secondly, in §§ 210 and 211 the BGB regulates what is known as *Ablaufhemmung*, a special form of suspension. It suffices to refer to § 210 BGB (legal capacity) as an illustration. If a person who is not legally competent, or who is restricted in his legal competence, is without a statutory representative, a limitation period running for or against that person will not start before the expiry of six months after the point in time at which the person becomes fully legally competent or the lack of representation is removed.

Thirdly, a more effective device is the measures of the creditor that entail a restart of the period of prescription (*Neubeginn der Verjährung*), previously known as 'interruption'. The restart means that the time that has elapsed before the interruption is not taken into consideration, and a new period of prescription can begin only on the termination of the interruption. The reasons leading to a restart of prescription are laid down in § 212 BGB, the most important among them being a restart by acknowledgement (*Anerkenntnis*, § 212 I Nr. 1 BGB).

It is important to realise that the *effect* of *Verjährung* or prescription is not to extinguish a claim; rather, it gives the person claimed to be liable only a countervailing right (or plea) to refuse performance (*Einrede der Verjährung*, § 214 I BGB). It is up to the defendant to plead *Verjährung*, for the court will not take notice of this fact *ex officio*. Another consequence of this approach is that a debtor, who has made payment even though the creditor's claim had already prescribed, has paid *cum causa*. If the debtor afterwards finds out that he could have refused payment, he cannot bring an action for the return of unjust enrichment (§§ 813 I 2, 214 II BGB). Moreover, if the creditor's claim is secured by a mortgage or pledge, he is not prevented from seeking satisfaction from the charged object by the prescription of his claim (§ 216 I BGB). In relation to the right of termination, special considerations apply.

The right to terminate a contract (*Rücktritt*) is not a 'claim' in the technical sense of the word. § 194 I BGB clarifies that only the right to demand a positive act or an omission from another is subject to prescription. This is also the only abstract definition of what in German law is the equivalent notion of 'claim', namely *Anspruch*. The right to terminate the contract is categorically a different right. It entails a power to affect the legal position of creditor and debtor by unilateral declaration (*Gestaltungsrecht*). Nevertheless, it would be inconsistent to subject the right to claim damages to prescription, yet to allow the innocent party indefinitely to hold the right to terminate the contract and satisfy his interest in the restitution of the counter-performance. In order to tackle this problem, § 218 BGB was introduced. It states as a general rule that the right to termination is excluded if the right to demand performance or to require that the performance be brought into conformity with the contract would be time-barred and the debtor has invoked prescription. It should be noted that this would also exclude the right, where applicable, to demand a price reduction.

10

Breach of Contract-Specific Contracts

1. INTRODUCTORY REMARKS

The cornerstones of liability for breach of contract under the BGB were the concern of chapter 9. Three main remedies were identified: enforced performance, termination and damages. These remedies are governed by the rules laid down in the General Part of the Law of Obligations (§§ 241 *et seq* BGB, *Allgemeines Schuldrecht*). These provisions are of general application. Some of them even apply to obligations other than contract, but the emphasis in this book is on contract law. The general rules are not confined to a particular instance of contract law. They are fundamental to the understanding of the system of remedies available for breach of contract.

Nevertheless, it would be misleading to conclude this book without an account of the most important special rules for breach of specific types of contract. These rules are idiosyncratic to particular instances of contract law and accordingly figure in the Special Part of the Law of Obligations of the BGB (*Besonderes Schuldrecht*, which begins with the contract of sale in § 433 BGB). It is the purpose of the present chapter to convey the extent and the nature of these special rules. An overview of the different types of contract and their specific rules has been already given in chapter 3, p 144. In the present chapter, the focus of attention must once again return to the Special Part. This time, the focus of the inquiry is on how far the Special Part contains deviations from the general principles of breach of contract presented in the previous chapter. It would serve no practical purpose to include all of the different types of contract and all of the possible variations of the general rules here. This must be reserved to specialised works. Instead, we will examine four types of contract, which we have selected because of their model character for the law of contract as a whole: the contract of sale (§ 433 BGB), the contract for work (§ 631 BGB), for services (§ 611 BGB) and leases (§ 535 BGB). Traditionally, due to the influence of Roman law, the contract of sale is seen as the paradigm instance of contract law. The contract for work is equally important in practice; it is also a model for construction contracts (insofar as they do not involve a contract of sale). The contract of service is not only crucial for all 'labour' contracts (*Arbeitsverträge*), but it also provides the model contract regime for the services provided by lawyers, medics and many other professionals.

The special rules for breach in the Special Part deviate from those contained in the General Part in two main ways.

The first type of deviation is the more radical one, because it singles out a particular type of irregularity of performance and subjects it to special rules. It is non-conforming performance (*Schlechtleistung*) that customarily requires special consideration in civil law systems. The paradigmatic case of a modern reciprocal contract—or to use the English terminology, a contract supported by consideration—is the provision of a thing or service (performance) against remuneration (counter-performance). German law differentiates between specific types of contract by distinguishing on the basis of the nature of promised performance. Traditionally, the remedies for non-conforming performance, ie, the breach of the performance obligation by bad performance, also mirrored the division between the different types of contract. Having a special regime of rules for non-conforming performance may be explained by reference to the actual differences between the performance obligations. Still, it tends to complicate matters and invariably necessitates the introduction of subtle meta-rules that determine the scope of application of the different sets of rules. As was explained in chapter 9, the main economising effect of the recent reform of the system of remedies for breach has been to reduce to an encouraging degree the number of special rules actually needed. Special rules for non-conforming performance have been retained, as we shall see shortly, but their differences from the general rules are quite limited. This simplifying effect is limited to the contract of sale and the contract for work. Even before the latest reforms, the contract of services did not involve a great number of special rules (with the notable exception of rules on termination). The rules on leases now are the main example of a more or less autarkic regime of remedies for non-conforming performance. Another example is the 'travel' contract, § 651a BGB, which historically evolved out of the contract for work (we do not discuss it further here, since the lengthy provisions are for most purposes self-explanatory).

The second type of special rules for breach of contract is made up of the amorphous batch of specific qualifications to the general rules applicable to remedies for breach. Normally, these qualifications are made irrespective of the type of irregularity of performance. The main example of this phenomenon is § 314 BGB. The remedy of termination by notice (*Kündigung*) is of central importance for continuing or long-term contracts. As we have seen (in chapter 9, p 436), generally speaking such termination is possible only with effects for the future. If a breach of contract is the condition for this remedy, it is referred to as 'extra-ordinary' termination and defined in abstract form in § 314 BGB. However, this provision is more a theoretical model than of practical relevance, for it is replaced in all important respects by the special rules applicable to individual types of contract.

2. SALE OF GOODS

Stefan Arnold and Unberath, 'Die Umsetzung der Richtlinie über den Verbrauchsgüterkauf in England' ZEuP 2004, 366; Bridge, *The Sale of Goods* (1998); Canaris, 'Die Nacherfüllung durch Lieferung einer mangelfreien Sache beim Stückkauf' JZ 2003, 831; Canaris, 'Die Neuregelung des Leistungsstörungs- und des Kaufrechts' in Egon Lorenz (ed), *Karlsruher Forum 2002* (2003), 5; Ernst and Gsell, 'Kaufrechtsrichtlinie und BGB' ZIP 2000, 1410; Guest (gen ed), *Benjamin's Sale of Goods* (6th edn, 2002); Grigoleit and Herresthal, 'Grundlagen der Sachmängelhaftung im Kaufrecht' JZ 2003, 118; Grundmann and Bianca (eds), *EU-Kaufrechtsrichtlinie* (2002); Grundmann, Medicus and Rolland (eds), *Europäisches Kaufgewährleistungsrecht*

(2000); Gsell, 'Nutzungsentschädigung bei kaufrechtlicher Nacherfüllung?' NJW 2003, 1969; Lorenz, 'Rücktritt, Minderung und Schadensersatz wegen Sachmängeln im neuen Kaufrecht: Was hat der Verkäufer zu vertreten?' NJW 2002, 2497; Lorenz, 'Selbstvornahme der Mängelbeseitigung im Kaufrecht' NJW 2003, 1417; Lorenz, 'Sachmangel und Beweislastumkehr im Verbrauchsgüterkauf–Zur Reichweite der Vermutungsregelung in § 476 BGB' NJW 2004, 3020; Oechsler, 'Praktische Anwendungsprobleme des Nacherfüllungsanspruchs' NJW 2004, 1825; Reinicke/ Tiedtke, *Kaufrecht*, (7th edn, 2004); von Sachsen Gessaphe, 'Der Rückgriff des Letztverkäufers—neues europäisches und deutsches Kaufrecht' RiW 2001, 721; Schubel, 'Das neue Kaufrecht' JuS 2002, 313; Sealey & Hooley, *Commercial Law: Text, Cases and Materials* (2003), Part III (chapters 7–13); Unberath, 'Die richtlinienkonforme Auslegung am Beispiel der Kaufrechtsrichtlinie' ZEuP 2005, 5; Westermann, 'Das neue Kaufrecht' NJW 2002, 241; Zimmer/Eckhold, 'Das neue Mängelgewährleistungsrecht beim Kauf' Jura 2002, 145.

(a) Preliminary Observations

Like the CISG, the Sale of Goods Act 1979 seeks to provide appropriate remedies for all typical types of breach of a contract of sale. Thus, for instance in Part VI of the 1979 Act on 'Actions for Breach of the Contract,' the rights of the buyer and the seller are set out, covering the non-payment of the price in section 49, the non-acceptance of the goods in section 50 and, in relation to the rights of the buyer, the non-delivery of the goods in sections 51 and 52 and breach of warranty in section 53. Similarly, the CISG offers a comprehensive solution for breach of the contract of sale (in its Article 45 *et seq*, dealing with the remedies of the buyer; Art. 61 *et seq* spelling out the remedies of the seller, etc). One would therefore be inclined to expect that in §§ 433 *et seq* BGB one would find a clarification of a similar sort of the respective rights of seller and buyer. It should be made clear at the outset however that this is not so. Of course, the main obligations of the parties to a contract of sale are defined in § 433 BGB, namely for the seller to deliver conforming goods and for the buyer to pay the price. However, while one particular type of irregularity of performance is given special attention, remedies in respect of other irregularities or types of breach follow the general principles (as explained in the previous chapter) and are not 'mirrored' in the Special Part of the Law of Obligations in the BGB. This naturally also explains why the present chapter can be comparatively short. The type of irregularity of performance that is specially regulated by the BGB is bad performance by the seller: that is, delivery of non-conforming goods or (in short) non-conforming performance. The remedies for this type of breach (commonly referred to as '*Gewährleistungsrecht*') are laid down in §§ 434–45 BGB which thus form a substantial part, and the part which is certainly the most important in practice, of the provisions in the BGB on the contract of sale. Directive 1999/44/EC on consumer sale adopts a similar (one-sided) approach and gives a first impression of the subject-matter of the special provisions on the contract of sale in the BGB (see now Part 5A of the Sale of Goods Act 1979, as inserted by reg 5 of the Sale and Supply of Goods to Consumers Regulations 2002, and note that the Directive is not concerned with the remedy of damages, which of course is of vital importance in German as much as in English law). In this section on breach of contract, we will therefore concentrate on non-conforming performance (for other aspects of the contract of sale, the reader may consult chapter 3). It may nevertheless be useful briefly to illustrate the application of the general principles on breach (*allgemeines Leistungsstörungsrecht*) to contracts of sale.

(b) Application of General Contract Principles to Breach of a Contract of Sale

The obligation of the *buyer* to *pay the price* is inherent in the contract of sale. It is laid down in § 433 II BGB and subject to the general contract rules (as set out in the previous chapter; see sections 27 and 28 of the 1979 Act: the buyer is bound to pay the price in accordance with the terms of the contract, but is only required to make payment if the seller is ready and willing to transfer possession in the goods in return for his payment of the price). The obligation can be specifically enforced. It should also be noted that if the buyer bears the so-called risk of counter-performance (*Preisgefahr*), the seller will retain the right to claim the price even if he is released from his obligation to perform because performance has become impossible (see § 447 BGB, also discussed in chapters 8, section 3(b) and 9, section 3(e), p 411).

According to § 288 BGB, the seller is entitled to interest if the buyer is in default of payment. This, it will be recalled, will normally be the case if a certain date has been fixed for payment (§ 286 II Nr. 1 BGB), or thirty days have elapsed since the buyer had notice of an invoice (the further conditions are regulated in § 286 III BGB) or if the debtor has been issued a *Mahnung* (§ 286 I BGB). The right to claim interest does not preclude the right to recover damages for any further loss resulting from a delay of payment according to §§ 280 II, 286 BGB, as § 288 IV BGB clarifies. For the right to claim interest in such circumstances in English law, see: section 54 of the 1979 Act (preserving any rights that the seller may have, apart from under the 1979 Act, to claim interest on the price), in conjunction with section 35A of the Supreme Court Act 1981. In practice, such interest is very regularly awarded in commercial claims for such debts. See also the Late Payment of Commercial Debts (Interest) Act 1998.

If a period for performance has been set to no avail, the seller may also terminate the contract (according to § 323 I BGB) and claim damages instead of performance (according to § 281 I BGB). The latter right depends on whether the buyer is answerable for the breach (§ 280 I 2 BGB); however, it will be recalled that the liability for money debts is generally regarded as 'strict'. On this point in English law, see the discussion in chapter 9, section 4 on termination: the ability of the seller to terminate the contract, treat himself as discharged from further performance and sue for damages for breach will fall to be determined by ordinary contract principles: see eg, *Bunge Corp v Tradax SA* [1981] 1 WLR 711, where the time stipulation was treated as a condition, entitling termination.

Furthermore, the *buyer* must *take delivery* of the goods according to § 433 II BGB. Loss resulting from failure to take delivery may be recoverable as damages for delay according to §§ 280 II, 286 BGB. In English law, see sections 50 and 51 of the 1979 Act: wrongful failure by the buyer to accept and pay for the goods gives rise to a claim in damages for the seller (see Sealey & Hooley, *Commercial Law: Text, Cases and Matierals* (3rd edn, 2003), pp 412–14 for details on the remoteness rule to be applied here). A delay in accepting the performance has the further consequences spelled out in §§ 293 *et seq* BGB (discussed in chapter 9, p 411. (In the US, compare § 2-709 UCC, where the buyer is obliged to take the goods only if the seller could not reasonably resell them.)

The *seller* is firstly under an obligation to *hand over the thing and transfer ownership* in the thing to the buyer, § 433 I 1 BGB (see sections 12(1) (implied condition that the seller has title to transfer the goods); 27 (delivery); and 28 (readiness and willingness to transfer possession in return for the price) of the 1979 Act). If the seller does not deliver at all, then in both English and German law the respective general principles on breach of contract apply. If the obligations of the seller and the buyer are to be fulfilled concurrently, as is normally the case, according to § 320 BGB (and section 28 of the 1979 Act), the buyer may withhold payment until the seller offers performance (discussed in chapter 8, p 349). The obligation of the seller may, as a general rule, be specifically enforced; contrast section 52 of the Sale of Goods Act 1979, where failure to deliver specific or ascertained goods may be remedied by an order of specific performance, but only where the court thinks it fit to do so. It is unlikely that the court's discretion under section 52 will be exercised to order specific performance where the goods are of an ordinary description and the buyer intends to resell them once received (see *Cohen v Roche* [1927] 1 KB 169, although whether today we would consider 'eight genuine Hepplewhite chairs' to be quite so 'ordinary' is another matter). There are also clear examples of when the court will order such specific performance: see eg, *Behnke v Bede Shipping Co Ltd* [1927] 1 KB 649 (concerning a ship designed specifically to meet the buyer's precise needs).

It will also be recalled that in German law the precise limits of the obligation of the seller to procure the subject-matter of the contract are somewhat controversial in relation to the sale of a specific thing. While some argue that the value of the counter-performance is the ceiling beyond which the seller is released from his obligation to perform according to § 275 II BGB, others maintain that the obligation of the seller is extinguished only if the costs are grossly disproportionate to the interest of the buyer (for more detailed discussion, see chapter 9, p 415 ff). The buyer may claim damages for delay (§ 280 II BGB), to cover loss caused by the delay of delivery, provided that the seller was in default according to § 286 BGB. As a general rule, this remedy is fault-dependent, ie the debtor must be answerable for the breach (§§ 280 I 2, 276 BGB); however, it will be recalled that the obligation to deliver generic goods is construed as a 'guarantee'-type liability (again discussed in section 3(e) of the previous chapter). If the buyer fixes a period for performance to no avail, he may also terminate the contract (§ 323 I BGB) and/or claim damages instead of performance (§ 281 I BGB, provided that the seller is answerable for the non-delivery). The normal qualifications apply: for instance, if the seller refuses to perform then the buyer may dispense with setting a period for performance (§ 323 II Nr. 1 BGB). In cases of impossibility, the right to claim damages instead of performance follows from § 311a II BGB in the case of initial impossibility and § 283 BGB in the case of subsequent impossibility. Note also that in cases of impossibility, the buyer may claim any substitute of performance independently of fault according to § 285 BGB.

Furthermore, the *seller* must deliver things that are *free from defects*, ie he must deliver conforming things, § 433 I 2 BGB. This result is achieved in English law by the use of a series of statutorily implied terms: see section. 13 (sale by description—implied condition that the goods correspond with their description), 14 (implied conditions as to the satisfactory quality of the goods and their fitness for any specified particular purpose) and 15 (terms implied in sales of goods by sample) of the 1979 Act. Note also that these rules derogate from the basic position in English law that the seller is otherwise deemed to give no such undertakings about the goods (unless by implication from usage: section 14(4) of the 1979 Act): *caveat emptor* is the basic rule (section 14(1) of the 1979 Act). (In the US, a similar position obtains with regard to the warranty of merchantability (§ 2-314 UCC) and the implied warranty of fitness (§ 2-315).) In German law, the conformity of performance is subject to a special regime of rules, which is set out in §§ 434–44 BGB. It is important to note from the outset however that these rules have a limited scope of application. Although this is not expressly stated, it is generally agreed that the special rules do not apply in respect of all cases of non-conforming performance. If the special rules are not applicable, the buyer may avail himself of the full range of remedies discussed in the previous chapter. In particular, the buyer may reject non-conforming performance and thereby take himself outside the scope of application of the special rules. He may demand conforming performance according to § 433 I 2 BGB, or he may set a period for performance and terminate the contract if the period lapses without the seller having offered conforming performance, § 323 I BGB. The qualification that the breach must not be 'minor' (§ 323 V 2 BGB) is immaterial, since the buyer has not received performance at all (see Faust in Bamberger and Roth (eds), *BGB* (2003), § 433 Rn. 15 with references also of the opposite view; the same applies in relation to claiming damages under § 281 BGB). The rejection in effect amounts to treating the case as one of non-delivery.

The precise dividing line between general principle and the special rules governing non-conforming performance is controversial at the fringes and the issue awaits clarification through court decisions. Some argue that the special rules presuppose that the subject-matter of the contract was actually 'delivered' (*geliefert*) to the buyer and that the latter accepted it (eg, Oetker and Maultzsch, *Vertragliche Schuldverhältnisse*, p 75; cf Article 3(1) of Directive 1999/44/EC). It is argued that only where performance has already been made is the rationale of the special rules to increase commercial certainty (eg, the objective short limitation period) fully justified. The majority opinion among commentators however would also apply the special rules if no delivery has taken place but the *risk* of the counter-performance has passed to the buyer (eg, Canaris, *Karlsruher Forum 2002*, p 72). At the latest, the transfer of risk occurs with delivery (§ 446 BGB) so the practical results of these two theoretical approaches will very often converge. The majority approach may make a difference however in cases where the delivery is to a carrier (§ 447 BGB) or if acceptance is delayed (§ 326 II 1 BGB).

It should be stressed that, within their scope of application, the special rules to a considerable extent refer back to the general principles (which indeed is the basic approach of the English provisions: where they apply and claim to be exclusive, then their operation is mandatory, but they also allow agreements to exclude certain terms that would otherwise apply and such terms are defined so as to reply on underlying contract law principles as to breach, termination and damages). This seems confusing at first but is quite sensible when the purpose of the special rules is considered. Their aim is merely to qualify the general principles introduced in the previous chapter, in the light of the peculiarities of the obligation of the seller to deliver conforming things, not to replace them completely. The recent reform has not abolished these special rules in their entirety, but it has considerably reduced the number and significance of the inconsistencies between general principles and the special rules. The remaining caveats are of limited importance, as will become apparent in the remainder of this section.

(c) Defining Conformity

The breadth of the notion of conformity (§§ 434 and 435 BGB) indirectly also determines the scope of application of the special rules. First, it should be noted that the provisions on the contract of sale cover not only sale of goods (ie, corporeal things) but (according to § 453 BGB) the sale of rights and other abstract entities, such as a commercial enterprise (ie, non-corporeal things). In what follows, the sale of goods will be discussed as the paradigm case. It should also be observed that the provisions of the contract of sale also apply to contracts that involve the production of the movable thing (the details on this topic are regulated by § 651 BGB). (Note that sales law in the US only applies to the sale of goods.)

The definition of 'conformity' is of great importance as far as the application of Directive 1999/44/EC is concerned, because it only aims to harmonise certain remedies for the delivery of non-conforming goods, and not more. It is interesting to observe that in implementing the Directive, the English legislator has not introduced a stand-alone definition of non-conformity for consumer sales. Instead, reg 3 of the Sale and Supply of Goods to Consumers Regulations 2002 has slightly altered the existing definition in sections 13 and 14 Sale of Goods Act 1979. These provisions imply certain terms by law into the contract of sale which by their very nature are subject to variation by agreement between the parties. However, the Directive (as well as the BGB) does not use an 'implied term' technique, but stipulates rules as to when 'objectively' performance does not conform to the contract requirements. The difference in approach is only apparent however and the assumed convergence in implementing the Directive real. The definitions of conformity in the BGB, as in the Directive, merely reflect the presumed intention of the parties (eg, Grigoleit and Herresthal, JZ 2003, 233; Canaris, *Karlsruher Forum 2002*, p 58). The parties remain free to define the requirements as to the performance as they think fit (on the Directive, see also below; it suffices here to note that the suggestion that an objective standard should be required, very much in the same manner as under the Product Liability Directive 1985/374/EEC [1985] OJ L210/29, ultimately was not followed in the adoption of Directive 1999/44/EC). The following remarks may thus, despite the slight difference in the theoretical explanation, safely be compared with section 12 *et seq* of the Sale of Goods Act 1979.

Conformity is defined as the absence of defects. Physical defects (§ 434 BGB) are distinguished from legal defects (§ 435 BGB). The requirements in relation to the physical condition of the thing are manifold. The relevant time is defined in § 434 I 1 BGB: the thing is free from physical defects if it has the agreed composition at the point when the risk passes. This provision also clarifies that, in the first instance, the parties define the standard which the thing has to satisfy. Insofar as the composition is not specifically agreed, § 434 I 2 BGB lists a number of factors which must be taken into account in deciding whether the thing is free from physical defects. First, (§ 434 I 2 Nr. 1), the things must be suitable for the use assumed according to the contract, and in addition (§ 434 I 2 Nr. 2), it must be suitable for the usual use and have a composition which is usual for things that kind and which the purchaser can expect in accordance with the type of thing (which two provisions correspond to the English rules contained, respectively, in section 14(3) and section 14(2) of the 1979 Act—the latter treats 'satisfactory quality' as containing the idea that goods sold should be fit for the purposes for which such goods are commonly used—see section 14(2A) and (2B) for the definition of 'satisfactory quality'. In the US, the concept of 'merchantability' performs a similar function: the goods must pass without objection in trade, must be of fair average quality, etc. See UCC § 2-314; in products liability law in the US, this is known as the 'consumer expectation' standard).

According to § 434 I 3 BGB, composition also includes those characteristics that the purchaser can expect according to the public statements of the seller, of the manufacturer (under the Product Liability Act) or his assistant, in particular in the advertising or in the marketing concerning particular characteristics of the thing, *unless* the seller did not know of the statement and also need not have known of it, it was corrected at the point in time of the conclusion of the contract in an equally valid manner, or it could not influence the decision to purchase. (In English law, see to the same effect the new section 14(2D) of the 1979 Act, inserted by reg 3 of the 2002 Regulations. In the US however see UCC § 2-313, which dispenses with any requirement of actual reliance to make out a claim of express warranty. Instead, the promise or representation must be a 'basis of the bargain': this issue has been hotly contested in the cigarette cases— eg, compare *Cipollone v Ligget Group*, 693 F Supp 208, 212–15 (DNJ 1988) (holding that smoker need not establish actual reliance under UCC § 2-313 to bring claim for breach of express warranty that smoking did not pose a health risk. '[A] statement in an advertisement becomes part of the basis of the bargain if, objectively viewed, the statement would tend to induce the purchase of the advertised product. Whether the statement actually induced a particular purchase is not relevant to a determination of whether the statement may constitute an express warranty') and *American Tobacco Co Inc v Grinnell*, 951 SW 2d 420 (Tex 1997) (holding that a claim for breach of an express warranty failed because the smoker could not establish reliance.))

Paragraph 434 II BGB contains what is commonly referred to as 'IKEA'-clause: a physical defect is also present if the agreed assembly has been carried out by the seller or his agent improperly or if the assembly instructions are incorrect (unless of course the thing is assembled correctly).

In order to avoid problems of distinguishing cases of non-conforming performance from other irregularities of performance, § 434 III BGB also treats (in a sweeping fashion) the following instances of failure of performance as non-conforming performance: if the seller delivers a different thing or too small a quantity; or if *generic goods* are promised (*Gattungskauf*) and the seller delivers goods that belong to a different kind (*Qualitätsaliud*). To come back to an example given above (in chapter 3, p 135): if whale-meat is promised and shark meat is actually delivered, the delivered shark meat is treated as 'defective' whale meat. Prior to the reform, it was necessary to distinguish between the different categories of generic goods in order to determine the scope of application of the special rules. This gave rise to serious uncertainty in the law, for there are no entirely clear boundaries between different sorts of products. § 434 III BGB has now alleviated this difficulty. If a *specific thing* is the subject-matter of the contract (*Stückkauf*) and a different object has been delivered, this also constitutes a case of non-conforming performance (*Identitätsaliud*). The issue is seen by some as controversial, for the aforementioned difficulty in discerning what is *aliud* (ie totally different goods) and what is *peius* (ie, 'merely' non-conforming goods) does not arise (eg, Canaris, *Karlsruher Forum 2002*, p 68; Lettl, JuS 2002, 866). However, the wording of the provision does not differentiate and the rationale is clearly one of assimilating the delivery of a different thing regardless of what were (at times subtle) distinctions between the sale of a specific thing and the sale of generic goods (eg, Faust in Bamberger and Roth (eds), *BGB* (2003), § 434 Rn. 107). If the seller delivers an object which is actually worth more than the promised thing, he may claim it back according to the rules of unjust enrichment (see Stephan Lorenz, JuS 2003, 36).

Legal defects are also included into this category of failure of performance. The relevant provision of the BGB is § 435: the thing is free from legal defects if third parties cannot claim any rights against the purchaser in relation to the thing or only those legal rights taken over in the purchase contract. It is equivalent to a legal defect if a right which does not exist is entered in the land register. In English law on this area, see section 12(1) of the 1979 Act, which implies a condition as to the seller's right to sell the goods in question (on which see eg, *Rowland v Divall* [1923] 2 KB 500 and *Niblett Ltd v Confectioners' Materials Co Ltd* [1921] 3 KB 387) and section 12(2)(a) and (b), which imply *warranties* as to the goods being free from encumbrances and as to quiet possession of the goods, respectively. Note that the latter are warranties only, so that breach of those implied terms can sound only in damages under English law. (In US law, this category would be covered by UCC § 2-312: the implied warranty of title and warranty against infringement.)

The rights of the buyer in respect of non-conforming performance depend on whether the buyer can be presumed unconditionally to have accepted the thing. This principle of *'caveat emptor'* is reflected in § 442 BGB, but it is subject to many qualifications (for instance, it does not apply to rights that figure in the land register). The rights of the buyer in respect of the conformity of the thing delivered are excluded if the buyer knew of the defect and did not reserve his rights on acceptance (see section 14(2C)(a) of the 1979 Act and *Bartlett v Sidney Marcus Ltd* [1965] 1 WLR 1013). The same applies if he was grossly negligent in failing to detect the defect, provided that the seller did not undertake a guarantee in respect of the conformity and that he did not wilfully conceal the defect. The key question in this context is the extent to which the buyer is required to examine the thing. As a general rule, the buyer is not required to do so but the courts have recognised a number of exceptions. More is expected of a buyer who has expert knowledge; the value of the transaction may also play a certain role. (See, for illustrations: Faust, *BGB* (2003), § 442 Rn. 20; who opposes the jurisprudence and argues in favour of limiting duties of inspection to extreme cases, otherwise transaction costs would be unduly increased: in many cases it would be easier for the seller to examine the thing.)

The English provisions on the extent of examination and care required of the buyer in such cases are to be found in section 14(2C) of the 1979 Act and should be read with the shift in language on conformity with the requirement of 'satisfactory quality' (which, until the reform in the Sale of Goods (Amendment) Act 1995, used to refer to 'merchantable quality': often, defects not discovered cost money to cure, which rendered the goods less valuable than the buyer had thought when he purchased them, and yet were still held to be of 'merchantable quality';—see eg, *Business Application Specialists Ltd v Nationwide Credit Corp Ltd* [1988] RTR 332, where £635 worth of repairs on a second-hand Mercedes that had been bought for £15,000 was not sufficient to deprive the car of 'merchantable quality' in the judgment of the court). Thus, section 14(2C)(b) makes clear that if the buyer has actually examined the goods, and that examination ought to have revealed the defect, then there is no claim for non-conformity with the implied condition as to satisfactory quality. Similarly, in the case of sales by sample, section 14(2C)(c) excludes the buyer's claim where the defect ought to have been apparent on a reasonable examination of the sample provided, although the wording here seems not require that any actual examination has taken place for the exclusion to operate. (See further, the presumptions as to defects in goods in consumer sales, introduced in section 48A(3) of the 1979 Act to implement Directive 1999/44/EC, discussed in section 2(i), p 515.)

In US law a buyer who accepts non-conforming goods with reason to know of the non-conformity loses the power to force the seller to take the goods back—UCC §§ 2-601 (acceptance), 2-607 (effect of acceptance) and 2-608 (power to revoke)—but he does not lose a claim for breach of warranty and damages unless he fails to give notice of the defect within a reasonable time: UCC § 2-607(3). The cases are decidedly in favour of buyers on what counts as a reasonable time: see eg, *Maybank v SS Kresge Co* 302 NC 129, 273 SE 2d 681 (1981), which is a striking example. The case holds that three years may not be too long for a consumer to notify manufacturer of flash bulb that in exploded an injured her eye because consumer would be unaware of duty to notify until they contacted an attorney. Compare *Aqualon Co v Mac Equipment, Inc* 149 F 3d 262, 36 UCC Rep Serv 2d 99, 89 ALR 5th 721 (4th Cir 1998), which holds that three years is too long for a business purchaser even when seller knew of the defect and the potential for a claim.

In dealings between commercial merchants, the German Commercial Code considerably increases the standard required of the buyer. In the interest of commercial certainty §§ 377 and 378 HGB impose a number of obligations on the buyer to notify the seller of any apparent defects and (as the case may be) also to examine the goods on receipt. It is not the place here to discuss this in detail, but it should be noted that in relation to commercial sales these provisions compel the buyer to act swiftly if he is to avoid losing his remedies in respect of non-conforming performance. So far as international sales are concerned, the buyer is required to examine the goods (Article 38 CISG) and to notify the seller of any defects discerned within a reasonable time (Article 39 CISG).

For the purposes of the remaining subsections, it will be assumed that the seller has delivered non-conforming goods, that the special rules are applicable, and finally that the buyer's rights in respect of the defect have not been excluded due to his imputed acceptance of the non-conformity. For an overview of the rights of the buyer (as provided for in the BGB) in respect of non-conforming performance, see Figure 4.

(d) Enforced Performance

§ 437 Nr. 1 BGB entitles the buyer to demand subsequent fulfilment or, in other words, to bring the performance into conformity with the contract (*Nacherfüllung*). The right to this variant of enforced performance no longer stems from § 433 I 2 BGB once the special rules are applicable. The right to demand subsequent performance is specially regulated by § 439 BGB. The prerogative of enforced performance is thus also maintained in respect of non-conforming performance. At the same time, the seller is granted a 'second chance' to fulfil the contract, for the buyer cannot as a general rule enforce any of his secondary rights before he has set a period of performance

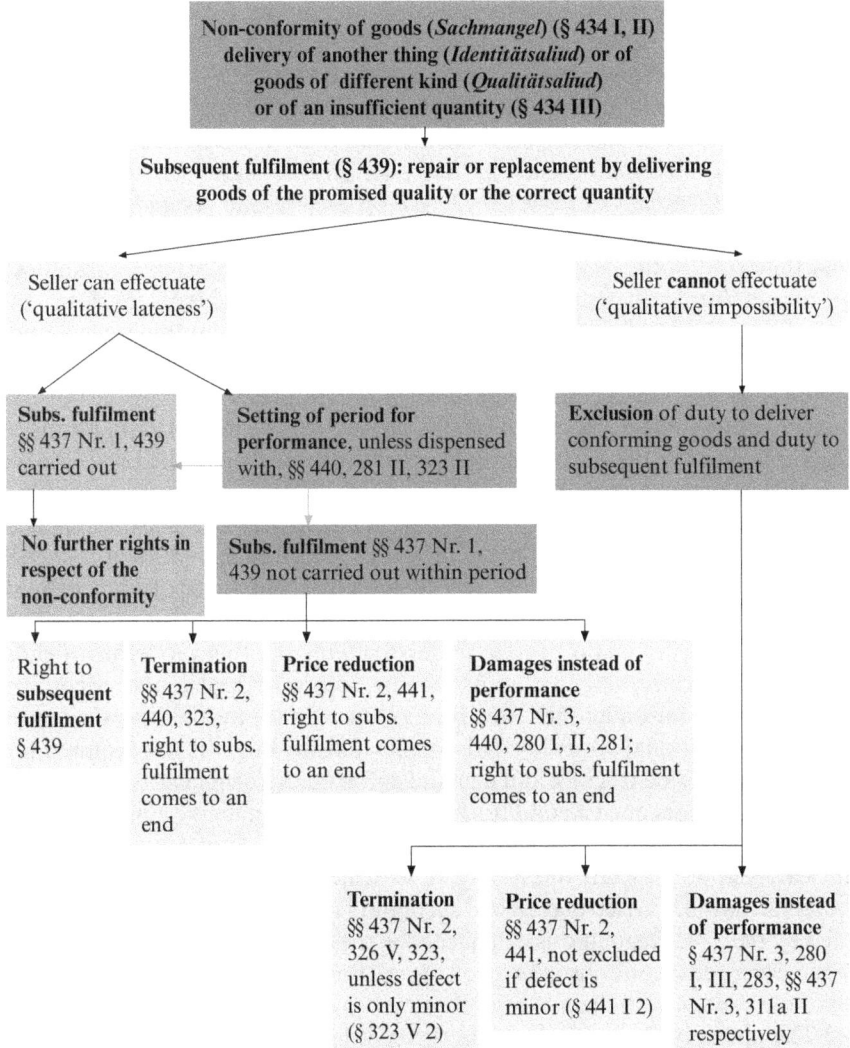

* Reproduced with kind permission of Professor Stephan Lorenz.

FIG. 4: Non-conforming goods (§§ 434 ff)*

which was to no avail: § 323 I BGB requires just that as a precondition to exercise the right to termination and § 281 I BGB is the parallel provision for the right to demand damages instead of performance. The special importance of § 439 BGB for German law therefore does not lie in the fact that it entitles the buyer to enforced performance, but rather due to the actual conditions and limitations to which this right is subjected under this provision. (In US law, the comparable provision is UCC § 2-508, which gives the seller a very limited right to cure any defects. However, this merely acts to limit the buyer's power to reject the goods and does not operate as a limitation on the buyer's power to enforce performance.)

Article 3(3) of the Consumer Sales Directive (1999/44/EC) contains an analogous right, on which § 439 BGB is modelled. The challenge posed by this prerogative of enforced performance was however a radically different one for English law (see, as to the manner of implementation, Bradgate and Twigg-Flesner, *Blackstone's Guide to Consumer Sales and Associated Guarantees* (2003), p 115 *et seq*; for a comparative discussion of the implementation in English law, see Twigg-Flesner and Howells, 'Much ado about nothing? The implementation of Directive 1999/44/EC into English Law' in Schermaier (ed), *Verbraucherkauf in Europa—Altes Gewährleistungsrecht und die Umsetzung der Richtlinie 1999/44/EG* (2003), pp 303–26 and Arnold and Unberath, ZEuP 2004, 366). The newly added section 48B of the Sale of Goods Act 1979 for the first time entitles the buyer to demand enforced performance in English law as a matter of right (rather than merely of the court's discretion). This comes close to a revolution of the remedies for breach of contract. It is probably for this reason, and due to the inertia of traditional reasoning, that in section 48E the court (to order specific performance or to give effect to a remedy which was not resorted to by the buyer) may make such orders either 'unconditionally or on such terms and conditions as to damages, payment of the price and otherwise as it thinks just.' The provision would seem to run contrary to the aim of the Directive to grant the consumer clear and unconditional rights. (See further, Arnold and Unberath, ZEuP 2004, at pp 377 and 382.) The challenge posed by the Directive to English orthodoxy was to a considerable extent further watered down and in fact avoided by the manner of implementation. First, the new remedy of enforced performance is limited to consumer sales. Unlike German law, English law thus (quite understandably for this very reason) chose to implement the Directive only within its (narrow) scope of application. Secondly, the remedies provided for under the Directive have been made available to the consumer alongside the traditional remedies. This means that the buyer is not required first to grant the seller a period of grace and demand enforced performance, but he can immediately claim damages or (if a condition is breached) terminate the contract. This may be possible to justify on the ground that it 'increases' the protection of the consumer, but it clearly shows how difficult it may be to achieve harmonisation of the civil and the common law in areas that show such fundamental differences. The solution adopted by the 2002 Regulations can hardly be regarded as entirely satisfactory, even from the perspective of consumer protection. For how is the consumer to decide which of the confusing multitude of options now available to him is suited best to his needs? The unresolved tension between the civil law-influenced European Directive and the traditional common law is bound to create further difficulties (which may yet to some extent be resolved by questions of the interpretation of the Directive and the new provisions of the 1979 Act being raised in UK courts and referred to the European Court of Justice under Article 234 EC—of course, this requires both that cases on the subject are brought in the national courts and that those courts are prepared to make such references to Luxembourg). It is for this reason that the approach adopted in Germany may hold a special interest for English law. It must be borne in mind however that the rules contained in §§ 433 *et seq* BGB reveal only part of the picture and must be understood as a comment on the general principles examined in the previous chapter.

Article 3(3) of the Directive on consumer sales recognises two ways of bringing the thing into conformity with the contract: the first is by curing the defect, ie by repairing the thing, and the second involves replacing them. It is left to the consumer to choose which he regards as the most appropriate in the circumstances. The CISG, by contrast, entitles the buyer to claim delivery of substitute goods only if the lack of conformity constitutes a fundamental breach (Article 46(2): this type of breach is discussed in the previous chapter; this is also the requirement for termination). Otherwise, the buyer may only require the seller to remedy the lack of conformity by repair (Article 46(3)). § 439 BGB has been, as alluded to above, modelled on the Directive in order to reduce the number of rules needed in domestic sales. The buyer is entitled to choose between having the defect cured by repair or by the delivery of substitute goods. However, the *Nachfrist* approach implied by the other remedies (termination and damages instead of performance, §§ 323, 281 BGB respectively) actually compels the buyer (in the ordinary case) to fix an additional period of time for performance (contrast Article 45 CISG). (Note that US law is famously different on this point because of the 'perfect tender' rule in UCC § 2-601, although again this goes to power to reject the goods and cancel the contract. White and Summers (*Uniform Commercial Code* (3rd edn, 1988), pp 355–7) have concluded that 'relatively little is left' of the UCC perfect tender rule because courts have used a variety of devices to prevent sellers from rejecting goods in bad faith to escape a disadvantageous bargain. But this is a far cry from requiring a material defect.)

It should be noted that it is not only physical defects that may be cured in this way, but legal defects: for instance, if the third party right is extinguished. If the buyer elects to demand substitute goods, he is under an obligation to make restitution in respect of the defective thing that was actually delivered, according to § 439 IV and §§ 346–8 BGB. § 439 II BGB clarifies that the cost incurred in bringing the thing into conformity with the contract must be borne by the seller. This is a 'carbon copy' of Article 3(4) of the Directive, which defines what 'free of charge' is supposed to mean in this context. The clarification was quite unnecessary, for it follows already from general principle that the debtor is not entitled to shift the cost of performing the contract on to the creditor unless this is expressly agreed.

An interesting question has arisen in German law as to the relationship between the right to demand the delivery of substitute goods and the content of the obligation of the seller. It is clear that where the obligation of the seller consists of making delivery of generic goods (*Gattungsschuld*, § 243 I BGB), the seller may create conformity with the contract by delivering other goods of the promised kind. However, if a specific thing has been sold (*Stückkauf*) it seems questionable that subsequent performance can consist in the delivery of another thing. The other thing is not owed under the contract and therefore its delivery cannot create conformity with the contract (eg, Faust, *BGB* (2003), § 439 Rn. 27). Yet this approach may be too formal. If the subject-matter of the contract is a specific thing which, according to the intention of the parties, is interchangeable with another thing then there seems to be no valid reason for restricting subsequent performance to effecting repairs (see Oetker and Maultzsch, *Vertragliche Schuldverhältnisse*, p 93, who stress that in this case the sale of a specific thing is 'functionally' equivalent to the sale of generic goods; cf Canaris, JZ 2003, 831). Others seem to prefer the view that in such a case one should characterise the sale as one of generic goods in the first place (Lorenz and Riehm, *Lehrbuch zum neuen Schuldrecht*, (2002), Rn. 505; it would seem that English law would be likely to take this approach as well, given the preceding discussion). It is clear from published sources that in the reform the legislator sought to reduce the significance of the distinction (*Bundestags-Drucksache* 14/6040, pp 209 and 232). Whether a particular sale is analysed as the sale of a specific thing may follow criteria other than the question whether the parties contemplated that, in the case of non-conforming performance, substitute goods may be delivered. A number of decisions of the lower courts indicate that the construction of the contract, and not the formal classification, is decisive. In OLG Braunschweig JZ 2003, 863, for instance, the sale concerned a nearly new Seat Ibiza which had been driven for 10 km. The court held that although the specific car was the object of the sale, subsequent performance could consist of the delivery of a comparable car with the same specifications. Recital 16 of the Directive suggests that, as a general rule, replacement may not be available in relation to 'second-hand goods'; this does not exclude the possibility that a right to a replacement may arise in exceptional cases.

One final point must be made in relation to subsequent performance. Since this is an instance of enforced performance, the limits of the right to demand (subsequent) performance must be given special consideration. Since the implementation of the Directive on consumer sales, these limits are also relevant to English law. There are two kinds of limits that exclude the right to subsequent performance.

First, the right to enforced performance is excluded if performance is impossible. § 275 I BGB also applies to a claim for subsequent performance. If it is impossible to cure the defect and it is not possible to deliver substitute goods, then curing the defect is impossible. This entails that the seller is automatically released from his obligation to cure the defect. It would serve no practical purpose to entitle the buyer to something that the seller cannot in fact provide. More difficult is the question as to when, according to § 275 II BGB, a seller is released from his obligation of subsequent performance. § 275 II BGB has been discussed in detail in chapter 9, p 413 ff. It suffices here to point out that so far as the obligation to deliver generic goods is concerned, there is widespread consensus that the seller cannot escape the duty of performance unless the cost of procuring the substitute goods is evidently and grossly out of proportion to the interest of the creditor in being provided with the thing. In relation to the sale of a specific thing, the precise limit is controversial. If the seller was not responsible for the impediment to performance, some argue that he should be released from the obligation of performance if the cost of procuring the thing exceeds the contract price (see eg, Huber, *Festschrift Schlechtriem* (2003), p 566). These commentators also adopt the same approach in relation to subsequent performance. § 439 III BGB refers to § 275 II BGB. In relation to the sale of a specific thing, and provided that the seller is not responsible for the defect, in bringing the performance into conformity with the contract he is not required to incur costs that exceed the value of the counter-performance, that is the price (see Huber, *Festschrift Schlechtriem*, p 540; cf Ackermann, JZ 2002, 378, 384). However, this is not the manner in which § 275 II BGB was intended to operate; the provision requires as a general rule a gross imbalance between the performance interest and the cost of performance. In the light of the Directive, the result is indeed questionable, for nowhere does the Directive limit the cost of effecting cure to the value of the counter-performance (see for this argument, Canaris, JZ 2004, 214, who suggests that § 275 II BGB is therefore limited to extreme cases of disproportionate outlays). It should be noted that the less strict the limits to enforced performance, the easier it becomes to establish fault of the seller: if the seller is not released from the obligation to cure and he fails to cure, he will invariably fail to meet the standard of objectively defined care under § 276 II BGB. If he is released from the obligation to bring the goods into conformity with the contract, he will be liable in damages only if he is answerable for the defect of the goods (this is more difficult to establish, as will be explained below).

Irrespective of § 275 BGB, the seller may refuse to cure the defect or deliver substitute goods if it is unreasonable. According to § 439 III BGB (cf Article 46 (3) CISG), subsequent performance can be denied if it involves disproportionate outlays. This is the second limit on the right to subsequent performance (and one which finds its English analogue in the new section 48B of the 1979 Act). The seller may refuse *one method* of subsequent performance if the other method is considerably more cost effective and does not entail any significant detriment to the buyer. This right to reject the demand for subsequent performance also arises if *both alternatives* of cure are unreasonably expensive or if only one method of cure is possible but too costly. (Whether this right to refuse performance in cases of so-called 'absolute unreasonableness' is compatible with the Directive is discussed below. See, for an overview of different ways of establishing unreasonableness, Oetker and Maultzsch, *Vertragliche Schuldverhältnisse*, p 97.) The leading English case on this issue is *Ruxley Electronics and Construction Ltd v Forsyth* [1996] AC 344, where the construction of a swimming pool by the defendant builders was only to a depth of six feet, nine inches (whereas the plaintiff had required it to reach sixteen feet, six inches). This disparity did not affect the safety of the pool, nor did it significantly reduce its value, yet the plaintiff claimed a right that the defendants should meet the cost of adding the extra nine inches to the depth of the pool. The House of Lords refused to sanction his claim, since the rebuild cost would have been wholly disproportionate to the benefit that its completion would have provided. (In the end result, the trial judge's £2500 award for 'loss of amenity' was allowed to stand: see Treitel, *The Law of Contract*, pp 947–8.) It is likely that German courts will adopt a similar approach that takes into account the interest of the creditor in the performance and balances it with the cost of curing the defect. The *Ruxley Electronics* case however concerned the right to recover the cost of cure by way of damages for breach of what in German law would be regarded as a contract for work (on which see section 3, below).

The prevalence of enforced performance, in combination with the corresponding limits thereon, determines the conditions of the other remedies available to the buyer. (See for an overview, Stephan Lorenz, NJW 2002, 2497. See also Figure 4, p 503.) If subsequent performance can be effected, as a general rule the buyer must first set a period of time for subsequent performance before he can resort to any secondary rights such as termination or damages instead of performance. By analogy to the general principles discussed in the previous chapter, this type of breach can be called 'qualitative late performance' because the seller is late in rendering subsequent performance. A grace period must also usually be set (§§ 437 Nr. 2, 323 I and §§ 437 Nr. 3, 281 I BGB). Furthermore, damages for delay (*mora debitoris*, §§ 437 Nr. 3, 280 II, 286 BGB) require that the seller be put on notice (*Mahnung*). If subsequent performance cannot be effected, or if the seller can rightfully reject it, then the setting of a period of time for performance would be futile. This type of breach can be called 'qualitative impossibility', for the seller's obligation to ensure conformity with the contract is excluded. The right to termination and the right to demand damages instead of performance do not depend on subsequent performance (§§ 437 Nr. 2, 325 V and §§ 437 Nr. 3, 283 respectively § 311a II BGB).

Since the *Nachfrist*-approach is also adopted in relation to non-conforming performance, it has become possible to define the remedies of the buyer in respect of non-conforming performance by analogy to the rules of the General Part of the law of contract. Non-conforming performance either involves late performance (when a period of performance must be set) or a subsequent performance that is impossible or that is rightly withheld (when secondary rights arise without the need to resort to subsequent performance first). It should be remembered however that the remedies of the buyer deviate in one crucial respect from the remedies contained in the General Part: they are subject to a special regime of prescription in § 438 BGB. We have discussed the details of this point in chapter 9, section 6, p 489.

(e) Termination

The right to terminate the contract for the delivery of a non-conforming thing follows from § 323 BGB. This is clarified in § 437 Nr. 7, Nr. 2 BGB, which also refers to a number of qualifications made in the section of the BGB on the contract of sale. In the previous chapter (p 415 ff), we discussed the general principles applicable to the right to terminate. The setting of a period of time for performance is necessary according to the general rule in § 323 I BGB. The buyer may however dispense with the grace period if, for instance, the seller refuses to cure the defect. This and further exceptions are set out in § 323 II BGB, discussed in the previous chapter. Likewise, if effecting cure or delivering substitute goods is impossible then the setting of a grace period may again be ignored, § 326 V BGB. § 440 BGB adds further qualifications to this *Nachfrist*-approach, all of which are derived from the special nature of the buyer's right to demand subsequent fulfilment of performance (§ 439 BGB). Clearly, if the seller is justified (according to § 439 III BGB) in refusing subsequent fulfilment because it would involve unreasonable cost, the setting of a period of grace is clearly inappropriate. Also, where within the period of performance the seller's second attempt to render subsequent performance has not been successful, the buyer need not await the lapse of the period of time set for this purpose (the details are regulated by § 440 sentence 2 BGB). A third instance concerns cases in which it could not be asked of the buyer to accept subsequent performance. If the seller deceived the buyer or if the delivered goods showed grave defects that destroy the buyer's faith in the seller's ability to fulfil the contract, this provision may apply, but it will always depend on the individual case (see also Article 3(5) of the Directive; and for details Faust, *BGB* (2003), § 440 Rn. 35 *et seq*).

Three further important points must be recalled at this stage, although they have already been examined in the previous chapter (see, also, Lorenz and Riehm, *Lehrbuch zum neuen Schuldrecht*, Rn. 519).

First, in the case of non-conforming performance the right to termination depends on whether the breach was not minor (*nicht unerheblich*). This is laid down in § 323 V 2 BGB and it will also be recalled that it is somewhat controversial how to set this threshold in concrete terms. Although the application of this exclusion of the right will depend on the circumstances in the individual case, it seems likely that the criteria will be considerably less strict than those applied in relation to the 'fundamental breach' approach of the CISG. In English law, rescission would be available on breach of condition (which ties in with the classification of the various implied terms as conditions or warranties, as discussed above in subsections (b) and (c)) or on breach of an intermediate term (as discussed in chapter 9, section 4(b), p 424) where a substantial failure of performance has occurred.

Secondly, we stated in the section on the general principles that the purpose of the right to terminate is to be relieved from the obligation to perform and, if the contract already has been performed, to be put the claimant into a position to claim back the performance. In cases of impossibility of performance of a reciprocal obligation, § 326 I 1 BGB fulfils a similar function. According to this provision, the debtor is automatically released from the obligation of counter-performance if performance is impossible under § 275 BGB. It is important to note again at this stage that this provision does not apply to non-conforming performance, as is expressly stated in § 326 I 2 BGB. The reason is that an automatic release would cut across the right of the buyer to elect which remedy to enforce: termination (§ 326 V BGB) or price reduction (§ 441 BGB) (the latter of which will be discussed in the next subsection). Price reduction is a remedy which in German law is typically made available in relation to bad performance and here we come across the first instance of application.

Thirdly, the effects of termination are set out in §§ 346–8 BGB. It suffices here to point out that restitution of the performance is owed under § 346 I BGB, and that a duty to compensate for the value of the performance arises where restitution cannot be made, § 346 II BGB. In sale of goods cases, the privilege of the 'innocent part' in § 346 III 1 Nr. 3 BGB acquires special importance. The starting point is as always that if the delivered defective thing perished in the hands of the buyer, the right to terminate is not excluded. § 346 II BGB provides for an obligation to monetary compensation instead. This obligation however is excluded by § 346 III 1 Nr. 3 BGB if the buyer was not answerable for the impossibility; the standard applied is that of the care the buyer applies in his own affairs (§ 277 BGB, gross negligence is not tolerated). If, for instance, the defective car was damaged in a traffic accident for which the buyer was not answerable, then he may terminate the contract without having to fear the obligation to compensate the seller for the value of the car. His right to the counter-performance is not diminished for this reason, but a certain deduction is to be made in respect of the actual use made of the car (for details, see chapter 9, section 5(d), p 432; there, we also discuss the issue of whether or not the situation is any different once the buyer knows or could have known of the defect).

(f) Price Reduction

Paragraph 437 Nr. 2 BGB mentions the right of the buyer to price reduction. This right is a peculiarity of the special parts of the law of contract and is, as already explained, customarily granted in respect of non-conforming performance (and in England it is a definite peculiarity of consumer sales law: see the new section 48C of the 1979 Act). We will come across it again in relation to the contract of work (§ 638 BGB) and leases (§ 536 BGB) (below, sections 3 and 5 respectively). It is however not recognised in relation to the contract of services (§ 611 BGB), which partly explains why it is not included in the general part of the law of contract. The right operates, just as in the case of termination, as a power to change the legal position by unilateral declaration. If the buyer has not yet paid, he is released from the obligation to pay to the extent that the price has been reduced. If he has already paid, he is entitled to restitution of the sum exceeding the price owed according to the rules on termination (§§ 441 IV, 346 I BGB). The function of the right to price reduction in effect amounts to a partial termination of the contract; however, the contract is not completely unwound—in particular, it is clear that the performance of the seller, the defective goods, are not to be returned to him.

The buyer can resort to price reduction instead of termination. The buyer will exercise this right if he intends to keep the defective thing or if the breach is not sufficiently serious to justify termination. The exclusion of § 323 V 2 BGB in relation to 'minor breaches' does not apply to the right to price reduction (§ 441 I 2 BGB). In all other respects, the right to price reduction has the same prerequisites as the right to terminate the contract. It is thus independent of fault of the seller; a period of grace must be granted as a general rule, § 323 I BGB; and the exceptions to the right to reduce the price are also identical to those in relation to the right to terminate and therefore need not be repeated here.

Paragraph 441 III BGB determines how the reduction is calculated: the purchase price is to be reduced in the ratio in which (at the time of the conclusion of the contract) the value of the thing in a condition free from the defect would have stood in relation to its real value. The reduced price is calculated by multiplying the actual value of the thing by the agreed price and dividing it by the value that the thing would have had, had it not been defective. At first sight, the procedure seems unnecessarily cumbersome, but it is sensible if its aim is considered: the amount of the price reduction ought to reflect whether the buyer made a good deal or a bad deal (a concern that one regularly sees reflected in the reasoning of the English courts in matters concerning frustration and the assessment of damages: see generally, chapters 7 and 9, above). (See Oetker and Maultzsch, *Vertragliche Schuldverhältnisse*, p 112; Lorenz and Riehm, *Lehrbuch zum neuen Schuldrecht*, Rn. 527.)

To give an example: if A buys a car that would be worth €15000 from B for the price of €10000 and because of a defect it is actually worth €12000, the price may be reduced by €2000 to a new price of €8000. If A had bought the car at a price of €16000, he would have been able to reduce the price by €3200. Where the price corresponds to the value without the defect, the amount less that the car is worth may be subtracted directly. In the example, if the price was €15000 then the reduction would amount to €3000. The prior existence of this material in German law may be of significant interest in developing the application of the newly introduced s. 48C of the 1979 Act in the UK in the years ahead. (Drawn from the US, *Chatlos Systems, Inc v National Cash Register Corp* 670 F2d 1304 (3d Cir 1982), is an extreme example. The price of a computer was $46,020. The value of the system delivered was $6,000. It was warranted to work as well as a $207,826 computer. Damages for breach of warranty were $201,828. Formula is value as warranted minus value as is (see § 2-714(2) ICC).)

(g) Damages

Before the reform, in German law the right to recover damages for non-conforming performance was subject to many qualifications and generally the approach was not regarded as satisfactory. The Code expressly regulated only the right to recover damages for breach of a guarantee undertaken in the individual case, and furthermore, only if the seller deliberately concealed the defect. Hence, the expectation interest was not fully protected by the means of an award of damages. Since the reform, the position has changed radically. The buyer is now entitled to damages in respect of non-conforming performance according to general principle, § 437 Nr. 3 BGB: ie if the seller is answerable for the breach. The buyer is entitled to damages instead of performance (§ 280 III BGB), damages for delay (§ 280 II BGB) and damages alongside performance (§ 280 I BGB), always provided that the seller is answerable for the breach (§ 280 I 2 BGB); in place of damages instead of performance, the buyer may recover for his wasted expenditure (§ 284 BGB). The conditions for exercising this remedy depend on the nature of the breach. (For a fuller discussion of the remedy of damages, see chapter 9, p 437 ff.)

If subsequent performance *is* possible—for instance, where the defect in the goods can be cured by effecting repairs—the right to claim damages instead of performance depends on fixing a period of time for subsequent performance. This follows, in accordance with general principle, from § 281 I 1 BGB and is a further example of the *Nachfrist*-approach. If the buyer demands damages instead of performance, his right to demand subsequent performance is extinguished (§ 281 IV BGB). The buyer is entitled to claim damages instead of the 'whole' performance only if the seller's breach was not 'minor' (§ 281 I 3 BGB; *großer Schadensersatz*); otherwise, the buyer must keep the defective thing and can recover damages only for the difference in value or the cost of curing the defect (*kleiner Schadensersatz*).

The right to damages thus follows the same pattern as the right to terminate or to price reduction. The important difference, of course, is that under German law the seller must be answerable for the breach for the right to damages to arise (§ 280 I 2 BGB). Normally, this requires that fault by the seller be shown (§ 276 BGB). Since subsequent performance is required of the seller (§ 439 BGB), he will be answerable for the ultimate failure of conforming performance if he was at fault in failing to render performance. Since vicarious performance of this obligation will normally be possible, and financial difficulties do not serve to exonerate the debtor, the seller is not likely to be able to rebut the presumption of fault. One must also bear in mind that a legal error only exceptionally eliminates fault (see chapter 9, p 447). Thus, if the seller gets it wrong and refuses to perform because, erroneously, he thinks that the threshold of unreasonableness of cost of cure in § 439 III BGB has been passed, he will be liable in damages. It is common ground that the seller need not, in addition, be answerable for the defect in the goods (whether it is *sufficient* that the seller *is* answerable for the defect in the goods is controversial: see Stephan Lorenz, NJW 2002, 2503, *contra* Hirsch, Jura 2003, 289).

The exceptions from the *Nachfrist* requirement contained in § 281 II BGB also apply. The setting of a period for performance may further be dispensed with under the same conditions as apply in relation to the right to terminate: § 440 BGB also stipulates further exceptions from enforced performance in respect of the right to recover damages. For instance, if subsequent performance involves disproportionate outlays and the seller refused to perform on this ground, the setting of a period for performance is not necessary. If subsequent performance is impossible, the seller also can claim damages instead of performance without first having to resort to enforced performance. As will be recalled, the right depends on whether the impossibility was initial (ie whether, for instance, the car was irreversibly defective already at the moment the contract was concluded; § 311a II BGB) or whether the impossibility accrued after the conclusion of the contract (§ 283 BGB). In the first case, the point of reference for determining whether the seller was answerable for the breach is the imputed knowledge of the seller of the impediment to conforming performance. In the latter case, the point of reference is whether the seller is answerable for the impediment to conforming performance. This will be the case, for instance, if the seller negligently caused the impossibility of curing the defect.

Damages for delay presuppose that the seller was in default in the technical sense of the word (*Verzug*, as defined in § 286 BGB). This regularly presupposes the issue of a special warning to the seller that subsequent performance is due. If, eg, the buyer rents a replacement car to use during the period in which the seller is making repairs, this loss may be recoverable as damages for delay according to § 280 II BGB (*Verzögerungsschaden*). Special difficulties are posed by the loss of profit caused by non-conforming performance, usually referred to as *Betriebsausfallschaden*. If the buyer cannot make a profit because the goods are not delivered, he is required to put the seller in default in order to be able to recover damages for delay. If the seller delivers defective goods and the buyer therefore fails to make a profit (eg, because he cannot use machinery for production or because he misses an opportunity to sell the goods on) the question arises whether this loss was due to the fact that the seller was late in curing the defect, or because he did not fulfil his obligation to deliver conforming goods. In the former case, the loss would be recoverable as damages for delay; in the latter, the loss could be recovered irrespective of whether the seller was in default. Ultimately, the question boils down to whether the buyer is required to issue a special warning (*Mahnung*, § 286 I BGB) in order to be able to recover. It is generally agreed that this is not appropriate and that the seller may therefore recover instantly for the loss of profit (provided of course the seller was answerable for the defect). (See chapter 9, p 467 for details.) There are no provisions in the Sale of Goods Act 1979 to deal with the possibility of claiming damages for goods delivered late but accepted by the buyer in spite of the delay: thus the matter falls to be considered under ordinary principles of contract law, which were discussed in chapter 9, section 5: note that the cases of *The Heron II* [1969] 1 AC 350 and *Victoria Laundry (Windsor) Ltd v Newman Industries Ltd* [1949] 2 KB 528 both concerned facts involving late delivery. Breach of stipulations as to time will often amount to a condition, the breach of which could be relied on to claim damages (again, see chapter 9).

Finally, the buyer may recover damages alongside performance in respect of any damage caused by the defective thing to his other rights or interests (under § 280 I BGB). This type of loss represented by the *Integritätsinteresse* is often referred to as consequential loss or *Mangelfolgeschaden*. If a latent defect causes physical damage to the person of the buyer or to other things owner by him, this loss has arisen irreversibly. To return to an example given in chapter 9 (at p 453): if horse fodder is infected and the horses that ate it then died, delivery of substitute fodder may create conformity with the contract but it will not revive the horses. Setting a period for performance would be futile and the loss is recoverable irrespective of subsequent performance.

Liability in damages depends on whether the seller is answerable for the defect (§ 276 BGB). This is presumed (§ 280 I 2 BGB) and will normally require that the seller is at fault. It should be noted that the seller is not normally required to inspect the goods before he sells them. Likewise, the producer of the goods is not his assistant within the meaning of § 278 BGB. In other words, the seller is not vicariously liable for the producer, nor indeed for any other person from whom he procured the goods (for references, see Faust, *BGB* (2003), § 437 Rn. 82). The seller may also be liable independently of fault if, for instance, he *guaranteed* the absence of the defect. This will depend on the construction of the contract in the individual case and should not be confused with the common law 'guarantee'-type of liability. (See, for the objective approach in § 157 BGB, chapter 3, section 3, p 133.) Normally, in the absence of express words to this effect, the courts are reluctant to infer from the circumstances that the seller intended to be liable independently of fault if the defect in question materialised. In respect of certain classes of transaction however the courts have been prepared to apply a strict approach. Arguably, this was less because the seller in these cases actually intended to be liable irrespective of fault, and more because the buyer was regarded as particularly worthy of protection. The paradigm case is the sale of second-hand cars by professional dealers. Here, the courts are prepared to infer a 'guarantee' more easily (see, eg, BGHZ 122, 256). Two further caveats must be entered at this stage. If generic goods were sold, the seller is assumed to have undertaken a 'guarantee' in respect of the risk of being able to *procure* the goods (*Beschaffungsrisiko*). This special 'guarantee' does not, as previously explained, cover defects in the thing that is actually delivered. By contrast, the 'guarantee' envisaged in § 443 BGB is of a more comprehensive nature and can be distinguished on that ground (often referred to as an 'independent guarantee'). It is not limited to the absence of a defect at the time when risk passes (§ 434 I BGB) but often concerns the durability of a product and furthermore may be undertaken by a third party (usually the producer).

(h) Relationship between Primary and Secondary Rights

At this juncture, it is useful to discuss an example that illustrates the importance in German law of subsequent performance for the exercise of secondary rights. Let us assume that a carpenter buys a chair from a furniture shop. The chair is defective, and instead of setting a period of time for the shopkeeper to have the chair repaired, the carpenter cures the defect himself and charges the seller the cost of having doing so. It would have cost the seller slightly less to repair the chair. In this example, the buyer skipped the level of primary enforcement and instead sought to rely on secondary rights straightaway. In English law, this would be a non-issue since in any event the buyer may immediately exercise his claim to a remedy in damages: the only issue would be if the diminution of value was accurately reflected by cost of cure (this also applies in consumer sales, for the buyer may resort to the traditional remedies alongside the rights provided for in the Directive).

In German law, while it is recognised that the buyer may in principle recover the cost of curing the defect as damages, the problem arises whether the buyer must first resort to the remedy of enforced performance. If he fails to do so, as in our example, what is the 'sanction' for this? Let us consider the example more closely. (See, for a comprehensive analysis, Lorenz, NJW 2003, 1417.)

When the chair was delivered to the buyer it was defective, § 434 I BGB. Hence, we are here faced with a typical case of non-conforming performance. The starting point for the remedies of the buyer in respect of the defect is § 437 BGB, which however refers back to the general principles for most intents and purposes. Since the carpenter, after having repaired the chair, will be likely to want to keep the chair, he may be interested in securing a price reduction (§ 441 BGB). Price reduction however is only possible if the conditions for termination are met, except for the fact that the breach may be minor. Setting a period of time for subsequent performance (ie, curing the defect, § 439 I BGB) would now be futile since the chair is already repaired. Hence, subsequent performance by the seller has become impossible. The right to terminate would then follow from § 326 V BGB, which in turn refers to § 323 BGB, except for the *Nachfrist*-requirement. § 323 VI BGB stipulates that termination is not allowed if the 'innocent' party was responsible for the circumstance giving rise to the right to terminate. The impossibility of subsequent performance was obviously caused by the buyer. As a result, he is not allowed to terminate the contract and furthermore he is also deprived of the right to price reduction. Recovering the cost of cure is a typical head of a claim to damages instead of (conforming) performance. However, § 281 I 1 BGB presupposes that subsequent performance is still possible; this is no longer the case since the chair is now repaired. The right to damages thus follows from § 283 BGB, which in turn requires that the seller was answerable for the impediment to (subsequent) performance. Obviously, the seller is not to be blamed for the fact that the buyer (prematurely, before awaiting the expiry of a period of grace) cured the defect. As a result, damages instead of performance are also excluded (note that the right to recover damages alongside performance under § 280 I BGB is not affected, but this notion does not cover the head of damages claimed here).

From the perspective of the common law this comes as something of a surprise. Is the buyer deprived of all rights in respect of the defect simply because he failed to enable the seller to cure the defect? This seems quite unsatisfactory; and the solution to this problem of 'self-help' (*voreilige Selbstvornahme*) is not immediately apparent and therefore controversial. The rationale of enforced performance is, as was explained in chapter 9, to afford the promisee as nearly as possible what he was entitled to expect under the contract. In relation to non-conforming goods, this means that the buyer is entitled to get conforming goods. The primary purpose of enforced performance is to protect the interest in the performance. An auxiliary purpose of enforced performance is to protect the interest of the debtor in being afforded a 'second chance' to perform. If the buyer immediately enforces (or seeks to enforce) his secondary rights, he deprives the seller of this protection. However, it would seem quite drastic if, as a result, the seller were to enjoy a total immunity in respect of the non-conformity of performance. Enforced performance is meant to protect the promisee in the first place and if he chooses not to rely on it, is the (appropriate) sanction really a total deprivation of the promisee's secondary rights? This conclusion does not seem necessary in order to protect the seller's interest in being given a second chance to perform. It suffices if the seller is not placed in a worse position than if the buyer had resorted to enforced performance. This means that the seller must pay the buyer what he saved as a result of not having to perform his obligation to repair. This right of the buyer is indeed provided for in the Code in § 326 II 2 BGB (for this argument, see Lorenz, NJW 2003, 1417). The effect of this provision is that the buyer is partially released from his obligation to pay the price and any excess amount already paid may be claimed back according to § 326 IV BGB. In our example the carpenter could, independently of fault, recover the cost of repair that the seller saved as a result of the fact that the buyer himself cured the defect. The buyer could not however recover the cost exceeding that amount, for he failed to enable the seller to effect a cure of the defect. (The issue of whether the buyer is entitled to secondary rights is controversial because, inter alia, § 326 I 2 BGB excludes the application of § 326 I 1 BGB in cases of non-conforming performance, although for entirely independent reasons, and § 326 II BGB could likewise be regarded as excluded. Some lower court decisions have indeed held that the buyer in such a case is not entitled to *any* remedy, eg, LG Gießen NJW 2004, 2906; similarly, see Dauner-Lieb and Dötsch, ZGS 2003, 250. The decision of the LG Gießen has now been affirmed by the BGH NJW 2005, 1348, on the ground that § 437 BGB stipulates for a 'closed' system of remedies which leaves no room for an analogous application of § 326 II 2 BGB.)

In the US, the issue is rather whether the buyer reasonably mitigated his damages. The cases are mixed on whether the duty to mitigate requires giving the defaulter another chance. (Hillman, 'Keeping the Deal Together After Material Breach— Common Law Mitigation Rules, The UCC, and the Restatement (Second) of Contracts' (1976) 47 *Colorado L Rev* 553 remains a good article on the topic.) Hillman's article challenges the many cases that state in categorical terms that there is no obligation to do further business with a defaulter. The most famous of these cases is *Canadian Indus Alcohol Co v Dunbar Molasses Co*, 258 NY 194, 200–201, 179 NE 383, 385 (1932) ('The plaintiff replied in substance that it had no longer any faith in the defendant's readiness or ability to live up to its engagements, and did not wish to add another contract to the one already broken. The law did not charge it with a duty to make such an experiment again.') See also *W-V Enterprises, Inc v Federal Sav & Loan Ins Corp*, 234 Kan 354, 367, 673 P2d 1112, 1122 (1983) ('there is no obligation to mitigate damages if the mitigation involves dealing with the defaulting party').

(i) Consumer Sales

Directive 1999/44/EC ([1999] OJ L171/12) on consumer sales covers the right to demand subsequent performance if non-conforming goods are delivered, the right to termination and the right to price reduction. It does not concern issues related to the passing of mercantile risk and the right to recover damages. The Directive is a minimum harmonisation measure, which means that the consumer may be protected more extensively than envisaged in the Directive but not less. The Directive has been used as a model for the recent German reform of the contract of sale (on the history and purpose of the reform, see chapter 9, p 381 ff.) Unlike the 2002 Regulations in England, the structural elements of the system of remedies envisaged by the Directive have been implanted into the very heart of the German law of obligations. As a result, relatively few and (some of them very much peripheral) provisions were necessary to deal with the special requirements of consumer sales. These provisions are §§ 474–9 BGB. This so-called 'grand solution' (*große Lösung*) has the advantage of reducing the number of overlapping regimes of rules, which is the main difficulty with the approach to implementation in English law (as has been already explained above). However, this '*große Lösung*' approach also means that European law flows particularly high up the rivers of domestic law (to borrow the metaphor of Lord Denning MR in *HP Bulmer Ltd v Bollinger SA* [1974] 2 WLR 202)—or, more precisely, the impact of European law extends beyond the areas to which it itself claims to apply and has a 'spill-over' effect on other (cognate and related) parts of national (private) law.

The Directive affects not only the contract of sale, but the remedies for breach of the contract of sale, since these remedies are to a great extent derived from the general principles for breach. For instance, the right to terminate the contract (§ 323 BGB, an essential aspect of the rights granted to the consumer in Article 3 of the Directive) is defined in the general part, which applies to all contracts and also to the delivery of non-conforming goods. Since the right to recover damages instead of performance follows the same pattern, it is also shaped by the approach adopted in the Directive, though only in an indirect way since it is not covered by the Directive itself. Two issues must be discussed in the present section. First, to what extent does the Directive determine the approach in those provisions of German law that are not limited to consumer sales? Secondly, we must also discuss the special rules applicable only to consumer sales.

The first issue—the wider impact of the Directive on the application of the German law of contract—is complex and we can only discuss some aspects here, by way of illustration. It will be recalled that Directives, as a general rule, do not have direct effect (and certainly not when relied on as a source of substantive rights by one private party against another: see eg, Case C–91/92 *Dori v Recreb Srl* [1994] ECR I-3325). They must be implemented by the national legislator. Three criteria must be met: the implementation must be effective, transparent and not discriminatory. Article 249(3) EC leaves Member States to choose the ways and means of ensuring that the Directive is implemented; however, that freedom must be exercised in the light of the obligation, imposed on all the Member States to which the Directive is addressed, to adopt, in their national legal systems, all the measures necessary to ensure that the Directive is fully effective, in accordance with the objective which it pursues. (See, from the rich case law of the ECJ: Case C–144/99 *Commission v Netherlands* [2001] ECR I-3541 (= NJW 2001, 2244) and Case C–180/95 *Draehmpaehl v Urania Immobilienservice* [1997] ECR I-2195 (= NJW 1997, 1839.) Furthermore, the relevant legislation must be sufficiently precise and clear, ie it must be such that the persons concerned are made fully aware of their rights and, where appropriate, afforded the possibility of relying on them before the national courts. The ECJ has emphasised that 'it is particularly important, in order to satisfy the requirement of legal certainty, that individuals should have the benefit of a clear and precise legal situation enabling them to ascertain the full extent of their rights and, where appropriate, to rely on them before the national courts' (Case C–236/95 *Commission v Greece* [1996] ECR I-4459, para 13). In addition, the ECJ has established the principle that national law should be so construed as to comply (so far as possible) with Community law. This approach is captured in the following statement of the court (Joined Cases C–240/98 and C–244/98 *Océano Grupo Editorial v Rocio Murciano Quintero* [2000] ECR I-4491 (= NJW 2000, 2571), para 30): '. . . it is settled case-law . . . that, when applying national law, whether adopted before or after the directive, the national court called on to interpret that law must do so, as far as possible, in the light of the wording and purpose of the directive so as to achieve the result pursued by the directive . . .'.

The 'safest' method of implementation is thus a 'carbon copy' of the Directive. However, even this approach can go wrong if certain traditional concepts sneak in by the back door. It has been already pointed out above that the wide discretion afforded to the English courts in section 48E of the Sale of Goods Act 1979 seems likely to fail the test set out in the previous paragraph. Whether the implementation of the

Directive in German law fully satisfies these requirements is also questionable, and due to the fact that the Directive has been implemented in a sweeping fashion, the assessment of the German law vis-à-vis the requirements of the Directive is made all the more difficult. We may give two examples at this stage. The first is that § 323 I BGB requires that the buyer must set a period of time for performance before the contract may be terminated. The Directive does not require as much as this: it suffices that curing the defect or delivery of substitute goods is requested from the seller and a reasonable time has passed (Article 3(3)). By comparison, the 2002 Regulations implemented this provision correctly (see section 48B(2) of the Sale of Goods Act 1979). The German rule in § 323 I BGB obviously demands more from the consumer. Construing German law in the sense envisaged by the Directive is not possible, for the Second Commission expressly rejected the removal of the requirement to set a period of time for performance. Applying the fall-back provision of § 323 II Nr. 3 BGB might provide a solution in consumer sale situations, but it is doubtful that this device is sufficient implementation, as it is not a fully transparent regulation of the rights of the consumer (see Unberath, ZEuP 2005, 5, 31, with references). Furthermore, it would distort the parallel between the remedy damages instead of performance and termination. The second example is also relevant to English law. As was explained above, under German law the seller may refuse to cure the defect or to deliver substitute goods if this would involve disproportionate outlays (§ 439 III BGB). A similar approach is adopted in section 48B(3)(c) of the Sale of Goods Act 1979 (as to which see Arnold and Unberath, ZEuP 2004, 379). By contrast, the Directive expressly deals only with the case that one remedy is disproportionate in relation to the other (Article 3 (3)). Whether this excludes the possibility that both remedies are rejected as unreasonable is uncertain. The implementation in English and German law will therefore be subject to the scrutiny of the ECJ, as and when an appropriate case arises in a national court and is referred to Luxembourg under Article 234 EC. (See, for a fuller discussion of these issues, Unberath, ZEuP 2005, 5; Stephan Lorenz in *Münchener Kommentar*, vol 3, Vor. § 474 Rn. 2 *et seq*)

We turn now to the second theme. The reform also inserted *special* rules for the contract of sale of goods between a dealer/seller and a consumer/buyer in §§ 474–9. This special regime of rules concerns, firstly, the binding nature of those provisions that are meant to protect the buyer, § 475 BGB. Secondly, they lay down a presumption as to the existence of defects, § 476 BGB, rights of redress of the dealer against his supplier, §§ 478–9 BGB, and a number of miscellaneous issues concerning guarantees which need not be discussed in detail here, § 477 BGB. Finally, § 474 I BGB defines the scope of application of the special rules and § 474 II BGB excludes the passing of risk with the handing over of the goods to a carrier (as to the thereby excluded § 447 BGB, see chapters 8 (p 357) and 9 (p 411).

Consumer protection in European legislation invariably entails the curtailment (to some extent) of freedom of contract. The Consumer Sales Directive is no exception (see its Article 7). § 475 I BGB follows suit and declares the relevant provisions to be binding to the benefit of the consumer. In effect, this means that a dealer cannot exclude these rights even if he was prepared to reduce the price in exchange for the waiver by the consumer of those consumer rights. (Public auctions where the consumer can attend personally are exempt.) The right to claim damages is not affected, although it should be noted that the rules on exclusion clauses in standard terms of business must be respected (§ 475 III BGB: as to these rules see chapter 3, p 163). § 475 II BGB stipulates that the length of the prescription period in relation to the remedies of the consumer may not be shortened below two years (and in the case of used goods, one year).

The definition of conformity in § 434 BGB is also mentioned, but it should be noted that the parties are free to determine the requirements with which the goods must comply. It is not the case that the Directive requires compliance with an objective standard (such as, for instance, according to the Product Liability Directive (see section 2(c), p 499, for this argument)). This is also recognised by the German courts in principle; however, the following example has given rise to differences of opinion as to the correct solution (OLG Oldenburg ZGS 2004, 75). The consumer bought a second-hand car that, unknown to the buyer, suffered from a serious physical defect, which made it unfit to drive. The seller objected to the termination of the contract by the buyer, arguing that the car had been described on its sale as a 'tinkerer's car' (*Bastlerfahrzeug*) and therefore did not need to be fit for driving. This rather clumsy attempt of the seller to escape liability failed. The court held that this clause in the contract was invalid, as it contravened § 475 I 2 BGB: ie, the clause served to circumvent the remedies granted to the consumer in relation to a defect. It is important to consider the factual circumstances of this case carefully: the price of the car was the actual market value of a second-hand car with the relevant specifications and it was common ground between the parties that the buyer, a sailor, did not buy the car for 'tinkering' purposes or the like, but rather to use it in the ordinary way. In this case, however, it seems unnecessary to rely on § 475 BGB or Article 7 of the Directive. The construction of the contract already provides the correct solution, namely that the description of the car as 'tinkerer's car' was not seriously intended (Lorenz, *Münchener Kommentar*, § 475 Rn. 8). § 475 BGB should be limited to cases in which the buyer is burdened with the risk of latent defects. If it is clear that the car is not fit to drive, the parties are clearly free to sell the car to be used for purposes other than driving (as a source for replacement parts, for instance). However, this is not what the parties intended in our example. Compare this analysis with the cases under the previous English rules as to 'merchantable quality' (eg, *Business Application Specialists Ltd v Nationwide Credit Corp Ltd* [1988] RTR 332) and the current approach to 'satisfactory quality' under section 14(2), (2A) and (2B), as well as the exceptions under section 14(2C)(a) and (b) where the buyer's knowledge of the defect or inspection of the car become significant. On the facts of the German case discussed here, it would seem likely that the result under English law would have been similar, given the quality normally expected of a car and the ambiguity of the description of the vehicle as one for 'tinkering'.

Another important rule is contained in § 476 BGB, which implements Article 5(3) of the Directive (corresponding to section 48A(3) and (4) of the Sale of Goods Act 1979). The provision stipulates that it is presumed that any defect that has become apparent within six months of the passing of risk existed at the time of the passing of risk, unless the presumption is incompatible with the nature of the goods or the nature of the lack of conformity. § 476 BGB chooses the passing of risk as the relevant point in time, instead of the time of delivery as laid down in the Directive, because the relevant time for conformity is the time when the risk passes (§ 434 I 1 BGB). This rule is necessary because normally, after the buyer has accepted the goods, it is for him to prove that the performance did not conform to the contract (as to this effect of acceptance on the burden of proof, see § 363 BGB). However, in the case of latent defects, the buyer will often have difficulties in proving that the defect already existed at the time at which the goods were handed over to him. § 476 BGB serves to overcome this difficulty.

This provision has been the subject of the first major decision of the *Bundesgerichtshof* on the reformed law of obligations (see BGH NJW 2004, 2299, case no 120). In this case, the consumer bought a second-hand car from the seller, a car dealer, for the price of €8500. The car was handed over to the buyer on 18 January 2002. On 12 July 2002, the engine of the car broke down. It was a matter of dispute between the parties what caused the engine problem. The buyer terminated the contract and sought restitution of the price (making a deduction of €657 for the total distance of 10,950 km that he had actually driven the car: see chapter 9, p 433, for this aspect of restitution). The Court of Appeal allowed the claim by applying § 476 BGB, while the *Bundesgerichtshof* quashed the decision and remanded the case. The right to terminate follows from §§ 437 Nr. 2, 323 BGB, provided that the car was defective at the time at which risk passed (here, at the time the car was handed over to the buyer on 18 January 2002). The buyer could not prove that the car was defective at that very moment. However, since this was a consumer sale and the defect of the engine showed itself within the six-month period, the question arose whether the buyer could avail himself of the presumption in § 476 BGB. In the view of the court, the presumption in § 476 BGB applied only to the defect that materialised. The difficulty in the present case was that the engine problem obviously had not existed at the time the car was handed over to the buyer. To the contrary, the buyer was able to drive the car for another 10,000 km before the engine gave way. The presumption that the court suggested does not help the buyer in relation to the question of whether or not a defect existed at all at the relevant time. The decision can be criticised in a number of respects.

First, the factual basis of the decision is somewhat unclear. The court emphasised that the defect may have been due to the careless behaviour of the buyer in the way in which he changed gears when driving. This in itself could justify not applying the presumption, for in such circumstances the presumption is incompatible with the nature of the defect. In other words, it is not sufficiently probable that the engine problem was due to a defect that existed at the time when the car was delivered to the buyer (for this point, see Stephan Lorenz, NJW 2004, 3022). A further objection concerns the conclusions drawn by the court concerning the findings of the lower courts. Even though the lower court had found that the drive belt was also loose, this defect might have well have existed at the time the car was handed over (see Gsell, EWiR § 437 BGB 1/04, 904).

Secondly, the approach of the BGH seems unduly restrictive in terms of general principle (see Lorenz, NJW 2004, 3021; *contra* Gsell EWiR § 437 BGB 1/04, 904). The approach of the court actually requires the seller to prove that a latent defect existed, which may also have existed at the time of the passing of risk. In many cases in which goods become defective in the course of their use, it will be difficult if not impossible to adduce such proof. Of course, the actual defect may be easy to prove, but this particular defect will often not have been present when the thing was handed over. It seems that the *Bundesgerichshof* is not willing to apply the presumption in such a case, thus depriving it of much of its importance in consumer protection in practice. This approach restricts the application of the presumption in those cases in which it is most pressingly needed. Whether this approach will survive the scrutiny of the ECJ seems at least questionable, given the goals of the Directive.

One final point must be made in this section on the special rules applicable to consumer sales. Article 4 of the Directive concerns the dealer's right of redress in relation to the supplier. The wording is quite vague ('the final seller shall be entitled to pursue remedies against the person or persons liable in the contractual chain') and the English legislator has (it seems rightly) adopted the view that no immediate action was required: the existing remedies of English law easily fulfil this function. The German legislator went a few steps further and expressly regulated the right of redress in §§ 478, 479 BGB. The details of these provisions cannot for reasons of space be discussed in full here. It suffices to make the following observations.

The rationale of these provisions seems sensible. If the dealer/seller is subjected to a mandatory regime of liability vis-à-vis the consumer/buyer, it seems fair that the law seeks to ensure that liability can in principle be passed on up the chain. This is achieved by avoiding so-called 'redress traps'. If, for instance, the seller bought the thing long before the defect materialised in the hands of the consumer/buyer, it is quite likely that the rights as against the supplier have become time-barred. To avoid this, § 479 BGB extends the time limits for prescription accordingly and § 478 III BGB applies the presumption in § 476 BGB along the chain. Likewise, between merchants it does not seem appropriate to insist on enforced performance; therefore, the seller may instantly resort to secondary rights in relation to the supplier (§ 478 I BGB). However, the German legislator ascribed these provisions binding force. This means they cannot be departed from unless the seller is adequately protected by 'other means', § 478 IV BGB (the open-textured nature of the exception is likely to create uncertainty). This is a quite unique feature of these provisions, for hitherto the modern legislator has on the whole abstained from interfering with freedom of contract in such a sweeping fashion in the commercial sphere. The assumption seems to have been that the seller/dealer will often be the 'weaker party' in comparison with the supplier. Whether this factual assumption is correct is open to doubt, but in any event it would not warrant such a radical departure from the liberal contract law model. (See, for criticism *Münchener Kommentar—*Lorenz, § 478 Rn. 7 with references.)

3. CONTRACT FOR WORK

Hertel, 'Werkvertrag und Bauträgervertrag nach der Schuldrechtsreform' DNotZ 2002, 6; Pause, 'Auswirkungen der Schuldrechtsmodernisierung auf den Bauträgervertrag' NZBau 2002, 648; Peters, 'Das Baurecht im modernisierten Schuldrecht' NZBau 2002, 113; Teichmann, 'Das neue Werkvertragsrecht' JuS 2002, 417; Schudnagies, 'Das Werkvertragsrecht nach der Schuldrechtsreform' NJW 2002, 396.

(a) Preliminary Observations

While the reform of the contract of sale was fundamental, the contract for work (*Werkvertrag*) has been affected only marginally by the new regime. The reason is that the general principles discussed in chapter 9 were already embodied in the sections on non-conforming performance of a *Werkvertrag* previous to the reform. Quite apart from the European input in the form of the consumer sales Directive discussed above, the traditional approach to non-conforming performance in the BGB—in the section on the contract for work—also served as a model for the contract of sale.

The special part of the BGB dealing with the contract for work (§§ 631 *et seq* BGB) does not reiterate the general principles discussed in the previous chapter. The focus of the qualifications made in the special part is on a particular type of irregularity of performance: non-conforming performance, which is regulated in §§ 633–9 BGB. This is a typical feature of the special part of the law of contract in the BGB and was also noted in relation to the contract of sale, above. (For other aspects of the contract for work, see chapter 3, p 155 ff.) It should be observed that, so far as construction contracts are concerned (for which see, eg, Peters, NZBau 2002, 113), the General Conditions for Building Works (*Verdingungsordnung für Bauleistungen* = VOB/B) are widely used in the building industry. They are on the whole to the same effect as the rules in the Code, but contain important variations meant to cater for the special position of construction works. In English building contracts, see the Joint Contract Tribunal (known as 'JCT') standard contracts, which are the most common form of contract used in the building industry (see further, Chappell, *Understanding JCT Standard Building Contracts* (7th edn, 2003) for discussion and explanation). It should be noted further that contracts for the production of movable things are on the whole subject to the rules of the contract of sale (§ 651 BGB, *Werklieferungsvertrag*).

Before we examine the remedies of the employer in respect of defective work in more detail, the central change of the recent reform should be mentioned. It concerns the approach to prescription periods for the remedies for non-conforming performance. Prior to the reform, two different regimes of prescription were applicable. The time limits were of different length and depended on whether the employer claimed damages for what was referred to as 'near' or 'remote' consequential loss. This distinction however was never convincingly drawn and therefore created significant uncertainty in the law. § 634a BGB now establishes a unitary approach to prescription of claims for defective work. (See *Bundestags-Drucksache* 14/6040, p 263.) The reform thus seeks to ensure that employers know in advance whether their claim is time-barred and reduces the incentive to rely on artificial reasoning so as to avoid the application of the shorter objective periods of the special part of the law of contract. Nevertheless, since the general period of limitation follows different rules (the point from which time starts to run being determined subjectively), the incentive to bring one's claim within the scope of application of one or the other regime of rules out of tactical considerations is not completely eliminated. (For a fuller discussion of the rationale of the rules on prescription, see chapter 9, p 486.)

(b) Application of General Contract Principles to Breach of a Contract for Work

The general principles examined in the previous chapter cover the area outside the scope of application of the special rules (contained in §§ 633 *et seq* BGB) for the *rights of the employer* in respect of non-conforming performance. However, the special rules as to bad performance are modelled on the general principles with only few qualifications (in particular, the approach to prescription is different).

As with the contract of sale, 'meta'-rules are necessary in order to determine the scope of application of the special rules. Two criteria are applied in order to determine whether the special rules apply. First, the performance must be a non-conforming performance. This is defined in § 633 BGB. Secondly, the special rules are applied only once the employer has accepted the work as, on the whole, being in conformity with the contract requirements (§ 640 BGB, *Abnahme*, discussed at pp 156, 353, 411). Thus, the general principles will apply if, for instance, the contractor performs late or fails to perform altogether. Even if the performance is not in conformity with the contract in the sense of § 633 BGB, the general rules will be applied before the *Abnahme* has taken place. The remedies available to the employer on the basis of general principle have been discussed in detail in chapter 9. It will be recalled that enforced performance is available, the contract may be terminated (§ 323 BGB) or damages may be claimed (§§ 280–4, 311a III BGB), any surrogate may be claimed if the conditions of § 285 BGB are fulfilled. In cases of impossibility, the obligation of counter-performance may automatically be extinguished according to § 326 I 1 BGB, although note that the contract of work contains special rules in §§ 644, 645 BGB on the passing of risk (discussed generally in chapter 9, p 409). Also, if performance remains outstanding, the obligation to pay the price may also be suspended according to § 320 BGB, although normally the contractor must perform first (§ 641 BGB: generally speaking, the obligation to provide remuneration becomes due only after acceptance of the work).

Finally, the *rights of the contractor* are not specially regulated (except for a limited number of individual elements) and otherwise follow general principle. Therefore, they need not be explained in detail at this stage. For instance, if the employer is late in paying the remuneration (§ 641 BGB regulates the time when it is due), then the contractor may recover interest according to § 288 BGB or any excess loss under § 280 II BGB. It suffices here to refer to a few peculiarities of the contract for work. Noteworthy are first, those provisions that seek to strike a balance between the duty of the contractor to perform first and his interest in obtaining security. This is achieved by granting the contractor certain limited proprietary interests in the subject matter of the contract, but this security can also take other, different forms (§§ 647–8a BGB).

Another of the interesting features of the provisions on the contract for work is the right of the employer to terminate the contract for work by notice (*Kündigung*) before the work is completed: § 649 sentence 1 BGB. This is mentioned here in the context of the rights of the contractor because the avoidance of the contract is not analysed in German law as a repudiation that can be accepted or not. The employer is not in breach if he avoids the contract prematurely. However, in such a situation the contractor retains his right to claim the remuneration according to § 649 sentence 2 BGB, subject of course to a deduction of the amount saved as a result of the premature termination of the contract or what he failed to earn as a result of a deliberate omission. The rationale of this approach is, on the one hand, that it would not be appropriate to impose on the employer the performance which he no longer wishes to obtain, but on the other hand, that the contractor should be entitled to make the profit he was entitled to expect from performing the contract. (US law is in accord with this position. *Rockingham County v Luten Bridge Co* 35 F 2d 301 (4th Cir 1929), is a famous illustration awarding the cost incurred up to the time of repudiation plus lost profit and not the contract price when plaintiff completed the construction of bridge after repudiation. *Bomberger v McKelvey* 35 Cal 2d 607, 220 P 2d 729 (1950) is a little known counter-example. McKelvey bought a lot from Bomberger and agreed to pay Bomberger $3500 to demolish a building on the lot. McKelvey planned to build a large drug store on several lots. McKelvey decided to delay construction of the store and ordered Bomberger not to proceed with demolition. Bomberger demolished the building anyway, claiming that he needed skylights salvaged from the building, which were worth around $540, to fulfil another construction contract. The demolished building was worth around $26,000 and was generating $300 monthly rent. The court held that Bomberger acted reasonably because to obtain substitute skylights might have delayed the completion of his other project by several months. The court made no effort to quantify or to balance the parties' respective losses.)

This provision, § 649 BGB, would elegantly have solved the problem in *White and Carter (Councils) Ltd v McGregor* [1962] AC 413 (noted by Goodhart (1962) 78 *LQR* 263 and Nienaber [1962] *CLJ* 213). In this case, M's agent contracted with White and Carter that the latter would display advertisements for M. On the same day, M asked White and Carter to cancel the contract. However, they refused to accept this cancellation and prepared the necessary plates for the display of the advertisements. In accordance with the term in the contract, that if an instalment remained unpaid for four weeks the whole sum due would be immediately payable, they also claimed the full amount due for performance of the whole contract. The claim was one for the debt—the contract price—and not for damages for breach. The House of Lords held that the repudiation of the contract by M did not bring it to an end but only entitled White and Carter to rescind it. White and Carter could affirm the contract, perform their part, and claim the contractual payment for doing so. In the words of Lord Reid, who gave the leading judgment for the majority, 'If one party to a contract repudiates it in the sense of making it clear to the other party that he refuses or will refuse to carry out his part of the contract, the other party, the innocent party, has an option. He may accept the repudiation and sue for damages for breach of contract, whether or not the time for performance has come; or he may if he chooses disregard or refuse to accept it and then the contract remains in full effect' (at 427). For obvious reasons, the plaintiffs preferred the contract price because in the instant case this was more profitable than a claim for damages, although it is questionable whether it is necessary to ascribe 'full effect' to the contract even after the employer has made it clear that he does not wish to obtain the performance. For discussion of this case, see Treitel, *The Law of Contract*, pp 1016–18; the key issue is to identify whether or not the injured party in such a situation has any 'legitimate interest' in completing performance of the contract (*per* Lord Reid, at 431)—if not, then the only remedy for breach will be in damages (see eg, *Attica Sea Carriers* [1976] 1 Lloyd's Rep 250 (and see Kerr (1978) 41 *MLR* 1, at 20–1), which raises the question of whether the claimant has satisfied the requirement to mitigate his loss (on which see Lomnicka (1983) 99 *LQR* 495 and Bridge (1989) 105 *LQR* 398).

(c) Defining Conformity

§ 633 BGB is the provision that defines, in a seemingly objective fashion, the requirements of conformity of the performance of the contractor. As is also the case with the parallel provision of § 434 BGB, these rules do not lay down an objective standard but merely reflect what is deemed to be the typical intention of the parties. It is for the parties to define the requirements as to performance. In construction law, for instance, lengthy lists of specifications are regularly used (the so-called '*Baubeschreibung*'). § 633 BGB also serves the additional purpose of providing a starting point for the special rules laid down in the BGB for defective work (eg, the different regime of prescription).

The general rule is that the work is free from physical defects if it has the agreed composition: § 633 II 1 BGB. Insofar as the composition is not agreed, then according to § 633 II 2 BGB the work is free from physical defects when it is appropriate for the assumed use under the contract, or otherwise for the usual use and has a composition which is usual for works of the same kind and which the customer can expect according to the type of work. § 633 II 3 BGB stipulates that it is equivalent to a physical defect if the entrepreneur produces a different work from that ordered or produces the work in too small a quantity. The work is free from legal defects, according to § 633 III BGB, if third parties cannot claim any rights against the customer in respect of the work or only those accepted in the contract. If the employer accepts the work even though he knows of the defect, he must reserve his rights if he is not to be deprived of them, § 640 II BGB. (For details on the requirements as to conformity, see Oetker and Maultzsch, *Vertragliche Schuldverhältnisse*, p 462 *et seq*, and for the changes brought about by the recent reform, see, eg, Schudnagies, NJW 2002, 396.)

In the following discussion of the possible available remedies, it is assumed that the work is defective and that the special rules of the BGB in relation to non-conforming performance are applicable. Structurally, these rules correspond to the approach described in the previous section on the contract of sale. We may thus limit our observations to the characteristic features of the contract for work.

(d) Enforced Performance

First, the employer is entitled to demand conforming performance: §§ 634 Nr. 1 and 635 BGB. This is referred to, in analogy to the contract of sale, as 'subsequent performance' or *Nacherfüllung*, but it should be observed that the right to choose between different methods of subsequent performance is given to the contractor. He is in a better position to decide whether curing the defect or the production of a new work is the more appropriate option. In relation to the contract of sale, the choice is given to the buyer.

The right to subsequent performance is another instance of enforced performance. The reason for its special regulation in the BGB is that it is subjected to stricter limits than the right to the primary performance under general principles. In the general part of the law of obligations, the most important limitation on enforced performance is impossibility (discussed in detail in chapter 9, p 406 ff). Where the promised result cannot be achieved (ie the defect cannot be cured either way), the contractor is released from his obligation to render subsequent performance according to § 275 I BGB. The contractor is also released if the conditions of § 275 II and III BGB are met and the contractor rejects performance. § 275 II BGB however requires that the expenditure for effecting cure is grossly out of proportion to the performance interest of the promisee. This provision will hardly ever come into play, for § 635 III BGB reduces the threshold considerably. The contractor is entitled to refuse to cure the defect if this would involve disproportionate outlays. In laying down this rule, the legislator had in mind cases where the cost of this effort would outweigh the contractor's interest in receiving conforming performance from the employer. Therefore, the BGB qualifies the demand for removal of defects by considerations of economic reasonableness. This applies of course with equal force to the claim for the production of a new work. The factors that are to be taken into account are primarily the nature of the defect and the interest of the promisee in receiving performance. (For illustrations of this principle, previously contained in the former § 633 II 2 BGB, see BGH NJW-RR 2002, 661; NJW-RR 1997, 1106; BGHZ 96, 111.)

In English law see *Ruxley Electronics Ltd v Forsyth* [1996] AC 344 (HL), discussed at p 507: the cost of reinstatement was an unreasonable claim in the circumstances. Typically, the measure of damages in such circumstances should be the diminution of value in the work; however, in *Ruxley* there was said to be no loss in value on the facts, although their Lordships did uphold the trial judge's award of a sum to reflect the 'amenity loss' of the claimant. The US law in this area is complicated. The contractor is entitled to be paid the contract price less damages (usually the cost of repair) if he 'substantially performs'. If he does not, then he has a claim in restitution for the value of performance. *Plante v Jacobs* 10 Wis 2d 567, 103 NW 2d 296 (1960), illustrates the interaction of the first rule and the rule measuring damages by loss in value when remedial cost is much greater. The builder, Plante, misplaced a living room wall by one foot on the narrow side. The court held that Jacobs had to pay the balance due on the contract for the work done (around $5000) and that they could not recover the price of moving the wall (around $4000) because narrowing the room did not lower their home's market value. Whatever loss the Jacobs suffered from having a smaller living room was uncompensated. (See Chomsky, 'Of Spoil Pits and Swimming Pools: Reconsidering the Measure of Damages for Construction Contracts' (1991) 75 *Minn L Rev* 1445, at 1451–60, where many similar cases are reviewed, the author concluding that the primary focus is the avoidance of economic waste.)

Before the secondary rights of the employer are examined, the relationship between primary and secondary rights must be clarified. The approach adopted in relation to non-conforming performance in principle is the same as that adopted in relation to any other breach under the general rules. The gist of this approach is encapsulated in the *Nachfrist*-notion. This means that before secondary rights can be enforced, the promisee (here the contractor) must be given the opportunity to bring the performance into conformity with the contract. For this purpose, the employer must as a general rule set a period of time for subsequent performance (§ 635 BGB) before he can avail himself of the secondary rights: recovery of the cost of reinstatement (§ 637 BGB), termination of the contract (§ 323 BGB), reduction in the price (§ 638 BGB) and the recovery of damages instead of performance (§ 281 BGB). The usual exceptions to this requirement apply (eg, § 323 II BGB). To this, § 636 BGB adds another set of exceptions, which reflect the special nature of the right to subsequent fulfilment: if the contractor is entitled to refuse reinstatement as unreasonable (§ 635 III BGB), then the employer's secondary rights obviously do not depend on setting a period of time for subsequent performance; likewise, if subsequent performance has failed or the employer cannot be expected to accept subsequent performance, the employer may instantly resort to his secondary rights.

(e) Recovery of Cost of Reinstatement

If the work is defective, the employer must generally set a period of time for subsequent performance. If performance is not forthcoming during this period, the employer may have the defect cured at his own expense and recover the cost of reinstatement from the contractor according to § 637 BGB. This right of the employer is analysed as a right to recover for expense (*Aufwendungsersatz*) and not as a right to claim damages. The conceptual difference is important, as since we are not dealing with a claim for damages, the right arises irrespective of whether the employer was answerable (§ 276 BGB) for the breach. The remedy is irrespective of fault. All costs that are objectively necessary prospectively can be recovered whether or not the cure was successful. Furthermore, § 635 III BGB entitles the employer to an advance on costs.

(f) Termination and Price Reduction

The right to terminate (*Rücktritt*) the contract for breach, if the breach consists of non-conforming performance, follows from § 634 Nr. 3 in conjunction with § 323 or § 326 V BGB respectively. If reinstatement is possible, the employer must first set a period of time for performance (§ 323 I BGB). The exceptions to this have been discussed above. The effects of termination have been discussed in chapter 9, p 432. (See also, Oetker and Maultzsch, *Vertragliche Schuldverhältnisse*, p 483.) If reinstatement is not possible, no such period of time must be set, § 326 V BGB. It should be recalled that the creditor is not automatically released from the obligation of counter-performance, § 326 I 2 BGB. If he seeks to extinguish his obligation to pay the remuneration, then he must terminate the contract or reduce the price.

Price reduction (*Minderung*) is governed by §§ 634 Nr. 3, 638 BGB and follows the same requirements as the right of termination, with the notable exception that the breach may be 'minor' (§ 638 I 2 BGB). Like the right to terminate the contract, the right to price reduction is a power to change the obligations of the parties to the contract by unilateral declaration. To the extent that the price is reduced, the buyer is released from his obligation to pay the remuneration and any amount already paid may be claimed back according to the rules of restitution, §§ 638 IV, 346 I BGB. The reduction is calculated in the same way as in relation to a contract of sale: § 638 III BGB (see section 2(f) p 510 for details and for an example of the required calculation).

(g) Damages

Again, we only consider here the right to recover damages for any loss caused by defects in the work. This is because the right to recover damages for loss caused by a defect is subject to a special regime of prescription in § 634a BGB.

The employer is entitled to recover damages instead of performance according to §§ 634 Nr. 4, 281 I 1 BGB, provided that the contractor has not cured the defect within the period of time set for this purpose. The exceptions discussed above apply (note in particular § 636 BGB). The expectation interest covers cost of cure, but as already pointed out the employer may recover such cost under § 637 BGB independently of any fault of the contractor. By contrast, the right to recover damages depends on whether the contractor is answerable for the breach (§ 280 I 2 BGB), which normally requires fault (§ 276 BGB). If the breach of contract consists of failing to effect cure (presupposing that the contractor is not released from that obligation), fault will easily be established considering that financial difficulties do not serve as an excuse and that cure can be performed vicariously. If reinstatement is not possible, the right to recover damages instead of performance does not depend on setting a period of time for subsequent performance. The conditions vary depending on when the impediment to subsequent performance accrued. In the case of initial impossibility, the right follows from § 311a II BGB and turns on whether the contractor could have known of the impediment. In cases of subsequent impossibility, the right follows from § 283 BGB and depends on whether the contractor is answerable for the impediment, ie the fact that reinstatement is impossible. Alternatively, the employer may recover for wasted expenditure according to §§ 634 Nr. 4, 284 BGB.

If the contractor is late in rendering subsequent performance, he is liable for what are known as moratory damages (*Verzögerungsschaden*—ie damages specifically representing the delay in performance) if the contractor is in default (*Verzug*). This follows from §§ 634 Nr. 4, 280 II, 286 BGB. However, if due to the defect the employer could not make an intended use of the work (loss of production or in selling it on), this is not analysed as loss caused by delay but is recoverable as simple damages alongside performance (§§ 634 Nr. 4 and 280 I BGB). The opposite view subsumes this type of loss under § 280 II BGB but dispenses with the requirement that the contractor ought to be issued a special warning (*Mahnung*, as § 286 I BGB would in fact require). The different categorisation of the loss therefore does not make a difference in practice (see chapter 9, p 467, for a fuller discussion).

If the defect causes damage to the other rights of interests of the employer, this loss is recoverable as 'simple' damages under §§ 634 Nr. 4, 280 I BGB. When a latent defect materialises, it would not be appropriate to require the setting of a period of time for subsequent performance. Subsequent performance (§ 635 BGB, curing the defect) would not have extinguished the loss. These *Integritätsschäden* accrue independently of whether performance ultimately fails. Liability depends on whether the contractor is answerable for the breach, ie (typically) whether he was at fault in relation to the defect (§§ 280 I 2, 276 BGB, this is presumed). It suffices to make two further remarks at this stage (see also chapter 9, p 469 ff). The contractor is vicariously liable for any assistants whom he employs in performing the contract: § 278 BGB. Generally speaking, the main contractor is liable for any fault of his sub-contractor. The contractor however is not liable for any fault of the suppliers of materials used for the work. (See, eg, Ulrich Huber, *Leistungsstörungen*, vol 1 (1999), p 680.) Furthermore, the degree of care required in relation to the subject-matter of the contract differs from that applicable under the contract of sale. While a seller is normally not under a duty to inspect the goods before he delivers them to the buyer, as a general rule it is the contractor who must perform such duties of inspection (for details, see *Staudinger*-Peters, § 634 Rn. 119 *et seq*).

4. CONTRACT OF SERVICES

Däubler, 'Die Auswirkungen der Schuldrechtsmodernisierung auf das Arbeitsrecht' NZA 2001, 1329; Henssler, 'Arbeitsrecht und Schuldrechtsreform' RdA 2002, 129; Katzenmeier, *Arzthaftung* (2002); Richardi, 'Leistungsstörungen und Haftung im Arbeitsverhältnis nach dem Schuldrechtsmodernisierungsgesetz' NZA 2002, 1004; Schiemann, 'Der freie Dienstvertrag' JuS 1983, 649; Spindler and Rieckers, 'Die Auswirkungen der Schuld- und Schadensrechtsreform auf die Arzthaftung' JuS 2004, 272; Vollkommer and Heinemann, *Anwaltshaftungsrecht* (2nd edn, 2003).

(a) Preliminary Observations

The contract of services is governed by §§ 611 *et seq* BGB and a number of special statutes. (For general provisions of English law, see sections 12–17 of the Supply of Goods and Services Act 1982.) Its main difference from the contract for work is that the provider of the service does not promise that he will ensure that a certain result comes about but merely that he will perform the service as promised (see also chapter 3, p 153, for this and other aspects of this type of contract).

The foregoing is easily apparent in the paradigm case of a contract with a medic. The latter owed the performance of an activity but normally does not promise to bring about a certain result, namely that the patient recovers. This contract is accordingly analysed as a contract for services. (Prior to the extension of damages for pain and suffering to contractual claims there was an incentive in German law to phrase claims in tort. However, see now § 253 II BGB which makes such damages available also in a contract claim. Typically, medical treatment will fall under the law of tort in England where the service is provided under the National Health Service, unless there is a contract for private treatment: see Grubb (ed), *Principles of Medical Law* (2nd edn, 2004), para 5.06 and Grubb & Kennedy, *Medical Law* (3rd edn, 2000), pp 272–7. On this 'guarantee' point in contracts for services, see the view of Nourse LJ in *Thake v Maurice* [1986] QB 644 (finding the usual position to be no more than a warranty that due care and skill would be used) and compare it with two cases on cosmetic surgery, where (respectively) US and Canadian courts have been prepared to find that a particular result was guaranteed, so that failure to achieve it amounted to a breach of contract: *Sullivan v O'Connor* (1973) 296 NE 2d 183 (Cal Sup Ct) and *LaFleur v Cornelis* (1979) 28 NBR (2d) 569 (New Brunswick).)

If the contract involves the management of the affairs of another person, § 675 BGB declares certain provisions from the law of mandate to be applicable. For instance, according to § 667 BGB the service provider must hand over everything he obtains in the course of and in connection with his service to the employer. A typical example of this type of contract (*Geschäftsbesorgungsvertrag*) is the contract to provide legal services. It will also be remembered that the contract of 'labour' (*Arbeitsvertrag*) is analysed as a contract of services. The great practical significance of the contract of services is therefore evident.

For the English position on employment contracts, which started from a common law development of a set of default rules via implied terms in the contract of employment, see Deakin, 'The Evolution of the Contract of Employment, 1900–1950: The Influence of the Welfare State' in Whiteside and Salais (eds), *Governance, Industry and Labour Markets in Britain and France* (1998) 212 ff and Collins, Ewing and McColgan, *Labour Law: Text and Materials* (2nd edn, 2005), chapter 2. One key element is the extent to which company rule-books and handbooks become incorporated as contract terms via the operation of implication of terms at common law: this may have significant consequences for the employee's contractual duties (see *Secretary of State for Employment v ASLEF (No 2)* [1972] ICR 19), although certain restrictions on the employer's freedom to change those rules without consultation may also result from the status of the rule-book under the contract (*French v Barclays Bank plc* [1998] IRLR 646). (For comparable US case law, see *Toussaint v Blue Cross & Blue Shield* 292 NW 2d 880 (Mich 1980), which is the leading case. The employee received oral assurances of job security and the manual said dismissal would only be 'for cause'. On the other side is *Fleming v AT&T Information Services, Inc* 878 F 2d 1472 (DC Cir 1989) (the presumption that an employee is hired 'at will' is not overcome by a written manual stating that employees will be treated fairly and will receive post-termination counselling).) Another important aspect is the extent and enforceability of collective agreements (see sections 179 and 180 of the Trade Union and Labour Relations (Consolidation) Act 1992 and cases such as *Alexander and Wall v Standard Telephones & Cables Ltd (No 2)* [1991] IRLR 287 (for employee attempts to enforce the agreement) and *Camden Exhibition & Display Ltd v Lynott* [1966] 1 QB 555 (for the employer's efforts to do likewise).

The present section can be comparatively short for the simple reason that, unlike many other specific contracts, the rules on the contract of services *do not contain a self-contained system of remedies for defective performance*. This entails that the general principles described in the previous chapter are also applied in respect of non-conforming performance. Nevertheless, it may be of interest to give a brief overview of the main aspects of liability for breach of a contract of services, because the application of the general principles is nevertheless qualified in certain respects and has been, to some extent, controversial in practice.

(b) Enforced Performance

The personal obligation to provide services cannot be specifically enforced (§ 888 III BGB: for details, see chapter 9, p 405). This corresponds to the basic position in English law: see *Johnson v Shrewsbury and Birmingham Railway* (1853) 3 DM & G 358 and section 236 of the Trade Union and Labour Relations (Consolidation) Act 1992, although note that the services must be of a personal nature—it will not suffice simply to claim that the contract is one for the provision of services. (See generally, Treitel, *The Law of Contract*, pp 1029–33.) As a general rule, the contract is to be performed personally and not by another on the promisor's behalf: § 613 BGB (see also chapter 8, section 4, p 361).

If the obligation to provide the service is impossible to perform, the promisee is released from that obligation by § 275 BGB. This may be the case in particular where the obligation has to be performed at a pre-defined time. For instance, under a contract of 'labour' the employee is required to be at the place of work and to provide the service as laid down in the contract during working hours. Lapse of time thus causes the provision of the service to become impossible. The service that was to be provided yesterday cannot be provided today. This is also presupposed by § 615 sentence 1 BGB, which—contrary to the general rule in § 326 I 1 BGB—preserves the right of the employee to demand remuneration if the employer is in delay of acceptance of the service. In cases in which the service must be personally performed, § 275 III BGB acquires special importance (see chapter 9, p 418; see § 616 BGB for the right to remuneration if the employee is personally unable to perform for 'insignificant' periods of time). The English approach to withholding pay will depend very much on the nature of the obligation undertaken by the employee: eg, under a time-service contract, the obligation is to be available and willing to work as directed during the relevant hours under the contract. See *Miles v Wakefield Borough Council* [1987] AC 539, where partial failure to perform may entitle the employer either to refuse all work offered and refuse to pay wages or to accept such performance as has been rendered and then pay for it on a pro rata basis. There are also certain statutory provisions that protect against such deductions being made by employers: see sections 13 (restrictions on deductions), 24 (statutory remedy of compensation for deductions) and 27 (definition of 'wages' and how this affects the notion of a 'deduction' therefrom) of the Employment Rights Act 1996 ('ERA 1996') (discussed in Collins, Ewing and McColgan, *Labour Law: Text and Materials*, chapter 2).

(c) Termination

Termination of a contract of service does not as a general rule have retroactive effects (contrast the effect of termination by *Rücktritt* in § 346 BGB). The contract of services is a so-called 'continuous contract' (*Dauerschuldverhältnis*), which means that it is not consumed in a singular exchange of performance. As a result, it is terminated by giving notice (*Kündigung*), ie a unilateral declaration which brings the contract to an end with effects for the future. The contract comes to an end either at the stipulated time or by ordinary notice of termination, which normally has to respect certain time limits (§ 620 BGB, see also chapter 3, p 154). (In the US however the 'employment at will' rule remains the governing principle in this area.)

In the present context of liability for breach of contract, the right to terminate the contract by notice 'extraordinarily' is of central importance (*außerordentliche Kündigung*). As we have seen previously (in chapter 9, p 436), the right is defined in abstract form in § 314 BGB, but in relation to the contract of service this provision is completely replaced by § 626 BGB. The provision applies to both parties and requires that the termination is justified by a reason of considerable weight ('*wichtiger Grund*'): clearly, this right is available only in exceptional cases and only in relation to serious breaches of contract. This accords with the default position under English employment law, where summary dismissal can only be justified (in the face of common law implied terms concerning reasonable notice; see, eg, *Nokes v Doncaster Collieries Ltd* [1940] AC 1014) and statutory protection (eg, section 86 of the ERA 1996) if the employer can show a serious breach of contract by the employee: see *Laws v London Chronicle (Indicator Newspapers) Ltd* [1959] 1 WLR 698 and *Wilson v Racher* [1974] ICR 428. Naturally, express terms as to dismissal, complaints and notice may also be included in the contract. Finally, at common law a different basic approach was taken to fixed-term contracts, but section 86(4) of the ERA 1996 prevents circumvention of the statutory minimum notice period by such devices.

Normally the parties are expected to terminate the contract by observing the relevant time limits or to await its agreed end. In the previous chapters we have also already mentioned the restrictive construction given to the provision by the labour courts and also referred to the many other specialised statutes, which must be complied with in relation to contracts of labour. It suffices here to mention that, according to § 628 I 2 BGB, the employee is deprived of the remuneration if, as a result of the breach of contract and the termination, the employer no longer has an interest in the services provided up to that moment.

It should not be concealed that it is controversial whether, in addition to termination by notice, the right to declare termination by *Rücktritt* under § 323 BGB is also available. (In this sense, eg, Oetker and Maultzsch, *Vertragliche Schuldverhältnisse*, p 412, although with the proviso that the contract is terminated with effects for the future. This runs contrary to § 346 BGB.) During the time before the performance has commenced, there seems no compelling reason not to apply § 323 BGB: here, no difficulties in winding up performance are to be expected. However, once the contract has been carried out, the right to terminate by notice (*Kündigung*) takes priority. (This also seems to be the view of the legislator, so far as it can be discerned from the preparatory works; cf *Bundestags-Drucksache* 14/6040, p 177. See *Münchener. Kommentar*- Ernst, vol 2a, § 323 Rn. 35–6, with references, who points out however that termination with retroactive effects may be appropriate in exceptional cases.)

(d) Damages

The right to recover damages for breach of contract follows the general principles examined in chapter 9 (see p 437 ff). If the employer is late with the payment of remuneration, he will become liable for interest and for damages for delay according to § 288 and § 280 II BGB respectively (for the calculation of interest in relation to contracts of labour see, eg, Richardi, NZA 2002, 1009: the matter is somewhat controversial). If the employee is late in providing the service, the classification of the right to recover damages depends on whether, due to the lapse of time, the performance has become impossible (then § 283 BGB applies, see above) or whether the service can be still performed, in which case the loss is likely to result out of the delay of the debtor and may be recovered under § 280 II BGB. Furthermore, if the contract was terminated according to § 626 BGB, § 628 II BGB stipulates a right to recover damages if the termination was due to a breach of contract by the other party (for an illustration, see BGH NJW 1984, 2093).

As mentioned previously, the provisions on the contract of service do not contain a special regime of rules for bad performance. The practical upshot of this is that the right to recover damages (as provided for in §§ 280–283 BGB) becomes central for the 'innocent' party. In particular, the employer cannot exercise a right to price reduction—which, it will be remembered, is independent of fault—if the service provided is not in conformity with the contract. This was recently confirmed in a case concerning the services of a lawyer (BGH NJW 2004, 2817). The court pointed out that a reduction in the remuneration could only be considered, by analogy to § 654 BGB, if the lawyer betrayed his client (in the sense of § 356 of the Criminal Code). Since this had not occurred in the instant case, the only way for the client to defend himself against the claim for the fees was to set off a claim for damages. Such a claim requires first, that the client suffered loss and secondly, that his loss was due to a non-conforming performance of the lawyer for which the latter was answerable (§ 280 I 2 BGB). (On the specific issue of wages deductions by employers under English labour law, see the discussion in sub-section (b), above.)

The standard of care required of professionals is determined objectively by reference to what is required in the respective trade or profession (§ 276 II BGB). This is generally regarded as a demanding standard. The breach of duty however must be proved by the innocent party, as the presumption of fault contained in § 280 I 2 BGB concerns only the question whether the guilty party can exonerate himself. Consider the following example (cf Ernst, (cited above), § 280 Rn. 158). If a medic negligently performed an operation and this resulted in injury to the patient, the patient may be able to recover damages according to § 280 BGB. As a general rule, it would be for the patient to show that the operation was not executed *lege artis* (this is the breach of contract founding liability, § 280 I 1 BGB) and for the medic to show that, nevertheless, he had not acted negligently (§ 280 I 2 BGB). Alternatively, the patient may seek to rely on a failure of the medic to obtain informed consent. Again, this would entail liability. Finally, it should be noted that after recent developments, damages for pain and suffering are also available in contract actions (§ 253 I BGB). This may shift the theoretical explanation of many medical malpractice cases from tort to contract (Spindler and Rieckers, JuS 2004, 272). For details on the standard of care required and the remarkable degree of 'strictness' of liability, see chapter 9, section 5(b); *The German Law of Torts*, p 330 *et seq*: legal malpractice; 536 *et seq*: medical malpractice (on which see further, Grubb & Kennedy, *Medical Law*, chapter 4).

More generally, under English law it should be noted that section 13 of the Sale and Supply of Goods Act 1982 provides that in 'a contract for the supply of a service where the supplier is acting in the course of business, there is an implied term that the supplier will carry out the service with reasonable care and skill'. However, section 16(3)(a) of the same Act makes clear that the Act does not exclude 'any rule of law which imposes on a supplier a stricter duty.' Thus, the final standard of care to be satisfied will depend on whether any pre-existing and stricter common law duty might apply to the provision of such services: if not, then we fall back on the section 13 fault standard. See chapter 9, p 447 ff, Treitel, pp 840–2 and Powell and Stewart (gen eds), *Jackson & Powell on Professional Negligence* (5th edn, 2001), paras 2-116–2-124 for further details. The last of these commentators suggest that the appropriate formulation for the test of the standard or 'reasonable care and skill' (whether expressed under the law of tort, the law of contract or statute) is: 'that degree of skill and care which is ordinarily exercised by reasonably competent members of the profession, who have the same rank and profess the same specialisation (if any) as the defendant' (para 2-120 (footnote omitted)). As the learned authors also point out (para 2-124), this standard will change over time as advances in skills, techniques, equipment and knowledge are made; many professional bodies attempt to provide further guidance for professional service providers and clients alike by means of the adoption of written standards of best practice in their particular profession (on this last point, see the discussion in *Jackson & Powell* (cited above) on particular professions such as surveyors (chapter 9, paras 9-23–9-25), solicitors (chapter 10, para 10-91) and accountants (chapter 15, paras 15-93–15-96).

The correct classification, in terms of duty, of non-conforming performance of a contract of service is controversial in German law. (See, for an overview, Oetker and Maultzsch, *Vertragliche Schuldverhältnisse*, p 413.) Some argue that the provision of the service as such suffices and if it was not performed according to the standard implied by the contract, this constitutes merely the violation of an auxiliary duty not to harm the interests of the other party (§ 241 II BGB; eg, Richardi, NZA 2002, 1011). The right to recover damages would thus follow from § 280 I BGB. The obvious objection to this approach is that, under the contract, the employer is entitled to expect not just the provision of a mere activity, but the provision of a service that conforms to the standard implied by the contract. Bad performance of a contract of service is non-conforming performance and not merely the violation of an auxiliary duty of protection. The right to recover damages would therefore follow from §§ 280 I and III, 283 BGB, since in most cases it will no longer be possible to rectify the bad performance, ie to restore conformity with the contract. This approach however would mean that if in exceptional circumstance the loss could nevertheless be avoided by curing the 'defect', this would have to be demanded first according to § 281 I 1 BGB. In relation to losses that would not be avoided by bringing the performance into conformity with the contract, the legal basis for damages would again be § 280 I BGB.

5. CONTRACT OF RENT

Derleder, 'Mängelrechte des Wohnraummieters nach Miet- und Schuldrechtsreform' NZM 2002, 676; Emmerich, 'Neues Mietrecht und Schuldrechtsmodernisierung' NZM 2002, 362; Gruber, 'Mietrecht und Schuldrechtsreform' WuM 2002, 252; Birgit Grundmann, 'Die Mietrechtsreform' NJW 2001, 2497; Hau, 'Reformiertes Mietrecht und modernisiertes Schuldrecht' JuS 2003, 130; Schmidt-Futterer, *Mietrecht* (8th edn, 2003); Unberath, 'Mietrecht und Schuldrechtsreform' ZMR 2004, 309.

(a) Preliminary Observations

The contract of rent or lease is regulated in §§ 535 ff BGB (*Mietvertrag*). Some important aspects of this type of contract have already been discussed (see especially, chapter 3, section 4(d), p 149). For present purposes, it is the remedies for breach of contract that are to the fore. The rules were subject to a major reform (in 2001, BGBl. I, 1149) which however was pursued independently of the reform of the law of obligations (BGBl. I, 3138) and followed different aims. The special rules for breach were not significantly changed and, more importantly, have not been fully adjusted to cohere and intermesh with general contract principles. This is also the reason why we need to return to the contract of tenancy, even if only briefly. This section of the special part of the law of contract traditionally contains a number of qualifications to the rules in the general part. Two main types of variations may be identified. The rules on non-conforming performance are heavily modified and the rules to terminate the contract by notice are exclusively dealt with in the special part.

(b) Application of General Principles to Breach of a Contract of Rent

If we look first at the *rights of the lessor*, it is apparent that the special part does not contain special rules for breach, except for the right to terminate by notice (*Kündigung*) and a special rule of prescription. The main obligation of the lessee is to pay rent: § 535 II BGB. This will normally be provided for in English law by the inclusion of a covenant to this effect, whether expressly or by the implied inclusion of 'the usual covenants,' of which the obligation to pay rent is one (*Propert v Parker* (1832) 3 My & K 280): see Harpum, *Megarry & Wade: The Law of Property* (6th edn, 2000), para 14-245 ff.

Late performance of the obligation to pay rent will result in liability for delay if the lessee is in default (*Verzug*, for which see § 286 BGB). Interest may be claimed from that moment onwards according to § 288 BGB, while § 280 II BGB covers any exceeding loss of delay (*Verzögerungsschaden*). The fault principle applies (embodied in § 276 BGB), yet it will be recalled that money debts are generally construed as involving 'guarantee' liability. Where payment of the rent is late, under the English law of leases of real property enforcement by the landlord can take the form of an action for the money owed, distress (by taking the defendant's goods from the property and selling them—a self-help remedy that does not require the sanction of the court) or the application of indirect pressure by threatening forfeiture of the lease (where the lease contains a forfeiture clause for non-payment of rent) (see, generally, Harpum, *Megarry & Wade: The Law of Property*, para 14-252 ff.).

The right to terminate the contract by notice is specially regulated (and will therefore be discussed in the next section): the general rule in § 314 BGB is thereby ousted. The right to terminate the contract with retroactive effects (§ 323 BGB) is as a general rule excluded for this type of 'continuous' contract (*Dauerschuldverhältnis*). (The problem is analogous to the contract of services, see p 531.) Under the English rules on leases of real property, a lease for a fixed term cannot be terminated by notice (in the absence of express contractual provision to the contrary). Periodic tenancies however can in principle be determined by notice: express provision can be made under the contract for such notice periods, but the default position is that, eg, a yearly tenancy can be determined by providing at least half a year's notice that will expire at the end of a completed year of the tenancy (*Sidebotham v Holland* [1895] 1 QB 378. Any periodic tenancy of less than one year requires notice of the full period to be given (*Lemon v Lardeur* [1946] KB 613). (See for details, Harpum, *Megarry & Wade: The Law of Property*, paras 14-068, 14-073, 14-076, 14-081 and 14-117.) These basic common law rules are subject to important statutory exceptions, which either restrict the landlord's right to determine the lease or allow the tenant to remain in the rented property even after the lease has been determined. These extremely detailed provisions vary in intensity depending on the precise nature of the tenancy at issue (business, agricultural or residential dwelling tenancies) and are beyond the scope of this book: for discussion, see Harpum, *Megarry & Wade: The Law of Property*, paras 22-062 ff (business tenancies); 22-086 ff (agricultural tenancies); and 22-128 ff (for residential dwellings).

By contrast, under German law the lessor's right to recover damages follows general principle. The lessee incurs obligations of protection or duties of care (*Schutzpflichten*, § 241 II BGB) in relation to the rented property. Their breach will give rise to liability according to § 280 I BGB, provided that the lessor suffered loss and the lessee was answerable for the breach (§ 276 BGB). In relation to duties of performance (other than the payment of rent), the *Nachfrist*-approach applies. This means that, according to § 281 I 1 BGB, a claim for damages instead of performance presupposes that the 'innocent' party has set a period of time for performance, and that no performance was forthcoming during that period. An important example in practice concerns the obligation to effect certain maintenance works (*Schönheitreparaturen*). It is the duty of the lessor to keep the rented thing in a condition suitable for the purpose of the contract, § 535 I 2 BGB. However, it is customary that this obligation is partially delegated to the lessee and the courts accept such clauses, provided that they are not unreasonably burdensome for the lessee (see, eg, Unberath, ZMR 2004, 313 with references). If the lessee is under a duty to keep the property in good repair (for instance, to paint the flat when moving out) and breaches this obligation, the lessor must first set a period of time for performance according to § 281 I 1 BGB before he can recover the cost of effecting the works. If the lessee in our example moves out without having painted the flat, this may in the individual case amount to a final and serious refusal of performance. In such a case, the setting of a period of time for performance can be dispensed with: § 281 II BGB. (If a deposit is taken by the landlord, as it will usually be as a matter of course at the outset of a residential lease under English law, then the typical practice is to deduct any such expenses from the amount of the deposit returned to the tenant when the lease comes to an end, although this is subject to the comments made in the next paragraph.)

See, for an illustration, BGHZ 49, 56, case no 118, which has been already referred to in the section on mitigation in the previous chapter. In this case, the lessees rented a house form the lessor. The obligation to keep the leased premises in a 'decorated' condition was shifted to the tenants. They failed to execute the redecoration works at the end of the tenancy and the landlord claimed for the cost of effecting the works as damages. Meanwhile however new tenants had executed the works at their own expense. The Court nevertheless refused to accept this as a reason to make a deduction in the damages claimed, because it 'would be unjustifiable to absolve the defendants just because the plaintiff was lucky in his further contractual negotiations.' The case has a parallel in *Joyner v Weeks* [1891] 2 QB 31. In this case, the plaintiff lessor sued on a covenant contained in a lease by which the defendant lessee promised to leave the premises in good repair. However, in breach of this covenant the premises were left in bad repair. The plaintiff had made a demise of the premises to a third person, which demise contained a covenant to repair. The defendant argued unsuccessfully that the plaintiff was only entitled to nominal damages. Note however that as a result of section 18 of the Landlord and Tenant Act 1927, the damages recovered for breach of a repairing covenant must not exceed the value by which the reversionary interest has been diminished (see Harpum, *Megarry & Wade: The Law of Property*, paras 14-281 and 14-282). See further section 147 of the Law of Property Act 1925 (allowing the court to release the tenant from internal decorative repairs liability where the landlord acted unreasonably) and the Leasehold Property (Repairs) Act 1938 (on which see Harpum, paras 14-285–14-287). The latter statute requires a notice to be served on the tenant by the landlord, informing the tenant of his right to serve a counter-notice on the landlord, exercising the tenant's rights under the 1938 Act. This counter-notice requires the landlord to gain the leave of the court to take any further action, and to do so he must show on the balance of probabilities that the breach needs to be remedied immediately to save him from substantial loss or damage (section 1(5) of the 1938 Act: see *Associated British Ports v CH Bailey Plc* [1990] 2 AC 703 (noted by Bridge [1990] *CLJ* 401).

For the sake of completeness, it is necessary to mention a special rule in this section on general principle. For the right to recover damages just set out is subject to a special regime of prescription in § 548 BGB, provided that the claim concerns a loss resulting out of a deterioration in the condition of, or damage to, the leased property. This special period of limitation will normally commence with the return of the object and only lasts for six months. This particular period of limitation is said also to apply to any concurrent delict claim, for otherwise the lessor could easily circumvent the rule. (For details, see Unberath, ZMR 2004, 313. Note that this drastic effect is *not* attributed to the other special regimes of prescription for breach of contract: ie to the contract of sale and the contract for works.)

The starting point for the *rights of the lessee* is § 535 I 1 BGB. The tenant is entitled to be enabled to make the agreed use of the subject matter of the lease. (See in English law the implied covenant by the landlord that the lessor will enjoy quiet enjoyment of the property subject to the lease: *Budd-Scott v Daniel* [1902] 2 KB 351. Note that the default position as to the safety or fitness for purpose of the rented real property is that the landlord makes no implied promise to that effect (see Harpum, *Megarry & Wade: The Law of Property*, para 14-210; this is an area in which US law has moved rapidly towards increasing a tenant's rights through first the doctrine of constructive eviction and then the implied warranty of habitability. *Javins v First National Realty Corp* 428 F 2d 1071 (DC Cir 1970), is a leading case on the latter point involving horrific housing conditions. An improvement innovation was giving tenants the right to withhold rent). There are exceptions to this general rule, however, both via the implication of terms at common law (see paras 14-211–14-214) and statutory protection for certain tenants under the Landlord and Tenant Act 1985 (Harpum, paras 14-216–14-225)).

If the performance of this obligation is impossible at the time at which the parties entered into the contract, the contract is deemed valid according to § 311a I BGB and the lessee may recover damages instead of performance (or wasted expenditure) according to § 311a II BGB. It should be noted that this depends on whether the lessor is answerable for the breach. This will be the case if he had actual or imputed knowledge of the impediment at the time of contracting (§ 311a II 2 BGB; for a fuller discussion see the previous chapter, p 456). Prior to the reform, the assumption was that the promisee 'guaranteed' his ability to perform the contract. In cases of initial impossibility, liability was thus treated as 'strict'. The present position of the law is different: the fault principle in § 276 BGB is applied. In relation to subsequent impossibility, liability for damages instead of performance is regulated by § 283 BGB and depends on whether the lessor was answerable for the impossibility (requiring application of the fault principle: see chapter 9, section 5, p 456, for a comparison with the English case of *Taylor v Caldwell*. Note that, after much uncertainty, the doctrine of frustration has been held in principle to be applicable to leases of real property: *National Carriers Ltd v Panalpina (Northern) Ltd* [1981] AC 675, which raises the prospect of the Law Reform (Frustrated Contracts) Act 1943 being applied to frustrated leasehold estates (see our general discussion of this Act in chapter 4, section 4, p 334).

Impossibility is of special importance in relation to leases because the performance must normally be offered at a particular time. If this is not satisfied, the performance becomes impossible (*absolutes Fixgeschäft*) simply due to the lapse of time. If the obligation of the seller under § 535 I 1 BGB is not fulfilled, the lessee is as a general rule released from his obligation of counter-performance: § 326 I 1 BGB. However, if the lessee was in delay of acceptance when the performance became impossible, the right to the rent is preserved (§ 326 II 1 BGB: see BGH NJW-RR 1991, 267 for an illustration—the result previously followed from the old § 324 II).

The liability of the lessor for defects in the leased object is subjected to a special regime of rules contained in §§ 536–536d BGB. These rules are self-contained and no serious attempt was made to adjust them to general contract principles, which general principles—as a result of the latest reform of the law of obligations—have changed considerably. The rules on non-conformity of performance must therefore be examined more closely below. At this stage, we must briefly state the rules that determine when each set of rules is applicable. Such 'meta'-rules are an inevitable complication of any system that maintains special and general rules for failure of performance. The courts proceeded hitherto on the following assumptions and it is to be expected that they will also adhere to them after the reform. (See, eg, BGHZ 136, 102; BGH NJW 1991, 3277; BGH NJW 1963, 804, case no 121. Academic writers tend to oppose the position of the jurisprudence on these issues: see, for a fuller discussion and references, Unberath, ZMR 2004, 310–11.) First, within the scope of application of the special rules the general rules are ousted. Secondly, the special rules in relation to physical defects apply from the moment that the leased object is handed over to the buyer. Thirdly, in relation to legal defects (§ 536 III BGB) the special rules as to non-conforming performance apply.

The definition of conformity in § 536 BGB therefore is also crucial to an understanding of the scope of application of the special rules. It suffices here to remark that, as in relation to the other types of contract, it is for the parties to define the requirements that performance must satisfy in order to be regarded as free from defects. Thus, the general rule is that the leased object must be suitable for the use presupposed in the contract: § 536 I 1 BGB. The need for adjustment between the various reforms can be seen from the fact that § 536 II BGB still refers to the 'guaranteed features' of the subject matter of the contract. Since the reform of the law of obligations, this type of limited 'guarantee' is also located in § 276 I BGB. However, the duplication is only a cosmetic flaw and does not create any difficulties in practical application. Finally, § 536b BGB governs the question as to when the lessee is deprived of his rights in relation to the defect on the ground that he had actual or imputed knowledge of the defect and did not reserve his rights.

(c) Enforced Performance

The contract of rent is a continuous contract. As a result, a defect in the leased object cannot be cured for the time it persisted. To this extent, 'subsequent' performance is impossible (§ 275 I BGB). It is curable, if at all, only with effects for the future. The obligation of the lessor to cure the defect follows from § 535 I 2 BGB. The lessee must enable the lessor to bring the performance into conformity with the contract, for otherwise he is deprived of his rights: § 536c BGB. As we have seen in relation to the contract of sale and the contract for works, the special regimes demanding that defects be cured also subjected the right to enforced performance to a 'reasonableness' test. Such cure could be refused if it involved disproportionate outlays (§§ 439 III, 635 III BGB). Somewhat surprisingly, no such special limit is laid down in the section on the contract of rent. The courts have nevertheless limited the obligation of the lessor arising from § 536 I 2 BGB (eg, BGH NJW-RR 1991, 204). If the cost of reinstatement would exceed a certain threshold (*Opfergrenze*), the defect of the leased object should no longer be regarded as a 'defect' in the technical sense of the term. This argument is evidently made to conceal the fact that a special test of reasonableness is missing from the list of provisions on the contract of rent. The test in § 275 II BGB is available only in extreme cases where the cost of reinstatement is grossly out of proportion to the performance interest. (See Unberath, ZMR 2004, 311; and Emmerich, NZM 2002, 365, who suggests that the rules as to the foundation of the transaction, § 313 BGB, ought to be applied instead.) Under English law, a breach of a landlord's obligation to repair is often the subject of an order of specific performance (eg, *Joyce v Liverpool City Council* [1996] QB 252; the court has inherent equitable jurisdiction to do this, but may rely instead on the statutory power laid down in section 17 of the Landlord and Tenant Act 1985) and may even lead to a mandatory injunction being issued by the court to compel the landlord to fulfil his obligation to maintain or repair the property (eg, *Parker v Camden LBC* [1986] Ch 162, at 173). Alternatively, if the tenant does the repairs himself after giving the landlord notice of the defect, he can then use his common law rights of set-off to reduce his rent payments by the amount expended on the repair (*Lee-Parker v Izzett* [1971] 1 WLR 1688; see the comments above on the US case of *Javins*—this approach is a recent innovation in the US). Note that where the equitable jurisdiction is invoked, its exercise will be at the court's discretion and thus subject to the traditional equitable restrictions on the grant of the remedy (which might be a way in which demands to put repairs in hand that will be excessively costly could be resisted by the landlord, although there does not appear to be any case law on this subject to date).

It should also be noted that enforced performance may be particularly important for the lessor who claims the leased object back from the lessee. The obligation of the lessee is laid down in § 546 BGB. The lessor is entitled to the rent for the period of time the object is withheld: § 546a I BGB (§ 571 BGB stipulates special rules for residential leases). Finally, §§ 721, 749a ZPO govern the execution of a judgment that orders a lessee to vacate residential premises and provide for special protection of the tenant (basically affording the tenant a period of grace).

(d) Termination by Notice and Price Reduction

If the leased object is defective, the rent is automatically reduced according to § 536 I BGB, and this applies whether or not the lessor is answerable for the breach. The right to price reduction therefore is not dependent on whether the lessee resorted to price reduction by unilateral declaration and does not presuppose that the lessee demanded removal of the defect first (contrast, eg, § 441 BGB). This is sensible, since the defect cannot be cured retroactively for the time it actually persisted. However, it will be recalled that the buyer must bring the defect to the attention of the lessor according to § 536c BGB. Rent that was paid in excess of the amount of the reduced rent can be claimed back according to the rules of unjustified enrichment (§ 812 BGB). (See BGH NJW 2003, 2601, as to the question whether unreserved payment extinguished the right to recover excess rent.) In order to preserve good relations between lessor and lessee and to avoid arguments over minor issues, § 536 I 3 BGB excludes the right to price reduction if the defect is 'minor' (only trivial breaches are covered by this exclusion. This is now in clear contrast with the rules on the contract of sale and for work, and probably will result in different approaches as to what constitutes a 'minor breach'). (On the issue of price reduction in English law, see the comments above relating to set-off by the tenant of expenses (incurred to remedy the landlord's breach of a covenant to maintain or repair) against rent owing to the landlord; equally, a damages claim may be brought for such breach, based on the loss of comfort and convenience resulting from disrepair (if the tenant remains in occupation) or on the reduction in the value of the lease (on assignment) or the rental (on sub-letting). Such damages may ultimately have an effect somewhat similar to a price reduction regime. See, generally, Harpum, *Megarry & Wade: The Law of Property*, para 14-280 and the references cited therein.)

Termination by notice (*Kündigung*) is one of the main remedies available for breach of contract to the parties to a contract for rent and is referred to as 'extraordinary' termination. Special rules apply. The right of the lessee to terminate the contract in cases of non-conforming performance follows from § 543 II 1 Nr. 1 BGB (§ 569 BGB contains qualifications as to the lease of residential premises; as discussed under subsection (b), above, English law has a similar series of qualifications to determination of the lease of residential premises by notice). The right of the lessor to terminate by notice if the lessee fails to perform follows from § 543 II 1 Nr. 3 BGB if the obligation to pay rent is breached (note § 569 III BGB applies to rent for residential premises) and from § 543 II 1 Nr. 2 and I 2 BGB in respect of other breaches.

(e) Damages for Non-conforming Performance

§ 536a BGB contains a comprehensive regulation of the liability of the lessor for non-conforming performance, which replaces §§ 280–3 BGB of the general part (note however that the right to recover for wasted expenditure instead of damages for non-performance is also granted to the lessee: § 284 BGB). § 536a I BGB entitles the lessee to recover damages for loss caused by a defect in the leased object. The provision extends to consequential loss as well. On these matters, beyond damages claims for breach of covenant as outlined above (where notice must be given to the landlord of such defect or disrepair), English law also applies the Defective Premises Act 1972 where the landlord is obliged to maintain or repair the premises (section 4(1)) or has a right to enter the premises to effect maintenance (section 4(4)). In such circumstances, the landlord owes a duty of care to all persons (including the lessee) who are affected by his failure to fulfil those duties and this duty can arise even in the absence of his actual knowledge of the relevant defects—see section 4(2), which covers the situation where the landlord should in all the circumstances have known of that defect. Thus, any defect that fell within the scope of the obligation to repair or that the landlord could have entered the premises to fix will be sufficient, and the duty will be breached if the landlord was negligent in not discovering that defect

Paragraph 536a II BGB entitles the lessee to recover the cost of curing the defect if the lessor is in default (*Verzug*) and has failed to do so himself; more importantly, the cost of cure is also available if the lessee was entitled to effect the cure himself because of a situation of necessity (in the latter case, the right exists independently of any fault on the part of the lessor; see the foregoing comments on set-off under English law, which would seem to operate more widely than merely in situations of necessity).

The right to recover damages under § 536a I BGB distinguishes between defects that existed at the time the contract was entered into and defects that have subsequently came into being. In relation to initial defects, the provision establishes a 'guarantee' liability. (See, for an illustration of this important instance of 'strict' liability in the BGB, BGH NJW 1963, 804, case no 121.) In relation to subsequent defects, the condition for recovery is that either the lessor was answerable for the defect (§ 276 BGB) or the lessor was in default (*Verzug*) in curing the defect, thereby also presupposing that the lessor was answerable for the breach (§ 286 IV BGB). Prior to the reform, the 'guarantee' liability envisaged by § 536a BGB for initial defects operated in harmony with general principle, for it was generally assumed that the contractual debtor 'guarantees' that, at least at the time of contracting, he is able to perform. However, as was explained above (in chapter 9, section 5(b) and (especially) (d), p 457), the Second Commission came to the view that the fault principle should apply also in relation to initial impediments to performance (see § 311a II BGB). The special rule of the contract of rent establishing 'guarantee' liability is thus now a true exception. This can create unsatisfactory results when applied in combination with the rules as to the scope of application of § 536a BGB. As explained earlier in this section, the provision only applies in relation to physical defects once the leased object has been handed over to the lessee. This has the unfortunate consequence that before this point, liability is fault-dependent (§ 311a II BGB), while from the moment the leased property is handed over, liability is strict (§ 536a I BGB in respect of initial defects: see further, Unberath, ZMR 2004, 312).

Appendix I: Cases

Chapter 2

Case 1
REICHSGERICHT (SIXTH CIVIL SENATE) 8 APRIL 1929
RGZ 124, 81

Facts

On 24 March 1919, the parties entered a 'precontract' (Vorvertrag) before a notary, by Clause II of which the plaintiff, at any time on the defendant's demand, undertook to enter a contract of sale with the defendant so as to vest in him ownership in house no 49 in P 'with all contents.' It was agreed and ordered that an entry should be made in the land register to secure this future claim. By Clause III 'the precise terms and conditions of the sale are to be finalised on the drawing up of the sale contract, the price of house and contents not to exceed M40,000.' By Clause IV the plaintiff's undertaking was to last until 24 March 1920.

The relevant entry in the land register was made on the defendant's behalf on 28 March 1919. On 12 March 1920 the defendant gave the plaintiff one week to perform his obligations but the plaintiff did nothing, in the belief that the contract was void because the parties' agreement regarding the price was inaccurately recorded. He sought a declaration to that effect, and an injunction requiring the defendant to consent to the erasure of the entry in his favour in the land register. The defendant counter-claimed for an injunction that the plaintiff transfer house and contents for M40,000 and agree to a change of ownership in the land register. The lower court rejected the claim and gave judgment on the counter-claim. On the plaintiff's appeal the counter-claimant cross-appealed for a judgment that the plaintiff sell him the property on the terms of the *Landgericht's* judgment. Judgment in the *Oberlandesgericht* was in the defendant's favour. The plaintiff's appeal was allowed.

Reasons

On the substance of the matter, the appellant rightly insisted on a point which he raised below, namely that the 'precontract' of 24 March 1919 is invalid for want of content.

It is familiar law that a precontract must meet not only the formal requirements (which is here the case—para 313 para 1 [311b I] BGB), but the substantive requirements of the main contract. In particular, the duties undertaken by the parties in the precontract must be certain or at least ascertainable, so that a court can determine the content of the ultimate contract (RGZ 66, 121; 72, 385; see also RGZ 106, 177). No such certainty or ascertainability exists in the 'precontract' of 24 March 1919. A sale contract, and consequently a precontract to a sale, requires agreement of the parties not only on the thing or right which constitutes the object of the contract but also on the price (para 433 BGB). We need not ask whether the seller's duty with regard to the contents was sufficiently certain or ascertainable under the contract of 24 March, since in any case the buyer's counterpart, the price, is left uncertain; the only thing fixed about the price is its upper limit, viz M40,000. The plaintiff could not on the basis of such a precontract have insisted on going through with a sale contract, let alone at a price of M40,000; nor can the defendant, even if he offers the highest sum mentioned. On the price alone, the agreement of 24 March lacks the quality of a pre-contract; it is simply a draft or sketch, not binding on either party, and capable at the very most of use in the interpretation of a subsequent precontract or main contract, if one were to be made. But there is the further point that the parties specifically agreed to postpone making the detailed terms of sale until the time of the later contract (compare para 154 para 1 BGB). It therefore depended on the free decision of both parties what these detailed terms should be, and such a decision could not imaginably be replaced or amplified by a judicial decision. Neither the *Landgericht* nor the *Oberlandesgericht* made any such attempt: both simply took M40,000 as the purchase price without even adverting to the matter or revalorisation, which they should have raised *proprio motu* (RGZ 106, 422; 107, 19, 129, 150; 109, 69).

The plaintiff's claim for a declaration that the contract of 24 March 1919 was void is therefore justified.

Case 2
OBERLANDESGERICHT HAMM 24 OCTOBER 1975
NJW 1976, 1212

Facts

By notarial contract the plaintiff sold the defendants a plot of land on which a single family house, designed for occupation by the plaintiff and his wife, had recently been erected. While the house was being built, and long before entering into the contract of sale, the plaintiff had purchased a large quantity of furniture and fittings, at a total price of about DM20,000, much of it being custom made, such as cupboards and kitchen cabinets. The furniture and fittings were installed in the house, but the plaintiff never occupied it, so he was eager to sell them with the property, as he had no real use for them. The defendants started using the furniture as soon as they moved into the house, and are still using it today. They gave the plaintiff a cheque for DM2000, but the plaintiff contends that a sale price of DM20,000 had been agreed, and now sues for DM18,000. The defendants deny that there was ever any contract about the furniture, as no agreement about the price ensued from the negotiations. The *Landgericht* gave judgment for the plaintiff, and the defendants' appeal was mainly unsuccessful.

Reasons

I. The plaintiff has a claim for DM18,000 under para 433 BGB. A contract for the sale of these fitments did come about between the parties.
1. The evidence does not make it absolutely clear that the parties expressly agreed on a price of DM20,000.

2. But under the special circumstances of this case the failure to agree on the price is not fatal to the formation of a contract of sale. It emerges from the whole evidence that the parties concluded a contract of sale with the peculiarity that it should be left for further negotiations to determine a fair price.

(a) It is true that in a case of doubt parties are held not to have made a contract until they have agreed on all the points which need agreement (para 154 BGB), and both parties here realised that there should be agreement on the price. But this principle applies only 'in cases of doubt' (para 154 BGB), ie it only gives rise to a presumption which is capable of being rebutted. It does not prevent the parties from entering into legal obligations although certain details of the transaction are still unregulated which one or both parties wish clarified (. . .). The principle of freedom of contract requires that people should be able to leave even essential points open, such as the purchase price in the present case (see BGH, NJW 1964, 1617), without impairing the contractual obligation which the parties wish to achieve.

(b) In the present case there was an agreement of this kind. It is common ground that the plaintiff wanted to sell the furniture along with the land, and as the defendants themselves say, they were in principle ready to take over the furniture, even if they had a somewhat different price in mind. It is not to be supposed that in such circumstances the plaintiff gave the defendants possession of the furniture, with all the risk of wear and tear, without there being any legal obligation between the parties at the time. Doubtless it would not have been easy for the plaintiff to sell the new furniture very favourably elsewhere, but he could hardly sell it at all once it was used. The plaintiffs letting the defendants possess and use the furniture before there was any agreement as to the price must, in good faith, be treated as an offer for sale at a price which remained to be determined, and the defendants accepted this offer by beginning to use the furniture. The circumstances were all well-known to them. They could not reasonably suppose that the plaintiff was selling them the house without any agreement about the furniture, or that he was letting them use it without any obligation to buy it at a price still to be fixed. It is worth noting that the price mentioned for these items was quite small in relation to the price of the house, only about 5 per cent.

Under these circumstances the defendants' taking possession of the furniture and making use of it is conduct which ranks as an acceptance of the plaintiff's offer (para 133 BGB). If this was not the defendants' intention, it was for them to make this clear to the plaintiff, and they did not do so. Any secret reservation the defendants may have had about buying the furniture when they took possession of it can be disregarded (para 116 BGB).

The court has also considered whether the agreement may not be merely a precontract with an obligation to conclude the sale contract later, but such a construction overlooks the point that the plaintiff has already performed one of the seller's essential obligations by putting the defendants in possession and giving them use of the chattels being sold.

The defendants can obtain no assistance from para 147 BGB, whereby an offer made to a person actually present must be accepted forthwith. The offeror may extend the period for acceptance at any time, and may do so implicitly (reference omitted). On a reasonable construction, the plaintiff's offer to sell the furniture to the defendants before any price was fixed was to last at least until the defendants moved into the house which had the furniture in it; proper acceptance duly took place. The view that a contract of sale was formed is further strengthened by the fact that the defendants have paid DM2000. This may not show that any price was agreed, but it does show that the parties agreed that the defendants be bound to buy the furniture at a price yet to be hit on.

(c) It is actually in the interests of both parties that the defendants should keep the furniture and pay a price still to be fixed. The defendants have often said that they were ready to keep the furniture, and the plaintiff cannot put it to any economic use. If no sale contract exists, the defendants will not only have to give up the furniture, but after being credited with the DM2000 they have paid, pay the plaintiff the value of the use of the furniture, which in the case of new furniture is very high, until such time as they call on him to remove it; furthermore, they will need to buy new furniture although, as has been said, they are quite happy with what they have. Both parties are experienced people and it must have been clear to them that unreasonable consequences of this kind would ensue if the furniture were used without there being any contract about it. This confirms the conclusion that the possession was handed over definitively and pursuant to a contract of sale.

3. There having been proof of the price which the defendants are thus bound to pay, it must be filled in by apt contractual construction (para 157 BGB; . . .). The parties must, as reasonable people, have intended to agree on a fair price. There is nothing to suggest that either party was to have a right of determination under para 315 BGB. As the defendant unanswerably argued, the purchase price was to be agreed, not laid down, especially not laid down by the plaintiff (para 316 BGB). If the parties do not agree, and if neither party nor any third party has a right of determination, the determination of the fair purchase price which the defendants are bound to pay can only be made by the court.

Case 3
BUNDESGERICHTSHOF (ANTI-TRUST SENATE) 2 APRIL 1974
BGHZ 41, 271

Facts

The plaintiff, a farmer with a large dairy herd, was bound by law to sell his milk, if at all, to the defendant dairy, which was required by provincial ordinance to pay less, by at least 2 pf per kilo, for milk from a non-TT herd like the plaintiff's. Suppliers were informed by circular that as from 1 May 1957 the differential would be 3 pf, subsequently raised to 5 pf and then to 10 pf. The plaintiff objected to these deductions but continued to supply milk, and now claims the sum of DM4040.91 as having been improperly deducted. The *Landgericht* rejected the plaintiff's claim and his appeal to the *Oberlandesgericht* was dismissed. On further appeal the judgment below was vacated, and the matter remanded to the Anti-Trust Senate of the *Oberlandesgericht*.

Reasons

1. The Court of Appeal was wrong in law to hold that notwithstanding the plaintiff's written protests his conduct evinced a declaration of consent to the defendant's published deductions.

2. But this does not really help the plaintiff, since the Court of Appeal went on to say in relation to para 315 BGB, that there was no need for the plaintiff to declare his consent to the deductions. This conclusion, at any rate, is supported by the following reasons:

(a) The 'dairy areas' laid down in para 1 of the Milk and Animal Fat Act (*Milch-und Fettgesetz*—MFG) determine which suppliers must deliver their milk to which dairy if they wish to sell it commercially at all. The contractual freedom of milk-producers is thus limited (*Kontrahierungsbeschränkung*): if they choose to dispose of their milk commercially they must deliver it to the specified dairy. For dairies, on the other hand, there is a total 'obligation to contract' (*Kontrahierungszwantg*) (BGHZ 33, 259, 262): para 1 para 4 MFG not only removes their freedom to choose their suppliers, but imposes on them an obligation to accept any milk tendered by the specified producers. In other respects however the rights and duties of milk producer and dairy regarding deliveries of milk remain unaffected by the provisions of para 1 MFG. Their legal relations are of a private law nature, as the Court of Appeal correctly held. The dairy may be a co-operative or a so-called 'private dairy', but this is irrelevant so far as its legal relations with a non-member are concerned. The relations between members of a co-operative dairy and the dairy itself may be affected by the constituent document or by subsequent resolutions, but relations between it and a milk producer who is not a member depend on the general private law of contract just like the relations between a producer and a private dairy. The contracts between producer and dairy regarding milk deliveries are sale contracts in the sense of paras 433 ff BGB. It is irrelevant, and therefore unnecessary, to decide whether a separate sale contract is made for the milk delivered on each occasion, as the Court of Appeal supposed, or whether this is a case of 'repeat obligations' (*Wiederkehrschuldverhältnisse*, [reference omitted] or of a long-term supply contract as the appellant maintains.

(b) Before a sale contract can be formed the parties must agree on the purchase price or at any rate on a method of determining it. There is no legal obligation to deduct more than 2 pf per kilo here, so to this extent the price paid for milk was dependent on the free bargaining of the parties. Given that bargaining is free, there are three obvious ways in which a contract could validly be made: if the price is expressly agreed between dairy and producer; if the price is determined unilaterally by the dairy and accepted by producers through appropriate conduct; or finally if the dairy is permitted, by either the express agreement or the implicit consent of the producers, to determine the price under para 315 BGB. But a valid sale can also come about even if producer and dairy are at variance over the price or its determination by the dairy, and even if, as in the present case, the producer expressly contests the dairy's determination of the price. Realism dictates, as indeed to the interests of the parties in this case, that people who are bound by law to enter into lasting relations as supplier and purchaser of goods, as the parties are here by para 1 MFG, should be treated as contractors, indeed as seller and buyer: otherwise they would be operating in a non-contractual framework, and the only rules to apply to their actions and obligations would be the provisions of paras 812 ff. BGB regarding the duty of restitution when there is no legal basis for an enrichment, rules which are not at all appropriate for such long-term relationships. Notwithstanding the failure of the present parties to agree on one point, namely an aspect of the purchase price related to the special factor of the source of the milk, it must be assumed, for it is in line with the will of the parties in other respects, that a contract came into existence, contrary to para 154 para II sentence 1 BGB, which is only a rule of construction. The lacuna in the contract must be filled in accordance with statutory provisions if the parties cannot agree among themselves [RGZ 60, 174, 178; other reference omitted]. In a case like ours the idea underlying para 315 BGB provides a method for filling the gap. Given the limitations on the freedom of contract imposed by para 1 MFG and expressly recognised by the Law against Restraints on Competition (*Gesetz gegen Wettbewerbsbeschränkungen—GWB*) para 100 para 8, para 315 BGB offers the best method of doing justice: para 315 para 1 recognises the just interests of the defendant by giving it the right to determine the price, and para 315 para 3 is designed to protect the just interests of the producer (for the application of para 315 BGB in similar cases, see RGZ 111, 310, 313 (electricity supply contract), and BGHZ 38, 183, 186 (unfair terms in general conditions of business); see generally Lukes in NJW 1963, 1897 ff). Since the dairy has a monopoly position it must treat its customers equally [reference omitted] and cannot be expected to adapt itself to the particular wishes of every individual supplier and pay him what he wants for his milk: it must have the right to fix what the contract has left open, unilaterally and in a fair and just manner, as set out in para 315 para 1 BGB. If the milk producer finds the dairy's unilateral determination unacceptable, he is sufficiently protected by para 315 para 3 BGB, for only if the dairy's determination is fair is he bound by it; if it is not, the determination is to be made by the court. To this extent the unilateral determination of the dairy is subject to contrary determination by the court.

3. The next step, as the Court of Appeal realised, is to see whether the defendant's 'industrial milk deductions,' as published in its circulars, were equitable in the sense of para 315 para 3 BGB, and then to check whether in adopting them the dairy had not abused its monopoly position under paras 1 and 2 MFG and so infringed the requirement of good morals and ethical behaviour in the sense of paras 138, 826 BGB [reference omitted]. In doing this however the court below applied too narrow a criterion, having inferred a general concept of abuse of monopolistic position from certain decisions of the Reichsgericht (RGZ 99, 107; 106, 386; 133, 388; 143, 24, 28), and furthermore, as the appellant rightly objects, it failed to consider whether the dairy had discriminated in breach of para 26 para 2 GWB.

(b) The producer may assert concurrently the rights which arise from para 315 para 3 BGB and from breach of para 26 para 2 GWB, as well as any other rights arising from paras 138, 826 BGB; independently of this, he can invite the anti-trust authorities to intervene under para 22 para 4 GWB in connection with para 3 [reference omitted].

Nor is there any essential difference regarding the burden of proof in cases arising under para 315 para 3 BGB and para 26 para 2 (second alternative) GWB, for in the former case the party fixing the performance must prove that he has done so in an equitable manner, and in the latter, the business which has discriminated is required to prove that it had objective justification for so doing [references omitted]. Thus there is no question, in a case like the present, of the court's fixing a 'just price' *proprio motu*, but simply of checking, from the point of view of para 315 para 3 BGB and para 26 para 2 (second alternative) GWB whether the party fixing the terms has established or proved that the terms he fixed (or any other terms which are to take their place) fall within the limits set by para 315 para 3 BGB and para 26 para 2 GWB.

Finally, the two provisions may give rise to similar remedies. While it is true that when the terms fixed by one party are not equitable, the determination under para 315 para 3 BGB is made 'by judgment,' meaning a constitutive judgment, a claim for performance may also be brought, the performance claimed being the performance which would be due had the terms been fixed fairly [reference omitted]; likewise, a claim for performance may be brought for what would have been due had there been no discriminatory conduct under para 26 para 2 GWB, at least where it is a question of indemnity under para 35 para 1 GWB and para 249 para 1 BGB [references omitted].

Case 4
BUNDESGERICHTSHOF (EIGHTH CIVIL SENATE) 7 NOVEMBER 2001
NJW 2002, 363

Facts

The parties are in dispute about whether they concluded a valid contract for the sale of a car in July 1999 in an internet auction. The r. .de AG in H (from now on called r. .de) carried out online auctions on its website under the description 'r. private auctions', in which the only people who could participate as sellers or buyers were those who had registered beforehand with r. .de, and had thereby approved the 'general conditions of contract for r. .de sale events' (from now on called the AGB). The following are extracts from the AGB:

'Preamble:

(3) § 156 of the BGB, § 34 b of the GewO (Trade Order) and the Regulations about Business Auctions do not apply to . . . *private auctions.*
§ 3 Description of the subject-matter of the purchase, offer of sale in private auctions
(1) R. .de enables participants to present to the public on offer pages objects in their ownership which are to be sold under the umbrella of *private auctions.*
(5) The participant who wants to sell is invited, as part of the process of the release of the offer page, to give the assurances and declarations mentioned in para 4 and § 5 para 4 to r. .de. R. .de acts in this connection as receiving agent for all other participants: § 164 (3) of the BGB. The release only takes place when the participant who wants to sell has given the required assurances and declarations.
§ 4 Contractual offer
(1) For objects offered under the umbrella of *private auctions* by . . . participants who want to sell, any participant (with the exception of the group of persons mentioned in para 2) can give a binding offer to purchase via the r. .de website during the offer period for the object in question (§ 6).

(4) Offers of purchase which are below the reserve price asked by . . . the participant who wants to sell are invalid.

(7) In the case of offers which are given under the umbrella of *private auctions*, r. .de acts as receiving agent for the participant who wants to sell: § 164 (5) of the BGB.

§ 5 Acceptance of a contractual offer

(4) In the case of *private auctions*, the participant who wants to sell declares, by the release of his offer page in accordance with § 3 para 5, his acceptance of the highest offer of purchase effectively given, taking into consideration § 4 paras 4 and 5. The participant who is selling will be informed by r. .de immediately when the contract of sale comes into existence, but at the latest before midnight on the second working day after the end of the offer period (§ 6) by email at the email address given by the participant who is selling.'

The defendant, who deals in EU reimported vehicles as a sideline, set up an offer page under his user name for the sale of a new VW Passat with a description of the vehicle. He stipulated the starting price (10 DM), the spaces between the bids, and the length of the auction. He gave the prescribed declaration which said, amongst other things: 'At this point in time I declare my acceptance of the highest offer of purchase effectively given.' The defendant did not stipulate a reserve price. The offer page was released for five days on the website of r. .de.

The claimant made the last and highest bid of DM26,350 under his user name eight seconds before the end of the auction. R. .de told the claimant by email that his bid was successful, informed him of the identity of the seller, and invited him to get in touch with the seller in order to arrange dispatch and payment.

The defendant refused to deliver the car to the claimant's order, on the ground that no contract had yet come into existence. He was however prepared to sell the vehicle at a price of 'about 39,000 DM'. As a precaution, he denied, on the ground of a mistake in the submission of the starting price, that he had made any declaration of will.

The claimant claimed from the defendant transfer of the car simultaneously with the payment of DM26,350. The *Landgericht* rejected the claim (LG Münster JZ 2000, 730). On the claimant's appeal, the *Oberlandesgericht* gave judgment against the defendant in accordance with the application (OLG Hamm JZ 2001, 764 = NJW 2001, 1142). By his appeal in law, which has been admitted by the appeal court, the defendant seeks the restoration of the judgment of the *Landgericht*.

Reasons

(. . .)

II. The appeal in law was unsuccessful. The parties have concluded a valid contract of sale in respect of the car offered by the defendant on the website of r. .de.

1. Contracts come into existence by declarations of will which correspond with one another and which envisage conclusion of a contract. As a rule they are an offer and an acceptance under §§ 145 ff BGB. In the case of auctions they are a bid and an acceptance (§ 156 BGB). These declarations of will can, as the appeal court has correctly stated, also be given and become effective by electronic communication of a file on the internet—online.

2. Conclusion of a contract under § 156 BGB is excluded in this case, because no acceptance has occurred of the claimant's bid. (. . .)

3. A contract has however come into existence under the general provisions of §§ 145 ff BGB.

(a) It is beyond doubt that the claimant's highest offer, given online, represents an effective declaration of will envisaging the conclusion of a contract of sale with the defendant. Contrary to the view of the appeal in law, there is also a corresponding declaration of will on the part of the defendant. According to the deliberations of the appeal court, which are correct, this lies in the fact that the defendant released the offer page set up by him for the auction of his car with the (express) declaration that he would at that point in time accept the highest offer of purchase effectively given.

Whether the defendant's declaration of will is, as the appeal court thought, legally to be classified as an offer of sale, and the subsequent highest bid of the claimant as its acceptance, or whether, as the wording of the declaration given by the defendant suggests (and this was accepted as a subsidiary point by the appeal court), the defendant's declaration of will represents a—legally permissible—acceptance declared beforehand of the highest bid which was given by the claimant can remain undecided. It has no significance for the legal consequences.

The reciprocal declarations of the parties have, according to the findings of the appeal court which are not challenged, in each case reached r. .de as the receiving agent of the parties (§ 164 (3) BGB) and therefore become effective (§ 130 (1) sentence 1 of the BGB). A contract of sale has thereby come into existence between the parties under §§ 145 ff BGB.

(b) The appeal court correctly assumes that the declaration given by the defendant, combined with the release of his offer page which was effected simultaneously, represents a declaration of will envisaging sale of the car which was on offer, and was not merely a non-binding invitation to treat (*invitatio ad offerendum*).

(aa) A declaration of will is a statement which envisages the effectuation of a legal transaction (see BGH judgment of the 24th May 1993—II ZR 73/92, NJW 1993, 2100 under I 1). Whether a statement or a piece of conclusive behaviour is to be understood as a declaration of will needs interpretation.

The appeal court, in assessing the effect on the claimant of the defendant's release of his offer page, was correct in not only taking account of the content of the offer page, which in online auctions appears on the screen. The court also considered the declaration which the defendant had to give on the release in order to effect the release (§§ 3 para 5, and 5 para 4 of the AGB), and which the defendant also actually gave by clicking on the appropriate preformulated declaration at the time of the release. This express declaration by the defendant, which admittedly did not itself appear on the offer page, but which reached r. .de as the claimant's receiving agent, represented, combined with the content of the offer page to which it referred, the defendant's declaration envisaging the conclusion of a contract of sale with the highest bidder.

The appeal in law objects that the appeal court had disregarded the unambiguous wording of the declaration given by the defendant on the release in an impermissible way. This only relates to the question—not significant for the decision—of whether the defendant's declaration of will should be classified as an offer or as an anticipated acceptance. It does not however affect its character as a declaration of will leading to a legal transaction.

(bb) The defendant's declaration of will was also, as the appeal court has correctly explained, sufficiently precise. Admittedly it was not directed at a person described in concrete terms (*ad incertam personam*). But it satisfied the requirement of precision, because the auction participant with whom the defendant wanted to contract could be identified without doubt, ie (only) the person who gave the highest offer within the offer period laid down [references omitted].

(cc) It is not necessary, as the appeal court thought, to refer to § 5 para 4 of the AGB in order to understand the defendant's declaration given on the release. It is true that general conditions of contract for internet auction can be called on as a basis for interpretation if declarations by the auctions participants are not comprehensible in themselves. Gaps in understanding can then be closed by referring to the mutual expectations of the auction participants, based on approval of the general conditions of contract and their common understanding of the way online auctions operate. The defendant's declaration given separately on the release ('At this point in time I declare my acceptance of the highest offer of purchase effectively given') however makes the defendant's intention to be bound unmistakably plain from its own terms, without any need to refer to the corresponding provision—worded in the same way—in § 5 para 4 of the AGB for an understanding of this declaration.

(dd) It does not matter whether the defendant was aware of the binding nature of his declaration when he gave his declaration of will and released his offer page. Even if there is no consciousness of making a declaration (an intention to be legally bound or to enter into a transaction), a declaration of will is present if the declarant—like the defendant—could, on applying the care necessary in human affairs, have realised that, in accordance with the principle of good faith and business custom, his statement might be regarded as a declaration of will, and if he could have avoided this result (BGHZ 91, 324; BGHZ 109, 171, 177). Reservation of an intention not to be bound which the recipient could not recognise should be ignored (§ 116 BGB). All that remains for the declarant is the possibility of avoiding his declaration of will under §§ 119 ff BGB within the limits set out there.

4. There are no grounds for saying that the defendant's declaration of will (and therefore the contract of sale) is ineffective. In particular such grounds do not arise, as the appeal in law claims, from the AGBG (General Conditions of Contract Act) [§§ 305–310 BGB]. (. . .)

Case 5
REICHSGERICHT (THIRD CIVIL SENATE) 12 JULY 1922
RGZ 105, 256

Facts

The defendant, who lived on the F estate in Mecklenburg, owned a parcel of woodland measuring 58.875 hectares. On 17 August 1919 he wrote to the plaintiff offering to sell him the timber on it at a price of M950 per Morgen and giving him until 25 August to accept. On 25 August the plaintiff telegraphed the defendant 'I accept 58.875 hectares at the price of M950 per Morgen'. That same day the telegram arrived in W, the telegraph office nearest to the F estate, but it was not delivered to the defendant until the next morning and then only by the normal postal delivery. Regarding the contract as having been duly formed on the basis—which the defendant denied—

that his telegram of acceptance had been brought to the defendant's knowledge by telephone on 25 August; the plaintiff sued for authority to remove the timber.

The *Landgericht* decided that the defendant must be put on his oath regarding the question whether or not the telegram was orally communicated to him, and made its decision dependent on what he swore to. The plaintiff's appeal to the *Oberlandesgericht* was dismissed. He appealed again, and his appeal was allowed.

Reasons

It is common ground that the telegram which arrived in the W Post Office on 25 August 1919 was not delivered to the defendant until the postman brought it with the morning delivery the following day. Now the defendant had arranged for telegrams addressed to him to be communicated to him by telephone under para 27 V 1 of the General Regulations for Postal and Telegraphic Services. The plaintiff seeks to conclude from this that his telegram should be treated as having 'reached' the defendant as soon as it arrived in W. Both tribunals of fact found against this contention, and rightly so. The transmission of telegrams by telephone—the method chosen by the defendant and expressly permitted by law (see para 19 II of the Telegraph Ordinance of 16 June 1904 (RZBl. 229))—is a method which anyone who sends a telegram, especially to an address in the country, must reckon with, and which is exactly like delivery by special messenger. Whichever method of communication is chosen, a telegram only reaches the recipient in the sense of para 130 BGB when the telegraph office makes it possible for him to learn of it. This certainly happens when the content of the telegram is communicated by telephone to the recipient's number and the message is taken by a member of the family of the household (RGZ 56, 262; 97, 336). The *Oberlandesgericht* did not find it proved that this had happened here, and consequently decided that the defendant must take a judicial oath regarding the oral communication of the telegram. But this is not a suitable case for such treatment. For even if the defendant's evidence under oath were against the plaintiff, and it was found that the plaintiff's declaration of acceptance came into the defendant's hands too late, it would not necessarily be right to dismiss the claim as the *Oberlandesgericht* proposes. The plaintiff sent off his declaration of acceptance in good time so that it would have reached the defendant on 25 August if it had been properly transmitted, that is, if the officials in W had done their duty. Furthermore, the defendant saw, or would have seen if he had been paying proper attention to the telegram form, that it had arrived in W at 9.50am on 25 August, and that the delay in transmission must therefore be due to some irregularity in the service. The defendant therefore came under a duty to inform the plaintiff without delay that the telegram had arrived late (para 149 BGB). He did not do this. It is true that he wrote on 26 August that he regarded his offer as having lapsed, since K had not appeared in person, as agreed, to conclude the matter; but as the *Oberlandesgericht* has found that there was no such agreement, this was not a ground of invalidity. What the defendant wrote was no substitute for the notice of delay provided for in para 149 BGB. The duty to make such notification arises from respect for good faith (*Treu und Glauben*), which requires that a person who uses a proper mode of transmission and can expect his acceptance to arrive in good time should be informed without any culpable delay if his expectations in a particular case have been frustrated by some unforeseen irregularity. He must therefore be in a position to discover that this is the reason for which the contract has gone off (I Motive for the BGB, p 171). An offeror who unjustifiably states that his offer has lapsed by reason of some irrelevant circumstance which would not have affected the conclusion of the contract if the declaration of acceptance had arrived in time, does not satisfy his duty to notify, for the risk remains that the acceptor may make further commercial arrangements in the justified belief that his declaration of acceptance arrived on time and so formed the contract. The consequence of a culpable failure to notify of delay is that, in derogation from the principle of paras 146, 150 para 1 BGB, the offer is deemed not to have lapsed but to have been accepted in due time, no account being taken of the delay which actually occurred. It is true that the plaintiff did not expressly invoke para 149, but in the circumstances of the case the Court of Appeal should have checked whether it was applicable or not.

But even if the defendant had satisfied para 149 BGB, the judgment under appeal could not stand. The *Oberlandesgericht* had misconceived the evidentiary value of the incoming telegram and its role in the burden of proof. We can leave aside for the moment the evidentiary value of the message for the recipient, for to that extent the telegram constitutes a private document and is in law to be treated as a written communication of the sender's will addressed directly to the recipient (see RGSt. 8, 92; 30, 238; 31, 42). But the incoming telegram also bears official statements regarding the place where it was handed in, the time when it arrived, and in the case of telegrams which are telephonically transmitted, the fact that it has been so communicated (para 27 para 10 V 6, General Regulations). Thus facts and events are indicated on it which are alien to the sender's declaration of intention but of considerable significance, or possible significance, to him and the recipient. This is especially true of the certification of oral communication. It cannot be said that para 27 para 10 is a purely internal service provision, since the telegraph service physically relinquishes the telegram on handing it to the addressee, and the entry in its arrivals book is quite sufficient to permit control of the staff. The annotation on the telegram cannot be made for the purpose of proof for or against the telegraph authorities, for they give no guarantee that telegrams will be delivered properly or on time and decline all liability in damages for delay in transmission (para 21 no 1 Telegraph Ordinance). But if the official annotation that the telegram has been orally communicated is not designed, mainly or at all, to serve the internal functioning of the service, it must in the nature of things be designed essentially for the benefit of the recipient: in requiring the official who communicates or processes the telegram to certify the fact, the telegraph authorities must intend to provide a means of proof of the fact and time of oral communication which is worthy of public credence and valid for or against any interested party. This is also in tune with the needs of commerce, given the important role a telegram can play in the formation of a contract under para 127 BGB.

If the telegram delivered to the defendant were before the court and bore a mark to the effect that it had been orally communicated, this would constitute good evidence of that fact under para 418 Code of Civil Procedure (ZPO), and the defendant would then have to prove that the act of communication so evidenced did not take place. The aforementioned General Regulations for the Telegraph Service state in para 27 para 10 V 6 that 'when telegrams have been orally communicated they are to be so marked and sent to the addressee by post in a closed envelope bearing the inscription . . . "Orally Communicated Telegram." ' In the light of (a) this provision, (b) the note in the arrivals book that the telegram had been orally communicated and (c) the failure to deliver it by special messenger (General Regulations for the Telegraph Service, para 27 para 12), one must conclude until it is shown otherwise, that the incoming telegram bore a mark of oral communication. The defendant should have realised that the telegraph service believed it to have been orally communicated, given the fact that the telegram which had arrived at W on Sunday morning was delivered to him only on Monday, and then only by normal postal delivery. Under these circumstances an averagely careful businessman who knew that the telegram had not in fact been orally communicated would immediately have got in touch with the telegraph service in order to clear up the matter. The defendant should have done this, and it would have been perfectly easy for him since he had a telephone. Having failed to do this forthwith, he should at any rate have done it when the plaintiff made it clear in his letter of 26 August that he regarded the contract as formed. Not only did the defendant omit to find out from the post office what had really happened, but he also failed to adduce the original telegram in evidence, and has not satisfactorily explained how he has come to lose it. Good faith (*Treu und Glauben*) made it his duty to preserve the telegram with care, for it was important for the legal relations of the parties. His breach of this duty must be accounted culpable.

The defendant's culpable omissions have made it impossible for the plaintiff to use the incoming telegram as evidence, indeed as proof under para 418 ZPO, of the timeous arrival of the telegram, which it was for him to establish. In consequence, under general principles (see RGZ 60, 152), the plaintiff's assertion that the telegram was communicated to the defendant on 25 August must be treated as true until the defendant proves otherwise. The Court of Appeal did not evaluate the matters of proof from this point of view: it will be necessary for it to do so if the plaintiff fails under para 149 BGB.

Case 6
REICHSGERICHT (FOURTH CIVIL SENATE) 3 MAY 1934
RGZ 144, 289

Facts

On 30 December 1931 the plaintiff tenant sent the defendant a notice of termination of the ten-year lease which they had entered into on 2 March 1926. The dispute was whether the notice reached the defendant in time, and if not whether she must be treated as if it had. The plaintiff claimed a declaration that the lease had been terminated by this notice.

The *Landgericht* dismissed the claim, but the *Oberlandesgericht* allowed the plaintiff's appeal. On the defendant's appeal, that decision was reversed and the case remanded to the trial court (judgment of 18 May 1933). The *Oberlandesgericht* made the final outcome dependent on the defendant's judicial oath. The plaintiff appealed, and the declaration he sought was granted.

Reasons

Regarding the defendant's contention that the notice was ineffective because it did not reach her, the following facts emerged. On 30 December 1931 the plaintiff posted a letter to the defendant's last known address in B. That was the defendant's last fixed abode, but she had left forwarding instructions with the post office at B. They were to forward mail to L, *post restante*. Accordingly the plaintiff's letter arrived at L on 31 December, where it was made available for collection. Meanwhile however on 12 December the plaintiff had given further forwarding instructions that mail arriving for her in L was to be forwarded to H, *post restante*, 'until further notice'. The post office form on which the defendant gave these further instructions contained the following footnote arising from the General Regulations for the Post and Telegraph Service, para V(1): '1. Instructions for inland forwarding lapse after fourteen days . . . and are, if necessary, to be renewed in advance.' Fourteen days having elapsed since the second forwarding instructions were given, the notice of termination was not forwarded by the L post office to H, but remained in L at the *post restante* counter awaiting collection. Then, since it was still not collected two weeks later, it was returned to the sender.

Is the letter to be regarded as having reached the defendant under these circumstances? As can be seen from para 130 BGB, it is not necessary that the defendant should actually have had knowledge of it: it is enough that it arrived in her area of control so that she could forthwith have knowledge of it. In its earlier decision it was unnecessary for this court to determine whether the letter could be treated as having arrived when it was made available for collection in L, since on the facts then found it was no part of the defendant's instructions that the letter should be kept in L at all. The disregard of her instructions may have been pursuant to Post Office Regulations, but this did not alter the fact that it was not her declared intention that the post office at L should act as her intermediary. On rehearing, the Court of Appeal held itself bound by this view of the law, but it was bound only so long as these findings of fact remained unaltered, and it failed to note that there had been a critical alteration in these findings of fact which underlay the *Reichsgericht's* decision. Previously the only information available was from the Post Office at L, and the *Oberlandesgericht* in its first judgment therefore assumed, as did this court, that there was no intrinsic time limit contained in the plaintiff's instructions for forwarding from L to H, and that it was only because of post office regulations, extrinsic to her forwarding declaration and unknown to the defendant, that her instructions for the letter in question were disregarded. In the renewed proceedings however it emerged that the two week limit was built in to the defendant's own forwarding instructions. Her declaration ceased to have effect after the lapse of these two weeks, and the prior situation then resumed: pursuant to the instructions left by the defendant in B, the post office in L was to hold any incoming mail for collection by her at the *post restante* counter there. It was therefore contrary to the findings of fact in the judgment of the Court of Appeal on the first occasion, in accordance with the defendant's declared intention that the L Post Office be once more the place to accept and hold incoming mail for her: it was in accordance with the declaration she herself had made that mail lay waiting for her in L. The defendant is bound by the terms in which she declared her intention, and cannot invoke her belief that by giving the second forwarding instructions in L she had cancelled for good, and not just for two weeks, that post office's power to accept and retain any mail which arrived for her.

We must now tackle the question left open by the *Reichsgericht* in its previous judgment, whether the letter is to be treated as having reached the defendant when it was put at the *poste restante* counter in the L post office. It is. The Reichsgericht has constantly held, in applying para 130 BGB, that a declaration of intention, especially one contained in a letter, is to be treated as having reached the distant addressee at the moment of time when the recipient could normally be expected to learn of it, given the general arrangements he has made for the receipt of such communications. In the application of this basic principle, the *Reichsgericht* has held that when people arrange to pick up their mail from a special locker in the post office, a declaration of intention is treated as having reached them on the day on which the letter containing it is placed in the locker, ie is made available for collection provided that it would normally be collected on that day [see RGZ 142, 402, 406; other references omitted]. The same must apply to *poste restante* arrangements where, as here, the addressee herself has instructed the post office to retain any mail addressed to her until she collects it.

The letter of termination of 30 December 1931 is accordingly to be seen as having reached the defendant on 31 December, or on 2 January 1932 at the latest. It is true that the defendant did not in fact learn of the declaration, though she could have, but this does not affect its efficacy, for as has already been said, it is the 'arrival' of the declaration of intention which is relevant under para 130 BGB, not the addressee's actual knowledge of it. It is just as if the letter had been placed in the mailbox at the defendant's home and then gone missing without her knowing anything about it.

The present findings of fact enable us to hold that the notice of termination 'reached' the defendant timeously and in proper form, so the judgment under appeal must be reversed and final judgment entered for the plaintiff in accordance with his claim.

Case 7
BUNDESARBEITSGERICHT (SECOND SENATE) 15 NOVEMBER 1962
NJW 1963, 554

Reasons

A notice terminating the employment of a pregnant woman is ineffective if the employer knew of the pregnancy at the time of giving notice or was informed of it within one week after the notice of termination arrived (Law for the Protection of Maternity—Mutterschutzgesetz (MSG) para 9 para 1). On 14 August 1961 the defendant employer, who was unaware of the plaintiff's pregnancy, sent her a notice of termination of employment. The fact of her pregnancy was communicated to him on 29 August. If this was more than one week after the notice of termination had arrived, it was too late for the statutory protection.

However, as the *Landesarbeitsgericht* correctly found, this was not the case. Information that a registered letter had been received for her and could be collected from the post office reached the plaintiff on 16 August, but the registered letter itself did not reach her then (compare *Reichsarbeitsgericht* in ARS 15, 354).

The appellant argues that since a person who is informed by the post office that a registered letter has been received for him can then put himself in possession of the letter, the arrival of such information is tantamount to the arrival of the registered letter itself. The court cannot accept this. The cases put forward an analogous, namely those in which the addressee has his mail placed in a special locker in the post office or where he asks for mail to be retained *poste restante*, are essentially different. It is true that in those cases also the addressee has to collect the mail from the post office, but it is located or dealt with there exactly as he has specified and chosen for the purpose. The locker in the post office and the poste restante counter are thus to be treated exactly like the letter box at his home. Items of mail which are placed in a special post office locker or kept at the *post restante* counter are already in the recipient's area of control just as much as mail put in his letter box at home, and have therefore 'arrived' in the sense of para 130 BGB. But it is different in the case of a registered letter. According to postal regulations, as is well known, a registered letter may be handed only to the addressee himself or to a person authorised to receive it on his behalf: there is no question of its being put in a mail box or in a post office locker or slipped through the door of a dwelling. Thus when the addressee is away, the registered letter does not come into his area of control at all, but remains in the possession of the post office. The only thing that comes into the addressee's area of control is the chit from the post office which tells him that a registered letter awaits him in the post office. This chit does not say who sent the registered letter, so the addressee has no means of knowing what it is about. The chit, therefore, cannot represent or stand in for the registered letter, and its arrival cannot represent or stand in for the arrival of the registered letter. Such arrival occurs only when the registered letter is fetched from the Post Office or is redelivered to some place within the recipient's area of control.

There is thus some risk in using registered mail when delivery must be made within a fixed period, but even the common assumption that this postal service is a very safe way of communicating important documents [reference omitted] cannot justify treating the arrival of the chit as the arrival of the registered letter itself. Since the chit says nothing about the sender or contexts of the registered letter, this would be to treat the letter as having arrived when it has not, and the recipient would be disadvantaged, for this would be to the benefit of the sender and to the detriment of the addressee.

Of course, the missive will be treated as having arrived if the addressee abuses his rights and fails to collect or delays the delivery of the registered letter. This court need not decide at what time the letter is deemed to arrive in such a case, for according to the findings of the *Landesarbeitsgericht* the plaintiff asked a friend to collect the registered letter for her. There is nothing abusive about that: not everyone can be expected to know the details of the postal regulations concerning the collection of registered letters by third parties. Again, the address given by the plaintiff did not indicate that the attic where she lived was a separate dwelling, and she had put her name on the mail box of the S family; but the information she gave was quite enough to ensure the delivery of a letter in the normal course of events, even a registered letter from her employer. It would be too much to expect a normal citizen to do more.

Case 8
REICHSGERICHT (SEVENTH CIVIL SENATE) 25 JUNE 1929
RGZ 125, 68

Facts

The plaintiffs' son, AZ Jr, who had taken out an insurance policy with the defendant company on 10 August 1925, had a fatal accident on his motor cycle on 6 October 1926. The plaintiffs claim RM10,000, the sum payable under the policy on the death of the insured. The defendant refused payment on the ground that at the time of the accident the insured was in default, having failed, notwithstanding proper notices of default, to pay the premiums due in February and August 1926. The plaintiffs deny that these notices of default reached their son. Both courts below held that they did, and dismissed the claim. The plaintiffs appealed; the judgments below were reversed and the case remanded.

Reasons

[Procedural]
II. [Adequacy of printed signature on notices of default?]
The Court of Appeal further held that the notice of 15 April 1926 'reached' the insured. It was sent by registered mail and was addressed to 'Mr AZ, Arendsee, Koloniestr.' The household at that address comprised the present plaintiffs, Mr AZ and his wife, their daughter, Miss EZ, and the insured. The insured had given his name as 'AZ Jr' in the application form, and was described as 'AZ Jr' in the certificate of insurance. When the postman made his rounds, he handed the letter in question to Miss EZ, as the certificate of delivery shows, for the receipt was signed by 'EZ', and the postman noted that he gave the letter to 'the daughter'. The *Oberlandesgericht* took the view that when the letter was delivered to the insured's residence to a member of his family it thereby came into his area of disposition so that he could learn of its contents. The court did not overlook the point that in the household to which the letter was delivered there were two people with the name of AZ, but it discounted the postman's belief that the letter was addressed to Miss EZ's father rather than her brother, and held that when the letter was handed to Miss EZ it came directly into the area of control of both the Messrs AZ, father and son.

We cannot accept this *in toto*. It is certainly irrelevant who the postman believed to be the correct addressee of the letter, but so long as it was uncertain which of the two Messrs AZ, father and son, the letter was for, it did not 'reach' either of them. While it was in doubt which was intended, each could say that he was not the addressee and could allow the letter to be returned in order that the ambiguity in the direction be cleared up

But while it might not be apparent from the way the letter was addressed that it was for the son and not the father, other indications on the envelope might have made this clear. For example, the envelope might have borne the name of the defendant company and it might have been generally known in the family that only the son had dealings with it; or perhaps the letter might have been opened by a member of the family and seen to have been for the son AZ. In these cases there would be no doubt that the letter had 'reached' Mr AS Jr.: a member of his family would have it in his hands and would know exactly to whom to give it. The address, originally ambiguous, would now have become unequivocal.

The defendant has led no evidence on the points just mentioned. The argument of the parties has essentially turned on the question whether the defendants' letter actually reached the hands of Mr AZ Jr—which would of course constitute 'arrival'—so the *Oberlandesgericht*, whose view of the law rendered it unnecessary, has not addressed itself to the relevant question.

Case 9
BUNDESGERICHTSHOF (EIGHTH CIVIL SENATE) 3 NOVEMBER 1976
BGHZ 67, 275

Facts

The suit concerns a piece of land in the city of M which is owned by the city itself, the third party. On 24 March 1972 the city leased two buildings on this land to the plaintiff HO who, like his co-plaintiff, is a waste paper merchant. The lease contained the following terms: 'para 8(2) Subletting or otherwise licensing the property to third parties is forbidden save with the written consent of the lessor. Any consent may be withdrawn by the lessor at any time. (3) Should the property be sublet or licensed to a third party without consent, the lessor may require the lessee to remove the third party from the premises within one month. If the lessee fails to do so, the lessor may determine this lease without notice.'

The plaintiffs subleased the buildings to the defendant. On 12 June 1972 the plaintiff HO wrote to the third party to inform it of the sublease and request consent. The third party replied in writing on 15 June to the effect that although it had reservations about such subleases, it was prepared to grant consent, revocable at any time. On 27 June there was a meeting between the plaintiff HO and the appropriate officer in the third party's property office. On 10 July the plaintiff HO wrote to the property office purporting to terminate the lease as from 31 October. The third party replied on 26 July saying that it could not accept this termination, that it revoked its consent to the sublease, and that the plaintiff must remove the sub-lessee from the premises by 31 August. The plaintiff HO wrote back on 3 August observing that his 'offer of termination' as from 31 October had lapsed because it had not been accepted by the lessor and that the lease consequently remained in force for the contractual period, but saying that he was ready to negotiate with the lessor on all points. On 10 August the third party replied to the plaintiff HO, terminating the lease 'without notice' as from 14 August, on the ground that the plaintiff HO was in breach of 'para 8 (3) of the lease by his refusal to terminate the sub-lease as of 31 August; the letter also stated that the third party intended to conclude a head lease with the defendant as from 15 August. The property office arranged for this letter to be served on the plaintiff HO by the postal service. As the addressee was not to be found at home, a written communication was left at his address, just as an ordinary letter would have been, informing him that the letter itself awaited him at the M post office. The third party concluded a lease with the defendant with effect from 15 August.

The plaintiffs now claim the rent on the under-lease for the months of September and October 1972, and the defendant counter-claimed, on appeal, for the repaying of half the rent which it had paid the plaintiffs for August 1972. The *Landgericht* dismissed the claim. The *Oberlandesgericht* dismissed the plaintiffs' appeal, and, treating the counter-claim as a cross-appeal, found the plaintiffs liable. The plaintiffs' further appeal was unsuccessful.

Reasons

1. In the Court of Appeal, the plaintiff's claim for the payment of the rent on the under-lease for September and October 1972 was dismissed under para 323 BGB, and the counter-claim for repayment of the rent for the second half of August was upheld because that same paragraph disentitled the plaintiffs from claiming the rent for that period. The reason rent could not be claimed under the sub-lease was because the written notice of termination given by the third party on 10 August had determined the lease between the third party and the plaintiff HO, making it impossible for the plaintiffs thereafter to fulfil their obligation under the sublease to guarantee the use of the premises to the sub-lessee.

2. We agree with the appellant that the Court of Appeal was wrong in this case to apply the rules regarding subsequent impossibility in bilateral contracts, for we adhere to the view we expressed on 30 October 1974 (BGHZ 63, 132, 137) that to the extent that the special provisions of paras 537, 538, 541 BGB apply, the rules relating to subsequent impossibility are ousted.

(a) But these provisions of the law of leases, like para 323 BGB, are only applicable if the notice of termination of 10 August was validly declared and substantially justified. If the declaration of immediate termination was effective and justified, the lease between the third party and the plaintiff HO came to an end. The third party would then have a claim for restitution against the defendant (paras 556 para 3 and 985 BGB), and this would constitute a 'right' in the sense of para 541 BGB. Furthermore, when the third party in its letter to the defendant [sic] of 10 August made it clear that it no longer accepted the defendant's possession under the sub-lease but would allow him to continue in possession only if he became head-lessee, this constituted a 'withdrawal of use' in the sense of that text (see BGH| 63, 138). If the notice of termination was valid, therefore, the defendant was freed by paras 541, 547 BGB from the obligation to pay rent under the sublease.

(b) The notice of termination was validly declared.

(aa) Notice of termination is a declaration of intention which needs to be received. If a declaration is made in the absence of the addressee it becomes effective at the moment at which it 'reaches' him (para 130 BGB). A declaration of intention reaches the addressee as soon as it comes within his area of control such that in normal circumstances he could be expected to learn of it [references omitted]. The written notice of termination of 10 August did not reach the plaintiff HO in this sense, for it lay in the M post office. Certainly the postal form stating that the letter was waiting for him in the post office came into the plaintiff's area of control, for the Court of Appeal was satisfied that the postman making the delivery left this form at the plaintiff's house just as if it had been a normal letter. This finding does not, however, justify the Court of Appeal in concluding that the letter of termination itself also reached the plaintiff HO The letter remained in the post office, and the chit informing HO that it was there simply put him in a position where he could bring the letter within his area of control (see BAG NJW 1963, 554; BGH VersR 1971, 262).

(bb) The declaration of termination must arrive: it is not enough that the addressee be informed that the letter containing it awaits him at the post office. (Rules of Bavarian administrative law permit bodies to effect service of documents by depositing them in the post office, but these are inapplicable to relations of private law; nor could the provisions of the BGB be ousted by the Postal Ordinance of 16 May 1963.)

(c) Para 132 BGB does not apply in this case. It is true that arrival may be deemed to have occurred under this paragraph, but only when a court official (*Gerichtsvollzieher*) is used to serve the document (para 132 para 1 sentence 1 BGB). It is only to such service that the reference made to the ZPO by para 132 para 1 sentence 2 BGB applies. Service by anyone other than a court official is not deemed to constitute 'arrival'. This is generally agreed by courts and writers alike [references omitted] and we see no reason to depart from that view. Legal certainty requires a narrow construction of provisions regarding the service of documents. Nor can the unequivocal wording of para 132 BGB be expanded by reference to the intention of the legislator. The legislator's intention was to provide a procedure whereby documents might be served by a judicial officer, an official commanding public trust and able to make an official certificate of service (I Motives to General Part paras 75, 76). The legislator accordingly intended that para 132 BGB, which deems arrival to have occurred, should never be applied unless a court official was involved in the process.

(dd) But in some cases para 242 BGB permits one to treat a declaration of intention as having arrived in due time although it did not reach the reception area of the person to whom it was directed (see BGH VersR 1971, 262; BGH NJW 1952, 1169— arrival precented or delayed). Here the reason the declaration did not reach the addressee was that, not having been at home when delivery was sought to be made, he failed to collect the envelope containing the declaration from the post office where it lay. It is true that in general there is no duty to take steps to obtain receipt of documents, and that a person who learns that a document has been deposited for him is not *ipso facto* bound forthwith to go and fetch it. But the legal relations between the sender and the addressee of the declaration may be so special that a situation arises where the addressee who fails to collect the deposited document may find himself treated as if it had actually reached his area of control. This is such a case.

The plaintiff HO had obtained from the lessor the consent which he needed under para 8(2) of the lease for the sublease which he had effected. Then when HO gave notice of termination, the lessor withdrew its consent and demanded the removal of the sub-lessee by 31 August. HO's response to this was that the lease remained on foot for its term, and that he was ready to negotiate on all points. For him to take no action whatever eight days later when he learnt that the letter, containing the notice to quit, awaited collection is irreconcilable with this last statement, especially as, according to the Court of Appeal's findings in another context, he implicitly refused in his letter of 3 August to remove the sub-tenant from the premises within the stipulated period. Even if he was expecting mail from other correspondents, he should have realised that the deposited envelope might well contain a declaration from the lessor in relation to the business in hand, since they had been in communication for six weeks. It is accordingly contrary to good faith (*Treu und Glauben*) for the plaintiff to take the point that the notice of termination did not actually reach him. It can therefore be disregarded.

(c) The notice of termination is furthermore justified.

3. In conclusion, the obligation of the defendant to pay rent to the plaintiff under the sublease came to an end on 14 August 1972.

Case 10
REICHSGERICHT (FIRST CIVIL SENATE) 8 FEBRUARY 1902
RGZ 50, 191

Facts

The defendant, a ticket agent in Hamburg for the Lübeck State Lottery, had sold the plaintiff a one-eighth lottery ticket, no 33412. On 31 October 1900 that ticket was drawn, with winnings of M166; the plaintiff was accordingly entitled to the sum of M17.29. The next day the defendant posted to the plaintiff a printed form, completed with the relevant figures and dates, informing him of his winnings. The document also stated that 'drawings in this main section' were to continue until 22 November and that 'the largest prize, perhaps of M500,000, as well as lots of large prizes and many thousands of smaller ones' were still on the wheel of fortune. Enclosed as a secondary lottery ticket was a one-eighth ticket no 33451 in the final section of the lottery, priced at M17.25. The document continued: 'If you propose to retain the enclosed lottery ticket, kindly send back your winning ticket in the enclosed stamped envelope immediately. I draw your attention to the fact that only if you send me your winning ticket immediately on receipt of this letter can I regard you as the rightful owner of the enclosed secondary ticket and recognise your right to any winnings it may make. Please use the enclosed form for your reply. I expect that you will want to retain the ticket I enclose, but if you do not, please send it back immediately so that I may have time to dispose of it elsewhere.'

The letter, in which the underlined words were printed with emphasis, was delivered to the plaintiff's lodgings (Vogelhüttendeich 164, Wilhelmsburg, Hamburg) on the morning of 2 November. The plaintiff had already gone to work, so it was accepted by another lodger and placed in the kitchen. According to the plaintiff, at about nine o'clock that morning the defendant received a telegram from Lübeck with the news that lottery ticket no 33451 had won M100,000, the winnings appropriate to a one-eighth ticket amounting to M10,416.07. On learning this the defendant sent his employee B to the plaintiff's lodgings where B persuaded the plaintiff's landlady—by lies, according to the plaintiff—to give him the letter addressed to the plaintiff, which was still lying on the kitchen table and had not yet come into the plaintiff's hands.

When the plaintiff returned home at noon, or possibly in the evening, he asked if there were any letters for him. He asserts, and is ready to swear, that he would have accepted the enclosed lottery ticket, and as evidence of this would prove that in previous cases when a ticket of his had been drawn, he had taken a further ticket in the same lottery and indeed in the same series. He also stresses that the defendant must have known, given the part of town where the plaintiff lodged, that he was dealing with a workman who would already have left for work before the first post was delivered.

The plaintiff claims M10,416.07, with interest at 4 per cent from the time of claim.

The *Landgericht* dismissed the claim, and the *Oberlandesgericht* dismissed the plaintiff's appeal. On the plaintiff's further appeal, the decision of the *Oberlandesgericht* is reversed and the case remanded for the following reasons.

Reasons

Because the court of appeal was of the opinion that the plaintiff must fail in either case, it did not decide whether he was bringing a 'contractual claim for the contractual sum or a tort claim for damages based on the defendant's preventing the plaintiff from acquiring the ticket.' The court held that if the plaintiff had accepted the lottery ticket which was sent to him, he would have been contracting for the chance of winning an uncertain amount; once the ticket was drawn, it represented the right to claim a specific amount, so it was an entirely different thing legally as well as economically; since the lottery ticket was drawn before it was accepted, the defendant was no longer bound by his offer.

This reasoning, which is essentially in line with that of the Landgericht, is unacceptable. It may in general be true that the offer of an undrawn lottery ticket lapses if it is drawn before the offer is accepted [references], but the first thing to consider must always be what the intention behind the offer of the ticket was in the individual case. According to the defendant's letter of 1 November 1900, the draw had begun and was to continue until 22 November, and his statement that he would regard the plaintiff as the rightful owner of the enclosed ticket and respect his claim to any winnings only if he sent back the previous winning ticket immediately on receipt of the letter was a quite unequivocal way of saying that although the plaintiff was to become owner of the ticket and entitled to its winnings only on the stipulated condition, yet if that condition were fulfilled he was to be the owner unconditionally, ie even if the ticket attracted winnings in the meanwhile. If this was not the defendant's intention, he was bound to make an express and appropriate qualification, and he did not do so.

The considerations which led the lower courts to decide against the plaintiff are thus not in point. But the respondent has argued that their decision can be justified on the following grounds. From the facts already established it emerges that the defendant repossessed himself of the letter he had sent before the plaintiff got to know of the contractual offer it contained; since, as the Reichsgericht (Fifth Civil Division) decided in its judgment of 26 October 1901 (see JW 1901, 866), an offer of a contract is held to 'reach' its addressee when it comes to that person's knowledge, the defendant was not yet bound by his contractual offer when he repossessed himself of the letter containing it. This conclusion is erroneous, for the premise is wrong. If a person chooses to communicate a contractual offer by means of a sealed letter, the true view is that the offer 'reaches' its addressee in the sense of para 130 BGB as soon as normal procedures bring the letter within the area of factual control of the addressee himself or of a person who represents him for the receipt of letters, and he is consequently in a position to acquaint himself with it [references].

There is nothing inconsistent with this in the decision cited by the respondent. As the reasons in that decision make abundantly plain, that case did not involve a situation where para 130 BGB fell to be applied; it was therefore enough to say that the contractual offer had come to the notice of the person for whom it was intended. In the present case, as the letter addressed by the defendant to the plaintiff was delivered to the dwelling of the plaintiff's landlady who, it can unhesitatingly be assumed, was qualified to accept letters, one must hold that the offer contained in the letter reached the plaintiff on the morning of 2 November and that the defendant became bound by his offer at that moment.

The plaintiff made no express acceptance of this offer meanwhile, and such acceptance as can be inferred from his bringing suit is clearly too late. But can the plaintiff not invoke para 823 BGB? The contractual offer which reached the plaintiff conferred on him a legal power to complete the lottery contract by accepting it and so to acquire the rights arising out of the contract. If the defendant intentionally or negligently caused the plaintiff to make no use of this legal power, he is guilty of an unlawful act in the sense of para 823 BGB. We need not ask whether one might not also invoke para 162 para 1 BGB, since no less is required for the application of that text here than for that of para 823.

It emerges from the plaintiff's own evidence that he would not have accepted the defendant's offer on 2 November before noon on that day, perhaps not before the evening, but it would be wrong to regard his claim as defeated by this consideration alone. Certainly the defendant had stipulated that only if the plaintiff sent back the 'winning ticket immediately on receipt of this letter' (and thereby communicated his acceptance of the offer) was he to be regarded as owner of the ticket which was sent to him and as the person entitled to any winnings. But this cannot have meant that the reply must be despatched by the very next post after the letter arrived. Such a construction is excluded: even in the normal case the defendant, in sending off his letter, could not expect the recipient to be able to make so speedy a response, but here the defendant must have known that he was dealing with a working man whose lifestyle would make it impossible for him to do what was required on the day of receipt before noon or even the evening.

The suit is not yet ripe for decision. Further elucidation of the facts is required before it can be said whether any tort has been committed under para 823 BGB.

Case 11
BUNDESGERICHTSHOF (ANTI-TRUST SENATE) 20 NOVEMBER 1975
NJW 1976, 801

Facts

Within Germany, the plainstiff is sole distributor of Rossignol skis. The defendant manages a leading specialist sports shop in Upper Bavaria. The parties had long-standing business connections. In the season 1972/73, the sale of Rossignol skis contributed DM100,000 to the defendant's overall turnover (skis) of DM 3 million. On 4 October 1973, the defendant ordered from the plaintiff 478 pairs of Rossignol skis. The plaintiff refused to accept the offer and informed the defendant that it would not deliver skis even after the current regime of resale price maintenance had fallen away.

The *Landgericht* rejected the action for a declaratory judgment stating that the plaintiff was not bound to accept the offer of 4 October 1973 or future orders from the defendant. After a change in plea, the *Oberlandesgericht* held that the defendant has no claim resulting from the refusal of his order of 4 October 1973 and that the plaintiff is not bound to accept future orders from the defendant for the supply of skis. The further appeal is successful in its main points.

Reasons

A. The claim for a declaratory judgment concerns the order of 4 October 1973. According to para 35 I 1 of the Cartel Act (GWB), the plaintiff must compensate the defendant for losses incurred, insofar as his refusal to supply the defendant according to his order of 4 October 1973 intentionally or negligently infringes legal provisions intended to protect the defendant. Para 26 II GWB prohibits an enterprise listed therein from unduly impeding another enterprise in business dealings normally open to similar enterprises or from treating that enterprise differently from like enterprises without sufficient reason. This provision intends to protect single enterprises (BGHZ 36, 91, 100 = NJW 1962, 196—Gummistrümpfe). A culpable infringement of this provision gives rise to a claim for damages under para 35 I 1 GWB.

I.

1. Para 26 II 1 GWB subjects enterprises operating price maintenance policies to a prohibition of discrimination. (. . .)

2. The Second Amendment Act extended the prohibition of discrimination expressed in para 26 II 1 GWB to enterprises and associations of enterprises insofar as their suppliers or customers of certain kinds of goods or commercial services depend on them to such an extent that they have insufficient and unacceptable means of switching to other enterprises. In order for this provision to apply, it is decisive to interpret what exactly is meant by 'insufficent and unacceptable means of switching to other enterprises' and where actual dependency occurs as outlined above (. . .)

(b) An interpretation of the intentions pursued by para 26 II 2 GWB leads to the following result:

(aa) By extending the range of addressees who are prohibited from discriminating, over and above the circle of enterprises listed in para 26 II 1 GWB, restrictions of unhindered competition effected by other kinds of commercially strong enterprises were to be prevented, whenever such disruptions were caused by an abuse of economic power. Even where not in a market-dominating position, an enterprise can hold such a strong position in the market that it can disrupt the markets in a manner which para 26 II GWB intended to prevent and to combat (BGHZ 49, 90, 96 = NJW 1968, 400— Jägermeister). In respect of enterprises operating price maintenance agreements, the legislator globally assumed such dangers to exist and therefore included them in the prohibition to discriminate. By the newly-added second sentence, additional enterprises are included which, although not market-dominating, hold such strong economic position in relation to other enteprises that their measures affect enterprises which depend on them in the same way as if they were operated by market-dominating enterprises. This additional group of enterprises is therefore subject to the same restrictions as regards contractual freedom. (. . .)

(cc) The dependency of one enterprise on another must be so strong that there are only insufficient or unacceptable other means of switching to third enterprises. Whether or not suffcent possibilities exist as envisaged by this provision is to be judged according to objective criteria, ie the possibilities provided by the relevant market for switching from the goods of the discriminating enterprise to those of other companies. Not every possible switch is 'suffcent' in the sense of section 26 II 2 GWB. Where an enterprise as supplier or customer of certain goods has very few competitors or where, in comparison to competitors, it holds a much stronger market position, it is market-domineering (para 22 I No 1, 2 GWB) and thus already falls under the prohibtion to discriminate as set out in para 26 II 1 GWB. Thus, para 26 II 2 GWB comes into play only insofar as an enterprise is exposed to considerable competition and does not hold a market-dominating position. The existence of considerable competition between suppliers is not the same as having sufficent possibilities to switch from an enterprise which discriminates between customers to another enterprise. The number of enterprises dealing in similar goods is likewise not decisive, at least not on its own. The overall decisive factor is the commercial value and market prestige of the goods in question. This factor determines whether or not sufficient possibilites exist to switch to other enterprises. Apart from their price, the actual value of particular goods is thus determined by their quality and the producer's advertising activities. These criteria significantly influence demand. In particular, it is advertising which can give branded goods a specific market position with the result that the customer feels unable to substitute the goods with other goods. (. . .)

Case 12
REICHSGERICHT (FIRST CIVIL SENATE) 5 APRIL 1922
RGZ 104, 265

Facts

In March 1920 the plaintiff sent the defendant a price-list of goods he had in stock. This was stated to involve no obligation (*freibleibend*). Crystallised tartaric acid, priced at M68.50, was included in the list. On 20 March the defendant sent the plaintiff a telegram: 'Request best price for 100 kilos Gries lead-free tartaric acid.' Two days later the plaintiff replied by telegram: 'Lead-free tartaric acid M128. per 100 kilos cash on delivery here.' Then the defendant telegraphed: '100 kilos lead-free Gries tartaric acid OK, confirmatory letter follows.' When the letter arrived it transpired that both parties intended to sell the goods and thought the other wished to buy them. The defendant refused to accept or pay for the goods and the plaintiff sold them at public auction. The plaintiff now claims as damages the difference between the price he thought had been agreed and the sum received at auction.

The *Landgericht* allowed the plaintiff only two-thirds of the claim, but the *Oberlandesgericht* allowed it in full. The defendant appealed, and his appeal was allowed.

Reasons

It is manifest that it nowhere appeared from the telegrams between the parties which of them was to be the buyer and which the seller. According to the evidence, both of them intended to be the seller.

The court below was of the view that as the plaintiff had only shortly previously offered the defendant crystallised tartaric acid in a price-list containing certain conditions as to payment, the defendant should have realised from the fact that the plaintiff's telegram contained the same conditions as to payment that the plaintiff wished to sell the goods; since the defendant must accept this construction of the plaintiff's telegram, a contract of sale arose.

The appellant objects that since both parties intended different things, there was no agreement. This fact could not be got round by saying, as the court below had done, that the defendant had committed a fault in misunderstanding the plaintiff's telegram, for it remained the fact that neither party wanted to buy and that therefore a contract had not been formed. It was quite another matter whether the supposed negligence gave rise to other consequences.

We cannot agree with the appellant on this point, for what the court below said was quite true: if the plaintiff's telegram was such that in all the circumstances it would be normal in the trade to give it a meaning going beyond the purely literal, the defendant must be held to such meaning; a contract would have been formed and the only possibility would be to seek to rescind it (*anfechten*). But we cannot agree with the court below that on its proper construction the plaintiff's telegram meant that he wanted to sell [explanation omitted in the text] . . . There is therefore a true lack of agreement. Both parties used words which seemed to match, but meant them in a different sense in such a way that there was no agreement. No contract of sale was formed.

In fact both parties are to blame for the misunderstanding, each having expressed himself unclearly, doubtless to save words. The defendant's telegram read: 'Request best price for . . . tartaric acid.' 'Best' implies a comparison, and can only be used where there is room for play, upwards in the case of a sale and downwards in the case of a purchase. What the defendant meant was that he wanted to know the lowest price for 100 kilos of tartaric acid. The same is true of the plaintiff. If instead of transmitting the words 'Tartaric acid 128 M.' he had said 'offer tartaric acid . . . 128', there would have been no doubt what he meant. As it was, neither party said clearly what he wanted. Both of them are at fault, but we agree with the Landgericht that the fault of the defendant was the greater: it was he who started the negotiations, and therefore should have taken particular care to express himself clearly.

Thus the plaintiff cannot demand performance. The question is whether on these facts there is room for a claim for damages. Some scholars say yes, others no. It is generally agreed that damages for *culpa in contrahendo* may be claimed if a contract comes about. When no contract eventuates, there are many cases where the Code allows a claim for the plaintiff's negative interest, ie reliance damages: so under para 122 (rescinding a declaration of will on the ground of error), para 179 (agent acting without proper authorisation), para 307 (impossible performance knowingly or carelessly undertaken), para 309 (formation of an unlawful contract). Writers are not agreed whether these principles can be extended to other cases, but in fact extension to similar cases has already been made by both courts and scholars. If both parties are to blame for the fact that an offer which was time-limited did not lead to a contract because the acceptance did not reach the offeror in time, then according to RGZ 97, 339, the loss suffered by the acceptor is to be split between the parties. If a carrier who offers his services publicly fails to reply to a request for carriage, he can be made liable for reliance damages under para 663 BGB [reference]. The considerations which led the legislator to make the provisions mentioned above can be found in the Protokollen. . . . In discussing the rescission of a declaration of will not seriously intended, it was said that equity requires the person making the declaration to pay for the reliance loss sustained by the other party if reasonably unaware that the declaration was not serious, the reason being that it was the declarer who caused the transaction to take place. Then it was said that this liability is imposed in the interests of security of transactions. Like reasons—equity and security of transactions—justify us in applying the same principles to the present case, one of so-called unapparent absence of agreement. Where one party has expressed himself so carelessly as to cause the other party to misunderstand him, equity and the security of transactions certainly require that he be saddled with the loss. Whether the same would apply in a case where there was no carelessness is a matter we need not now decide. As has already been stated, the plaintiff here was at fault as well as the defendant, so one must ask whether the plaintiff's claim is not barred by his own carelessness. The answer is that it is not. The plaintiff's claim would fail if he was at fault in mistaking the other party's declaration (as under paras 122, 179, 307, 309), but that is not the present situation. Here the plaintiff could well believe that the defendant wanted to buy acid. The fault of the plaintiff was rather that he also expressed himself badly and caused the defendant to misunderstand him. In a case like this the personal fault of the victim does not destroy his claim, because it cannot be said, in the words of the Code, that he 'should have known' the defendant's true meaning; it only has the effect that the loss is to be borne by both parties in proportion to their carelessness, since the fault of both of them contributed to the harm. But the harm which is to be so divided between them is not the value of performance, but only the so-called negative interest. Equity does not require that the plaintiff recover the profit he would have made if the contract had come into existence, but only that he be compensated—either wholly or, as in this case, partially only—for the harm he suffered from being of the good faith belief, due to the defendant's faulty mode of self-expression, that the defendant wanted to effect a purchase. No other solution accords with the statutory provisions mentioned above, in the case of rescinding for error and so on. If the plaintiff proves his assertions, his negative contractual interest consists of the difference between the auction price and the market price or other possible price on the day that the plaintiff learnt that the defendant wanted to sell rather than to buy, that being the day on which the plaintiff could sell off the goods.

Case 13
BUNDESGERICHTSHOF (THIRD CIVIL SENATE) 8 APRIL 1957
NJW 1957, 1105

Facts

The plaintiff and his father, who had been a customer of the defendant's for some time, had bought six one-eighth tickets in the Twelfth North-West German Class Lottery. The draw in the sixth class began on 1 July, and one of these tickets won DM24. The defendant so informed the plaintiff on a printed form, crediting him with his winnings and charging him the price of the follow-up ticket which was enclosed. It requested the recipient to return the attached acceptance form by the first post or, in the unexpected event he did not wish to take it, to send the follow-up ticket back on the same day. The plaintiff and his father did nothing. On 19 July the follow-up ticket won DM40,300, and the defendant wrote to the plaintiff asking him to return it forthwith since he had not accepted it on 2 July when it was sent to him. On 20 July the father of the plaintiff sent the defendant a letter which he said he had written four days earlier and in which he accepted the follow-up ticket.

The plaintiff now claims his winnings. The two lower courts dismissed the claim. On the plaintiff's appeal those judgments were vacated and the case remanded.

Reasons

I. The court of Appeal was right to hold that no contract could be formed by the plaintiff's declaration of acceptance in his letter of 20 July. It is to acquire a chance of winning that one buys a lottery ticket, but once the ticket has been drawn this chance has gone, and with it the object of the contract. We need not dwell on this point, since even the appellant accepts the Court of Appeal's judgment on it.

II. Nor, according to the Court of Appeal, was there any contract between the parties before the follow-up ticket was drawn: there was no possibility of acceptance under para 151 BGB, and in the circumstances of the case no implicit declaration of acceptance for the purposes of para 148 BGB could be inferred from 'the silent retention of the follow-up ticket.' Here the essential question is: when a lottery agent makes such an offer to a customer with whom he has already had dealings, does para 157 BGB, with its reference to the good faith observed by businessmen, make it right to treat the customer as agreeing to the contract so proposed, although he does nothing whatever? The answer is 'no'.

The interests of the parties speak against treating the customer's silence as agreement. If the customer wants to continue playing, all he need do is send in the printed form of acceptance; this at least he can be expected to do in order to clarify the rights of the parties. The interests of the ticket agent point to the same conclusion. If the customer's inactivity were to be treated as a declaration of acceptance, the agent who received no reply 'by return of post' would immediately find himself bound by a contract which prevented him from disposing of the follow-up ticket elsewhere. This would be intolerable, since the agent whose customer has failed to respond to his proposal or request must in all equity be allowed to make his legal position clear and safe. Of course the agent will often act on the assumption that the customer does agree to his offer, and either retain the ticket for him or, if time presses, play it on his account; but in cases where the agent's reliance is justified, he can be protected without holding that a contract has been formed (*negotiorum gestio*, negligence of the customer in fresh dealings in an existing relationship).

Most importantly, there is no general business practice (*Verkehrssitte*) inconsistent with the conclusion we have reached. A general business practice in the sense of para 157 BGB includes a professional opinion held by all those involved in the business in question (see RGZ 114, 9; 135, 340), but the Court of Appeal has found that there is no unanimity on the effect of a customer's silence when he is invoiced for the price of a follow-up ticket enclosed with a statement of his recent winnings. Nor did the parties to the present litigation believe that there was any such unanimity.

2. Regarding the possible formation of a contract under para 151 BGB, the Court of Appeal did not consider whether before the follow-up ticket was drawn, any intention to accept was evinced by the plaintiff or his father, the statutory representative with whose consent he played. This was because it believed that no contract could come

about by an uncommunicated acceptance under para 151, given that the defendant had not dispensed with the need for communication and that it was not normal practice to regard a declaration of acceptance as superfluous.

So far as the substantive law is concerned, the Court of Appeal was right to hold that the way the defendant conducted his business might imply a waiver (*Verzicht*) of the need to communicate acceptance, such as para 151 BGB refers to. Since the form letter, as the Court of Appeal correctly held, does not make it absolutely clear that the customer would not be entitled to take further part in the lottery with the follow-up ticket unless he returned the acceptance form, it is necessary to construe it in the light of paras 133, 157 BGB, and to take into account not only what the defendant wrote, but what he did.

The essential question here is whether the plaintiff could honestly and realistically conclude from the way the defendant had behaved when customers, including his father, had done nothing, that the defendant was content with an uncommunicated acceptance of its offer under para 151 BGB. When it was considering the two instances put forward by the plaintiff, the Court of Appeal did not ask itself this question, and so went wrong in law.

In a letter which the defendant wrote to the plaintiff's father on 20 March 1953 the defendant had said 'I now realise that you did not receive the follow-up ticket which I sent you and accordingly [emphasis added] I hold your winnings at your disposal.' From this the plaintiff argues that the defendant had treated his offer as accepted despite the absence of any declaration of acceptance, and had charged him the price by setting it off against the winnings he held; indeed, that would have been the end of the matter had the customer not established that he never received the substitute ticket. It is not enough to ask, as the Court of Appeal did, whether there really was a contract under para 151 in this case. The critical question is whether by his conduct the defendant could have induced the other party to believe that he would hold a contract formed on the failure to return the follow-up ticket.

Then in a letter of 19 March 1954, the defendant stated in terms that since the plaintiff's father had not sent back the follow-up ticket, the defendant had had to assume that he was ready to accept it and play. Whether the defendant 'stuck' to this position—which is all that occupied the Court of Appeal—is irrelevant. Here, too, the question is whether, in view of the terms of the 1954 letter and his understanding of the letter of the previous year, the plaintiff not having made any express declaration of acceptance, could suppose that the defendant, given his particular attitude, might treat his failure to send back the follow-up ticket as implicit acceptance of his offer.

It cannot be said to be futile to evaluate the defendant's conduct from this point of view. If the Court of Appeal concludes, after reviewing the evidence, that the two instances mentioned are simply 'isolated cases, not amounting to any declaration of waiver in the sense of para 151 BGB, it still has to check the plaintiff's assertion that the defendant had adopted the general position that a contract could be formed under para 151 BGB; for if that were the defendant's practice and it was generally recognised, his statements to the plaintiff's father would cease to stand on their own, and could be seen as expressing an intention which was to apply in all similar cases.

Whether this is in fact the case is another matter. One must concede to the appellant that the fact that the plaintiff's father sent off the form of acceptance on 20 July does not show that he and the plaintiff had dismissed the possibility of a contract having come about under para 151 BGB (para 286 ZPO). It is not true that the intentions for forming a contract under para 148 or under para 151 BGB are mutually exclusive: both possibilities concur, and a person who believes that it is not in law necessary that his declaration of acceptance reach the offeror may nevertheless send such a declaration with the aim of giving formal expression to a contract which in his view is already concluded.

Case 14
BUNDESGERICHTSHOF (EIGHTH CIVIL SENATE) 16 DECEMBER 1964
NJW 1965, 387

Reasons

B.
I. The Court of Appeal held that, from 1 August 1959 when the defendant's buses started to use the bus station, a contract for the use of the bus station against payment, a contract of private law, had existed between the parties. The defendant knew from the time it had previously used the bus station in the summer of 1956 (admittedly for another route, but that was immaterial), that the plaintiff exacted a fee for its use. Its renewed use of the bus station since 1 August 1959 was therefore in the full knowledge and consciousness of the legal implications of its conduct. By using the bus station it accepted the plaintiff's offer of a contract; the plaintiff having in the circumstances waived the need for the declaration of acceptance to reach it. Furthermore, a contract was also formed under the principles of the factual contractual relationship (*faktische Vertragsverhältnis*) for which it was not necessary that the defendant should have refused to make any payment for using the bus station.

The Court of Appeal proceeded to say that it was quite lawful to make a private law charge for the use of the bus station, for the use in question was not just a public use, but a special use, given the facilities which had been provided near the station and the circumstances in which the use was taking place. The judges viewed the area and confirmed that the use being made by the defendant went beyond public use. The bus station was entirely different from the normal bus stops and simple stopping bays which are in public use, for it was equipped with all the advantages of platforms, bus lanes, the timetable board, the waiting room with its refreshments and the toilets.
II. The appellant has not successfully impugned these views.
1. In principle no one need pay for making use of public property (BVerwGe 4, 342, 345—NJW 1957, 962). But if the owner of a public thing wishes, consistently with it being used by the public, to afford a kind of user which goes beyond public use, a so-called special use, he can in the absence of statutory regulation make such use conditional on the user's contracting to pay a fee for it. This is in line with our previous holdings (BGHZ 19, 85, 92; BGHZ 21, 319, 330).
2. The appellant accepts that it was making a special use of the bus station and its facilities, but maintains that it did not contract for this special use. It wanted to make use of it like the general public; it never asked for special use; the special use was forced on it against its will by the plaintiff; and it is a principle of the private law of obligations that no contract can arise unless the recipient of an offer is willing to accept it. We disagree.

(a) The Court of Appeal held, as a subsidiary argument, that when the essentials of life are being provided on a large scale, a contract arises from the mere acceptance of such a service, just because it is typically social behaviour. On this view it would be irrelevant whether or not the defendant intended to accept the special usage afforded to it by the plaintiff. Supporters of this doctrine do not regard the factual public offer of a service and the factual acceptance of this service as constituting declarations of intention which trigger given legal consequences, but as congruent conduct whose typical social significance produces the same rights and duties as a transaction at law. The basis of the obligations lies in the *opinio juris* that a person who acts in this socially typical manner, by knowingly and willingly accepting or using a service, thereby becomes bound in law regardless of whether he entertained or expressed any intention to be so bound (Larenz, NJW 1956, 1897). We need not adopt any position regarding this concept of a 'contract arising through socially typical conduct' nor consider the appellant's objection to it that it is inapplicable on the facts of the case before us, for even the adherents of the traditional view that no contract can come about unless there are matching declarations of will concede that the normative force of general practice can attribute to 'typically social' conduct the import of a true declaration of will. In particular, when one accepts an essential service it is not the will of the individual that is the significant feature, but the standard implications of his conduct: there is no room for the individual will here, so it recedes into the background. In construing the declaration of will which the acceptance of such a service entails, the intention of the particular individual no longer counts. If a person so conducts himself that in accordance with good faith and general practice he can only be understood as expressing a certain intention, his verbal disclaimer of such a meaning of his conduct can be ignored. His words are contradicted by his acts (*protestatio facto contraria*); through his own conduct he has forfeited any other construction [references omitted].

On either of the views stated, it follows from the facts, as conclusively found by the Court of Appeal, that the defendant knew that the plaintiff insisted on payment for the use of the bus station, that the defendant used the bus station in this knowledge, and that such use is, in accordance with normal practice, treated as an expression of agreement, and that it is irrelevant that the defendant did not wish to enter into any contract with the plaintiff regarding the use of the bus station, or even that he expressly objected to doing so.

Nor did the defendant's notice of termination free him, as the appellant maintains, from any contract which arose. In a case like this, a declaration of termination is futile. The defendant did not want to stop using the bus station, but to carry on using it, as in fact it did. A notice of termination by the defendant would, like its declaration that it was unwilling to contract, be contradicted by its actual behaviour.

Case 15
BUNDESGERICHTSHOF (EIGHTH CIVIL SENATE) 27 JANUARY 1965
NJW 1965, 965

Facts

In early March 1961, R, the proprietor of the defendant firm, went to the plaintiff's place of business with M, the engineer who managed the defendant's branch at D.

There they had negotiations with H, the plaintiff's partner and general agent, concerning the purchase of a tractor and trailer from the plaintiff. On 28 March M and H inspected the trailer and then went to H's home where H drafted a contract of sale on one of the plaintiff's invoices, which both H and M signed. The document was addressed to 'The Firm of R, pipe construction, via the factory at D,' and ran as follows: 'Purchased, after agreement and inspection, one caterpillar tractor with Deutz 175-PS motor, and one trailer, as is, at a lump sum price of DM20,000. Collection against payment in cash to be made between 25 and 30 April 1961 . . .'

R was away at a spa at the time, and when he returned at the end of April 1961 he took delivery of the tractor but not the trailer, and paid the plaintiff DM7200.

The plaintiff sued for DM13,000 with interest against delivery of the trailer, claiming that at the time of the original negotiations between the parties in early March 1961 R had empowered M to continue negotiations with the plaintiff after verifying certain details about the trailer and to enter an agreement for the purchase of both vehicles. The defendant contended that M's signature to the document of 28 March was subject to R's approval.

Both lower courts rejected the claim; on the plaintiff's further appeal their judgment is vacated and the case remanded.

Reasons

The appellant maintained that his claim may be based on a matter which the court of appeal did not consider, namely the acceptance without protest of a commercial letter of confirmation. He was right. Since it emerges from several of the documents submitted by the plaintiff that the defendant did not protest the sale contract of 28 March until 30 August, this should have been considered, notwithstanding that the plaintiff did not expressly invoke the rules of law on commercial letters of confirmation.

1. A commercial letter of confirmation is a document addressed by one contractor to the other in which he communicates his version of the conclusion and content of a contract which has been formed orally, telephonically or telegraphically. It is the normal method used by businessmen to establish evidence of the content of a transaction so formed [reference omitted]. In order to serve as a letter of confirmation the document must be designed *ex facie* to reflect the dealings or at least their gist (BGH, 5 December 1960, BB 61, 271).

Since the document of 28 March satisfies these basic requirements, it is a commercial letter of confirmation. Not only was it obviously apt to establish the terms agreed between M and H on 28 March, but it was also clearly designed to put the defendant in the picture as to the terms to which its representative had agreed, with resulting obligations for the defendant. That this was the plaintiff's purpose is evident from the fact that the document was addressed to the defendant. Furthermore, its content satisfies the requirements of a commercial letter of confirmation, notwithstanding that it does not contain the expression 'confirmation' or 'confirm'; for usual though it may be for the draughtsman of such a document to 'confirm' the formation of the contract in so many words, this is not an essential feature of a confirmatory letter. Nor does the fact that the document is signed by M as the representative of the defendant addressee count against its being given the effect of a letter of confirmation. Indeed, M's signature gives the document a higher evidentiary value than a document signed by the sender alone, as is usual. There are therefore no objections to regarding this letter in law as a letter of confirmation.

2. The recipient of a letter of confirmation is required by good faith (*Treu und Glauben*) and commercial practice to make an immediate protest if he does not wish to be bound by its contents. If he makes no protest, the contract is treated as formed with the content as confirmed. The Reichsgericht and the Bundesgerichtshof have constantly held that this is the result in law even if no firm contract ensued from the transactions preceding the letter of confirmation. It is therefore irrelevant whether the negotiator, here the employee M, had the power to conclude a contract or not (see RGZ 103, 401, 405; RG JW 38, 1902; BGHZ 7, 187, 189; BGH NJW 64, 1951). What produces the contract in such a case is not the conduct of the representative, which may be unauthorised, but the silence following on the confirmatory letter (BGH NJW 64, 1951).

3. But the addressee's duty to protest arises only when he learns of the letter of confirmation or at the earliest when it 'reaches' him in the sense of para 130 BGB. This is for the person who sends the letter of confirmation to prove. The document is taken to have arrived as soon as 'normal procedures bring the letter within the area of factual control of the addressee himself or of a person who represents him for the receipt of letters, and he is consequently in a position to acquaint himself with it' (RGZ 50, 191, 194).

The plaintiff has not yet asserted in terms that the document of sale dated 28 March came to the attention of R immediately or after his return from the spa. Indeed, M gave evidence that he left the document which the plaintiff handed him in the D branch office which he managed for the defendant and that he later destroyed it when he thought the matter was closed. We must therefore see whether M had power to accept the document of sale so as to affect the defendant.

It is possible that M was qualified to receive the document *qua* manager of the D branch of the defendant's business. The decisive question here is whether businessmen would regard the branch office as a proper place to which to deliver written communications directed to the defendant's head office. The question cannot be conclusively answered on the facts as found by the Court of Appeal. One must start from the fact that a branch of a business is not *ipso facto* to be regarded as a 'proper place of acceptance' for written communications directed to the head office. The important thing is what impression the branch office gives to the outside world. If a branch has a degree of independence, especially in matters of commerce, it may be right to treat it as empowered to accept documents, and it may be relevant whether the communication relates to matters with which that branch regularly deals. If it emerges that the D branch was in general occupied only with construction work or other technical matters, this would militate against its being a proper place for the acceptance of documents addressed to the defendant.

Quite apart from this, one must see whether M had power under the special agency granted to him by the defendant in connection with the purchase of both vehicles to accept the document of 28 March so that it must be treated as having reached the defendant. Here one must consider not only whether M was granted a power of receipt in the sense of para 164 para 3 BGB, but whether the defendant told him to act as a messenger. In either case the document would have 'reached' the defendant. If M had a power of receipt, the document 'arrived' as soon as it was handed to him (para 164 para 3 BGB). If he was simply a messenger the document arrived at the moment at which in the normal course of events it could be expected to reached the defendant's head office or come to R's attention. The answer to these questions depends largely on the content and scope of the mandate pursuant to which M negotiated with the plaintiff on 28 March. Here also more findings of fact are required. It is true that the Court of Appeal has found that the mandate was only 'to clear up a few preliminary questions relating to the machines being purchased', but in view of the plaintiff's assertion that M was empowered to conclude the contract, all this may mean is that while it was common ground that the mandate went that far, it was not proved that it went any further. However, the Court of Appeal was reading the conflicting evidence only in the light of the question whether M was empowered to conclude the contract; if it had examined the scope of the mandate from the point of view of M's power to accept documents, it might well have reached a different conclusion, especially as in his evidence M did not accept that it was beyond his powers to conclude the contract subject to R's approval. Nor has the defendant expressly stated that M acted beyond his mandate in negotiating with the plaintiff for the purchase of both vehicles in the name of the defendant, in concluding the contract in the name of the defendant subject to its approval, and in co-operating in the written confirmation of the agreed terms. On the other hand, it may be necessary, by way of construction, if need be, to examine whether the mandate to negotiate was wide enough to entail a power to accept a document of confirmation regarding the conclusion of a contract on behalf of the defendant.

4. The rules on acceptance of a commercial letter of confirmation without protest are designed to protect proper commercial conduct (RGZ 129, 347, 349). They therefore do not apply unless the person uttering the document is in good faith. In a case where the contract has been concluded through an intermediary and the draughtsman knew that the intermediary had no authority to represent the principal, he can draw no comfort from the recipient's failure to protest the letter of confirmation (compare BGH NJW 64, 1951). This must be taken into consideration when the case is finally decided.

Case 16
OBERLANDESGERICHT COLOGNE 19 MARCH 1980
RBRK 1980, 270

Reasons

This being a claim for damages for non-performance, the appropriate venue under paras 17, 29 ZPO, 270 para 1 BGB, would normally be the court at K. The Landgericht at A, where the claim was brought, can therefore only be the correct venue if the parties have validly agreed on its competence. The plaintiff's general conditions of business do provide for such a venue, but . . . there will be no agreement to that effect unless those conditions are incorporated into the contract between the parties. The Landgericht held that they were not, and we agree.

I. The rules relating to letters of confirmation do not apply when the recipient of an order 'confirms' his acceptance of it with variations of the contractual offer it contains [reference omitted]. A proper commercial letter of confirmation reflects the content of a contract formed orally or by telephone or telegraph and is written in order to avoid misunderstandings, uncertainties or differences. Despite its description as 'confirmation of order,' the plaintiff's letter of 6 January does not satisfy these requirements. It did not rehearse the terms of a contract resulting from prior negotiations; on the contrary, its function was to conclude a contract, none having yet been formed (on this see GBHZ 61, 285).

II. The conduct of the defendant after receiving the plaintiff's letter of 6 January does not make for a contractual adoption of the plaintiff's general conditions of business. It is true that by reason of para 24 no 1 AGBG (Law on General Conditions of Business—Gesetz zur Regelung des Rechts der Allgemeinen Geschäftsbedingungen—AGBG) the constricting provisions of para 2 do not apply in the present case, but it still remains necessary for general conditions of business to be incorporated in a contract between merchants. It is true that even as between merchants the validity of jurisdictional clause has been questioned on various grounds [references omitted], but we need not examine this view, which we would be unlikely to endorse, as there are other reasons for denying the efficacy of the plaintiff's general conditions of business in this case. By making its written order of 28 December 1976 refer to its general conditions of business and including a copy of them with it, the defendant made it unmistakably clear that it was not going to be forced into dealing on anyone else's terms. For one thing, it made any alteration in its terms ineffective without a specific written agreement; for another, it expressly adverted to the fact that the ordering of goods was an explicit acknowledgement of the exclusive applicability of its own conditions of delivery and payment, and of the inapplicability of any other terms. It is quite true that the defendant's conditions of delivery and payment were ill-adapted to the transaction in question: for example, they referred to the 'purchasing conditions of the buyer' as if it were the other party, when he himself was to be the buyer—but this does not affect the conclusion that the defendant gave unequivocal and unmistakable expression to its intention to bar any other general conditions of business. The plaintiff did likewise on 6 January in its confirmation of the plaintiff's order; it referred to its own general conditions of business, and sought to make them bind the defendant. The defendant did not respond to this demand of the plaintiff's that his general terms of business control the transaction, but this silence could not by itself in any way amount to an implicit declaration of acceptance, for silence rates as refusal rather than acceptance, given the inapplicability of the rules of commercial letters of confirmation [reference omitted]. The only conduct of the defendant which could possibly be construed as a declaration of acceptance in the instant case is its acceptance of part of the goods in question. This court does not, however, view such acceptance of the goods as amounting to a declaration by the defendant that he was ready to submit to the plaintiff's general conditions of business.

1. When two sets of general conditions of business conflict, as they frequently do, the tendency is, so far as possible, to prevent the abortion of the contract. The courts originally started from para 150 para 2 BGB, whereby an acceptance in terms differing from those proposed, whether broader or narrower, was treated as a rejection, coupled with a fresh offer. The last contracting party to refer to his own conditions of business could therefore insist on them if the other party proceeded to perform the contract without dissent. Under this theory of the last word, as it was called, it all

depended on which contracting party had made the last reference to his conditions (see eg, BGHZ 18, 212). In practical terms, the result was that if you accepted goods without dissent, you were treated as accepting the other party's general conditions of business.

In its recent decisions the *Bundesgerichtshof* has restricted this approach, without casting much doubt or light on the underlying principle. It takes the view that the mere absence of dissent does not entitle the last person to refer to his conditions of business to assume automatically that the other party agrees to such alterations. This is to maintain the principle that among merchants silence is not tantamount to agreement (thus already in BGHZ 1, 355). On the contrary, there will normally be no agreement when the customer has made it clear that he is only going to take goods on his own general conditions of business and not on the supplier's terms [BGHZ 61, 282; further references omitted]. All we learn from the decisions of the BGH is that when a purchaser accepts goods without dissent, one may in a particular case find that he has implicitly accepted the supplier's general conditions of business, reference to which makes it a new offer under para 150 para 2 BGB (NJW 1973, 2106). In BGB BB 1974, 1136, where the customer had included a qualified clause of refusal to deal on the other party's terms, it was accepted that it was for the supplier to get an unequivocal declaration in writing from the customer. While the *Bundesgerichtshof* has not yet explained how to deal with an unqualified acceptance of goods when the parties' general conditions of business are in conflict [reference omitted], there is no mistaking its concern for legal security and clarity in commercial transactions. Thus in one recent case (WM 1977, 451, 452) where a person had modified the terms of the order in confirming it, he was held disentitled to treat the other party's acceptance without demur as an expression agreement with the contract as modified. This viewpoint alone 'meets the need for legal security and clarity in those typical cases where each negotiating party refers to his own contracting terms, and tries to make them part of the contract; often there is no discussion, let alone any agreement, whose terms are to apply, a matter on which their reciprocal rights frequently depend, should anything go wrong with performance. This should not unduly hamper commercial dealings. Modern communications are so good that even when time is short and the distance long, the parties can easily and quickly resolve the question whose terms of business are to apply. Anyone who fails to do this or starts performing before reaching agreement acts at his own peril.'

The *Bundesgerichtshof* went on to hold that the customer had not implicitly accepted the altered offer by accepting part of the goods. It agreed that when an order is modified on confirmation, this new offer (para 150 para 2 BGB) can be accepted implicitly, for example, by the acceptance of performance without demur, but said that this was the case only when in all circumstances it would be proper business practice to regard such conduct as clearly evincing consent. The *Bundesgerichtshof* further pointed out that paras 146, 147 BGB are applicable to a fresh offer under para 150 para 2 BGB, with the result that it can only be accepted within the period during which the offeror could normally expect a reply. If no goods are accepted within this period, then it is doubtful, to say the least, whether the subsequent acceptance of performance by the customer can be treated by the supplier as an implicit endorsement of his conditions of sale and payment, and, on the other side, whether the customer should have such meaning attributed to his action.

This decision of the *Bundesgerichtshof* may not lay down any precise tests, but at least we think it shows the right way to proceed. We must now pay much more attention to the way that businessmen actually do business. It is common experience that parties negotiating a contract are very reluctant to let the deal go off because of a conflict between the conditions of business [references omitted]. This is why the conflict of terms is often deliberately left unresolved. It is only when problems arise in the course of performance that the parties resort to the point in order to reinforce their own legal position at that time. Then, for tactical purposes, the matter is treated as clear although up until that time it had intentionally been left unclear. Indeed, one of the reasons why parties include in their general terms a clause whereby they refuse, absolutely or conditionally, to deal on any other terms, is to provide ammunition in such cases. Thus when there is a conflict between general terms of business one should only find agreement on them when one party has unequivocally submitted himself to the other party's demand for the exclusive application of the latter's terms [reference omitted]. It is for the person confirming the order 'to ensure, by making his position absolutely clear, that the alterations he is proposing in the terms become part of the contract' (BGHZ 61, 286). In our case an express clause stated that silence would be taken as agreement. Such a clause cannot however satisfy the requirement of clarity which is essential in legal transactions for the avoidance of disputes. That requirement would be flouted if acceptance of goods without protest were treated as a conclusive declaration of assent. It would therefore be quite wrong for a court to treat some subsequent conduct as an implicit declaration of intention simply in order to resolve the uncertainty about the validity of conflicting terms which had been left unresolved by the parties themselves. Thus some cases have held that the unconditional acceptance of goods did not constitute acceptance of a qualified 'our terms only' clause which the other party had introduced in confirming the offer (OLG Karlsruhe, BB 1973, 816; LG Hagen, BB 1976, 723; perhaps also OLG Frankfurt, BB 1975, 1606).

If silence in the face of an 'our terms only' clause does not amount to submission, then it must be immaterial whether the clause is more or less rigorously formulated. We see no reason to make the validity of contracts depend on the drafting skill of one party or his draftsman [references omitted]: the form of such a clause cannot be crucial. Even the most drastic clause is typical of general conditions of business, just as typical as a less drastic clause, and it is their common typicality which is important, not the different degrees of rigour in their formulation. Were it otherwise, prophylactic draftsmanship would take the place of law.

Nor can it be relevant whether a specific objection has been made to the conditions of business proposed by the partner. To say that an objection to the application of the other party's conditions of business amounts to a new offer under para 150 para 2 BGB if it is made separately by letter, but not if one just refers to one's own conditions of business, would simply add a new twist to the old problem. The foreseeable response would be to make all future protests in an 'individualised form,' just as appropriate clauses were drafted when the courts started treating the acceptance of goods without protest as an implicit declaration of consent (for example, 'Acceptance of the goods is not to be taken as consent to other terms,' and so on). The real problem ought not to be masked by finding an implied declaration of consent, and the real problem is that the parties never reached any clear and unequivocal agreement, and generally—for fear of endangering the deal —never really meant to. But if the parties conduct themselves in this manner, why should we invest juristic constructions and make hair-splitting distinctions in order to absolve them from the legal consequences, especially if the result is to subject one of them entirely to the other's terms? In any case it does not square with the habits of tradesmen to treat the acceptance of goods as implicit submission to the other party's terms. Such behaviour really betokens an intention to ignore the conflict of terms, lest the contract be aborted, rather than any intention to accept the terms of the other party. Businessmen are more concerned with receiving goods and payment than with problems which may well not manifest themselves during the performance of the contract. The legal principle to apply in such a situation is as follows: a person who delivers goods before it has been determined which of the conflicting terms are to apply, waives his right to any such determination and cannot treat the acceptance of the goods as an indication of consent, ie of submission to his terms.

Flume has criticised the *Bundesgerichtshof* for not adopting a clear position and for not forthrightly abandoning the doctrine that the acceptance of goods may amount to a declaration of acceptance of an offer (*Das Rechtsgeschäft* (ed. 3, 1979, 675). We agree with him that it is time to stop making these difficult and confusing distinctions in individual cases and to start from the principle that if both parties refer to their own terms of business, the terms which conflict are invalid. Each contractor has it in his power to require the other to take a clear position. If he does not do so, usually for fear of losing the deal, then it is that. Flume's description of the economic and legal situation (at p 676) is apt: 'The essential feature of cases where both contractors refer to their own general conditions of business is that the question whose conditions are to apply is not brought out into the open. Neither party is prepared to let the contract abort on this point. Neither insists that the other recognise the exclusive validity of his terms. Since the contracting parties have not resolved the question, one should not use para 150 para 2 BGB to deem agreement to have been reached when it has not. When both parties have referred to their terms of business, each can raise the question whose conditions are to apply when the contract is being concluded. If this question is not raised, and if neither manages to get the validity of his own terms of business accepted, the inconsistent terms are not incorporated.'

Finally, there is a certain element of inconsistency and shuffling, almost of bad faith, in a person who is now trying to profit from the confusion surrounding the terms of the contract which he could easily have resolved but consciously permitted to subsist.

The whole contract is not, of course, rendered invalid by failure to resolve the confusion and reach agreement on which terms are to apply: the parties do not intend that the contract should fail just because there is no agreement on that point (reference omitted). Those parts of the general terms which are not in conflict take precedence over dispositive law, which replaces only those clauses which are invalidated by the unresolved conflict (reference omitted). The same result would be achieved by analogical application of para 6 para 2 AGBG, which on this point contains a general principle of law (reference omitted).

2. In applying these principles to the case in hand, we conclude that the venue clause in the plaintiff's general terms of business, which is prejudicial to the defendant, is not binding on him. The defendant did not accept it. What happened was that there was an exchange of mutually conflicting stereotyped declaration with no further negotiations about them. In such a case one needs a clear written agreement by the defendant,

and there is none here [reference omitted]. This conclusion is all the more necessary because in this case the plaintiff had appreciated the defendant's unwillingness to trade on the plaintiff's terms, and had indeed raised the problem in his letter of 6 January 1977. In such a conflict it was not enough for the plaintiff to refer to his own conditions of business and say that he would treat the defendant as accepting them if he did not protest: it was not in the plaintiff's power to bypass the rule that in commercial dealings silence counts as rejection. The subsequent negotiations about the price of the goods contain nothing approaching a declaration by the defendant that he submitted to the plaintiff's terms of business. On the contrary, the more or less intentional failure to go into the question despite the evident need for clarification shows that basically neither party wanted to put the formation of the contract at risk by insisting on an answer. Nothing could have been easier for the plaintiff than to state in one of its letters that the defendant had not yet accepted in writing the validity of his terms of business, but there is no sign of any such attempt at clarification in the plaintiff's correspondence.

As a subsidiary argument, the court notes that as the acceptance of the goods by the defendant took place after a substantial interval and not within the period within which the plaintiff was entitled to expect a reply from the defendant to his letter of 6 January under para 147 para 2 BGB, it could not have any positive value as a declaration of consent [reference omitted].

Case 17
BUNDESGERICHTSHOF (SEVENTH CIVIL SENATE) 9 JULY 1970
BGHZ 54, 236

Reasons

The defendant supplied the plaintiff with a contraflow heat-exchanger for installation in a customer's brewery. It had to be removed shortly after it was installed, allegedly because it did not work properly or have the guaranteed attributes. The original negotiations between the parties effectively started on 19 November 1954, when the defendant sent a telegram to the plaintiff offering to supply the heat-exchanger. This was followed by telephone conversations for a week. Then on 26 November the plaintiff wrote the defendant a letter whose terms differed from those of the defendant's original telegram. Four days later the defendant replied with a brief 'Confirmation of Order', which contained, for the first time, the clause 'Conditions of Delivery: VDMA.' Those were the conditions of the German Machine Builders Association, which included a clause limiting the supplier's liability.

The plaintiff claimed damages of DM25,558.28. The Landgericht ordered the defendant to refund the price, viz DM7921.30 with interest. The *Oberlandesgericht* dismissed the plaintiff's appeal, and his further appeal was equally unsuccessful.

2. The appellant contests the Court of Appeal's view that the VDMA conditions were incorporated into the contract. His objections are unfounded.

(a) It must certainly be granted that the Court of Appeal misunderstood the plaintiff's evidence about the parties' telephone communications between 19 and 26 November. The plaintiff did not assert that the contract was formed during those telephone communications but that the defendant then made a new offer, varying his offer of 19 November so as to meet the wishes of the plaintiff, and that the plaintiff, after consulting his customer, wrote its letter of 26 November in acceptance of this telephonic offer of the defendant's.

(b) But even if one accepts the plaintiff's evidence as accurate, one must agree with the Court of Appeal's conclusion that the VDMA conditions became incorporated in the contract.

This is not, as the Court of Appeal thought, because the defendant's letter of 30 November constituted a fresh offer and the plaintiff's subsequent conduct an acceptance of it. The VDMA conditions became part of the contract because the defendant's letter of 30 November is in law a proper 'commercial letter of confirmation' to which the plaintiff took no exception, and this is true although it was described as a 'confirmation of order' and did not expressly refer to prior oral or telephonic negotiations [on commercial letters of confirmation, see BGHZ 7, 187; 11, 1; 18, 212; 40, 42; BGH NJW 1965, 965; BGH NJW 1966, 1070; other references omitted].

(aa) The fact that the defendant called its letter of 30 November a 'Confirmation of Order' rather than a 'Letter of Confirmation' does not prevent its being regarded in law as a 'commercial letter of confirmation.' The name the parties give to the document is not critical. Nor is it absolutely necessary that the letter should expressly mention or refer to prior oral or telephonic agreement. What is important is that the document should be substantially designed to avouch the result of prior contractual negotiations in a binding manner [references omitted]. Here the plaintiff could have been in no doubt that this was the purpose of the defendant's letter of 30 November. So far, it is only in cases where the negotiations have been oral, telephonic, telegraphic or by telex that the court have found a 'commercial letter of confirmation' and held that its content became part of the contract in the absence of protest by the addressee [reference omitted]. The *Bundesgerichtshof* has never decided whether a commercial letter of confirmation might not exist in other cases: the question was expressly left open in our judgment of 25 May 1970.

The question falls for decision now, for, treating the plaintiff's assertions as correct for the purposes of the appeal, we have here a contract where the defendant's offer was made by telephone (between 19 and 26 November) and the plaintiff's acceptance was made in writing (letter of 26 November).

The plaintiff's letter of 26 November cannot itself be a commercial letter of confirmation, for on his own view the contract was not yet formed, there having been no acceptance prior to that letter. Thus of the two declarations of will which formed the contract, one of them (the defendant's) was telephonic, and the other (the plaintiff's) was in writing. In such a case it is right to apply the rules concerning 'commercial letters of confirmation' and the addressee's failure to object. This is implicit in the scope and purpose of the judge-made rules on the matter, which are rooted in the practice of tradesmen. Tradesmen have an interest in clarifying their contractual relations and in avoiding disputes over the content of contracts; in pursuit of this interest they habitually draw up a document in writing to confirm and fix the content of agreements which have been reached otherwise than in writing. If such a confirmatory document is unacceptable to the other party, he must, within the limits that good faith requires, make an immediate protest. If he fails to do so, the terms of the letter of confirmation take effect as the terms of the contract.

The clarification provided by a letter of confirmation is just as necessary in cases like the one here assumed, where the contract is concluded by a telephonic declaration on one side (the defendant's) and by a declaration in writing on the other (the plaintiff's). At least this is true for the party, here the defendant, whose contractual declaration has so far been only oral or telephonic. In such cases the single written declaration of will is insufficient to fix the terms of the contract so as to avoid disputes in the future, since the nature and terms of the other party's telephonic declaration remain uncertain.

The present case is a striking example of such uncertainty. The parties are in dispute over the range and substance of their telephone conversations between 19 and 26 November, and cannot agree whether the defendant made an offer on terms like those of the plaintiff's letter of 26 November. This uncertainty greatly affects the effect of the plaintiff's letter of 26 November, for depending on whether the plaintiff's assertion is true or false, that letter is either the acceptance of an offer or a new offer in itself, linked with a rejection of the offer in the defendant's original telegram. In the midst of such uncertainty the defendant, on receiving the plaintiff's letter of 26 November, had every reason to finalise and clarify the terms of the contract, and it must have been evident to the plaintiff that this was the purpose of the defendant's letter of 30 November.

(cc) The relative brevity of the letter of 30 November does not prevent its being treated as a 'commercial letter of confirmation.' The defendant in it referred to the plaintiff's letter of 26 November, and could thus dispense with an iteration of the details without forfeiting the necessary specificity.

(dd) The letter of 30 November also makes it sufficiently clear that the defendant was not prepared to contract except on VDMA terms.

(ee) It is not at all unusual for a machine shop such as the defendant's to import VDMA conditions into a contract. As a dealer in such machinery the plaintiff should have expected this, and cannot therefore now maintain that he had no need to protest because he had no reason to expect any such term in the defendant's letter of confirmation.

Case 18
BUNDESGERICHTSHOF (EIGHTH CIVIL SENATE) 20 MARCH 1974
NJW 1974, 991

Facts

The plaintiff manufactures French fried potatoes which he sells to wholesalers such as the defendant. On 19 August 1970 the defendant telephoned the plaintiff to ask him for his prices. The rest of the telephone conversation is in dispute. After the telephone call the plaintiff sent the defendant a 'confirmation of order' for a specific quantity of French fries. The defendant did not reply to this document, but obtained French fries from another firm and accepted none from the plaintiff.

The plaintiff claims damages for non-acceptance in a partial amount of DM10,000 plus interest. The *Landgericht* dismissed the claim, but the Court of Appeal allowed it. The defendant's appeal was unsuccessful.

Reasons

I. The Court of Appeal found that no contract of sale was concluded on the telephone on 19 August, but that because the 'confirmation of order' was accepted without protest, the plaintiff's contractual claim was nevertheless well grounded. This document was in law a commercial letter of confirmation, and the defendant had failed to prove, the burden being on his, that its terms differed substantially from those of the telephone conversation or that the plaintiff had deliberately 'confirmed' something he knew to be incorrect.

II. The appellant's objections to the finding that the confirmation of order of 19 August was a commercial letter of confirmation are without merit. This court has only a limited power to review the construction of such an individual and atypical declaration as this document; we can only ask whether the Court of Appeal infringed any principles of logic, rules of construction or canons of procedure, or whether it misconceived the nature of a commercial letter of confirmation. This is not the case.

1. The fact that a document is described as a confirmation of order is no obstacle to its being treated as a commercial letter of confirmation. It is established law that the description which a party gives to his document is not conclusive. Frequently trades-men pay little attention to this matter [reference omitted]. It is also immaterial that the document neither mentions nor refers to a previous telephonic agreement (BGHZ 54, 236, 249), but since there had only been one telephone conversation between the parties, on the very day on which the letter was sent, it is clear that this letter could only refer to the telephone conversation of 19 August. The external appearance of the document was also consistent with its being intended to reflect the essentials of the telephone conversation.

2. A further requirement for a commercial letter of confirmation is that it be preceded by contractual negotiations [BGH NJW 1963, 1922, 1925; other reference omitted].

(a) It is essential to the concept of a commercial letter of confirmation that it reflects the real or supposed outcome of prior contractual negotiations. This is what distinguishes it from a confirmation of order which, instead of communicating the result of previous contractual negotiations, constitutes the acceptance of an offer in the form of a confirmation, or sometimes even an offer in itself (BGHZ 18, 212, 214). Since on general principles of proof the plaintiff must establish the salient elements of a commercial letter of confirmation, it is for him to prove that contractual negotiations preceded the 'confirmation of order.'

(b) We do not agree with the appellant that the Court of Appeal was wrong in law to find this proved. The Court left it an open question whether the parties actually came to an agreement on the telephone about the purchase of French fries, or whether the defendant simply wanted a quotation and made it clear that he did not want to buy, but it did find that there was no disagreement over the details of the quantity to be supplied, the price or the method of payment, and that at the end of the conversation there was talk of a confirmation of order. Given these facts, the Court of Appeal was entitled to conclude that contractual dealings had taken place, for the plaintiff had made a precise offer and the defendant had concerned himself with its terms. It is immaterial whether or not a contract was actually formed on the telephone, because a document may be a commercial letter of confirmation even though no contract was formed in the prior contractual negotiations [reference omitted].

III. If the 'confirmation of order' of 19 August is a commercial letter of confirmation, the defendant was bound to object to it if he objected to being bound by it.

1. The reason is that one tradesman who sends a letter of confirmation to another so as to fix and record the result of antecedent contractual negotiations assumes that the recipient will forthwith check the document to see whether it correctly reflects his view of the content of the negotiated agreement. If he makes no protest, the sender is in principle entitled to rely on the transaction proceeding in the form in which he confirmed it (BGH NJW 1972, 45).

2. But this does not apply when the terms of the confirmatory document deviate so widely from the terms of the discussions that the person sending it could not reasonably count on the recipient's agreeing to it or when the person sending it knew that it was inaccurate and so infringed the principles of good faith (BGHZ 40, 42, 44–5).

IV. The Court of Appeal was right in holding that the burden of proof of these matters is on the recipient of the letter of confirmation.

1. On general principles of proof the person who sends a 'confirmation of order' must prove all that is necessary for the application of the rule which justifies his claim. This means that he must prove that his letter is a commercial letter of confirmation and that it reached the other party. If the recipient asserts that no obligation resulted on him because the document deviated seriously from the content of the prior negotiations or intentionally misrecorded them, it is for him to prove all that is necessary for this defence to apply. Since as a general rule a failure to object to a commercial letter of confirmation has binding results, a person who claims that exceptionally this binding result did not ensue must prove why the rule does not apply [reference omitted].

2. It must be added that it is mercantile practice to expect the recipient of a commercial letter of confirmation which does not reflect the prior dealings or what was agreed to make an immediate protest [reference omitted]; thus if a commercial letter of confirmation does not agree with the prior negotiations, the recipient who fails to protest has not behaved in the manner required of businessmen. He must therefore demonstrate that he was not required to behave in the normal and indicated manner, and that no protest against the letter of confirmation was called for because it deliberately or seriously misrepresented the prior negotiations.

3. Even under the *Reichsgericht*, therefore, the recipient of a letter of confirmation had the burden of proving that the person who sent it had infringed the principles of good faith by intentionally making it reflect something other than had been expressed in the prior negotiations.

4. It might possibly be different where the person sending the letter of confirmation had the intention of trapping the recipient or of taking him unaware, but the facts of the present case to not raise that question in any way.

Case 19
BUNDESGERICHTSHOF (EIGHTH CIVIL SENATE) 20 MARCH 1985
NJW 1985, 1838

Facts

On 27 October 1980, the debtor in bankruptcy ordered from the claimant clocks operating as time switches which were to be fitted into electrical stoves; the contract was subject to the general conditions of trade printed on the back of the claimant's order forms. Under no 14 the order form states that changes in the order must normally be in writing and that the purchasing conditions of the debtor in bankruptcy applied. No 16 of these conditions states: 'Differing conditions of trade. By accepting our order, the supplier agrees to our purchasing conditions. Where our order is confirmed by the supplier using conditions deviating therefrom, our conditions of purchase will continue exclusively to apply, even if we do not expressly raise any objections. Deviations will thus only apply where they have been expressly agreed by us in writing. If the supplier objects to this practice, he must immediately and specifically state his objections in a separate letter. In such cases we retain the right to cancel the order and no claims against us will result from such action. Our conditions will also apply for future transactions, even where they are not specifically referred to, as long as they have reached the customer in the course of an order confirmed by us.'

On 11 February 1982, the debtor in bankruptcy placed with the claimant a follow-up order for the supply of further thermostats. The claimant confirmed the order referring to his General Conditions of Supply and Payment according to which his written confirmation of the order in conjunction with these Conditions were to apply exclusively. Any amendments or additions to the contractual clauses were only valid in written form; no 7 of these general conditions contains an extended and expanded retention of proprietary rights for goods delivered. The claimant supplied the time switches and thermostats of a total value of DM454 245.58. On 21 May 1982, the debtor in bankruptcy requested that conciliation proceedings be started. At that time, out of the above-mentioned and still unpaid deliveries, he still had in stock switches not yet installed of a total value of DM47 789.05 had already been installed in finished stoves which were still at the debtor's premises. During July/August 1982, the debtor in bankruptcy paid the equivalent price for the pieces which were not yet installed. On 29 October 1982, 'follow up' bankruptcy proceedings were started in respect of the debtor's assets and the defendant appointed as receiver in bankruptcy. The claimant demanded from the defendant payment of the value of the appliances which, on 21 May 1982, had already been installed in stoves which were still with the bankrupt debtor. He also requested information as to what claims the bankrupt had on 21 May 1982 stemming from sales of stoves containing the switches and energy regulators supplied by him. The *Landgericht* rejected the claim. The claimant's appeal and further appeal were also unsuccessful.

Reasons

I. The solution to the legal problem of the litigation depends on whether No 7 of the General Conditions of Trade (AGB) had become part of the contract. If this is the case, the claimant's claim for payment can be justified on the basis of para 46 of the Bankruptcy Order (*Konkursordnung*/KO) or on paras 989 et seq BGB, para 59 1 No 1 KO or para 812 et seq BGB, para 591 No 4 KO (see Senate, NJW 1982, 1749 = WM 1982, 486). As a result of the assignment of future claims, the claimant would also be entitled to any outstanding claims which the debtor in bankruptcy has against his customers and which were subject to such an assignment, so that the request for information would also be justified (para 402 BGB). But if No 7 of the claimant's General Conditions of Trade has not become part of the contract, the demand for payment and for information are unfounded. It is possible that the claimant transferred ownership in the switches only under the suspensory condition of full payment of the purchase price. The debtor in bankruptcy had to assume such retention of title given his knowledge of the claimant's general conditions of trade when the contract was concluded (see Senate, NJW 1982, 1749 = WM 1982, 486). But in this case this fact does not lead to a successful further appeal since the claimant, even before he made a request for a settlement during composition proceedings, had lost the ownership of the switches at the latest point when they were fitted into the stoves (para 947 11 BGB). He thus only had an ordinary claim in bankruptcy which could not be made outside of bankruptcy proceedings. Since claims from the sales of these stoves had not in advance been assigned to the claimant, he likewise had no right to demand information as to the sales.

II.

1. Following the decision of the *Landgericht*, the court of appeal assumed that the claimant's General Conditions of Sale and Payment, and thus condition No 7, had not become part of the contract. They had not been agreed on by separate contract. A tacit inclusion into the contract is barred by the debtor's conditions of purchase known to the claimant. The defensive clauses contained in No 16 of these conditions are not invalid according to para 9 of the Act on General Conditions of Trade (AGB-Gesetz). By this clause, the debtor in bankruptcy intended to secure for all of his transactions as uniform contractual conditions as possible and especially to preclude suppliers' retention of title. This aim cannot be objected to, since any retention of title impedes at least any transfer of ownership by way of security which is normally linked to business arrangements for bank loans.

2. These arguments can withstand legal scrutiny, at least as far as their result is concerned.

(a) In commercial business transactions, the inclusion of general conditions of trade in single contracts requires that the contractual partners tacitly or specifically agree on their application [Senate, WM 1979, 19 (20) and NJW 1978, 978 with further references].

Without any legal error, the Court of Appeal has rejected the existence of an explicit agreement on the applicability of the claimant's general conditions of trade for this particular contract. The further appeal does not refute this argument. The Court of Appeal furthermore correctly assumed that the debtor in bankruptcy had not tacitly agreed to a total inclusion of the claimant's general conditions of trade. The assumption that the debtor in bankruptcy tacitly agreed to the claimant's conditions of sale is countermanded by the unequivocal statement contained in his conditions of purchase that he intended exclusively to conclude contracts according to his conditions and that differing conditions contained in a confirmation of orders will only apply once they have been agreed by him in writing. In this context it is irrelevant, whether or not the defensive clause has itself become part of the contract, a clause which was intended to make it clear during contractual discussions, ie before the contract was signed, that the purchaser will not be bound by any clauses contained in the seller's trading conditions except for those enumerated in the defensive clause itself. What matters is solely the debtor's intentions as expressed in the defensive clause after the claimant had confirmed the order, though with reference to his own general conditions and such change is not discernible from the facts of the case. As the appeal court assumes and the further appeal obviously does not dispute, in view of the—advance—objection to the application of the claimant's general conditions as explicitly stated in the debtor's defensive clause, and in the absence of other circumstances, such a change of intention cannot be thought to have taken place, especially not from the fact that the debtor failed once more to reject the claimant's conditions of sale and accepted the goods without reservation (see Senate, WM 1977, 451 (452)). Without a contractual agreement between the partners concerning the claimant's conditions of sale, these have not altogether become part of the contract. The further appeal acknowledges this point.

(b) However, the further appeal submits that the debtor in bankruptcy's defensive clause which bars a wholesale inclusion of the claimant's conditions of sale in the contract, does not preclude the fact that certain clauses of these conditions of sale have nonetheless become part of the contract. The defensive clause only excludes the claimant's conditions of sale insofar as these deviate from the debtor's purchasing conditions; it does not also exclude additional conditions to which the debtor had not expressedly objected, such as No 7 of the Sales Conditions containing rules on an extended retention of ownership with a clause on processing and advance assignment of rights, all the more where such additional conditions are customary for this particular line of business. The court cannot uphold this reasoning.

(aa) Where a contract, as here, has been concluded without agreement on the application of the general conditions of trade of one party, this does not mean that the corresponding optional legal rules automatically apply (see Bunte ZIP 1982, 449 (450) with overview over the various legal opinions; Wolf in: Wolf-Horn-Lindacher AGB-Gesetz para 2, note 77; Ulmer, in: Ulmer-Brandner-Hensen AGB-Kommentar, 4. ed., para 2, note 101; Erman-Hefermehl BGB, 7. ed., para 2 AGB-Gesetz, note 48) in such a case and instead of the rules contained in the general conditions. From the intentions of the parties it can rather be deduced that such rules deviating from or supplementing optional legal rules will apply which have been set out in the general conditions of either party and where these conditions are of identical content and where their application has thus been intended by both parties.

(bb) Such apparent consensus is however missing, where one party's general conditions of trade contain 'additional' rules which have no equivalent in the other party's conditions, such as, the use of clauses on the retention of ownership The question as to whether in such a case a tacit consent can be assumed of one party to the unilaterally fixed additional conditions of the other contractual partner, even where both parties' general conditions do not result in a consensus of intentions, can only be answered according to the intention of the party opposing the clause, insofar as this can be discerned from all other circumstances of the case (see Ulmer, para 2, note 104; Löwe-Graf von Westphalen-Trinkner, AGB-Gesetz, para 2, note 47). In this case, no intention of the debtor in bankruptcy can be ascertained to indicate that his defensive clause was merely meant to exclude the claimant's sales conditions insofar as they run counter to his own conditions of purchase but not also other additional rules. By his defensive clause, the debtor clearly and unequivocally expressed his intention that for any orders placed only his own purchase conditions applied and that, without his expressed written acknowledgement, any other conditions would not become part of the contract even where he fails formally to object to them. The debtor in bankruptcy thereby unequivocally expressed his intention that his own conditions of purchase only leave room for the claimant's conditions of sale where and insofar as their contents are either identical with his own or where they have been agreed by him in writing (for a similar case see: Senate NJW 1979, 2199 = WM 1979, 805). There was therefore no need for the debtor to raise a specific objection against the retention of ownership clause contained in the claimant's conditions of sale in order to prevent the clause from becoming part of the contract.

No other result can be reached in respect of this clause on the retention of ownership just because it possibly is part of customary law applicable for this line of business as the further appeal alleges (. . .)

Case 20
BUNDESGERICHTSHOF (NINTH CIVIL SENATE) 29 FEBRUARY 1996
BGHZ 132, 119 = NJW 1996, 1467

Facts

The first defendant (from now on called the defendant) and two other persons were members and directors of the A-Autovermietung (car hire) GmbH with its registered office in Frankfurt a M. They negotiated a current account credit with the claimant at the beginning of January 1992, which was to be for the benefit of the Dresden branch of A. The claimant made the credit dependent on every director entering into a guarantee, and gave to its representatives conducting the negotiations a blank form of guarantee for the defendant without limit on time or amount. The defendant signed the document. Later his name and address were noted in the place provided for the description of the guarantor in the form. Besides this, the place and date of the declaration were entered. The stamp of A-Autovermietung appears next to the defendant's signature. The defendant claims that he put it there himself in order to show that it was the company, and not himself personally, who was entering into the guarantee for the branch in Dresden. The document was returned to the claimant. The claimant completed the form with the missing details of the creditor and the principal debtor. In 1993 bankruptcy proceedings were commenced against the company. The claimant claimed against the defendant, as joint debtor with the other directors, for the amount of the credit balances of DM42, 271.77 plus interest.

The *Landgericht* rejected the claim but the appeal court gave judgment against the defendant in accordance with the application. The defendant by his appeal in law sought restoration of the decision at first instance. The appeal in law was successful.

Reasons

I. The appeal court, after assessing all the circumstances alleged by the parties, and on the basis of the evidence obtained, came to the conclusion that the defendant's declaration was, from the point of view of the recipient, a personal guarantee, in spite of the company stamp appearing on it. This interpretation, which in principle is the responsibility of the judge of fact, is a possible one and does not reveal any legal error (. . .)
II. The guarantee must be in the form set out in § 766 sentence 1 BGB (. . .). The appeal court considers that the guarantee satisfies the requirement of written form if the guarantor signs it, and the document is completed immediately afterwards in

accordance with his intentions by a third party orally empowered to do so inserting the details necessary under § 766 sentence 1 of the BGB. This view corresponds with the consistent case law of the highest courts [references omitted]. Accordingly the guarantee is regarded as being given in accordance with the formal requirements as soon as the creditor is in possession of a document which contains all the details necessary under the statute. This view cannot however be followed. A document signed in blank does not become a formally effective guarantee under § 766 sentence 1 of the BGB by completion of the document on the basis of an oral authority.

1. The provisions of § 766 BGB are exclusively to protect the guarantor. They are supposed to encourage him to exercise greater care, and protect him from making declarations which he has not sufficiently considered [references omitted]. Because the provisions are to warn the guarantor about the liability associated with his declaration, the requirement for written form is only satisfied if the document contains, besides the intention to guarantee the debt of another, a description of the creditor, the principal debtor and the demand which is being guaranteed [references omitted]. The warning function is accordingly not satisfied simply by the guarantor signing a piece of paper which shows his intention of providing a guarantee. The document should also delimit the risk which he undertakes, and thereby bring it to his attention when he makes his declaration [references omitted].

2. If the statute prescribes written form for a declaration, § 126 sentence 1 of the BGB merely requires that the document is signed personally by the person who issues it. Accordingly, the text does not need to be completed when the signature is made. The declarant can sign the paper in blank, and written form is in this case maintained by completion of the document [references omitted]. The case law so far is based on this idea. It cannot however convince, because it does not sufficiently take into account the sense and purpose of the strict requirements as to form in guarantee law.

(a) Admittedly it cannot be deduced from the provisions of § 766 BGB that the guarantee must be provided by the guarantor himself with those details of the identity of the creditor and the principal debtor and the content of the obligation which are compulsorily required. Even when statute prescribes written form for a declaration of will, the party can use an agent (§ 167 (2) BGB) or make the signature in blank and empower someone else to complete the document to the necessary extent [references omitted]. There is no basis in statute for saying that this possibility must be generally excluded in the case of guarantees. The case law until now (and the unanimous opinion in the academic literature) that the guarantor may use an agent to give his declaration [references omitted] or can empower the creditor in accordance with § 181 of the BGB to complete the parts of the declaration which are still missing [references omitted] should therefore basically be followed [references omitted].

(b) § 766 BGB places special requirements on the written form by saying that the features of the contractual content mentioned above at 1 should be made known 'in black and white' to the guarantor before he makes his signature. These requirements are only to protect the guarantor from undertaking liability too hastily. If a form is signed the contents of which unambiguously indicate that it is a guarantee, but which does not mention the creditor, the principal debtor or the liability which is to be secured, the subject matter and scope of the risk are not usually identified to the extent which statute considers to be necessary for the person who incurs liability by signing.

(c) § 167 (2) BGB, which says the declaration does not need to be in the form laid down for the legal transaction to which the authority refers, is interpreted restrictively by the case law for transactions which need authentication under § 313 BGB. According to the consistent case law of the highest courts, a corresponding authority must be notarially authenticated, in spite of the provisions of § 167 (2) BGB, if the legal power given is to be irrevocable [references omitted]. But if the authority can be revoked, it is in fact binding in accordance with the principal's intention, because the legal transaction serves the agent's interests exclusively. It allows him to exploit immediately the authority given to him, even though the case law of the highest courts affirms the need for form [references omitted].

§ 313 sentence 1 [§ 311b sentence 1] BGB which guarantees protection from ill-considered dealings, guarantees the buyer expert advice from the person providing authentication, and is meant to bring about clarity and security in legal transactions generally. In contrast to this, § 766 sentence 1 BGB only protects the guarantor, whose liability as a rule only benefits others: the creditor and the principal debtor. Between the guarantor and the agent, there therefore usually exists a division of interests, which in the area of land transactions needing authentication under § 313 [§ 311b sentence 1] BGB, requires an authority complying with formal requirements. In the case of guarantees needing special form, it is therefore generally justified to require written form for the authority for giving the appropriate declaration of will, or the power to complete the blank form. The purpose of the protective provisions of § 766 BGB, ie to bring clearly to the guarantor's attention the content and scope of his liability, would be eroded if the guarantor could put his signature on a piece of paper which does not contain all the necessary components of the declaration, and orally empower a third party—in particular the principal debtor, or the creditor—to fill in the missing details, and this was allowed to suffice. If such a regime is permitted, the statutory formal provisions cannot fulfil their purpose of warning the guarantor. (. . .) This is especially the case where the guarantor empowers another person—in particular the creditor, at the same time releasing him from the provisions of § 181 BGB—to complete the document.

(d) If the signature in blank combined with an oral authority is allowed to suffice, the decision about the effectiveness of the guarantee is virtually exclusively dependent on facts which are not evident from the document. The protection intended by § 766 BGB is thus almost destroyed. This is demonstrated particularly clearly if the parties are also in dispute about who completed the document and made the addition to the signature indicating the liability of another person. Besides this, the view propounded so far by the case law of the highest courts exposes the guarantor to a considerable extent to the danger of misuse of a blank form. If the signature is genuine, the presumption applies under § 440 (2) ZPO (Civil Procedure Code) that the text above it corresponds with the intention of the person issuing the document. He therefore has to prove that completion of it was not as agreed [references omitted]. The requirements which § 766 sentence 1 of the BGB places on the form of a guarantor's declaration are to avoid such risks. (. . .)

III. As the guarantee does not satisfy the formal requirements of § 766 sentence 1 BGB, the contract is void (§ 125 sentence 1 BGB).

1. The defendant is not violating the principle of good faith (§ 242 BGB) by relying on formal ineffectiveness.

(a) The absence of form in respect of a legal transaction can only in quite exceptional cases be ignored on the basis that it amounts to impermissible exercise of a right. Otherwise, the formal provisions of civil law would be eroded [references omitted]. Admittedly the conduct of a party can be contrary to good faith if he has drawn benefits from an important contract over a lengthy period, and now wants to withdraw from his obligations by appealing to the lack of form. In relation to a guarantor, this needs in particular to be considered when he has drawn indirect benefits as a shareholder in the principal debtor from the granting of credit over a period of years, and has by his actions caused the creditor to place justified trust in the effectiveness of the contract, and the creditor has performed his obligations with this in mind [references omitted].

(b) Such prerequisites are lacking in this case. (. . .)

2. The alteration made by this judgment to case law of the highest courts which has existed for decades not only has implications for the future. It likewise affects legal relationships which have been entered into but not yet concluded. There are no constitutional grounds which militate against this.

(a) Judgments of the highest courts are not to be equated with statutes and do not achieve comparable binding legal effect. By deviating from a previously held legal opinion, the judge is not in principle violating Article 20, para 3 of the Basic Law. In particular, he does not need proof that factual relationships or general views have changed in a certain respect [references omitted]. A court decision which concerns the effectiveness of a legal transaction is a finding evaluating an act, and has effect, simply by its nature, on a set of facts existing in the past and not yet concluded. This so-called false retrospective effect is, in the same way as for statutory provisions, in principle unobjectionable from a legal point of view [references omitted]. The rules developed in the constitutional court case law about limiting retrospective alteration of statutes [references omitted] cannot simply be carried over to the case law of the highest courts. This is because the courts are not as a rule bound to an established case law which in the light of better knowledge is shown to be no longer tenable [references omitted]. It follows from this that limitations of false retrospective effect are more seldom required for judicial decisions than for statutes.

(b) The Federal Constitutional Court has not so far established any generally valid rules in this respect [references omitted] and has contented itself with decisions in individual cases. Accordingly, limits on retrospective effect can arise from the constitutional state principle of legal certainty. For the citizen this means primarily protection of trust. (. . .) In the balancing exercise which must accordingly be carried out, it should in particular be borne in mind that substantive justice embodies a component of the constitutional state principle which is at least equal in importance to the principle of legal certainty [references omitted].

(c) Besides this, in private law the general clause of § 242 BGB guarantees that the judge can never limit himself to looking at the matter in a formal way, if this is inconsistent with the principle of good faith. In this connection, a party's trust in the continued existence of a right must be given appropriate consideration if it is worthy of protection. The case law of the highest courts has worked out a string of legal concepts for this purpose (eg, impermissible exercise of a right, absence or disappearance of the basis of a transaction, forfeiture) which in general facilitate sufficient consideration of the justified interests of both parties. (. . .)

False retrospective effect as a result of a change in the case law of the highest courts has therefore for good reason been so far limited in the realm of private law only in cases of the continued existence of a long-term obligation relationship, frequently of a care or maintenance nature, and the retrospective effect had consequences for the persons affected by it which possibly threatened their existence (. . .).

(d) Protection of trust of a kind comparable with those cases should not be granted to the claimant in this case. At the point in time of the legal transaction, the decisions of the highest courts which were significant for a correct understanding of § 766 sentence 1 BGB and of §§ 126 and 167 BGB had been issued a long time before [references omitted]. The case law had merely delayed in expressing the legal consequences suggesting themselves here in the case of guarantees in blank. (. . .) The effect is limited in this case to one of three guarantees given for the same loan contract. The decision has no 'knock-on effect' for the claimant, because it has itself stated that in its business there is in principle no signing in blank.

Case 21
REICHSGERICHT (FIFTH CIVIL DIVISION) 21 MAY 1927
RGZ 117, 121

Facts

In February 1920 the plaintiff was engaged as a manager by the defendant company, the managing director of which was the second defendant. In June 1922 the plaintiff left the service of the first defendant as a result of a disagreement.

By a contract of employment dated 13 August 1920, which was to run for three years, the plaintiff was allotted the house, 6 K. Street in O. as his official residence rent-free. The defendant company had bought it shortly before for M120,000. When a new contract of employment was drawn up on 20 February 1922, to run until 30 September 1924, the second defendant signed a document on behalf of the first defendant, the company, whereby the plaintiff was granted a right of pre-emption in respect of the official residence at the price of M120,000.

The plaintiff sued both defendants demanding that the house be conveyed to him; alternatively he claimed damages resulting from the failure to convey the house.

The defendants pleaded that the promises had not been made notarial form or before a court as required by para 313 [311b I] BGB and were not binding. Alternatively they denied that any such promises had been made.

The Court of Appeal found that in 1920 the second defendant had congratulated the plaintiff on his performance and had stated that the house was to be his in lieu of Christmas bonuses in cash in 1920 and 1921. Shortly afterwards the second defendant had repeated the statement, adding that the plaintiff had requested the second defendant to convey the house to him, but the second defendant had assured him on his word as a nobleman that the notarial conveyance could take place at any time, but was unnecessary between the parties. The Court of Appeal also found that no fraudulent intention of the defendants existed not to perform the contract and to rely on its formal invalidity. Instead the defendants originally had the intention to fulfil their obligations and had only changed their minds subsequently. The second defendant, in giving the assurances set out above, had caused the agreement not to be made in official form; it was contrary to good faith if the defendants now refused to convey the house.

The District court and the Court of Appeal of Dusseldorf gave judgment for the plaintiff. The judgment was quashed for the following reasons.

Reasons

The courts below . . . held that the defendants in their negotiations had the serious intention to perform the contract which was invalid in form and that they only decided subsequently not to do so. The courts below held as a matter of law that it is contrary to good faith and against the sentiments of decency entertained by all fair and just people if the defendants now refuse to execute the conveyance contrary to their previous promises 'made in such a solemn form.'

In view of the statutory requirement of form laid down by para 313 section 1 [311b I] BGB neither the plea that a present violation of good faith (of present malice [references] had been shown nor any other violation of bonus mores can be said to have been made out.

As regards the first plea, the practice of the *Reichsgericht* [references] requires that a party who opposes a plea of lack of form must have been mistaken concerning the legal requirement of form and that this mistake was caused wilfully or negligently (para 276 BGB) by the other party to the transaction. The facts as found do not disclose the existence of these two prerequisites. Instead, the pleadings show that both parties were aware of the need to observe the formalities; no deception or even an attempt to this effect has occurred. Nor can the defendants be said to have acted culpably at the time when the disputed promises were made, seeing that the Court of Appeal has found that the defendants had the serious intention at that time to honour their promises and made the promises with this intention in mind. If it is correct that both parties knew of the need to observe the formalities, it is also due to the consent of the plaintiff that the formal recording of their agreement was postponed, and he must bear the consequences of this postponement without being able to shift the burden on the other party. The mistake concerning the legal need to observe the formalities which is necessary to support the plaintiff's complaint cannot be replaced by a factual mistake as to whether in the circumstances the promise, even though informal, would be kept. The complaint raised here, as developed by the practice of the *Reichsgericht* and as featuring in the broader context of blameworthiness at the conclusion of the contract (*culpa in contrahendo*) does not support the claim . . . [references].

A violation of good morals has not occurred either which might bind the defendant in virtue of para 826 BGB in conjunction with para 249 BGB to execute a conveyance (reference). If the promises 'upon the word of a nobleman' were inspired by the honest intention to perform them when they were made, the 'solemn declaration' alone cannot by itself be regarded as a violation of good morals; it can only be said to exist if the fact of these promises were denied in the course of the proceedings and their performance was refused. Since however the defence of lack of form in accordance with para 313 section 1 [311b I] BGB constitutes, in principle, an admissible plea of an existing legal remedy a violation of good morals which obliges the defendant to pay damages held to have occurred in the special circumstances of the case, can only be found in the present situation, if the previous attitude can be said to have created a legal obligation. This must be denied in the present case, having regard to the basic facts found by the Court of Appeal. It is the essence of a legal provision requiring form that if the form is not observed, a declaration of an intention to conclude a legal transaction is not binding. It does not bind, even if the intention is manifested by especially emphatic words in solemn form. The statutory requirement of form cannot be replaced by some other solemn expression chosen by the parties. The form required by the statute cannot be rendered superfluous by these means, and it is not possible by way of awarding damages to accord legal effects to an informal declaration, if the statute denies it any effect.

Accordingly the claim for the performance raised by this action, which cannot be supported on the ground of blameworthiness at the conclusion of the contract (*culpa in contrahendo*) cannot be justified either on the ground that good morals have been violated. The claim must therefore be rejected.

Case 22
BUNDESGERICHTSHOF (FIFTH CIVIL DIVISION) 27 OCTOBER 1967
BGHZ 48, 396

Facts

The defendant sold to the plaintiff a parcel of land by a contract in writing, but not before a notary or court, as required by para 313 [311b I] BGB. The plaintiff's claim that the defendant be condemned to convey the premises was allowed by the *Landgericht* Bielefeld and the *Oberlandesgericht* Hamm. A second appeal by the defendant was rejected for the following reasons.

Reasons

The plaintiff contends, first of all, that since both parties were aware of the need for the written contract of 20 June 1958 to be in proper form, and therefore had both knowingly failed to observe the statutory provisions on form, neither of them could assert that it was contrary to good faith to claim that the contract was void for lack of form. With this argument the plaintiff relies on the practice of the *Reichsgericht*, affirmed by this Division, that no party may raise the defence of malice, if the facts show only that knowingly or unknowingly the parties acted contrary to para 313 [311b I] BGB [references]. As the Court of Appeal has found, these prerequisites are not present in this case. It is true that the plaintiff, too, knew that the contract had to be in proper form, because he suggested that it should be drawn up by a notary. On the other hand, the defendant did not act knowingly in contravention of para 313 [311b I] BGB.

He attempted, and attempted successfully, to persuade the plaintiff not to insist on notarial form for inasmuch as by referring to his signature and thereby to his commercial reputation he declared that the written contract was equivalent to a notarial contract. In these circumstances and also because the managing partner of the defendant who had been his chief in the past, was in his eyes endowed with special authority, it was practically impossible for the plaintiff to insist on compliance with the statutory formalities.

The defendant contends further, as regards the substantive law, that the arguments set out in the decision if the court below do not rule out the possibility that the Court of Appeal was not aware of the difference between a harsh and an unbearable result, as developed by the practice of this Division. Since the Court of Appeal mainly supports its opinion that the defendant may not rely on the absence of form by a general reference to the practice of this court, the defendant's criticism provides the occasion for setting out this practice in brief. Faced with the question as to whether in certain circumstances the seller of land is bound according to good faith by a contract of sale which is void for lack of form, the practice is that this is only the case if not to recognise the contract as valid would lead to a result which would be unbearable for the purchaser and would not only affect him harshly [references]. These conditions were regarded as fulfilled by this Division, if one contracting party has given up his own way of life in reliance on the promise by the other party or has assumed a new way of life, which he would have to give up, if the existence of contractual ties were to be denied. Such is the case if a special fiduciary relationship or duty of protection exist (eg, in connection with a contract for a homestead) or if the seller who has spent the purchase price is no longer able to repay with the result that the purchaser cannot recover his money [references]. Moreover, the practice of the *Reichsgericht* already admitted the plea of bad faith, if the party which opposes the invalidity of the contract for lack of form was mistaken regarding the legal need to comply with formalities and if this mistake was caused culpably, or at least negligently, by the other party to the transaction [references], if the party who relies on the violation of the provisions on form has adopted an attitude which is incompatible according to good faith with his previous behaviour [reference] or if a party, albeit unintentionally, has induced the other party to disregard the need for the necessary conclusion of a contract which is formally invalid, with the result that the latter assumed that informal agreements were sufficient [references].

In the present case the principle expressed by the *Reichsgericht* [reference] must lead to the conclusion that according to good faith the defendant is bound by the written contract of 20 June 1958. As the Court of Appeal has found, the managing partner of the defendant, with whom the plaintiff had served his commercial apprenticeship, had brushed aside the doubts of the plaintiff at the time when the contract was concluded as to the need to call in a notary by pointing out with a certain pride that the contract bore his signature. When the plaintiff reminded him that every person is mortal, the representative of the defendant stated in addition that he had also signed the contract in the name of the defendant firm and that therefore the contract was equivalent to a notarial contract. Similarly the defendant stated also in its subsequent letter of 15 February 1963 addressed to the plaintiff that it was his custom to honour his obligations no matter whether made orally, in writing, or in notarial form. Thus the defendant has announced in such an emphatic manner his intention to perform the contract, which was invalid in form, by pledging his status and reputation and by referring to his business practice that he cannot resile free from contract without offending against good faith. Reliance subsequently on the formal invalidity of the contract, constitutes an admissible exercise of his right, irrespective of the fact that the plaintiff was not in error as to the formal requirements.

Case 23
BUNDESGERICHTSHOF (FIFTH CIVIL DIVISION) 21 APRIL 1972
NJW 1972, 1189

Facts

On 21 October 1963, the plaintiff and the defendant, a co-operative charitable housing corporation, concluded a written contract on (1) an option to buy a double-occupancy house, to be erected by the defendant on real property owned by the corporation, and (2) the purchase of two shares in the co-operative. The plaintiff paid in cash the purchase price of DM1000 for the shares in the co-operative and DM77,000 as part of the final price for the house, preliminarily estimated at DM78,500; he also made personal contributions which he values at DM2000, but which the defendant values at DM885.50. The plaintiff refuses to pay the remaining DM7047.58 which the defendant demands in respect of the final house price (DM83,900), until the defendant has removed defects in the building.
The plaintiff has lived in the house since August 1965.

The *Landgericht* and *Oberlandesgericht* have ordered the defendant to convey the title in the property and to allow the plaintiff to be registered in the land register. With this further appeal the defendant pursues his claim to have the plaintiff's claim rejected.

Reasons

I. As the *Oberlandesgericht* correctly stated, under para 313 [311b I] BGB the contract needed to be recorded by a notary and is null and void for formal defects (para 125 BGB). But this result is altogether unacceptable for the plaintiff. The general rule that un-notarised contracts on the transfer of real property are null and void must here exceptionally give way to the principle of good faith (para 242 BGB):

According to the established case law of this Division, such deviation from the general principle can only be tolerated in quite exceptional circumstances. The buyer of a private house who fails to have his purchase contract notarised can normally only claim monetary compensation, even where he has paid the full purchase price and has lived in the house for quite some time (judgment of this Division of 29 January 1965—V ZR 53/64, NJW 64, 812, 1014 = WM 65,315; see also judgment of this Division of 29 October 1965—V ZR 96/563, ZMR 66, 202 = WM 66, 89 and of 21 March 1969—V ZR 87/67, LM No 37 to para 313 BGB = WM 69, 692 = NJW 69, 1167). However, the court held this result to be intolerable where a party's very existence was at risk (see the references in the judgment of 21 March 1969 and of 27 October 1967—V ZR 153/65, BGHZ 48, 396 = NJW 68, 39). The Court of Appeal correctly held this case to be exceptional:

(. . .)

Indeed, this case shows exceptional features: The prospective buyer of the owner-occupied house, already elderly when concluding the contract and occupying the house, purchased it as home for his old age. He spent his entire savings, for him a quite considerable amount (ie, DM77,000 in cash, DM100 for shares in the co-operative and at least DM885 as own contributions = in total almost DM80,000) to acquire the house and had paid in cash the overwhelming part of the purchase price. In view of apparent defects in the building, the parties are in dispute over the remaining part of the purchase price of about DM7000. Contractual partner of the plaintiff, an ordinary craftsman and member of a co-operative, was the housing co-operative to which he belonged, a recognised charitable institution which he, given its organisational structure, trusted with the choice of a correct and legally sound form for their contract. This trust was furthermore underpinned by the following 'additonal' typewritten agreement inserted into the printed contract form:

'As a cost-saving exercise, both parties will forego having this contract notarised, but acknowledge that it is valid.'

This clause expressly declares the contract to be legally binding, which is different from the clause which the court considered in the above-cited judgment of 21 March 1969.

Under these circumstances, the fact that a prospective buyer is forced to relinquish his home and to look for another old-age residence very nearly equals losing the entire basis of his existence. Thus, in view of para 242 BGB, the *Oberlandesgericht* rightly held such a result to be insufferable.

The counterclaims brought by the further appeal will not succeed:

(a)–(d) . . .)

(e) The unacceptable consequences arising from the contractual nullity for lack of formal requirements are not removed by the fact that, according to the defendant, the plaintiff still owes part of the purchase price, amounting to some thousand Deutschmark, even if, in this context, this fact must be presumed to be correct (but see II and III).

II. In so far as the appeal court affirmed that under para 242 BGB the parties were bound by the provisional purchase contract despite its non-compliance with formal requirements, this court upholds this decision in respect of the extent to which the parties are bound. However, some reservations still remain.

From the binding nature of the contract the *Oberlandesgericht* concludesd that, as a matter of course, the plaintiff now had a claim against the defendant for the transfer of ownership The non-payment of the residual purchase price was held as no impediment, since the plaintiff had a right of retention because of various detected building defects (para 273 I BGB).

However, it must first be examined whether or not the contract, deemed to be valid, gives the plaintiff a right to conveyance. The result depends on an interpretation of the contract. Since a standard contract was obviously used which is or was in general use throughout the Land North-Rhine Westphalia and thus beyond the territorial jurisdiction of just one *Oberlandesgericht*, the Court of Further Appeal has jurisdiction for its own interpretation of that contract. The Court holds:

A contract for the purchase of an option to buy a house is intended as a mutually binding preliminary purchase contract. According to its wording, both parties are bound 'at a given time' to conclude a (notarised) purchase contract using a specific standard form (Part 2 of the preliminary contract); the plaintiff was only entitled to claim 'registration of transfer of ownership' 'once the envisaged final purchase contract was concluded and he had fulfilled all his obligations towards the building corporation as set out in the contract' (Part 3.3). In an earlier case, this Court interpreted a comparable preliminary contract to the effect that the applicant's claim for transfer of ownership did not already arise from the preliminary contract but rather only from the main contract which was still to be concluded (judgment of 30 June 1967—V ZR 104/64, BB 67, 1394). Where for instance a duty to transfer ownership existed by law as a result of a previously concluded agency contract (para 667 BGB), the Court interpreted clauses in preliminary contracts, using the same terminology, to mean that the due date of the claim for transfer of ownership was postponed until the main contract was concluded and all obligations from the purchase contract had been fulfilled. In respect of cases which, on the basis of para 242 BGB were acknowledged to be exceptional, the Court deemed the postponement of the due date to be irrelevant and acknowledged that the claim for transfer of ownership was thus due (judgment of 26 April 1968—V ZR 74/67, WM 68,1014 = BBauBl. 68, 571, and the contemporaneous judgments V ZR 75/67 and V ZR 76/67). As a result, this Division now holds that even in cases such as this one, where an obligation to transfer ownership does not arise until the preliminary contract has been concluded, an obligation nonetheless exists. The result is based on a sensible interpretation of the preliminary contract and the interests of the parties (paras 133, 157 BGB). The Court's previous considerations, originally only needed to be made in respect of the maturity of the claim, can now also be used strongly to advocate an interpretation of the preliminary contract to the effect that it gives rise to a claim for transfer of ownership

The Court must weigh up the basic interests of publicly-funded building corporations in a safe recovery of expenditures from prospective buyers and the danger of losses arising from a transfer of ownership against the interests, likewise to be protected, of applicants in becoming full owners of the real property as soon as the building work is completed, since their own funds have normally been invested prior to completion of the building and these funds often represent the entire family savings, accumulated over many years. The buyer thereby intends to save additional administrative costs and like expenditures and to be protected from heavy losses should the building corporation run into financial difficiulties. The building corporation's need for security is safeguarded by the contractual clause on the transfer of ownership whereby such transfer is postponed until a final contract has been concluded under the law of obligations, in which the final price and other outstanding payments are fixed.

Case 24
BUNDESGERICHTSHOF (FIRST CIVIL SENATE) 22 JUNE 1956
BGHZ 21, 102

Facts

The K Speditionsgesellschaft mbH (transport company) (KSG), a sister company of the defendant, commissioned the claimant (who carries on a haulage business) as haulier by arrangement with the Association of Road Traffic Hauliers (loading area distribution point) for the dispatch of certain goods to H. When the claimant's lorry and trailer were already laden, the claimant's husband, who was driving the vehicle, suffered a fatal accident while coupling the lorry and the trailer. The head of the Association, the haulier Q, acting on the claimant's behalf turned to an employee F of

KSG for the provision of a driver. F then contacted the defendant's employee S. The driver H employed by the defendant was thereon made available to the claimant and carried out the transportation with the claimant's vehicle. On the journey back, the vehicle broke down as a result of engine damage and had to be towed away.

The claimant seeks reimbursement of repair costs and loss of profit from the defendant. She considers that the defendant is liable for H as its assistant in performance (*Erfüllungsgehilfe*), but at least for the fact that it had provided an unreliable driver in breach of its duty.

(. . .)

The *Landgericht* ordered the defendant to pay part of the sum. The *Oberlandesgericht* rejected the claim. The claimant's appeal in law led to reference of the case back to the appeal court.

Reasons

I. (. . .)

II. On the other hand there are severe legal difficulties about the appeal court's assumption that the assignment of the driver H did not produce any legal obligation on the part of the defendant. (. . .)

The very concept of a favour assumes that the service in question will not be paid for. But the mere fact that the service will not be paid for does not permit the conclusion that it does not have the character of a legal transaction. The statutory regime about grace and favour transactions (eg, §§ 516, 598, 662 and 690 BGB) shows this. On the other hand, the giving of advice or a recommendation on a pure grace and favour basis produces no legal effect (§ 676 [§ 675 (2)] BGB). The unselfishness of the person acting does not in itself suffice to refute the assumption that legal relationships may possibly arise from the circumstances. Legal obligations for the person performing the service can arise from favours he promises or provides, although this is not inevitable.

If the person providing the service is obliged to provide it (§ 241 BGB) the effectuation of the service is bound to take place in the realm of legal transactions (in particular that of § 242). However, the absence of such an obligation does not in any way exclude the possibility of a favour exhibiting the character of a legal transaction [references omitted]. The defendant, in rejecting liability on the basis that it was not obliged to make the driver available, fails to recognise this.

A favour shown to someone will only have the character of a legal transaction when the person providing the service intends that his actions should be legally recognised [references omitted] and if he thus intends to create a legal commitment [references omitted] and the recipient has received the service in this sense. If this is not—whether because no intention to be bound can be assumed due to the type of favour involved or the circumstances under which it was given, or because such an intention was expressly or tacitly excluded—the matter cannot be assessed from the angle of a legal transaction. The question of whether there is an intention to be legally bound should not be decided according to some inward intention of the person giving the service which has not been made apparent. It should be determined by whether the recipient of the service should have concluded from the actions of the person providing the service that there was such an intention in the given circumstances according to the principle of good faith and having regard to business custom. It is therefore a question of how the actions of the person providing the service appear to the objective observer [references omitted].

The type of favour, its basis and purpose, its significance in a business and a legal sense (in particular for the recipient), the circumstances in which it is provided, and the state of the interests of the parties at the time can raise the favour above the level of pure factual events. These factors are therefore relevant when assessing the issue of an intention to be bound and the nature of any possible legal transaction. Favours in everyday life are as a rule outside the scope of legal transactions. The same applies to favours which are rooted in purely social relationships [references omitted]. The value of a item which has been entrusted to someone, the business significance of a matter, the recognisable interest of the recipient of the favour and the danger he might run—which he cannot recognise but the person providing the service can—if the service is performed defectively, can lead all to the conclusion that there was an intention to be legally bound [references omitted]. Information given within the framework of a business relationship must therefore be on the basis of a legal obligation of conscientiousness [references omitted]. If the person providing the service has himself a legal or business interest in the assistance given to the person receiving the favour, this will as a rule argue in favour of him being legally bound [references omitted]. As with contractual negotiations, liability is usually based in cases of this kind on the violation of a duty of care (*Sorgfaltspflicht*) which has arisen through establishment of legal relationships or a relationship of trust similar to a contract [references omitted].

If these legal principles are applied to the case to be decided, the result is as follows. The defendant was not obliged to provide a driver, and KSG, which had given the transportation order to the claimant, did not have such a duty. But when the defendant made a driver available at the request of the claimant or of the Association for Road Traffic Hauliers (which, according to the finding of the appeal court, was acting in her name) it had a legal duty to send a reliable driver. The favour requested by the claimant was something which concerned the economic and business activities of both parties. The appeal court judgment in its subsidiary reasoning speaks of an event in legal relationships between the road traffic business undertakings concerned. The claimant was in a predicament as a result of the death of her husband. If she found no driver, she not only lost profit from the freight business; she also possibly had to bear the costs—small though they were—of reloading the goods. It was obvious, and S could also recognise, that sensibly the claimant was not prepared to carry out the freight business whatever the circumstances, and even accepting the risk associated with the employment of an unreliable driver. For the claimant, the vehicle represented not only an object of quite substantial value, but also a significant source of income. The claimant could and was allowed to place confidence in the defendant allocating a reliable driver to her, and the defendant was not permitted to disappoint this reliance. If it had no appropriate driver available, it should have refused the claimant's request. If it did not want to do that, then it should at least have drawn the claimant's attention to the doubts which existed about the intended use of driver H, in order to escape legal consequences. (. . .)

The defendant is therefore responsible for the choice of a reliable driver.

III.

These considerations not only provide the basis for the defendant being legally bound, but they also answer, in substance, the question of the degree of fault-based liability.

(. . .) The view is put forward in the academic literature [references omitted] that liability for favours is limited, as a rule, to intention and gross negligence. Whether such a principle can be established can be left undecided. The statutory regime for fault-based liability in the case of gratuitous contracts is formulated in differing ways (§§ 521, 599 BGB: liability for gross negligence; § 690 BGB: liability for the care one takes in one's own affairs; § 662 of the BGB (with § 276 of the BGB), giving of information in the context of an existing binding relationship: liability for slight negligence). In the case of statutory liability for grace and favour journeys, the case law has expressly rejected the establishment of such a principle [references omitted]. The question of the scope of the liability in grace and favour relationships which are of legal significance must be decided according to the circumstances and the form which the individual case takes. Where the grace and favour activity springs from a relationship of trust, and the subject-matter concerned is of economic and business importance, as a rule, in correspondence with the statutory regime for liability in the case of a mandate (*Auftrag*), observance of the care necessary in human affairs is expected of the person providing the service. This is especially so if there is a particular business commitment on the part of the parties. The individual circumstances mentioned above, and the fact that the claimant's request was transmitted by the Association for Road Traffic Hauliers as the technically competent authority for both parties, justify the analogous application to the present case of the provisions about mandates applying for gratuitous contracts to procure services.

There is also no cause for limiting the liability under the statutory provisions by assuming a more or less fictional agreement to limit liability, as the claimant has stated through her expert representative Q that she asked for a reliable driver and in the circumstances was permitted to assume that the defendant would comply with this request. (. . .)

IV.

(. . .) Accordingly it can be assumed that the defendant, on the basis of an obligation arising from a legal transaction, could have only have sent H without violating the care necessary in human affairs if it had pointed out to the claimant the substantial doubts existing about his responsible control of the vehicle on a long-distance journey.

Case 25
RECIHSGERICHT (SIXTH CIVIL SENATE) 7 DECEMBER 1911
RGZ 78, 239

Reasons

According to the findings of the appeal court, the claimant, after she made various purchases in the defendant's department store, proceeded to the linoleum store in order to buy some linoleum flooring. She explained this to the assistant W, who was serving there, and selected from the samples which he produced the one which she wanted for the flooring. When he was obtaining the roll indicated by the claimant, W put two other rolls to one side. The rolls fell over, striking the claimant and her child, who had both come nearer, and dragging them both to the ground. The purchase of the flooring did not take place, because the fall put the claimant, as she said, in too much of a state.

The appeal court assumed, without any error in law, that there was fault on the part of W in relation to the claimant's accident because he had put the rolls on one side without securing them, instead of giving them lateral support, or leaving them against the wall. Because the area of their base was proportionately small, they were insufficiently stable. W could have foreseen that the claimant, as the purchasing public usually do, would come closer to the place where the goods she had asked him to produce to her were stored.

(. . .)

The appeal court's view that the defendant was liable under § 278 BGB for W's fault is, despite challenge by the appeal in law, not legally open to objection, and is in harmony with the case law of this senate. W entered into sale negotiations with the claimant on the defendant's behalf (§ 164 BGB and § 54 HGB (Commercial Code)). The claimant had asked for linoleum flooring, which she wanted to inspect and buy, to be produced to her. W complied with the request, in order to make a sale. Requesting production of the flooring and acceptance of the request were for the purpose of effecting a sale which is a legal transaction. This was no mere factual event, as a pure act of favour might be, but a legal relationship, similar in character to a contract, in preparation for the sale arose between the parties. It has produced legal obligations, in so far as a duty arose for both the seller and the would-be purchaser to observe the care required for the health and property of the other party in the production and inspection of the goods.

(. . .) in the case law of the *Reichgericht* it is recognised in numerous decisions that duties of care for the life and property of the other party can arise from a contractual or obligation relationship These have nothing to do with the legal nature of the relationship in the narrower sense, but necessarily follow from its factual form [references omitted].

The defendant used W to fulfil the obligation described, for the benefit of the would-be purchaser. It is therefore responsible for his fault. The legal concept in § 278 BGB is entirely appropriate here, (. . .). It would conflict with general feelings about the law if, in cases in which the employee of a business causes harm to the would-be purchaser through carelessness in producing goods for inspection, for testing, or to carry out an experiment or something similar, the proprietor of the business—with whom the would-be purchaser intended to conclude the purchase—was only liable under § 831 BGB and not unconditionally. The injured party would then, if exculpatory proof succeeded, be referred to the employee who in most cases has no money. (. . .)

Case 26
BUNDESGERICHTSHOF (EIGHTH CIVIL DIVISION) 28 JANUARY 1976
BGHZ 66, 51 = NJW 1976, 712 = JZ 1976, 776

Facts

The plaintiff, who at the time of the accident was fourteen years of age, went with her mother to a branch of the defendant's, a small self-service store. Whilst her mother, after selecting her goods, stood at the till, the plaintiff went round to the packing counter to help her mother pack the goods. In doing so she fell to the floor and suffered an injury which necessitated lengthy treatment. Alleging that she had slipped on a vegetable leaf, she sued the defendant for breach of his duty to provide safe access. The Court of Appeal having dismissed as time-barred the claim for damages for pain and suffering, the parties are now in dispute only on the question whether the defendant is obliged to compensate the plaintiff for her economic loss as well as prospective damage.

The *Landgericht* rejected the claim as time-barred. The Court of Appeal granted it—after deducting one-fourth for contributory fault. The defendant's further appeal was unsuccessful for these reasons.

Reasons

I. The Court of Appeal found as proved that the plaintiff slipped on a vegetable leaf lying on the floor near the packing counter and suffered injuries which necessitated the expenditure in question and may possibly lead to future loss. These findings disclose no legal error, they are in fact undisputed on appeal.

II. According to the Court of Appeal's opinion the defendant had not furnished the proof incumbent on him that he had taken all necessary care for the safety of movement in his store and that the accident could only be attributed to the fact that another customer had shortly before let a vegetable leaf fall to the floor. These findings also cannot be faulted legally. They conform to the settled case law of the BGH (NJW 1962, 31; cf also RGZ 78, 239) both on the duty of a shopkeeper to ensure safety of movement and on the reversal of the burden of proof required by para 282 [280 I 2] BGB in cases of claims for damages based on *culpa in contrahendo*. This point also is not contested on appeal.

III. The defendant therefore is liable—so continued the Court of Appeal—after taking the contributory fault of the plaintiff into account, for three-quarters of the existing and prospective loss, and that not only in delict, but also for fault in concluding contract, since in opening the self-service store he infringed the contractual duty of protection and care which he had undertaken to the plaintiff. Moreover, the plaintiff also has a claim for damages under a contract with protective effects towards a third party because her mother was during the accident preparing to contract with the defendant and the plaintiff was being included as an assistant within the scope of that contract-like obligation. For claims however arising from fault in concluding a contract the limitation period is thirty years, so that the claim was brought in good time.

IV. These explanations stand up to examination—at least in result. Admittedly the main line of the Court of Appeal's reasoning, that the defendant is directly liable to the plaintiff for fault in concluding the contract, irrespective of whether a contract with protective effects towards a third party needs to be brought into the picture, gives rise to doubts. Liability for *culpa in contrahendo*, which in cases like the present one is more favourable to a plaintiff than the general liability in delict for breach of the duty to provide safe access—because of the increased liability for employees (para 278 BGB in contrast to para 831 BGB), the longer limitation period (para 195 BGB in contrast to para 852 [repealed] BGB), and the reversal of the burden of proof (para 282 [280 I 2] BGB)—rests on a legal obligation created by way of supplement to the

written law. It arises from the process of bargaining for a contract and is largely independent of the actual conclusion or efficacy of a contract (BGHZ 6. 330, 333). The liability for a breach of the duties of protection and care arising from this obligation
finds, in cases of the present kind, its justification in the fact that the injured party
entered the other party's sphere of influence for the purpose of negotiating for a contract and can therefore rely on enhanced carefulness in the other party to the negotiation (cf also BGH NJW 1960, 720). This is borne out exactly by the present case in
which the mother entered the sales department of the defendant for the purpose of
making a purchase and in doing so had to subject herself to a risk involved in the
increased congestion, especially near the till, in a self-service store. It is however
always a presupposition of liability for *culpa in contrahendo* in this type of contract of
sale that the injured party enters the sales department with the purpose of contracting
or of entering into 'business contracts'—and therefore at least as a possible customer,
though perhaps without a fixed intention to purchase (cf BGH NJW 1962, 31). It need
not be decided whether it is enough, in view of the peculiarities of sale in a self-service
store, for a customer (when entering the sales department) to have intended at first
only to have a look at the objects offered and be possibly stimulated to buy or only to
make a preliminary comparison of prices with those in competing enterprises. In any
case there is insufficient justification for a contractual liability for *culpa in contrahendo*
stretching beyond liability for delict when the person entering the store never intended
to buy, perhaps because—leaving aside the shop-lifter mentioned by the court of
Appeal—he is sheltering from a shower or using the store as a way through to another
street or even only to meet other persons. The line may be difficult to draw in particular cases, above all because it depends on the difficult proof of unexpressed intention.
In the present case however it is beyond dispute that the plaintiff from the start did not
intend to make a contract herself but only to accompany her mother and help her in
buying. A direct application of liability for fault in concluding a contract with the
defendant is therefore excluded.

V. Nevertheless the appellate judgment is proved right in result, because it is supported by supplementary considerations.

1. If the plaintiff's mother had been injured in the same way as her daughter, there
would have been no objection to making the defendant liable for *culpa in contrahendo*—as is also clearly stated in the appeal. In that case nothing need be said about
the question, disputed in academic circles, whether in a self-service store the display of
the goods constitutes an offer and the contract of sale is concluded by the buyer's
accepting it in presenting the selected goods at the till—thus reserving a final decision
until that moment—or whether the display of the goods constitutes only an invitation
to make offers, which the customer for his part makes by showing them to the cashier
and the latter accepts by registering it on behalf of the self-service store. In any case
the general run of the reasons for the judgment, even though it contained no express
statement by the Court of Appeal, makes it obvious that at the moment of the accident the goods intended for the purchase had already been finally chosen and a legal
obligation already existed between the defendant and the plaintiff's mother justifying
liability for *culpa in contrahendo*.

2. It is on the legal obligation that the plaintiff can rely to justify her contractual
claim for damages. It accords with the long-standing case law of this Senate in
particular that in special circumstances even bystanders who do not themselves

participate in a contract are included in the protection afforded by it, with the consequence that although they have no claim to have the primary contractual duty performed, they are entitled to the protection and care offered by the contract and can
make good in their own name claims for damages arising from the breach of those
subsidiary duties . . . It is not necessary to consider here the theoretical question
whether such a contract with protective effects towards third parties, on which the
courts have proceeded hitherto, is derived from the supplementary interpretation of a
contract incomplete to that extent (paras 133, 157 BGB), or whether, as is increasingly
accepted in the literature, direct quasi-contractual claims arise on grounds independent of the hypothetical intention of the parties, perhaps from customary law, or on
the basis of legal developments by the courts. In any case, according to both views it
is essential that the contract, according to its sense of purpose and the requirements of
good faith, demands an inclusion of third parties in its sphere of protection; and that
one party to the contract can in honesty—and in a manner discernible by the other
party—expect that the cares and protection owed to it will be equally extended to a
third person. There is no good reason to exclude sales in general from this legally possible configuration as this is shown in particular by sales in shops to which buyers, in
certain circumstances, must enter the sphere of influence of the seller. And that is also
the view of the Sixth Senate in BGHZ 51, 91, 96.

3. Admittedly the inclusion of third persons in the sphere of protection of a contract—if the contract between contractual and delictual liability established by the
legislator is not to be destroyed or blurred—needs to be confined to narrowly
defined cases. Whether the mere fact that the customer makes use of a third person
in initiating and concluding a purchase in a self-service store is enough for the protected effect to be accepted as possible may be left undecided; for in the present case
it must be added that the plaintiff's mother was responsible for her daughter 'for
better or worse' (BGHZ 51, 91, 96) and therefore—and this should be known to the
defendant also—for that reason alone it could reasonably be inferred that the
daughter accompanying her should enjoy the same protection as herself. In such a
close family relationship the courts have always seen themselves justified in extending contractual protection.

4. That in the present case the sale was not concluded at the moment of the accident
is, in the result, unimportant. If one looks on the duty of protection and care as the
determining element of the legal obligation based on negotiating for a contract, and if
one considers that the other party owes this duty of care both before and after the
conclusion of the contract, the inclusion of third persons (who are equally worthy of
protection) in the obligation follows. Moreover, there would be no rational ground
for making the contractual liability depend on the chance of whether the negotiations
had already led to a contract when the damage occurred; that is impressively shown
by the present case, where the 'sale negotiations' had, in essence, been completed and
the conclusion of the contract—possibly subject to a delay on the mother's part in
completing it at the till, and for which the plaintiff's mother was not responsible—was
in any case imminent. The appellant's contention that a cumulation of liability for
culpa in contrahendo and inclusion of a third party in the protective effect of a contract
would lead to an unforeseeable widening of the risk on a seller, is directed in principle
against justification of both institutions in general. The danger of a flood of litigation,
which cannot be dismissed out of hand, has, as has already been explained, long

been taken into account by the courts, which have imposed strict requirements on the inclusion of third parties in the protective sphere of a contract. As regards to merely precontractual relations some reservation may be indicated. But in any case with so narrow a limitation there is no objection to an extension of protection if—as here— the person causing the damage could not reasonably have opposed any desire expressed by the mother, when negotiating for a contract, to have from the start the same protection expressly given to the child who was subsequently injured herself. Finally, in so far as the appellant contends that the long limitation period—combined with the reversal of the burden of proof—would intolerably worsen the evidentiary position of anyone sued for damages in such situations, the remedy must be found in laches (*Verwirkung*) of the existence of which there is no indication in this case.

Case 27
BUNDESGERICHTSHOF (SEVENTH CIVIL SENATE) 12 NOVEMBER 1986
BGHZ 99, 101 = NJW 1987, 639

Facts

In 1981, the claimant intended, together with his business partner at that time as shareholder of a company M which had not been entered in the trade register, to develop a chain of various types of fast food restaurant, and have it run under a franchise system. On 25 June 1981, M (as seller) and the defendants (a married couple) concluded a contract of sale in which the seller agreed to set up a restaurant 'Sch' completely ready for business in the shopping centre B-T which was under construction at that time, and the defendants agreed to pay a total price which was expected to be between DM200,000 and DM250,000 plus VAT. The defendants were to provide DM60,000 plus VAT, and the rest of the purchase price was to be financed. (. . .)

Reasons

I. (. . .)
II. (. . .)
1. It is necessary to proceed on the basis of the appeal court's (. . .) opinion that:
(1) The franchise contract is void as a whole (§ 138 (1) BGB). This is because of a number of provisions which benefit the franchiser unilaterally, and excessively limit the defendants' economic freedom of action, and for which they have not even been given only approximately reasonable compensation.
(2) The purchase contract is also included in this invalidity (§ 139 BGB).
This assessment which the appeal in law adopts, and which is not called in question by the reply to the appeal in law, does not reveal any legal error.
2. It follows from the invalidity of these contracts that the claimant has obtained the sum of DM87,800 paid to him by the defendants without legal grounds. He is obliged, in so far as he has been enriched, to hand over what he has received (§ 812 (1) sentence 1 BGB). (. . .)
3. The appeal court has correctly examined whether the defendants have benefited from anything which diminishes their claim to repayment—whether by way of

restitution for the enrichment or because of a counterclaim which could be set off by the claimant against their claim. (. . .)

(b) The claimant however did not have a restitutionary claim, as the appeal court recognised, if he was obliged because of fault committed in the contractual negotiations, to release the second defendant from his liability to pay the purchase price.

(aa) The appeal court's starting proposition was that it was possible for a person who concludes with his partner a contract drafted and used by him, but which is ineffective, to be liable for fault in conclusion of the contract. The reply to the appeal in law is wrong to challenge this. The case law has always taken the line on certain factual situations that, when a contract is ineffective, the party who is responsible for the ground of invalidity can be obliged to pay compensation because of fault in contractual negotiations [references omitted]. This can arise for instance in case of a failure to give an explanation about the absence of a valid authority under the law relating to communes (BGHZ 6, 330, 333), about the need for permission for a transaction in foreign exchange law (BGHZ 18, 248, 252 f), about the absence of statutory or contractual form for a contract (BGH judgment of 29 January 1965—V ZR 53/64 = NJW 1965, 812, 814; judgment of the senate of 19 April 1967—VII ZR 8/65 = WM 1967, 798), and about the invalidity of a transaction because of illegality (OLG Düsseldorf BB 1975, 201); or in a case where so-called 'hidden disagreement' is culpably induced (RGZ 104, 265, 267 f). (. . .) It cannot be otherwise in the case of the culpable use of a contract which is contrary to good morals under § 138 (1) BGB because of disadvantage to the other party [references omitted]. The objection made by the reply to the appeal in law that the liability of the user of a contract which benefits him unilaterally (and is therefore contrary to good morals under § 138 (1) BGB) should be limited to the definition in § 826 BGB cannot be followed. The basis of liability consists of the violation of the pre-contractual duty to show consideration to the other contracting party (BGH judgment of 28 May 1984), in whom trust in the existence of a contractual relationship is induced. Fault is admittedly required here, as in comparable cases of liability for pre-contractual conduct, but not intention to inflict harm in a manner contrary to good morals.

(bb) Likewise the objection in the reply to the appeal in law that the appeal court had not established fault by the claimant is unsuccessful in the end result. The deliberations of the appeal court to the effect that the claimant was responsible for the invalidity of the contract independently of whether he was conscious of the legal effects of the formulation of the contract are open to objection when expressed with this degree of generality. But the appeal court did not have to express itself more exactly in the present case, because the claimant had never said in any of his submissions that he did not realise and had no reason to realise the one-sided nature of the formulation of the contract in violation of good morals, and why he claimed this was so. The claimant had a duty of explanation here. In the area of liability for fault in contractual negotiations, the case law has admittedly not proposed any general reversal of the burden of proof of the kind contained in § 282 [§ 280 (1) sentence 2] BGB. But in relation to individual pre-contractual legal relationships, in particular in the case of the violation of duties of protection and explanation, it has divided the burden of explanation and proof according to areas of organisation or risk [references omitted]. The position is the same here. When deciding whether the claimant could regard the franchise contract as effective in spite of the numerous provisions which burdened the defendants unilaterally, the only potentially important matters (eg, possible legal advice to the claimant, or use of a pre-formulated contract recommended by a respected association) are ones on which the defendants cannot be expected to make factual statements, but on which the claimant must be in a position to give information. In the absence of explanations of this kind, the appeal court could assume that the claimant was responsible for the pre-contractual violation of duty.

(. . .)

Case 28
BUNDESGERICHTSHOF (FIFTH CIVIL SENATE) 20 JUNE 1952
BGHZ 6, 330

Facts

In 1946 the claimant, a scrap metal company, contacted the defendant, a borough council, in order to lease an industrial site. By letter of 28 June 1946, the chief executive of the borough council told the claimant that the site, measuring about 10,00 square metres, was 'awarded' to the claimant at an annual leasehold rent of RM0.25 per square metre, subject to the town council's approval. The defendant drafted a leasing contract which was unanimously accepted at the planning committee's meeting of 5 July 1946 and sent to the claimant on 9 July. On 22 July 1946, the claimant sent his own draft contract, on which the defendant, by letter of 30 July 1946, sent the claimant a lease contract 'in its final form' with the remark that the town council refused any amendments to it; the claimant was asked to sign the contract and to send it back to the chief executive of the town; on approval by the town council, the claimant was to be informed and to receive back the official copy of the contract. Thereon the claimant signed the submitted lease contract. On 23 August 1946, the town council approved the lease contract with the restriction that ' no right of pre-emption was to be granted, the duration of the lease—previously fixed for 20 years—was to be reduced and the defendant's liability for damages created from a drop in the canals' water level was to be excluded.'

With the defendant's approval, the claimant started to use the site to deposit scrap The parties then discussed repairs to the connecting rail siding and the installation of necessary points. With the defendant's approval, the claimant obtained the points; the defendant helped in providing the federal railway with wood in exchange for the necessary sleepers.

By letter of 18 November 1947 the claimant sent the defendant confirmation that the defendant's building supervisor had given his permission to start with the depositing of scrap. At the beginning of April 1948, the claimant was informed by the defendant's town planning officer K that a large company was interested in the site. By letter of 5 April 1948 the claimant pointed out that he had taken the site on a lease and asked 'pro forma' to sign the lease contract. The defendant rejected the view that specific agreements had actually been reached and then told the claimant that it had not leased any site to the claimant nor given permission for its use; thereafter, in its council meeting of 21 May 1948, the defendant finally refused to lease the site to the claimant and ordered him to vacate the site.

The claimant demands damages from the defendant for *culpa in contrahendo*.

The *Landgericht* has rejected the claim; the *Oberlandesgericht* held the claim for damages to be justified in principle. The defendant's further appeal is unsuccessful.

Reasons

I. The Court of Appeal held that:

A valid lease contract was not concluded, since the formal requirements set out in para 37 II of the DGemO (German Borough Council Order) (in its version valid for the British Zone, Amtsbl. der MilReg. No 7, p 127 et seq) had not been met and any reference to the principles of good faith cannot lead to a different result. However, statutory bodies are not exempt from liability for *culpa in contrahendo*. The town council had approved the lease contract between the parties and the town's building inspector S had informed the claimant, based on a corresponding authorisation from the town council, that the contract was to be deemed to have been concluded if the claimant were to renounce any right of pre-emption and agreed to a reduction of the period of lease. Once the claimant's owner had signed a corresponding lease contract, S. declared that the claimant could now start using the site. The defendant's constitutionally appointed representative bodies had thus been bound to issue a contract complying with all formal requirements. The defendant culpably failed to inform the claimant that the contract had not been finally concluded. Instead, and with the obvious intention of not being legally bound, in order if possible to offer the site to a more suitable party, it had delayed giving the contract its final form. By the defendant's statements that the matter was in order and the lease contract was deemed to be concluded, the defendant had created the claimant's trust in the fact that the lease contract had indeed become legally binding and that the written form was of no further legal significance. According to the defendant's statements and behaviour, the claimant relied, and should have been able to rely, on the fact that the lease contract was to be concluded. By the fact that the defendant had unrestrictedly permitted the claimant to start with the depositing of scrap and left him with the difficult task of constructing the sidings leading to the leased site, the claimant must have got the impression that this was done as part of the execution of the lease contract which required these operations to be carried out.

The claimant has at least suffered damages from the unnecessary expenditures on levelling the site. Only during a final procedural assessment of damages can it be established whether this also applies to the transport of the scrap

II.

1. The further appeal erroneously disputes that statutory bodies are at all liable for *culpa in contrahendo*. The further appeal is correct in so far as it holds that legal provisions imposing special requirements for acts of statutory bodies are more than formal requirements, and are rather intended to protect these statutory bodies from rash and dangerous acts of persons acting for these bodies by restricting the authority of these persons [references]. (. . .) On the other hand, there is insufficient reason for safeguarding statutory bodies from any kind of liability for *culpa in contrahendo*. (. . .) Liability for *culpa in contrahendo* is a form of liability which is based on a statutory obligation created in addition to those listed in the legislation and which has its origin

in the start of contractual discussions which require that both parties observe the usual care in their dealings with each other. (. . .)

3. The statement made by the witness S that the lease contract should be deemed to have been concluded, and that the claimant could start to use the site once he had agreed to the amendments to the lease contract, was in line with the authorisation which the town council had given to the witness. But in fact the contract had not become valid because of failure to conform to the formal requirements of para 37 II DGO, a fact which both the witness and the town council should have known. Instigating such an error constitutes fault as far as the town council and the witness S are concerned; and the defendant is vicariously liable under paras 31, 89, 278 BGB, while any possible obligation which the town bodies may have to execute the town council's resolution by concluding a contract complying with all formal requirements is not an obligation towards the claimant and is thus irrelevant for the question of fault. The claimant has thus a claim for damages against the defendant, although the claimant cannot demand, as set out above, to be put in a position which would have existed if the contract had in fact been concluded. The claimant makes no such demand. The claimant can however request to be compensated for the damage suffered from relying on the validity of the contract.

Case 29
BUNDESGERICHTSHOF (TENTH CIVIL DIVISION) 12 JUNE 1975
NJW 1975, 1774

Facts

The plaintiff claimed damages on the ground that the defendant had failed to conclude a licensing agreement with the plaintiff, although a director of the defendant had made a promise to this effect.

The District Court rejected the claim, but the Court of Appeal of Hamm allowed it in principle. A second appeal by the defendant was unsuccessful for the following reasons.

Reasons

I.
2. (a) The Court of Appeal has allowed, in principle, a claim by the plaintiff for damages on the ground of blameworthy conduct in concluding a contract. It held that by the manner of his negotiations the defendant's director had caused justified expectations that a licensing would be concluded with the plaintiff. The reliance of the plaintiff on this expectation deserved protection.

(b) The appellant has objected . . . that the Court of Appeal had applied too low a standard in gauging the expectations in reliance on the negotiations for a contract resulting in liability to compensate the damage suffered in reliance on the conclusion of a contract, the negotiations for which had been broken off.

3. The basis of liability for blameworthy conduct in negotiating a contract is to be found in disappointed expectations [reference]. Looked at from this angle, if negotiations for a

contract are broken off without good reasons, the party breaking off the negotiations may be liable in damages, if by his conduct he has previously raised or maintained the expectation that a contract was certain to be concluded [references]. This obligation is the consequence of the liability for the effects of a situation of confidence towards another who has been induced to believe that the proposed contract will become a reality [reference]. In so far as the proposed contract was to be concluded with a company still to be formed, it must depend on the circumstances whether, in the light of the negotiations, a company formed subsequently could expect that the proposed contract would be concluded with it. It is true that in such a situation the other party may have an interest to reserve its full power decision until he has obtained more detailed information about the character and composition of the company to be formed. On the other hand, if a new company is to be formed by the contracting party, the other party may allow his co-contractor a certain freedom of action and curtail his own liability of decision, if he can be sure that the contract will be concluded. The Court of Appeal has held that the latter is the case. This finding of fact . . . binds the present court. It justifies the conclusion . . . that the plaintiff has claims based on the blameworthy conduct in the conclusion of the contract, having regard to the situation of confidence established towards him.

Case 30
BUNDESGERICHTSHOF (FIFTH) CIVIL SENATE) 29 MARCH 1996
NJW 1996, 1884 = JZ 1997, 467

Facts

The claimant had rented rooms on the ground floor and in the cellar of a house in B Street in L for a printing business. In the summer of 1989, the defendant acquired the land. To achieve a more economic use, he planned to alter the building to increase the size of an extension, and to divide it into shared ownership. In this connection negotiations between the parties took place in early 1991 about the sale of the rooms used by the claimant and further rooms at the price of DM750,000. This gave rise to the claimant carrying alterations from the end of April 1991 to February 1992. In October and December 1991, conversations took place between the parties about a date for authenticating the sale. The sale fell through in the end, because the defendant was only prepared to proceed at the price of DM1,000,000. After the defendant terminated the letting, the claimant vacated the property in the summer of 1992. Against the defendant's rent demand for the period from April 1992, the claimant set a claim for reimbursement of the costs of his building measures, the costs for moving and repair of machines because of the defendant's building measures and, with these in mind, overpaid rent in the sum of 20,150 DM—after reduction. By his claim he demanded payment of the balance of DM154,716.34 from the defendant. He claimed that the parties were of one mind about the sale. Its authentication was not to take place until late in 1991, but only because the defendant wished to avoid tax disadvantages. The claimant's building measures had taken place with the defendant's consent. The defendant was liable for the reimbursement of the costs which had arisen from this on the ground of unjustified enrichment, and fault in the contractual negotiations. The defendant denied the existence of agreement about the sale and his consent to the claimant's works, and counterclaimed for the remainder of the rent, compensation for use, and reimbursement of costs for the removal of part of the alterations.

The *Landgericht* allowed the claim by a partial judgment about the principles. The defendant's appeal was unsuccessful. By his appeal in law he seeks rejection of the claim. The claimant applies for rejection of the defendant's appeal in law. The defendant's appeal in law has not been accepted by the senate in so far as it is directed against the claimant's entitlement, which has been established in principle, to reduction of the agreed rent in a total sum of DM20,150. In other respects the appeal in law led to quashing and reference back.

Reasons

I. (. . .)

II.

1. (a) Because of contractual freedom, every contractual partner has the right until conclusion of the contract to walk away from the contract under consideration. Expenditure which is made in the expectation of conclusion of the contract is therefore in principle incurred at one's own risk [references omitted]. Only if the conclusion of the contract can, in the light of the negotiations between the parties, be assumed to be certain, and expenditure for the implementation of the contract is made before its conclusion in reliance on this, is it possible for this expenditure to be reimbursable by the partner in the negotiations on the ground of fault in contractual negotiations, if he later declines to conclude the contract without any valid ground [references omitted]. A duty founded in this way to compensate for loss incurred through reliance amounts however to an indirect compulsion to conclude the contract. This compulsion runs counter to the purpose of the formal provisions of § 313 sentence 1 [§ 311b (1)] BGB, according to which a commitment without the observation of form is to be prevented because of the objective peculiarity of the subject-matter of the contract [references omitted]. In the area of legal transactions which must be authenticated under § 313 sentence 1 BGB, breaking off contractual negotiations, the consequence of which could be assumed to be certain, by a partner to the negotiations therefore does not trigger claims to compensation for loss, even if there is no valid ground for breaking off [references omitted].

(b) The invalidity which results from a violation of the formal provisions of § 313 sentence 1 [§ 311b (1)] BGB is however displaced, if it simply cannot, in all the circumstances, be reconciled with the principle of good faith, for example because it endangers the existence of the other party to the contract [references omitted] or because claiming invalidity represents a particularly serious violation of the duty of good faith [references omitted].

It is also necessary to proceed on the basis of these principles when deciding whether a partner to negotiations is obliged to reimburse the expenditure of the other party on the grounds of *culpa in contrahendo* when contractual negotiations are broken off. (. . .) In so far as this follows from the defendant's conduct being a particularly serious breach of good faith, only an intentional violation of the duty of good faith can as a rule be considered as a basis for a claim to compensation for harm under *culpa in contrahendo*, as it amounts to a person pretending to be ready to conclude a contract when he is not [references omitted].

That has so far not been established. (. . .) The quashing of the disputed judgment gives the parties in this respect an opportunity to make further submissions.

(c) A person pretending to be prepared to conclude a contract on certain conditions, in particular at a certain price, when he is not is, on the principle of good faith, comparable with the case where a partner to negotiations was at first so prepared, and said so, but in the course of negotiations changed his mind without revealing it [references omitted]. This is especially so if the potential seller had said he was in agreement with the extension and alteration works proposed by the person interested in buying. In all such cases, the statement of final preparedness to contract on certain conditions communicates the impression of a special negotiation position to the partner to the negotiations. This exposes him to the increased danger of disadvantageous disposition of his wealth. This special position of danger creates a relationship of increased reliance, which obliges the person conducting the negotiations to have greater regard to his partner's interests. This also gives rise to an obligation to protect the partner from making a mistake about the (continued) existence of a stated final preparedness to conclude the contract on certain conditions, if this does not exist (any longer).

The defendant may have violated such a duty of explanation here. He has claimed in another connection that in late 1991 it had become evident that the cost calculated for his alteration and extension proposals of DM1,500,000 was insufficient, and it would in fact amount to about DM3,000,000. Therefore he could not keep to his original calculation. But he alleges that, from this point in time onwards, the basis of the claimant's assumption that the contract would come into existence between the parties had disappeared. This was the latest date at which the defendant's preparedness to enter into the contract (assumed as certain by the claimant following the negotiations) was present. The uncertainty which had now arisen remained concealed from the claimant, but the defendant knew about it. His prior conduct and his knowledge of the claimant's current works therefore obliged him to inform the claimant without delay of the change in his ideas about price, in order to give the claimant the opportunity to refrain from further investment in the alteration and extension of the rooms made over to him. In this respect also there has been no submission which enables an exact chronological determination and classification of the expenditure.

2. Contrary to the view of the appeal in law, the claimant's claim to compensation for loss should not be reduced on the basis of contributory fault, in so far as it is based on expenditure which the claimant made before he learnt of the change in the defendant's asking price. The claimant's expenditure in reliance on the contract coming into existence is only to be reimbursed if the defendant has represented conclusion of the contract as certain in spite of his reservations, and has therefore acted deceitfully. Contributory fault on the claimant's part (which would in any case be assessed as negligent) would be overridden by the defendant's intentional behaviour [references omitted].

On the other hand, the defendant is not responsible for the expenses which the claimant has incurred after he could no longer be certain that the proposed contract about the shared ownership would be concluded. Investment which he made after the defendant had revealed the increase in his asking price should therefore not be reimbursed. It was not based on reliance on the contract coming into existence, but on mere speculation. In this respect also the necessary categorisation of the expenditure asserted by the claimant is lacking. (. . .)

Case 31
BUNDESGERICHTSHOF (SEVENTH CIVIL SENATE) 5 APRIL 1971
BGHZ 56, 81

Facts

The married couple, St, had a six-storey business and residential complex erected in H, but before it was completed they ran into financial difficulties. After calling a meeting of creditors, they commissioned the defendant, a financial and real estate agent, to look after further financial issues in relation to the building, as well as the sale of the business units and the residential accommodation. They gave him comprehensive powers. Among other things, it was agreed that further building works were only to be carried out with his agreement. But in the ensuing period the client and his architect made further efforts to allocate these works. After several tradesmen had stopped their activities, they obtained an offer from the claimant for the continuation of the metal building work. The defendant learnt about this and let the intended written contract be signed by the client. The claimant carried out the work he had taken over, but did not receive any payments.

The claimant now claims compensation from the defendant for the loss (which it calculates as totalling 19,007.58 DM) which it alleges it has suffered because, in view of the consent given by the defendant, it relied on being able to take on the work to be carried out without any guarantee of payment for it.

The *Landgericht* rejected the claim. The *Oberlandesgericht* allowed it. The defendant's appeal in law was unsuccessful.

Reasons

I. (. . .)
II.
1. The initial position taken in law by the appeal court is in harmony with the consistent case law of the *Bundesgerichtshof*. According to this, the duties from the statutory obligation relationship based on the initiation of contractual negotiations by an agent apply in principle to the person the agent represents. But under special circumstances the agent himself must also be responsible for the violation of these duties, in particular such as a duty of explanation. This occurs if special reliance was placed on him personally by the other contracting party, or if he had an economic interest of his own in the conclusion of the transaction. (. . .)
3. The decisive issue is therefore whether the principles developed by the case law and doctrine about an agent's own liability from the angle of fault in contractual negotiations may be applied to the defendant because he has claimed personal trust from the claimant to a special extent, and has thereby influenced the contractual negotiations.
(a) In these cases letting an agent be liable for his own fault on conclusion of a contract appears to be justified when he has gone beyond the normal trust in negotiations which always exists in the initiation of business relationships—or at least ought to exist. This is because he has thereby offered the partner in the negotiations an additional guarantee by himself personally (and possibly even the only such guarantee) for the existence and fulfilment of the prospective legal transaction; and this guarantee

was a significant factor in the other party's decision. Such special reliance placed in the agent can, for instance, be based on his special technical knowledge of the subject matter of the contract. But it can also be based on his personal reliability, or the power which he has to influence the implementation of the contract. This is particularly at issue when serious doubts exist about the financial capacity of the principal (see eg, BGH LM no 4 at § 276 (Fa) BGB). Above all, this special case of reliance must be applied to a person who appears as a sort of financial adviser who seeks to bring the most diverse interests into harmony with one another.

This kind of claim to personal trust by the agent does not however in any way assume that the agent conducts the negotiations himself. He can also act through a sub-agent, who is then to be regarded as his assistant in performance (*Erfüllungsgehilfe*) in the sense of § 278 BGB for possible pre-contractual duties applying to him. The senate has already decided this in a case in which an architects' association had engaged a project manager who negotiated with the tradesmen for the removal of defects (LM no 37 on § 278 BGB). It is thus decisive that the special situation of trust has been created by the agent himself, or is in some way attributable to him, and that it has decisively influenced the conduct of the other negotiating partner.

(b) But then it is impossible to see why, according to the principles mentioned, liability should only attach to the person who claims the special trust of the negotiating partner as required in the case law by appearing as agent of a party in the negotiations. There are no effective objections to applying these principles also to the adviser of a contracting party who keeps himself in the background during the negotiations, and only establishes his own relationships with the other negotiating party indirectly via the negotiating partner who is his client. This occurs when he consents to the intended conclusion of the contract, his declaration to this effect is brought to the knowledge of the other party, and it is the determinative factor inducing him to conclude the contract.

This is because from the viewpoint of the other party to the contract, it makes no difference whether he was induced to conclude the contract by special reliance on an agent of the other party to the negotiations who met him face to face, or whether he relied on the agreement to the intended transaction, produced by his direct contracting partner, of an adviser appointed by him. In both cases the co-operation of a third party who has a particular claim to personal trust has decisively influenced the decision of the other party.

But from the viewpoint of the third party the position appears to be the same. Whether he conducts the negotiations himself, or he leaves them to his client with his own express agreement to the intended conclusion of the contract, he always—if he is in the position of trust required by the case law—has to take into account the possibility that the other party to the negotiations will orientate himself to his, the third party's, attitude. This is especially true if it appears to be the only determinative one in all the circumstances.

A third party may be involved in the conclusion of a contract and he may know (or should know) that particular reliance is placed in him by the negotiating partners. They may both make their actions depend on his agreement. It would not be reconcilable with the principle of good faith if he could simply withdraw from his consequential responsibility by not appearing as his client's agent, but letting the client conclude the contract himself with the third party's express consent.

In such cases, the interests are the same so the legal assessments must be the same. Therefore the duties from the obligation relationship based on the initiation of contractual negotiations apply to an adviser of a contracting party who has a particular claim to the trust of the other party, and on whose decision in the given circumstances the conclusion of the intended legal transaction finally depends. It does not matter whether he appeared as agent of one party in the contractual negotiations or whether he merely gave his agreement to the conclusion of the contract and this was communicated to the other party to the negotiations.

4. The appeal court assumes that the defendant, after the further financial supervision of the extensive and ailing building project had been transferred to him, acquired a special position of trust not only as against the client, but in the relationship with the building tradesmen and the client's creditors. There is no objection to this on legal grounds. In this connection the persons involved were entitled to assume that the defendant would cope with his task of overcoming the financing difficulties which had arisen so far and effecting completion of the building work with all the care to be expected, but also in such cases required, from a financial expert, which he is.

Full approval should therefore be given to the appeal court's view that all the persons involved were entitled to rely on the defendant agreeing to further building works only if he had previously scrupulously examined them, found them to be necessary and regarded them as financially achievable in the ordinary course of events. For the building tradesmen and the claimant who were to co-operate in the completion of the building, the defendant was therefore much more important than the client and his architect. (. . .)

5. The appeal court was therefore correct to assume that the duty to explain all the circumstances which were of substantial importance for the claimant's decision to take on the works, which would otherwise only have applied to the direct contracting partner (the client in this case), applied also to the defendant himself as a result of the special trust which the claimant showed towards him personally. According to the recognised case law [references omitted], the facts which should be revealed under the principle of good faith include the probability of hindrances to fulfilment of the prospective contract, or its fulfilment within a time limit. (. . .)

Case 32
BUNDESGERICHTSHOF (SECOND CIVIL SENATE) 17 JUNE 1991
NJW-RR 1991, 1241

Facts

The claimant was the owner of the motor yacht 'G VI' which had been bought at a price of DM40,000. In September 1985, he placed an 'application for total watersports insurance' with the defendant insurance company with which he maintained a number of other insurances. A comprehensive insurance policy for an insured sum of DM400,000 made out 'by authority of the companies involved' by P, a specialist broker for yacht insurance, was forwarded to him. The claimant paid the premiums due to the firm P After carrying out comprehensive alteration works, the claimant asked the defendant in July 1987 for an employee to visit him. He told this employee that he wanted to change the fully comprehensive insurance to partially comprehensive, and to increase the insured sum to DM 1 million. The defendant's employee S then inserted 'HP' at the start of a form provided by the defendant headed 'Notice of Amendment,' noted the claimant's wishes for amendment, inserted 'immediately' for the date of commencement of the insurance, and had this form signed by the claimant. In August 1987, S telephoned the claimant twice to tell him that the firm P needed a valuation or shipyard opinion about the value-enhancing works. The claimant applied for this, but before it was obtained, the yacht was burnt out. The claimant received DM400,000 for the fire damage from the firm P which, in the name of the insurer which it represented, refused further payments. In the current action, the claimant has demanded payment of DM600,000 from the defendant on the ground that, even it if was not under a duty to him as contracting partner to enter into a contract, it should be responsible as negotiator for the fact that he had no temporary cover, as no proper explanation had been given.

The *Landgericht* rejected the claim but the *Oberlandesgericht* allowed it. The defendant's appeal in law led to restoration of the judgment of the *Landgericht*.

Reasons

1. The *Landgericht* and the *Oberlandesgericht* have denied the existence of a comprehensive insurance contract between the parties. (. . .)
2. The appeal court was wrong to find that the defendant had a liability of its own as negotiator of the comprehensive insurance, which is the only kind of liability that accordingly falls to be considered.

(a) According to the consistent case law of the *Bundesgerichtshof*, the duties arising from the statutory obligation relationship based on initiation of contractual negotiations by an agent apply in principle to the person the agent represents, and only exceptionally and in special circumstances to the agent as well [references omitted]. Even if a contract for a comprehensive ship insurance already existed in the present case, and it was therefore not a question of initiating a contract for the first time, these principles must nevertheless be applied. This was because the actions of the defendant, instigated by the claimant, had the objective of concluding another insurance contract—which among other things would be a partial instead of a fully comprehensive insurance, and for which the insured sum would be raised from DM400,000 to DM 1 million.

The exceptional cases in which the agent's own liability can arise are usually so described as to require that the agent has a special economic interest in the conclusion of the contract, or that he has laid claim to personal trust to a special extent [references omitted]. Such exceptional cases have been found to be present on many occasions in the case law in respect of prospectus liability [references omitted] and used car dealers [references omitted]. Otherwise the case law of the highest courts is in general restrained, which takes account of the exceptional character of the liability [references omitted].

(b) The defendant had no special economic interest in the conclusion of the contract between the claimant and the insurance pool represented by the firm P.

The appeal court's starting point, that not every economic interest—and in particular not one which is merely indirect—suffices for personal liability, is admittedly correct. Therefore it has repeatedly been stated that, for example, the interest which the person acting has in obtaining a commission cannot fulfil these prerequisites [references omitted]. What is necessary is a relationship to the subject-matter of the contract which is so close that the person negotiating is, so to speak, acting in his own affair: that he is to be regarded as the economic master in the transaction [references omitted].

That cannot be assumed from the findings of the appeal court in the present case. A possible interest by the defendant in obtaining a commission—on which the claimant has partly relied at second instance—is not sufficient for this. In this connection, it has not even been established whether the defendant has received a commission from the comprehensive insurance pool at all. (. . .)

(c) The appeal court's view that the defendant laid claim to special personal trust should also not be followed. In this respect the appeal court's requirements are insufficient. It does not suffice for the personal liability arising on this basis that the contracting partner *places* special trust in the person negotiating. The case law of the highest courts requires that trust be *claimed* by the person negotiating [references omitted]. The agent must therefore by his conduct influence the other person's decision. A general allusion to the specialist knowledge which he had does not suffice here [references omitted]. The agent must provide, over and above the general trust which arises in negotiations, an additional guarantee coming from him personally for the seriousness of the transaction and its fulfilment [references omitted]. These special prerequisites are not present as a rule in respect of employees [references omitted] and insurance agents [references omitted].

In the present case, the defendant did no more than respond to the claimant's intimation that he wanted to change an insurance, which he did not describe in any more detail, by sending an employee to his office to obtain his wishes about amendment and to forward the 'Notice of Amendment' to the broker acting for the insurance pool. Even if the claimant had turned to the defendant in relation to all his insurance affairs, this would not give rise to a claim to special trust in the sense of the case law mentioned above. (. . .)

Case 33
BUNDESGERICHTSHOF (SEVENTH CIVIL SENATE) 5 OCTOBER 1961
BGHZ 36, 30

Facts

In 1958 the plaintiff building contractors did the gross construction work for a dwelling on land belonging to the defendant. They now sue for DM6134.60, the price of the work done.

The dispute is whether there was any contract between the parties for this work.

In the written 'building contract' to which the defendant was a signatory, his contractor was described as 'Idealheim, Hans W, Architect.' Idealheim was entered as a limited company in the commercial register after the contract was formed.

The contract recited, *inter alia*, that the defendant commissioned Idealheim to build to build a two-family house at a ready-to-move-in price, guaranteed by Idealheim, of DM32,000.

According to the defendant, this contract showed that his only legal relations were with Idealheim; it was Idealheim that had commissioned the plaintiffs to build the house, acting in their own name through architect W. The plaintiffs should accordingly have claimed payment from Idealheim.

The plaintiffs counter by saying that they negotiated the building contract with W, acting as the defendant's architect and representative, and that the defendant had empowered him to do so.

The *Landgericht* dismissed the claim, but the *Oberlandesgericht* allowed it in major part. The defendant appeals, and the case is remanded.

Reasons

I.

1. According to the Court of Appeal, the plaintiffs have no contract claim; they did however have a claim for unjustified enrichment.

According to the Court of Appeal, no contractual rights accrued to the plaintiffs from their negotiations with the architect W, either against the defendant or against Idealheim (or indeed against W personally). This is because the plaintiffs believed they were dealing with the defendant through W. As there was no evidence that W had intended to act as the defendant's representative, there was a misunderstanding which prevented the formation of any contract. Since there was no contract, the enrichment conferred on the defendant by the building work executed by the plaintiffs was without legal ground.

2. These reasons are insufficient for holding the defendants liable to the plaintiffs in unjust enrichment.

(a) The Court of Appeal accepts that the defendant had a valid contract with Idealheim, whereby the latter was to build a dwelling for him ready for occupation and he was to pay Idealheim the stipulated sum.

Now for an enrichment claim under para 812 BGB there must be a direct transfer of value between the plaintiff and defendant. One the stated hypothesis, that is lacking in this case. It is true that the defendant's land is enhanced in value by the plaintiff's work, but he is not enriched at their expense, because for him the enhancement is not the result of the plaintiffs' activity but of Idealheim's performance of its contract with him, under which he became Idealheim's debtor for the price.

If the defendant had a valid contract with Idealheim which obliged him to pay Idealheim, it is irrelevant to him whether or not there is a valid contract between Idealheim and the plaintiffs, whom Idealheim commissioned to do the work. Even if the contract between the plaintiffs and Idealheim is invalid, Idealheim is still the only person the plaintiffs can sue; the suit would have to be an enrichment claim, Idealheim's enrichment consisting of its being freed from its contractual obligation to the defendant to the extent that the building was completed [references omitted].

(b) The only way the plaintiffs would have an enrichment claim against the defendant would be if nullity affected both the relations between the plaintiffs and Idealheim and the relations between Idealheim and the defendant; this is so whenever a benefit is conferred through an intermediary [RG JW 1945, 2459; other references omitted]. No such double nullity has been established by the Court of Appeal.

For this purpose it is unnecessary to decide whether misunderstanding did in fact prevent the formation of a contract between the plaintiff's and Idealheim, although, as is shown below under II. 1, the Court of Appeal was wrong in law to hold that it did.

But certainly the findings of the judgment in question afford no basis for holding that the contract between Idealheim and the defendant was void or avoided, so as to relieve the defendant of his obligation to pay Idealheim.

II. But the plaintiffs' claim is not necessarily unfounded just because no enrichment claim lies.

1. The Court of Appeal's reasons for holding that no contractual claim arose because of the misunderstanding are also affected by error.

The Court of Appeal finds that the plaintiffs believed they were contracting with thee defendant through W as his representative. Further details in the judgment indicate that the plaintiffs could conclude that W was acting for the defendant from the way he behaved and the role he played. W's declarations must therefore be construed as the declarations of a representative. Now whether a person is acting as a representative or in his own name depends, as always when it is a matter of construing declarations of intention in legal transactions, on the objective meaning of his declarations, ie what in all good faith they meant to the recipient. The Court of Appeal made everything turn on whether W was minded to act as representative or in his own name. That is wrong. His internal intention is not conclusive. It is true that there is some support in the literature for the Court of Appeal's view that a person must have intended to act as agent before a contract can be formed through him [reference omitted], but this conflicts with the general principle that what counts in legal transactions is the will as declared (reference omitted). There is no reason why the general principle should not apply in the law or agency, too. Evidence that it does is provided by the terms of para 164 para 2 BGB. By that text the effects of representation ensue if the intention to act in the name of another is apparent; if it is not, the declarer must treat the transaction as having been concluded in his own name and cannot rely on the fact that he had no intention of so contracting. In the contrary case, where the declarer is apparently acting in someone else's name but means to act for himself, there can be no reason for treating his inner intention, at odds with appearance, as crucial.

The error of law just pointed out must materially have influenced the conclusion of the Court of Appeal that the plaintiffs' agreement with W was invalid by reason of this misunderstanding. It must therefore reinvestigate the contract which emerged from the plaintiff's negotiations with W, and see whether the plaintiffs' declarations and those of W coincide, be it on a contract with the defendant, represented by W, or a contract with W in his own name or in that of Idealheim.

2. If it then emerges that the plaintiffs contracted with Idealheim, they have no claim against the defendant, not even a claim for enrichment [reference omitted].

3. (a) But if the Court of Appeal finds that the plaintiffs contracted with W as the defendant's representative, it does not necessarily follow that the defendant is liable. It would also have to be shown that the defendant was bound by W's declarations as those of his representative.

The Court of Appeal held—and there was no legal error in so holding—that W was not specifically authorised by the defendant to contract with the plaintiffs on his behalf. But it has not asked . . . whether the defendant may not be estopped from disowning the conduct of W on the ground of ostensible or apparent authority (*Duldungsvollmacht, Anscheinsvollmacht*), doctrines invoked by the plaintiffs. Further investigation of the facts is needed before this question can be decided.

(b) It is possible that W acted in the name of the defendant without having any power to bind him, whether arising from actual, ostensible or apparent agency. W would then be liable to the plaintiffs under para 179 BGB, since the defendant has not ratified the contract, but the plaintiffs would have no claim against the defendant, not even a claim for enrichment. No doubt one may have a claim against the party represented as well as a claim against the unauthorised representative under para 179 BGB; this was laid down by the *Reichsgericht* [reference omitted], has met with general approval [references omitted] and is in principle unobjectionable. But it remains true that no enrichment claim lies against the party represented if (1) he himself has concluded a contract with the person who appeared as his representative, though unauthorised, and (2) he had, arising from this contract, a right as against the unauthorised agent to the performance rendered by the third party, and (3) he is obliged to pay the unauthorised agent. In such a case he would not be enriched at the expense of the third party (see above I. 2 (a)), whose legal relations with his contractor are quite immaterial to him. Thus even if the facts which trigger para 179 BGB are given, there can be no claim for enrichment, provided, as the Court of Appeal held, that there was a valid contract between Idealheim and the defendant which obliged the latter to pay the former.

Case 34
BUNDESGERICHTSHOF (FIRST CIVIL SENATE) 12 FEBRUARY 1952
BGHZ 5, 111

Facts

On 17 and 18 April 1949, at two days on which football was being played. the claimant filled in three football pool coupons from Sport-Toto GmbH, the defendant, and handed them over with the corresponding stake money of DM15 to the owner of the restaurant Sch in K. Mrs Sch had not been appointed by the defendant as a betting office, but had been commissioned by W, the defendant's betting office in W near K, to accept bets. She accepted the coupons, affixed the respective stake stickers unto them and marked them with the defendant's stamp She handed over to the claimant the A sections of the coons for the participant to keep Sections B and C of the coupons for two entries, intended for the defendant were forwarded by her, but those for the third remained at her place and were found there after Sport-Toto's final accounting for the event. This third entry had won a total of DM22,500. By registered letter of 22 April 1949, the claimant sent the defendant the A sections of the coupons for this entry in his possession and demanded payment of his share in the winnings. The defendant refused payment, since the coupon parts B and C had not been received in time by the central office in Koblenz and not gone through the proper checks as set out in the agreed betting terms. The then applicable betting terms as printed in excerpts on the reverse of the coupons stated:

'Art 5 As long as in special cases no other provisions have been agreed, the stake and the coon must be in the possession of Sport-Toto GmbH no later than Friday, 6 pm. All coupons received thereafter are invalid.

Art 8 The risk and hazard inherent in correct receipt of the coupons by Sport-Toto GmbH is borne by the participant.

Art 9 Without any right of defence, coupons will not participate in the event which

(a) . . .

(b) . . .

(c) have not yet been received by Sport-Toto GmbH by the close of the counting of all participants in each event. . . .

(d) . . .

Art 13 All appeals against the determination of winners must have been received by the Central Office within 10 days after the day of the event. . . .'

These conditions were later amended.

The claimant brought an action for payment of his partial amount totalling DM6,100. The defendant refers to the fact that receipt of the coupon sections by the central office is a precondition for any claim for a win and that the risk and hazard involved in such receipt taking place lies with the participant. A receipt by the betting office alone does not suffice. Furthermore, Mrs Sch had no authority to accept bets.

Both lower courts have rejected the claim. The further appeal results in a quashing of the judgments; the case is referred back for further deliberations.

Reasons

The appeal court bases its decision on the assumption that a valid betting contract was concluded by the parties. It leaves undecided whether the restaurant Sch had been a betting office recognised by the defendant, or the defendant had generally prohibited the setting-up of sub-offices or had known of Mrs Sch.'s activities. It merely states that the defendant had in any case accepted and treated as valid coupons to which Mrs Sch had affixed with the stake stickers and which she had subsequently stamped. From this fact the court deduces that the defendant must therefore accept the consequences arising from the appearance that an authority legally existed. The appeal court also presumes a timely receipt of the claimant's coupon in the sense of Art 5 of the betting conditions, but it holds that the claimant's right to his win has lapsed since the pre-requisites of Art 9 c are not fulfilled as the particular part of the coupon had not reached the defendant's central office in time. In view of Art 8, the appeal court rejects the award of damages for vicarious liability. The participant had accepted all risks and hazards for a timely arrival of the betting coupons at the defendant's office. The defendant had thus excluded any vicarious liability in respect of the coupons' transmission.

Presuming initially, as the appeal court does, that it appeared as if Mrs Sch, the landlady of the restaurant, had been legally authorised, and that a legally valid betting contract had been concluded, the interpretation of the respective betting conditions on which the appeal court bases its decision can however not be followed. These conditions are typical terms of contract on which the defendant without exception based all its betting contracts. They were printed on the contract forms. The court of further appeal has the unrestricted right to interpret such terms of contract.

If the landlady Sch must be regarded as one of the defendant's betting offices with full powers of agency, then in the absence of any expressed limitation, her apparent authority covered receipt of all declarations to be made to the defendant and also the performance of all actions which were necessary in order to claim a win. A restriction of such authority can especially not be deduced from the fact that the defendant, in Arts 5, 8 and 9 of the betting conditions, sometimes refers to the Sport-Toto betting offices and sometimes to Sport-Toto GmbH as recipients for the betting coupons. There is no apparent intention to differentiate between these two kinds of recipients. According to Art. 5 in particular, the betting offices are empowered to accept the entire coupons with all their sections, as the appeal court rightly presumed. It is only in Art13 that the period of time, during which any objections may be raised, is clearly linked to the receipt of the coupons by the central office.

A sufficiently clear distinction can also not be derived from the fact that the provisions of Arts 5, 8 and 9 would partially overlap if one were to assume that the Toto betting offices and Toto GmbH are on an equal footing. General conditions of contract like these are not always the result of a full and correct legal study of the situation and thus do not *per se* justify the application of strictly logical principles of interpretation, as is necessary in the case of legal provisions. They are directed at a wide audience of contractual partners most of whom are unfamiliar with the law, for which reason they must be precise and clear without recourse to logical deductions. Furthermore, there is still scope for the application of Art 9 c in addition to Art 5, even if one equates the Toto betting offices with Toto GmbH, ie in those cases, which are exempt from the general rules of Art 5; and Art 8 remains applicable for cases in which the participant does not use the betting offices for the transmission of the coupons. In any case, the wording of Art 8 does not make it absolutely clear that the defendant, by this provision, intended to exclude liability for his own fault and those of his agents in respect of the transmission of coupons, a task which he had taken on himself and over which the participant had no influence whatsoever. If the defendant intended that these provisions meant something else, he has not made this sufficiently clear. The defendant carries the risks for any possible doubt in respect of the wording, since he could have phrased the provisions more precisely (see RGRKomm, note 3 to para 157, 9. ed, p 343; RGZ 120,18 [20]; RGZ 145, 21 [26]). Given the present wording of the betting conditions, the participant could assume that he had fulfilled all preconditions for claiming a win once he had handed in the betting coupon at the betting office in time.

Nonetheless, the claim is not yet ready for a decision along the line of the court of further appeal's reasoning. The appeal court's findings insufficiently prove the landlady Sch's authority as a result solely of the appearance of such a right. Against the principal, the contractual partner can plead such apparent authority in cases, where he could assume in good faith that the principal knew and tolerated the behaviour of the agent who acted for him. The appeal court held without error in law that this was so in respect of the claimant, who not only received the betting coupons from the landlady Sch, but also recognised that she held the defendant's stake stickers as well as the stamp to cancel them. But the court fails to realise, that a further pre-requisite must be present on the part of the principal, ie that he, if using all necessary care, should have realised what the agent was doing and could have prevented it (see RG HRR 1931, 529; Düringer-Hachenburg HGB Part I, 479; Staudinger, 10 ed, note 9 to para 167).

Case 35
BUNDESGERICHTSHOF (ELEVENTH CIVIL SENATE) 29 JUNE 1999
NJW 1999, 2883

Facts

The claimant demands from the defendant the remainder of a savings account credit balance, which the defendant paid out to a person authorised by the claimant. The claimant, who was at that time aged 70, had a savings account at the S savings bank which, in early 1992, showed a credit balance of about DM150,000. In April 1992, she opened a savings account with the defendant, for which she gave a full power of attorney to her doctor, Dr D. According to her evidence, he had offered to the claimant that he would invest her savings at a higher rate of interest with a bank in Luxembourg, and claimed that a minimum sum of DM200,000 was necessary for this. The credit balance invested in the S savings bank was transferred in May 1992 to the new savings account with the defendant. Besides this, the claimant took out a loan in the sum of DM50,000 from the S savings bank. The claimant gave the amount of the loan to Dr D, who paid it into the claimant's savings account with the defendant. The savings account therefore showed a credit balance of a total of DM203,041.90. A few days after the transfer of the credit balance, Dr D's wife terminated the savings account. She arranged for DM3040.90 to be paid to her in cash. She paid DM200,000 immediately to the defendant to discharge loans owed to it by her husband. Dr D, who had intended to use the money in this way in breach of the agreement from the start, was amongt other things given a total sentence of three and a half years for deceit in respect of it. In an action between the claimant and Dr D, Dr D made a commitment in a settlement to pay a part sum of DM80,000, and this payment was made. The claimant demands from the defendant reimbursement of the remainder of her loss in the sum of DM121,040.90. The claimant is of the view that the defendant should not have made the payments to Mrs D, so her (the claimant's) claims to repayment of the credit balance continued to exist. The defendant claims that the payment out of the credit balance had effected a release, because the claimant had granted Dr D a comprehensive power of attorney in respect of the newly opened savings account.

   The *Landgericht* rejected the claim. The appeal court amended the judgment of the *Landgericht*, ordered the defendant to pay DM50,260.22 and rejected the claimant's appeal in other respects. The claimant is pursuing her case further in the appeal in law. The defendant by its cross appeal seeks the complete rejection of the claim. The claimant's appeal in law was well founded. The defendant's cross appeal was unsuccessful.

Reasons

I.
1. (. . .)
2. These deliberations do not stand up to legal examination. The claimant, as creditor in respect of the credit balance, has a claim to the payment out of her credit balance (§ 607 BGB). The appeal court did not take into consideration the fact that the claimant was not obliged to let the withdrawal by Dr D's wife, on the instructions of

Dr D as the person authorised to operate the account, take effect against her, the claimant, as he misused his authority.

(a) According to the consistent case law of the *Bundesgerichtshof*, the principal must in principle bear the risk of misuse of an authority. The contracting partner does not have a duty to examine whether and to what extent the agent is bound in the internal relationship (with the principal) only to make limited use of his agency power—which is *unlimited* as against third parties. The principal is however protected in his relationship with the contracting partner against a recognisable misuse of the agency power, if the agent has made use of his agency power in an obviously dubious manner, so that the contracting partner must have well-founded suspicions of a violation of good faith by the agent against the principal. A substantial incriminating circumstance is necessary here, presupposing objective evidence of misuse [references omitted]. The objective evidence will in particular be present when, in the given circumstances, the need for the other party to the transaction to query this with the principal is simply unavoidable [see Schramm in Bankrechts-Hdb § 32 marginal no 24 with further references].

(b) These prerequisites are present here. It is true that establishing them is a matter for assessment by the judge of fact, and can only be examined to a limited extent in appeal in law proceedings. But, in any case, the issues of whether the concept of objective evidence was misunderstood, and whether significant circumstances were left out of account in the assessment, are subject to examination. If that is the case, the court determining the appeal in law can undertake the assessment itself, if the findings of the appeal court give—as here—a completed picture of the facts (see, on this, Senate NJW 1992, 316 [317] = LM H 6/1992 Art 16 WG no 5).

The defendant knew that the credit balance invested by the claimant with it had been increased by DM50,000 to DM200,000 by the take-up of a loan to the claimant. The claimant gave to her doctor (and not, for instance, to a member of her family) a comprehensive power of attorney. This was used only a short time after the opening of the account (and only a few days after the crediting of the main sum of 150,000 DM) to terminate the savings account in order to discharge personal loan obligations by the attorney to the defendant. As the appeal court correctly emphasises, if the claimant had wanted to discharge the personal debts of her doctor with the credit balance, there would have been simpler ways of doing it. This is not a question of a normal everyday event in banking business. The event is so striking that suspicion of a misuse of authority should have forced itself on the defendant as the claimant's contractual partner. The use of an authority for one's own purposes as a rule gives cause for paying attention. In the circumstances present here, there were strongly suspicious elements which indicated a diversion of the sums of money withdrawn, and suggested that the agent wanted to siphon these away from the principal in abuse of his authority. The defendant should have in particular been distrustful because it was a savings account which had built up a substantial credit which the person entitled usually intends to use for his own investment purposes, and not to discharge the debts of the person with power to operate his account. These doubts necessitated the raising of questions with the claimant. The defendant should, in view of this, have set aside its own financial interest in the discharge of the loan granted to the attorney.

(c) As this is a case of misuse of authority, the defendant does not deserve protection for its reliance on the existence of the agency powers. The claimant as principal does not have to permit the agent's legal transactions to take effect against her (consistent case law—see senate [references omitted]). The claimant's claim to have the contents of the account paid out to her was not extinguished by the withdrawal by the attorney, and still exists.

(d) There is a single case in which the view was put forward that, on misuse of an authority, the disadvantageous results of the agency were to be split in accordance with the fault existing on both sides, applying the legal concept in § 254 of BGB [references omitted]. There is no need to decide whether this view should be followed. The claimant's grant of a power of attorney cannot by itself be rated as a culpable co-operation in the misuse of the authority. (. . .)

3. (. . .) The whole of the claim should be allowed. (. . .)

Chapter 3

Case 36
REICHSGERICHT (EIGHTH CIVIL SENATE) 2 FEBRUARY 1931
RGZ 131, 274

Facts

The defendant owned two adjoining houses in Hamburg, K St. nos 66 and 67. In no 66 the plaintiff had been running a jewellery shop since 1921, when he had taken it over at a premium from a stamp dealer. At the end of 1929 the defendant rented a shop in no 67, two shops away from the plaintiff's, to L, another jeweller, who has been selling jewellery there since then. The plaintiff now seeks an injunction against the defendant, forbidding him to allow any jeweller but the plaintiff to do business on his premises, and ordering him to make L quit, on pain of a judicial penalty.

The *Landgericht* dismissed the claim, but on the plaintiff's appeal, the *Oberlandesgericht* allowed it, though with no judicial penalty. On the defendant's appeal, the decision below was reversed and the case remanded.

Reasons

The Court of Appeal was right to hold that the plaintiff was the defendant's tenant, even though the tenancy agreement was never put in writing as was envisaged when the plaintiff moved in. The rent of M6000 per month, which was to have been put in the written contract, was agreed between the parties, and all other statutory requirements were met. The court therefore held that the question whether the defendant was free to allow competitors of the plaintiff on his premises depended on para 536 BGB. In applying this text, one must take account of normal commercial practice and the special circumstances of the case; but the court added that it was the 'correct' legal view that mattered, not the law and practice as it was at the time of the lease.

This approach, as the appellant argues, misconceives the role played in the construction of contracts by the normal commercial practice referred to in para 157 BGB, and overlooks the fact that in the law of obligations, terms implied by statute can normally be ousted by the actual agreement which the parties, in agreement with normal commercial practice, have formed. Likewise, it was in breach of paras 133, 157 BGB, as well as para 286 ZFO, that the Court of Appeal ignored evidence pertaining directly to the position of the parties on the matter of competition when they were concluding the contract: the defendant asserted that at the time the plaintiff moved in, he had drawn his attention to the fact that Th had a jewellery shop in the same building, and that the plaintiff had replied that that was beneficial rather than the reverse, for there were already quite a few jewellery shops in K St, and the customers this brought to the street always went wherever the best bargain was to be had. In saying that this evidence only showed that the plaintiff could not complain of the shop being run by Th, the court ignored its most vital part, namely the plaintiff's answer.

Furthermore we must agree with the appellant that the Court of Appeal pitched the statutory obligations of the landlord too high. The *Reichsgericht* has never said that the landlord's obligations to provide a thing fit for contractual use (paras 535, 537 BGB) necessarily include the duty to protect the commercial tenant from real competition, not just on the rented premises but on all premises under the landlord's control. In RGZ 119,353, the tenant had taken a 25-year lease of premises in a building under construction; he was to use it as a cigar shop, and at the time of the contract the landlord had expressly undertaken that there would be no other cigar shop in the building. The landlord's successor then built a kiosk for the sale of cigars and other commodities directly in front of the shop rented to the plaintiff, and blocking the public view of it. Although in that case the competition was taking place on land outside the rented premises, the landlord's successor was held to be in breach of his duties under para 242 BGB in encouraging competition in this manner. This decision does not however justify the generalisation made by the Court of Appeal below.

In the case of a contractual licence it is quite clear that, provided it remains possible for the commercial tenant to use the premises for the permitted purposes, the landlord is not bound to promote or protect the advantage which the tenant expects from them (HGZ 91, 54; 91, 310; 94, 267). With particular reference to competition, the judgment in LZ 1914, 1028 states that the tenant is not normally entitled to have competitors kept out of the *leased premises*. Only if the contract is a special one, as evidenced by its express terms, the arrangement of the premises (as in the case of a public house) or some other consideration [reference omitted] will the landlord come under any such duty under paras 157, 242 BGB, and indeed, if the circumstances are very special, as they were in RGZ 119, 353, he may be in breach of contract (in the sense of para 242 BGB) if he permits competition, *outside the leased premises*. But a landlord who owns several pieces of property does not normally, in letting one of them, promise not to permit competition in any other: to hold otherwise would make for difficulties in view of the fact that on the sale of any property, the landlord's duty devolves separately to its purchaser under para 571 BGB.

The Court of Appeal was therefore in error; the statutory duty to afford the tenant the use of the leased property does not of itself embrace an obligation to protect him from competition, although in a special case such an obligation may arise under para 242 BGB, as well as paras 133, 157 BGB. But in applying paras 157 and 242 BGB, one must take into account all the relevant circumstances and not, as the Court of Appeal did, just the needs of the contractual licensee; it would be a severe restriction on the rights of the owner of property in a street devoted to one kind of business if he could not let his property to the practitioners of that very business.

In this case we cannot establish and define the defendant's duty without a fresh evaluation of the interests of both parties, and an examination of the way the contract between them came into being. If it appears that the defendant should have taken some account of the plaintiff's interests when he was letting no 67, then one must look into his contract with L in order to see whether he can really be expected to terminate it, and perhaps pay L an indemnity. While the appellant is wrong to say that such a remedy lies only for faulty breach of contract and not in specific performance, it would nevertheless be an unacceptable extension of the landlord's duty to protect his tenant from competition to hold that although the defendant was not guilty of any faulty breach of contract, he was nevertheless bound, as against the plaintiff, to terminate his contract with L, no matter what the cost. On the question of breach of contract, the appellant is right to point out that the letters of the parties in September 1929 must be taken in to account. The case must be decided afresh in the light of these observations.

Case 37
BUNDESGERICHTSHOF (FIRST CIVIL DIVISION) 15 JUNE 1956
BGHZ 21, 66

Facts

Both parties were engaged in selling books through book clubs. They advertised by using abbreviations of their firm name. The plaintiff called itself 'German Home Library,' the defendant chose the name of 'Stuttgart Home Library.'

A book club bearing the name of 'German Home Library' existed from 1916 until 1945. Since its owner at that time had been the official publisher of the National Socialist Party, the business was taken over by the Allied Control Commission and was continued subsequently in reduced form under the name of 'Hamburg Book Circle.' In 1949 the business of the 'German Home Library,' including all its assets and liabilities, was transferred to a German trade union, which founded a new firm which began operations on 2 July 1950 and advertised under the name of 'German Home Library.'

The defendant was established on 4 June 1949 and took on the firm name of 'Stuttgart Home Library' on 24 August 1949.

The plaintiff contended that he was the successor of the business established in 1916, that the term 'Home Library' had acquired the reputation of a slogan identifying it with the plaintiff and had been accepted as such by the book trade and by the reading public. He alleged that 12 BGB (name and para 16 of the Law of Unfair Competition and para 25 of the Trademark Law) had been violated.

The defendant denied that the plaintiff was the successor of the original business carrying the name 'German Home Library.' He also claimed that the plaintiff could not claim the name 'Home Library' as his own, but, at best, only that of 'German Home Library.' However, no danger of confusion existed between that name and the name of the defendant. In any event, due to laches the plaintiff had lost any right to complain about a possible confusion, seeing that, as a result of several years of advertising the defendant had acquired a valuable position which was protected in law.

The District Court of Hamburg gave judgment for the plaintiff. The Court of Appeal of Hamburg rejected the claim. On a second appeal by the plaintiff the case was referred back for the following reasons.

Reasons

. . . Among the points to be considered by the Court of Appeal in respect of the remaining question of laches (Verkwirkung) . . . the following must be noted:

I. As this Court had stated several times, following a constant practice of the *Reichsgericht* [references] the doctrine of laches starts from the notion that the person committing the injurious act was entitled to assume in the particular circumstances of the case that the injured party was prepared to tolerate the permanent use of the description in issue with the result that a belated claim based on tradeM, get-up or other rights of identification of the injured party was contrary to good faith. Contrary to earlier practice the *Reichsgericht* in its later discussions required no longer for a defence of laches to be successful that the party committing the injury must have obtained common acceptance of his use of the description; instead it is regarded as sufficient if the party committing the injury is in a state of possession which deserves protection [references]. This practice has been attacked by a number of writers especially in the post-war period [references]. This Division has not taken a final position on this question. In so far as the present facts should give rise to the Court of Appeal to consider this question the following general observations should be noted.

This Division does not regard it as necessary in every case that the description in issue must have obtained at least a geographically limited public acceptance [references]. Also the protagonists of the opposite view must admit that the acquisition of a public reputation cannot, as such, justify the defence of laches. Thus Reimer [references], among others, requires that the injured party must have tolerated the injurious act in the knowledge, or in the culpable ignorance, of the public recognition does not matter by itself; it matters, in addition, whether or not a balancing of interests in the particular case, having regard to all the circumstances governed by the principles of good faith in accordance with para 242 BGB, justifies the rejection of the defence of laches. It becomes clear that satisfactory results can only be achieved by this method if a situation is envisaged in which the injured party behaved unquestionably in a manner which entitled the injuring party to believe that his acts were being tolerated; in this case he cannot be blamed under any circumstances for having built up a valuable possession [references]. Simply to deny the injuring party the defence of laches in such a case on the ground that public recognition had not yet been acquired would not be in accordance with equity. This is so, in particular, if having regard to the size of his business and the extent of his advertising campaign determined thereby, the injured party could not even acquire public recognition of the disputed description if only in a limited area, or could only do so after a comparatively long time. In order to allow the defence of laches it is therefore unnecessary as a rule that the injuring party should enjoy a full right; instead it is sufficient, following the more recent practices of the Reichsgericht, that a more continuous, honest and undisturbed use of a description has created a situation which is of important value for the customers, which should be retained by him according to good faith and which even the injured party cannot context, if he had facilitated it by his conduct [references]. The observation [references] to the effect that it is unjust if the registered owner of a mark may have to give way, even if the injuring party cannot even assert his right against a third party, does not suffice to support the opposite view. The notion of laches applies not only in the law of trade M and of Unfair Competition, but constitutes an aspect of the admissible exercise of rights, which is valid in all branches of law. The decision must not rely on absolute standards, in the present case on the acquisition of an exclusive right towards third parties. Instead it may accord entirely with equity if the injuring party is not restricted in his defence against a careless holder of a right, even if the injured party is unable to proceed against third parties on the strength of an exclusive right of his own. It is evident that in considering the prerequisites outlined here for admitting the defence of laches judicial discretion may be exercised broadly and that the parties feel a certain element of uncertainty as to the outcome of the dispute. In this respect matters are not different in all other branches of law where the notion of good faith is in issue, that is to say when the facts in their manifold variety do not lend themselves to be judged by a system of rules which are fixed once and for all. Consequently there is no reason why the defence of laches should be judged by different standards and made to depend on different conditions, in the law of TradeM and Names, which may lead to grave injuries in individual cases. On the other hand, it would be wrong to assume that the continuation of the more recent practice of the *Reichsgericht* may be intended to facilitate a successful plea of the defence of laches. No such effect is either intended or to be feared if the courts weigh and examine all these circumstances which are required according to the principles developed by the practice of the courts, before the defence of laches can operate.

Case 38
BUNDESGERICHTSHOF (FIFTH CIVIL DIVISION) 25 MARCH 1965
BGHZ 43, 289

Facts

The Area Court (Amstgericht) in Liebenburg, acting as special court in agricultural matters (*Landwirtschaftsgericht*) by an order of 29 June 1948 gave its consent, as required by the Procedure Regulations in Agricultural Matters of 1 January 1948 (LVO) to a contract whereby the owner of a farm agreed to transfer it to her two brothers in order to be divided into two separate farms. The conveyance never took place. Instead, pending an exchange of parcels, the brothers took a tenancy of the farm.

The Court's consent was communicated informally to the two District Agricultural Offices (*Kreislandwirtschaftsamt*) in whose area the farm was situated and to the notary acting for the parties. In the course of a dispute in which the validity of the local court's consent had been challenged the local court served, on 11 April 1963, the order embodying its consent on the Agricultural Chamber (*Landwirtschaftskammer*) which was the superior authority in agricultural matters, competent to receive the notice in question. The latter appealed in time to the competent court, the Court of

Appeal in Braunschweig, which dismissed the appeal on the ground that it was an abuse of legal process. On a second appeal in point of law the order to the Court of Appeal was quashed and the case was referred back for the following reasons.

Reasons

... The decision depends on whether the lodging of the appeal constitutes an abuse of legal process. Contrary to the opinion of the Court of Appeal this is not the case.

It is recognised in practice and in the literature that the principle of good faith which permeates substantive law (para 242 BGB) applies also in the law of procedure, not only in litigious proceedings, but in non-contentious litigation (*Freiwillige Gerichtsbarkeit*) and therefore also in proceedings involving agricultural holdings [references]. There are cases in which appeals not limited in time cannot be lodged after a disproportionately long interval. The late lodging of an appeal may offend against good faith which justifies the treatment of the appeal as inadmissible. In such cases it is also said that the right of appeal has been lost through laches (*Verwirkung*), which constitutes a special case of abuse of right. The passage of time must be accompanied by other circumstances, if a late entry of an appeal is to be regarded as final the situation created by the decision appealed against in the absences of an appeal, and were justified in so thinking [references].

The appeal in proceedings concerning agricultural holdings must be lodged within two weeks, beginning with the day when the order was served [references]. An ... appeal which is lodged after the time limit has passed is inadmissible.

According to the practice of the courts the loss of a right to appeal due to laches is not restricted to appeals which are unlimited in time but has also been allowed where the appeal was subjected to a time limit [references]. The question of laches may arise, for instance, if the service of the order was invalid owing to some omission and if therefore the time for lodging an appeal had not started to run, with the result that the appellant knew of the decision and delayed lodging an appeal for such a long time that in the particular situation it is contrary to good faith to lodge it now. Here also the mere fact that a long period of time has passed is insufficient to constitute laches. No general principle is embodied in the legislation to the effect that a decision can no longer be appealed against after a certain time has passed irrespective of whether the decision has been served nor not. Instead a time limit for appealing against judicial decision must be provided for expressly, as it was done for certain situations [references] which issue need not be considered here [references]. The fact that the parties to the agreement assumed at all times that the contract had been approved with legal effect is of no decisive importance, if only for the reason that the planned division of the farm has not taken place hitherto and that after the conclusion of the contract it has been run by the two brothers of the owner together. The fact is decisive that the Agricultural Chamber only came to know of the approval of the contract when the decision was served on it as late as 11 April 1963. For this reason alone the appeal which has been lodged in time cannot be regarded as an inadmissible exercise of legal process, even if many years have passed since the decision was pronounced ... It is also not possible to agree with the Court of Appeal that the Agricultural Chamber must be deemed to have cognisance of the decision of the area court for along time. The question is irrelevant as to whether the Agricultural Chamber could have obtained cognisance without difficulties of the decision which should have been served on it. The Agricultural Chamber was under no obligation to make any such enquiries. The Court of Appeal fails to consider that it is the duty of the court to serve judicial decisions. The Agricultural Chamber [references] could assume that decisions which had not yet been served on it [reference] would be served on it subsequently.

Case 39
BUNDESGERICHTSHOF (EIGHTH CIVIL SENATE) 22 FEBRUARY 1984
BGHZ 90, 198

Facts

The claimant is the German marketing company of an Italian manufacturer of construction cranes. It sold to the defendant, which carries on a building enterprise, a revolving tower crane of Type E 231 produced by these manufacturers for stationary deployment. In discharge of the purchase price of DM84,399.70, the defendant paid DM25,000 as a down payment and by agreement traded in its used crane, the value of which the parties have accepted as DM45,200. The defendant refuses to pay the remainder of the purchase price of DM14,199.70, which the claimant claims in the present action along with other demands. It relies on (. . .) the absence of a type approval for the crane delivered on 5 July 1979. (. . .)

Reasons

II.
1. The appeal court considers the defendant's claim to rescission to be justified, because the crane as delivered was defective (§ 459 (1) [§ 434] BGB). (. . .)
2. These deliberations of the appeal court do not stand up to legal examination in every respect.

(a) A mistake in the sense of § 459 (1) [§ 434] BGB occurs when the factual condition of the sold object deviates from what was agreed in the sale contract, and this deviation destroys or lessens the value of the object, or its fitness for its usual use or its use assumed under the contract. What was contractually assumed here was the delivery of a crane which had already undergone a type examination on the part of the manufacturer in the sense of § 25 (2) of the UVV ('cranes'), and was therefore immediately ready for use. The appeal court assumed, as did the defendant, that there was a duty of this kind. That is not challenged by the appeal in law, because the claimant itself has not at any time denied such a duty. On the contrary it made an attempt—admittedly doomed to failure—to fulfil its contractual duty in this respect at the time when the crane was delivered by handing over a type examination approval of 2 August 1977.

(aa) The appeal court has correctly assumed that the claimant could not fulfil its duty by handing over this document. (. . .)

(bb) Nevertheless it has not been established that the crane was also defective (. . .) at the point in time of delivery. (. . .)

(b) If on the other hand the appeal court's view that there was a defect in the thing were to be accepted, the defendant would acquire a right of rescission (. . .). It could not however rely on this after the supply by the claimant during the course of the first stage of the legal proceedings of a valid type approval of 22 January 1980 for the model of crane delivered.

It is admittedly disputed (as, in the nature of things, a case of this kind seldom arises) whether the right of rescission comes to an end if a defect which is present when the risk passes has disappeared by the time rescission is effected [references omitted]. This question has not been decided by the *Bundesgerichtshof*, and does not need a conclusive discussion here either. This is because the defendant's insistence on the right of rescission appears to be an impermissible exercise of a right in violation of the principles of good faith (§ 242 BGB).

(aa) According to the findings of the appeal court the defendant took the crane into service following on its delivery on 5 July 1979, and used it until the beginning of December 1979. The fact mentioned in its reply of 22 October 1979 that the permission number of the 'TUEV' (Technical Surveillance Association) (. . .) was not impressed on the crane has not deterred the defendant from further use of the crane nor caused it to make an immediate declaration of rescission to the claimant. It made up for failing to do the latter only by its written statement of 30 January 1980. This was however at a time when the original uncertainty about the validity of the type approval of 2 August 1977 was objectively removed by the supplementary certificate given to the manufacturer on 22 January 1980, and there were no longer any obstacles to the further use of the crane. In such a case, further pursuit of a possible right of rescission amounts to an impermissible use of a right under § 242 BGB.

(bb) It is not possible to draw any different conclusion from the fact that the defendant, when it made its rescission declaration, possibly still had no knowledge of the supplementary certificate of 22 January 1980. (. . .) This is because in a case like this in which the defect did not consist of an impairment of the substance of the thing, and has been removed without any risk of untoward consequences by the supplementary certificate, it is only a question of the objective circumstances. The purchaser is not accused of consciously dishonest conduct. Exercise of the right is only impermissible because it would no longer correspond to a proper protection of the interests involved. That applies even if claims against the claimant to compensation for delay (§ 286 BGB) or for positive breach of contract might have accrued to the defendant because of delayed supply of the supplementary certificate. In these proceedings this admittedly is not to be proved because the defendant has not raised such claims. But possible claims to compensation could exist independently of the right of rescission. Their existence would therefore not be linked with denial of the defendant's access to the right of rescission by the principle of good faith. (. . .

Case 40
REICHSGERICHT (SEVENTH CIVIL DIVISION) 3 DECEMBER 1920
RGZ 101, 47

Facts

The plaintiff ussed the defendant for transactions with end-of-month settlement. Arising from this business relationship, in February 1916 the plaintiff owed the defendant RM34,111.50. By notarised certificate of indebtedness of 26 February 1916, he acknowledged this debt and undertook to repay it by an agreed schedule of instalments (details on dates of instalments due). As collateral security he pledged some securities, among them 25 shares of the Petersburg Internationale Handelsbank, abbreviated to Peter Inter. He agreed to an immediate execution of the title should this become necessary. On 12 December 1917, the plaintiff ordered the defendant to sell the Peter Inter in his possession since, as a result of the troubles which had started in Russia, a sharp slump in the share price was to be expected. He also ordered the purchase of shares in Phönix (RM 5,000) and Norddeutsche Lloyd (RM 5,000) as replacement, likewise to act as collateral security. The defendant refused to carry out the instruction. The plaintiff submits that the defendant's behaviour was in breach of good faith and led to considerable losses. The plaintiff was not able to redeem the Peter Inter shares before 12 August 1918, when he could sell them at a price of only RM112, whereas on 12 December 1917 a price of RM149 1/2 could have been obtained. Furthermore, if the Phönix shares had been bought on 12 December 1917 a 40 per cent profit could have been made, since in May 1918 the plaintiff had sold other Phönix shares he held at a price which was 40 per cent higher than the December 1917 price. After deduction of an undisputed claim which the defendant has against him, the plaintiff demands payment of RM4581.50 plus interest. In addition, he requests a declaratory judgment to the effect that the defendant has no further claims from their business contacts and that he is therefore not entitled to execute the document of 26 February 1916.

Both lower courts have found according to the plaintiff's claim. The defendant's further appeal was rejected for the following reasons.

Reasons

The legal findings of the *Kammergericht* are to be upheld which state that the defendant needed to comply with the plaintiff's request, ie to exchange 25 shares of Peter Inter, which the defendant held as security, for RM5000 worth of shares in Phönix and Norddeutscher Lloyd, each worth RM5000.

It is an established fact that in December 1917, as a result of a price slump, a considerable reduction in the value of Peter Inter shares could have been expected. Based on para 1218 BGB, the plaintiff as pledger of the share certificates could demand to have these shares returned in exchange for other securities. If at that time the plaintiff had offered the defendant RM5000 worth of Phönix shares and RM5000 of Norddeutsche Lloyd shares against the return of the Peter Inter, the defendant could not have refused the exchange since, as the Court of Appeal ascertained, these exchange documents represented at least the same amount of security as the Peter Inter. No slump in prices was to be expected in respect of the substitute shares. The defendant had no claim to greater security than the one represented by the Peter Inter shares in December 1917. In particular, he had no claim to have these exchanged for gilt-edged securities. In commercial terms the same result would have been achieved if the defendant had himself carried out the substitution which the plaintiff had requested, ie if he had sold the Peter Inter on the stock exchange and bought the replacement shares with the proceeds and then kept these as collateral security. The defendant alleges that he was under no obligation to accept the instruction since a banker is not committed to accept orders for share dealings. However, this is not the point here. Whether or not and to what degree, in view of commercial usage, a banker is permitted to refuse share-dealing orders can be left unanswered. In this context the only question that needs to be answered is whether the holder of a collateral security, whether a banker or not, must co-operate when a risky security is to be exchanged for a safer one of equal value, and, as here, in the manner as instructed by the plaintiff. The plaintiff's order was addressed to the banker not only in his professional capacity but also in his capacity as contractual partner and plaintiff's pledgee. It was this contractual relationship with the plaintiff which gave rise to special obligations. By his unreasonable refusal to accept the plaintiff's commission, the defendant has culpably infringed his contractual obligations.

There is no need for further reasoning that a contract of pledge gives rise to obligations for the pledger as well as the pledgee. Similarly, the principle of good faith (para 242 BGB) applies to the way in which the pledgee meets his contractual obligations. Para 1218 sets out the pledgee's obligation to return the pledged documents in return for other securities where a considerable reduction in the value of the pledged documents is to be expected. This provision is in itself a practical application of para 242 (RGZ 74, 151). Although para 1218 does not explicitly state that the pledgee needs to co-operate in the legal transactions required for a substitution of the pledged documents, in the light of the principle of good faith, circumstances such as these can demand a duty to co-operate.

The principle of good faith is mainly a question of weighing up both parties' interests. Where the defendant's co-operation in the exchange of the pledged documents was required because of the plaintiff's urgent needs and where this could be achieved without any risk to the pledgee, it was a breach of good faith for the defendant to refuse to co-operate. The plaintiff's urgent interest in the sale of the Peter Inter shares was evident as these were threatened by a further reduction in value as a result of the troubles in Russia. On the other hand, not only were the defendant's interests unaffected by the substitution of the Peter Inter by sound German securities of at least equal value, likewise held by him as pledge; but such an exchange also served his own interests. Moreover, compliance with the order did not encumber the pledgee with unreasonable effort. The sale and purchase of securities was part of his usual commercial activities. The banker could charge the usual fee for carrying out the instruction. It is true that the banker had a greater interest in merely selling the Peter Inter and to offset the proceeds against his claim for which the plaintiff had given the pledge. But no such right existed under the parties' contract and the defendant had no right to refuse the instruction in order to force the plaintiff to agree to the sale of the Peter Inter shares merely as a means of settling the debt from the proceeds. In breach of the contract, the defendant would thereby have obtained an unmerited advantage.

The further appeal submits that the defendant had not been under any obligation to assist in the plaintiff's speculative transactions in respect of the pledged securities and that the possibility could not have been ruled out that the share prices may have fluctuated in a different way. In theory, both points are valid. But what the plaintiff intended was not a speculative share dealing. He had no interest in making a profit from the exchange of the shares but rather intended to avert the threat of considerable losses. The defendant did not refuse to carry out the commission because the substitute shares were likely to fall in price or to become worthless. The appeal court rightly assumed that in view of the political and economic situation in Germany at that time as far as the substitute share were concerned, such a considerable drop in share prices as forecast in respect of Russian securities could not have been foreseen. In the proceedings before the lower court, the defendant submitted no facts to justify doubts he may have had at that time.

It can also be left undecided whether the defendant could have rejected the plaintiff's instruction if the latter had been able otherwise to obtain substitute securities, since the appeal court had in fact ascertained that the plaintiff had no ready cash with which to acquire substitute shares. The further appeal's submission must be rejected.

The defendant also cannot submit that he had been prohibited from accepting instructions other than for cash transactions. The case only concerns cash dealings. The Phönix shares and the Norddeutscher Lloyd shares, each worth RM5000, were to be purchased with the cash proceeds from the sale of the Peter Inter shares. The plaintiff needed no credit. The defendant has not been able to show that the cash proceeds from the shares to be sold would not have been sufficient to meet the purchase price for the substitute shares.

Finally, the further appeal alleges that even if the defendant needed to carry out the order to sell the Peter Inter shares, he would not have been under an obligation to acquire the substitute shares and that he was therefore not responsible for the loss which the plaintiff sustained from the missed increase in value of the Phönix shares. This submission is wrong. The plaintiff's instruction was made in respect of one single indivisible transaction intended, under para 1218 BGB to substitute the threatened Peter Inter shares by other shares, equally given as pledge. The commission could only be carried out as intended, ie in its entirety. As a result, the defendant must compensate the plaintiff for the entire loss arising from the defendant's breach of contract through failure to carry out the instruction as a whole. The lost profit from the RM5000 worth of Phönix shares and the loss in price of the Peter Inter shares are adequately connected with the defendant's culpable breach of contract.

Case 41
REICHSGERICHT (SECOND CIVIL DIVISION) 4 MAY 1932
RGZ 108, 1

Facts

The plaintiff, owner of a chemical factory and oil refinery, who also produced and sold machinery and articles for the maintenance of machinery such as lubricants, was the proprietor of six tradeM in pictorial form, registered between 1915 and 1924 with the competent German authorities. All of these show a laughing face in opposition to a crying face. The faces are located in the surrounds of axle bearings and at shaft ends.

The defendant, who also dealt in lubricants for machinery, made use of a prospectus in order to advertise its own products. This showed a complete human figure, the laughing head of which forms the end of a bearing and supports it; above it appeared the words 'Keystone-Hanks', below it the words 'Permanent Lubricant'. The figure kicks away in disgust an oil can which displays a crying face.

The plaintiff claimed that the defendant has consciously imitated the motif of the laughing and the crying face in advertising its own competing goods so as to cause confusion, because it had become known in the trade as indicating the plaintiff's products. He alleged a violation of para 1 of the Law against Unfair Competition (UnlWG) in conjunction with para 826 of the Civil Code and asked that the defendant be condemned, (a) to desist from using the motif of a crying and a laughing face in opposition to each other in any advertisements or communications; (b) to lay accounts of all sales of lubricants before and after the use of the motif employed in the plaintiff's trademark and (c) damages caused by the use of the plaintiff's motif in his trademark.

The *Landgericht* Dortmund and the *Oberlandesgericht* Hamm dismissed the claim. On the plaintiff's further appeal, the decision of the *Oberlandesgericht* reversed for the following reasons.

Reasons

In order to determine the three claims it is essential to ascertain whether the general impression of the respective pictorial designs is likely to confuse the average purchaser of the goods in question which are undoubtedly the same or similar so as to attract the operation of para 20 of the Trade Mark Act. In order to solve this question which, contrary to the courts below must be answered in the affirmative, it is decisive that the trademark registered in the plaintiff's name are marks bearing particular strong characteristics, seeing that they embody a highly individual motif. The satisfaction with the quality of the lubricant produced and distributed by the plaintiff is expressed by the laughing face figuring at the point of the machinery where the lubricant operation, while dissatisfaction with the lubricants of lower quality, produced and distributed by others, is contrasted by the crying face. The better or worse quality of machinery is thereby indicated simply and effectively . . .'

This special motif bearing particularly strong characteristics . . . has been treated in commerce as an essential characteristic of the trademark, as the Court of Appeal has found on grounds which cannot be faulted. It has therefore imprinted itself generally on the memory of the average purchaser.

A trademark consisting of an image, is characterised both by its external form and the execution of the picture as well as by the substantive content, the meaning and significance of the pictorial display. If, therefore, the motif, the meaning of the picture, fulfils the function of pointing to a particular industrial or commercial undertaking, it follows that any mark which embodies the same motif pictorially may result in confusion, even if the pictorial display differs in form, provided that the motif appears in its pure form [references]. This is the case here . . . The pictorial display in the prospectus of the defendant is based on the same motif. The centrepiece of the display is made up of the laughing face at the place of the machinery where the lubricant of the defendant is applied. Moreover, the defendant has taken over the contrast between satisfaction with the good and dissatisfaction with the bad merchandise. He uses the same idea as that expressed by the plaintiff in his trademark in order to draw attention to the difference between his own lubricants, alleged to be better and others which are less effective . . . The Court of Appeal failed to appreciate that in protecting the motif it does not matter . . . whether the imitation includes every detail of the display, and that it must suffice, instead if the principal features of the motif are taken over and reproduced by the imitation. Therefore, even if the respective pictorial displays may differ in form, nevertheless the defendant's display retains the characteristic motif, no new motif has been created by the addition of other conceptual elements of equal value.

The danger of confusion exists therefore notwithstanding the fact that the pictorial displays differ in their execution, that the words 'Keystone-Hanks' have been added, which refer to the firm of the defendant . . . The plaintiff's claim for an injunction is thus justified within the limits set by paragraph 12 of the Trademarks Act . . .

To this extent this court can determine that issue on the merits by quashing the judgment under appeal.

In addition the plaintiff asks that the defendant be condemned to lay accounts as to which sales of lubricants were concluded before and after the use of the above-mentioned motif and to pay compensation for the loss still to be ascertained, caused to the plaintiff through the use of the motif. The plaintiff bases his claim on the intentional imitation of his trademark by referring to the correspondence between the parties before the action was brought, whereby the plaintiff asked the defendant to desist from imitating the plaintiff's trademark by supplying the defendant with the numbers of their registration. The right to compensation is derived from paras 12, 14 and 20 of the Trademarks Act in conjunction with para 826 of the Civil Code and para 1 of the Law against Unfair Competition. This claim . . . must clearly be treated as one for a declaration, in case the plaintiff should not succeed in obtaining an order to lay accounts . . . Since the Court of Appeal did not examine at all the question as to whether the defendant is liable to having intentionally imitated the plaintiff's mark, ie for the intentional violation of a trademark, the judgment had to be quashed also to this extent and the case remanded to the Court of Appeal.

The same applies to the claim for an account . . . the appellant alleges a violation of para 687 of the Civil Code. The Court of Appeal held that this provision does not apply [references] on the ground that a person who intentionally and without a legal right employs a trademark belonging to another in order to identify his own goods admittedly interferes with a legal right of another unlawfully, but that he acts on his own account and not on behalf of another. However, according to the constant practice of this court [references], where a patent, design or copyright has been violated, a claim for an account, in addition to a claim for the payment over of all gains made by the imitator has been allowed according to the principles governing the conduct of business for another (*negotiorum gestio*). The reason is that any object which has been created in contravention of a patent, design or intellectual property right represents the protected idea of an innovation or of a protected creative form and that therefore the commercial trade in such objects without a legal right is to be treated at the same time as the exploitation of one's own account of a business concerning another in the meaning of para 682 (2) of the Civil Code. It is true that in the decisions of this Division [references] the analogous application of these provisions to the law of designs and get-up was rejected on the ground that the use of a design or of a get-up without a legal right in the course of selling goods of one's own was not a transaction which involved a right of the owner of the mark, and because the right of the injured party for compensation according to paragraphs 14 and 15 of the Trademarks Act, while constituting compensation for the complete, the actual damage and the loss of gains, did not create a direct obligation to hand over the illegal profits. On reconsideration of this question this

Division cannot maintain the opinion expressed in the decisions [references] but now holds that a claimant under paras 14 and 15 of the Trademarks Act is entitled not only to damages but also to an account according to paragraph 260 of the Civil Code—thus following in the result the opinion of the First Division formulated for violations of Patents, Designs and Artistic Property rights . . . Of course the application of the rules of the Civil Code concerning unjustifiable enrichment are excluded as a matter of principle, seeing that the Trademarks Act (paras 14 and 15), as distinct from the Copyrights Acts, regulates the duty to pay compensation to the exclusion of all other claims and limits it to intentional or reckless violations of marks [references]. Equally it is correct that the duty to pay compensation under paras 14 and 15 of the Trademarks Act—contrary to that arising from violations of patents under para 35 of the Patents Act [references] and of the duty to pay compensation for violations of rights in designs under para 9 of the Act of 1 June 1891 [references]—is not directed towards the return of the profits obtained by the defendant as a result of the use of the protected invention or of the protected design, if the injured party himself was not able to make profits to the same extent [references]. Thus the application of para 687 (2) of the Civil Code, according to which anybody who knowing that he is not entitled to treat as his own another person's business is liable to hand over any profits he may have made (paras 687 (2), 681 (2), 667 of the Civil Code) is also excluded where a design or get-up has been violated. However, as early as 24 June 1904 [reference] this Division has held that in cases such as the present it is difficult for the plaintiff to specify and for the court to determine the amount of damages, unless the defendant is obliged to lay an account. Paragraph 287 of the Code of Civil Procedure . . . does not offer a sufficient means for obtaining full compensation. Paragraph 687 (2) of the Civil Code . . . is not, however, the only device for applying para 260 of the Civil Code. In those cases in which a right to information by the debtor greatly facilitates the prosecution of rights and often is the only means of making the latter possible, the principle of good faith—leaving aside any conduct of business on behalf of another without authority—requires that a claimant who is excusably unaware of the existence and extent of his rights be given that information from the debtor who has easy access to it.

Such is the case here [references]. The obligation to provide information is sometimes more extensive and sometimes more restricted. The most extensive duty is that of having to lay accounts. According to para 259 (1) of the Civil Code it is discharged by providing accounts, if an administration is involved which has an income and expenses. This is not the case here. However, according to para 260 of the Civil Code the duty to give information may be limited to the presentation of an inventory of a plurality of assets (objects, rights of claims) which the plaintiff, who claims rights on the comprehensive ground that the defendant has intentionally or recklessly violated a mark, cannot specify in detail . . .

Case 42
BUNDESARBEITSGERICHT (SECOND SENATE) 23 JUNE 1994
NZA 1994, 1080

Facts

The defendant employed the claimant on 1 February 1991 as an outdoor worker for dressings and cotton wool. A period of six months' probation was agreed in the employment contract during which the employment relationship could be ended by both sides on one month's notice terminating at the end of the month. The defendant ended the employment relationship on 30 April 1991 by a letter of 21 March 1991 and released the claimant from work. The claimant made claims against the defendant for compensation because of premature termination of the employment relationship by a lawyer's letter of 4 April 1991. (. . .) After no agreement was reached about the claims, the claimant sued for a declaration that the termination was ineffective. The claimant asserts that the termination had only been made because of his homosexual tendencies.

The *Arbeitsgericht* rejected the claim. The claimant's appeal was unsuccessful. The claimant's appeal in law succeeded.

Reasons

The appeal in law leads to quashing of the appeal court judgment and reference back, in which connection the senate has made use of the option in § 565 (1) sent 2 of the Civil Procedure Code (ZPO).

The reasons of the *Landesarbeitsgericht* for its decision were in substance as follows: (. . .) Even if it were assumed that termination had only been effected because of the claimant's homosexuality, it was effective. It was not invalid under § 134 BGB, because the exercise of the claimant's general right of personality was not violated by the termination. The termination was merely realisation of a risk to which every employee was exposed in the first six months of his employment. (. . .)

II. The appeal in law is well founded.

1. (. . .)

2. The judgment of the *Landesarbeitsgericht* cannot however be maintained on the basis of the facts which it hypothetically assumed, ie that the termination had only been made because the claimant's homosexuality and of the reasoning given by it. The *Landesarbeitsgericht* did not examine whether, on the facts assumed by it, the termination violated the general principle of good faith (§ 242 BGB). In this connection, according to the view of the senate, there is no need—and this is something which the *Landesarbeitsgericht* takes into account as a matter of priority—to discuss whether the termination is even to be regarded in these circumstances as contrary to good morals (§ 138 BGB) (see on the strict prerequisites of § 138 BGB: BAGE 16, 21 (25) = NJW 1964, 1542 = AP no 5 on § 242 of the BGB Termination (I)). Likewise it is necessary to go into the question of the direct application of basic rights claimed by the claimant (Art 1 para 1, Art 2 para 1, Art 3 para 3 and Art 12 of the Basic Law) (derived from Kühling, AuR 1994, 126 (127) with further references).

(a) The provisions of § 242 BGB are only applicable to a limited extent alongside those of § 1 of the Protection against Termination Act (KSchG). The KSchG has concretised and conclusively regulated the prerequisites and effects of the principle of good faith so far as protecting the existence of the employee's place of work is concerned, and his interest in its maintenance. Circumstances which must be assessed within the framework of § 1 of the KSchG, and which could cause termination to appear to be socially unjustified, do not fall to be considered as violations of good faith. A termination violates § 242 BGB, and is invalid if it contravenes the principles of good faith for reasons which are not covered by § 1 of the KSchG. The same applies for terminations to which the KSchG does not apply as the six months waiting period under § 1 (1) of the KSchG is not fulfilled because, for these cases, the protection against termination excluded by statute would still be preserved via § 242 BGB [references omitted]. Typical situations of termination contrary to good faith are, in particular, inconsistent behaviour on the part of the employer, expression of termination in an offensive form or at an inappropriate time (BAGE 28, 176 (184) = NJW 1977, 1311 = AP no 1 at § 1 of the KSchG 1969 Waiting Period (at II 2); BAG NZA 1986, 97 = NJW 1987, 94 L = AP no 88 at § 626 of the BGB (at II 4)).

(b) The principle of good faith (§ 242 of the BGB) forms a constraint on content which is immanent in all rights, legal situations and legal norms. The exercise of a right violating § 242 BGB or the exploitation of a legal situation by going beyond the right is regarded as impermissible according to the above case law. The requirements which arise from the principle of good faith can only be decided here in the light of the circumstances of the individual case. On this legal basis the *Bundesarbeitsgericht* has applied § 242 BGB in those cases, among others, where termination notices were given within the probation period and where the KSchG therefore did not apply. (. . .) On the other hand, the *Bundesarbeitsgericht* (BAGE 44, 201) ruled that a notice given within the probation period was ineffective under § 242 BGB as well as § 102 (1) of the BetrVG (Constitution of Businesses Act) because the employer had dismissed the claimant on the basis of unconfirmed hearsay evidence by a witness, without giving him a prior opportunity to comment, on suspicion of consumption of hashish. This termination was expressly stated to be ineffective because of violation of § 242 BGB. In BAGE 61, 151, in the case of an employee who had made a suicide attempt after an infection with HIV and was therefore incapable of work (with associated costs of continued wage payments) for several months, § 242 BGB was examined, and its application in the actual case only denied because it involved termination grounds which were typically to be assessed within the framework of § 1 of the KSchG. On the basis of the employer's economic considerations, which were held to be defensible, it was accepted that termination was not contrary to good faith. Finally, reference must also be made to the decision of the senate of 12 July 1990 (BAG NZA 1991, 63) in which termination is likewise discussed from the point of view of a violation of good faith, and with regard to the point in time when the termination arrived. Breach of good faith was not derived from this alone as—so the Senate argues—an infringement of justified interests of the recipient of the termination had to be present as well, in particular of regard for his personality. The seventh Senate (BAG NZA 1986, 97) had already decided to the same effect in a case in which a termination was assessed which was delivered on Christmas Eve without the justified interests of the recipient of the declaration, in particular for respect for his personality, being thereby established as violated.

(c) In continuation of this case law [references omitted], from which only extracts have been reproduced, the senate considers even a termination given during the probation period to be contrary to good faith if it is given when (according to the claimant's convincing submissions, assumed by the *Landesarbeitsgericht* to be correct) the employee's performance has been confirmed to be good, and only because of the employee's homosexuality.

(aa) It has already been referred to in the introduction (at II 2a) that the principle of good faith forms an immanent limitation to the content of all rights, legal situations and legal norms. That also applies for the power of formulation exercised by means of termination, which—and this is inherent in the law about termination as a whole—is subject to judicial control [references omitted]. In the concretisation of such a general clause as the principle of good faith, regard must be had, according to the consistent case law of the Federal Constitutional Court (BVerfGE 7, 198 (204f); BVerfGE 42, 143 (148); BVerfGE 89, 214), to the basic right guarantee of private autonomy, the right to regard for human dignity and the general right of personality (BAGE 89, 214 is also similar to this). Since § 242 BGB refers quite generally to custom (*Verkehrsitte*) as well as good faith, a concretisation is required from the courts which measures up to conceptions of value which are primarily determined by the decisions of principle in the Constitution. In the interpretation and application of this provision regard is to be had to the basic rights as 'guidelines' (BVerfGE 7, 198 (206)).

(bb) It follows from this first of all that it is not inconsistent with custom (*Verkehrsitte*) and good faith if the defendant, as the person entitled to receive the services which the claimant is obliged to render, makes use within the probation period of the right of termination granted to it by the principle of private autonomy. The formulation of legal relationships by the individual in accordance with his own will is a part of the general freedom of action. Art 2 para 1 of the Basic Law guarantees private autonomy as 'self-determination of the individual in legal life' (BVerfGE 89, 214 = NJW 1994, 36). Private autonomy is however necessarily limited. Rights of equally ranking holders of basic rights are ranged against its exercise. The claimant has for his part a right to the free development of his personality (Art 2 para 1 of the Basic Law). This basic right also incorporates the freedom to formulate one's private sphere in the area of sex life according to one's own decision (BVerfGE 60, 123 (146) with further references). It is true that the termination does not directly affect the claimant's right to choose a partner of the same sex and to live with this person in a relationship similar to marriage. But the termination takes away his economic base for this reason only, in conditions unequal to those applying to a heterosexual orientated employee, whose employment the defendant would not have terminated in the probation period where he worked successfully alongside others. It therefore restricts the possibility of conducting his life as he chooses because he has homosexual tendencies. As the *Landesarbeitsgericht* assumes the facts to be correct, namely that the claimant's employment was only terminated because of his homosexuality, and the claimant amplifies this to the same effect, even though he had fulfilled the work-related expectations placed in him, this amounts to disciplining of his sexual conduct. (. . .) In this situation, possibly justified needs on the part of the defendant—for instance because of the effects of the claimant's way of life on work with fellow employees, the peace of the business, customer relationships—cannot be accepted. The defendant has also not relied so far on anything of this kind. The duties of an employee against his employer end in principle at the point where his private sphere begins.

The formulation of the area of private life is outside the employer's sphere of influence, and is only limited by duties under the employment contract in so far as private behaviour has an effect on the business realm and leads to disruption there [references omitted]. If conduct outside employment does not affect the sphere of duties under the employment contract, the employer is not entitled to express his disapproval about matters which have become known to him from the employee's private sphere by effecting termination of the contract. This is all the more so when these matters can be classified as part of the employee's intimate sphere. The employer is not called by the employment contract to be keeper of the morals of the employees who are active in his business (LAG Düsseldorf DB 1969, 667 (668)). In the present case it must be further assumed in the claimant's favour—in the absence of elucidation of the facts by the *Arbeitsgericht* and the *Landesarbeitsgericht*—that the defendant has 'sounded out' the claimant by means of a fellow employee and, using the information obtained in this way, relied on the freedom to terminate. This represents a disregard of the claimant's personality—the fellow employee concerned is said to have described himself as 'used'—and therefore contains an exploitation of a legal position which is contrary to good faith (as in BAGE 10, 207) or—in the words of the Federal Constitutional Court—an implementation of the 'right of the stronger party.' This use of private autonomy represents an impermissible exercise of a right: § 242 of the BGB. (. . .)

Case 43
BUNDESGERICHTSHOF (NINTH CIVIL SENATE) 7 JUNE 1984
BGHZ 91, 324 = NJW 1984, 2279

Facts

The claimant, which manufacured steel buildings, had demanded from its customer the firm SVG GmbH ('SVG') bank securities to guarantee obligations arising from supplies. The director of SVG also agreed to this. He accepted a bill of exchange made out by the claimant on 4 September 1981 and drawn on SVG for DM259,046.83 for this firm. On 8 September 1981, the defendant savings bank sent the following letter to the claimant:

'Our security for the sum of DM150,000 in favour of SVG GmbH
Ladies and gentlemen
For the benefit of SVG GmbH, we have taken up directly enforceable security in the sum of DM150,000 to your firm in favour of SVG GmbH.
We would be very obliged to you for a brief indication of the extent of the obligations of SVG GmbH to you at the moment. . . .'
The claimant replied on 17 September 1981:
' Thank you for your letter of the 8th September 1981. We are pleased to note that you have taken up in respect of SVG GmbH . . . directly enforceable security to our firm in the sum of DM150,000.
Our claims against the firm mentioned above amount to 1,652,717.83 Austrian schillings at today's date which is equivalent to DM236,102.54. . . .'
On 24 September 1981, the defendant wrote to the claimant:

'In reply to your letter of the 17th September 1981, we are informing you that we have not taken up directly enforceable security in the sum of DM150,000 in your favour as against the above mentioned firm (SVG GmbH). The details quoted in your letter are not therefore correct. . . .'

After the claimant had referred on 28 September 1981 to the contradiction with the letter of 8 September 1981, the defendant replied on 6 October 1981:

'. . . In the letter of the 8th September 1981, our branch office proceeded on the basis that a security exists as against Sch Hallen Bau GmbH. This assumption was based on a mistake. In December 1980 the taking up of a security as against the firm Sch was under discussion. This security never came into existence . . .'

By a letter of 17 November 1981, the defendant avoided 'as a precaution, once again on the grounds of mistake, a security declaration it had possibly given.'

On 8 December 1981 the bill of exchange for DM259,046.83 was protested because it had not been paid by the drawee.

The *Landgericht* awarded the claimant DM150,000, together with procedural interest, by a reservation judgment of 12 August 1982. It declared this judgment to be without reservation on 11 November 1982. The *Oberlandesgericht* rejected the appeals, which were combined for joint proceedings and decision. The appeal in law by the defendant was unsuccessful.

Reasons

I. The following has been established on the basis of the assessment (reserved for the judge of fact) of the undisputed circumstances. The claimant was permitted to interpret the letter of 8 September 1981 to the effect that, by this letter, the defendant wanted as against the claimant to enter into a directly enforceable security of up to DM150,000 for the obligations of SVG arising from the deliveries of steel buildings. The debt arising from the bill of exchange of 4 September 1981, which was accepted by this company and not honoured, also belongs to these obligations. The claimant also understood the letter in this way, and accepted the contractual offer recognised in it. In this respect the appeal in law raises no objections.

1. As it correctly states, however, it is necessary, according to the assumption of the judge of fact, to proceed for the purposes of the appeal in law on the basis that the defendant's representatives only intended by their letter of 8h September 1981 to make a factual communication; and thus, by signing and sending it, they did not have the intention or even the consciousness of making a binding declaration in relation to a legal transaction. But then, as the appeal in law claims, the prerequisites for a declaration of will were absent. Its nullification by avoidance under § 119 para 1 BGB was therefore not needed. In any event harm arising from reliance (which had not been demonstrated) was compensatable by analogy with § 122 BGB if the defendant could have recognised the possible interpretation of its conduct as a declaration of will by application of the care which it had a duty to show.

The challenge is unfounded.

(a) The view that consciousness of making a declaration was a constitutive requirement for a declaration of will, and that therefore its absence would result in invalidity without the need for avoidance (and in any event, by analogy with § 122 BGB or under *culpa in contrahendo*, liability of the declarant for compensation for harm arising from reliance fell to be considered) is held in particular by [references omitted]. The view that a declaration given without that consciousness, which its recipient might understand as relating to a legal transaction, was at first effective, but could be avoided as a declaration mistake in accordance with §§ 119 paras 1, 120, 121 BGB is principally held by [references omitted].

The *Bundesgerichtshof* has not so far decided the question conclusively. It has expressly left it open in the judgments of 20 October 1952 [reference omitted] and 11 July 1968 [reference omitted]. It cannot be unambiguously deduced from the decision of 10 May 1968 [reference omitted] that the *Bundesgerichtshof* considered the consciousness of making a declaration to be constitutive. It is stated there that the belief in a legal transition taking effect by virtue of statute law could not replace the intention to enter into a legal transaction and its declaration. On the other hand, the judgment concerning a grace and favour transaction [reference omitted] and the decisions of the Federal Labour Court in [references omitted] accept that it does not depend on the internal intention of the declarant, which remains hidden, but on how the recipient of the declaration could understand the statement in accordance with good faith and considering all the accompanying circumstances. In its judgment of 14 March 1963 [reference omitted], the *Bundesgerichtshof* apparently regards the consciousness of making a declaration as a prerequisite for a declaration of will, but also states that a person who creates the impression by decisive conduct that he had and expressed an intention to enter into a legal transaction, without actually having it, must under § 242 BGB let himself be treated as if he had such an intention. According to the judgment of the *Bundesgerichtshof* of 23 February 1976 [reference omitted], the signing of a trade register notification by a member of a firm for the remaining members is as a rule to be understood as meaning that he approved for the internal relationship what he had there declared. In this connection, the question of whether there is an intention to be legally bound is not to be assessed according to the internal intention of the member making the declaration, which remained hidden, but according to whether his conduct appears in the eyes of his fellow members, according to the principle of good faith and having regard to business custom, to be the expression of a certain intention. In this judgment, avoidance under § 119 para 1 BGB is also regarded as possible. The principles developed there, though, have not until now, so far as is evident, been carried over to declarations which are not appropriate to alter company law relationships externally and internally.

(b) This senate, proceeding from the deliberations of the second civil senate, is of the view that the effectiveness of the security obligation does not depend on whether the defendant's agents had the intention or even the mere consciousness, in the signing and sending of their letter of 8 September 1981, of giving a declaration in relation to a legal transaction. The following reasons are decisive for this, following [references omitted]. In §§ 116 ff BGB the concept of the declaration of will is not defined. In particular nothing can be derived from the wording of § 119 BGB against the view held here. It is not only the person who thought the content was a different legal transaction who has no intention to give 'a declaration with this content.' The same applies to the person who did not intend to give any declaration in relation to a legal transaction at all. It should not be concluded from § 118 BGB that lack of consciousness of making a declaration (or lack of intention to enter into a transaction) would always lead to invalidity without the need for avoidance. If the declarant, as is presupposed in § 118 BGB, consciously intends not to be bound, in the expectation that this will also be recognised, invalidity is what he intends. He does not need to be given the choice of making what has been declared apply both against him and in his favour, or avoiding it under § 119 BGB. There is no comparison between this and a declaration made without the consciousness that it will be understood to be in relation to a legal transaction. The latter is much closer to the declaration which is intended to be legally effective, but which is mistaken. A person who makes a declaration that he will buy, but who is thinking of a sale, finds himself in a quite similar situation to the person who gives the usual indications for a purchase, but is not thinking of a purchase. In both cases it appears appropriate to leave the choice to the declarant of whether he wants to avoid under § 119 para 1 BGB and then have to compensate in respect of the reliance interest under § 122 BGB, or whether he wants to stand by his declaration and receive a possible counter-performance which could put him in a better position than his unilateral obligation to compensate for harm resulting from reliance.

This possibility of choice also excludes the objection that, without the consciousness of making a declaration, there is no personal autonomous formulation by way of self-determination, and this cannot be replaced by personal responsibility alone. The law about declarations of will is not only based on the right of self-determination of the holder of the right. In §§ 119, 157 BGB, it protects the trust of the recipient of the declaration, and certainty in the affairs of life, in that it also binds the declarant to legal consequences which were not imagined and (which is to be considered as equivalent) not consciously brought into effect. The power of the declarant, who in both cases did not intend the legal consequences actually expressed in his declaration, to annul these consequences by retrospective avoidance (§ 142 para 1 BGB), or leave them to apply, takes sufficient account of the concept of self determination [reference omitted].

A declaration of will when consciousness of making a declaration is lacking is only present, though, if it can be attributed as such to the declarant. That assumes that, on the application of the care necessary in the affairs of life, he could have recognised that his declaration or his conduct might have been interpreted, in accordance with the principle of good faith and having regard to business custom, as a declaration of will and avoided this consequence [references omitted].

2. The appeal in law further objects from this legal standpoint that the appeal court made no findings from which it would follow that the defendant's representatives could, exercising the care that they were under a duty to show, have recognised the interpretation of their conduct as a declaration of will. This objection does not succeed. In the light of the wording of the letter of 8 September 1981 composed by the defendant's representatives, by which it first made contact with the claimant, no grounds were needed by the judge of fact for saying that the defendant's representatives would have been compelled to recognise that the recipient would understand their letter as a binding offer for the conclusion of a contract for giving security. This is because in the declaration, which satisfies the formal requirements of § 766 BGB, the creditor and debtor are described, the commitments which are to be guaranteed are sufficiently determined and the intention to guarantee is expressed objectively. In any case, a savings bank or bank which allows such a declaration to reach a creditor of its customer must, on applying the care necessary in the credit business, take into

account that the recipient will interpret the declaration, according to its content, as a security obligation. The fact that the defendant, as the appeal in law has claimed in this connection, in accordance with business custom, uses a form on the taking up of a security, is not inconsistent with this. This is because it must be known, even to the managers of a branch of the defendant savings bank who are authorised to represent it, that declarations of will do not have to be given on forms to be binding, and in particular a businessman (§ 1 para 2 no 4 of the Commercial Code) can take up a security without a form (§ 350 of the Commercial Code).

II. The appeal court's decision that the defendant had not effectively avoided its declaration of 8 September 1981 does not, contrary to the challenges of the appeal in law, reveal any mistake of law.

1. The defendant's letter of 24 September 1981 does not fulfil the prerequisites of a declaration of avoidance in the sense of § 143 para 1 BGB. A declaration of avoidance is any declaration of will which lets it be known unambiguously that the legal transaction is to be retrospectively set aside. In this connection, the express use of the word 'avoid' is not necessary. According to the circumstances, it can completely suffice if an obligation, taken up according to the objective declaratory value of the expression of intention, is disputed, or not acknowledged, or if it is contradicted. But in each case it is necessary that the intention is unambiguously revealed that the transaction is not intended to be left in existence simply because of the absence of intention [references omitted].

Starting from this point, the appeal court correctly emphasises that the letter of 24 September 1981 does not satisfy these requirements because it contains no sort of reference to an absence of intention. The judge of fact correctly understood absence of intention as including the lack of consciousness of making a declaration. The appeal in law considers, on the other hand, that in the special case of avoiding an act undertaken without the consciousness of making a declaration, the letter of 24 September 1981 was sufficient as a declaration of avoidance. But that is not so. Even if a person who is the subject of a claim based on a statement has acted without consciousness of making a declaration, a lack of intention, however described, must be recognisable in the avoidance, as in other cases of avoidance for mistake. This is because the honest recipient of the declaration has an interest worthy of protection in discovering without delay whether the other party wants to set aside his declaration retrospectively because of an absence of intention [reference omitted]. The appeal in law does not claim that the defendant's letter of 24 September 1981 had done more than merely deny the taking up of a security.

2. The appeal court assumes that the defendant, by its letter of 6 October 1981, had avoided belatedly, ie not without culpable delay (§ 122 para 1 BGB). This only happened 15 days after knowledge of the ground for avoidance. Admittedly the mistaken party had as a rule to be allowed a reasonable period for consideration. It facilitated sensible consideration of the question of whether the mistaken party really wanted to avoid or to be content with the declaration given in spite of the mistake. But as the defendant did not in any case want to adhere to the security obligation, it did not need a longer period to consider whether it wanted to avoid or not. Therefore the defendant had delayed. This delay had been at least negligent. The defendant had neither explained nor proved a defence. Its answering letter of 24 September 1981 showed that its considerations had been concluded at this point in time.

Against this, the appeal in law objects that the defendant should have been given a longer period for consideration than was allowed by the appeal court, because it had not been conscious of having entered into a security obligation in favour of the claimant. It was therefore necessary for it to examine the factual and legal situation thoroughly. The avoidance in the letter of 6 October 1981 was accordingly in time.

The objection is unfounded. The defendant has itself stated in the grounds of appeal that it recognised the ground for avoidance from the claimant's letter of 17 September 1981, which arrived on 21 September 1981. The appeal in law accordingly proceeds on the basis that the defendant obtained knowledge by this letter of the ground for avoidance, that is to say that it discovered that, contrary to its impression, the claimant had interpreted the letter of 8 September 1981 as a security declaration and was also permitted to interpret it in this way. There is therefore no evident reason why the defendant, which had concluded its considerations by the compositon of the answer of 24 September 1981 at the latest, should have waited until 6 October 1981 for the sending of the avoidance declaration. Under these circumstances, the accusation of the judge of fact that the defendant had negligently delayed cannot be objected to. He has not exaggerated the requirements for an avoidance without delay.

Case 44
REICHSGERICHT (SECOND CIVIL SENATE) 8 JUNE 1920
RGZ 99, 147

Facts

On 18 November 1916 the defendant sold to the claimant around 214 barrels of Haakjöringsköd by the steamer Jessica, unloaded at M4.30 per kilo c.i.f. Hamburg for net cash against the bill of lading and policy. (. . .) On arrival in Hamburg the goods were confiscated by the *Zentral-Einkaufsgesellschaft mbH* (central purchasing company) in Berlin who took delivery of them shortly afterwards. The claimant claims that the goods had been sold to him as whale meat when they were shark meat. As whale meat, they would not have been subject to confiscation. The defendant, who had delivered goods which were not in accordance with the contract, therefore had to reimburse him for the difference between the purchase price and the confiscation price paid by the *Zentral-Einkaufsgesellschaft* which was substantially lower. He claimed payment of M47,515.90. The *Landgericht* declared the claim to be justified in principle. It established that both parties had assumed on conclusion of the contract that Haakjöringsköd was whale meat and deduced from this that the claimant could demand a refund of the price paid less the confiscation price received from the *Zentral-Einkaufsgesellschaft* just because the defendant had delivered shark meat. (. . .) The appeal in law was unsuccessful.

Reasons

(. . .) As the *Oberlandesgericht* has established in a manner free from doubt, both parties mistakenly assumed on the conclusion of the contract of 18 November 1916 that the goods forming the subject-matter of the contract and defined in it—214 barrels of

Haakjöringsköd loaded on the steamer Jessica—were whale meat. The goods were in reality shark meat and as such were correctly described by the Norwegian word Haakjöringsköd, the meaning of which the parties did not know. This finding does not however justify the view that what was sold, ie Haakjöringsköd had also been delivered and that the claimant, after the goods had been transferred to him by the delivery of the bills of lading, could have avoided the purchase contract for mistake about characteristics of the type of product which are important in human affairs, in accordance with § 119 (2) BGB. Instead, it follows from this finding that both parties wanted to conclude a contract about whale meat, but that in declaring their contractual intention, they mistakenly used the description Haakjöringsköd which does not correspond to this intention. The legal relationship which exists between them should be assessed just as if they had used the description whale meat which did correspond with their intention [reference omitted]. Accordingly whale meat should have been delivered in accordance with the contract, and the claimant should be directed to the legal remedies provided for in §§ 459 ff [§ 437] BGB after shark meat had been delivered to him [reference omitted]. This was because the goods delivered lacked the characteristic of being whale meat, (. . .) which was so substantial that its absence represented a defect in the thing in the sense of § 459 (1) [§ 434]. The claimant is therefore entitled to rescind, and as a consequence he can demand a sum of money from the defendant—the amount of which is yet to be established—which is equal to the price paid by him to the defendant less the confiscation price granted to him by *Zentral-Einkaufsgesellschaft* (. . .)

Case 45
BUNDESGERICHTSHOF (FIFTH CIVIL SENATE) 1 OCTOBER 1999
NJW 1999, 3704

Reasons

(. . .)
II. The appeal court propounds the view that the defendants had refused to approve the sale contract of 3 March 1995 by a document of 24 March 1995; and this made the contract appear in the end to be invalid. The approval declared on 13 April 1995 therefore had no effect. No confirmation or novation of the purchase contract by further notarised declarations of 24 March 1995 and 10 April 1995 had occurred. (. . .)
III. This does not stand up to legal examination.
1. The appeal court is admittedly not mistaken in law in assuming that the legal transaction, which had up to that point been potentially (*schwebend*) ineffective, became finally invalid with the refusal of approval to the notarised purchase contract of the 3 / 6 March 1995 on the part of the defendants by their declarations on the morning of 24 March 1995. (. . .)
2. The appeal court's view that the claimant and the first defendant had not by the notarially authenticated declarations of 24 March 1995 and 10 April 1995 confirmed the legal transaction which finally became invalid should not be followed. The appeal court's interpretation is defective.

(a) The interpretation of rules for individual contracts by the appeal court can be examined by the court dealing with the appeal in law in so far as statutory rules of interpretation, recognised principles of interpretation, conceptual rules, empirical principles or procedural provisions have been violated [references omitted]. A recognised principle of interpretation is regard for the situation of the contractual partner's interests (BGH, BGHR BGB § 157 interpretation rule 1). The appeal court has violated this. Its interpretation amounts to saying that the declarations mentioned appear to be pointless. This is because approval of the contract of 3 / 6 March 1995 was no longer possible due to expiry of the relevant period. But according to general experience of life it must be assumed that it is the parties' intention that a contractual provision should have a legally significant content. Therefore if there are several possible interpretations, preference must be given to the one which gives real significance to the contractual norm, if it would otherwise appear to be (partially) pointless (BGH WM 1998, 1535). One possible interpretation here is that the claimant and the first defendant intended to confirm the sale contract of the 3 / 6 March 1995 in the sense of § 141 (1) BGB. This provision admittedly does not apply directly, because the sale contract was not void but ineffective in the end due to refusal of approval. But there are no difficulties about application of § 141 (1) BGB by analogy to such ineffective legal transactions. The sense and purpose of the statutory regime do not dictate that confirmation of a void legal transaction should be permitted but not confirmation of a legal transaction which was ineffective in the end. The parties can have an interest in the implementation of such a transaction if the grounds which led to ineffectiveness have disappeared.

(. . .)

Case 46
REICHSGERICHT (SECOND CIVIL DIVISION) 31 MAY 1927
RGZ 117, 176

Facts

The plaintiff and L were partners in a business for the manufacture of ambulances under the firm name of L. By a contract dated 24 January/26 March 1923 they sold the business to the D.O.W. company which continued the business under the original name of L. Clause 1 of the contract dealt with the sale of the machinery and the raw materials. Clause 2 provided that in view of the assignment of the patents and similar rights together with all non-pecuniary assets, such as business connections, sales opportunities etc., the plaintiff and L were to receive for ten years a share in half the sales volume of ambulances produced after the sale of the business, which share was to amount to 7 per cent in the first year and to 5 per cent thereafter. Clause 3 provided that the plaintiff was to be taken over by the new firm and was to be employed in a leading position. The business was transferred on 1 March 1923, and the plaintiff was engaged as commercial manager by a contract dated 14 April 1923. He left the defendant's employment on 31 December 1923 and received 6 months' salary as compensation.

The plaintiff alleged that the accounts supplied to him of sales completed had been defective and that since 1 May he had not received the payments stipulated by clause

2 of the contract. He claimed, first, M4352.66 plus interest and an account of the sales of ambulances concluded since 1 January 1924 and, secondly, payment of 2— per cent of the sales value of the ambulances as evidenced by the accounts to be delivered.

The defendant contended the plaintiff had started again to manufacture ambulances in competition with the defendant after he had left the defendant's employment. This activity was in violation of clause 2 of the contract while, in breach of the contract, the plaintiff could not claim his share in the turnover; instead he was liable in damages. The plaintiff replied that clause 2 did not prohibit him from competing. Moreover, after he had been given notice by the plaintiff he had no choice but to resume work in an area in which he was an expert.

The District Court of Berlin gave judgment for the plaintiff, and the judgment was affirmed by the *Kammergericht*. On a second appeal by the defendant the judgment of the court below was quashed and the case referred back for the following reasons.

Reasons

'. . . The contracts of 24 January/26 March 1923, apart from dealing with the sale of the business, also contains the provision that the plaintiff is to be taken on a leading capacity by the firm which was to be set up, subject to conditions still to be fixed. He was so employed by the contract of 14 April 1923. It does not contain a provision in restraint of trade in respect of the time after the plaintiff has left the defendant's employment. The defendant does not rely on an agreement in restraint of trade concluded between a merchant and his commercial assistant, to be governed by para 74 ff, HGB [Commercial Code]. Instead he contends that the competition by the plaintiff constituted a violation of clause 2 of the contract of sale, since by engaging in competing activities he acted contrary to his obligation to assign to the defendant all the non-pecuniary assets of the business.

The *Kammergericht* proceeds correctly from the principle that a restraint of trade imposed on the vendor as part of a sale of a business may also be agreed on tacitly . . . the interpretation of clause 2 of the contract by the District Court and by the *Kammergericht* is open to criticism, since it adheres excessively to the literal meaning of this contractual clause and overlooks its importance according to good faith.

Clause 2 provides that the plaintiff and L must assign to the defendant all non-pecuniary assets of the firm, in particular patents and similar rights, business connections and sales opportunities in consideration of a percentage share of the plaintiff and L for a period of ten years in the sales value of all ambulances sold during this time. The defendant has stated . . . that [certain governmental authorities] were and are the principal customers, and that it is in the business with these that the plaintiff has competed with the defendant since May 1924 by producing and delivering the same type of car. If this should be true, the plaintiff has complied with his contractual duty to transfer the sales opportunities to the defendant to the extent that he has introduced the defendant to [the governmental authorities] as a supplier. The question is, however, whether this exhausts his contractual obligation or whether after he had left the defendant's employment—even if no prohibition to compete had been imposed on him in his capacity as a commercial assistant—he was under a duty not to compete at all with the defendant, as long as he was to have and to retain a share in the profits . . .

A merchant who promises as a consideration to the opposite party in a contract for the transfer of a business and its customers . . . a share in the profits for the duration of ten years assumes that during this period in which the vendor is to participate in the results of the business, he will obtain the benefit of the custom of those clients which the vendor would have obtained, if he had retained the business. The vendor cannot reasonably expect that the buyer will permit him to recover by starting a competing business, the customers whose transfer to the buyer was to lead to the profit to be shared, while claiming nevertheless his share of the profits in the business which had been sold. The opposite view would demand of the defendant that he must supply a competitor continuously with money, thus enabling the latter to undercut him and possibly to drive him out of business. Such a result would not accord with the presumed intention of reasonable and honest merchants. Consequently, according to good faith, clause 2 of the contract . . . can only be interpreted to mean that the plaintiff's share of the profits for the duration of ten years is balanced by his contractual duty, limited to the same period and independent of his remaining in the employment of the defendant firm, not to deprive the defendant of the non-pecuniary assets assigned to the latter, in particular of the customers, or to reduce them in their value. To act otherwise would frustrate the purpose of the contract, which was to transfer to the defendant the profit from the business to the same extent as it had been enjoyed by the plaintiff and L.

Case 47
REICHSGERICHT (FIFTH CIVIL DIVISION) 5 OCTOBER 1939
RGZ 161, 330

Facts

The heirs of Z owned a big area of land ready for building development at the foot of a wooded mountain situated in an angle formed by the A and the L street. The defendant bought a strip
running along L street in order to develop it. His plan, which included the area retained by the heirs of Z, provided for seven building plots on part of the land between the A and L streets, the foot of the mountain and another street to be laid out subsequently. Five plots bordered on the L street, while the remaining two were situated further back immediately at the foot of the mountains behind the two plots along the L street which were furthest to the right and to the left. The area behind the intervening three plots in the middle was to remain open. The contract of sale was approved by the local administration on the basis of the building scheme as a whole.

On 30 June 1936 the plaintiff bought from the defendant the central plot situated along the L street and built a dwelling house on it. The plaintiff contended that he had acquired this particular plot because he was anxious to have a clear view of the wooded mountain slopes and because the defendant had assured him by reference to the building scheme that no buildings would be erected between the three plots in the middle and that the central plot enjoyed the best view. The written contract did not contain any such assurance and the defendant denied having given it. The contract excluded any liability for physical defects.

On 5 January 1937, the defendant acquired from the heirs of L in addition the land up to the foot of the mountain behind the strip along the L street acquired previously, to be developed with access by a new road leading to the L street. The defendant applied for and obtained the necessary administrative approval for the alteration of the original scheme. The defendant built the road and one house together with a separate garage on one of the plots behind the plaintiff's land.

The plaintiff contended that the new building obscured his view of the mountain and that the value of his property had been reduced. He demanded that the defendant be condemned to desist from erecting another structure on the remaining plot and to pay damages of at least 6100 Reichmark. The Landgericht Bonn and the Court of Appeal of Cologne rejected the claim. On the plaintiff's further appeal the decision of the Court of Appeal has reversed for the following reasons.

Reasons

I. The Court of Appeal holds . . . that it is not a defect of the land purchased by the plaintiff (para 459 section 1 BGB) if the area at the rear of it can be built on. It is unable to deduce from the pleadings that the defendant had warranted, in the meaning of the second section of the above mentioned provision, that the land sold by him was bordered by an area which could not be built on. The Court of Appeal also holds that fraud has not been proved and that therefore the defendant can also not be held liable on the legal ground that he has fraudulently asserted a quality of the object (para 463 BGB as interpreted by the *Reichsgericht* in a constant practice). Furthermore, the Court of Appeal denied that the plaintiff's claims could be justified on the facts, if the principles concerning the failure of the basis of the transaction (*clausula rebus sic stantibus*) (para 242 BGB) were to be applied. The Court of Appeal also could not find that a tort had been committed . . .
II. The appeal . . . is directed against the rejection of the claim based on warranties and conditions under the contract of sale and for damages in tort.

As regards the claims based on warranties and conditions the appellant contends that, contrary to the opinion of the Court of Appeal, it is a defect of the land purchased, if the area at its rear can be built on, resulting in a reduction of the value and suitability of the purchased land for normal use or at least for the use envisaged by the contract. He contends that this defect existed at the time when the risk passed . . . since the defendant was already able at that time to develop the area by providing the access road. The appellant contends that the defect so defined suffices to justify his claims. In addition he contends also that the defendant has warranted as a feature of the land sold that the area at the rear could not be developed . . .
1. Features of an object sold include, first of all, everything which pertains to its natural corporal nature. Thus it is a feature of land destined for development that the soil permits building. In addition, relations exist with the environment of the object which are of a factual, economic and also of a legal nature and which may constitute features of the object. This is the case if relations of this kind are based on the nature of the object itself, emanate from it and affect its value or suitability for use according to their substance or duration, having regard to the opinion of ordinary people. Thus the actual situation of the land, the relationship of one plot to others, is a feature because this relationship is relevant for its value and possible uses . . .

In the result the appeal is justified. The circumstance that the strip between the purchased land and the wooded slope of the mountain was not to be built on was only the means of retaining for the purchased land the advantage of its beautiful situation without restriction. This situation constitutes the essential feature. According to the pleadings both parties assumed at the time of the conclusion of the contract that the situation created the relationship between the purchased land and its environment. Having regard to the assumption that the strip in question would remain open land owing to lack of access and the building scheme approved by the authorities, this relationship between the purchased land and its environment was of such duration in the contemplation of the parties as to constitute according to the opinion of ordinary people one of the factors determining the value and suitability for use of the purchased plot. Accordingly it was a feature of the purchased land that it should provide an unimpeded view of the wooded slopes of the neighbouring mountain and that this view could not be curtailed by the erection of buildings on the intermediate strip

2. A purchased object is defective, if it lacks a quality essential for normal use, or for a different use, stipulated by the contract. The seller is liable for such a defect, if the usefulness or value of the object is thereby extinguished or not insignificantly reduced (para 459, section 1: paras 462, 463, section 2, 480 BGB).

According to the appellant the fact alone that the strip behind his land can be developed has reduced significantly the value or the suitability of the purchased land for normal use. This is not so . . .

Different considerations apply if, so the appellant contends, the parties provided in the contract that the strip behind (the appellant's land) was to remain permanently free of structures which obstruct the view. According to the recent practice of the *Reichsgericht* [references] . . . a defect exists only if the object is unsuitable for its contractual purpose, and if the contract assumes a certain use, it is this use which determines the features of the object which the buyer can demand.

An object is therefore defective if it lacks a feature or even an advantage which the parties assumed to exist when they concluded the contract . . .

Contrary to the opinion of the courts below the fact that the strip behind the appellant's land can be developed, may well constitute a defect of the purchased land . . . the possibility that it might be developed, as it was subsequently, existed already at the time when the risk passed.

However, the claims cannot be founded on the sole ground that the purchased land was defective. This would only lead to a claim for rescission or for a reduction of the price (paras 462, 472 BGB), and no such claim has been made.

3. A claim for damages, as raised by the plaintiff, could only be based on the seller's duty of warranty, if the seller had fraudulently concealed the defect or if he had given an assurance or had fraudulently asserted falsely that the area behind (the plaintiff's land) could not be developed (para 463 BGB). Fraud need not be considered . . .

As regards the question of an assurance . . . the Court of Appeal states correctly that the plaintiff has not explained satisfactorily why the written contract is silent about the assurance, alleged to be almost fundamental, that no development would take place and why this assurance should only have been given in the preliminary negotiations, but, as is undisputed, was not raised when the contract was concluded before the notary. It is true that tacit assurances are legally possible, but in fact they are only rarely presumed to exist; in any case, features which are assumed by the contracting parties to exist are not deemed to have been assured, seeing that the law distinguishes between them [references] . . .

III. If the liability of the defendant, asserted the plaintiff, falls within the area of liability of a seller for defects of the object sold, it cannot be examined whether the claim could be supported totally or in part on the ground that the basis of the contract had disappeared (para 242 BGB) or that the defendant had been at fault in the course of the conclusion of the contract [references]. However, if—as is the case here—no claim to the same effect exists according to para 463 BGB, a claim for a positive breach of contract may lie (para 276 BGB) [references] and, irrespective of any contractual liability for defects, a claim in tort (para 826 BGB) . . .

1. A positive breach of contract exists when, in consequence of a culpable violation of his duty to perform, the debtor causes damage to the creditor which exceeds the amount equal to the value of the performance or if he endangers the performance of the contract to such an extent that the creditor cannot be required to continue with the contract [references]. The second case is excluded here since it is principally concerned with continuing contractual relations, but in both cases the debtor has violated his obligation; liability arises under the contract. However, normally at least, a contractual obligation terminates with the performance of the contract; in the present case the defendant's acts, which the plaintiff regards as a positive violation of the contract, occurred at a time after the contract had been completely performed. For when the defendant acquired the area in the rear, opened it up for development by building an access road and obtained administrative consent, the purchased land had been paid for, handed over and conveyed. Thus no contractual obligation existed any longer which the defendant could still violate. However, even if a contract has been brought to an end by complete performance, certain after-effects may remain, just as at the initiation of negotiations for a contract may have pre-contractual effects. The requirement that a contract must be performed according to good faith and in accordance with common practice (para 242 BGB) may impose on the debtor the duty to carry out, or to desist from carrying out, certain acts . . . Thus . . . a lessor who has let a flat to a medical practitioner must permit a notice of change of address during an adequate period after the tenancy has come to end [references]. Where the transaction involves a single, quickly executed exchange of goods, the continuation of a duty on the part of the debtor to act constantly in agreement with the contractual purpose of the other party cannot normally be assumed without further reasons and for an indefinite period . . . Matters are different however when land is sold and conveyed. There the special circumstances of the individual case must be determined. In the present case the plaintiff . . . has bought his plot precisely on the assumption, shared by the defendant, that the land at the rear would not be developed. Consequently, the defendant is not necessarily relieved of the charge that he has acted positively in contravention of duties as a debtor according to good faith in as much as he proceeded to develop the area at the rear as early as one year after the plaintiff, relying on the assumption that this area would not be developed, had built a dwelling house on the purchased land. According to para 276 BGB even a clause in the contract of sale exempting him from any liability under the warranty would not, according to para 276 section 2 BGB relieve the defendant from liability for an intentional contravention.

It might be objected against the legal conclusions advanced here that the defendant (who did not act fraudulently or gave an express warranty) is at most liable to reduce the purchase price, on the ground that the possibility of development and not the subsequent building operation constitutes a defect of the object sold but that he is not liable to pay damages for having failed to perform his obligation or even to pay more . . . Such an approach would however underestimate the effects of the contract concluded between the parties and would equate to a great extent the factual consequences that the area can be developed with those that it has been developed. It is true that if, in agreeing on the sale, the parties proceeded from the assumption that the area in the rear could not be developed, the absence of the feature assumed by the contract to exist constituted a defect of the plot sold and if a third party without the assistance of the defendant had developed this area and placed a building on it, the plaintiff would not have been able to sue either the defendant or the third party for compensation of the damage not made good by the reduction of the price—leaving aside the remedies available under para 226, 826 BGB. However, in relation to the plaintiff, the defendant was not in the position as any third party. Between the two the contract created a legal relationship, the binding obligation of which based on the general conviction, rooted in morals, that a word, once given, must be kept. As long as the area in the rear remained in fact undeveloped, the plaintiff could only be said to suffer damage exceeding the reduction due to defect, due to the danger that the area might be developed one day. As long as the defendant continued to adhere to the contract, this danger . . . was not to be treated seriously. Only because the defendant acted contrary to the spirit of the contract, a mere danger became . . . actual damage. It would be contrary to the natural sense of justice if a contracting party were not to be held liable for the damaging effects of such a conduct which is contrary to the contract and cannot be excused on legally relevant grounds. Of the provisions on tort only para 826 could be applicable. This states that a person who intentionally causes damage to another *contra bonos mores* is liable to pay compensation. The Court of Appeal has accepted that the plaintiff has suffered damage. The pleadings, which the Court of Appeal found not to be untrue, show that the damage was caused intentionally. The duty of the defendant to pay damages depends therefore on the answer to the question whether his conduct at the time of the conclusion of the contract or the fact that he subsequently built on the area at the rear is contrary to *bonos mores*. As to the former, the defendant is absolved, since the Court of Appeal did not find any fraud. As to the latter, any act *contra bonos mores* could only be founded on any previous activities of the defendant at the time when the contract was concluded. For the pleadings do not show conclusively that the defendant, in developing the land proceeded with the considered intention of damaging the plaintiff, and the findings of the Court of Appeal refute it. The violation of a contractual duty, considered by itself, does not however constitute an act *contra bonos mores* [references] . . . In these circumstances the justified interests of the plaintiff are satisfied by referring him to his remedy based on a positive breach of the contract.

Case 48
BUNDESGERICHTSHOF (SECOND CIVIL DIVISION) 7 FEBRUARY 1957
BGHZ 23, 282

Facts

The plaintiff, born in 1904, was appointed a co-director of the defendant savings bank. By a contract of 25 August 1936 he was appointed sole director until the end of July 1946. The contract provided that in certain circumstances (death, incapacity) he was to be entitled to a retirement pension without having served for any qualifying period. In 1945 he was dismissed on the ground that his national-socialist past excluded him from further employment.

The plaintiff claimed a pension on the basis of the contract of 1936.

The Court of Appeal of Hamburg denied that the plaintiff was entitled to a pension under the contract but held that he could not be denied all rights to a pension and awarded him one half of what he would have received as a pension had he become incapacitated. The Court of Appeal reached its decision by means of supplementing the contractual terms with the help of an interpretation which took account of good faith. It argued that plaintiff's past service merited an adequate provision. No facts had emerged which had shown any disgraceful behaviour. The defendant was without doubt able to pay an adequate, permanent pension. The defendant's plea that, by granting him a pension, the plaintiff would be in a better position than employees relying on collective agreements was rejected on the ground that the claim was based on an individual contract. Since the plaintiff was only a little over forty years old when he was dismissed and since his health and the capacity to work and to adapt himself corresponded to his age, a pension amounting only to one half of what he would have obtained had he been incapacitated was to be considered as adequate. It would be unfair to make an award which would only make provision for payments as his need arose. In the words of the Court of Appeal, the result was 'a pension which is only modest, measured by his former position and potential increases after 1945 owing to age, but which runs since June 1953 irrespective of any other remuneration.'

On a second appeal by the defendant the judgment of the court below was reversed and the claim dismissed for the following reasons.

Reasons

... A supplementation of the contract by way of interpretation is only possible if the contract is incomplete [references]. In the present case it is doubtful whether a lacuna existed in the contract or whether the latter contained an intentional restriction of the contactual pension rights which is therefore incapable of an extension. In any event, a contract can only be supplemented by way of interpretation in accordance with the principles of good faith [references]. The plaintiff has argued that the legal ethos at the time when the contract was concluded must be decisive. This is incorrect [references]. In principle it must be ascertained what the parties would have stipulated had they foreseen the subsequent chain of events [references]; moreover, any supplementation of the contract by way of interpretation must not result in a modification, or limitation of the contractual intention or in an addition to it, nor in a change of the contract, but only in a supplementation of the substance of the contract [references]. However, if accordingly the intention of the parties must be taken into account, as it is expressed in the contract, ie as it existed at the time of the conclusion of the contract, nevertheless in cases were the lacuna in the contract to be supplemented, did not exist from the beginning but arose only afterwards in consequence of further developments, any subsequent event must be disregarded [references]. If the event is one which is affected by a change in the political situation, or if it occurred after a change in the legal ethos, then either the contract cannot be supplemented by interpretation, because the event cannot be interpreted according to the intention of the parties which was based on a situation and or legal ethos which were entirely different, or the application of good faith, which para 157 BGB requires to be observed also when a contract is to be supplemented by interpretation, must bring about that the change in the legal ethos is taken into account. In the present case only the first possibility must be considered . . . Because of his political past the defendant could not employ him and, as subsequent events have shown, the plaintiff was precluded for years from providing his services. The defendant had to replace the plaintiff by another full time employee. In normal circumstances it seems out of the question that the plaintiff would have been conceded a pension in similar circumstances, unless he is in distress . . . The payment of a pension to a healthy person, capable of work, aged forty-one cannot be expected from a savings bank—leaving aside, perhaps, the case of an extraordinary wasting away of his powers—if the right to a pension is connected with the premature dismissal caused by a disability to work in the person of a servant and necessitates the appointment of another full time employee to fill the vacant position. If the plaintiff had been promised a pension for this contingency, he would claim for himself advantages beyond the reign of National Socialism, which he would never have obtained, had he not been connected with National Socialism. Any such agreement would be void according to para 138 section 1 BGB.

Until now and at present the plaintiff cannot either claim a pension on grounds of fairness. The plaintiff receives in his present employment a net annual income of DM25–30,000. If he were to receive a pension in addition he would be better off than if he had remained in the defendant's employment. The fall of National Socialism would therefore have yielded him an advantage in addition to the advantages he obtained through National Socialism. It is not equitable to grant him such an advantage, while the defendant must fill the position by a salaried replacement and the plaintiff is not in want.

It is irrelevant that the defendant can afford pension judgments to the plaintiff, but it is relevant that equity does not support a solution whereby, having been dismissed for personal reasons, he would receive a pension in addition to any salary for services to another after his obligations towards the plaintiff had ceased, although in normal circumstances he would never have received a pension in the event that happened . . .

Case 49
BUNDESGERICHTSHOF (SEVENTH CIVIL SENATE) 9 OCTOBER 1986
NJW-RR 1987, 144

Reasons

The appeal court leaves open the question of the claimant's authority for the claim, and considers all the claims to be time-expired on 29 September 1982. It assumes that there was a guarantee period of two years in accordance with § 12 (1) of the contract and that the period commenced with the inspection and approval of the building work in accordance with § 8 (1) of the General Conditions of Contract for Architects' Contracts (AVA). It regards the length and commencement of the guarantee period as 'negotiated' (*ausgehandelt*). The appeal in law successfully challenges this.

1. According to § 12 (1) of the architects' standard form of contract, a period of 2 years is agreed as the limitation period for the liability of the architect in accordance with § 8 of the AVA. This number is, like other entries in the form—with the exception of the hand written correction of a description of house types and the date of the document—inserted with a typewriter. The contract document therefore appears, as the appeal court also accepts, to be general conditions of contract put forward by the defendant. In such conditions of contract, the statutory guarantee period cannot be effectively shortened (. . .). General conditions of contract are not however present in so far as the contractual conditions have been 'negotiated' individually between the parties (§ 1 (2) of the AGBG (General Conditions of Contract Act) [§ 305 (1) sentence 3 BGB]).

2. The appeal court bases its finding that the length and commencement of the guarantee period had been 'negotiated' on the evidence of the civil engineer A interrogated by it, who had concluded the architect's contract with the defendants on behalf of F. A has stated:

He knew the form of contract brought by the first defendant to the negotiations as the standard form of the Architect's Association, and had therefore had no doubts about its use. The points which were to be individually determined had been talked through. In so far as the form had needed to be completed, these issues had been very intensively discussed, as well as the limitation issue. He had had in mind first of all to get a five-year period accepted. But then he had discovered that the developer R would only be liable under its guarantee for two years. The limitation period for the liability of architects should to run in tandem with the period for the developer's liability. The participants were in agreement here in assuming that the period should begin with the inspection and approval of the building for the defendants as well. Apart from the level of the fee, where he had had to make concessions to the defendants, the contract had corresponded with his wishes in every respect.

The course of dealings thus described does not support the appeal court's finding that the length and commencement of the guarantee period were 'negotiated'.

(a) 'Negotiate' means more than 'treat' (*Verhandeln*) [references omitted]. So it does not suffice for a finding that the contract or individual clauses were 'negotiated' that the form put forward is known to the negotiating partner and does not meet with objections, or that the content is merely explained or discussed and corresponds with the wishes of the partner [references omitted].

(b) It is only possible to speak of 'negotiation' when the user first seriously puts 'on the table' the core content which is contrary to statute law in his general conditions of contract, ie the provisions which amend or supplement the substantial content of the statutory regime, and gives the negotiating partner freedom of formulation for protection of his own interests, with at least a real possibility of influencing the shaping of the content of the contractual conditions [references omitted]. He must therefore clearly and seriously declare himself prepared to make the desired amendment to the individual clauses. As a rule, such preparedness also leaves its mark in identifiable amendments to the pre-formulated text. In special circumstances a contract can however be rated as the result of a 'negotiation' even if in the end, after thorough discussion, it stays in the form of the original draft [references omitted].

(c) Neither the defendants' submissions nor the description of the course of dealings by the user's contracting partner give any ground for thinking that the defendants here would have been seriously prepared to amend the pre-formulated contractual conditions at the wish of the negotiating partner. The civil engineer A appearing for F and the future clients' association has neither requested nor secured any amendment to the text as pre-formulated with the gaps already filled in, in spite of exhaustive discussion. Instead, he has agreed to all the contractual conditions. His unsuccessful attempt to bring the fee down did not concern the pre-formulated contractual conditions. It is true that he had 'in mind' at first get a five-year guarantee period accepted. But he abandoned this of his own accord when he had discovered—and this can only have happened from his firm—that the developer R associated with F was only to provide a guarantee for two years, which he apparently saw as irreconcilable. Nothing in his description of the dealings suggests that the two-year period provided for by the defendants for their liability had seriously been put 'on the table' by them. A has only given evidence about his own considerations which caused him to accept the two-year period required by the defendants. For this, he could not even get a reduction of the remuneration accepted, even though this was at that time inherently possible. Thus it can in any event be deduced from his representation of the results of the dealings that he gave way to a supposedly better insight and thereby submitted to the contractual conditions.

Case 50
BUNDESGERICHTSHOF (TENTH CIVIL SENATE) 18 MAY 1995
BGHZ 130, 19

Facts

The claimant, a savings bank, granted continuous credit to the building company U-GmbH & Co KG (from now on called the principal debtor or KG). On 18 January 1984, the defendant, which was a member of the KG with a limited liability share in the sum of DM100,000, accepted liability as guarantor on the basis of a form without limitation in time or amount and which was unconditionally enforceable [ie under which the person granting it cannot raise the objection that there has not yet been an unsuccessful execution against the principal debtor] for the credit granted to the KG. According to no 1 sentence 1 of the 'Guarantee Conditions,' the guarantee was taken up 'for the securing of all existing and future demands by the savings bank against the principal debtor, including conditional or fixed term ones. . .from their business relationship (in particular from current account, credits and loans of every kind and bills of exchange) as well as from bills of exchange which are submitted by third parties, guarantees, transfers or statutory transmissions of debts'. At the same time, the defendant committed itself not to charge currently held real property. The defendant latter breached this duty. Shortly afterwards, in October 1985, it left the KG in return for a pay-off in the sum of DM150,000. There is dispute as to whether this took place as a result of pressure from the claimant. In January 1986, the claimant raised the current account credit allowed to the principal debtor to DM 2.5 million. At the same time it granted two loans for 2 million and DM 1.5 million. By a letter of 19 February 1990 which reached the claimant on 22 February 1990, the defendant terminated the guarantee. At this point in time, the principal debtor's bankruptcy was already imminent, and it occurred shortly afterwards. The claimant claimed against the defendant as guarantor for a sum of over DM 10 million. By the present claim it demands payment of a part sum of DM 1 million. The *Landgericht* and the *Oberlandesgericht* allowed the claim in principle. The defendant's appeal in law led to quashing and reference back.

Reasons

A. The appeal court has stated that the guarantee contract was effectively created. (. . .)

B. These deliberations do not stand up to legal examination in certain important respects. The wide declaration of purpose is partially ineffective. It is therefore uncertain whether the guarantee was still securing demands when the defendant terminated it.

I. Admittedly the guarantee contract was—if one ignores the general conditions of contract problem—effectively concluded, and was not affected by the defendant leaving the company.

1. The declaration of the purpose of the security in no 1 sentence 1 of the 'Guarantee Conditions' according to which a guarantee is taken up 'for the securing of all existing and future demands, including conditional or fixed term ones, from their business relationship (in particular from current account, credits and loans of every kind, and bills of exchange)' satisfies the requirements as to certainty of content under § 765 BGB. (. . .)

2. The guarantee was not limited in time in such a way as only to apply for the length of the defendant's membership of the company and to be extinguished when it left the company. Nor was it limited to those demands by the claimant which had arisen up to the point when the defendant left. It says expressly in the contract that the defendant was providing a guarantee without limitation in time. In its regime there are no gaps to be closed by supplementary contractual interpretation for the case of the guarantor's membership of the company ending (. . .). This is because the defendant could— and the appeal court correctly refers to this—take its exit as a cause for terminating the guarantee by notice. Under Guarantee Condition no 5 a termination for the future was always possible, without this needing to be based on any grounds. The defendant has not taken this route, although it would have been reasonable for it to do so (. . .).

II. However, the declaration of the purpose of the security violates § 9 of the AGBG (General Conditions of Contract Act) [§ 307 BGB] and possibly § 3 of the AGBG [§ 305c (1) BGB].

1. The extension of the guarantee to all existing and future demands by the claimant in the preformulated declaration of purpose, which should be regarded as a general condition of contract [reference omitted], must be measured against the General Conditions of Contract Act. There is no individual agreement with priority which could remove the significance of the declaration of purpose (§ 4 of the AGBG [§ 305 (1) sentence 3 of the BGB]). (. . .)

2. A guarantee declaration in a form by which liability is widened to all existing and future obligations of the principal debtor arising from a banking business relationship can be surprising—with the result that it has not become a component of the contract (§ 3 of the AGBG [§ 305c (1) BGB])—if the guarantee is taken up for the purpose of securing a current account credit. (. . .)

(b) A regime in general conditions of contract has the character of surprise if it clearly deviates from the expectations of the contracting partner, who should not sensibly need to take it into account in the circumstances. The contracting partner's expectations here are determined by the general and the individual circumstances accompanying the conclusion of the contract [references omitted]. The general accompanying circumstances include the degree of deviation from the dispositive statute law and the usual formulation for that area of business. The special accompanying circumstances include the course and content of the contractual negotiations as well as the outward character of the contract [references omitted]. According to the view put forward by the senate so far, a clause in a bank's or savings bank's form-based contract is not surprising, if in it a guarantor secures all existing and future claims from the banking business relationship against the principal debtor, even though the cause for taking up the guarantee was only a particular claim by the credit institution against the principal debtor. (. . .) The senate had given as its reasoning that, according to § 765 (2) BGB, it was included in the rules of the statutory provision that a guarantee could also be taken up for future demands against the principal debtor of undetermined amounts. None of the provisions of §§ 765 ff BGB (and in particular not § 767 BGB) provide for the limitation of the guarantee to a determined maximum when it had been taken up from the outset for future claims arising from a determined business relationship In the light of this statutory regime, and the goal pursued by it of unilaterally securing a creditor, the guarantor could not be protected, released or otherwise relieved simply because he had taken up the global guarantee in respect of the establishment or extension of a particular obligation of the principal debtor.

(c) The senate does not adhere to this case law, which has partly met with agreement [references omitted] and partly with disapproval in the academic literature [references omitted]. In contrast to its previous view, the senate deduces from § 767 (1) sentence 3 BGB a requirement for limitation of the guarantee. The provision states that a guarantee obligation is not widened by a legal transaction which the principal debtor enters into after the taking up of the guarantee. This regime should not only be applied when a limitation is actually agreed. The statute assumes it to be self-evident that, besides the certainty of the demands to be secured, there should for the guarantor's protection be a limitation of the guarantee by reference to a sum of money. In this manner, unilateral extension of the scope of the guarantee by the principal debtor and the creditor on their own authority is to be prevented. An unlimited extension of liability by the legal transactions of others contradicts the fundamental protection of the guarantor's private autonomy [references omitted]. He will not generally expect such a deviation from dispositive statute law. As the relationship with the bank is a business relationship with an open content, the objective limitation of the guarantor's liability to demands from the banking business relationship does not suffice to protect the guarantor [references omitted]. In so far as the guarantor's expectations are not determined by the statutory model but by the course and content of the contractual negotiations, the senate adheres to the case law of the fifth and eleventh civil senates of the *Bundesgerichtshof*. In the case of mortgages on land for security purposes for repayment loans, these senates consider the extension of the real (*dinglich*) liability to all existing and future obligations of the third party to be in principle 'surprising' in so far as they go beyond the cause for the security contract [references omitted: 'causal case law']. (. . .) the guarantor who enters into a guarantee because of a particular credit which is limited in amount should not [need] to take into account a clause in a form under which the guarantee extends to all existing and future demands from the banking relationship, without any limitation as to amount [references omitted]. Admittedly the surprise presupposed in § 3 of the AGBG [§ 305c (1) BGB] cannot arise if the guarantor, when taking on the guarantee, does not actually think about the level of the debts for which he promises to assume responsibility. (. . .) It is different however if the guarantor when giving a guarantee declaration orientates himself to the granting of a particular credit, or to the extension of an existing credit by a certain sum, or to the prolongation of a particular credit, and it is permissible for him to do so. No substantial change is needed to this assessment if the credit which forms the actual cause for the guarantee is granted on current account. (. . .)

(d) Widening the guarantor's liability to all existing and future obligations of a company by means of a form will not as a rule be 'surprising' for a guarantor who as director, or sole or majority shareholder of the principal debtor can determine the type and level of its obligations. He does not need the protection of § 767 (1) sentence 3 BGB (. . .).

(e) In the present case the surprise effect of the wide declaration of purpose cannot be assessed conclusively. (. . .)

3. This is because the extension of the guarantee to all demands—even future ones—under the banking relationship without limitation of amount is ineffective because it infringes § 9 of the AGBG [§ 307 (2) BGB]. (. . .)

(b) The extension of the guarantee liability by means of a form beyond the demand which was the cause of the guarantee to all present and future obligations of the principal debtor is not reconcilable with the main statutory decision behind § 767 (1) sentence 3 of the BGB (see above 2c) (§ 9 (2) no 1 of the AGBG [§ 307 (2) no 1 of the BGB]). At the same time, it so limits important guarantor's rights which arise from the contract's nature that the attainment of the contract's purpose is endangered (§ 9 (2) no 2 of the AGBG [§ 307 (2) no 2 of the BGB]). On both grounds an unreasonable disadvantage to the guarantor must be assumed [references omitted].

(aa) A wide declaration of purpose expects the guarantor to take on an incalculable risk. The guarantor has no influence over the creation and proper discharge of new debts. If he has to be responsible for them, his liability can suddenly amount to many times the amount he had reckoned for in the worst case. This could threaten him with ruin. He is supposed to be protected from such consequences by § 767 (1) sentence 3 of the BGB. He should not run the risk, without his agreement, of incurring an incalculable liability though the uncontrollable steps of third parties—the principal debtor and the creditor.

(bb) Furthermore, if a private person takes on a guarantee, limited liability follows as a rule from the purpose of the contract. The prohibition contained in § 9 (2) no 2 of the AGBG [§ 307 (2) no 2 of the BGB] is supposed to prevent contractually important rights and duties being undermined by general conditions of contract [references omitted]. The legal issues which are contractually important depend, in the case of contracts shaped by statute, on the statutory type of contract. The subjective horizon of the contracting parties' expectations takes second place to this. In the case of a guarantee, the prohibition of dispositions by other parties is contractually important because of § 767 (1) sentence 3 of the BGB.

(c) Within the framework of § 9 of the AGBG [§ 307 BGB] the cause of the guarantee is to be understood primarily in an objective sense. This is different from § 3 of the AGBG [§ 305c (1) BGB] which is predominantly geared to the parties' subjective concepts of purpose (. . .). Even a guarantor who intends unthinkingly to be responsible for the principal debtor's 'obligations' as a whole is unreasonably disadvantaged if it is required of him in a form to be jointly liable for other debts than those which were the objective cause of the guarantee. The objective cause is the current need of the creditor for security, but preserving the prohibition of dispositions by other parties. (. . .)

4. The fact that extension by the form of the guarantee liability to all demands arising from the banking relationship has not become part of the contract does not lead in the present case to its ineffectiveness. The declaration of purpose should instead be preserved in the form that the guarantee secures all existing and future demands, including conditional and fixed term ones, by the defendant against the principal debtor under the credit relationship as at the time of the giving of the guarantee declaration. The decisive factor is therefore in principle the credit limit at that time.

(a) The legislator has in principle decided in § 6 (1) of the AGBG [§ 306 (1) BGB] that—in contrast to § 139 BGB—the legal consequences of the control of general conditions of contract are limited to the clauses or parts of clauses affected in each case. The whole clause, or even the whole contract, including the parts not directly affected by the control of general conditions of contract, would only exceptionally be ineffective if adhering to the regime—possibly supplemented under § 6 (2) of the AGBG [§ 306 (2) BGB—is unreasonable for a contracting partner (§ 6 (3) of the AGBG [§ 306 (3) BGB]). When there are objections to a clause or part of a clause in general conditions of contract, the preservation of the contract in other respects in principle assumes of course that the provision can be split into a permissible and an impermissible part. For this, division would need to be possible into components which would each be comprehensible in themselves and meaningfully separable from each other [references omitted].

(b) The declaration of purpose here is divisible in its content and subject matter (see above 3(a). Over against this, perfect linguistic separation is not possible. (. . .) Although a version of the clause which is free from objections can only be achieved by rewording rather than by leaving out individual sections, this does not amount to an impermissible reduction in order to maintain validity (. . .) The ban on reductions to maintain validity (. . .) is supposed to protect the contracting partner of the user from unfair clauses, and ensure that the content of general conditions of contract does justice to the interests on both sides. It would be inconsistent with this to permit the user, when he puts forward his conditions, to go beyond the boundary of what is permitted in an unscrupulous way, with nothing more to fear than that the court would move the detriment to his partner in the transaction back to a permissible level. It is not a question of that here. On the contrary, the rewording of the clause should facilitate the retention by the contract of a performance content: the very content which corresponds to the guarantor's conceptions when giving his guarantee declaration, so that his justified interests are taken fully into consideration. The total invalidity of the guarantee would—measured by the protective purpose of the General Conditions of Contract Act—be an excessive legal consequence (. . .). To separate linguistically (a) the taking up of the guarantee for the demand the securing of which was the cause for the guarantee from (b) the extension of the guarantee to all existing and future obligations of the principal debtor, it would have sufficed to divide the declaration of purpose accordingly into two sentences. In this case it was beyond question that the part of the declaration of purpose concerning the main obligation can exist after elimination of the other part, and the guarantee can remain effective as such. Therefore there is no prohibition existing for the guarantor's protection against producing the same result by the rewording of a unified clause (. . .)

Chapter 4

Case 51
BUNDESARBEITSGERICHT 21 OCTOBER 1966
NJW 1967, 173

Reasons

I. . . .
A widow's claim against the former employer of her divorced husband for payment of a pension can only be based on the contract of employment between her divorced husband and the defendant, his former employer. . . .
II. The Landgericht correctly interpreted the defendant's undertaking to pay a pension to Mr R, the divorced husband of the plaintiff, as not giving rise to rights in the person of the plaintiff. . . .
1. It is not correct, as the appeal court assumes, that pension undertakings must be interpreted restrictively. It is correct that no claim for a company pension can legally be derived from the contract of employment alone, but rather requires a separate legal basis (*BAGE* 4, 360, 367 = *NJW* 56, 1732; *BGHZ* 16, 50, 51 = *NJW* 55, 501). This does not mean however that there needs to be an *explicit* undertaking to provide a pension. It is generally accepted that as well as individual contracts or collective agreements, even a so-called tacit agreement or a customary practice within a business or

even the principle of equal treatment can act as the legal basis for a pension claim [references]. The general rules on interpretation apply throughout. Like the contract of employment, pension undertakings which generally form part of that contract are subject to the same rules on the interpretation of civil contracts as those found in §§ 133, 157, 242 BGB.

2. When applying the general rules on interpretation the same result is reached as that of the *Landesarbeitsgericht* (LAG).

(a) In No 5 of the pension undertaking the 'wife' of the deceased employee is promised a lifelong pension. As correctly stated by the LAG, the general linguistic use of the word 'wife' does not include a divorced wife. Legislation uses this term in the same way. Legal provisions generally contain an addition where the legislator intends to express that the provisions apply not only to spouses but also to divorced partners . . . §§ 58 et seq of the Marriage Act (EheG) which variously refer to 'spouses' when including divorced former spouses do not lead to a different conclusion since the title of that section of the Act is called 'consequences of divorce' which clarifies that it deals with divorced partners. (Other examples listed) . . .

(c) The legal provisions of the law on civil servants and on social security in favour of divorced spouses provide no generally binding legal principle applicable for contractual pension undertakings made by private employers. Under the principle of contractual freedom, a private employer promising his employees old age and widows/widowers pensions is not bound to use the general public law principles of, and provisions on, civil servants and social security. Nor must an employer include divorced spouses who had a maintenance claim against the deceased employee, in the group of persons entitled to a widow's pension. It is not up to the court to decide whether or not such practice would be desirable. An explicit inclusion of a relevant provision in the contract is an indispensible precondition for such claim. The current legal provisions provide no legal basis for a former employee's pension claim against his former employer, and where such a pension claim is agreed by contract, the law does not grant a divorced spouse who had been entitled to maintenance a direct claim for a widow's pension. Such a claim by a divorced spouse must have been specifically agreed on, for instance by naming the entitled person in the contract. This was not the case here. The defendant's pension undertaking contains nothing which could be construed as a reference to regulations which apply for civil servants or to provisions on social security . . .

Case 52
BUNDESGERICHTSHOF (THIRD CIVIL SENATE) 10 MAY 1951
BGHZ 2, 94

Facts

The plaintiff was leaving the hospital where his wife was a private patient when he fell and suffered concussion, a fractured skull, and a cerebral haemorrhage. He alleged that the accident was due to the dangerous condition of the main entrance of the hospital, and claimed damages from the defendant. So far as his action was based on breach of contract it was dismissed at all levels of jurisdiction.

Reasons

The Court of Appeal held that the defendant was not liable on its contract with the plaintiff for the hospitalisation of the plaintiff's wife. It accepted that under a contract of *lease* the tenant's family have a contractual claim against the landlord if there is a defect in the leased dwelling or its approaches which is attributable to him and they suffer harm thereby; and it agreed that the hospitalisation contract is like a lease in certain respects; it found however that the lease features of a hospital contract are really very subsidiary: the patient has no claim to any particular room, and the primacy of the medical treatment reduces the significance of the premises as compared with a contract of lease. Therefore no contractual liability of the defendant arose under § 278 BGB.

In contesting these views, the appellant emphasises the fact that he himself made the contract whereby his wife was taken in by the defendant as a private patient. The contract bound him to pay the hospital bill and bound the defendant not only to care for his wife (§ 328 BGB), but as a subsidiary duty, to enable him to visit his wife in safety. Given that he was a principal contracting party, it is irrelevant, says the plaintiff, whether, had he not been, the defendant would be liable to him under § 328 BGB in the way the landlord is liable to the tenant's family.

Contrary to the appellant's view, the contractual liability of the defendant for the accident which the plaintiff suffered as he was leaving the hospital by the front steps cannot depend on whether it was the plaintiff himself or his wife who entered into the hospitalisation contract. It is true that a contract is formed when a private patient is taken into a hospital, even a hospital run by a public body (RGZ 64, 231; 83, 72; 111, 263; see also RGZ 108, 87), and that the plaintiff as husband acquired contractual rights against the defendant (RGZ 64, 233); yet it is not from the formation of the contract but from its content that a duty to take care of the plaintiff's safety must arise. If in addition to the primary obligation towards the patient to give him medical treatment, the terms of the contract include an obligation towards certain third parties, the hospital would be contractually liable to those third parties regardless of whether they had participated in the formation of the contract or not.

The hospitalisation contract is doubtless a contract of services (*Dienstvertrag*) [(RG JW 1938, 1246; other references omitted], whereby the patient is to be provided with bed and board as well as with medical treatment and care. The medical treatment is however the essential and critical element, the bed and board being by contrast rather subsidiary [see RGZ 112, 60; other references omitted]. There is thus no occasion to infer any subsidiary contractual duty to ensure that the patient's husband be safe in visiting the hospital. But the result would be just the same even if one held, in view of the purpose of the hospitalisation contract, that there was an independent contract for lodging and meals collateral to the main contract for medical services; the result would be the same, too, if a separate contract with different terms were made with a doctor (RG JW 1936, 3182 no 6), for example, if the patient were taken into the hospital on the referral of the doctor treating her so that the treatment could be continued there. For even if there were a separate contract with the hospital for lodging and meals, the plaintiff as husband would have no contractual claim to safe access to his sick wife, despite the lease features of the contract. It is true that under the law of lease the tenant's family have the same rights against the landlord regarding the safety of the premises as the tenant himself [RGZ 91, 21, 24; 102, 232; 152, 175, 177; 169, 87; other references omitted]. In accordance with the purpose of the contract, rights are granted under § 328 BGB to those who belong to the tenant's household, members of the family and domestic help; but no such rights are granted to guests: the precondition is living together in the rented premises. The tenant intends (and his intention, though inexplicit, is perceptible by the landlord) to have the lease include the members of his family and respect their needs; to persons outside the home who stand in no particular relationship to the leased premises, this does not apply. The recognition of the tenant's implicit contractual purpose to put his family in the optimum legal position may have led to giving a child a direct claim for proper medical treatment when the treatment is arranged by its statutory representative (RGZ 152, 175), but even so it is only the child being treated who has a direct claim for the contractual performance arising out of the contract. When the husband takes the wife to hospital, he admittedly has a contractual claim that she be properly treated, but apart from that he is in no special relationship with the hospital and has no contractual claim for care towards his own person; he therefore cannot demand safe access to his wife in the hospital on the basis of the hospitalisation contract. We need not decide whether it would make any difference if the husband, with the consent of the hospital management, had stayed in the hospital, even overnight, in order to be near his wife. On the facts, the plaintiff had no claim against the defendant for breach of a contractual duty of care.

Case 53
BUNDESGERICHTSHOF (SEVENTH CIVIL DIVISION) 9 NOVEMBER 1966
BGHZ 46, 198

Facts

The plaintiff's grandmother (the testatrix) died on 13 March 1962 when the plaintiff was ten years old. She left her estate to her three daughters. One of them was the defendant, and aunt to the plaintiff. The testatrix left two savings bank books, one of the *Stadtsparkasse* (municipal savings bank) the other of the *Kreissparkasse Köln* (Cologne Disctrict Savings Bank) both made out in the name of the plaintiff. The defendant took both savings books. After the start of the court action, she relinquished one of these to the plaintiff. This litigation concerns the *Kreissparkasse* savings book. There is DM9554.17 in the account. The lower courts have rejected the claim for surrender of the book. The plaintiff's further appeal is successful.

Reasons

. . .

3. In assessing the evidence, the only question that arose was whether or not the testatrix and the District Savings Bank concluded a contract in favour of the plaintiff (§ 328 BGB) with the effect that the plaintiff *ab initio* owned the claim against the bank in respect of the funds, ie both the opening balance and later payments. The facts raised the question of whether the testatrix only intended to leave the savings account as a bequest to her granddaughter with the result that she became owner of the

savings account only at the death of the testatrix, unless of course the testatrix had otherwise disposed of it.

(a) The fact that such a bequest is possible through a contract between living persons and without the need for the formal requirements requested for wills and testaments can directly be deduced from §§ 328 II, 331 I BGB (RGZ 106, 1 et seq; BGHZ 41, 95; BGH NJW 1965, 1913; BGB-RGRK § 516, No 29). There is no need once again here to discuss the counter-arguments put forward by Boehmer (Staudinger/Boehmer, *Erbrecht*, 11. ed. Introd. § 27), Coing (Kipp/Coing *Erbrecht*, 11. ed., § 81(IV) and (to a certain degree) by Lehmann (Staudinger/Lehmann, *BGB*, 11. ed., before s 1937, No 14). But in order to assume that the opening of a savings account in a third person's name constitutes a case as envisaged by § 331 BGB, the contract between the saver and the savings bank must show that the saver wishes to bequeath the funds on his/her death. The savings bank must also have intended this effect. There is however no need for very strict demands in respect of this point. When a savings contract is concluded, the savings bank allows the saver to decide which person is entitled to the savings and at what point, and does not influence the decision. Savings banks accept any instructions from the saver as to who shall have a claim to the funds (see RG LZ 1932, col 955). According to § 808 BGB, by payments made to the holder of the savings book, the savings bank is freed from any claims brought by the person actually entitled to the funds. In deviation from other contracts, for instance giro accounts, where, in the interests of the contractual party who enters an obligation, it must be unambiguously clear who in fact is entitled under the contract, in the case of savings contracts it is sufficient that the person entitled to the savings is somehow identifiable from the contract, though not necessarily clearly and specifically, so long as it is eventually possible to identify without doubt who the beneficiary is and under which conditions he/she becomes entitled. Where later on several persons make a claim for the funds, the savings bank can rid itself of any obligation by payments made to the holder of the book. But the bank can leave it to the various claimants to settle the question of entitlement amongst themselves or if necessary with the aid of the courts, and then to pay the person which the court decision names as successful claimant.

(b) The typical feature of this case lies in the fact that a close relative (grandmother) opened the savings account in the name of her relative, who was still a child (grandchild), without handing over the savings book and, as must be assumed, without informing the beneficiary that a savings account had been opened in her favour.

As already explained in detail (see above under 2(c)), such behaviour must normally be interpreted as indicating that the saver wishes to retain the right of disposition until her death. On the other hand it cannot normally be assumed that the grandmother's intentions to name her granddaughter as entitled party should have no legal consequences whatsoever (see Mordhorst, 'Spareinlagen auf fremden Namen' *MDR* 1956, 4 6; Ritter, *Der Sparvertrag auf den Namen eines Dritten*, Erlanger Diss., 67 et seq). Unless the circumstances of the case indicate otherwise, by opening the savings account in the grandchild's name, the grandmother expresses her intention, irrespective of her continued right of disposition, to bestow the savings bank deposits, or what is left in the account at the time of her, ie the grandmother's death on her granddaughter and that she therefore intends to give her granddaughter preferential treatment to the detriment of her other heirs. It could have been precisely for this reason that the testatrix, immediately before her death, announced her intention of bestowing DM40,000 on the plaintiff a fact which, for the purposes of this further appeal can be assumed as proven. In view of this aspect of the case, the court of appeal needed to consider the plaintiff submissions to this point.

(c) It is possible to bestow funds on a third person under § 331 BGB by opening a savings account in that other person's name (see OLG Kiel, LZ 1919, 971). It is not prohibited just because the saver and the recipient did not conclude a legally valid agreement clarifying the rights in the savings account (*Valutaverhältnis*) with the result, as far as the heirs are concerned, the entitlement to the savings account was received without legal basis and consequently gives rise to the heirs' claim for unjust enrichment. However, in its decision, reprinted in NJW 1965, 1913, at 1914 (= WM 1965, 748), the *Bundesgerichtshof* has pointed out that the naming of the beneficiary can constitute the saver's offer to the beneficiary to bestow funds on him/her (promise to make a gift or conditional gift) which the beneficiary can accept even after the saver's death (§§ 130 II, 153 BGB); an offer which, under § 518 II is not subject to any formal requirements, since the gift was already made when the offer was accepted (see also Erman/Westermann, *BGB*, 3. ed.; § 331, note 4.)

4. Under § 564 ZPO, the appeal court's decision had to be quashed. The court of further appeal cannot give a final ruling, since it cannot itself establish exactly for which purposes the testatrix opened the savings account in the name of the plaintiff. This point needs clarified by the court of appeal to whom the case is returned under § 565 ZPO. In further hearings, the parties will be given the opportunity to make supplementary submissions and to raise further claims in the light of the above findings. Whether or not the testatrix, by opening the savings account, intended to make a disposition under § 331 BGB can only finally be ascertained by close inspection and interpretation of the relationship between the relatives, especially the relationship between the testatrix and her daughters (the heirs) and, on the other hand, her relationship to the plaintiff, her granddaughter. Any ill effects from remaining doubts and uncertainties must be borne by the plaintiff.

Case 54
REICHSGERICHT (FOURTH CIVIL SENATE) 8 FEBRUARY 1923
RGZ 106, 1

Facts

The claimant, sole heir according to the will of the deceased HE who died in 1918, demands from the defendant the surrender of several saving bank books allegedly forming part of the inheritance. During her life, the testatrix had personally paid in the savings amounts and the books had been made in the names of her siblings that of the defendant among others. As requested by the deceased, each book contained a stipulation according to which the testatrix, during her life, was entitled to withdraw capital and interest without consent from the 'owners of the books' or to make other provisions in respect of the capital and the interest. The testatrix later on handed over the books to the defendant which are now in her possession. The *Landgericht* decided in favour of the claimant, the court of appeal rejected the claim. The further appeal is unsuccessful.

Reasons

The decisions is based on the finding that an agreement had been reached between the testatrix and the administration of the savings bank according to which on the testatrix's death or at the later time as specified in the books, the 'persons entitled as shown by the books' have a direct claim against the savings bank for payment of the amount of the credit in the savings account. As a result of the agreement, the defendant and her siblings (or children of her siblings) under §§ 328, 331 of the Civil Code (BGB) became creditors of the savings accounts set up in their name as from the date specified in the books, whereby they also became owners of these books according to § 925 BGB. Simultaneously, the agreement replaced a formal assignment of the savings-bank deposits which was not carried out by simply issuing the books and their re-registration under the new names (RGZ, 60, 143; 73, 221; 89, 402).

The legal validity of the agreement cannot be disputed under § 331 BGB. There were no particular formal requirements which had to be observed, even though payments to third persons were to be made free of charge. In the case of a contract for the benefit of third persons, the question of possible formal requirements can only be relevant for the relationship between promisor and promisee (see Warn. 1914, No 243, p 341; judgment of 22 January 1920; IV 397/19). In this case the promise of a gift was not made directly to the third person and was not directed at that third person, so that neither the formal requirements of § 518 nor those of § 2301 apply. The relationship between the testatrix and the savings bank is a contract for a loan on interest which does not require a special form in order to become valid.

Reservations as to the legal validity of agreements such as this one can arise solely from the fact that by using this kind of agreement there is—indisputably—a danger that the formal requirements set out for testaments are circumvented. However, no such illegal circumvention can be assumed where the law itself in its § 331 which contained no restrictions whatsoever, provides legitimate means of avoiding formal requirements in respect of wills and testaments. Moreover, the misgivings are not as grave as it initially appears. The Inheritance Tax Act (*Erbschaftssteuergesetz*) of 20 July 1922 (RGBl. 1922, 695) in its § 2 (1) (No 4) makes provision for the taxation of such transactions. According to §§ 214 et seq, and § 32 KO (Bankruptcy Act), the creditors of the estate can challenge such transactions. In this context it can be left undecided whether or not heirs entitled to a compulsory portion of the inheritance (*Pflichtteilsberechtigte*) can defend themselves against their creditors by using § 2329 BGB. Possible misgivings must also take second place to the demands of commercial life which, in ever more frequent cases, use such transactions in order, amongst other purposes, to meet a considerable economic interest of the parties. The majority of legal writers and the case law (see in particular Hellwig, *Verträge auf Leistung an Dritte* p 350 et seq; Endemann, *Bürg. Recht*, 8, ed., vol 3, § 30, vol. 4, § 87 IV, no 6) favour the recognition of such contracts and the *Reichsgericht* in the decision of its III. Senate (RGZ 88, 137) has followed this opinion in a case not unlike the present one, as has the II. Senate in an earlier decision (RGZ 80, 177). There seem to be no dissenting decisions of the *Reichsgericht* and this is particularly true of the decision reproduced in RGZ 83, 223. The case to be decided does not concern a contract in favour of a third person, since the testator's contractual partner merely held the legal position of a messenger acting on the testator's instructions. Finally, there is no discrepancy between the court's opinion as stated above and the one held by this Senate and cited by the further appeal (RGZ 98, 279), since in that case the legal question to be solved in respect of the current case was deliberately left undecided. In RGZ 98, 297 the court merely refers to the above-mentioned reservations concerning the legal validity of agreements of this kind; but as shown above and on repeated reflection, such reservations cannot be given the weight of a decisive factor. The above-mentioned decision dealt with an agreement of the testatrix's death. The heir's action against these third persons to agree to the surrender of the securities to the estate was successful because—a legal point which must be followed—the contract which is subject to the law of obligations and which is concluded with the bank in favour of third persons, could not transfer ownership to these third persons. A second study of this decision as to whether or not the reason given in that decision suffices to uphold it, or whether the heirs, despite the lack of an effective transfer of ownership in the securities, were bound by an obligation *in rem* and thus barred from exercising their claim of ownership, is not needed in deciding this case (for this point see in particular Kipp in *Festschrift für Luitpold*: 'Wer kann mit Vermaächtnissen beschwert werden?' p 141).

The further appeal also submits that the testatrix, in exercising her right of disposition over the credit balance which she had retained for the duration of her life had, by appointing the claimant as her sole heir, legally validly transferred to that heir her own claims against the savings bank. However, it follows from the stipulations in the savings books that the testatrix had retained the right to demand the capital and the interest be paid to her only as against the savings bank. In this way, ie by a declaration to the contractual partner (the savings bank) the contractor could at any time be partially or completely cancelled by the testatrix A unilateral cancellation through the appointment in her will of a third person as her heir was not envisaged and not permissible.

Finally, the appeal court correctly assumes that the claimant cannot claim the surrender of the books to her as heir on the basis of the contract of its deposit allegedly concluded between the testatrix and the defendant. According to the appeal court's view, the purpose and content of the contract was that the holder of the books (the bank) surrendered these books after the testatrix death to the persons entitled as shown by the entries in the books. In respect of the savings book intended for the defendant herself, a possible claim for surrender in favour of the claimant and based on the contract for deposit has lapsed because the defendant, according to the above reasons, has become creditor of the credit balance and thus, according to § 925 BGB owner of the book already in her possession. The claimant was likewise no claim for the retransfer of the other books stemming from the contract of deposit, because that contract had been concluded, as the appeal court ascertained, in favour of the other relatives and grants them, according to § 331 BGB which in this context also applies, a direct claim under the law of obligations for possession of the books in exclusion of the heiress.

Case 55
BUNDESGERICHTSHOF (FIFTH CIVIL SENATE) 29 JANUARY 1964
BGHZ 41, 95

Facts

The parties are joint heirs of a woman who died in 1953. Shortly before her death the decedent wrote to her bank 'After my death please give my niece [the defendant] . . . the share certificates lodged in my safe-deposit box and the money in my account . . .' After her aunt's death the defendant obtained the share certificates from the safe-deposit box and sold them. The plaintiff now claims part of the proceeds as belonging to the estate.

The *Landgericht* and the *Oberlandesgericht* gave judgment for the plaintiff, but on the defendant's appeal the decision was reversed and the case remanded.

Reasons

The only question the Court of Appeal dealt with was whether the defendant had obtained joint ownership in the share certificate. As the appellant points out, it should also have asked whether she did not have at least a personal claim against the estate to have joint ownership vested in her.

The court below was quite right to hold that the decedent's instruction to the bank created no real right in the defendant: real contracts for the benefit of third parties are not recognised by the courts as a matter of positive law (RGZ 66, 97, 99–100; 98, 279, 281–3; 106, 1, 3). Nor is there a case for anything like a right of expectancy or *Anwartschaftsrecht* (such as was mentioned in RGZ 106, 1, 3, as against RGZ 98, 279, 281–3), less far-reaching than a full vested right, but imposing a real obligation on the heirs.

But the decisions are uniform on the following point: a person who wishes to make a gratuitous grant of a right against another which is to vest only on his death (§§ 328, 331 BGB) may do it by means of a contract for the benefit of that third party (here the donee) even without observing the formal requirements for a *donatio mortis causa* [§ 2301 BGB) (RGZ 80, 175, 177–8; 88, 138–9; 106, 1, 2–3; 128, 187–9; other references omitted]. This certainly applies where the right granted is a right to claim money from a bank. Why should it be different when it is a question of a right to claim a share certificate? In both cases the grant under §§ 328, 331 BGB is of a personal claim which the third party (here the defendant) automatically acquires on the death of the promisee (here the decedent) against the promisor (here the bank). In both cases performance consists of a conveyance (transfer of ownership in the money or the share certificate) which the bank is obliged by its legal relationship to the promisee (the decedent: the *Deckungsverhältnis*) to effect for the third party. How the promisee's heirs are ultimately affected by the real transfer of rights which arises through this performance-transaction depends on the legal relationship between the third party and the decedent (the *Valutaverhältnis*). If it is a question of gift, it may be effected in two ways: the account-holder can make a promise of gift direct to the beneficiary (which quite probably happened here, given that the parties lived together), or he may make a contract with the bank for the benefit of the third party donee, containing an offer of his promises gift for onward transmission by his contractor, the bank, to the beneficiary, which the beneficiary can accept by silence, since this is what the account-holder wants (RGZ 128, 187, 189). Any informality in the gift promise is thus cured by performance (§ 518 BGB; RGZ 128, 187, 189), and the third party is entitled to receive and retain, even against the heirs of the promisee, what the bank now owes him. Accordingly in German law the result of this case depends entirely on whether the decedent wanted the defendant to have the shares as a gift, or only in order to defray expenses. This is also the right preliminary question as to the defendant's liability in tort (was her dealing with the share certificate contrary to law in the sense of § 823 BGB?) Indeed, in both cases, even if she had no real right in the shares, a personal claim for the transfer of ownership would entitle her to win by the *exceptio doli (dolo petit qui petit quod redditurus est)*.

Case 56
BUNDESGERICHTSHOF (SIXTH CIVIL DIVISION) 24 JUNE 1969
BGHZ 52, 194

Facts

As general agents for Europe, the defendant sold H installations, produced by company S in M (USA), and used for simplifying the feeding of animals. In order to advertise for these installations, he had organised a working trip to the USA in the summer of 1960 to inspect the installations operating on American farms. He had invited mainly farmers and agricultural consultants. For the flight out and back he chartered a plane from an American airline. In September 1961, he organised a second similar fact-finding trip for which he had gathered 74 participants. For this trip he had again chartered a plane from the 'PA' company. The overall flight costs were charged to the participants. On 9 September 1961, the participants departed from Düsseldorf for the USA in a plane belonging to the chartered airline. After a stop-over in Shannon (Ireland), the plane started to cross the Atlantic. A few minutes later it crashed. All passengers were killed.

Under the Warsaw Convention for the Unification of Certain Rules Relating to the International Carriage by Air of 12 October 1929 (in the following: WC) (RGBl. 1933 II, 1039), their surviving dependants, among them the plaintiff, received from the third-party insurer of the 'PA' the maximum sum of liability insurance. However, the dependants were not satisfied with this sum. They brought an action for a judicial declaration that the defendant was liable to compensate them for current and future losses from the death of their breadwinners.

The *Landgericht* (High Court) rejected the claims, the *Oberlandesgericht* (Court of Appeal) found in their favour. The defendant's further appeal resulted in the latter decision being quashed and the matter being referred back to the court of appeal for the following reasons.

Reasons

The appeal court interprets the contract concluded by the defendant with the participant to the effect that the defendant had personally become liable for transporting the participants by air to the USA and back. Since he had thus become an air carrier in the sense of the Warsaw Convention (WC), and the transportation had not been free of charge (Art 1 WC), he was liable under Art 17 WC. He could not rely on the maximum amount set out by Art 22 WC. The appeal court did not decide whether or not the plaintiff could deduce the defendant's unlimited liability from Art 25 WC, since the court held such liability already to be founded by the the defendant's breach of Art 3 II 2 WC, as he failed to issue air tickets. His letter to the participants could not be construed as air tickets.

There are fundamental legal doubts in respect of the appeal court's decision (VersR 1968, 583) declaring the defendant unrestrictedly to be liable under Art 3 II 2 WC.
(. . .)
B.
I. The appeal court's findings are correct that the defendant acted as air carrier and is thus liable under the Warsaw Convention.
1. The application of the Convention presupposes that this is a case of international air transport in the sense of its Art 1 (see § 51 of the Air Transport Act—LuftVG), and that the defendant acted as air carrier in the sense of the Convention. The decisive question is whether the participants had concluded a transport contract with the defendant o whether the latter had only been bound by the participants' mandate to arrange for their transportation by an airline, whereby only that carrier, ie the 'PA' was liable.

(a) The appeal court rightly proceeds from the letter of invitation which the defendant sent on 4 July 1961 to numerous farmers, agricultural consultants, etc as possible purchasers or advisors on purchases of the ensilage installation. This letter, accompanied by a registration form, stated:

> 'The great interest which active farmers, scientists and professional journals show in the H process for rationalising the feeding of animals has caused us to organise a second working trip to the USA this autumn to which we cordially invite you.
>
> We shall probably leave Düsseldorf on 8 September 1961 and fly to Chicago. The return flight will take place on 30 September 1961 from New York.
>
> The costs, including bus trips and accommodation, will probably run to DM1900. All in all there will be 76 participants. . . .
>
> In Germany, the trip will be organised by us and in the USA by the S company . . .'

The appeal court rightly finds that this letter is not yet an offer to conclude a contract but rather an invitation to apply to the defendant for participation in the trip The deceased passengers did so by filling in and returning the registration form and by sending DM1900. By his letter of 23 August 1961, the defendant accepted the offers. It said:

> 'Concerning: Second H study trip to USA
> Dear Mr . . . (followed by name)!
> We confirm with thanks receipt of DM1900 and inform you that we have made a firm booking for you for the second H. study trip to the USA. Attached you will find a circular with further instructions regarding the trip.'

The appeal court holds that the participants could only understand this letter to mean that the defendant wanted to be liable for organising the air transport although by using an airline (§ 278 BGB), since the defendant retained the right personally to select the participants. All applications needed to be directed to the defendant who was to receive payment. The trip was an advertising trip organised by the defendant for his own purposes. Although he instructed the participants that a Lockheed was to be used, he did not indicate with which airline the participants needed to conclude a contract. They knew that the defendant himself was not an airline and that he did not own a plane. However, in 1961, it was already customary that companies organised air transport on planes which they chartered from airline companies.

(b) The further appeal submits that the appeal court's reasoning infringes general rules of interpretation and fails to consider vital circumstances. There are, however, no such indications.

The assessment of the contents of the contract, which the appeal court reached after interpreting the parties' expressed and tacit declarations of intent (§§ 133, 157 BGB), is feasible. It infringes no principles of logic or experience. The further appeal incorrectly submits that the case concerns an interpretation of typical clauses of model contracts. The fact that the defendant concluded identical contracts with all participants does not alter the fact that individual declarations needed to be interpreted.

The Court of Appeal investigated the defendant's allegation that he did not intend to be personally liable for transportation but rather only intended to arrange the conclusion of a contract for transport between the participants and an airline company enlisted by him. The appeal court does not wish to rule out that the defendant intended merely to act as intermediary, but it holds that he should have clearly expressed this intention to the participants.

(aa) As repeatedly submitted by the defendant, his legal position in relation to the participants was not that of a travel agent. Normally, when air transport is offered, a travel agent merely intends to act as an agent. It is not the travel agent but rather the airline, whose ticket he sells, who is eventually liable as air transport operator (Schleicher/Reymann/Abraham, *Das Recht der Luftfahrt*, 3. ed., Art 1 WC, n 28, p 274; Riese, ZLW 1962, 8; Bodenschatz, VersWi 1957, 358; Georgiades, RFDA 1953, 16 et seq; decision of the Court de Cassation, Paris, RFDA 1956, 217). The same applies where several air passengers get together (group travel) and one of them deals with an airline with whom he then concludes a group transport contract, so for instance the chairman of a sports club, or a company acting for its employees. In such cases it is the operating airline alone who acts as air carrier and not the chairman or the company owner (see Schleicher/Reymann/Abraham, above, Art 1 WC, n 26; Bodenschatz, above, p 360; Riese, ZLR 1958, 7; Meyer ZLR 1957, 328, at 330). The case before the court cannot, however, be compared to those cases. Contrary to the position of a travel agency, this case concerns a trip organised by an enterprise which is part of a worldwide corporation and which could be trusted to be able to organise its own air travel in respect of a trip which benefitted its own commercial interests.

(bb) The defendant's liability as carrier of his air passengers would be excluded, if he merely intended to be and indeed acted as agent of an air carrier. The appeal court correctly rejects the submission that this was the case.

The defendant made no submissions as to how the participants had commissioned him in their name to conclude a contract with an airline. The fact that, when concluding the charter contract, he did not name the participants speaks against such interpretation. Above all, the appeal court's reasoning is strengthened by the fact that the defendant never informed the participants with which airline they were to fly, ie with which contractual partner the defendant should conclude the contract in their name . . .

The 'agent-clause' in Art 17 of the charter-party concluded between the defendant and the airline does not point out that the defendant intended, and was expected, merely to act as the participants' agent. Although this clause, used by many companies which are members of the IATA (International Air Traffic Association) when planes are chartered, states that the charterer concludes the contract 'both on his own behalf and as agent for all persons carried in the aircraft' (see to this point Sundberg, Air Charter, 1961, 359 et seq), it is doubtful whether the word 'agent' used in this clause means an agent in the sense of § 164 BGB or merely an intermediary, as will be shown below (see Grönfors, *Air Charter and the Warsaw Convention* (1956), p 115, n 4; Schweickhardt, ZLW, 1964, 13). This question does not need to be answered in this context. No inference to the participants' detriment can be drawn from the contract concluded by the defendant with the airline, for instance that they, by returning the completed application forms, had given the defendant power of agency.

(cc) In detailed submissions the further appeal tried to substantiate the fact that the defendant, when concluding an air charter-party with the chartered company for his participants, merely acted under a mandate from the participants (contract for services—*Geschäftsbesorgungsvertrag*). As a result and as against the participants, he was not liable for transport. Like a forwarding agent (see § 407 BGB) who arranges transportation through a carrier, he simply undertook carefully to select the company chartering out the plane.

The further appeal correctly holds that such a construction is possible (see Guldimann, *Internationales Lufttransportrecht* (1965), Art 1 WC, n 8; Schweickhardt, ZLW 1964, 23; Riese, ZLW 1962, 8; Rudolf, ZLW 1960, 146) and could have been envisaged for these particular circumstances. But, in the sphere of commercial law, the answer to this question already poses grave difficulties, ie the point whether an agent who concludes a contract with a third person in the interests of his principal does so as an agent only (commission agent, forwarding agent) or whether he acts on his own account (own business). The present case presents the same difficulties. Its solution depends entirely on the circumstances and on the interpretation of the statements made by the parties (Schleicher/Reymann/Abraham, above, Art 1 WA, n 28; Schweickardt, *Schweizerisches Lufttransportrecht* (1954), pp 50, 51) . . .

Decisive here is the general principle according to which any interpretation of declarations of intent is not governed by what the party possibly intended to declare but rather by what was in fact declared. The recipient is not responsible for any uncertainties; their effects need to be borne by the person who failed clearly to express himself. The appeal court applied this principle. In so far as it concludes that the defendant was not merely a 'forwarding agent' but had rather undertaken to carry out transportation himself, this result cannot be faulted. The defendant had fixed the price at DM1900. There was never any mention of the fact that he needed to provide his 'principals' with an account on how these sums had been spent. The participants had not approached him with the order to arrange for them a trip to the USA. It was he who advertised a working trip to be organised by him and in his interests.

The further appeal alleges that this was 'merely' a contract in favour of third persons (§ 328 BGB). This allegation misses the vital point. It is possible that the 'Aircraft Charter Contract' concluded between the American airline (chartered company) and the defendant (charterer) was also concluded in favour of the 'group' listed in the con-tract as persons to be transported (so Art 8 of the contract), as is often the case in such charter contracts (see Drion, *Limitation of Liabilities in International Air Law* (1954), No 120, n 3). However, the decision in this case does not hinge on the relationship between the defendant and the airline (the covering contract) but rather on the underlying debt relationship (*Valuta-Verhältnis'*) between the defendant and the par-ticipants. As held by the appeal court, in case of a transport charter this can again take the form of a transport contract, ie a sub-contract on transportation, which the char-terer concludes with the travellers whom he has attracted, and for the performance of which contract he has concluded a further transport contract with the operating air-liner (von Bodenschatz, VersWi, 1957, 358 so-called 'real charter contract; similarly Pelichet, *Responsabilité Civile en Cas d'Affrètement et de Location d'Aéronef* (1963), p 40). Where such a triangular relationship exists, the charterer is the air carrier in relation to his passengers and liable under Art.17 WC (Schleicher/Reymann/Abraham, above, Art 1 WC, n 26; Riese, ArchLuftR, 1939, 138; Bodenschatz, above, 360; Goedhuis, *National Air Legislations and the Warsaw Convention* (1937), p 134; Shawcross/Beaumont, on Air Law, 2. ed, 1951, n 513 = 3. ed., 1966, 603). Contrary to the further appeal's opinion, the 'agent-clause' in Art 17 of the charter-party is not the decisive point which is decisive. This clause intends to create a direct legal relationship between the chartered company and the passengers assembled by the charterer, so that the chartered company, as against the passengers, acts as air carrier in the sense of Art 1 WC with the result that when claims for dam-ages are brought against him, he can draw on the restrictions on liability set out in Art 22 WC, even where initially he did not know who his passengers were ('undisclosed principal'; see Sundberg, above, 360; Shawcross/Beaumont, above, 2. ed., No 351 = 3. ed., 480; Drion, above, No 120; Rudolf, ZLW 1960, 146; Dutoit, *La Collaboration entre Compagnies Aériennes* (1957), p 101). Thus, this 'agent' clause can have the effect that the passengers also acquire a personal, direct claim for transportation against the chartered company (§ 328 BGB). This does not however change the fact that the pas-sengers first and foremost have concluded a contract for transport with the charterer acting as their 'agent'. An interpretation of this internal relationship between charterer and air passengers does not depend on the interpretation of the outer rela-tionship between charterer and chartered company, ie the contents of the charter-party. The decisive question is whether or not the defendant concluded the contract not only in his own name, but for his own interests and as air carrier for the passen-gers gained through advertising. The appeal court has correctly answered the question in the affirmative . . .

II. The court of appeal correctly ascertained that the defendant is basically liable under Art 17 WC . . .

III. (But) the facts on which the appeal court bases its decision only justify the finding that the defendant's liability is limited by the maximum amount set out in Art.22 WC. But since 'PA''s insurance company has already paid the maximum amount, addi-tional liability requires the existence of other claims.

1. The plaintiffs submit that the defendant's liability is unlimited under the rules on breach of contract (§ 325 BGB, positive breach of contract, contract with protective effect in favour of the surviving dependants) and on tort under §§ 823 et seq BGB. This is not correct. Once it has been ascertained that the defendant acted as air carrier, ie

was liable under Art 17 et seq. WC; all other bases for liability are thereby excluded (Art 24 WC).

2. Thus, the claim for unrestricted liability can only be well founded if the dependents' allegation is correct that the defendant or the 'PA' company and its staff acted so negligently that their behaviour amounted to intentional breach of contract (Art 25 WC). The appeal court has not answered this question. Since this point can only be ascertained by a court which considers the facts, this case is referred back to the appeal court for further deliberations and decision.

Case 57

BUNDESGERICHTSHOF (SEVENTH CIVIL SENATE) 17 JANUARY 1985

BGHZ 93, 271

Facts

The defendant, an airline company, chartered seats to company T for a return flight from Frankfurt/Main to Santa Lucia (Antilles, Caribbean) planned for 9 and 16 December, 1980. Company T passed on a number of these seats to company O, Fernreisen GmbH, a travel agent, for air package tours. On 15 December 1980, company T stopped payments.

On 16 December 1980 employees of the defendant refused to let a Mrs H take the return flight to Frankfurt, although she had booked with company O air tickets for the trip to Santa Lucia between 9 and 16 December 1980 for herself and her companion. As the reason for their refusal the employees stated that company T had not paid for the flight. Mrs H and her companion then flew back with another airline. The resulting costs of US$1,783.60 plus interest were successfully claimed by Mrs H against company O.

The plaintiff, an insurance company structured as a public limited company, indemnified company O for the claim of the court action plus interest amounting to DM44,575,64 in addition to the legal fees and court costs amounting to DM1397.32. The plaintiff now claims the entire amount of DM5972.96 plus interest from the defendant. Both the *Landgericht* and the *Oberlandesgericht* have granted the claim for DM4575.69 plus interest. The further appeal, though admissible, was unsuccessful for the following reasons.

Reasons

The Court of Appeal (*Berufungsgericht*) is of the opinion that the charter contract between company T and the defendant constituted a true contract in favour of a third party as set out in § 328 BGB, by which Mrs H had obtained against the defendant a right to transport. By refusing to transport Mrs H, the defendant became liable to pay Mrs H damages under § 325 BGB. In divergence from the provisions of § 334 BGB, the defendant could not raise against Mrs H the possible defence of breach of contract for outstanding payments, which he has against company T. As far as the relationship between the chartered company and the benefiting traveller goes, one must assume that the plea of unpaid charter fees was tacitly excluded since the traveller relies on having acquired a claim of transportation against the airline free from any pleas.

As against Mrs H, the defendant and company O were joint debtors. As company O has satisfied Mrs H's claim for damages, this claim transferred to company O under § 426 (2) BGB. Although both joint debtors are in principle liable in equal proportions, in this case § 254 BGB comes into play *mutatis mutandis*. The defendant must therefore solely bear the loss, since he has caused the client H further transport costs by refusing transportation. Company O thus has a claim against the defendant amounting to the payments made to Mrs H and this claim has passed on to the claimant.

The further appeal is unsuccessful.

1. As a result of the travel contract concluded between Mrs H and company O as tour operator, Mrs H had a claim for transportation from Frankfurt/Main to Santa Lucia and back against company O (§ 651(a)(1) BGB). As the Court of Appeal rightly held, this claim for transport also existed as against the defendant. It is true that there existed no direct contractual links between Mrs H and the defendant and, in particular, company O as tour operator did not act as the defendant's agent. But when concluding the travel contract for herself and her companion, Mrs H had at the same time booked two of the tickets chartered to company T by the defendant. The charter contract concluded between the defendant company T constitutes a contract for transport in favour of Mrs H (see BGHZ 52, 194, 201/202; LG Frankfurt/Main [1983] *NJW* 52; Ballhaus in *BGB-RGRK*, 12. ed. 328, note 50; MünchKomm/Gottwald, § 328, note 39; Schwenk [1970] *BB* 282, 284).

(a) Contrary to the opinion of the further appeal, such a contract in favour of Mrs H. cannot be denied for the reasons that (1) the charter contract does not contain an agency clause; (2) the air tickets had been issued by company T and not by the defendant and (3) the defendant did not know the persons to be transported. It is true that the decision in BGHZ 52, 194, 202 and the legal literature following this ruling (see Ballhaus, above; Schwenk, above) are of the opinion that when a contract in favour of third persons is to be assumed, special significance is to be attached to such an 'agency' clause, whereby the charter contract is concluded in the name of the charterer as well as for the benefit of various air passengers to be transported. However, such a clause is not the determining factor in the classification of the charter contract as contract in favour of third parties. Likewise, the place where the air tickets were issued is not decisive.

A charter contract obliges the chartered party to make available to the corridor seats on the flight organised by him. He knows that the persons to be transported are normally only named after the charter contract has been concluded, by the charterer or by a third person empowered to act for him, once package travel contracts have been signed. Thus under § 328 (2) BGB it is the main purpose of a charter contract to transport air passengers who are identified to the chartered party only when the charterer or the third person insert their names on the air ticket. The contractual partners had intended that the contract had this particular aim. It is thus appropriate to assume that the air passengers who, at the time the charter contract was concluded would normally not be known, and *in whose interests* the charter contract was concluded, have direct contractual claim for transportation against the chartered party even where the charter contract does not contain an agency clause and their air tickets are not issued by the chartered party himself.

(b) Contrary to the opinion of the further appeal the provisions of § 651 (a) BGB also contain nothing against the assumption that a contract in favour of a third party was concluded. It is true that under § 651 (a) BGB the traveller who has concluded a tour contract in principle only has the tour operator as his contractual partner; but when executing specific tour services that tour operator can make use of other persons or bodies providing services to carry out his obligations. This arrangement, merely concerning the relationship between the tour operator and the passenger, does not rule out that the passenger, as a result of the specific form of the contract, *in addition to* his claim against the tour operator also has a claim against these third persons so employed. The opinion held by most legal writers contractually holds that it is possible to construct the contract between the tour operator and the person providing the service as a contract in favour of a third party which provides the passenger with direct claims against the provider of the service (see Beuthien in *Studienkommentar zum BGB*, 2. ed., § 651 (a) Note 3; Brox [1979] *JA* 493, 494; Erman/Seiler *BGB*, 7. ed., § 651 (a), note 11; MünchKomm/Lowe, before § 651 (a), note 15; Palandt/Schwerdtner, *BGB*, 12. ed., § 651 (a), note 27 et seq., see also Bartl *Reiserecht*, 2. ed., note 269).

(c) Finally, the various interests of the parties are best served if the charter contract is seen as a contract in favour of the passenger. Especially in the case of air package tours, the passenger depends to a large degree on the services of the chartered party as the case before the court shows. His interest in a journey which is as trouble-free as possible therefore demands that he is able to direct his claim for transportation not only against the tour operator, but against the airline. The interests of the chartered party in only being liable to the tour operator for the provision of the services are comparatively slight.

2. The appeal court's opinion is also to be upheld where it finds that in respect of the relationship between Mrs H and the defendant the charter contract excludes the application of § 334 BGB. It correctly assumes that the defendant could not counter Mrs H's claim for transportation by the plea that company T had not fulfilled the contract.

(a) The rule contained in section 334 BGB according to which the promisor can use pleas arising from the main contract against demands from the third party can—even tacitly—be excluded (see Gottwald, above, § 334, note 2). In particular, the very nature the main contract can mean that the debtor cannot use all pleas from this contract against the third party (see BGH [1980] *NJW* 450; LG Frankfurt/Main [1983] *NJW* 52, 53; Palandt/Heinrichs, above, § 334 Note 1; Staudinger/Kaduk, above, § 334 Note 8).

This is the case here. The defendant concluded the charter contract with company T—a tour operator—which then transferred the chartered airline seats to company O—against a tour operator. For this reason the defendant had to assume that the seats were used as part of travel contracts concluded by the tour operators with travellers and that these travellers would already have paid the costs of the flight, included in the overall price for the journey, before the start of the journey irrespective of whether they had been obliged to do so. The defendant had also agreed that company T issued air tickets for the seats which he had chartered out. Under these circumstances the defendant must have known—as the appeal court rightly assumes—that passengers booking an air package tour and who are not aware of the specific legal form of the transport contract, expected and could expect that their claim for transportation against the defendant was free from pleas. As chartered party, the defendant could not oppose Mrs H's claim by pleading that the charter contract had not been fulfilled. Rather, it is part of his area of risks to ensure that payments which passengers made for the flight are received by him in time.

(b) The argument raised by the further appeal cannot be followed, according to which it was up to company O to fulfil the customer's expectations and to make appropriate arrangements with the defendant. The charter contract concluded between the defendant and company T is a contract in favour of air passengers. The air passengers' interests were thus adequately protected as set out above; there was no need for any further agreements between company O and the defendant. Mrs H, customer of company O could also rely on the fact that the defendant would provide her with transportation, once she had paid the fare for the journey.

(c) The defendant also had no other reasons for refusing to transport Mrs H. The appeal court correctly assumes that the defendant, as against Mrs H could not plead an overbooking allegedly made by company T. Even where the defendant's claim is correct that: first, company T had regularly overbooked flights, and secondly, that on 16 December 1980 the defendant had accepted a number of company T's passengers in Santa Lucia, this provides no explanation as to why Mrs H in particular could not have been given transport for reasons of overbooking. In this respect the appeal court rightly points out that Mrs H had not been refused transport for *that* reason but rather because company T had allegedly not paid for the air ticket.

3. As a result of the defendant's unjust refusal to provide return transport, Mrs H had a claim for damages against company O under § 651 (f) BGB, since company O as tour operator was vicariously liable for the defendant's fault. On the basis of the charter contract concluded in her favour and broken by the defendant, Mrs H had an *additional* claim for damages against the defendant, arising out of § 352 BGB. Since in respect of this claim, as the appeal court rightly assumes, the defendant and company O are liable as joint debtors, and company O has in the meantime settled Mrs H's claim, under § 426 (2) BGB her claim against the defendant has passed onto company O.

The appeal court's reasoning can also not be faulted according to which, as far as the relationship between the defendant and company O was concerned, the defendant in analogous application of § 254 BGB, was not merely liable for his portion of the performance of the contract but was rather liable in full. By unjustly refusing to provide return transport, the defendant has caused the additional transport costs incurred by Mrs H. There is no reason to assume that company O caused this damage, since company O fulfilled its duty to provide Mrs H with return passage by booking the chartered flight seats. Furthermore, company O had no way of putting pressure on the defendant to fulfil his duty to transportation. It is thus appropriate that the defendant, according to the degree of his own fault, is liable in full for the entire damage [see decision of the Senate in BGHZ 59, 97, 103 with references].

4. The claimant indemnified company O their insured, for the damage stemming from Mrs H's claim. According to § 67 (1)(1) of the Insurance Contracts Act (WG) Mrs H's claim against the defendant has thus passed to the claimant.

Case 58
REICHSGERICHT (SEVENTH CIVIL DIVISION) 4 JUNE 1902
RGZ 51, 403

Reasons

On 29 October 1900, the merchant Karl W obtained a personal life assurance worth DM10, 000 for the benefit of his wife, the plaintiff. After his death on 22 May 1901, a bankruptcy petition was filed in respect of his inheritance and the defendant appointed as receiver in bankruptcy. He objected to the payment of the insurance sum to the plaintiff who now by this action demands his approval to the payment. The receiver bases his objection on the fact that the insurance contract constituted a gratuitous transfer in the sense of § 32 II of the Bankruptcy Order (KO) which is subject to rescission under these provisions. Both lower courts have ruled in favour of the plaintiff. The appeal court held that there is in fact a gratuitous transfer subject to rescission, according to § 32 II KO, if funds were disposed of which formed part of the deceased bankrupt person's estate. Here, this was not the case. Under § 330 BGB, when the life assurance contract was concluded, the plaintiff on the death of her husband directly acquired an entitlement to demand payment of the insurance sum from the insurance company. The husband himself had of course never owned the right to be paid by that company.

The defendant bases his further appeal on § 331 I BGB which states:

'Where the obligation is to be performed to a third person after the death of the person to whom it was promised, in case of doubt that third person acquires the right to performance of the undertaking on the death of the recpient of the undertaking.'

The further appeal could not succeed.

According to § 330 BGB, in cases as here, where a contract was concluded in favour of a third person and where there is doubt, that third person acquires a directly actionable claim if the life assurance contract made provision for payment of the insurance sum to the third person. In respect of all contracts in favour of a third person § 331 I BGB, as quoted above and cited in the further appeal provides that where an obligation to a third person is be performed after the death of the recipient of the undertaking, that third person acquires the claim only at the point of death. This result equally applies to insurance contracts. Unless otherwise agreed, up to that point the beneficiary of such an insurance contract merely acquires an expectation to receive the insurance sum but not yet a conditional right. (see Dernburg *Bürgerliches Recht*, vol. 2, § 106, n II, 1; Planck, *Bürgerliches Gesetzbuch*, n 1 to § 331).

However, the following points need to be considered in respect of the manner of acquisition at the above specified point in time: The beneficiary acquires assets which the deceased had provided to be transferred at the point of his death; but since this point of death is decisive for the acquisition, the assets are not part of the inheritance and do not stem from the testator's estate. Instead, at the point of death, the beneficiary acquires the respective claim directly as a result of the insurance contract. Contrary to other provisions dealing with the transfer of rights in case of death, legislation here provides for a direct acquisition *mortis causa*. Since a right acquired in such manner is not part of the estate, it cannot be touched by the creditors of the estate (see Endemann, *Bürgerliches Recht*, 3 to 5 ed., vol. 3, § 66, 287).

In respect of § 331 I BGB, Jaeger and Hellwig come to a different conclusion. Jaeger holds that: 'In case of doubt, the third person acquires the claim at the point of death directly from the testator' (*Kommentar zur Konkursordnung*, n 28 to § 32). Hellwig deduces that at the point of death 'the assets are shifted directly at the expense of the stipulator's estate' (*Die Verträge auf Leistung an Dritte*, § 57, 367). In view of their opinion that at that specific point in time a transfer of property occurred, both writers presume that, where a bankruptcy petition was filed in respect of the estate of the person who received the undertaking, under the preconditions set out in §§ 30 to 32 KO the receiver in bankruptcy can rescind the bequest to the third person and the event of death acts as point of acquisition of that bequest.

But this court cannot follow these arguments for the above-stated reasons. When the BGB entered into force, the outcome remained the same. The *Reichsgericht* previously held (see Seuffert, *Archiv*, vol. 48, 452) that in a case like this, acquisition in favour of a third person directly although conditionally occurred when the contract in favour of the third person was concluded. The result was that at the point when the bankruptcy order was made in respect of the insured testator's estate, rescission of the testator's respective legal dispositions was excluded, because, as stated above and regarding the claim for payment of the insurance sum, no assets were distributed which were part of the estate to which the creditors in bankruptcy were entitled. Under the provisions of the BGB rescission is likewise excluded since, according to these now applicable provisions, the assets which are subject to the bankruptcy petition were not reduced by acquisition of the now unconditional claim for payment of the life assurance proceeds.

Case 59
BUNDESGERICHTSHOF (EIGHTH CIVIL SENATE) 19 SEPTEMBER 1973
BGHZ 61, 227

Facts

The plaintiff claims damages for the harm caused to the house of its insured, B (the landlord), to whose rights it is subrogated (§ 67 Insurance Contract Act— *Versicherungsvertragsgesetz*—VVG).

The first defendant had rented one floor of B's house since 1966, as well as a further room which he used as a store-room. On the ground outside the house he kept a single-axle motor-trailer, equipped for the sale of food and drink and containing two cylinders of propane gas which fuelled some cooking apparatus and two lights. The second defendant was a salesman employed by the first defendant.

On the early morning of 21 December 1967 there was an explosion due to escaping propane gas. This explosion destroyed the vehicle and damaged doors and windows in the landlord's house as well as the paintwork outside and in. On 22 December 1967 the landlord gave immediate notice to quit, and the first defendant moved his vehicle to another plot of land which he rented.

The plaintiff indemnified the landlord and now claims payment of the sum of DM3718.98, first demanded on 11 October 1969, on the basis that on the evening of 20 December 1967 the second defendant carelessly failed to turn off the taps of the propane gas cylinders.

The *Landgericht* gave judgment for the plaintiff, but the *Oberlandesgericht* reversed on the ground that the claim was time-barred, a point which the defendants had raised in their second ground of appeal. The plaintiff's appeal is dismissed.

Reasons

I. . . . II. Claims against the first defendant.

1. The Court of Appeal assumed, without detailed investigation, that the landlord (to whose rights the plaintiff is subrogated) had concurrent claims against the first defendant in tort and under the contract of lease. It found these claims time-barred under § 558 BGB [now § 548 BGB]. The Court held that no claim arose under § 7 Road Traffic Act (*Strassenverkehrsgesetz*—StVH) because the trailer-shop was not a 'motor vehicle' in the sense of § 7 of that enactment, nor was it 'in operation' at the time, as required by that provision.

2. In the circumstances of the case there is much to be said for this last point, but we need not determine it now for, as we shall explain, the applicability of § 558 BGB means that if any claim did arise under the Road Traffic Act it would in any case have prescribed.

The *Reichsgericht* and the *Bundesgerichtshof* have always held, with virtually no dissent from commentators, that the short prescriptive period of § 558 BGB applies to all damages claims, regardless of their basis, which the landlord can bring in respect of alteration to or deterioration of the leased property. This includes claims under the Road Traffic Act, at any rate when, as here, the garaging, keeping, or parking of the vehicle is envisaged by the lessee and the harm results from such a use of the leased property. To hold otherwise would frustrate the purpose behind § 558 BGB, namely that the parties should be prompt in finalising the landlord's claims for damages, for § 14 StVG has a two-year prescriptive period which the landlord could invoke in order to displace § 558 BGB.

3. The main damage caused by the explosion, according to the Court of Appeal, was to parts of the property that were neither demised by the lease nor, like the front door, the entrance hall, and the staircase, provided for common use by people including the first defendant. The Court of Appeal, following the *Reichsgericht* in RGZ 75, 116, was right to hold that this is no obstacle to the application of§ 558 BGB to all claims for damages arising out of harm caused by the explosion.

(a) It is true that the six-month prescriptive period of § 558 para 1 BGB applies by its terms only to claims in respect of alteration to and deterioration of the *leased* property, and of itself this applies only to the property which the lessee may use under the lease contract, exclusively or in common with others. To this extent, at any rate, the statutory rule is unequivocal: all claims in respect of such harm prescribe in six months. Desirable as it might be to have a single prescriptive period for claims for damage to leased and to unleased property, the binding nature of § 558 as a special rule of the law of leases makes it impossible to say that where damage to unleased property occurs as well, claims for damage to the leased property prescribe in thirty years (§ 195 BGB).

(b) Quite the contrary. It frequently happens that a tenant causes simultaneous harm to leased and unleased parts of the property. If in such cases one part of the claim prescribed in six months and the other only in thirty years, the aim of § 558

BGB, namely to procure that the landlord's claims be swiftly and finally dealt with, would only be partially achieved. We must therefore follow the *Reichsgericht* in holding that in such mixed cases the uniform short prescriptive period of six months applies. To construe § 558 BGB in this manner causes no juridically unacceptable disadvantage to the landlord, at any rate where he is in immediate possession of the unleased parts which are damaged, for then he can forthwith ascertain the nature and extent of the damage just as he can when the tenant returns the leased property (see this Senate 2 October 1968, NJW 1968, 2241). We must take it that that is the situation here, for the plaintiff has not asserted that those parts of the dwelling which were not leased to the first defendant were leased to anyone else and thus inaccessible to him. We therefore need not investigate when the period of prescription begins to run in respect of harm to property leased not to the defendant but to other tenants, supposing that one could in law have different start-points for the six-month period of prescription depending on when the damages parts of the property were returned to the landlord (compare § 558 para 2 BGB).

(c) We must also reject the idea of having different periods of prescription depending on whether the harm is caused predominantly to the leased property (as in RGZ 75, 116) or to parts of the property not included in the lease. To handle such mixed cases in that way would lead to legal uncertainty, as the Court of Appeal pointed out, and would leave open the question how to deal with a case where the harm caused to leased and unleased property was equal in extent.

(d) Nor can it matter how extensive the harm caused to the parts of the property not leased may have been; for the clear intention of the statute is that the landlord is bound by the short prescriptive period even when very considerable harm is caused to the leased part of the premises. All this flows from the legislator's concern that the landlord's claims for damages be dealt with quickly and definitively.

(e) Another factor which tells in favour of having a uniform short period of prescription is that the duty of care incumbent on the tenant of premises applies to the whole premises and not just to those parts which are leased to him, for, leaving aside other concurrent claims which the landlord might have, the tenant could hardly be liable for damaging the leased property unless he were in breach of this duty. The tenant has a contractual obligation to take care that his use of the leased property causes no harm to other parts of the property. There can hardly be any overwhelming reason for having separate periods of prescription when the tenant causes harm to leased and unleased parts of the property by a single act or omission in breach of his duty of care. It can be left open what the decision should be if the only harm caused by the tenant's breach of his duty of care is to objects not included in the lease, since the question does not arise here.

(f) The appellant does attempt to split the lease into two, one object being the land on which the sale-trailer was kept, and the other the store room. Had there been two contracts of lease between the first defendant and the landlord, such a division might arguably be acceptable, but even the plaintiff makes no such assertion. If there is but only contract of lease, § 558 BGB applies to all parts of the property which are leased, and also those, such as the external stairway, the front door, and the foyer, which are in common use and provide a necessary link between the various parts which have been leased. It is thus impossible to say, as the appellant tries to do, that none of the damage due to the explosion in front of the house was to 'leased things' under § 558 para 1 BGB.

5. The appellant raises no objection to the manner in which in which the period of pre-scription was computed, and no error of law is to be found therein. The Court of Appeal was consequently right to dismiss the claim against the first defendant.

III. Claims against the second defendant.

1. Here, too, the Court of appeal allowed the defence of prescription, in reliance on the decision of this Senate in BGHZ 49, 278. As in that case, the person from whom dam-ages were claimed here was an employee and agent for performance of the tenant who, being drawn into the protective ambit of the contract of lease, could invoke the short prescriptive period of § 558 BGB just as the tenant himself could. There was the further ground, as in the decision cited, that the second defendant was engaged in a 'dangerous activity' on behalf of the first defendant, and was thus entitled, if sued, to be indemnified by him; but if the second defendant was liable and the first defendant was liable to indemnify him, the first defendant would then lose the protection of § 558 BGB.

2. The appellant objects to this that the second defendant was not engaged in any dangerous activity: there are gas cookers in every house, but housemaids and cooks are not engaged in a dangerous activity. The concept of dangerous activity was devel-oped in relation to truck drivers and agents of that kind whose employment was inher-ently dangerous. There is much to be said for this, but we need not decide whether in the end of the day we agree with it for, as can be inferred from the cited decision, the tenant's assistant is entitled to invoke the short period of prescription if he falls within the protective ambit of the contract of lease. The Court of Appeal was right to hold that this was true of the second defendant.

(a) This Senate has repeatedly explained that contracts of lease are a prime exam-ple of the application of the legal doctrine of contracts with protective effects for third parties (see BGHZ 49, 278, 279; 49, 350, 353). The courts include a third party in the protective ambit of a contract if the creditor owes him a duty of care and protection. In the case of leases this applies not only to the tenant's family but also to domestic servants and other assistants who, consistently with the lease, share in the use of the leased property or indeed, as here, use it on behalf of the tenant.

(b) It is therefore beyond doubt that the second defendant was included in the pro-tective ambit of the contract of lease. The question then arises whether this entitles him to invoke the defence under § 558 BGB in his own right. As was explained in BGHZ 49, 278, 279, the primary effect of the protection is that the third party, if injured by the landlord's breach of contractual duty, may sue him for damages. But if the third party has the right to sue the landlord for damages, it is difficult to see why, when he has damaged the landlord, he should not be able to invoke the short pre-scriptive period, just like the tenant himself. Ultimately, the third party is given a claim for damages because it would be unjust, when the tenant has a claim, to deny a like claim for contractual damages to the third party who uses the leased property as envisaged and comes to harm thereby or thereon. If this is so, it would be no less unjust to deny the protection of § 558 BGB to a tenant's assistant when he has caused harm to the leased property while using it on behalf of the tenant or pursuant to a con-tract with him. If the contract of lease can extend its protective ambit to a third party in appropriate cases like the one before us, there can be no doctrinal reason why its protective effects should be limited to granting a claim for damages. On the contrary, it is entirely appropriate to extend it so as to curtail liability by means of the short pre-scriptive period [reference omitted].

(c) As this Senate said in the two decisions cited, it is extremely important not to over-extend the circle of persons who fall within the protective ambit of the contract, but there can be no objection to including, along with the tenant's family, at least those employees who are, consistently with the lease, using the leased property with the tenant or on his behalf. *Here*, at any rate, the main idea is not so much that the ten-ant was under a duty of care and protection for the third party, and thus to a certain extent responsible for his well- or ill-being (see BGHZ 51, 91, 96) as that the third party was using the leased property consistently with the lease and that this involved the risk, equally evident to the third party and the tenant, of his damaging the leased property and being sued for it. This inclusion of the third party in the contract is the real justification for giving him the defence of prescription under § 558 BGB, the same benefit that the tenant enjoys (Gernhuber reaches the same result for the more extreme case of contractual exemption clauses in JZ 1962, 553).

(d) In NJW 1969, 1469, Boeck objects to the decision in BGHZ 49, 278 as being incompatible with the rules regarding common debtors. This is unjustified. It is true that under § 425 BGB one common debtor cannot invoke the prescription which benefits another, but here, even assuming that the defendants are common debtors of the landlord, the second defendant has the defence under § 558 BGB not in any acces-sory capacity deriving from its availability to the first defendant as tenant, but rather in his own right, this being precisely the protective effect of the contract of lease.

Case 60
BUNDESGERICHTSHOF (EIGHTH CIVIL SENATE) 15 FEBRUARY 1978
BGHZ 70, 327

Facts

Two storage sheds on the defendant's property were joined along their length by a common wall. The defendant used one of these sheds for his own business; the other he had let on 6 September 1972 to the firm K to equip and use as a depot. As from 1 February 1974 the defendant had sublet this shed to the plaintiff by an oral agreement.

On 16 July 1974 it rained very heavily; rainwater came through the wall between the two sheds, flooded parts of the plaintiff's business premises and damaged the furni-ture he displayed there. The plaintiff alleged that the flooding had made it impossible to continue using the shed, and quit as from the end of September 1974. K refused to accept this, and sued the plaintiff for the rent until the end of 1974, when the sublease could be terminated. K obtained judgment.

The plaintiff now seeks damages for the harm due to the flooding, on the ground that, as the defendant knew when he entered into the headlease, the downpipes and the valley between the two sheds were inadequate to contain and carry off the rainwater from the two roofs. Not only was the defendant liable in tort (§ 823 BGB); he was liable to the plaintiff for breach of the lease contact also, for although the plaintiff was not a party to the lease, he fell within its protective ambit.

The plaintiff's claim was dismissed in both lower courts, and his appeal was also dismissed.

Reasons

I. The Court of Appeal rejected the plaintiff's claim in tort (§ 823 BGB) on the ground that the defendant had not been at fault. This cannot be impugned, since there is no error of law in the Court of Appeal's evaluation of the evidence and findings of fact.

II. The plaintiff only has a contractual claim for damages on the lessor's 'guarantee' (for which fault is not a prerequisite—§ 538 BGB), if he comes within the protective ambit of the head lease between the defendant and the firm K. The Court of Appeal held that he does not; in reliance on the judgment of the Oberlandesgericht Celle of 4 October 1974 (VersR 1975, 838) it said that the plaintiff did not need such protection because it had a claim on the sublease against its own contractor, k, and 'therefore does not need any additional 'contractual' debtor'. We agree with this.

1. We have regularly held that in certain circumstances it is possible for a third party to acquire rights under a contract between two other persons, rights which give rise to contractual claims and whose content depends on what the principal parties have agreed (BGHZ 49, 278; 61, 227; NJW 1976, 1843). The third party can only be properly included in the protective effect of ambit of the contract if he can be expected to come into contact with the performance or the object of performance (here the property leased: see BGHZ 49, 350, 354; 61, 227, 234). This requirement is satisfied in the present case, because although the defendant's written agreement to the sublease was not obtained as required by 4 para 2 of the lease between the defendant and K, there is no doubt that the defendant knew of the sublease to the plaintiff and acquiesced in it. There can thus be no suggestion that the plaintiff's use of the leased property was unauthorised (see BGHZ 49, 350, 355 f).

2. That does not mean that the plaintiff sub-lessee was drawn within the protective ambit of the contract between the defendant and the firm K. It is perhaps doubtful whether the sub-lessee was using the rented property in the way that the tenant's family or employees do, that is, regularly (*bestimmungsgemäss*). This was regarded as critical for the decision in BGHZ 61, 227, and NJW 1976, 1843, but it need not be discussed further here. The critical factor, as the Court of Appeal saw, is that the plaintiff had no such need of protection as would justify giving it a direct contractual claim against the defendant: the plaintiff already had a contractual claim against its own landlord, K, a claim with the same content as the claim it urges against the defendant. In particular, it can claim damages from K, its contractor, under § 538 BGB, given appropriate facts. Now the reason why a third party is granted a claim for damages is that it would be unjust if, when the tenant automatically has a claim, he, the third party, were denied one when he regularly and *without any contract* comes into contact with the leased property and comes to harm through it or on it. Ultimately it is based on the principle of good faith (see BGHZ 49, 350, 351; 51, 91, 96; 61, 227, 233). But if the victim has his own contractual claim with identical content, albeit against another debtor, he has no need to invoke the protection of a contract concluded between others. To allow a claim in a case like this on the basis of a contract with protective effect for third parties would conflict with the frequently expressed concern of the courts to avoid an endless extension of the protected class (BGHZ 49,

354; 61, 234). This reinforces our view that it would be wrong to include the subtenant in the protective effect of the main lease.

This is not in conflict with the decision in BGHZ 49, 350, where the question whether the subtenant was a so-called 'creditor for purposes of protection' was expressly left open (at p 355).

Case 61
REICHSGERICHT (SEVENTH CIVIL SENATE) 25 FEBRUARY 1921
RGZ 102, 65

Facts

A merchant called F had a giro account at the head office of the defendant bank in H. On 27 January 1919 he went with the plaintiff to its Altona branch, and told them that the firm H & T, which had an account at that branch, had issued an instruction to credit him with DM8200. The bank teller ascertained by telephone that this was true. F then instructed him to transfer the sum of DM8200 to the plaintiff's account in a Hamburg bank. The transfer by H & T in F's favour was duly executed, but that by F in the plaintiff's favour was not. The plaintiff now claims payment of DM4200, with interest (F, who has now fled, having paid him DM4,000 in cash of the DM8200 owing) on the basis that the defendant bank was contractually—and also tortiously— liable for this sum.

Both lower courts rejected the claim. The plaintiff's appeal is dismissed.

Reasons

The Court of Appeal accepted the plaintiff's account of what happened at the Altona branch of the defendant bank, namely that the bank teller first checked by telephone that H & T's instructions to transfer were under way, and F then instructed him to credit the DM8200 to the plaintiff's account in the Hamburg Privatbank. On receiving F's chit instructing them to make this transfer, the teller turned to the plaintiff and said 'That's all right. We will credit this sum to your account.'

The Court of Appeal rejected the plaintiff's argument that this statement by the defendant's teller created a contract between him and them whereby they were bound to credit his account in the Hamburg Privatbank with DM8,200. The plaintiff was a complete stranger, and the teller was not one of the officers who alone had authority under the bank's constitution to enter into any such obligation. This is correct in law.

[The court then rejected the appellant's claim that he was assignee of F's rights against the defendant, and that the defendant bank was liable to him in tort].

The Court of appeal proceeded to say that although F had a right against the defendant, arising from the transfer instructions he had given them, to have the DM8200 transferred to the plaintiff's account, no such right vested in the plaintiff, for a giro transfer is not a contract for the benefit of a third party (§ 328 BGB) so as to enable the third party to make a direct claim against the bank.

The respondent denies that F himself had any claim against the defendant because the credit instructions he had given the teller in the branch office in Altona where F had no account could not result in any contract between F and the head office in H; *a fortiori* the plaintiff could have no claim. But the respondent is in error. The Altona branch of the defendant is not an independent legal person, but simply an office of the defendant which is empowered to do independent banking business. Moreover, if the Altona branch accepted F's credit transfer instructions and communicated them to the head office where F did his business, the defendant was bound under F's contract with the head office to honour his instructions. Thus F certainly had a right that the defendant credit to the plaintiff's account the DM8200 which F had transferred in his favour.

We must therefore decide the question whether the Court of Appeal was correct to hold that the plaintiff obtained no direct claim against the defendant bank from the credit transfer instructions in his favour given to it by F. The Sixth and Fourth Civil Senates (RGZ 84, 354; 91, 119 . . .) have held otherwise, but this court has investigated the matter in depth and cannot in principle follow those decisions. Admittedly the reasons given by the *Oberlandesgericht* in the present case are not convincing, for it is not true that a contract for the benefit of a third party can only arise if it is the intention of both parties that he should have an unconditional and irrevocable right to the sum whose transfer is in question: the third party's right may perfectly well be conditional, dependent, for example, on the non-exercise of a power of revocation. The Court of Appeal's view can however be supported on other grounds.

The simple giro transfer (the red cheque of the *Reichsbank*) has not elicited a view, much less a closely reasoned view, from many commentators. There used to be much dispute on whether the holder of a white cheque had any claim for payment against the drawee bank, but the discussion was terminated by the enactment of the Cheques Act of 11 March 1908 which provides that the holder has no such claim (§§ 15, 18; RGZ 99, 77). As to the red cheques, some writers have denied that it is a contract which gives the third party a direct claim against the bank [references omitted], while at least one author would grant such a claim, though he does not argue that point closely. Nor do we find much legal basis for the opinion of the Sixth and Fourth Civil Senates of the *Reichsgericht* in the decisions cited; in any case what was there said was *obiter*.

The answer must depend in the first instance on § 328 para 2 BGB: in the absence of specific provision, it is a matter of inference from all the circumstances, especially the purpose of the contract, whether the third party is to have a direct right to claim performance. Also relevant is the rule of construction in § 329 BGB: a person who agrees with another to satisfy the latter's indebtedness but without assuming the debt is not to be supposed, in cases of doubt, to have conferred on the creditor a right to bring a direct claim against him for satisfaction. It is therefore a question of the will of the parties whether the third party is to have a direct claim for performance. If no such intention is expressed in the contract, it is a question whether it may be inferred from all the circumstances, especially the purpose of the contract; where there is nothing more than an undertaking to perform, there is a presumption against such in inference.

In the normal case a credit transfer instruction is simply a direction to the bank to transfer a certain sum from the credit of the mandator to a third party. The bank is not normally informed of the transaction underlying the transfer. If the mandator's account is in credit or if it is prepared to allow him an overdraft, the bank executes the instruction by taking the amount from the mandator's account and putting it in that of the third party, and then informing both parties of what it has done. If the third party's account is at a different bank, the bank receiving the instruction does not enter into any relations with him at all, but transfers the sum to the other bank to be credited to him, it is then that bank which informs the third party of the credit. Nothing whatever in the purpose of the contract makes it necessary to assume that the parties intend to give the third party a claim against the bank for the execution of the transfer. On the contrary, we must agree with Düringer-Hachenburg [reference omitted] that banks which enter into Giro contracts have, at least in the normal case, no such intention. Much less is such an intention to be inferred if the third party is not even its customer. We have seen that the Cheques Act refuses to allow the holder of a white cheque to sue the bank; the reason is that if the third party, the holder, had a direct claim against the bank, the bank would be exposed to litigation with total strangers with whom they had had no dealings (reference omitted), the legal relationship between the transferor and the third party being as unknown to the bank as the relationship between the transferor and the bank is unknown to the third party. The same consideration applies in the present case, and the Cheques Act gives a valuable indication of the principles on which it should be decided. If in the case of a white cheque, which is handed directly to the third party by its maker, and which has the quality of an order bill, indeed usually a bearer bill, the holder obtains no direct claim to payment against the drawee bank, such a claim by the third party must surely be rejected in the case of a red cheque, which generally never comes into the hands of the third party; indeed, he commonly remains in complete ignorance of the proceeding it triggers until he is told that the sum has been credited to him, and he may never learn of it at all if the maker stops the instruction before it is carried out or if he has no funds to meet it.

This is not to deny that under very peculiar circumstances it might be possible exceptionally to conclude that the parties had a different intention. But there are no such circumstances here. In particular, the teller's remark, quoted at the outset of this opinion, is no basis for finding any different intention, quite apart from the fact that he had no authority to bind the defendant to anything in the least unusual.

There was no need to convene the United Civil Senates to discuss this question of law since the decisions of the Sixth and Fourth Civil Senates which we have mentioned were on basically quite different facts, and the view of the law which they gave and we do not accept was given *obiter* and was unnecessary to the decisions.

Case 62
BUNDESGERICHTSHOF (SEVENTH CIVIL SENATE) 24 FEBRUARY 1972
BGHZ 58, 184

Facts

The B GmbH H & Co (hereinafter 'the developers') was building private dwellings in Sch, and entered into preliminary contracts of sale (*Kaufanwärterverträge*) with the plaintiffs in 1968. Negotiations with the plaintiffs were principally conducted by the defendant, then an assistant director of the developers, charged, *inter alia*, with the sale of these dwellings. In the course of the negotiations the plaintiffs had received from the developers a document called 'Instructions for Sale': it gave a detailed description of the properties for sale, referred to the need to take a brokerage fee of 3 per cent into account in the individual prices and stated that any interested party could refer for further particulars to the defendant, who was empowered by the developers to enter into transactions concerning land.

The defendant then, in the name of the developers, concluded preliminary contracts of sale with the plaintiffs. In each case he gave them three copies of the contract for signature, two of which (one for the plaintiffs and one for the defendant) contained the following clause: '6. Financing: the total cost, exclusive of architect's fee, of these ownership apartments is guaranteed as being DM . . ., plus 3 per cent brokerage fee to be paid to the H.I.-K. GmbH.' The third copy, which the defendant gave to the developers, did not contain the addition about the brokerage fee.

Some time after the contracts were signed, the plaintiffs were billed for payment of the fee on invoices headed 'H.I.-K.' and signed by the defendant. The plaintiffs paid the sums to the account indicated in the invoices, but in fact the firm 'H.I.-K. GmbH.' was a figment, and the sums paid by the plaintiffs passed to the defendant.

Feeling that they had been taken in by the defendant, the plaintiffs had the brokerage agreements rescinded for fraud, and in the present proceedings reclaim the sums they paid to the defendant on the ground that they unjustifiedly enriched him.

The *Landgericht* gave judgment for the plaintiff, but the *Oberlandesgericht* allowed the defendant's appeal (JZ 1971,424, noted Lorenz). The plaintiff was permitted to appeal, and the appeal was successful.

Reasons

I

1. The Court of Appeal held that the plaintiffs had no claim under the rules of unjust enrichment (§ 12 BGB) for the return of the sums which the defendant had received. The Court inferred from the plaintiffs' own evidence that they were unaware that the defendant was identical with the payee of the brokerage fee, and that their payments were not in purported performance of any brokerage contract between themselves and him. The plaintiffs' duty to pay arose solely from the brokerage clauses in their contracts with the developers, genuine contracts for the benefit of third parties which conferred a right on the third party, here the defendant.

The Court of Appeal of course realised that the plaintiffs had had the brokerage agreements with the developers rescinded for fraud, the defendant having had no authority to make any such contracts. It nevertheless held that in a case such as the present, where the *Deckungsverhältnis* (or relationship between promisor and promisee) is defective the promisor cannot claim back from the third party what he has rendered, but must turn to the promisee, even in a case of double nullity, as it is called, when he *Valutaverhältnis*, the link between the promisee and third party, is also baseless. Admittedly, if the promise had intended to make a gift to the third party and the gift was effective in law, the promisor might have an enrichment claim against the third party analogous to that provided by § 822 BGB, but this was not such a case.

2. . . .

3. We cannot agree that the defendant was an obviously inappropriate person for the plaintiffs to sue in restitution.

(a) It sometimes happens where there is a genuine contract for the benefit of third parties, that is, where the third party acquires a claim of his own, that the legal relationship between the promisor and the promisee (the *Deckungsverhältnis*) proves to be ineffective or defective. It has long been a matter for dispute how the principles of restitution operate in such a case (reference omitted). This is not the moment to resolve all the problems involved or to provide an answer to all the questions.

In a case concerning a credit transfer where the mandate to transfer was invalid this court stated its agreement with von Caemmerer (JZ 1962, 385, 386) that a just and realistic appraisal of the restitutionary significance of situations in which more than two people are involved depends on the peculiarities of the particular case (BGHZ 50, 227, 229). This is true whenever a third party is implicated in the performance, for, as von Caemmerer rightly emphasises, there are many different ways in which obligations and performance may be made dependent on the existence of legal relationships. This applies also to genuine contracts for the benefit of third parties, that is, contracts which give the third party an independent right [reference omitted]: it is still critical what purpose the parties had in mind, given the intentions they expressed.

(b) This inevitably determines which party is to be regarded as rendering the performance and which as receiving it under the law of enrichment, for it is now established that by 'performance' (*Leistung*) § 812 para 1 BGB means a conscious act which is *intended* to increase the wealth of another [BGHZ 40, 272, 277; 48, 70, 73; 50, 227, 230 ff.; other reference omitted]. The purpose of the act is inferred from the will of the parties; if there is a mismatch between the intentions of the transferor and the transferee we look at the matter objectively from the viewpoint of the recipient (BGHZ 40, 272, 278), but if the intentions of the parties coincide, their purpose in effecting the transfer alone determines what the 'performance' is in terms of enrichment law.

(c) The Court of Appeal recognised this basic principle but did not apply it correctly.

(aa) The Court of appeal obviously assumed that *whenever* there is a genuine contract for the benefit of a third party, a transfer made by the promisor to the third party is *always* intended to constitute both performance by promisor to promisee (in the *Deckungsverhältnis*) and also performance by promisee to third party (in the *Valutaverhältnis*): only by taking the exchanges in these two legal relationships together could one explain who, in 'real economic' terms, was eventually to benefit from the performance. Now his may be so in many cases (for example, where there is 'shorthand performance' (*abgekürzte Leistung*), using the contract for the benefit of a third party), but not necessarily in all. On the contrary, it can make sense, even economic sense, to see the transfer by the promisor to the third party as intended so exclusively for the third party that the transfer constitutes in enrichment law a performance to the third party whose validity depends only on that of the *Deckunsverhältnis*. Apart from the example of the life-care contracts covered by § 330 BGB (see von Caemmerer JZ 1962, 385, 387) one can imagine cases of other kinds in which it would be the intention of the parties that the third party acquire his own claim against the promisor based *exclusively* on the *Deckungsverhältnis* between promisor and promisee and entirely independent of any *Valutaverhältnis* between promisee and third party. The first class of case that comes to mind is those in which (contrary to § 335 BGB, which is not mandatory) *only* the third party is to have a claim against the promisor or those in which the creation of such a right exhausts the *Valutaverhältnis* (reference omitted). In such cases it is quite just to hold that the performance relationship of enrichment law exists only as between third party and promisor.

(bb) The present case shows this peculiarity. The brokerage fee agreement in favour of 'H.I.-K.' (that is, the defendant) was made by the plaintiffs within their preliminary sale contracts with the developers, represented by the defendant. But the parties to the brokerage fee agreement omitted the relevant clauses from the copy of the preliminary sale contracts which went to the developers; this omission symbolised the splitting of the fee agreement from the preliminary sale contract and rendered the one independent of the other.

But the parties' own evidence already showed that they were independent. According to the defendant, the parties acted as they did in order that the legal relationship between the developers and the plaintiffs remain unaffected by the brokerage fee agreement. Again, even the plaintiffs said that they did not suppose that the agreement in question was in satisfaction of any debt owed by the developers to 'H.I.-K.'; they took it that they themselves owed the fee to the beneficiary for services rendered. Indeed, the plaintiffs' only dealings regarding the brokerage fee were with H.I.-K. It was in H.I.-K's name that the defendant invoiced them and received payment from them. With these proceedings the developers had absolutely nothing to do. Thus although the plaintiffs made the brokerage agreement with the developers, its economic centre of gravity lay in their legal relationship with the third party.

On these facts the only possible inference is that the sole purpose of the plaintiffs in paying the defendant was to satisfy *as against him* their debt to 'H.I.-K.' which arose from the preliminary sale contracts, the sole basis of that debt in law. This was also the defendant's understanding and could not be otherwise. Given such a common purpose, the relationship of the parties was that of party rendering and party receiving a performance in the sense of enrichment law, such that if the sale contracts proved defective an adjustment fell to be made.

(cc) This holding is not in conflict with prior holdings of this court. The case decided by the Fourth Civil Senate on 20 March 1952 (BGHZ 5, 281) is an example of so-called 'shorthand performance' not here in issue. The case before the Eighth Civil Senate of 4 April 1962 (NJW 1962, 1051) did not involve any contract for a third party at all. So far as can be seen, this is the first time that the *Bundesgerichtshof* has had to decide a case with the features of the present one.

Case 63
BUNDESGERICHTSHOF (SEVENTH CIVIL SENATE) 7 NOVEMBER 1960
BGHZ 33, 247

Facts

On 11 April 1953 two adjacent stressed concrete panels in the roof of the Siemens-Martin steel foundry in W fell some fifty to sixty feet to the ground and struck two persons working there. S, an engineer, was killed on the spot, leaving a widow and two children; L, a workman, was badly injured.

The roof had been constructed by the defendant between October 1952 and March 1953. The old framework of the roof had been retained, but the one-piece concrete skin was replaced by the stressed concrete panels which the defendant had developed. The plaintiff, as statutory insurer, paid L and the dependants of S, and now claims an indemnity, based on tort and on positive breach of contract (§§ 328, 618 BGB, in connection with § 1542 RVO (Imperial Insurance Ordinance)).

The defendant denies that its work under the building contract with the steel foundry was unworkmanlike; as a subsidiary point it asserts that if there were any fault in the construction of the roof, the steel foundry was also to blame, and the plaintiff is affected thereby; finally, the defendant raises the defence of prescription.

The *Landgericht* dismissed the claim, but on the plaintiff's appeal the *Oberlandesgericht* gave judgment for the plaintiff. On the defendant's appeal, this decision was reversed and the case remanded.

Reasons

1(a) The court of Appeal did not decide whether the victims' (and consequently the plaintiff's) claims in tort, if any, were prescribed. It held that the victims had a direct claim against the defendant for positive breach of contract under §§ 328, 618 para 1 and 3, 844 BGB. Its building contract with the steel foundry put the defendant under a subsidiary duty to avoid causing harm to the contractor in the execution of the work. In a case falling under § 618 par 1 BGB this duty of the defendant was owed also to the customer's employees; for breach of these contractual duties such people could sue the defendant directly in contract.

(b) This is in line with the doctrine developed by the *Reichsgericht* and the *Bundesgerichtshof*; the basis of this liability is a contract for the benefit of third parties, in the sense that it protects those third parties towards whom the creditor himself owes duties of care and protection.

(c) The Court of Appeal was quite correct to include the victims of this accident in the circle of those who are protected by the building contract. Of course this circle must not be unduly large, but in the present case it was sufficiently constricted. The two victims were among the workers and staff who were permanently employed in the factory whose roof the defendants had built. There was thus a group, numerically limited and spatially compact, towards whom the employer had a special duty of care under § 618 BGB regarding the safety of the work place. This was the only group which the Court of Appeal included within the protective ambit of the building contract; it did not, as the appellant asserts, include the foundry's entire workforce of several thousand people.

2. The Court of Appeal was quite right to hold that the victims' claims passed to the plaintiff under § 1542 RVO. It has already been held (BGHZ 26, 365) that § 1542 RVO applies to contractual claims for damages as well as to claims in tort.

3. The Court of Appeal was right to hold that the defendant's fault was a contributory cause of the accident and that therefore it was liable for positive breach of contract . . .

4. The Court of Appeal believed that it was irrelevant whether any fault on the part of the steel foundry contributed to the accident, so it did not investigate this question. The appellant is right to criticise this.

The question is whether in a case like this the contributory fault of the defendant contractor affects the injured third party by reason of § 254 BGB. The only cases before the *Reichsgericht* and the *Bundesgerichtshof* so far have been those where the contractor was the victim's statutory representative or his agent for performance. In these cases the fault has been imputed to the victim (BGHZ 9, 316; 24, 325).

According to the commentators, the party in breach should always be able to face the injured third party with the contributory fault of its contractor under § 254 BGB, and not just when the contractor is the statutory representative or an agent for performance.

Unlike the Court of Appeal, we agree with this. As in all contracts for the benefit of third parties, it is only out of the contractual relations of the main contractors that the protected third party obtains his rights against the person who injures him. This being so, it is logical that his rights against the party injuring him be no grater than those of the main contracting party. This can be inferred from the juridical basis of § 334 BGB, whereby contractual defences good against the promisee are good against the third party as well. Some time ago the *Bundesgerichtshof* said 'the extension of the plaintiff's legal protection by his inclusion in the protected contractual sphere' involves that 'he must accept the concomitant legal disadvantages.' This points to the solution we wish to adopt, and also shows that it is quite equitable.

Since the judgment in issue took no account of any contributory fault of the steel foundry, it cannot be upheld.

5. If the plaintiff's claim could be based on tort, as it might possibly be, the defendant's liability would be unaffected by any contributory fault on the part of the steel foundry. The Court of Appeal did not find it necessary to investigate this question, and it has not decided whether any such claim has prescribed. Since this court does not have the requisite facts to make such a decision itself, the judgment under appeal must be vacated and the matter remanded to the Court of Appeal.

Case 64
REICHSGERICHT (THIRD CIVIL SENATE) 5 OCTOBER 1917
RGZ 91, 21

Facts

The male plaintiff is a senior assistant on the railways. When he was moved to J, he was provided with accommodation which had previously been used by Dr, the station supervisor. A few months after moving in, his daughter, the female plaintiff, contracted tuberculosis, and had to go on a voyage for her health. The plaintiffs attribute this illness to the fact that the dwelling was infested with tuberculosis bacilli, Dr's wife having had pulmonary trouble, and that the defendant state failed to disinfect the dwelling until five or six days after they moved in. They therefore claim damages for the loss attributable to the disease, not all of which may have manifested itself.

The *Landgericht* allowed the claims. The *Oberlandesgericht* rejected the defendant's appeal in respect of the male plaintiff's claim, but allowed it in respect of that of the female plaintiff, whose claim was therefore dismissed. The female plaintiff's appeal was allowed, and the defendant's appeal was dismissed.

Reasons

On the basis of the evidence, the Court of Appeal concluded that the female plaintiff became ill because the service dwelling in which she lived had been infected with tuberculosis bacilli during the illness of Mrs Dr, but it held that the only person to whom the defendant was liable was the male plaintiff: he had a claim, based on an analogous application of §§ 618, 278 BGB, for the damage he had suffered through his daughter's illness. The Court said that the delay in disinfecting the house was due to the fault of Dr D, the railway doctor appointed by the defendant who attended to Mrs Dr. It was the duty of Dr D to inform the railway authorities of all cases of tuberculosis which came to his notice in his capacity as railway doctor, and if he had performed this duty, the house would have been disinfected at the right time. But the Court of Appeal disallowed the female plaintiff's claim for damages on the ground that she had no contractual or similar relationship with the defendant, and that her claim in tort failed because the defendant, having adduced exculpatory proof under § 831 BGB, was not liable for Dr D.

So far as the male plaintiff's rights are concerned, the Court of Appeal was correct in the result but wrong in the reasons, and so far as the female plaintiff's rights are concerned, it was wrong in both regards.

Since the male plaintiff is an official, the solution must be looked for in public law; and since there are no relevant texts, it must depend on the principles which emerge from the nature of the case in the light of the legal ideas which control decisions in analogous relationships subject to private law. It is established by the *Reichsgericht* that the state and other bodies of public law owe their officials a duty of care such as is implied into the contract of employment by § 618 BGB. Thus it has been held that under the Prussian Law on Conditions of Service of Teachers in Public Schools of 3 March 1897, local authorities are bound to ensure that the accommodation they provide for teachers are safe and properly maintained, and that they are liable for any injury or illness caused to the teacher by culpable breach of this duty (RGZ 71, 243). This duty of care is closely related to the fact that the accommodation is provided so as to enable the occupant to perform his service obligations or to perform them more easily. Being required to use the service dwelling for the performance of his duties, the official can expect the local authority to protect him adequately against defects in the dwelling which imperil his health. This leads to the conclusion that in respect of official accommodation the state owes the same duty of protection to the dependants whom the official is entitled to lodge in the dwelling as to the official himself. For if the official is bound to use the accommodation provided, so, too, are they, in the interests of maintaining the family community.

So far as the official himself is concerned, the protective duty owed to him means that he can hold the state responsible for its breach, not only when his own health suffers, but when he suffers loss through injury to the health of a dependant. Just as the official's entitlement to compensation when his own health is affected is based on the application of § 618 BGB by analogy, so when a dependant's health is affected, private law powerfully suggests that the dependant has a claim for damages as well as the official himself. If a landlord is responsible for unhealthy conditions on the leased premises and a member of the tenant's family suffers thereby, the tenant can sue the landlord under § 538 BGB for the consequent harm he may suffer (RGZ 77, 99, 101).

But in addition the dependant himself can normally sue the landlord for his own harm (though not for his pain and suffering). Unless very peculiar circumstances indicate a different conclusion, the tenant of a family dwelling who concludes a lease must be taken, as the landlord must know, to intend to obtain the maximum protection for the members of his household and to acquire for them the same rights in relation to the safety of the premises as he himself enjoys against the landlord (§ 328 BGB). If the landlord's contractual duties are not extended in this manner, injured dependants would be restricted to claiming in tort, and would not have the benefit afforded to the tenant by §§ 278, 538 BGB, that the landlord is strictly liable for any defects in the premises existing at the time of the contract. To give such different rights to the tenant and to his dependants is offensive to proper legal sentiment and false to the tenant's purpose in contracting, for, as the landlord is bound to know, he wants his dependants to be as well placed as himself to sue for damages. So, too, in the contract of employment of private law where the employer provides the employee with a family house so as to facilitate the rendering of the contractual services, the employee must be taken to intend the employer to assume the duty, as regards the condition and maintenance of the living quarters, to protect his dependants from danger to life and limb to the same extent as himself (§ 618 BGB) and to have them acquire rights of their own to this effect. Now if an official who is directed to live in service quarters could not claim from the state protection against dangerous defects in the living premises for those dependants who are entitled to stay in the dwelling, and if his dependants did not have a claim of their own to that effect, there would be an intolerable difference in the treatment of cognate legal relationships in public and in private law. Such differential treatment would be all the more unjustifiable as the official and his dependants do not have the freedom of choice which is open to the tenant or employee and their dependants, but are bound to use the accommodation provided. This extension to the dependants of the state's duty of care is also in line with the development in public law of the state's duty to look after the family of its officials. It is one of the benefits to which officials are entitled, not by way of contractual counter-performance for their services, but as a means of assuring their position in life.

In the case for decision the state has failed to satisfy its duty of care, since it failed to take steps to ensure that its service accommodations were disinfected sufficiently soon after the departure of an occupant in whose family tuberculosis had broken out. The rules certainly provide that in such a case the station master is to undertake the disinfection. A duty is also imposed on railway doctors and supervisors to inform the railway authorities of any cases of tuberculosis in the family of railway employees which come to their knowledge. If this duty is performed, the railway authorities would be in a position to give the station master due notice of any required disinfection. But if no such notification is given, as may easily happen, the regulations make no provision for securing the object in question. The dangers to which officials are exposed in the absence of such notification is such that the defendant should have provided for steps to be taken which would permit the premises to be disinfected at the right time, possibly by making inquiry of the station doctor before assigning accommodation to a new occupant.

Case 65
OBERLANDESGERICHT DÜSSELDORF 3 OCTOBER 1974
NJW 1975, 596

Facts

The plaintiff's son was stabbed in a brawl and was taken to the defendant's hospital where the chief surgeon saw to the stab wound in the skin and stomach lining. The youth died. At the post-mortem it transpired that there were other wounds which had not been cared for, in the rear stomach lining, in the upper and lower intestine, and in the left kidney. The plaintiff asserted that the chief surgeon had caused her son's death by failure to attend to these wounds, and claimed damages for loss of support.

The *Landgericht* rejected the claim. Before the *Oberlandesgericht* the plaintiff sought to answer the defendant's proof of exculpation under § 831 BGB, first by asserting that the defendant was itself to blame in failing to provide an assistant surgeon for the operation, and then by arguing that the defendant was personally liable in contract and must answer for the fault of the chief surgeon as its agent for performance. The plaintiff's appeal was dismissed.

Reasons

The plaintiff has no claim for damages against the defendant. There can be no claims under §§ 242, 276 BGB for breach of contractual duty since there was no contract between the parties. The hospitalisation contract with the defendant under which the plaintiff's son received medical treatment and care in the hospital was made not with the plaintiff but with the local medical union (AOK). It is true that AOK did not actually refer the plaintiff's son to the hospital—this was an emergency case—but the contract was formed later when AOK agreed to pay the bill. It is not alleged that any contractual negotiations took place between the parties, and it is clear that there were none.

Nor did this contract have any protective effect for the plaintiff. Such protective effect only applies to the insured and not to his dependants (RG JW 1937, 926; BGHZ 2, 94). Normally the protective effect of a contract is limited to those persons who, by their connection with the creditor, come into contact with the debtor's performance, and whose safety is, to the debtor's knowledge, as important to the creditor as his own. This requirement is normally met only when the creditor has a joint responsibility for the protection and care of the third party (BGHZ 51, 91, 96; BGHZ 56, 269; BGH NJW 1959, 1676; 1970, 38). This is not the case with the plaintiff here. The decision of the *Bundesgerichtshof* to which the plaintiff refers (NJW 1959, 1676) is of no assistance to her, for in that case the third party was one of the plaintiff's employees, ie a person who came into contact with the debtor's performance through the creditor and to whom the creditor owed a duty of care and protection. These preconditions are not satisfied here: the defendant's performance did not affect the plaintiff and AOK is not bound to afford her care and protection. Nor can it be said that the plaintiff was 'close to the performance' (*Leistungsnähe*). The performance which was owed by the defendant, namely medical care and attention in its hospital, did not affect the plaintiff. She was not the patient. Furthermore, the plaintiff in this case was in no relationship with the creditor AOK. She cannot acquire a claim against the defendant by founding on her own relationship with the third party, her son (under § 328 BGB), or on *his* duties towards her.

Case 66
BUNDESGERICHTSHOF (SECOND CIVIL SENATE) 11 APRIL 1951
BGHZ 1, 383

Facts

The plaintiff, who had ingrowing toenails, was referred for outpatient treatment to the defendant city's hospital by the local medical union of which he was a member. He was made to sit down on a three- piece settee, about 30 inches high, designed for gynaecological examinations but used as an auxiliary operating table, the back part having been fixed in a horizontal position. The second defendant, who had been the hospital's chief doctor for many years, gave the plaintiff a local anaesthetic, an injection of 2 per cent Novocaine solution, in either one big toe or both. While waiting for this to work, the plaintiff suddenly lost consciousness and fell off the settee. He injured his cervical column in the fall, and has since experienced severe stiffness and loss of function in both arms. At the time of the accident the second defendant was standing at the door of the small operating theatre, speaking to his chauffeur, and the operating sister was quite close to the plaintiff, treating a patient for burns.

The plaintiff claims that the defendants are liable on the following grounds. No one had told him to lie down after the injection, so he was still sitting when he suddenly became unconscious. Had he known he should lie down, he would have done so, and not fallen. The second defendant should have realised and guarded against the risk of a sudden faint, in particular by making him lie down, but instead of taking any such steps he left the plaintiff to his own devices after giving him the injection. This was the sole reason for the accident, which had rendered him wholly and, as it seemed, permanently unfit for work. The plaintiff claims an annuity for lost earnings and damages for pain and suffering from both defendants.

The *Landgericht* rejected the claim, but the *Oberlandesgericht* held the plaintiff entitled to a monthly sum for loss of earnings and damages for pain and suffering. The defendants' appeal was successful only in part.

Reasons

The plaintiff has a good contractual claim against the first defendant. The *Reichsgericht* always held that when a medical union refers a member to a hospital, the contract it makes with the hospital is one in favour of the patient whereby, under § 328 BGB, the patient acquires a direct claim to proper treatment against the operator of the hospital (RGZ 165, 106). The first defendant entrusted to the second defendant the treatment of the union patient referred to it, so he became the first defendant's agent for performance and the first defendant is accordingly responsible to the plaintiff under § 278 BGB for any fault committed by the second defendant in the execution of his professional medical activity.

Between the plaintiff and the second defendant there were no direct contractual relations. A hospital doctor's duty to undertake the proper treatment of union patients is normally owed only to the hospital which appoints him. But if a hospital doctor actually does embark on the treatment of a union patient and injures him in his health by infringing widely recognised rules of medical science, he is liable to the patient under §§ 823 ff. BGB, whether or not he has any contract with the patient. It is immaterial whether the fault of the doctor is one of commission or of omission. The doctor may be under no obligation to the patient to treat him at all, but if he does so, he must avoid injuring him in body of health by breach of the rules of medical science [reference omitted].

In the instant case the Court of Appeal was right to find that it was the second defendant's fault that the plaintiff did not lie down after the injection; he should have told him himself or got the operating sister to do so.

The appellant contends that the failure to tell the plaintiff to lie down was not an adequate cause of the consequent harm. This is not so. The decisions of the *Reichsgericht* cited by the appellant on consequences for which the actor is not responsible because the causal connection is not adequate, refer to consequences which occur only under extremely peculiar circumstances and through quite improbable concatenations of events, and which can be ignored in the normal course of things. The consequences here, according to the expert, are not of this kind. On the contrary, the expert expressly emphasised that the reason for the good old rule that a patient should always be prone or supine during all manipulations and injections is precisely the possibility of a faint and a fall; it may be true that this rule cannot always be observed in practice and often is not, but such practical considerations cannot relieve the doctor of the charge that he ignored a duty of care. In such a case there can be no question of any interruption of the adequate causal connection. The appellant is also wrong to say that the Court of Appeal pitched the doctor's duty of care too high. The Court was right to follow the expert, whose evidence was based on his knowledge of the rules of the medical art, and who stated in terms that there was undeniable negligence in this case unless perhaps it could be proved that the sister had been enjoined to attend to the patient and that the patient had disobeyed her instruction to lie down.

It follows that the plaintiff's claim for monthly payments is established against the first defendant under §§ 276, 278 BGB and against the second defendant under § 823 BGB. However, the second defendant alone is liable for the damages for pain and suffering under § 847 BGB. Only under § 831 BGB could the first defendant be held liable for such damages. The defendant city asserts that it has satisfied the requisite exculpatory proof. We agree. It was common ground that the second defendant had been chief doctor in the first defendant's hospital for many years and that the nurse had served as operating sister for nine years without any criticism. The plaintiff did not even assert, much less prove, anything that tended to show that the second defendant had been guilty of any fault during his twenty years' service in the defendant city's hospital. Under such circumstances the hospital management cannot be expected to adduce any further exculpatory proof.

Case 67
BUNDESGERICHTSHOF (SIXTH CIVIL SENATE) 19 JANUARY 1977
NJW 1977, 2073

Facts

The defendant is an attorney who represented the plaintiff's father in divorce proceedings. In January 1972 the plaintiff's father and mother met in the defendant's office, where they signed a divorce agreement drawn up by the defendant. It contained the following clause: '§ 6. As to the house, the parties agree that the half belonging to Mrs M is to be transferred to the three children in equal parts. Mr M hereby agrees not to sell his half but to transfer it to his present legitimate children. An appropriate notarial contract to this effect is to be concluded immediately after the divorce is final. Mr M further promises that once the divorce is final he will indemnify Mrs M against any liabilities arising from the house or its construction . . .' A divorce decree was granted in February 1972, and the defendant, in the name of the plaintiff's father, thereon waived any rights of appeal, as did the mother's attorney. The plaintiff's mother now refuses to transfer her interest in the property to the plaintiff and his siblings.

The plaintiff claims damages for breach of the defendant's duty as attorney. The *Landgericht* rejected the claim but the *Oberlandesgericht* allowed it. The defendant was permitted to appeal, but his appeal was dismissed.

Reasons

I. [The reasoning of the Court of Appeal].
II. Despite the appellant's contentions, this reasoning is sound in law.
1. [The defendant was in breach of his duty as attorney].
2. Nor is there anything wrong in law with the Court of Appeal's holding that although there was no contract between the plaintiff and the defendant, the plaintiff could sue the defendant for damages for his faulty breach of contract.

(a) The Court of Appeal found that there was here a contract with protective effect for third parties and that the plaintiff's claim arose therefrom. We do not have to decide whether this is so.

(aa) Certainly an important factor pointing in that direction is that the plaintiff was the son of the attorney's client and was entitled to care and protection from him (compare BGHZ 61, 227, 233). The usual problem in cases of contracts with protective effects for third parties is whether the victim was someone the debtor could expect to be harmed by a breach of the contract. That is not the problem here. The very words of § 6 of the divorce agreement drawn up by the defendant show that the children were its sole beneficiaries, the only people apt to suffer if the agreement proved invalid.

The only question here is how far the protective effect of this contract works in favour of the children, in particular whether they have any claim for damages for breach of contract in their own right. Now the contract between client and attorney is such, given its nature and structure, that it can only be very seldom, whether one interprets the contract extensively or invokes § 242 BGB (see BGHZ 56, 269, 273; NJW

1975, 977), that the duties it generates can be sued on by third parties, for the fiduciary relationship between client and attorney makes it strongly bilateral and self-contained [references omitted]. Thus the fact that third parties have an interest in what an attorney does will not normally lead to any extension of his liability, even if those persons are named or known to him. However, an exception must be made where a contract drafted by the attorney is designed to vest rights in third parties specified therein, especially third parties who, as in the present case, are represented by the client. It is true that most of the cases where the courts have granted third parties a claim for damages arising out of a contract to which they were not parties have involved personal injury or property damage and its consequences [BGHZ 49, 350, 355; NJW 1955, 257; other references omitted], but it is not impossible for a third party to have a personal claim for economic loss caused by breach of subsidiary contractual duties (NJW 1968, 1929; BGH NJW 1975, 344). In drawing the line here one must certainly apply an especially stringent test: the circle of persons to whom the protective effect of a contract extends is to be narrowly drawn, so as to avoid blurring the line between contractual and tortious liability in an unacceptable manner (BGHZ 66, 51, 57; NJW 1974, 1189). It must always be borne in mind, in claims for purely economic loss, that the debtor is not to be made liable for the mere ricochet effect of his conduct on third parties.

(bb) Despite this, we cannot, on the special facts of the present case, fault the Court of Appeal's holding that the plaintiff was drawn into the protective ambit of the attorney's contract. The respondent invokes a decision of this court of 6 July 1965 (NJW 1965, 1955), but this is not quite in point. The court there did allow the daughter of a client to sue the attorney although she was not herself a party to the contract, but the court was reluctant to categorise the contract as one with protective effect for third parties [references omitted]. Contracts with protective effect for third parties are concerned with breach of subsidiary duties by the contractor (see BGH NJW 1975, 344), whereas in that case the question was really whether the attorney could be made liable towards the client's daughter, the third party, for a breach of specific duties of performance (reference omitted). Our case is clearly distinguishable.

(b) The plaintiff might also base his claim here on the concept of *Drittschadensliquidation*, a doctrine which borders on, if it does not actually overlap, the area of application of the doctrine of contracts with protective effect for third parties (see BGHZ 49, 350, 355). It would have been quite proper for the defendant's client to indemnify his son, the plaintiff, for the harm he had suffered, and one could then infer from the fact that he brought suit as his son's statutory representative that he was making an assignment of his own claim which the plaintiff, on the threshold of majority, could implicitly accept. But we need not pursue the matter here.

(c) In whatever legal or doctrinal category one puts the present litigated facts, the result must be that the plaintiff has a direct claim against the defendant attorney for compensation for the harm which he suffered as a result of the defendant's failure to tell his father of the need to implement the agreement in § 6 of the divorce document. Any other conclusion would be inconsistent with the meaning and purpose of the attorney's contract here and of the father—son relationship between the client and the plaintiff of which the defendant was well aware.

Case 68
BUNDESGERICHTSHOF (EIGHTH CIVIL SENATE) 16 OCTOBER 1963
NJW 1964, 33

Facts

The defendant lets out most of his house. The plaintiff rents business premises on the ground floor and sells carpets there. Most of the rooms on the floor above are let to a teacher of commerce, K, who runs a trade school there (hereinafter called the K trade school). The two toilets already on that floor were included in the lease to K, which provided that K was to instal two more, so that there should be four toilets in all near the K trade school. It was agreed that the two toilets at the end of the corridor (each having an outer room with a wash hand basin as well as the toilet proper) should be available for use by other tenants on that floor.

The defendant himself was one of those who made use of the toilets. He is an optician who practises his profession in the rooms on the first floor which were not leased to the K trade school, and which he adapted for that purpose. A door leading from his surgery into the corridor gives access to the toilets. The second floor was let to an insurance company, and the defendant lived on the third floor.

In the night of 3–4 November 1958 (after one of the defendant's evening surgeries) the plaintiff's business premises on the ground floor were flooded. Large quantities of water came through the ceiling under the common toilets on the first floor and damaged the premises below. The plaintiff claims damages for the harm caused by the water to the carpets and other goods he had stored there. The *Landgericht* dismissed the claim, but the *Oberlandesgericht* gave judgment for the plaintiff and the defendant's appeal is dismissed.

Reasons

I. The Court of Appeal found that a tap had been left running in one of the common toilets and that this was the cause of the damage. It was unknown who had left the tap running, or even whether it was one of the students at the K trade school or one of the defendant's patients. It was quite possible that a tap was just dripping at the time when Mr and Mrs K made their evening round along with B, one of the staff of the K trade school. But it was an evening when the defendant had an evening surgery, and he could not swear that he had no patients that evening. One of the defendant's guests or patients might have forgotten to turn the tap off. The appellant does not contest these findings of fact.

On these facts the Court of Appeal found the defendant and the owner of the K trade school liable to the plaintiff as joint debtors. It said that a lease of rooms in a building in which other rooms are let to other tenants is a contract for the benefit of third parties, namely the other tenants, and is to be treated like a contract with protective effects for them. Thus if by breach of the duty of care which he owes in the first instance only to the landlord, a tenant causes damage to other tenants of the same building, he is liable to them. To the extent that he was using the toilets, the defendant should be equated with a tenant: he was under the same duty of car as a tenant. The plaintiff could therefore claim the same protection as if the first floor had been let to

K and another tenant. Several tenants would be liable as joint debtors in respect of damage caused by breach of their duties of care, both towards the landlord and towards the plaintiff, and each would be responsible for the fault of the other without possibility of exculpation, despite the rule of construction of § 425 BGB. The same must apply to the liability of the defendant towards the plaintiff by reason of his use of the common toilets.

II. The result is right, despite the appellant's objections.

1. It must be granted to the appellant that exception can be taken to the Court of Appeal's view that the contract of lease is a contract with protective effect for the fellow tenants. It is true that the *Bundesgerichtshof* has accepted the doctrine, advanced especially by Larenz and Gernhuber [references omitted], that where the contractual duties of care and protection should in accordance with good faith and the purpose of the contract be owed to certain other persons as well as to the main contracting party, such a third party can sue the person whose breach of such a contractual duty causes him harm (NJW 1959, 1676). But the circle of persons entitled to enjoy the protective effects of a contract has been drawn very narrowly by the *Bundesgerichtshof*. The decision cited explains that such contracts are certainly not intended to give a contractual claim for damages to everyone who may suffer harm as a result of the debtor's breach of a duty of care. It accords with the sense and purpose of the contract and the principle of good faith that the only persons to whom the debtor owes his contractual duty of care and protection are those who are brought into contact with his performance by the creditor and in whose welfare the creditor has an interest because he himself is bound to take care and protect them, like the members of a man's family or the employees of an entrepreneur. To extend the contractual debtor's responsibility in this way is justified because he must know that the safety of the limited and compact group of persons to whom the contractual protection ensures is of as much concern to the creditor as his own. Thus Larenz (NJW 1960, 77, 80) emphasises that it is only towards those whose wellbeing affects the creditor so closely that he would obviously want them as well protected as himself that responsibility can justifiably be imposed. Gernhuber (JZ 1962, 553, 555) speaks of a rule of customary law whereby a third party is to a certain extent included in the obligational relationship of others if the risks inherent in the performance of the obligation affect him at least as much as the creditor, or if the risks connected with a want of safety in the creditor's sphere affect him like the debtor, because, consistently with the contract, he is performing in lieu of the debtor. No such close links generally exist between landlord and tenant in leases of rooms in a building. The landlord is not normally jointly responsible for the 'weal or woe' of his tenant, and he has no occasion to be as concerned with the tenant's security as with his own. Furthermore, as Gernhuber notes (JZ 1962, 553, 556), the courts have not yet granted protective effects to third parties who have suffered only property damage.

2. But it is not necessary to come to a final conclusion on this matter because the judgment of the Court of Appeal can be supported on other grounds.

(a) Had it been the defendant himself who failed to turn off the tap, he would have been liable to the plaintiff, not only as user or joint-user of the toilets, as the Court of Appeal held, but also as landlord under the contract of lease: for in addition to his principal duty to afford the tenant the use of the leased premises, the landlord is also under a duty to take care to avoid having an adverse or damaging effect on the tenant while the tenant is using the leased property [RGZ 159, 27, 33; other references omitted]. If breach of this duty of care causes harm to property brought on to the premises by the tenant, the landlord is liable. There is a converse case, though similar in law, where a tenant by breach of his duty to take care of the leased property causes water damage to property not comprised in the lease but belonging to the resident landlord; here the Reichsgericht held that the tenant's liability extends to all the harm which he has caused to the landlord through culpable breach of the contract of lease, not just to the harm he causes to the leased property (RGZ 84, 222, 225). The decision of the *Bundesgerichtshof* of 14 October 1955 is based on the same view. Here a tenant was claiming damages from his landlord for flood damage to property he had brought on to the rented premises. The water came into the rented premises from the store room above them, which was evidently not leased. The BGH explained that the claim lay under §§ 276, 278 BGB, in connection with § 536 BGB: the landlord was bound to maintain the tenanted premises in such a condition as to enable them to be used without disturbance, and he is liable if he or anyone authorised by him fails to deploy the necessary care to perform this duty.

It is immaterial whether the breach of the duty of care arose from the landlord's actual use of the building in which the tenant leased the rooms. A tenant who is damaged by a cause emanating from the premises leased by a fellow-tenant in general has no contractual action against him, but this does not mean that he cannot sue the landlord if the harm emanates from premises which the landlord has reserved. It is possible to make the landlord liable because he is in a contractual relationship with the tenant, whereas there is normally no such contract between different tenants. That a landlord who uses rented premises may come under contractual duties is shown by the decision where the *Reichsgericht* held the landlord bound to take care to close the gate to the courtyard in common use (RGZ 103, 372).

Nothing contrary to this follows from the decision of the *Reichsgericht* in RGZ 103, 9. It is true that in that case the *Reichsgericht* held that the mere fact that the rooms had been leased did not generate any responsibility on the part of the landlord for property brought on to the premises by the tenant, but the peculiarity of that case was that the landlord had no connection whatever with the property so brought in: the tenant kept the room he rented unlocked, and property was stolen from it without the landlord having been in any way to blame. That case is very far removed from the present case.

If the landlord uses rooms in the tenanted building his duty is so to conduct himself that the tenant is not damages. In the present case therefore the defendant should have taken care that the taps were turned off and that water could not get into the plaintiff's business premises.

The defendant is equally liable if it was one of the defendant's relatives or patients that left the tap running: such persons count as agents for performance under § 278 BGB, because they are engaged with his consent in satisfying the duty of care he owes to the plaintiff. Furthermore, in such a case the defendant would himself have been at fault, because if he makes the toilets available to his patients, he is bound to check, or get someone else to check, that they have been left in a proper condition once the surgery is over.

(b) This duty of care was objectively breached. The condition of the leased room was such that the property brought on to the premises by the plaintiff was put at risk.

Water from toilets which were used in part by the defendant came through the ceiling into the plaintiff's business premises and damaged the goods which were stored there. It was the duty of the defendant to prevent any such happening. It is admittedly uncertain on the findings of the Court of Appeal whether the person who failed to turn off the water tap was one of the defendant's patients or employees: the omission might be attributable to one of the persons attending the K trade school. If so, should the defendant have been aware of the danger thus threatening the tenanted premises? Was he to blame for not preventing it? Did his surgery outlast the classes in the trade school? These questions are unanswered but, contrary to the view of the appellant, it is not for the plaintiff to answer them. Where damage may occur to the beneficiary of a contract from a whole range of dangers emanating from the debtor, courts and writers agree that when damage occurs it is for the obliged party to exculpate himself rather than for the entitled party to bring proof on matters which fall outside his area of control, and usually outside his knowledge as well. [BGHZ 23, 288, 290; 27, 236, 238; 28, 251, 254; NJW 1962, 31; other reference omitted]. It is true that this principle, stemming from §§ 282, 285 BGB, was first developed in relation to contracts of services, employment and lodging, and there may perhaps be limits to its application to contracts of lease, but its application is certainly justified on the special facts of this case. In the exercise of their professions, both the defendant and K permitted a large number of virtually uncontrollable persons to use the toilets. This increased the danger that some negligence on the part of a user might damage the premises which the plaintiff leased and the property he had brought on to them. This danger fell outside the plaintiff's control and surveillance. The defendant made it even more difficult to establish responsibility because he himself used the toilets in common with K. In a case such as the present where the guilty person must come from the circle of one or two parties, each of whom blames the other, the plaintiff can hardly ever prove whose negligence caused the harm; such difficulty of proof, as the Court of Appeal was right to observe, is unjust. The defendant must be charged with proving what steps he took to prevent danger arising to the plaintiff's rented premises and why he is not to blame. This is the principle which underlies the rule of the division of proof which we have mentioned, and it squares with the view of Raape, who says that the rule should apply to cases of positive breach of contracts of lease as well. He gives an example which is quite close to the present case: while an attic is being cleared, so many heavy objects are placed in a room that the floor gives way, and property belonging to the tenant of the rooms below is damaged. All the tenant need prove is that the floor which collapsed was overloaded. Then it is for the landlord to prove that he knew nothing whatever about the overloading, perhaps because the clearance was being done by another tenant.

Because the defendant has not adduced the proof which is required for his exculpation, the Court of Appeal was right in law to allow the claim.

Case 69
REICHSGERICHT (THIRD CIVIL SENATE) 3 JUNE 1921
RGZ 102, 232

Facts

The plaintiff and her husband lived on the third floor of a house belonging to the defendant and rented from him by the husband. On the morning of 23 October 1918 her husband was found dead and she was found unconscious in their bedroom. This was due to gas poisoning, the gas having come, according to the plaintiff, from the floor below. On the floor below the defendant was having gas replaced with electricity, and had retained G, a master plumber, to remove the gas pipes. At the end of his work on 21 October, one of G's workmen failed to plug the gas pipe leading from the gas metre to the apartment of one Gr, a publican. The gas metre was turned off at the time, but it was turned on by Gr on 22 October, and gas then flowed out of the unstopped pipe and filtered through the ceiling into the living quarters above, those of the plaintiff and her husband as well as those of Gr himself.

The plaintiff claimed compensation for her own illness and for the loss she suffered through her husband's death, the claim being based on the contract of lease which her husband had entered as well as on tortious negligence. The defendant denied the plaintiff's assertions about the gas poisoning and contended that the accident had occurred because a gas tap in their apartment had carelessly been left on either by the plaintiff or by her husband.

Both lower courts dismissed the claim, but the plaintiff's appeal was allowed.

Reasons

The Court of Appeal accepted the plaintiff's version of the cause of the gas poisoning. It held, in accordance with decisions of this court (see, eg, RGZ 91, 24), that the contract of lease concluded by the plaintiff's husband was one for the benefit of the plaintiff under § 328 BGB and that therefore the plaintiff had a personal contractual claim against the landlord for breach of his contractual duty of care under §§ 536, 538 BGB. It also held, correctly, that the landlord was contractually bound to each of his tenants not to damage them by works being effected on the premises and to indemnify them for any harm due to culpable breach of this duty. The Court nevertheless rejected the plaintiff's claim because the defendant was neither personally at fault nor liable for the negligence of an agent for performance (§ 278 BGB). There was no personal fault in the defendant because the person to whom he had entrusted the work, the master plumber G, was a specialist. He had thereby fulfilled his duty of care to see that the works were carried out properly and in a manner not involving risk to the occupants of the house, all the more so since what was involved was a simple and easy task which the chosen specialist could be expected to carry out properly. It was not common practice for the landlord himself to supervise specialist tasks which he was in no position to evaluate, nor to appoint a representative to do so for him. It therefore could not be expected that the defendant should supervise G's work. Nor was the defendant liable under § 278 BGB, because the work being done on the gas pipes was not in execution of any duty owed by the defendant to the plaintiff, but of a duty owed by the defendant to the occupant of the lower apartment: G and his workmen could therefore not be regarded as the defendant's agents for performance vis-à-vis the plaintiff.

The appellant criticises the Court of Appeal's opinion on both points. Criticism of the finding that the defendant was not personally at fault is without merit. In the case of work such as was here entrusted to the master plumber G, the defendant was under no duty, either personally or through a clerk of works, to see that the work was being carried out properly or to check it as soon as it had been completed. A subsequent inspection, perhaps in the defendant's own interests, would not have prevented the accident.

On the other hand, the appellant is right to say that there has been misapplication of §§ 2778, 536, 538 BGB. The Court of appeal itself recognised that the landlord has a contractual duty to all his tenants not to injure them by work being done on the premises. This duty stems directly from the basic duty imposed on the landlord by § 536 BGB, which is not simply to make the rented property available at the outset of the lease in a condition suitable for use in accordance with the contract, but also to maintain it in this condition for the duration of the lease. But this is not a duty merely to avoid doing harmful work on the premises, it is a positive duty to see that the rented property is maintained in a condition suitable for contractual use. It therefore includes the duty to take care that the tenant's uses of the premises is not unacceptably affected by any work being done on the premises, including work done in parts of the building other than those demised to the tenant for his exclusive use. If the landlord allows work to be done in the house which runs the risk of affecting the tenanted premises, he is bound under the contract of lease so to effect these works that this danger is averted, regardless of where in the house or why the work is being done. The landlord of a house whose ground floor needed strengthening or whose gas or water supply was defective at any point would clearly be contractually bound as against tenants anywhere on the premises who were endangered thereby to do any repairs properly. If he entrusts the work to someone else he is using that other person for the performance of his duty towards all such tenants: he must therefore answer for his assistant's fault under § 278 BGB as if it were his own. The same is true if the danger arises from works undertaken in rooms rented to others. For example, suppose a supporting wall on the ground floor is to be removed in order to enlarge the windows. The landlord's contractual duty to do these works is owed only to the tenant of the ground floor and not to other tenants, but if he actually engages on the work, he owes to all the tenants in the house a contractual duty so to manage it that the rooms they rent are not adversely affected. To this extent therefore the workmen whom the landlord employs for modification of the building are his agents for performance under § 278 BGB not only as against the tenants whose rooms could be affected by the work of reconstruction. So here, taking the plaintiff's assertions as true, although the defendant was indeed under no contractual duty towards the plaintiff to replace the gas pipes by electric wiring, he was responsible to the plaintiff and to the other tenants in the house for seeing that the gas pipes were removed without risk of gas flowing into their rooms. Those persons to whom the defendant entrusted the removal of the gas pipes were consequently his agents for performance vis-à-vis the plaintiff too.

Such an application of § 278 BGB in respect of the landlord's obligation to maintain the leased property so that it remains fit for contractual use is correlative to the tenant's liability for his employees arising from his duty to treat the leased property properly: those whom the tenant engages in the business he runs on the tenanted premises are his agents for performance of his duty to treat the premises properly, even if he owes the landlord no duty whatever to run the business in which those persons are employed (see RGZ 84, 222). . . .

Case 70
BUNDESGERICHTSHOF (SIXTH CIVIL SENATE) 18 JUNE 1968
NJW 1968, 1929

Reasons

I. The Court of Appeal held that the firm D had no contractual claim. This is correct in law.

1. The firm D bought the machine from the firm R, not from the defendant. The Court of Appeal was correct in holding that there were two separate sale contracts— one between the defendant, who manufactured the machine, and its Swiss general agent, R, and the other between R and the purchaser, D (compare RGZ 87, 1, 2). The appellant's contention that R was the commercial agent of the defendant and had sold the machine to D in the defendant's name is in conflict with the admitted facts on which the Court of Appeal based its judgment. It is agreed that R regularly bought the defendant's machines on its own account and sold them on its own account to Swiss customers. Consistently with this, it was R and not the defendant who on 19 December 1961 offered D the machine which was later bought, a purchase which D confirmed on 12 February 1962 to R, not to the defendant. Then on 21 February R ordered the machine from the defendant, an order which the defendant confirmed on 22 March 1962 to R, and not to D. On 30 September 1963 the defendant sent its invoice to R, which then, on its own account, invoiced D.

On these facts the Court of Appeal was right to conclude that even if R called itself 'general agent,' it was a merchant acting as a principal rather than as a commercial agent. The fact that R constantly acted for the defendant and, so far as possible, for no one else, does not mean that it sold in the name of the defendant any more than the fact that it referred to the defendant in its accounts as 'our house.' What was said in the negotiations by R's manager and what was written by Dr L, the firm's administrative adviser, is immaterial here. In support of the Court of Appeal's conclusion it may be noted that in its confirmation of order of 22 March 1962 the defendant allowed R '10 per cent rebate for onward sale.'

2. If R was the buyer of the machine, then D can only claim on the contract of sale if it can sue on the contract between R and the defendant. The Court of Appeal committed no error of law in saying that this was not possible.

(a) According to the Court of Appeal, the plaintiff did not claim to be assignee of any claims for damages which R might have had against the defendant on the contract between them. There was therefore no occasion to check whether R had any claim against the defendant in respect of harm suffered by it, or, pursuant to the transfer of risk of carriage, by D (compare § 447 BGB; BGHZ 40, 99, 101). The appellant now says that the fact that R had received the purchase price from D entailed a silent transfer of any claim for damages it might have. The Court of Appeal did not investigate this question. Nor did it need to do so, since the plaintiff made no mention of an express or implicit assignment in either head of claim. It consistently founded on D's own claims and not on any assigned claims of R, doubtless because R, as the defend - ant's general representative, was unlikely to transfer any claims it might have against 'our house.'

(b) The Court of Appeal also denied that D had any personal claim for damages on the footing that the sale to R by the defendant was arranged as a genuine contract for the benefit of third parties. That is quite correct in law.

The Court of Appeal recognised that a sale by manufacturer to his 'contract dealer' (*Vertragshändler*) whereby the manufacturer is to deliver the goods directly to the sub-vendee (*Streckengeschäft*) can be interpreted so that the sub-vendee obtains a direct right to have the goods delivered or rather, in this case, properly loaded. It nev- ertheless found no good reason to treat the contract of sale between R and the defend- ant in this manner. Contrary to the view of the appellant, there is no legal error in such a construction, especially as the Court of Appeal highlighted the fact that the machine was not collected from the defendant by D, the supposed beneficiary, but by a carrier arranged by R.

(c) The only remaining question is whether D is included within the protective ambit of the sale contract between R and the defendant. This depends on the meaning and purpose of the contract. The Court of Appeal held not and, despite the appel- lant's objections, this is the right result.

(aa) The defendant delivered the machine to R 'ex works,' the place of perfor- mance, according to the confirmation of order, being the defendant's place of business at G. The parties are agreed that the defendant's liability is to be determined by German law. Now it is to be noted that the provision of § 447 BGB (which is rendered applicable in certain cases by §§ 651, 644 § 2 BGB) does not apply as between the defendant and R: it was not the defendant who, at R's request, had the machine car- ried by a forwarding agent or carrier for whom it had itself arranged: it was R who had the machine collected from the defendant.

It was not the defendant's obligation to arrange for the delivery of the machine. It was certainly bound to hand it over to the carrier or agent sent by the purchaser in such a condition that the carrier could deliver it to the purchaser unharmed (RGZ 115, 162, 164; further references omitted). The duty to load the thing in a profes- sional manner is part of the vendor's duty to deliver the purchased object to the purchaser (§ 433 para 1 BGB), and the Court of Appeal was right to describe this duty as a subsidiary one. If the vendor is in breach of it he cannot rely on any trans- fer of risk under §§ 446, 447 BGB, which unburden him only of risks incidental to the carriage of the goods. If he fails to pack them properly or load them in a profes- sional manner on to the vehicle of the carrier or agent, he is responsible for the consequent destruction or deterioration of the goods [see RG, JW 1901, 725 no 19; other references omitted]. It is wholly immaterial that harm attributable to such a breach of contract arises only after the vendor has handed the goods over to the carrier (reference omitted).

The defendant has not denied that although it sold the machine 'free ex works' it undertook to load the machine on to the truck. If its workmen committed a fault in this, then it would be answerable under § 278 BGB; the damage to the goods would not be 'accidental' so the defendant could not rely as against R on the provisions of §§ 446, 447 BGB. The rules of §§ 323 ff BGB would remain applicable, and the defendant would be liable in damages and would in particular forfeit its right to claim the price.

(bb) But this helps the plaintiff only if the defendant's duty to load the machine properly was owed to D as well as to its purchaser, R. The Court of Appeal did not regard this as established.

The appellant, as against this, relies on the decisions of this court to the effect that third parties are to be drawn within the protection of a contract if the debtor's duty of care should be respected not only as towards his contractor, but as against others (NJW 1959, 1676; VersR 1959, 1009; also BGHZ 33, 247, 249). In addition to personal injury cases, this court has allowed the third party a personal claim for damages for property damage and even for merely economic loss (NJW 1965, 1955; BGHZ 49, 350). We need not here ask whether this expansion of liability results from an extensive construction of the contract based on the principle of good faith [reference omitted] or from some other source [reference omitted]. This line of decisions has been criticised in some quarters, but the *Bundesgerichtshof* has adhered to it (BGHZ 49, 278; BGHZ 49, 350).

Still, this court has frequently emphasised that it is only within narrow limits that contractual duties of care are to be extended outside the circle of the actual parties to the contract [VersR 1962, 86; other reference omitted]. The distinction between direct and indirect victims should be maintained. The general rule is that contractual liability is annexed to the tie that binds the creditor to his contractual partner. If these principles are forgotten, a contractor will be unable to tell, and so calculate, what risk he is undertaking, and it will be difficult to justify holding him liable. Thus it is by no means enough that third parties 'come into contact' with the performance of the debtor through the creditor. In modern commercial transactions involving long chains of dealers this is almost always the case. The concept of 'contract with protective effect for third parties' must be restricted not only as regards the subjects, ie those third parties who are drawn into the protected area, but as regards its objects, ie the terms of the contract from which it is sought to draw such protective duties. The meaning and purpose of a contract, once it is construed in accordance with the principle of good faith (§ 157 BGB), will only justify the extension of the duties of care and protection to third parties if the principal creditor himself owes them protection and care and is in some sense responsible for their 'weal and woe' (see BGHZ NJW 1964, 33). This will normally be so only in rather personal situations, such as exist in the family or in employment or in tenancy. An especially strict test must be applied if the protective effect is to apply to property damage and economic loss.

This is not the place to decide in detail what people deserve and need to be included. The Court of Appeal essentially relied on the above principles of law and asked whether the contract between the defendant and R could be construed in such a way as to give D a place in the protective purpose of the contract, at any rate so far as the duty to load the gods with care was concerned. The Court did not misapprehend the fact that the machine was clearly produced in accordance with D's wishes, and was to be delivered directly to D, but it saw in this fact no sufficient reason for giving D a personal right to claim damages. From the legal point of view this is perfectly right. It is essentially just a question of the construction of the contract, a matter over which a court of review has only limited control. Doubtless tradesmen do think it important to take care of their customers' interests, but not in the sense of owing them 'protection and care' [reference omitted]. In a *Streckengeschäft* like the present, the goods are packed and loaded so as to reach the ultimate purchaser, but this just helps to decide how they are to be packed and loaded: it is not a sufficient reason for bringing the sub-purchaser within the protection of the contractual subsidiary duty.

(cc) The appellant says that good faith demands his inclusion in the protection of the contract, for otherwise the result would be inequitable. The considerations it adduces are only partially correct.

It is true that R could claim damages from the defendant because, as we have said, the defendant is not relieved by § 447 BGB. If so, says the appellant, it would be unjust if D were 'saddled with' the loss since the risk of carriage had passed to it (§ 447 BGB; compare art 185, Swiss Code of Obligations (OR)). But this is wrong. There was surely a contract of sale and delivery between R and D, but it relieved R only of the true risks of carriage, whereas here we have harm due to improper loading. The seller, R, had to see to the loading, and since it had the loading done by the defendant, it must answer for the defendant's fault in this regard, as the Court of Appeal correctly said by invoking § 278 BGB and the comparable rule in Swiss law (Art 101 OR). D may well have good claim against R (for damages or for refund of the purchase price) wherein R could assign to D its claims for damages against the defendant (compare § 281 BGB and the similar rule in Swiss law).

No further consideration of these factors is needed to show that the results of the decision of the Court of Appeal are not necessarily inequitable or such as to constrain us to grant D the right to claim damages directly from the defendant.

II. The Court of appeal was right to hold that D had no claim for damages against the defendant on the basis of *negotiorum gestio* (*Geschäftsführung ohne Auftrag*). In loading the machine the defendant was neither executing a mandate from R nor yet performing a task for D for which it had no mandate: it was doing its own duty as seller to deliver the machine to the purchaser [reference omitted]. The appellant's proposals on this matter are based on a misconception of the law.

III. Nor did the firm D have any claim in tort against the defendant on the ground that the defendant caused 'its' machine, the machine of D, to be loaded in an unprofessional manner. D had already paid DM30,000 towards the purchase price, but that did not make it 'owner by Vorbehalt' as the Court of Appeal rightly held. Nor was D in indirect possession of the machine during the carriage. The carrier was in possession of the machine during the carriage. The carrier was in possession of the machine for R, not for D.

1. As we have explained there were here two sale contracts which must be kept legally distinct. We must also distinguish the transfer of ownership from the defendant to R from the further transfer to D. When the machine was handed to the carrier sent by R, the risk passed to R and the risk of carriage passed simultaneously to D, regardless of the fact that here R was delivering directly from the factory rather than from his own place of business or place of performance (BGHZ 24 March 1965, NJW 1965, 1324). But the transfer of risk has nothing to do with the transfer of ownership (nor with the acquisition of a vested right of future ownership) (RGZ 93, 330, 331; 85, 320). In a contract for sale and delivery ownership only passes to the purchaser when the purchased property comes into his hands (RGZ 108, 25, 27–8; 102, 38, 40; 99, 56, 57;

NJW 1960, 1952), although it may happen earlier in exceptional cases, for example if the vendor, in handing the goods to the carrier, untypically intends to vest them in the purchaser and the carrier is authorised by the purchaser to acquire ownership in them as his agent [see RGZ 84, 320, 322; other reference omitted].

In the present case it may be assumed that on handing the machine to the carrier the defendant was ready to transfer his ownership in it to R (probably conditionally on the outstanding price being paid). The carrier commissioned to deliver the machine to R had been chosen not by the defendant but by R. The carrier and forwarding agent were therefore in possession of the machine as intermediaries for R. It does not follow from this that R would have been ready to transfer ownership to D before the machine actually arrived at it destination, let alone immediately. So far as the relationship between R and D goes, one should maintain the principle already mentioned, that when there is a contract for the sale and delivery of goods, the property passes only on the delivery of the goods to the purchaser. In the relationship between D and R the carrier was ordered by the seller, not by D, to whom the carrier was unknown until the accident. The carrier could not acquire ownership directly for D without some special authorisation (see RGZ 103, 30, 32; 102, 41; 84, 320, 322).

2. After investigating all the circumstances, the Court of Appeal found that there was no such authorisation here. The appellant's objections to this are without merit.

The Court of Appeal did not overlook the possibility that in view of the particularly close interfusion of the two sales contracts the defendant might have transferred the property directly to D, through the intermediacy of the carrier, but it decided that this had not happened, especially since the loading chit which the defendant gave to the carrier said 'To the order of the Firm R & Co.' This is legally unassailable. Nor was the Court of Appeal wrong to ignore the fact that the invoice which the defendant sent to R on 30 September 1963 stated, under the heading '"Delivery". To be collected by truck belonging to K in Z, for delivery to D in N.' Such a delivery note is a feature of every *Streckengeschäft* and it did not evince any intention on the part of the defendant to transfer ownership directly to D.

Case 71
BUNDESGERICHTSHOF (EIGHTH CIVIL SENATE) 10 JULY 1963
BGHZ 40, 91

Facts

The plaintiff, who makes belts, had done business for many years with the defendant, who processes leather. The defendant sold the plaintiff 36 pieces of natural suede, dyed green, for DM581.93, having obtained it from the firm H. The plaintiff made the leather into belts for women's dresses and sold most of them to the firm K-F, which delivered them to a mail order house. Many of these dresses then developed yellow stains at the points where the belt and the material met. K-F withdrew some 395 of these stained dresses.

The plaintiff claims damages from the defendant on the basis that the stains were caused by the faulty dyeing of the leather supplied by the defendant. K-F had suffered a loss of DM10,375.50, but it was common ground that K-F had made no claim for this sum against the plaintiff, and the plaintiff did not contend that it was liable to K-F. The plaintiff nevertheless claimed to be entitled to sue for the damage suffered by its purchaser as if it were a loss.

The *Landgericht* held that the defendant must pay for the harm suffered by K-F, and the *Oberlandesgericht* dismissed the defendant's appeal. The defendant's further appeal is now allowed.

Reasons

A.   . . .

B.

1. The appellant's criticism of the Court of Appeal's view that the plaintiff may claim damages for the loss suffered by its purchaser is well-founded.

According to the Court of Appeal, it must be assumed that at the time they made the contract of sale, the parties implicitly agreed that the plaintiff should be entitled to sue for any loss suffered by its purchasers, whether or not those purchasers could claim compensation from the plaintiff.

II.

1. This initial assumption is already open to doubt. An implicit declaration of intention denotes conduct which, while not apparently constituting a declaration at all, is treated, by reason of its factual context, as evincing an intention to produce specific legal results. An implicit declaration is accordingly a genuine declaration of intention. Here the parties themselves did not allege that it was their agreed intention (expressed by their conduct, here silence) that the plaintiff should be able to sue for any loss suffered by its purchasers; nor did the Court of Appeal adduce any facts in support of its conclusion. It is plain therefore that when the court speaks of an implicit agreement, it means only that it feels that the plaintiff should have the right in question and that this can be achieved by the method of creative implication.

2. We cannot agree with this. It is true that the courts, with the approval of the commentators, have under certain circumstances made exceptions to the general principle that damages can only be claimed by the person who has suffered the loss; a contracting party has then been granted the right to claim as damage suffered by itself a loss actually accruing to a third party. This is called *Schadensliquidation im Drittinteresse* [reference omitted]. The cases in which such a right has been allowed to take various forms, but their common feature is that the entitlement under the contract and the interest protected by the contract are vested in different persons, and that therefore the harm caused by a breach of contract strikes the third party rather than the contractual creditor. That such a shifting of interest (*Interessenverlagerung*) or shifting of loss [references omitted], as writers call it, should not benefit the person causing the harm is generally agreed.

(a) One line of cases involves indirect representation: a party concludes a contract in his own name but at the instance of and on the account of a third party. The *Reichsgericht* and the *Bundesgerichtshof* have always held, as a firm principle, and without any nice reasoning, that the person executing the order can sue for damage suffered by the person giving it (RGZ 90, 240, 246; 113, 250, 254; 115, 419, 425; BGHZ 25, 250, 258).

(b) In another line of cases there is an 'unburdening of the risk' [references omitted]: it sometimes happens that a person who is bound to deliver a chattel to another is relieved from his obligation if the chattel is destroyed by the fault of someone else. One example arises when a chattel which has been sold on the terms that it is to be handed over to the purchaser somewhere else has been delivered to a carrier such as the railways. Then § 447 BGB makes the risk pass to the third party purchaser, who remains bound to pay the price. Although the only person to suffer is the third party purchaser, the vendor is held entitled to claim this loss from the party causing it (RGZ 62, 331). The same is true when a chattel which is the object of a bequest is destroyed before it is handed over to the legatee: the heir is relieved of liability under § 275 BGB, but he may claim the loss suffered by the legatee from the person causing it [references omitted].

(c) The final class of case in the area of *Schadensliquidation im Drittinteresse* is those where one person is looking after the goods of another. A party's contractual obligation to care for and protect the goods applies where the property has been put at the bailor's disposal by a third party who owns it. If the owner is damaged as a result of a breach of this contract, the bailor is allowed by the courts to bring a contractual claim for the compensation of the harm which has been suffered by the owner, especially if the bailee could meet the owner's claim in tort by relying on § 831 BGB. The *Reichsgericht* used to invoke the cases on indirect representation in order to justify this holding, and said that in both situations the interests of contractor and third party were very intimately connected (RGZ 93, 39).

A different basis for *Liquidation des Drittschadens* was offered by the *Reichsgericht* in its judgment in RGZ 170, 246. Suppletive contractual construction was employed there in order to hold that the defendant, who had contracted to repair a city refrigerator, had granted the city the right to sue it for any loss suffered by butchers whose meat in the cold store was spoiled as a result of careless repair work. This is also the basis given by the *Bundesgerichtshof* for its decision in BGHZ 15, 224, 227. In this case a carrier had contracted with a forwarding agent, and owing to the fault of the latter a truck which belonged to the carrier's wife had been confiscated by the authorities in the Soviet zone. In another decision of the *Bundesgerichtshof* on 27 January 1958 [reference omitted], a steamer which was under charter was damaged by the carelessness of the person supplying it with water. Although the harm was suffered by the owner of the ship, the charterer was allowed to claim this loss from the supplier of the water. In so deciding, the *Bundesgerichtshof* invoked RGZ 93, 39 and BGHZ 15, 224.

3. Commentators have strenuously opposed the use of contractual construction as the way to grant the right to claim damages for a loss suffered by a third party, on the ground that to impute any such intention to the parties is to do violence to their true will [reference omitted]. We need not go into this question here since the case before us does not fall within any of the types of case we have mentioned. It is common ground that the plaintiff did not buy the leather from the defendant at the instance of and on the account of its purchaser. Nor is there any intimate linkage of interests in the sense of the decisions regarding the duty to look after someone else's goods. It may be, as the Court of Appeal held, that the purchaser has an interest in having smooth business relationships with its customers, but this fact by no means satisfies the precondition of an intimate connection of interests as laid down in the decisions cited. It cannot be suggested that the seller is under any duty to promote the advantageous development of the buyer's business relationships with its sub-vendees.

Nor does anything said by the parties justify the Court of Appeal's implication into the contract of a clause that the plaintiff should be able to sue for damage suffered by its purchasers regardless of whether they themselves could sue the plaintiff. For one thing there is no gap or lacuna in the contract which calls for any such implication. It is not true that whenever a contract fails to regulate a certain matter there is a gap which needs to be filled. The decisions of the courts make it plain that such a gap exists only when the factual setting or the real agreed intention of the parties shows that the express terms are obviously inadequate. The courts must not, in completing the contract, extend its object. To the extent that the parties have not explicitly deviated from what is laid down by the case, they leave the completion of their contract to its statutory provisions [BGHZ 9, 273, 277; other references omitted]. Thousands of sale contracts are made every day which contain no provision about whether the purchaser is to be entitled to sue if a defect in the goods causes harm to his sub-purchasers. Not all these contracts have a gap: on the contrary, the parties operate on the basis that the statutory rules shall apply. But the Code proceeds on the principle that, apart from exceptional cases such as §§ 618 para 3, 1298 BGB, the only damage one must pay for when one breaks one's contract is damage caused to the other contractor himself. It may be different where the contract gives rise to a duty to protect the third party, but that is a special case which does not arise here.

The Court of Appeal offered no basis for its conclusion that if the parties had thought about the possibility that the plaintiff's customers could suffer if the leather were badly dyed, they would, as decent businessmen, have agreed that the defendant should be liable to the plaintiff, even if the plaintiff was not or could not be sued by his customers. On the contrary, experience suggests that in reality businessmen are much more interested in protecting themselves from such damages claims by using exemption clauses, so far as the courts will let them, for such claims are unpredictable in their extent, incapable of being covered in an economically satisfactory manner by increasing the sale price or taking out insurance, and apt, as in the present case, greatly to exceed the value of the goods sold.

There is the further requirement that any contractual gap should be capable of being filled by suppletive interpretation. That requirement is not met here. A term cannot be implied into a contract unless it is a compelling and self-evident conclusion from the agreement as a whole such that unless such a term is implied, the result would obviously be in conflict with what was in fact agreed (BGHZ 12, 337, 343; 29, 107, 110). The Court of Appeal has not said why the plaintiff's customers have refrained from suing. They may have omitted to obtain a guarantee from the plaintiff of the quality of the dyeing of the belts, or they may believe that the plaintiff is not liable in damages for any faulty and positive breach of contract. But claims for damages based on defects in purchased goods have been restricted by the legislator, and with good reason. If the Court of Appeal were right, the plaintiff's customers would have a claim for damages here if the defendant were guilty of a positive breach of contract as against the plaintiff, although the law of sales would deny them one in their own right. They would be in as good a position as if the defendant had committed a positive breach of contract as against them, not just as against the plaintiff. Such a rule can hardly be said to be necessary in order to advance the general purpose of the contract or to save the plaintiff from intolerable hardship

In a judgment of 7 August 1959 (Betrieb 1959, 1083) this senate held that a plaintiff who had bought goods in order to incorporate them with goods belonging to a customer could sue for the harm suffered by his customer owing to a defect in the purchased goods. The court was by no means saying that the principles of *Drittschadensliquidation* apply within the chain of purchasers. It emphasised that it all depended on the construction of the contract between the parties, and that if the intention and purpose of the contract make it clear that the interest of the third party is to be protected, the person whose contractual rights have been infringed may be entitled to sue for the damage to the third party. The peculiarity of that case was that, according to the construction of the contract made by the court below and binding on this court, the seller had agreed to assume the buyer's risk as against the buyer's customer, and had bound itself to pay for damage which third parties might suffer from using the goods which had been sold. The decision is not as far-reaching as Erman suggests [reference omitted]. In the case before us however it is quite plain, even on the findings of the Court of Appeal, that the defendant was not bound to stand in for harm suffered by the plaintiff's purchasers and sub-purchasers.

4. *Schadensliquidation im Drittinteresse* is sometimes allowed by courts and commentators on other grounds than contractual interpretation, but those grounds have no application here either. A claim may be available where all the damage due to the harmful conduct of the obligor is suffered by a third party rather than by the person with title to sue. There must be only *one* damage, one which the claimant would have suffered if the protected interest had been vested in him. The third party is harmed *instead* of the person with the claim [reference omitted]. So, in the types of case that we find in the reports and the books, as between the plaintiff and the third party, the harm is suffered only by the person represented, not by the person representing him, only by the person to whom the risk has passed, not by the person from whom it has passed, only by the owner of the thing, not by the person who bailed it by contract to the defendant. The doctrine is not triggered by the mere fact that in addition to the person with title to sue a third party has suffered harm. Allowing a person to sue for damage to a third party must not be permitted to bring about any extension of liability founded in law or contract by duplicating the victims whom the person causing the harm must satisfy. The *Reichsgericht* stressed this vital point in its decision in RGZ 170, 246, where butchers' meat was spoilt in the city cold-store badly repaired by the defendant. It emphasised that the damage must be one and the same, whichever party, city or butcher, had the title to sue. The only harm involved was the damage to the meat, and, as the *Reichsgericht* explained, no 'multiplication' of the harm resulted from granting the city a right to claim for the loss suffered by the butchers.

No such simple displacement of loss or interest in this sense occurs when a buyer resells the thing and his sub-buyer suffers harm through a defect in it, since it is quite possible that the first buyer himself also suffers a loss. That is why Tegert [reference omitted] is right to deny that the seller is contractually liable for harm caused by defects in the thing to subsequent acquirers in a chain sale. Another reason for not applying *Schadensliquidation im Drittinteresse* in chain sales is that if the first seller were liable to eventual sub-buyers for his breach of contract, he would be faced with an accumulation of loss which is intolerable and contrary to the basic principles of contract law [reference omitted]. The judgment of the Reichsgericht in DR 1941, 637 clearly supports this, because although it held that the first purchaser had the right to sue for the loss suffered by his sub-purchaser, it based its decision on the fact that he had bought the thing on the instructions and for the account of that person. The *Reichsgericht* thus decided the case on the basis of indirect representation, as it was called, and this would not have been necessary had the court thought a purchaser enti-tled as such to sue for the loss suffered by his sub-vendee.

Nor can the original seller be made liable on the general principle of respect for good faith. It is not inequitable that a sub-purchaser's claims should depend on the contract of sale he himself has made. If the terms of his own contract afford him no claim for damages, equity does not require us to let him claim damages from the original seller through his vendor, simply because the original seller is liable in damages to his vendor. There is no general principle that a person who causes harm must pay for it even if his creditors suffers no damage. To this extent at least Werner [reference omit-ted] is right to emphasise that damages are in principle payable only for harm actually sustained by the claimant, not as a kind of penance due from the person responsible.

We need not enquire whether a different conclusion might not be called for, on the grounds of justifiable reliance, in a case where the producer of goods vaunts their mer-its through advertisements and thereby induces an ultimate consumer to buy them through an 'anonymous' chain of distributors. No such fact situation is present here.

Case 72
BUNDESGERICHTSHOF (SIXTH CIVIL SENATE) 12 JULY 1977
NJW 1977, 2208

Facts

The defendant was carrying out the earth removal operations required in the con-struction of an aqueduct and reservoir for the city B and the local water authority. In the course of the works a mechanical digger operated by one of the defendant's men damaged an electric cable which supplied several concerns. As a result current to the plaintiff's business was interrupted for 32 minutes, and the work of its 1385 employ-ees brought to a halt.

The *Landgericht* and the *Oberlandesgericht* dismissed the claim for damages. The plaintiff's appeal was also dismissed.

Reasons

I.

1. The Court of Appeal held that the plaintiff had no tort claim under § 823 para 1 BGB, since no legal interest protected by this rule had been invaded: in having to pay wages when no work could be done owing to the lack of current the plaintiff suffered a purely economic loss. The Court also held that there had been no invasion of an estab-lished and operative business. Furthermore, no claim arose under § 823 para 1 BGB, for although there was a provincial regulation regarding the safeguarding of electric cables during building operations (§ 18 para 3 Provincial Building Ordinance of Baden-Wurttemberg—BadWurttBauO), it did not have the character of a protective law (*Schutzgesetz*) in favour of customers supplied from the national electricity grid.

2 This is perfectly in line with the decisions of this court.

(a) This court has frequently stated the preconditions which must be met before damages are payable for affecting a business (BGHZ 29, 65; 41, 123; 66, 388, 393).

Those principles involve the conclusion that the damage done by the defendant's mechanical digger to the electric cable was not an invasion of the plaintiff's business as such, since there is lacking the requirement of intimate connection with the business (*Betriebsbezogenheit*). In a similar case (BGHZ 29, 65, 74) the court said that the breaking of an electric cable supplying a factory is no more intimately connected with the business than injury to its employees or damage to its vehicles: it is not an essential characteristic feature of an established and operative business that it have an uninterrupted supply of electricity, especially as all the other customers connected to the same cable have the same legal relationship with the utility that supplies the current. We need not dwell on this point since even the appellant does not contest it.

(b) Although it had previously held otherwise (see, eg, NJW 1968, 1279), this court in its decision of 8 June 1976 (BGHZ 66, 388) stated that § 18 para 3 BadWurttBauo (and the similar provisions of the building ordinances of other Länder) are not protective laws in favour of subscribers who suffer economic loss through a lack of current due to damage to a cable. Accordingly there are no legal objections to the view of the Court of Appeal, which evidently was unaware of that decision. Nor, indeed, does the appellant himself contest this part of the judgment.

II. The plaintiff also puts forward a contractual claim both in his own right and by assignment. The Court of Appeal rejected this. The underlying facts are that representatives of the parties had a meeting on site with representatives of the water authority and the city, that the plaintiff's business manager and the city representative drew attention to the presence of the main electric cable where the earthworks were about to begin and stressed how vital it was for the plaintiff's business, and that the defendant's clerk of works was then told that any digging in the neighbourhood of the cable must be done by hand rather than by machine. The Court of Appeal analysed these facts correctly, and its holding that the plaintiff was not drawn into the protective ambit of the contract of services between the water authority and the defendant cannot be faulted.

1. The case law recognises that persons not immediately involved in a contract may yet be drawn within its protective ambit, with the result that although they cannot bring a claim for performance, as would be the case if it were a true contract for the benefit of third parties under § 328 par 1 BGB, they may nevertheless have a contractual claim for damages if they suffer harm owing to faulty conduct by the debtor in breach of contract (on this see BGHZ 49, 350; NJW 1975, 344; NJW 1954, 874; BGH VersR 1955, 750; NJW 1956, 1193; NJW 1959, 1676; BGHZ 51, 91, 96). The cases agree that whether third parties are to be included in the protective area of a contract when they were not involved in its formation and have not been expressly covered by the parties, depends on the meaning and purpose of the contract and its construction in accordance with the principle of good faith (§ 157 BGB) (see BGHZ 56, 269, 273); in the long run what is critical is not so much the relationship between the contractors themselves as the special relationship between the creditor and the third party whose inclusion is in question (see especially BGHZ 51, 91, 96). In order to avoid an intolerable extension of contractual duties of care beyond what the principle of good faith can demand of the debtor of the contractual performance, the court has frequently observed that the duties of care and protection can only be extended beyond the actual parties to the contract if the principal creditor, here the water authority has some responsibility for the well-being of the third party, as owing him protection and

care (see especially BGHZ 51, 91, 96; NJW 1974, 1189). This requirement, which is needed so as to avoid blurring the line between contractual and tortious liability in an insupportable manner and contrary to the will of the legislature, is normally present only when there is a legal relationship of a personal nature between the contractual creditor and the third party, such as commonly arises in family relationships, in employment, and in landlord and tenant cases (see BGHZ 51, 91, 96).

2. Contrary to the appellant's contention, the Court of Appeal acted consistently with these principles in holding that the requirements for including the plaintiff in the protective area of the contract for work between the defendant and the water authority were not satisfied in this case.

(a) In particular the water authority here was in no way responsible for the wellbeing of the plaintiff. For the contractual creditor, the plaintiff was only one of a large number of subscribers that might be affected by damage to the cable. As this court said in its judgment of 3 November 1961 (VersR 1962, 86, 88), contractual duties must not be extended in cases where faulty work or failure to take security measures could cause harm to people of all kinds—house-owners, tenants, entrepreneurs and so on— for then the class of people protected by the contract would be unlimited and unforeseeable. The mere fact that the plaintiff's business was apt to suffer a considerable economic loss through interruption of the electricity supply does not justify holding that the water authority, which could itself suffer if the plaintiff was damaged, must look out for its wellbeing. Even if it is true that the contractual creditor had a certain interest in the safety of the cable, this interest was only a general one, and not one solely or predominantly related to the needs of the plaintiff for which the plaintiff could claim protection from the creditor.

(c) Nor can it be said that the meeting on site modified the contracts of works between the defendant and the water authority. The water authority was bound to give such instructions before the work started in order to enable the defendant to take the necessary steps to protect the utility cables (including telephone cables—§ 317 StGB), and the special reference to the harm the plaintiff might suffer if the current were interrupted was insufficient to bring it within the protective area of the contract contrary to the principles already stated. It is important that at the time he concludes the contract, the contractual debtor should be able to see what risk he is undertaking, and this would be impossible if the creditor could later determine what third parties were to be included in its protective area by making a unilateral declaration to the debtor or to some unauthorised employee.

3. The Court of Appeal was also right to hold that the plaintiff had no assigned claim for damages from the water authority. The requirements of *Drittschadensliquidation* are not met (BGHZ 51, 91, 93, ff). There is no special legal relationship between the plaintiff and the water authority, the defendant's contractual creditor, such as would justify holding that in law it was not the creditor but the plaintiff who suffered the harm. Only if, at the time of the wrong, the creditor's interest is vested in, or has passed to, the third party, does the party liable have to make good to the creditor what is lost by reason of the creditor's legal and economic relations with the third party. Apart from a few exceptional cases (eg, BGHZ 40, 91, 100) this only applies when the creditor has contracted on the third party's account (eg, BGHZ 40, 91, 100) this only applies when the creditor has contracted on the third party's account (for example, BGHZ 25, 250, 258) or when the object which the debtor was to safeguard belonged

not to the creditor but to the third party (as in BGHZ 15, 224). No such fact situation is present here (see also NJW 1959, 479). We need not now enquire what the case would be if the defendant contractor had undertaken by contract a specific duty of care towards the third party, since as has been stated, no such agreement is shown to have been made.

Case 73

BUNDESGERICHTSHOF (SECOND CIVIL SENATE) 29 JANUARY 1968
BGHZ 49, 357

Facts

The plaintiff chartered a Rhine barge, *The Avanti*, belonging to the first defendant and captained by the second defendant, to carry a load of sheet metal from Basel to the Ford Works in Cologne. The metal was owned by Cornigliano, which had sold it to Ford and had arranged with Panalpina to take it to Cologne. Panalpina entrusted the arrangements for the Rhine journey to the Schweizerische Reederei AG, its parent company, who had the plaintiff, another daughter company, effect it.

The cargo was damaged en route owing to unseaworthiness and bad stowage. Cornigliano allowed Ford to deduct the amount of the damage from the purchase price, and then passed this loss to Panalpina, whence it passed through Schweizerische Reederei to the plaintiff; along with the debit in each case went an assignment of all claims in respect of the damage. The plaintiff was thus exercising, *inter alia*, the rights of Cornigliano, the owner.

The plaintiff's claim was dismissed by the *Landgericht*, but the *Oberlandesgericht* allowed it, and the defendants' appeals were unsuccessful.

Reasons

I. . . .
II. . . .
1. The appellant contests the view of the Court of Appeal that Cornigliano (the vendor and principal of the forwarding agent) could claim for the harm suffered by Ford (the purchaser and consignee) under the doctrine of *Schadensliquidation im Drittinteresse*. We need not take a position on this question for, as we shall see the decision does not depend on it.

The risk of damage to property is normally borne by its owner. However, when there is a contract for sale and delivery, ownership and risk are split. The vendor owns the thing, but the purchaser bears the risk, the vendor having shifted to him any damage which may be caused to the thing. Suppose the object sold is destroyed or damaged during the carriage. One thing, at any rate, ought to be crystal-clear, namely that the person who causes the harm should not benefit from the split between title and risk. Only sheer conceptualism could lead to the unacceptable conclusion that the person responsible is liable neither to the vendor, because the vendor, who is still able to claim the price from the purchaser, has suffered no loss, nor to the purchaser, although he has suffered economic loss, because he has no ownership to be protected by § 823 par 1 BGB. It is common ground that whereas the vendor as owner is entitled to sue for damages, the purchaser is not. What is disputed is whether in such a suit the owner may claim for his own loss or for the loss suffered by the purchaser. The view that the owner is claiming for his own loss rests on the consideration that since the tortfeasor has nothing to do with the special legal relationship between vendor and purchaser, the owner can claim for his loss as if the risk had not passed to the purchaser. On this view, the purchaser's economic loss cannot be relevant because § 823 para 1 BGB does not protect the purchaser's contractual right to have the property transferred to him. But there is another view. It would allow damage tortiously caused to the object of a contract of sale and delivery to be recovered under the doctrine of *Liquidation im Drittinteresse*, a theory which was first deployed in cases of breach of contract, eg, in the case of indirect representation. In the present case we need not decide which view to adopt. The difference of opinion is only important when the purchaser's loss exceeds the loss the vendor would have suffered had it not been shifted. But that does not arise in this litigation. Cornigliano, the vendor, has indemnified the purchaser, Ford, by allowing a reduction of the purchase price. So the loss in suit is the loss suffered by Cornigliano itself, the loss of part of the purchase price (the deduction for the damage suffered by the sheet metal). The facts do not suggest that the agreed price was out of line with the market value of the damaged cargo.

Although Cornigliano was under no duty to make any allowance to Ford for the loss Ford suffered it was not, in so doing, in breach of its duty to mitigate its loss (§ 254 para 2 BGB). If the loss in suit were Ford's loss—as it is under the doctrine of *Schadensliquidation im Drittinteresse* which the Court of Appeal applied—§ 254 para 2 BGB would be irrelevant because that loss was immitigable; and on the assumption that Cornigliano is claiming for its own loss, § 254 para 2 BGB does not apply, because the legal relations between vendor and purchaser (here the transfer of the risk) are *res inter alios acta quoad* the wrongdoer.

Case 74
BUNDESGERICHTSHOF (FIRST CIVIL SENATE) 29 JANUARY 1969
NJW 1969, 789

Facts

A collection of jewellery owned by the plaintiff was being carried in the boot of a car by their traveller K, then a general agent and now a partner in the firm. In the middle of June 1965 K hired a room in the defendant's hotel, as he had often done before. On returning to the hotel one evening at about 10pm, he gave the night porter the keys of the car (including the key of the boot) and told him to have the car garaged. The garage in question was nearby but it was not part of the hotel: it belonged to B, a firm which serviced and rented cars. If a guest wished his car garaged, this was the garage which the defendant hotel used. The porter called B and had the car fetched by one of its employees. There were notices in the hotel rooms about this service in June 1965. They said 'Contract Garaging. Day and Night. Cars Fetched and Returned.'

One of B's employees collected the car and the porter handed him the keys of the car and its boot. The car was returned next morning by a different employee at about

9am and left in front of the hotel. In the middle of the afternoon K and his colleague T drove to H to see a customer, and when T went to the boot to collect the jewellery he found it locked. K and T then looked through the collection and saw that a number of wrist watches had been stolen from it. The lock of the boot was undamaged, and police enquiries proved fruitless.

The plaintiff claims compensation both in his own right and as assignee of the rights of K. The *Landergericht* dismissed the claim and the *Oberlandesgericht* dismissed the appeal. On the plaintiff's appeal, the judgment below is reversed and the case remanded.

Reasons

I. . . .

II. 1. . . 2. . .

3 (a) The Court of Appeal clearly assumed that if the defendant were liable in contract for the loss of the wrist watches the plaintiff could claim for its loss on the basis of an assignment to it by K. This is correct. The principle of *Schadensliquidation des Drittinteresses* is applicable. It is implicit in the agreement between the defendant and K, already a contractual guest in the defendant's hotel, for the deposit of the car for reward, that the defendant's contractual liability for the protection of the car applies even if the car belongs to a third party, it being irrelevant whether the defendant knew or should have known or had any ground of supposing that it did so belong (BGHZ 15, 224, 228).

(b) On the other hand, there are objections in law to the view of the Court of Appeal that the contract of deposit in this case did not cover the contents of the boot. By its very nature the contract of deposit applies to the moveable which is handed over to the depositee for protection as an entirety, whether it consists of a single object, a collection of objects which are legally or physically discrete, or of one single thing which contains a number of objects which are legally or physically separate. So far as can be seen, this has never been doubted before (see BGH NJW 1968, 1718). Thus the defendant's contractual duty extended to safeguarding the contents of the boot.

Given the findings made by the Court of Appeal, that the watches were stolen while the car was in B's garage, the defendant had the burden of proving that its inability to return the property was not due to matters for which it was responsible (§ 282 BGB). It is not enough for the defendant to prove that it took all necessary care, which in any case it has not yet done. The circumstances here (the boot being opened without harming the lock, the removal of the more valuable objects from the collection, the employment in the garage of a person who, according to the district attorney was 'well-known to be a burglar and confidence-trickster') strongly suggest that it was the fault of the defendant or one of its agents for performance (§ 278 BGB) that the goods have gone, so the defendant can exculpate himself only by proving what in fact caused their loss (RGZ 149, 284 ff.; BGH NJW 1952, 1170). This has not been done.

(c) The outcome of the case now depends on whether the defendant has a total or partial defence on the ground that the plaintiff or its partner K was at fault under § 254 BGB. This defence was raised by the defendant, but the Court of Appeal naturally did not consider it.

As will be seen, this court cannot conclusively apportion responsibility for the harm under § 254 BGB, since the requisite facts have not been found by the Court of Appeal. The judgment of that court must therefore be vacated and the matter remanded to it for further proceedings and decision on the merits and on costs, taking the following considerations into account.

4. The Court of Appeal will have to verify whether fault on the part of K or the plaintiff contributed to the loss in issue, so as to reduce, perhaps to nothing, the damages payable by the defendant (§ 254 BGB). Given such a fault, then the amount of responsibility to be attributed to K and therefore to the plaintiff depends in the first instance on how far the harm was preponderantly caused by one or other party; the critical factor here is whether the conduct of one party not only enabled the harm to occur but made its occurrence substantially more probable than did the behaviour of the other party. The temporal order of the events which caused the harm is not critical (BGH NJW 1952, 537, 539; NJW 1963, 1447, 1449). Only if one cannot conclude from the respective causal efficacy of the conduct of both parties that the harm was preponderantly caused by either of them should the degree of fault of the two parties be considered. Then the first thing to do, before proceeding to apportionment, is to determine the amount of the fault of each party.

The first factor to consider is that K left the jewellery in the boot of the car without telling the porter or anyone else on the defendant's staff that it was valuable and that the risk of loss was consequently very high (§ 254 par 2 sentence 1 BGB). If the boot had a separate key—this is not clear—the fact that K gave it as well as the car key to the porter would increase the plaintiff's contribution.

K's behaviour seems intrinsically to be grossly negligent of his own interests, but various considerations, some undisputed, others inferable from the plaintiff's evidence, make it seem less grave. There is the standing of the hotel to be considered and the quality of service which the guests would expect. Guests want to be spared the bother of parking their car, but they also expect it to be safeguarded as they themselves would do. According to the defendant, the garage ticket states that no liability is accepted for the contents of the boot, but since the plaintiff's evidence is that the ticket was not handed to K before, or even at the time when, the car was handed over, the defendant would not be showing the careful service to be expected of such a hotel unless he told K that the garage owner's exclusion of liability made it risky to leave things in the boot. There is the further fact in this case, according to the plaintiff, that K had been a frequent guest in the defendant's hotel in recent years. It was known to the hotel staff who looked after him that he carried a valuable collection of jewellery with him in the car and they never sought to dissuade him from leaving it in the boot, as he sometimes did. Furthermore, on the present occasion the staff knew that K had the jewellery with him. It is true that K did not always leave the jewellery in the car, but he may have been induced to believe that when the car was securely garaged the jewellery in its boot would also be safe. It is not clear on the evidence whether K knew where the car was garaged or how it was secured, so he could perhaps infer from the information provided in the hotel that his car would be looked after in a manner appropriate to its standing. The Court of Appeal will have to investigate these circumstances, determine the causal potency of the conduct of both parties, and apportion the responsibility between them.

Chapter 5

Case 75
BUNDESGERICHTSHOF (FIFTH CIVIL SENATE) 9 JULY 1980
BGHZ 78, 28

Reasons

I.

The parties are carrying out the transfer of the half share in the co-ownership of a flat. The proprietor of this right is the first party. The second party is his minor son. The first party—described as the 'transferor'—'transferred' this share in the co-ownership by way of gift to the second party—described as the 'transferee—by a notarially authenticated contract between the parties dated the 1st April 1978. The parties declared in the contract that they were agreed about the transfer of the right and furthermore the transferor consented to and the transferee applied for, the entry of the change in ownership in the Land Register. It says in parag VI 5 of the document that the transferee knew of the existing communal and house rules in relation to the residential property and entered into these.

These communal rules have been made the content of special ownership in accordance with the provisions of §§ 8 (2), 5 (4) and 10 (2) of the WEG (Ownership of Flats Act).

On receipt of the application for registration at the Land Registry, the registrar of the *Amtsgericht* took the view in an interim decision on 10 October 1978 that the appointment of a supplementary administrator (*Ergänzungspfleger*) was necessary for the transfer, as the gift did not merely provide a legal advantage for the second party. This was because of his entry into the management contract (no 5 of the document).

The registrar and the *Amtsgericht* have not amended the decision in response to the objection entered against it. The *Landgericht* has rejected the appeal (which now is counted as a complaint) as unfounded.

The Bavarian Oberste Landesgericht wishes to reject the further complaint by the parties. But it considers itself to be prevented from doing so by the judgment of the *Bundesgerichtshof* published in BGHZ 15, 168, and has therefore put the matter before the *Bundesgerichtshof* for decision, in accordance with § 79 (2) of the GBO (Land Registry Regulations).

II

. . .

III

The further complaint, which is admissible, is unsuccessful in this case.

The transfer of ownership applied for can, in accordance with § 20 of the GBO, be allowed only in the case of a conveyance which has been effectively declared in law. But there is no such legally effective conveyance according to § 107 BGB, because the second party does not merely obtain a legal advantage by the conveyance of the half share in the flat ownership, and it therefore required the interpolation of a guardian:

1. The question of whether there is a legal disadvantage simply because of the public burdens associated with every kind of acquisition of land can, in relation to the gift being discussed here of a share in a flat ownership, be left undecided, as in the cases in

which the *Bundesgerichtshof* concerned itself with the gift of land [reference omitted]—eg BGHZ 15, 168. Nor is it necessary to discuss whether the fact that ownership of the flat which has been transferred by way of gift is burdened by a legal charge (*Grundschuld*) could play a role in this connection.

The acquisition of ownership of a flat (or a share in this) exhibits, in comparison with the acquisition of a piece of land, the special feature that the transferee, by acquiring a real property right, enters simultaneously into the community of owners of the accommodation. He enters into the many kinds of duties connected with this by statute law (§§ 10 ff of the WEG), and is subjected to the statutory provisions about the administration of the communal property (§§ 20 ff of the WEG). However, it can be left undecided here whether a legal transaction by which a minor acquires ownership of a flat is to be regarded as one which is not exclusively beneficial if no provisions have been made amending the statutory model for the community relationship of the owners of the accommodation between each another and for the administration of the communal property [references omitted]. This is because, in the case for discussion here, a legal disadvantage which—independently from the entry into the communal order agreed in para VI no 5 of the notarised document—is, according to §§ 8 (2), 5 (4) and 10 (2) of the WEG, directly associated with the acquisition of the real property right, can in any case be seen in the fact that in the communal order agreed between the owners (up to this point in time) of the accommodation, the duties applying to the individual owners by virtue of statute law have been increased—and not just insignificantly.

Not is it possible to dispute the view that the acquisition in the present case cannot be a pure legal advantage by claiming that the legal disadvantages mentioned are not independent duties but—as the communal order has been made the content of special property—obligations inherent in the ownership itself. This is because in contrast to, for instance, the case of the gift of land burdened with the rights of a mortgagee (*Grundpfandrechte*) (which, according to the widely held opinion, can only be assessed as a gift of unburdened land [BayObLGZ 1979, 49, 53 with references]), the transferee is liable here for the duties imposed on him not just as real property obligations with the acquired property but also personally.

2. As therefore, according to § 107 BGB, the minor second party's own declaration could not lead to any legally effective conveyance (§ 4 (1) of the WEG), the contract needed the consent of the statutory representative in accordance with § 108 (1) of the BGB. The declaration of the first party, the second party's father, in the conveyance cannot amount to a simultaneous declaration of such consent because the first party was prevented from representing the second party by § 181 of the BGB.

The court submitting the case correctly assumes that the provisions of § 181 of the BGB are not inconsistent with an act here by the first party on behalf of the second party because the conveyance only fulfils the first party's obligation validly based on the gift contract (§ 181 (last half sentence) of the BGB).

. . .

What is decisive however is that it would not be reconcilable with the protective purpose of § 107 BGB, in the case of a gift of flat ownership by the statutory representative to a minor who is over seven years old, to undertake the assessment of whether the gift merely gives the minor a legal advantage separately on the one hand for the obligation contract and on the other hand for the real property transaction fulfilling it. The result of such a split approach would be that, where the basic transaction [the obligation contract] has a beneficial character, ignoring legal disadvantages which are associated with the transfer of the real property right, the statutory representative is authorised in the light of § 181 (last half sentence) of the BGB to represent the minor in accepting the conveyance, or in approving the acceptance declared by the minor himself. In so far as such a split approach is recommended in BGHZ 15, 168 (there in relation to a gift of (unburdened) land and without any conclusive opinion on the question of whether in such a case the fulfilment [real property] transaction also is only legally advantageous for the minor), the second civil senate, as it has stated when questioned, will not follow it.

The protection of minors which § 107 of the BGB seeks to achieve would, if the exceptional provisions of § 181 (last half sentence) of the BGB were permitted to apply in relation to the fulfilment transaction, be largely excluded for gifts by statutory representatives. The question of whether in an actual case the acquisition of a real property right by way of gift brings with it legal disadvantages in the sense of § 107 of the BGB is not influenced by whether the gift is made by a third party or by a statutory representative. (The question of the 'benevolence' of the donor also plays no role here). But if, on acquisition from a third party, the interests of the minor are to be protected by the required incorporation of the statutory representative precisely because of such disadvantages, the minor's interest demands the incorporation of a guardian on an acquisition from the statutory representative according to the general principle of law contained in § 181

BGB. Otherwise the issue (which is decisive according to the sense and purpose of § 107 BGB) of whether the legal transaction turns out in the end to be legally burdensome to the minor would be left out of consideration [references omitted].

The question of the legal advantage or disadvantage of a gift is therefore to be assessed from consideration of the obligation contract and the real property contract as a whole, in accordance with this balancing of interests indicated by statute. Account is therefore taken in the same way of the case of a gift by a statutory representative as well as of a gift by a third party. . . . According to the sense and purpose of § 107 BGB, such an interpretation is justified, even taking into account that the provisions are related to 'a (one) declaration of will,' when according to the view put forward here, several declarations of will are to be combined for an overall assessment. There is in any case a corrective against too narrow a treatment of § 107 BGB, as the court submitting the case has also recommended. This is that even the concept of exclusive benefit is to be seen subject to the protective purpose of § 107 BGB (without however going as far as saying that the 'legal' advantage here would be replaced by the 'economic').

Case 76
BUNDESGERICHTSHOF (SEVENTH CIVIL SENATE) 31 MAY 1990
BGHZ 111, 308

Facts

The claimant demands from the defendant on the basis of a transferred right the remainder of his payment for work in the sum of DM20,505 and interest. The claimant's husband, the witness S, carried out skilled trade work for the defendant in 1985 and 1986 without being entered in the Skilled Trade Register and without having registered a business. Both these things were known to the defendant. He has paid at least DM4500 to S for his services. S has not paid taxes and social insurance contributions. S has transferred to the claimant the remainder of the demands for payment for work asserted by him.

The *Landgericht* has ordered the defendant to pay to the claimant DM11,880 and interest. In other respects it has rejected the claim. The *Oberlandesgericht* has rejected the claim entirely. The claimant's appeal in law, which has been admitted, led to quashing of the appeal court judgment and reference of the matter back to the *Oberlandesgericht*.

Reasons

1. The appeal court accepts that not only the defendant, but also his contracting partner S, had violated the Act to Combat Illegal Labour (SchwArbG). S had carried out a skilled trade independently without being entered in the Skilled Trade Register (§ 1 para 1 no 3 of the Act to Combat Illegal Labour). He had at the same time acted in order to obtain economic advantages of a substantial extent. These endeavours sufficed for fulfilment of the definition. He therefore had neither contractual nor statutory claims which he could have transferred to the claimant.

2. That is correct as a starting point.

. . .

3. The contracts concluded by S and the defendant were therefore void according to § 134 of the BGB. As the Senate [reference omitted] has explained in more detail, the Act to Combat Illegal Labour is intended simply to forbid illegal labour by the threat of financial penalties against the contractor as well as against the client and to prevent the exchange of performances between the 'contractual partners'. This in itself is an important indication that the legal order intends to deny effectiveness to a contract which disregards the prohibition of illegal labour. In particular—as the senate has explained in detail [reference omitted]—the purpose of the Act to Combat Illegal Labour can only be attained if contracts of this kind are regarded as not legally effective. That applies at least when, as here, both parties have violated the Act to Combat Illegal Labour. In the individual case, though, the 'appeal to invalidity' in respect of a legal transaction which violates a statutory provision can violate good faith, so that the contract must be treated in the end result as effective [reference omitted].

4. The claimant can therefore, because of the invalidity of the concluded contracts, derive rights if need be from the dismantling of them. According to the case law of the senate, §§ 677 ff BGB are in principle applicable in cases of this kind [reference omitted]. But the 'expenditure' of S consisted here of an activity which was prohibited by statute. He could not 'consider this to be necessary according to the circumstances'; simply for this reason a claim to reimbursement in accordance with §§ 683, 670 BGB does not apply.

5. But the claimant can, contrary to the view of the appeal court, successfully refer to the provisions on unjustified enrichment. The assumption of a claim under § 812 para 1 sentence 1 1st alternative of the BGB does not fail here in the end result because of the provision in § 817 sentence 2 of the BGB. This provision applies in principle for

case formulations of the kind present here. It can also be used against the creditor's successor [reference omitted].

In the present case, the assignor S has violated the Act to Combat Illegal Labour by his skilled trade activity. According to the findings of the appeal court, both parties intended to implement their contracts as illegal labour. There can therefore be no doubt that S was aware of the violation and intended it all the same.

6. Enrichment claims belong however to fairness law and are therefore subject to a special degree to the principles of good faith [reference omitted]. It would not be reconcilable with these principles if the defendant did not have to restore the value of what he had unlawfully received, but could keep it without paying for it. The *Reichsgericht*, in the case of prior performance in respect of the purchase of a brothel, has described the purchaser's intention not to pay but to refuse to hand over the house which he had acquired by referring to § 817 sentence 2 BGB as deceitful conduct not protected by the legal order [reference omitted]. The position is similar here. When applying the prohibition in § 817 sentence 2 BGB [reference omitted] on demanding back, which affects the creditor harshly, it is not possible to leave out of account the purpose pursued by the prohibiting statute in question [reference omitted]. Accordingly a restrictive interpretation of the provision (which is problematic from the point of view of legal policy and disputed in the area of its application) can be required in the individual case. The Act to Combat Illegal Labour does not primarily pursue the protection of either one or both contracting partners, but principally the safeguarding of public interests. In particular labour market policy considerations were in the foreground when the Act was enacted. According to the official reasons, illegal labour leads to increased unemployment in many branches of the vocational world, causes tax losses and harms the social insurance fund; it also endangers the independent business proprietor, who cannot work so cheaply as the illegal worker. The client should only secondarily be protected from having no guarantee claims in respect of defective work peformance [reference omitted]. The Act was formulated as a protective statute in the sense of § 134 BGB because the goals pursued could only be attained by the invalidity of the forbidden transactions [reference omitted]. But on the other hand, by excluding contractual claims, the objective of the Act, which is principally the policy of preserving order, is largely complied with. It is not irrefutably required, for the implementation of the aims of the Act, for the customer in a case of illegal labour to be allowed to keep the performance without payment, at the cost of the illegal worker who performs first. This is because the exclusion of contractual claims (combined with the risk of a criminal prosecution and the subsequent payment of taxes and social welfare contributions when the illegal labour becomes known) is sufficient on its own to provide the general preventative effect desired by the legislature. The guarantee of a settlement in enrichment law—especially in the limited scope required (see further below on this)—is in the view of the senate not inconsistent with this general preventative effect. According to the view of the legislature, the client, who is generally stronger economically, should moreover on no account be treated more favourably than the economically weaker illegal worker [reference omitted]. Under these circumstances a view based on good faith acquires decisive importance, ie that it would not correspond with fairness to leave unpaid for an unjustified advantage to the customer who has benefited from the prior performance [references omitted]. According to § 818 para 2 BGB the enrichment claim provides compensation for

the value which has accrued to the defendant without legal ground. When valuing what has been obtained by the illegal labour, it is necessary first to bear in mind that the illegal worker can on no account receive any more by way of an enrichment settlement than he had agreed—in an invalid way—as payment with his client [reference omitted]. However as a rule quite susbstantial reductions from this will be appropriate because of the risks associated with illegal labour. A particular consideration which strongly reduces the value of the claim is that contractual guarantee claims are not present from the outset because of the invalidity of the contract. If defects have already shown themselves, these are additionally to be included into the calculation of the settlement within the framework of the balancing exercise.

Case 77
BUNDESGERICHTSHOF (SEVENTH CIVIL SENATE) 22 SEPTEMBER 1983
NJW 1984, 230

Facts

In 1976 the defendant entrusted the claimant, who had made an appropriate offer in the name of 'H-Metallbau (Metal Construction),' with the delivery and installation of windows and doors and with the execution of other metal work for the construction of a office block. The claimant in her claim demanded the balance due. Having regard to the defendant's numerous complaints about defects, the parties agreed in an exchange of letters of 1 December 1978, 9 January 1979 and 26 January 1979 that an expert opinion should first be obtained regarding the defects complained of by the defendant in proceedings for the preliminary gathering of evidence; and then the claimant should eliminate the defects, and after this the defendant should pay the balance of the sum demanded for the work. After receipt of the expert's opinion, the claimant stated that it was prepared to eliminate the defects. The defendant however declined this, and referred to the fact that it was entitled to have the defects removed by a third party. The claimant, who was also technically unsuited for the work, had not only not made any serious efforts for several years to put the work right, but she was also—as the defendant had first discovered in 1979—not legally in a position to do so, as she was not a member of the Chamber of for Skilled Trade but merely a member of the Chamber of Industry and Commerce. She therefore lacked the authority to carry out the skilled work to be dealt with here.

The *Landgericht* found the defendant liable in accordance with the application. The appeal and the appeal in law were unsuccessful.

Reasons

As the appeal court. . .considers,. . .the necessary elimination of defects has admittedly still not been effected. The defendant could not however derive any rights from this, as it had 'consistently refused and prevented' the remedial works which had been repeatedly offered. The fact that the claimant and her husband were not entered as managers in the register of skilled tradesmen did not permit the defendant to free itself from the agreement which had been made. The appeal in law is unsuccessful in challenging this.

1. First it takes the view that the work contract concluded between the parties is void in accordance with § 134 of the BGB as only a master tradesman entered in the register of skilled tradesmen was allowed to undertake the services put out to tender. After it had discovered that the claimant had not been entered, it (the defendant) had been able to avoid the consequential agreement of December 1978 / January 1979. This was conclusively seen by the fact that it had rejected any remedial work by the claimant. That is wrong simply because the prerequisite assumed by the appeal in law for the avoidance declaration (invalidity of the work contract) is not present. It is necessary to proceed on the same basis as the appeal court that the fact that the claimant is not entered in the register of skilled tradesmen has no influence on the effectiveness of the contracts in question, even if the claimant's business falls under the provisions of the Skilled Trade Order.

She ought then in principle not to carry out any skilled trade services, because neither she nor her husband had the master tradesman's certificate necessary for the entry or an appropriate approval of an exception (§§ 7 ff of the HandwO (Skilled Trade Order)). Nevertheless a violation—as assumed here—of this statutory prohibition would not of itself lead to ineffectiveness of civil law contracts which deviate from it.

(a) The question of whether legal transactions which contravene the prohibition are void under § 134 BGB is to be answered according to the sense and purpose of the prohibiting provision in question. The decisive issue is whether the statute is not only opposed to the conclusion of the legal transaction but also its effectiveness in private law and therefore its economic consequence [references omitted]. Even the fact that an act is made punishable or is threatened with a fine as an administrative offence (see § 117 (1) no 1 of the Skilled Trade Order) does not irrefutably cause the invalidity of the civil law transaction. That applies above all when the prohibition only concerns one of the parties concluding the contract (the claimant in this case): as a rule such a contract is valid [references omitted]. In special cases invalidity admittedly can also follow from the violation of unilateral prohibitions, if the purpose of the statute cannot be otherwise attained and the regime created by the legal transaction cannot be accepted ([reference omitted] for a violation of the

Legal Advice Act; [reference omitted] for banned advertising of medicines; [references omitted]). Such an exception is present, for example, if the statute creating the prohibition is to serve the protection of the individual consumer and therefore also that of the particular contractual partner [references omitted]. If on the other hand it is a question of a mere administrative provision which forbids an otherwise unobjectionable legal transaction on the grounds of regulation of trade or a policy of preserving order, the validity of a contract which is concluded contrary to the prohibition remains unaffected [references omitted].

(b) The *Bundesgerichtshof* has not so far decided what consequences in civil law a violation of § 1 of the Skilled Trade Order carries with it. The opinions in the case law and the literature—few in

number—refer to the purely public law function of preserving order which this provision has, and therefore unanimously assert the effectiveness of contracts which contravene the prohibition

[references omitted]. The Senate endorses this view, having regard to the purpose of the Skilled Trade Order.

The legislator has made permitting the independent carrying on of a skilled trade dependent on proof of vocational knowledge and skills, in order to maintain the high level of performance and

peformance capacity of skilled tradesmen in the interests of business as a whole. At the same time he wanted to ensure the proper training of new recruits for skilled trade, as also for the rest of the business world. He saw an appropriate and necessary means for the attaining of this goal in the introduction of proof of qualifications and entry in the skilled trade register (BverfGE 13, 97 [107ff.] = NJW 1961, 2011 with extensive references to the story of the origin of the Skilled Trade Order; [reference omitted]). On the other hand, averting dangers for the general public or the individual from an improper exercise of a vocation were of no concern to him. Instead the decisive factor was interest in the maintenance and promotion of a sound capable level of trade as a whole [reference omitted]. Sufficient account can be taken of this by measures in vocational law or public law sanctions (§§ 16, 118 of the Skilled Trade Order), without it being necessary to deny effectiveness in civil law to an individual legal transaction which had come into existence within the framework of the prohibited carrying on of a trade [references omitted]. A further argument in favour of this result is the fact that § 3 of the Skilled Trade Order allows subsidiary or auxiliary services to skilled trades to be carried out by a different main enterprise, and § 4 of the Skilled Trade Order even permits the continued conduct of the business of a deceased master tradesman for a certain period by his surviving dependant who does not have vocational knowledge and training. It follows from this that the contract for building works concluded between the parties is not invalid under § 134 BGB.

2. Nevertheless the appeal in law considers that the defendant was not bound to the agreements of December 1978 / January 1979. The defendant had—so it now claims—made a mistake about the skilled trade law status of the claimant and effectively made a declaration of avoidance immediately after revelation of the true state of affairs. The appeal in law is likewise unsuccessful here.

(a) It is doubtful whether the defendant has given a proper declaration of avoidance at all in the sense of § 143 BGB by its refusal of the offer of remedial work by the claimant. It is true that the express use of the word 'avoid' is not necessary for this. But it is always necessary for there to be a statement or conclusive conduct from which it unambiguously follows for the recipient of the avoidance that the declarant wishes to overturn the legal transaction retrospectively because of lack of intention [references omitted]. Here the defendant has merely referred to the fact that it considered the carrying out of remedial works by the claimant to be unreasonable because of the extensive defects and the lack of proof of the skilled trade qualification. The fact that this was lacking in the clarity necessary for a declaration of avoidance argues strongly in favour of the above view. In the end the Senate does not however need to go into this question in greater detail, as the defendant in any case has no ground for avoidance worth considering.

(b) The only kind of avoidance which comes into consideration is one in accordance with § 119 (2) BGB according to which a mistake about the characteristics of a person which are of importance in the affairs of life is to be regarded as a mistake about the content of the declaration. This includes the natural features of personality as well as those factual and legal circumstances which, as a result of their nature and assumed duration would, according to the general view of things, usually influence the assessment of a person in all or in certain legal relationships [reference omitted]. This can—depending on the circumstances—quite reasonably include the qualification of the contracting partner in vocational law, as is necessary for an entry in the register of skilled tradesmen. But whether a mistake about this justifies avoidance of a legal transaction is dependent on the special circumstances of the individual case. In this respect account must be taken of the transaction avoided and its objectives [references omitted]. If the concept of mistake about a characteristic is not to become too trivial and to give rise to intolerable legal uncertainty [reference omitted], only those characteristics of a person may be considered as of significance in the affairs of life which the declarant has made the basis of the contract in some recognisable manner (without him needing actually to turn them into part of the content of his declaration) [references omitted].

That—so far as concerns the entry of the claimant in the register of skilled tradesmen—has not happened in the present case. The defendant may admittedly on the conclusion of the building contract and of the later agreement for remedial work unconsciously have proceeded on the basis that the claimant fulfilled the prerequisites in vocational law for her trade activity. It has however never expressed the view that this circumstance was to be of importance for the commissioning of the work. It only seemed to matter to it that the claimant's business enterprise was in a position to carry out the contractual services with the necessary expert knowledge and reliability [reference omitted]. The issue of whether the business was legally a skilled trade one or an industrial one with a subordinate skilled trade sideline was however unimportant. As the appeal court correctly established, the claimant has at no time given the impression that she was proprietor of a skilled trade enterprise. She described her trade in a neutral manner as metal construction, was a member of the Chamber of Industry and Commerce and took part in business life under this designation for many years, without any objection from the competent authorities. If the defendant nevertheless only intended to conclude the work contract with a registered skilled trade business, it would have had to make its intention clear in an appropriate manner. As it has not done this, avoidance of the

agreement of December 1978 / January 1979 is excluded, without regard to whether the claimant actually violated the provisions of the Skilled Trade Order or not.

3. Finally the defendant has also not behaved unreasonably subsequently in adhering to that agreement. (Details are given).

4. As a result of the defendant's refusal in respect of the claimant's repeated offers of remedial work, the claim for payment for the remainder of the work has in the meantime become due.

(Details are given).

Case 78
BUNDESVERFASSUNGSGERICHT (FIRST SENATE) 22 MARCH 2004
NJW 2004, 2008

Facts

The constitutional complaint concerns inheritance certificate proceedings, the subject matter of which is succession to the former Crown Prince Wilhelm of Prussia (the testator) who died in 1951, and was the oldest son of the former Kaiser Wilhelm II, who died in 1941. In 1938, the testator concluded an inheritance contract with his second son LF, with the participation of Wilhelm II. It appointed LF as the sole first heir (*Vorerbe*) (heir appointed in such a way that a subsequent heir (*Nacherbe*) will inherit in the future). The estate included among other things a substantial part of the so-called house assets (*Hausvermögen*) situated in Germany of the former Prussian royal house.

In connection with the inheritance contract, Wilhelm II renounced his rights to the house assets in favour of the testator.

In his will in 1950 the testator explained among other things that he would support 'the contract of 1938,' and also appointed his son LF as his 'universal heir' of the assets which are not included 'in the assets which passed from my father to me.' LF, who died in 1994, drew up a will in 1981 in which he appointed his grandson GF, the son of his third son who had died in 1977, as sole heir of all his assets. This appointment of an heir was also to take place if LF had become the full heir of the former house assets.

The complainant is the oldest son of LF. After LF's death, he applied for the issue of an inheritance certificate as sole subsequent heir of the testator. He had previously among other things declared in a notarised document in 1961 with reference to the house statute (*Hausgesetz*) of 1920 and § 1 of the inheritance contract of 1938 that, if he concluded a marriage which was not with someone of equal rank in birth according to the principles of the old house constitution (*Hausverfassung*) he 'irrevocably renounced all rights which I have as possible successor.' He repeated this renunciation in notarised documents of 1967 and 1976, in each case on the occasion of marriages which were described in these documents as not being with persons of equal birth. GF applied for the issue of an inheritance certificate that he had become sole heir of the testator after the death of the first heir. He made an ancillary application for issue of an inheritance certificate for LF stating that LF was the sole heir of the testator.

The Probate Court declared by an interlocutory order of the 7 September 1995 that it intended to grant an inheritance certificate for LF as sole heir of the testator. The equal birth clause in § 1 of the inheritance contract was, according to modern standards, void for violation of good morals under § 138 BGB. This led to the invalidity of the succession by the subsequent heir which had been directed, but not to the ineffectiveness of the appointment of LF as sole heir. The complaint lodged against this by the complainant was rejected by a decision of the Landgericht of Hechingen of 17 February 1997. It agreed with the view of the Probate Court and regarded the equal birth clause as void for violation of § 138 of the BGB. The court reached the conclusion, by way of supplementary interpretation of the inheritance contract, that LF had been appointed as sole full heir. On a further complaint by the complainant, the Oberlandesgericht of Stuttgart by a judgment of 19 August 1997 submitted the case to the *Bundesgerichtshof* for decision (ZEV 1998, 185 = FGPrax 1997, 230). The *Oberlandesgericht* considers the further complaint to be unfounded because in any case the objection based on § 242 BGB of impermissible exercise of a right prevents appeal to the equal birth clause. However, the *Oberlandesgericht* considered itself to be prevented by the decision of the Bavarian Oberstes Landesgericht (BayObLGZ 1996, 204) from rejecting the complaint.

The *Bundesgerichtshof* by its decision of the 2 December 1998 quashed the decision of the *Landgericht* and referred the case back to the *Landgericht* for different treatment and fresh decision. It regarded the equal birth clause in § 1 of the inheritance contract as effective (NJW 1999, 566).

If at the relevant point in time none of the male descendants satisfied the requirements of the equal birth clause, there would be no appointment of a subsequent heir, so the first heir might retrospectively have become full heir. After obtaining a legal historian's opinion on the question of whether the complainant's wife was of equal birth, the *Landgericht* rejected his complaint by a decision of 7 December 2000. The Probate Court was instructed to issue an inheritance certificate to GF which showed him as subsequent heir of the testator. The court came to the conclusion that the complainant was not in an equal birth marriage. He was therefore excluded from succession. The complainant's further complaint was rejected by a decision of the *Oberlandesgericht* of the 21 November 2001 (FamRZ 2002, 1365). The disputed decision of the *Landgericht* did not reveal any error in law.

The complainant is contesting the decision of the *Bundesgerichtshof*, and the decisions of the *Landgericht* and the *Oberlandesgericht* submitted to it, by his constitutional complaint, which has been lodged within the time limit. He complains, among other things, of a violation of his basic rights under Art 6 para 1 and Art 3 paras 1 and 3 of the Basic Law. The Federal Constitutional Court allowed the complaint, quashed the decisions challenged, and referred the matter back to the *Landgericht*.

Reasons

The chamber accepts the constitutional complaint for decision, because this is necessary for implementing the complainant's basic right under Art 6 para 1 of the Basic Law (§§ 93b sentence 1, 93a (2) b of the Federal Constitutional Court Act). The prerequisites for a decision by the chamber allowing the complaint are present (§ 93c (1) sentence 1 of the Federal Constitutional Court Act). The disputed decisions violate the complainant's basic right to freedom of marriage (Art 6 para 1 of the Basic Law).
1. The Federal Constitutional Court has already decided the constitutional law questions which are determinative for the assessment.

According to the consistent case law of the Federal Constitutional Court, an objective order of values is embodied in the basic rights provisions of the Basic Law, which applies as a basic decision in constitutional law for all areas of law, and which also primarily acquires decisive significance in the interpretation of general clauses in civil law. In so far as § 138 and § 242 BGB refer quite generally to good morals, custom (*Verkehrssitte*) and good faith, they require concretisation by the courts according to standards of value concepts which are primarily determined by the decisions of principle in the Constitution [references omitted].

This however does not change the fact that the Federal Constitutional Court does not in principle have to examine the interpretation and application of simple law. It merely has to secure the observance of basic right norms and standards by the ordinary courts.
. . . The threshold of a violation of objective constitutional law which the Federal Constitutional Court has to correct is only reached if the decision reveals mistakes in interpretation which are based on a view of the meaning of a basic right which is in principle incorrect, in particular in the scope of its protective area, and which are also of

some weight in their material significance for the actual case. The Federal Constitutional Court's examination in relation to the application of the general clauses of §§ 138 and 242 BGB is limited to the question of whether the courts have correctly recognised the meaning and scope of the basic right to freedom of marriage, and balanced it against the testator's freedom of testamentary disposition by a comprehensive assessment of the particular circumstances of the individual case [reference omitted]. . . .

2. Taking these standards as a basis, the decisions which are being challenged do not stand up to examination in constitutional law. The *Bundesgerichtshof* in its decision in relation to the assessment of the equal birth clause has failed to recognise the significance of the complainant's basic right to freedom of marriage (Art 6 para 1 of the Basic Law). . . .

(a) The starting point is the testator's freedom of testamentary disposition as a determinative element of the guarantee of the right of inheritance protected by Art 14 para 1 sentence 1 of the Basic Law. As a power of disposition for the owner which goes beyond his death, it is closely associated with the guarantee of ownership and, like it, enjoys especially emphasised protection as an element in the securing of personal freedom [reference omitted]. It gives the testator the opportunity to regulate succession himself by a disposition on death largely in accordance with his personal wishes and ideas [reference omitted]. In particular, the testator is not compelled by the Constitution to treat his descendants equally [reference omitted]. The freedom of testamentary disposition also embraces the freedom not to have to arrange succession to one's assets by the general convictions of society or the views of the majority [reference omitted].

(b) The testator's freedom of testamentary disposition protected by Art 14 para 1 sentence 1 of the Basic Law is set against the complainant's basic right under Art 6 para 1 of the Basic Law. Art 6 para 1 of the Basic Law guarantees the freedom to enter into marriage with a partner chosen by oneself [reference omitted]. The equal birth clause contained in the inheritance contract of 23 November 1938 is apt indirectly to influence the freedom of marriage of the testator's descendant who was appointed as the subsequent heir. Because complete exclusion from succession is linked to entering into a marriage which is not of equal birth in the sense of the house constitution, the descendant is confronted with the alternatives of not concluding such a marriage or losing his position as the subsequent heir. The interference continues even after the conclusion of a marriage which is not of equal birth in the sense of the house constitution. This is based on the fact that the descendant could possibly still be appointed as subsequent heir if he was at least in a marriage which accorded with the house constitution at the time the subsequent heir became entitled. Pressure was therefore indirectly exerted on the complainant, even after entering into a marriage which was not of equal birth in the sense of the house constitution, to dissolve this marriage. As marriage is protected by Art 6 para 1 of the Basic Law as a life partnership which is in principle indissoluble [reference omitted], there is an indirect continuing interference by the equal birth clause.

(c) The *Bundesgerichtshof* has admittedly looked at the question of whether the equal birth clause exceeds the limits drawn by the order of values in the Basic Law within the framework of §§ 138 and 242 of the BGB. But the balancing exercise undertaken by it does not satisfy the requirements of constitutional law that the balancing should be comprehensive and take into account the special circumstances of the individual case.

. . .

(bb) Finally the question of whether the concept of equal birth in the sense of the house statute was still appropriate, after the abolition of the monarchy, to justify interferences with the freedom of marriage of the claimant to the inheritance was not sufficiently considered within the framework of the balancing exercise.

The succession to the throne in the German Reich and in Prussia is determined according to the house statute of the Brandenburg Hohenzollerns. The office of the German Kaiser was indissolubly linked with the Prussian Kingdom under Art 11 of the Constitution of the German Reich of 16 April 1871 (RGBl, 64 [69]). The provisions relating to the Prussian crown determined the acquisition and loss of the office of Kaiser in the Reich (see Laband, Deutsches StaatsR, vol I, 6th edit [1912], § 10 II). Art 53 of the Constitution for the Prussian State of 31 January 1850 provided that the crown, in accordance with the house statutes, is inheritable (*Gesetz-Sammlung für die königlich Preußischen Staaten* [Collection of statutes for the royal Prussian states], p 17 [24]). Those provisions of the house statutes which regulate who belongs to the royal house thereby became a component of the Constitution. Descent from an equal birth marriage in the sense of the house statutes became a decisive criterion for capacity to succeed to the throne (see Bornhak, *Preußisches StaatsR*, 2nd edit [1911], § 29, Hubrich, *Preußisches StaatsR*, 1909, § 9).

When the Weimar Reich Constitution of 11 August 1919 (RGBl, 1383) and the Prussian Constitution of the 30 November 1920 (*Preußisches Gesetzsammlung* [Collection of Prussian statutes], p 543) came into effect, the republican form of state was introduced. The Constitution of the German Reich of 16 April 1871 was abolished (Art 178 para 1 of the Constitution of the Weimar Reich). Art 81 para 1 of the Prussian Constitution abolished the Constitution of 31 January 1850. The house statutes of the former ruling imperial and royal houses thereby simultaneously became superfluous in the context of the law of the state.

Since the Basic Law came into effect, Art 20 para 1 and Art 28 para 1 sentence 1 of that Law prevent the reintroduction of the monarchy. The marriage and family traditions of noble families have no meaning today for determining the head of state (see Herzog, in: *Maunz/Dürig*, GG, Stand: September 1980, Art 20 note III marginal notes 5–8; Stern, *Das StaatsR der BRep Dtschld*, vol I, 2nd edit [1984], § 17 II 2).

Against the background of changed circumstances in the law of the state, the *Bundesgerichtshof* should on constitutional grounds have considered, within the framework of the balancing exercise whether an appointment of an heir linked with the preservation of the equal birth principle can still justify interferences with the heir's freedom of marriage, and whether a substantial basis of justification for an appointment of an heir on such conditions has ceased to exist. This principle cannot fulfil today its original function in the law of the state—the regulation of the succession to the throne in an inherited monarchy.

Case 79

BUNDESGERICHTSHOF (TWELFTH CIVIL SENATE) 19 FEBRUARY 2003
NJW 2003, 1860

Facts

The parties are a divorced couple. They are in dispute about the validity of a contract
for the purchase of land which was concluded between them. The parties married in
1985, and the marriage produced two children, born in 1986 and 1989. In 1994, the
claimant entered into an extramarital relationship with R, an asylum seeker of
Algerian nationality. From this relationship, the claimant gave birth to a child on
13 February 1996. The parties concealed its true parentage in their circle of relations
and acquaintances. After R's application for asylum had been rejected with legal
effect in May 1996, his deportation was set for March 1997. The claimant thereon
asked the defendant for consent to an immediate divorce which would enable her to
marry R, and thereby prevent his deportation. After lengthy discussions, the parties
concluded a notarially authenticated contract on 13 December 1996 in which the
claimant transferred to the defendant her half share in the co-ownership of the land on
which the family home was built, at the price of DM132,000. On 4 February 1997 the
parties' marriage was dissolved. On 17 March 1997 the claimant declared her avoidance of the land purchase contract. The claimant seeks a declaration that the contract
of 13 December 1996 is void. . . . In substance she claims that the transfer of the half
share in the co-ownership was contrary to good morals, because its value was
DM250,000 and therefore there was a gross disproportion to the agreed price of
DM132,000. Conscious of the relationship between these values, and exploiting the
claimant's emotional predicament, the defendant had obtained a financial advantage
from the contract which could not be approved.

   The *Landgericht* rejected the claim. The *Oberlandesgericht* rejected the claimant's
appeal. The claimant in her appeal in law seeks what she demanded at first instance.
This appeal led to quashing and reference back.

Reasons

According to the view of the *Oberlandesgericht*, the contract concluded by the parties
is effective even if it is assumed in favour of the claimant that her share in the land
which was transferred to the defendant for DM132,000 was worth DM250,000, and
that in acquiring it the defendant had exploited her emotional predicament to his
advantage.

   . . . These deliberations do not stand up to legal examination in all respects.

1. The *Oberlandesgericht* was in the end result correct to deny the presence of the prerequisites of § 138 (2) BGB.

   (a) It is true that fulfilment of the definition of extortion is not prevented, as is stated
in the disputed judgment, by the absence of 'special circumstances' which give the
agreement an 'objectionable character.' As the wording of § 138 (2) BGB indicates ('in
particular'), a legal transaction 'by which someone, exploiting the predicament . . .
of another, causes financial advantages to be promised or granted . . . in return for a
performance which are in conspicuous disproportion to the performance,' is always

void. Reference to § 138 (1) BGB is not needed for this [reference omitted]. There is therefore no room for an examination of whether special—additional—circumstances give the agreement an objectionable character. . . .

(b) In the case to be decided here, there is however no extortionate transaction. This is because the defendant did not, as is required by § 138 (2) BGB, exploit a predicament of the claimant by concluding the purchase contract in respect of the land. The *Oberlandesgericht* has admittedly assumed, in the claimant's favour, that the defendant has exploited the claimant's emotional predicament to his advantage. But this assumption does not bind the court dealing with the appeal in law, because it is obviously based on an understanding which is wrong in law of the characteristics of the definition which have been set out.

It is admittedly true that even psychological distress can represent a predicament in the sense of § 138 (2) BGB [reference omitted]. But the claimant's anxiety that future life together with R would be frustrated in the case of his deportation does not fulfil this prerequisite. As the *Bundesgerichtshof* has explained, the predicament which, when exploited, leads to invalidity of the exploitative legal transaction must arise from the present situation of the exploited partner. The fear of the partner to the transaction that his future plans could come to nothing if the transaction does not take place cannot form the basis of such a predicament [BGH NJW 1994, 1275 [1276]; prevailing opinion, references omitted]. A present predicament for the claimant could admittedly be founded on the fact that, in the case of the impending deportation of R, her child would have to grow up without his natural father. Whether the claimant felt this prospect to be a predicament is not beyond question, as the parties had passed the claimant's child off in their circle of relatives and acquaintances as the legitimate child of them both, and received it into the family with the other two children they had both had. The question can however remain undecided, as it does not appear that the defendant had exploited any such possible predicament which the claimant had by concluding the land purchase contract. The extortionate exploitation of a predicament assumes that the partner to the transaction who is acting extortionately is to provide the exploited partner with a payment or performance in kind (see, as to this requirement, BT-Dr 7/3441, p 40), and the exploited partner is dependent on this for the resolution of his predicament [references omitted]. There are no grounds for this in regard to the land purchase contract concluded by the parties. It is not apparent that the claimant was dependent on the payment of the purchase price by the defendant for the resolution of her possible predicament. Whether the claimant was dependent on the defendant's consent for the divorce has no significance for the definition of extortion. For one thing, consent to the divorce is not an element of the contract about the transfer of the claimant's share in the co-ownership to the defendant. For another, this consent is not a performance of economic value, and the definition of extortion assumes this to be necessary for a transaction involving exchange when it asks for a conspicuous disproportion between the—to introduce the necessary supplementary word: economic—value of the performance to be provided by the partner to the transaction who is acting extortionately and the financial advantage promised or granted to him for it [reference omitted].

2. The denial by the *Oberlandesgericht* of the presence of the prerequisites of § 138 (1) BGB is not supported by the factual findings in the disputed judgment, because there are no special circumstances which would give the agreement an objectionable

character. A legal transaction which does not fulfil the definition of extortion in § 138 (2) BGB can nevertheless be void under § 138 (1) BGB if a conspicuous disproportion exists between the performance and counter-performance, and further circumstances are present, in particular that the person benefiting has acted out of reprehensible frame of mind [reference omitted]. If the disproportion between performance and counter-performance is especially blatant, the conclusion that there has been intentional or grossly negligent exploitation of a circumstance inhibiting the contracting partner (and therefore a reprehensible frame of mind) can be justified [reference omitted]. An especially gross disproportion can be assumed if the market value of a piece of land is almost twice as high as the purchase price [reference omitted]. The *Oberlandesgericht* has assumed in the claimant's favour that the half share in the co-ownership in the parties' land which had until then been jointly held, though sold to the defendant for DM132,000, had been worth DM250,000. It is therefore necessary to proceed on the basis of this value relationship for the purpose of the appeal in law proceedings. Admittedly no finding can be obtained from this on the question of whether the defendant has violated good morals by concluding the land contract with the claimant. On a contract for the purchase of land which is concluded between spouses in the context of divorce proceedings, it will not in any case be possible to deduce a conspicuous disproportion leading to the immorality of the transaction merely from the relationship of the value of the land and the purchase price, if the purchase price—as the defendant has submitted here—is part of a more comprehensive financial settlement. A land value which exceeds the purchase price may be reflected in other economic concessions by the person making the acquisition. Likewise the judge of fact will take into consideration the new orientation of their circumstances in life which is necessary for both spouses in the case of divorce. He will have to apply strict requirements before finding a reprehensible frame of mind arising from the exploitation of the distressed situation of a spouse who wants to secure an early divorce. It will be necessary, for instance, to consider the fact that—as the defendant claims here—the parties wanted by their agreement to preserve for their children the property which had so far been held jointly, and therefore to come up with a purchase price for the acquiring spouse which was capable of being financed. Although in contracts for an exchange of services or goods a flagrant disproportion between performance and counter-performance may in the individual case suggest the assumption that the contracting partner thereby benefited has intentionally exploited this to the disadvantage of the other, the principles of law developed on this issue cannot in any case be transferred to family law contracts [reference omitted]. . . . In particular the legal order could not accept—as the deliberations of the *Oberlandesgericht* suggest—a spouse making false statements in divorce proceedings about the expiry of the year of separation (§ 1565 (2) BGB), and in this way paving the way for the other spouse to obtain the 'quick' divorce which this spouse wants, and using this 'concession' to negotiate a sale by the spouse who wants the divorce of her property to him at half price.

3. The disputed judgment cannot accordingly stand, at any rate on the basis of the reasoning which it gives. The senate cannot make a conclusive decision in the case.

. . .

Case 80
BUNDESGERICHTSHOF (TENTH CIVIL SENATE) 13 MARCH 1990
BGHZ 110, 336

Facts

The claimant granted an instalment loan to the defendant on 2 December 1981 which
was negotiated by a third party and which was based on the following calculation:

Amount of loan: 25,000.00 DM
Agent's fees: (5 per cent) 1,250.00 DM

Financing sum 26,250.00 DM
Interest (1.1 per cent per month) 17,325.00 DM
Handling fee (4 per cent) 1,050.00 DM

Total loan 44,625.00 DM

The 'effective rate of interest (bank) incl handling fee' was given in the loan application as 26.2 per cent pa and the 'credit costs (incl agents)' as 29.3 per cent pa.
The loan was to be repaid from 1 January 1982 by a first instalment of DM729 and
DM59 subsequent instalments of DM744 a month. The defendant paid a total of
DM38,229.10 up until January 1987 after several warnings and respites. He refused
further payments on the ground that the loan contract was void due to interest so high
that it was contrary to good morals.

The claimant appropriated a part of the payments to interest for delay, fees and
interest for periods of respite, and out-of-court legal action costs. By the action, it has
claimed a balance of DM12,766.40 plus 21.6 per cent interest on DM12,184.90 since 1
December 1986. The claim has been rejected at both previous instances. The
claimant's appeal in law, which has been admitted, was unsuccessful.

Reasons

I
The appeal court regarded the instalment loan contract as void under § 138 (1) of the
BGB, and gave as its reasoning:
II
This assessment withstands examination under the appeal in law. The prerequisites of
§ 138 (1) BGB are subject to this in their full scope [reference omitted].
1. According to the case law of the third civil senate of the *Bundesgerichtshof*, which
this senate has followed, and on the basis of which the appeal court has also acted, a
conspicuous disproportion between performance and counter-performance is part of
the objective definition of an extortionate instalment loan transaction. The most
important basis of evaluation here is a comparison of the effective contractual rate of
interest with the effective market rate [reference omitted].
   (a) According to the calculations of the appeal court, the contractual rate of
interest of 29.3 per cent exceeded the market rate of 16.64 per cent relatively by 76.08
per cent and absolutely by 12.66 percentage points. . . .

(b) A relative difference in rate of 76.08 per cent does not suffice, as the appeal court has recognised, to establish a violation of § 138 (1) BGB. The *Bundesgerichtshof* considers that a conspicuous disproportion between performance and counter-performance in principle only exists when the contractual rate of interest is around twice as high as the market rate [reference omitted]. As exceeding by 100 per cent is not a hard and fast limit but only a guideline, the application of § 138 (1) BGB should still be approved if the relative difference in rates is between 90 per cent and 100 per cent, and the other credit conditions laid down by the bank bring the burden imposed on the borrower into the intolerable area (BGHZ 104, 102, 105 with further references). On the other hand, if the contractual rate of interest exceeds the market rate relatively by less than 90 per cent, the *Bundesgerichtshof* has routinely denied a conspicuous disproportion (BGHZ 99, 333, 336; 104, 102, 105). In the present case, the relative difference in rates is, at 76.08 per cent, clearly beneath this limit.

(c) The appeal court has therefore correctly based the assumption of a conspicuous disproportion between performance and counterperformance not on the relative, but on the absolute difference in rates of 12.66 percentage points.

(aa) The *Bundesgerichtshof* has not so far expressed a definitive opinion on the question of whether in the case of instalment loan contracts, besides the relative difference in interest rate of about 100 per cent, a predetermined absolute difference in interest rate can serve as a guideline for the comparison of interest rates, and at what percentage the limit should be. It has merely decided that such an additional standard limit would not in any case be set at 11.5 per cent [reference omitted] but that in an individual case an absolute difference of 13.58 per cent, with a relative difference in rate of 83.72 per cent, can suffice for application of § 138 (1) BGB if, in addition, substantial parts of the loan serve to discharge other loans with more favourable rates of interest (BGHZ 104, 102, 106). The question has been answered in differing ways by first instance courts and the literature.

(bb) According to the view of the senate, an absolute difference in interest rates of 12 per cent acquires a similar guideline function to the relative difference of about 100 per cent. The degree by which the average rate of interest (*Schwerpunktzins*) is exceeded is, in high interest periods in which the absolute difference in interest rates is of greater importance [reference omitted], an insufficient criterion for the finding of a conspicuous disproportion between performance and counter-performance. High average interest rates (*Schwerpunktzins*), where the percentage by which they are exceeded is about 100 per cent (which should be regarded as allowed in principle), make absolute differences in interest rates appear permissible, even though they do not have a reasonable relationship to the higher refinancing costs and the growing insolvency risk for the instalment loan banks. The calculation of the contractual rate of interest is determined not only by the expenses of refinancing, enforcement of payment and risk reserves, but also, to a substantial extent, by the relatively constant operating costs and the profit margin. Exceeding the market rate of interest by 12 per cent or more therefore clearly goes beyond the increased costs, even in the case of a generally high level of interest, and allows instalment loan banks an enhancement of their profits at the cost of borrowers. These are, as a rule, of limited financial capacity, and are in any case exposed by the high credit fees to especially heavy burdens. In cases of this kind, a conspicuous disproportion between performance and counter-performance is therefore present even if the relative percentage by which the average rate of interest is exceeded does not reach the critical limit.

2. In this case, the contractual rate of interest exceeds the market rate absolutely by 12.66 per cent, and is therefore above the guideline mentioned. The conspicuous disproportion between performance and counter-performance which is accordingly present, as the appeal court has stated, in the end result correctly, is further increased by the regime relating to the consequences of delay contained in the claimant's loan conditions, which excessively burdens the defendant. . . . Bearing that in mind, as well as, in particular, the conspicuous disproportion between performance and counter-performance which has been explained, the appeal court has, within the framework of the overall balancing exercise undertaken, correctly regarded the loan contract as contrary to good morals (§ 138 (1) BGB).

. . .

Case 81
BUNDESVERFASSUNGSGERICHT (FIRST SENATE) 19 OCTOBER 1993
BVERFGE 89, 214=NJW 1994, 36

Facts

The constitutional complaints concern the question of how far the civil courts are obliged on constitutional grounds to subject guarantee contracts with banks to control of content when relatives with no income or assets of recipients of credit undertake high liability risks as guarantors. Bank contract law is not regulated by special statutes. It is governed by the contract law of the BGB, and by the AGB (general conditions of contract) in which credit institutions have almost completely and uniformly regulated their services. In granting credit, they use contractual forms which are largely the same. A central credit committee, to which the associations of the credit institutions belong as members, achieves co-ordination. In the security practice of credit institutions, it has become usual in the case of consumer credit and business credit with medium sized undertakings to conclude guarantee contracts with family members. Their income and assets are frequently left uninvestigated. The purpose of such contracts is not exclusively to increase the assets available for liability. It is also to deal with transfers of assets, and to make recipients of credit exercise care in their business dealings by bringing in their relatives (opinion of the Federal Association of German banks). For the last ten years the civil courts have been increasingly concerned with cases in which young adults have become hopelessly overburdened with debt because they had provided guarantees for high bank loans to their partners or parents, even though they only had tiny incomes.

(a) The courts of first instance at first subjected the above contractual practice to extensive content control. . . .

(b) The control of the content of contracts by first instance courts was largely rejected by the ninth civil senate of the *Bundesgerichtshof* [reference omitted]. The third civil senate has agreed with this in substance [reference omitted]. Guarantee contracts could not be regarded as contrary to good morals just because they would probably lead to overburdening with debt. The freedom to formulate contracts included, for everyone of full legal capacity, the legal power to take on obligations which could only be fulfilled under especially favourable conditions. The business inexperience of a guarantor was no ground for imposing duties of explanation and advice on credit institutions. A person of full age knew in general, even without special indication, that the giving of a guarantee declaration represented a risky transaction. The bank could therefore assume that a person who took on a guarantee obligation knew the significance of his action, and assessed his risk on his own responsibility. Different considerations would apply if the bank by its own action (and in a way which it could recognise) caused the guarantor to make a mistake by which the risk of liability was increased. This case law has partly found reserved approval in the academic literature [references omitted]. But it was predominantly rejected [references omitted]. Even some first instance courts have failed to follow it [references omitted]. The criticism is to the effect that the *Bundesgerichtshof* had carried out the task of judicial control of content in too inflexible and indiscriminatory a manner, and had thereby failed to fulfil the basic decision in the Constitution. . . .

The proceedings 1 BvR 567/89: The complainant's father operated at first as a real estate broker; he erected and sold flats for owner occupation. In 1982 he asked the city savings bank C for a doubling of his credit limit of DM50,000 to DM100,000. When the city savings bank demanded a security, the complainant, who was at that time 21 years old, signed a pre-printed guarantee document on 29 November 1982 with a maximum sum of DM100,000, plus additional obligations, which included among other things: . . .

The increase in credit was accordingly granted. The complainant received a right of signature for her father's credit account, but had no assets herself. She had no vocational training, was mainly unemployed, and at the time of the guarantee declaration earned DM1150 net per month in a fish factory. In October 1984, the complainant's father gave up his real property business and operated as a shipowner. The city savings bank financed the purchase of a ship with DM 1.3 million. In December 1986, it terminated the outstanding credit (about 2.4 million DM), and informed the complainant that a claim would be made against her under the guarantee. The complainant at first claimed a declaration that her guarantee was invalid. After the city savings bank had raised a counterclaim for payment of DM100,000 with interest, the parties to the initial proceedings declared the claim for a declaration to be settled. The *Landgericht* allowed the counterclaim by the judgment which is being challenged. On the complainant's appeal, the *Oberlansdesgericht* changed the decision of the *Landgericht*, and rejected the counterclaim (WM 1988, 1436 (1438)): The city savings bank was obliged on the ground of fault in contractual negotiations to release the complainant from the guarantee, as it had violated its duties of provision of information. It was true that in general the creditor did not have to explain to the guarant or what risk he incurred. But an exception from this principle was required when the creditor's conduct recognisably caused the guarantor to make a mistake. It was equivalent to this when a credit institution trivialised the type and scope of guarantee liability to a guarantor who was obviously unskilled in business, and thereby influenced his decision. This was the case here. It was established by the evidence that the gist of what the representative of the city savings bank had said when the guarantee document was signed was: 'Here, please, just sign this. It doesn't mean you're entering into any big obligation; I just need it for my records.' He had thereby substantially 'glossed over' and trivialised the actual risk for the complainant. It could not be assumed that she would have been prepared, on a realistic assessment, to take on the guarantee. The *Bundesgerichtshof* quashed the decision of the *Oberlandesgericht* by the judgment which is being challenged, and rejected the complainant's appeal against the judgment of the *Landgericht* (BGH NJW 1989, 1605 = LM § 765 BGB no 67 = ZIP 1989, 629): Guarantees are legal transactions creating one-sided obligations for which the creditor as a rule has neither a duty of explanation nor a duty to obtain information about the state of the guarantor's knowledge. A person who is aged over 18, and therefore of full age according to statute law, knew in general, even without special experience in business matters, that a guarantee declaration gave rise to liability risks. A guarantor's expectation that he would not have a claim made against him could not be the basis of a business transaction. The representative of the city savings bank had done nothing which would have influenced this assessment. At the time of the guarantee declaration, the principal debtor's credit was good, and the information given by the bank employee was therefore correct. The complainant as guarantor should herself have kept an eye on the further development of the father's business affairs and therefore her future liability risk. Express reference had been made in the guarantee form to the possibility of giving notice of termination.

The complainant by her constitutional complaint objects to the violation of her basic rights under Art 1 para 1 and Art 2 para 1 of the Basic Law, in combination with the principle of the social state. . . . At the time of the guarantee declaration her available (*pfändbar*) income consisted of DM413.70. Since October 1991 she had been the single mother of a son. She lived on social assistance and child benefit (*Erziehungsgeld*). Up to January 1992 a debit balance calculated at DM160,000 had accumulated. It could not therefore be expected that she could ever pay off an obligation of this kind.

The proceedings 1 BvR 1044/89: The complainant entered into a guarantee in 1979 with the claimant bank which was unconditionally enforceable [ie, under which the person granting it cannot raise the objection that there has not yet been an unsuccessful execution against the principal debtor] for the securing of a so-called 'insurance loan,' which had been granted to her husband for a total of DM30,000. At the time of the guarantee declaration she had no income or assets. As a housewife, she cared for her two children born in 1971 and 1978. As her husband fell into delay with interest payments, the bank gave notice terminating the loan in 1988. The debit balance at that time amounted to DM32,140.31. It was reduced to DM16,274.02 by realisation of the repurchase value of the life insurance. The bank made a claim against the complainant for this sum. The *Landgericht* allowed the claim by the judgment which is being challenged: No doubts existed about the effectiveness of the guarantee promise. § 310 BGB was not applicable, as obligations which became due in future, however high and unfulfillable, did not represent transfer of future assets. The guarantee contract was also not void under § 138 of the BGB. When the guarantee was taken on, it was possible that the complainant would take up employment before the liquidation of the credit, or would obtain other income. If her husband should become unemployed, he could take over the care of the household and the children. But even long-term inability to perform did not lead to immorality of the guarantee contract. No claim had been made that the bank was culpable in relation to the giving of advice. The *Oberlandesgericht* rejected the complainant's appeal on the same grounds as the decision of the *Landgericht*, by a judgment which is also challenged. The complainant by her constitutional complaint objects to the violation of her basic rights under Art 1 and Art 2 of the Basic Law. It was known to the bank that as a mother of two small children she would not be able to take up employment in the foreseeable future. With such employment as could at the moment reasonably be expected of her, she would never be in a situation to release herself from the guarantee obligation. In fact, the indebtedness would be bound to increase continually, despite regular payments. The consequent destruction of any prospect for the future resulted in a violation of the Constitution.

Reasons

B. . . .

C. In so far as the first complainant's constitutional complaint is permissible, it is also successful. But the second complainant's constitutional complaint is unfounded.

1. Both constitutional complaints are directed against civil court judgments for the payment of money. The normative foundations which support the judgments are not challenged: no objection is made to the determinative provisions of the BGB. The complainants' objections are concerned instead with the interpretation and application of those general clauses which require control of the content of obligation contracts by the civil courts, primarily §§ 138 and 242 BGB. In the concretisation of these clauses, the basic right guarantee of private autonomy and the general right of personality had to be considered, and the civil courts had failed to recognise this in the initial proceedings. This reasoning includes the significance of those basic rights to which concretisation of general clauses in civil law applies.

The Basic Law contains in its basic rights section fundamental decisions in constitutional law for all areas of the law. These fundamental decisions develop through the medium of those provisions which directly control the area of law in question, and above all have significance in the interpretation of general clauses in civil law (see BVerfGE 7, 198 (205f) = NJW 1958, 257; BVerfGE 42, 143 (148) = NJW 1976, 1677). When § 138 and § 242 BGB refer quite generally to good morals, custom (*Verkehrsitte*) and good faith, they require concretisation by the courts by the standard of value concepts which are primarily determined by decisions of principle in the Constitution. Therefore the civil courts are constitutionally obliged to have regard to the basic rights as 'guidelines' in the interpretation and application of the general clauses. If they fail to recognise this, and therefore make a decision which is to the disadvantage of a party to the proceedings, they violate that party's basic rights (see BVerfGE 7, 198 (206f) = NJW 1958, 257; consistent case law).

However, the Federal Constitutional Court does not in principle have to examine the interpretation and application of simple law. It is merely obliged to secure the observance of the basic right norms and standards by the ordinary courts. It cannot therefore oppose a legally effective civil court decision just because it would itself have put the emphasis elsewhere in the assessment of conflicting basic right positions, and therefore decided otherwise. The threshold at which a violation of the Constitution takes place which the Federal Constitutional Court has to correct is only reached when the disputed decision reveals mistakes in interpretation which are based on an opinion which is in principle incorrect of the significance of a basic right (in particular the scope of its protective area). These mistakes must also be of some importance in their material significance for the actual case (BVerfGE 18, 85 (93) = NJW 1964, 1713; BVerfGE 42, 143 (149) = NJW 1976, 1677; consistent case law). Measured by this standard, the judgment of the *Bundesgerichtshof* cannot subsist in the case of the first complainant (II). On the other hand, it does not appear in the case of the second complainant that the civil courts, in the decisions which have been challenged, have failed in principle to recognise the significance of the basic rights (III).

II. 1. The guarantee contract which the *Bundesgerichtshof* had to assess differed significantly from everyday credit securities. The first complainant undertook an extraordinarily high risk in it, without having an economic interest of her own in the credit secured. Renouncing almost all those protective provisions of the BGB which could be removed by agreement, she gave an unconditionally enforceable guarantee of her father's entrepreneurial risk to an extent which went far beyond her economic circumstances. It was foreseeable from the start, and easy for the credit institution to establish, that if liability arose the complainant would probably not be in a position right to end of her life to free herself by her own power from the burden of indebtedness which she had undertaken. In this situation, the question of the prerequisites and reasons for the conclusion of the contract had to be dealt with, especially as the party's submission concentrated on this. The complainant had claimed in the trial courts that the city savings bank had violated pre-contractual duties of showing consideration, and had pursued its own interests in exploiting her business inexperience. The *Oberlandesgericht* followed this view in the end result. However, the *Bundesgerichtshof* saw no cause to exercise control over the content of the guarantee contract. The *Bundesgerichtshof* did not ask itself the question of whether and how far both contracting partners could actually freely decide about the conclusion and content of the contract. This contains a misunderstanding of private autonomy as guaranteed by the basic rights.

2. (a) According to the consistent case law of the Federal Constitutional Court, formulation of legal relationships by the individual in accordance with his intentions is a part of the general freedom of action (see BVerfGE 8, 274 (328) = NJW 1959, 475; BVerfGE 72, 155 (170) = NJW 1986, 1859). Art 2 para 1 of the Basic Law guarantees private autonomy as 'self determination by the individual in the legal world' (Erichsen in: *Isensee/Kirchhof*, Hdb d StaatsR VI, p 1210 marginal no 58). Private autonomy is necessarily limited, and needs legal formulation. Private legal regimes therefore consist of a calibrated system of rules and methods of formulation, co-ordinated with each other, which must fit into the constitutional order. But this does not mean that private autonomy can be dealt with by the legislature as it pleases, and its guarantee in the basic rights can lose its content as a result. The legislature is bound in the necessary formulation by the objective law guidelines of the basic rights. He must open up an appropriate area of activity in the legal world for the self-determination of the individual. According to its regime content, private autonomy must be implemented by the state. Its guarantee so to speak follows justitial realisation, and is therefore the basis of the legislature's duty to make available methods of formulation of legal transactions which must be treated as legally binding and, in the case of a dispute, form the basis of enforceable legal positions.

(b) The duty to shape the private legal system gives the legislator a problem of practical concordance. Equally ranking holders of basic rights take part in civil law transactions and they pursue differing interests and (frequently) opposing goals. As all participants in civil law transactions enjoy the protection of Art 2 para 1 of the Basic Law, and can appeal to the basic right guarantee of their private autonomy to the same extent, it is not only the right of the stronger party which should apply. The conflicting basic right positions should be seen in their reciprocal effect on each other, and should be limited in such a way that they are effective for all participants as extensively as possible. In procedural law, the proper reconciliation of interests follows from the coinciding intentions of the contracting partners. They both bind themselves, and therefore together make use of their individual freedom of action. If one of the contracting parties has such a strong ascendancy that he can in fact unilaterally determine the contractual content, this results, so far as the other contracting party is concerned, in determination *by another* (see BVerfGE 81, 242 (255) = NJW 1990, 1469). Admittedly the legal system cannot provide for all situations in which equilibrium in negotiations is more or less impaired. Simply on grounds of legal certainty, a contract ought not subsequently to be put in question or corrected for every disturbance of equilibrium in negotiations. However, if it is a question of a categorisable case which reveals a structural inferiority of one of the contracting parties, and if the consequences of the contract are unusually burdensome for the inferior contracting party, the civil law system must react to this and facilitate corrections. This follows from the basic right guarantee of private autonomy (Art 2 para 1 of the Basic Law) and the social state principle (Art 20 para 1 and Art 28 para 1 of the Basic Law).

(c) Current contract law satisfies these requirements. The authors of the BGB admittedly proceeded on the basis of a model of formally equal participants in private law transactions, even if they created various protective norms for the weaker party in legal transactions. But even the *Reichsgericht* gave up this way of looking at the matter, and 'changed it back into a material ethic of social responsibility' (Wieacker, *Industriegesellschaft und Privatrechtsordnung* [The Industrial Society and the Private Legal System] 1974, p 24). Today there is extensive agreement that contractual freedom only works in the case of an approximately balanced relationship of the strengths of the partners as the means for an appropriate reconciliation of interests, and that the reconciliation of disturbed contractual parity is one of the chief tasks of current civil law (see the overview by Limbach, JuS 1985, 10 with further references; finally Preis, *Grundfragen der Vertragsgestaltung im ArbeitsR* [Fundamental questions on the formation of contracts in labour law] 1993, p 216 ff). Large parts of the BGB can be interpreted in the sense of this task (Hönn, *Kompensation gestörter Vertragsparität* [Compensation for disturbed contractual parity] 1982). In this connection the general clauses of the BGB have central significance. The wording of § 138 (2) BGB expresses this particularly clearly. It describes typical circumstances which automatically lead to the inferiority of one contracting party in negotiations, and which include his inexperience. If the superior party exploits this weakness in order to promote his interests unilaterally in a conspicuous manner, this leads to invalidity of the contract. § 138 (1) BGB links invalidity quite generally to a violation of good morals. Calibrated legal consequences arise from § 242 BGB. Civil law jurisprudence is in the end result united in taking the view that the principle of good faith describes an inherent boundary to the contractual power of formulation, and forms the basis of the authority for judicial control of the contract's content (see finally, *Fastrich, Richterliche Inhaltskontrolle im*

PrivatR [Judicial control of content in private law] 1992, p 70 ff; Preis, p 249 f). There is admittedly disagreement in the academic literature about the prerequisites for and the intensity of this control of content. However, for the assessment in constitutional law, it is sufficient to establish that current law in any case has instruments available which make it possible to react appropriately to structural disturbances of contractual parity. For the civil courts, a duty follows from this to ensure, in the interpretation and application of the general clauses, that contracts do not serve as a means for determination *by another*. If the contracting partners have agreed a regime which is in itself permissible, a more extensive control of content will as a rule be unnecessary. But if the content of the contract is unusually burdensome for one party, and obviously inappropriate as a reconciliation of interests, the courts ought not to content themselves with saying: 'Contract is contract.' Instead they must resolve whether the regime is a consequence of structurally unequal negotiating strength, and if necessary intervene to correct it, within the framework of the general clauses of current civil law. How they must proceed here, and what conclusion they should reach, is primarily a question of simple law, to which the Constitution leaves a wide margin. But it is necessary to consider whether there is a violation of the basic right guarantee of private autonomy if the problem of disturbed contractual parity is not noticed at all, or its resolution is sought by unsuitable methods.

3. The disputed decision of the *Bundesgerichtshof* is marked by such a violation. The guarantee declaration which is in dispute was assessed as if a normal contract with corresponding interests and comprehensible risks had been made. All the arguments by which the first complainant tried to prove her weakness in negotiations were rejected by reference to the fact that she was of full age and should have ascertained the risks arising herself. That is not sufficient. The risk of liability which the first complainant undertook by the guarantee contract in dispute, without having any economic interest of her own, was—as already explained—unusually high. Besides this, it was extraordinarily hard to evaluate. The guarantee sum laid down only described a maximum for the main demand; the considerable costs and interest on the credit were to be added to this, without the basis of their calculation having been shown in the guarantee contract. Above all however there was no limitation on the business obligations secured. Besides, when the removal by negotiation of the protective provisions in guarantee law is considered, it becomes clear that the first complainant was to be liable practically as a partner of her father. Even people experienced in business could scarcely have evaluated the meaning and the extent of this risk. For the 21-year-old first complainant, who had no skilled vocational training, the meaning and extent were practically incomprehensible. In a case of such pronounced inferiority of a contracting partner, the decisive issue is the way in which the contract came into existence, and in particular how the superior contracting partner has behaved. However, the *Bundesgerichtshof* denies any duty of explanation or guidance on the part of the credit institution. The *Bundesgerichtshof* even regards the pressure exerted by the bank employee with the words 'You're not entering into any big obligation' as insignificant. It merely sees in this—contrary to the findings of the *Oberlandesgericht*—provisional information about creditworthiness, which could have no influence on the negotiating position of the complainant. That does not do justice to the problematic nature of this case, and fails to meet the basic right guarantee of private autonomy so fundamentally that the decision cannot stand. Whether a

violation of the general right of personality also falls to be considered can accordingly be left undecided.

III. In the case of the second complainant, it is not a question of taking on a high entrepreneurial risk which it is hard to evaluate. The guarantee concerned a consumer loan, which was not unusually high if the initial cost for the setting up of a household is considered. The recipient of the loan was the second complainant's husband, so it might be assumed that she was herself directly interested in the grant of the loan. According to the findings of the disputed judgments, the circumstances accompanying the conclusion of the contract also gave no cause for suspicion that the second complainant had been forced to make her guarantee declaration, or that her freedom of decision had been infringed in some other way. There are likewise no grounds for finding any possible fault in relation to advice by the credit institution. The bank has admittedly made the grant of the loan dependent on the security of a guarantee, but according to the findings of the *Landgericht*, it has not violated any duties to give information here, and in particular has not glossed over the risk of liability. In assessing these facts, the *Landgericht* has dealt thoroughly with the general clauses in §§ 138 and 242 BGB. It is not evident that it had misunderstood the basic right guarantee of private autonomy. The *Landgericht* and the *Oberlandesgericht* admittedly refused to declare the guarantee contract to be invalid just because the second complainant did not have an income or assets of her own. But having regard to the kind and level of the loan, that is not open to objection on constitutional grounds.

Likewise the complaint of a violation of the general right of personality does not succeed. It can be left undecided whether and how far this undesignated freedom developed by the case law is affected if there is hopeless indebtedness when a credit or guarantee contract is made. It cannot be deduced from the findings of the judge of fact in the initial proceedings that such a danger had existed. Nor is it sufficiently demonstrated in the constitutional complaint.

Case 82
BUNDESGERICHTSHOF (ELEVENTH CIVIL SENATE) 14 MAY 2002
BGH NJW 2002, 2228

Facts

The parties are disputing about the validity of a guarantee. The claimant savings bank concluded five loan contracts on the 13/14 April 1994 with the R-Bau-GmbH (R-GmbH), the former first defendant and a further member of the R-GmbH. Among these was a current account credit contract for a maximum sum of DM200,000 at a rate of interest of 12.5 per cent pa. At the same time the second defendant (the defendant), the wife of the former first defendant, took on an unconditionally enforceable guarantee [ie, under which the person granting it cannot raise the objection that there has not yet been an unsuccessful execution against the principal debtor] up to a maximum sum of DM100,000 for securing all existing and future demands by the claimant against the borrowers, including conditional and time limited ones. Previously the B-Bank GmbH had arranged a deficiency guarantee for 80 per cent for the credit granted. After the opening of total execution proceedings regarding the property of R-GmbH on the 31 May 1996 had been refused for want of assets, the claimant terminated all the loan contracts instantly. In the following period the B-Bank GmbH paid the claimant a sum of DM207,471.01 and empowered it to commence court proceedings in respect of the demands which it had as deficiency guarantor against the borrowers and the defendant as co-guarantor. After realising various securities, the claimant has made a claim for payment.

The *Landgericht* allowed the claim against the former first defendant in part. It allowed it against the defendant in accordance with the application in a sum of DM100,000 plus interest. The defendant's appeal was largely unsuccessful. The appeal in law was successful, and led to quashing of the disputed decision and reference of the case back to the appeal court in so far as the decision was to the defendant's disadvantage.

Reasons

I. The appeal court regarded the taking up of the guarantee by the defendant as effective, giving its reasons in substance as being: . . .

II. These deliberations do not stand up to legal examination in crucial respects. Contrary to the view of the appeal court, the parties' guarantee contract (according to the defendant's disputed submission, from which it is necessary to proceed for the purpose of the appeal in law) violates good morals, and is consequently void.

1. According to the case law of the ninth and eleventh civil senates of the *Bundesgerichtshof*, which has now coincided, the application of § 138 (1) BGB to guarantee or joint liability contracts concluded by credit institutions with private providers of security as a rule depends crucially on the disproportion between the scope of the obligation and the financial capabilities of the guarantor or joint debtor who is personally close to the main debtor [references omitted]. It is true that the mere fact that the person affected probably cannot even bear the interest fixed by the parties to the loan contract out of the available (*pfändbar*) part of his income or assets in the long term at the time when the security takes effect is not as a rule enough for making the negative value judgment of immorality. Where such a blatantly excessively demand is made there is however (unless there are additional circumstances) a rebuttable presumption based on general experience of life, that he has taken on the ruinous guarantee or joint liability only because of emotional attachment to the main debtor, and the provider of credit has exploited this in a morally objectionable manner [consistent case law, see Senate, references omitted].

2. Contrary to what the appeal court has assumed, the defendant was, according to her submission, probably not in a position when she took on the guarantee to bear alone, and long term, the interest agreed in the credit contracts which were the cause of the guarantee declaration, with its maximum sum of DM100,000, from her own available income and/or assets. There is therefore a factual presumption, which would have to be refuted by the claimant, that the defendant took on the guarantee only because of emotional attachment to her husband.

(a) According to her evidence, which remains unchallenged, the defendant earned DM1470 net per month as a part time teacher at the time she took on the guarantee in March 1994. This income was, considering her duty to maintain her son who was at that time seven years old, unavailable (§ 850c (1) of the ZPO (Civil Procedure Order)).

Her income from the letting of a sub-divided house in the sum of DM1232.50 monthly was subject, according to her disputed submission, to expenses of DM2143, for interest and repayment of the mortgage loan, allegedly valued at around DM300,000. These expenses were, as the appeal court recognises, necessary to produce the rental income. It has not been established that less than DM1232.50 per month of the expenses related to interest, nor is this evident in the light of the amount of the mortgage loan. In fact, according to the defendant's submission, it is necessary to assume that not even part of her rental income was available for servicing the current interest on the guaranteed loan sum of DM100,000. The appeal court's assumption that the defendant was in a position, with the assistance of her salary and her rental income, to create wealth therefore has no basis.

(b) According to her evidence, the defendant does not even have available assets for consideration when assessing her capacity to pay. According to her submission, for which proof has been provided, and which the appeal court in breach of procedural rules (according to the justified objection of the appeal in law) has not investigated, her sub-divided residential property has a market value of only DM300,000, and is mortgaged to the full extent of its value. This mortgage liability must be considered when assessing the guarantor's ability to pay. The ninth civil senate of the *Bundesgerichtshof* has admittedly put forward the opposite view in two older decisions [references omitted]. But in the light of the opinion now also shared by the ninth civil senate, that the effectiveness of a guarantee is only determined by the guarantor's actual economic capacity [references omitted], this view is out of date. According to this new case law, it is simply logical to reduce the guaranteed risk only by the value of the security effectively available in the individual case of the committed real asset, ie to take the value of real mortgages into account so as to reduce assets. Not to consider them would contradict the usual practice of banks, and would, in particular in the case of real mortgages for the full amount of a property's value, lead to a guarantor having to be treated as able to pay even though he obviously is not (Nobbe/Kirchhof, BKR 2001, 1 [9f]). It is not therefore possible to adhere to the older case law of the ninth civil senate mentioned above. This (ie, the eleventh) senate is, in accordance with § 132 of the GVG (Constitution of the Courts Act) in a position to amend the case law without invoking the Grand Senate for Civil Cases, as it has competence for guarantee issues, in place of the ninth civil senate, under the plan for division of the business of the *Bundesgerichtshof* applying since 1 January 2001.

(c) From the viewpoint of a credit institution acting in a rational manner (which is the determinative viewpoint here) on the take up of the guarantee in March 1994, it was not possible to count on an immediate, substantial and long-term improvement in the defendant's income and assets. In view of the age of the seven-year-old son that she was caring for, full-time vocational activity by the defendant in the near future appeared rather improbable. It has neither been alleged and substantiated nor established that the situation regarding the income and assets had turned out more favourably than was to be expected when the guarantee was taken on. The controversial issue argued by the reply to appeal in law of whether the guarantor's financial situation at the time the guarantee arises must also be considered when assessing the issue of immorality therefore does not present itself.

3. Contrary to the assumption of the appeal court, which referred to the case law of the ninth civil senate of the *Bundesgerichtshof* (which was formerly competent for

guarantee law), the creditor's interest in protecting itself from transfers of assets between married couples does not affect the immorality of a guarantee which creates blatantly excessive financial demands on the spouse entering into it. Besides this the appeal court has overlooked the fact that a claim against a spouse entering into a guarantee creating blatantly excessive financial demands should be rejected even according to the case law of the ninth civil senate, as unfounded at that time, if no transfer of assets has taken place—as is the case here [references omitted].

(a) As this senate has already stated in its decision on 29 June 1999 submitted to the Grand Senate for Civil Cases [references omitted], the goal of preventing possible transfers of assets does not on its own justify an unlimited demand for joint liability. Without special grounds, which must be explained by the provider of credit and if necessary proved, it is not in principle possible to assume that a guarantee (or the taking on of joint liability) for a blatantly excessive demand exists from the outset merely to prevent a substantial transfer of assets between the main debtor and the provider of the security. Such an agreement, which would give personal security a quite special meaning, is not in any way usual practice, or to be deduced from circumstances outside the contractual document. A person who proposes such a restricted interpretation of the guarantee or joint liability agreement by appealing to the real intention of intelligent contracting parties puts himself outside generally recognised principles of interpretation. Besides this, he violates the prohibition on a reduction of guarantees or joint liability contracts contained in forms in such a way as to retain their validity. If the provider of credit claims against the person concerned (as here) without asserting even only as a starting point that (and to what extent) a transfer of assets has taken place which is substantial in relation to the amount of the credit, this post-contract behaviour, which is to be considered within the framework of contractual interpretation [references omitted], also shows that assumption of a tacit limitation of liability is not justified.

(b) This opinion is meanwhile also shared in principle by the ninth civil senate of the *Bundesgerichtshof*. But it regards itself as prevented from applying the principles recognised by it for the future to guarantee contracts dating from the period before 1 January 1999 as well [references omitted]. This was because it considered that it had not been sufficiently apparent to the credit institutions to what extent they had to safeguard their interest in a protection which was as effective as possible from transfers of assets through appropriate contractual regimes over and above the mere taking up of a guarantee. This senate cannot follow this differentiated way of looking at the matter.

It can remain open here whether and to what extent the trust of a party to proceedings in the continued existence of the case law of the highest courts is worthy of protection [see on this Schimansky, WM 2001, 1889 with further references]. This case does not crucially depend on the answer to this question, because for an intelligent creditor the trust which is essential for protection for dispositions could not arise. The idea that preventing transfers of assets by the main debtor was an element which could prevent a finding of immorality was considered for the first time by the ninth civil senate of the *Bundesgerichtshof* [references omitted] in reaction to the decisions of principle by the Federal Constitutional Court of 19 October 1993 (BVerfGE 89, 214 [229ff] = NJW 1994, 36) and 5 August 1994 (BVerfG NJW 1994, 2749). The ninth civil senate has in this connection expressly contradicted the differing case law of the eleventh civil senate [references omitted]. The eleventh civil senate has also in the ensuing period continually adhered to the view that the mere goal of preventing possible transfers of assets does not in principle justify an economically pointless demand for joint liability by the provider of credit [references omitted]. There could therefore be no question of established case law of the highest courts in favour of considering the creditor's interest in protection from transfers of assets without the guarantee being expressly limited to this purpose [references omitted].

III. The appeal court judgment should therefore be quashed (§ 564 (1) of the ZPO, old version). The case is not ready for a final decision, in particular there are no findings by the judge of fact on the value of the defendant's sub-divided house, on the valuation of the mortgage loan and on the defendant's monthly interest and repayment obligations when the guarantee contract was concluded. The case therefore had to be referred back to the appeal court for further elucidation of the facts (§ 565 (1) sentence 1 of the ZPO, old version).

Case 83
BUNDESGERICHTSHOF (TWELFTH CIVIL SENATE) 11 FEBRUARY 2004
BGH NJW 2004, 930

Facts

The parties, who are divorced, are in dispute about maintenance after marriage and settlement of the accretion (*Zugewinn*) [ie, increase in spouses' assets during marriage]. The applicant, who was born in 1948, and the respondent, who was born in 1955, married on 22 November 1985. The children M and V were born from this marriage on 24 March 1986 and 21 May 1989. The applicant has worked as consultant to a business since 1985. The respondent, has passed master's degree examinations in ancient history, history of art and German philology, and led archaeological excavations in 1984 and 1985, but gave up this activity because of pregnancy. At the wish of her husband she did not pursue her intention of obtaining a doctor's degree; she devoted herself to the household and bringing up the children. On 17 February 1988 the parties concluded a notarised marriage contract. In it they renounced 'reciprocal claims to any . . . maintenance after marriage, with the exception of the wife's claim for maintenance for looking after the children . . . in the case of a divorce.' Besides this they agreed a division of assets for the future. They declared that no accretion had arisen so far. As a precaution they mutually renounced any possible settlement claims in respect of accretion which had arisen. They excluded any pension settlement. The respondent's renunciation was made on the condition that the applicant should (a) effect from June 1988 at the latest a private life insurance for the respondent for the capital sum of DM80,000 on the completion of her sixtieth year, with the option of a pension instead, and (b) pay the premiums regularly on this during the existence of the marriage. In the case of divorce he was to pay to her three times the annual premium on the insurance in one sum in settlement. He would not then be liable for any further payments. On 27 April 1988, a life insurance of DM80,000 was effected with L for the respondent, and the applicant subsequently made payments on this. On 13 November 2001 in the divorce proceedings before the *Amtsgericht*, he committed himself, as an amendment to the original contract, to pay the instalments continuously until the insurance matured on 1 May 2015. The applicant obtained, according to the findings of the *Oberlandesgericht*, a monthly average income 'in the final years' of DM27,000 net from subordinate and independent work. The respondent has carried on an 'alternative' toy shop, latterly together with a post office, at her place of residence since 1994. Her monthly income from this activity amounts—according to her—to DM1084 before taxes. The parties lived in a house in A with a living area of 200 square metres on a plot of about 1200 to 1300 square metres, which the parties had rented from the applicant's brother for a total monthly rent of DM2548. The respondent received from the applicant monthly housekeeping money of DM2692, and compensation for her assistance in his office at the house of DM500 monthly. Besides this, the nature of their marital economic circumstances, so far as concerned clothing, furnishings and fittings, was modest, according to the findings of the *Oberlandesgericht*. The parties have been living separately on a permanent basis since February 1999. In accordance with the agreed wishes of the parties, the children usually live with the respondent. The applicant pays maintenance for them in accordance with the highest level on the Düsseldorf table.

The *Amtsgericht* dissolved the parties' marriage by a combined judgment, and established that there would be no pension settlement. Besides this, it ordered the applicant to pay DM3671 basic maintenance to the respondent, and DM1081 old age pension maintenance. It rejected the respondent's applications for further maintenance and for information and payment of an accretion settlement within the framework of a step action (*Stufenklage*). The judgment of the Amtsgericht is legally effective since 13 April 2002 in relation to the pronouncement on the divorce and the pension settlement. On the respondent's appeal, the Oberlandesgericht ordered the applicant to pay basic maintenance of 2897 euros to the respondent monthly in advance, as well as pension maintenance of 952 euros. Apart from this, it rejected her appeal in relation to the claim for maintenance. Likewise it rejected the applicant's cross appeal by which he contested the judgment for payment of maintenance exceeding DM2500 (= 1278.23 euros) monthly. In relation to the accretion settlement, it ordered him to provide information about his assets at the end [of the marriage] and in other respects it referred the case back to the Amtsgericht (NJW 2003, 592 = FPR 2003, 130 = FamRZ 2003, 35 with a note by Bergschneider, Fam RZ 2003, 39). The applicant appealed against the appeal judgment, in so far as it is adverse to him, by an appeal in law which has been admitted. The appeal led to partial quashing of the disputed judgment, and reference of the case back to the *Oberlandesgericht*.

Reasons

I. In the view of the *Oberlandesgericht*, the respondent is entitled, besides care maintenance, to a claim for top-up maintenance as well as to the giving of information for the purpose of the accretion settlement. The notarised contract between the parties of 17 February 1988 did not exclude these claims as—measured by standards mentioned by the Federal Constitutional Court in its decisions of 6 February 2001 (NJW 2001, 957) and 29 March 2001 (NJW 2001, 2248)—it should be regarded as ineffective. . . . These deliberations do not stand up to legal examination.

II. Statute law gives married couples the opportunity by agreements made during (or by way of precaution before) marriage to regulate in a binding manner maintenance after marriage or other matters in relation to pensions and assets for the case of a subsequent divorce (§§ 1408 (1), (2), 1585c BGB).

1. According to the case law of the senate so far, full contractual freedom existed in principle for agreements of this kind. There was no special control of content based on whether a regime was reasonable (Senat, NJW 1997, 192; see also NJW 1991, 913)— apart from agreements under § 1587o of the BGB. Giving up maintenance after marriage did not affect a core area of marriage (Senat, NJW 1985, 1833). It was also not an element in the nature of marriage that an 'economic life partnership' would arise or that the spouses would participate on the dissolution of the marriage in the changes in assets which had occurred during the marriage (Senat, NJW 1985, 1833).

The only limitations to the validity of such an agreement arose from §§ 134 and 138 BGB. Whether an agreement violated good morals in the individual case depended on its overall character, to be deduced from its content, motives and purpose. In this connection further insights could be gained from the time elapsing before a divorce which was not intended but only considered to be possible (Senat, NJW 1985, 1833, and NJW 1991, 913). It was not sufficient on its own that the agreement had been concluded in an effort to escape all the disadvantageous consequences of a divorce (Senat, NJW 1991, 913). Nor did it suffice that the regime could have an effect which was exclusively or predominantly to the disadvantage of one of the spouses (Senat, NJW 1997, 192). Finally, the immorality of the agreement could also not be derived merely from the circumstance that the woman concluding the contract had been pregnant by the man, and he had made the conclusion of the marriage with her dependent on the conclusion of this contract. As the man could have refrained from marrying regardless of the woman's pregnancy, and could have confined himself to the legal obligations of a father not married to the mother, it was not possible to assume a reprehensible exploitation of the woman's predicament (Senat, FamRZ 1996, 1536 [1537] and FamRZ 1997, 156 [157f]). Admittedly renunciation of the right to maintenance could be contrary to good morals, and therefore be void, if the parties had regulated their family burdens based on the marriage in a way which was objectively to the disadvantage of social welfare (Senat, BGHZ 86, 82 [88]; FamRZ 1985, 788 [790], and FamRZ 1992, 1403). Awareness on the part of the parties that they were harming the social welfare authority by their agreement would not be absolutely necessary for this. The fact that they had shown gross negligence in closing their minds to such knowledge could suffice (Senate, NJW 1985, 1833). Also the divorced party against whom a claim for maintenance was made was in certain cases prevented from appealing to a renunciation of maintenance by the other party under the principle of good faith (§ 242 of the BGB). This could be the case if the circumstances existing at the time of renunciation of maintenance had developed afterwards in such a way that paramount interests of the children of the marriage which deserved protection were inconsistent with reliance on the renunciation (Senate, NJW 1985, 1835, and NJW 1987, 776) This was so even if the parties had considered the development which then actually arose— ie, divorce when the children's need for care and control was continuing—when concluding the renunciation of the maintenance (Senate, FamRZ 1992, 1403 [1404]). The duration and level of the duty of maintenance was admittedly limited in such a case in so far as the child's welfare did not require the continued existence of a claim to maintenance [references omitted]. So far as the level was concerned, the spouse having care and control only had a claim to maintenance in so far as she was reliant on it to cover her own necessary living expenses in order to fulfil her duties of care and control. The spouse with care and control should only be granted more than the necessary maintenance if special grounds relating to child welfare demanded this (Senate [references omitted], FamRZ 1997, 873 [874f]).

2. The decisions of the Federal Constitutional Court of 6 February 2001 (NJW 2001, 957) and of 29 March 2001 (NJW 2001, 2248) give cause for examination of the case law set out above.

(a) By its senate decision of 6 February 2001 [reference omitted] the Federal Constitutional Court has followed to its case law on the control of the content of guarantee contracts (NJW 1994, 36) and on the prohibition on competition by trading agents (*Handelsvertreter*) without compensation (NJW 1990, 1469). The court carried the principles developed there over to marriage contracts and agreements about maintenance. According to these, the private autonomy guaranteed by Art 2 para 1 of the Basic Law assumed that the prerequisites of self-determination were in fact present. The mutual intention of the contracting parties expressed in the contract would as a rule permit the conclusion that a proper adjustment of interests had been effected by the contract, and the state had in principle to respect this. However, it might be evident on the basis of a one-sided imposition of contractual burdens, and of a substantially unequal negotiating position of the contracting partners, that in a contractual relationship a partner carried such weight that he could effectively determine the contractual content unilaterally. It was then the task of the law to work towards the preservation of the basic right positions of both contracting partners in order to prevent self-determination for one contracting partner turning into determination by someone else. This also applied to marriage contracts by which married people regulated their highly personal relationships for the period of their marriage or afterwards. Art 6 para 1 of the Basic Law gave them the right here freely to formulate their partnership internally for the time being in accordance with marital and family responsibility and considerations. Admittedly it was only a marriage in which the man and woman were related to each other in a partnership with equal rights which was protected in constitutional law. The state had as a result to set boundaries to the freedom of the spouses to formulate their marital relationships and reciprocal rights and duties with the assistance of contracts. These boundaries had to be set at the point where the contract was not an expression of a life partnership with equal rights, but reflected a one-sided dominance of one marriage partner based on unequal negotiating positions. This had as a rule to be assumed when an unmarried pregnant woman was faced with the future alternatives of either caring for the child alone, or of involving the child's father in responsibility by marriage, although at the price of concluding a marriage contract with him which imposed heavy burdens on her. Whether such a contract clearly burdened the woman more than the man also substantially depended on the family structure which the contracting partners sought to achieve and on which they based their contract. If the partners to the marriage mutually renounced their statutory claims to maintenance after marriage, this did not create an unequal burden in the case of marriages in which both partners pursued careers of equal value and shared the tasks of home and family. However if the life plans of the partners provided that one of the married partners should give up a career to dedicate himself substantially to looking after the children and the household, the renunciation of maintenance after marriage disadvantages this spouse. The more statutory rights in the marriage contract were negotiated away, or additional duties were undertaken, the stronger this effect of unilateral disadvantage became. It was the task of the courts to subject the content of the contract in cases of disturbance to contractual parity to control via the general clauses of civil law and, if necessary, to correct it in order to preserve basic right positions of a partner to the marriage contract which were infringed. Such control of content is not inconsistent with freedom of marriage, because the latter does not justify unlimited freedom in formulation of marriage contracts, nor, in particular, a one sided allocation of burdens in such a contract. Accordingly, part of the law of marriage is conventionally compulsory law.

(b) The senate decision mentioned above only directly concerned the effectiveness of a marriage contract made before the marriage in which a pregnant woman had committed herself, among other things, partially to release the husband and child's father from claims to maintenance of the expected child in the case of divorce. But the Federal Constitutional Court in its chamber decision of 29 March 2001 [reference omitted] developed this case law, and objected to an appeal court decision which had awarded only the necessary care maintenance to the wife, but had rejected her further applications for maintenance, and accretion and pension settlements. Prior to their marriage, the spouses had contractually excluded maintenance subsequent to the marriage, as well as accretion and pension settlements. The *Oberlandesgericht* should— according to the Federal Constitutional Court—have taken the special situation in which the wife found herself at the conclusion of the contract, as a pregnant woman who already had a severely disabled child from another relationship (and this alone was a clear indication of her inferior position as a contracting partner), as a cause for subjecting the whole content of the contract to control. In this connection it should have investigated the question of whether the marriage contract burdened the wife unilaterally and unreasonably—especially in her constrained family and economic circumstances.

3. The question of what consequences follow from these decisions for the assessment of marriage contracts in general—and thus also for cases in which the wife is not pregnant at the conclusion of the contract—is answered in different ways in the literature and in the specialist publicity.

(a) Differences exist in assessing when—in general—it is possible to speak of a one-sided allocation of burdens for the case of a divorce. . . .

(b) The significance which should be attributed to an imbalance existing between the contractual partners is also differently evaluated. . . .

(c) The Federal Constitutional Court has expressly left open the question of the instruments with which the specialist courts should carry out the control of content given to them. The literature on this subject which considers sanctions differentiates between §§ 138 (1) and 242 BGB according to the extent of the disadvantage . . .

III. According to the senate's view, it is not possible to give a general answer which is conclusive for all conceivable cases about the conditions under which an agreement— by which spouses regulate their maintenance rights or assets for the case of a divorce in a manner which deviates from the statutory provisions—is ineffective (§ 138 BGB) or makes an appeal to all or individual contractual rules impermissible (§ 242 BGB). What is necessary is an overview of the agreements made, the reasons for which and the circumstances in which they came into existence, and the shaping of married life, both as intended and realised. It is necessary to proceed here from the following principles:

1. The statutory regimes about maintenance, accretion and pension settlement after marriage are in principle subject to contractual amendment by the spouses. The current law does not recognise an irreducible minimum content in the consequences of divorce in favour of the spouse entitled.

(a) The legislator has admittedly set against the principle enshrined in § 1569 of the BGB—of personal responsibility of each spouse for his own maintenance after marriage—an almost complete system of maintenance claims. These ensure the protection of the socially weaker spouse after the divorce, and are in particular to compensate for the disadvantages caused by marriage which that spouse has suffered because of the marriage or the bringing up of children in progressing in his own career and building up a corresponding pension for old age. On the other hand, the legislator has in §§ 1353, 1356 of the BGB guaranteed the right (protected in the Basic Law; see Art 6) of spouses to shape their married life together on their own responsibility and free from statutory handicaps, in correspondence with their individual ideas and needs. The contractual freedom in relation to the consequences of divorce is in this respect a necessary complement to this guaranteed right, and originates from the legitimate need to agree deviations from the statutorily regulated consequences of divorce so as to suit the individual picture of the spouses' marriage better. . . .

(b) The accretion settlement is less an emanation of post-marriage solidarity than an expression of distributive justice which can certainly compensate for disadvantages related to marriage in the individual case. But in its standardisation it reaches far beyond this goal, and, not least for this reason, is subjected by § 1408 (1) of the BGB to the disposition of the spouses. . . .

(c) These considerations apply—at any rate in principle—for the pension settlement as well, which admittedly is to be understood in accordance with its objective as anticipated maintenance for old age, but on the other hand is copied from the mechanism of the accretion settlement. § 1408 (2) BGB therefore expressly permits modifications by way of marriage contract to the pension settlement as well, up to the point of its total exclusion, although these become ineffective if a spouse applies for divorce within a year.
. . .

2. The basic negotiability of the consequences of divorce may not however lead to the possibility of the protective purpose of the statutory rules being avoided at will by contract. That would be so if it gave rise to an allocation of burdens which was evidently one-sided and not justified by the individual formulation of marriage relationships, and which it seems unreasonable for the burdened spouse to accept on a sensible assessment of the nature of the marriage. This assessment should be made following reasonable consideration of the interests of the other spouse and his trust in the validity of the agreement made. When statutory rules are negotiated away by contract, the burdening of the one spouse will weigh all the more heavily and the interests of the other spouse will need to be examined all the more closely, as the intrusion into the core area of the law about the consequences of divorce become more direct.

(a) This core area includes primarily care maintenance (§ 1570 BGB), which is not subject to the free disposition of the spouses in view of its connection with the interest of the child. It is true that it is not exempt from *any* modification. So cases could nevertheless be imagined in which the mother's job permits her to combine care of the children with gainful employment without the child's upbringing suffering. All-day care by the mother does not seem to be an unalterable prerequisite for a good upbringing, so the spouses could reach an agreement to bring in third parties to take on care when the child reaches a certain age, in order to facilitate the mother's return to her career as soon as possible.

Besides this, in relation to the core area of the consequences of divorce it will be possible to undertake an order of ranking for their negotiability which is primarily regulated by the significance which the individual rules relating to the consequences of divorce have for the person entitled in his current situation. Thus the securing of the current need for maintenance for the person entitled is as a rule more important than, for example, the accretion settlement or later pension settlement. Within the definitions of maintenance, after care maintenance (§ 1570 BGB), illness maintenance (§ 1572 BGB) and maintenance because of old age (§ 1571 BGB) will have priority. . . .

(b) Pension settlement is ranked at the same level as maintenance because of age.
. . .

(c) The accretion settlement proves to be the most accessible to disposition by marriage contract. The understanding of marriage does not require, as Schwab has correctly indicated (DNotZ 2001, 9 [16]), a definite co-ordination of the assets acquired in the marriage. Life partnership in marriage was and is—even as a partnership between a man and a woman with equal entitlements—not necessarily also an assets partnership Even the equal weighting of career activity and family work emphasised—for the purpose of the law about maintenance after marriage—by the Federal Constitutional Court (FamRZ 2002, 527 [529]) does not result in definite structuring of the marriage assets sphere. . . .

3. Whether an evidently one-sided allocation of burdens arises from an agreement which deviates from the statutory law about the consequences of divorce, and which it seems unreasonable for the burdened spouse to accept, must be examined by the judge of fact. This task is not made otiose by the fact that the burdened spouse was sufficiently advised by a notary about the content and consequences of the contract (a A Langenfeld, DNotZ 2001, 272) especially as in any case such examination and advice only takes place for agreements in notarial form, as prescribed by § 1408 (1) in combination with §§ 1410, 1587o (2) sentence 1 BGB. It does not occur with maintenance agreements which are made by private writing or without formal requirements—as permitted by § 1585c BGB.

(a) The judge of fact must in this connection first examine—within the framework of control of *validity*—whether the agreement, at the point in time when it came into existence, obviously leads to such a one-sided allocation of burdens in the case of divorce that—detached from future developments with the spouses and the circumstances of their lives—it should be wholly or partially denied the recognition of the legal order because of violation of good morals, with the consequence that the statutory rules take its place (§ 138 (1) of the BGB). An overall assessment is necessary here, in the context of the individual circumstances at the conclusion of the contract, in particular those relating to income and assets, the style of marriage as planned or already realised, and the effects on the spouses and the children. Subjectively, it is necessary to consider the goals pursued by the spouses in the agreement, and the other motives which caused the spouse who benefited to want to shape the marriage contract in this way, and induced the disadvantaged spouse to comply with this wish. The verdict of immorality will as a rule only fall to be considered if rules from the core area of the statutory law about the consequences of divorce are negotiated away by the contract entirely, or at any rate in substantial parts, without this disadvantage being mitigated for the other spouse by other advantages, or justified by the special relationships of the spouses, by the type of marriage which they either sought for or lived, or by other important interests of the benefited spouse.

(b) In so far as a contract accordingly subsists, the judge must then—within the framework of the control of its *exercise*—examine whether and to what extent a spouse is misusing the legal power granted to him by the contract if, in the case of divorce, when faced with a statutory consequence of divorce desired by the other spouse, he appeals to the fact that this was effectively negotiated away by the contract (§ 242 BGB). It is not only the circumstances at the time of the conclusion of the contract which are determinative for this. What is decisive is whether now—at the point of the breakdown of the relationship—an obviously one-sided allocation of burdens arises from the agreed exclusion of a consequence of divorce, and it would be unreasonable for the burdened spouse to accept it. This needs to be so even when appropriate regard is paid to the interests of the other spouse and his trust in the validity of the agreement which has been made, and when the nature of the marriage is rationally assessed. That can in particular be the case if the formulation of the marital relationships actually agreed deviates fundamentally from the original life plan on which the contract is based. A spouse will as a rule not be able to demand post-marriage solidarity here, when he for his part has violated marital solidarity. However, in so far as there is a reasonable settlement of disadvantages related to the marriage, issues of culpability will take second place. Overall, the balancing exercise required must be orientated to the order of rank of the consequences of divorce. The higher the rank of the consequence of divorce which is contractually excluded but is now being claimed, the more weighty must be reasons which—considering the factual style of the marriage which has in the meantime materialised by agreement—argue for its exclusion. If a spouse's appeal to the contractual exclusion of the consequence of divorce does not stand up to judicial control of the exercise of rights, this does not lead, within the framework of § 242 BGB, to the invalidity of the contractually agreed exclusion. Nor does it necessarily lead to the implementation of the consequence of divorce provided for by statute but contractually excluded.

The judge must instead order a legal consequence which takes account in a calibrated manner of the justified interests of both parties in the situation which has now arisen. The more central the legal consequence provided for by statute is to the core area of statute law about the consequences of divorce, the more closely the judge will have orientate himself to that legal consequence.

IV. The disputed decision does not satisfy the above requirements for judicial control over the validity and exercise of agreements relating to maintenance or marriage contracts.

1. The Oberlandesgericht regarded the contract as invalid as a whole because the respondent had renounced maintenance claims under §§ 1571 to 1576 BGB to accretion and pension settlements, and an unreasonable one-sided regime to her disadvantage had therefore been made. The fact that the parties had allowed the care maintenance under § 1570 BGB to stand changed nothing in this assessment as this

was only a question of the minimum maintenance which was in any case to be left to a parent bringing up a child, in the interests of children needing care, according to the case law of the Bundesgerichtshof under § 242 BGB. This view of the *Oberlandesgericht* is not supported by the factual findings in the disputed judgment. Such invalidity could, as explained, only arise from § 138 (1) BGB—within the framework of an overall consideration of the agreed rules (validity control). The prerequisites for a violation of good morals are however neither explained nor are they otherwise evident.

(a) The reasons which caused the parties to conclude their agreement are not obvious. In particular it has not been established what motives induced the respondent contractually to renounce part of the rights she has in the case of a possible divorce. The *Oberlandesgericht* assumes the respondent was in a position of inferiority when the contract was concluded, and that the applicant misused this. In the light of the limitation of § 138 (1) BGB to serious violations of the moral order, there is no factual basis for such an evaluation. At the conclusion of the contract, the respondent had already been married to the applicant for more than two years, and was not pregnant again. She had an academic education which she had already used successfully in her career. The interruption of her career which had accompanied the birth of her (first) child was little more than two years behind her. Full economic dependence of the respondent on the applicant of the kind on which the assessment of the *Oberlandesgericht* was based has therefore not been demonstrated. The fact emphasised by the *Oberlandesgericht*, that the respondent in the context of her pregnancy did not, at the applicant's wish, pursue a promotion which she had sought, has no importance for the question of the immorality of her renunciation of the statutory consequences of divorce. That also applies to the applicant's good situation so far as income and assets are concerned, which the *Oberlandesgericht* stresses, but without establishing that it existed at the time when the contract was concluded. In particular, no 'predicament' for the respondent can be derived from the applicant's favourable financial situation which could have caused her to embark on a partial renunciation of the rights which were granted to her by statute law in the case of divorce, and which were especially valuable where income was above average—as the *Oberlandesgericht* explains.

(b) The objective content of the notarised contract made by the parties cannot, according to the findings so far, form the basis of an accusation of violation of good morals either. This is because the direct core area of the statutory consequences of divorce is not affected by the agreement. The parties have not negotiated away the maintenance to the extent that 'a claim to maintenance by the wife for care of the children' is in question. . . .

The parties have admittedly negotiated away important consequences of divorce in respect of maintenance for illness and old age. This could—in connection with the further rules—however form a basis for an accusation of immorality if the parties, in planning their lives at the time that they concluded the contract, had proceeded in agreement on the basis that the respondent should completely withdraw from her working life on a permanent basis, or at least long term, and should devote herself to work for the family. This is because it is only in this case that the respondent would be prevented from building up her own security permanently against the risks of old age or illness, and a constant dependence on the applicant would be formed. But no such agreed life plan has been established. . . .

The exclusion of the duty of maintenance agreed by the parties for the case of unemployment, and the renunciation of top-up maintenance (for the period after caring for the children) and fairness maintenance do not—simply from their significance in the system of the law on the consequences of divorce—justify the verdict of immorality. Nor does any different conclusion arise from the exclusion of statutory property status. 2. In so far as it follows that the agreements made by the parties—even in a subjective respect—withstand judicial validity control by the standard of § 138 (1) BGB, it remains to be examined whether and how far the applicant is prevented by § 242 BGB from appealing to the agreed exclusion of individual consequences of divorce (control of exercise). . . .

The other points of view cited by the *Oberlandesgericht* also cannot support the accusation of misuse of a right. The applicant's particularly high income—at least in the later years—does not need to be shared by the respondent in contradiction of the property status agreement made. This also applies for the assumption (which is not more precisely verified) that the respondent—working all day in her shop business— had enabled the applicant, by her conduct of the household and care of the children, to devote himself fully to his career activity. The interests of their children are not affected by the co-ordination of the parents' assets. Other circumstances of significance for § 242 BGB are not evident.

V. The disputed decision cannot after all stand. The senate cannot make a final decision on the basis of the findings made by the *Oberlandesgericht* in the case. The case therefore had to be referred back to the *Oberlandesgericht* so that it could finish making the findings necessary for the required control of validity and exercise. . . .

Chapter 6

Case 84
BUNDESARBEITSGERICHT (SECOND SENATE) 27 NOVEMBER 2003
NZA 2004, 597 = DB 2004, 1208

Facts

The parties are in dispute about the validity of a notice of termination of appropriate length and a 'declaration renouncing the claim to notice protection' signed by the claimant, and about a dissolution application made by her. The claimant had worked for the defendant as a cleaner since e 14 April1995. She was finally employed in the DRK (German Red Cross) care home B. Her tasks included, among other things, the cleaning of the guest room and the outer surface of the nurses' cupboards. On 30 March 2002 another worker at the DRK noticed how the claimant was standing in front of a nurses' cupboard which she had opened. The further details are disputed between the parties. On 3 April 2002, a conversation took place between the claimant, the manager of the establishment and the defendant's attorney, after DRK had refused further co-operation with the claimant. The claimant was accused of attempted theft. Another DRK worker had seen how the claimant had held that worker's handbag and opened it. In the course of the conversation, the defendant threatened the claimant with an extraordinary notice of termination, and stated that the employment relationship could also be terminated by agreement by a notice of appropriate length. The claimant consented to this. The defendant gave the claimant written notice on 3 April 2002, by which the claimant's employment relationship was terminated by a notice of appropriate length on 31 May 2002. After this the claimant signed the 'declaration renouncing the claim to notice protection,' formulated and signed by the director, which says: 'The employee declares: I, BF, received on 3 April 2002 the appropriate period of notice terminating my employment on 31 May 2002. I raise no objections against the business related termination of my employment, and will not, on whatever grounds, avail myself of my right to claim continued existence of my employment, or pursue a claim raised with this objective. The contents of the declaration were known, approved and signed by us'. The claimant has disputed the notice of termination by her claim which reached the *Arbeitsgericht* (labour court) on 24 April 2002, and which seeks the dissolution of her employment in return for a compromise payment. She has avoided her signed declaration under § 123 BGB, in particular for the impermissible threat of an extraordinary notice, and the failure to grant an appropriate period for reflection. . . . Besides this, she revoked her declaration under § 312 of the BGB, new version. As an employee, she was a consumer. The typical situation of a doorstep transaction was present. The agreement was concluded at her workplace, and she had not been advised about the legal consequences of the renunciation declaration, nor about a possible right of revocation. . . .

The *Arbeitsgericht* rejected the claim. The *Landesarbeitsgericht* (state labour court) rejected the claimant's appeal. The claimant is pursuing her claim by her appeal in law, which has been admitted by the *Landesarbeitsgericht*. The appeal was unsuccessful.

Reasons

The employment relationship of the parties has been ended with legal effect by the termination agreement of 3 April 2002–31 May 2002. The claimant's application for dissolution is therefore pointless.

A. . . .

B. . . .

I. The claimant has not effectively avoided the termination agreement.

1. The claimant could not effectively avoid her declaration under § 119 (1) of the BGB on the ground of lack of consciousness of making a declaration, or of a mistake about the contents of the declaration based on 'absence' of glasses. This claim has not been pursued by her anyway, and is not included in the appeal in law. This is because she has not declared the possible avoidance without delay in the sense of § 121 (1) BGB. The avoidance declared by the statement of claim of the 24 April 2002 only occurred after three weeks had elapsed, and therefore not without delay in the sense of the norm mentioned.

2. The claimant has also not effectively avoided her declaration under § 123 (1) BGB.

(a) According to § 123 (1) BGB, a person who has been induced unlawfully by threat to give a declaration of will can avoid the declaration with the consequence that it becomes invalid under § 142 (1) BGB. A threat in the sense of this norm assumes objectively the intimation of a future evil, the infliction of which is in some way represented as dependent on the power of the person making the intimation. An employer's threat to end the employment by an extraordinary notice of termination, if the employee is not prepared to accept an ordinary notice and to renounce the right to raise a claim to notice protection, represents the intimation of a future significant evil, the realisation of which lies within the power of the employer making the intimation [consistent case law of the senate, references omitted]. The threat of an extraordinary notice is unlawful if a sensible employee could not take such a notice seriously into consideration. The threat of the notice can, as a rule, only be unlawful because of the mismatch of method and purpose. If the person making the threat has no justified interest in the attainment of the goal pursued (acceptance of a notice of termination of appropriate length by the employee or giving up the right to testing by the court) or if the threat should not be regarded as an appropriate method for the attainment of this goal according to the principle of good faith, the threat is unlawful [references omitted]. It is not necessary that the threatened notice of termination, if given, would have been found valid in notice protection proceedings [references omitted].

(b) In this connection it cannot be generally expected of a sensible employer that, in his consideration of the matter, he should 'guess' the assessment of the court of fact. The only case in which the employer cannot contemplate giving an extraordinary notice declaration (as a means of inducing the employee to give in and accept a notice of termination of appropriate length—giving up the right to a claim for notice protection— or to conclude a termination agreement) is if he would have to assume, considering all the circumstances of the individual case, that the threatened notice, if it was given, would very probably not stand up to testing by an *Arbeitsgericht* [references omitted].

(c) The disputed judgment stands up to this limited standard of testing. The defendant's threat of an extraordinary notice to terminate the claimant's employment was not unlawful. According to the deliberations of the *Landesarbeitsgericht*, which are correct, a sensible employer in the defendant's situation might consider giving an extraordinary notice. On the basis of the incident on 30 March 2002, there was a suspicion, based on facts, that the claimant had substantially violated her contractual duties. These facts were the co-workers' cupboard door, which had indisputably been opened, the claimant's admission that she had opened the cupboard door out of curiosity, the opening of someone else's handbag asserted by a witness, and the DRK's wish for the claimant's recall. . . .

II. The claimant has not effectively revoked the termination agreement of 3 April 2002 under §§ 312 (1), 355 BGB (new version). The statutory prerequisites are not fulfilled.

1. Under § 355 (1) sentence 1 BGB (new version) a consumer is no longer bound by a declaration of will aimed at the conclusion of the contract if a right of revocation has been granted to him by statute law, and he has revoked his declaration of will in time. § 312 (1) sentence 1 no 1 BGB (new version) grants a right of revocation to the consumer under § 355 BGB (new version) in the case of a contract between an undertaking and a consumer which has as its subject matter a performance in return for payment, and the consumer has been induced to conclude it by oral negotiations at his workplace (door step transaction).

2. . . .

3. The claimant does not however have a right of revocation under §§ 312 (1), 355 BGB (new version). The termination agreement of 3 April 2002 is not a doorstep transaction in the sense of § 312 (1) sentence 1 no 1 BGB (new version).

(a) It can remain undecided whether the claimant is a consumer in the sense of § 312 (1) in combination with § 13 BGB [new version, references omitted]. It can also be left undecided whether a termination agreement has as its subject matter a performance in return for payment in the sense of the norm at all—or whether this is only so when a compromise payment or something similar is made—or whether it is a question of a disposition transaction not encompassed by the norm (confirming a performance in return for payment—referring to the 'actus contrarius' [references omitted]; denying it [references omitted]).

(b) In any case, the parties' termination agreement is not a doorstep transaction. It is true that the agreement was concluded 'at the workplace' in the sense of the norm, and the wording of § 312 (1) sentence 1 no 1 BGB (new version) appears therefore at first sight to include a termination agreement concluded on the employer's business premises [references omitted]. The concept of the workplace in the sense of this norm is generally widely understood, and encompasses the whole of the business area, including the staff section [references omitted]. But a different result follows—as the *Landesarbeitsgericht* has correctly recognised—from the structure of the statute, its sense and purpose and the history of its origin.

(aa) It contradicts the structure of statute law to apply § 312 BGB (new version) to employment termination agreements. The doorstep right of revocation under §§ 312 ff BGB (new version) is a consumer protection right which is related to the type of contract [references omitted]. It only includes 'special forms of sale.' The statutory right of revocation has no application to contracts which are not sale transactions—like employment contracts, and cancellation contracts in employment law [references omitted].

(1) § 312 BGB (new version) is part of the second book of the BGB, third section, first title, second sub-title. The second sub-title is headed 'Special forms of sale.' Besides doorstep transactions, distance sale contracts and electronic transactions—and therefore special forms of sale—are brought together and regulated in this sub-title. However, neither employment contracts nor employment termination contracts fall within the forms of sale mentioned, as the consumer mentioned in the norms must be a recipient of appropriate goods or services [references omitted].

(2) The second sub-title implements the Directive for the protection of consumers for cases of contracts concluded outside business premises. According to Art 1 of Directive 85/577/EC, only those obligations are covered by it which a consumer enters into, within the framework of a doorstep transaction, as against a person carrying on a business, as a counter-performance for goods or services (ECJ 17. 3. 1998, [1998] ECR I-1199 = EuGH NJW 1998, 1295). No grounds can be deduced from the statutory provision for saying that the German legislature, in implementing the Directive, wanted to make a right to revocation available in employment termination contracts above and beyond the sphere of the Directive's application.

(3) Besides this, it follows from § 312 (3) no 2 BGB (new version) that only (certain) *sale* transactions in §§ 312 ff BGB (new version) can be intended, ie when the exercise of the right of revocation is made dependent on a minimum sum of 40 euros.

(4) . . .

(5) Finally there is the fact that a right of revocation for an indefinite period under § 355 (3) sentence 3 BGB (new version) in the absence of proper advice would not be compatible with the general interest in expediting employment termination disputes, as is expressed for instance in §§ 4, 7 KSchG (Notice Protection Act), § 17 TzBfG (Part

Time and Fixed Term Act) [references omitted].

(bb) The history of the origin [of the statutory provision] also argues against applying the statutory right of revocation to employment termination agreements.

(1) . . .

(2) It is recognisable from the statutory materials that only the three special forms of sale were included under the second sub-title: doorstep transactions, distance sale contracts and contracts concluded electronically. The second sub-title is intended first to gather together the material regulated until now in individual statutory provisions to facilitate practical application of the law. Secondly, it was intended to systematise the regulated material in order to avoid contradictions in evaluation. These goals argue unambiguously for regulating merely the special forms of sale known and mentioned so far in §§ 312 ff of the BGB (new version). . . . .

(3) . . .

(cc) Finally the sense and purpose of the regime in § 312 BGB (new version) argue decisively against extending the right of revocation to employment termination agreements. Contrary to the claimant's view, a situation comparable to the doorstep transaction is not in principle present when a termination agreement is concluded on business premises.

(1) §§ 312 ff BGB (new version), serve the protection of the consumer. They are supposed to protect the consumer from the dangers associated with the so-called direct sale. The consumer is to be preserved on the one hand in the preparation and in the conclusion of a transaction from infringement of his freedom of decision in legal transactions, and from a surprise in the conclusion of a transaction in certain situations (BT-Dr 10/2876, p 6f; BGH [26 March 1992], NJW 1992, 1889 [1890]; BGH [25. 10. 1989], BGHZ 109, 127 [133]). But, on the other hand, he should not simply be protected by the right of revocation under § 312 BGB (new version) from unwise legal transactions, or those which are unfavourable to him. This is clear from the fact that, eg, a right of revocation does not exist in respect of transactions at the workplace if the negotiations originate from an initiative on the part of the consumer (§ 312 (3) no 1 BGB (new version)).

(2) A certain type of sale and marketing is common to the doorstep transactions enumerated in § 312 (1) sentence 1 nos 1 to 3 BGB (new version). This makes the statutory second sub-title 'Special forms of sale' clear. It is common to the statutory definitions that the conclusion of the contract takes place outside business premises, ie outside fixed selling and shopping areas, publicly accessible to the consumer [references omitted]. The result of the legal transactions mentioned in § 312 BGB (new version) is based for the supplier essentially on a special situation for concluding the contract, in which it is suggested to the consumer that the offer is a limited one which could only be accepted immediately [references omitted]. Because of this situation the consumer has no opportunity to compare the quality and price of the offer with other offers (BT-Dr 10/2876, p 6). There is insufficient information available for him to make a rational decision. If he does not want to lose the deal, he must contract. § 312 BGB (new version) is accordingly intended to provide the consumer with the opportunity of obtaining comparative information. The intention is thereby to correct the asymmetry of information—in retrospect—by a claim to information and a time limited right of revocation [references omitted]. § 312 BGB (new version) accordingly creates protection for the consumer which is situation related [references omitted]. § 312

(1) sentence 1 BGB (new version) differentiates here according to individual typified situations. While in the case of § 312 (1) sentence 1 no 1 and no 3 BGB (new version) the danger of surprise is the prominent feature, no 2 of § 312 (1) sentence 1 takes account primarily of the fact that the consumer is not in a position to withdraw from the negotiations. For § 312 (1) sentence 1 no 1 BGB (new version) the situation (ie, the location) mentioned in the statutory provision in which preparation for the contract takes place is crucial for creating the effect of surprise. It is only for this typified case that the legislature considers a general protection of customers to be necessary. Therefore a right of revocation for termination agreements under § 312 (1) sentence 1 no 1 BGB (new version) cannot be affirmed by reference to the fact that the employee could only withdraw from contractual negotiations which take place at his workplace with difficulty [references omitted]. If preparation for the contract or conclusion of the contract take place in 'normal' business premises, ie in a place which is typical for the contract, § 312 BGB (new version) does not protect the consumer, not even from superior knowledge or special 'negotiating skills' on the part of the contracting partner.

(3) The employee concluding a termination agreement on business premises therefore does not, as a rule, find himself in a situation encompassed by the protective purpose of § 312 BGB (new version).

The contractual negotiations and the conclusion of the contract do not occur in an atypical place which is alien to the employee and to the legal transaction to be concluded, which is a 'termination agreement in employment law.' The 'workplace' in the sense mentioned is in fact typically the place in which questions relating to the employment relationship are discussed and regulated. Accordingly, there is in principle no surprise element which is typical of the situation. The employee must and will assume 'at his workplace'—in fact in the staff areas—that the employer (or a superior) will discuss questions and problems of his employment with him, and if necessary, regulate them by way of a legal transaction. The workplace is not only the area in which the employment contract commitments come into existence, but also the place in which they are dissolved [references omitted]. For this very reason it is impossible to assume any surprise about the place of negotiations. In fact it would be strange to conduct conversations about the employment relationship and its termination not on the business premises but in a 'neutral place' (lawyer's office or somewhere similar).

(4) Admittedly the employee is sometimes only presented with an offer of cancellation to be accepted 'now, today.' But this cannot generally lead to the statutory revocation rules which typify particular situations being applied en bloc to employment cancellation contracts. §§ 312 ff BGB (new version) assume a double need for protection—related to the type of situation and to the type of contract [references omitted]. Therefore the objection that the consumer would in part be more strongly protected on concluding economically substantially less important contracts than an employee on concluding a cancellation contract, by which, as a rule, the whole basis of his life's existence would be affected [references omitted] leads nowhere. It cannot form the basis of a right of revocation which does not exist in statute law.

(5) . . .

III. The claimant's declaration is also not—as the appeal in law considers it to be— ineffective just because the defendant had given the claimant no time for reflection before signing the termination agreement [references omitted]. In particular the reliance on § 242 BGB (new version) which the claimant claims, is not appropriate according to the case law of the senate to form the basis of such a weighty invasion of private autonomy as granting a right of revocation not statutorily provided for would represent, especially as the claimant had not even claimed to have sought for an appropriate period for reflection. . . .

IV. Contrary to the view of the appeal in law, the termination agreement by the parties of 3 April 2002 is not ineffective because of an inappropriate disadvantage to the claimant under §§ 307, 310 (4) BGB (new version) either. The agreement is not subject to control of content under § 307 (2) BGB in combination with § 310 (3) BGB (new version).

. . .

V. As the employment relationship has been effectively ended on the basis of the termination agreement by the parties on 31 May 2002, no further testing is needed as to whether the notice of termination on 3 April 2002 is socially justified in the sense of § 1 (2) of the KSchG, and whether the claimant could, if necessary, have effectively dissolved the employment relationship under §§ 9, 10 of the KSchG in return for a compromise payment.

Case 85
LANDGERICHT HANAU (FIRST CIVIL SENATE) 30 JUNE 1978
NJW 1979, 721

Facts

The defendant, the deputy head teacher of a girls secondary modern school, ordered as its agent '25 Gros rolls' of toilet paper from the claimant. The defendant signed an order form filled out by the claimant's representatives on which the designation 'Gros = 12 x 12' appears near other details. When the claimant tried to deliver the goods, the girls school refused acceptance of the predominant part of them. The claimant then claimed against the defendant, and arranged for a demand for payment to be delivered to her, which she contested. Besides this, she avoided the legal transaction. She disputes having had knowledge of the meaning of the quantitative designation 'Gros'. She claims merely to have ordered 25 double packs of toilet paper, which the school had accepted and paid for. Admittedly the designation 'Gros' had been mentioned in the order. The agents had however described this, in combination with the statement of quantity 12 x 12, as a type of packaging.

The claim to payment for the toilet paper was unsuccessful.

Reasons

The claimant has no claims under § 179 BGB against the defendant. It is true that the school, represented by the defendant, has not approved the majority of the legal transaction. Fulfilment of the contract by the defendant is inapplicable however because the contract has been effectively avoided by the defendant. The defendant in giving her declaration of will was mistaken about the content of her statement (§ 119 (1) BGB). She definitely did not want to buy 25 x 12 x 12 = 3600 rolls of toilet paper, but merely 25 large (große) rolls. The claimant asserts that the defendant would have known precisely what content would have been attributed to her declaration. It is not however possible to assume such a fact. It is completely contradictory to experience that someone, as the agent of a school which can only be described as a small institution, should order at one time 3600 rolls of toilet paper each with 1000 sheets. This is a quantity which would have covered the needs of the establishment for several years. Apart from the fact that this scarcely appears conceivable on the grounds of financial control, which normally takes place annually, storage difficulties alone for such a quantity of goods lead to the assumption that any deliberate action of this kind should be excluded. Nor does the argument that the defendant as a teacher must have been conversant with the meaning of the expression of quantity used inevitably mean she knew it. Apart from the fact that it has not been established which subjects she teaches, the description of quantity 'Gros' is today quite unusual and archaic, so it can no longer be regarded as an unquestionable part of teaching material. Besides this, the information 'Gros = 12 x 12' gives no clarity here, as the number of rolls cannot be conclusively deduced from it. Other units of measurement could quite well be intended, in particular having regard to the spelling mistakes made by the claimant's agents on the order form.

Case 86
BUNDESGERICHTSHOF (NINTH CIVIL SENATE) 27 OCTOBER 1994
BGH NJW 1995, 190

Facts

The claimant bank is claiming against the defendant, an Iranian woman, on the basis of a guarantee. The defendant visited her father Dr M in N on a number of occasions since 1980. He came from Iran and has acquired German citizenship In August 1980, the defendant opened a savings account with the claimant, which had a business relationship with Dr M On 8 March 1985, Dr M and his wife bought a house for DM800,000. The purchase price was to be financed by the claimant. On 5 March 1985 the defendant, who was accompanied by Dr M, signed a guarantee form worded in German, produced by the claimant on its business premises. The claimant did not explain or translate the contents of the form before signature. According to the document, the defendant provided a guarantee which was unconditionally enforceable (ie, the person granting it could not raise the objection that there had not yet been an unsuccessful execution against the main debtor) and without a limit as to time or amount, for all existing and future demands by the claimant arising from its business relationship with Dr M and his wife. On 10 April 1985, the claimant granted the main debtors a loan of DM800,000. The claimant, which has given further credit to the main debtors, claims a remaining total demand of more than DM400,000 under the business relationship

The claimant demands from the defendant the payment of a liability on the part of the main debtors in the sum of DM251,783.91, and submission to an execution arising from a charging order (*Arresthypothek*) for DM255,000 on an owned residence which the defendant acquired in the middle of 1985. The claim was successful at the lower instances. The defendant's counterclaim for an order directing the claimant to approve the cancellation of this charging order was dismissed. The defendant's appeal in law led to quashing of the disputed judgment and reference back.

Reasons

I. The appeal court accepted that there was a legally effective guarantee by the defendant (§§ 765 ff BGB) . . .
II. These deliberations do not stand up to legal examination in all respects.
1. . . .
   (c) Contrary to the doubts expressed in the appeal in law (but not explained in any more detail), the written form of the guarantee declaration, which is necessary according to § 766 BGB, has been observed. The document expresses the guarantor's intention to assume liability for another person's obligation, and describes the creditor, the main debtor and the guaranteed obligation [see BGH NJW 1993, 1261 (1262) = LM H. 7/1993 § 766 BGB no 25 with further references]. The defendant has disregarded the warning function of written form: she signed the document without finding out its content and realising the significance of the step she was taking.
2. The appeal in law is however successful in its objection to the appeal court denying any right by the defendant to avoid her contractual declaration on the ground of mistake about its content, and thereby to remove the legal efficacy of the guarantee contract retrospectively (§§ 119 (1), 121, 142 (1), 143 (1) BGB).
   (a) Contrary to the view of the appeal court, the defendant has demonstrated conclusively and without possibility of contradiction that, when she gave her declaration of will, she had been mistaken about its content (§ 119 (1) case 1 BGB). Her last assertion, that she assumed at that time—on the basis of a corresponding communication by the main debtor—that it was a question of a formal signature in respect of her investment with the claimant (a savings account), is decisive. She states that she did not know at this point in time that the main debtors had bought a house seven days previously, and that the claimant was to finance the purchase price. Admittedly it had originally been submitted on behalf of the defendant that she knew that she was to guarantee the financing of the main debtors' purchase price debt on the house purchase. But the defendant dropped this submission before the oral hearing, because according to her statement—until now unrefuted—it did not originate from her, but was based on allegations by the main debtor to her attorney. Her case is accordingly not contradictory in this respect (see § 138 (1) of the ZPO (Civil Procedure Code)). If her submission is correct, the defendant was mistaken about the content of her declaration. Even the person who has signed a document without reading it can avoid if he has formed a certain, although incorrect, concept of its content (BGH BB 1956, 254; BAG NJW 1971, 639 (640)). If the defendant assumed that by her signature she was approving a factual event in relation to her savings account, she did not know that she was giving a declaration in respect of a legal transaction. Or if the defendant assumed that by her signature she was undertaking a legal transaction in relation to her savings account, then she did not know that she was entering into a guarantee liability. In both cases the defendant, without perceiving it, expressed something different from what she had in reality intended to declare; she was mistaken about the meaning that her declaration acquired in the sphere of legal transactions (see BGH, LM § 119 BGB no 21).

(b) This mistake was a causal factor in relation to the signature of the document, according to the defendant's further submissions (§ 119 (1) of the BGB; see BGH NJW 1988, 2597 = LM § 119 BGB no 29 = BGHRBGBB § 119—Causality 1). The defendant has asserted that she would not have signed a guarantee obligation if she had known the true state of affairs. This amounts to claiming that this is how she would have behaved on a rational assessment of the case. Admittedly the defendant, according to her submission, felt under an obligation of gratitude to the main debtor, because he had arranged a pain relieving back operation for her. But for the defendant to be responsible for the main debtors' obligations to the sum of DM800,00 for the house purchase, and beyond this for their further debts arising from the financed acquisition of three owned residences, was out of proportion to such a debt of gratitude.

(c) The appeal court has left open whether the defendant has avoided her contractual declaration without delay in accordance with § 121 BGB. According to the defendant's submission, that cannot be ruled out. The declaration of avoidance in the lawyer's statement of 3 July 1991, which was delivered to the claimant on 12 July 1991, could not succeed on the basis of the reasoning given in it that the defendant had known when signing the guarantee document that she was to guarantee the credit to be used to pay the purchase price for the main debtors' house; she had, as a result of lack of knowledge of the language, not known that she was giving a guarantee declaration by her signature. If this submission is correct, the defendant would not have been mistaken in the legal sense, as her intention and her declaration would have been in agreement. On the other hand the defendant's assertion, made for the first time in the statement of 16 September 1991, that she had not known when signing the document that she was giving a guarantee for the main debtors, is legally significant. She had assumed instead that her signature concerned her investment with the claimant. It can be left undecided whether the defendant, as the reply to the appeal in law claims, has by this submission put in a new ground for avoidance in an impermissible manner (see on this BGH NJW 1966, 39 = LM § 143 BGB no 4). The defendant has at least, by claiming a different ground of avoidance in place of the original one, made a new declaration of avoidance. The question of whether this is in time is to be assessed according to the point in time at which it was given (see BGH NJW 1966, 39 = LM § 143 BGB no 4; NJW-RR 1993, 948). The appeal court will have to test whether the declaration of avoidance in the statement of 16 September 1991, which was forwarded to the claimant by the court on the same day, occurred without culpable delay (see BGH WM 1962, 511 (513)). This cannot be ruled out, according to the defendant's submission, in the special circumstances of the present case. The defendant acquired knowledge of the grounds of avoidance at the earliest when her attorney learnt about the basis of the claim by seeing the court documents. This occurred at the beginning of July 1991. According to her submission, the defendant discussed the factual and legal position at the beginning of September 1991 with her attorney.

(d) . . .

3. . . .

4. As a guarantee obligation on the part of the defendant is not established, she could not be ordered to submit to the execution on the basis of the charging order (§ 932 of the ZPO, §§ 1147, 1184 BGB). On the same ground, the appeal court could not reject the defendant's counterclaim that the claimant should be ordered to co-operate in the cancellation of this charging order.

Case 87
BUNDESGERICHTSHOF (FIRST CIVIL SENATE) 28 FEBRUARY 2002
BGH NJW 2002, 2312

Facts

The parties are in dispute about whether a remuneration agreement made between them includes VAT. In 1993, the parties and the B newspaper made an agreement about the production and sale of a video film. According to this, the net income from the sale of the film, which was to be marketed by the B newspaper, was to be divided between the three partners in equal shares. The question of the claimant's VAT responsibilities was neither addressed in the agreement nor otherwise between the parties. The claimant has had a total of DM71,030.57 paid out to it by the defendant for the period from December 1993 to October 1995 on the basis of the agreement. He was therefore called on to discharge VAT, for which the tax rate was, in response to his objection, reduced from the original rate of 15 per cent to 7 per cent. The claimant now demands reimbursement by the defendant of the sum arising from this of DM4972.14 by his claim which was partially withdrawn at first instance after reduction of the tax rate. He claims that the defendant had assumed, just as he himself had, that he was not subject to VAT. The defendant has contested this. She has in particular disputed being under a mistake about the claimant's VAT liability.

The appeal court has allowed the claim which had been rejected by the *Landgericht*. The defendant's appeal in law, which has been admitted, is directed against this decision. It led to rejection of the claimant's appeal against refusal of the claim by the Landgericht.

Reasons

I. The appeal court considered the defendant to be contractually bound to reimburse the VAT to the claimant. . . .
II. The challenges in the defendant's appeal in law directed against this judgment are successful. The appeal leads to quashing of the decision challenged, and restoration of the judgment of the *Landgericht* rejecting the claim. The claimant is not entitled to the claim made in this action from any legal point of view.
1. According to the case law of the *Bundesgerichtshof*, the agreed price for a performance also in principle settles the expenditure for the purposes of the VAT to be paid by the person making the performance. The settlement of the expenditure is a dependent component of the payment to be made ['gross price'; references omitted]. . . . Different considerations apply if the parties have agreed a 'net price', for which a trade usage or custom (*Verkehrsitte*) can be determinative [references omitted]. The claimant has not however claimed any circumstances which could justify a corresponding contractual interpretation in this case. Nor has the appeal court established such circumstances. The claimant has instead relied on an identical mistake by both parties in relation to the duty to pay VAT on the shares of the proceeds paid out by the defendant to him (see on this presently at 2). The appeal court has among other things explained in the reasons for its decision (no I 4) that the question of the (claimant's) duty to pay turnover tax had indisputably not been asked in the first place.

2. The question of who has to bear the VAT which has actually arisen can admittedly be susceptible to a supplementive contractual interpretation, if nothing can be deduced from the wording of the contract in this respect—as in this case. It is a prerequisite for this however that the parties assumed by way of identical mistake that a turnover effected between them is not subject to the duty to pay VAT [references omitted]. This prerequisite is not fulfilled in this case. . . .

The appeal court has admittedly allowed the claim in its decision, which was issued before the two last quoted judgments of the *Bundesgerichtshof*. But its deliberations, which ultimately only take account of considerations of fairness, allow no doubt about the fact that, on the basis of the claimant's submissions and of the documents to which he referred, it likewise could not convince itself that the defendant as well as the claimant had been mistaken about the obligation to pay VAT on the shares of the proceeds paid out by her to the claimant. The appeal court has therefore assumed from a factual angle, in the same way as the *Landgericht*, a so-called internal or hidden calculation mistake [references omitted]. But a mistake of this kind represents a mere mistake of motive which, as such, is legally insignificant.

It can be left undecided whether a different assessment would ensue if, as the claimant has claimed in the oral proceedings in the appeal in law, both the parties had not thought about the question of the duty to pay VAT. For one thing, the claimant's subsidiary submission, to which he has referred in this connection, is in irreconcilable conflict with his main submission that he was mistaken in relation to the obligation to pay turnover tax on the payments which had been made to him. Furthermore, in the legal action the defendant has always denied being under a misapprehension—even only an unconscious one—in respect of the VAT liability on these payments; and the claimant has not produced proof for his assertion to the contrary.

3. Furthermore, the claim does not appear to be well founded according to the rules about the absence of a foundation for the transaction either (§ 242 BGB). The foundation for the transaction assumes a common conception on the part of the parties to it. This can admittedly also be found if there is a unilateral conception of the foundation of the transaction, and the other party has recognised it and has not objected to it [references omitted]. But it is not possible to assume this merely because one party has revealed his calculation principles to the other party to the transaction [references omitted]. Accordingly, even in such a case, the risk of a defective evaluation in relation to the tax liability on turnover remains with the person making performance and cannot on the basis of good faith be shifted to the other contracting party [references omitted]. Moreover, since in this case, according to the claimant's own (supplementary) submission, the defendant had no ideas about the tax side of the matter, the idea that the purchase price should still be received by the claimant undiminished is ruled out as a foundation of the transaction [references omitted]. Accordingly the claimant has no claim on principle from the legal angle of absence of a foundation for the transaction either. . . .

Case 88
OBERLANDESGERICHT HAMM 8 JANUARY 1993
NJW 1993, 2321

Facts

The claimant's husband concluded a life annuity insurance with the defendant in August 1984. It provided for a yearly premium of DM1454.20 to be paid for seven years. That produced an agreed yearly annuity of DM800 or a capital settlement of DM10797 . The due date was 1 August 1991. In September 1985 the claimant's husband, who had paid two yearly premiums, died. The contract was converted to a non-contributory one in the ensuing period at the claimant's wish. On 30 September 1986 the defendant announced that because of the non-contributory nature of the contract, the minimum annuity had not been reached and that the life annuity insurance was therefore converted, in accordance with the agreed insurance conditions, into a non-contributory endowment insurance. The endowment sum amounted to DM3098 and was due on 1 August 1991. Because of a change in rates, the claimant received, with a covering letter of 14 December 1990, a new insurance certificate dated 31 December 1990 which showed a yearly annuity of DM3099 instead of DM800. According to the defendant, the changes caused by the resetting of the rates were entered into the main frame installation via a special application which showed about 240 data fields in 49 screen pages. On manual input of the individual items of information from the separate contracts, in this case the final lump sum of DM3098 was accidentally entered into the data field for the yearly life annuities. The defendant informed the claimant by a letter of 18 July 1991 that the capital settlement amounted to DM47,433.45 . Actually however the defendant calculates that the capital settlement should only be DM4225.54, and it paid out this sum to the claimant. The claimant claims the remaining sum of DM43,207.91 in the action.

The Landgericht allowed the claim in full. The defendant's appeal, which claims that there had been a declaration mistake and in any event a relevant calculation mistake, is directed against this decision. The defendant's appeal was successful.

Reasons

The claimant is not entitled to the claim made in the action, as the defendant has effectively avoided its declaration of will, which led to the conclusion of the contract, in accordance with § 119 (1) alternative 2 of the BGB.
1. The defendant by its letter of 14 December 1990 submitted a contractual offer which in accordance with the enclosed insurance certificate involved a yearly life annuity of DM3099. However, the defendant did not intend to submit a declaration with these contents.

(a) According to the defendant's version of events, which the senate is following in accordance with § 286 of the Civil Proceedings Order (ZPO), on the manual input of the data and the entries into the main frame installation, the amount of the endowment sum was accidentally entered into the space for the yearly annuity. On the basis of these data, the insurance certificate was then drawn up Such a mistake cannot be assessed any differently from the case where the person responsible types something incorrectly when drawing up the insurance certificate. Such a mistake is subject to the rules about declaration mistake [references omitted].

Contrary to the claimant's view, the mistake does not relate to action merely preparatory to a declaration of will which is then individually drawn up It is true that the insurance certificate has been separately drawn up in accordance with the previously altered data. But the mistake in the input of data did not only continue to have an effect in the drawing up of the insurance certificate, but went into this document unaltered. The incorrect annual life annuity was reproduced in the insurance certificate in the sum of DM3099 unchanged. The case is not therefore different from when the declarant writes his offer incorrectly or makes a typing mistake. But that would be a declaration mistake [reference omitted]. It is therefore not a case here of an internal calculation mistake in which the declarant works internally with incorrect data and then submits a contractual offer based on it in error, which does not however repeat these defective calculation data.

The decisive factors for the assessment of a mistake are the ideas and intentions of the person acting in the last 'human decision'. This took place when the manual entries into the approximately 240 data fields were made. The person responsible made a mistake—he recorded something incorrectly—which then had an effect on the factually incorrect communication without further human involvement.

(b) If the declaration of will leading to conclusion of the contract is therefore effectively avoided, there is no claim by the claimant because there is no contract. The defendant's letter of 18 July 1991 does not on the other hand form the basis of any claim by the claimant and in particular it does not amount to an acknowledgement. It is merely concerned with the notification of the level and due date of the capital settlement.

This letter is not confirmation of the legal transaction avoided (§ 144 (1) BGB). That would assume that it could be deduced from the letter that the sender wanted to adhere to the legal transaction in spite of its voidability [reference omitted]. That is not the case here. This letter is recognisably based on the insurance certificate of 31 December 1990. There is no evidence to indicate that the defendant would already have recognised the incorrectness of the annuity sum which was stated at too high a figure.

2. As in the present case a declaration mistake is present, it can remain open whether on a different legal assessment the same result would have had to be reached because of an extended mistake as to content, because of § 119 (2) BGB or because of § 242 BGB [reference omitted].

Case 89
BUNDESGERICHTSHOF (EIGHTH CIVIL SENATE) 8 JUNE 1988
BGH NJW 1988, 2597

Facts

The claimant demands from the defendant primarily delivery of the oil painting 'Portrait of a young man' by a claim submitted in July 1985. On 19 March 1984, the claimant sold the picture belonging to him to the defendant for the price of DM6000.

A receipt on the same day contains a declaration by the claimant that the 'Oil paint-ing, Man's head by Frank Duveneck' had been examined by Dr S and reported as a definite original by Frank Duveneck. The picture was given to the defendant, and the purchase price paid. The defendant had the painting investigated by the curator Dr R in August 1984, who attributed it to the painter Wilhelm Leibl. The defendant trans-ferred the picture, according to his account, on 2 August 1984 together with a number of other *objets d'arte* and antiques to a gallery A-GmbH at a total price of DM6,220,000. DM25,000 of this was allotted to the painting which was the subject of the dispute, which was described in a 'list for the purchase contract of 2 August 1984' as 'attributed to Frank Duveneck (1848–1919) (Wilhelm Leibl or Leibl's circle).' On 19 June 1985, the claimant discovered the picture in an exhibition on Wilhelm Leibl and his artist's circle at the City Gallery R. It was exhibited there as a work by Wilhelm Leibl. The claimant avoided the purchase contract and the transfer declara-tion of 19 March 1984 for mistake, by a lawyer's letter of 26 June 1985. By this letter he also demanded return of the picture with simultaneously repayment of the DM6000 paid. The defendant refused this.

The claim for handing over was allowed at the previous instances. The defendant's appeal in law led to quashing and reference back.

Reasons

I. The appeal court has explained: . . .
II. These observations of the appeal court do not stand up to the challenges by the appeal in law in all respects.
1. The appeal in law is certainly incorrect in objecting to the appeal court's opinion that the claimant had effectively avoided the purchase contract.

(a) The claimant's right to avoidance is not excluded, as the appeal in law consid-ers it to be, by the provisions of §§ 459 ff BGB [now § 437 BGB].

(aa) Admittedly, according to the case law of the *Bundesgerichtshof*, the guarantee provisions under the law of sale exclude avoidance by the purchaser for mistake about such characteristics of the item sold as can be the basis of guarantee claims [references omitted]. On the other hand, there can be no question of a 'competition' between claims relating to defects and a right of avoidance by the seller in accordance with § 119 (2) BGB, because the seller never has any guarantee rights [references omitted]. Contrary to a minority opinion [references omitted], this does not however mean that the seller could always make use of a right of avoidance under § 119 (2) BGB. If that were so, the seller who erroneously assumes the thing to be free from defects, could by avoidance for mistake free himself from his duty of guarantee, by accepting the duty to compensate under § 122 BGB which is directed at the negative interest. It should instead be assumed, along with the view overwhelmingly held in the academic litera-ture, that the seller is prevented, in accordance with the concept of abuse of rights, from making use of the right of avoidance, if the consequence would be that he would evade statutorily prescribed attributions, ie his duty of guarantee [references omitted].

(bb) It follows from this that the claimant's right of avoidance is not excluded in the present case. This is because the defendant has no intention of seeking the legal consequences of a guarantee claim which would be capable of being prevented by avoidance.

(i) The appeal court has established as a judge of fact that the painting originates not from Duveneck but from Leibl. This is not disputed by the appeal in law, and does not reveal any legal errors. Where there is a purchase of specific goods, as here, the fact that the picture, contrary to the content of the contract, does not originate from the painter Duveneck does not lead to the assumption of a false delivery, but represents a defect in the sense of § 459 (1) BGB [see now § 434 BGB] [references omitted]. Nothing is changed here, according to the view of the Reichsgericht (RGZ 135, 339 (342 f)) by the fact that the 'Leibl' is—as the claimant asserts—worth substantially more than a 'Duveneck' would have been. If the defendant therefore had a claim to rescission, that would not prevent the claimant from avoiding. This is because the defendant is not in agreement with the dismantling of the purchase contract, which is a pre-action issue for him offered by the main application in the action and would also be the legal consequence of a rescission (§§ 467, 346 ff [323] BGB). The seller's prevention of something cannot be contrary to good faith if the buyer does not want it. . . .

(cc) It is true that the view is held in the academic literature that the seller only has a right of avoidance in accordance with § 119 (2) BGB in the case of delivery of a thing which is better than that which is the subject of the obligation [references omitted], or in the case of a special subjective interest on the part of the seller in the subject matter [references omitted].

(i) . . .

(ii) The question does not however need a conclusive decision. This is because the claimant is not prevented from avoiding, even if the value relationship asserted by the defendant existed. The view set out above (at cc) is admittedly suitable as a rule of thumb for the normal case—because it is then, when the thing, as a result of its 'being different,' is of no more value than if it had the characteristic presupposed by the contract, that the seller will, by avoiding, only as a rule be pursuing the purpose of releasing himself from the buyer's guarantee claims. But the view needs limiting in cases like the present one, where this result excludes the seller's avoidance (see on this II 1 (a) (bb) above). The only thing which can in the end be decisive is whether the seller has delivered a thing with different characteristics than were presupposed in the contract. It cannot—subject to the limits of the prohibition on abuse of rights—be crucial whether the performance produced is of a value higher than or equal to the contractually assumed one. There is no evident reason why, over and above this, the seller's statutory right of avoidance under § 119 (2) BGB should be denied to him.

(dd) . . .

(ee) Finally it can be left undecided whether the claimant, had he recognised the authorship of the picture, would still have sold it—but merely at the higher price corresponding to a work by Leibl. Whether the buyer should be given the right to contradict avoidance by the seller in accordance with § 242 BGB and to offer to pay the increase in price [references omitted] does not need any decision, because the defendant claims no such right and has not stated that he wants to pay the real value of the picture.

(d) The prerequisites of a mistake about a characteristic in accordance with § 119 (2) BGB are present.

(aa) The authorship of the painting is a characteristic which is significant in human affairs (*verkehrswesentlich*) [references omitted]. The fact that a picture by Duveneck can, according to the defendant's submission, be worth as much as a picture by Leibl changes nothing here. . . .

(bb) The appeal in law is incorrect in claiming that the claimant's right to avoid was excluded because he had suffered no disadvantage economically by the avoided declaration [references omitted]. It is true that this applies for the usual case [references omitted], and serves as a criterion [references omitted] for the boundary between a significant mistake and mere 'obstinacy, subjective moods and foolish views' (RGZ 62, 201 (206)) where 'on a sensible assessment of the case' (§ 119 (1) BGB) the mistake had no influence on the giving of the declaration. In sales of *objets d'arte* however it is not only the economic value which is crucial. The appeal court has said in this connection that in Munich a picture by Leibl acquires a greater esteem—and this means *publicly*: for the claimant as well, as his actions and the witness statement by his wife demonstrate—than a painting by Duveneck, even independently of the pure financial value. This cannot be objected to as legally incorrect.

2. Following all this, the defendant was in principle under an obligation, after effective avoidance of the purchase contract by the claimant, to give back the picture which he had acquired from him (§ 812 (1) BGB). . . .

3. . . .

Case 90
BUNDESARBEITSGERICHT (SECOND SENATE) 6 FEBRUARY 2001
BAG NZA 2003, 848

Facts

The parties are in dispute about an avoidance of an employment contract declared by the defendant for deceit about an existing pregnancy. The parties concluded an employment contract of indefinite length on 3 May 2000, which provided for the employment of the claimant as a worker in a laundry. Under the contract, the claimant was to perform all the usual work of a laundry assistant. Under § 8 of the contract it says, among other things:

§ 8 The employee affirms . . . that there is no pregnancy.

According to the certificate of the claimant's gynaecologist produced by the claimant, it had already been established on 8 June 2000 that the claimant was pregnant. The defendant avoided the employment contract for deceit by a letter of 11 April 2000. . . . The defendant has submitted that it has no work suitable for pregnant women. In such a case, it had to have the right to ask about the existence of a pregnancy, and to avoid the employment contract if the question was incorrectly answered.

The *Arbeitsgericht* (labour court) and the *Landesarbeitsgericht* (state labour court) have decided in favour of the claim. In its appeal in law, the defendant seeks rejection of the claim. The appeal in law was unsuccessful.

Reasons

A. The Landesarbeitsgericht has assumed the following: . . .

B. The senate has followed this in the end result and, in substantial parts, in the reasoning. In so far as the senate has until now held a contrary view, it no longer adheres to it.

I.

1. The employment relationship of the parties still exists. The avoidance for deceit declared by the defendant is ineffective. The question about the pregnancy addressed to the claimant before she was hired violated § 611a (1) sentence 1 BGB. This provision should be interpreted in conformity with European law, to the effect that a question about pregnancy is as a rule impermissible, even if the applicant is applying for a post of indefinite length which she cannot for the time being take up because of the intervention of statutory prohibitions on employment.

2. Only an answer which is contrary to the truth to a question which is put in a permissible manner will give the right to avoidance under § 123 (1) BGB. Such a question assumes a legitimate interest, which is worthy of approval and protection, in the answer. If this is not present, then an answer which is contrary to the truth is not unlawful [reference omitted]. The *Landesarbeitsgericht* has also assumed this and has correctly decided that a question about pregnancy in this case was impermissible, because it violated the statutory prohibition of § 611a BGB.

(a) According to § 611a (1) sentence 1 BGB, the employer may not disadvantage an employee on account of his sex in the formation of an employment relationship.

(b) Admittedly the senate has assumed so far—as the appeal in law correctly claims—that a question about pregnancy was permissible, if a statutory prohibition on employment (§ 4 of the MuSchG (Protection of Mothers Act)) by the employer would have intervened from the start (BAG [1. 7. 1993], NZA 1993, 933 = AP BGB § 123 no 36 = EzA BGB § 123 no 39).

(c) But the senate does not adhere to this view.

(aa) The provisions of § 611a of the BGB are based on the implementation of Directive 76/207/EC (ABl no L 39/40) by the German legislature. A national court must as far as possible orientate the interpretation of the internal law of the state to the wording and purpose of the relevant Directives, in order to attain the goal pursued by them (BAG [2. 4. 1996], BAGE 82, 349 = NZA 1996, 998). This principle follows from the priority of community law over national law. The case law of the ECJ acquires special importance here.

(bb) According to the case law of the ECJ, disadvantage to a pregnant applicant on hiring under an employment relationship of indefinite length is impermissible because of violation of Directive 76/207/EC if the applicant can take up her work again after expiry of the statutory protected periods. This applies even if she cannot be employed at the start of the employment relationship because of a statutory prohibition on employment. The disadvantage would in these cases be based on sex.

According to the ECJ's decision of 5 May 1994 (ECR [1994] I-1657 = NZA 1994, 609 = AP EC Directive 76/207 Art 2 no 3—Habermann-Beltermann), Art 2 para 1 in combination with Art 3 para 1, Art 5 para 1 of Directive 76/207/EC excludes avoidance of an employment contract by the employer under § 119 (2) BGB if an employee who is hired for an indefinite period cannot pursue her activity for part of the time because of a prohibition on night working applying during pregnancy and breast-feeding. The ECJ has regarded it as crucial here that it was a question of a contract of indefinite length, and that the prohibition on night working for pregnant women only took effect for a period which as against the total length of the contract was limited. A different way of looking at the matter would, according to the case law of the ECJ, run counter to the protective purpose of the Directive, and would take away its practical effectiveness.

Besides this, Art 2 para 1 in combination with Art 5 para 1 of Directive 76/207/EC excludes the dismissal of a employee who was hired for an indefinite period to stand in for another employee for the time being during her maternity leave, and who cannot guarantee this deputisation because she herself becomes pregnant shortly after being hired (ECJ [14. 7. 1994], ECR [1994] I-3567 = NZA 1994, 783 = AP MuSchG 1968 § 9 no 21—Webb). Dismissal cannot, according to the case law of the ECJ, be based on the woman's incapacity to take up her work (ECR [1994] I-3567; NZA 1994, 783 marginal no 26—Webb). The termination of the contract can also not be justified by the fact that the employee is only temporarily prevented from doing the work for which she had been hired (ECR [1994] I-3567; NZA 1994, 783).

According to the ECJ's decision of 3 February 2000 (ECR [2000] I-549 = NZA 2000, 255 = AP BGB § 611a no 18—Mahlburg), Art 2 paras 1 and 3 of Directive 76/207/EC does not prohibit hiring a pregnant woman for a post of indefinite length just because she cannot be employed in this post from the commencement onwards for the length of her pregnancy due to a statutory prohibition on employment resulting from her condition (see also ECJ [4 October 2001] AP EC Directive 76/207 no 27). In agreement with this established case law of the ECJ, the senate assumes that in the case of (planned) employment relationships of indefinite length, a question about pregnancy as a rule violates Directive 75/207 (see APS/Linck, § 611a BGB marginal no 54; Pfeifer, in: KR 6th edit, § 611a BGB marginal no 33; Kamanabrou, comments on ECJ [4. 10. 2001], NZA 2001, 1241 = EzA BGB § 611a no 17—Brandt-Nielsen). The decisive factor is that the applicant in the case of an employment relationship of indefinite length, is in a position after expiry of maternity protection to pursue the activity contractually provided for. The transitory hindrance to employment takes second place, taking into account and evaluating the Directive's protective purpose. A particular sex is not an 'indispensable prerequisite' (§ 611a (1) sentence 2 BGB) for the activity to be carried out. This is because after expiry of the protective periods, the woman can perform the agreed work. The long-term equilibrium assumed under an employment contract of indefinite length is not crucially disturbed by the prohibition on employment, which is in any case time limited. The recognisable objective of a question about pregnancy is that the applicant will not be hired if the question is answered in the affirmative, simply because of the pregnancy, and therefore because of sex. It is precisely this which § 611a (1) sentence 1 BGB seeks to prevent.

Case 91

BUNDESGERICHTSHOF (EIGHTH CIVIL SENATE) 6 DECEMBER 1996
BGH NJW-RR 1996, 429

Facts

The claimant sells computer goods through local branches, and provides services. At the end of January 1990, it sold its R base to the first defendant, which was at that time still in the formation stage, but has in the meantime been entered in the trade register. The founding members at that time, the second to fourth defendants, took up a guarantee which was unconditionally enforceable (ie, the person granting it could not raise the objection that there had not yet been an unsuccessful execution against the main debtor) for a part of the purchase price amounting to DM891,200 (plus VAT) in each case. The first defendant paid off the purchase price of DM1,300,968, leaving a residue of DM433,796.56. It refused to make further payments on the ground that it had been deceived by the claimant when concluding the purchase contract. The defendants were ordered by the earlier instances to pay the remainder still outstanding of the purchase price as joint debtors. The appeal in law by the first to fourth defendants led to quashing and reference back.

Reasons

I. The appeal court has in substance explained: . . .
II. These observations do not stand up to examination by the appeal in law in every respect.
1. The appeal court has correctly found that there are no claims by the defendants in guarantee law. Incorrect information about turnovers and profits of the undertaking sold cannot as a rule form the basis of a defect in a thing, nor do they represent a promised characteristic (note that the issue is controversial in relation to the reformed § 434 BGB).
2. The appeal court assumes, without any legal error, in the context of the discussion of fault on conclusion of the contract, that a duty to provide information applies to the seller of an undertaking, if shortly before the conclusion of the contract, more than 40 per cent of the service turnover which was previously normal was lost due to the giving of notices of termination. This corresponds with the case law of the *Bundesgerichtshof*. According to this, there is admittedly no duty on the part of the seller to provide the buyer with information about all the circumstances which are important for him. The decisive factor is instead whether such provision of information might be expected in the individual case, according to good faith and taking into consideration perceptions in human affairs (*Verkehrsanschauung*). In particular information must be given about those circumstances which could frustrate the purpose of the contract, and which therefore are of substantial importance for the other party [references omitted].

In this case, the decline in the level of service contracts by more than 40 per cent within half a year was of substantial importance for the buyer. That follows simply from the fact that a substantial loss of gross yield accompanied it. If the gross yield amounted to about 43 per cent of the turnover, as the parties have agreed, the defendant could, in the case of a turnover of only DM299,000 instead of the assumed DM580,000, merely obtain a gross yield of DM129,000 instead of the expected DM252,000. An annual gross yield of DM252,000 had formed the basis for the determination of the purchase price, as the witness B has stated in accordance with the findings at the previous instance. . . .

Case 92
BUNDESGERICHTSHOF (FIRST CIVIL SENATE) 31 JANUARY 1979
LM § 123 BGB Nr. 52

Facts

The claimants are film companies and are concerned, among other things, with the sale of serialised films to television organisations. The defendant's business is in the area of negotiating licences for American television films and serialised films. From 1965 to 1967, and in 1969, the first claimant and the defendant concluded contracts about the acquisition of television rights in the American serialised films 'Daktari' and 'F'. The licence period for both serialised films was five years, running in each case from the delivery of the dubbing material for each individual episode. The licences permitted three broadcasts in Austria and the Federal Republic in each case. On 16 January 1969, the first claimant and the defendant agreed in two contracts that the licence periods would be lengthened by a further five years for the two serialised films mentioned. At the same time, the defendant was granted a 50 per cent share in the net income which would be obtained in the case of a sale within the second licences, ie on a further sale to a television organisation in the Federal Republic. The first claimant committed itself to account half yearly for the net income acquired. On 17 November 1969, the first claimant and the defendant agreed to settle the defendant's 50 per cent share in the proceeds in these second licences by a lump sum payment of US$10,000. In order to facilitate a sale of the serials beyond 1979, the second claimant acquired from the defendant the rights in both serialised films up until 1 January 1988 by a contract of 10 March 1970. The defendant avoided the 'agreement to extend' the licences for 'deceit and, as a precaution, for mistake as well' on 10 June 1974. This was on the basis of publication in a magazine of the sale of the second licences in the television serials 'Daktari' and 'F' to ZDF at a price of DM 8.3 million. The claimants regard the agreements as legally effective, and are applying for a declaration to this effect.

The *Landgericht* allowed the claim. The defendant's appeal was unsuccessful. . . .

The defendant's appeal in law results in quashing and reference back.

Reasons

According to the appeal court's opinion, the avoidance of the 'licence extensions' declared by the defendant is ineffective. The appeal in law is successful in so far as it is directed against the decision about avoidance for deceit.

1. The *Landgericht* regarded the avoidance of the 'licence extensions' of 10 June 1974 as avoidance of the agreements of 17 November 1969 and 10 March 1970. The appeal court, which has referred to the observations of the *Landgericht* on avoidance, has followed this view, which cannot be objected to on legal grounds.

2. The appeal court has, without violating the law, not allowed the avoidance of these agreements for mistake to take effect on the ground that, at the most, it is a mistake about the appropriateness of the price, which is not for consideration under § 119 BGB. Contrary to the view of the appeal in law, the presence of an actual offer of purchase by ZDF cannot be regarded as a characteristic of the film exploitation rights in question which is significant in human affairs. Admittedly factual and legal

circumstances which influence the usefulness and value of a thing or a right also fall to be considered as characteristics of the thing or right which are significant in human affairs in the sense of § 119 (2) BGB. But they must always be circumstances which characterise the thing or the right itself, and not circumstances which may only exercise an indirect influence on the valuation of the thing or right (RGZ 149, 235 [238]). The mere possibility of economic exploitation by the contracting partner is not a characteristic of significance in human affairs (see BGHZ 16, 54 [57] = NJW 1955, 340), because it does not confer a value characteristic which adheres to the right itself.

3. On the other hand, the appeal court could not consider the avoidance for deceit to be unfounded simply because the claimants had not been obliged to inform to the defendant before the conclusion of the agreements of 17 November 1969 and 10 March 1970 that, at these points in time, actual offers by ZDF to acquire the exploitation rights in the serialised films had already been made. The appeal court was admittedly correct in assuming that deceit by silence can only come into consideration if the claimants had been obliged to provide such information to the defendant. A general duty to inform does not generally exist in individual transactions in which the contracting partners pursue opposing interests. It cannot simply be expected that the better-informed contracting partner will reveal unasked all the facts known to him which can be of significance for the actual contract concluded. Nevertheless the principle of good faith, which also governs the law of purchase, can give rise to a duty on the part of one contracting partner (usually the seller) in the individual case to communicate facts to the other (usually the purchaser) which are obviously of significance for his decision (see BGH NJW 1971, 1795 [1799] with comment by Giesen on commercial purchase; BGH NJW 1970, 653 [655] with comment by Putzo on purchase by undertakings; BGH LM § 123 BGB no 45 on land purchase, all with further references). It is of particular importance here, as is recognised in the case law quoted (see also BGH LM § 276 [Fb] BGB no 1), whether a special relationship of trust existed between the contracting parties, and the less well-informed contracting partner recognisably trusted the specialist knowledge of the other. The appeal court has not sufficiently taken account of these aspects. On the one hand, it established that the parties had been in intensive long-standing business relationships, and besides this in relationships of personal friendliness; and, until the conclusion of the agreements of 17 November 1969, had pursued the exploitation of the serialised films in the common interest. But then, on the other hand, the appeal court considers that, following the conclusion of the agreement of 17 November 1969 only opposing interests had been pursued, so that there had no longer been room for a duty by the claimants to provide information. The appeal court thereby overlooks the fact that the principles quoted have been developed precisely for those cases in which the contracting parties, by concluding the contract, pursue interests which are opposed to each other. The mere fact that the parties pursue opposing interests can therefore not exclude the duty by one contracting party to give information arising from a special situation of trust. A special situation of trust of this kind, leading here to a duty by the claimants to give information, arises from the appeal court findings which have already been quoted, that the parties had been in intensive long-standing business relationships, and besides this in relationships of personal friendliness, and had pursued the exploitation of the serialised films in the common interest on the basis of the participation of both sides in the proceeds, even though this film exploitation was exclusively in the claimants'

hands. The defendant could thus neither influence the exploitation, nor have know-ledge of the exploitation measures or actual offers already received. Whether in this respect it is possible to assume a partnership (*Gesellschaft*) relationship, or a relation-ship, similar to a partnership can be left open. In any case, according to the findings of the appeal court, there was such a close relationship between the parties in respect of the serialised films in dispute here, that the defendant (who, according to the con-tract formulation so far, already had to rely on information from the claimant about the film exploitation) could on conclusion of the agreement of 17 November 1969 place trust in being informed of those essential facts which were obviously of significance for his decision. It was obviously of decisive importance in relation to the conclusion of this agreement (by which the defendant's share in the proceeds of the exploitation—which had so far been 50 per cent—was to be satisfied by a lump sum settlement of US$10,000) that, at this point in time, actual offers by ZDF existed about acquisition of the exploitation rights at a price of 8.3 million DM . . .

The appeal court judgment could not therefore stand. The case had to be referred back for a different hearing and decision. The appeal court will now have to look into the applications for evidence. In this connection, having regard to the fact that, according to the contract formulation, details of the film exploitation which were in the claimant's hands had to remain unknown to the defendant, the appeal court will not be able to place demands which are too excessive on the necessary substantiating of the evidence offered.

Case 93
BUNDESGERICHTSHOF (EIGHTH CIVIL DIVISION) 25 MAY 1977
BGHZ 69, 53

Facts

When in 1961 the construction engineering firm of B was in financial difficulties the defendant came to its rescue financially and by participating in the management. The firm took the new form of a limited partnership consisting of a private company (Gesellschaft mit Beschränkter Hasftung) and of limited partners. The defendant sub-scribed to 51 per cent of the capital contributed by each. In 1962 the defendant wished to dispose of his participation in the limited partnership and made an offer to this effect to the plaintiff. In the course of the negotiations he supplied a consolidated bal-ance sheet which showed a profit of DM10,444 on 31 August 1962, bought the greater part of the defendant's holding for DM1,090,500.

The plaintiff alleged that the defendant had fraudulently alleged, by falsifying the balance sheet sent on 31 August 1961, that the partnership had made a profit, however modest, and was on the way to recovery while in fact it was experiencing serious and ever-increasing losses. He added that he had been forced, *inter alia,* to inject nearly DM8,000,000 of his own. The defendant had assured him—a fact which was uncon-troversial—shortly before the conclusion of the contract that the situation as set out in the balance sheet of 31 August 1961 had not changed. The plaintiff stated that, had he known the true position of the finances and the revenues of the partnership, he would not have participated in it. He claimed DM1,750,000 as part of his damage.

The District Court of Munich dismissed the claim. The Court of Appeal of Munich condemned the defendant to pay DM705,018,32. On appeal by both parties the judgment of the Court of Appeal was quashed and the case referred back for the following reasons.

Reasons

I.

1. According to the Court of Appeal the evidence was insufficient to show that the defendant had fraudulently deceived the plaintiff. It held however that the plaintiff was entitled in principle to damages on the ground of blameworthy conduct in concluding the contract.

2. These conclusions of the Court of Appeal cannot be faulted—as the defendant seeks to argue—at least in the result.

II.

1. As regards the *amount* of damages the Court of Appeal has allowed the claim to an amount of DM705,018,32 only.

2. In coming to this conclusion the Court of Appeal has erred in law.

(a) The Court of Appeal is correct in holding that a person who has suffered damage in consequence of blameworthy conduct in the course of negotiations for a contract is entitled to reliance damages; the upper limit is not set by the value of damages for non-performance but may even exceed it in a particular case [references]. The party which suffered the damages may therefore demand compensation to be restored to the position in which he would have been, but for the blameworthy conduct [references]. The question as to what kind of damage is to be compensated is determined by the criterion [reference] . . . whether the damaging conduct was the cause of the damage in the individual case having regard to the great variety of forms of blameworthiness in concluding a contract [references].

(b) The present situation represents the typical case in which no contract would have come into being without the injurious conduct . . . namely the incorrect information concerning the loss at the time of the conclusion of the contract . . . In these circumstances the damages must be assessed as a rule by reference to the expenses—assuming that the mutual performances had to be returned—the injured party had incurred needlessly in reliance on the information supplied by the injuring party [reference].

(c) The present case is special inasmuch as the buyer now adheres to the contract, as he may, although he would not have entered in the contract of sale, had he know the real position initially. It may be that he regards this course as indicated for economic reasons, or it may be, as is the case here, that at the time when he became aware of the inaccuracy of the seller's information, the enterprise which he had acquired had been integrated into his own choice of businesses to such an extent that to restore the original situation could only have been effected with very great difficulty. In such a case the calculation of damages set out above cannot lead to an appropriate assessment of the damage to be compensated, for the obvious reason that the mutual performances are not being returned . . .

(d) If the damage is to be assessed at all realistically in such a case, the purchaser who adheres to the contract must be treated as if he had succeeded in concluding the contract of sale at a more favourable price in the knowledge of the true facts [reference]. No evidence—hypothetical and factually almost impossible—is required to show that at the time the seller would have agreed to the conclusion of a contract under those conditions. Here, too, the damage consists of the amount representing the excess of the purchase price which the plaintiff paid in the mistaken faith in the accuracy of the defendant's account of the balance sheet . . .

Case 94
BUNDESARBEITSGERICHT (EIGHTH SENATE) 22 OCTOBER 1998
BAG NJW 1999, 2059

Facts

The defendant demands compensation from the claimant. The parties are in dispute about, in particular, whether the claimant has effectively avoided a corresponding acknowledgement of a debt because of an unlawful threat. The defendant is a retail grocery undertaking with numerous branches. The claimant, who was born in 1952, was employed by it from September 1987 to 18 December 1995 as a salesperson and cashier in the K branch. According to a cash till instruction which was contained in the claimant's employment contract, purchases by relatives should not to be deducted. On 18 December 1995, at about 10.10, the deputy marketing manager B observed the claimant serving her husband at the cash till. She immediately informed her superior, the district sales manager S, and informed him that the claimant had not charged her husband for two packets of cigarettes at DM4.85 each and a packet of coffee at DM5.99. The claimant had already deducted items for her husband frequently in the past, and even then the suspicion had arisen that she had only charged for a part of the goods. At 11 o'clock the district sales manager had a conversation with the claimant at the branch, which the parties have reported in different ways. At any rate, Herr S finally put before the claimant the alternatives of either agreeing to a cancellation contract and giving an acknowledgement of debt, or allowing the police to be called. At this point, the claimant said she did not want the police involved, but she wanted in the first instance to confer with her husband. After he had been consulted, he said he would now take his wife away with him. Herr S replied that he could do so, but that the matter would then in his opinion have to be cleared up in another way. The claimant then asked that the police should not be sent for, and gave her husband to understand that she wanted to stay. Shortly afterwards, Herr S sent the claimant's husband off the premises on the ground that he had behaved vociferously and improperly. The claimant then signed the following debt acknowledgement: 'I admit the following facts: In the period from: 1. 7. 1993 to 18. 12. 1995 in the branch: K where I was employed as: cashier I have caused the firm P loss in the sum of DM5750 by not having rung up goods for my husband and my sister at the cash till (1 x DM50 per week). I hereby acknowledge of my own free will that I owe the firm P a sum of DM5750 (in words: five thousand seven hundred and fifty) + 7.25 per cent interest. I undertake also to give to the firm P a notarised acknowledgement of debt for the amount of this loss. If a precise scrutiny should reveal that the amount of loss is higher than the sum acknowledged by me, I undertake to give an additional acknowledgement of debt for the excess sum. On the basis of the facts under consideration I must expect instant dismissal. Repayment of the sum is agreed as follows: The sum will be paid back in 11 instalments of DM480 and one instalment of DM470. Interest at the rate of 7.25 per cent = DM416.88 will be paid in addition with the first instalment. If this agreement is not observed, I must expect court proceedings . . .'

The claimant waited while Herr S tried in vain for about an hour and half to obtain an immediate appointment with a notary for the notarial authentication of the debt acknowledgement. The parties then signed a cancellation contract, by which the employment relationship 'was dissolved with effect from the 18. 12. 1995, with the agreement of both side.' By a lawyer's letter of 22 December 1995, the claimant declared avoidance of the debt acknowledgement and the cancellation contract because of threat. She started a claim on 22 January 1996 for a declaration that the employment relationship was still existing, but later withdrew this claim. . . .

The *Arbeitsgericht* (labour court) and the *Landesarbeitsgericht* (state labour court) allowed the counterclaim. The claimant's appeal in law, which was admitted by the *Landesarbeitsgericht*, was unsuccessful.

Reasons

The defendant has a claim against the claimant for compensation corresponding to the acknowledgement which has been given.
I. The basis of the claim is positive violation of a demand (now §§ 280 (1), 611 BGB).
1. The claimant was obliged as a cashier by her contract of employment to deduct completely the goods which customers placed before her. She was not allowed to let customers have goods without deduction and payment. An intentional violation of this contractual duty gives the defendant a claim to compensation. That also applies to purchases by relatives which the claimant should definitely not have deducted. The loss corresponds to the purchase price for the goods which the defendant lost. It is not a question of whether or not a purchase contract has come into existence, and whether the customer would have bought the goods in a proper manner.
2. . . .
3. . . .
4. The claimant is, on the basis of her debt acknowledgement of 18 December 1995, excluded from making the objection she has raised.
  (a) The *Landesarbeitsgericht*, by merely discussing the question of avoidance, has assumed the existence of a legally effective declaration. This assessment is correct. The claimant has not merely given a declaration of knowledge (*Wissenserklärung*) which is not legally binding (reference omitted). . . .
  (b) The parties have concluded a contract confirming a debt (a so-called declaratory, causal or confirmatory debt acknowledgement). A so-called constitutive (abstract or independent) debt acknowledgement in the sense of § 781 BGB is not however present. The claimant evidently did not in any case intend to acknowledge a debt as existing independently of its basis. It was instead a confirmation of a demand for compensation. The recital of the factual foundations for the demand is the principal argument in favour of this. The parties were pursuing the purpose of determining the actions which inflicted the loss, and the loss itself, in order to establish clarity about these. The purpose could only be to remove doubt about the length of time during which the loss was inflicted, and the weekly level of the loss, and to establish the

total demand in this respect in a binding manner. No doubt could exist for the claimant about this content of the declaration. The defendant also saw it in this way.

(c) The interpretation of the debt acknowledgement therefore shows that, in so far as the claimant now raises objections, the parties reached a binding agreement. The causal debt acknowledgement excludes all objections which were known to the claimant at this point in time, or which she reckoned for [see only BGH NJW 1995, 961 with further references]. The claimant knew that, in the given situation, the frequency of her actions and the respective individual sums needed elucidation and ought to be explained. The debt acknowledgement extends precisely to this (see only Staudinger/Marburger, § 781 marginal nos 11 ff).

(d) The claimant has not effectively avoided the debt acknowledgement. The only ground for avoidance which falls to be considered is unlawful threat under § 123 (1) BGB, which is not present.

(aa) A person who has been induced unlawfully to give a declaration of will by threat can avoid the declaration (§ 123 (1) BGB). Threat is a warning of a future evil which is taken seriously by the other party, and which can be, and is to be brought about by the person making the threat according to his statement and in the other party's view, if the person threatened does not give the expected declaration of will [references omitted]. The claimant has been induced to give a debt acknowledgement by a threat by the district sales manager S. He indisputably warned that the police would be called in, and, at least impliedly (*konkludent*), a criminal charge laid if the claimant did not give the debt acknowledgement. Without this warning the claimant would not have signed the debt acknowledgement.

(bb) A threat is unlawful according to the general view if the means, ie the threatened behaviour, or the purpose, ie the declaration of will extorted, or in any case the combination of both, is unlawful [references omitted].

(cc) In this case the threaten to call in the police for explanation, as well as the threat of laying a criminal charge, was permitted, and therefore not unlawful. The defendant—if its submissions are taken as a basis—had sufficient grounds to accuse the claimant of suspected long-term manipulations. This clearly follows from the claimant's answers in the conversation with the district sales manager on 18 December 1995. The legal order simply provides for the threatened means in appropriate cases. No other conclusion can be drawn on the basis of the allegations in the claim. It is not only the undisputed statements of the deputy marketing manager to the district sales manager on 18 December 1995 which argue in favour of this. The claimant's answers about the content of her conversation with Herr S demonstrate that sufficient suspicion existed that the claimant had committed criminal acts over a long period, and not just on one occasion. The calling in of the police is the appropriate means here. The defendant did not in any sense threaten haphazardly. The claimant also gave no later answer to the effect that she had insisted on the day in question that it was a question of a 'one-off' event, and that she had nevertheless been compelled to give an acknowledgement which went beyond this.

(dd) The goal sought to be attained, ie the giving of the debt acknowledgement, was likewise lawful. A debt acknowledgement is in any case not forbidden, or contrary to good morals, if the recipient of the declaration may assume the existence of the debt. The defendant was allowed to assume here from the circumstances as a whole that the claimant had behaved as in her acknowledgement, and the demand for DM5750 was justified. It was not merely a question of a preliminary suspicion. The statement of claim is insufficiently substantiated in the light of the precise description of the course of events by the defendant. The claimant should have taken a detailed position about the course of the conversation. Her view that an explanatory conversation had not taken place is not comprehensible without more exact explanation. There is also no offer of evidence. Contrary to the assumption in the appeal in law, the level of the loss has not been assessed arbitrarily. It was instead based on the content of the conversation of 18 December 1995 about which the claimant has made no substantiated submissions. The agreed level of loss laid down cannot be objected to in the given circumstances. Doubts do not arise either in respect of the weekly level of loss of DM50, or in respect of the calculation of a lump sum in the context of the long period of infliction of loss. It is not of importance that the defendant had no legal right to the giving of a debt acknowledgement. The existence of a legal right directed towards the result sought after is not a prerequisite for the lawfulness of this result [BGH NJW 1997, 1980 (at II 2b) with further references].

(ee) The combination of means and purpose (the so-called purpose-means relationship) was not inappropriate (*unangemessen*) and therefore does not make the defendant's conduct unlawful. The threat of a criminal charge only served the purpose of causing the claimant to make good the defendant's loss. The defendant was not, for instance, exploiting a crime by the claimant which had become known coincidentally in order to pursue civil law claims of a different kind against her. There was an internal connection between the crime to be prosecuted and the loss to be made good, because the loss arose from the crime. The defendant could consider the compensation sum allowed as accurate. In these cases, employment of the means of threat of a criminal charge for the purpose of settlement of loss in civil law is overwhelmingly regarded as appropriate (*angemessen*) [references omitted]. This should be approved. The person making the threat cannot be denied a justified interest in settlement of the loss. If it is only a question of settlement of the loss arising from the crime, and if no advantage is taken of the debtor, the threat of a criminal charge does not violate the principle of good faith. The fact that the police called in would hardly have been in a position to establish the real loss does not mean that any advantage has been taken here. The objections of the *Landesarbeitsgericht* to this in principle are ineffective. The criminal proceedings are not being instituted in a manner contrary to their function. Police and state prosecution inquiries definitely also serve the interest of the victim of the crime in obtaining a settlement [references omitted]. Thus, for instance, criminal files can be used in the civil proceedings (§§ 273, 432 of the ZPO (Civil Procedure Order)) and suspension of civil proceedings must be considered until the completion of criminal proceedings (§ 149 of the ZPO) or adhesion proceedings (where a civil claim by the victim is added to criminal proceedings) (§§ 403 ff of the StPO (Criminal Procedure Order)). From the point of view of the victim, a criminal prosecution can be made completely superfluous by provision of compensation in civil law. The latter will often be more important to him than the punishment of the perpetrator. The fact that a criminal prosecution can take place independently of a charge by the person making the threat will not as a rule make that person's conduct inappropriate (*unangemessen*). This is because criminal prosecution in practice nevertheless depends on his making a criminal charge. On the other hand, violation of the principle of good faith, which has the consequence of unlawfulness would fall to be considered if the person making the threat expected action of the part of the criminal prosecution organisations anyway. But there are no grounds for saying that in this case. Contrary to the view of the *Landesarbeitsgericht*, the principles about avoidance of a cancellation contract for threat of. an immediate notice of termination [references omitted] should not be transferred to cases of the present kind. Instead it should be determined in both groups of cases what can be assessed as suitable and socially appropriate conduct.

(e) Finally the debt acknowledgement is not void because of violation of good morals (§ 138 BGB). A debt acknowledgement can be contrary to good morals because of the circumstances as a whole at the conclusion of the contract, in particular the content, motive and purpose of the legal transaction. It is partially accepted that the threat of a criminal charge ought not to force the perpetrator into making a precipitate decision. Above all, he ought not to be deprived of any period for consideration if the level of the loss to be made good is first to be fixed by a comparison [references omitted]. In the case of an obligation which far exceeds income and assets, immorality must be considered if additional circumstances attributable to the creditor lead to a intolerable disequilibrium of the contracting parties. Such burdens can in particular arise from the fact that the creditor exploits the debtor's inexperience in business matters, or his emotional predicament, or impermissibly violates his freedom of decision in some other way [BGH NJW 1997, 1980 (at II 3) with further references].

The claimant has admittedly asserted that she was 'put under massive pressure.' But her actual submission as to the facts does not justify the assumption that she had no suitable period for consideration, that there was an intolerable disequilibrium between the parties when the contract was concluded, or that the defendant had impermissibly violated the claimant's freedom of decision. The defendant in particular complied with the claimant's wish to call in her husband for the purpose of a discussion.

II. . . .

Chapter 7

Case 95
REICHSGERICHT (THIRD CIVIL DIVISION) 4 MAY 1915
RGZ 86, 397

Facts

By a contract dated 28/31 October 1913 the defendant gave the plaintiff the option to hire the defendant's circus building for the year from 6 September 1914 to 31 August 1915 and for any of the following four years subject to certain conditions. It was agreed that the tenant would also assume the lessor's obligations towards the catering and cloakroom concessionaries, to arrange for performances or other events on at least 150 days or nights during a year, so as to enable them to exploit their concessions or to pay for each day less M300 to the catering concessionaire and M60 to the cloakroom concessionaire. The plaintiff, by a declaration made in time, exercised the option for the year running from 1 September 1914 to 31 August 1915. He believes, however, that he is not bound by the lease thus created, seeing that which has broken out. He brought an action for a declaration . . . that his withdrawal from the contract was justified.

The Landgericht Berlin and the Kammergericht rejected the claim. On the plaintiff's second appeal the judgment below was confirmed for the following reasons.

Reasons

Since according to the provisions of the present law the judge is not empowered to adjust the relations between the parties to a contract in order to mitigate the hardships of war, the only question is whether the plaintiff has a right to withdraw from the contract for the lease of the defendant's circus building because war has broken out. The answer must be in the negative.

The plaintiff argues in the first place that, as a result of the war he is precluded from the exercise of his contractual right of use for reasons which are not attributable to his person and is therefore relieved from the payment of rent in accordance with the principle expressed in s 552 BGB. This argument fails, apart from other objections, because both courts below have found as a fact that the operation of the circus had not been rendered impossible by war. This finding does not disclose any error of law . . . The assertion of the plaintiff in the pleadings relied on in the second appeal actually disclose only, as the court of appeal assumes, that it is doubtful whether the circus can be run for a profit or that it is impossible to do so. That this conclusion is factually correct follows also from the fact, which the plaintiff now admits, that at present circus performances are being staged in his own circus either by himself or by his brother.

A right to withdraw from a contract because of changed circumstances is . . . not granted generally by the Civil Code and could only be allowed in the present circumstances, if it could be regarded as tacitly agreed [reference]. The court below was right in holding that even by applying the principles of ss 133, 157 most extensively the contract cannot be interpreted to allow the plaintiff to withdraw from it, if he can no longer use the circus building with profit because of the war. Good faith and common practice do not justify in any circumstances that the plaintiff should shift to the defendant the loss which the war has caused to the plaintiff.

Case 96
REICHSGERICHT (THIRD CIVIL DIVISION) 21 SEPTEMBER 1920
RGZ 100, 129

Facts

In 1912 the plaintiff let business premises to the defendant for a period ending on 1 April 1915 in a building in Berlin belonging to the plaintiff. The lease was however extended to the end of March 1920 since the defendant has availed himself of an option to renew the tenancy. Under para 20 of the contract the defendant was entitled to the supply of steam for industrial purposes. The plaintiff considers that he is entitled to demand payments, in addition to that made under para 20 of the contract, for the steam supplied between 6 September 1917 and the end of July 1919 because the market conditions for coal and labour have changed substantially. By way of a subsidiary plea the plaintiff asks for a declaration that the contract for the delivery of steam is invalid or that henceforth he is only bound to supply steam at a reasonable price. The claim was rejected by the Landgericht Berlin and by the Kammergericht. On a second appeal by the plaintiff the judgment of the Kammergericht was reversed for the following reasons.

Reasons

The Court of Appeal was right in rejecting the plaintiff's contention that properly interpreted, the words in para 420 number 6 of the contract 'the prices for industrial steam are as follows' as well as the additional contents of this arrangement disclose a contractual agreement to the effect that a fundamental change in conditions will also result in a change in the price of steam. The relevant observations of the Court of Appeal are mainly of a factual nature and do not disclose any error in law. Nor can objections be raised against the arguments of the Court of Appeal rejecting the attempt of the plaintiff to base his claim on the ground that the obstinate insistence of the defendant on the contract price constituted a violation of good morals (*boni mores*) according to para 138 BGB with the result that the contractual clause concerning the price of steam was void at the present time, thus opening up the possibility of fixing an adequate price for the steam in accordance with paras 632 or 812 BGB. However, the plaintiff's demand appears justified from the point of view of the so-called *clausula rebus sic stantibus*. The Civil Code recognises this principle only in a limited number of special cases, and the *Reichsgericht*, as this Division said recently in a decision of 8 July 1920 [references], has not recognised it as a general principle. On the other hand, the *Reichsgericht* has recognised in a series of decisions of this and other Divisions delivered during the last few years, that the unexpected course and result of the War, leading to a collapse and radical change of economic conditions, may exceptionally have had such an effect on existing contracts as to justify the request of a contracting party for a dissolution of the contractual relationship, if that party cannot any longer be expected for economic reasons to adhere to the contract given the new, completely changed conditions. The principle was and is based on positive law as expressed in para 242 and 325 BGB. If, according to the first of these provisions, good faith governs the debtor's duty to perform as also the creditor's right of performance—his right to performance—then having regard to this aspect, performance of a contract can no longer be owed or demanded if, as a result of a complete change of conditions, the contractual performance has become completely different from that originally contemplated or intended by both parties. And if in para 325 BGB impossibility means not only factual but also economic impossibility the *clausula rebus sic stantibus* features clearly in the Code. In the cases decided earlier, the situation was such that one party to the contract demanded a dissolution of the entire contractual relationship on the ground that the conditions had changed completely. In the present case both parties continue the contract intentionally or have continued it. Now one of them, in the present case the plaintiff, demands an increase in the counter performance while the contract continues. The plaintiff asserts that, from an economic point of view, his own performance has become different from what it was at the time of the conclusion of the contract to such an extent that the substance of the counter-performance, if not changed, would be unbearably disproportionate in economic terms compared with his performance to such a degree as to require a modification of the counter-performance according to good faith. This Division cannot refuse to recognise that the plaintiff's demand is justified, assuming that his assertion is correct. In the decision of 8 July of this year (referred to above), this Division held that in such a case fairness requires a corresponding modification of the contractual performance of the other party [references]. It is true that in its decision of 4 May 1915 [references], reiterated subsequently on 3 July 1917 [reference], this Division stated that the judge cannot adjust relations between the parties in order to mitigate the hardships of war. The first and noblest task of the judge is, however, to satisfy in his decisions the imperative demands of life and to allow himself in this respect to be guided by the experiences of life. The statement (quoted above) of this Division, as this Division believes now, cannot be maintained in its strict generality. It has been superseded by the experience of this Division during the subsequent course of the war, and especially as a result of its unexpected outcome and the ensuing, equally unexpected turbulent changes of all economic conditions. These conditions require imperatively that the judge should intervene in existing contractual relations if otherwise a manifestly unbearable situation would arise which would be an insult to good faith and to every principle of fairness and justice. The foundation in positive law, regarded as desirable and necessary, is provided by the provisions of the Civil Code cited above. If these provisions support even the dissolution of the entire contractual relationship at the request of one of the parties, it appears all the more admissible to modify an individual contractual clause forming part of a contractual relationship which the parties wish to continue, if good faith, fairness and justice so require. Moreover, it may also be possible to rely on the idea that when a contractual performance has become impossible as a result of changed conditions, a gap arises in the contract which the judge must fill in by his own determination, as in the case of other contractual gaps.

In order however to prevent at the outset any misuse of the above mentioned principle, three factors must exist if it is to apply.

First, as has already been said repeatedly, both parties must wish to continue the contractual relationship cases where the continuation is compulsory are not to be considered for this purpose.

Secondly, only very special and quite exceptional transformation and change of circumstances, as it has been brought about by the war, can bring about the result outlined above. The fact alone that a subsequent change in the conditions is not foreseeable and could not be foreseen does not suffice.

Thirdly, in a case such as the present, an adjustment of the interests of both parties must take place. A change cannot only take place in favour of that party which suffers or has suffered as a result of the new conditions if the contract continues. The interests of the other party, whose duty of performance will be increased or altered, will also have to be considered. The whole disadvantage must not be placed on him, with the result that his situation would become unbearable and would offend against fairness and justice. Instead the loss must be fairly apportioned between them. How to make the proper adjustment depends on the experience of the judge and his sensitive appreciation of both sides.

If the present case is considered from this point of view little supports the reasons of the decision by the court below. The plaintiff has pleaded that having regard to the contractual price paid to the defendant for the supply of steam he had to pay an additional sum of M89,000 during the period between 1 September 1917 and the end of July 1919, due to the immense increase in the price of coal etc. In other words he has clearly made a loss of this amount. In this connection it must be noted that the yearly rental for the premises let to the defendant amounted only to M9362. The situation in question is illustrated glaringly by the fact that the Rent Control Officer in Berlin, on 21 February 1920 raised by more than ten times of the contract price the price of the steam to be supplied by the plaintiff to the defendant during the period from 31 March 1920, the end of the contract, until 31 March 1921, the time up to which the Rent Control Officer had extended the lease, which the plaintiff had terminated. In view of this fact and the other clearly apparent conditions, the statement of the Court of Appeal that the plaintiff merely miscalculated when he concluded the contract inasmuch as he did not take the consequences of a war into consideration, does not agree at all with reality. Wrong calculations at the time when the contract was concluded cannot, naturally, constitute a basis for modifying agreed prices. Even if the train of thought of the Court of Appeal were to be followed to this extent, that the plaintiff should perhaps have taken the effects of a possible war into consideration, it is out of the question that the plaintiff, when he concluded the contract in 1912 should have envisaged even remotely, in view of the state of the German Reich at that time, a war of such a size, such an outcome and such consequences, and could have included such a war in his calculations. Nobody in Germany foresaw such an event or could have foreseen it; what happened was beyond any human imagination. The Court of Appeal, therefore, clearly wronged the plaintiff in placing the burden of the consequences of this war on him alone, as against the defendant, on the grounds that the plaintiff did not consider the consequences of a possible war. Obviously the fact that no war clause was included in the contract must not be held against the plaintiff.

In conclusion the following observations must be made. In a decision of the First Division of the Court dated 9 March 1918 [references] the following statement occurs: 'The plaintiff does not wish to be released from the contract but wants instead the contract to continue, though with the changed content in that either the price be raised or that the plaintiff be relieved of the duty to perform until peace is concluded. This result cannot be achieved having regard to the reasons set out here.' Clearly this statement was intended to apply only to the contractual relationship and the situation at that time (1918). There is thus no reason for applying para 137 BGB, all the more so because the First Division in a decision of 18 February 1920 [references] expressed an opinion which, in its general tendency, agrees with the present decision.

Case 97
REICHSGERICHT (SECOND CIVIL DIVISION) 3 FEBRUARY 1922
RGZ 103, 328

Facts

The defendant W and E were partners owning a spinning mill. The defendant terminated the partnership agreement with effect from 31 May 1919 and entered into negotiation with the plaintiff K in order to safeguard his share in the partnership assets. On 21 May 1919 a notarial contract was concluded between the plaintiff and the defendant which contained the following stipulations by the defendant:

1. 'If in the course of a dissolution of a partnership I acquire the land, buildings and other fixtures and appurtenances owned at present by the firm B & W for a price up to 600,000 M, I assign to Mr K the entire complex at the same price at which I acquired it. Between us the account will be settled on the basis of M600,000 so that Mr K must pay me the price at which I acquired the complex and, in addition, half of the sum by which the purchase price exceeds M600,000.

2. If, in agreement with Mr X I acquire the land, buildings and fixtures owned at present by the firm of B & W for a price exceeding M600,000 I assign the entire complex to Mr X for the price of M600,000. In this case Mr K pays the price of M600,000 and promises, in respect of the excess over M600,000, to pay in addition the half share due to Mr B.

3. If Mr B. acquires the land with all fixtures and appurtenances at a price exceeding M600,000 I receive out of the purchase price to be paid by him the share due me up to M600,000; the excess between M600,000 and the highest bid payable to me by Mr B is to be paid to Mr K.'

The agent of the plaintiff promised to pay the price at the time of the conveyance, as to one third in 5 per cent war loans at a price of 98 per cent. The plaintiff was also to take over the existing raw materials at the fixed maximum prices to be assessed at the time of payment. In addition it was provided:

'If Mr K thereby acquires the assets of the firm of B & W he will be prepared to employ Mr W as manager of the factory for a salary to be agreed on later on, to be fixed by a contract of employment. Mr X will regard himself as bound by the contract until 31 December 1919.'

On 12 January 1920 the plaintiff's agent wrote that the plaintiff regarded himself as bound by the agreement beyond 31 December 1919 and that he insisted on his contractual rights. The defendant replied that he regarded the matter as closed. Thereon the plaintiff brought an action for a declaration, *inter alia*, that the contract of 21 May 1919 remained lawfully in existence and that the defendant continued to be bound by it:

The Landgericht, Zwickau rejected the claim but the Oberlandesgericht Dresden allowed it. On a second appeal the case was referred back to the Court of Appeal for the following reasons.

Reasons

. . . The appellant objects rightly that the defence of the so-called *clausula rebus sic stantibus* has not been taken into account sufficiently. The Court of Appeal contented itself with the observation that it would lead to complete lawlessness in the realm of contracts if the defendant were to be accorded the right to rescind the contract because the economic conditions had changed. This fear is unfounded; it is only necessary to delimit the boundaries within which the defence deserves to be noted. The pleadings of the defendant in this respect can be regarded as correct without further proof to the following extent the sum of M600,000 which recurs in clauses 1–3 of the contract was chosen because the price of the factory undertaking was estimated at approximately this sum, with the result that the appropriate price of the defendant's share amounted to 300,000 M.

The Court takes official notice of the depreciation of money which began in the autumn of 1919 and multiplied the price of land, machinery and shares. The plaintiff insisted already in the courts below that according to the contract the defendant was not bound to purchase anything which might cost him more later on: the performance of neither party had become more onerous; only the relative value of the mutual obligations had been altered. However, this argument does not refute the defendant's objection. It is true that the Civil Division of the *Reichsgericht* [references] still held in April 1921 that the offer of sale by the owner of a house, made in 1912 with binding effect until 1922, was valid despite the depreciation of the currency. This decision— which, it should be noted, was criticised by writers [references]—must not be interpreted to mean that a fundamental change of prices of itself, which does not simultaneously render the performance more onerous, never suffices to justify the defence according to para 242 BGB of the disadvantaged party. The decision is formulated entirely with regard to the special circumstances of the particular case, which may have shown speculative features; no general principle was established, nor could it be established. In general, to use the words of Oertmann's *Geschäftsgrundlage* (1921) it is relevant whether the basis of the transaction, understood as the assumption at the time of the conclusion of the transaction by the parties, of the existence of certain determining circumstances, has ceased to exist. This may also happen if the balance of values is disturbed, provided that the continued equivalence of performance and counter performance was assumed. The question as to whether this occurred in the present case must be examined, and it must be done by the Court of Appeal, since in the absence of findings of fact the *Reichsgericht* itself is unable to decide the question. Even if the consideration will suffice normally that a depreciation of money, such as it occurred in 1919, came as a surprise for the world of commerce and could not be foreseen, it must be note that plaintiff's counsel has claimed once more in the course of the second appeal that the contract was of a gambling nature and that each party had accepted the danger of an unfavourable change of values, no matter what its causes may be.

The judgment under appeal must therefore be quashed and the case must be referred back to the Court of Appeal. For the purposes of the renewed proceedings attention must be drawn to the fact that even the Court of Appeal should hold, after a renewed examination of the facts, that the basis of the transaction had ceased to exist, it does not follow necessarily that the defendant is entitled to be released from the contract as a whole.

The first question must be whether or not the plaintiff has already performed a part of his obligation. According to the defendant, the performance of the contract by the execution of the mutual obligations is to take place in the future.

At present no more has happened than the conclusion of the contract itself; only when the partners dissolve the partnership, the plaintiff was to provide the defendant with 300,000 M, and the defendant was to assist the plaintiff to acquire the business or to give to him the excess above M300,000 of the sale price of his share in the partnership This point of view does not tally with the facts as the plaintiff sees them. He contends that on 21 May 1919, when the parties concluded the contract, it was uncertain whether as a result of the dissolution of the partnership, either by a private sale of the business to one or the other of the partners or by public auction, the share of the defendant would reach an adequate price. The fear that it might not be reached had been the motive for the defendant to enter into the contract, which had protected the defendant against this danger. If this is correct, the plaintiff, even if he should adhere definitely to a sum of M300,000 as the upper limit between himself and the defendant, and if as the result of the subsequent depreciation of money, perhaps already since the autumn of 1919, a purchase price of less than M300,000 was not to be envisaged any longer, would certainly have protected the defendant, for a time at least, against a dissipation of his fortune. It cannot be doubted that this is a performance. Regarded from this point of view the obligation of the plaintiff would constitute a continued obligation, which he had performed in part. If the defendant were to be released in consequence of a change of circumstances, he could not be allowed a right to rescind *ex tunc* but only a right to terminate the agreement for the future. He would remain contractually bound to pay an adequate remuneration in return for the performance which he received in fact.

Moreover, even if it should be held that the basis of the transaction had ceased to exist, an attempt must be made to maintain the contract with the necessary modification. This Division does not share the view that the court is empowered to interfere with the content of a transaction by means of a constitutative judgment in cases other than those in which the statute allows it exceptionally. However, before the debtor resiles from the contract or terminates it by notice because a fundamental shift has taken place of the value between performance and counter performance, he must invite the creditor to increase his performance; the debtor is only free, if the creditor refuses. This follows from the provision of para 242 BGB, according to which the consideration of good faith is the principle yardstick of a contractual debtor. A step as serious as that of resiling from a contract of long duration on the occasion of a change of circumstances which occurred independently of the intention of both parties must not take place without giving the other party an opportunity to adapt himself to the new situation. Naturally, no such invitation need be issued, if the other party declares unequivocally that he declines to increase his performance. However, this is not yet established in the present case . . . If the contract should be modified the price would have to be increased corresponding to the present depreciation of money, if a resilation of the defendant is to be avoided. Any increase in the value of the business due to any other reasons (increased demand) would constitute an advantage for the plaintiff and need not be compensated by him.

Case 98
REICHSGERICHT (SIXTH CIVIL DIVISION) 30 NOVEMBER 1922
RGZ 105, 406

Facts

The parties, both German nationals, met in Moscow in 1920. The plaintiff lent the defendant, a former prisoner of war, 30,000 Soviet rubles in return for two promissory notes dated 16 and 17 May 1920, whereby the defendant undertook to pay the plaintiff M5000 and M2500 within two months of his return to Germany. When the plaintiff claimed M7500 the defendant contended and the plaintiff admitted that at the time when the loan was made the equivalent of 30,000 Soviet rubles was only 300 M.

The District Court found that at the time when the loan was made, the parties assumed that a Soviet ruble was equivalent to 25 pf and that neither party was aware at the time that the value of the ruble was much lower. Accordingly it gave judgment for the plaintiff, which was upheld by the Court of Appeal. On further appeal the judgment of the Court of Appeal was quashed for the following reasons.

Reasons

The approach of the Court of Appeal is open to doubt as to whether the defendant may claim to annul his two promissory notes on the ground of mistake . . . had in fact sought to avoid them, his attempt was ineffective in law seeing that according to his own pleadings he had not been in error in respect of the substance of his own declaration and had not intended to make a declaration different from that which he had made; instead his error concerned the value of the Soviet ruble and therefore constituted a motive for his declaration.

The appellant rightly objects that this view cannot be sustained in law . . . The loan was made in Soviet rubles; therefore, according to para 607 s 1 BGB it must as a rule be repaid in the same currency. By a special agreement, embodied in the promissory notes, the defendant undertook however to repay M7500 . In making this agreement . . . the parties assumed that in Germany a Soviet ruble was worth 25 pf. Consequently the declaration of the defendant that he intended to owe the plaintiff M7500 in lieu of the original sum of money lent represents a manifestation of intent, clearly apparent to the plaintiff, that he proposed to convert the money lent into German currency at this rate of exchange. It is true that this intention, which was directly influenced by the mistaken belief that the ruble was worth not 1 pf but 15 pf determined the decision of the defendant. However, it did not refer to those circumstances which preceded his declaration forming part of the transaction and did not merely represent subjective considerations. Instead, this intention was part of the declaration itself and was communicated to the other party in the course of the negotiations for a contract. It was not necessary to incorporate it in the documents or to make an express oral statement. The intention to apply the rule of conversion, assumed to be correct, was expressed as such in the declarations exchanged in connection with the special agreement . . .

Accordingly, the mistake was not one of motive, which is irrelevant in law, but constituted a mistake concerning the basis of the legal transaction. It must be regarded as a mistake affecting the declaration which may be annulled in accordance with para 119 s 1 BGB.

Case 99
REICHSGERICHT (FIFTH CIVIL DIVISION) 28 NOVEMBER 1923
RGZ 107, 78

Facts

The plaintiff is the owner of land entered on the land register of the former German District Court in Luderitzbucht (former German South-West Africa). The defendant has been, since 1913, the holder of a mortgage of this property for M13,000 which was noted on the land register. The debt fell due on 1 April 1920. The plaintiff paid to the defendant by bank transfer the sum of M18,980 in discharge of the principle obligation and of overdue interest. The plaintiff therefore asks that the defendant be condemned to hand over the document representing the mortgage and to agree that the entry in the land register be expunged. The defendant refused to comply on the ground that the debt must be paid either in the hard currency which was formerly in force in what was then the German Protectorate of South-West Africa or moneys of corresponding value. The Landgericht Berlin gave judgment for the plaintiff, which was upheld on appeal by the Kammergericht. On the defendant's second appeal the judgment below was reversed for the following reasons.

Reasons

'. . . In this case it was necessary to determine the question as to whether according to this (ie, German) law the defendant as holder of the mortgage can demand a revaluation of his claim which is secured by a mortgage, having regard to the extensive devaluation of the German paper currency.

It is true that in the present case the defendant did not expressly raise in the courts below the question of revalorisation. But in his reply to the claim he stated already that the could not be expected to accept payment in depreciated German paper currency since this would mean that he would have to renounce a considerable part of the value of his claim. The defendant added: it would be pure mockery if the owners of the land in South-West Africa were entitled to satisfy their mortgage creditors in almost worthless German paper currency and to reserve for themselves the accrued value resulting from the change of political circumstances. He has indicated clearly thereby that he regarded himself as entitled according to the law in force at present, to demand payment of a larger sum than the nominal value of his claim, if payment were made in paper currency. The court was bound, accordingly, to examine this demand in the light of all relevant legal considerations . . .

It cannot be . . . assumed that the depreciation of the currency was so insignificant when the mortgage fell due (on 1 August 1920) as to exclude from the outset the legal possibility of a revalorisation of the claim. The cost of living index had at that time already increased ten fold . . . The purchasing power had therefore already diminished considerably on 1 April 1920. It will be for the Court of Appeal to determine first of all, whether the factual conditions for a revalorisation of mortgage debts . . . were present at that time . . .

If the Court of Appeal should reach the conclusion that the factual conditions for a revalorisation of the claim were not present in the spring of 1920 and that the defendant defaulted in his duty to accept payment by refusing to accept the proffered amount in paper money, it will then have to examine whether the defendant has thereby lost the right to demand the revalorisation of his claim, having regard to the subsequent, very severe depreciation of the German currency [references].

The legal possibility of a revalorisation of mortgage debts is to be recognised according to present German law, especially according to para 242 BGB. In the case of mortgage debts in particular it must be taken into account that normally the debtor has received a corresponding compensation having regard to the much increased value of the land—at least when paper money is made the unit of account . . .

It is irrelevant, as the plaintiff emphasises, whether it was recognised in legal theory and practice as early as 1920 that it was admissible to revalorise mortgage or whether this realisation only prevailed later on under the influence of constantly growing depreciation of money. Incorrect legal notions in the year 1920 can no longer be decisive today.

According to para 242 BGB it must be considered what good faith (*Treu und Glauben*) requires, having regard to current practice. A fair consideration of the interests of both parties is called for. It follows that no general principles can be established requiring the revalorisation of every mortgage claim as such, nor that they must all be revalorised to the same extent . . . Instead, it will be necessary to take into account not only the increase in the value of the land—measured according to paper marks—which will be the principal factor, but also the other circumstances of the case, such . . . the economic strength of the debtor, whether agricultural, industrial or urban land is involved. Also the charges, especially of a public character which burden the land must be taken into account; in the case of land let on tenancies the reduction of income as a result of measures for the protection of tenants also deserve consideration.

The provisions of German currency law do not preclude a revalorisation. It is true that the Law modifying the Banking Act of 1 June 1909 [references] declares that the notes of the *Reichsbank* are legal tender [references] . . . But all these provisions rested at the time of their promulgation . . . on the justified assumption that the notes . . . had a value equal to hard money . . . The legislator, in enacting these provisions, had not envisaged the possibility of a considerable depreciation of the value of paper currency, let alone of the extent . . . that has occurred increasingly. After the paper mark had collapsed, a conflict arose between these currency provisions, on the one hand, and the various other statutory provisions on the other hand, designed to prevent a debtor from discharging his obligations in a manner inconsistent with the requirements of good faith and common practice. The principal provision to this effect is para 242 BGB which applies to all legal relationships. In such a conflict the latter provision must take precedence over the provisions dealing with currency because, as has been shows, at the time of their promulgation the possibility had not been envisaged of a collapse of the currency to such an extent, as a result of which the consequences of the currency legislation are no longer compatible with the principles of good faith and with equity. Consequently rigid adherence to the currency legislation in this case was not foreseen. In fact legislation by the Reich in recent times has shown increasingly that the principle 'mark equals mark' is no longer maintained without some exceptions. The reason is that, faced with requirements of commercial life and the effect of the changed economic conditions, it is no longer possible to adhere to the currency legislation in so far as it placed the paper mark on an equal footing with the gold mark

. . . [references]. The great number of these adjusting provisions [references] indicates clearly that they were not intended to establish special regulations, deviating from the general law, to govern special situations. Thus it cannot be concluded therefrom that in other cases revalorisation is inadmissible. On the contrary, these regulations show clearly that the legislator has undermined the principle that the paper mark can be used at its nominal value to pay off a debt effectively. The principle had to be abandoned in face of the actual economic conditions. The practice of the Reichsgericht has moved in the same direction to an ever-increasing extent [references].

It is true that the above-mentioned decisions of the Civil Divisions of the *Reichsgericht* deal with claims arising from bilateral contracts while the present case involves a loan secured by a mortgage. However, following the observations made above, there can be no serious doubt in holding that according to para 242 BGB the admissibility of revalorisation of contractual claims, recognised by these decisions, extends also to loans secured by mortgages. In the case of loans, too, their nature presupposes an equivalence between performance and counter-performance; here too, the substance is to be preserved for the creditor . . . In the case of loans of money, too, the debtor is bound (usually it is also the intention of the parties) not only to repay the same amount of money, but also to repay it in money of the same value. When the parties stipulate that the repayment is to be made in their national currency, they do so in the belief that this currency constitutes a firm and constant standard, within the limits of some normal variations. Accordingly the principle that the recipient of a loan of money must return an equivalent amount has been breached by currency legislation . . . For the legislator, in conferring on legal tender a nominal value, has indicated that, at least in normal economic conditions, a payment by means of legal tender is to be treated as payment of the 'same value.' But this principle must be disregarded for the reasons given above, if as a result of an especially heavy depreciation of legal tender, not foreseen at the time when the currency legislation was passed, it would lead to results which can no longer be reconciled with para 242 BGB. It will be necessary to determine in each case in accordance with the principle of good faith what degree of monetary depreciation is necessary before a creditor's claim must be revalorised.

The conclusion that revalorisation is permissible can also be reached by way of the supplementary interpretation of the contract, if the court examines what the parties, acting according to the precept of god faith (para 157 BGB), would have agreed in view of the purpose of the contract as a whole, if they had foreseen the possibility of an especially severe depreciation of money . . . The provisions of the currency legislation do not prohibit an agreement by which the effect of the statutory value of paper money is excluded by the parties and that this can be done tacitly.

In view of these considerations it can be stated affirmatively that a revalorisation of a loan secured by a mortgage is legally admissible having regard to the heavy depreciation of German paper money.

Case 100
OBERLANDESGERICHT BREMEN 18 MARCH 1952
NJW 1953, 1393

Facts

The defendant by a contract dated 22 May 1950 let to the plaintiff a sports hall for the period from 30 May 1950 until and including 6 June 1950 for the express purpose of staging a guest performance of the play 'Two Hours for You' featuring Marika Rökk in accordance with the annexed programme. The rent was to be 15 per cent of the gross profit but not less than DM1500, which were to be paid and were paid at the time when the contract was concluded. The guest performance could not take place since Mrs Rökk had suffered an injury. The plaintiff demanded the return of DM1500, which had been paid when the contract was concluded and 5 per cent interest.

The Court of Appeal of Bremen gave judgment for the plaintiff for the following reasons.

Reasons

The claim is justified in view of para 323 ss 1 and 3 in conjunction with paras 812 ff BGB. The district court proceeded correctly from the principle that—leaving aside the special rule embodied in paras 552 BGB—the tenant need not pay rent, if circumstances for which neither party is responsible render impossible the contractual use of the object which has been let: para 323 s 1 BGB. According to a constant practice of the *Reichsgericht* [reference] the general principles of para 275, 323 BGB can also be applied in the law relating to tenancies.

In order that para 323 s 1 can apply, the performance due by the defendant must have become impossible. The obligation of a landlord of commercial premises may be of very different kinds. A shop, for instance, can be let for carrying out all kinds of businesses, or for a strictly defined branch of business. To the extent that the use of the rented premises is limited, the danger increases that the performance of the contract may become impossible because the contract does not permit a switch to another use. The question as to whether the obligation of the landlord has become impossible must therefore depend on the respective purpose of the contract.

In the case decided by the *Reichsgericht* [references] the plaintiff had let a shop for the exploitation by a certain sales outlet in return for a rent geared to the turnover, with provision for a minimum rental. The *Reichsgericht* held that it was a purpose of the contract that this sale outlet should operate in the rented premises. The tenant was only permitted to use the premises for running this sales outlet, while on his part the landlord was only bound to make the premises available for running this sales outlet. This followed from the manner in which the rent was fixed. In the decision of the *Reichsgericht* relied on by the district court [references], the content of the contract led to the conclusion, on the other hand, that the tenant was completely free as to the use of the premises and was not precluded from employing them for purposes other than a multiple store. The right of the tenant to sublet and to alter and extend the premises, to assign his contractual rights and the landlord's own statement all supported it. Consequently it is necessary to ascertain the purpose of the contract in each individual case, what type of use of the rented premises was agreed on and whether the obligation of the landlord so found became impossible to perform as a result of subsequent circumstances. If the subsequent circumstances do not impede the use of the premises as envisaged by the contract, the claim would have to be rejected clearly for the reason that the prerequisites for applying para 323 BGB are absent. In finding that the appearance of Mrs Marika Rökk at the first performance was not included in the contract, the District Court should have dismissed the claim on the ground that the contractual use had not become impossible, and it would have been unnecessary to consider the special provisions of para 552 BGB.

Contrary to the opinion of the District Court the substance and the purpose of the contract in issue lead to the conclusion that the appearance of Mrs Rökk at the guest performance was part of the contract . . .

If, therefore, the guest performance of 'Two Hours for You' with the appearance of Marika Rökk had become part of the contract, the performance owed by the defendant according to the lease to the effect that the sports hall was to be made available for producing the said guest performance has become impossible as a result of the illness of Mrs Marika Rökk. Thus the prerequisites exist for applying para 323 s 1 BGB . . .

Case 101
BUNDESGERICHTSHOF (FIRST CIVIL DIVISION) 16 JANUARY 1953
MDR 1953, 282

Facts

The defendant in West Berlin, who had been doing business with the plaintiff for some time, ordered from the latter 600 drill hammers by a letter dated 31 May 1948. In it the defendant stated 'delivery as quickly as possible' 'we will fetch it ourselves by long distance lorry' and 'payment through our office in West Germany.' As the plaintiff knew, the drill hammers had been ordered from the defendant by the office for Foreign Trade of the Eastern Zone of Germany and were intended for the mines in that zone. The order reached the plaintiff only on 18 April 1948, since it had first to be passed by the authorities in the Eastern Zone.

In the meantime the so-called 'Berlin Blockade' had begun, which lasted from 24 June 1948 until 21 May 1949. The plaintiff, replying on the order, manufactured first 200 hammers and, by an invoice dated 30 November 1948, invited the defendant to take delivery. Subsequently he produced 74 more hammers and prepared the remaining 326 hammers up to a semi-finished state. The defendant did not fetch the hammers and did not pay for them either.

The plaintiff sued for payment of the order. The Court of Appeal gave judgment for the plaintiff against delivery of the hammers. The defendant's second appeal was rejected for the following reasons.

Reasons

The Court of Appeal was correct in holding that the purpose of the contract for the production and sale in dispute, namely to forward the drill hammers to the Eastern

Zone, never became part of the contract as a real condition in the meaning of para 158 BGB. Neither the wording of the defendant's written order nor the plaintiff's letter of acceptance disclose that the validity of the contract was to 'depend on the possibility of delivery to the Eastern Zone.' As the defendant himself states, the drill hammers which have been ordered represented a type which was no longer sufficiently modern for the advanced mining technology in the Western Zone. When the plaintiff received the written order, the Berlin Blockade was already in force and it was completely uncertain whether and when it would be lifted. It would have been of extreme consequence for the plaintiff, who had to incur considerable costs for the manufacture of the hammers, the object of the order, if the validity of the contract had been made to depend on the condition, completely outside his control, that the delivery of the hammers to the Eastern Zone could be carried out . . . the plaintiff had no personal interest as to the manner in which the defendant intended to deal with the drill hammers. The plaintiff's own interest was only that the defendant should take delivery and make payment in accordance with the contract. With these interests in mind, it would only have been justified to regard the intended use of the hammers as a genuine condition of the contract, if an intention to this effect by the parties had been clearly expressed in the terms of the contract. This was not done.

The performance of the contractual obligations is also not contrary to the legal provisions which forbid exports into the Eastern Zone or require a permit. Since there is no doubt that the parties did not intend to evade the prohibitions of export when they concluded the contract and would not have achieved it by a delivery of the hammers to the defendant at the contractual place of delivery . . . the appeal fails in so far as it alleges that the contract is contrary to para 134 BGB.

At the same time the performance by the defendant has not become impossible in law. It is true that the payment of the contract price would mean a financial sacrifice for the defendant, resulting from the supervening difficulties of disposing of the goods, which the defendant has not foreseen at the time when the contract was concluded. It need not be decided here whether to this extent an economic impossibility exists in the meaning of the previous practice of the *Reichsgericht* [references]. At a time when the doctrine of the fundamental basis of transactions (*Geschäftsgrundlage*) had not yet been developed, the *Reichsgericht* formulated the concept of economic impossibility and equated it to true impossibility in the meaning of para 275 ff, 323 ff, BGB. The purpose was to facilitate a release from contractual obligations in case of an increase in the burden of the performance appearing after the conclusion of the contract which exceeds the limit of financial loss which the debtor can be expected to bear. In its later decisions the problem of the economic impossibility of contractual performance was treated by the *Reichsgericht*, not on the basis of an analogous application of the rigid legal consequences of true impossibility but of a concept of a fundamental basis of transactions viewed within the wide and loose framework of para 242 BGB [references]. The questions which are raised by the concept of economic impossibility also concern in reality the problem as to whether the performance of a contract can be expected of the debtor. This is a problem which, having regard to the usually opposing interests of the parties, can only be solved in reliance on para 242 BGB which makes it possible to adopt the substance of the contract to present circumstances by balancing the opposing interests of the parties from the point of view of what can be expected from them [references]. The Court of Appeal has correctly examined the question as to the extent of the performance of the contract which can be expected of the defendant by relying on para 242 BGB, though it did so from the legal aspect of the failure of the fundamental basis of the transaction and not of economic impossibility.

The Court of Appeal agrees with the District Court that the delivery of the drill hammers into the Eastern Zone and its sale to the users had become a basis of the transaction. This cannot be challenged on legal grounds. It is true that as far as a rule in a contract for the production and sale of goods the intention of the person placing the order to forward the semi-finished or finished products to a particular client does not render this purpose of concluding the contract a basis of the transaction which affects both parties. Reasons of contractual certainty require that in principle each party must bear the risk that the purposes intended by him in concluding the contract cannot be achieved. However, both parties proceeded from the assumption that the delivery of the drill hammers into the Eastern Zone would become possible within the foreseeable future, despite the blockade existing at the time of the conclusion of the contract. This hope of the parties did not materialise, however . . . It need not be determined . . . whether the basis of the transaction has disappeared after the conclusion of the contract or . . . whether it did not exist at the time when the contract was concluded, because it is undisputed that even at that time the hammers could not be sent to the Eastern Zone. For even if the basis of the transaction was absent from the beginning, though its absence was only realised afterwards, the legal consequence is not that the transaction is invalid, but that it must be adapted to the actual situation, having regard to para 242 BGB; it is true that good faith may also require a total release from the contactual liabilities [references]. Thus, also from the point of view of an initial failure of the basis of the transaction, it is correct in law when the Court of Appeal held that the impossibility of disposing of the drill hammers in the Eastern Zone did not result in a complete release of the defendant from his contractual duties, but—in so far as the entire contract is in issue—proceeded from the need to adopt the contractual duties to the real situation, having regard to the circumstances in the light of good faith.

If the basis of the transaction has failed and if having regard to the purpose of the transaction a party cannot be expected to remain bound by the contract, it must be examined first whether it is possible to adapt the contract to the real situation [references]. This examination must cover in each case the individual content of the particular contractual relationship, including all accompanying circumstances; the interference with the contractual relationship must be limited to such modifications as are necessary to avert unbearable consequences according to the demand of justice [references].

If in a contract for the delivery and payment of a series of objects, all the individual claims arising out of the contractual relationship are in issue, the court must adapt the entire contractual relationship as a unit to the factual situation, unless a complete release from all obligations is indicated. This adaptation may lead to a modification, especially a reduction, of the individual claims, or to a *partial* maintenance of the contract in accordance with the existing terms of the contract coupled with the elimination of far-reaching obligations. The decision of the Court of Appeal is not open to legal challenge when in the present case, having balanced the interests and the risks involved of both parties, it held in the exercise of its judicial powers of adjustment flowing from para 242 BGB that the defendant could be expected to be bound by the contract in issue at least up to the amount of the payment for work done, equal approximately to one quarter of the total sum due under the contract. It cannot be overlooked that this decision leaves the fate of all other contractual duties of the defendant completely open. Since, however, the Court of Appeal . . . believes that it is in accordance with good faith to hold the defendant to a part of the contract and since this part of the contract exceeds what is demanded in the claim and the counter-claim—it is only the consequence of the fact that in their statements of claim they have merely submitted a segment of the entire legal relationship to the contract of the courts.

Case 102
BUNDESGERICHTSHOF (FIFTH CIVIL SENATE) 14 OCTOBER 1959
NJW 1959, 2203

Facts

A claim for an increase in the amount of the dead rent fixed in a contract for the extraction of saltpetre at the turn of the century cannot be upheld on the ground that the intervening decline in the purchasing power of money has caused the collapse of the basis of the transaction.

Reasons

1. . . .
2. . . .
3. The court below held that the landowners had no claim for any increase in the amount of the dead rent, and did so on the ground that the 'equivalence' between per-formance and counter-performance had not really been disturbed by intervening events. The court held that although the contract of 1898 for the extraction of salt-petre was a reciprocal contract, and the agreed dead rent was the mining company's counter-performance for the right of extraction granted to it by the landowner and the agreement of the latter not to dispose otherwise of the minerals during the period of the contract, it was impossible to say why the dead rent was set at M1200 per annum: that sum was not related to the current price of saltpetre, since the parties in 1898 did not refer to it, and indeed did not know, because there was technically no means of finding out, whether there were any extractable saltpetre at all in the area covered by the contract or if so, how much of it there might be. Nor could the landowners' claim for an increase in the amount of the dead rent be based on the view that revaluation was justified because the original basis of the transaction had collapsed owing to gen-eral changes in the economy. According to the jurisprudence of the supreme court, it was only in very exceptional cases that there was any scope for adapting a long-term contract to altered circumstances, ie when the relationship between performance and counter-performance had shifted so fundamentally that it would be inconsistent with the requirements of good faith and fair dealing and the principle of fidelity to contracts to maintain the original allocation of rights and duties. That was not the

situation in the present case. The dead rent was not part of a direct exchange, and cannot be seen as a sufficient counterpart for the landowners' contractual duty. To grant the requested increase in the agreed amount would be to make an impermissible revaluation of a debt in marks; the mark was set at par by the *Aufwertungsgesetz* of 1925 and again at par for DM by UmstG para 18 par 1 no 1, and the official indexes and other publications show that there has been no revolutionary change in the general economy since that currency reform.

The appellant claims that these views are wrong in law.

(a) To a certain extent the appellant is right. We cannot agree with the court below on all the points related to collapse of the basis of the transaction on which it rejected the landowners' claim for an increase in the dead rent. It is indeed possible that in the course of a long-term contractual relationship the balance between performance and counter-performance may become so upset that it would no longer be fair to keep the disadvantaged party to what was originally agreed. If that be so, then the principle of good faith and fair dealing which dominates the whole of our law (para 242 BGB) requires either that the reciprocal obligations be adapted to the changed situation, supposing that the maintenance of the contract is in the interests of the parties as properly conceived, or that the contract be completely cancelled. Actually, this was the position from which the court below started. It first asked whether there was a relationship of equivalence between the obligation the landowners undertook in the contract of 1898 and the agreed dead rent. They held that there was. This was correct, since the question is not whether performance and counter-performance were objectively equivalent in value, but whether the parties treated them as being so. But the court went on to say that no *disturbance* of this relationship of equivalence could be found because the agreed annual sum of M1200 was an 'arbitrary figure' which bore no relation to the current price of saltpetre or the amount extractable from the land in question. This is very dubious, and the appellant is right to argue that even an arbitrary sum may in the minds of the contractors have been geared to the general condition of the economy and the current purchasing power of money. If such circumstances have changed very materially in the intervening period one could no more exclude the possibility of a shift in the relationship of equivalence in the case of an 'arbitrary' sum than in the case of a sum fixed in relation to concrete factors in the situation.

Again, the lower court's reasoning is dubious in that it first asked whether the plaintiff had a claim for the 'reinstatement of the relationship of equivalence' as such, that is, as an independent ground of claim, and only then asked as a subsidiary question whether 'the change in the basis of the transaction' entitled the landowners to demand an increase in the dead rent under para 242 BGB on the ground of the alteration in the economic situation. In reality, though the court below does not seem to have seen this, these are one and the same question: the shift in the balance between performance and counte-rperformance ('disturbance of the relationship of equivalence') is simply an instance of the destruction or collapse of the basis of the transaction, that is, of a situation which may lead to a cancellation of the contract or its adaptation to the new situation, under the very narrowly defined conditions laid down in the jurisprudence of the *Reichsgericht* and *Bundesgerichtshof*.

(b) Despite these defects in the decision of the court below, the outcome is correct. One of the stated requirements for the application of the theory of the collapse of the basis of the transaction, and one which is especially important in cases of this kind, is that the intervening change be of a critical nature and affect the interests of the parties to a significant degree. Not every adverse modification of the prior relationship of equivalence, unforeseen by the parties at the time of the contract, justifies a departure from the principle that contracts must be adhered to (*'pacta sunt servanda'*).

What is really required is such a fundamental and radical change in the relevant circumstances that it would be an intolerable result quite inconsistent with law and justice to hold the party to the contract [references]. This test is crucial in this case. The court below recognised this and was right to apply this test. In doing so it went thoroughly into the facts and after considering the interests of both parties came to the conclusion that the stated preconditions for breaking with the principle that contracts must be kept were not satisfied.

This court is in entire agreement. The imbalance between the duties of the parties which is in issue in this case is the result of the fall in the purchasing power of money since the contract was formed. According to the calculations in the expert opinion of Larenz, which we can unhesitatingly accept, the value of money diminished by two-thirds during the period in question; thus the sum agreed as dead rent in the contract has only about one third of the purchasing power today it had in 1898. But the plaintiff is quite wrong to say that the landowners are now entitled to claim three times the original sum, namely DM3600. Simple arithmetic does not answer the question whether a reduction in purchasing power produces a situation which is intolerable by the test of good faith and fair dealing. The expert opinion just mentioned, which itself proposes a rise of only 75 per cent rather than 200 per cent, pays too much attention to the figures in stating that if in 1898 M1200 was fair compensation to the owners for their performance (ie, agreeing not to exploit the minerals) the fall in the value of money in the ensuing sixty years was so great that it would be inequitable not to increase that sum.

The very writer of the opinion in his book *Geschäftsgrundlage und Vertragserfüllung* (2nd edn, 1957) is right to emphasise the basic principle that contracts must be adhered to, and states that the law should only intervene under para 242 BGB in cases where holding the party to his contract would be *manifestly* and *grossly* contrary to its spirit (p 165), and that a rigorous standard should be applied: it is not every serious shift in equivalence that justifies departing from the contract, but only such a shift as a reasonable person would see as going far beyond the risk assumed and as negating nearly the entire interest which the affected party had in the transaction [references]. We agree with these principles, and if one keeps them in mind it is clear that the claim in the instant case is unjustified. The court below rightly saw the critical question as being whether the dead rent as originally fixed 'must now be regarded as a wholly inadequate return', and did not fall into any legal error in concluding that it could not. This finding alone justified the court in dismissing the claim.

Whether it would make any difference to the decision if the landowners, contrary to the actual fact, were in urgent need of the money and would face economic ruin if the payments of dead rent were suppressed or seriously reduced is a question we need not answer. Nor need we take a position on the question whether it falls within the so-called 'normal risk of contracting' when recurrent payments under a long-term contract or a contract of indefinite duration, such as this one, which the court below held contained no 'speculative element', lose two-thirds of their value because of the ever-increasing cost of living [references]. For even on a very generous view of *Treu und Glauben* it would be impossible to justify granting the plaintiffs another increase in the dead rent when the contractual sum was fully revalued at the end of the First World War and then in 1948 converted at par into the present currency. Otherwise the effect of the doctrine of the foundation of the transaction would be to imply into long-term contracts a sort of 'gold clause,' and this, as the court below was right to observe, would be contrary to the currency legislation and would be apt to impair faith in the currency. The courts are not free to depart from the law on grounds of equity; only the legislator can effect any further adjustment of long-term contracts to situations produced by inflation.

(c) The appellant invokes para 7 d of the Law on Agricultural Leases which permits the courts to adjust a contract when radical changes occurring in the surrounding circumstances have produced a gross imbalance between reciprocal obligations, and argues that it can be applied by analogy to the present case. That is not so. The court below explained that this legislation is very specific and not to be extended to contracts of other types. That is right. It is true that contracts for the extraction of soda are in many respects similar to long-term leases of land [reference], but at any rate as regards the dead rent they do not have those features of long leases of land which led the legislature to enact para 7 LPG.

This provision is just the most recent example of special legislation on long-term leases of farms, going back now for many years, passed in the public interest for reasons having to do with agriculture, and it cannot be extended by analogy or construed by the courts as applying to contracts of types other than long-term farming leases, which are distinctive, especially because the effect of their terms alters over time [references]. The legislation applies only to such leases. The aim of the legislator is to see that the return of agricultural land is fairly divided between owner and tenant farmer despite changes in economic circumstances, so that both may make their contribution to the maintenance and increase of its productivity—the tenant-farmer by good farm management and the owner by performing his contractual duties to keep the buildings in good repair and improve the land. If either party lacked the means to perform his part, the harvest would suffer, and if the owner were not properly protected against economic changes he would be reluctant to enter into long-term leases of his farmland, although they conduce to its optimal use [references]. Such considerations are not central to contracts for the extraction of minerals: they were mainly entered into half a century ago; if new contracts are entered into today the parties are free to adopt appropriate terms whereby their obligations will be adjusted to future developments. At any rate there appears to be no public interest beyond that of the parties to mineral extraction contracts such as to call for special legislation.

A further reason for not applying this statute in the present case, whether directly or by analogy, is that that enactment empowers the courts to make law for the parties, whereas when a court applies para 242 BGB, as is suggested in this case, it is simply finding the law, not making it; the judge does not reconstruct the legal relation of the parties but simply declares what alterations in the legal relationship have already been produced, according to good faith and fair dealing, by changes in the surrounding circumstances [references].

Case 103
BUNDESGERICHTSHOF (FIFTH CIVIL DIVISION) 31 JANUARY 1967
BGHZ 37, 44

Facts

By a contract dated 13 February 1959 the plaintiff purported to sell to the defendants three plots of land amounting to 13766 square metres as well as a part measuring 500 square metres of a fourth plot of land. In return the defendant was to build, within eight weeks of receiving the official building permit, on a plot of the plaintiff an apartment house of 2,700 cubic metres containing twelve flats or, if permission for the project should not be forthcoming, two houses of corresponding size. If no permission at all should be obtainable, the defendant was to erect the building or buildings on one of the plots purchased by himself and to re-transfer the plot so built on to the seller.

The three plots so sold were registered in the name of the defendant, and a caution was registered for the benefit of the defendant in respect of the portions of the fourth plot. The defendant had not obtained the necessary permission to build when the action was brought, nor had he erected a building.

The plaintiff demanded that the three plots should be reconveyed to him and that the caution should be cancelled; in addition he asked for a declaration that the contract was invalid, either because it had been impossible from the beginning since neither the plot sold by him nor those remaining to him could be built on as intended, seeing that no such official permission could possible be forthcoming. Moreover, the plots could not be built on in the absence of a proper sewage connection, nor was such a connection to be forthcoming in the foreseeable future.

The District Court of Munich rejected the claim; the Court of Appeal of Munich allowed it. On a second appeal the decision of the Court of Appeal was quashed and the case was referred back for the following reasons.

Reasons

The Court of Appeal believes that the contract is void because, so far as the defendant's duty to build on the land was concerned, its performance was impossible from the beginning. As the court below found, the plots in question—both those still owned by the plaintiff as well as those which he sold to the defendant—can only be built on when it becomes possible to connect them with the sewerage system; this situation, in the absence of which no building permit could be obtained, would probably not materialise before 1968; possible this uncertainty might remain even longer. At least until 1964 no general building plan had been in existence and it was therefore impossible to predict what kinds of building would be permitted, once the land had become ready for development and open to building operations; in particular it was not possible to forecast whether the future building plan would allow houses of the size agreed on in the contract or perhaps only single family houses. In assessing these facts as found, the Court of Appeal held that the contractual performance in question was not permanently impossible; instead the impossibility was tempered only. At the time when the contract was concluded it was reasonable to assume that, one day, the plots would become open to building, and it was still reasonable to assume it today. The Court of

Appeal held however that the case before it was one where a temporary impediment of performance must be treated as if it were permanent, because it was doubtful whether the purpose of the contract could be achieved. For this reason the plaintiff was entitled according to good faith to regard himself as no longer bound by the contract [reference].

. . . the point of departure of the Court of Appeal is open to far-reaching legal objections . . .

Para 306 BGB [old version] regulates the legal consequences of an initial impossibility of a contractual performance, ie of an objective impossibility existing already at the time when the contract was concluded; in such a case the contract is void. The judgment under appeal states that this rule applies not only if the impossibility is permanent, but when an impediment which rendered performance impossible for the time being can again be removed later on. In so holding it proceeds from the principles which the practice of this court has developed for the case where the performance which is owed becomes impossible as a result of an event which occurred *after* the obligation came into being para 275 BGB. It is true that in this connection 'impossibility' must be understood, as a rule, to indicate a situation where the performance of the obligation it precluded for ever [references]. Exceptionally, however, also a merely temporary impediment is equated to a permanent impossibility, especially in the case of obligations of long duration—namely if it puts in doubt the achievement of the purpose of the contract and if the other contracting partner cannot be expected, according to good faith, to comply with the agreement [references]. The fact that a performance which is owed becomes impossible subsequently does not destroy the contract as such. Instead the legal relationship between the parties is determined by the loss of far-reaching provisions of para 275 ff, 323 ff BGB [references]. It is doubtful whether the identical treatment of temporary and permanent impossibility, which is permissible in the case of subsequent impediments to performance, can be extended to para 305 BGB—which alone sanctions to the serious consequence that the contract is void.

In this general formulation the question need not be decided here. Even if in the case of an initial impossibility in the meaning of para 306 BGB it should not be excluded in principle also treat an impediment which impedes performance temporarily on the same footing as one which is permanent, nevertheless it is not possible to do so where the contracting parties know of the existence of the present impediment but assumed mistakenly that it could be removed. In such cases, if it turns out later on that it will take considerably more time before the impediment is got out of the way than all the parties assumed when they concluded the contract, a mutual mistake has occurred, the legal consequences of which are not determined by para 306 BGB. Instead they must be considered from the aspect as to whether the basis of the transaction has disappeared (para 242 BGB); it is necessary to examine whether and to what extent as a result of the unforeseen delay in fixing the date of performance the situation as seen originally by the contracting parties has been changed so fundamentally that according to good faith the contract can no longer be executed in the manner envisaged at the beginning [references]. The application of the principles concerning the failure of the basis of a transaction results only exceptionally in the total destruction of the contractual relationship; normally reasons of contractual fidelity and commercial security demand that the contract be maintained as far as possible and that it is to be adjusted in a form which takes into account the legitimate interests of both parties [references].

In the present case a mutual mistake has occurred concerning the basis of the transaction. Both parties in concluding the contract . . . assumed that the contract would be carried out within a foreseeable time and, in particular, that the apartment house to be erected by the defendant would be built soon; certainly the construction was not to take place in the distant future. The parties were aware of the planning difficulties, but hoped nevertheless to obtain a building permit soon, even before a connection could be established with the sewerage system. The parties only realised later on that their hopes were unfounded. At the moment when the original hope that the plots could be built on within a comparatively short period was disappointed, the legal relationship between the parties entered a new phase; henceforth it became uncertain what the waiting period would be before building could begin. This state of uncertainty remained in the ensuing period and persisted still at the time of the last hearing in the Court of Appeal. At that time, at least, it could seem doubtful whether the time which had elapsed as well as that which was likely to pass in the future before the plots would be right for development constituted such an important factor that the parties could no longer be expected to adhere to the substance of their previous agreement [reference]. The Court of Appeal has failed hitherto to examine this question.

Case 104
BUNDESGERICHTSHOF (SECOND CIVIL DIVISION) 28 MAY 1973
BGHZ 61, 31

Facts

The plaintiff became a director of the defendant company in 1926. By a contract of employment dated 18 February 1935 he received a fixed salary of RM50,000 and a percentage of the profits. The contract provided further that his pension was to be calculated as follows: after ten years' service 25 per cent of DM40,000 with annual increase of 1 per cent with a maximum of 60 per cent after 35 years. After 20 years' service the basic standard was to be increased to 50,000 REM.

The plaintiff retired in 1951 and received from then onwards an annual pension of DM15,000 equal to monthly payments of DM3,083.33. In the 1969 plaintiff asked for an increase, which was refused. He claimed an additional pension at the monthly rate of DM804.17 on the ground that wages and salaries and the general cost of living had increased considerably.

The District Court of Hanover dismissed the claim. The Court of Appeal of Celle allowed it. The defendant's second appeal was dismissed for the following reasons.

Reasons

I. The Court of Appeal regards the claim as justified because para 242 BGB requires the adjustment of the pension to the changed condition, especially because the cost of living rose by 45.2 points between 1950 and 1970 [references]. This division agrees as to the result.

II. It is true that in its previous practice this Division has refused to increase a pension on the grounds of the depreciation of money in the absence of a contractual adaptation clause, at least in cases in which the agreed pension could still be regarded as a performance in accordance with the contract [references]. This practice was identical with that of the Federal Supreme Labour Court which held on 12 March 1965 [reference] that, while contrary to earlier decision [references] the adjustment of contactual pension payments to the increased cost of living was no longer excluded in principle, it could only be considered if, as a result of the rise in prices, the agreed payments can no longer be regarded as a performance which provides a living in accordance with the purpose of the contract [reference].

III. Meanwhile the development has continued. The constant increase in the cost of living in the Federal Republic which . . . up to 1960 amounted on average to little more than 1 per cent per year, has since gained momentum . . . All in all the cost of living has increased between 1958 . . . and 1971 . . . by approximately 53.6 per cent. This corresponds to an internal devaluation of approximately 34.9 per cent.

IV. In the light of this recent development the Federal Supreme Labour Court in two decisions of 30 March 1973 [references] abandoned the practice of restricting the adjustment of pensions to cases in which as a result of increase prices the purpose of the agreed performance to provide a living has been frustrated altogether. The Federal Supreme Labour Court now holds that, at least when the cost of living has risen by more than 40 per cent, the value of a pension no longer corresponds to what was promised originally to such an extent that the limit has been reached where the pensioner can be expected according to good faith to observe a standstill and where to deny any adjustment would offend the sense of justice intolerably. In so holding the Federal Supreme Labour Court distinguished between other contractual obligations and promises of maintenance, the special characteristic of which are to assure the livelihood of the beneficiary, or at least to make a contribution thereto. The payments are made out of the profits of the enterprise, the foundations of which the pensioner has helped to create during his activity on behalf of the enterprise. The Federal Supreme Labour Court takes into account, in addition, that the provision of maintenance by the enterprise is also a remuneration for the pensioner's loyalty towards it and for the sum total of his services. These services had been rendered by the pensioner in advance, trusting that he could plan the later stages of his life on the basis of a maintenance promised to him. If this expectation should be disappointed as a result of the depreciation of the currency, a pensioner would have no longer the means of bargaining for an adjustment, contrary to other sections of the population whose income would have kept up with the increase in prices.

The Federal Supreme Court observes that in these circumstances it was first of all a matter for the enterprise to examine the question of such a compensation by adjusting the maintenance payments to the economic development, and to offer an equitable and legal settlement, having regard to the existing situation. Many enterprises had done so already and were doing so continuously. In the case of provision for old age by enterprises, considerable differences existed in the size of the payments, in the gradations among the individual groups of employees and in the conditions for payment as well as in the ability of enterprises to afford payments. Moreover, the reflex effect on other duties of support owed by the enterprise and the total cost arising from each of these could not be established easily. Consequently, the courts could not prescribe in advance the measure and the form of any adjustment. No automatic increase of pension payments without a contractual promise to this effect could be based on para 242 BGB.

If the party owing the pension had not yet met the creeping inflation by an adequate increase of the pension, he should first of all negotiate with the pensioner or pensioners. If no agreement could be reached, the debtor would have to decide on his own in his reasonable discretion in accordance with para 315 BGB. If he failed to do so, or if his decision was not reasonable, the courts would have to determine the performance due in accordance with para 315 (3). In this connection the facts put forward by the parties for and against an adjustment of a retirement pension were particularly relevant. The extent of the rise in prices must be the standard for fixing the extent of the adjustment. No attention should be given in principle to any other aspects of the pensioner's assets or income, except possibly any increase in income arising from any statutory insurance. Equally, the question of need should not be taken into account as a rule. On the other hand, the profitability of the enterprise and the principle of equality of treatment might be relevant.

V. This Division agrees in all matters of principle. In so far the special circumstances of cases coming before it should make it necessary to deviate in certain respects, each individual case will have to be decided on its own.

1. The fact that this Division is not concerned with pension claims by employees in the meaning of labour law, but only by organs of enterprises—namely directors and managers—does not in principle call for a different decision from that of the Federal Supreme Labour Court. Normally both contracting parties envisage that the pension provided to a director or manager will serve, either alone or with other revenues, to assure for the beneficiary a standard of living commensurate to his position hitherto in case of old age, premature incapacity to work or of dismissal without any expectation of an equivalent means of livelihood of another kind. Here, too, the pension can be regarded as part of the remuneration for services which the beneficiary has given before he retired and which contributes to the prosperity of the enterprise, the profits of which now feed the pension. This balance, assumed to exist when the obligation to pay a pension is incurred, is seriously disturbed if, as a result of a fall in the purchasing power as compared with that outlined previously, the pension can no longer fulfil by its agreed amount its intended function which is to guarantee the previous standard of living completely or in part. The enterprise, on the other hand, is not affected in the result by the depreciation of money, for generally the revenues have at least kept up with the increase in prices or they have even overtaken it as a result of economic growth. It is true that costs, especially wages and salaries, have increased as well. The proportion of the individual pension obligations, however, the nominal value of which has remained the same, has decreased correspondingly.

The special features set out here preclude a comparison with other obligations of long duration which are not concerned with maintenance (eg, for the production of potash) as the practice of this court cited by the appellant has underlined expressly [references].

2. The pensions for directors and managers which have been in issue before this Division exceed in most instances the average amount paid by enterprises. This Division, agreeing with the Federal Supreme Labour Court and rejecting the opinion of the appellant, does not, however, regard this fact as decisive, at least given the

extent of the increase in costs as it has occurred at present. A pension is intended as a rule not only to guarantee a minimum of subsistence in old age, but to enable the beneficiary to maintain the standard of living reached in his professional life, either completely or in part.

Different considerations may apply however if the promise of a pension is made, not in order to provide for the future but for other reasons (for instance as a cloak for a payment of profits to a managing partner).

3. . . .

4. This Division, like the Federal Constitutional Court [reference], The Federal Supreme Court [reference], and the Federal Supreme Labour Court [reference] regards the principle of nominalism (Mark equals Mark) as one of the fundamental bases of our legal and economic organisation. In the light of the facts before it, this Division does not however attribute decisive importance to the objection that this principle would be undermined or lead to a further devaluation by an adjustment of contractual claims, in accordance with the prerequisites of para 242 BGB, with reference to the greatly increased cost of living, even if limited to pensions arising out of contracts of employment [references]. The pensions provided by the Statutory Insurance Scheme have been increased about two and a half times . . . between 1957 and 1970 [references]. The salaries of employees in commerce and in the service of public authorities; based on collective agreements, rose . . . by 120.4 per cent between 1958 and 1971, that is to say by more than doubt. The increase in the wages of industrial workers is even higher . . . old age pensioners paid by enterprises which do not contain an index clause are frequently adjusted from time to time on a voluntary basis [reference].

Considering, finally, that ordinary contracts for the exchange of goods, not involving any personal element also contain not infrequently clauses about the price, whereby the debtor of the industrial or commercial product safeguards himself against any increase in the cost of materials and wages, the argument does not convince that the protection of the currency requires strict adherence to an amount of a pension which no longer suffices to provide maintenance as envisaged by the contract owing to the increase in prices. Instead, the adjustment of such pensions intended to provide a living is to be regarded only as a late and inevitable consequence of a development which the State and the economy have taken in to account long ago, but to which pensioners of enterprises as distinct from other sectors of the population, were exposed without protection, unless they had been astute enough to safeguard themselves by index clauses.

VI.

1.

2. The appellant's view cannot be accepted that the plaintiff, while working for the defendants, had received a very high salary and that such a salary was also intended to enable the recipient to a accumulate capital or to provide otherwise for his retirement. Although the plaintiff received a salary and a share of the profits which were high in the circumstances, the parties agreed in 1935 on a pension which was appropriate at that time in order to assure the plaintiff in any event of maintenance corresponding to his standard of living at that time. The parties assumed that in his old age the plaintiff should not have to rely on his savings alone. Conversely nothing suggests that they regarded the pension as the sole resource of maintenance for the plaintiff.

It follows that the present economic situation of the plaintiff is irrelevant. Clearly the holder must not suffer disadvantage because by his own effort he has built up a multiple and particularly good nest egg for his old age. All the more it is not the intention of a promise of a pension that in his old age the beneficiary must have recourse for his maintenance to the substance of any capital he may have saved.
VII. . . .

Case 105
BUNDESGERICHTSHOF (THIRD CIVIL DIVISION) 13 NOVEMBER 1975
NJW 1976, 565

Facts

On 24 June 1971 the defendant, a football club and a member of the German Football League transferred W, one of the players, to the plaintiff for the fee of DM40,000. Both parties were unaware of the fact when he appeared for the defendant that in a League match against Arminia Bielefeld on 29 May 1971 he had accepted a bribe. After having played three times for the plaintiff W confessed. The plaintiff dismissed W with immediate effect and he was barred from playing by the German football league.

The plaintiff contended that the contract of transfer was void and demanded repayment of the transfer fee. The courts below gave judgment for the plaintiff. A second appeal by the defendant was rejected for the following reasons.

Reasons

I. The Court of Appeal has allowed the claim for the repayment of the transfer fee on the ground of a mutual mistake of the parties concerning the basis of the transaction when they concluded the transfer contract on 24 June 1971 and that the plaintiff had validly rescinded the contract because the basis of the transaction was absent.
II. The Court of Appeal started from the proposition that both parties were mistaken about the basis of the transaction when they concluded the contract of transfer and therefore applied to the present case the principles concerning the legal consequences of the absence of the basis of a transaction. This means that in the case of a mutual mistake of the contracting parties concerning the basis of the contract the legal consequences are governed by para 242 BGB [references]. In such a case it may be contrary to good faith, if one party seeks to hold the other party to the contract [references].
1. The view of the Court of Appeal that a mutual mistake concerning the basis of the transaction had occurred in the present case cannot be questioned, contrary to the opinion of the appellant.
   (a) The basis of a transaction consists of the common notions of the parties, which did not become part of the contract as such but had manifested themselves at the conclusion of the contract, or it consists of the notions of one of the parties which the other parties could recognise and did not question concerning the existence or future emergence of certain circumstances on which the intention of the parties to transact business is founded [references]. The Court of Appeal started from this rule.

(b) The Court of Appeal found that the plaintiff wishes, by concluding the contract of transfer, to be able to engage the player W and to employ him during the coming seasons as a member of its team in a regional league. The court found also that it was a matter of course for the parties to assume that the player was not subject to a charge which might endanger his licence to play for the club of his transfer. These findings . . . of a factual kind bind the court and also support the view of the Court of Appeal . . .

2. If . . . two football clubs, such as the plaintiff and the defendant, agree on the payment of a transfer fee in order to create the condition, required by the statutes of the German Football League, to enable a player to receive permission to apply for the club to which he is transferred, the parties in making a reasonable assessment of their mutual interests assume as a basis of their contractual intention that the player does not possess any personal characteristics which render him objectively unfit to receive a player's licence.

3. The Court of Appeal has not overlooked that not very disturbance of the basis of a transaction is significant. In view of the paramount importance in the law of contracts of the principle that contracts must be carried out, reliance on the fundamental disturbance of the basis of a transaction is only admissible in exceptional cases, if it appears imperative in order to avoid an unbearable result which cannot be reconciled with law and justice and which the party concerned cannot be expected to accept according to good faith [references] . . . If a football player accepts bribes in order to tamper with the results of a game, he offends severely against the recognised rules of the sport and against the principles of decency in sport. As a rule he is no longer suitable to receive a licence to play for clubs of the German Football League. To pay a transfer fee for such a player is to make payment in a legal vacuum. As shown above (2) the agreement concerning a transfer fee only makes sense if the player fulfils the personal prerequisites that he can receive a player's licence according to the statutes of the German Football League. These prerequisites are lacking, as a rule, if a player has been prepared to accept money in order to influence the results of competition in sport through fraudulent activities.

Thereby a financial obligation between the clubs engaged in the contract of transfer loses its material justification. A player who is subject to such a serious charge has, objectively, also lost his value for his previous club because, after his defect has become known, he cannot play for any club at all. It does not appear justified to grant compensation to the transferring club for a loss which it would have suffered also if the player had not moved to another club, and to burden the club to which the player was transferred with a corresponding duty to pay compensation, although it cannot derive any benefit from the player, either financially or in sport. In these circumstances the basis of the transaction has been undermined to such an extent that the club which owes the money cannot be expected to adhere to the contract of transfer which was concluded in ignorance of the bribery. Nor can it be doubted that not only the plaintiff, but also every other club, would have refrained from concluding a contract, if informed of the situation.

4. The Court of Appeal has also delimited correctly the respective spheres of risk. As the appellant points out correctly, the distribution of the risk is especially important for determining the question of the legal consequences of the disappearance of the basis of the transaction. It is established by the practice of the courts that

circumstances which according to the purpose of the contract clearly fall within the sphere of risk of one of the parties do not as a rule entitle that party to rely on the collapse of the basis of the transaction [references]. This is not, however, the case here . . .

(c) In the present case it is decisive that player W, having been involved in an act of bribery at the time when he changed clubs, could no longer be considered a licensed or contractual player for personal reasons in accordance with the rules established by the German Football League and recognised as binding by the parties. In consequence of his entanglement in the scandal in the Federal League he was afflicted with a personal defect which excluded him altogether as a player, for *any* club, as the legal outcome of the matter in the German Football League shows. It is irrelevant that the parties were ignorant of this when they concluded the contract. What matters is the objective situation, not the subjective knowledge of the parties. W lost his personal qualification as a football player within the area of the German Football League when he acted contrary to the rules of sport and not only when this became known to the public. Consequently already at the time when he changed clubs he lacked the legal pre-requisites for being used by a club belonging to the German Football League. Such a player also loses his objective 'value' for his original club as a result of an act contrary to the rules of sport. If the defect adhering to the player is only discovered after the contract for a transfer has been concluded, this only discloses that the player had already lost the qualities which rendered him valuable for a club in the German Football League. Such a defect is to be attributed, as a rule, to his *old* club, for it originated in the latter's sphere.

(d) The Court of Appeal regarded as decisive for the distribution of the risk to what extent the misconduct with which the player must be charged touches in essence his internal relations with the club which employs him. It held that the nature of the obligation of a licensed player towards his club consisted in playing for and not against his club; accordingly it has placed the burden of the risk of any violation of this obligation on the club that employed him, even if the player migrates to another club later on. The Court of appeal has rightly placed the risk on the defendant as being the club which is 'more closely involved', having regard to the circumstances of the case, than the plaintiff. The fact that the player W was bribed in connection with the league match of the defendant in Bielefeld on 29 May 1971, which constitutes the cause of the disruption of the basis of the transaction represented by the contract of transfer, belongs to the 'sphere of risk' of the defendant not only from the point of view of time. The misconduct of the player is also directly connected with his activity for the plaintiff in sport and as an employee. In the light of such a situation it cannot be assumed according to good faith that the plaintiff assumed the risk.

5. The Court of Appeal held that as a result of the absence of the basis of the transaction the plaintiff is entitled to withdraw from the contract and has allowed the claim for the full repayment of the transfer fee. This too cannot be faulted on legal grounds.

(a) The absence or the failure of the basis of a transaction does not, of course, result in the complete elimination of the contractual relationship The release of one or of both parties to a contract from their contractual obligations must only be allowed in so far as good faith so requires. The first question is, therefore, whether the contract cannot be modified so as to accord with reality in a manner which takes into account the legitimate interests of both parties [references]. The Court of Appeal has observed these principles. It has held that a modification of the contract is excluded because the counter-performance of the defendant in releasing the player W prematurely was worthless in practice and, in particular, because an apportionment of the financial damage among both parties was ruled out in view of the obvious distribution of the risk. This conclusion, too, cannot be faulted . . .

Case 106
BUNDESGERICHTSHOF (EIGHTH CIVIL SENATE) 8 FEBRUARY 1984
NJW 1984, 1746

Facts

In 1977 the plaintiff, an Iranian importer, ordered from the defendant, a German brewery, 12,000 cases of export beer, 24 cans per case, at a price of DM15.36 per case. The price of DM184,320 was paid by draft on a bank in Teheran in July 1977. The goods were to be delivered c.i.f. Teheran, and were shipped in August 1977 from Bremen to a port in Iran, whence they were largely distributed inland. Investigations disclosed that about 40 per cent of the goods were damaged and unusable, and on 7 November 1978 the parties reached the following compromise: 'Until 31 May 1980 the plaintiff may buy cases of beer at a reduced price of DM9.30 . . . Payment of DM20,000 will shortly be made to the plaintiff's account in Teheran. The balance of the sum demanded as damages, a further DM20,000, will be paid on receipt of a draft in respect of 20,000 cases of beer . . .' The first DM20,000 was paid to the plaintiff by the defendant, but no more deliveries of beer were made nor was the further DM20,000 paid to the plaintiff. In January 1979 the Shah fled and Ayatollah Khomeini seized power in Iran. Since then, according to the plaintiff, the Islamic Republic has a total prohibition, on pain of death, of trade in alcoholic products and the importation of alcohol into Iran. The plaintiff wished to negotiate a further extra-judicial settlement, but the defendant would not consent, so the plaintiff in the present litigation claimed damages in respect of the useless beer in the amount of DM53,728 (ie, 40 per cent of DM184,320 = DM73,728 less DM20,000 already received).

The Landgericht gave judgment for the full amount, the Oberlandesgericht only in the sum of DM37,000. The [defendant's] appeal was dismissed.

Reasons

II.
1. . . .
(c) According to the court below, this was not a case of impossibility of performance, since the prohibition of importing alcohol into Iran did not affect the defendant's duty to make compensation for the harm it had caused. The parties do not challenge this, and the court was correct so to hold, at any rate in the result, since the plaintiff's obligations under the compromise were performed by the very act of making it (partial release, granting of delay, modification of the debt) and the defendant's obligations thereunder, namely to pay the further DM20,000 and to deliver discounted beer f.o.b. German ports as agreed in 1977, were perfectly capable of being

performed. The plaintiff was not bound to order any beer or to set up a credit line; these were options of the plaintiff and preconditions of the defendant's obligations.

(d) The court below was right—as the parties accept—to deny that the compromise was invalidated by para 779 BGB. Under this provision a compromise is invalid only when the actual underlying facts differed from those supposed by the parties. If, by contrast, expectations as to future events which the parties entertained at the time of the compromise are falsified by subsequent occurrences—such as here the political developments in Iran and their effect on the contract—para 779 BGB cannot invalidate the compromise [references].

(e) The court below was correct to start from the position that the basis of the transaction [*Geschäftsgrundlage*] of 7 November 1978 subsequently collapsed.

(aa) Even the appellant admits that, quite apart from para 779 BGB, para 242 BGB is applicable to a compromise. [reference].

(bb) The basis of a transaction consists of the common assumptions entertained by the parties at the time of the contract, or of an assumption of one of the parties, ascertainable by the other and not objected to by him, regarding the existence or future occurrence of circumstances, to the extent that the parties' intention to make the transaction is based on such assumptions [reference]. The court below held that the possibility of further deals between the parties was the basis of the transaction. The appellant's objection to this is misconceived. This was not simply a wish of the parties, even though it was frequently expressed, for only further dealings could achieve the economic purpose of the compromise, to make good the losses suffered by the plaintiff. The discount on the price of the beer could make sense only if the plaintiff could dispose of any beer it ordered. The finding that this assumption by the parties formed the basis of the compromise is not in conflict with the principle that a party may not, by invoking matters which fall within his own area of risk, claim that the basis of the transaction has collapsed [reference]. It is true that in commercial matters the risk of being unable to dispose of the goods normally falls within the purchaser's area of risk [reference], but the court below was right to point out that this was not a contract of sale but a transaction by which the defendant was to compensate the plaintiff for its losses. There is nothing to suggest that if the compensation envisaged by the compromise failed to materialise, the parties intended the loss to be borne by the plaintiff alone.

(cc) The basis of the compromise has collapsed. The court below found that trade in alcoholic drinks in Iran is forbidden. The appellant's objections are without merit . . .

(dd) This court has always held that the collapse of the basis of a transaction can only be invoked when otherwise there would be manifestly intolerable consequences inconsistent with law and justice and such as cannot be imputed to the party affected [references]. Nevertheless, the basis of a transaction may be held to have collapsed if the balance of the reciprocal obligations has been gravely disturbed by some intervening event [reference]. In this compromise the plaintiff, in return for waiving its right to sue in respect of the delivery of defective beer in August 1977, was to receive a given benefit in exchange, and is entitled to more than a fraction of that benefit.

The appellant objects in vain that the plaintiff should have foreseen the political developments in Iran. The parties' expectations—here of their future cooperation—may constitute the basis of a transaction even if they are aware that their expectations may not be answered. According to the findings of the court below, to which the appellant makes no procedural objections, the possibility that these expectations might be frustrated was not so manifest as to prevent the plaintiff from invoking the collapse of the basis of the transaction.

(ee) Notwithstanding the collapse of the basis of the transaction, the court below upheld the compromise, but altered its terms. It was right to do so [references]. Only exceptionally do the rules of collapse of the basis of the transaction make the contract disappear *in toto*; the general rule is that the contract should be maintained so far as possible and simply adjusted to the changed situation so as to do justice to the justified interests of both parties [references]. The evidence does not suggest that if they had known how matters would develop, the parties would have refused to enter any compromise at all. After all, when the plaintiff notified him that the goods were defective, the defendant originally proposed a deal which made no reference whatever to further deliveries of beer. If the compromise is to be upheld, the prior legal situation is irrelevant, so it is immaterial how seriously the defendant questioned the size of the plaintiff's claim or whether the compromise was a very generous one on his part.

The way the court below set about adapting the contractual duties of the parties to the altered circumstances represents an exercise of an *ex officio* discretion of the judge of fact [reference]. The court divided the loss resulting from the collapse of the basis of the transaction equally between the parties. Such a division is quite in order when there is no reason to adopt a different division, and when the loss due to the disturbance cannot be loaded on to one of the parties only [references]. Nothing in the procedure suggests that either party has been burdened with more than half of the risk that the compromise might not be executed. Given the inadequacy of the evidence, the court below had to make a lump-sum estimate of some matters, such as the profit to be made from further sales of beer, but this lies within the area of the fact-finders and certainly does not suggest that adaptation of the contract is impermissible.

(ff) The precise way the court adapted the contract is also legally acceptable.

(gg) In order to work out the profit the plaintiff would probably have made had the compromise been executed, the court assumed that during the period when a discounted price was on offer it would have ordered 60,000 cases and made a profit of DM0.90 per case. Neither finding is irrational, as the appellant asserts. para 287 I ZPO, possibly by analogy, provides a basis for the court's estimate of the amount that might well have been ordered. In estimating the gain the plaintiff would have made had the compromise been carried out, the court arrived at an estimate of the amount of the plaintiff's loss. Since in fact the compromise was not carried out and no exact proof of the amount is available, para 287 I ZPO permits an estimate to be made [reference]. There is no reason not to allow a similar estimate when a contract is being adjusted after its basis has collapsed. The courts have constantly held that estimates made by judges of fact under para 287 I ZPO may be reviewed on appeal only to the extent that the evaluation has been made on obviously false or fundamentally irrelevant grounds or if facts with a critical bearing on the decision have been ignored. The estimate made by the court below survives such a review: . . .

Case 107
BUNDESGERICHTSHOF (EIGHTH CIVIL SENATE) 14 OCTOBER 1992
NJW 1993, 259

Facts

The parties were 'people's enterprises' in the former German Democratic Republic (DDR), now transformed into limited liability companies. Under the DDR's Economic Plan for 1990 the plaintiff was required to buy a large piece of machinery from an Austrian supplier, and the defendant was to pay the plaintiff the sum of 1,706,000 DDR M, half of which the defendant was to receive from general state revenues and the other half through a bank credit. Nothing was forthcoming from the general state revenues, and the bank credit, which the defendant transferred to the plaintiff, amounted to only DDR M376,806.90. The Contract Law of the DDR which was applicable to the contract at the time of its formation was repealed on 1 July 1990, but, according to the *Bundesgerichtshof*, remained applicable in so far as consistent with the new market economy. When the DDR was absorbed into re-united Germany, DDR-M were converted into DM at the rate of two for one.

The plaintiff claimed the unpaid balance. The *Kammergericht* ordered the defendant to pay DM451,346.55 with interest. Both parties appealed, and the case was remanded to the *Kammergericht*.

Reasons

The defendant's appeal:
The parties are agreed that under the contract of January 1990 the plaintiff had a claim against the defendant for 1,706,000 DDR-M, which was reduced in amount by the 376,806.90 DDR-M paid on 26 June 1990. The plaintiff accordingly had a claim against the defendant in the amount of 1,329,193.10 DDR-M.

This outstanding claim has been neither met by payment nor extinguished by statute, but must be adapted in accordance with the principles of the collapse of the basis of the transaction, given that the state failed to provide the envisaged finance . . .
2. The Contract Law of the DDR gives the defendant no claim for cancellation or modification of its duty to pay. The wording and purpose of para 78 of the law, which might be thought applicable, make it clear that an economic contract can only be affected by reason of overwhelming social interests, which neither existed nor were suggested in this case . . .
5. The *Kammergericht* was of the following view. The defendant could claim a reduction in the price under para 242 BGB, for the maxim of good faith and fair dealing was an ethical principle of law which is applicable throughout the whole system. It is therefore applicable even to contracts formed in the DDR prior to the entry into force there of the BGB, to the extent that novel circumstances external to the contract and not arising from its own terms are involved. The change of the currency from DDR-M to DM was irrelevant . . . It was also irrelevant that the defendant had not received the full amount of the credit envisaged by the plan. It may have been true that on forming the contract the parties counted on the sale being financed as to 50 per cent by the bank credit, but a debtor cannot successfully invoke the occurrence of

unexpected difficulties in obtaining finance or the failure of a planned credit to materialise. However, it was relevant under para 242 BGB that the defendant did not receive the promised amount from the DDR's general revenues. When the sale contract was entered into, both parties operated on the basis that the state plan provided for 50 per cent of the finance. The intervening collapse of the state plan and the consequent impossibility of obtaining payment from the state amounted to a collapse of the basis of the transaction. After the parties were transformed into stock companies it would not be consistent with good faith and fair dealing for the defendant alone to be burdened with the loss. Thus the contract had to be modified, so that each party bore half of the loss due to the failure of the state to provided the promised moneys.

(a) These observations are not in every respect correct in law.

Certainly the Kammergericht was right to hold that the rules relating to the collapse of the basis of the transaction, which follow from the principle of good faith and fair dealing, were applicable in this case. This principle is a legal principle transcending statute and immanent in all legal systems; for example, its effect may be seen in A 1 no 2, sentence 2 of the common Protocol on the leading principles of the Treaty between the DDR and the Federal Republic for the Creation of a Monetary, Economic and Social Union, which is binding by reason of Art 4 I 1.

(b) The basis of a transaction is constituted by the common assumptions entertained by the parties at the time of the contract, or by an assumption of one of the parties, ascertainable by the other and not objected to by him, regarding the existence or future occurrence of circumstances, to the extent that the parties' intention to make the transaction is based on such assumptions [references].

(aa) We need not decide whether the court below was right to hold that the change of currency in itself or the abandonment on 1 July 1990 of the provisions regarding prices in the DDR were not events such as to justify adaptation of the contract, for the court rightly held that the leading occurrence which justifies such modification is the failure of the state to provide the allocated finance, that is, an event prior to the change of currency and the repeal of the price regulations.

(bb) The court below held that at the time the contract was formed the parties assumed that the 'Reconstruction A' plan was a state plan which was to be financed, in accordance with the provisions of the state, as to 50 per cent from state revenues ... It is uncontested and decisive that the plaintiff as well as the defendant assumed at the time of the contract that the financial needs would be fully met from state sources. In this sense the contractual will of the parties (in so far as one can speak of such a thing when a planned economy is in force) rested on this common assumption.

(c) The court below was also right to hold that the parties' common expectations were also frustrated in regard to the provision of the bank credit, but it proceeded to deny the defendant's invocation of the rules of collapse of the basis of the transaction, on the ground that a debtor is in principle not allowed to found on unexpected difficulties in obtaining finance when a source on which he had counted fails to materialise, this being a risk which falls within the debtor's area of risk.

On the special facts of this case this court cannot agree.

(aa) The case law certainly recognises that circumstances which clearly fall within the area of risk of one or other party, given the contractual purpose, do not entitle that party to claim that the basis of the transaction has disappeared [reference]. Thus the *Bundesgerichtshof* has decided that the failure of expected finance to materialise is not normally to be seen as a collapse of the basis of the transaction, since this falls within the debtor's sphere [reference]. But it must not be overlooked that these decisions were rendered against the background of a functioning market economy. In the context of a socialist planned economy matters are different. The economic units of the DDR ran no financial risk if they adhered to the plan, as it was guaranteed by the total state direction of the economy, including control of the banks. The defendant had no choice: it had to adhere to the stipulations of the plan, buy the machine and rely on the provision of the finance allocated by the plan. This was the situation at any rate at the end of 1989 and the beginning of 1990, when the contract was formed, and at that time the very quick succession of events, the collapse (mid-1990) and the speedy unification (October 1990), was not to be foreseen. Thus the defendant cannot be charged with having taken any risk at the time of the contract even with regard to the provision of credit envisaged by the plan. It had no power to influence the allocation between general revenues and credit. To refuse to adapt the contract in relation to the part that was to come from the credit, as the court below has done, would be to make the individual business's ability to claim adaptation depend on a capricious distinction drawn in the state's financing plan.

(bb) The facts here, where the claimant took no risk, distinguish this case from those decided by the *Bundesgerichtshof* after the collapse of 1945 [references]. The appellant overstates the effect of those cases in saying that no account may be taken of the collapse of the basis of the transaction when fundamental political, economic or social changes have occurred . . .

(d) The defendant cannot be expected to continue to adhere to the contract with the plaintiff on the existing terms. In respect of machinery costing DM376,806 the defendant, who already paid 376,806.90 in DDR-M in June 1990, is now being sued for a further DM664,597. It would be inconsistent with law and justice to grant the claim, and contrary to good faith and fair dealing to insist on it.

(e) In effecting the necessary modification of the contract it must be borne in mind that it is only exceptionally that the doctrine of the collapse of the basis of the transaction leads to a total cancellation of the contractual duty; generally the contract is to be maintained so far as possible and simply adapted until it accords with the justified interests of the parties [references]. In the case of a contract formed by autonomous parties it may be right to ordain a disposition which reasonable parties would have adopted had they foreseen the eventual situation [reference], but that does not apply where the contract was imposed by the state [reference]. In cases like the present the only consideration is to effect a fair resolution of the respective losses of the parties.

The modification must take place as of the time when the basis of the transaction collapsed, that is, as of the time when it was clear that the finance was not going to be forthcoming. That was in June 1990. . .

We agree with the court below that it accords with the facts and the interests of the parties to effect an equal split of the loss resulting to the defendant from the collapse of the basis of the transaction. Any other modification more favourable to the defendant would be unfair to the plaintiff, for it had to obtain credit for the requisite import of the machinery in the full amount of the stipulated price . . .

Chapters 8–10

Case 108
BUNDESGERICHTSHOF (SEVENTH CIVIL SENATE) 8 JULY 1982
NJW 1982, 2494

Facts

On 10 February 1977 the defendant commissioned the claimant to carry out clinker brick-cladding work on 60 houses at a price of DM70.80 per square metre. Work came up on further houses. The parties agreed that the VOB/B (1973) (General Conditions on Building Contracts) would apply. A formal approval on inspection did not take place. On 16 August 1978 the claimant submitted a final invoice of DM692, 397.04, minus sums already paid totalling DM544, 059.11. The defendant made deductions in respect of certain items, alleged higher interim payments than stated and deducted an agreed security figure of 5 per cent = DM31, 890. The defendant also retained the outstanding amount of DM46, 474.77 on grounds of defective work on four houses (F,G, L, and B). He estimated the costs of correcting the defects at DM32,742. In reply, the claimant alleged that these costs were sufficiently covered by the security sum retained for the five-year term of warranty. By court action the claimant now demands DM148,337.93 residual payments for wages plus interest.

By partial judgment, the lower instance courts granted the claimant the mathematically undisputed outstanding amount of DM46, 474.77 plus interest. The defendant's further appeal was admitted and resulted in the quashing of the judgment and a referral back to the *Landgericht*.

Reasons

I. The Appeal Court, like the *Landgericht*, holds that the retained security sum must be included when assessing the defendant's right to refuse performance of the contract because of proven claims for improvements.

There is no reason to grant the defendant further security. The security retained is also not to be divided into partial amounts attached to each house; the period of warranty commenced with the approval of the work as a whole, for which reason the calculation is to be based on the entire amount retained, ie DM31,890. This sum covers the assessed costs for the removal of the defects found in houses F and G in respect of which the claimant intends to retain at least DM23,000. Insofar as the defendant, in appeal proceedings, for the first time bases his right to refuse payment amounting to a further DM26,000 on defects in the houses stemming from damp, his counter-claims must be rejected for being belatedly submitted.

The further appeal successfully refutes these arguments.
1. According to the contract of 10 February 1977, in the final accounts '5 per cent of the net building costs will be retained for the duration of the term of warranty, ie for five years from the date of approval'. Such an agreement on a security sum to be retained will basically not prevent the principal from refusing payments due because of defective workmanship While the security is intended to ensure a contractually correct performance and the preservation of the warranty rights (para 17 No1 II VOB/B

[1973]), the refusal to perform contractual duties under para 320 BGB is intended, apart from safeguarding claims, to put pressure on the contractor to perform his duties immediately (*Senat, NJW* [1958] 706 No4; [1981] 2801; BauR [1978] 398 [400] = ZfBR [1978] 25 [26]). The defence based on para 320 BGB can thus not be averted by granting a security (para 320 I 3 BGB). The retention after approval of residual wage payments already due aims to induce the contractor immediately to rectify the defects as set out in para 13 No5 VOB/B. As long as there is a right to claim removal of defects, and the parties are thus not obliged *to make final settlements after* the term of warranty *has expired* and the sums retained as security *have become due,* the defendant is in principle entitled, over and above his right to the security, to refuse payment for reasons of defective work (italics as per original).

2. Fixing a quite considerable sum as security may have an impact on the amount to which performance can justifiably be refused; but the principal is not *solely* restricted by that amount when he alleges faulty workmanship and the costs for repairs are covered by the security sum. Instead, he can retain a *further* considerable amount which he deems necessary to pressurize the contractor into a speedy correction of the defects. The latter may not plead that the principal can only exercise his right to refuse performance insofar as he has a claim to have defects repaired which in monetary terms exceed the security (BGH, *NJW* [1981] 2801). The amount of the sum which the principal may retain under para 320 BGB depends on the actual circumstances and the principle of good faith. This Division of the Court has already pronounced that two or three times the sum of expected costs for repairs are adequate [BGH, *NJW* [1981] 2801 with further references]. Thus the appeal court's reasoning can only be followed insofar that the security should be taken into consideration and must be included when calculating the amount up to which payments can be validly refused. Nonetheless, the fact that the expected costs for repair are or are not covered by the security cannot be decisive. The point is not 'to grant the defendant a further safeguard', as the appeal court holds. Refusal to perform the contractual duties is, rather, intended to put adequate pressure on the claimant speedily to repair the defects in the work done.

3. Although it cannot be right to allot the retained security schematically in equal amounts of DM362 to each of the 88 houses, it nonetheless cannot be forgotten that the defendant exercises his right to refuse performance for reasons of defects which occurred in four houses and as early as during the first year of the warranty period. But the retained sums are meant to safeguard the claimant's rights in respect of *all* houses and for a period of up to five years. In the case of large-scale building projects such as this one further defects and damage resulting from such defects are to be expected. Moreover, the term of warranty has not expired. Thus the sums retained as security can only be included to a very limited degree in the calculation of the amount up to which performance of contractual duties may be refused.

According to the substantiated facts on which the further appeal is to be based, the right to refuse payments up to the sum of DM23,000 for alleged costs for repair amounting to DM15,114 for the houses F and G is an adequate remedy. The same is true in respect of a further and subsequently substantiated right to refuse payment up to the sum of DM26,000 because of alleged costs for repairs totalling DM17,628 for the houses L and B. In this respect, it is immaterial at which point the defendant became aware of the defects in these houses. The right to refuse performance as set out in para 320 BGB does not depend on the opponent's knowledge but rather on whether the other party's performance was not carried out at all, or insufficiently or with defects, so that the debtor's default is partially or totally excluded (see: BGH, *NJW* [1966,] 200; *WM* [1974] 369 [370]). Where the right to refuse performance is asserted during court proceedings, once acceptance of the work has taken place, this will not however lead to a (partial) dismissal of the claim but merely to a judgment ordering simultaneous performance, ie of payment and of repair of defects. [Para 322 I BGB; see BGHZ 61, 42 [45] = *NJW* [1973] 1792 with further references; BGH *BauR* [1980] 357; see also BGHZ 73, 140 [144] = *NJW* [1979] 650].

. . .

Case 109
BUNDESGERICHTSHOF (EIGHTH CIVIL SENATE) 16 JULY 2003
NJW 2003, 3341

Facts

On 6 June 2001 the claimant ordered a Camcorder DV Panasonic NV-DS 38 EG at the price of DM1999 by email from the defendant, who carries on, among other things, a mail order business in electronic equipment in M. The purchase price was paid by the credit bank which was brought in. On 28 June 2001, the defendant gave the properly addressed package to a parcel service for dispatch to the claimant. The claimant alleges that he has not yet received the camera. He had not signed the delivery slip of 29 June 2001 submitted in this legal action by the defendant; the signature ('M U') was a forgery.

In his claim, the claimant demands that the defendant be ordered to hand over a camcorder of the type described, and to transfer ownership of this camera. The defendant claims that, by handing over the package to the parcel service, it had done what was necessary on its side for fulfilment, as there was a duty to send, and § 447 of the BGB was to be applied. The claimant had also received the parcel; the signature on the delivery slip was his.

The *Amtsgericht* has rejected the claim, and the *Landgericht* has rejected the claimant's appeal directed against this. The claimant is pursuing his claim to its full extent by his appeal in law which has been admitted by the appeal court.

Reasons

I. In its decision, which satisfied the requirements of § 540 of the ZPO (Civil Procedure Order), the *Landgericht* has assumed that the present case was concerned with a mail order purchase in the sense of § 447 BGB, and the defendant had therefore complied its obligations arising from the purchase contract by handing over the camcorder to the parcel service on 28 June 2001. The provisions of § 447 BGB were also to be applied to modern forms of sale, as the legislature, in spite of critical opinions in the literature, had not taken the reform of the law of purchase as an opportunity to regulate these forms of sale in a different way.

II. The decision of the Landgericht stands up to legal examination in the end result.

1. The appeal court has obviously admitted the appeal in law in accordance with § 543 (2) no 2 of the ZPO because it considered it necessary to settle the legal question of whether, under the reform of the law of purchase, the provisions of § 447 BGB 'can and should apply to modern forms of sale.' This question does not however need settlement by the highest courts for cases of the present kind, as the legislature has already answered it by the insertion of § 474 (2) BGB. According to this provision, application of § 447 BGB to contracts for the purchase of consumer goods is—compulsorily— excluded (§ 475 (1) BGB). There is no doubt that, according to the statutory definition in § 474 (1) sentence 1, first half sentence of the BGB, a case of the kind which is present here represents a purchase of consumer goods. Although the admission of the appeal in law formulated by the appeal court accordingly has no valid subject matter, the court dealing with the appeal in law is bound by it (§ 543 (2) sentence 2 of the ZPO).

2. The reasoning for the admission of the appeal in law reveals that the appeal court intended already to apply the law of purchase in its new version which came into force on 1 January 2002. That is certainly legally incorrect, because in the present case the relevant provisions are the version which still applied until 31 December 2001 (Art 229 § 5 sentence 1 of the EGBGB (Introductory Statute to the BGB)). But as § 447 of the BGB remained unamended, and the *Landgericht* overlooked the new exclusionary provision in § 474 (2) BGB, the legal error has in this respect no consequences as it depends on the provision—subject to the following observations.

3. The appeal court has, in the end result, correctly assumed that the defendant is not obliged to deliver another camcorder of the same type under § 433 (1) BGB, even if the claimant did not receive the camcorder and it disappeared in an unexplained fashion en route after dispatch.

   (a) In this respect it certainly does not matter whether, according to the special provisions of § 447 (1) BGB applying to a mail order purchase, the risk had transferred to the claimant. The defendant's duty of delivery had already lapsed under the general provisions of § 275 BGB, old version, when the camcorder disappeared after it was handed over to the parcel service. According to these provisions, the creditor is released from the duty to perform in so far as performance becomes impossible as a result of a circumstance arising after the commencement of the obligation relationship for which he is not responsible. These prerequisites are fulfilled here; in particular nothing has been alleged or is otherwise evident to suggest that the defendant has violated its duties to show care (*Sorgfaltspflichten*) in the choice of the parcel service entrusted with the dispatch of the camera. Besides this, it is not inconsistent with release from the duty to perform that an obligation as to class *(Gattungsschuld)* was agreed when the camera was ordered (§ 279 of the BGB, old version). By the choice of an actual piece of equipment and the delivery of it by the defendant to the parcel service, the obligation relationship was limited under § 243 (2) BGB to the camcorder handed over. By delivery of the piece of equipment to the carrier, the defendant has done what was necessary on its side in the sense of this provision for the effectuation of the performance owed, and this also follows from § 447 (1) BGB. The place for performance for the actions to be undertaken by the defendant to effect performance was its place of business (§ 269 (1) and (3) BGB).

   (b) The place for performance of the obligation owed by the seller to hand over the item purchased to the buyer and to transfer ownership in it (§ 433 (1) sentence 1 of the BGB, old version) is, in case of doubt, the seller's place (of residence). Admittedly this only applies if no (other) place for performance can be deduced, either from a determination by the parties or from the circumstances, in particular from the nature of the obligation relationship (§ 269 (1) BGB). The claimant does not claim, nor is it otherwise discernible, that the parties have expressly or tacitly agreed a place for fulfilment for delivery of the camcorder which is different from the defendant's address (*Sitz*). Nor does such a thing follow from the circumstances, for instance from the nature of this purchase contract. The fact that in the mail order business it is typically the task of the seller to effect the sending of the item purchased—at his own cost or that of another—is no basis on its own for the assumption that the place for receipt should also be the place for performance (place for fulfilment) for the seller's duty of delivery (argument from § 269 (3) BGB). The presumption in § 269 (1) BGB, according to which the defendant's address *(Sitz)* was the place for fulfilment of the seller's duties which it owed, therefore remains (likewise Bamberger/Roth/Grüneberg, § 269 marginal no 10, 33; Soergel/Wolf, 12th edn, § 269 marginal no 16; contra OLG Stuttgart, NJW-RR 1999, 1576; MünchKomm/Krüger, 4th edn, § 269 marginal no 20; Palandt/Heinrichs, 62nd edn, § 269 marginal no 12).

(c) Whether the defendant, as it claims, also makes it possible for its customers to collect goods from its branch businesses can be left undecided (see judgment of the senate of 5 December 1990—VIII ZR 75/90, NJW 1991, 915 on dispatch to another place than the place for fulfilment). Even if the defendant sells goods exclusively by mail order, this does not change the fact that the customer's order at least contained a conclusive declaration that the item purchased was to be delivered to him at his residential address *(Wohnanschrift)* or another address given for dispatch.

(d) No different conclusion follows from § 447 BGB. This provision allocates to the buyer the risk, associated with the dispatch, of accidental destruction of or damage to the item, if the seller dispatches the item sold to another place than the place for fulfilment at the request of the buyer. In this case the risk of counter-performance passes to the buyer as soon as the seller hands the thing over to the person entrusted with the dispatch (but see, after the new law for the consumer goods purchase, § 474 (2) BGB). The place for performance to be determined in accordance with § 269 BGB is not affected by the regime in § 447 (1) BGB. The definition in § 447 (1) BGB assumes instead that the place for the action of performance to be undertaken by the seller (place of performance), and the place at which the consequence of performance occurs, are separate (Soergel/Huber, BGB 12th edn, § 447 marginal no 14; Bamberger/Roth/Faust, BGB, § 447 marginal no 5).

4. In the end it no longer matters whether the parcel service actually handed over the package to the claimant and he signed the delivery slip, as the defendant has alleged, The claimant cannot demand the (fresh) delivery of a camcorder of the type purchased. His appeal in law must therefore be rejected.

Case 110
REICHSGERICHT (SIXTH CIVIL SENATE) 7 JUNE 1915
RGZ 87, 64

Facts

On 20 July 1913, there was a collision between a tram belonging to the plaintiff and a taxi belonging to the first defendant and driven by the second defendant. The passengers in the taxi, Sch, an accountant, and his wife and daughter, were injured. They claimed damages from the plaintiff tram company under the Imperial Law of Liability. The plaintiff now alleges that the accident was entirely due to the fault of the second defendant, for which the first defendant is responsible, and seeks a declaration that the defendants are bound to indemnify it for all loss arising from the accident.

The lower courts granted the claim and the defendant's appeal is dismissed.

Reasons

1. The court below did not misapply § 278 BGB, as the appellant contends. Doubts may certainly be entertained about the reasoning of the Court of Appeal that in a case like the present the taxi driver may regard all his passengers as contractors, and may look to each of them for the fare. We need not decide this however since in any case there is no doubt that a contract was made with the accountant Sch, who boarded the taxi at the same time as his wife and daughter. But that does not mean that he is the only person with a contractual claim arising out of the contract of carriage. On the contrary, the contract of carriage is a contract in favour of the wife and daughter who were travelling with him; they were 'third parties' under § 328 BGB, and acquired a direct right to demand performance, namely proper and safe carriage. There is therefore no reason to doubt the Court of Appeal's conclusion that the first defendant was liable under the contract of carriage to all three passengers, and the he must answer for the fault of the second defendant, who in this respect was his agent for performance under § 278 BGB.

Case 111
BUNDESGERICHTSHOF (EIGHTH CIVIL DIVISION) 24 OCTOBER 1979
BGHZ 75, 221

Facts

On 2 January 1973, the defendant sold B seven lorries, under retention of title until final payment of the purchase price, and delivered the vehicles to B.

As part of two agreements on the provision of collateral of 14 January 1974 and 24 July 1975, B and the plaintiff concluded agreements on the transfer by way of security of the expectancy, *in rem*, in respect of five of the vehicles still under retention of title. This transfer was meant to safeguard all other outstanding and future claims the defendant might have against B from existing invoices and other legal titles. The plaintiff and B concluded a concurrent agreement on the loan of the vehicles to B.

On 20 November 1975, the defendant and B amended their purchase contract of 2 January 1973 to the effect that the lorries should remain the defendant's property as security for all current and future main and ancillary claims stemming from the entire existing business relationship Thereafter the defendant granted B several loans.

On 19 December 1975, the defendant demanded that the vehicles be returned, since B had allegedly failed to meet his obligations in respect of payments. On the same day, the defendant fetched the vehicles from B and sold them to third persons.

The plaintiff was of the opinion that he had obtained ownership of five vehicles, since B had paid the full purchase price; He claimed damages from the defendant.

The *Landgericht* and the *Oberlandesgericht* ruled in favour of the plaintiff. The further appeal is unsuccessful.

Reasons

I.

1. The appeal court held that by the contract of 2 January 1973, B had acquired an expectant right of ownership in respect of the lorries. As a result of further contracts, concluded between B and the plaintiff on 17 January 1974 and 24 July 1975 regarding five of the vehicles, the defendant could no longer transfer full ownership. The latter contracts must be interpreted to mean that the plaintiff acquired an expectant right, *in rem*, in respect of the five lorries. The court's findings are correct and not the subject of this appeal.

2. The appeal court's assumption can be followed that prior to 20 November 1975 the condition was not met under which the plaintiff, as a person entitled under an expectancy *in rem* could acquire full ownership of the five vehicles named in the contracts as collateral security. The appeal court found that the purchase price for the vehicles had not been fully paid at that time, ie when B and the defendant amended the purchase contract of 2 January 1973 by agreeing on an extended retention of ownership (. . .)

3. The appeal court found and the further appeal does not dispute that B's obligation to pay the purchase price for all vehicles had fully been met on 10 December 1975. Any further claim thereafter raised by the defendant was not based on the purchase contract of 2 January 1973.

4. Whether or not on 10 December 1975 the plaintiff became owner of the five vehicles which had been assigned to him as collateral and whether or not, as a result, he can claim damages from the defendant for breach of ownership through the sale of the vehicles depends on whether the defendant and B needed the plaintiff's approval for their amendment agreement of 20 November 1975 on the suspensive condition of full payment of the purchase price, ie on the condition by which, according to the purchase contract of January 1973, the point in time was determined at which the expectancy *in rem* developed into a full title. The question had to be answered whether the plaintiff's approval was needed for the result that, according to the amendment, the change of ownership in the five vehicles could only take place once all other claims which the defendant had against B were met.

II. The appeal court held that B, when reaching the agreement of 20 November 1975, acted without authority when he dealt with the plaintiff's expectancy in respect of the five vehicles. Extending the retention of title not only amounted to an amendment of the purchase contract but also directly resulted in a change of the agreement between the plaintiff and B (*Erfüllungsgeschäft*). The provisions made by B in respect of the plaintiff's expectancy *in rem* are null and void. Once the purchase price had been fully paid, ie on 10 December 1975, the expectant right transferred to the plaintiff had matured to a full right of ownership

The appeal brought against this result must fail.

1. As correctly held by the appeal court, it is basically possible subsequently to extend a retention of title thereby allowing the vendor of goods sold under retention of title to use his rights in the goods for other claims against the purchaser. When goods are sold under retention of title, as long as the condition for full transfer of title has not yet been met, vendor and purchaser can alter their agreement. They can rescind or change it by adding further conditions. Ownership then transfers once all conditions are met, including the one subsequently added (BGHZ 42, 53, 58).

2. The validity of the claims here brought by the plaintiff against the defendant depend on whether or not such an agreement on the conditions for transfer of ownership is still at the disposition of the transferor, ie the first purchaser, once the latter has transferred his expectancy *in rem* to a third person (the second purchaser of the expectancy *in rem*).

(a) The further appeal alleges that this question is to be answered in the affirmative. It thereby follows the opinion held in particular by Serick (*Eigentumsvorbehalt und Sicherungsübertragung*, 1963, vol I, 251 et seq, 253), according to which the second acquirer of the expectancy obtains a legal position of which he cannot be unilaterally deprived by the vendor who retained ownership in the goods. But he can so be deprived by an arbitrary act of the conditional purchaser who transferred his expectancy to him, since it still depends on the purchaser whether the original condition is met. The original contractual relationship, ie the underlying contract, continues until both parties have fulfilled all obligations under it. The acquisition of the expectancy by a third person does not mean that the acquirer becomes a party to that contractual relationship Thus the conditional purchaser remains entitled, without consent of the second acquirer of the expectancy, to influence the purchase contract. With approval from the vendor who retained ownership in the goods, he can rescind the contract with the result that the condition, ie full payment, can no longer be fulfilled and that the expectancy *in rem* expires. He is also entitled to agree changes in the methods of payment with the vendor (see also Raiser, *Dingliche Anwartschaften*, 1961, 31; Schlegelberger/Hefermehl, HGB, 4. ed., § 368, addendum, n 34; Esser, Fälle und Lösungen zum *Schuldrecht*, 1963, 54, n 14). The further appeal also submits that the second acquirer of the expectancy must accept an agreement between the parties to the purchase contract in respect of an extension of the retention of ownership

(b) This court cannot follow the reasoning submitted in the further appeal. Like the appeal court, it holds that an extension of the retention of ownership as affected by the agreement of 20 November 1975 constitutes an invalid disposition by B in respect of the plaintiff's expectancy.

(aa) it is correct that even after transfer to a third person, the existence of an expectancy is linked to the underlying purchase contract, the outcome of which is determined by the contractual partners, to whom the second acquirer of an expectancy does not belong. This view was held by the court of appeal. Thus, no expectant right comes into being where the contract under the law of obligations does not exist, is null and void or has no effect. In such cases, even acquisition in good faith is impossible, since good faith in the existence of the claim for the purchase price is not protected (Raiser, above, 38; Serick, above, 271). The second acquirer's expectant right also directly expires where the vendor retaining title rescinds the contract because the purchaser is in default (BGHZ 35, 85, at 21) or where the contract is successfully rescinded for other reasons. The existence of the expectant right, a precursor to ownership (BGHZ 28, 16, at 27), as a personal right *in rem* (*subjektiv-dingliches Recht*) is weakened by its dependancy on the underlying contract which is subject to the law of obligations (schuldrechtlicher Vertrag) (see Serick, above). This dependency affects any second acquirer, who must accept any effects on the existence of his rights stemming from the performance of the purchase contract. He must, for instance accept that the purchaser rescinds the contract which eliminates the condition under which the expectancy turns into a full right. In these instances the purchaser exercises no right to which he is not entitled.

(bb) On the other hand, the appeal court's reasoning must be followed that the dependency of the expectant right on the underlying contract does not necessarily mean that the second acquirer of the expectancy must tolerate any arbitrary behaviour of the first conditional purchaser which affects his expectancy *in rem* .

Without approval by the second acquirer of an expectant right, the conditional purchaser cannot arbitrarily make provisions in respect of the expectancy. 'Making provision' in this context means any legal transaction by which a person directly affects a right, ie by transfer to a third person, or by encumbering the right or by relinquishing it or changing its contents (BGHZ 1, 294, at 304). Where the retention of title originally agreed on as part of the purchase contract is later on extended in such a way that the agreement on the transfer of ownership, previously merely conditional on full payment of the purchase price, now includes a further condition, ie the performance of additional obligations from an overall pending business relationship whereby the purchased goods act as collateral for financing other claims which are not based on the original purchase contract, this further agreement directly results in a change in the contents of the expectant right, ie the conditional right to acquire ownership in the goods (BGHZ 35, 85, at 93).

The conditional purchaser is no longer capable of altering the contents of the expectancy, for lack of entitlement (§ 185 BGB), after he has transferred this right to a third person. In so far as the further appeal stresses that the third person (second acquirer of the expectancy) has not become part of the original contract and must therefore accept any effects on the condition which originate from a change of the underlying contract, it fails to grasp that the conditional purchaser is not entitled to make any legal provision affecting the expectancy which is not part of the performance of his original purchase contract concluded under the law of obligations. It is not decisive that the conditional purchaser still has rights and obligations from the original purchase contract. The important point is that he, after transfer of the expectancy, can no longer make provision in respect of this right and that he, as a result of the close link (dependency) between the expectancy and the contract under the law of obligations, can no longer arbitrarily affect a change in the agreed conditions for a transfer of ownership which directly affects the contents of the expectancy *in rem* to the detriment of the second acquirer of this expectancy,unless this change is founded on the conditions of the original purchase contract (see Ermann/Weitnauer,

BGB, 6. edn, § 455, n 28; Flume AsP 161, 385, 394).

(cc) The appeal court rightly pointed out that jurisprudence and legal doctrine have given the acquirer of an expectancy *in rem* a strong legal position, enabling him to use its value for credit purposes, expressed as the opportunity to acquire a full title (BGHZ 20, 88, at 98; 35, 85, at 89). In particular, it is recognised that the holder of an expectancy *in rem* under paras 929, 930 BGB can transfer it as collateral to a creditor (BGHZ 28, 16, at 18 and 25). It would therefore be inconsistent and contradictory to the justifiable interests of commercial life if the provider of a collateral (conditional purchaser) without the consent of the recipient of his collateral (second acquirer of the expectancy) could re-use that expectancy as personal collateral for a credit agreement with his conditional vendor thereby, for instance, extending the latter's retention of title. In practice, he thus commercially devalues the right which he transferred to the first recipient of the collateral (see BGHZ 28, 16, as above; 35, 85, as above).

The following considerations also give rise to strong misgivings in respect of the further appeal's opinion: Under § 267 BGB, the acquirer of an expectancy can pay up the purchase price for and on behalf of the conditional purchaser, thereby acquiring ownership The purchaser, ie his debtor (§ 267 II BGB) cannot raise any objection (decision by this Senate of 31 May 1965—VIII ZR 302/63 = WM 1965, 701, 703), since he has transferred his expectancy and lost his power of disposition even under § 267 II BGB (see BGH decision of 24 May 1954—IV ZR 184/53 = NJW 1954, 1325, 1328). The chance that the acquirer of an expectancy by his payments under § 267 BGB can acquire full ownership, even without consent from the conditional purchaser who lost his power of disposition, could be undermined if the conditional purchaser agrees with the vendor, to the detriment of the acquirer of the expectancy, that this expectancy will now only mature once further claims are met which the vendor who retained his title in the goods has against the conditional purchaser.

(dd) Contrary to the view held by the further appeal, the result, arrived at for doctrinal and commercial considerations, that any later extension of the retention of title, for instance a further use of the retention of ownership as means of safeguarding credits received by the first acquirer of the expectancy *in rem* over and above what had been agreed in the original purchase contract, requires the consent of the acquirer of the expectancy, does not have the effect that the acquirer is thereby given the position of an owner before the condition is met, thereby curtailing the vendor's legal position. As before, the vendor can exercise his right of ownership Thus, by rescinding the contract, he can annul the expectancy if the purchase price is not paid (§ 455 BGB). But, as against the conditional purchaser and first acquirer of the expectancy, the vendor cannot unilaterally alter the original conditions for the transfer of ownership, for instance because he later on intends to link his right to retain the tile to further claims. No reason can be found why the vendor should be allowed to extend his legal position as regards the second acquirer of the expectancy, even with the consent of the purchaser who already relinquished his power of disposition. Far less can a justifiable interest of the conditional purchaser be discerned to re-use the transferred expectancy as a means of securing further credit. The second acquirer of the expectancy obtained no stronger position than that of the conditional purchaser since the conditional vendor retains all rights from the purchase contract and from his retention of ownership as set out in the original agreement.

3. (. . .)

Case 112
BUNDESGERICHTSHOF (TWELFTH CIVIL DIVISION) 28 NOVEMBER 1990
BGHZ 113, 62

Facts

The plaintiff is a company specialising in professional liability insurance. In a previous court action, its client, an architect, had been held liable for damages. The insurance company had paid out to a shareholder of a limited liability company (W GmbH), the successful claimant of the first action. According to the company's structure the shareholder was, as against the other shareholders, unreservedly liable for the company's debts and he had actually made payments for the company which experienced financial difficulties. Now, and by this second action, the claimant (the insurance company) demands repayment of the insurance sum for reasons of unjust enrichment by alleging that (a) the defendant (the shareholder) and the architect had fraudulently led the insurance company to believe that there had indeed been an event insured against, and (b) that the defendant had not been entitled to receive insurance payments, since these could only have been due to the W GmbH, not the defendant, since the W GmbH had not assigned their claim for damages to the defendant, which, in any case, should have been lower.

The *Landgericht* rejected the claim. According to its findings, the defendant did not know of any reason why the insurance claim should have been lower. The claim for unjust enrichment failed because the plaintiff knew of the circumstances on which the defendant based his right to receive payments. The plaintiff's appeal was unsuccessful in so far as it was directed against the defendant of the previous action, ie the architect. On appeal, the *Oberlandesgericht* found in favour of the plaintiff. The defendant's further appeal is unsuccessful for the following reasons.

Reasons

I. The appeal court rightly held that the plaintiff has a claim for unjust enrichment against the defendant. This claim is based on § 812 I 1 BGB (*condictio indebiti*).
1. The transfer of the indemnity payments amounting to DM44,456.26 constitutes a performance by the plaintiff to the defendant.

The appeal court held that it was not the plaintiff but rather the former second defendant (the architect) who carried out the obligation. He used the plaintiff merely as 'recipient of his order.' This opinion cannot be shared. There was no order to make payments to a third person (see the BGH decision of 20 June 1990, BGHZ 111, 382). According to the appeal court's correct and unopposed findings, the plaintiff intended, by his payments, to meet an obligation which the architect had to the W GmbH, ie to settle a claim based on his third party liability. The insurer thought that he was bound to indemnify his client because of the valid underlying insurance contract. As is normal for third party liability insurers who pay creditors, the insurance company did not pay its own debt to the recipient but rather paid in respect of the insured person's obligation. . . .

Contrary to the appeal court's opinion, this does not mean that the plaintiff made payment as a result of an instruction from the architect, who only informed him that the defendant demanded damages; in other words, he notified his insurance company that an event had occurred for which he had obtained insurance cover. The architect had stated that in his opinion the claim for damages was justified. This does not amount to a formal order, nor even to an instruction. The insured has no right to give such instruction and the insurer would not need to comply. It is up to the insurer, prior to making payments to a third person (the creditor), to check the insurance contract and to investigate the legitimacy of the creditor's claim against the insured. The insurer meets his client's obligation only once the investigation of this underlying debt relationship establishes that the creditor has in fact a claim as made. This was the case here. When the architect informed his insurer of the defendant's claim for damages, the plaintiff investigated the existence of that claim. He had doubts in respect of the defendant's entitlement. After the defendant had provided additional information, the plaintiff had no further qualms and decided to pay the defendant.

2. The defendant received payments without legal justification . . .

According to the court's findings, the plaintiff made the payments as a performance of the architect's own obligation under third party liability. Performance of an obligation could not take place if the architect was in fact under no such obligation towards the W GmbH. But if such obligation in fact existed, the defendant, ie the shareholder would only have a claim against the architect, where the original claim of the W. GmbH had been assigned to him, the shareholder, making him the creditor of the claim for damages. According to the defendant's own submissions, this was not the case here.

(a) Where a personally liable shareholder of a limited liability company (GmbH) which experiences financial difficulties is called on to provide cover for instance for the company's banking debts because of his joint liability under the law of obligations, this does not have the effect that company claims against third persons are legally transferred to that shareholder.

The appeal court correctly held that payments made by the plaintiff to the defendant did not bring about the intended result, ie that the claim for damages held by the W GmbH was met, either because no such claim existed or because the claim did not belong to the defendant. The defendant received payments without legal justification.

3. As a result, the preconditions for a claim for unjust enrichment against the defendant under § 812 I 1 BGB are here fulfilled . . .

In the absence of an order (see above under 1), restitution under the rules on unjust enrichment is not subject to the established rules for cases or orders for payment but rather is subject to the rules which apply for other types of payments by third persons. In the case of performance by a recipient of an order for payment, the order to indemnify a third person for a claim which the third person, the creditor, has against the debtor, ie the instructing party, originates from the debtor. In this case, however, it is the third person, the payer, who decides to meet the claim. He alone performs the obligation.

Payment by a third person as set out by § 267 BGB is also made where the person who makes the payments in respect of another person's liability deems himself to be obliged so to pay the debtor (MünchKomm/Lieb, 2. ed., § 812, n 100). In such a case, payment is made, as here by the third party liability insurer, *solvendi causa*, ie in respect of the claim for damages (*Valutaschuld*) (see Staudinger/Lorenz, BGB, 12. ed.,

§ 812, n 45). By payment to the creditor, the third party liability insurer normally pays off another person's debt, although he thereby also performs his own obligation to indemnify the insured person (underlying contractual relationship), he makes payments in respect of a third person's obligation, ie his insurance client's duty to pay damages. (On the relationship of third party insurance and claims for damages see the BGH decision of 8 October 1969, IV ZR 633/68—NJW 1970, 134). This is one of the important practical cases of payments made in respect of a third party's debts (*Drittzahlung auf fremde Schuld*) (see Lorenz, JuS 1968, 441, 446 et seq).

According to the predominant legal opinion, restitution under the law of unjust enrichment in cases of payments made by third parties is governed by the principle that the person who made the payment has a direct claim for restitution against the supposed creditor, where in fact there was no underlying obligation to pay [extensive references]. This result applies at least where, as here, the prerequisite is met that the supposed debtor did not at all, or not in a way which makes him liable, order the payer to make the payments [references] . . .

A person who performs another person's obligation has a direct *condictio indebtii*, ie a claim for unjust enrichment against the recipient, if and in so far as there has been no underlying obligation. The fact that the obligation was met without an order from the 'debtor' whose debt did not in fact exist, is insufficient reason for the assumption that payment was made not by the payer but rather by the debtor himself. There is therefore no reason why the debtor should become involved in the restitution.

Case 113
BUNDESGERICHTSHOF (SEVENTH CIVIL SENATE) 11 APRIL 1957
BGHZ 24, 97

Facts

By contract dated 28 April 1952, the defendant's son-in-law, K, took over the sole proprietorship of a business which he had previously run in commercial partnership with the plaintiff: 'I personally guarantee payment of the sum still owed by K under the sale contract of 28 April 1952.'

K had paid the plaintiff DM15,000 in May 1952, but the balance remained unpaid. On 1 December 1954 final default judgment was given against K for DM10,000. Execution against him is unavailing.

The plaintiff sues the defendant as guarantor for the balance due and his legal costs. The defence is that K had counterclaims against the plaintiff which K set off after judgment was rendered against him, and that the plaintiff's claim was thus extinguished.

The *Landgericht* held the defendant liable. The *Oberlandesgericht* rejected his appeal. His further appeal is now allowed.

Reasons

The Court of Appeal was of opinion that since any counter-claims which K might have had against the plaintiff arose before 4 May 1952, they could not be set off against the sum claimed. It therefore did not decide whether any such counterclaims were good in law.

The appellant is right to criticise this (. . .)

The fact that there is final judgment against K, the principal debtor, does not mean that the defendant guarantor's objections need not be investigated. Of course it is true that while § 768 BGB permits a surety to use defences available to the principal debtor, this does not apply to cases falling under §§ 387 ff BGB: a surety may not declare a set-off when the principal debtor might; all he can do is to defer payment under § 770 II BGB for as long as the creditor can satisfy himself by making a set-off against a due claim by the principal debtor. However, the surety is not limited to this defence of his, for once the principal debtor or creditor had duly declared a set-off, this extinguishes the claim for which the surety was liable, and he is thenceforward free.

(a) In the present case the principal debtor did declare a set-off, but only after he had been held liable by final judgment. At that time he no longer had any power to declare a set-off.

§ 767 II Code of Civil Procedure (ZPO) allows K to raise against the claim which had been confirmed by judgment only such defences as arose after the end of the oral proceedings. It is irrelevant that the declaration of set-off was made after this time. What is critical is when the valid counterclaims arose (see, *inter alia*, RGZ 64, 228); on the defendant's own testimony they arose before the end of the preliminary oral proceedings.

The significance of § 767 II ZPO is not purely procedural: once a debt has been confirmed by judgment, a purported set-off is *substantially* invalid unless the counterclaim could be raised in the execution proceedings (RG HRR 1935, 691). Such a purported set-off, being invalid, cannot benefit the defendant surety. There is nothing inconsistent with this in the decision in RGZ 122, 146, 148, for there the principal debtor declared a set-off in the suit brought against him, and did so, even though in vain, *before* the end of the oral proceedings.

(b) But while the judgment issued in the preliminary trial prevented any subsequent set-off by K, the principal debtor, the plaintiff as creditor remained as free as ever to use this legal remedy. The actual wording of § 770 II BGB is literally satisfied here, since it only refers to the power of set-off vested in the *creditor*, but some commentators are of the opinion that the surety can only rely on the dilatory exception of § 770 II BGB if the creditor is *bound* to accept a set-off declared by the principal debtor, and cannot do so if the debtor no longer has a power of set-off [references omitted]. It is not necessary for us to decide whether or not this view is correct, for in the case before us K's counterclaims, if valid, would give him the principal debtor, a *ius retentionis* under § 273 BGB (RGZ 137, 34, 38), and this defence is one which the defendant guarantor may use under § 768 BGB, unaffected by the fact that K himself is now prevented from relying on it by the judgment issued against him: to this extent the defendant is not barred by the legal force of the judgment (see, *inter alia*, RG JW 1909, 419 no 13). On the facts of the case there can be no doubt that the mutual claims here arose from the same legal relationship in the sense of § 273 BGB.

Case 114
BUNDESGERICHTSHOF (EIGHTH CIVIL SENATE) 25 NOVEMBER 1970
NJW 1971, 421

Reasons

I. The Court of Appeal found that the parties did indeed enter into contracts of supply, and dismissed as unproved the plaintiff's contention that these contracts were subsequently cancelled. Since the appellant does not contest this finding, we must proceed on the basis that the plaintiff was bound to perform the contracts.

II. The defendant's claim for damages thus depends on whether the plaintiff was in default in performing his obligations. The courts below have found, quite correctly, that the terms of the defendant's letter of 17 October 1960 were sufficient to put the plaintiff in default. The appellant seeks to rebut this by invoking his General Conditions of Business, but we need not decide whether these conditions were incorporated into the relevant contracts, since the plaintiff himself does not claim that the circumstances under which Clause 6 of these Conditions would excuse delay in delivery by the plaintiff had occurred.

III. The Court of Appeal was right to accept that there would have been no default on receipt of the letter of 17 October 1960 if the plaintiff had previously asserted a right to withhold performance under § 273 BGB on the ground of the defendant's delay in paying sums due under previous contracts, but it was unable to conclude that the plaintiff had done so. The witness A could not recall the proceedings which the plaintiff said had taken place in H, and could not say precisely when the plaintiff had told the defendant in Milan that it would only deliver if the defendant satisfied the claims outstanding against it. It was quite possible, therefore, that the plaintiff's reservations concerned contracts of supply antedating those in dispute. This finding is legally unassailable. The Court of Appeal was thus right to hold that on receipt of the letter of 17 October 1960 the plaintiff was in default (§ 286 BGB).

The appellant contends that the default was terminated by the plaintiff's subsequent assertion of a right to withhold performance. This cannot be accepted. For one thing, it is very doubtful whether there is any factual support for the appellant's view, since in its letter of 12 November 1960 the plaintiff categorically refused to perform the supply contracts of 1959, and such an outright refusal to perform can hardly be construed as an assertion of a defence under § 273 BGB. Nor is there any basis, even on the appellant's view, for holding that the defence was raised before 12 November 1960. It has already been decided on several occasions that when a debtor who has been put in default subsequently acquires, out of the same legal relationship a counterclaim which gives him the right to withhold performance, neither his acquisition nor his assertion of this right cures the default in which he has been put. In order to terminate his default for the future, the debtor must take steps to cure the delay, in other words, he must, if possible, as it was here, establish a *Zug-um-Zug* relationship by offering to perform *pari passu* with counter-performance (RGZ 93, 310; 120, 193, 197; . . .)

It makes no difference if, as here, the claims of the debtor who is in default (here the plaintiff) arose before those of the creditor (here the defendant). Thus it does not help the appellant to suggest that the defendant was also in default, even if there were any findings of fact to substantiate this assertion. The result is the same even on the assumption that the defendant was in default regarding payment of sums due under the 1958 contracts.

The mere fact that the defendant was in breach of contract could not prevent the plaintiff's being in default, for the obligations arising out of the different contracts were basically independent. The plaintiff could have taken steps to acquire rights from the defendant's delay just as the defendant later did from the plaintiff's delay. In particular, he could have asserted a right to withhold performance, a step which would, as has already been stated, have prevented him being in default himself. Furthermore, it may be possible in a case of this sort where the duties arising from one contract are balanced by duties from another contract in the same business relationship, to hold that non-performance of one contract constitutes a breach of the other. On this basis the defendant might be barred by the principle of good faith from relying on the plaintiff's delay in performance when he himself was in breach. But this would call for special circumstances which the appellant has failed to adduce. The Court of Appeal's finding that the plaintiff was in default from 17 October 1960 and that this default was not terminated proves unassailable even from the point of view represented by the appellant.

In a case like the present, a subsequent assertion of the right to withhold performance would not terminate the default: default can be ended only by performance or by a real tender of due performance (see OLG Karlsruhe NJW 1955, 504).

This does not mean that a subsequent assertion of the right to withhold performance is without significance. Although it does not put an end to the default, since it is in no way a substitute for performance, yet it does bring about a *Zug-um-Zug* relationship: it gives the debtor a power to put an end to the default by making an offer to perform *Zug-um-Zug* against counter-performance. In this indirect manner a debtor who has been put in default may still exact performance from the other party.

Case 115
BUNDESGERICHTSHOF (SIXTH CIVIL SENATE) 7 MARCH 1972
NJW 1972, 1045

Facts

R, a pensioner, owed money to both parties. The plaintiff's claims against him were secured by a notarial contract dated 23 October 1961, whereby R pledged to the plaintiff his share of a certain inheritance. The defendant, which had a claim of about DM24,000 against R for costs, obtained a judicial order for security and payment against R on 16 October 1962, which attached R's share in the same inheritance for payment to the defendant up to that amount. On 12 July 1963, the real property belonging to the inheritance was auctioned with a view to division among the heirs. In the division proceedings a representative of the defendant opposed the payment out to the individual heirs and to the plaintiff, and the net proceeds were put on deposit by order of the execution court. The portion of the estate falling to R remained on deposit thereafter. Both parties applied to the depositee for payment out to them of R's part, but without success. The plaintiff then raised a claim against the defendant for an order requiring him to give his consent to the payment out to the plaintiff of the sum on deposit. The Landgericht Duisburg gave judgment for the plaintiff, and the defendant appealed. In the appeal proceedings the defendant counter-claimed, and on 13 March 1967 the Oberlandesgericht Dusseldorf ordered the plaintiff to give his consent to payment out to the defendant of the sum on deposit. The plaintiff's appeal against this judgment resulted in the reinstatement of the judgment at first instance (BGHZ 52, 99), and on 25 July 1969 the depositee finally paid out to the plaintiff the sum which had fallen due to R.

The plaintiff now claims damages for loss of interest, on the basis that the defendant had infringed his security right and had been at fault in doing so.

The *Landgericht* dismissed the claim and the plaintiff's appeal was dismissed also. The plaintiff was allowed to appeal further, and that appeal is now dismissed.

Reasons

I. The only basis of claim which the Court of Appeal considered was the claim in tort. In the long run, however, it left unanswered the question whether any delictual injury had occurred, for it was unpersuaded either that the harm was unlawfully caused or that the defendant had been at fault. The Court of appeal found against unlawfulness because it is in principle permissible and entirely lawful to institute legal proceedings in pursuance of supposed rights. Furthermore, there was no fault because the defendant could not be blamed for being wrong in law as he was. Until the final decision of the BGH in the prior proceedings, the defendant was entitled to believe in the correctness of its view of the law, namely that its own charge attached to the proceeds due to R and that the plaintiff's contractual pledge interest did not, for this was in line with the decisions of the *Reichsgericht* and the opinion of most commentators.

II. The appellant has not been able to fault this reasoning

1. It is not necessary to determine whether the requirements for tort are present here or not. The prior proceedings have made it clear that it was wrong to deposit the money in issue in favour of the defendant as well as of the plaintiff. This being so, the defendant was enriched without legal ground at the expense of the plaintiff; he was therefore bound under § 812 BGB to make a declaration of release (BGH NJW 1970, 463 . . .). If the defendant delayed doing so for a reason for which it is answerable (§§ 284–286 BGB [now §§ 286 et seq]) it must be liable in damages.

In these circumstances the defendant will be responsible for its failure to perform its duty to release the money in good time unless it made an error of law for which it is not to blame. As will be seen, the courts are reluctant to find that an error of law was made without fault; the criteria they apply are very strict, especially when it is a question of seeking to avoid the consequences of delay. If the criteria are satisfied, there can clearly be no finding of fault such as is required for liability in tort. Thus, like the Court of Appeal, we may leave aside the question whether any tort was committed or not, because as will be explained presently, the defendant was not at fault and is not answerable for its failure to fulfil its duty to release the money.

2. The *Reichsgericht* was originally opposed to treating any non-negligent error of law as an excuse for delay and it only modified its position in RGZ 146, 144. The *Bundesgerichtshof*, on the other hand, has always accepted this (see BGH NJW 1951, 398) but it has attached very strict preconditions to the excuse; in particular, it insists that the situation be such that a reasonable person exercising the care required in

social intercourse would have expected the debtor to win the lawsuit in question. Although its position has attracted some criticism [references omitted], the BGH has adhered to this view. What this court said in its decision on 4 March 1969 (LM to § 276 (Bd) BGB no 2) was concerned with whether the error of law on the actual facts of that case connoted fault or not, and is not in conflict.

But strict though the requirement of care is, one must not treat it as meaning that an unfavourable outcome on the legal question must have been positively inconceivable to the debtor; were this so, there would hardly ever be any room for the excuse. It remains true, nevertheless, that the debtor may not burden the creditor with the risk of a simply doubtful point of law [references omitted].

3. The strict criteria are satisfied in this case by the factors mentioned by the Court of Appeal as excusing the [defendant]. The legal position adopted by the defendant in the prior trial was that a contractual security right in part of a joint inheritance did not, when the community of heirs was divided, attach by way of real subrogation to the objects which replaced the undivided part of the joint inheritance. This was in accord with the wording of § 1258 par 3 BGB, the decisions of the *Reichsgericht* and also the views generally entertained by commentators then and since (RGZ 84, 395, 397; other references omitted). The court was therefore right to find no want of care in the [defendant's] conviction that it was entitled to the amount on deposit on the basis of its attachment, it being generally accepted that such a charge does attach by way of real subrogation to the division of an inheritance (BGHZ 52, 99, 105).

Nor was the Court of Appeal wrong in holding that under these circumstances the defendant could not be blamed for adhering to its view of the law although the *Landgericht* had decided against it and although the plaintiff had referred to a decision of the Oberlandesgericht Saarbrücken. As the Court of Appeal observed, invoking the comments of the Oberlandesgericht Dusseldorf in its judgment in the prior proceedings of this case of 13 March 1967, neither of these decisions is very cogently argued, and while they agree in the result with the *Bundesgerichtshof's* eventual decision in the prior suit, the reasoning is not the same.

4. The appellant is right to say that in view of the very low interest which is paid on sums on public deposit, it would have been better had the parties agreed to deposit the sum in issue elsewhere until the legal position was cleared up But the defendant was not obliged to agree to this under any rule of law then in force, much less was it bound to make the sum in issue available to the plaintiff while reserving the right to reclaim it later.

Case 116

BUNDESGERICHTSHOF (EIGHTH CIVIL SENATE) 25 SEPTEMBER 1968
BGH NJW 1968, 2238

Facts

On 7 June 1960 the plaintiff, a civil engineering and demolition firm, ordered 15,000 litres of diesel fuel from the defendant for use in its trucks. The defendant had a chain contract (*Streckengeschäft*) with its supplier, and procured the supplier to deliver the oil directly to the plaintiff, without passing through the defendant's depot. After paying the defendant the price of DM6,452.50 the plaintiff discovered that the engines of its vehicles had suffered damage allegedly due to noxious qualities in the diesel fuel. The plaintiff notified the defendant of this on 29 June 1960, and the defendant transmitted the complaints to its supplier, the K Co in H. After interlocutory proceedings to obtain evidence in December 1960, the defendant brought suit against the supplier in November 1961, and this action is still pending before the *Landgericht* in H.

The plaintiff now sues the defendant for its repair costs of DM18,253 plus further costs and damages for loss of business, a total of DM26,678 plus interest. Both lower courts dismissed the claim: the plaintiff's appeal was unsuccessful.

Reasons

I. The Court of Appeal made no finding as to the quality of the diesel fuel, or whether it met the minimum requirements of DIN (*German Industrial Standard*) 51,601. It also left open the question whether the damage in issue was caused by the fuel oil ordered from the defendant. It dismissed the claim on the ground that the defendant had given no assurance that the goods were 'DIN-standard' (§ 480 par 2 BGB [now § 276 I]), and that the defendant was not responsible for any noxious qualities the fuel might have. This was because the defendant was not bound to make any chemical or physical inspection of the fuel it had procured to be delivered directly to the plaintiff under a chain contract. The defendant had had no adverse experiences with its supplier, the K Co in H, and was thus entitled to assume that the goods supplied would match the requirements. The court of appeal therefore held that no liability in damages arose under paras 276, 326, 480 par 2 BGB [now §§ 437 Nr. 3, 280 I BGB] or in *delict*.

II.

1. The appellant first of all criticises the court of appeal's view that he has no claim for positive breach of contract, and argues that it was wrong to hold that the defendant was under no duty to inspect the goods.

(a) We do not accept the appellant's view that by making no finding as to the quality of the fuel the court of appeal dealt inadequately with the question of liability. Indeed, since the court assumed that the fuel was defective and caused the harm to the engines, it did not overlook any essential fact on the question whether the defendant was under a duty to inspect the goods.

(b) Contrary to the view of the appellant, the fact that the defendant obtained the fuel not from its producer but from an importer who imported it from Holland, is immaterial to the question of the defendant's duty to inspect. The defendant acted as an intermediary, and as such, contrary to the view of the appellant, was not as a general rule, that is, in the absence of special circumstances, bound to inspect the goods he sold on to the consumer. The view of the court of appeal to this effect is in line with well-established opinion both in the courts and in the books [references]. In the case of sales of specific goods the rule certainly applies, but it is also applicable to sales of generic goods unless the circumstances indicate otherwise [references]. Admittedly in RGZ 125, 78 the *Reichsgericht* did find a duty to inspect in the circumstances. There the defendant had supplied the plaintiff steelworks with scrap metal whose chromium content damaged the plaintiff's Martin furnaces. However, most of the defendant's stock of scrap metal had been acquired during the period of inflation when he knew that much of the scrap in circulation contained chromium, so the case was a special one, and shows that there is normally no presumption that the seller of generic goods is under any duty to inspect them.

A duty to inspect goods for possible damaging features might arise from trade practice, if such a practice were established. Again, the duty of care which attaches to any advice given along with the goods may call for an inspection of the goods prior to the giving of the advice (BGH NJW 1958, 866). In that case the seller of lime had given carelessly false information to the customer about its fitness for a given purpose, so there was a breach—not a positive breach of the contract of sale, but a breach of the contract of advice. The court accepted that in principle the seller of generic goods is under no duty of inspection even if their fitness for a particular purpose has been mentioned in the negotiations. We agree with that view. In the present case no special duty to inform was undertaken, so a duty to inspect the fuel could only arise from a trade practice or from the special circumstances of the case.

Since the plaintiff alleged no such trade practice, that point disappears.

The mere fact that the defendant obtained the goods not from the producer but from their importer, and that they were of foreign origin does not, contrary to the view of the appellant, show that in the absence of a relevant trade practice the middleman was under any duty to inspect, especially when, as here, the customer knew that a chain contract was involved and that the seller had no opportunity to make any inspection.

If the defendant had had reason to doubt the quality of the goods it would be different, but the unassailable findings of the court below show that this was not the case.

If there was no duty to inspect, the plaintiff cannot complain that the defendant should have told him that no inspection had been made. The plaintiff could not expect to receive an analysis from a defendant who was under no duty to inspect, especially as he knew that this was a chain contract.

(c) The court below committed no error in holding that the oil was not contaminated during the carriage, so no fault of the defendant could be based on such an event. Of this the appellant makes no complaint.

(d) Nor can the court below be criticised for holding that the defendant was not liable for any fault committed by his supplier, for according to the general view of courts and writers a seller's supplier is not to be regarded as one of those whose services he uses in order to fulfil his own obligations (*Erfüllungsgehilfen*) (BGHZ 48, 119,120). The appellant does not question this.

(e) No extra-contractual liability on the part of the defendant arises on these facts, and no liability in *delict*. The Court of Appeal was right so to hold, and the appellant does not criticise it.

2. The appellant does maintain that the guarantee which he alleges the defendant received from his supplier, namely a guarantee that the fuel was up to standard, was impliedly passed on to him by the defendant and that the defendant is accordingly liable under § 480 II BGB.

The Court of Appeal, like the appellant himself, accepts that the defendant gave no *express* assurance in the sense of § 480 II [now § 276 I] BGB that the diesel fuel was at least of the quality stipulated by DIN 51,601. The court was also right to deny that there was any *implied* assurance.

The appellant does not specify from what circumstances it is to be inferred that the K Co gave this guarantee to the defendant. We can leave aside the question whether the transmission of an analysis entails a guarantee of the appropriate quality, for since it was only the defendant, and not the plaintiff, who received the analysis, the plaintiff cannot complain that he was assured that the goods delivered would match the analysis. In reality the plaintiff is making a quite different case, namely that the defendant impliedly assured him that the goods he was to deliver would match the standard (DIN 51,601), and that he did not keep his word.

We accept the appellant's contention that an assurance need not be express [references]. It can be inferred from the circumstances of the individual case, so that in the end it is a question of fact for the judge who interprets them. Such a finding is only to a limited extent reviewable on appeal.

On this point the court of appeal stated that the mere use of the term 'diesel fuel' did not amount to an assurance that the fuel was at least of the quality called for by DIN 51,601. It was only a term descriptive of the goods. Nor did it hold it relevant that the sale arose because the defendant approached the plaintiff and invited him to obtain supplies for his numerous vehicles from the defendant. No trade practice could be established that the supply of diesel oil entails a guarantee of its freedom from defect. It is true that according to the official report of the Chamber of Commerce and Industry of K it is usual for documents of sale to refer to the goods being marketable and of the quality normal in the trade; but this only means that the fuel meets the minimum standards of DIN 51,601, and it is only an implied precondition of the transaction and not an assurance in the sense of § 480 II [§ 276 I] BGB. The court therefore concluded that while it was indeed part of the contract that the delivery be of diesel fuel of proper quality, this agreement did not amount to an assurance in the sense of § 480 II [§ 276 I] BGB. There in no error of law in the court's reasoning.

The court was right to distinguish between a mere description of the goods, ie the determination in the contract of what was being sold, and an assurance which evinced the seller's intention to give a guarantee. We agree that nothing in the facts of the case suggests that the parties impliedly included any such assurance, so at the end of the day the outcome depends on whether there was a trade practice of the kind asserted by the plaintiff or whether the existence of the DIN-standard with its minimum specifications for commercial diesel oil can serve as a substitute for such a trade practice. It is true that in its decision of 9 December 1963 (VersR 64, 541) the Oberlandesgericht of Cologne held that at a pinch one could find an implied assurance, based on trade practice, that heating oil contained no abnormal amount of water, but nothing of the sort applies to diesel oil. The presence of the DIN-standard in the contractual agreement has no such effect on the contract itself, as the court of appeal was right to hold.

There are some special circumstances where the seller of goods is held to have given an assurance in their description. This is so in the case of the sale of seeds. The basis for this is the Seeds Law of 27 June 1953 (BGBl. I 450) which provides:

'If recognised or permitted seeds are advertised or offered or sold or otherwise brought into commerce, the minimum requirements under § 54 para 1 and any statements about them will be held, in case of doubt, to be guarantees.'

There is a special need to protect the buyer of seed, for he cannot tell till long after the sowing whether the right seed has been delivered. The courts were quick to see this need, and this provision responds to it. This is why the qualities of seeds of a given variety are held to be guaranteed as a trade usage [references]. But the *Reichsgericht* refused to hold that a seller who described the goods as 'Cognac-Kirsch' was giving a guarantee of its qualities, or that the use of the description amounted to an assurance that the goods were pure and free from dye-stuffs. Their reason was that while the statute provided that Cognac must contain no dye-stuffs apart from a small quantity of sugar colouring, there was no prohibition of so describing goods which did not have that quality.

The DIN-standards are recommendations (of the German Committee on Standards) and people are expected to adhere to them voluntarily. They therefore contain no statutory presumption that the seller guarantees that the goods meet the standard. Thus the plaintiff cannot hold the defendant liable under § 480 II ([now § 276 I) simply because standard DIN 51,601 was part of the basis of the contract: the presence of the standard does not have the further effect that the defendant was bound to deliver conforming goods.

This view is not in conflict with the decision of this court on 21 June 1967 [BGHZ 48, 118 f] which said that it might be possible to conclude from the way the producer advertised artificial fibre and the way it was processed in industry that the processing industry had guaranteed its quality. But there are no comparable facts in our case here. In particular the reference to the DIN-standard was unconnected with any advertising or any trade mark or mark of quality, not to mention the fact that the presence of the maker's trade mark would not normally give rise to any guarantee on the part of the middleman.

Accordingly, there can be no question of the defendant having given any assurance that the diesel fuel had any particular qualities. Since we are concerned only with the liability of the middleman, the rules rendering the producer liable for harm done by his products are irrelevant.

Case 117
BUNDESGERICHTSHOF (SIXTH CIVIL SENATE) 18 DECEMBER 1952
BGHZ 8, 239

Facts

Corrugated iron was being carried in the defendant's truck pursuant to a contract of carriage with the plaintiff, who was riding in the passenger's seat. At a moment on the return journey when it was being overtaken by another lorry, the truck struck a tree standing on the near side of the highway. The plaintiff was seriously injured and now claims damages from the defendant and the driver.

The defendants' attributed the accident to the fact that the truck was struck on its off-side by the lorry which was overtaking it. The *Landgericht* and *Oberlandesgericht* dismissed the claim. The plaintiff's appeal was allowed, and the case was remanded.

Reasons

I. . . .

II. The court below was correct to hold that when a vehicle on the highway collides with a tree in conditions of good visibility, that is prima facie proof that the driver was in breach of his duty to observe the care requisite in the conduct of his vehicle and that this fault caused the accident. [references]

The courts have always held that prima facie proof of this kind is rebutted only when the defendant proves the existence of facts which counteract a judicial finding that what actually happened was what typically happens [references]. The facts suggesting the possibility of an untypical occurrence have to be fully established [references]. It is true that the decisions which so hold are all cases of damage occurring in marine or river transport, but the principle they enunciate is of general application and applies in the present case. In order to disarm the prima facie proof against him, the defendant must prove the occurrence of facts which bespeak a serious possibility that the truck struck the tree without any fault on his part.

The Aurt of Apeal held that the fact that immediately before the accident the truck was being overtaken by another lorry was sufficient to neutralise the prima facie proof. It was not. The court below approached the question of evaluating the facts with an incorrect view of the principles established by the courts regarding prima facie proof. The prima facie proof could only be neutralised by proof that the overtaking lorry did actually strike the defendant's truck or obstructed its forward movement by cutting in too sharply after overtaking. The rejection of the claim against the driver therefore cannot stand.

III. The plaintiff's claim for damages against the contractual carrier is based on both the contract of carriage and on tort (§ 831 BGB).

The courts have constantly held that the contractor who undertakes the carriage of persons (or any similar contract of services such as the accommodation of a guest) has the burden of disproof when the facts at first sight justify the conclusion that he was in breach of the duty of care imposed on him [references]. Indeed in its later decisions the *Reichsgericht* so held in cases where the cause of the accident fell within the area of risk for which, in case of doubt, the contractor was answerable [references]. In RGZ 148, 148, 150, a case like the present of a positive breach of contract in the execution of the contract, it left aside the question of the proper impact of § 282 (now § 280 I 2) BGB. The question need not be investigated here either, for whether one applies § 282 (now § 280 I 2) BGB or the principles developed by the courts, the result is the same: in either case the contractor in situations like the present is bound to prove that he was free from fault [references]. The carrier's contractual duty is to see that the passenger is properly transported to the agreed destination. Should the passenger be injured by an event appertaining to the carriage or some feature of the vehicle, one may justifiably conclude that the carrier has not performed his contractual duty. In such a case he must therefore lead evidence to the contrary, that the damaging event was due to a cause for which he is not answerable [references].

The Court of Apeal did proceed, in adherence to the later jurisprudence of the *Reichsgericht*, to review the facts in order to see whether or not the cause of the accident arose from a risk within the defendant carrier's area of responsibility, and so whether he must adduce proof of the absence of fault.

But instead of investigating whether the unexplained cause of the accident arose in the area of risk attaching to the operation of a truck in the defendant's business, the court below required the plaintiff to elucidate the occurrence at least to the extent of making it appear on all the facts that the defendant was guilty of carelessness.

When dealing with the question of prima facie proof the court below held that a driver who in conditions of good visibility collides with a tree has prima facie fallen short of the care requisite in operating a truck: since it cannot consistently be doubted that in such a case the contractual carrier would be answerable for the cause of the accident, it is therefore somewhat contradictory for the court below to have held that the cause of the accident did not arise from the area of risk for which the defendant carrier is answerable.

If the court below does not hold the carrier liable on the ground of prima facie proof, as discussed earlier, it must again check whether, in relation to his contractual liability, the carrier is bound to prove, and whether he has in fact proved, that no fault attached to himself or to his driver in connection with the accident. Even if it is proved that the other lorry did while overtaking strike or otherwise obstruct the defendant's truck, it would still be necessary to ask whether that finding alone is sufficient to establish a lack of fault on the part of the carrier or his driver.

2. Given that the defendant driver had been in the service of the defendant carrier for quite a time when he was charged with the journey in question, it would not be enough for the carrier to show that at the time of the driver's original appointment he took all requisite care: the carrier would need to show that at the time he asked the driver to undertake the journey in question he was so convinced of the driver's reliability that he could do so without any breach of his duty of care. So in addition to proving care in the original appointment, he must prove care in subsequent supervision of the driver, and absence of reason to doubt his aptitude for the journey in question. [references]

Furthermore, in order to escape liability, the carrier must prove that he took the requisite care to see that the truck was fit for the journey or that even if he had done so, the harm would in any event have occurred.

Case 118
BUNDESGERICHTSHOF (EIGHTH CIVIL SENATE) 15 NOVEMBER 1967
BGHZ 49, 56

Facts

The defendants, a married couple, had had a service tenancy of a house belonging to the plaintiff at a monthly rent of DM100. § 5 of the tenancy agreement ran as follows: '2. The tenant must bear the cost of decorating the leased premises and of maintaining them in a decorated state: redecoration includes making good any harm caused to the finish of walls, ceilings and floors by the fault of the tenant. The landlord may require the tenant to execute any appropriate redecoration in a proper manner. 5. Should the tenant fail to execute necessary repairs without delay on the written demand of the landlord, the land- lord may have the redecoration done at the tenant's expense' § 14 no 1 provided that at the end of the tenancy the premises were to be delivered up in proper condition. The defendants occupied the premises for six years and moved out at the end of December 1962 without having done any redecoration at all.

By contract dated 10 and 14 February 1963 the plaintiff leased the dwelling to another married couple, Mr and Mrs JR, at a monthly rent of DM200; the new tenants contracted to execute the necessary redecoration at their own expense and actually did so. The plaintiff claims the sum of DM1,146.60 damages for breach of § 5 no 2 of the lease contract. Both lower courts gave judgment for the plaintiff, and the defendants' appeal is now dismissed.

Reasons

I. The Court of Appeal held that the claim must be for damages for non-performance; no claim in debt could be based on the ground that if the plaintiff had made a fruitless written demand for performance, it had the right under § 5 no 5 of the lease to undertake the redecoration and charge the defendants with the cost. He need not decide whether this is right, since the judgment under appeal is correct in the result even if the plaintiff's claim is one for performance rather than for damages.

II.

1. The defendants argue that they were not in breach of contract, and are therefore not liable in damages. The tenanted premises had been used in a perfectly normal manner, as the experts agreed, so if there was any harm, it was not due to any use which was in breach of the contract (§ 548 BGB), and it followed that the dwelling was in proper condition as required by § 14 no 1 of the contract when it was vacated.

But whether or not the dwelling was used or overused by the defendants in breach of contract is neither here nor there. The Court of Appeal found, and its findings have not been attacked, that the premises urgently required redecoration when the defendants vacated them; in other words, redecoration was necessary to put them in a habitable condition as called for by the contract. This being so, the defendants were under a duty, by § 5 no 2 of the tenancy agreement, to make the necessary redecoration by the time they left, at the latest; when a tenant undertakes to redecorate, this agreement is designed to relieve the landlord not only of the expenses arising during the currency of the lease (in derogation of the rule laid down by § 536 [535 I 2] BGB), but from the necessity of incurring the expense of redecoration when the next tenant is to move in. Simply put, it is the tenant rather than the landlord who has to maintain the premises in a habitable condition (reference omitted), a duty which is neither reduced nor elided by the sitting tenant's readiness to endure a low standard of comfort. This at any rate is the case when the landlord had a right under the contract to require the tenant to redecorate during the tenancy (§ 5 no 2 sentence 3) and to do the redecoration himself, if necessary, on written notice to the tenant and at the tenant's expense (§ 5 no 5). Of course the tenant's duty to redecorate does not mean that the dwelling must be in pristine condition when he moves out. The purpose of the shifting of the cost of redecoration is achieved, and the resulting duty of the tenant fulfilled, if at the end of the tenancy the rooms are such that they can properly be offered to a new tenant. Thus the dwelling does not, at least in principle, have to be completely reinstated. Questions may arise in some cases whether and to what extent the tenant has to redecorate before moving out, but in a case like the present, where it is certain that the premises were in urgent need of redecoration because no decorations at all had been done during the six years of the tenancy, the tenant cannot, by quitting, avoid the duty of redecoration which he has neglected during the currency of the contract: he must at the end of the contract pay the sums he would have spent earlier if he had conducted himself as the contract required.

2. The *Landgericht* started off by saying that the defendants had refused to perform

their duties under § 5 no 2 of the tenancy agreement, and the Court of Appeal agreed. (. . .) In a case like the present, it would be sheer formalism to require any such declaration after the defendants' conclusive refusal to perform had made it clear that there was no chance whatever that contractual performance would be forthcoming. (This result now follows from § 281 II BGB.) (. . .)

3. (a) The harm suffered by the plaintiff as a result of the defendants' positive breach of contract consists in the fact that when their tenancy ended, redecoration was required in order to make the dwelling lettable at the full market rent it would have commanded had the contractual redecoration been effected, that is, to avoid any reduction in the plaintiff's chances of obtaining a proper rent from the new tenant, this being the purpose of § 5 of the tenancy agreement. Now the real property market may still be rather tense, but it runs contrary to all experience to suppose that a new tenant would pay a rent appropriate to a dwelling in proper order if the premises required redecoration and he had to bear its cost. The case might be different if the dwelling were subject to rent control and could easily be let at the highest legal rent despite the need for redecoration, but we need not decide that point now, for there is no suggestion that this dwelling was rent-controlled. It is true that the plaintiff was able to let the dwelling to Mr and Mrs R. at twice the rent paid by the defendants but this is no evidence that the loss did not occur, for on the one hand, the defendants' tenancy, unlike that of Mr and Mrs R, was a service tenancy, where the rent is characteristically affected by the existence of an employment relationship between the parties, and on the other hand, five years had elapsed since the tenancy was granted to the defendant, during which period the market had changed materially. The plaintiff's claim for damages for non-performance is a money claim so the defendant tenants must bear in full the necessary cost of redecoration.

(b) The appellant argues that the fact that Mr and Mrs R did the redecoration neutralised the harm, and that the plaintiffs therefore have no claim for damages. Some courts and commentators are indeed of the view that the landlord has no claim for damages if the incoming tenant contracts to do the redecoration and actually does it [references omitted], but this view has been criticised by other courts and commentators, and this court finds it unacceptable [references omitted].

Once economic harm has occurred and arguably been offset, the question whether the claim for damages subsists is to be determined on the principle of what is called 'balance of advantages' (*Vorteilsausgleich*), whereby a circumstance is only to be taken into account if it stands in an adequate causal relationship with the cause of the harm. Here it suffices if the advantage which later arises is of a kind which the harmful event was generally apt to trigger. The Court of Appeal in this case found that there was no such causal relationship: the new tenants undertook the work of redecoration not because the defendants had failed to do it but because they themselves had contracted in the tenancy agreement to do it. Whether the reasoning is sufficient to justify the conclusion need not be decided now, for the existence of an adequate causal relationship between the event which causes the harm and the event which neutralises it is not a sufficient, but only a necessary condition of its relevance to the continued existence of the claim for damages. Only if it would not be inequitable to absolve a defendant from his duty to repair the harm he has caused can he be absolved by an event which diminishes or neutralises that harm (BGHZ 10, 107, 108; 30, 29, 33). But the party causing the harm would certainly be receiving an unjustified bonus if one credited him with an action which a third party took by reason of a contractual agreement with the victim with which the party causing the harm had nothing to do (BGHZ 7, 30, 49;NJW 1963, 1051). That is the case here. It was the plaintiff, and not the defendants, who found the new tenants. As the Court of Appeal expressly found, Mr and Mrs R undertook the redecoration in their own interests and without any intention of conferring a benefit on the defendants (compare § 267 BGB). The same is true of the plaintiff: in making his agreement with Mr and Mrs R he had no intention of relieving the defendants. Thus the defendants cannot be credited with the contract between the plaintiff and the new tenants whereby the latter undertook to redecorate, even if in economic terms their redecoration made good the loss in value of the dwelling. To decide otherwise would be unfair to the plaintiff, for to make the agreement with Mr and Mrs R regarding the redecoration was an act in reduction of the damage which it was no part of the plaintiff's duty to do (reference omitted) and it would presuppose that he had exacted a rent from the new tenants which was not warranted by the condition of the dwelling as well as an undertaking to bear the cost of its renovation. We have already said that no tenant can be expected to do this, so if the plaintiff had insisted on an undiminished rent plus an obligation to redecorate, he would have had a very restricted choice of new tenants.

It follows from what we have said that a landlord who succeeds in finding new tenants who are ready to undertake the necessary redecoration at their own expense is not simply performing his duty to mitigate his loss under § 254 II BGB; this provision therefore does not justify his having to account for the new tenants' act. III. The outcome would be the same on the view, put forward by the plaintiff in oral argument, that § 5 no 5 of the tenancy agreement gave rise to a claim in debt, and that this debt claim had not been changed into a claim for damages. A claim for performance can lapse if its object has been achieved and the creditor's interest has disappeared [references omitted], but that would not have occurred here. There is some dispute about the circumstances under which a claim lapses by this doctrine of achievement of object, but Lehmann is certainly right to say that the creditor's claim only lapses if the result achieved is really the same as if the debtor himself had performed properly. Now here the plaintiff had only acquired the right, as against the defendants, to have the property reinstated under the contract at the cost of performing his own contractual obligation, namely maintaining the use of the premises for many years, so there would only have been a true achievement of the object if third parties had gratuitously reinstated the dwelling. But the performance by Mr and Mrs R resulted from a new contract under which the plaintiff assumed new obligations of his own. Thus this is not a case of achievement of the object which makes the claim for performance lapse. Just as in the balancing of advantages in the case of a claim for damages, what is decisive here is that the new tenants which undertook the redecoration were found by the plaintiff. It would be unjustifiable to absolve the defendants just because the plaintiff was lucky in his further contractual negotiations. In view of the fact that the defendants here refused to perform, we need not decide whether the decision would be different if the defendants had been ready to perform and the plaintiff had anticipated their performance by getting the new tenants to redecorate quickly, nor whether the plaintiff's claim for performance would have lapsed if the new tenants had been introduced by the defendants, especially if they had taken over the old tenancy arrangements and had done the redecoration on the basis of the obligation contained therein.

Case 119
BUNDESGERICHTSHOF (SIXTH CIVIL SENATE) 24 MARCH 1959
BGHZ 30, 29

Facts

The defendant, a wife who since 1949 had lived with her husband, the co-defendant, under the matrimonial property regime of community of property, on 1 April 1956 intentionally set ablaze the agricultural property of her adjoining neighbours. For this crime she has been bindingly sentenced. The fire caused extensive property damage to buildings and movables.

The parties now only dispute the amount of compensation payable for the buildings partially destroyed and partially damaged in the blaze. The Bavarian Chamber of Insurance has calculated the costs of repair of the buildings at DM27, 120 and fixed the compensation according to the current value at DM21, 463. The claimant demands from the defendant payment of the difference amounting to DM5, 5657.

The *Landgericht* has awarded the claimants only DM250 for the damage to the buildings and otherwise rejected the claim, reasoning that through the compensation the claimants, ie the victims, should not financially be placed in a better position than they were in before the damaging event occurred; they must therefore allow a deduction under the heading 'new for old,' since the reconstructed buildings are more valuable than at the time of the damage. Applying para 287 ZPO (Code of Civil Procedure), the *Landgericht* has assessed this deduction to be as high as the Bavarian Chamber of Insurance's calculation of the amount of compensation due. The claimant's appeal failed as did the further appeal, admitted by the Court of Appeal.

Reasons

1. The appeal court correctly assumes that a deduction is basically to be made for the difference between old and new in cases when compensation is to be calculated for the damage or destruction of goods whose original value has fallen through use and lapse of time or which had even already been damaged, and that this method is to be applied in the case under consideration.

a) According to para 249, first sentence BGB, a person liable to pay damages must restore the situation as it would be if the circumstance making him liable had not occurred. Where damages are to be paid for the injury to a person or, as here, for damage to property, instead of repair the claimant can demand under para 249, sentence 2 BGB payment of funds needed for such repair. Here, the claimants chose to make such claim. In fact, the claim for monetary compensation is a claim for restoration, although not directly through the debtor's performance but rather by providing satisfaction for the creditor through the debtor's payments (RGZ 71, 212, 214).
It applies to both alternatives set out in para 249 BGB that the restoration of the previous state of affairs means that the victim whose property has been damaged must be placed in the same position economically as he was in before the event took place which led to the liability for damages (RGZ 91, 104, 106; 126, 401, 403). The law is not guided by the restoration of exactly the same conditions as had existed before the damaging events took place but rather by the victim's economic situation as it would

have been without the damaging event (see RGZ 131, 158, 178; 143, 267, 274). The therefore necessary comparison of the economic situations mirrors the basic principle of the law of damages, ie to ensure that compensation does not render the victim richer or poorer. Although the further appeal is justified in claiming that the Civil Code does not contain provisions on how to make allowances for the difference between old and new when calculating compensation, it is none the less incorrect, as the further appeal alleges, to assume that the Civil Code did not intend to have this difference taken into account. Rather, the legislator did not find it necessary to make legal provisions in this respect since, as is expressed in the motivations for the draft of a Civil Code (Amtliche Ausgabe, vol. II 1888 to s. 218, p 18 et seq). This practice had already found satisfactory solutions to this question and is expected also to do so in future. The relevant passage runs:

The solution to the question whether and to what extent in cases of claims for damages the advantage which the victim has obtained from the damaging event must be deducted from the compensation (*compensatio lucri et damni*) must be left to jursiprudence and practice. . . . It goes without saying, . . . that where from one and the same action or a complex of actions for which the same person is liable, damaging and profitable consequences arise, these cannot be seperated and the result as a whole must be looked at. Even an attempt to solve this question by express legal provisions would be dubious, particularly in the case of tort. Its solution is intrinsically linked to the determination of the term of 'damage', which in any event cannot be done by law for all cases and for all their possible and perhaps dubious differences. . . . Unimpeded by legal provisions, legal practice will continue to find solutions for each particular case.

At that time the decision of the *Reichsoberhandelsgericht (ROHG XXIII, No 116)* was already available—and cited in the motives to the BGB (above, p 19, note 1) which principally favours a consideration of the difference between old and new where damages are claimed. Where it thus transpires that such offsetting of advantages was already envisaged by the legislator of the Civil Code and is an inherent part of civil law [RGZ 54, 137, 14o et seq; OLG Hamburg *MDR* [1952] 224 and further references from literature], it can be left undecided whether or not the rules on the consideration of a loss in value resulting from the differences between old and new, as set out in paras 710 (3), 872 HGB (Commercial Code); paras 86, 141 (2) VVG (Act on Insurance Contracts); para 85 BSchG (Act on Shipping on Inland Waterways), contain a general basic principle (as held by Fischer in respect of paras 710, 872 HGB in his *Der Schaden nach dem Bürgerlichen Gesetzbuch*, Jena 1903, p 203) or whether these sections are special provisions restrictively dealing with their specific matter which cannot elsewhere be applied analoguously.

(b) The further appeal is wrong where it holds that in this case an equalisation of advantages in the form of a deduction 'old for new' cannot apply because it was not the same event which lead to the claimants' advantage and disadvantage, since the loss resulted from the arson and the advantage from the reconstruction of the buildings. The adjustment of advantages is a component in the calculation of the damage (see RGZ 103, 406,408). In this respect it is unnecessary that the damaging action has also directly brought about the advantage; rather, it suffices that damage and advantage stem from several events, which are separate as to their outward appearance as long as, according to the natural flow of affairs, the damaging event was generally capable of bringing about such advantages and that the connection is not too tenuous, in which case and according to a reasonable person's understanding, it no longer merits further consideration (BGHZ 8, 325, 329; RGZ 133, 221, 223; 146, 275, 278; see also Cantzler, *AcP* [156] 42, who talks of a causal connection between the conditions). Seen in this light, there are no objections against holding that the advantage which the claimant accrued from the reconstruction of the buildings damaged or destroyed in the fire as a result of the change from old to new, was created by and is adequately causally linked to the damaging action, ie the arson.

(c) In its decisions BGHZ 8, 325 and 10, 107 this Senate has already pointed out that the legislator, as stated in detail above under 1 (a), has left it to the case law to decide which advantage to take into account. In these two decisions it was furthermore stated that it must be considered in each case whether or not an allowance is consummate with the meaning and aim of the liability for damages. But this does not mean that this is a question as to the facts of the case, as the claimants allege when they—erroneously—question the appeal court's admission of the further appeal. The point is rather that when deciding the legal question as to whether or not an advantage can be taken into account, an overall view must be taken of the various interests as they exist between the victim and the tortfeasor as a result of the damaging event. This is because the principle that an advantage, which is adequately causally created by the damaging action, must always be taken into account, cannot be applied in all cases. The limits as to what is reasonable must be observed. On the one hand, damages should in principle not result in a financial improvement of the victim, but on the other hand the tortfeasor should not unjustly be favoured (BGHZ 10, 107, 108; Ennecerus/Lehmann, *Recht der Schuldverhältnisse* 15. edn 1958, para 17 II 1 a (p 85); see also SchlH OLG *MDR* [1952] 747). Countrary to the opinion expressed in the further appeal, making an allowance for the advantage resulting from the change from old into new is not already unacceptable in cases where the victim is forced to incur expenditures which he would otherwise not have had, because the repair or reconstruction of the damaged goods can only be done by increasing their value compared with the situation at the time of the damage. The contribution to the costs which the claimant must make in respect of the reconstruction of the buildings damaged by fire is mirrored by the added value of the buildings, their increased life expectancy and the deferment of future necessary repairs to them. There are here no special circumstances and the further appeal has not raised any which could be decisive for the question of reasonability, as for instance that the claimant is financially unable to meet the necessary extra costs.

2. There is apparently no reason why the question as to the taking into account of advantages gained from the change from old to new should be decided on differently for durable economic goods and short-lived goods. First, such distinction of economic goods according to their life span has not found entry in the system of civil law but is rather the result of an economic, though in this context important, point of view and has found its way into tax law. As the appeal court rightly stated, for considerations under civil law the difference is one of degree and not of principle. Insofar as the further appeal alleges that in respect of durable economic goods the owner is more concerned with the value in use than the trade value and thereby perhaps wishes to indicate that in the case of short-lived economic goods the trade value is decisive, it must be counter-argued that even in the case of these goods it is not merely the retail

value of the (old) goods as it stood before the damage occurred, from which to proceed but rather their special value to the victim. An exchange of old goods by new ones has an effect both in the case of goods with long or short life spans, ie in the form of added property value, an enrichment of the victim, where an allowance is not made under the auspices of 'new for old'. Increased costs for material and labour must, however, be attributed to the tortfeasor when the amount of damages is calculated under para 249 (2) BGB (RGZ 98, 55; 102, 143); but this does not alter the fact that the victim's enrichment which is expressed in the increased economic value of the reconstructed buildings, which are now new instead of old, must be equalised, since otherwise the victim has received a compensation exceeding the damage (differently Oertmann, *LZ* [1916] 1512, changing his previous opinion).

Whether and to what extent disadvantages arising from the need for the victim to contribute part of the costs for reconstructing the buildings, such as interests for loans taken up, losses in interests for accumulated capital, tax disadvantages and other items are seperately to be taken into account when calculating a discount under the principle 'new for old' need not be decided in this case, since no substantiated claims were made in this respect.

3. One can think of circumstances in which the repair of a building after the damage does not result in an increased value and thus not in a financial gain made by the victim. Such a case was admitted by the Oberlandesgericht Oldenburg in its decision published in *VersR* [1954] 182, on which case the further appeal bases its reasoning. In this context the further appeal criticises the claimant's specific submission that the restoration of the buildings to the condition in which they were before the damage occurred would have cost DM27, 120, ie the same amount as that which the Bavarian Chamber of Insurance calculated as being necessary for the repair of the buildings and that the appeal court had not dealt with this submission.

However, the *Landgericht* had already held this submission to be inconclusive, as a restoration to the old state, ie with all the wear and tear from use over the course of years is quite impossible. The appeal court has—as set out in the reasons to its decision—upheld the opinion of the *Landgericht* and stated that in the case of destruction of or damage to old goods or goods worn from use and thus devalued, the recreation of the same condition as before is impossible. The claimants' submission in respect of possible ways and means of reconstructing or, respectively of constructing the fire-damaged buildings, for which the further appeal has not requested any further evidence, can be appraised by the judge dealing with the facts of the case, since such appraisal is within the limits of free evaluation of evidence pertaining to the case (para 286 ZPO) and cannot be opposed for legal reasons.

Case 120
BUNDESGERICHTSHOF (EIGHTS CIVIL SENATE) 2 JUNE 2004
NJW 2004, 2299

Facts

On 15 January 2002, the claimant bought an Opel V at a price of 8450 euros for his private use from the defendant, a motor vehicle dealer. The vehicle, which was first registered in December 1996, showed at this point in time a kilometre reading of 118,000. In November 2001, when the kilometre reading was 117,950, the defendant had renewed the timing belt. The vehicle was handed over to the claimant on 18 January 2002 in return for payment of the purchase price.

On 12 July 2002, when the kilometre reading was 128,950, the vehicle suffered engine damage, the cause of which is disputed between the parties. The vehicle has been with the defendant since then. The defendant refused to carry out a repair free of charge. The claimant thereon declared his withdrawal from the purchase contract by a letter of 26 July 2002.

In the present legal action, the claimant demands from the defendant repayment of the purchase price, subject to a deduction for benefit enjoyed, which he estimates at 657 euros (0.06 euros x 10,950 km since delivery). Altogether he accordingly seeks payment of 7,793 euros, together with interest for delay, simultaneously with retransfer of the vehicle. Further, the claimant has applied for a finding of delay in acceptance by the defendant. The *Landgericht* rejected the claim after obtaining an expert's opinion. On appeal by the claimant, the *Oberlandesgericht* allowed the claim. By its appeal in law, which has been admitted by the appeal court, the defendant seeks the restoration of the first instance judgment.

Reasons

I. The appeal court has explained:

The claimant was entitled in accordance with § 437 BGB in combination with §§ 440, 323 and 326 (5) BGB to withdraw from the purchase contract. The cause of the engine damage, which occurred on 12 July 2002, according to the findings of the expert employed at first instance, was that a timing belt, which was too loose, disengaged from the camshaft sprocket, which had caused a malfunction of the intake valves in the first cylinder head. The expert had attributed the loosening of the timing belt to defective material, and inappropriately high wear and tear on the timing belt. He was of the opinion that a longer durability should be expected from a timing belt than a mere life of eight months and about 10,000 km. The claimant had thereby proved that the engine damage could not be attributed to normal wear and tear, and had occurred within six months since the passing of the risk on 18 January 2002.

Therefore it was presumed under § 476 BGB in favour of the claimant as buyer that the vehicle was already defective when the risk passed. The defendant as seller had not proved any facts over against this which were irreconcilable with this presumption in relation to the type of vehicle sold, or the type of defect which had occurred. After the expert had also described a defective gear change at high engine speed by the claimant as a possible cause of the loosening of the timing belt and therefore a driving defect as a possible cause of the harm, the defendant had made this part of his case. However, there was no ground or proof whatever for the presence of a driving defect by the claimant, who had contested this. The mere assertion of such a driving defect did not suffice to refute the presumption in § 476 BGB.

Taking as a starting point the undisputed performance of 10,950 km since handing over and a total life to be expected of 250,000 km, compensation for use was calculated to be 0.06 euros per kilometre travelled, and therefore 675 euros altogether (this should be 657 euros). As the defendant refused to carry out a cost-free repair of the engine from the outset until today, the claimant did not have to set any period for the defendant.

II. This does not stand up to legal examination.

1. The objection by the appeal in law that the appeal court judgment violated § 540 ZPO (Civil Procedure Order) as it did not reproduce the application in the defendant's appeal is admittedly unsuccessful (. . . details are given).

2. But the objection by the appeal in law that the appeal court reached the assumption that there was a material defect in the sense of § 434 (1) BGB (which entitles the claimant to withdraw from the purchase contract of 15 January 2002 in accordance with § 437 no 2 BGB) by means of a procedural defect is successful.

(a) The appeal court correctly assumed that the BGB (Civil Code) is to be applied in the version applying since 1 January 2002 because the purchase contract was concluded on 15 January 2002 (Art 229 § 5 sentence 1 EGBGB (Introductory Statute to the Civil Code)). According to § 434 (1) sentence 1 and sentence 2 no 1 BGB, a thing is free from material defects if it has the agreed composition when the risk passes. In so far as composition was not agreed, the thing is free from material defects if it is suitable for the use which is presupposed under the contract. If the buyer claims, as the claimant does here, rights under § 437 BGB, by referring to the presence of a material defect after he has received the item bought, the burden of explanation and proof of the facts which form the basis of the material defect apply to him, even under the new law of obligations (Bamberger/Roth/Faust *BGB* § 434 marginal no 119; Palandt/Putzo *BGB* 63rd ed § 434 marginal no 57/59; see also *Begründung zum Entwurf eines Gesetzes zur Modernisierung des Schuldrechts* [Reasons for Draft Statute for Modernising the Law of Obligations], BT Drucks 14/6040 p 245). In so far as § 476 BGB reverses the burden of proof in favour of the buyer for the consumer goods purchase—as here—that does not affect the question of whether a material defect is present at all. The provisions assume instead that a material defect has arisen within six months since the passing of the risk and contain a presumption taking effect merely from a time angle that this defect was already present at the time the risk passed.

(b) Contrary to the view of the reply to the appeal in law, the appeal court has correctly not taken account of the engine damage to the vehicle which occurred on 12 July 2002. The engine damage was not yet present according to the undisputed facts at the time of the risk passed—the determinative time according to § 434 (1) BGB—on 18 January 2002. Accordingly the appeal court has correctly laid emphasis on the question of whether the engine damage which occurred on 12 July 2002 should be attributed to a cause already present at the time the risk passed and based on the composition of the vehicle.

On this subject, the appeal court has first established that the engine damage should be attributed to defective material and unreasonably high wear and tear of the timing belt, which was renewed before the conclusion of the purchase contract in November 2001. In so far as it uses this cause as an established basis, the appeal court is relying on the observations of the expert employed at first instance. The appeal in law is correct in objecting to this. The finding rests on a procedural error. The appeal court has violated the requirement following from § 286 ZPO to assess the results of the evidence completely, because it has ignored a substantial part of the expert's observations.

(aa) It is true that the expert has stated in summary in his written opinion submitted to the court of first instance that the cause of destruction of the engine was the disengaging of the timing belt from the camshaft sprocket, which had caused a malfunction of the intake valves in the first cylinder head, on which the valve disk of the fourth cylinder was broken off, and caused a fracture of the connecting-rod above the pistons. This again could be attributed to a timing belt which was too loose. According to his—the expert's—opinion, the causes for this loosening were a material defect and unreasonably high wear and tear of the timing belt. According to the position today, a longer durability and functional capacity could be expected from a timing belt than merely eight months in this case where there was a life of about 10,000 km. However, under the previous section 'Assessment', the expert has mentioned the engaging of a lower gear at high engine speed as a further possible cause of the loosening of the timing belt. In agreement with this, the expert stated, according to the transcript, when explaining his opinion in the oral proceedings before the *Landgericht* on 27 March 2003, that he could not say with hindsight exactly how the disengaging of the timing belt had arisen; he could still not rule out the possibility of damage due to a defective gear change. Accordingly, it says in the reasons for the judgment of the *Landgericht* that the expert had (as had also been shown in the oral proceedings) not meant to make any statement in the written opinion as to whether the engine damage could not also have arisen because of the claimant's driving. On the basis of the observations of the expert, who could only make presumptions about the cause of the disengaging of the timing belt, it was therefore not possible to assume with sufficient certainty that there was a material defect. A defect in driving causing the damage could not be adequately excluded.

(bb) The appeal court has admittedly mentioned the possibility of a defect in driving in the form of a defective gear change, which could not, according to the expert's explanation, be ruled out, in its further observations when examining whether a material defect was present which had been left out of consideration. But it only considered this possibility afterwards in the context of an examination of § 476 BGB, and observed there were no grounds or proof for the presence of defect in the claimant's driving, which he disputed. The mere assertion by the defendant of such a defect in driving did not suffice to rebut the presumption in § 476 BGB. The possibility of a defective gear change causing the damage, in the case of a gearbox functioning properly in other respects, should however already have been included in the assessment of the evidence in the context of examination of a material defect—and it had to be explained and proved by the claimant (see above under II 2 (a)).

(cc) The judgment is based on this procedural error (§ 545 (1) ZPO).

It cannot be ruled out that the appeal court would have regarded a material defect as not proved (§ 286 ZPO) if, when considering the division of the burden of proof under § 434 BGB, it had considered the possibility of a defective gear change which was pointed out by the expert.

(c) When considering this division of the burden of proof, the appeal court also ought not to have ruled out the possibility of defective driving without the taking of further evidence. The appeal court must in any case take evidence from the expert himself in writing or orally (§§ 402, 398 ZPO)—as the appeal in law correctly points out—if it intends to assess his observations in a different way from the court of first instance (BGH judgment of 8 June 1993— VI ZR 192/92, NJW 1993, 2380 under II 2 a; BGH judgment of 12 October 1993—VI ZR 235/92, NJW 1994, 803 under II 1 (b); in relation to the hearing of a witness, see senate, judgment of 17 July 2002—

VIII ZR 151/01, NJW-RR 2002, 1649 under II 2 (b)). That is the case here. As already explained above (under II 2 (b) (aa)), the *Landgericht* has understood the expert, after an oral hearing, to say that defective driving could not be ruled out as a cause of the engine damage. In contrast to this, the appeal court has based its assumption that there was a material defect on the fact that the expert had attributed the loosening of the timing belt exclusively to a material defect and unreasonable wear and tear.

3. Futhermore, the appeal in law correctly objects to the fact that the appeal court, in calculating the value of the benefit enjoyed by the claimant through use of the vehicle (§ 346 (1), (2) sentence 1 no 1 BGB), has violated § 286 ZPO by simply assuming, following the claimant's submissions, an expected total life of 250,000 km. It cannot be deduced from the judgment whether the appeal court recognised that the defendant, as the appeal in law correctly points out, disputed this assertion by the claimant and why it, if so, nevertheless used the total life mentioned as a basis (on estimating the value of the benefit enjoyed through use of the vehicle, by analogy with § 287 ZPO, see BGHZ 115, 47, 49 ff; senate judgment of 17 May 1995—VIII ZR 70/94, WM 1995, 1145 = NJW 1995, 2159 under III 2: further, Reinking/Eggert, Der Autokauf [The car purchase], 8th ed, marginal no 321, 322).

III. In the end, the disputed judgment cannot stand. The legal action is not ready for a final decision, as it needs further factual findings. Therefore the judgment on appeal must be quashed, and the matter referred back to the appeal court.

Case 121
BUNDESGERICHTSHOF (EIGHTH CIVIL SENATE) 16 JANUARY 1963
NJW 1963, 804

Facts

In December 1959 the first defendant purchased a plot of land on which an apartment block was being built. The basic construction work had been completed, though the building inspectorate had not yet approved it, and a start had been made with the internal decoration. On 22 February 1960 the defendants leased one of the apartments to the plaintiffs, the lease to run from 1 March 1960, or at the latest from 1 April. The plaintiffs moved their furniture into the apartment when it was apparently ready, but they could not move in themselves because on 29 March the building inspectorate having ascertained that, *inter alia*, the reinforced concrete ceilings were not up to specifications, prohibited further work and declared, under § 79 para 2 of the Hesse Building Regulations, that the building should not be occupied until final approval. In the expectation that the objections could soon be allayed and final approval obtained, the parties agreed that the plaintiffs should temporarily move into a hotel at the defendants' expense, but by early May 1960 it had become clear that in view of the inadequacy of the foundations, extensive support works would be required before final approval could be granted. On 27 May 1960 the defendants informed the plaintiffs in writing that it was impossible for them to honour the contract of lease, and refunded the building cost premium. The plaintiffs rented another apartment, and moved into it on 18 June 1960. The defendants paid the plaintiffs' expenses up to this point, but refused to pay anything in respect of the higher building cost premium, extra expenses of moving and so on.

The plaintiffs have put in an itemised claim amounting to DM5,893.92. The *Landgericht* held that claim justified in principle, and the defendant's appeal from this holding was dismissed. The defendant's further appeal is now dismissed.

Reasons

I. The Court of Appeal held that the plaintiffs' claim for damages for non-performance could be supported by the meaning, if not by the terms, of § 538 para 1 BGB in connection with § 537 BGB (now §§ 536, 536a BGB).
II.
II. No legal error to the detriment of the defendant was committed by the Court of Appeal. Indeed, it was unnecessary for the Court of Appeal to invoke the principle underlying the decision of the *Bundesgerichtshof* in BGHZ 9, 320, whereby § 538 BGB can be construed so as to entitle the lessee of property yet to be produced to claim damages for non-performance if defects in the sense of § 537 BGB are present at the time when the property is made ready for delivery, whether or not the lessor was at fault. In our case the defects which rendered the leased property incapable of contractual use were already present at the time when the contract was made. The plaintiffs were to move in on 1 April, if not on 1 March, and the building was essentially ready on 22 February. It is beyond dispute that an apartment is defective in the sense of § 537 BGB if the concrete ceilings in the building are not up to official specifications and if its foundations are so defective that extensive support work is required before the building regulations are satisfied The appellant puts forward far too narrow a conception of 'defect' in this connection, especially in its contention that a defect in the foundations of the building does not constitute a defect in the leased apartment. We need not here decide whether every trivial defect in the rest of the building which could have an effect on the apartment actually leased, such as a defective water pipe in an adjacent apartment (reference omitted), should be treated as a defect in the leased property, but it is perfectly evident that an apartment is defective in the sense of §§ 537, 538 BGB if there are defects in the foundations or the roof or other parts of the building which are essential for the leased apartment. It was a certain, or at least a probable, result of the building fault which admittedly existed at the time of the lease that the building inspectorate would prohibit occupation and refuse the approval required for it to be used as a dwelling. That approval had not yet been refused at the time of the lease is immaterial: it is sufficient that the building defects on which the refusal was based were already present. It follows that § 538 BGB can be applied directly. Nor is it necessary that the defendant should have been at fault, for his liability flows from the guarantee, implied by law into the lease, that the property is free from defect.
III. The appellant contends that §§ 275, 323 BGB (see now §§ 275, 326, 283 BGB) are applicable here rather than §§ 537, 538 BGB, and that the claim should therefore be dismissed It is generally agreed that §§ 275, 323 BGB, which deal with subsequent impossibility, are capable of application to a contract of lease, but it is nevertheless the clear intention of the legislator that they should be subordinated to the special provisions of §§ 537, 538 BGB if these provisions are applicable [references omitted]. That is the case here. As we have said, this is a typical instance of the strict liability of the

lessor for defects existing in the leased property at the time of the lease, a liability based on §§ 537, 538 BGB, not a case of subsequent impossibility in the sense of §§ 273, 323 BGB, for which the landlord is not responsible.

The appellant's reference to the jurisprudence of the *Reichsgericht* is wide of the mark. The cases cited (RGZ 82, 203, 207; 146, 60, 64; 157, 363, 367) involved situations where, after the lease was concluded, reasons for which the lessor was not responsible rendered it impossible for him to fulfil the contract. In RGZ 82, 203, 207, the premises were leased before the First World War for use as a dance hall, a use which was rendered impossible by a wartime ban on dancing in public. In RGZ 146, 60, 64, premises had been leased for use as a retail outlet, and could no longer be used for that purpose after the enactment of the statute for the protection of retail trade on 12 May 1933. In RGZ 157, 363, 367, the restaurateur's licence which the lessee needed was withdrawn owing to the fault of a sub-lessee for whom he was responsible: here, too, the lessor was held not liable because it was not his fault that the performance of the contract had become legally impossible.

The situation before us is different in that the plaintiffs' inability to occupy the apartment because of the refusal of building approval was due to defects of construction which already existed at the time the contract was formed. Nor was it, as the appellant contends, legally impossible for the defendants to let the plaintiffs have the leased premises. There was nothing impossible about proceeding with the requisite support works and so on, and thus obtaining official approval. The defendants may not have had the funds to do this, but that does not affect the plaintiffs' claims under §§ 537, 538 BGB, any more than the fact that the defendants had been deceived by the architect who sold them the property. It is against him that they must seek recourse.

Appendix II:

The German Civil Code†
*Bürgerliches Gesetzbuch**
Extracts

First Book
General Part

First Section
Persons
[. . .]

§ 2

Attainment of majority
Majority occurs at completion of the eighteenth year of a person's life.
[. . .]

§ 13

Consumers
A consumer is any natural person who concludes a legal transaction for a purpose which can neither be attributed to his business nor to his independent vocational activity.

§ 14

Undertakings
(1) An undertaking is a natural or legal person or a legally competent company (Gesellschaft) of persons who or which, in concluding a legal transaction, acts in exercise of his or its business or independent vocational activity.
(2) A legally competent company of persons is one which is equipped with the capacity to acquire rights and enter into obligations.
[. . .]

Third Section

Legal transactions

First Title

Legal competence

† Translated by Raymond Youngs.
* Of 18 August 1896 (RGBl., p 195), as published on 2 January 2002 (BGBl. I, pp 42, 2909) and amended.

§ 104

Lack of legal competence

A person lacks legal competence if he:

1. has not completed the seventh year of his life
2. is in a state of disturbance of mental activity through disease which would exclude free determination of the will, in so far as the state is not by its nature a transitory one.

§ 105

Invalidity of declaration of will

(1) A declaration of will by a person who lacks legal competence is invalid.

(2) A declaration of will is also invalid if it is given in a condition of unconsciousness or a transitory disturbance of mental activity.

[. . .]

§ 106

Limited legal competence of minors

A minor who has completed the seventh year of his life is limited in his legal competence in accordance with §§ 107 to 113.

§ 107

Consent of statutory representative

A minor needs the consent of his statutory representative for a declaration of will by which he does not merely obtain a legal advantage.

§ 108

Conclusion of contract without consent

(1) If a minor concludes a contract without the necessary consent of the statutory representative, the effectiveness of the contract depends on ratification by the representative.

(2) If the other party invites the representative to make a declaration about the ratification, the declaration can only take effect as against him; a ratification or refusal of ratification declared to the minor before the invitation becomes ineffective. The ratification can only be declared up until the expiry of two weeks after the receipt of the invitation; if it is not declared, it is deemed to have been refused.

(3) If the minor has acquired unlimited legal competence, his ratification takes the place of the representative's ratification.

§ 109

Right of revocation for other party

(1) The other party is entitled to revoke until the contract is ratified. Revocation can also be declared as against the minor.

(2) If the other party knew about the minority, he can only revoke if the minor has claimed that the representative consented when this is untrue; he cannot revoke even in this case if he knew of the absence of consent at the conclusion of the contract.

§ 110

Effecting performance with own means

A contract concluded by a minor without the approval of the statutory representative is deemed to be effective from the start if the minor effects performance in accordance with the contract with means which have been given to him for this purpose or for his free disposition by the representative or, with his approval, by a third party.

§ 111
Unilateral legal transactions
A unilateral legal transaction which a minor undertakes without the necessary consent of the statutory representative is ineffective. If the minor undertakes such a transaction with this consent in favour of another person, the transaction is ineffective if the minor does not produce the consent in written form, and the other person rejects the transaction on this ground without delay. Rejection is excluded if the representative had apprised the other person of the consent.

[. . .]

Second Title

Declaration of will

§ 116
Secret reservation
A declaration of will is not void just because the declarant secretly makes the reservation of not having intended what was declared. The declaration is void if it is to be given as against another person and he knows of the reservation.

§ 117
Sham transaction
(1) If a declaration of will which is to be given as against another is only given as a sham with that person's agreement, then it is void.
(2) If another legal transaction is concealed by a sham transaction, the provisions effective for the concealed transaction will be applied.

§ 118
Lack of seriousness
A declaration which is not seriously intended and which is given in the expectation that there will be no failure to recognise the absence of seriousness is void.

§ 119
Avoidability for mistake
(1) A person who, when he gave a declaration of will, was mistaken about its content, or did not intend to give a declaration with this content at all, can avoid the declaration if it is to be assumed that he would not have given it if he had known the state of affairs and on a rational assessment of the case.
(2) A mistake about those characteristics of a person or a thing which are regarded as significant in human affairs is deemed to be a mistake about the content of the declaration.

§ 120
Avoidability for incorrect communication
A declaration of will which has been incorrectly communicated by the person or facility used for the communication can be avoided under the same prerequisite as a declaration of will given by mistake according to § 119.

§ 121

Period for avoidance

(1) Avoidance must in the cases of §§ 119 and 120 occur without culpable delay (promptly) after the person entitled to avoid has acquired knowledge of the ground for avoidance. Avoidance as against an absent person counts as occurring punctually if the declaration of avoidance has been dispatched promptly.

(2) Avoidance is excluded if ten years have elapsed since the giving of the declaration of will.

§ 122

Duty of person avoiding to compensate for harm

(1) If a declaration of will is void under § 118 or avoided on the basis of §§ 119 or 120, the declarant must, if the declaration had to be given as against another, compensate this other person, or otherwise any third party, for the harm which the other person or the third party suffers as a result of trusting in the validity of the declaration, but not however beyond the amount of the interest which the other person or the third party has in the validity of the declaration.

(2) The duty to compensate for harm does not arise if the party suffering harm knew of the ground of invalidity or avoidability or did not know of it as a result of negligence (ought to have known it).

§ 123

Avoidability because of deception or threat

(1) A person who has been caused to make a declaration of will by fraudulent deception or unlawfully by threat can avoid the declaration.

(2) If a third person has practised the deception, a declaration which was to be given as against another is only avoidable if he knew of the deception or ought to have known of it. In so far as a person other than the one to whom the declaration was to be given has acquired a right directly from the declaration, the declaration is avoidable as against him if he knew of the deception or ought to have known of it.

§ 124

Period for avoidance

(1) Avoidance of a declaration of will which is avoidable under § 123 can only take place within a year.

(2) The period begins in the case of fraudulent deception at the point in time at which the person entitled to avoid discovers the deception and in the case of threat at the point in time at which the state of compulsion ceases. The provisions of §§ 206, 210 and 211 applying to limitation of actions apply correspondingly to the running of the period.

(3) Avoidance is excluded if ten years have elapsed since the giving of the declaration of will.

§ 125

Invalidity because of absence of form

A legal transaction which lacks the form prescribed by statute law is void. The absence of form provided for by a legal transaction likewise results in invalidity in case of doubt.

§ 126
Written form
(1) If written form is prescribed by statute law, the document must be signed by the author with his own hand by the signature of his name or by means of a notarially attested mark.
(2 In the case of a contract, the signatures of the parties must be made on the same document. If several documents in identical terms are drawn up in respect of the contract, it suffices if each party signs the document intended for the other party.
(3) Written form can be replaced by electronic form unless a different conclusion follows from statute law.
(4) Notarial authentication can take the place of written form.
[. . .]

§ 126b
Text form
If text form is prescribed by statute law, the declaration must be given in a document or in another manner appropriate for permanent reproduction in written characters, the declarant must be named and conclusion of the declaration must be made recognisable by reproduction of the signature or otherwise.

§ 127
Agreed form
(1) The provisions of § 126, § 126a or § 126b also apply in case of doubt for form provided for by a legal transaction.
(2) Transmission by telecommunication and exchange of letters in the case of a contract suffice for the observance of written form provided for by a legal transaction, in so far as a different intention is not to be assumed. If such a form is chosen, an authentication corresponding with § 126 can be demanded afterwards.
(3) [. . .]

§ 128
Notarial authentication
If notarial authentication of a contract is prescribed by statute law, it is sufficient if first the offer and then the acceptance of the offer is authenticated by a notary.
[. . .]

§ 130
Declaration of will becoming effective as against absent persons
(1) A declaration of will which is to be given as against another is, when it is given in that person's absence, effective at the point in time at which it reaches him. It is not effective if a revocation reaches the other person previously or at the same time.
(2) It has no influence on the effectiveness of the declaration of will if the declarant dies or becomes legally incompetent after it is given.
(3) These provisions also apply if the declaration of will is to be given as against an authority.
[. . .]

§ 133
Interpretation of declaration of will
In the interpretation of a declaration of will the real intention is be ascertained and the literal sense of the statement is not to be followed.

§ 134
Statutory prohibition
A legal transaction which violates a statutory prohibition is void unless a different consequence is to be deduced from the statute.
[. . .]

§ 138
Immoral legal transaction; extortion
(1) A legal transaction which violates good morals is void.
(2) In particular a legal transaction is void by which someone through exploitation of the predicament, inexperience, lack of judgement or significant weakness of will of another person causes to be promised or granted to himself or a third party in return for a performance economic advantages which are conspicuously disproportionate to the performance.

§ 139
Partial invalidity
If part of a legal transaction is void, the whole transaction is void unless it can be assumed that it would have been undertaken even without the void part.

§ 140
Conversion
If a void legal transaction corresponds to the requirements of another legal transaction, the latter is valid if can be assumed that its validity would have been desired on knowledge of such invalidity.
[. . .]

§ 142
Effect of avoidance
(1) If an avoidable legal transaction is avoided, it is to be regarded as void from the start.
(2) A person who knew of the avoidability or ought to have known of it will, when the avoidance occurs, be treated as if he had known of the invalidity of the transaction or ought to have known of it.

§ 143
Declaration of avoidance
(1) Avoidance occurs by declaration as against the opposing party.
(2) The opposing party is, in the case of a contract, the other party, and in the case of § 123 paragraph 2 sentence 2 the person who has acquired a right directly from the contract.
(3) In the case of a unilateral legal transaction which was to be undertaken as against another person, the other person is the opposing party. The same applies to a legal transaction which was to be undertaken as against another person or against an authority, even if the transaction has been undertaken as against the authority.

(4) In the case of a unilateral legal transaction of a different kind, the opposing party is everyone who has obtained a legal advantage directly on the basis of the transaction. If the declaration of will was to be given as against an authority, the avoidance can however take place by way of a declaration as against the authority; the authority must communicate the avoidance to the person who has been directly affected by the transaction.

§ 144
Confirmation of avoidable legal transaction
(1) Avoidance is excluded if the avoidable legal transaction is confirmed by the person entitled to make the avoidance.
(2) The confirmation does not need the form determined for the legal transaction.

Third Title

Contract

§ 145
Binding effect of offer
A person who offers to another that he will conclude a contract is bound by the offer, unless he has excluded this binding effect.

§ 146
Extinguishment of offer
An offer lapses if it is refused as against the offeror, or if it is not accepted in time as against him under §§ 147 to 149.

§ 147
Time for acceptance
(1) An offer made to a person who is present can only be accepted immediately. This also applies to an offer made by telephone or other technical apparatus from person to person.
(2) An offer made to an absent person can only be accepted up to the point in time at which the offeror may expect arrival of the answer in usual circumstances.

§ 148
Determination of period for acceptance
If the offeror has determined a period for the acceptance of the offer, acceptance can only occur within that period.

§ 149
Declaration of acceptance arriving belatedly
If a declaration of acceptance reaching the offeror belatedly has been sent in such a way that it would have reached him in time on regular dispatch, and if the offeror ought to have recognised this, he must notify the delay to the acceptor promptly after receipt of the declaration in so far as this has not already occurred. If he delays in sending the notification, the acceptance does not count as delayed.

§ 150

Delayed and conditional acceptance

(1) Delayed acceptance of an offer counts as a new offer.

(2) An acceptance with extensions, limitations or other amendments counts as a refusal combined with a new offer.

§ 151

Acceptance without declaration as against the offeror

A contract will come into existence by acceptance of an offer without acceptance needing to be declared to the offeror if such a declaration is not to be expected in accordance with custom (Verkehrssitte), or if the offeror has renounced his right to it. The point in time at which the offer lapses is determined by the intention of the offeror which is to be deduced from the offer or the circumstances.

§ 152

Acceptance by notarial authentication

If a contract is notarially authenticated without both parties being present simultaneously, the contract comes into existence by authentication of the acceptance occurring in accordance with § 128, if no other provision is made. The provisions of § 151 sentence 2 apply.

§ 153

Death or legal incompetence of offeror

The formation of the contract is not prevented by the offeror dying or becoming legally incompetent before acceptance, unless a different intention on the part of the offeror must be assumed.

§ 154

Patent lack of agreement; absence of authentication

(1) As long as the parties have not agreed on all points of the contract about which an agreement is to be made according to the declaration of even only one party, the contract is not concluded in case of doubt. An understanding about individual points is not binding even if a record has been made.

(2) If authentication of the intended contract has been arranged, in case of doubt the contract is not concluded until the authentication has occurred.

§ 155

Hidden lack of agreement

If the parties have, in relation to an agreement which they regard as concluded, not in reality agreed about a point as to which agreement should be made, what has been agreed is valid in so far as it is to be assumed that the contract would have been concluded even without a provision about this point.

[. . .]

§ 157

Interpretation of contracts

Contracts are to be interpreted as required by good faith and having regard to custom (Verkehrssitte).

Fifth Title

Agency and Power of Attorney

§ 164
Effect of agent's declaration

(1) A declaration of will which someone, within the agent's authority which he has, gives in the principal's name takes effect directly for and against the principal. It makes no difference whether the declaration is made expressly in the name of the principal or whether the circumstances indicate that it is made in his name.

(2) If the intention to act in the name of another is not evident, the absence of an intention to act in one's own name should not be considered.

(3) The provisions of paragraph 1 apply correspondingly if a declaration of will to be given as against another is made to that person's agent.

§ 165
Agent with limited legal competence

The effectiveness of a declaration of will given by or to an agent is not impaired by the fact that the agent has limited legal competence.

§ 166
Absence of intention; attribution of knowledge

(1) In so far as the legal consequences of a declaration of will are influenced by absence of intention or by the fact that certain circumstances are known or ought to be known, it is the situation of the agent and not of the principal which should be considered.

(2) If in the case of an agent's authority (a power of attorney) given by a legal transaction the agent has acted in accordance with certain directions of the donor of the power, the latter cannot in respect of those circumstances which he knew himself rely on the agent's lack of knowledge. The same applies in respect of circumstances which the donor of the power ought to have known in so far as the fact that he ought to have known can be equated with knowledge.

§ 167
Creation of power of attorney

(1) A power of attorney is created by way of a declaration to the person to be authorised or to the third party against whom the agency is to take place.

(2) The declaration does not need to be in the form which is determined for the legal transaction to which the power of attorney relates.

§ 168
Extinguishment of power of attorney

The extinguishment of the power of attorney is determined in accordance with the legal relationship on which its creation is based. The power of attorney is revocable even if the legal relationship continues to exist, in so far as no different consequence is to be deduced from this relationship The provisions of § 167 paragraph 1 apply correspondingly to the revocation declaration.

§ 169
Power of attorney of delegate and executive member of company (Gesellschaft)
In so far as the extinguished power of attorney of a delegate or an executive member of a company is deemed still to be existing under §§ 674, 729, it does not operate in favour of a third party who knows or ought to know of the extinguishment when undertaking a legal transaction.

§ 170
Period of effect of power of attorney
If the power of attorney is created by a declaration as against a third party, it will remain in effect as against this person until the extinguishment is notified to him by the donor of the power attorney.

§ 171
Period of effect in case of announcement
(1) If someone has announced by special communication to a third party or by public advertisement that he has authorised another person, this person has the authority of agency on the basis of the announcement in the former case as against the third party and in the latter case as against every third party.
(2) The agent's authority continues to exist until the announcement is revoked in the same manner as it was made.

§ 172
Power of attorney
(1) It is equivalent to special communication of an authorisation by the donor of a power of attorney when he has handed over a power of attorney to the agent and the agent produces this to a third party.
(2) The agent's authority continues in existence until the power of attorney is given back to the donor or is declared to be ineffectual.

§ 173
Period of effect in case of knowledge or negligent lack of knowledge
The provisions of § 170, § 171 paragraph 2 and § 172 paragraph 2 do not apply if the third party knows of the extinguishment of the agent's authority when the legal transaction is undertaken or if he ought to know of it.

§ 174 Unilateral legal transaction by attorney
A unilateral legal transaction which an attorney undertakes as against another is ineffective if the attorney does not produce a power of attorney, and the other person rejects the legal transaction on this ground without delay. Rejection is excluded if the donor of the power of attorney had apprised the other party of the power of attorney.

§ 175
Return of power of attorney
After the extinguishment of the power of attorney, the attorney must give back the power of attorney to the donor; he does not have a right of retention.
[. . .].

§ 177
Conclusion of contract by agent without agent's authority
(1) If someone concludes a contract in the name of another person without any agent's authority, the effectiveness of the contract for and against the principal depends on the latter's ratification.
(2) If the other party invites the principal to make a declaration about ratification, the declaration can only take place as against him; a ratification or refusal of ratification declared as against the agent before the invitation is ineffective. The ratification can only be declared up until the expiry of two weeks after receipt of the invitation; if it is not declared, it is deemed to have been refused.

§ 178
Right of revocation by other party
Until ratification of the contract the other party is entitled to revoke, unless he knew of the lack of agent's authority on conclusion of the contract. Revocation can also be declared as against the agent.

§ 179
Liability of agent without agent's authority
(1) A person who has concluded a contract as an agent is, in so far as he does not prove his agent's authority, obliged to the other party to effect fulfilment or compensate (according to that party's election), if the principal refuses to ratify the contract.
(2) If the agent did not know of the lack of agent's authority, he is only obliged to compensate for that harm which the other party suffers as a result of relying on the agent's authority, but not beyond the amount of the interest which the other party has in the effectiveness of the contract.
(3) The agent is not liable if the other party knew of the absence of agent's authority or ought to have known of it. The agent is also not liable if he had limited legal competence, unless he acted with the consent of his statutory representative.

§ 180
Unilateral legal transaction
In the case of a unilateral legal transaction, agency without agent's authority is not permissible. If however the person as against whom such a transaction was to be undertaken has not objected to the agent's authority asserted by the agent when the transaction was undertaken, or if he was in agreement with the agent acting without agent's authority, the provisions about contracts apply correspondingly. The same applies if a unilateral legal transaction is undertaken as against an agent without agent's authority with that person's agreement.

§ 181
Transactions with oneself
An agent cannot, except in so far as he is permitted to do otherwise, undertake a legal transaction in the name of the principal with himself in his own name or as agent of a third party, unless the transaction is exclusively in fulfilment of a commitment.

Sixth Title

Consent and ratification

§ 182
Approval
(1) If the effectiveness of a contract or of a unilateral legal transaction which is to be undertaken as against another is dependent on the approval of a third party, the giving and the refusal of the approval can be declared as against the one as well as against the other party.
(2) Approval does not need the form determined for the legal transaction.
(3) If a unilateral legal transaction the effectiveness of which depends on the approval of a third party is undertaken with the consent of the third party, the provisions of § 111 sentences 2, 3 apply correspondingly.
[. . .]

§ 184
Retrospective effect of ratification
(1) Subsequent approval (ratification) takes effect retrospectively at the point in time when the legal transaction was undertaken, in so far as no other provision is made.
(2) Retrospective effect does not render dispositions prior to ratification ineffective if they have been made in respect of the subject matter of the legal transaction by the ratifier or have occurred by way of execution or seizure or by the insolvency administrator.

Fifth Section

Limitation

First Title

Subject matter and length of limitation period

§ 194
Subject matter of limitation
(1) The right to demand that another person shall do or refrain from doing something (a claim) is subject to limitation.
(2) Claims from a family law relationship are not subject to limitation in so far as they are aimed at the restoration for the future of the situation corresponding to the relationship.

§ 195
Standard limitation period
The standard limitation period is three years.

§ 196
Limitation period in respect of rights in land
Claims to transfer of property in land as well as to the creation, transfer or termination of a right in land or to the alteration of the content of such a right as well as claims to counterperformance are subject to a limitation period of ten years.

§ 197
Three year limitation period
The following are subject to a 30-year limitation period in so far as no other provision is made:
1. Claims to delivery arising from property and other rights in rem,
2. Family and inheritance claims,
3. Claims established in a legally binding way,
4. Claims arising from directly enforceable settlements or directly enforceable documents, and
5. Claims which have become enforceable by a finding which has been made in insolvency proceedings.
(2) In so far as claims under paragraph 1 no 2 have regularly recurring services or support services as their content and claims under paragraph 1 nos 3 to 5 have regularly recurring services becoming due in the future as their content, the standard limitation period takes the place of the limitation period of 30 years.

§ 198
Limitation in case of succession
If a thing in relation to which a claim in rem exists enters the possession of a third party by succession, the successor has the benefit of the limitation period which elapsed during the possession of the legal predecessor.

§ 199
Commencement of standard limitation period and maximum periods
(1) The standard limitation period commences with the end of the year in which
1. the claim arises, and
2. the creditor acquires knowledge of the circumstances forming the basis of the claim and the identity of the debtor, or would have done so had he not been grossly negligent.
(2) Claims to compensation which are based on violation of life, body, health, or freedom have a limitation period (without regard to when they arose and knowledge, or absence of knowledge due to gross negligence) of 30 years from the commission of the act, the violation of duty or the other event giving rise to the harm.
(3) Other claims to compensation
1. without regard to knowledge, or absence of knowledge due to gross negligence, have a limitation period of ten years from when they arise, and
2. without regard to when they arise and knowledge, or absence of knowledge due gross negligence, have a limitation period of 30 years from the commission of the act, the violation of duty or the other event giving rise to the harm,
whichever period ends soonest.
(4) Claims other than claims to compensation have a limitation period of ten years from the date they arise without regard to knowledge, or absence of knowledge due to gross negligence.
(5) If the claim relates to an omission, the contravention takes the place of the arising of the claim.

§ 200
Commencement of other limitation periods
The limitation period for claims which are not subject to the standard limitation period begins with the date when the claim arises in so far as no other date for commencement of the limitation period is determined. § 199 paragraph 5 applies correspondingly.

§ 201
Commencement of limitation period for established claims
The limitation period for claims of the kind described in § 197 paragraph 1 nos 3 to 5 begins with the date the decision becomes legally effective, the establishment of the directly enforceable title or the finding in the insolvency proceedings, but not before the date when the claim arose. § 199 paragraph 5 applies correspondingly.

§ 202
Impermissibility of agreements about limitation
(1) Limitation periods cannot be reduced in advance by a legal transaction in the case of liability based on intention.
(2) Limitation periods cannot be increased by a legal transaction beyond a period of 30 years from the statutory commencement of the limitation period.

Second Title

Suspension, expiry of suspension and recommencement of limitation period

§ 203
Suspension of limitation period in case of negotiations
If negotiations about the claim or the circumstances forming the basis of the claim are proceeding between the debtor and the creditor, the limitation period is suspended until one or other of the parties refuses to continue with the negotiations. Expiry of the limitation period occurs no sooner than three months after the end of the suspension.

§ 204
Suspension of limitation period by pursuit of right
(1) A limitation period is suspended by
1. the commencement of an action for performance or for declaration of existence of a claim, for granting of an execution clause or for issue of an execution judgment,
2. the submission of an application in simplified proceedings about the maintenance of minors,
3. the submission of a warning decision in warning proceedings,
4. the instigation of notification of a conciliation petition which is delivered at a conciliation office set up or recognised by the state (Land) justice administration or, if the parties make an attempt to reach an agreement conjointly at another conciliation office which manages conflict settlements, and if the notification is instigated following the delivery of the application, the suspension of the limitation period occurs with the delivery,
5. the assertion of set off to the claim in the proceedings,
6. the submission of an announcement of the dispute,

7. the submission of an application for the carrying out of independent evidence proceedings,

8. the commencement of agreed expert opinion proceedings or the commissioning of an expert in the proceedings in accordance with § 641a,

9. the submission of an application for the issue of a detention warrant, of an interim order or an interim injunction or, if the application is not submitted, its delivery, if the order for the detention, the interim order or the interim injunction is submitted to the debtor within a month of announcement or submission to the creditor,

10. the notification of the claim in insolvency proceedings or in shipping law allocation proceedings,

11. the beginning of arbitration proceedings,

12. the delivery of an application to an authority if the permissibility of the action is dependent on a prior decision of this authority and the action is brought within three months after the making of the request; this applies correspondingly for applications to be made to a court or to a conciliation office described in no 4, the permissibility of which depends on the prior decision of an authority,

13. the delivery of an application to the higher court, if this court has to determine the competent court and the action is brought, or the application for which the determination of the place of jurisdiction has to occur is made, within three months after the making of the request, and

14. the instigation of notification of the first application for granting of assistance for the cost of proceedings; if the notification is instigated following the submission of the application, the suspension of the limitation period occurs with the submission.

(2) The suspension under paragraph 1 ends six months after the legally binding decision or other termination of the proceedings initiated. If the proceedings come to a halt as a result of the parties not pursuing them, then the last step in the proceedings by the parties, by the court, or by the other office concerned with the proceedings is substituted for the termination of the proceedings. The suspension begins again when one of the parties pursues the proceedings further.

(3) §§ 206, 210 and 211 have corresponding application to the period under paragraph 1 nos 9, 12 and 13.

§ 205
Suspension of limitation period in case of right to refuse performance
The limitation period is suspended as long as the debtor is entitled temporarily to refuse performance on the basis of an agreement with the creditor.

§ 206
Suspension of limitation period in case of supervening force (force majeure)
The limitation period is suspended as long as the creditor within the last six months of the limitation period is prevented from pursuing his rights by supervening force (force majeure).

§ 207
Suspension of limitation period on family and similar grounds
(1) The limitation period in respect of claims between married couples is suspended as long as the marriage exists. The same applies for claims between

1. life partners as long as the life partnership exists,
2. parents and children and the spouse of a parent and that person's children during the minority of the children,
3. the guardian and the ward during the period of the guardianship,
4. the person supervised and the supervisor during the length of the supervision relationship, and
5. the charge and the carer during the length of the care relationship
The limitation period for claims of a child against the advisor is suspended during the length of the advisor relationship
(2) § 208 remains unaffected.

§ 208

Suspension of limitation period in relation to claims for violation of sexual self-determination
The limitation period in respect of claims for violation of sexual self-determination is suspended until the creditor attains the age of 21 years. If the creditor in respect of claims for violation of sexual self-determination lives with the debtor in the same household at the beginning of the limitation period, the limitation period is also suspended until the termination of these household arrangements.

§ 209

Effect of suspension
The period of time during which the limitation period is suspended is not included when calculating the limitation period.

§ 210

Expiry of suspension in case of persons who are not fully legally competent
(1) If a person who is not legally competent, or who is restricted in his legal competence, is without a statutory representative, a limitation period running for or against that person will not start before the expiry of six months after the point in time at which the person becomes fully legally competent or the lack of representation is removed. If the limitation period is shorter than six months, the period determined for limitation purposes takes the place of six months.
(2) Paragraph 1 does not apply in so far as a person with limited legal capacity is competent in relation to legal proceedings.

§ 211

Expiry of suspension in estate cases
The limitation period in respect of a claim which belongs to an estate or is directed against an estate does not start before the expiry of six months after the point in time at which the inheritance is accepted by the heir, or the insolvency proceedings regarding the estate are opened, or from which the claim can be made by or against a representative. If the limitation period is shorter than six months, the period determined for limitation purposes takes the place of six months.

§ 212

Recommencement of limitation period
(1) The limitation period begins again if

1. the debtor acknowledges the claim to the creditor by an interim payment, an interest payment, the giving of security, or in some other way, or

2. an execution by a court or by an authority is undertaken or proposed.

(2) The fresh commencement of the limitation period as a result of an execution does not count as having occurred if the execution is annulled on the application of the debtor or because of absence of the statutory prerequisites.

(3) The fresh commencement of the limitation period through application to carry out an act of execution does not count as having occurred if the application is not granted or the application is withdrawn before the execution or the act of execution obtained is annulled in accordance with paragraph 2.

§ 213

Suspension, expiry of suspension and fresh commencement of limitation period in relation to other claims

Suspension, expiry of suspension and fresh commencement of the limitation period also apply for claims arising from the same ground which exist either in addition to the claim or instead of it, as desired.

Third Title

Legal consequences of limitation

§ 214

Effect of limitation

(1) On expiry of the limitation period the debtor is entitled to refuse performance.

(2) Any performance rendered in satisfaction of a time expired claim cannot be demanded back, even if the performance was rendered in ignorance of the fact that it was time expired. The same applies for a contractual acknowledgement as well as for a giving of security by the debtor.

§ 215

Set off and right of retention after expiry of limitation period

The expiry of a limitation period does not exclude set off and the claiming of a right of retention if the limitation period for the claim had not yet expired at the point in time at which there could first be set off or the performance could be refused.

§ 216

Effect of limitation on secured claims

(1) The expiry of the limitation period in respect of a claim for which a mortgage, a ship mortgage, or a right of pledge exists does not prevent the creditor from seeking his satisfaction from the encumbered object.

(2) If a right has been procured for the securing of a claim, retransfer cannot be demanded on the basis of the expiry of the limitation period for the claim. If property is reserved, withdrawal from the contract can occur even if the limitation period in respect of the secured claim has expired.

(3) Paragraphs (1) and (2) do not apply to the expiry of the limitation period in respect of claims to interest and other recurring performances.

§ 217
Limitation in respect of subsidiary performances
The limitation period in respect of the claim to subsidiary performances dependent on the main claim expires with that of the main claim, even if the special limitation period applying to the former claim has not yet expired.

§ 218
Ineffectiveness of withdrawal
(1) Withdrawal because performance was not effected or not effected in accordance with the contract is ineffective if the limitation period in respect of the claim to the performance or the claim to subsequent fulfilment has expired and the debtor refers to this. This also applies if the debtor does not need to perform under § 275 paragraphs 1 to 3, § 439 paragraph 3 or § 635 paragraph 3 and the claim to performance or the claim to subsequent fulfilment would be time barred. § 216 paragraph 2 sentence 2 remains unaffected.
(2) §214 paragraph 2 applies correspondingly.
[...]

Second Book

Law of obligation relationships

First Section

Content of obligation relationships

First Title

Duty to perform

§ 241
Duties arising from obligation relationship
(1) By virtue of the obligation relationship, the creditor is entitled to demand performance from the debtor. Performance can also consist in an omission.
(2) The obligation relationship can, according to its content, oblige each party to have regard to the rights, legal entitlements and interests of the other party.

§ 242
Performance in accordance with good faith
A creditor is obliged to effect performance in the manner required by good faith, having regard to custom (Verkehrsitte).

§ 243
Obligation relating to class
(1) A person who is obliged to provide a thing determined only according to its class must provide a thing of average type and quality.
(2) If a debtor has done what is necessary on his side to provide such a thing, the obligation relationship is limited to this thing.

§ 244

Debt in foreign currency

(1) If a money debt expressed in another currency than the euro is to be paid within the country, the payment can be made in euros, unless it is expressly agreed that payment is to be in the other currency.

(2) The conversion will take place according to the currency value which is determinative at the time of the payment for the place of payment.

§ 246

Statutory rate of interest

If a debt is to bear interest according to statute law or a legal transaction, four per cent per annum is to be paid in so far as no other rate has been determined.

§ 247

Basic rate of interest

(1) The basic rate of interest is 3.62 per cent. It changes on the 1st January and 1st July each year by the percentage points by which the base factor rose or fell since the last change of the basic rate of interest. The base factor is the rate of interest for the most recent major refinancing operation of the European Central Bank before the first calendar day of the half year concerned.

(2) The Deutsche Bundesbank will publish in the Bundesanzeiger the applicable basic rate of interest without delay after the points in time mentioned in paragraph 1 sentence 2.

[. . .]

§ 249

Type and scope of compensation

(1) A person who is under a duty to provide compensation has to restore the state of affairs which would exist if the circumstance giving rise to the duty to compensate had not arisen.

(2) If compensation for harm is to be provided because of injury to a person or because of damage to a thing, the creditor can instead of restoration demand the sum of money necessary for this. In the case of damage to a thing the sum of money necessary under sentence 1 only includes turnover tax if and in so far as it has actually become payable.

§ 250

Compensation in money after setting of time limit

A creditor can determine for the person obliged to compensate an appropriate period for restoration in kind by a declaration that he will refuse restoration in kind after expiry of this period. After the expiry of the period, the creditor can demand compensation in money if the restoration in kind does not take place in time; the claim to restoration in kind is excluded.

§ 251

Compensation in money without setting of time limit

(1) In so far as restoration in kind is not possible or is not sufficient for indemnifying the creditor, the person obliged to compensate must indemnify the creditor in money.

(2) The person obliged to compensate can indemnify the creditor in money if restoration in kind is possible only with disproportionate expenditure. Expenses which have arisen from medical treatment of an injured animal are not disproportionate simply because they substantially exceed its value.

§ 252
Lost profit
The harm for which compensation is to be made also includes lost profit. Profit is deemed to be lost if it could be expected with probability in the usual course of things or the special circumstances, in particular the arrangements and provisions which have been made.

§ 253
Non-material harm
(1) In the case of harm which is not financial harm, compensation in money can only be demanded in the cases determined by statute law.
(2) If compensation is to be provided because of injury to the body, health, freedom or sexual self-determination, fair compensation in money can also be demanded for harm which is not financial harm.

§ 254
Contributory fault
(1) If fault on the part of the victim has contributed to the origin of the harm, the duty to compensate as well as the extent of the compensation to be provided depends on the circumstances, and in particular on the extent to which the harm has been predominantly caused by the one or the other party.
(2) This also applies if the victim's fault is limited to the fact that he has omitted to draw the debtor's attention to the risk of an unusually high level of harm of which the debtor neither knew nor ought to have known, or that he has omitted to avert the harm or to reduce it. The provisions of § 278 apply correspondingly.

§ 255
Transfer of claims to compensation
A person who has to provide compensation for the loss of a thing or a right is obliged to compensate only in return for transfer of the claims which belong to the person entitled to compensation on the basis of property in the thing or on the basis of the right against third parties.
[. . .]

§ 266
Partial performances
The debtor is not entitled to make partial performances.

§ 267
Performance by third parties
(1) If the debtor does not have to perform in person, a third party can also effect performance. The consent of the debtor is not necessary.
(2) The creditor can refuse performance if the debtor objects.

§ 268
Right of discharge by third party
(1) If the creditor carries out an execution against an object belonging to the debtor, everyone who runs the risk of losing a right in the object through the execution is entitled to satisfy the creditor. The same right belongs to the person in possession of a thing if he runs the risk of losing possession through the execution.
(2) Satisfaction can also occur by deposit or by setting off.
(3) In so far as the third party satisfies the creditor, the demand transfers to him. The transfer cannot be claimed to the creditor's disadvantage.

§ 269
Place of performance
(1) If a place for performance is neither determined nor can it be deduced from the circumstances, in particular from the nature of the obligation relationship, performance must occur in the place in which the debtor had his residence at the time the obligation relationship arose.
(2) If the obligation arose in the carrying out of the debtor's business and if the debtor had his business establishment in another place, the place of establishment is substituted for the place of residence.
(3) It should not be deduced from the mere fact that the debtor has agreed to pay the costs of dispatch that the place to which the dispatch must be made should be the place of performance.

§ 270
Place of payment
(1) In case of doubt the debtor should transmit money at his own risk and cost to the creditor at his residence.
(2) If the demand arose in the carrying out of the creditor's business and if the creditor has his business establishment in another place, the place of establishment is substituted for the place of residence.
(3) If, as a result of a change in the creditor's residence or business establishment after the obligation relationship arose, the costs or the risk of transmission increase, the creditor must bear the additional costs in the former case and the risk in the latter case.
(4) The provisions about the place of performance remain unaffected.

§ 271
Time for performance
(1) If a time for performance is neither determined nor can it be deduced from the circumstances, the creditor can demand performance immediately and the debtor can effect it immediately.
(2) If a time is determined, it is to be assumed in case of doubt that the creditor cannot demand performance before this time, but the debtor can effect it earlier.
[. . .]

§ 273
Right of retention
(1) If the debtor has a claim which has fallen due against the creditor from the same legal relationship on which his obligation is based, he can, in so far as no different

conclusion is to be drawn from the obligation relationship, refuse the performance owed until the performance which is due to him has been effected (right of retention).

(2) A person who is obliged to hand over an object has the same right if he is entitled to a claim which has fallen due for expenditure on the object or because of harm caused to him by it, unless he has obtained the object by a tort committed deliberately.

(3) The creditor can prevent the exercise of the right of retention by a providing a security. Security by a guarantee is excluded.

§ 274
Effects of the right of retention

(1) The claiming of a right of retention only has, as against the creditor's claim, the effect that the debtor must be ordered to perform in return for the performance which is due to him (simultaneous fulfilment).

(2) On the basis of such an order the creditor can pursue his claim by way of execution without effecting the performance which he owes if the debtor is in delay in acceptance.

§ 275
Exclusion of duty to perform

(1) The claim to performance is excluded in so far as this is impossible for the debtor or for anyone.

(2) The debtor can refuse performance in so far as this requires expenditure which is in gross disproportion to the creditor's interest in performance, having regard to the content of the obligation relationship and the requirement of good faith. When determining the efforts to be expected of the debtor, consideration must also be given to whether the debtor is responsible for the hindrance to performance.

(3) The debtor can further refuse performance if he has to effect performance personally, and on balancing the hindrance to his performance, together with the creditor's interest in performance, the debtor cannot be expected to do this.

(4) The creditor's rights are determined in accordance with §§ 280, 283 to 285, 311a and 326.

§ 276
Responsibility of debtor

(1) The debtor is responsible for intention and negligence if no stricter or more lenient liability is either determined or to be deduced from the other content of the obligation relationship, in particular from the adoption of a guarantee or a risk of production. The provisions of §§ 827 and 828 apply correspondingly.

(2) A person acts negligently if he does not have regard to the care necessary in human affairs.

(3) The debtor cannot be released in advance from liability for intention.

§ 277
Care in own affairs

A person who only has to take responsibility for that care which he is accustomed to apply in his own affairs is not freed from liability for gross negligence.

§ 278

Responsibility of debtor for third parties
The debtor has to answer for fault on the part of his statutory representative and of the persons whom he uses for the fulfilment of his obligations to the same extent as for his own fault. The provisions of § 276 paragraph 3 do not apply.
[. . .]

§ 280

Compensation for violation of duty
(1) If the debtor violates a duty arising from an obligation relationship, the creditor can demand compensation for the harm arising from this. This does not apply if the debtor is not responsible for the violation of duty.
(2) The creditor can only demand compensation for delay in performance under the additional prerequisite of § 286.
(3) The creditor can only demand compensation instead of performance under the additional prerequisites of § 281, § 282 or § 283.

§ 281

Compensation instead of performance, because of non-performance or performance not in accordance with obligation
(1) In so far as the debtor does not effect the performance which is due or does not effect it in accordance with the obligation, the creditor can, under the prerequisites of § 280 paragraph 1, demand compensation instead of performance if he has set a reasonable period for the debtor for the performance or subsequent fulfilment, but without result. If the debtor has effected a partial performance, the creditor can only demand compensation instead of the whole performance if he has no interest in the partial performance. If the debtor has not effected performance in accordance with the obligation, the creditor cannot demand compensation instead of the whole performance if the violation of duty is not substantial.
(2) The setting of a period can be dispensed with if the debtor refuses performance seriously and finally, or if special circumstances are present which, on balancing the interests of both sides, justify the immediate making of a claim to compensation.
(3) If, because of the kind of violation of duty, the setting of a period does not come into consideration, then a warning will take its place.
(4) The claim to performance is excluded as soon as the creditor has demanded compensation instead of performance.
(5) If the creditor demands compensation instead of the whole performance, the debtor is entitled to demand back what has been performed in accordance with §§ 346 to 348.

§ 282

Compensation instead of performance because of violation of duty under § 241 paragraph 2
If the debtor violates a duty under § 241 paragraph 2, the creditor can demand compensation instead of performance under the prerequisites of § 280 paragraph 1 if performance by the debtor can no longer be expected of the creditor.

§ 283
Compensation instead of performance on exclusion of duty to perform
If the debtor does not need to perform according to § 275 paragraphs 1 to 3, the creditor can demand compensation instead of performance under the prerequisites of § 280 paragraph 1. § 281 paragraph 1 sentences 2 and 3 and paragraph 5 apply correspondingly.

§ 284
Reimbursement of abortive expenditure
In the place of compensation instead of performance the creditor can demand reimbursement of expenditure which he has made in reliance on receiving the performance and could fairly make, unless its purpose would not have been attained even without the debtor's violation of duty.

§ 285
Handing reimbursement over
(1) If the debtor obtains replacement or a claim to replacement for the object which is the subject of the obligation as a result of the circumstance on the basis of which he does not need to effect performance according to § 275 paragraphs 1 to 3, the creditor can demand the handing over of what has been received as replacement or the transfer of the claim to replacement.
(2) If the creditor can demand compensation instead of performance, this will reduce by the value of the replacement obtained or the claim to replacement if he makes use of the right provided for in paragraph 1.

§ 286
Delay by debtor
(1) If the debtor does not perform in response to the creditor's warning which takes place after performance has become due, then he will be in delay as a result of the warning. The raising of a claim to performance as well as the submission of a warning order in warning proceedings are equivalent to a warning.
(2) A warning is not needed if
1. a time is determined for the performance according to the calendar,
2. an event must precede the performance and an appropriate time is determined for the performance in such a way that it can be reckoned from the event onwards according to the calendar,
3. the debtor refuses performance seriously and finally,
4. the immediate commencement of delay is justified on special grounds on balancing the interests of both sides.
(3) The debtor in respect of a demand for payment will be in delay at the latest if he does not perform within 30 days after the due date and an account or an equivalent payment statement is received; this only applies as against a debtor who is a consumer if his attention has been particularly drawn to these results in the account or payment statement. If the point in time of the arrival of the account or payment statement is uncertain, the debtor who is not a consumer is in delay at the latest 30 days after the due date and receipt of the counterperformance.
(4) The debtor is not in delay as long as performance fails to occur as a result of a circumstance for which he is not responsible.

§ 287
Responsibility during delay
The debtor is responsible for all negligence during the delay. He is liable with regard to the performance even for chance events unless the harm would also have occurred on punctual performance.

§ 288
Interest during delay
(1) A money obligation bears interest during the delay. The rate of interest during delay for the year is five percentage points above the basic rate of interest.
(2) For legal transactions in which no consumer participates, the rate of interest for demands for payment is eight percentage points above the basic rate of interest.
(3) The creditor can demand higher interest on a different legal ground.
(4) A claim for further loss is not excluded.
[. . .]

Second Title

Delay by creditor

§ 293
Delay in acceptance
The creditor falls into delay when he does not accept the performance offered to him.

§ 294
Actual offer
The performance must be actually offered to the creditor as it is to be effected.

§ 295
Verbal offer
A verbal offer by the debtor suffices if the creditor has declared to him that he will not accept the performance or if action by the creditor is necessary for the effecting of the performance, in particular if the creditor has to collect the thing owed. An invitation to the creditor to undertake the necessary action is equivalent to an offer of performance.

§ 296
Dispensability of offer
If a time is determined in accordance with the calendar for the action to be undertaken by the creditor, an offer is only needed if the creditor carries out the action punctually. The same applies if an event has to precede the action and a reasonable time for the action is determined in such a way that it can be reckoned from the event onwards according to the calendar.

§ 297
Inability on part of debtor
The creditor does not fall into delay if the debtor is not in a position to effect performance at the time of the offer or, in the case of § 296, at the time determined for the action by the creditor.
[. . .]

§ 300
Effects of delay by creditor
(1) The debtor only has to answer for intention and gross negligence during delay by the creditor.
(2) If a thing is owed which is only determined by its class, the risk transfers to the creditor at the point in time at which he falls into delay by not accepting the thing offered.
[. . .]

§ 304
Reimbursement of additional expenditure
The debtor can in the case of delay by the creditor demand the reimbursement of the additional expenditure which he had to incur for the unsuccessful offer as well as for the preservation and maintenance of the object owed.
Second Section
Formulation of obligation relationships in legal transactions by general conditions of business

§ 305
Incorporation of general conditions of business into contract
(1) General conditions of business are all contractual conditions formulated before-hand for many contracts which one contracting party (the user) places before the other at the conclusion of a contract. It does not matter whether the provisions form an outwardly separated component of the contract or are taken into the contractual document itself, what their scope is, in what kind of written form they are composed and what form the contract takes. General conditions of business are not present in so far as the conditions of contract are negotiated individually between the contracting parties.
(2) General conditions of business will only be a component of a contract if the user on conclusion of the contract
1. refers the other contracting party expressly to them or, if an express reference is only possible with disproportionate difficulties because of the way in which the contract is concluded, by a clearly visible notice at the place of conclusion of the contract, and
2. provides the other contracting party with the opportunity of becoming acquainted with their content in a reasonable manner which also takes appropriate account of any physical disability of the other contracting party which the user can recognise and if the other contracting party is in agreement with their applicability.
(3) The contracting parties can agree the applicability of certain general conditions of business in advance for a certain kind of legal transaction, provided they observe the requirements described in paragraph 2.

§ 305a
Incorporation in special cases
Even without observance of the requirements described in § 305 paragraph 2 nos 1 and 2, there will be included, if the other contracting party is in agreement with their applicability:

1. the tariffs and implementation provisions of the railways issued with the approval of the competent transport authority or on the basis of international treaties and the transportation conditions of trams, buses and motor vehicles providing regular services approved in accordance with the Transportation of Persons Act in the transportation contract,

2. the general conditions of business published in the official journal of the regulatory authority for telecommunications and post and kept available in the places of business of the user

a) in transportation contracts which are concluded outside business premises by the insertion of postal packets in letterboxes,

b) in contracts about telecommunication, information and other services which are effected at once directly by employment of methods of communication from a distance and during the effecting of a telecommunication service if the general conditions of business can only be made accessible to the other contracting party before the conclusion of the contract with disproportionate difficulty.

§ 305b
Priority of individual arrangement
Individual contractual arrangements have priority over general conditions of business.

§ 305c
Surprising and ambiguous clauses
(1) Provisions in general conditions of business which in the circumstances, in particular the outward appearance of the contract, are so unusual that the contractual partner of the user does not need to take them into account are not part of the contract.
(2) Doubt about the interpretation of general conditions of business will be resolved to the disadvantage of the user.

§ 306
Legal consequences of non-incorporation and ineffectiveness
(1) If general conditions of business have wholly or partially not become part of the contract or are ineffective, the contract remains effective in other respects.
(2) In so far as the provisions have not become part of the contract or are ineffective, the content of the contract will be determined in accordance with the statutory provisions.
(3) The contract is ineffective if adhering to it, even taking into account the alteration provided for in paragraph 2, would represent an unreasonable hardship for a contracting party.

§306a
Prohibition of circumvention
The provisions of this section apply even if they are circumvented by other formulations.

§ 307
Control of content
(1) Provisions in general conditions of business are ineffective if they unreasonably disadvantage the user's contracting partner in a manner contrary to the requirements

of good faith. An unreasonable disadvantage can also arise from the fact that the provision is not clear and comprehensible.

(2) An unreasonable disadvantage is to be assumed in case of doubt if a provision

1. cannot be reconciled with essential basic concepts of the statutory regime from which there is a deviation, or

2. so limits essential rights or duties which arise from the nature of the contract that the attainment of the purpose of the contract is endangered.

(3) Paragraphs 1 and 2 as well as §§ 308 and 309 only apply for provisions in general conditions of business by which rules are agreed deviating from legal provisions or supplementing them. Other provisions can be ineffective under paragraph 1 sentence 2 in combination with paragraph 1 sentence 1.

§ 308

Prohibition on clauses with possibility of discretion

In general conditions of business, the following in particular are ineffective

1. (Periods for acceptance and performance)

a provision by which the user reserves unreasonably long or insufficiently determinate periods for the acceptance or refusal of an offer or the effecting of performance; reservation of performance only after expiry of the period for revocation or return under § 355 paragraphs 1 and 2 and § 356 is excepted from this;

2. (Additional period)

a provision by which the user, deviating from the legal provisions, reserves an unreasonably long or insufficiently determinate additional period for the performance to be effected by him;

3. (Reservation of right of withdrawal)

agreement of a right by the user to release himself from his duty to perform without a ground which is objectively justified and given in the contract; this does not apply for long term obligation relationships;

4. (Reservation of right of alteration)

agreement of a right by the user to alter the promised performance or to deviate from it, if the agreement of the alteration or deviation, taking into consideration the interests of the user, cannot be expected of the other contracting party;

5. (Fictitious declarations)

a provision according to which a declaration by the contractual partner of the user is, on the undertaking or omission of a certain act, to count as given or not given by him, unless

a) the contractual partner is allowed an appropriate period for giving an express declaration and

b) the user commits himself especially to draw the attention of the contractual partner at the beginning of the period to the significance of his conduct as provided for;

this does not apply to contracts in which Part B of the Order regarding public works contracts (Verdingungsordnung) for building services is included as a whole;

6. (Fictitious arrival)

a provision that a declaration by the user of particular importance is to count as having reached the other contracting party;

7. (Winding up of contracts)

a provision under which the user can demand, for the case in which a contracting party withdraws from the contract or terminates the contract by notice,
a) an unreasonably high recompense for the exploitation or use of a thing or a right or for services effected or
b) an unreasonably high reimbursement of expenses;
8. (Non-availability of performance)
an agreement permissible under no 3 of a reservation by the user to release himself from the duty to fulfil the contract in the case of non-availability of the performance, if the user does not commit himself,
a) to inform the contractual partner without delay about the non-availability and
b) to restore counterperformances of the contractual partner without delay.

§ 309
Prohibition of clauses without possibility of discretion
Even in so far as a deviation from the statutory provisions is permissible, the following are ineffective in general conditions of business:
1. (Price increases on short notice)
a provision which provides for increase of the payment for goods or services which are to be delivered or carried out within four months after the conclusion of the contract; this does not apply for goods or services which are delivered or carried out within the framework of long term obligation relationships;
2. (Rights to refuse performance)
a provision by which
a) the right to refuse performance which belongs to the contractual partner of the user under § 320 is excluded or limited, or
b) a right of retention belonging to the contractual partner of the user, in so far as it is based on the same contractual relationship, is excluded or limited, and in particular is made dependent on the recognition of defects by the user;
3. (Prohibition of set off)
a provision which takes away the power from the contractual partner of the user to set off an undisputed demand or one established in a legally binding way;
4. (Warning, setting of a period)
a provision by which the user is released from the statutory obligation to warn the other contracting party or to set him a period for performance or subsequent fulfilment;
5. (Lump sum for claims to compensation)
the agreement of an all-inclusive claim by the user to compensation or to recompense for a diminution in value, if
a) the lump sum exceeds the harm to be expected in the cases regulated according to the usual course of events or the diminution in value usually arising, or
b) the other contracting party is not allowed expressly to prove that harm or a diminution in value did not occur at all or is substantially lower than the lump sum;
6. (Contractual penalty)
a provision by which the user is promised payment of a contractual penalty for the case of non-acceptance or delayed acceptance of the performance, of delay in payment or for the case where the other contracting party releases himself from the contract;
7. (Exclusion of liability on violation of life, body or health and in case of gross fault)
a) (Violation of life, body or health)

an exclusion or a limitation of liability for harm from violation of life, body or health which is based on a negligent violation of the user's duty or an intentional or negligent violation of the duty of a statutory representative or agent of the user;

b) (Gross fault)

an exclusion or limitation of liability for other harm which is based on a grossly negligent violation of duty by the user or on an intentional or grossly negligent violation of duty of a statutory representative or agent of the user;

a and b do not apply for limitations of liability in the conditions of transport and tariff provisions of trams, buses and powered vehicles on regular services authorised in accordance with the Transportation of Persons Act, in so far as they do not deviate from the Regulation on general conditions of transportation for tram and bus traffic and regular services with powered vehicles of the 27th February 1970 to the disadvantage of the passenger; b does not apply for limitations of liability for state authorised lottery or raffle contracts;

8. (Other exclusions of liability on violation of duty)

a) (Exclusion of right to be released from contract)

a provision which excludes or limits the right of the other contracting party to be released from the contract in the case of a violation of duty for which the user is responsible and which does not consist in a defect in the object purchased or in the work; this does not apply for the transportation conditions and tariff provisions described in no 7 under the prerequisites mentioned there;

b) (Defects)

a provision by which in relation to contracts about deliveries of newly manufactured things and about work services

aa) (Exclusion and reference to third parties)

claims against the user because of a defect are excluded altogether or with reference to individual parts, limited to the granting of claims against third parties or are made dependent on prior court claims against third parties;

bb) (Limitation to subsequent fulfilment)

claims against the user are limited altogether, or with reference to individual parts, to a right to subsequent fulfilment in so far as the right is not expressly reserved to the other contracting party on failure of subsequent fulfilment to reduce or, if the defects liability does not relate to building services, at his option to withdraw from the agreement;

cc) (Expenses on subsequent fulfilment)

the duty of the user is excluded or limited to bearing the expenses, in particular costs of transportation, road tolls, work and materials, necessary for the purpose of subsequent fulfilment;

dd) (Withholding of subsequent fulfilment)

the user makes subsequent fulfilment dependent on the prior payment of the full sum due or of a part of the sum due which is disproportionately high, taking the defect into consideration;

ee) (Exclusive period for notification of defects)

the user sets the other contracting party an exclusive period, which is shorter than the period permissible under ff, for the notification of defects which are not obvious;

ff) (Reduction of limitation period)

the limitation period for claims against the user in respect of a defect in the cases of § 438 paragraph 1 no 2 and § 634a paragraph 1 no 2 is reduced or, in the other cases, there is a limitation period consisting of less than a year from the statutory commencement of limitation; this does not apply for contracts in which Part B of the Order regarding public works contracts (Verdingungsordnung) for building services is included as a whole;

9. (Effective period of long term obligation relationships)

in respect of a contractual relationship which has as its subject matter the regular delivery of goods or the regular effecting of services or work by the user,

a) an effective period for the contract binding the other contracting party for longer than two years,

b) a tacit lengthening by, in each case, more than a year of the contractual relationship binding the other contracting party, or

c) a longer period of notice of termination than three months before the expiry of the contractual duration provided for initially or extended tacitly and which is to the disadvantage of the other contracting party;

this does not apply to contracts for the delivery of things sold as related to each other, for insurance contracts and for contracts between the proprietors of copyright rights and claims and exploitation companies in the sense of the Act on the exercise of copyright rights and related protective rights;

10. (Change of contracting partner)

a provision according to which in purchase, service or work contracts a third party steps, or can step, into the rights and duties arising from the contract in place of the user, unless

(a) the third party is described by name in the provision, or

(b) the provision grants to the other contracting party the right to release himself from the contract;

11. (Liability of agent concluding contract)

a provision by which the user imposes on an agent who concludes the contract for the other contracting party

a) a personal liability or duty to indemnify without an express and separate declaration directed at this, or

b) in the case of an agency without authority, a liability going beyond § 179;

12. (Burden of proof)

a provision by which the user alters the burden of proof to the disadvantage of the other contracting party, in particular by

a) imposing on this person the burden of proof for circumstances which lie within the area of responsibility of the user, or

b) causing the other contracting party to confirm certain facts;

b does not apply for acknowledgements of receipt which are signed separately or are provided with a separate qualified electronic signature;

13. (Form of notifications and declarations)

a provision by which notifications or declarations which are to be given to the user or a third party are to be in a stricter form than written form or subject to special requirements as to receipt.

§ 310
Area of application

(1) § 305 paragraphs 2 and 3 and §§ 308 and 309 do not apply to general conditions of business which are used as against an undertaking, a legal person under public law or

a special fund under public law. § 307 paragraphs 1 and 2 also apply in cases within sentence 1 in so far as this leads to the ineffectiveness of the contractual provisions mentioned in §§ 308 and 309; appropriate account is to be taken of the customs and usages applying in trade.

(2) §§ 308 and 309 do not apply to contracts by electricity, gas, district heating and water supply undertakings for the supply of special consumers with electrical energy, gas, district heating and water from the supply network in so far as the conditions of supply do not deviate to the disadvantage of the buyer from the Regulations about general conditions for the supply of tariff customers with electrical energy, gas, district heating and water. Sentence 1 applies correspondingly for contracts about the disposal of sewage.

(3) In relation to contracts between an undertaking and a consumer (consumer contracts) the provisions of this section apply with the following provisos:

1. general conditions of business count as being inserted by the undertaking, unless they were introduced by the consumer into the contract;

2. § 305c paragraph 2 and §§ 306 and 307 to 309 of this Code as well as Article 29a of the Introductory Act to the Civil Code also apply to preformulated contractual conditions when these are only intended for use on one occasion and in so far as the consumer could not have any influence on their content because of the preformulation;

3. in assessing the unreasonable disadvantage under § 307 paragraphs 1 and 2, the circumstances accompanying the conclusion of the contract must also be considered.

(4) This section does not apply to contracts in the area of inheritance, family and company law or to tariff contracts or business or service agreements. In its application to labour contracts, the special features applying in labour law are to be considered as appropriate; § 305 paragraphs 2 and 3 are not applicable. Tariff contracts and business and service agreements are equivalent to legal provisions in the sense of § 307 paragraph 3.

Third Section

Obligation relationships arising from contracts

First Title

Formation, content and termination

First Sub-title

Formation

§ 311

Obligation relationships arising from legal transactions and similar obligation relationships

(1) A contract between the participants is necessary for the formation of an obligation relationship by a legal transaction as well as the alteration of the content of an obligation relationship, in so far as statute law does not prescribe otherwise.

(2) An obligation relationship with duties under § 241 paragraph 2 also arises from

1. the opening of contractual negotiations

2. the initiation of a contract, in which initiation one party, having regard to a possible relationship in the nature of a legal transaction, grants to the other party the possibility of exerting an effect on his rights, legal entitlements and interests, or entrusts these to him, or

3. similar business contacts.

(3) An obligation relationship with duties under § 241 paragraph 2 can also arise in favour of persons who are not themselves to be contracting parties. Such an obligation relationship arises in particular when the third party claims reliance for himself to a special extent and thereby substantially influences the contractual negotiations or the conclusion of the contract.

§ 311a
Hindrance to performance on conclusion of contract

(1) It is not inconsistent with the effectiveness of a contract that the debtor does not need to perform under § 275 paragraphs 1 to 3 and the hindrance to performance is already present on conclusion of the contract.

(2) The creditor can demand compensation instead of performance or reimbursement of his expenses to the extent determined in § 284, according to his choice. This does not apply if the debtor did not know of the hindrance to performance on conclusion of the contract and is also not answerable for his lack of knowledge. § 281 paragraph 1 sentences 2 and 3 and paragraph 5 apply correspondingly.

§ 311b
Contracts about land, property and estates

(1) A contract by which one party commits himself to transfer or acquire the property in a piece of land needs notarial authentication. A contract concluded without regard to this formality is valid in its entire content if it is followed by transfer and entry in the Land Register.

(2) A contract by which one party commits himself to transfer his future property or a fraction of his future property or to encumber it with a usufruct is void.

(3) A contract by which one party commits himself to transfer his present property or a fraction of his present property or to encumber it with a usufruct needs notarial authentication.

(4) A contract about the estate of a third party who is still alive is void. The same applies to a contract about the part of an estate which must go to the closest relation or a legacy from the estate of a third party who is still alive.

(5) Paragraph 4 does not apply to a contract which is concluded between future statutory heirs about the statutory inheritance or the part of the estate of one of them which must go to the closest relation. Such a contract needs notarial authentication.

§ 311c
Extension to accessories

If someone commits himself to transfer or encumber a thing, this duty extends in case of doubt to the accessories to the thing.

Second Sub-title

Special forms of sale

§ 312
Right of revocation in front door transactions
(1) In a contract between an undertaking and a consumer which has as its subject matter a performance in return for money and which the consumer has been induced to conclude
1. by oral negotiations at his workplace or in the area of a private dwelling,
2. on the occasion of a leisure time event carried out by the undertaking or by a third party at least also in the undertaking's interests or
3. following on a surprise approach on a vehicle or in a publicly accessible area
(front door transaction), the consumer has a right of revocation in accordance with § 355. The consumer can be allowed a right of return in accordance with § 356 in place of the right of revocation, if in connection with this or a later transaction a continuous association is to be maintained between the consumer and the undertaking.
(2) The necessary information about the right of revocation or return must refer to the legal consequences of § 357 paragraphs 1 and 3.
(3) Without prejudice to other provisions, the right of revocation or return does not exist for insurance contracts, or if
1. in the case of paragraph 1 no 1 the oral negotiations on which the conclusion of the contract is based have been conducted on the previous order of the consumer, or
2. the performance is effected and paid immediately on conclusion of the negotiations and the payment does not exceed 40 euros, or
3. the consumer's declaration of will has been authenticated by a notary.

§ 312a
Relationship to other provisions
If the consumer is entitled at the same time in accordance with other provisions to a right of revocation or return under § 355 or § 356 of this statute or under § 126 of the Investment Act, the right of revocation or return under § 312 is excluded.

§312b
Distance sale contracts
(1) Distance sale contracts are contracts about the delivery of goods or about the effecting of services, including financial services, which are concluded between an undertaking and a consumer by the exclusive use of distance communication methods, unless the conclusion of the contract does not take place within the framework of a sales or services system organised for the distance sale. Financial services in the sense of sentence 1 are bank services and services in connection with a grant of credit, insurance, pensions for individuals, investment and payment.
(2) Distance communication methods are methods of communication which can be employed for the initiation or the conclusion of a contract between a consumer and an undertaking without the simultaneous physical presence of the contracting parties, in particular letters, catalogues, telephone calls, faxes and emails as well as radio, tele and media services.
(3) The provisions about distance sale contracts do not apply to contracts

1. about distance learning (§ 1 of the Distance Learning Protection Act),
2. about time share use of residential buildings (§ 481),
3. about insurances, as well as their negotiation,
4. about the transfer of land and rights in the nature of land, the formation, transfer and termination of rights in rem in respect of land and rights in the nature of land as well as about the construction of buildings,
5. about the delivery of food, drinks or other household objects of daily need, which are delivered at the residence of a consumer, or the place where he stays or works, by undertakings within the framework of frequent and regular journeys,
6. about the effecting of services in the areas of accommodation, transport, delivery of food and drinks as well as use of leisure time when the undertaking commits itself on conclusion of the contract to carrying out the services at a determined point in time or within a period of time which is exactly stated,
7. which are concluded
a) by use of automatic vending machines or automised business premises or
b) with the operators of telecommunication services on the basis of the use of public telephones in so far as they have the use of such telephones as their subject.
(4) In the case of contractual relationships which include an initial agreement with transactions connected to it following on one another or a sequence of separate transactions of the same kind connected to it, and in a temporal relationship, the provisions about distance sale contracts only apply to the first agreement. If transactions of this kind follow one another without such an agreement, the provisions about the undertaking's duties to provide information only apply to the first transaction. If however no transaction of the same kind takes place for longer than a year, the next transaction is deemed to be the first transaction in a new sequence in the sense of sentence 2.
(5) More extensive provisions for the protection of the consumer remain unaffected.

§ 312c
Advice to consumer in case of distance sale contracts
(1) The undertaking must make the information (which is provided for in the Regulation under article 240 of the Introductory Statute to the Civil Code) available to the consumer clearly and comprehensibly in time before he gives his contractual declaration, in a manner corresponding to the distance communication method employed, and giving the business purpose. The undertaking must, in telephone conversations instigated by it, disclose its identity and the business purpose of the contact expressly at the beginning of each conversation.
(2) The undertaking must further communicate to the consumer the contractual provisions, including the general conditions of business, and the information provided for in the Regulation under article 240 of the Introductory Statute to the Civil Code in the scope and manner determined there in text form, and
1. in the case of financial services punctually before the giving of his contractual declaration, or, if at the wish of the consumer the contract is concluded by telephone (or by use of some other method of distance communication which does not allow the communication in text form before the conclusion of the contract) without delay after the conclusion of the distance sale contract;

2. in the case of other services and in the case of the delivery of goods, immediately, and at the latest by the complete fulfilment of the contract, and in the case of goods at the latest by delivery to the consumer.

A communication under sentence 1 no 2 can be dispensed with in the case of services which are furnished directly by employment of methods of distance communication, in so far as these services occur instantaneously and are deducted through the supplier of the method of distance communication. The consumer must however in this case be able to inform himself of the address of the undertaking's establishment at which he can make objections.

(3) In the case of financial services the consumer can demand from the undertaking at any time during the period of the contract that it makes available to him in a document the contractual provisions including the general conditions of business.

(4) Further limitations on the use of distance communication methods and further duties to supply information on the basis of other provisions remain unaffected.

§ 312d
Right of revocation and return in relation to distance sale contracts

(1) The consumer has a right of revocation under § 355 in respect of a distance sale contract. The consumer can be granted a right of return under § 356 instead of a right of revocation in the case of contracts about the delivery of goods.

(2) The period for revocation does not, deviating from § 355 paragraph 2 sentence 1, begin before the fulfilment of the duties to give information under § 312c paragraph 2, nor in the case of the delivery of goods before the day of their arrival with the recipient, nor in the case of recurring delivery of goods of the same kind before the day of arrival of the first partial delivery, nor in the case of services before the day of conclusion of the contract; § 355 paragraph 2 sentence 2 does not apply.

(3) The right of revocation in respect of a service lapses in the following cases also:

1. in the case of a financial service, if the contract has been completely fulfilled by both sides at the express wish of the consumer before the consumer has exercised his right of revocation,

2. in the case of another service, if the undertaking has begun to carry out the service before the end of the period for revocation with the express consent of the consumer, or the consumer has brought this about himself.

(4) The right of revocation does not exist, in so far as no different provision has been made, in relation to distance sale contracts

1. for the delivery of goods which are prepared according to a customer specification or are clearly tailored to personal needs or which are not appropriate for return on the basis of their composition or which can perish quickly or the expiry date of which would be exceeded,

2. for the delivery of audio or video recordings or of software in so far as the data carriers delivered have been unsealed by the consumer,

3. for the delivery of newspapers, journals and magazines,

4. for the carrying out of betting and lottery services,

5. which are concluded in the form of auctions (§ 156), or

6. which have as their object the delivery of goods or the provision of financial services, the price of which is subject on the financial market to fluctuations over

which the undertaking has no influence, and which can occur within the period for revocation, in particular services in connection with shares, share certificates which are issued by a capital investment company or a foreign investment company, and other negotiable securities, foreign currency, derivatives or instruments on the money market.

(5) The right of revocation also does not exist in the case of distance sale contracts in which the consumer already has a right of revocation or return under §§ 355 or 356 on the basis of §§ 495, 499 to 507. In the case of such contracts paragraph 2 applies correspondingly.

(6) In the case of distance sale contracts about financial services, the consumer, deviating from § 357 paragraph 1, only has to provide reimbursement for the value of the service provided under the provisions about statutory withdrawal if he has been referred to this legal consequence before giving his contractual declaration and if he has expressly agreed that the undertaking should begin to carry out the service before the end of the period for revocation.

§ 312e
Duties in electronic business

(1) If an undertaking uses a tele or media service for the purpose of the conclusion of a contract about the delivery of goods or about the carrying out of services (contract in electronic business), it must

1. make available for the customer appropriate, effective and accessible technical methods with the assistance of which the customer can recognise and correct mistakes in submission before the giving of his order,

2. communicate to the customer clearly and comprehensibly the information provided for in the Regulation under Article 241 of the Introductory Act to the Civil Code in time before the giving of his order,

3. confirm to the customer the arrival of his order without delay by electronic means, and

4. provide to the customer the possibility on conclusion of the contract of calling up the contractual provisions, including the general conditions of business, and storing them in a form capable of being reproduced.

The order and confirmation of receipt in the sense of sentence 1 no 3 count as having arrived when the parties for whom they are intended can call them up in usual circumstances.

(2) Paragraph 1 sentence 1 nos 1 to 3 do not apply if the contract is concluded exclusively by individual communication. Paragraph 1 sentence 1 nos 1 to 3 and sentence 2 do not apply if something different is agreed between contracting parties who are not consumers.

(3) More extensive duties to give information on the basis of other provisions remain unaffected. If the customer has a right of revocation under § 355, the revocation period does not begin, deviating from § 355 paragraph 2 sentence 1, before the fulfilment of the duties regulated in paragraph 1 sentence 1.

§ 312f
Divergent agreements

No deviation may be made from the provisions of this subtitle to the disadvantage of the consumer or the customer in so far as no different provision is made. The provisions of this subtitle apply even if they are circumvented by different formulations, in so far as no different provision is made.

Third Sub-title

Adaptation and termination of contracts

§ 313
Disturbance of foundation of transaction
(1) If the circumstances which have become the foundation of the contract have seriously altered after the conclusion of the contract and if the parties would not have concluded the contract, or would have concluded it with a different content if they had foreseen this alteration, then adaptation of the contract can be demanded in so far as adherence to the unaltered contract cannot be expected of one party taking into consideration all the circumstances of the individual case and in particular the contractual or statutory division of risk.
(2) It is equivalent to an alteration of the circumstances if essential preconceptions which have become the foundation of the contract turn out to be wrong.
(3) If an adaptation of the contract is not possible or cannot be expected of a party, the disadvantaged party can withdraw from the contract. For long term obligation relationships, the right to terminate by notice takes the place of the right of withdrawal.

§ 314
Termination of long term obligation relationships by notice on substantial ground
(1) Long-term obligation relationships can be terminated by any contracting party on a substantial ground without observing a period of notice. A substantial ground is present if, taking into consideration all the circumstances of the individual case and balancing the interests of both sides, the continuation of the contractual relationship until the agreed termination or until the expiry of a notice period cannot be expected of the party giving notice.
(2) If the substantial ground consists of the violation of a duty under the contract, termination by notice is only permissible after the expiry without result of a period determined for the taking of remedial action or after a warning without result. § 323 paragraph 2 applies correspondingly.
(3) The person so entitled can only terminate by notice within a reasonable period after he has obtained knowledge of the ground for termination.
(4) The entitlement to demand compensation is not excluded by termination by notice.
[. . .]

Second title

Mutual contract

§ 320
Objection of unfulfilled contract
(1) A person who is under an obligation in a mutual contract can refuse the performance which is incumbent upon him until the effectuation of the counterperformance, unless he is obliged to effect performance beforehand. If the performance has to occur

in favour of several people, refusal can be made to an individual of the part which is due to him until the whole counterperformance has been effectuated. The provisions of § 273 paragraph 3 are not applicable.

(2) If performance has been partially effected by one party, counterperformance cannot be refused in so far as refusal would in the circumstances violate the principles of good faith, in particular because of the relative triviality of the part remaining to be performed.

§ 321

Objection of uncertainty

(1) A person who is obliged to effect performance beforehand under a mutual contract can refuse the performance which is incumbent upon him if it is evident, after conclusion of the contract, that his claim to counterperformance is endangered by the lack of ability to perform on the part of the other party.The right to refuse performance lapses when the counterperformance is brought about or security is provided for it.

(2) The person obliged to effect performance beforehand can determine an appropriate period in which the other party must effect counterperformance simultaneously with performance or provide security, according to his choice. After expiry of the period without result, the person obliged to effect performance beforehand can withdraw from the contract. § 323 applies correspondingly.

§ 323

Withdrawal because performance not carried out or not carried out in accordance with contract

(1) If the debtor in a mutual contract does not effect performance which is due, or does not effect it in accordance with the contract, the creditor can withdraw from the contract, if he has determined for the debtor an appropriate period for performance or subsequent fulfilment but without result.

(2) The setting of a period can be dispensed with, if

1. the debtor refuses performance seriously and finally,

2. the debtor does not effect performance on a date determined in the contract or within a determined period and in the contract the creditor has made the continued existence of his interest in performance dependent on the punctuality of the performance or

3. special circumstances are present which justify immediate withdrawal, on balancing the interests of both parties.

(3) If the setting of a period does not come into consideration because of the type of violation of duty, then a warning will takes its place.

(4) The creditor can withdraw even before performance becomes due, if it is obvious that the prerequisites for withdrawal will occur.

(5) If the debtor has effected partial performance, the creditor can only withdraw from the whole contract if he has no interest in partial performance. If the debtor has not effected performance in accordance with the contract, the creditor cannot withdraw from the contract if the violation of duty is insignificant.

(6) Withdrawal is excluded if the creditor is solely or overwhelmingly responsible for a circumstance that would entitle him to withdraw or if a circumstance for which the debtor is not responsible occurs at a time at which the creditor is in delay in acceptance.

§ 324
Withdrawal because of violation of duty under § 241 paragraph 2
If the debtor in a mutual contract violates a duty under § 241 paragraph 2, the creditor can withdraw if adherence to the contract can no longer be expected of him.

§ 325
Compensation and withdrawal
The right to demand compensation in respect of a mutual contract is not excluded by withdrawal.

§ 326
Release from counterperformance and withdrawal in case of exclusion of duty to perform
(1) If the debtor does not need to perform under § 275 paragraphs 1 to 3, the claim to counterperformance lapses; in the case of partial performance § 441 paragraph 3 applies correspondingly. Sentence 1 does not apply if the debtor does not need to effect subsequent fulfilment under § 275 paragraphs 1 to 3 in the case of performance not in accordance with the contract.
(2) If the creditor is solely or overwhelmingly responsible for a circumstance on the basis of which the debtor does not need to perform under § 275 paragraphs 1 to 3 or if this circumstance for which the debtor is not responsible occurs at a time when the creditor is in delay in acceptance, the debtor retains the claim to counterperformance. He must however allow to be reckoned against him what he saves as a result of release from performance or acquires by some other use of his power to work or wilfully refrains from acquiring.
(3) If the creditor demands the handing over under § 285 of the replacement obtained for the object owed or transfer of the claim to replacement, he remains obliged to effect counterperformance. This is however reduced in accordance with § 441 paragraph 3 in so far as the value of the replacement or of the claim to replacement falls short of the value of the performance owed.
(4) In so far as a counterperformance which is not owed under this provision is effected, what is performed can be demanded back under §§ 346 to 348.
(5) If the debtor does not need to perform according to § 275 paragraphs 1 to 3, the creditor can withdraw; on withdrawal § 323 applies correspondingly with the proviso that the setting of a period can be dispensed with.
[§ 327 is repealed.]

Third Title

Promise of performance to third party

§ 328
Contract for benefit of third party
(1) Performance towards a third party can be stipulated for by contract with the effect that the third party acquires the right directly to demand performance.
(2) In the absence of a special provision, it must be deduced from the circumstances, in particular from the purpose of the contract, whether the third party is to acquire the right, whether the third party's right is to arise immediately or only subject to certain

prerequisites, and whether power should be reserved to the persons concluding the contract to cancel or amend the third party's right without his consent.

§ 329
Rule of interpretation on taking over of fulfilment

If one party commits himself in a contract to satisfy a creditor of the other party without taking over the obligation, in case of doubt it is not to be assumed that the creditor is to acquire the right directly to demand satisfaction from him.

§ 330
Rule of interpretation in case of a life insurance or life annuity contract

If stipulation is made for the payment of the insured sum or the life annuity in a life insurance or life annuity contract to a third party, it is to be assumed in case of doubt that the third party is to acquire the right directly to demand performance. The same applies if in the case of a gratuitous transfer a performance towards a third party is imposed on the beneficiary or in the case of a transfer of assets or property a performance is promised by the transferee to a third party for the purpose of the settlement.

§ 331
Performance after death

(1) If performance towards a third party is to take place after the death of the person to whom it is promised, in case of doubt the third party acquires the right to the performance on the death of the recipient of the promise.

(2) If the recipient of the promise dies before the birth of the third party, the promise to perform towards the third party can only still be cancelled or amended if authority for this has been reserved.

§ 332
Alteration by disposition on death in case of reservation

If the recipient of a promise has reserved to himself the power to put another person in the place of the third party described in the contract without the consent of the promisor, this can take place in case of doubt in a disposition on death as well.

§ 333
Rejection of right by third party

If the third party rejects the right acquired from the contract as against the promisor, the right is deemed not to have been acquired.

§ 334
Objections by debtor against third party

Objections arising from the contract also belong to the promisor as against the third party.

§ 335
Right of demand by recipient of promise

The recipient of the promise can, in so far as no different intention on the part of the persons concluding the contract is to be assumed, also demand performance towards the third party if this person has the right to the performance.

Fifth Title

Withdrawal, and right of revocation and return in respect of consumer contracts

First Sub-title

Withdrawal

§ 346
Effects of withdrawal

(1) If a contracting party has contractually reserved for himself the right of withdrawal or if he is entitled to a statutory right of withdrawal then in the case of withdrawal the performances received are to be retransferred and the benefits taken are to be handed over.

(2) The debtor has to provide compensation for value instead of retransfer or handing over in so far as

1. retransfer or handing over is excluded by the nature of what has been obtained,

2. he has consumed, transferred, encumbered, converted or transformed the object received,

3. the object received has deteriorated or is destroyed; however, deterioration which has arisen by proper operation is left out of consideration. If a counterperformance is determined in the contract, it is to be taken as a basis in the calculation of the compensation for value; if compensation for value for the advantage of use of a loan is to be provided, it can be proved that the value of the advantage of use was lower.

(3) The duty to provide compensation for value lapses:

1. if the defect giving rise to the entitlement to withdraw has shown itself for the first time during the conversion or transformation of the object,

2. in so far as the creditor is responsible for the deterioration or destruction or the harm would likewise have occurred in his hands,

3. if in the case of a statutory right of withdrawal the deterioration or the destruction occurred in the hands of the person entitled even though he observed that care which he usually applies in his own affairs.

A remaining enrichment must be handed over.

(4) The creditor can demand compensation for violation of a duty under paragraph 1 in accordance with §§ 280 to 283.

§ 347
Benefits and uses after withdrawal

(1) If, contrary to the rules of a proper business, the debtor does not obtain benefits even though he could have done so, then he is obliged to provide the creditor with compensation for value. In the case of a statutory right of withdrawal, the person entitled only has to take responsibility in relation to the benefits for that care which he usually uses in his own affairs.

(2) If the debtor gives the object back, provides compensation for value, or his duty to provide compensation for value is excluded in accordance with § 346 paragraph 3 no 1 or 2, then he is to be compensated for necessary expenditure. Other expenses are to be reimbursed in so far as the creditor is enriched by these.

§ 348
Simultaneous fulfilment
The obligations of the parties arising from withdrawal are to be fulfilled simultaneously. The provisions of §§ 320, 322 apply correspondingly.

§ 349
Declaration of withdrawal
Withdrawal takes place by a declaration as against the other party.

§ 350
Extinguishment of right of withdrawal after setting of period
If a period has not been agreed for the exercise of the contractual right of withdrawal, a reasonable period for the exercise can be determined for the person entitled by the other party. The right of withdrawal is extinguished if the withdrawal is not declared before the expiry of the period.

§ 351
Indivisibility of right of withdrawal
If there are several participants on the one or the other side in respect of a contract, the right of withdrawal can only be exercised by all and against all. If the right of withdrawal is extinguished for one of the persons entitled, it is also extinguished for the remainder.

§ 352
Set off after non-fulfilment
Withdrawal because of non-fulfilment of an obligation is ineffective if the debtor could free himself from the obligation by set off and declares the set off without delay after the withdrawal.

§ 353
Withdrawal in return for forfeit
If the right of withdrawal is reserved in return for payment of a forfeit, the withdrawal is ineffective if the forfeit is not paid before or at the time of the declaration and the other party rejects the declaration on this ground without delay. The declaration is however effective if the forfeit is paid without delay after the rejection.

§ 354
Forfeiture clause
If a contract is concluded with the reservation that the debtor is to lose his rights under the contract if he does not fulfil his obligations, the creditor is entitled to withdraw from the contract when this occurs.
Second Sub-title
Right of revocation and return in respect of consumer contracts

§ 355
Right of revocation in respect of consumer contracts
(1) If a right of revocation is granted to a consumer by statute in accordance with this provision, then he is no longer bound by his declaration of will to conclude the contract if he has revoked it within the period. The revocation does not have to contain any reasons and must be declared in text form or by sending the thing back within two

weeks to the undertaking; punctual dispatch suffices for the observance of the period. (2) The period begins with the point in time at which a clearly formulated warning about his right of revocation has been communicated to the consumer in text form, which makes his rights clear to him according to the requirements of the method of communication employed, and which also contains the name and address of the person against whom the revocation must be declared and an indication of the beginning of the period and the regime of paragraph 1 sentence 2. If the warning is communicated after conclusion of the contract, the period is one month, deviating from paragraph 1 sentence 2. If the contract must be concluded in writing, then the period does not begin to run before a contract document, the written application of the consumer or a copy of the contract document or of the application is made available to the consumer. If the commencement of the period is in dispute, the burden of proof falls on the undertaking.
(3) The right of revocation lapses at the latest six months after the conclusion of the contract. For the delivery of goods the period does not begin before the day of their arrival with the recipient, and further not in the case of distance sale contracts about financial services if the undertaking has not properly fulfilled its duties of communication under § 312c paragraph 2 no 1.

§ 356
Right of return in respect of consumer contracts
(1) The right of revocation under § 355 can, in so far as this is expressly permitted by statute, be replaced by an unlimited right of return in the contract in respect of conclusion of a contract on the basis of a sale prospectus. It is a prerequisite that
1. a clearly formulated warning about the right of return is contained in the sale propectus,
2. the consumer could obtain detailed knowledge of the sale prospectus in the absence of the undertaking and
3. the consumer is granted the right of return in text form.
(2) The right of return can be exercised within the period for revocation (which does not however begin before the receipt of the thing) and only by sending the thing back or if the thing cannot be sent back as a packet, by a demand to take it back. § 355 paragraph 1 sentence 2 applies correspondingly.

§ 357
Legal consequences of revocation and return
(1) The provisions about statutory withdrawal apply correspondingly to the right of revocation and of return in so far as no different provision is made. § 286 paragraph 3 applies for the obligation to reimburse payments under this provision correspondingly; the period determined there begins with the consumer's declaration of revocation or return. In this connection the period with respect to an obligation of reimbursement on the part of the consumer begins with the giving of this declaration, and with respect to an obligation of reimbursement on the part of the undertaking with its arrival.
(2) The consumer is obliged to send the thing back when exercising the right of revocation, if it can be sent by a packet. Costs and risks of sending back are born by the undertaking in the cases of revocation and return. If a right of revocation under § 312d

paragraph 1 sentence 1 exists, the regular costs of return may be contractually imposed on the consumer if the price of the thing to be sent back does not exceed a sum of 40 euros or if, in the case of a higher price for the thing, the consumer has not yet provided the counterperformance or a part payment at the time of the revocation, unless the goods delivered do not correspond to those ordered.

(3) The consumer must, deviating from § 346 paragraph 2 sentence 1 no 3, provide compensation for value for a deterioration which has arisen through proper operation of the thing, if he has been referred in text form, at the latest at the conclusion of the contract, to this legal consequence and the possibility of avoiding it. This does not apply if the deterioration is to be attributed exclusively to the testing of the thing. § 346 paragraph 3 sentence 1 no 3 does not apply if the consumer has been properly warned about his right of revocation or has obtained knowledge of this in some other way.

(4) More extensive claims do not exist.

§ 358
Connected contracts

(1) If the consumer has effectively revoked his declaration of will to conclude a contract regarding the delivery of goods or the provision of another service by an undertaking, then he is also no longer bound by his declaration of will to conclude a consumer credit contract connected with this contract.

(2) If the consumer has effectively revoked his declaration of will to conclude a consumer credit contract then he is also no longer bound by his declaration of will to conclude a contract connected with this consumer credit contract about the delivery of goods or the provision of another service. If the consumer can revoke the declaration of will to conclude the connected contract in accordance with this subtitle, paragraph 1 alone applies and his right of revocation under § 495 paragraph 1 is excluded. If the consumer nevertheless declares the revocation of the consumer credit contract in the case of sentence 2, this counts as revocation of the connected contract as against the undertaking in accordance with paragraph 1.

(3) A contract about the delivery of goods or the provision of another service and a consumer credit contract are connected if the credit wholly or partially facilitates the financing of the other contract and both contracts form an economic unity. An economic unity is in particular to be assumed when the undertaking itself finances the counterperformance of the consumer, or in the case of financing by a third party if the provider of credit makes use of the co-operation of the undertaking at the preparation or the conclusion of the consumer credit contract. In the case of a financed acquisition of land or a right in the nature of land, an economic unity should only be assumed if the lender provides the land or the right in the nature of land himself or if he, over and above making the loan available, promotes the acquisition of the land or the right in the nature of land by co-operation with the undertaking, by adopting its transferor's interests wholly or in part, by taking over functions of the transferor in the planning, advertising or execution of the project, or by favouring the transferor one-sidedly.

(4) § 357 applies correspondingly for the connected contract. In the case of paragraph 1 claims for payment of interest and costs against the consumer from the winding up of the consumer credit contract against the consumer are however excluded. The provider of credit steps into the rights and duties of the undertaking under the connected contract in the relationship to the consumer in respect of the legal

consequences of the revocation or the return if the credit has already gone to the undertaking when the revocation or return comes into effect.

(5) The necessary warning about the right of revocation or return must refer to the legal consequences under paragraph 1 and paragraph 2 sentences 1 and 2.

§ 359
Objections in respect of connected contracts

The consumer can refuse to pay back the credit in so far as objections under the connected contract would entitle him to refuse his performance as against the undertaking with whom he has concluded the connected contract. This does not apply if the financed payment does not exceed 200 euros as well as in respect of objections which are based on a contract amendment agreed between this undertaking and the consumer after conclusion of the consumer credit contract. If the consumer can demand subsequent fulfilment, he can only refuse payment back of the credit if the subsequent fulfilment has failed.

[. . .]

Fourth Section

Extinguishment of obligation relationships

First Title

Fulfilment

§ 362
Extinguishment by performance

(1) An obligation relationship is extinguished when the performance owed is effected in favour of the creditor.

(2) If performance is made to a third party for the purpose of fulfilment, the provisions of § 185 apply.

§ 363
Burden of proof in case of acceptance as fulfilment

If the creditor has accepted as fulfilment a performance offered to him as fulfilment, the burden of proof falls on him if he wants the performance not to be counted as fulfilment because it was a performance different from the one owed or because it was deficient.

[. . .]

Third Title

Settling of accounts

§ 387
Prerequisites

If two people owe each other performances which are analogous in their subject matter, each party can set off his demand against the demand of the other party as soon as he can demand the performance due to him and effect the performance which he owes.

[. . .]

Fifth Section

Transfer of demand

§ 398
Assignment
A demand can be transferred (assignment) by the creditor to another person by a contract with this person. The new creditor takes the place of the former creditor at the conclusion of the contract.
[. . .]

§ 404
Debtor's objections
The debtor can set against the new creditor the objections which were established at the time of the assignment of the demand against the former creditor.
[. . .]

§ 407
Legal dealings towards former creditor
(1) The new creditor must allow a performance to take effect against himself which the debtor effects in favour of the former creditor after the assignment, as well as any legal transaction which is undertaken after the assignment between the debtor and the former creditor in respect of the demand, unless the debtor knows of the assignment at the time of the performance or at the time of the undertaking of the legal transaction.
(2) If a legally effective judgment about the demand has been issued in an action which has started between the debtor and the former creditor after the assignment, the new creditor must allow the judgment to apply against him, unless the debtor knew of the assignment when the action began.

§ 408
Multiple assignment
(1) If an assigned demand is assigned again by the former creditor to a third party, if the debtor performs in favour of the third party or if a legal transaction is undertaken between the debtor and the third party or an action has started, the provisions of § 407 apply correspondingly as against the former transferee in favour of the debtor.
(2) The same applies if the demand which has been already assigned is transferred by judicial decision to a third party or if the former creditor acknowledges to the third party that the demand which has already been assigned has passed by virtue of statute law to the third party.

§ 409
Notification of assignment
(1) If the creditor notifies the debtor that he has assigned the demand, he must allow the notified assignment to have effect against himself in his relationship with the debtor, even if it did not occur or is not effective. It is equivalent to notice if the creditor has issued a document about the assignment to the new creditor described in the document who produces it to the debtor.
(2) The notice can only be withdrawn with the consent of the person who has been described as the new creditor.
[. . .]

§ 412
Statutory transmission of demand
The provisions of §§ 399 to 404, 406 to 410 apply correspondingly to the transfer of a demand by virtue of statute law.

Sixth Section

Taking over of obligation

§ 414
Contract between creditor and transferee
An obligation can be taken over by a third party by a contract with the creditor in such a way that the third party takes the place of the former debtor.

§ 415
Contract between debtor and transferee
(1) If the taking over of the obligation by the third party is agreed with the debtor, its effectiveness depends on the creditor's ratification. Ratification can only take place when the debtor or the third party has informed the creditor of the taking over of the obligation. Until ratification the parties can alter or cancel the contract.
(2) If ratification is refused, the taking over of the obligation is deemed not to have taken place. If the debtor or the third party invites the creditor to make a declaration about ratification and determines a period, the ratification can only be declared up until expiry of the period; if it is not declared, it is deemed to have been refused.
(3) As long as the creditor has not given the ratification, the transferee in case of doubt is obliged as against the debtor to satisfy the creditor punctually. The same applies when the creditor refuses ratification.
[...]

§ 417
Objections by transferee
(1) The transferee can set objections against the creditor which arise from the legal relationship between the creditor and the former debtor. He cannot set off a demand belonging to the former debtor.
(2) The transferee cannot derive objections against the creditor from the legal relationship between the transferee and the former debtor which forms the basis of the taking over of the obligation.
[...]

Seventh Section

Multiplicity of debtors and creditors

§ 421
Joint debtors
If several people owe a performance in such a way that each is obliged to effect the whole performance, but the creditor is only entitled to demand the performance once (joint debtors), the creditor can demand the performance, as he wishes, entirely or in

part from each of the debtors. All the debtors remain under an obligation until the effectuation of the whole performance.

§ 422
Effect of fulfilment
(1) Fulfilment by a joint debtor is also effective for the remaining debtors. The same applies to performance in place of fulfilment, and to deposit and set off.
(2) A demand which belongs to a joint debtor cannot be set off by the remaining debtors.
[. . .]

§ 426
Duty to settle and transmission of demand
(1) The joint debtors are in their relationship with one another under the obligation in equal fractions, in so far as no other provision has been made. If it is not possible to obtain from one of the joint debtors the contribution which falls to him, the deficit must be born by the remaining debtors who are obliged to settle.
(2) In so far as a joint debtor satisfies the creditor and can demand settlement from the remaining debtors, the creditor's demand against the remaining debtors passes to him. The transmission cannot be claimed to the creditor's disadvantage.
[. . .]

Eighth Section

Individual obligation relationships

First Title

Purchase and exchange

First Sub-title

General provisions

§ 433
Typical contractual duties in purchase contract
(1) The seller of a thing is obliged by a purchase contract to hand the thing over to the purchaser and to provide the property in the thing. The seller has to provide the thing to the purchaser free from physical and legal defects.
(2) The purchaser is obliged to pay the agreed purchase price to the seller and to take the purchased thing.

§ 434
Physical defects
(1) The thing is free from physical defects if it has the agreed composition when the risk passes. In so far as the composition is not agreed, the thing is free from physical defects
1. if it is suitable for the use assumed according to the contract, or otherwise

2. if it is suitable for the usual use and has a composition which is usual with things of the same kind and which the purchaser can expect in accordance with the type of thing.

Composition according to sentence 2 no 2 also includes characteristics which the purchaser can expect according to the public statements of the seller, of the manufacturer (§ 4 paragraphs 1 and 2 of the Product Liability Act) or his assistant, in particular in the advertising or in the marking about particular characteristics of the thing unless the seller did not know of the statement and also need not have known of it, it was corrected at the point in time of the conclusion of the contract in an equally valid manner, or it could not influence the decision to purchase.

(2) A physical defect is also present if the agreed assembly has been carried out by the seller or his agent improperly. Further a physical defect is present in a thing intended for assembly if the assembly instructions are defective unless the thing is assembled correctly.

(3) It is equivalent to a physical defect if the seller delivers a different thing or too small a quantity.

§ 435
Legal defects

The thing is free from legal defects if third parties cannot claim any rights against the purchaser in relation to the thing or only those taken over in the purchase contract. It is equivalent to a legal defect if a right which does not exist is entered in the Land Register.

§ 436
Public burdens on land

(1) In so far as nothing different is agreed, the seller of a piece of land is obliged to bear development contributions and other residents' contributions in respect of adjoining land for the steps in construction which have been begun up to the day of the conclusion of the contract, independently of the point in time when the contribution obligation arises.

(2) The seller of a piece of land is not liable for its freedom from other public taxes and from other public burdens which are not appropriate for entry in the Land Register.

§ 437
Rights of purchaser in respect of defects

If the thing is defective, the purchaser can, if the prerequisites of the following provisions are present and in so far as no different provision is made,

1. demand subsequent fulfilment under § 439,
2. withdraw from the contract under §§ 440, 323 and 326 paragraph 5 or reduce the purchase price under § 441 and
3. demand compensation under §§ 440, 280, 281, 283 and 311a or reimbursement of abortive expenditure under § 284.

§ 438
Limitation of claims in respect of defects

(1) The limitation period for claims described in § 437 nos 1 and 3 expires
1. in 30 years if the defect consists of

a) a right in rem of a third party on the basis of which handing over of the purchased thing can be demanded, or

b) another right which is entered in the Land Register.

2. in five years

a) in the case of a building and

b) in the case of a thing which has been used for a building in accordance with its usual manner of use and has caused the building's defectiveness, and

3. in two years in other cases.

(2) The limitation period begins in relation to pieces of land with the transfer and in other cases with the delivery of the thing.

(3) Deviating from paragraph 1 nos 2 and 3 and paragraph 2, claims expire after the regular limitation period if the seller has deceitfully kept the defect secret. In the case of paragraph 1 no 2 the limitation does not however take effect before the expiry of the period determined there.

(4) § 218 applies for the right of withdrawal described in § 437. The purchaser can in spite of ineffectiveness of the withdrawal under § 218 paragraph 1 refuse payment of the purchase price in so far as he would be entitled to do so on the basis of the withdrawal. If he makes use of this right, the seller can withdraw from the contract.

(5) § 218 and paragraph 4 sentence 2 apply correspondingly to the right of reduction described in § 437.

§ 439
Subsequent fulfilment

(1) The purchaser can demand as subsequent fulfilment according to his choice the removal of the defect or the delivery of a thing free from the defect.

(2) The seller has to bear the expenditure necessary for the purpose of subsequent fulfilment, in particular transport, road tolls, work and materials costs.

(3) The seller can refuse the kind of subsequent fulfilment chosen by the purchaser regardless of § 275 paragraphs 2 and 3 if it is only possible with disproportionate cost. In this connection in particular the value of the thing in a condition free from the defect, the significance of the defect and the question of whether it would be possible to resort to the other kind of subsequent fulfilment without substantial disadvantages for the purchaser are to be taken into consideration. The purchaser's claim in this case is limited to the other kind of subsequent fulfilment; the right of the seller to refuse even this under the prerequisites of sentence 1 remains unaffected.

(4) If the seller delivers a thing which is free from the defect for the purpose of subsequent fulfilment, he can demand from the purchaser the retransfer of the defective thing in accordance with §§ 346 to 348.

§ 440
Special provisions for withdrawal and compensation

Except in the cases of § 281 paragraph 2 and § 323 paragraph 2 it is not necessary to set a period even if the seller refuses both kinds of subsequent fulfilment in accordance with § 439 paragraph 3 or if the kind of subsequent fulfilment to which the purchaser is entitled has failed or cannot be expected of him. A repair counts after the second unsuccessful attempt as having failed if nothing different follows in particular from the kind of thing or the kind of defect or the other circumstances.

§ 441
Reduction

(1) Instead of withdrawing, the purchaser can reduce the purchase price by declaration made to the seller. The exclusionary ground of § 323 paragraph 5 sentence 2 does not apply.

(2) If there are several participants on the purchaser's side or on the seller's side, the reduction can only be declared by all or against all.

(3) In a case of reduction, the purchase price is to be reduced in the ratio in which at the time of the conclusion of the contract the value of the thing in a condition free from the defect would have stood to its real value. The reduction is, so far as is necessary, to be ascertained by valuation.

(4) If the purchaser has paid more than the reduced purchase price, the surplus is to be reimbursed by the seller. § 346 paragraph 1 and § 347 paragraph 1 have corresponding application.

§ 442
Knowledge of purchaser

(1) The rights of a purchaser in respect of a defect are excluded if he knows of the defect on conclusion of the contract. If a defect remains unknown to the purchaser as a result of gross negligence, the purchaser can only claim rights because of this defect if the seller has deceitfully kept the defect secret or has undertaken a guarantee for the composition of the thing.

(2) The seller has to remove a right entered in the Land Register even if the purchaser knows of it.

§ 443
Guarantee of composition and durability

(1) If the seller or a third party undertakes a guarantee for the composition of the thing or for the fact that the thing will keep a certain composition for a certain length of time (durability guarantee), the purchaser in a case covered by the guarantee has, regardless of the statutory claims, the rights from the guarantee to the conditions given in the guarantee declaration and the relevant advertising against the person who has granted the guarantee.

(2) In so far as a durability guarantee has been undertaken, it is presumed that a physical defect arising during its period of validity is the basis of the rights under the guarantee.

§ 444
Exclusion of liability

The seller cannot refer to an agreement by which the purchaser's rights in respect of a defect are excluded or limited in so far as he has deceitfully kept the defect secret or has undertaken a guarantee about the composition of the thing.

§ 445
Limitation of liability in case of public auctions

If a thing is sold on the basis of a right of lien in a public auction under the description "lien", then the purchaser only has rights in respect of a defect if the seller has deceitfully kept the defect secret or has undertaken a guarantee about the composition of the thing.

§ 446
Transfer of risk and burdens
The risk of accidental destruction and of accidental deterioration passes to the purchaser with the handing over of the thing sold. From the handing over onwards the benefits are due to the purchaser and he bears the burdens of the thing. It is equivalent to handing over if the purchaser is in delay in acceptance.

§ 447
Passing of risk in case of postal purchase by dispatch
(1) If the seller sends the thing sold to another place than the place of fulfilment at the purchaser's demand, the risk passes to the purchaser as soon as the seller has delivered the thing to the forwarding agent, the carrier or the other person or institution determined for the carrying out of the dispatch.
(2) If the purchaser has given special instructions about the kind of dispatch and if the seller deviates from the instructions without compelling reasons, the seller is responsible to the purchaser for the harm arising from this.

§ 448
Costs of handing over and comparable costs
(1) The seller bears the costs of the handing over of the thing and the purchaser the costs of the acceptance and the dispatch of the thing to a place other than the place of fulfilment.
(2) The purchaser of a piece of land bears the costs of recording the purchase contract and of the transfer, the entry in the Land Register and of the declarations necessary for the entry.

§ 449
Reservation of property
(1) If the seller of a movable thing has reserved the property until payment of the purchase price, it is to be assumed in case of doubt that the property will be transferred under the condition precedent of complete payment of the purchase price (property reservation).
(2) On the basis of the property reservation the seller can only demand the thing if he has withdrawn from the contract.
(3) Agreement of a property reservation is void in so far as the passing of the property is made dependent on the buyer fulfilling the demands of a third party, in particular of an undertaking connected with the seller.

§ 450
Excluded purchasers in respect of certain sales
(1) In relation to a sale by way of execution, the person commissioned with the undertaking or management of the sale and the assistants called in by him inclusive of the person recording the proceedings are not permitted to buy the object to be sold either for themselves personally or by someone else as agent for another.
(2) Paragraph 1 also applies on a sale outside execution, if the order for the sale has been given on the basis of a statutory provision which empowers the customer to have the object sold for the account of another, in particular in the cases of lien sale and of sale permitted in §§ 383 and 385 as well as on a sale from an insolvent estate.

§ 451
Purchase by excluded purchaser

(1) The effectiveness of a purchase which occurred contrary to § 450 and of the transfer of the object purchased depends on the consent of those participating as debtor, owner or creditor in respect of the sale. If the purchaser challenges a participant to make a declaration about the permission, § 177 paragraph 2 applies correspondingly.

(2) If as a result of the refusal of the permission a new sale is undertaken, the earlier purchaser must answer for the costs of the new sale as well as for the smaller proceeds.

§ 452
Purchase of ships

The provisions of this subtitle about the purchase of land apply correspondingly to the purchase of registered ships and ship construction work.

§ 453
Purchase of rights

(1) The provisions about the purchase of things apply correspondingly to the purchase of rights and other objects.

(2) The seller bears the costs of the establishment and transfer of the right.

(3) If a right is sold which gives entitlement to possession of a thing, the seller is obliged to hand the thing over to the purchaser free from physical and legal defects.

Second Sub-title

Special types of purchase

First Chapter

Purchase on approval

§ 454
Occurrence of purchase contract

(1) On a purchase on approval or on inspection, the approval of the purchased object is a matter entirely in the purchaser's discretion. In case of doubt, the purchase is concluded subject to the condition precedent of approval.

(2) The seller is obliged to permit the purchaser to investigate the object.

§ 455
Period for approval

The approval of an object purchased on approval or on inspection can only be declared within the agreed period and in the absence of such a period only until the expiry of a reasonable period determined by the seller for the purchaser. If the thing was handed over to the purchaser for the purpose of approval or inspection, his silence counts as approval.

Second Chapter

Repurchase

§ 456
Occurrence of repurchase
(1) If the seller has reserved the right of repurchase in the purchase contract, the repurchase comes into existence with the seller's declaration to the purchaser that he is exercising the right of repurchase. The declaration does not need to be in the form for the purchase contract.
(2) The price at which the sale takes place applies in case of doubt for the repurchase as well.

§ 457
Liability of reseller
(1) The reseller is obliged to hand over to the repurchaser the purchased object with its accessories.
(2) If before the exercise of the right of repurchase the reseller is to blame for deterioration, destruction or impossibility of handing over the purchased object arising for some other reason, or if he significantly changes the object, he is responsible for the harm arising from this. If the object has deteriorated without fault on the part of the reseller or if it has only changed insignificantly, the repurchaser cannot demand reduction of the purchase price.

§ 458
Removal of rights of third parties
If before the exercise of the right of repurchase the reseller has exercised his right of disposal over the object purchased, he is obliged to remove the rights of third parties founded on this. A disposition which occurs by way of execution or the implementation of a detention warrant or by the insolvency administrator is equivalent to a disposition by the reseller.

§ 459
Reimbursement of expenditure
The reseller can demand reimbursement of expenditure which he has made in respect of the purchased object before the repurchase in so far as the value of the object is raised by the expenditure. He can take away any equipment which he has provided to the thing to be handed over.

§ 460
Repurchase at valuation
If the assessed value which the object purchased has at the time of repurchase is agreed as the repurchase price, the reseller is not responsible for deterioration, destruction or impossibility of handing over the object arising for some other reason, and the repurchaser is not obliged to reimburse expenditure.

§ 461
Several persons entitled to repurchase
If the right of repurchase belongs to several people jointly, it can only be exercised as a whole. If is has been extinguished for one of the persons entitled or if one of them

does not exercise his right, the remaining ones are entitled to exercise the right of repurchase as a whole.

§ 462
Exclusive period
The right of repurchase can only be exercised in relation to land until the expiry of 30 years and in relation to other objects until the expiry of three years after the agreement of the reservation. If a period is determined for the exercise, this takes the place of the statutory period.

Third Chapter

Pre-emption

§ 463
Prerequisites for exercise
A person who is entitled to a right of pre-emption in respect of an object can exercise the right of pre-emption as soon as the person under the obligation has concluded a purchase contract with a third party about the object.

§ 464
Exercise of right of pre-emption
(1) The right of pre-emption is exercised by a declaration made to the person under the obligation. The declaration does not need the form determined for the purchase contract.
(2) On the exercise of the right of pre-emption the purchase comes into existence between the person entitled and the person under the obligation under the provisions which the person under the obligation has agreed with the third party.

§ 465
Ineffective agreements
An agreement by the person under the obligation with the third party by which the purchase is made dependent on the non-exercise of the right of pre-emption or a right of withdrawal is reserved to the person under the obligation for the case of exercise of the right of pre-emption is ineffective as against the person entitled to the right of pre-emption.

§ 466
Subsidiary performances
If the third party has committed himself in the contract to a subsidiary performance which the person entitled to the right of pre-emption is not in a position to effect, the person entitled to the right of pre-emption must instead of the subsidiary performance pay its value. If the subsidiary performance cannot be valued in money, the exercise of the right of pre-emption is excluded; the agreement of the subsidiary performance does not however come into consideration if the contract with the third party would be concluded even without it.

§ 467
Total price
If the third party has purchased the object to which the right of pre-emption relates with other objects at a total price, the person entitled to the right of pre-emption must

pay a proportionate part of the total price. The person under the obligation can demand that the right of pre-emption be extended to all things which cannot be separated without disadvantage to him.

§ 468
Deferment of payment of purchase price
(1) If the purchase price has been deferred for the third party in the contract, the person entitled to the right of pre-emption can only claim deferment if he provides security for the deferred sum.
(2) If a piece of land is the subject of the right of pre-emption, it does not need the provision of security in so far as the reservation of a mortgage on the land has been agreed for the deferred purchase price or a debt for which a mortgage on the land exists has been taken over and set against the purchase price. Corresponding provisions apply if a registered ship or ship construction work is the subject of the right of pre-emption.

§ 469
Duty to communicate, period for exercise
(1) The person under the obligation must without delay communicate to the person entitled to the right of pre-emption the content of the contract which has been concluded with the third party. Communication by the person under the obligation can be replaced by communication by the third party.
(2) The right of pre-emption can be exercised in respect of land only until the expiry of a period of two months and in respect of other objects only until the expiry of the period of a week after the receipt of the communication. If a period is determined for the exercise of the right, this takes the place of the statutory period.

§ 470
Sale to statutory heir
The right of pre-emption does not in a case of doubt extend to a sale which occurs with regard to a future right of inheritance to a statutory heir.

§ 471
Sale on execution or insolvency
The right of pre-emption is excluded if the sale occurs by way of execution or from an insolvent estate.

§ 472
Several persons entitled to right of pre-emption
If the right of pre-emption belongs to several people jointly, it can only be exercised as a whole. If it has been extinguished for one of the persons entitled or if one of them does not exercise his right, the others are entitled to exercise the right of pre-emption as a whole.

§ 473
Non-transferability
The right of pre-emption is not transferable and does not pass to the heirs of the person entitled in so far as no different provision is made. If the right is limited to a certain period, then in case of doubt it is inheritable.

Third Sub-title

Purchase of consumer goods

§ 474
Concept of purchase of consumer goods
(1) If a consumer buys a moveable thing from an undertaking (purchase of consumer goods), the following supplementary provisions apply. This does not apply to second hand things which are sold in a public auction in which the consumer can take part personally.
(2) §§ 445 and 447 do not apply to the purchase contracts regulated under this sub-title.

§ 475
Divergent agreements
(1) The undertaking cannot rely on an agreement made before the communication of a defect to the undertaking if that agreement deviates from §§ 433 to 435, 437, 439 to 443 as well as from the provisions of this subtitle, to the disadvantage of the consumer. The provisions described in sentence 1 apply even if they are circumvented by other formulations.
(2) Limitation of the claims described in § 437 cannot be reduced by a legal transaction before the communication of a defect to the undertaking, if the agreement leads to a limitation period from the statutory commencement of limitation of less than two years, or in respect of second hand things of less than one year.
(3) Paragraphs 1 and 2 do not apply for the exclusion or limitation of the claim to compensation, notwithstanding §§ 307 to 309.

§ 476
Reversal of burden of proof
If a physical defect shows itself within six months from the passing of the risk, it is presumed that the thing was already defective at the time the risk passed, unless this presumption is irreconcilable with the kind of thing or defect involved.

§ 477
Special provisions for guarantees
(1) A guarantee declaration (§ 443) must be framed simply and comprehensibly. It must contain
1. reference to the statutory rights of the consumer as well as to the fact that they are not limited by the guarantee and
2. the content of the guarantee and all significant information which is necessary for the claiming of the guarantee, in particular the length and the territorial area of validity of the guarantee protection as well as the name and address of the provider of the guarantee.
(2) The consumer can demand that the guarantee declaration be communicated to him in text form.
(3) The effectiveness of the guarantee obligation is not affected by the fact that one of the above requirements is not fulfilled.

§ 478
Right of recourse by undertaking

(1) If the undertaking had to take back a thing sold as newly manufactured as a result of its defectiveness or the consumer has reduced the purchase price, the setting of a period (which would otherwise be necessary) because of the defect claimed by the consumer is not needed for the rights of the undertaking described in § 437 against the undertaking who had sold him the thing (the supplier).

(2) The undertaking can in respect of a sale of a newly manufactured thing demand from its supplier reimbursement of the expenditure which the undertaking had to bear in the relationship to the consumer under § 439 paragraph 2 if the defect claimed by the consumer was already present on the passing of the risk to the undertaking.

(3) In the cases of paragraphs 1 and 2, § 476 applies with the proviso that the period begins with the passing of the risk to the consumer.

(4) The supplier cannot rely on an agreement made before the communication of a defect to the supplier which deviates from §§ 433 to 435, 437, 439 to 443, as well as from paragraphs 1 to 3 and from § 479 to the disadvantage of the undertaking, if no settlement of equal value is granted to the person who is creditor in respect of the right of recourse. Notwithstanding § 307, sentence 1 does not apply for the exclusion or limitation of the claim to compensation. The provisions described in sentence 1 apply even if they are circumvented by other formulations.

(5) Paragraphs 1 to 4 apply correspondingly to the claims of the supplier and of the remaining purchasers in the supply chain against the seller in question if the debtors are undertakings.

(6) § 377 of the Commercial Code remains unaffected.

§ 479
Limitation of recourse claims

(1) The claims to reimbursement of expenses provided for in § 478 paragraph 2 expire two years from delivery of the thing.

(2) The limitation period in respect of the claims of the undertaking provided for in §§ 437 and 478 paragraph 2 against its supplier because of the defect in a newly manufactured thing sold to a consumer commences at the earliest two months after the point in time at which the undertaking has fulfilled the consumer's claims. This suspension of the expiry of the period ends at the latest five years after the point in time at which the supplier has delivered the thing to the undertaking.

(3) The above paragraphs apply correspondingly to the claims of the supplier and of the remaining purchasers in the supply chain against the seller in question if the debtors are undertakings.

Fourth Sub-title

Exchange

§ 480
Exchange

The provisions about purchase apply correspondingly to exchange.

Second Title

Time-share residence rights contracts

§ 481
Concept of time-share residence rights contract
(1) Time-share residence rights contracts are contracts by which an undertaking creates the right (or promises to create it) for a consumer in return for payment of a total price for a period of at least three years to use a residential building in each case for a determined period (or a period to be determined) of the year for the purposes of recreation or residence. The right can be a right in rem or other right and can in particular also be granted through membership of an association or shares in a company.
(2) The right can also consist of choosing the use of a residential building in each case from a stock of residential buildings.
(3) A part of a residential building is equivalent to a residential building.

§ 482
Prospectus duty in respect of time-share residence rights contracts
(1) A person who as an undertaking offers to conclude time-share residence rights contracts must hand out a prospectus to every consumer who expresses interest.
(2) The prospectus described in paragraph 1 must contain a general description of the residential building or of the stock of residential buildings as well as the information provided for in the Regulation under Article 242 of the Introductory Act to the Civil Code.
(3) The undertaking can undertake an amendment in relation to the information contained in the prospectus before the conclusion of the contract in so far as this becomes necessary on the basis of circumstances on which it could have no influence.
(4) In every advertisement for the concluding of time-share residence rights contracts it must be stated that the prospectus is obtainable and where it can be requested.

§ 483
Contract and prospectus language in respect of time-share residence rights contracts
(1) The contract is to be formulated in the official language (or, if there are several official languages there, in the official language chosen by the consumer) of the member state of the European Union or of the contracting state of the Treaty on the European Economic Area in which the consumer has his domicile. If the consumer belongs to another member state, he can also choose the, or one of the, official languages of the state to which he belongs instead of the language of his state of domicile. Sentences 1 and 2 also apply for the prospectus.
(2) If the contract has to be authenticated by a German notary, §§ 5 and 16 of the Authentication Act apply with the proviso that a certified translation of the contract in the language chosen by the consumer under paragraph 1 is to be handed over to him.
(3) Time-share residence rights contracts which do not comply with paragraph 1 sentences 1 and 2 or paragraph 2 are void.

§ 484

Written form in respect of time-share residence rights contracts

(1) The time-share residence rights contract needs written form in so far as a stricter form is not prescribed in other provisions. The conclusion of the contract in electronic form is excluded. The information contained in the prospectus described in § 482 handed over to the consumer becomes part of the content of the contract in so far as the parties do not expressly (and making reference to the deviation from the prospectus) make some different agreement. Such amendments must be communicated to the consumer before the conclusion of the contract. Notwithstanding the applicability of the prospectus information under sentence 3, the contract document must contain the information provided for in the Regulation described in § 482 paragraph 2.

(2) The undertaking must hand over to the consumer a contract document or copy of the contract document. It must also hand over to him, if the language of the contract and the language of the state in which the residential building is situated are different, a certified translation of the contract in the language (or in a language included in the official languages of the European Union or of the Treaty for the European Economic Area) of the state in which the residential building is situated. The duty to hand over a certified translation does not arise if the use right refers to a stock of residential buildings which are situated in different states.

§ 485

Right of revocation in respect of time-share residence rights contracts

(1) The consumer is entitled to a right of revocation under § 355 in respect of a time-share residence rights contract.

(2) The necessary warning about the right of revocation must also give the costs which the consumer has to reimburse in the case of revocation in accordance with paragraph 5 sentence 2.

(3) If the prospectus described in § 482 has not been handed over to the consumer before the conclusion of the contract, or is not in the language prescribed in § 483 paragraph 1, the period for exercise of the right of revocation is one month, deviating from § 355 paragraph 1 sentence 2.

(4) If one of the pieces of information which are provided for in the Regulation described in § 482 paragraph 2 is missing from the contract, the period for the exercise of the right of revocation only begins when this piece of information is communicated in writing to the consumer.

(5) Compensation for the services performed as well as for the transfer of the benefit of the residential buildings is excluded, deviating from § 357 paragraphs 1 and 3. If the contract needed notarial authentication, the consumer must reimburse to the undertaking the costs of the authentication, if this is expressly provided for in the contract. In the cases of paragraphs 3 and 4, the duty to reimburse costs does not exist; the consumer can demand from the undertaking reimbursement of the costs of the contract.

§ 486

Prohibition on deposit in respect of time share residential rights contracts

The undertaking is not permitted to demand or accept payments from the consumer before the expiry of the revocation period. Provisions more favourable to the consumer remain unaffected.

§ 487
Divergent agreements

No deviation may be made from the provisions of this title to the disadvantage of the consumer. The provisions of this title apply, in so far as no different provision is made, even if they are circumvented by other formulations.

Third Title

Credit contract; financial assistance and instalment delivery contracts between undertaking and consumer

First Sub-title

Credit contract

§ 488
Typical contractual duties in credit contract

(1) By a credit contract, a lender is obliged to make available to a borrower a sum of money of an agreed amount. The borrower is obliged to pay any interest which is owed and to repay the credit made available when it is due.

(2) In so far as no different provision is made, the agreed interest is to be paid after the expiry of each year, and, if the credit is to be repaid before the expiry of a year, on the repayment.

(3) If no time is determined for the repayment of the credit, the due date depends on the lender or the borrower giving notice. The period of notice is three months. If interest is not owed, the borrower is entitled to make repayment even without notice.

§ 489
Ordinary right to give notice by borrower

(1) The borrower can give notice terminating wholly or partially a credit contract for which a fixed rate of interest is agreed for a determined period

1. if the commitment to pay interest ends before the time determined for the repayment and no new agreement about the rate of interest has been made, provided he gives a notice period of one month, at the earliest for the expiry of the day on which the commitment to pay interest ends; if an adaptation of the rate of interest in certain time periods of up to a year has been agreed, the borrower can give notice in each case only for the expiry of the day on which the commitment to pay interest ends;

2. if the credit is granted to a consumer and is not secured by a mortgage on land or a ship, after the expiry of six months from complete receipt, provided he gives a period of notice of three months;

3. in any case after the expiry of ten years from complete receipt, provided he gives a period of notice of six months; if a new agreement is made about the time of repayment or the rate of interest after the receipt of the credit, the point in time of this agreement replaces the point in time of the payment out.

(2) The borrower can give notice at any time terminating a credit contract with a variable rate of interest, provided he gives a period of notice of three months.

(3) Notice by the borrower under paragraphs 1 or 2 does not count as having been given if he does not pay back the sum owed within two weeks after the notice has become effective.

(4) The borrower's right to give notice under paragraphs 1 and 2 cannot be excluded or made more onerous contractually. This does not apply in respect of loans to the Federation, a special fund of the Federation, a state (Land), a commune, a group of communes, the European Communities or foreign regional bodies.

§ 490
Extraordinary right to give notice

(1) If a substantial deterioration occurs or threatens to occur in the financial circumstances of the borrower or in the value of a security lodged for the credit, by which the repayment of the credit, even using the security, is endangered, the lender can give notice having immediate effect terminating the credit contract, in case of doubt always before the paying out of the credit, and after paying out only as a rule.

(2) The borrower can terminate prematurely a credit contract in respect of which a fixed rate of interest is agreed for a determined period and the credit is secured by a mortgage on land or a ship, observing the periods in § 489 paragraph 1 no 2, if his legitimate interests require this. Such an interest is in particular present if the borrower has a need for a different utilisation of the thing lent for security for the loan. The borrower has to compensate the lender for the loss which he incurs as a result of the premature notice (compensation for early termination).

(3) The provisions of §§ 313 and 314 remain unaffected.

§ 491
Consumer credit contract

(1) The following provisions do not apply to consumer credit contracts
1. in respect of which the credit to be paid out (net amount of credit) does not exceed 200 euros;
2. which an employer concludes with his employee with interest below market rates;
3. which are concluded within the framework of the furtherance of housing and of town planning on the basis of public law grant awards or on the basis of subsidies from public budgets directly between the public law institution awarding the means of furtherance and the borrower at rates of interest which are below market rates.

(2) The following are also not to be applied:
1. §§ 358, 359, § 492 paragraph 1 sentence 5 no 2, § 495, § 497 paragraphs 2 and 3 and § 498 to consumer credit contracts in respect of which the granting of the credit is made dependent on securing by a mortgage on land and which takes place on conditions which are usual for credit contracts secured by mortgages on land and their intermediate financing; it is equivalent to securing by a mortgage on land if no such security is given in accordance with § 7 paragraphs 3 to 5 of the Building Savings Bank Act;
2. § 358 paragraphs 2, 4 and 5 and §§ 492 to 495 to consumer credit contracts which are drawn up in a court record established in accordance with the provisions of the Civil Proceedings Order or are notarially authenticated if the record or the notarial document contains the annual interest, the costs of the credit taken into account on conclusion of the contract and the prerequisites under which the annual interest or the costs can be changed;
3. § 358 paragraphs 2, 4 and 5 and § 359 to consumer credit contracts which finance the acquisition of securities, foreign currency, derivatives or precious metals.

§ 492

Written form and contractual content

(1) In so far as no stricter form is prescribed, consumer credit contracts are to be concluded in writing. Conclusion of the contract in electronic form is excluded. The requirement of written form is satisfied if the offer and acceptance are declared by the contracting parties separately in writing in each case. The declaration of the lender does not need to be signed if it is drawn up with the assistance of automatic equipment. The contractual declaration to be signed by the lender must give

1. the net credit sum or the maximum limit of the credit;

2. the total sum of the instalments to be paid by the borrower for the repayment of the loan, as well as payment of the interest and other costs, if the amount of the total sum is established on the conclusion of the consumer loan contract for the total loan period, and, for loans with variable conditions which are repaid in instalments, a total sum on the basis of the loan conditions which are determinative at the conclusion of the contract;

3. the method of repayment of the loan or, if an agreement about this has not been provided for, the regime for termination of the contract;

4. the rate of interest and all other costs of the loan which, in so far as their amount is known, are to be described individually and in other respects are to be given according to their basis, inclusive of possible negotiation costs to be borne by the borrower;

5. the effective annual interest or, if an alteration of the rate of interest or other price determining factors is reserved, the original effective annual interest; together with the original effective annual interest there must also be stated the prerequisites under which the price determining factors can be altered and over what period burdens which arise from an incomplete payment out or from an addition to the credit are to be taken into account in the calculation of the effective annual interest;

6. the costs of a remaining debt insurance or other insurance which is concluded in connection with the consumer credit contract;

7. securities to be arranged.

(1a) Deviating from paragraph 1 sentence 5 no 2, no total sum is to be stated in the case of loans which can be utilised up to a maximum limit, or for loan contracts for immovables. Loan contracts for immovables are consumer loan contracts for which making the loan available depends on its being secured by a mortgage and occurs on conditions which are usual for loan contracts secured by mortgage and their bridging financing; it is equivalent to securing by a mortgage if securing in accordance with § 7 paragraphs 3 to 5 of the Building Savings Banks Act is ignored.

(2) Effective annual interest is the total burden per year, to be given as a percentage rate of the net credit sum. The calculation of the effective and the original effective annual interest is determined in accordance with § 6 of the Regulation of Price Information Order.

(3) The lender must make a copy of the contract declarations available to the borrower.

(4) Paragraphs 1 and 2 also apply for the authority which a borrower gives on the conclusion of a consumer credit contract. Sentence 1 does not apply for an authority relating to court process and an authority which is notarially authenticated.

§ 493

Overdraft credit

(1) The provisions of § 492 do not apply for consumer credit contracts in respect of which a credit institution grants to a borrower the right to overdraw his current account to a certain amount, if, apart from the interest for the credit claimed, no further costs are taken into account and the interest is not charged in shorter periods than three months. The credit institution has to inform the borrower before the claiming of such a credit about

1. the maximum limit of the loan;
2. the annual interest applying at the point in time of the information;
3. the conditions under which the rate of interest can be changed;
4. the regulation of the termination of the contract.

The contract conditions in accordance with sentence 2 nos 1 to 4 are to be confirmed to the borrower at the latest after the credit is first claimed. The borrower must further be informed while the credit is being claimed about every alteration of the annual interest. The confirmation in accordance with sentence 3 and the information in accordance with sentence 4 must take place in text form; it suffices if they take place on a statement of account.

(2) If a credit institution allows a current account to be overdrawn and if the account is overdrawn for longer than three months, the credit institution must inform the borrower of the annual interest, the costs and the amendments in this connection; this can occur in the form of a notice on a statement of account.

§ 494

Legal consequences of defects in form

(1) The consumer credit contract and the authority given by the consumer for the conclusion of such a contract are void if written form is not entirely observed or if one of the items of information prescribed in § 492 paragraph 1 sentence 5 nos 1 to 6 is absent.

(2) Notwithstanding a defect under paragraph 1, the consumer credit contract is valid in so far as the borrower receives the credit or claims it. However the rate of interest (§ 492 paragraph 1 sentence 5 no 4) which is used as a basis for the consumer credit contract reduces to the statutory rate of interest if it, the effective or original effective annual interest (§ 492 paragraph 1 sentence 5 no 5) or the total sum (§ 492 paragraph 1 sentence 5 no 2, paragraph 1a) is not given. Costs not stated are not owed by the borrower. Agreed instalments are to be calculated afresh taking into consideration the reduced interest or costs. If the prerequisites under which price-determining factors can be altered are not stated, these can not be altered to the disadvantage of the borrower. Securities cannot be demanded if information about them is absent; this does not apply if the net credit sum exceeds 50,000 euros.

(3) If the effective or the original effective annual interest is given at too low a level, the rate of interest on which the consumer credit contract is based reduces by the percentage rate by which the effective or the original effective annual interest is understated.

§ 495
Right of revocation

(1) The borrower has a right of revocation under § 355 in respect of a consumer credit contract.

(2) Paragraph 1 does not apply to the consumer credit contracts mentioned in § 493 paragraph 1 sentence 1 if the borrower can pay back the credit at any time after the contract without observing a notice period and without additional costs.

§ 496
Renunciation of objections, prohibition on bills of exchange and cheques

(1) An agreement by which the borrower renounces the right to raise against the creditor in respect of a transfer (the transferee) in accordance with § 404 objections which he has against the lender, or to set off also against the creditor in respect of a transfer in accordance with § 406, a demand which he has against the lender, is ineffective.

(2) The borrower cannot be obliged to enter into a commitment by way of a bill of exchange for the claims of the lender under the consumer credit agreement. The lender cannot accept a cheque from the borrower for the securing of his claims under the consumer credit agreement. The borrower can demand from the lender at any time the handing over of a bill of exchange or cheque which has been issued contrary to sentence 1 or 2. The lender is liable for all harm which is suffered by the borrower as a result of such an issue of a bill of exchange or cheque.

§ 497
Treatment of interest for delay, attribution of partial payments

(1) In so far as the borrower falls into delay with payments which he owes on the basis of the consumer loan contract, he must pay interest on the sum owed under § 288 paragraph 1; this does not apply for loan contracts for immovables. The rate of interest for delay in respect of these contracts is two and a half percentage points per year above the basic rate of interest. In an individual case the lender can prove a higher or the borrower a lower level of loss.

(2) Interest falling due after commencement of delay must be credited to a special account and may not be put into an open account with the sum owed or other demands of the lender. § 289 sentence 2 applies in relation to this interest with the proviso that the lender can demand compensation only to the limit of the statutory rate of interest (§ 246).

(3) Payments by the borrower which do not suffice for the repayment of the total debt due are attributed (deviating from § 367 paragraph 1) firstly to legal costs, then to the remaining sum owed (paragraph 1), and lastly to interest (paragraph 2). The lender may not reject instalments. The limitation period for claims to reimbursement of the credit and interest is suspended from the commencement of the delay (in accordance with paragraph 1) onwards to its establishment in a manner described in § 197 paragraph 1 nos 3 to 5, but not for longer than ten years from when it arises. § 197 paragraph 2 does not apply to claims for interest. Sentences 1 to 4 do not apply in so far as payments are made in respect of an execution the chief demand under which is for interest.

(4) Paragraph 2 and 3 sentence 1, 2, 4 and 5 do not apply to loan contracts for immovables.

§ 498

Complete repayment in respect of instalment credit

(1) The lender can only terminate the consumer credit contract by notice because of delay in payment by the borrower in the case of a credit which is to be paid off in instalments, if

1. the borrower is in delay with at least two consecutive instalments wholly or partially and at least with ten per cent or, for a consumer credit contract period of over three years, with five per cent of the nominal amount of the loan or of the instalment price and

2. the lender has set the borrower a two-week period for payment of the outstanding amount by a declaration that he demands the total remaining debt on non-payment within the period, but without result.

The lender is to offer to the borrower, at the latest with the setting of a period, a discussion about the possibilities of a regime based on agreement.

(2) If the lender terminates the consumer credit contract by notice, the remaining debt reduces by the interest and other costs of the credit dependent on the period of the credit which, on an apportioned calculation, are allocated to the period after the notice becomes effective.

(3) Paragraphs 1 and 2 do not apply to loan contracts for immovables

Second Sub-title

Financial assistance between an undertaking and a consumer

§ 499

Deferred payment, other financial assistance

(1) The provisions of §§ 358, 359 and 492 paragraphs 1 to 3 and of §§ 494 to 498 apply (subject to paragraphs 2 and 3) correspondingly to contracts by which an undertaking grants to a consumer in return for money deferral of payment of more than three months or other financial assistance in return for money.

(2) For finance leasing contracts and contracts which have as their object the delivery of a certain thing or the carrying out of a certain other service in return for instalments (instalment transactions), the special features regulated in §§ 500 to 504 apply, subject to paragraph 3.

(3) The provisions of this subtitle do not apply to the extent determined in § 491 paragraphs 2 and 3. The cash payment price takes the place of the net credit amount mentioned in § 491 paragraph 2 no 1 in respect of an instalment transaction.

§ 500

Finance leasing contracts

Only the provisions of §§ 358, 359, 492 paragraph 1 sentences 1 to 4, § 492 paragraphs 2 and 3 and § 495 paragraph 1 as well as §§ 496 to 498 apply correspondingly to finance leasing contracts between an undertaking and a consumer.

§ 501

Instalment transactions

Only the provisions of §§ 358, 359, 492 paragraph 1 sentences 1 to 4, § 492 paragraphs 2 and 3, § 495 paragraph 1 as well as §§ 496 to 498 apply correspondingly to instalment transactions between an undertaking and a consumer. In other respects the following provisions apply.

§ 502

Necessary information, legal consequences of defects in form in respect of instalment transactions

(1) The contractual declaration to be signed by the consumer in respect of instalment transactions must give

1. the cash payment price;

2. the instalment price (total amount of deposit and all instalments to be paid by the consumer inclusive of interest and other costs);

3. amount, number and due date of the individual instalments;

4. the effective annual interest;

5. the costs of an insurance which is concluded in connection with the instalment transaction;

6. the agreement for a reservation of property or another security to be lodged.

The giving of a cash payment price and effective annual interest are not needed if the undertaking delivers things or carries out services only in return for instalments.

(2) The requirements of paragraph 1, § 492 paragraph 1 sentences 1 to 4 and § 492 paragraph 3 do not apply for instalment transactions for distance sales, if the information described in paragraph 1 sentence 1 nos 1 to 5, with the exception of the amount of the individual instalments, is communicated to the consumer in text form in sufficient time for him to take cognisance in detail of the information before the conclusion of the contract.

(3) The instalment transaction is void if the written form of § 492 paragraph 1 sentences 1 to 4 is not observed or if one of the items of information prescribed in paragraph 1 sentence 1 nos 1 to 5 is absent. Notwithstanding a defect under sentence 1, the instalment transaction is valid if the thing is handed over to the consumer or the service is carried out. The cash payment price is however to bear interest at the statutory interest rate at the most, if the instalment price or the effective annual interest has not been supplied. If a cash payment price is not mentioned, then in case of doubt the market price applies as cash payment price. The lodging of securities cannot be demanded if no information is given on this subject. If the effective or the original effective annual interest is given at too low a level, the instalment price reduces by the percentage rate by which the effective or the original effective annual interest is understated.

§ 503

Right to return and withdrawal in respect of instalment transactions

(1) Instead of the right of revocation which belongs to the consumer under § 495 paragraph 1, the consumer can be granted a right to return in accordance with § 356.

(2) The undertaking can only withdraw from an instalment transaction because of the consumer's delay in payment under the prerequisites described in § 498 paragraph 1. The consumer must also reimburse the undertaking for the expenses incurred as a result of the contract. In measuring the reimbursement of benefits from a thing which has to be given back, regard must be had to the diminution in value occurring in the meantime. If the undertaking takes back the thing which was delivered on the basis of the instalment transaction, this counts as the exercise of the right of withdrawal,

unless the undertaking agrees with the consumer to reimburse him for the ordinary sale value of the thing at the point in time that it was taken away. Sentence 4 applies correspondingly if a contract for the delivery of a thing is connected with a consumer credit contract (§ 358 paragraph 2) and if the lender appropriates the thing; in the case of withdrawal, the legal relationship between the lender and the consumer is determined in accordance with sentences 2 and 3.

§ 504
Early payment in respect of instalment transactions
If the consumer fulfils his obligations under the instalment transaction early, the instalment price reduces by the interest and other costs dependent on the operative period of the transaction which, on an apportioned calculation, are allocated to the period after the early fulfilment. If a cash payment price is not to be given in accordance with § 502 paragraph 1 sentence 2, the statutory rate of interest (§ 246) is to be taken as a basis. The undertaking can however also demand interest and other costs dependent on the operative period of the transaction for the first nine months of the operative period originally provided for, even if the consumer fulfils his obligations before the expiry of this period.

Third Sub-title

Contracts for delivery by instalments between undertaking and consumer

§ 505
Contracts for delivery by instalments
(1) The consumer is entitled, subject to sentence 2, to a right of revocation in accordance with § 355 in respect of contracts with an undertaking in which the consumer's declaration of will is directed to the conclusion of a contract which has as its object
1. the delivery by way of partial performances of several things sold as belonging together and in respect of which the payment for all the things is to be made in instalments, or
2. the regular delivery of things of the same kind, or
3. the obligation repeatedly to acquire or to purchase things.
This is inapplicable to the extent determined in § 491 paragraphs 2 and 3. The sum of all the instalments to be paid by the consumer until the earliest possible point in time for termination by notice corresponds to the net credit sum mentioned in § 491 paragraph 2 no 1.
(2) The contract for delivery by instalments under paragraph 1 needs written form. Sentence 1 does not apply if the possibility is created for the consumer to call up the provisions of the contract, inclusive of the general conditions of business, on conclusion of the contract and to store them in a form capable of being reproduced. The undertaking must communicate the content of the contract to the consumer in text form.

Fourth Sub-title

Unalterability, application to new start businesses

§ 506
Divergent agreements
No deviation may be made from the provisions of §§ 491 to 505 to the disadvantage of the consumer. These provisions apply even if they are circumvented by other formulations.

§ 507
Application to new start businesses
§§ 491 to 506 also apply to natural persons who have credit, deferral of payment or other financial assistance granted to them to take up a commercial or independent vocational activity or conclude a contract for delivery by instalments for this purpose, unless the net amount of the credit or cash payment price exceeds 50,000 euros.
[. . .]

Eighth Section

Individual obligation relationships

Fourth Title

Gift

§ 516
Concept of gift
(1) A donation by which someone enriches another out of his assets is a gift if both parties are in agreement that the donation should occur without payment.
(2) If the donation occurs without any intention by the other party, the donor can invite him to declare his acceptance, and set a reasonable period for this. After the expiry of this period, the gift is deemed to be accepted if the other party has not previously refused it. In the case of a refusal, the handing over of what has been donated can be demanded in accordance with the provisions about the handing over of an unjustified enrichment.
[. . .]

§ 518
Form for promise of gift
(1) Notarial authentication of the promise is necessary for the validity of a contract by which a performance is promised by way of gift. When a promise of an obligation or an acknowledgement of an obligation of the kind described in §§ 780 and 781 is given by way of gift, the same applies to the promise or declaration of acknowledgement.
(2) The lack of form is cured by the effectuation of the performance promised.
[. . .]

§ 521
Liability of donor
The donor only has to answer for intention and gross negligence.
[. . .]

§ 528
Demand for return because of impoverishment of donor
(1) In so far as the donor is not in a position after the completion of the gift to pay for his reasonable maintenance and to fulfil the duty to maintain his relatives, his spouse, his life partner or his former spouse or life partner imposed on him by statute law, he can demand the handing over of the subject matter of the gift from the donee in accordance with the provisions about the handing over of an unjustified enrichment. The donee can avoid the handing over by payment of the sum necessary for the maintenance. The provisions in § 760 and the provisions of § 1613 applying to the duty to maintain relatives, and (in the case of the donor's death) the provisions of § 1615, apply correspondingly to the donee's duty.
(2) Amongst several donees, the earlier donee is only liable in so far as the later donee is not under the obligation.
[. . .]

§ 530
Revocation of gift
(1) A gift can be revoked if the donee is guilty of severe ingratitude by a serious misdemeanour against the donor or a near relative of his.
(2) The donor's heir only has a right of revocation if the donee has intentionally and unlawfully killed the donor or prevented his revocation.
[. . .]

Fifth Title

Hiring contract and lease contract

First Sub-title

General provisions for hiring

§ 535
Content and principal duties in hiring contracts
(1) The hirer is obliged by the hiring contract to grant to the hiree the use of the hired object during the hiring period. The hirer must let the hiree have the hired object in a condition appropriate for use in accordance with the contract and maintain it in this condition during the hiring period. He must bear the encumbrances to which the hired object is subject.
(2) The hiree is obliged to pay the hirer the agreed hiring charge.

§ 536
Reduction in hiring charge in case of physical and legal defects
(1) If at the time it is made over to the hiree the hired object has a defect which deprives it of its fitness for use in accordance with the contract, or if such a defect

arises during the hiring period, the hiree is freed from payment of the hiring charge for the period in which it is deprived of its fitness. For a period during which its fitness is reduced, he only has to pay an appropriately reduced hiring charge. An insignificant reduction in fitness should be left out of consideration.

(2) Paragraph 1 sentences 1 and 2 also apply if a promised characteristic is absent or later ceases to exist.

(3) If the hiree is wholly or partly deprived of use of the hired object in accordance with the contract by the right of a third party, paragraphs 1 and 2 apply correspondingly.

(4) In a hiring relating to residential accommodation, an agreement which diverges to the disadvantage of the hiree is ineffective.

§ 536a

Claim by hiree to reimbursement of expenses and loss because of a defect

(1) If a defect in the sense of § 536 is present at the conclusion of the contract or if such a defect arises later because of a circumstance for which the hirer must answer or if the hirer delays in removing a defect, the hiree can demand compensation without prejudice to the rights under § 536.

(2) The hiree can remove the defect himself and demand reimbursement of the necessary expenses if

1. the hirer is in delay in removing the defect or

2. the immediate removal of the defect is necessary for the maintenance or restoration of the continued existence of the hired object.

[. . .]

§ 537

Payment of hiring charge in case of personal hindrance by hiree

(1) The hiree is not released from payment of the hire charge by the fact that he is hindered in the exercise of his right of use for a reason relating to himself personally. The hirer must however permit the value of expenditure saved and of those advantages which he obtains by some other exploitation of the use to be charged against him.

(2) As long as the hirer is not in a position to grant use to the hiree because the hirer has let a third party have such use, the hiree is not obliged to pay the hire charges.

[. . .]

§ 542

End of hiring

(1) If the hiring period is not determined, any contracting party can terminate the hiring by notice in accordance with the statutory provisions.

(2) A hiring which is entered into for a determined period ends with the expiry of this period in so far as it is not

1. terminated by extraordinary notice in the cases permitted by statute law, or

2. extended.

§ 543

Immediate termination by extraordinary notice for substantial reason

(1) Any contracting party can terminate the hiring by extraordinary notice immediately for a substantial reason. A substantial reason is present if the person giving

notice cannot be expected to continue the hiring until the expiry of the notice period or until some other termination of the hiring, having regard to all the circumstances of the individual case, in particular fault of the contracting parties, and balancing the interests of both sides.

(2) A substantial ground is in particular present if

1. use of the hired object in accordance with the contract is wholly or partly not granted to the hiree punctually or is taken back again,

2. the hiree violates the rights of the hirer to a substantial degree by substantially endangering the hired object through neglect of the care which he owed or by letting a third party have it without authority, or

3. the hiree

a) is in delay with payment of the hire charge, or a not insubstantial part of the hire charge, for two consecutive charge periods, or

b) in a period which extends over more than two charge periods is in delay with payment of the hire charge by a sum which amounts to the hire charge for two months.

In the case of sentence 1 no 3, termination by notice is excluded if the hirer has previously received satisfaction. It becomes ineffective if the hiree could release himself from his obligation by setting off, and declares the setting off without delay after the termination notice.

(3) If the substantial ground consists in the violation of a duty in the hiring contract, termination by notice is only permissible after the ineffectual expiry of a reasonable period determined for redress or after an ineffectual warning. This does not apply if

1. a period or warning obviously promises no result,

2. an immediate termination notice on special grounds is justified, balancing the interests on both sides, or

3. the hiree is in delay with the payment of the hire charge in the sense of paragraph 2 no 3.

(4) §§ 536b and 536d are to be applied correspondingly to the right of termination by notice belonging to the hiree under paragraph 2 no 1. If there is dispute as to whether the hirer has granted use of the hired object punctually or has effected redress before the expiry of the period determined for this purpose, the burden of proof falls on him.

[. . .]

Second Sub-title

Hirings of residential accommodation

[. . .]

§ 550

Form of hiring contract

If a hiring contract for a longer period than a year is concluded otherwise than in written form, it is deemed to be for an indeterminate period. Termination by notice is however permissible at the earliest at the expiry of a year after the handing over of the residential accommodation.

[. . .]

§ 557

Increase of hire charge under agreement or statute law

(1) During the hiring the parties can agree an increase of the hire charge.

(2) The parties can agree future alterations of the level of the hire charge in steps under § 557a or as index-linked under § 557b.

(3) Otherwise, the hirer can demand increases in the hire charge only in accordance with §§ 558 to 560, in so far as an increase by agreement is not excluded or the exclusion follows from the circumstances.

(4) An agreement which deviates from this to the disadvantage of the hiree is ineffective.

[. . .]

§ 558

Increase of hire charge to comparable hire charge usual for locality

(1) The hirer can demand consent to an increase of the hire charge up to the comparable hire charges usual for the locality if the hire charge has been unchanged for 15 months at the point in time at which the increase is to take place. The demand for increase in the hire charge can be claimed one year after the last increase in the hire charge at the earliest. Increases under §§ 559 to 560 are not to be taken into account.

(2)–(5) [. . .]

(6) An agreement which deviates from this to the disadvantage of the hiree is ineffective.

[. . .]

§ 566 Purchase does not override hiring

(1) If the residential accommodation which is hired out is transferred by the hirer to a third party after it has been handed over to the hiree, the transferee takes the place of the hirer in respect of the rights and duties arising from the hiring during the period of his ownership

(2) If the transferee does not fulfil the duties, the hirer is liable for the harm which the transferee has to make good like a guarantor who has renounced his right to the Vorausklage objection (that there has been no execution against the main debtor). If the hiree is informed of the transmission of ownership by the hirer, the hirer is released from liability if the hiree does not terminate the hiring by notice at the first date at which such termination is permissible.

[. . .]

§ 568

Form and content of termination notice

(1) Termination of the hiring by notice needs written form.

(2) The hirer must inform the hiree punctually of the possibility, the form and the period for objection in accordance with §§ 574 to 574b.

[. . .]

Second Sub-chapter

Hirings for indefinite period

§ 573
Ordinary termination notice by hirer
(1) The hirer can only terminate by notice if he has a justified interest in the termination of the hiring. Termination by notice for the purpose of raising the hiring charge is excluded.
(2) A justified interest on the part of the hirer in the termination of the hiring is present in particular if
1. the hiree has culpably and not insubstantially violated his contractual duties
2. the hirer needs the accommodation as a residence for himself, members of his family or members of his household or
3. the hirer would be prevented from an appropriate economic utilisation of the property by the continuation of the hiring, and would thereby suffer substantial disadvantages; the possibility of obtaining a higher hire charge by a further hiring out as residential accommodation remains out of consideration; the hirer can also not rely on the fact that he wants to transfer the hired premises in connection with an intended establishment of residential ownership or one occurring after handing over to the hiree.
(3) The grounds for a justified interest on the part of the hirer are to be given in the written termination notice. Other grounds will only be considered in so far as they have arisen subsequently.
(4) An agreement which deviates from this to the disadvantage of the hiree is ineffective.
[. . .]

Fourth Sub-title

Lease contract

§ 581
Typical contractual duties in lease contract
(1) The lessor is under a duty in a lease contract to grant to the lessee the use of the leased object and the enjoyment of its products, in so far as they are to be regarded as yield according to the rules of proper economics, during the term of the lease. The lessee is under a duty to pay the agreed rent to the lessor.
(2) The provisions about hiring contracts are to be applied correspondingly to lease contracts (with the exception of land lease contracts), in so far as no other conclusion follows from §§ 582 to 584b.
[. . .]

Sixth Title

Loan

§ 598
Typical contractual duties in relation to loan
The lender of a thing is under a duty in a loan contract to allow to the borrower the use of the thing without payment.

§ 599
Liability of the lender
The lender only has to answer for intention and gross negligence.

§ 600
Liability for defects
If the lender is deceitfully silent about a defect in law or a fault in the thing loaned, he is under a duty to compensate the borrower for the harm arising from this.
[. . .]

Seventh Title

Contract for loan of thing

§ 607
Typical contractual duties in contract for loan of thing
(1) By a contract for loan of a thing, the lender is obliged to hand over to the borrower an agreed fungible thing. The borrower is obliged to make payment for the loan and on the due date restitution of things of the same kind, quality, and quantity.
(2) The provisions of this title do not apply to the handing over of money.

§ 608
Notice
(1) If no period is determined for the return of the thing handed over, the due date depends upon the lender or the borrower giving notice to terminate.
(2) A contract for the loan of a thing concluded for an indefinite period can be wholly or partially terminated by notice at any time by the lender or the borrower, in so far as nothing different has been agreed.

§ 609
Payment
The borrower must make payment, at the latest on return of the thing handed over.
[. . .]

Eighth Title

Service contract

§ 611
Typical contractual duties in service contract
(1) The person who promises services is under a duty by a service contract to perform the services promised and the other party to pay the agreed remuneration.
(2) The object of the service contract can be services of any kind.
[. . .]

§ 612
Remuneration
(1) Remuneration is deemed to be tacitly agreed if in the circumstances the service should only be expected to be given in return for remuneration.

(2) If the level of the remuneration is not determined, when a rate exists remuneration in accordance with the rate should be regarded as agreed, and when there is no rate the usual remuneration.

(3) In the case of an employment relationship remuneration cannot be agreed for the same work or work of equal value which is smaller because of the sex of the employee than for an employee of the other sex. Agreeing a smaller remuneration will not be justified by the fact that because of the employee's sex special protective provisions apply. § 611a paragraph 1 sentence 3 is to apply correspondingly.

[. . .]

§ 618

Duty to take protective measures

(1) The person entitled to the service must so arrange and maintain premises, apparatus or implements which he has to provide for the carrying out of the services and so regulate services which are to be undertaken under his direction or management that the person under the duty is protected against risk to life and health in so far as the nature of the service allows it.

(2) If the person under the duty is taken into the domestic establishment, the person entitled to the service must in respect of living and sleeping accommodation, board and work and recreation time make those facilities and arrangements which are necessary having regard to the health, morality and religion of the person under the duty.

(3) If the person entitled to the service does not fulfil the obligations he owes in respect of the life and health of the person under the duty, the provisions of §§ 842 to 846 applying for torts apply correspondingly to his obligation to provide compensation.

[. . .]

§ 619a

Burden of proof in respect of liability of employee

Deviating from § 280 paragraph 1, the employee must provide compensation to the employer for the harm arising from the violation of a duty under the work relationship only if he is responsible for the violation of duty.

§ 620

Termination of service relationship

(1) The service relationship ends with the expiry of the period for which it is entered into.

(2) If the length of the service relationship is neither determined nor capable of being deduced from the nature or the purpose of the services, each party can terminate the service relationship by notice in accordance with §§ 621 to 623.

(3) The Part Time and Fixed Term Act applies for employment contracts which are concluded for a determined period.

[. . .]

§ 623

Written form for termination notice

The termination of employment relationships by notice or by a termination contract requires written form to be effective; electronic form is excluded.

[. . .]

§ 626
Immediate termination by notice on a substantial ground
(1) The service relationship can be terminated by notice by any party on a substantial ground without the observance of a period for the notice, if facts are present on the basis of which it cannot reasonably be expected of the person giving the notice that the service relationship should continue until the expiry of the notice period or until the agreed termination of the service relationship, taking into consideration all the circumstances of the individual case and balancing the interests of both contracting parties.
(2) Notice can only be given within two weeks. The period begins at the point in time at which the person entitled to give notice obtains knowledge of the facts which are crucial for the notice. The person giving notice must on request inform the other party in writing of the ground for the notice without delay.
[. . .]

Ninth Title

Work contract and similar contracts

First Sub-title

Work contract

§ 631
Typical contractual duties in work contract
(1) The undertaking is obliged by a work contract to produce the work promised and the client is obliged to pay the agreed remuneration.
(2) The subject matter of a work contract can be the production or alteration of a thing as well as another result to be brought about by work or a service.

§ 632
Remuneration
(1) Remuneration is considered to be tacitly agreed if the production of the work is, in the circumstances, only to be expected in return for remuneration.
(2) If the level of the remuneration is not determined, if a valuation exists remuneration in accordance with the valuation is to be regarded as agreed and in the absence of a valuation the usual remuneration.
(3) In case of doubt an estimate of costs is not to be remunerated.

§ 633
Physical and legal defects
(1) The undertaking must provide the client with the work free from physical and legal defects.
(2) The work is free from physical defects if it has the agreed composition. In so far as the composition is not agreed, the work is free from physical defects
1. when it is appropriate for the assumed use under the contract, or otherwise
2. for the usual use and has a composition which is usual for works of the same kind and which the client can expect according to the type of work.

It is equivalent to a physical defect if the undertaking produces a different work from that ordered or produces the work in too small a quantity.

(3) The work is free from legal defects if third parties cannot claim any rights against the client in respect of the work or only those accepted in the contract.

§ 634
Rights of client in respect of defects

If the work is defective, the client can, if the prerequisites of the following provisions are present and in so far as no different provision is made

1. demand subsequent fulfilment under § 635,
2. demand under § 637 the right to eliminate the defect himself and reimbursement of the necessary expenses,
3. withdraw from the contract under §§ 636, 323 and 326 paragraph 5 or reduce the reimbursement under § 638 and
4. demand compensation under §§ 636, 280, 281, 283 and 311a or reimbursement of abortive expenditure under § 284.

§ 634a
Limitation of claims in respect of defects

(1) The limitation period for claims described in § 634 nos 1, 2 and 4 expires

1. subject to no 2, in two years in respect of work the result of which consists in the production, servicing or alteration of a thing or in the carrying out of planning or surveillance services for this,
2. in five years in respect of a building and work the result of which consists in the carrying out of planning or surveillance services for this, and
3. in other cases in the ordinary limitation period.

(2) The limitation period begins in the cases of paragraph 1 nos 1 and 2 with the acceptance.

(3) Deviating from paragraph 1 nos 1 and 2 and paragraph 2, the limitation period for the claims is the ordinary limitation period, if the undertaking has deceitfully kept the defect secret. In the case of paragraph 1 no 2 limitation does not however occur before the expiry of the period determined there.

(4) § 218 applies for the right of withdrawal described in § 634. The client can in spite of ineffectiveness of the withdrawal according to § 218 paragraph 1 refuse payment of the remuneration in so far as he would be entitled to do so on the basis of the withdrawal. If he makes use of this right, the undertaking can withdraw from the contract.

(5) § 218 and paragraph 4 sentence 2 apply correspondingly to the right of reduction described in § 634.

§ 635
Subsequent fulfilment

(1) If the client demands subsequent fulfilment, the undertaking can according to its choice remove the defect or produce new work.

(2) The undertaking must bear the expenses necessary for the purposes of the subsequent fulfilment, in particular costs of transport, road tolls, work and materials.

(3) The undertaking can refuse subsequent fulfilment notwithstanding § 275 paragraphs 2 and 3 if it is only possible with disproportionate cost.

(4) If the undertaking produces new work, it can demand from the client the return of the defective work in accordance with §§ 346 to 348.

§ 636
Special provisions for withdrawal and compensation
Except in the cases of §§ 281 paragraph 2 and 323 paragraph 2, the setting of a period is not necessary even if the undertaking refuses subsequent fulfilment in accordance with § 635 paragraph 3 or if subsequent fulfilment has failed or cannot be expected of the client.

§ 637
Self help
(1) In the case of a defect in the work, the client can remove the defect himself after the expiry without result of an appropriate period determined by him for subsequent fulfilment, and demand reimbursement of the necessary expenses, unless the undertaking justifiably refuses subsequent fulfilment.
(2) § 323 paragraph 2 applies correspondingly. The determination of a period is not necessary even if subsequent fulfilment has failed or cannot be expected of the client.
(3) The client can demand from the undertaking an advance for the expenditure necessary for the removal of the defect.

§ 638
Reduction
(1) Instead of withdrawing, the client can reduce the remuneration by a declaration to the undertaking. The ground for exclusion in § 323 paragraph 5 sentence 2 does not apply.
(2) If there are several participants on the client's side or on the undertaking's side, the reduction can only be declared by all or against all.
(3) In a case of reduction, the remuneration is to be reduced in the ratio which, at the time of the conclusion of the contract, the value of the work in a defect-free state would have had to the real value. Reduction is, so far as is necessary, to be ascertained by valuation.
(4) If the client has paid more than the reduced remuneration, the additional amount is to be reimbursed by the undertaking. § 346 paragraph 1 and § 347 paragraph 1 apply correspondingly.

§ 639
Exclusion of liability
The undertaking cannot refer to an agreement by which the rights of the client in respect of a defect are excluded or limited in so far as it has deceitfully kept the defect secret or has assumed a guarantee for the composition of the work.

§ 640
Acceptance
(1) The client is obliged to accept work produced in accordance with the contract in so far as the acceptance is not excluded because of the composition of the work. Acceptance cannot be refused because of insignificant defects. It is equivalent to

acceptance if the client does not accept the work within a reasonable period determined for him by the undertaking even though he is obliged to do so.
(2) If the client accepts defective work in accordance with paragraph 1 sentence 1 even
though he knows of the defect, he only has the rights described in § 634 nos 1 to 3 if on
the acceptance he reserves his rights in respect of the defect.

§ 641
When remuneration is due
(1) Remuneration is to be paid on acceptance of the work. If the work is to be
accepted in parts and the remuneration is determined for the individual parts, the
remuneration is to be made for each part on its acceptance.
(2)–(4) [. . .]
[. . .]

§ 644
Bearing of risk
(1) The undertaking bears the risk until acceptance of the work. If the client falls into
delay in acceptance, the risk passes to him. The undertaking is not responsible for
accidental destruction and an accidental deterioration of the material delivered by the
client.
(2) If the undertaking dispatches the work at the client's request to a different place
than the place for fulfilment, the provisions of § 447 which apply to purchase apply
correspondingly.

§ 645
Responsibility of client
(1) If the work has been destroyed, has deteriorated or has become impracticable
before acceptance as a result of a defect in the material delivered by the client or as a
result of a direction given by the client for the execution without the contribution of a
circumstance for which the undertaking is responsible, the undertaking can demand
the part of the payment corresponding to the work performed and refund of the
outlay not included in the payment. The same applies if the contract is cancelled in
conformity with § 643.
(2) Further liability on the part of the client on the basis of fault remains unaffected.

§ 646
Completion instead of acceptance
If acceptance is excluded because of the composition of the work, completion of the
work takes the place of acceptance in the cases of § 634a paragraph 2 and §§ 641, 644
and 645.

§ 647
Undertaking's right of lien
The undertaking has a right of lien for its demands under the contract in respect of the
client's moveable things produced or repaired by it if they have come into its possession in connection with the production or for the purpose of the repair.

§ 648

Security mortgage for building undertaking

(1) The undertaking in respect of a building or an individual part of a building can ask for the grant of a security mortgage on the client's building site in respect of its demands under the contract. If the work is not yet completed, it can ask for the grant of the security mortgage for a part of the remuneration corresponding to the work performed and for the expenses not included in the remuneration.

(2) The proprietor of a shipyard can ask for the grant of a ship's mortgage in the client's ship or ship under construction in respect of his demands for the construction or the repair of a ship; paragraph 1 sentence 2 applies in accordance with its sense and § 647 does not apply.

§ 648a

Skilled building worker security

(1) The undertaking in respect of a building, an external structure or a part thereof can ask for a security from the client for the prior performances to be provided by it, inclusive of the subsidiary claims appertaining to them, by determining for the client a reasonable period for the provision of the security by a declaration that it will refuse his performance after the expiry of the period. Security can be demanded up to the level of the foreseeable claim for remuneration as it arises from the contract or a subsequent additional order as well as for subsidiary claims; the subsidiary claims are to be fixed at 10 per cent of the claim to remuneration which is to be secured. The security is to be regarded as sufficient even if the provider of the security reserves the right to revoke his promise in the case of a significant worsening of the client's financial circumstances with effect for claims for remuneration from the building services which the undertaking has not yet performed at the time of arrival of the revocation declaration.

(2) The security can also be provided by a guarantee or other promise of payment by a credit institute or credit insurer authorised to carry on business in the area of application of this statutory provision. The credit institute or credit insurer may only make payments to the undertaking in so far as the client recognises the undertaking's claim to remuneration or has been ordered to pay the remuneration by a provisionally executable judgment and the prerequisites are present under which the execution may be begun.

(3) The undertaking must reimburse the client for the usual costs of the provision of the security up to a maximum rate of 2 per cent per annum. This does not apply in so far as a security must be maintained because of the client's objections to the undertaking's claim to remuneration and the objections show themselves to be unfounded.

(4) In so far as the undertaking has obtained a security for its claim to remuneration under paragraphs 1 or 2, the claim to the grant of a mortgage security under § 648 paragraph 1 is excluded.

(5) If the client does not provide the security within the specified period, the rights of the undertaking are determined under §§ 643 and 645 paragraph 1. If the contract accordingly counts as cancelled, the undertaking can also ask for compensation for the harm which it has suffered as a result of having trusted in the validity of the contract. The same applies if the client terminates the contract in accordance with paragraph 1 at a point in time associated with the demand for the security, unless the

notice was not given in order to escape the placing of the security. It is presumed that the harm consists of 5 per cent of the remuneration.

(6) The provisions of paragraphs 1 to 5 do not apply if the client

1. is a legal person under public law or a special fund under public law, or

2. is a natural person and is having the building works carried out for the construction or repair of a single family house, with or without a subsidiary apartment; this does not apply in the case of supervision of a building project by a building supervisor authorised to dispose of the client's financial means.

(7) An agreement deviating from the provisions of paragraphs 1 to 5 is ineffective.

§ 649
Client's right to give notice

The client can terminate the contract by notice at any time until the completion of the work. If the client gives notice, the undertaking is entitled to ask for the agreed remuneration; it must however allow what it saves in expenditure or acquires (or wilfully refrains from acquiring) by other use of its power to work as a result of the cancellation of the contract to be charged against it.

§ 650
Estimate of costs

(1) If an estimate of costs formed the basis of the contract, but without the undertaking taking on a guarantee for the correctness of the estimate, and if it occurs that the work cannot be carried out without a significant exceeding of the estimate, the undertaking only has the claim determined in § 645 paragraph 1 if the client terminates the contract by notice on this ground.

(2) If such an exceeding of the estimate is to be expected, the undertaking must inform the client without delay.

§ 651
Application of law of purchase

The provisions about purchase apply to a contract which has as its subject matter the delivery of movable things to be manufactured or to be produced. § 442 paragraph 1 sentence 1 also applies in respect of these contracts if the defect is attributable to the material delivered by the client. In the case of moveable things to be manufactured or to be produced, in so far as it is a question of things which are not fungible, §§ 642, 643, 645, 649 and 650 are also to be applied with the proviso that the determinative point in time under §§ 446 and 447 takes the place of acceptance.
[. . .]

Second Sub-title

Travel contract
[. . .]

§ 651f
Compensation

(1) The traveller can, without prejudice to the right of abatement or termination by notice, demand compensation for non-fulfilment unless the defect in the travel is based on a circumstance for which the travel organiser is not responsible.

(2) If the travel is frustrated or substantially impaired, the traveller can also demand an appropriate indemnification in money for holiday time spent fruitlessly.
[. . .]

Tenth Title

Brokerage contract

Subtitle 2

Credit negotiation contract

§ 655a
Credit negotiation contract between undertaking and consumer
The following provisions apply subject to sentence 2 for a contract under which an undertaking undertakes to negotiate for a consumer a consumer credit contract in return for money or to indicate to him the opportunity to conclude a consumer credit contract. This does not apply to the extent determined in § 491 paragraph 2.

§ 655b
Written form
(1) The credit negotiation contract needs to be in written form. In particular, subject to other information duties, the remuneration of the credit negotiator must be given in the contract as a percentage of the credit; if the credit negotiator has also agreed remuneration with the undertaking, this must also be given. It is not permissible for the contract to be connected with the application for giving of the credit. The credit negotiator must communicate the contents of the contract to the consumer in text form.
(2) A credit negotiation contract which does not satisfy the requirements of paragraph 1 sentences 1 to 3 is void.

§ 655c
Remuneration
The consumer is only obliged to pay the remuneration if, as a result of the negotiation or the indication of the credit negotiator, the credit has been provided to the consumer and a revocation by the consumer under § 355 is no longer possible. In so far as the consumer credit contract facilitates the early redemption of another loan (debt conversion) and this is known to the credit negotiator, a claim only arises to the remuneration if the effective annual interest or the original effective annual interest does not increase; in calculating the effective or originally effective annual interest for the loan to be redeemed, possible negotiation costs are left out of consideration.

§ 655d
Ancillary payments
The credit negotiator is not permitted to agree a payment for services which are connected with the negotiation of the consumer credit contract or the indication of the opportunity to conclude a consumer credit contract, except the remuneration under § 655c sentence 1. It is however possible to agree that the credit negotiator is to be reimbursed for necessary expenses which have actually arisen.

§ 655e
Divergent agreements, application to new start businesses
(1) It is not permissible to deviate from the provisions of this subtitle to the disadvantage of the consumer. The provisions of this subtitle apply even if they are circumvented by other formulations.
(2) This subtitle also applies for credit negotiation contracts between an undertaking and a new start business in the sense of § 507.
[. . .]

Twelfth Title

Mandate and contract for transacting business

First Sub-title

Mandate

§ 662
Typical contractual duties in relation to mandate contract
On the acceptance of a mandate, the delegate commits himself to transact business entrusted to him by the delegator on the delegator's behalf without payment.
[. . .]

§ 667
Duty to hand over
The delegate is under a duty to hand over to the delegator everything which he receives for the carrying out of the mandate and which he obtains from transacting the business.
[. . .]

§ 670
Refund of expenditure
If the delegate, for the purpose of carrying out the mandate, incurs expenditure which in the circumstances he may regard as necessary, the delegator is obliged to refund it.

Second Sub-title

Contract to transact business

§ 675
Transacting business without payment
(1) The provisions of §§ 663, 665 to 670, 672 to 674 and, if the person under the duty has the right to terminate by notice without observing any notice period, the provisions of § 671 paragraph 2 as well apply correspondingly to a service contract or a work contract which has transaction of business as its object, in so far as no different provision is made in this sub-title.
(2) A person who gives advice or a recommendation to another person is, without prejudice to the responsibility arising from a contractual relationship, a tort or another statutory provision, not obliged to compensate for the harm arising from following the advice or the recommendation.
[. . .]

Thirteenth Title

Conduct of business without mandate

§ 677
Duties of person conducting business
A person who conducts business for another without either a mandate from or being otherwise entitled to do so as against him must conduct the business in the manner required by the interest of the person in control of the business, having regard to his actual or presumed intention.
[...]

§ 683
Refund of expenditure
If taking over conduct of the business corresponds with the interest and the actual or presumed intention of the person in control of the business, the person conducting the business can demand refund of his expenses in the same way as a delegate. In the cases mentioned in § 679 the person conducting the business has this claim even if taking over conduct of the business is in conflict with the intention of the person in control of it.
[...]

Twentieth Title

Guarantee

§ 765
Typical contractual duties in relation to guarantee
(1) In a guarantee contract the guarantor commits himself to the creditor of a third party to be responsible for the fulfilment of the liability of the third party.
(2) The guarantee can also be taken on for a future or a conditional liability.

§ 766
Written form for guarantee declaration
The guarantee declaration must be given in writing for the guarantee contract to be valid. Giving the guarantee declaration in electronic form is excluded. In so far as the guarantor fulfils the main obligation, the defect in form is cured.

§ 767
Scope of guarantee obligation
(1) The existence for the time being of the main obligation is crucial for guarantor's obligation. This applies in particular if the main obligation is altered by fault or delay on the part of the main debtor. The guarantor's obligation will not be increased by a legal transaction which the main debtor takes on after the guarantee is taken on.
(2) The guarantor is liable for any costs of a termination notice and legal action which are to be refunded by the main debtor to the creditor.

§ 768
Objections by guarantor
(1) The guarantor can claim any objections which the main debtor has. If the main debtor dies, the guarantor cannot rely on the fact that the heir has only limited liability.

(2) The guarantor does not lose an objection by the main debtor renouncing it.
[...]

§ 774
Statutory transmission of demand

(1) The creditor's demand against the main debtor transfers to the guarantor in so far as he satisfies the creditor. The transmission cannot be claimed to the creditor's disadvantage. Objections (Einwendungen) by the main debtor from a legal relationship existing between him and the guarantor remain unaffected.

(2) Co-guarantors are liable to each other only under § 426.
[...]

Twenty-sixth Title

Unjustified enrichment

§ 812
Claim to handing over

(1) A person who obtains something without a legal ground by the performance of another or in some other way at his cost is obliged to hand it over to him. This obligation also exists if the legal ground later disappears or the result intended by the performance according to the content of the legal transaction does not occur.

(2) The recognition of the existence or non-existence of an obligation relationship occurring by way of a contract also counts as a performance.

§ 813
Fulfilment in spite of objection

(1) What is provided (das Geleistete) for the purpose of fulfilment of an obligation can be demanded back even if there was an objection against the claim by which the making of the claim was permanently excluded. The provisions of § 214 paragraph 2 remain unaffected.

(2) If a time-limited obligation is prematurely fulfilled, a demand for its reversal is excluded; refund of interim interest cannot be demanded.

§ 814
Knowledge of absence of obligation

What is provided for the purpose of fulfilment of an obligation cannot be demanded back if the person making the performance knew that he was not obliged to make it or if the performance corresponded to a moral duty or regard to propriety.
[...]

§ 817
Violation of statute law or good morals

If the purpose of a performance was determined in such a way that the recipient has by acceptance violated a statutory prohibition or good morals, the recipient has an obligation of handing over. Demand for return is excluded if the person providing the performance may likewise be charged with such a violation, unless the performance consisted of entering into an obligation; what is provided in fulfilment of such an obligation cannot be demanded back.

§ 818

Scope of claim for enrichment

(1) The duty to hand over extends to the benefits derived as well as to what the recipient obtains on the ground of an acquired right or as compensation for the destruction, damage or removal of the object obtained.

(2) If handing over is not possible because of the nature of what is obtained or if the recipient is on some other ground not in a position to hand over, he must compensate for its value.

(3) The duty to hand over or to compensate for value is excluded in so far as the recipient is no longer enriched.

(4) From the point in time when the case becomes pending the recipient is liable in accordance with the general provisions.

§ 819

Increased liability in case of knowledge and violation of statute law or morals

(1) If the recipient knows of the absence of the legal ground at the time of receipt or if he discovers it later, he is obliged to hand over from the time of receipt or the obtaining of knowledge as if the claim to handing over had become pending at this time.

(2) If the recipient violates a statutory prohibition or good morals by acceptance of the performance, he is under the same obligation from receipt of the performance onwards.
[. . .]

§ 821

Objection of enrichment

A person who enters into an obligation without legal ground can refuse fulfilment even if the claim to release from the obligation is time barred.

§ 822

Duty of third party to hand over

If the recipient transfers what has been obtained to a third party without payment, the third party is obliged, in so far as the recipient's duty to hand over the enrichment is excluded as a result, to hand over as if he had received the transfer from the creditor without legal ground.

Twenty-seventh Title

Tort

§ 823

Duty to compensate

(1) A person who deliberately or negligently unlawfully injures the life, body, health, freedom, property or other right of another is obliged to compensate the other for the harm arising from this.

(2) The same duty applies to a person who violates a statutory provision which has as its purpose the protection of another. If, according to the content of the statutory provision, a violation of it is possible even without fault, the duty to compensate will only arise in the case of fault.
[. . .]

§ 825
Provision on sexual acts
A person who induces another by deceit, threat or abuse of a relationship of dependency to carry out or suffer sexual acts is obliged to compensate him from the harm arising from this.
[. . .]

§ 828
Minors; deaf mutes
(1) A person who has not completed the seventh year of his life is not responsible for harm which he inflicts on another.
(2) A person who has completed his seventh but not his tenth year is not responsible for the harm which he inflicts on another in an accident with a motor vehicle, a railway or a hover rail. This does not apply if he has caused the injury deliberately.
(3) A person who has not yet competed his eighteenth year is, in so far as his responsibility is not excluded under paragraphs 1 or 2, not responsible for the harm which he inflicts on another if, on the commission of the action causing the harm, he does not have the necessary intelligence to realise his responsibility.
[. . .]

§ 831
Liability for work assistants
(1) A person who employs another for work is obliged to compensate for the harm which the other unlawfully inflicts on a third party in carrying out the work. The duty to compensate does not arise if the employer observes the care necessary in human affairs in the selection of the person employed and, in so far as he has to provide apparatus or implements or has to supervise the carrying out of the work, in such provision or supervision; or if the harm would still have arisen despite application of this care.
(2) The same responsibility applies to a person who takes over for an employer by contract the control of one of the matters described in paragraph 1 sentence 2.
[. . .]

§ 839
Liability on violation of official duty
(1) If an official intentionally or negligently violates an official duty which is incumbent on him as against a third party, he must compensate the third party for the harm arising from this. If the official can only be charged with negligence, a claim can only be made against him if the victim cannot obtain compensation in another manner.
(2) If an official violates his official duty by a decision in a legal issue, he is only responsible for the harm arising from this if the violation of duty consists of a criminal act. This provision has no application to a refusal or delay which is contrary to duty in exercise of the office.
(3) The duty to compensate does not arise if the victim has intentionally or negligently refrained from averting the harm by the use of a legal remedy.

§ 839a
Liability of court expert

(1) If an expert appointed by the court presents an incorrect opinion intentionally or with gross negligence, he is obliged to compensate for the harm which is incurred by a party to the proceedings through a judicial decision which is based on this opinion.

(2) § 839 paragraph 3 is to be applied correspondingly.

[. . .]

§ 852
Claim for handing over after expiry of limitation period

If the person obliged to make compensation as a result of a tort has acquired something at the cost of the victim, he is obliged even after expiry of the limitation period for the claim to compensation for the harm which has arisen from a tort to make restitution in accordance with the provisions about handing over an unjustified enrichment. This claim expires ten years after it arises and, without regard to the time when it arises, 30 years from the commission of the act causing the injury or the other event giving rise to the harm.

[. . .]

Third Book

Law of Property

Second Section

General provisions about rights to land

§ 873
Acquisition by agreement and register entry

(1) Agreement of the person entitled and the other party about the coming into existence of the alteration in rights and the entry of the alteration in the Land Register is necessary for transfer of ownership in land, for encumbering land with a right, and transfer or encumbering of such a right, in so far as statute law does not provide otherwise.

(2) Before the register entry the parties are only bound to the agreement if the declarations are notarially authenticated, given before the Land Registry Office or handed in at this office, or if the person entitled has handed to the other party a permission for register entry corresponding with the provisions of the Land Register Order.

[. . .]

§ 892
Public faith in Land Register

(1) The contents of the Land Register are deemed to be correct in favour of the person who acquires a right to land or a right to such a right by a legal transaction, unless an objection to such correctness is entered or the incorrectness is known to the transferee. If the person entitled is restricted in disposing of a right entered in the Land Register in favour of a certain person, the restriction is only effective against the transferee if it is evident from the Land Register or known to the transferee.

(2) If a register entry is necessary for the acquisition of the right, the time of making the application for entry (or, if the agreement necessary under § 873 only comes into existence later, the time of agreement) is crucial for the transferee's knowledge.
[. . .]

Third Section

Ownership

First Title

Content of ownership
[. . .]

Second Title

Acquisition and loss of ownership in land

§ 925
Conveyance
(1) The agreement of the transferor and the transferee (conveyance) to the transfer of ownership in land which is necessary under § 873 must be declared when both parties are simultaneously present before a competent authority. Any notary is competent for the acceptance of a conveyance, without prejudice to the competence of other authorities. A conveyance can also be declared in a court settlement or in an insolvency plan which is confirmed with legal effect.
(2) A conveyance which takes place subject to a condition or a provision as to time is ineffective.

Third Title

Acquisition and loss of ownership in movable things

First Sub-title

Transfer

§ 929
Agreement and delivery
For the transfer of property in a movable thing it is necessary that the owner delivers the thing to the transferee and both are in agreement that the ownership should pass. If the transferee is in possession of the thing, agreement about the transmission of ownership suffices.
[. . .]

§ 932
Acquisition in good faith from person not entitled
(1) The transferee becomes the owner by a transfer occurring under § 929 even if the thing does not belong to the transferor, unless he did not act in good faith at the time at which he would acquire ownership under these provisions. However, this applies in

the case of § 929 sentence 2 only if the transferee had obtained possession from the transferor.

(2) The transferee is not acting in good faith if he knows that the thing does not belong to the transferor (or his ignorance of this is due to gross negligence).

Index